For Reference

Not to be taken from this room

ENCYCLOPEDIA OF
Special Education

THIRD EDITION

THIRD EDITION

VOLUME 3

ENCYCLOPEDIA OF
Special Education

A Reference for the Education of Children, Adolescents, and Adults with Disabilities and Other Exceptional Individuals

Edited by

Cecil R. Reynolds

Elaine Fletcher-Janzen

JOHN WILEY & SONS

ISBN-13: 978-0-471-67798-7 (VOL. 1); ISBN-10: 0-471-67798-1 (VOL. 1)
ISBN-13: 978-0-471-67799-4 (VOL. 2); ISBN-10: 0-471-67799-X (VOL. 2)
ISBN-13: 978-0-471-67801-4 (VOL. 3); ISBN-10: 0-471-67801-5 (VOL. 3)

ISBN-13: 978-0-471-67802-1 (SET); ISBN-10: 0-471-67802-3 (SET)
Printed in the United States of America.
10 9 8 7 6 5 4 3 2 1

PREFACE TO THE THIRD EDITION

It has been 20 years since we first set foot on the journey that has become the third edition of the *Encyclopedia of Special Education*. If someone has told us then that we would end up chronicling the evolution of special education, we probably would not have believed him or her. It was enough, at that time, to have created the first *Encyclopedia of Special Education;* nearly 2,000 pages, thousands of entries, and more than 400 authors coming together to cement this fledgling field that was full of hope and imagination.

So, here we are more than 20 years later, near the end of our guardianship of the *Encyclopedia*. It is our old friend, and it has been our mentor, our judge, and our inspiration. During the editing of the second and third editions, we are well aware of how life, research, and standards have changed for those of us who practice in special education. It is an interesting process to look back and see how the *Encyclopedia* has changed over the years and how it has really provided a mirror of the zeitgeist of the times in which we live.

The first edition was full of new ideas such as profile analysis, direct instruction, and terms such as "trainable" and "educable." The field had license to imagine and try ways to rewire the brain that was having trouble in school. Not so now! The third edition clearly marks the federal and state demands for evidence-based practices, perhaps reflecting the end of imagination and the beginning of an era of proof or accountability. Hence, we see behavioral terms and behavioral-oriented credentials enjoying resurgence because they allow for documentation of behaviors that are easy to observe. Accountability is a force to be noticed as it infiltrates and guides current practice.

The first edition was full of laws that were still new and somewhat unexplored: We were still trying to interpret Public Law 94-142! Now we have visited those laws, reauthorized (and revised) them many times, and joined them with support such as the ADA and Technology acts. Individuals with disabilities have never enjoyed the protections of as many laws and regulations as we have today. There are also so many more consumer protection groups and organizations around today that fight for the rights of those who have disabilities. In fact, current beliefs about advocacy are also focusing on assisting full participation by the individual with the disability in planning and transitions. Years ago, parents got together and had to forge an

organization and eventually laws that gave their children the right to an appropriate education. Their voices were heard and their legacy has been grand indeed as we see the very same children advocating for themselves.

The advocacy network that surrounds special education students today is vast, connected, and accessible. The Internet has exponentially changed the individual's abilities to learn about support organizations and to reach out to others who have similar concerns and conditions. This movement is not just on a national level, the World Health Organization is rallying the international community to connect the daily living experiences of individuals with disabilities in the *International Classification of Functioning, Disability, and Health*. This classification system was designed to describe the *individual* with a disability, not just to classify the disability itself. Indeed, we remember that in the first edition of the *Encyclopedia,* it was acceptable to label individuals via the disability; therefore, individuals with Schizophrenia were schizophrenics and individuals with Mental Retardation were the mentally retarded. The disability came first and the individual came second. In the second edition of the *Encyclopedia,* we remember stressing heavily with all of our editors and authors that all language referring to clinical populations would have to reflect the individual first and his or her handicapping condition second. This was a major literary turn at the time!

Many years ago, special education students were all too often relegated to isolated classrooms in secluded areas of school buildings. Not so now. The third edition (and somewhat in the second edition) of the *Encyclopedia* fully reflects that concepts such as "mainstreaming" are now archaic. Inclusion is the rule unless it is not in the best interests of the student. Disability and ability now live side by side. Humanness is central and our similarities outweigh our differences, even in special education.

The three editions of the *Encyclopedia* have also reflected the evolution of test construction and interpretation. The level of psychometric design is outstanding right now. Consumers have come to enjoy new tests that have specificity, such as tests about executive functions, trauma, study skills, and so on. The major broadband assessment batteries that measure cognitive abilities and psychological constructs are excellent, theory-based measures that have imaginative and careful design. Therefore, our ability to include well-designed tools in the assessment process has never been better. The third edition of the *Encyclopedia* catalogues many new tests and revisions of old and true instruments.

The demand for "countable" accountability of special education outcomes is upon these days. For the past 20 years, the *Encyclopedia* reflected exploration, and now exploration is passé and counting and demanding results is the zeitgeist of the times. Renegades as we are, we have included more and more neuropsychological principles and terms into the various editions of the *Encyclopedia* as we have paid homage to the vast mystery of the human brain and personality that will most likely never be reduced down to accountable facts. Herein lies the rub for those with interests in brain-behavior relationships, the very thing that we seek is unattainable and therein provides continuous wonder, curiosity, and frustration! We are confident that the most important aspect of future research that seeks to improve the daily lives of children with disabilities lies in the study of the brain and its relationship to learning and daily living skills. This process will always be a study of one, and not given to group statistics. Therefore, regardless of the political zeitgeist, we have expressed our desire to support clinical excellence throughout the third edition of the *Encyclopedia* and minimize old ideas that have been parceled out as new and redesigned to fit ends that are not apolitical. The original *Encyclopedia* was bursting with curiosity and wonder about a new field. We wish to maintain this tribute in the current edition and support the continued innocence of true scientific exploration.

So, what is new in the third edition of the *Encyclopedia*? Very little information these days is entirely new; however, there are some entries that reflect a resurgence or future directions, such as Response to Intervention, Highly Qualified Teachers, Diffusion Tensor Imaging, and Positive Behavior Supports. Tom Oakland, our "International Special Education entries" Contributing Editor provided us with many entries from new areas of the world such as Estonia, Albania, sub-Saharan Africa, and other exciting places reflecting his expertise in international special education and the trend of professionals to think more globally these days.

All of the laws and legal entries were completely and competently updated by our Contributing Editor, Kimberly Applequist, JD. The final regulations for the Individuals with Disabilities Education Improvement Act of 2004 are not out at this time and so the exact nature of the guidelines is not known, but we look forward to seeing how they take shape. Randall DePry updated many entries related to teaching and behavioral supports and provided new entries on the exacting process of applied behavior analysis. Lee Swanson focused on entries pertaining to the latest developments in reading and reading remediation. These entries will provide the reader with the most up-to-date information on a topic that is being urgently stressed all over the United States at this time. His expertise is very evident in these entries.

Rachel Toplis spent many hours updating information on organizations and journals so the readers will be able to get current information that they can apply immediately. She also wrote to all of the biographees and asked what they had been up to for the past few years. It was nice to have contact with them again.

Ron Zellner and Cynthia Riccio were Contributing Editors hailing from Texas A&M University who provided us with current information on technology, assistive, devices, and current trends in special education guidelines. Contributing Editor Sam Goldstein brought us up to date on the latest imaging devices that are assisting in the investigation of autism spectrum disorders, reading interventions, and learning in general. In addition, James Kaufman had a very creative time refreshing entries on theories of creativity and intelligence; the reader will enjoy his unique perspectives on these topics. Last but not least, the Drs. Ron Dumont and John Willis provided a completely new thread of reviews of standardized assessments throughout the *Encyclopedia*; their expertise in assessment reviews are legendary and we are please to have them as part of our effort.

Please allow us to apologize to our authors if their affiliations or names have changed over the past 20 years and the most recent changes are not incorporated into the third edition. We have tried to keep up with the changes but are sure that we have missed a few and promise to remediate in future editions! We also had to make editorial decisions about giving credit where credit was due for updates of entries. Therefore, the reader will notice that we have taken painstaking efforts to list the authors and to which editions they contributed. In some cases, an entry needed some tiny editing and in that case, Cecil and Elaine took tiny liberties and corrected dates or added a current reference here and there. We, again, apologize if our tiny contributions were bigger than the author would wish. In most of these cases, the article was so well written it would have been a waste of time to try to rewrite.

There are, as usual, many individuals to thank for assisting with the creating and preparation of this volume of work. First, let us thank the contributing editors to the previous and current editions. These individuals took on the responsibilities of looking at where the field has been and where it is going in their respective areas of expertise. They then shepherded many authors into taking on smaller parts to reflect important aspects of the basics and documenting growth. Without their commitment and dedication, we would be bereft of hope for a renovation of this size of work! We would also like to thank the individual authors for their cheerful attitude and dedication to their contributions: They are representatives of the best the field has to offer and we are very grateful for their efforts.

Cecil would like to thank Julia, as he does so untiringly, for her support in so many ways, and his long-deceased Dad, who gave him the gift of a model of service. Elaine would like to take this opportunity to thank David, Emma, and Leif for putting up with her being obsessed one more time; and her father, Peter C. Fletcher, who has modeled insatiable curiosity and a love of life's work that will stay with her always.

Lastly, we would like to thank the editors at John Wiley & Sons, Inc., Tracey Belmont and Lisa Gebo for their supervision of the work, and publisher Peggy Alexander for making a lifetime commitment to this endeavor. What started as a description of the field of special education became a history of special education and a chronicle of its life and times. We have been honored to witness this process and, as always, look forward to future growth.

P

PAKISTAN, SPECIAL EDUCATION IN

Special education was established formally in 1972. Nine years later, in 1981, the federal government promulgated an ordinance, Disabled Persons (Employment and Rehabilitation) Ordinance, 1981. In 1985, the office of the Directorate General of Special Education was established as a division of the Department of the Ministry of Women's Development, Social Welfare, and Special Education. Innumerable governmental and nongovernmental organizations currently are providing special education services.

Pakistan is comprised of four provinces: Punjab, Sindh, North West Frontier Province, and Balochistan. Punjab has a population of 73,621,290, among whom 1,826,623 (2.4 percent) have disabilities. Among Sindh's population of 30,439,893, 929,400 (3 percent) have disabilities. Among the North West Frontier Province's population of 17,735,912, 375,448 (2.1 percent) have disabilities. Among Balochistan's population of 6,565,885, 146,421 (2.2 percent) have disabilities.

Thus, the total populations of persons with disabilities is 3,293,155, among whom 265,398 are visually impaired, 243,683 are hearing impaired, 625,785 are physically impaired, 210,854 are mentally handicapped (i.e., those who are totally dependent on others), 250,184 are mentally impaired (i.e., those who display greater independence), 270,451 have multiple disabilities, and 1,426,800 have other disabilities (e.g., autism, Down syndrome, and ADHD)

Among the total population of persons with disabilities living in urban (or rural) areas, 10.7 percent (and 12.2 percent) are between ages 0 and 4, 14 percent (and 15.3 percent) between 5 and 9, 10.7 percent (and 9.7 percent) between 10 and 14, 9.5 percent (and 7.8 percent) between 15 and 19, 8.4 percent (and 5.7 percent) between 20 and 24, 7 percent (and 5.7 percent) between 25 and 29, 6.2 percent (and 4.7 percent) between 30 and 34, 5.1 percent (and 3.7 percent) between 35 and 39, and 4.9 percent (and 3.9 percent) between 40 and 44 years

REFERENCES

Department of Special Education, University of the Punjab Lahore: www.pu.edu.pk

Education statistics, Ministry of Education Government of Pakistan: www.moe.gov.pk

Ministry of Women Development, Social Welfare and Special Education. (2002). *Handbook.* 2002 Statistics Division, Ministry of Economic Affairs and Statistics, Government of Pakistan. Retrieved from http://www.statpak.gov.pk

SHAHID WAHEED QAMAR
Lahore, Pakistan

PALESTINIAN CHILDREN AND YOUTH IN THE GAZA STRIP, SPECIAL EDUCATION AND

Historical Context of the Gaza Strip

The Gaza Strip, a rectangular shaped parcel of land, hugs the southeastern corner of the Mediterranean Sea. It is approximately 25 miles long and 5 miles wide at its widest location. The landmass of Israel is approximately 8,000 square miles. The Occupied Territories comprise 2,400 square miles, of which the Gaza Strip comprises 136 square miles, or less than 1.3 percent of Israel and the Occupied Territories combined (Marsden, 1995). Its modern neighbors are Israel to the north and east and Egypt to the south. During the last 2,000 years Palestine and its people have been ruled by a succession of foreign powers: chronologically, the Romans, Turks, Byzantines, Crusaders, Turks, Ottomans, British, Egyptians, and most recently, Israelis. The Gaza Strip, Israel, the West Bank, and Jordan are modern-day remnants of the historic state of Palestine.

The British rule, starting in 1918 under a League of Nations mandate, ended when the 1948 War lead to the creation of the state of Israel. This war forced thousands of Palestinians living in what is now Israel to flee north into Lebanon, east into Jordan, or south into Gaza. Their intent was to remain in these sanctuaries for a brief period of time (e.g., a week or two) and then return to their homes and land. Their fate was different. They were not allowed to return and instead became permanent refugees. Those who fled to Gaza were made to settle largely in eight camps. Refugees now constitute approximately 75 percent of the Palestinian population in the Gaza Strip.

The Gaza Strip and the West Bank emerged as residual territories separate from Israel. From 1948 to 1967 the Gaza Strip was held in trust by Egypt—a condition viewed internationally as having a provisional character pending a political settlement in the area. Egyptian educational methods were implemented into the Gaza Strip.

In 1950, the United Nations created the United Nations Relief and Works Agency for Palestinian Refugees in the New East (UNRAW) to provide humanitarian assistance and social services together with educational services to displaced Palestinian refugees (Roberts, Joergensen, & Newman, 1984). Its regional headquarters is in Amman, Jordan

In 1967, during the Six Day War, Israel advanced into and remained in the Gaza Strip. Israel destroyed more than 400 villages in the Occupied Territories to open the way for Jewish settlements, further increasing the refugee population. Israel interpreted this victory as justification to formally annex the Occupied Territories and reestablish a "Greater Israel" that closely followed Old Testament biblical boundaries. In contrast, the international community interpreted the role of Israel in these territories to be that of an occupying power, with all associated rights and duties (Roberts et al., 1984). In 1994, Israeli military occupation subsided, Yasser Arafat returned to the Gaza Strip and West Bank, and the Palestinian Authority began to establish governments and to rule. Political infighting and resulting political instability have occurred following Arafat's death.

The Social and Political Context for Education in the Gaza Strip

The population within the Gaza Strip is estimated to be approximately 1.2 million and growing. Gaza has one of the highest birthrates in the world, approximately 5 percent annually. Half of its population is under 15 (Human Resources and Social Policy, 1993). Overpopulation was exacerbated further by the return of expatriates.

Israel, as the occupying force in this region, feared educational activities could strengthen Palestinian nationalism and efforts to unify and thus posed a threat to its security. The first Intifada (i.e., uprising) served to strengthen these fears. Thus, Israel exerted control over education. It closed two universities in Gaza, banned the use of most textbooks (e.g., those with three of the four colors within the Palestinian flag) and censored others, banned the use of maps that made reference to Palestine (preferring to use the Biblical names of Judea and Samaria), closed schools frequently (e.g., thirty-six closures between September 1988 and January 1989) and often for months, prohibited schools from issuing educational materials parents could use at home during school closures, used roadblocks to monitor and disrupt the passage of children to school, detained students for alleged infractions without charge, arrested students prior to and released them after the final examinations (resulting in widespread cheating on final exams), restricted groups to no more than two when under curfew (conditions

that often extended for weeks), tear-gassed schools, making them inaccessible for weeks, stormed schools and damaged property, and beat students and teachers.

On occasion, these and other conditions elicited stone throwing by students on their way to school and disruptive behavior once in school. Conditions outside of the classroom, including students' physical survival, became more important than learning the three Rs. Military officials bulldozed all cinderblock fences surrounding schools because students used them as barriers between them and the military.

Education in the Gaza Strip

From 1967 until 2004, schools were subject to control by Israeli military authorities. Public schools have a 6-days-a-week, 9-months-a-year schedule, with no school on Friday, the Muslim Sabbath. Public preschool education and special education services for children with handicapping conditions were unavailable (see Abu Ghazaleh, Abu Ghazaleh, & Oakland, [1990] for a discussion of services provided to mentally disabled infants, children, and youth in the Gaza Strip. Also see Oakland [1997] for a discussion of efforts to address the needs of young children with mental retardation). Students enter school at age six. Nine years of schooling are compulsory. Students who elect to attend secondary school enter at age 15 and, until recently, had to pass the Egyptian-administered tawjihi exit examination to receive high school credit. An Egyptian curriculum was used throughout this region.

Two main educational systems prevail: local, government-administered schools, comprising 31 percent of the students, and U.N. Relief and Works Agency-administered schools for children from refugee families, comprising approximately 62 percent. Classrooms are overcrowded. The average class size is 40; some have 60 students. Classes typically are offered in double shifts, the first from 7 AM to 11 AM and the next from 11 AM to 3 PM. Gender segregation is longstanding (e.g., due to both religious conservatism and colonial heritage) and widely practiced within the 22 Arab countries, including Gaza. Fewer than 10 percent attend one of four private schools. They have a low teacher: pupil ratio (i.e., about 1:16) and employ the best-prepared teachers.

Local Government-Administered Schools

Educational facilities generally are lacking and substandard. No new schools were built during 1967 and 1977. The few that have been constructed have not kept pace with the region's burgeoning population of children. Few government-supported schools have libraries or science laboratories.

Teachers' educational backgrounds also generally are substandard. Teachers are not required to have teacher training. Most have a 2-year diploma from a community or teacher's college. Their salaries are low, generally less than $100 per month. The lack of adequate standards for becoming a teacher and their low salaries contribute to low prestige and associated lack of respect by students and their families. Most teachers are female. Males are most likely to teach math and science at the secondary level.

Until somewhat recently, families were required to pay for tuition and books. Many families were unable to pay these fees, given their severe economic problems. Unemployment rates for men typically exceed 40 percent. Women rarely work outside of their homes and thus do not contribute directly to the family's economic resources. In addition, in reference to girls, poor families must decide whether to use their limited resources for their education or for establishing a dowry. Marriage and preparation for it generally are thought to be more important than education for their future.

United Nations Relief and Works Agency-Administered Schools

The U.N. Relief and Works Agency is the largest provider of education in the Gaza Strip. Its 159 schools and support facilities generally are substandard. For example, there are more classes than classrooms. About one quarter of high schools have a science laboratory. The ability of this agency to educate refugee students has been attenuated by the large increase in children among Palestine refugee families, a 33 percent increase between 1987 and 1994. Its elementary schools have both mixed and gender-segregated classrooms. All secondary schools are segregated by gender.

Various differences existed between local government-administered and U.N. Relief and Works Agency-administered schools. The U.N. Relief and Works Agency controlled its own finances, administration, employment, and teacher preparation. Parents were not charged for tuition or books. Teachers and administrators came from refugee families. U.N. Relief and Works Agency teachers are paid about twice as much as their colleagues working in locally administered schools.

Education After the Intifada

The Declaration of Principles on Interim Self-Government Arrangements was signed by the Israeli and Palestinian Liberation Organization in Washington, DC, on September 13, 1993, establishing a pathway for Palestinian self-rule. Eight months later the Agreement on the Gaza Strip and Jericho Area (i.e., the Cairo Agreement) was signed. Israel withdrew its troops from the Occupied Territories in May 1994, allowing Palestinians to assume some degree of self-rule following 27 years of Israeli occupation.

The Palestinian Ministry of Education and Higher Education was established in September 1994. This Ministry, along with the Department of General and High Education, are working with the U.N. Relief and Works Agency and the local education authorities to increase the number of schools, improve teacher quality (e.g., 12,000 teachers received in-service continuing education), and in other ways improve educational services. A locally developed curriculum, together with new textbooks, has replaced those from Egypt.

Special education services generally are unavailable in schools. Moreover, many families are reluctant to identify their children as displaying special education needs, in part due to a lack of services for them. The U.S. Agency for International Development-sponsored Sun Day Care Center, established in 1982, developed an elaborate and effective infrastructure for the provision of services to children with mental retardation and their families. Services to children with hearing and language disorders also were provided. The Sun Day Care Center closed in 1996, shortly after the institution of the new Arafat government.

Educational leaders face significant challenges due to financial and personnel shortages, continued Israeli military incursions, and lack of political stability and respect for government. The need for social and psychological changes among students may be more subtle yet no less real.

During the Intifada, teachers often were seen as being distant from and enemies of students. Teachers often feared student's undisciplined nature. The change from surviving in a society daily impacted by harsh military occupation to one that allows greater self-rule requires the need to make fundamental social and attitudinal changes. For example, principles of self-authority and self-discipline need to replace principles of self-protection and belligerence. Students must move from life under forms of anarchy to one of self-control and respect for education. The continued restrictions on movement of persons beyond the Gaza Strip by the Israelis serve to reinforce in Palestinians the long-held reality that education is less important than efforts that help ensure more basic needs are met.

REFERENCES

Abu Ghazaleh, H. A., Abu Ghazaleh, K. A., & Oakland, T. (1990). Primary and secondary prevention services provided to mentally handicapped infants, children, and youth in the Gaza Strip. *International Journal of Special Education, 5*(1), 21–28.

Gumpel, T., & Awartani, S. (2003). A comparison of special education in Israel and Palestine: Surface and deep structures. *Journal of Special Education, 37,* 33–48.

Human Resources and Social Policy. (1993). *Developing the Occupied Territories: An investment in peace* (Vol. 6). Washington, DC: Author.

Marsden, H. (Ed). (1995). *Whitaker's almanac.* London, England: J. Whitaker and Sons.

Oakland, C., (1995). *Primary-and secondary-school education in the Gaza Strip during the Israeli Occupation: 1967–1994.* Master's thesis, Department of Social Anthropology, Cambridge University.

Oakland, T. (1997). A multi-year home based program to promote development on young Palestinian children who exhibit developmental delays. *School Psychology International. 18,* 29–39.

Roberts, A., Joergensen, B., & Newman, F. (1984). *Academic freedom under Israeli military occupation: Report of WUS / ICJ Mission of Inquiry into higher education in the West Bank and Gaza.* London, England and Geneva, Switzerland: World University Service (UK) and International Commission of Jurists.

CHRISTOPHER OAKLAND
New York City, New York

PALMAR CREASE

Human palms are covered by creases of different depths, lengths, and directions. The flexion creases are formed during early intrauterine life and are thought to be influenced by factors causing anomalies in the embryo. Variations in appearance of the palmar creases have been linked to certain medical disorders. Therefore, alterations have medical diagnostic value and usually are included in dermatoglyphic analysis. The three main creases have been the primary focus of most investigations. They are the radial longitudinal or thenar crease, the proximal transverse, and the distal transverse. Alter (1970) measured differences in the space between palmar creases, noted abnormalities, and described variations in a normal population.

A single crease across the palm of the hand frequently is described as characteristic of Down syndrome (Robinson & Robinson, 1965; Telford & Sawery, 1977). The proximal and distal transverse creases are replaced or joined into a single crease that transverses the entire palm. This has been referred to as a single palmar crease, single transverse fold, four finger line, or simian crease. The term simian crease, although frequently used, is not appropriate. The frequency of the single palmar crease ranges between 1 and 15 percent in controlled populations and possibly higher in groups with developmental defects (Schaumann & Alter, 1976). Researchers noted that the variability in appearance makes determination difficult and may partially account for the wide range in reported frequency.

REFERENCES

Alter, M. (1970). Variation in palmar creases. *American Journal of Diseases of Children, 20,* 424.

Robinson, H. B., & Robinson, N. M. (1965). *The mentally retarded child: A psychological approach.* New York: McGraw-Hill.

Schaumann, B., & Alter, M. (1976). *Dermatoglyphics in medical disorders.* Heidelberg, Germany: Springer-Verlag.

Telford, C. W., & Sawery, J. M. (1977). *The exceptional individual.* Englewood Cliffs, NJ: Prentice Hall.

SALLY E. PISARCHICK
*Cuyahoga Special Education
Service Center*

DOWN SYNDROME PHYSICAL ANOMALIES

PANDAS

See PEDIATRIC AUTOIMMUNE NEUROPSYCHIATRIC DISORDERS ASSOCIATED WITH STREPTOCOCCUS INFECTIONS.

PARAPLEGIA

Paraplegia is a term used to describe a physical condition in which the individual is unable to functionally use the lower extremities of the body. The term describes the topography of the impairment and does not suggest the etiology of the physical limitations, which may be of varied origin (Best, 1978).

Paraplegia results from many disorders that interfere with the brain or spinal cord's ability to transmit stimuli to the motor effectors (muscles) of the legs, or from the inability of the larger muscles of the legs themselves to act in a functional manner. It may result from cerebral palsy, which is a nonprogressive disorder of the central nervous system where the brain is involved, or from orthopedic disorders that involve the musculoskeletal system such as muscular dystrophy. In the former condition, the neurological input to the muscles may be impeded at the level of the brain. The latter involves an asymmetrical deterioration of muscle fibers, depriving the legs of the necessary activity for gross muscular action. Conditions such as spina bifida, in which there is often a physical interruption in the continuity of the spinal cord, may also cause impairment of the body's function below the level of the lesion (injury). The origin of the paraplegia can be congenital (either the disorder or predisposition is present from birth) or adventitiously (accidentally) acquired. The former may include genetically transmitted disorders such as Werdnig-Hofmann disease, where the anterior horn cells (those cells of the spinal cord having motor function) deteriorate and lose function early in the child's development, or traumatic injury, which can occur at anytime in life.

While the disease underlying the paraplegia often suggests additional concerns for management, many of these diseases are more of a concern for medical intervention than for educational. Educational management and teaching, however, must take into consideration the limitations imposed on the individual with paraplegia, as well as safety and health considerations. When paraplegia results from neurological impairment, sensory deficits to the lower segments of the body may also be sustained as well as functional deficits (Capildeo & Maxwell, 1984). These deficits, which may include bowel and bladder incontinence (Staas & La Mantina, 1984a), also require assistance from both a psychological and hygienic perspective. The paraplegic who manifests sensory deficits and maintains a sitting posture for most of the day should avoid remaining in one position in school, at home, or in other settings for a prolonged period of time. Since sensitivity to pain may be impaired, prolonged placement in one position may increase skin irritation that goes unrecognized by the individual until sores or descubiti develop (Kosiak, 1982; Kottke et al., 1982).

In the nonsensorily impaired individual, discomfort usually accompanying skin erosion allows for the independent shift in positioning that facilitates, avoiding injury. If the primary means of movement is accomplished by use of a wheelchair, a firm seat or wheelchair insert providing a firm seat and lateral support should be used. Reliance on the webbed or sling seat often found in portable folding chairs does not allow for adequate uniform support. The paraplegic may begin to favor one side of the supportive webbed seat, asymmetrically tipping the body. To regain a vertical perspective to the environment, compensation of the spine in the opposite direction is likely to be forced, resulting in a scoliosis (lateral curvature of the spine) over time. Aside from orthopedic implications, infringement on the diaphragm may reduce vital capacities by reducing pulmonary (lung) function. This can result in shallow, rapid cycles of breathing that increase tendencies toward respiratory problems. These shallow, rapid cycles further impede reducing body noise, making localization of low-amplitude sounds more difficult and interfering with the controlled expiration necessary to speech production.

Management must also include an understanding of the nutritional needs of the individual with paraplegia. Since activities may be circumscribed, caloric intake for the active nonparaplegic is not an accurate gauge for determining diet. Such a diet would provide excess nutritive support resulting in weight gain. Diet should, therefore, be provided on an individual basis, taking into consideration the specific activity level of the individual.

The environmental experience, as regarded as part of the educational process, will be impaired if provision for available alternatives to independent ambulation are not provided. The younger child with paraplegia who is deprived of free exploration of the environment may be impeded in concept development (Connor et al., 1978). For the toddler, a device such as a scooter board or crawl-a-gator may assist in active environmental exploration. This device consists of a board on which casters are mounted. The child lies prone on the device and propels himself or herself around the floor by pushing the ground with the upper extremities. The older child may begin to use a wheelchair or a parapodium. The latter device allows the child and preadolescent with paraplegia to ambulate in an upright position to more freely explore and learn. Training in donning (putting on) and duffing (removing) the parapodium is essential to increasing the independent functioning of the individual. With developed upper extremities, the parapodium can also be used to climb stairs.

Within the classroom, a standing table may be used to support the child in an upright position, freeing the upper extremities for manual exploration of learning materials, and concomitantly avoiding static positioning. This table is ideal for use in the classroom where academics may require writing and other skills requiring hand use and lower body support. Thus for the special educator to accommodate the needs for education and management of the individual with paraplegia, a comprehensive understanding of methods and materials necessary to circumvent the functional impairedness becomes essential. This management includes positioning, locomotion, and the ability to attend in a learning situation, free from the distraction imposed by the disability. This also must occur on a case-by-case method to be successful (Mulcahey, 1992), and prevent further health complications (Herrick, Elliot & Crow, 1994).

REFERENCES

Best, G. A. (1978). *Individuals with physical disabilities: An introduction for educators.* St. Louis, MO: Mosby.

Capildeo, R., & Maxwell, A. (Eds.). (1984). *Progress in rehabilitation: Paraplegia.* London: Macmillan.

Connor, F. P., Williamson, G. G., & Siepp, J. M. (1978). *Program guide for infants and toddlers with neuromotor and other developmental disabilities.* New York: Teacher's College Press.

Herrick, S. M., Elliott, T. R., & Crow, F. (1994). Social support and the prediction of health complications among persons with spinal cord injuries. *Rehabilitation Psychology, 39*(4), 231–250.

Kosiak, M. (1982). Prevention and rehabilitation of ischemic ulcers. In F. J. Kottke, G. K. Stillwell, & J. F. Lehman (Eds.), *Krusen's handbook of physical medicine and rehabilitation.* Philadelphia: Saunders.

Kottke, F. J., Stillwell, G. K., & Lehman, J. F. (Eds.). (1982). *Krusen's handbook of physical medicine and rehabilitation.* Philadelphia: Saunders.

Mulcahey, M. J. (1992). Returning to school after a spinal cord injury: Perspectives from four adolescents. *American Journal of Occupational Therapy, 46*(4), 305–312.

Rushkin, A. P. (Ed.). (1984). *Current therapy in physiatry.* Philadelphia: Saunders.

Staas, W. E., & La Mantina, J. (1984a). The neurogenic bladder: Physiologic mechanisms and clinical problems of bladder control. In A. P. Ruskin (Ed.), *Current therapy in physiatry* (pp. 396–410). Philadelphia: Saunders.

Staas, W. E., & La Mantina, J. (1984b). Descubitus ulcers. In A P. Ruskin (Ed.), *Current therapy in physiatry* (pp. 410–419). Philadelphia: Saunders.

ELLIS I. BAROWSKY
Hunter College, City University of New York

CEREBRAL PALSY
MUSCULAR DYSTROPHY
SPINA BIFIDA

PARAPROFESSIONALS

Various descriptors have been used to identify the paraprofessional in special education. MacMillan (1973) has identified as potential paraprofessionals, nonprofessional adults, older children in the role of tutor, and parents. Tucker and Horner (1977) identify a paraprofessional as any person other than the teacher who is engaged in providing educational opportunities for children with disabilities. While not considered a fully trained professional, the paraprofessional is one who is expected to possess certain competencies that will promote a higher quality and more effective educational program for individuals with disabilities.

Interest in the use of paraprofessionals in special education programs has largely been based on three issues: relieving the special education teacher from nonprofessional duties; increasing the quality of the instructional program; and meeting the needs of a burgeoning number of special education programs.

The use of paraprofessionals in the special education classroom was first reported in the 1950s (Cruickshank & Haring, 1957). The conclusions drawn from this investigation were that the teachers who had paraprofessionals assigned to their classrooms felt that they were able to do a better job of teaching. The administrators of these programs concurred with this opinion, as did the parents of the children, who felt their children had profited from the presence of a paraprofessional in the classroom. In the 1960s, as a result of professional and legislative efforts, there emerged an increased interest in the establishment of a number and variety of educational services for students with disabilities. As a result of this, there was an immediate critical shortage of professional personnel to meet the rapid expansion of special education programs (President's Panel on Mental Retardation, 1962). The paraprofessional was viewed as a potential solution to this problem (Blessing, 1967).

In the ensuing years, the concept of paraprofessionals as an answer to manpower problems and improved quality of classroom instruction gained considerable acceptance. Roos (1970) recognized the need for less sophisticated trained personnel as an answer to the shortage of trained special educators. MacMillan (1973) also felt that the use of paraprofessionals in special education programs was an appropriate means for closing the manpower gap. In addition, various authors (Hanson, 1969; Karnes, Teska, & Hodgins, 1970) concluded that the instructional program in the special classroom was enhanced by the presence of paraprofessionals. Karnes and Teska (1975) determined that the use of paraprofessionals was not only effective, but that in some instances, paraprofessionals were as capable as professional teachers in carrying out instructional programs. The available evidence supported the concept that paraprofessionals can and do serve a meaningful and significant role in special education programs. However, there emerged a further concern relative to the type of training that is necessary to produce effective paraprofessionals, and their role in the classroom remains an issue for discussion.

Competency to function as an effective paraprofessional is, in many ways, directly related to the perceived role of the paraprofessional in the program. Competencies have been identified at various levels of sophistication. Tucker and Horner (1977) feel that training should be directly related to skills that would assist the paraprofessional in changing student behavior. They feel that this should include training in areas such as curriculum, task analysis, and even parent counseling. Greer and Simpson (1977) take a somewhat more generic approach by defining the paraprofessional as a tutor. In training for this role, they enumerate a number of competencies that are indigenous to a variety of teaching functions (e.g., assessment, programming, scheduling and teaching). Other authors (Fimian, Fafard, & Howell, 1984; Gartner, 1972) have been more specific in the identification of areas or topics that they feel are necessary to produce a competent paraprofessional. These topics entail many of the traditional child development and curriculum/method sequences, as well as characteristics, behavior management techniques, and routine clerical skills. In summary, the training program for paraprofessionals may vary depending on the individual's qualifications and experience as well as the perceived role of the paraprofessional in the assigned special education program.

The position of the paraprofessional in special education programs has usually been one of a subordinate. The paraprofessional is expected to carry out his or her assigned duties in tandem with the fully trained professional. The assumption is that while paraprofessionals may be a valuable addition to the overall program, the teacher must be regarded as the one ultimately responsible for the teaching function. However, paraprofessionals have been used in a variety of ways in the educational setting. Their duties have usually encompassed activities such as clerical work, supervision of nonacademic activities, housekeeping, acting as parent surrogates, and sometimes even as active teachers engaged in the instructional process under the supervision of the trained teacher (Blessing, 1967; French & Pickett, 1997; Greer & Simpson, 1977; MacMillan, 1973).

Concerns for the extension of educational programs to a population of individuals with disabilities that has been unserved in an educational setting (e.g., the severely and profoundly disabled) has created a potential new role for the less than baccalaureate trained (paraprofessional) teacher. Although Sontag, Burke, and York (1976) feel that teachers working with the severely disabled should be rigorously trained and possess a number of specific and precise competencies, Burton and Hirshoren (1979) view the use of well-trained paraprofessionals as teachers as a resolution of problems that are indigenous to this level of programming (e.g., available manpower, individualization of instruction, and teacher burnout). Tucker and Horner (1977) have acknowledged the need for well-trained paraprofessionals in programs for the severely disabled and agree that it is impractical to rely on fully trained teachers to provide the individualized instruction that is necessary in these programs.

While enjoying considerable discussion, the paraprofessional role in special education has not been clearly defined. However, the role continues to be evaluated, especially in light of inclusive practices (Doyle, 1997).

REFERENCES

Blessing, K. R. (1967). Use of teacher aides in special education: A review and possible application. *Exceptional Children, 34*, 107–113.

Burton, T. A., & Hirshoren, A. (1979). The education of the severely and profoundly retarded: Are we sacrificing the child to the concept? *Exceptional Children, 45*, 598–602.

Cruickshank, W., & Haring, N. (1957). *A demonstration: Assistants for teachers of exceptional children.* Syracuse, NY: Syracuse University Press.

Doyle, M. B. (1997). *The paraprofessional's guide to the inclusive classroom: Working as a team.* Baltimore: Brookes.

Fimian, M. J., Fafard, M., & Howell, K. W. (1984). *A teacher's guide to human resources in special education.* Boston: Allyn & Bacon.

French, N. K., & Pickett, A. L. (1997). Paraprofessionals in special education: Issues for teacher educators. *Teacher Education and Special Education, 20*(1), 61–73.

Gartner, A. (1972). The curriculum: Issues in combining theory and practice in training teacher aids. *Journal of Research & Development in Education, 5*, 57–68.

Greer, B. B., & Simpson, G. A. (1977). A demonstration model for training noncertified personnel in special education. *Education & Training of the Mentally Retarded, 12*, 266–271.

Hanson, F. M. (1969). Aides for the trainable mentally retarded. *Journal of the California Teachers Association, 65*, 23–26.

Karnes, M. B., & Teska, J. (1975). Children's response to intervention programs. In J. J. Gallagher (Ed.), *The application of child development research to exceptional children.* Reston, VA: Council for Exceptional Children.

Karnes, M. B., Teska, J. A., & Hodgins, A. S. (1970). The successful implementation of a highly specific preschool instructional program by paraprofessional teachers. *Journal of Special Education, 4*, 69–80.

MacMillan, D. L. (1973). Issues and trends in special education. *Mental Retardation, 11*, 3–8.

President's Panel on Mental Retardation. (1962). *A proposed program for national action to combat mental retardation.* Washington, DC: U.S. Government Printing Office.

Roos, P. (1970). Trends and issues in special education for the mentally retarded. *Education & Training of the Mentally Retarded, 5*, 51–61.

Sontag, E., Burke, P. J., & York, R. (1976). Considerations for serving the severely handicapped in the public schools. In R. M. Anderson & J. G. Greer (Eds.), *Educating the severely and profoundly retarded.* Baltimore: University Park Press.

Tucker, P. J., & Horner, R. D. (1977). Competency based training of paraprofessionals training associates for education of the severely and profoundly handicapped. In E. Sontag, J. Smith, & N. Certo (Eds.), *Educational programming for the severely and profoundly handicapped.* Reston, VA: Council for Exceptional Children.

THOMAS A. BURTON
University of Georgia

TEACHER BURNOUT
TEACHER EFFECTIVENESS

PARENTAL COUNSELING

Counseling parents of children with disabilities has taken a number of different forms. Variations in counseling strategies reflect diverse professional orientations as well as differing family dynamics and needs. Because new challenges often arise as the child's disability interacts with increased demands at different developmental stages, counseling is frequently a recurrent need.

Parental counselors include teachers, guidance counselors, educational evaluators, social workers, psychologists, physicians, and other parents. Counseling can range from informal and infrequent teacher/parent exchanges to long-term programs that involve all family members. Counseling approaches can be grouped into three broad categories, those providing information about the nature of the child's disability, those offering psychotherapeutic insight into the often conflicting emotions that accompany recognition of the disability, and those providing training to improve parent/child interactions and to manage the child's behavior.

Counseling aimed at educating parents about the nature of their child's disability is probably the most common. In order for parents confronted with a disabled child to make appropriate and realistic adjustments, they need various sources of accurate and pragmatic information. The information-focused counseling provided by physician, psychologist, and/or evaluator when the child's disability is first identified is clearly crucial for parents. Information-centered counseling is also provided when teachers share their insights, goals, and expectations and when parent organizations (e.g., ACLD, ARC, Closer Look) offer pamphlets, telephone hotlines, and parent support groups.

Psychotherapeutic approaches to parent counseling focus on helping parents to work through and resolve emotional stresses and conflicts often precipitated by the presence of a disabled child in the family. Such counseling can occur with parents and counselor alone, jointly with the disabled child, or with all active family members, including siblings and even caretaking grandparents. With advances in the understanding of the complex interrelations within families, the trend has been in the direction of including more family members in psychotherapeutic counseling (Foster & Berger, 1979). Sibling relationships represent one of those significant complexities that recently has spawned nationwide sibling support groups as well as greater consideration of siblings within the context of counseling (Grossman, 1972).

A third category of counseling is parent training programs. Through such programs, parents learn more effective means of communicating with their children and methods for better managing their children's problem behaviors. Parent training programs teach techniques such as active listening and problem solving (Gordon, 1975), ways to function as filial therapists (Guerney, 1969), methods for becoming behavioral change agents (McDowell, 1974). Numerous research studies demonstrate that parents can be effective in working with and modifying their children's behavior and that such parent involvement is generally positive (McDowell, 1976).

Increasingly, two theoretical notions, or frameworks, have informed many of the counseling approaches available to parents of children with disabilities: stages of grief theory and family systems theory. Regardless of the particular approach (educational, psychotherapeutic, or parent training), many of those who counsel parents have been guided by, or at least sensitized by, one or both of these frameworks. The first reflects the prevalent view that many, if not all, parents of handicapped children undergo some version of a mourning process in reaction to their child's disability. To varying degrees, this represents a loss of the hoped for intact, healthy child. Variations on Kubler-Ross's (1969) stages of grief theory have been proposed to explain parents' emotional journey toward productive adjustment to their child's handicapping condition (Seligman, 1979). These mourning stages include denial of the existence, the degree, or the implications of the disability; bargaining, often evident in the pursuit of magical cures or highly questionable treatments; anger, often projected outward onto the spouse or the helping professional or projected inward, causing feelings of guilt and shame; depression, manifest in withdrawal and expressions of helplessness and inadequacy; and acceptance, the stage in which productive actions can be taken and positive family balances maintained. It is commonly believed that any of the earlier stages can be reactivated by crises or in response to the child's or the family's transitions from one developmental stage to another.

Family systems theory, particularly Minuchin's structural analysis (Minuchin, Rosman, & Baker, 1978) and Haley's (1973, 1976, 1980) strategic approach provides another highly valued conceptual framework for counseling. Within this framework, families are seen as interdependent systems whose problems are relational. This view offers concepts and techniques for considering the effects on all parts of the family of intervention with one member or with one subsystem. By focusing on the dynamics of a family's structure, hierarchy, and stage in the family life cycle, family systems theory offers a more complex, and therefore more accurate, understanding of the functioning, development, and needs of a particular family with a disabled child (Foster, Berger, & McLean, 1981).

Both family systems theory and stages of grief theory are widely applicable conceptual influences within family counseling. Neither of these frameworks mitigates against using any of a wide variety of other educational, psychotherapeutic, or parent training methods to promote growth in families with children with disabilities.

REFERENCES

Foster, M., & Berger, M. (1979). Structural family therapy: Applications in programs for preschool handicapped children. *Journal of the Division for Early Childhood, 1,* 52–58.

Foster, M., Berger, M., & McLean, M. (1981). Rethinking a good idea: A reassessment of parent involvement. *Topics in Early Childhood Special Education, 1*(3), 55–65.

Gordon, T. (1975). *Parent effectiveness training.* New York: Plume.

Grossman, P. (1972). *Brothers and sisters of retarded children.* Syracuse, NY: Syracuse University Press.

Guerney, B. G. (1969). Filial therapy: Description and rationale. *Journal of Consulting Psychology, 28,* 304–310.

Haley, J. (1973). *Uncommon therapy.* New York: Norton.

Haley, J. (1976). *Problem-solving therapy.* San Francisco: Jossey-Bass.

Haley, J. (1980). *Leaving home.* New York: McGraw-Hill.

Kubler-Ross, E. (1969). *On death and dying.* New York: Macmillan.

McDowell, R. L. (1974). *Managing behavior: A program for parent involvement.* Torrance, CA: Winch.

McDowell, R. L. (1976). Parent counseling: The state of the art. *Journal of Learning Disabilities, 9*(10), 48–53.

Minuchin, S., Rosman, B., & Baker, L. (1978). *Psychosomatic families.* Cambridge, MA: Harvard University Press.

Seligman, M. (1979). *Strategies for helping parents of exceptional children.* New York: Free Press.

KATHERINE GARNETT
*Hunter College, City University
of New York*

FAMILY COUNSELING
PSYCHOTHERAPY WITH INDIVIDUALS WITH DISABILITIES

PARENT EDUCATION

A child's first and lasting teacher is his or her parents. Parents help prepare the next generation to function effectively in our increasingly global and interdependent society by rearing, nurturing, and shaping their children's attitudes, beliefs, and confidence (Smith, Perou, & Lesesne, 2002). Parents often are not prepared for their demanding and time-consuming roles. Parents have little formal training or education in how to raise children. Thus, based on parents' limited training, parent education experts have sought to develop parent education programs to help parents and other adults rear children (Hamner & Turner, 2001).

Parent education programs provide information and empower parents to fulfill their responsibilities more effectively (Smith et al., 2002). They provide parents knowledge, guidance, and understanding about their children and ways to respond to them in a positive, nurturing, and proactive manner (First & Way, 1995). Parent education programs help increase parents' confidence that they are performing their job successfully. Parent education programs may be most valuable in assisting parents who are at risk of harming or damaging their child's healthy development (Keller & McDade, 2000). Helping parents raise their children more effectively can produce positive outcomes for the child and parent and promote the general welfare of our society.

Parent education programs have been promoted through various books, manuals, and seminars (Campbell & Palm, 2004; First & Way, 1995; Smith et al., 2002). Program content differs in its theory and principles (First & Way, 1995; Smith et al., 2002). Programs often are rooted in reflective listening, Adlerian, and/or behavioral methods (Hamner & Turner, 2001; Smith et al., 2002). Reflective listening utilizes receptive and expressive communication skills. Specifically, parents increase their ability to accept and understand their child's perspective of problems or circumstances without assigning blame. The expressive language aspects of parent training involve expressing personal responsibility for a contentious issue or problem. Parents utilize "I" messages to convey feelings and to describe the child's behavior and its effects on the parent (Hamner & Turner, 2001; Smith et al., 2002). Additionally, this method seeks to explore alternative conflict resolution approaches (Hamner & Turner, 2001; Smith et al., 2002).

Adlerian methods advocate developing families in which individuals take responsibility for their behaviors, promoting self-confidence and courage in their children, establishing active communication channels, and promoting a democratic family unit (Hamner & Turner, 2001).

Behavioral methods typically are used in families with children who display behavioral problems (Thompson, Grow, Ruma, Daly, & Burke, 1993). The goal is to help parents reduce or remove undesirable behavior patterns in their children and to replace these patterns with desirable behaviors (Smith et al., 2002). For example, methods attempt to reduce or remove a child's negative behavioral patterns by better managing the child's environment and thus changing his or her behavior that exacerbates and maintains the conduct (Cheng Gorman, & Balter, 1997).

Research has not demonstrated the superiority of one method. Nevertheless, the belief that participation in a program may be effective in promoting change is somewhat widely held (First & Way, 1995). Parent training programs may be somewhat effective with middle and low income parents who have children with developmental, learning, and behavioral programs (Thompson et al., 1993). However, most parent education programs have been unsuccessful in producing measurable and longlasting effects with families from diverse ethnic, cultural, and socioeconomic backgrounds. The ineffectiveness of parent education programs may be attributed to professionals and parent experts having insufficient knowledge or experience dealing with ethnically and culturally diverse families (McDermott, 2001). Empirically based research projects demonstrate a weak support for the efficacy of culturally sensitive parent education programs (Cheng Gorman & Balter, 1997). Thus, professionals may remain unaware of how culture may impact parenting behaviors (Smith et al., 2002).

REFERENCES

Campbell, D., & Palm, G. F. (2004). *Group parent education: Promoting parent learning and support.* Thousand Oaks, CA: Sage.

Cheng Gorman, J., & Balter, L. (1997). Culturally sensitive parent education: A critical review of quantitative research. *Review of Educational Research, 67,* 339–369.

First, J. A., & Way, W. L. (1995). Parent education outcomes: Insights into transformative learning. *Family Relations, 44,* 104–109.

Hamner, T. J., & Turner, P. H. (2001). *Parenting in contemporary society* (4th ed.). Needham Heights, MA: Allyn-Bacon.

Keller, J., & McDade, K. (2000). Attitudes of low-income parents toward seeking help with parenting: Implications for practice. *Child Welfare League of America, 29,* 285–312.

McDermott, D. (2001). Parenting and ethnicity. In M. J. Fine & S. W. Lee (Eds.), *Handbook of diversity in parent education* (pp. 315–336). San Diego, CA: Academic Press.

Smith, C., Perou, R., & Lesesne, C. (2002). Parent education. In M. H. Bornstein (Ed.), *Handbook of parenting: Vol. 2. Biology and ecology of parenting* (2nd ed., pp. 389–410). Mahwah, NJ: Erlbaum.

Thompson, W. R., Grow, C. R., Ruma, P. R., Daly, D. L., & Burke, R. V. (1993). Parent education: Evaluation of a practical parenting program with middle- and low-income families. *Family Relations, 42,* 21–25.

Tiffany D. Sanders
University of Florida

FAMILY COUNSELING
PARENT EDUCATION
PSYCHOTHERAPY WITH INDIVIDUALS WITH
  DISABILITIES

PARENTING SKILLS

Parenting can provide some of the most stimulating, gratifying, and rewarding life experiences. Parenting is not an innate ability. Parenting involves a set of skills and attitudes that must be developed and practiced to achieve a level of proficiency. The development of effective parenting skills can be challenging without the presence of good models and guidance from family, friends, and parenting experts. Many parents try to expand their parenting skills by attending seminars, reading handbooks and manuals, trial and error, by talking with other parents, or obtaining information from reliable sources (Taylor, 2004). The acquisition of effective parenting skills may be more critical, complex, and prolonged when caring for a child with special needs (Taylor, 2004). Most parents plan to rear a child with no special needs and thus generally make various adjustments when rearing a child with special needs (Hamner & Turner, 2001).

Parents alter the nature of their parenting styles in order to mold and shape their child to function successfully in different environments and society. Parents adjust their parenting style based on the child's needs, temperament, and disposition, as well as different environmental circumstances. For example, compared to early childhood, when parents often are more direct, the adolescence stage of development, characterized by hormonal and puberty changes and frequent mood swings, often demands parents to function more as counselors who provide support and nurturance during difficult times. This stage also necessitates less physical guidance and setting limits, and more encouragement to become independent and self-sufficient individuals (Hamner & Turner, 2001).

Mothers and fathers with special-needs children often encounter special challenges that result in increased stress and conflicts as to how best to parent their child. Low income and minority parents of special-needs children face additional challenges and stressors. For example, they are less likely to have time to attend to the child's special needs, more difficulty accessing professional resources, and less money to purchase needed equipment. In addition, they are likely to have lower levels of educational attainment and thus have less knowledge about specialists to assist them and their special-needs child (Keller & McDade, 2000). Thus, they are likely to need more support, information, guidance, and professional advice to learn skills necessary to address their children's normal and special needs.

Parents and educators share responsibility for educating and socializing children to enable them to acquire good mental health and to contribute to society. However, the relationship between parents and educators may be contentious and riddled with animosity and distrust (Moriarty & Fine, 2001). The need for parents, educators, and parenting experts to create relationships that are collaborative and empower parents of children with exceptionalities is apparent (Lancaster, 2001). This relationship is characterized by all parties displaying care and concern for the welfare of the child (Moriarty & Fine, 2001). That is, parents and

professionals recognize that each is partner on a team, and work together to establish goals of success for the child (e.g., effective social skills). Having established achievable goals, the team would then develop a plan of action to help ensure the child is taught appropriate social skills and allowed the opportunity to practice them with peers.

The role of educators in promoting parenting skills includes serving as a role model while providing a quality education to the special-needs child, motivating and reinforcing parents' participation in their child's education process (if needed), augmenting the parents' knowledge and skills surrounding educational issues concerning their child, working collaboratively with other professionals, and informing parents of other available resources (Lancaster, 2001). Additionally, educators and parents collaborate on their child's academic and social progress, and encourage them to develop realistic expectations and goals for the child's future. Teachers are able to offer parents strategies or skills that transfers needed educational programs to the home and community (Taylor, 2004). In turn, parents can provide educators with relevant information about their child's disability, previous experiences and techniques implemented that were and were not successful in promoting academic and social success, and support school-related efforts to improve collaboration between the school and parent.

REFERENCES

Hamner, T. J., & Turner, P. H. (2001). *Parenting in contemporary society* (4th ed.). Needham Heights, MA: Allyn-Bacon.

Innocenti, M., Huh, K., & Boyce, G. (1992). Families of children with disabilities: Normative data and other considerations on parenting stress. *Topics in Early Childhood Special Education, 12,* 403–427.

Keller, J., & McDade, K. (2000). Attitudes of low-income parents toward seeking help with parenting: Implications for practice. *Child Welfare League of America, 29,* 285–312.

Lancaster, P. E. (2001). Parenting children with learning disabilities. In M. J. Fine & S. W. Lee (Eds.), *Handbook of Diversity in Parent Education* (pp. 231–252). San Diego, CA: Academic Press.

Mahoney, G., O'Sullian, P., & Robinson, C. (1992). The family environments of children with disabilities: Diverse but not so different. *Topics in Early Childhood Special Education, 12,* 386–402.

Moriarty, M. L., & Fine, M. J. (2001). Educating parents to be advocates for their children. In M. J. Fine & S. W. Lee (Eds.), *Handbook of Diversity in Parent Education* (pp. 315–336). San Diego, CA: Academic Press.

Taylor, G. R. (2004). *Parenting skills and collaborative services for students with disabilities.* Lanham, MA: Scarecrow Education.

TIFFANY D. SANDERS
University of Florida

PARKHURST, HELEN (1887–1973)

Helen Parkhurst devised the Dalton Plan and founded the Dalton School in New York City. The essence of the Dalton Plan, based on Parkhurst's concept of the school as a laboratory where students are experimenters and not just participants, was individualization of instruction through student contracts, with each student working individually at his or her own pace to carry out contracted assignments.

Early in her career, Parkhurst studied with Maria Montessori in Italy; from 1915 to 1918 she supervised the development of Montessori programs in the United States. She left the Montessori movement to put her own educational plan into practice at schools in Pittsfield and Dalton, Massachusetts. She founded the Dalton School in 1920 and served as its director until her retirement in 1942. Parkhurst lectured throughout the world and established Dalton schools in England, Japan, and China. Her book, *Education on the Dalton Plan* (1922), was published in 58 languages. After retiring from the Dalton School, Parkhurst produced radio and television programs for children and conducted a discussion program in which she gave advice on family life.

REFERENCES

Parkhurst, H. (1922). *Education on the Dalton Plan*. New York: Dutton.

Parkhurst, H. (1951). *Exploring the child's world*. New York: Appleton-Century-Crofts.

PAUL IRVINE
Katonah, New York

PARTIALLY SIGHTED

The term partially sighted was used to classify and place students in special classes whose distance visual acuity was between 20/70 and 20/200 in the better eye after correction (Hatfield, 1975). In 1977 the classifications of levels of vision adopted by the World Health Organization omitted the use of partially sighted in its system (Colenbrander, 1977). As a result, this term has virtually disappeared from the literature (Barraga, 1983).

REFERENCES

Barraga, N. C. (1983). *Visual handicaps and learning*. Austin, TX: Exceptional Resources.

Colenbrander, A. (1977). Dimensions of visual performance. *Archives of Ophthalmology, 83*, 332–337.

Hatfield, E. M. (1975). Why are they blind? *Sight Saving Review, 45*, 3–22.

ROSEANNE K. SILBERMAN
Hunter College, City University of New York

BLIND
LOW VISION
VISION TRAINING
VISUAL IMPAIRMENT

PARTIAL PARTICIPATION

The principle of partial participation entails the position that all students with severe disabilities (including the profoundly mentally retarded and the severely physically disabled) can acquire a number of skills that will enable them to function at least partially in a variety of least restrictive school and nonschool environments or activities (Baumgart et al., 1980). Because of the severity of their sensory or motor impairments as well as deficits in attentional and learning processes, some severely disabled students have difficulty in learning skills needed to function independently in current and subsequent least restrictive environments. Rather than denying access to these environments, proponents of the principle of partial participation believe adaptations can be implemented that will allow students to participate in a wide range of activities (Demchack, 1994) as well as experience inclusive programming. The latter, however, may not always be the least restrictive environment for students with severe disabilities.

Adaptations via modes of partial participation can take on a variety of dimensions in the activities of severely disabled learners (Baumgart et al., 1982; Wehman, Schleien, & Kiernan, 1980). Materials and devices can be used or created in an effort to adapt tasks (e.g., using an enlarged adaptive switch to operate kitchen appliances, using picture communication cards to communicate needs in a restaurant, using a bus pass instead of coins when a student is unable to count coins for bus fare, using frozen waffles rather than a waffle iron and batter when preparing breakfast). The sequence of steps in skills being taught can be modified (e.g., dress in a bathing suit before going to community pool if extra time is needed to manipulate clothing; sit on the toilet first, then pull pants down if unsteady on feet in the bathroom). Personal assistance can be provided for part or all of a task (e.g., peers push wheelchair to help deliver attendance records to office, teacher takes bread out of bag and places it in toaster prior to having student press lever on toaster). Rules can be changed or adapted to meet the needs of individual students (e.g., allow student to eat lunch in two lunch periods in cafeteria if he or she is a slow eater owing to physical disabilities). Societal or attitudinal as well as physical environments can be adapted (e.g., installing wheelchair ramps in public places, installing electronic doors in public buildings to make them more accessible for wheelchair users).

The classroom teacher will need to follow a number of steps to implement partial participation strategies successfully. These include: (1) taking a nondisabled person's inventory of steps/skills used in a particular task; (2) taking a severely disabled student's inventory of steps used or skills exhibited for the same task; (3) determining the skills that the student with disabilities probably can acquire; (4) determining the skills the disabled student probably cannot acquire; (5) generating an adaptation hypothesis; (6) conducting an inventory of adaptations currently available for use; (7) determining individualized adaptations to be used; and (8) determining skills that can probably be acquired using individualized adaptations (Baumgart et al., 1982).

Several considerations are recommended when using individualized adaptations for severely disabled students. These include: (1) empirically verifying the appropriateness and effectiveness of adaptations in the criterion or natural environment; (2) avoiding allowing students to become overly dependent on adaptations; and (3) carefully selecting adaptations to meet needs of individual students in critically functional environments (Baumgart et al., 1980). Appropriate applications of the principle of partial participation will enhance the access of severely disabled individuals to integrated environments available to the nondisabled population at large (Brown et al., 1979; Ferguson & Baumgart, 1991).

REFERENCES

Baumgart, D., Brown, L., Pumpian, I., Nisbet, J., Ford, A., Sweet, M., Messina, R., & Schroeder, J. (1982). Principle of partial participation and individualized adaptations in education programs for severely handicapped students. *Journal of the Association for Persons with Severe Handicaps, 7*(2), 17–27.

Baumgart, D., Brown, L., Pumpian, I., Nisbet, J., Ford, A., Sweet, M., Ranieri, L., Hansen, L., & Schroeder, J. (1980). The principle of partial participation and individualized adaptations in education programs for severely handicapped students. In L. Brown, M. Falvey, I. Pumpian, D. Baumgart, J. Nisbet, A. Ford, J. Schroeder, & R. Loomis (Eds.), *Curricular strategies for teaching severely handicapped students functional skills in school and nonschool environments* (Vol. 10). Madison: Madison Public Schools and the University of Wisconsin.

Brown, L., Branston-McClean, M. B., Baumgart, D., Vincent, L., Falvey, M., & Schroeder, J. (1979). Using the characteristics of current and subsequent least restrictive environments in the development of curricular content for severely handicapped students. *Journal of the Association for Persons with Severe Handicaps, 4*, 407–424.

Demchak, M. A. (1994). Helping individuals with severe disabilities find leisure activities. *Teaching Exceptional Children, 27*(1), 48–52.

Ferguson, D. L., & Baumgart, D. (1991). Partial participation revisited. *Journal of the Association for Persons with Severe Handicaps, 16*(4), 218–227.

Wehman, P., Schleien, S., & Kiernan, J. (1980). Age appropriate recreation programs for severely handicapped youth and adults. *Journal of the Association for Persons with Severe Handicaps, 5*, 395–407.

Cornelia Lively
University of Illinois, Urbana-Champaign

HUMANISM AND SPECIAL EDUCATION

LEAST RESTRICTIVE ENVIRONMENT

PASAMANICK, BENJAMIN (1914–1996)

Benjamin Pasamanick began his professional studies at Cornell University, where he received his BA in 1936. During this period, he began studying physiology and biochemistry, and was accepted as the sole undergraduate advisee of Nobel Laureate James Sumner. In 1937, he attended the University of Maryland School of Medicine, earning his MD in 1941. His internship psychiatry was completed at Brooklyn State Hospital and Harlem Hospital, both in New York City. Following his psychiatric residency at the New York State Psychiatric Institute in 1943, Pasamanick became an assistant at the Yale Clinic of Child Development, where he was accepted to study under Arnold Gesell.

He subsequently held numerous faculty, research, and clinical positions at medical schools and clinics throughout the northeastern United States. He was the Sir Aubrey and Lady Hilda Lewis professor of social psychiatry at the New York School of Psychiatry, professor of psychiatry at the New York University College of Medicine, and research professor of psychiatry at the State University of New York, Stony Brook. At the time of his death in 1996, he was research professor emeritus of pediatrics at Albany Medical College.

Throughout his illustrious career as a mentor, scholar, and clinician in child psychiatry, Pasamanick maintained an interest in exceptional children, particularly those with

Benjamin Pasamanick

mental retardation. He challenged conventional practices, frequently promoting change and innovation, and sought a melding of basic research in child development with the practice and promotion of a clear conceptual framework for treatment.

Pasamanick is perhaps best known for his research on the multidimensional, multifactorial influences on children's development (Kawi & Pasamanick, 1979), particularly his longitudinal studies of the development of black infants (Granich, 1970). He was the first to demonstrate that the behavioral development of black infants, as an indicator of intellectual maturity, was indistinguishable from that of white infants. He ultimately came to believe that, early in life, intelligence and related cognitive skills are primarily biologically determined but become increasingly chronologically and socially influenced with age, eventually being driven by socioeconomic factors.

Pasamanick extensively studied mental disorders and the continuum of reproductive casualty and epidemiology (Davis, Dinitz, & Pasamanick, 1974). His research in the 1950s and 1960s focused on prenatal factors involved in mental illness and treatment of mental disorders, with his work in this area finding that at least 80 percent of serious cases of mental illness were treatable at home using drug therapy. His investigation into the state of mental health in large cities, conducted on behalf of the American Public Health Association, indicated that at least one in ten of those living in American cities, while appearing normal, had mental problems.

In the 1960s and 1970s Pasamanick served as associate state commissioner for research in the Department of Mental Hygiene, and later became associate commissioner for research and evaluation in the Division of Mental Retardation and Child Development. His work substantially influenced service delivery to children with disabilities in a variety of settings.

Among his numerous contributions, he served as president of the American Orthopsychiatric Association (1970–1971), president of the American Psychopathological Association (1967), and president of the Theobald Smith Society (1984). Pasamanick was a familiar figure at professional gatherings where he presented scientific papers, and he authored or edited numerous books and articles in scholarly journals, with more than 300 publications to his credit. His service on editorial boards included *Child Development,* the *American Journal of Mental Deficiency,* the *Merrill-Palmer Quarterly,* and the *Journal of Biological Psychiatry.*

REFERENCES

Davis, A., Dinitz, S., & Pasamanick, B. (1974). *Schizophrenics in the new custodial community: Five years after the experiment.* Columbus, OH: Ohio State University.

Granich, B. (1970). Benjamin Pasamanick. *American Journal of Orthopsychiatry, 40,* 368–372.

Kawi, A., & Pasamanick, B. (1979). *Prenatal and paranatal factors in the development of childhood reading disorders.* Millwood, NY: Kraus.

CECIL R. REYNOLDS
Texas A&M University
First edition

TAMARA J. MARTIN
The University of Texas of the Permian Basin
Second edition

AMERICAN ORTHOPSYCHIATRIC ASSOCIATION

PASE v. HANNON

PASE (Parents in Action on Special Education) v. *Hannon* (Joseph P. Hannon, superintendent of the Chicago public schools at the time this case was filed) was a class-action suit on behalf of African American students who were or who might be classified as educable mentally retarded (EMR) and placed in self-contained special classes. PASE was established by a parent advocacy group assisted by the Northwestern School of Law Legal Assistance Clinic and the Legal Assistance Foundation in Chicago. The U.S. Department of Justice filed an *amicus curiae* (friend of court) brief on behalf of the plaintiffs. Defendants in the case were various officials employed by the Chicago Board of Education as well as the Board of Education of the State of Illinois. *PASE* resulted in a 3-week trial conducted by Judge Grady, who issued an opinion deciding the case on July 7, 1980.

The issues and expert witness testimony in *PASE* were virtually identical to those presented in *Larry P.* v. *Riles,* heard by Federal District Court Judge Peckham in California in a trial concluded in May 1978. The fundamental allegations were that overrepresentation of African American students in EMR special class programs constituted discrimination, and that overrepresentation was caused by the defendants' use of biased IQ tests. The plaintiffs claimed the overrepresentation from biased IQ tests violated constitutional and statutory protections, particularly the Equal Protection Clause of the Fourteenth Amendment and the nondiscrimination protections in the Education for All Handicapped Children Act of 1975 (PL 94-142) and Section 504 of the Rehabilitation Act of 1973. The plaintiffs and defendants agreed that African American students constituted about 62 percent of the total school population in Chicago, but 82 percent of the EMR population. The actual percentage of African American students classified as EMR was 3.7 percent; in contrast, 1.3 percent of Anglo American students were classified as EMR.

In a 3-week trial in 1979, the plaintiffs relied heavily on

several of the witnesses who appeared just under 2 years earlier in the *Larry P.* trial in California. In particular, the plaintiffs relied on Leon Kamin's analysis of the historical pattern of racist attitudes and beliefs among early developers of intelligence tests in the United States (Kamin, 1974). Robert Williams, a prominent African American psychologist, provided testimony concerning the differences in the cultures of Anglo American and African American students and identified a few examples of biased items. Although other witnesses appeared for the plaintiffs, the testimony of Kamin and Williams was noted prominently in Grady's decision.

Witnesses for the defendants contended overrepresentation reflected the genuine needs of African American students, who were claimed to have a higher EMR incidence owing to the effects of poverty. This emphasis on socioeconomic status as an explanation for overrepresentation was also relied on by *Larry P.* defendants, though unsuccessfully. The association of EMR with poverty has been reported for many decades throughout the western world for diverse racial and ethnic groups. The defendants also contended that any biases that might exist in IQ tests were neutralized in the placement process through the use of procedural protections such as parental informed consent, the development of a multifactored assessment that focused on educational needs, and decision making by a multidisciplinary team.

Judge Grady clearly was dissatisfied with the evidence presented by both the plaintiffs and the defendants. He noted, somewhat testily, that only cursory information on the testing question was presented in the evidence. He questioned attorneys for both sides and learned that no one relied heavily on careful analysis of each of the test items in preparing for the case. He then concluded that an analysis of each of the items on the three tests in question, the Wechsler Intelligence Scale for Children, the Wechsler Intelligence Scale for Children–Revised, and the Stanford Binet, was required for him to decide on claims of bias. Judge Grady then undertook an item-by-item analysis of the questions on the three tests.

Approximately two thirds of the space in Judge Grady's lengthy opinion was devoted to his analyses of the intelligence test items. Judge Grady provided the exact wording of the item, the correct answer, and the scoring criterion, where appropriate, for determining whether a response was awarded one or two points. This unprecedented breach of test security was initially shocking to many professionals, but no known harm or serious threat to normative standards has been reported.

Judge Grady concluded from his personal analysis of the IQ test items that only eight of several hundred items were biased. He noted that four of those eight items were not on current versions of the tests, and that those that were generally appeared at the upper limits of the test. Items that appeared at the upper limits of the test typically would not be given to students who might be considered for classifica-

tion as EMR. Grady concluded that any biases that existed on the test exerted a very small influence on classification and placement decisions, and agreed with the defendants that other safeguards, mentioned earlier, compensated for these negligible biases.

The sharply different opinions in *PASE* and *Larry P.* did not go unnoticed in the professional literature (Bersoff, 1982; Sattler 1980). The trial opinions were markedly different despite virtually identical issues and similar evidence. The reason different conclusions were reached can best be understood from an analysis of the different approaches taken by the federal court judges. Judge Grady required that a direct connection be established between biased items and misclassification of African American students as EMR. He found no such connection in Kamin's testimony about historical patterns of racism, in Robert Williams' descriptions of differences in cultural backgrounds of Anglo American and African American students, and in his own analyses of items. Grady then ruled that the absence of a clear connection between biased items and misclassification prevented the plaintiffs from prevailing. In contrast, Judge Peckham in *Larry P.* accepted allegations of item bias and concluded that the other protections in the referral, classification, and placement process were insufficient to overcome these biases. Both decisions have been criticized; *PASE* because of the method used by Judge Grady (Bersoff, 1982) and *Larry P.* because of conclusions concerning item biases that did not reflect available evidence (Reschly, 1980; Sandoval, 1979).

The plaintiffs appealed the *PASE* trial decision. However, before the appellate court ruled, the issues in the case were rendered moot by the decision of the Board of Education in Chicago to ban the use of traditional IQ tests with African American students being considered for classification and placement as EMR. This ban was part of a negotiated settlement in still another court case concerning the desegregation of the Chicago public schools. The appeal was then withdrawn by the plaintiffs. The *PASE* decision is an interesting contrast to that in *Larry P.,* but it does not have the impact of *Larry P.* for a variety of reasons.

REFERENCES

Bersoff, D. (1982). *Larry P.* and *PASE;* Judicial report cards of the validity of individual intelligence tests. In T. Kratochwill (Ed.), *Advances in school psychology* (Vol. 11, pp. 61–95). Hillsdale, NJ: Erlbaum.

Kamin, L. J. (1974). *The science and politics of IQ*. New York: Halsted.

Reschly, D. (1980). Psychological evidence in the *Larry P.* opinion: A case of right problem-wrong solution. *School Psychology Review, 9,* 123–135.

Sandoval, J. (1979). The WISC-R and internal evidence of test bias with minority groups. *Journal of Consulting & Clinical Psychology, 47,* 919–927.

Sattler, J. (1980, November). In the opinion of . . . *Monitor*, pp. 7–8.

DANIEL J. RESCHLY
Peabody College, Vanderbilt University
First and Second edition

KIMBERLY F. APPLEQUIST
University of Colorado at Colorado Springs
Third edition

DIANA v. STATE BOARD OF EDUCATION
LARRY P.
MARSHALL v. GEORGIA
NONDISCRIMINATORY ASSESSMENT

PATH ANALYSIS

Path analysis is a technique developed in the 1930s by Sewell Wright (1934) for the purpose of studying causal relationships among variables. Path analysis provides mathematical models expressing the direct and indirect effects of variables assumed to have causal status on variables assumed to be affected by the causal variables. A direct effect occurs when one variable influences another in the absence of mediation by a third variable. For example, one might assume that a particular educational intervention had a direct effect on student achievement. An indirect effect exists when a causal variable affects a dependent variable by influencing a third variable, which in turn affects the dependent variable directly. For example, teacher training might be assumed to affect teaching behavior, which would influence student achievement. Under these conditions, teacher training would have an indirect effect on student achievement. Its influence on achievement would occur through its effect on teaching behavior.

The mathematical models used to express causation in path analysis have their origins in regression analysis. The simplest path model is one involving the regression of a dependent variable on one or more variables assumed to explain variation in the dependent variable. For instance, student achievement might be regressed on an educational intervention assumed to affect achievement. Under this model, the intervention would have a direct effect on achievement. The residual term in the regression equation would also be included in the model. It is assumed to be uncorrelated with other variables in the equation. The residual would be treated as a causal variable indicating the effects of variables not explicitly included in the model on achievement. For instance, intelligence is a variable not explicitly identified in the model that might account for part of the variation in achievement. Many other variables that might affect achievement could be identified.

Models involving indirect effects require more than one regression equation. For instance, the example given involving the indirect effect of teacher training on achievement would require two regression equations. The first would include the regression of achievement on teacher training and teacher behavior; the second would include the regression of teacher behavior on teacher training. The general rule governing the number of equations is that one equation is needed for each dependent variable.

The two models discussed to this point assume unidirectional causation. For instance, in the indirect effects model, teacher behavior is assumed to affect achievement, but achievement is not assumed to affect teacher behavior. Models assuming unidirectional causation are called recursive. Ordinary least squares (OLS) regression can be used with recursive models. Nonrecursive models assuming bidirectional causation between one or more pairs of variables require procedures that go beyond OLS regression. Duncan (1975) provides an excellent discussion of nonrecursive models.

Causal relations may be expressed in path analysis not only through mathematical models, but also through path diagrams such as the one shown in the following Figure. Variables A and B in the diagram are called exogenous variables. An exogenous variable is a variable whose variation is explained by factors outside of the causal model. The curved double-headed arrow indicates that variables A and B are related and that no assumption is made regarding the direction of the relationship. Variables C and D are endogenous variables. Endogenous variables are affected by exogenous variables and/or other endogenous variables.

The Ps in the model represent path coefficients. In a recursive model, these are standardized regression weights. Each path coefficient is interpreted as that fraction of the standard deviation in the dependent variable for which the causal variable is directly responsible. For instance, P_{da} indicates that fraction of the standard deviation in variable D for which variable A is directly responsible. The standardized regres-

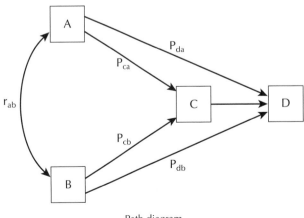

Path diagram

sion weights functioning as path coefficients in path models are no longer widely used in causal modeling. The assumption that all variables in a causal model should be placed on the same scale has been challenged. Unstandardized weights are now typically used. See Duncan (1975) for a discussion of the problems associated with standardized weights.

Path analysis may be regarded as a special case of a more general technique called structural equation modeling (Bentler, 1980; Joreskog & Sorbom, 1979). The major difference between path analysis as it was developed by Wright and structural equation models is that structural equation models may include latent as well as manifest variables. A latent variable is a variable that is not observed directly, but rather is inferred from two or more manifest indicators. For example, student achievement could be treated as a latent variable to be inferred from scores on two or more achievement tests. A structural equation model expresses the effects of one set of variables on another set of variables. The variables in the model may include both latent variables and manifest variables. For instance, a model might include the effects of sex on student achievement in mathematics. Sex would be a manifest variable in this model and mathematics achievement could be a latent variable inferred from two or more test scores. Structural equation modeling represents a powerful extension of Wright's pioneering work in path analysis. With structural equation techniques, it is possible not only to represent a broad range of causal relations among variables, but also to represent a wide variety of latent variables that may be of concern in educational and psychological research.

REFERENCES

Bentler, P. M. (1980). Multivariate analysis with latent variables. In M. R. Rozenweig & L. W. Porter (Eds.), *Annual review of psychology* (Vol. 31). Palo Alto, CA: Annual Review.

Duncan, O. D. (1975). *Introduction to structural equation models.* New York: Academic.

Joreskog, K. G., & Sorbom, D. (1979). *Advances in factor analysis and structural equation models.* Cambridge, MA: Abt.

Wright, S. (1934). The method of path coefficients. *Annals of Mathematical Statistics, 5,* 161–215.

JOHN R. BERGAN
University of Arizona

MULTIPLE REGRESSION
REGRESSION (STATISTICAL)

PATH-REFERENCED ASSESSMENT

Path-referenced assessment (Bergan, 1981, 1986; Bergan, Stone, & Feld, 1985) is an approach that references ability to position in a developmental sequence. The path-referenced approach has been applied in the Head Start Measures Battery (Bergan & Smith, 1984; Stone & Lane, 1991), a set of six cognitive scales designed to assist in planning learning experiences to promote the development of Head Start children. Within the path-referenced framework, ability is defined as a latent (unobserved) variable estimated from overt performance on test items. The ordering of skills in a developmental sequence is indicated by variations in item difficulty. Items of low difficulty reflect tasks related to lower levels of development, whereas items of high difficulty are associated with higher levels of development. The examinee taking a path-referenced test obtains a latent ability score referred to position in a developmental sequence and used to indicate the probability of performing the various tasks in the sequence correctly. For example, a child taking the math scale of the Head Start Measure Battery might receive a latent ability score indicating high probabilities of performing simple counting tasks correctly and low probabilities of performing more complex addition tasks correctly.

The path-referenced approach applies latent trait models (Bock & Aitkin, 1981; Lord, 1980) to the problem of referencing ability to position in a developmental sequence. The general latent trait model asserts that the probability of performing a test item correctly is a function of latent ability and certain item parameters. Item parameters that may be reflected in a latent trait model include item difficulty, item discrimination (which gives the strength of the relationship of the item to the underlying latent ability), and a guessing parameter. Latent ability and item difficulty are placed on the same scale in the latent trait model. The path-referenced approach uses the latent ability parameter to estimate an individual's ability, described as his or her developmental level. Item difficulty parameters are used to quantify developmental sequences. The fact that latent ability and item difficulty are on the same scale is used to reference developmental level to position in a developmental sequence. For example, suppose that a child taking a math test including a set of counting items receives a developmental level score of 50. Assume that the difficulty of counting to 5 was 48 and the difficulty of counting to 10 was 52. The child's position in the counting sequence would lie between counting to 5 and counting to 10.

The construction of path-referenced tests requires the testing of hypotheses about the developmental sequencing of skills constituting an ability. The hypothesis testing orientation links path-referenced assessment to cognitive research and theory. Embretson (1985) has pointed out that psychometric practice generally is far removed from the hypothesis testing tradition of cognitive psychology. Hypothesis testing is typically restricted to studies of test validity and does not include the testing of hypotheses about items based on assumptions about underlying cognitive processes. The construction of developmental sequences in path-referenced tests requires that hypotheses be advanced related to the cognitive processes associated with tasks in a sequence. In particular, the demands associated with the processes involved in task performance must be identified so that the hypothesized ordering of skills in a sequence can be established. The sequence must then be empirically validated. Cognitive theory and research provide the basis for forming hypotheses about sequencing.

Path-referenced assessment differs in significant ways from both norm-referenced assessment and criterion-referenced assessment. Norm-referenced assessment references test performance to position in a norm group. An ability score is given indicating where the individual stands in the group. Ability is defined in terms of group position. In the path-referenced approach, ability is estimated from test performance using a latent trait model. Latent ability is then referenced to position in a developmental sequence. Path referencing indicates where the individual is in a sequence and in so doing specifies the competencies that have been mastered in the past and those that lie ahead as development progresses.

Criterion-referenced assessment references test performance to the mastery of objectives (Glaser, 1963; Nitko, 1980). The objectives may or may not reflect tasks that are sequenced (Nitko, 1980). Although latent trait models have been used in criterion-referenced assessment (Nitko, 1980), they have not been integrated into the theory underlying criterion-referenced tests. The criterion-referenced approach ignores the ability construct altogether. Overt test performance is linked directly to the mastery of objectives. In path-referenced assessment, overt performance is used to estimate ability. Ability is then related to position in a developmental sequence and used to establish the probability of correct performance of tasks in the sequence. Use of the ability construct requires that individual skills be part of an empirically validated system of knowledge. Each skill in the system contributes to ability. When one teaches a set of skills that are part of a knowledge system, ability is affected. The educator operating from a path-referenced perspective is concerned with teaching ability. The mastery of specific objectives is related to ability. The educator operating from a criterion-referenced framework is concerned with the mastery of objectives. No assumptions are made about the relationship of objectives to ability.

Path-referenced tests may be used in a number of ways. One major use has to do with the management of instruction. Information on path position can be used in establishing individualized learning experiences in educational settings. For example, the Head Start Measures Battery is used by teachers in the Head Start program to provide individualized learning experiences for children. Teachers use planning guides reflecting skills measured by the battery to plan learning experiences appropriate to each child's developmental level in each of the content areas measured by the battery.

A second use of path-referenced assessment involves placement in a special program. Norm-referenced instruments are typically used in making placement decisions. However, path-referenced instruments also may make a useful contribution in determining placement. The major goal of placement is typically to provide a program that is appropriate to the learning needs of the student. To assist the decision-making process, information associated with path position can be related to information about the kinds of learning opportunities available in a special program. A decision to place would imply that learning opportunities congruent with path position can be provided better in the special program than in other available alternatives.

A third use of path-referenced instruments involves evaluating learner progress. Path-referenced instruments provide quantitative ability scores reflecting a continuous ability scale. Gains can be described in terms of the difference between pretest and posttest ability. Path-referenced instruments are better suited to measuring gains than frequently used norm-referenced technology because path-referenced scores do not depend on group position (Bergan, in press). Moreover, since path-referenced ability scores are linked to path position, it is possible to determine changes in the performance of specific skills that accompany progress.

A fourth important use of path-referenced instruments has to do with curriculum design. Path-referenced instruments can provide information about the structure of knowledge in specific content areas. For example, a path-referenced math scale may provide information on the developmental sequencing of math skills. Information on the sequencing of skills can be used in formulating curriculum sequences in math. It should be noted that this does not imply that the sequence of instruction should be the same as the sequence of development.

Because the path-referenced approach is new, it is too early to specify the full variety of applications that it may find in assessment. However, it is worth noting that the need for assessment providing information related to skill sequences has been recognized for many years. This need was thoroughly articulated in Gagne's (1962, 1970, 1977) work. Latent trait technology affords a practical approach to the construction of assessment instruments that are developmental in character. Latent trait technology has been widely used in assessment (Hambleton, 1983), and it is reasonable to expect that it will find increasing application in the assessment of development.

REFERENCES

Bergan, J. R. (1980). The structural analysis of behavior: An alternative to the learning hierarchy model. *Review of Educational Research, 50,* 225–246.

Bergan, J. R. (1981). Path-referenced assessment in school psychology. In T. R. Kratochwill (Ed.), *Advances in school psychology* (Vol. 1). Hillsdale, NJ: Erlbaum.

Bergan, J. R. (1986). Path-referenced assessment: A guide for instructional management. In C. A. Maher (Ed.), *Special services
in the schools.* New York: Haworth.

Bergan, J. R., & Smith, A. N. (Eds.). (1984). *Head Start Measures
Battery.* Washington, DC: Department of Health and Human
Services.

Bergan, J. R., Stone, C. A., & Feld, J. K. (1985). Path-referenced
evaluation of individual differences. In C. R. Reynolds & V. L.
Willson (Eds.), *Methodological and statistical advances in the
study of individual differences.* New York: Plenum.

Bock, R. D., & Aitkin, M. (1981). Marginal maximum likelihood
estimation of item parameters: Application of an algorithm.
Psychometrika, 46, 443–459.

Embretson, S. E. (Ed.). (1985). *Test-design: Developments in psychology and psychometrics.* Orlando, FL: Academic.

Gagne, R. M. (1962). The acquisition of knowledge. *Psychological
Review, 69,* 355–365.

Gagne, R. M. (1970). *The conditions of learning* (2nd ed.). New York:
Holt, Rinehart, & Winston.

Gagne, R. M. (1977). *The conditions of learning* (3rd ed.). New York:
Holt, Rinehart, & Winston.

Glaser, R. (1963). Instructional technology and the measurement
of learning outcomes: Some questions. *American Psychologist,
18,* 519–521.

Hambleton, R. K. (Ed.). (1983). *Applications of item response theory.*
Vancouver, British Columbia: Educational Research Institute
of British Columbia.

Hambleton, R. K., & Eignor, D. R. (1979). *A practitioner's guide to
criterion referenced test development, validation, and test score
usage.* Washington, DC: National Institute of Education and
Department of Health, Education, and Welfare.

Lord, F. M. (1980). *Applications of item response theory to practical
testing problems.* Hillsdale, NJ: Erlbaum.

Nitko, A. J. (1980). Distinguishing the many varieties of criterion-
referenced tests. *Review of Educational Research, 50,* 461–
485.

Stone, C. A., & Lane, S. (1991). Use of restricted item response
theory models for examining the stability of item parameter
estimates over time. *Applied Measurements in Education, 4*(2),
125–141.

JOHN R. BERGAN
University of Arizona

**DEVELOPMENTAL DELAYS
HEAD START**

PATTERNING

Patterning is also known as the Doman-Delacato treatment method for children with neurological disabilities.
The center for the treatment program is located in Philadelphia under the name Institutes for the Achievement

of Human Potential. The central theory of the Doman-
Delacato treatment method is the neurological organization of the individual. The theory posits that the individual progresses through four neurological developmental
stages: medulla and spinal cord, pons, midbrain, and
cortex. The stages finalize in hemispheric dominance.
The theory further proposes that mankind develops in an
orderly manner. The rationale stresses that an individual's
development in mobility, vision, audition, and language
follows specific neurological stages that are correlated
with anatomical progress. In this treatment method, a
specific program of patterning is developed for each client. The patterning features definite time sequences for
selective exercises that can be imposed either actively or
passively on the nervous system. It is claimed that these
exercises lead to improvement in the sensory motor functions of the individual.

The Doman-Delacato treatment was popular during the
1960s. Advocates of the treatment program have reported
success with a wide range of disabilities, including mental
retardation, brain damage, learning disabilities, physical handicaps, aphasia, language disorders, and dyslexia.
Numerous reports from professionals, paraprofessionals,
and parents have confirmed the success of the treatment
program. The widespread acceptance of neurological exercises was enhanced through articles published in popular magazines such as *Good Housekeeping* and *Reader's
Digest.*

Medical teams, educators, and persons serving in the human services field have studied, evaluated, and researched
the claims of the advocates of neurological organization
theories. The numerous studies and carefully controlled
research reviews do not support the purported achievements
of the patterning approach.

REFERENCES

Bower, G. (1966). *Neurophysiology of learning* (3rd ed.). New York:
Appleton-Century-Crofts.

Doman, G. (1966). *Neurological organization and reading.* Springfield, IL: Thomas.

Glass, G., & Robbins, M. (1967). A critique of experiments on the role
of neurological organizations in reading performance. *Reading
Research Quarterly, 3,* 5–51.

Money, J. (Ed.). (1962). *Reading disabilities: Progress and research
needs in dyslexia.* Baltimore: Johns Hopkins Press.

Robbins, M. (1966). A study of the validity of Delacato's theory of
neurological organization. *Exceptional Children, 32*(8), 517–
523.

PAUL C. RICHARDSON
Elwyn Institutes

**NEURODEVELOPMENTAL THERAPY
NEUROLOGICAL ORGANIZATION
NEUROPSYCHOLOGY**

PDR

See PHYSICIANS' DESK REFERENCE.

PEABODY DEVELOPMENTAL MOTOR SCALES

The Peabody Developmental Scales (PDMS; Folio & Fewell, 1983) is an early childhood motor development test for children birth through 7 years 11 months. The instrument includes a Gross-Motor Scale, which tests reflexes, balance, nonlocomotor, locomotor, and receipt and propulsion of objects; and a Fine-Motor Scale, which tests grasping, hand use, eye-hand coordination, and finger dexterity. The Gross-Motor Scale contains 170 items divided into 17 age levels, with 10 items at each level. The Fine-Motor Scale contains 112 items divided into 16 age levels, with 6 or 8 items at each level. Items are scored on a three-point system that distinguishes among mastered skills, emerging skills, and skills clearly beyond the child's reach.

The PDMS was normed on 617 children that were representative of the nation as a whole with regard to gender, race, ethnicity, geographic region, and urban/rural residence. Raw scores are converted into scaled scores (z-scores, T-scores, developmental motor quotients) and age scores.

Reviewers (Compton, 1996; Reed, 1985; Venn, 1986) have been generally complimentary of the PDMS, finding the instrument a comprehensive measure of a fundamental aspect of child development. Weaknesses noted include the cumbersome nature of test administration.

REFERENCES

Compton, C. (1996). *A guide to 100 tests for special education.* Upper Saddle River, NJ: Globe Fearon.

Folio, M. R., & Fewell, R. R. (1983). *Peabody developmental motor scales and activity cards.* Austin, TX: PRO-ED.

Reed, H. B. C. (1985). Review of the Peabody Developmental Motor Scales. In J. V. Mitchell, Jr. (Ed.), *The ninth mental measurements yearbook* (p. 1119). Lincoln: Buros Institute of Mental Measurements, University of Nebraska Press.

Venn, J. J. (1986). Review of the Peabody Developmental Motor Scales. In D. J. Keyser & R. C. Sweetland (Eds.), *Test critiques: Volume V* (pp. 310–313). Austin, TX: PRO-ED.

TADDY MADDOX
PRO-ED, Inc.

PEABODY INDIVIDUAL ACHIEVEMENT TEST–REVISED/NORMATIVE UPDATE

The Peabody Individual Achievement Test–Revised (PIAT-R; Markwardt, 1989) is an individually-administered measure of academic achievement designed for children and adults, ages 5 to 22. The PIAT-R assesses six academic content areas with the following subtests: General Information, Reading Recognition, Reading Comprehension, Mathematics, Spelling, and Written Expression. The subtests are combined to yield a Total Reading score, Total Test score, and a Written Language Composite score. Administration time is approximately 60 minutes.

All subtests except for Written Expression are dichotomously scored. Detailed scoring criteria are provided for both levels of the Written Expression subtest. All subtests except Written Expression yield standard scores, percentile ranks, age equivalents, and grade equivalents. Computerized scoring software is also available for the PIAT-R.

The PIAT-R was recently renormed, and is referred to as the PIAT-R Normative Update (PIAT-R/NU; Markwardt, 1997). A sample of 3,429 children stratified according to 1994 U.S. Census data comprised the standardization sample. Reliability of the PIAT-R/NU was demonstrated with split-half reliability coefficients of the subtests ranging from the low to mid 0.90s. The PIAT-R/NU was shown to be stable with test-retest values in the low to mid 0.90s. Validity was established by demonstrating strong correlations to other achievement measures such as the K-TEA (Kaufman & Kaufman, 1985), KeyMath-R (Connolly, 1988), and PPVT-R (Dunn & Dunn, 1981).

Reviews of the PIAT-R are generally quite favorable. Rogers (1992) comments that the test appears to be a useful instrument to both practitioners in the schools and to researchers. The subtest that continues to be the most difficult to score is the Written Expression subtest. The PIAT-R manual provides specific categories with many examples for scoring, but many examiners may find it difficult to categorize an individual child's writing nonetheless. This particular subtest is one that could utilize further research.

REFERENCES

Connolly, A. J. (1988). *KeyMath Revised: A Diagnostic Inventory of Essential Mathematics.* Circle Pines, MN: American Guidance Service.

Dunn, L. M., & Dunn, L. M. (1981). *Examiner's manual for the Peabody Picture Vocabulary Test–Revised edition.* Circle Pines, MN: American Guidance Service.

Kaufman, A. S., & Kaufman, N. L. (1985). *Kaufman Test of Educational Achievement.* Circle Pines, MN: American Guidance Service.

Markwardt, F. C. (1989). *Peabody Individual Achievement Test–Revised.* Circle Pines, MN: American Guidance Service.

Markwardt, F. C. (1997). *Peabody Individual Achievement Test–Revised / Normative Update.* Circle Pines, MN: American Guidance Service.

Rogers, B. G. (1992). Review of the Peabody Individual Achievement Test–Revised. In J. J. Kramer & J. C. Conoley (Eds.), *The eleventh mental measurements yearbook.* Lincoln, NE: Buros Institute of Mental Measurements.

ELIZABETH O. LICHTENBERGER
The Salk Institute

ACHIEVEMENT TESTS

PEABODY PICTURE VOCABULARY TEST–THIRD EDITION

The Peabody Picture Vocabulary Test–Third Edition (PPVT-III; Dunn & Dunn, 1997) is an individually administered test of listening comprehension in the English language for children and adults ages 2 years 6 months to 90. This test is an achievement test of receptive vocabulary as well as a screening test of verbal ability for individuals who use the English language as their dominant language. The test consists of two forms, Form III A and Form III B. Each form contains four training items and 204 test items. The test items are broken down into 17 sets of 12 items each. Most examinees complete 5 sets, or 60 items. This untimed test takes an average of 11–12 minutes to complete.

Examinees are shown four black-and-white pictures, and are instructed to point to the picture that best represents the meaning of the stimulus word said by the examiner. Examinees are only required to use nonverbal responses. The starting point is determined by the age of the test taker. However, if the examinee's level of functioning is found to fall below the 25th percentile or above the 75th percentile, he or she can begin the test at the more appropriate level. Test descriptions and history, testing and scoring procedures, and standardizations or statistics can be found in the examiner's manual. A norms booklet is also included in the test for scoring purposes. Test responses and scores are recorded on performance record forms that are included with the test. (There are separate forms for Form III A and Form III B).

Standardization data for the PPVT-III were collected in 1995–1996. The sample of 2,725 individuals represented the U.S. Census data from March 1994. The sample consisted of 1,441 females and 1,284 males as well as 2,000 children and 725 adults over the age of 19. All persons in the sample were between the ages of 2.5 and 90. The following disability categories were represented in normative sample: Learning Disabled, 5.5 percent, Speech Impaired, 2.3 percent, Mentally Retarded, 1.2 percent, Hearing impaired, .13 percent, Gifted and Talented, 2.9 percent. Raw scores are converted to age equivalents, percentiles, normal curve equivalents, w-scores, and stanines using a scoring table in the test kit.

The alternate forms reliability coefficients computed from standard scores for the PPVT-III ranged from .88 to .96 with a median of .94. Internal consistency ranged from .86 to .97 with a median reliability of .94. Test-retest reliability among all forms and age groups for the PPVT-III were in the .90s. Criterion validity was examined by looking at the correlations between the PPVT-III and other tests of intelligence and verbal abilities. The correlations between standard scores of the Peabody and the WISC-III ranged from .82 to .92 for children between the ages 7 years 11 months and 14 years 4 months. The correlations between the PPVT-III and the Kaufman Adolescent and Adult Intelligence Test were .76 to .91 for ages 13 to 17 years 8 months, and .62 to .82 using the Kaufman Brief Intelligence Test for ages 18 to 71 years 1 month. The correlations between the Oral and Written Language Scales and the PPVT-III ranged from .63 to .83 for ages 3 to 5 years 8 months and 8 years 1 month to 12 years 10 months.

The PPVT-III appears to be a reliable and valid test of receptive vocabulary. The easy administration and short testing time also add to its appeal.

REFERENCES

Bell, N. L., Lassiter, K. S., & Matthews, T. D. (2001). Comparison of the Peabody Picture Vocabulary Test–Third Edition and Wechsler Adult Intelligence Scale–Third Edition with university students. *Journal of Clinical Psychology, 57,* 417–422.

Campbell, J. (1998). Test reviews. *Journal of Psychoeducational Assessment, 16,* 334–338.

Campbell, J. M., Bell, S. K., & Keith, L. K. (2001). Concurrent validity of the Peabody Picture Vocabulary Test–Third Edition as an intelligence and achievement screener for low SES African American children. *Assessment, 8,* 85–94.

Dunn, L. M., & Dunn, L. M. (1997). *Examiner's manual for the Peabody Picture Vocabulary Test–Third edition.* Circle Pines, MN: American Guidance Service.

Plake, B. S., & Impara, J. C. (Eds.). (2001). *The fourteenth mental measurements yearbook.* Lincoln, NE: Buros Institute of Mental Measurements.

Washington, J., & Craig, H. (1999). Performances of at-risk, African American preschoolers on the Peabody Picture Vocabulary Test–III. *Language, Speech, and Hearing Services in Schools, 30,* 75–82.

RON DUMONT
Fairleigh Dickinson University

JOHN O. WILLIS
Rivier College

PEABODY REBUS READING PROGRAM

The Peabody Rebus Reading Program is a representational symbol system designed to teach early reading skills to children. A basic vocabulary of pictographic symbols known as rebuses represent entire words or parts of words; they provide a foundation for developing reading and comprehension skills. Rebus symbols may be classified into four basic categories: combination symbols, which primarily depict objects or actions (e.g., ball = ⊘); relational symbols, which depict locations or directions (e.g., in = ▣, on = ⬚); and abstract symbols, which are primarily arbitrary symbols representing ideas such as "at" = ◆ and "too" = ⌇). The fourth category combines symbols with alphabet letters, affixes (e.g., doing = ⬚ ing), and other rebuses (e.g., into = ▣ ⌇).

The Peabody Rebus Reading Program includes two levels. The reading level is designed as an alternative, complementary, or supplementary program for traditional readiness programs (Woodcock, Clark, & Davies, 1969). Two workbooks each containing 384 exercise frames are introduced to children. As a student marks an answer using a moistened pencil eraser, a special "invisible ink" indicates the accuracy of the selection. On completion of this level, a child will have developed several prereading skills such as matching spoken words to printed words, reading in a left-to right direction, and comprehending rebus words and sentences. At the second level, the transition level, students progress from reading rebuses to reading spelled words. Teaching materials include one workbook and two rebus readers, emphasizing systematic substitution of spelled words for rebuses. Initially, the spelled words are paired with their corresponding rebus symbols. The symbols are gradually faded to effect transition to standard orthography. On completion of the transition level, a student will be able to read 122 spelled words, sound out words, recognize punctuation, and read stories.

The Peabody Rebus Reading Program is designed to introduce children to reading by first having them learn a vocabulary of rebuses in the place of spelled words. The program has additional application for facilitating the development of language skills.

REFERENCE

Woodcock, R. W., Clark, C. R., & Davies, C. O. (1969). *The Peabody Rebus Reading Program*. Circle Pines, MN: American Guidance Service.

SUSAN MAHANNA-BODEN
TRACY CALPIN CASTLE
Eastern Kentucky University

PEACE CORPS, SPECIAL EDUCATION IN

The Peace Corps is a volunteer program that was established in 1961 by President John Kennedy. Its goal is to help the people of interested countries and areas of the world in meeting their needs for trained manpower through the help of American volunteers. The promotion of a better understanding of Americans on the part of the people served, and a better understanding of other people on the part of Americans, are also basic goals of the program (Shute, 1986). During the 1960s, goodwill among nations was advocated by early Peace Corps participants. During the 1970s, individuals in both the host countries and the United States recognized the need for technically skilled individuals familiar with local needs in food, job, health, and schooling areas. Thus in recent years, programs for volunteers cover such diverse assignments as work in agriculture, industrial arts/skilled trades, and health and education (Peace Corps, 1986). Over 5,200 volunteers in 63 countries now offer their services in three major world regions: Africa (Sub-Saharan Africa), Inter-America (Central and South America), and NANEAP (North Africa, Near East, Asia, and the Pacific). Training is provided to the volunteers in the language, history, customs and social-political systems of the host country.

The Peace Corps offers a program for individuals interested in special education. Volunteers can be assigned specific placements working with children displaying mental retardation, learning disabilities, emotional disturbances, blindness or visual impairments, deafness or hearing impairments, multihandicaps, or speech problems. Assignments in special education cover teacher training and direct classroom teaching. Volunteers in the teacher-training program conduct needs assessments, organize and implement workshops and seminars, develop teaching aids using locally available materials, give demonstration lessons, establish criteria for evaluation, observe teachers, and monitor teachers' progress. Those participating in the direct-teaching program help to screen and assess the special child's abilities and progress; teach classes in academics, extracurricula areas, and self-help skills; and structure activities to facilitate interactions of the special child with the family and community.

To qualify as a special education volunteer, an individual must be a U.S. citizen and be at least 18 years of age. There are also medical and legal criteria. Finally, the special education volunteer should possess a four-year degree with some preservice teaching in special education (actual teaching experience is preferred but not obligatory). All volunteers receive a monthly allowance to cover housing, food, and spending money. On completion of the two-year service commitment required of all volunteers, an allotment for every month served is provided as a readjustment allowance on return to the United States (Shute, 1986).

REFERENCES

Peace Corps. (1986). *The toughest job you'll ever love*. Washington, DC: ACTION.

Shute, N. (1986). *After a turbulent youth, the Peace Corps comes of age*. Washington, DC: ACTION.

LAWRENCE J. O'SHEA
University of Florida

COMMUNITY-BASED SERVICES
VOLUNTARY AGENCIES

PEDIATRIC ACQUIRED IMMUNE DEFICIENCY SYNDROME

Since the first cases of Acquired Immune Deficiency Syndrome (AIDS) were reported in 1981, the human immunodeficiency virus (HIV) that causes AIDS has presented an epidemic unknown in modern history. Worldwide, over 20 million people have died from AIDS since the first cases were identified in 1981. In 2003, approximately 2.9 million people worldwide died of AIDS—490,000 were children. This amounts to approximately 1,350 AIDS deaths in children per day.

According to the *Global AIDS Epidemic / UNAIDS Fourth Global Report* of July 2004, more than 1,900 children worldwide are infected with HIV each day. In 2003, an estimated 4.8 million people became newly infected with HIV—630,000 of them were children. The vast majority of them were infected antepartum (20 percent before childbirth; during pregnancy); intrapartum (40 percent during childbirth), or during breastfeeding (40 percent). Antiretroviral treatment for children presents special challenges. Few HIV medicines are produced in pediatric formulations, and those available as syrups have limitations. They have a short shelf life, children sometimes object to the taste, and they remain very expensive.

In the United States approximately 25 percent of infants born to HIV-infected mothers each year are born HIV-infected. Approximately 89 percent of all children with AIDS are perinatal cases—children who contracted the virus from their mother during pregnancy or birth. Other causes of pediatric AIDS include transmission through breast-feeding, tainted blood transfusions before 1985, and sexual abuse.

The average age for diagnosis of perinatal cases is 4.1. Only 54 percent of all perinatal cases are diagnosed by the age of 7.

Children with AIDS have special needs and concerns, as the variety of manifestations that occur with pediatric AIDS is larger than with adult AIDS. Children with HIV and AIDS often suffer from central nervous system complications, the inability to combat childhood diseases, and failure of growth and development (Children's Hope Foundation, 1998).

Newborns infected with HIV live an average of less than 18 months. Presently, hemophiliacs represent the largest HIV-positive school age group, but this number is declining due to an increasing safe blood supply (Adams, Marcontel, & Price, 1989). The school environment has one of the lowest exposure rates of HIV in terms of normal contact among children. This also applies for school personnel (Adams et al., 1989). However, 25 states have mandated health education prior to graduation, and specifically education on HIV transmission and prevention (Kerr, 1989). The CDC and American Academy of Pediatrics have developed guidelines for school and day care attendance. The guidelines call for consideration of exclusion of the HIV-infected child from regular classrooms or group day care only if the child lacks control of body secretion; practices frequent hand- and object-mouthing behavior; is known to be a frequent biter; or has oozing skin lesions.

Curricula on HIV/AIDS education for special education populations have been focusing on defining health and prevention strategies (New Mexico State Department of Education, 1991). Unfortunately, it appears that very few school districts alter the HIV/AIDS curriculum to meet the needs of students with learning issues (Strosnider & Henke, 1992).

To date, nearly every court decision regarding the status of HIV-infected students and personnel attending school, has allowed the individual to stay in school in the absence of evidence that HIV can be spread by casual contact. Therefore, it is essential that school boards, administrators, and general personnel are thoroughly educated and repeatedly updated with information about AIDS. CDC guidelines recommend a team approach to decisions regarding type of educational setting for HIV-infected children. The team should be composed of the child's physician, public health personnel, parents, and personnel from the educational settings (Kirkland & Ginther, 1988). One other factor that should be addressed within the team approach is the involvement of the school's administration, counselor, psychologist, and social worker in providing emotional and social support to the HIV-infected child and children who make up his or her peer or support group, or classmates (Walker, 1991). It is crucial that at this stage of development of the AIDS disease, health policies and disease control concerns do not violate the individual's rights to privacy (Bruder, 1995) and an appropriate education.

REFERENCES

Adams, R. M., Marcontel, M., & Price, A. L. (1989). The impact of AIDS on school health services. *Journal of School Health, 58,*(8), pp. 341–343.

Bruder, M. B. (1995). The challenge of pediatric AIDS: A framework for early childhood special education. *Topics in Early Childhood Special Education, 15*(1), 83–99.

Children's Hope Foundation. (1998). *Children and AIDS*. Retrieved from http://www.childrenshope.org

Kerr, D. L. (1989). Forum addresses HIV education for children and youth with special needs. *Journal of School Health, 59*(3), p. 139.

Kirkland, M., & Ginther, D. (1988). Acquired immune deficiency syndrome in children: Medical, legal and school related issues. *School Psychology Review, 17*(12), 304–310.

New Mexico State Department of Education. (1991). *HIV/AIDS guidelines for special education populations*. Sante Fe; NM: Author.

Strosnider, R., & Henke, J. (1992). *Delivery of AIDS prevention education to students with disabilities: Implications for preservice education.* (ERIC Clearinghouse No. EC303726)

Walker, G. E. (1991). Pediatric AIDS: Toward an ecosystemic treatment model. *Family Systems Medicine, 9*(3), 211–227.

ELAINE FLETCHER-JANZEN
*University of Colorado at
Colorado Springs*

AIDS DYSMORPHIC SYNDROME

PEDIATRIC AUTOIMMUNE NEUROPSYCHIATRIC DISORDERS ASSOCIATED WITH STREPTOCOCCUS INFECTIONS

Pediatric Autoimmune Neuropsychiatric Disorders Associated with Streptococcal Infections (PANDAS) is a fairly recent phenomenon wherein Obsessive Compulsive Disorder and tic disorders are originated or exacerbated by a streptococcal infection. PANDAS is thought to occur when antibodies from a streptococcal infection cross-react with the brain's basal ganglia (Larson, Storch, & Murphy, 2005; Snider & Swedo, 2004). In other words, the antibodies produced by the body to ward off the bacterial streptococcal infection erroneously attack the individual. Furthermore, abnormalities in the basal ganglia are linked to behavioral and emotional problems such as Obsessive Compulsive Disorder and tics.

Five clinical criteria were identified for PANDAS (Swedo et al., 1998). First, there must be symptoms of an Obsessive Compulsive Disorder and/or tic disorder. Secondly, symptom onset must occur prior to puberty (ages 3 through 13). Third, the course of PANDAS must be distinguished by an episodic course exemplified by acute and severe onset. This sudden onset usually is described as an explosion of symptoms, unlike what is generally seen with pediatric Obsessive Compulsive Disorder. PANDAS also must be associated with neurological abnormalities such as unusual muscular movements and motoric hyperactivity. Finally, and most importantly, a group A beta-hemolytic streptococcal (GABHS) infection is or was present. In order for PANDAS to be considered, the National Institute of Mental Health suggests there be at least two Obsessive Compulsive Disorder and/or tic incidents (Larson et al., 2005; March, 2004; Swedo et al., 1998).

As case studies illustrate, children with PANDAS face many of the same pervasive impairments as those with Obsessive Compulsive Disorder and tic disorders (Allen, Leonard, & Swedo, 1995; Gabbay & Coffey, 2003; Larson et al., 2005). Further, children with PANDAS experience at least a 40 percent rate of psychiatric comorbidities. Thus, the seriousness of the disorder warrants the need for special educators, psychologists, and others to be cognizant of both the symptoms and preferred treatments.

Treatment research for PANDAS has focused primarily on antibiotics and/or immunomodulatory therapies (e.g., IV immunoglobulin and plasma exchange). However, neither of these two treatment approaches has a strong empirical basis. More recently, Storch and colleagues (2004) found cognitive behavioral therapy to be an effective treatment approach. Despite these preliminary findings, more research is needed to test the effectiveness of cognitive behavioral therapy, clearly define its diagnostic criteria, gather additional data on treatment responses, and examine the benefits of using antibiotics and immunotherapies (Larson et al., 2005)

Further, those close to the child should be aware of sudden out-of-character behaviors following a sore throat such as obsessive thinking, muscular and coordination problems, repetitive behaviors, and signs similar to those seen in Attention-Deficit/Hyperactivity Disorder. As mentioned earlier, atypical behaviors commonly subside and then spontaneously reoccur.

REFERENCES

Allen, A. J., Leonard, H. L., & Swedo, S. E. (1995). Case study: A new infection-triggered, autoimmune subtype of pediatric OCD and Tourette's syndrome. *Journal of the American Academy of Child and Adolescent Psychiatry, 34,* 307–311.

Gabbay, V., & Coffey, B. (2003). Obsessive-Compulsive Disorder, Tourette's Disorder, or Pediatric Autoimmune Neuropsychiatric Disorders Associated with Streptococcus in an adolescent? Diagnostic and therapeutic challenges. *Journal of Child and Adolescent Psychopharmacology, 13,* 209–212.

Larson, M. J., Storch, E. A., & Murphy, T. K. (2005). Is it PANDAS? How to confirm the sore throat/OCD connection. *Current Psychiatry, 4,* 33–48.

March, J. S. (2004). Pediatric Autoimmune Neuropsychiatric Disorders Associated with Streptococcal Infections (PANDAS): Implications for clinical practice. *Archives of Pediatrics & Adolescent Medicine, 158,* 927–929.

Snider, L. A., & Swedo, S. E. (2004). PANDAS: Current status and directions for research. *Molecular Psychiatry, 9,* 900–907.

Storch, E. A., Gerdes, A. C., Adkins, J. W., Geffken, G. R., Star, J., & Murphy, T. (2004). Behavioral treatment of a child with PANDAS. *Journal of the American Academy of Child and Adolescent Psychiatry, 43,* 510–511.

Swedo, S. E., Leonard, H. L., Garvey, M., Mittelman, B., Allen, A. J., Perlmutter, S., Lougee, L., Dow, S., Zamkoff, J., & Dubbert, B. K. (1998). Pediatric Autoimmune Neuropsychiatric Disorders Associated with Streptococcal Infections: Clinical description of the first 50 cases. *American Journal of Psychiatry, 155*(2), 264–271.

JASON GALLANT
ERIC A. STORCH
University of Florida

OBSESSIVE-COMPULSIVE DISORDER
TOURETTE SYNDROME

PEDIATRICIAN

A pediatrician is a medical doctor or osteopathic physician who has completed a residency in pediatrics. In addition to the medical care of the newborn, infant, child, and adolescent, the pediatrician is trained in many areas important to the overall growth and development of the child: motor development and coordination, sensory development, psychosocial maturation, and moral and cognitive development.

A wide variety of medical conditions may handicap a child's ability to learn. Some may be due to hereditary factors. Others may be prenatal and relate to the health of the mother or to direct dangers to the fetus such as infections or drugs. Some may be perinatal, occurring during or immediately following the birth process. This group includes complications resulting from the mechanics of labor and delivery. Some conditions may occur or be diagnosed only after the infant has gone home. Thus it is clear that the pediatrician has an important role in special education.

First, the pediatrician may be able to diagnose a condition that could have an adverse effect on the child's ability to learn and estimate the approximate extent of the handicap. Based on this and other relevant information, a plan for intervention and education can be developed. Second, school performance may be the first valid indication that a child is not developing normally. A comprehensive pediatric examination is a vital part of the overall assessment of such developmental problems so as to identify or rule out contributing medical factors, such as visual problems. If needed, detailed remedial measures may then be implemented (Berlin, 1976).

When necessary, the pediatrician can help by referral of the child to other specialists whose expertise may be needed to identify or treat the precise problems in question. Examples of medical specialists to whom such referral may be made include ophthalmologists for disorders of the eyes, neurologists for conditions related to the brain or other parts of the central nervous system, and ear, nose, and throat specialists for children with hearing impairments. Children's health problems may manifest themselves at school. If there is a medication or other treatment program in force, teachers can both monitor and encourage compliance with this program. Over 50 percent of all American parents have sought help from a pediatrician for school-related problems (American Academy of Pediatrics, 1978). For this reason, it is important that pediatricians and teachers maintain open lines of communication so that they may assist one another in helping children with both school-related and health problems.

REFERENCES

American Academy of Pediatrics. (1978). *The future of pediatric education.* Washington, DC: Author.

Berlin, C. M. (1975). Medical bases of exceptional conditions. In R. M. Smith & J. T. Neisworth (Eds.), *The exceptional child: A functional approach.* New York: McGraw-Hill.

WILLIAM J. SHAW
LOGAN WRIGHT
University of Oklahoma

PEDIATRIC PSYCHOLOGIST

The past two decades have been a period of significant professional growth for pediatric psychology. In general, the number of psychologists in medical settings has increased rapidly and the scope of their activities has widened enormously. Wright (1967) first used the term pediatric psychologist to refer to "any psychologist who finds himself dealing with children in a medical setting which is nonpsychiatric in nature" (p. 323). A year later, in 1968, the Society of Pediatric Psychology was founded; it eventually became a section of the Division of Clinical Psychology of the American Psychological Association. The *Journal of Pediatric Psychology* was established by the society in 1976; it has since become a major source of clinical and research publication for the field (Wright, 1993).

There are three major types of pediatric settings in which pediatric psychologists work: (1) the pediatric hospital or multispecialty general hospital inpatient unit, (2) the ambulatory care facility (outpatient clinic or private pediatric office), and (3) the comprehensive care center (e.g., kidney dialysis center, burn hospital) for chronic illnesses or chronic medical conditions, which may provide outpatient and/or inpatient services. The primary clinical responsibilities of the pediatric psychologist in these settings are basically twofold: to provide direct psychological services to patients and to consult to a variety of pediatric medical subspecialties including nephrology, cardiology, hematology-oncology, endocrinology, neurology, genetics, and surgery.

The longest history of association between psychology and primary health care is that between psychologists and pediatricians. This association has been strengthened recently by several groups involved in the training and certification of pediatricians. First, the educational role of pediatric psychologists has been highlighted by recommendations of the Task Force on Pediatric Education (American Academy of Pediatrics, 1978), which placed an increasing emphasis on training in the area of behavioral pediatrics. Second, the Committee on Psychosocial Aspects of Child and Family Health of the American Academy of Pediatrics (1982) noted the important role of the pediatrician in the evaluation and treatment of common behavioral and developmental disorders as well as somatic disorders with psychosocial etiology. This committee also stressed the value of a collaborative relationship between pediatricians and clinical psychologists in the treatment of these problems. Therefore, an increasing recognition of the role of health-related behaviors in the prevention, development, and maintenance or exacerbation of illness has helped to foster the expansion of pediatric psychology as a subspecialty within clinical psychology.

Pediatric psychologists work with a wide range of health-related and developmental problems in children and adolescents (Magrab, 1978; Varni, 1983). They are called on to deal with many common childhood problems and issues of child-rearing that are presented frequently to the pediatrician. Among these common problem areas are eating and sleeping difficulties, toilet training and bed wetting, learning and developmental disorders, and problems in child management.

Over the past 20 years, pediatricians have increasingly focused on the prevention of disease and the management of chronic childhood illnesses for which there are no known cures, such as cystic fibrosis, sickle cell disease, and juvenile diabetes. This shift in the practice of pediatrics has placed a new emphasis on patients' problems of daily living, issues of quality of life, and problems related to compliance with therapeutic regimens. It has further supported the active involvement of pediatric psychologists in the comprehensive delivery of health care to children.

Many children present in medical settings with physical symptoms of unclear origin or with symptoms having significant psychosocial components, including headaches, chronic abdominal pain, and failure to thrive. The psychosocial concomitants of physical illness in children represent a major source of referrals to pediatric psychologists.

Behavioral treatment procedures have shown considerable promise as an approach to alleviating or reducing the symptomatic behaviors associated with a number of somatic disorders in children (Siegel, 1983). Pediatric psychologists have used a variety of behavioral techniques such as biofeedback, relaxation training, and various operant conditioning procedures to successfully modify the symptoms associated with such disorders as asthma, ruminative vomiting, and enuresis.

Pediatric psychologists have also been concerned with the prevention of health-related problems. Among the problems that have received considerable attention in this area are the reduction of stress associated with hospitalization and painful medical procedures and the management of behaviors (e.g., overeating) that are associated with the development of physical disorders such as high blood pressure.

Finally, pediatric psychologists who work in hospital settings are often called upon to provide emotional support to health-care personnel who deal with children having life-threatening conditions. Professional burnout is a significant problem with staff who provide medical care to terminally ill children. The pediatric psychologist may consult with the staff to help them cope with the emotionally draining experiences that they encounter in these settings.

REFERENCES

American Academy of Pediatrics, Committee on Psychosocial Aspects of Child and Family Health. (1982). Pediatrics and the psychosocial aspects of child and family health. *Pediatrics, 79,* 126–127.

American Academy of Pediatrics, Task Force on Pediatric Education. (1978). *The future of pediatric education.* Evanston, IL: Author.

Magrab, P. R. (1978). *Psychological management of pediatric problems.* Baltimore: University Park Press.

Siegel, L. J. (1983). Psychosomatic and psychophysiological disorders. In R. J. Morris & T. R. Kratochwill (Eds.), *The practice of child therapy.* New York: Pergamon.

Varni, J. W. (1983). *Clinical behavioral pediatrics: An interdisciplinary biobehavioral approach.* New York: Pergamon.

Wright, L. (1967). The pediatric psychologist: A role model. *American Psychologist, 22,* 323–325.

Wright, L. (1993). The pediatric psychologist: A role model. In M. C. Roberts & G. Koocher (Eds.), *Readings in pediatric psychology.* New York: Plenum.

LAWRENCE J. SIEGEL
*University of Texas Medical
Branch at Galveston*

**PARENT EDUCATION
PEDIATRICIAN
PSYCHOSOCIAL ADJUSTMENT
PSYCHOSOMATIC DISORDERS**

PEER RELATIONSHIPS

When the topic of peer relationships is discussed in the literature, it is usually characterized as the interaction of students with disabilities with their nondisabled classmates. This is an important and relevant topic in light of the impact IDEA has had in ensuring that students with disabilities be educated in the regular classroom whenever appropriate.

Current research suggests that students with disabilities are often not included in many activities in the regular classroom. It has been shown that the classroom teacher sometimes fails to include the child with disabilities into many typical academic activities. For example, one study (Brophy & Good, 1974) found that regular classroom teachers tended to initiate more negative interactions with low-status, learning-disabled students than with high-status, nonlearning-disabled students. Other researchers have demonstrated that this type of nonproductive negative interchange between the classroom teacher and the student with disabilities will have a significant impact on the relationship between that child and his or her regular class peers (Weinstein, Marshall, Brattaseni, & Middlestadt, 1982). The negative interaction between the student and the teacher seems to solidify the low status of the low-performing student.

The relationship between students with disabilities and their peers is a complex phenomenon that is molded by many factors. Several of the more noteworthy factors are age of the child with disabilities, attitudes and behavior of the classroom teacher, type of handicapping condition affecting the student, self-concept and skill level of the student, and whether or not the regular class students have been prepared to understand the specific needs of some mainstreamed students. For example, it has been suggested that beginning in the early elementary grades

(Rubin & Coplan, 1992), the influence of the peer group increases as the child gets older. In other words, during the early years of a disabled child's school experience, parent and teacher acceptance are more important than peer approval or acceptance.

Methods to improve the peer relationships of the child with disabilities can be found in the literature. As an example of one such approach, Schwartz (1984) provides a checklist for regular class teachers to follow when preparing for the arrival of a mainstreamed child. Among other activities, teachers are asked to give regular class peers information about handicapping conditions and allow for any questions students might have. Such procedures help increase the frequency of positive interaction between the disabled child and his or her peers. This approach is particularly important with physically disabled students. Some research suggests that the physically disabled child is the least likely to be accepted by his or her nondisabled peers.

REFERENCES

Brophy, J., & Good, T. (1974). *Teacher-student relationships: Causes and consequences.* New York: Holt, Rinehart, & Winston.

Rubin, K. H., & Coplan, R. L. (1992). Peer relationships in childhood. In M. H. Bernstein and M. Lamb (Eds.), *Developmental psychology: An advance textbook* (3rd ed., pp. 519–528). Hillsdale, NJ: Erlbaum.

Schwartz, L. L. (1984). *Exceptional students in the mainstream.* Belmont, CA: Wadsworth.

Weinstein, R. S., Marshall, H. H., Brattaseni, K., & Middlestedt, S. E. (1982). Student perceptions of differential treatment in open and traditional classrooms. *Journal of Educational Psychology, 74,* 679–692.

CRAIG DARCH
Auburn University

MAINSTREAMING
PEER TUTORING

PEER TUTORING

Peer and cross-age tutoring procedures have been identified in the literature as having success in the instruction of children with disabilities. Tutoring programs have been successful in improving a wide variety of academic skills. Peer tutors have been effective in teaching math (Bentz & Fuchs, 1996; Johnson & Bailey, 1974) and spelling (Harris, 1973), but have most often been applied for reading skills (Chaing, Thorpe, & Darch, 1980). Many authors identify the need to carefully prepare children before they perform as tutors (Martella, Marchand-Martella, Young, & Macfarlane, 1995; Schloss & Sedlak, 1986). Procedures for preparing children to function as tutors have not been extensively discussed in the literature. There are few sources readily available for a comprehensive description of tutor preparation techniques that have been successfully implemented.

Although there is little research that has been conducted on particular training procedures, anecdotal information leads to the conclusion that carefully designed interactions and tutor preparation are important for the success of a tutoring program. If peer tutoring programs are to be beneficial to everyone involved, the teacher must invest time in the development, implementation, and evaluation of these instructional sessions.

One issue that designers of tutoring programs should consider is the identification of potential peer tutors. This is difficult because research has not given teachers definitive answers as to the characteristics of good peer tutors.

Some studies in special education that have shown tutoring to be effective have older students tutoring younger students (Parson & Heward, 1979). Other reports indicate that large age differences are not critical to an effective peer tutoring program (Dineen, Clark, & Risley, 1977). In fact, one peer tutoring study demonstrated that learning-disabled (LD) elementary-age students were effective in teaching other elementary LD students placed in the same resource room (Chiang et al., 1981). Therefore, based on information currently available, it is safe to conclude that tutor-tutee age difference is not in itself critical to the success of a peer tutorial program.

It appears that tutors can be selected from most special education programs. Research has demonstrated that effective peer tutors can come from either able or less able students. While studies within regular classrooms are common, low-achieving and special classroom students have also been effective tutors (Paine et al., 1983). Several studies have shown higher functioning LD students to be effective tutors for lower functioning LD classmates.

For several reasons, student assignments as tutors can be justified. Tutoring can improve self-concept, be used as a means of practicing previously learned skills, and reinforce academic or social performance. The peer tutoring program can be instrumental in helping special education students develop a more positive attitude and self-image. The success that tutees achieve in these carefully designed programs can contribute to important changes in previously unmotivated students.

REFERENCES

Bentz, J. L., & Fuchs, L. S. (1996). Improving peers' helping behavior to students with learning disabilities mathematics peer tutoring. *Learning Disability Quarterly, 19*(4), 202–215.

Chaing, B., Thorpe, H., & Darch, C. (1980). Effects of cross age tutoring on word recognition performance of learning disabled students. *Learning Disability Quarterly, 3,* 11–19.

Dineen, J. P., Clark, H. B., & Risley, T. R. (1977). Peer tutoring among elementary students: Educational benefits to the tutor. *Journal of Applied Behavior Analysis, 10,* 231–238.

Harris, V. W. (1973). Effects of peer tutoring, homework, and consequences upon the academic performance of elementary school children (Doctoral dissertation, University of Kansas, 1972). *Dissertation Abstracts International, 33,* 11-A, 6175.

Johnson, M., & Bailey, J. S. (1974). Cross-age tutoring: Fifth graders as arithmetic tutors for kindergarten children. *Journal of Applied Behavior Analysis, 7,* 223–232.

Maher, C. A. (1984). Handicapped adolescents as cross age tutors: Program description and evaluation. *Exceptional Children, 51,* 56–63.

Martella, R. C., Marchand-Martella, W. E., Young, K. R., & Macfarlane, C. A. (1995). Determining the collateral effects of peer tutoring training on a student with severe disabilities. *Behavior Modification, 19*(2), 170–191.

Paine, S., Radicchi, J., Rosellini, L., Deutchman, L., & Darch, C. (1983). *Structuring your classroom for academic success.* Champaign, IL: Research.

Parson, L. R., & Heward, W. L. (1979). Training peers to tutor: Evaluation of a tutor training package for primary learning disabled students. *Journal of Applied Behavior Analysis, 12,* 309–310.

Schloss, P., & Sedlak, R. (1986). *Instructional methods for students with learning and behavior problems.* Boston: Allyn & Bacon.

CRAIG DARCH
Auburn University

DIRECT INSTRUCTION
PEER RELATIONSHIPS
SOCIAL SKILLS INSTRUCTION
TEACHER EFFECTIVENESS

PENNSYLVANIA ASSOCIATION FOR RETARDED CITIZENS v. PENNSYLVANIA (1972)

Commonly known as the *PARC* decision, the case of the *Pennsylvania Association for Retarded Citizens* v. *Pennsylvania* is one of two landmark court decisions granting educational rights to the handicapped (the other is *Mills* v. *Board of Education of Washington, D.C.*). *PARC* and *Mills* were instrumental in the passage of state and federal laws guaranteeing equal access for the handicapped to all educational programs.

The *PARC* case was a class action suit (the suit was certified by the court as representing all similarly situated individuals in Pennsylvania) brought by the Pennsylvania Association for Retarded Citizens and 13 mentally retarded students. The suit was brought because three students had been denied attendance in the public schools of Pennsylvania. The case was brought under the equal protection and due process clauses of the Fourteenth Amendment to the U.S. Constitution. In *PARC,* the plaintiffs argued that allowing the state to provide a free public education to some of its citizens while denying others of its citizens the right to attend the same schools or to receive an appropriate education at state expense was unfair and denied equal protection of the law. They also argued that handicapped children were excluded from public education without access to due process. (The Fourteenth Amendment does not deny the ability of a state to deprive a citizen of any fundamental right; however, before an individual can be deprived of life, liberty, or property by a state, the state must demonstrate a compelling interest and must grant the citizen a hearing and other such protection as may be deemed necessary under the due process clause.)

In deciding for the plaintiffs, the court clearly acknowledged that admitting seriously disturbing, profoundly retarded, physically handicapped children would be difficult and expensive at all levels; however, the court ruled that the interests of the handicapped were protected by the Fourteenth Amendment and that this protection outweighed the difficulties created by providing an education to the handicapped. The decision was extensive in its requirements and many of its provisions are routinely included in present statutes such as the Individuals with Disabilities Education Act and its predecessor, the Education of All Handicapped Children Act of 1975 (PL 94-142). The *PARC* decision required the state to provide a free, appropriate education to all handicapped children regardless of the nature or extent of their handicaps; to educate handicapped children alongside nonhandicapped children to the extent possible; to conduct an annual census to locate and serve handicapped children; to cease and desist from applying school exclusion laws, including prohibition of serial suspension practices; to notify parents before assessing a child to determine the presence of a handicap and prior to placement in a special education program; to establish procedures to meet the due process requirements of the Fourteenth Amendment should disagreements arise regarding the school's decision about a handicapped child's educational placement or program; to reevaluate handicapped children on a systematic basis; and to pay private school tuition if the school refers a child to a private school or cannot reasonably meet the needs of a handicapped child in a public setting. Later interpretations of the *PARC* decision by other courts have concluded that the schools must also use proven, state-of-the-art teaching methods with the handicapped (under the requirement of providing an appropriate education).

Following the *PARC* decision and the subsequent ruling in *Mills,* a flood of suits in various states came forth arguing for the rights of the handicapped to equal educational opportunities. Few of these cases were even litigated, however, as most states during the period 1972 to 1974 passed and funded legislation requiring local school districts to provide special education programs for the handicapped.

The *PARC* decision and related cases had a profound effect on special education as currently practiced. *PARC* fostered a rapid change in American schools, bringing into local schools, for the first time in many cases, children with severe disabilities, including profound levels of mental retardation, deafness, blindness, multiple handicaps, and severe orthopedic impairments.

CECIL R. REYNOLDS
Texas A&M University
First and Second editions

KIMBERLY F. APPLEQUIST
*University of Colorado at
Colorado Springs*
Third edition

CONSENT DECREE
EQUAL EDUCATIONAL OPPORTUNITY
EQUAL PROTECTION
**INDIVIDUALS WITH DISABILITIES EDUCATION
    IMPROVEMENT ACT OF 2004 (IDEIA)**
LEAST RESTRICTIVE ENVIRONMENT
MAINSTREAMING
**MILLS v. BOARD OF EDUCATION OF DISTRICT OF
    COLUMBIA**

PEOPLE FIRST

People First is a self-advocacy organization run by and for people with mental retardation. It has the dual purpose of assuring the availability of the services, training, and support needed to maintain and increase the capabilities of people with developmental disabilities for leading independent and normal lives; and of demonstrating to society that the disabled are people first and handicapped second (People First, 1984). Groups of mentally retarded people are taught to organize their affairs, run meetings, and make decisions and carry them through. All of this is accomplished with minimal help from nonhandicapped advisers. To a large extent, these groups are not only concerned with the needs and problems of mentally retarded people, but also the needs and problems of all handicapped people. Statewide and national conventions of self-advocacy groups have been held and an international self-advocacy movement of People First groups is emerging.

One of the first self-advocacy groups was Project Two, which operated in Nebraska. In 1968 many institutionalized mentally retarded individuals were moved to community-based facilities; hence Project One was deinstitutionalization. Deinstitutionalized people felt they needed a sounding board—a self-help group; hence Project Two. Similar developments occurred in Oregon, where there were self-help groups. Three mentally retarded members and two non-handicapped advisers attended a conference for mentally handicapped people in British Columbia, Canada. They returned inspired with the idea of starting an organization of people with mental retardation who would put together such conferences. This was the beginning of the People First movement in America. What is interesting is that the movement started up 2 years after Project Two but was unaware of the other group's existence.

Self-advocacy groups have sprung up in America and Britain. Such groups are challenging traditional views of mental handicaps, handicapped people, and mentally retarded persons who can speak for themselves. Self-advocacy groups stretch nonhandicapped people's expectations and attitudes, thereby helping to create a new independence for mentally handicapped persons. In California, People First was contracted by the State Council of Developmental Disabilities to critique the current service system for the developmentally disabled. The unique aspect of this project is that it was entirely conducted by the consumers of the services and was not the work of professionals.

REFERENCES

People First of California. (1984). *Surviving the system: Mental retardation and the retarding environment.* Sacramento, CA: State Council on Developmental Disabilities.

Williams, P., & Shoultz, B. (1982). *We can speak for ourselves.* Bloomington: Indiana University Press.

MILTON BUDOFF
*Research Institute for
Educational Problems*

ADVOCACY FOR CHILDREN WITH DISABILITIES
ADVOCACY ORGANIZATIONS

PERCENTILE SCORES

A percentile score is a score derived from the relative position of a raw score in the entire distribution of raw scores. The raw score must possess at least rank information; i.e., raw scores must be able to be ranked. Usually we assume at least intervals for the raw scores, so that a one-point difference has the same meaning for all possible scores. Percentile scores lose this interval quality.

The calculation of a percentile score is based on the number of scores lower than the raw score being changed or transformed. A percentile score of 50 means that half (50 percent) of the scores in the raw score distribution fall below the score under consideration. This percentile score is also called the median. A percentile score of 10 means 10 percent of the scores are lower, and a percentile score of 90 means 90 percent of the scores are lower.

Percentile scores are not equal intervals. That is, a 10 percentile point difference has a different meaning when examined for a score of 10 or 50. The difference between percentile scores of 10 and 20 may represent many raw score points, while the difference between 50 and 60 may represent only a few. This is because raw score distributions typically have most scores clustered around the average score, perhaps two thirds of the scores within one standard deviation, so that 10 percent of the scores will occur within a few points of each other. At the extremes of the score distribution there are few people, and 10 percent may represent a large raw score range. Percentile scores should not be treated as interval scores. They cannot be routinely added, subtracted, divided, or multiplied to obtain anything sensible. Their primary use is to inform the user of the relative position of a raw score with respect to all other raw scores. In standardized testing, in which a norm sample has been carefully sampled, the percentile score tells us how an observed raw score compares with the norm group distribution of raw scores.

VICTOR L. WILLSON
Texas A&M University

GRADE EQUIVALENTS
MEASUREMENT

PERCEPTUAL AND MOTOR SKILLS

Perceptual and Motor Skills (titled *Perceptual and Motor Skills Research Exchange* in 1949) is published bimonthly. Two volumes a year total between 2,000 and 3,000 pages. About 30 percent of the articles are submitted from outside the United States. The purpose of this journal is to encourage scientific originality and creativity from an interdisciplinary perspective including such fields as anthropology, physical education, physical therapy, orthopedics, anesthesiology, and time and motion study. Articles are experimental, theoretical, and speculative. Special reviews and lists of new books received are carried. Controversial material of scientific merit is welcome. Submissions are examined by multiple referees, and critical editing is balanced by specific suggestions as to changes required to meet standards.

A survey made in the 35th year of publication showed that *Perceptual and Motor Skills* was listed for the preceding decade in the top 5 percent of psychology journals for numbers of citations elsewhere of its articles and total numbers published of refereed, selected archival articles. For more than 30 years this journal has consistently maintained a policy of being highly experimental, open to all defensible points of view, encouraging of new and often unpopular ways of approaching problems, and protective of authors by careful but open-minded refereeing and editing.

REFERENCES

Ammons, C. H., & Ammons, R. B. (1962). Permanent or temporary journals: PR and PMS become stable. *Psychological Reports, 10,* 537.

Ammons, R. B., & Ammons, C. H. (1962). Permanent or temporary journals: Are PR and PMS stable? *Perceptual & Motor Skills, 14,* 281.

C. H. AMMONS
*Psychological
Reports / Perceptual and
Motor Skills*

PERCEPTUAL CONSTANCY

Perceptual constancy refers to the ability to perceive objects possessing invariant properties such as size, shape, and position in spite of changes in the impression on the sensory surface. Essentially, this means that one recognizes a chair as not only a chair but as the same chair regardless of the viewing angle. Even though an object may have been seen only from a single point of view, we are often able to recognize that object from different distances and from nearly any angle of view.

Perceptual constancy seems to be largely an innate skill (Martindale, 1981). For example, when we observe from a great distance a man who is 6 feet in height, he may appear to be only an inch tall; however, he will be perceived as roughly his correct height nevertheless. Normal individuals can easily perform such tasks with objects not previously seen whenever any other environmental cues are present.

Perceptual constancy is an integral part of overall visual perception and is involved heavily in the early reading process. Disorders of perceptual constancy are relatively rare, but they do occur and can wreak havoc with early learning. Children learn to recognize letters and words even though they see them printed in a variety of orthographic representations. Much variability of printing by children and their teachers occurs during the early learning stages as well, yet children master these various representations with relative ease. The generalization necessary to performing such tasks of visual pattern recognition requires perceptual constancy. Children with mild disturbances of perceptual constancy or higher order visual pattern recognition will have great difficulty with many school tasks, but especially with reading. The disorder is low enough in incidence, however, that accurate estimates of its prevalence are unavailable.

REFERENCE

Martindale, C. (1981). *Cognition and consciousness.* Homewood, IL: Dorsey.

CECIL R. REYNOLDS
Texas A&M University

DEVELOPMENTAL TEST OF VISUAL PERCEPTION–SECOND EDITION
PERCEPTUAL DEVELOPMENT, LAG IN
PERCEPTUAL TRAINING

PERCEPTUAL DEFICIT HYPOTHESIS

The perceptual deficit hypothesis, a once widely accepted view of learning disabilities exerted a dominant influence on special education teaching and evaluation practices from the early 1960s to the mid-1970s. While the perceptual deficit hypothesis encompasses a number of variants, its central notion is that learning disabilities arise from perceptual-motor dysfunction of neurological origin (Cruickshank, 1972). Learning-disabled children are viewed as having deficient form perception and/or visual analysis, and these deficiencies are believed to be the central feature of their difficulties in learning to read.

This view of learning disabilities widely influenced special education practice through the writings and programs of Kephart (1960), Getman (1962), Barsch (1965), and Frostig (1961). Remedial programs reflected this orientation by emphasizing gross and fine-motor training, ocular exercises, spatial orientation, balance board training, visual discrimination, sequencing, closure exercises, etc., as necessary prerequisites to more direct teaching of academics. It was believed that such foundation training in sensory-motor functions would remediate underlying processing deficits and was a required prerequisite to higher order, conceptual, or symbolic learning.

Proponents of the perceptual deficit hypothesis were influenced by Piaget's theories concerning the role of maturation and motor functioning in perception, by gestalt psychology's emphasis on perceptual development, and by Strauss and Lehtinen's (1947) work with brain-injured children. In their programs for learning-disabled children, these pioneers of special education translated stage theories of learning literally into hierarchies of preacademic remediation activities that sought to develop motor, visual, and visual-motor skills prior to focusing on academic learning. In theory, the development of academic skills required mastery of these lower-level functions.

By the mid-1970s, the perceptual deficit hypothesis and its concomitant remedial programs began to receive severe and substantial criticism. Aspects of the underlying theory were questioned and fault was found with the early foundation research. The overly simplified and literal translation of theory into practice was decried as an essential misinterpretation of the concept of perception. New research indicated that learning disabilities, and reading disabilities in particular, were attributable more to problems in the verbal realm than to perceptual deficits (Vellutino et al., 1977).

Tests used to diagnose specific aspects of perceptual deficit came under particularly heavy fire. The most commonly used, the Frostig Developmental Test of Visual Perception (DTVP; Frostig, 1961), was criticized for its weak theoretical foundation. In addition, the DTVP was found to have insufficient factorial validity, meaning that its subtests do not actually tap distinct and separate perceptual functions and therefore cannot be validly used to specify different remedial activities. Thus the widespread use of this test for diagnostic/prescriptive purposes was resoundingly invalidated. Additionally, perceptual training based on the Frostig test was found to have no relation to academic progress and only a negligible effect on DTVP performance itself (Hammill, Goodman, & Wiederholt, 1974). There arose the ethical issue of spending children's limited classroom time on pseudo prerequisite exercises with no validated relationship to academic achievement.

Remediation based on the perceptual deficit hypothesis, along with remediation based on the Illinois Test of Psycholinguistic Abilities (ITPA), continues to be debated under the broader rubric of underlying process training. Underlying process training has come to represent a genre of emphasis within special education in general, and within the study of learning disabilities in particular. Proponents of one or another of the process orientations seek to psychologically parse special students into a variety of processing strength/weakness categories in order to pinpoint areas of underlying need. While this effort has had appeal to many special educators because of the puzzling performance discrepancies of learning-disabled students, its basic assumptions have been seriously questioned.

The assumptions of a process orientation are that human performance can, in fact, be parsed into psychologically distinct categories, that any given parsing categories are valid compartments, that valid tests exist with which to parse, and that remediation based on underlying processing profiles will transfer to functional and academic learning. Currently, the state of the art in psychology and special education does not support any of these assumptions.

REFERENCES

Barsch, R. H. (1965). *A movigenic curriculum* (Publication No. 25). Madison: Wisconsin State Department of Instruction.

Cruickshank, W. M. (1972). Some issues facing the field of learning disability. *Journal of Learning Disabilities, 5,* 380–383.

Frostig, M. (1961). *The Marianne Frostig Developmental Test of Visual Perception.* Palo Alto, CA: Consulting Psychologists.

Getman, G. (1962). *How to develop your child's intelligence.* Luverne, MN: Announcer.

Hammill, D., Goodman, L., & Wiederholt, J. L. (1974). Visual-motor processes: Can we train them? *Reading Teacher, 27,* 469–480.

Kephart, N. (1960). *The slow learner in the classroom.* Columbus, OH: Merrill.

Strauss, A. A., & Lehtinen, L. E. (1947). *Psychopathology and education of the brain-injured child.* New York: Grune & Stratton.

Vellutino, F. R., Steger, B. M., Moyer, S. C., Harding, C. J., & Niles, J. A. (1977). Has the perceptual deficit hypothesis led us astray? *Journal of Learning Disabilities, 10,* 54–64.

KATHERINE GARNETT
*Hunter College, City University
of New York*

PERCEPTUAL DEVELOPMENT, LAG IN

PERCEPTUAL DEVELOPMENT, LAG IN

Lag in perceptual development has been hypothesized as a major cause of learning difficulties in children by Kephart, Delacato, and Getman, among others. In general, these theorists believe there is a sequential series of strategies children use to process information from the environment; if learned incompletely at any stage, these strategies will cause learning difficulties at higher levels. These theorists maintain that proficiency in perceptual functioning provides an essential foundation for academic learning. Furthermore, they presume children experience academic failure because of developmental lags in these perceptual systems, lags that can and must be ameliorated before academic learning can occur. Although varying somewhat in theoretical orientation, these researchers, as well as Frostig, Barsch, Ayres, Doman, S. Kirk, and W. Kirk, advocate perceptual training to both establish the necessary foundation for and enhance the acquisition of academic learning. Their research provides much of the foundation for current work in the field of learning disabilities (Smith, 1984).

An early proponent of perceptual-motor training, Kephart (1971) believed that motor learning underlies all learning. Basing his theory on works of Hebb, Strauss, Werner, Piaget, and Montessori, Kephart hypothesizes that perceptual development occurs through motor activity and corresponding sensory feedback. Once developed, the perceptual system functions without sole reliance on motor response. It is only through completion of this developmental sequence that the child can readily acquire concepts necessary for academic learning. To ameliorate the underlying developmental limitations and distortions that Kephart believed result in academic failure, he developed a training program based on gross motor activities such as posturing and balancing, locomotion, and throwing and catching balls.

Delacato believes training specific locomotor tasks will influence various centers in the brain and other perceptual and cognitive functions controlled by these centers. One critical aspect of his theory is the establishment of hemispheric dominance to improve speech and other sensory functions. He advocates training the child in unilateral hand use and monocular activities and removing music from the child's environment (Cratty, 1979). Maintaining that unmastered stages of neurological development result in reading and other academic difficulties, Doman and Delacato (Ayres, 1975) emphasize remedial activities designed to recapitulate their hypothesized sequence of neurological developmental. In an effort to establish the unilateral cerebral dominance believed critical in treating reading difficulties, they prescribe training to attain sleep posturing, crawling, and activities that foster unilateral hand, eye, and foot dominance.

Getman holds a position similar to Kephart. Like Kephart he proposes movement as a prerequisite to learning. Unlike Kephart, he emphasizes the importance of vision in the learning process and uses vision in a global sense. He hypothesizes that deficiencies in some visual components will lead to learning difficulties (Cratty, 1979). Designed to enhance academic success, particularly reading, Getman's training program includes locomotor and balancing activities as well as eye-hand coordination and other tasks to enhance ocular function.

Frostig (Frostig & Horne,1964) maintains that poor perceptual development precludes conceptual learning, resulting in academic difficulties. Focusing on visual-perceptual learning, training in gross motor activities and paper and pencil tasks follows assessments using Frostig's Developmental Test of Visual Perception (DTVP). According to Frostig, when integrated with regular academic tasks, these activities promote sensorimotor development, ameliorating dysfunctional perceptual processes and enhancing academic performance.

Barsch's (1967) movigenics curriculum emphasizes the academic value of efficient cognitive and physical movement. Like previous theorists, Barsch views the child as a perceptual-motor being whose successful development depends on proper spatial orientation. Movigenics emphasizes activities that enhance visual-perceptual and motor development.

Ayres' (1975) sensorimotor integration theory posits that the foundations to learning are established through the integration of sensory feedback to the brain. Maintaining that perception and movement are dependent on proper sensory integration, Ayres postulates numerous deficits resulting in poor perceptual-motor functioning. To increase integration and facilitate academic learning, Ayres advocates sensory stimulation through activities such as rolling, spinning, and swinging exercises.

Kirk and Kirk (1971) advocate a different approach to the diagnosis and remediation of learning difficulties. Focusing on the communication abilities of the child, Kirk and Kirk provide psycholinguistic evaluation and training to facilitate academic learning. Although training focuses on auditory and visual perception, Kirk and Kirk advocate training focusing on the individual's weak areas.

Although numerous perceptual-motor theories and training programs exist, research findings to support the theories on which they are based or validate their efficacy have not been found. Hammill, Goodman, and Wiederholt (1974) reviewed studies investigating the effects of the perceptual training programs of Frostig, Kephart, and Getman on readiness skills, intelligence, and academic achievement. Of the studies reviewed, positive effects of training on intelligence and academic achievement were not demonstrated and readiness skills improved in only a few cases. In a study of the effects of Delacato's training method on reading ability and visual-motor integration, O'Donnell and Eisenson (1969) found no improvements in either visual-motor integration or reading ability. Further, a number of researchers, professional groups, and parent groups have severely criticized Delacato's theory and program (Aaron & Poostay, 1982).

Finally, in an evaluation of 38 studies employing Kirk and Kirk's psycholinguistic training model, Hammill and Larsen (1978) found only six demonstrating positive results and concluded that the efficacy of psycholinguistic training remains nonvalidated. Although perceptual and psycholinguistic training theorists maintain the efficacy of their treatment programs, others question the large amounts of time and money expended on these unsubstantiated perceptual-training programs (Hammill et al., 1974). Research may validate their value in certain cases, but general use appears unwarranted.

REFERENCES

Aaron, I. E., & Poostay, E. J. (1982). Strategies for reading disorders. In C. R. Reynolds & T. B. Gutkin (Eds.), *The handbook of school psychology* (pp. 410–435). New York: Wiley.

Ayres, A. J. (1975). Sensorimotor foundations of academic ability. In W. M. Cruickshank & D. P. Hallahan (Eds.), *Perceptual and learning disabilities in children* (Vol. 2, pp. 301–360). Syracuse, NY: Syracuse University Press.

Barsch, R. H. (1967). *Achieving perceptual motor efficiency*. Seattle, WA: Special Child.

Cratty, B. J. (1979). *Perceptual and motor development in infants and children*. New York: Macmillan.

Frostig, M., & Horne, D. (1964). *The Frostig program for the development of visual perception: A teacher's guide*. Chicago: Follett.

Hammill, D., Goodman, L., & Wiederholt, J. L. (1974). Visual-motor processes: Can we train them? *Reading Teacher, 27*, 469–478.

Hammill, D., & Larsen, S. (1978). The effectiveness of psycholinguistic training: A reaffirmation of position. *Exceptional Children, 44*, 402–414.

Kephart, N. C. (1971). *The slow learner in the classroom* (2nd ed.). Columbus, OH: Merrill.

Kirk, S. A., & Kirk, W. D. (1971). *Psycholinguistic learning disabilities: Diagnosis and remediation*. Chicago: University of Illinois Press.

O'Donnell, P. A., & Eisenson, J. (1969). Delacato training for reading achievement and visual-motor integration. *Journal of Learning Disabilities, 2*, 441–447.

Smith, C. R. (1984). *Learning disabilities: The interaction of learner, task, and setting*. Boston: Little, Brown.

SHIRLEY PARKER WELLS
ELEANOR BOYD WRIGHT
University of North Carolina at Wilmington

NEUROLOGICAL ORGANIZATION
REMEDIATION, DEFICIT-CENTERED MODEL OF

PERCEPTUAL DISTORTIONS

Perceptual distortion is a clinical term referring to aberrant reception and interpretation of stimuli by one or more of the five basic senses: vision, hearing, smell, taste, and touch. Perceptual distortion typically occurs in conjunction with schizophrenia, severe depression, and psychomotor and ideopathic epilepsies. Schizophrenics are particularly susceptible to perceptual distortion and often process incoming sensory information abnormally via attenuation or reduction. Schizophrenics traditionally have been thought to underestimate tactile, auditory, and visual stimuli in particular. Related to perceptual distortion is evidence that schizophrenics have a defective sensory-filtering mechanism that does not allow them to focus on the most relevant of stimuli at any given time (Pincus & Tucker, 1978). Perceptual distortions that mimic the schizophrenic's perceptual distortions also may be induced by various psychoactive drugs. Prolonged sensory deprivation can also produce perceptual distortions and full-blown hallucinations.

In contrast to schizophrenics, depressed and epileptic individuals exaggerate the intensity of incoming stimuli. Psychomotor seizures produce the most specific of the perceptual distortions but they tend to be ideopathic. Perceptual distortions may also be considered a soft sign of neurological impairment and may occur with learning disabilities, though the latter is far less frequent than commonly believed.

REFERENCE

Pincus, J. H., & Tucker, G. J. (1978). *Behavioral neurology* (2nd ed.). New York: Oxford University Press.

CECIL R. REYNOLDS
Texas A&M University

CHILDHOOD SCHIZOPHRENIA
PERCEPTUAL DEVELOPMENT, LAG IN
SEIZURE DISORDERS

PERCEPTUAL-MOTOR DIFFICULTIES

Perceptual-motor development is recognized as a basic foundation for later learning. The perceptual deficit hypothesis holds that academic difficulties underlie perceptual deficits (Daves, 1980) and that improving the perceptual processes will bring about improvement in academic achievement. Frequently, children with serious learning disorders have difficulty with spatial orientation, eye-hand coordination, and body image. The early work of Strauss and Lehtinen (1947) described such disorders using the term brain-injured, but later such disorders were labeled the Strauss syndrome by Stevens and Birch (1957). They described the child with perceptual-motor difficulties as one who showed disturbances (separately or in combination) in perception, thinking, and emotional behavior.

Kinsbourne (1968) drew an analogy between the developmental syndrome of cognitive deficits and the acquired Gerstmann syndrome in some adults with parietal lesions in the dominant hemisphere. In both syndromes, he noted selective delay in the ability to recall and use information regarding relative position of items in spatial or temporal sequence; selective difficulty in learning to read and write; spelling errors characterized by errors of letter order and script malorientation; delayed acquisition of finger order sense; inability to discriminate between right and left; and difficulty in arithmetic. He concluded that the developmental syndrome probably represented a developmental lag rather than an indication of localized or lateralized cerebral damage.

There is little question regarding the importance of the development of perceptual-motor skills. Cratty (1975) notes that a child with perceptual-motor difficulties cannot translate thoughts into written and printed form with the same precision as a normally developing child. Such a child also may possess various perceptual deficits within one or more modalities (touch, kinesthesia, vision, audition) that may combine as evidence of a defective nervous system and lead to learning problems. Cruickshank (1979) also emphasized that perceptual processing deficits or neurological dysfunction underlie learning problems. Such problems are related to receiving, processing, and responding to information from outside the environment and from inside the child's own body. The ability to understand, remember, think, and perform perceptual-motor skills all precede the ability to read, write, or master arithmetic. Strategies to assist children in the overall learning process were developed (Kephart, 1963) based on the notion that perceptual-motor deficits are primarily organic in nature, and further, that they can be remediated by the development of specific skills such as form perception, eye-hand coordination, and temporal-spatial relationships.

Both Frostig (1975) and Kephart (1975) emphasized the need to develop skills in their natural order. They stressed the effect of motor processes on perception and the effects of perception on cognitive processes (i.e., the use of vision and motor skills or activities in the formation of a concept). In a similar manner Barsh (1963) developed a curriculum, movigenics, involving a progressively more complex sequence of activities in which children explore and orient themselves in space. Barsh's emphasis was on the development of muscular strength, dynamics, balance, space, body awareness, and rhythmics.

Controversy exists regarding the efficacy of such programs. Much of the research to replicate beneficial results linking perceptual motor training to academic achievement (Balow, 1971; Goodman & Hammill, 1973; Zigler & Seitz, 1975) suggests that the claims are unwarranted. Little evidence has been found to support the use of perceptual-motor activities in the treatment or prevention of disabilities in reading or other specific school subjects. However, other research tends to confirm earlier claims (Ayres, 1972; Gregory, 1978; Masland, 1976; Neman, 1974). There is continued interest in and support for determining the benefits of specific sensory-motor training.

REFERENCES

Ayres, A. (1972). *Sensory integration and learning disorders.* Los Angeles: Western Psychological Services.

Balow, B. (1971). Perceptual-motor activities in the treatment of severe reading disabilities. *Reading Teacher, 24,* 513–525.

Barsh, R. H. (1963). *Enriching perception and cognition: Techniques for teachers* (Vol. 2). Seattle, WA: Special Child.

Cratty, B. J. (1975). *Remedial motor activities for children.* Philadelphia: Febiger.

Cruickshank, W. M. (1979). Learning disabilities: Perceptual or other? *Association for Children with Learning Disabilities Newsbriefs, 125,* 7–10.

Daves, W. E. (1980). *Educator's resource guide to special education: Terms-laws-tests-organizations.* Boston: Allyn & Bacon.

Frostig, M. (1975). The role of perception in the integration of psychological functions. In W. Cruickshank & D. Hallahan (Eds.), *Perceptual and learning disabilities in children* (Vol. 1, pp. 115–146). Syracuse, NY: Syracuse University Press.

Goodman, L., & Hammill, D. (1973). The effectiveness of the Kephart-Getman activities in developing perceptual-motor and cognitive skills. *Focus on Exceptional Children, 4*(9), 19.

Gregory, R. L. (1978). Illusions and hallucinations. In E. C. Carterette & M. P. Friedman (Eds.), *Handbook of perception: Vol. 9. Perceptual processing* (pp. 337–358). New York: Academic.

Kephart, N. C. (1963). *The brain injured child in the classroom.* Chicago: National Society for Crippled Children and Adults.

Kephart, N. C. (1975). The perceptual-motor match. In W. Cruickshank & D. Hallahan (Eds.), *Perceptual and learning disabilities in children* (Vol. 1, pp. 63–70). Syracuse, NY: Syracuse University Press.

Kinsbourne, M. (1968). Developmental Gerstmann syndrome. *Pediatric Clinics in North America, 15*(3), 771–778.

Masland, R. (1976). The advantages of being dyslexic. *Bulletin of the Orton Society, 26,* 10–18.

Neman, R. (1974). A reply to Zigler & Seitz. *American Journal of Mental Deficiency, 79,* 493–505.

Stevens, G. D., & Birch, J. W. (1957). A proposal of clarification of the terminology and a description of brain-injured children. *Exceptional Children, 23,* 346–349.

Strauss, A. A., & Lehtinen, L. E. (1947). *Psychopathology and education of the brain-injured child* (Vol. I). New York: Grune & Stratton.

Zigler, E., & Seitz, V. (1975). On an experimental evaluation of sensory motor patterning: A critique. *American Journal of Mental Deficiency, 79,* 483–492.

SALLY E. PISARCHICK
*Cuyahoga Special Education
Service Center*

MOVIGENICS
VISUAL-MOTOR AND VISUAL-PERCEPTUAL PROBLEMS
VISUAL PERCEPTION AND DISCRIMINATION

PERCEPTUAL SPAN

Perceptual span is the amount of information that is acquired during the eye fixation. In reading our visual field can be divided into three different regions with respect to fixation: foveal, parafoveal, and peripheral. Although acuity is very good in the foveal (the central 2 degrees of vision), it is not nearly as good in the parafovea (which extends to 5 degrees on either side of fixation), and it is even poorer in the periphery (the region beyond the parafovea). Therefore, on tasks such as reading, we move our eyes to place the fovea on that part of the text we want to see clearly.

An important finding in reading research is that the size of perceptual span is not constant and varies as a function of text difficulty. The size of the span is smaller when the level of difficulty is high.

Eye-contingent display change techniques (e.g., moving window technique, moving mask technique, or boundary technique) were developed and are used to determine how much information can be obtained in a given eye fixation (Rayner, 1998). All studies using these techniques have shown that perceptual span is limited and asymmetric. It extends from about 4 character spaces to the left of the currently fixated character to a maximum of about 15 character spaces to the right. However, for the orthographies, such as Hebrew, that are printed from the right to left, perceptual span is asymmetric to the left of eye fixation. The asymmetry is not "hard-wired": it varies from language to language. Bilingual readers can alter the area from which they extract information when they switch from language to language.

Characteristics of the writing system influence not only the asymmetry of the span but also the overall size of it. Thus, perceptual span of Japanese readers is about 13 characters when the print is arranged horizontally. When reading vertically, the span is about five to six characters. Readers of Chinese have an asymmetric perceptual span extending from 1 character space to 3 character spaces to the right. Not only can the characteristics of the writing system but reading skill as well influence the size of the perceptual span. Beginning readers have smaller spans (about 12 letter spaces to the right of fixation) as compared to skilled readers (14 to 15 letter spaces).

Research has also focused on the perceptual span of blind people (Bertelson, Mousty, & D'Alimonte, 1985). The most common system for alphabetic languages is known as Braille. For the majority of Braille readers the size of perceptual span is just one letter. They read with one finger (almost always an index finger) one letter at a time. Some skilled Braille readers use two index fingers to read, increasing their reading speed by almost 30 percent.

Although total perceptual span is limited to about 15 letter spaces, the area within which word identification takes place is even more limited. Generally this word identification span does not exceed 7 to 8 character spaces to the right of fixation, and readers can recognize a word to the right or sometimes two short words.

A question as to whether readers are able to acquire information from below the line that they are reading has been examined (Rayner, 1998). The results revealed that readers typically focus on the currently fixated line. The information below the fixated line is not comprehended, unless it is the specifics of a task or characteristics of the orthography.

REFERENCES

Bertelson, P., Mousty, P., & D'Alimonte, G. (1985). A study of Braille reading: Patterns of hand activity in one-handed and two-handed reading. *Quarterly Journal of Experimental Psychology, 37A,* 235–256.

Inhoff, A. W., & Topolski, R. (1992). Lack of semantic activation from unattended text during passage reading. *Bulletin of the Psychonomic Society, 30,* 365–366.

Rayner, K. (1998). Eye movements in reading and information processing: 20 years of research. *Psychological Bulletin, 124,* 372–422.

OLGA JERMAN
*University of California,
Riverside*

PERCEPTUAL TRAINING
VISUAL EFFICIENCY

PERCEPTUAL TRAINING

Many theorists believe that perception is a learned skill; therefore, it is assumed that teaching or training can have an effect on a child's perceptual skills (Lerner, 1971). Once perceptual abilities have been assessed, there are various teaching procedures and programs that can be used to improve perceptual skills.

Some of the most frequently used educational programs for children with learning disabilities have focused on perceptual training activities. While many of these perceptual training programs have emphasized visual or visual-motor training, there are also perceptual training activities in the areas of auditory perception, haptic and kinesthetic perception, and social perception. In spite of all the available material on these perceptual training programs, many researchers have questioned their effectiveness as a way to improve school learning (Hallahan & Cruickshank, 1973; Hammill & Larsen, 1974).

Since similar perceptual training activities have been used in many different programs, it is often unclear who first used them (Hallahan & Kauffman, 1976). However, most of these training activities are based on theories that began with the work of Werner and Strauss (1939). The following descriptions of some of these perceptual training programs provide an overview of these theories and activities.

Newell Kephart worked closely with Werner and Strauss and derived many of his educational techniques from them. This perceptual-motor theory of learning disabilities stresses that perceptual-motor development helps the child establish a solid concept of his or her environment and that perceptual data only become meaningful when they are connected with previously learned motor information (in Kephart's terms, when a perceptual motor match occurs). Children with learning problems are viewed as having inadequate perceptual-motor development, manifested by motor, perceptual, and cognitive disorganization. Kephart argues that these children are unable to benefit from standard school curricula (Lerner, 1971).

The book *The Slow Learner in the Classroom* (Kephart, 1971) presented Kephart's perceptual-motor training program, which included activities involving chalkboard training, sensory-motor training, ocular-motor training, and form-perception training. The chalkboard training activities were recommended for promoting directionality, crossing the midline, orientation, tracing, copying, and eye-hand coordination. The activities presented in the sensory-motor training portion of the program were designed to help the child coordinate the movements of his or her body. Balance beams, balance boards, "angels in the snow" exercises, and trampolines are used to develop total body coordination in the gross motor systems. Ocular-motor training was proposed to help children gain control over their eye movements; it includes activities for ocular pursuit in which the child follows objects visually. Because of Kephart's belief that motor activities influence visual development, the activities in the form-perception training include assembling puzzles, constructing designs from matchsticks, and putting pegs in pegboards (Hallahan & Kauffman, 1976).

Getman (1965) also proposed a model that attempts to illustrate the sequences of children's development of motor- and visual-perceptual skills. This model, called the visuomotor complex, is applied in a manual of training activities. *The Physiology of Readiness: An Action Program for the Development of Perception in Children* (Getman, Kane, Halgren, & McKee, 1964). The program described in this model has activities in the following six areas: general coordination, balance, eye-hand coordination, eye movements, form perception, and visual memory. The exercises in the general coordination section deal mainly with movements of the head, arms, and legs; they are designed to provide children with practice in total body movement. A balance beam is used for most of the activities in the balance section; the activities emphasize the use of visual perception for the acquisition of better balance.

The eye-hand coordination program involves the children in chalkboard exercises that are designed to increase their ability to coordinate eyes and hands. Activities in the eye-movement program are aimed at increasing children's ability to move their eyes rapidly and accurately from one object to another, while the form-perception program has children using templates to trace shapes on the chalkboard and on paper, eventually leading to the drawing of the figures without templates. The final part of the program, the visual-memory activities, uses a tachistoscope or slide projector to flash slides of figures for children to name, trace in the air, circle, trace on worksheets, or draw. The purpose is to develop children's visual imagery skill by showing more complex figures for shorter periods of time as the children become more proficient.

Frostig and Horne (1964) have a visual-perception training program designed for remediation or readiness training. The Frostig Program for the Development of Visual Perception has activities in the areas of eye-motor coordination, figure ground, perceptual constancy, position in space, and spatial relations. Each of these areas has worksheets for the teacher to use with the children. The eye-hand exercises focus on coordinating eye and hand movements by having the children draw lines between boundaries. The figure-ground exercises have the children find and trace figures embedded within other lines and figures. Perceptual generalization is emphasized in the perceptual constancy exercises; the children are trained to recognize that objects remain the same even if presented in different forms, colors, sizes, or contexts. The position in space exercises have the children place themselves in various positions (e.g., over or under) in relation to objects in the room; worksheets are also provided that require the children to discriminate objects in various positions. Finally, the spatial-relations exercises have the children do worksheets to observe spatial relationships.

Barsch's movigenic theory proposes that difficulties in learning are related to the learner's inefficient interaction with space. The training program that evolved from this theory has a series of activities that are a planned developmental motor program (Barsch, 1965). There are three main components to this curriculum: postural-transport orientations, which include muscular strength, dynamic balance, body awareness, spatial awareness, and temporal awareness; percepto-cognitive modes of gustatory, olfactory, tactual, kinesthetic, auditory, and visual activities; and degrees of freedom of bilaterality, rhythm, flexibility, and motor planning. Chapters on each of these aspects of the program are included in the curriculum along with exercises to use with learning-disabled children.

Several books and training manuals that focused on training motor skills were written and developed by Cratty (1973). These materials present exercises similar to those found in physical education programs for the purpose of enhancing motor skills and improving a child's cognitive abilities.

REFERENCES

Barsch, R. (1965). *A movigenic curriculum* (Bulletin No. 25). Madison, WI: Department of Instruction, Bureau for the Handicapped.

Cratty, B. (1973). *Teaching motor skills.* Englewood Cliffs, NJ: Prentice Hall.

Frostig, M., & Horne, D. (1964). *The Frostig program for the development of visual perception.* Chicago: Follett.

Getman, G. (1985). The visuomotor complex in the acquisition of learning skills. In J. Hellmuth (Ed.), *Learning disorders* (Vol. 1). Seattle, WA: Special Child.

Getman, G., Kane, E., Halgren, M., & McKee, G. (1964). *The physiology of readiness: An action program for the development of perception in children.* Minneapolis: Programs to Accelerate School Success.

Hallahan, D., & Cruickshank, W. (1973). *Psychoeducational foundations of learning disabilities.* Englewood Cliffs, NJ: Prentice Hall.

Hallahan, D., & Kauffman, J. (1976). *Introduction to learning disabilities.* Englewood Cliffs, NJ: Prentice Hall.

Hammill, D., & Larsen, S. (1974). The relationship of selected auditory perceptual skills and reading ability. *Journal of Learning Disabilities, 7,* 429–436.

Kephart, N. (1971). *The slow learner in the classroom* (2nd ed.). Columbus, OH: Merrill.

Lerner, J. (1971). *Children with learning disabilities.* Boston: Houghton Mifflin.

Werner, H., & Strauss, A. (1939). Types of visuo-motor activity and their relation to low and high performance ages. *Proceedings of the American Association of Mental Deficiency, 44,* 163–168.

DEBORAH C. MAY
State University of New York at Albany

MOVIGENICS

PEREIRE, JACOB R. (1715–1780)

Jacob R. Pereire, an early educator of the deaf, was the originator of lip reading and the creator of the first manual alphabet for the deaf that required the use of only one hand. Pereire also demonstrated that speech can be understood by using the tactile sense to perceive the vibrations and muscular movements produced by the voice mechanism.

Pereire conducted schools for the deaf in Paris and Bordeaux, and his methods were further developed by de l'Epée and Sicard at the National Institution for Deaf-Mutes in Paris. In recognition of his work, Pereire received an official commendation of the Parisian Academy of Science, was made a member of the Royal Society of London, and was awarded a pension by King Louis XV.

REFERENCE

Lane, H. (1984). *When the mind hears.* New York: Random House.

PAUL IRVINE
Katonah, New York

PERFORMANCE-BASED STANDARDS

Performance-based standards describe the knowledge and skills that a teacher must demonstrate with an acceptable level of competency (Interstate New Teacher Assessment and Support Consortium [INTASC], 1992). A performance-based standard goes beyond a description of the requisite knowledge or skill. Rather, it describes the application of the knowledge and skills and the degree of competency expected, specifying both the nature of the evidence (i.e., a test, videotaped lesson) and the quality of expected performance (Marzano & Kendall, 1997). Performance-based standards differ from curriculum standards, statements that describe what will happen in the classroom, and content standards, statements that describe what a learner should know and be able to do (Elliott, 1996; Marzano & Kendall). Performance-based standards for teachers should be aligned with content standards for students and be consistent with state licensing requirements (Elliott). For example, this student content standard, "Students read and understand a variety of materials" (Colorado Model Reading and Writing Standards Task Force, 1995) is aligned with the performance-based standard, "The teacher has demonstrated the ability to plan and organize reading instruction based on ongoing assessment" (Colorado Department of Education, 2000).

Performance-based standards are an outgrowth of the standards movement of the 1980s and 1990s (Marzano & Kendall, 1997). This educational initiative began with the publication of *A Nation at Risk* (National Commission on Excellence in Education, 1983), a report on the state of education in the United States. This report included among its recommendations standards of performance for both students and teachers (National Commission on Excellence in Education). Diane Ravitch, former U.S. Assistant Secretary of Education, is considered by many educators to be the primary force behind the standards movement. She defined standards as "clearly defining what is to be taught and what kind of performance is expected" (Ravitch, 1995).

With the publication of *A Nation at Risk,* political and

educational leaders began to rethink what K–12 students and their teachers should know and be able to do. In 1989, the National Council of Teachers of Mathematics became the first of many specialty associations and state departments of education to publish content standards for students (Marzano & Kendall, 1997). In 1986, the Carnegie Task Force on Teaching as a Profession released its report, *A Nation Prepared: Teachers for the 21st Century* (Carnegie Corporation of New York, 1986), which urged the teaching profession to set standards of performance for teachers and called for the establishment of the National Board of Professional Teaching Standards (NBPTS). The creation of the NBPTS in 1987 prompted discussions of standards for teachers and resulted in the initial development of performance-based standards for accomplished veteran teachers (INTASC, 1992). These performance-based standards have since become the model for initial state licensure standards for beginning teachers (INTASC, 1992) and accreditation standards for university teacher preparation programs (National Council for Accreditation of Teacher Education, 2004).

At the dawn of the twenty-first century, performance-based standards provide a nationally unified focus throughout the entire teacher career continuum (Quatroche, Duarte, Huffman-Joley, & Watkins, 2002). For experienced teachers, performance-based standards for National Board Certification recognizes advanced levels of competence (NBPTS; 2005). For initial state licensure, performance-based standards reflect the "knowledge, dispositions, and performances deemed essential for all beginning teachers" in order to help all students achieve state content standards (INTASC, 1992, p. 3). In the early 1990s, the National Council for Accreditation of Teachers (NCATE) required that all its specialty associations, including the Council for Exceptional Children (CEC), to revise its standards to be performance-based (NCATE, 2004). In 2001, NCATE required accredited university teacher preparation programs to use performance-based standards in place of the traditional approach of listing required courses (NCATE, 2004).

Performance-based standards require a method of evaluation that assesses performance as well as knowledge and skills. The NBPTS pioneered the use of portfolios to evaluate teacher performance for National Board Certification (Quatroche et al., 2002). These portfolios include videotapes of teacher-student interaction, student work samples, and teacher analyses and commentaries. The INTASC performance-based assessments are modeled after the NBPTS portfolios and contain similar artifacts (Weiss & Weiss, 1998). Assessments are based on evidence provided by the teacher that shows how teaching behavior directly contributes to student learning. Accredited university teacher education programs must align with state and national performance-based assessments, which demonstrate that the teacher candidate "knows the subject matter and can teach it effectively so that students learn" (Wise, 2000b). As of 2000, NCATE expects accredited institutions to use performance-based assessments to evaluate teacher candidates (Wise, 2000a).

There is a growing consensus among educators that performance-based standards and assessments have improved the preparation of teacher candidates, the licensing requirements of novice teachers, and the recognition of accomplished veteran teachers. In turn, this ultimately helps ensure that K–12 students receive a higher quality of instruction (Douglas & Fennerty, 1994; Quatroche et al., 2002; Wise, 2000a). For preparing and licensing new teachers, performance-based standards and assessments provide a more effective way of evaluating what prospective teachers know and can do than can be gleaned from examining course syllabi and grades (Douglas & Fennerty, 1994; Quatroche et al.; Wise, 2000a). The rigorous performance-based standards and assessments for accomplished teachers developed by the NBPTS have helped teaching become "a profession more comparable to others such as medicine, law, and engineering" (Quatroche et al.). Finally, a growing body of converging evidence suggests that veteran teachers who attain high NBPTS performance-based standards have consistently superior performance than their peers who do not have Board Certification, and produce more knowledgeable and skillful students (Quatroche et al.).

REFERENCES

Carnegie Corporation of New York. (1986). *A nation prepared: Teachers for the 21st century. The report of the Task Force on Teaching as a Profession* (ED268120). New York: Author.

Colorado Department of Education. (2000). *Performance-based standards for Colorado teachers.* Denver, CO: Author.

Colorado Model Reading and Writing Standards Task Force. (1995). *Colorado model content standards for reading and writing.* Denver, CO: Colorado State Department of Education.

Douglas, L. D., & Fennerty, D. C. (1994). *Teacher candidate performance-based assessment* (ED367634). Denver, CO: Colorado State Department of Education.

Elliott, E. (1996). What performance-based standards mean for teacher preparation. *Educational Leadership, 53*(6), 57–58.

Interstate New Teacher Assessment and Support Consortium (INTASC). (1992). *Model standards for beginning teacher licensing, assessment, and development: A resource for state dialogue* (ED369767). Washington, DC: Council of Chief State School Officers.

Marzano, R. J., & Kendall, J. S. (1997). *The fall and rise of standards-based education.* Mid-continent Research for Education and Learning (McREL). Retrieved June 10, 2005, from http://www.mcrel.org/PDF/Standards/5962IR_FallAndRise.pdf

National Board for Professional Teaching Standards (NBPTS). (2005). *About NBPTS: History & facts.* Retrieved June 10, 2005, from http://www.nbpts.org/about/hist.cfm

National Commission on Excellence in Education. (1983). *A nation at risk: The imperative for educational reform.* U.S. Department of Education. Retrieved June 10, 2005, from http://www.ed.gov/pubs/NatAtRisk/title.html

National Council for Accreditation of Teacher Education (NCATE). (2004). *NCATE at 50: Continuous growth, renewal, and reform.* Retrieved June 15, 2005, from http://www.ncate.org/public/aboutNCATE.asp

Quatroche, D. J., Duarte, V., Huffman-Joley, G., & Watkins, S. (2002). Redefining assessment of preservice teachers: Standards-based exit portfolios. *Teacher Educator, 37*(4), 268–281.

Ravitch, D. (1995). *National standards in American education: A citizen's guide.* Washington, DC: Brookings Institute.

Weiss, E. M., & Weiss, S. G. (1998). *New directions in teacher evaluation.* (ERIC Digest ED429052). Washington, DC: Office of Educational Research and Improvement.

Wise, A. E. (2000a). Performance assessment in progress. *Quality Teaching: Newsletter of the National Council for Accreditation of Teacher Education, 9*(2), 4–5, 8.

Wise, A. E. (2000b). Performance-based accreditation: Reform in action. *Quality Teaching: Newsletter of the National Council for Accreditation of Teacher Education, 9*(2), 1–2.

ELAINE A. CHEESMAN
*University of Colorado at
Colorado Springs*

HIGHLY QUALIFIED TEACHER

PERFORMANCE INSTABILITY

Performance instability refers to inconsistent functioning on a given task across time. As a characteristic of children with disabilities, performance instability often is confused with a second type of variability referred to by O'Donnell (1980) as intraindividual discrepancy. Whereas performance instability denotes changeability within a single domain across time, intraindividual discrepancy refers to variability across different performance areas within a similar time frame.

Historically, performance instability has been viewed as a distinctive characteristic of learning-disabled children. Strauss and Lehtinen (1947) reported dramatically unstable performance among their pupils. Similarly, Ebersole, Kephart, and Ebersole (1968) indicated that learning-disabled children inconsistently retained previously learned materials. More recently, Swanson (1982) typified the learning-disabled population as performing in a fragmented, inconsistent manner. In addition, performance instability is included explicitly and implicitly in well-known classification schemes for identifying learning-disabled students, such as the Strauss syndrome (Stevens & Birch, 1957), Clements' symptoms of minimal brain dysfunction (Clements, 1966) and attention-deficit/hyperactivity disorders (American Psychiatric Association, 1994). Moreover, learning disabilities teachers appear to agree on the importance

of performance instability as a descriptor of their students (Aviezer & Simpson, 1980).

Nevertheless, the validity and usefulness of performance instability as a salient learning disabilities characteristic is weakened by at least two facts. First, work in two areas that are conceptually related to performance instability—attention disorders and impulsivity—demonstrates that learning-disabled children do not behave distinctively when compared with pupils with different labels of exceptionality. Second, research exploring performance instability among normal and mildly handicapped learning-disabled and behavior-disordered students indicates that the three groups are essentially comparable in the extent to which they manifest performance instability on academic tasks (Fuchs, Fuchs, & Deno, 1985; Fuchs, Fuchs, Tindal, & Deno, 1986).

REFERENCES

American Psychiatric Association. (1994). *Diagnostic and statistical manual of mental disorders* (4th ed.). Washington, DC: Author.

Aviezer, Y., & Simpson, S. (1980). Variability and instability in perceptual and reading functions of brain injured children. *Journal of Learning Disabilities, 13,* 41–47.

Clements, S. D. (1966). *Minimal brain dysfunction in children: Terminology and identification* (NINDS Monograph No. 3, U.S. Public Health Service Publication No. 1415). Washington, DC: U.S. Government Printing Office.

Ebersole, M., Kephart, N. C., & Ebersole, J. B. (1968). *Steps to achievement for the slow learner.* Columbus, OH: Merrill.

Fuchs, D., Fuchs, L. S., & Deno, S. L. (1985). Performance instability: An identifying characteristic of learning disabled children? *Learning Disability Quarterly, 8,* 19–26.

Fuchs, D., Fuchs, L. S., Tindal, G., & Deno, S. L. (1986). Performance instability of learning disabled, emotionally handicapped, and nonhandicapped children. *Learning Disability Quarterly, 9,* 84–88.

O'Donnell, L. G. (1980). Intra-individual discrepancy in diagnosing specific learning disabilities. *Learning Disability Quarterly, 3,* 10–18.

Stevens, G. D., & Birch, J. W. (1957). A proposal for clarification of the terminology used to describe brain-injured children. *Exceptional Children, 23,* 346–349.

Strauss, A., & Lehtinen, L. (1947). *Psychopathology and education of the brain-injured child.* New York: Grune & Stratton.

Swanson, H. S. (1982). In the beginning was a strategy: Or was it a constraint? *Topics in Learning & Learning Disabilities, 2,* x–xiv.

DOUGLAS FUCHS
LYNN S. FUCHS
*Peabody College, Vanderbilt
University*

ATTENTION-DEFICIT/HYPERACTIVITY DISORDER
IMPULSE CONTROL

PERINATAL FACTORS IN HANDICAPPING CONDITIONS

A number of perinatal factors increase the risk of handicapping conditions in the newborn. Social factors include lack of prenatal care; maternal age; inadequate maternal nutrition; use of alcohol, tobacco, or drugs (Alcohol, Drug Abuse, and Mental Health Administration, 1992); stress; work; handicapping condition (Lord, 1991); and fatigue. Maternal disease factors such as hypertension, diabetes, and heart disease may also affect fetal condition at birth. However, alterations in the birth process itself may contribute to the development of fetal handicapping conditions. Preterm labor, postterm labor, premature rupture of membranes, multiple births, antepartum hemorrhage, breech presentations, Caesarean sections, and forceps deliveries all add to the risk of unfavorable fetal outcomes and handicapping conditions (Avery & Taeusch, 1984).

The purpose of prenatal care is to provide ongoing education and evaluation during pregnancy. Serial evaluations permit the physician or midwife to uncover actual or potential morbid states and institute timely interventions with the potential for improved fetal outcome. Early detection of urinary tract infections, hypertension, heart murmurs, protein or sugar in the urine, too little or too rapid uterine growth, or swelling of extremities provides the health-care team with the opportunity to arrest the development of the more serious maternal cardiac or renal disease, hypertension, premature labor, or complications of unexpected multiple births. Therefore, lack of good prenatal care can and often is associated with poor fetal and/or maternal outcome (Harrison, Golbus, & Filly, 1984).

Maternal age represents a nonspecific influence on fetal outcome at birth. Adolescent women 15 years and younger have increased incidences of newborns with neurologic disorders and low birth weights. Women 40 years and older are at increased risk for stillborns or infants with chromosomal abnormalities (Avery & Taeusch, 1984).

Inadequate maternal nutrition and insufficient maternal weight gain of less than 14 pounds have been associated with low infant birth weight. The heavy use of alcohol during pregnancy increases the newborn's risk for growth retardation, microencephaly, cardiac anomalies, and renal anomalies. Tobacco use during pregnancy increases the newborn's risk for low birth weight, prematurity, and even stillbirth. Prescribed, over-the-counter, or recreational drugs may have an adverse effect on the neonate. The probability of a drug causing harm is dependent on the drug itself, the dose, route of administration, stage of gestation, and the genetic makeup of the mother and fetus. Drugs increase the risk of low birth weight, chromosomal abnormalities, organ anomalies, and even fetal death. Further, drugs can create problems with resuscitation and potential withdrawal phenomenon in the newborn (Hobel, 1985).

Stress, work, and fatigue have been associated with an increased risk for poor fetal outcome. The association between stress, work, fatigue, and pregnancy complications is not clear, but it is related to growth retardation and/or low birth weight of the neonate (Creasy, 1984).

Maternal disease factors associated with poor fetal outcome and handicapping conditions include hypertension, diabetes, and heart disease. Hypertension is the most frequently identified maternal problem associated with growth retardation. Hypertension is also associated with preterm labor, low birth weight, cerebral palsy, mental retardation, and fetal death (Avery & Taeusch, 1984).

Poorly controlled maternal diabetes with associated high blood sugars is related to poor fetal outcome. The risk for growth retardation, congenital defects, and brain damage is increased by the complications of diabetes. Maternal heart disease with associated reduced cardiac output is also associated with the increased risk of prematurity and low birth weight (Hobel, 1985).

Prematurity with its complications is associated with many handicapping conditions. Postterm pregnancy refers to pregnancy lasting longer than 42 weeks. Postterm pregnancy is associated with an increased risk for growth retardation, distress, and even death of the neonate (Hobel, 1985).

The premature rupture of membranes is associated with an increased risk of premature birth and an increased risk for neonatal infection (Oxorn, 1986). Multiple births, antepartum hemorrhage, breech presentation, Caesarean section, and forcep deliveries also increase the risk of handicapping conditions to the newborn. These alterations in the birth process increase the risk for neonatal mortality, central nervous system hemorrhage, asphyxia, and long-term neurologic disability (Avery & Taeusch, 1984).

REFERENCES

Alcohol, Drug Abuse, and Mental Health Administration. (1992). *Identifying the needs of drug-affected children: Public policy issues.* OSAP Prevention Monograph II. Rockville, MD: Office of Substance Abuse Prevention.

Avery, M. E., & Taeusch, H. W. (Eds.). (1984). *Schaffer's diseases of the newborn* (5th ed.). Philadelphia: Saunders.

Creasy, R. K. (1984). Preterm labor and delivery. In R. K. Creasy, & R. Resnik (Eds.), *Maternal-fetal medicine, principles and practice* (pp. 415–443). Philadelphia: Saunders.

Harrison, M. R., Golbus, M. S., & Filly, R. A. (1984). *The unborn patient, prenatal diagnosis and treatment.* Orlando, FL: Grune & Stratton.

Hobel, C. J. (1985). Factors during pregnancy that influence brain development. In J. M. Freeman (Ed.), *Prenatal and perinatal factors associated with brain disorders* (NIH Publication No. 85-1149, pp. 197–236). Bethesda, MD: U.S. Department of Health and Human Services.

Lord, C. (1991). Pre and perinatal factors in high-functioning females and males with autism. *Journal of Autism and Developmental Disorders, 21*(2), 197–209.

Oxorn, H. (1986). *Human labor and birth* (5th ed.). Norwalk, CT: Appleton-Century-Crofts.

ELIZABETH R. BAUERSCHMIDT
University of North Carolina at Wilmington

MICHAEL BAUERSCHMIDT
Brunswick Hospital

ETIOLOGY
INTERVENTION
LOW BIRTH WEIGH INFANTS
MARCH OF DIMES
NEONATAL BEHAVIORAL ASSESSMENT SCALES
PREMATURITY

PERKINS-BINET TESTS OF INTELLIGENCE FOR THE BLIND

The Perkins-Binet Tests of Intelligence for the Blind (Davis, 1980) were designed to assess the intellectual functioning (verbal and performance) of visually impaired children. Shortly after their appearance it became evident that there were a number of significant flaws in the tests. Reviewers (e.g., Genshaft & Ward, 1982) found the test manual lacking in technical information. Instructions for administering were vague, and in some instances, incomplete. The tests were lengthy and difficult to administer, and scoring criteria were unclear. There were also concerns about psychometric adequacy and the lack of reliability and validity data (Gutterman, Ward, & Genshaft, 1985). The tests have since been withdrawn from the market.

REFERENCES

Davis, C. J. (1980). *The Perkins-Binet Tests of Intelligence for the Blind.* Watertown, MA: Perkins School for the Blind.

Genshaft, J., & Ward, M. (1982). A review of the Perkins-Binet Tests for the Blind with suggestions for administration. *School Psychology Review, 11*(3), 338–341.

Gutterman, J. E., Ward, M., & Genshaft, J. (1985). Correlations of scores of low vision children on the Perkins-Binet Tests of Intelligence for the Blind, the WISCR-R and the WRAT. *Journal of Visual Impairment & Blindness, 79*, 55–58.

ROBERT G. BRUBAKER
Eastern Kentucky University

BLIND
VISUALLY IMPAIRED

PERKINS SCHOOL FOR THE BLIND

The Perkins School for the Blind was the first private residential school for the blind chartered in the United States. It was founded by Samuel Gridley Howe in 1832 to serve two blind students and was originally called the New England Asylum for the Blind. At that time asylum was all that even the most fortunate blind person could expect out of life. However, Howe, a strong believer in education, changed the name to the New England Institution for the Education of the Blind. Today, it is known as the Perkins School for the Blind, after Thomas Perkins, a prominent Boston merchant and one of the school's early benefactors. Probably one of its most well-known students was Helen Keller, who attended Perkins from 1887–1892.

The Perkins programs are comprehensive and serve a wide variety of blind, visually impaired, deaf-blind, and multiimpaired children, teenagers, and adults. The programs include preschool services, ages 0–5; primary and intermediate services, ages 6–15; secondary services, ages 15–22; deaf-blind program, ages 5–22; severely impaired program, ages 16–22; adult services, ages 18 and up; and community residence and independent living services, ages 18 and up. The philosophy is to prepare students and clients to meet everyday life to the best of their abilities emotionally, socially, physically, vocationally, and avocationally (Annual Report, 1998).

Perkins also provides other services besides direct care, including the Samuel P. Hayes Research Library, which collects print material about the nonmedical aspects of blindness and deaf-blindness. In addition, it houses a museum on the history of blind and deaf-blind and a historic collection of embossed books for the blind. The Howe Press is located at Perkins. It is the developer and manufacturer of the Perkins Brailler, used throughout the world. The Howe Press also distributes children's books, brailling accessories, and other aids and materials for blind and low-vision students.

REFERENCE

Perkins School for the Blind Annual Report. (1998). Watertown, MA: Author.

ROSANNE K. SILBERMAN
Hunter College, City University of New York

BLIND
VISUAL IMPAIRMENT

PERMANENT PRODUCT RECORDING

Permanent product recording is an observation method where student products are measured and recorded. This method is the most common technique that teachers use to collect and record student data (Cooper, Heron, & Heward, 1987). Alberto and Troutman (2006, p. 62) write that permanent products are "tangible items or environmental effects that result from a behavior." This method, also known as outcome recording, allows a teacher or researcher to count a result of a behavior after it has been omitted (Wolery, Bailey, & Sugai, 1988). Examples of behaviors that are suitable for permanent product recording include homework completion, answers on a test, pencil marks left on a desk, audio or video recording of student behavior, and school vandalism.

Permanent product recording has many advantages, including (1) having the option to count the behavior right after it occurred or waiting until a later time to count and record the behavior (Sulzer-Azaroff & Mayer, 1991); (2) being able to maintain a durable sample of the targeted behavior (Alberto & Troutman, 2006); and (3) being able to focus on teaching, instead of systematically observing a student during instruction (Maag, 1999). As with all direct observation systems, collecting interobserver reliability data is critical. The formula for calculating interobserver reliability for permanent product recording is taking the number of agreements and dividing by the agreements plus disagreements, then multiplying by 100. This formula will give you the percentage of agreement between the primary observer and an independent observer.

REFERENCES

Alberto, P. A., & Troutman, A. C. (2006). *Applied behavior analysis for teachers* (7th ed.). Upper Saddle River, NJ: Pearson Merrill Prentice Hall.

Cooper, J. O., Heron, T. E., & Heward, W. L. (1987). *Applied behavior analysis.* New York: Macmillan.

Maag, J. W. (1999). *Behavior management: From theoretical implications to practical applications.* San Diego, CA: Singular.

Sulzer-Azaroff, B., & Mayer, G. R. (1991). *Behavior analysis for lasting change.* Fort Worth, TX: Harcourt Brace.

Wolery, M., Bailey, D., Jr., & Sugai, G. (1988). *Effective teaching: Principles and procedures of applied behavior analysis with exceptional students.* Boston: Allyn & Bacon.

RANDALL L. DE PRY
*University of Colorado at
Colorado Springs*

BEHAVIORAL ASSESSMENT

PERSEVERATION

Perseveration is used in special education to describe behavior that is continued by a child beyond the normal (Cuneo & Welsch, 1992) end point of the behavior and that is accompanied by difficulty in changing tasks. Perseveration is considered to be a soft neurologically sign and is believed to be most common among learning-disabled and brain-injured children. Lerner (1971) discusses perseverative behavior as one of the four major behavioral characteristics of learning-disabled children.

In formal assessment, perseveration is often noted on such tasks as the Bender-Gestalt, in which the child is required to reproduce a series of nine drawings. Figures one, two, and six of this series require lines or rows of circles, dots, and repeating curves. Once started on the task of making dots, circles, or repeating curves, some children have great difficulty in stopping and subsequently distort their drawings greatly. Such children seem to get carried away by a specific activity, repeating it over and over, unable to stop. Perseveration is most commonly seen in motor tasks, but it can also be present in verbal behavior and even in thought patterns.

On intelligence tests such as the Wechsler Intelligence Scale for Children–Revised, children may display verbal or ideational perseveration. Although not formally scored as perseveration, this behavior lowers children's intelligence test scores significantly. On tasks such as telling how two everyday, common objects are alike (the similarities subtest of the WISC-R), some children will give the same fundamental answer to each pair of items; they seem unable to alter their mental set once established. Anxiety may also promote perseverative behavior.

Levine, Brooks, and Shonkoff (1980) have presented an interesting, useful view of perseveration and have provided some excellent clinical examples. They note that transitional events, or even minor changes in routine, constitute common impediments to many children with learning disorders, many of whom are perseverative. At the same time, some of these children are impersistent at academic or other tasks, a finding that seems paradoxical on the surface. However, as Levine et al. note, there may be a fine line between impersistence and perseveration, and the two traits coexist in some children.

Difficulties with adaptability may be a component of a general biological predisposition to inefficient attentional strategies. Children who cannot shift tasks, activities, or mental sets may be reflecting anxiety linked to issues of loss or fear of failure, or may be demonstrating neurological abnormalities associated with frontal lobe or possibly reticular function. Persevactive responses to occur more frequently in the case of frontal lobe dysfunction (e.g., see Reynolds & Horton, 2006). Koppitz (1963, 1975) has reviewed a number of studies in which children with brain damage demonstrate higher levels of perseverative behavior than do normal children of the same age. Perseveration is one of the best indicators of neurological impairment on the Bender-Gestalt Test (Koppitz, 1963, 1975) and is one of the least subjective scoring categories.

The following clinical illustrations from Levine et al. (1980) are useful in understanding the different features of perseveration as well as its relationship to impersistence.

1. A child may find the daily progression of routines difficult to manage. Getting up in the morning, dressing, eating breakfast, and preparing for school may present problems. The youngster may linger over each activity. The same pattern may appear when the youngster returns from school; there may be problems initiating routines, coming in from play, disengaging from the television set, and preparing for sleep. Parental efforts to induce a shift of activities may result in severe temper tantrums and unbridled anger.

2. A child may persist at an activity, wishing to sustain it beyond a reasonable period. Such a youngster has difficulty in suspending a project for continuation. Sometimes the behavior reflects a child's wish to pursue some enterprise that is likely to yield success rather than to move on to a riskier endeavor that might culminate in failure; such tenacity may be an avoidance response. At other times perseveration may be a consequence of cognitive inertia with regard to shifting sets. For example, some children with memory deficits or difficulties in establishing object constancy may experience change as overwhelming.

3. A child may resist any changes in daily routine. His or her behavior may deteriorate at the prospect of an unexpected visit to a relative. The youngster may be upset by the arrival of cousins for an overnight visit or by having to give up his or her own bed for the night. Some children crave consistency, or a sameness that helps provide order in a world that seems chaotic. They do not appreciate surprises and instead insist on knowing exactly what is going to happen each day (pp. 240–241).

Painting (1979) has commented, appropriately, that perseveration may occur because a particular response is so gratifying to a child that it is repeated primarily for the pleasure involved. A child with learning problems who gets a test item correct or who has mastered a particular activity may perseverate in the behavior because it promotes feelings of success and aids the child's self-esteem.

Perseveration may occur for a variety of reasons. Good diagnosis must go beyond designation of the presence of perseveration to explaining why the child perseverates. Treatment choices are likely to be impacted significantly by etiology in the case of perseverative behavior.

REFERENCES

Cuneo, K., & Welsch, C. (1992). Perseveration in young children: Developmental and neuropsychological perspectives. *Child Study Journal, 22*(2), 73–92.

Lerner, J. (1971). *Children with learning disabilities.* Boston: Houghton Mifflin.

Levine, M. D., Brooks, R., & Shonkoff, J. P. (1980). *A pediatric approach to learning disorders.* New York: Wiley.

Koppitz, E. M. (1963). *The Bender Gestalt Test for Young Children.* New York: Grune & Stratton.

Koppitz, E. M. (1975). *The Bender Gestalt Test for Young Children. Vol. II. Research and application, 1963–1973.* New York: Grune & Stratton.

Painting, D. H. (1979). Cognitive assessment of children with SLD. In W. Adamson & K. Adamson (Eds.), *A handbook for specific learning disabilities.* New York: Halstead.

Reynolds, C. R., & Horton, A. M. (2006). *Test of verbal conceptualization and fluency.* Austin, TX: PRO-ED.

CECIL R. REYNOLDS
Texas A&M University

BENDER-GESTALT TEST

PERSONALITY ASSESSMENT

There are numerous personality theories, definitions, and perspectives that incorporate a variety of individual traits. In general, personality is thought to include characteristics such as attitudes, interests, emotional reactions, impulses, behavior, temperament, and social interaction styles that are stable over time. Developmental influences of personality are thought to include hereditary predispositions, conscious and preconscious motivations, as well as environmental experiences (Fadiman & Frager, 2005). A clinician's theoretical orientation often influences which personality components are emphasized and which assessment methods are used.

Evaluation procedures are determined by the intended purpose of the assessment. The goals of psychological evaluation within school systems typically are to diagnosis, determine need for educational support services, and design appropriate interventions. Within clinical settings, the goals of assessment for children may include trauma stabilization, diagnoses of pathology common to psychotic disturbances (e.g., schizophrenia hallucinations), and treatment planning. Neuropsychological assessments for children also include measures of personality that may have implications for brain injuries, lesions, and diseases known to produce profound emotional changes (e.g., disinhibition, euphoria) related to specific anatomical structures (Lezak, 1995). In some cases, children may receive personality assessments from multiple providers in collaboration with special education personnel to design comprehensive school- and community-based intervention (e.g., a bulimic adolescent who is receiving family therapy in a clinical setting while simultaneously receiving individual counseling and behavioral modification services at school to address purging behaviors).

Psychologists conducting individual personality assessments are expected to be knowledgeable of national, state, and school district laws, policies, and guidelines applicable to psychoeducational assessment. The Individuals with Disabilities Education Improvement Act (2004), state statutes, state board of education rules, and state department of education technical papers provide directives pertinent to such issues as the qualities that need to be assessed, under what conditions students may be provided special education services, and the degree of restrictiveness in educational settings. Diagnostic symptomology for personality disorders is delineated in the *Diagnostic and Statistical Manual of Mental Disorders,* fourth edition (American Psychiatric Association, 2000). Best practices in psychological assessment dictate careful consideration in selecting evaluation methods and an understanding of validity and reliability issues (American Educational Research Association, 1999).

Assessment methods include clinical interviews, behavioral observations, and psychological measurement instruments. Clinical interviews may be conducted with students and caregivers, including teachers. Objectives of the interview include gathering information on: developmental and medical history; establishing onset, severity, and the chronic nature of problem behaviors; understanding social, economic, and cultural contexts; and identifying support systems (Sattler, 2002). Interviews may be unstructured or follow a protocol (e.g., Behavior Assessment System for Children Structured Developmental History, Semistructured Clinical Interview for Children and Adolescents).

Behavioral observations strive to provide objective and quantifiable data in a systematic manner. Specific behaviors are identified and defined (e.g., yelling that disturbs classroom instruction). Then occurrences are documented across settings. These data can be analyzed to establish the frequency, duration, pattern, time-of-day, and location of particular behaviors (Kelley, Noell, & Reitman, 2003). School personnel may design charts, graphs, or tables to collect and summarize these data. There are also numerous published observational coding systems (e.g., Classroom Observation of Conduct and Attention Deficit Disorders) tailored to specific diagnoses' symptoms (Sattler, 2002). However, these observation measures typically do not offer national norm comparison data for a wide range of behaviors (e.g., on/off task, disrupting others).

Psychological measurement instruments for personality can be divided into two categories, objective and projective. Objective measures, often in the form of rating scales, provide quantitative scores and strive to adhere to rigorous validity and reliability standards. This is accomplished through expert review of test item content, statistical analysis of theoretical constructs, comparisons of score stability, standardized administration, and establishing national norms for scores. Personality rating scales may provide test items across a broad range of behaviors from internal-

izing (e.g., anxiety, depression) to externalizing (e.g., Oppositional Defiant) disorders (e.g., Minnesota Multiphasic Personality Inventory, Millon Adolescent Personality Inventory). Instruments (e.g., Brown ADD Scales) also may be narrow in scope, focusing on specific syndrome symptoms such as Attention-Deficit/Hyperactivity Disorder or skill sets such as social skills (e.g., Social Skills Rating System). Rating scales also may measure positive characteristics for specific traits such as extroversion, introversion, or learning style preferences in temperament (e.g., Student Styles Questionnaire).

Projective personality measures typically are less standardized, utilize more open-ended response methods, rely more heavily on clinical interpretation, may not be normed, and thus may not include national comparison scores. Some recent projective instruments and scoring systems strive to provide greater standardization in administration and scoring (e.g., Roberts Apperception Test for Children, Exner scoring for Rorschach). Projective measures may include story-telling techniques, drawings, or sentence completions (e.g., House-Tree-Person Drawing Technique) that often are interpreted based on theory. The use of projectives measures is somewhat controversial, especially in regard to their validity and reliability (Kamphaus & Frick, 2000). Best practices in all psychological assessment require the integration of multiple methods and multiple sources of information across multiple settings and over multiple time periods considering multiple traits when making diagnostic or placement recommendations.

REFERENCES

American Educational Research Association. (1999). *Standards for educational and psychological testing.* Washington DC: Author.

American Psychiatric Association. (2000). *Diagnostic and statistical manual of mental disorders* (4th ed.). Washington, DC: Author.

Fadiman, J., & Frager, R. (2005). *Personality and personal growth* (6th ed.). Upper Saddle River, NJ: Prentice Hall.

Individuals with Disabilities Education Improvement Act of 2004. 20 U.S.C. § 1400 et seq. Retrieved August 28, 2005, from http://www.ed.gov/policy/speced/guid/idea/idea2004.html

Kamphaus, R. W., & Frick, P. J. (2000). *Clinical assessment of child and adolescent personality and behavior.* Needham Heights, MA: Allyn & Bacon.

Kelley, M. L., Noell, G. H., & Reitman, D. (2003). *Practitioner's guide to empirically based measures of school behavior.* New York: Kluwer Academic.

Lezak, M. D. (1995). *Neuropsychological assessment* (3rd ed.). New York: Oxford University Press.

Sattler, J. M. (2002). *Assessment of children: Behavioral and clinical applications* (4th ed.). La Mesa, CA: Author.

DIANA JOYCE
University of Florida

BEHAVIOR ASSESSMENT SYSTEM FOR CHILDREN–
    SECOND EDITION
MMPI
PERSONALITY INVENTORY FOR CHILDREN

PERSONALITY INVENTORY FOR CHILDREN–SECOND EDITION

The Personality Inventory for Children–Second Edition (PIC-2) is a multidimensional, objective questionnaire for use in the evaluation of children and adolescents ages 5 to 19. It assesses both broad and narrow dimensions of behavioral, emotional, cognitive, and interpersonal adjustment and is completed by parents or parent surrogates. The PIC-2 consists of a Standard Form with 275 descriptive statements with a true-and-false response format; it takes about 40 minutes for the parent to complete. There is also a 96-item Behavioral Summary derived from the longer Standard Form that takes about 15 minutes to complete. This version can be used for screening, research, or monitoring behavior change.

Basic instructions for the respondent are printed in the Administration Booklet and on the Answer Sheet. The respondent is informed that the inventory contains statements that will help describe his or her child's feelings, behavior, and family relationships. The respondent is directed to mark T if the statement is true or mostly true and F is the statement is false or not usually true. There are three response validity scales that are part of the PIC-2, including Inconsistency, Dissimulation, and Defensiveness. The nine adjustment scales include Cognitive Impairment, Impulsivity and Distractibility, Delinquency, Family Dysfunction, Reality Distortion, Somatic Concern, Psychological Discomfort, Social Withdrawal, and Social Skills Deficits. There are 21 subscales of the adjustment scales. The manual that accompanies the PIC-2 contains all of the information needed for effective use of both the Standard Form and Behavioral Summary versions of the questionnaire.

The standardization sample of the PIC-2 included 2,306 students in the United States, from kindergarten through the 12th grade. The sample was representative of the 1998 U.S. census with respect to gender, age, geographic region, ethnic background, and parents' educational level, and included a spectrum of socioeconomic status conditions. The scales of the PIC-2 provide T scores that have a mean of 50 and a standard deviation of 10.

The internal consistency reliability for the longer and more stable adjustment scales ranges from .75 to .91, with a median of .84. The adjustment scale retest reliability ranges from .66 to .90, with a median of .82, for a 1-week interval. Criterion validity was evidenced by moderate cor-

relations between adjustment scales of the PIC-2 and other instruments, including the Clinician Symptom Checklist, Personality Inventory for Youth (PIY), and the Student Behavior Survey (SBS), with the majority of correlations ranging from .30 to .60.

REFERENCES

Impara, J. C., & Plake, B. S. (Eds.). (1998). *The thirteenth mental measurements yearbook.* Lincoln, NE: Buros Institute of Mental Measurements.

Mitchell, J. V. (Ed.). (1985). *The ninth mental measurements yearbook.* Lincoln, NE: Buros Institute of Mental Measurements.

RON DUMONT
Fairleigh Dickinson University

JOHN O. WILLIS
Rivier College

PERSON-CENTERED PLANNING

Teaching youth with disabilities the skills necessary to become self-determined individuals has become an increasing priority for educators, adult service professionals, and families. With the help of a supportive group of people, person-centered planning (PCP) has emerged as a powerful mechanism for facilitating self-determined futures for youth with disabilities (O'Brien & O'Brien, 2000; Whitney-Thomas & Timmons, 1998). Person-centered planning is considered a "process-oriented approach" (Condon, Fichera, & Dreilinger, 2003) that empowers people with disabilities by viewing them as the primary director of their life. The planning process encourages an individual to involve personal and community networks in planning for the future. The process includes articulating a vision and coordinating resources and supports to make the vision a reality. By encouraging youth and their families to identify and express preferences and assume responsibility for personal goal setting and taking action on their goals, PCP is clearly aligned with the objectives of transition planning and interagency collaboration (Condon, Fichera, & Dreilinger).

Person-centered planning is an approach for learning about people with disabilities and, through an ongoing process of social change (O'Brien & O'Brien, 2000) focuses on creating a lifestyle that can help people contribute in community life. PCP is a way of planning together with people to express and live according to the values of contribution, community inclusion, and choice. According to Mount (1997, p. 8), "this form of planning is a powerful tool because it provides the capacity to develop new visions for people, reimagine what is possible for them, and reevaluate their own roles and investments in making these ideals livable."

Table 1

Characteristics of traditional systems	Characteristics of person-centered systems
Goals focus on decreasing specific negative behaviors.	Images of the future are grounded in the belief that the person will experience positive, empowering changes in their life.
Program categories and service options that are often segregated are identified.	Positive changes are centered on specific community settings and engaging in valuable roles within those settings.
Many goals and objectives reflect minor accomplishments that can be attained in existing programs without making changes.	Ideas that seem unrealistic and impractical indicate that major changes are needed within existing systems, not the person.

Traditional forms of transition planning for individuals with disabilities are based on the developmental model; that is, emphasizing the deficits and needs of the individual with disabilities and viewing them as needing to be fixed (Smull, 1997). Responsibility for decision making is assigned to professionals who, in turn, inundate the individual with disabilities and his or her family with endless program goals and objectives.

Person-centered planning reflects an alternative set of values and messages by basing its procedure on the promise of community inclusion for everyone. Rather than assume the lead with responsibilities, professionals must instead listen to, and take direction from, individuals with disabilities and their families (Lehr & Brown, 1996). Many of the activities, people, and experiences these individuals enjoy should provide professionals with clues on which specific interest areas need to be expanded and increased. Similarly, situations that frustrate individuals with disabilities should convey the message to the professional that the setting, environment, activity, or people in the situation need to change (Butterworth & Strauch, 1994).

Person-centered planning helps the professional to change from the superior role of expert to a more humble role as a partner whose motto is: "work so that people have many ways to be a part of community life" (Mount, 1997, p. 57). Professionals must work to negotiate organizational changes to remove barriers that may stand in the way. Table 1 provides a summary of the differences between traditional views and person-centered planning views (Smull, 1997) on supporting individuals with disabilities.

Common Approach to Person-Centered Planning

Personal futures planning. Personal futures planning is based on two core contexts (O'Brien & Lovett, 1997): (1) pro-

viding support to people with disabilities and their families and friends and (2) providing assistance to service providers who want to transform the system they work within. The process focuses on developing a personal profile of the individual with disabilities by identifying strengths within the individual, the individual's significant others, and within the community (O'Brien & Lovett, 1997). Next, the Personal Futures Planning process engages the participants in creating images of a desirable future, identifying obstacles and opportunities, designing strategies, committing to next steps, and identifying needed systems changes. Finally, the participants are asked to commit to various responsibilities necessary toward ensuring that the desired future becomes reality. Personal futures planning calls on all its participants to work together as equal contributors in meeting the focus individual's needs and goals (O'Brien & Lovett).

MAPS (Making Action Plans) developed from efforts to assist families to include their children with disabilities in ordinary school classrooms (Pearpoint & Forest, 1997). MAPS brings together the key players in a child's life to identify a roadmap for working toward and achieving goals for the focus child (Forest & Lusthaus, 1989). The MAPS process identifies where the child currently is, what the goals are for the child, and how the team will work together to reach the goals. MAPS addresses the child's history, identity, strengths, gifts, and the team's dreams and nightmares for the child. The child's needs and actions steps for the plan are also identified. The MAPS process is most effective when the team has a general idea of what the goals are for the focus child (Kincaid & Fox, 2002).

PATH (Planning Alternative Tomorrows with Hope) is an effective process for bringing together a team that may already know a child well and has made a commitment to supporting the child in the future (Pearpoint & Forest, 1997). PATH is ideal for addressing short-term and long-term planning and achieving goals through achievable and measurable steps. As with most person-centered plans, the PATH process ensures that each team participant is assigned particular responsibilities for completing the identified action steps with the plan.

Essential lifestyle planning. Essential Lifestyle Planning developed from efforts to assist people to move from institutions into community agencies. The process focuses on gathering information about the focus person's core values, preferences, and nonnegotiables toward identifying the ideal match between the individual and a particular service agency (O'Brien & Lovett, 1997). Essential Lifestyle Planning also takes into account the person's disability and safety and health needs when developing a vision for the future and mobilizing and changing community services.

Each of the four approaches previously described share the common philosophical tenet of empowering individuals with disabilities through the formation of powerful alliances with families, friends, and service providers. The person with disabilities is the focus of planning and, in conjunction with their significant others, considered the primary authority on their life. Furthermore, each approach to person-centered planning encourages people to appreciate the dignity of risk by trying new things in order to help the person with disabilities realize their desired future. Finally, each approach aims at changing the traditional landscape of the community (Smull, 1997) by confronting and reducing the segregation of, and congregation among, people with disabilities.

Conducting a Person-Centered Planning Meeting

Participants in a person-centered planning meeting search for a common vision of a desirable future with the focus person and identify ways to use their vision to guide everyday action (O'Brien & O'Brien, 2000). The person responsible for leading the development of this common vision is the meeting's facilitator. The facilitator leads the group through the planning process by setting the agenda, assessing equal opportunity for all to participate, handling conflict when necessary, and accurately recording the comments and process. This person should be a neutral, unbiased person. The facilitator should be someone who is familiar with the person-centered planning process. During the planning process, it is important that the facilitator be able to reflectively listen, and provide short feedback phrases.

Preparing the meeting. Before the meeting, the facilitator should ensure that the room is designed in way that is free of distractions and allows the participants to feel comfortable. Chairs should be arranged in a manner that encourages interaction among participants. O'Brien and O'Brien (2000) suggest that the facilitator post chart paper around the room so that notes can be recorded and viewed easily by the participants.

Design of the meeting. The facilitator should begin the meeting by orienting participants to the structure and purpose of the meeting as well as delineating the ground rules. Sample ground rules may include (O'Brien & Lovett, 1997): (1) the facilitator keeps the meeting on track and will adjourn at the agreed-upon time; (2) everyone should be an active listener and speaker; (3) avoid disrespectful behavior; (4) maintain an open mind toward unconventional methods for helping the focus person accomplish their goals; (5) disagreements are expected and will be addressed but will not be resolved at the meeting; and (6) reminding everyone that the meeting doesn't require anyone to do anything; instead, it offers an invitation for participants to commit themselves to supporting the accomplishment of the focus person.

Following the agenda. Once the preliminary steps of welcoming participants and establishing the ground rules are accomplished, the facilitator proceeds to the essence of the meeting by gathering information on the focus person's goals for the future. All participants are asked to provide responses to the following commonly asked questions (O'Brien & Lovett, 1997; O'Brien & O'Brien, 2000): (1) what is the quality of the focus person's present life experiences?; (2) what is changing for the focus person, or in the surrounding environment, that is likely to influence the quality of the focus person's life?; (3) what are the most important threats to the person's quality of life?; (4) what is our image of a desirable future for the focal person?; (5) what are the most critical barriers to our moving toward the desirable future we've described?; (6) how will we most effectively manage these critical barriers and move toward the future we've defined?; and (7) what are the next steps?

Follow-up. Shortly after the meeting, all participants receive a written report that describes, in detail, the information gathered during the person-centered planning process. O'Brien and O'Brien (2000) recommend that, 2 weeks after the meeting, the people directly responsible for managing the person's schedule meet briefly to review the focus person's progress in light of the direction they set at the meeting. They consider the type, the number, and the balance of activities the person is involved in as well as the way the person presently performs the activities. One month after the meeting, the person who convened the planning process should review the commitments that were made during the "next steps" part of the meeting by either gathering the people who accepted responsibility for action or contacting each person individually (O'Brien & O'Brien). The purpose of this check-in is to share what has happened, what has been working well, and what needs improvement.

Conclusion

Person-centered planning enables individuals with disabilities to have a community presence and choice and influences change by creating a compelling image of a desirable future (Whitney-Thomas & Timmons, 1998). Those considered significant in the person's life are invited to join forces in helping him/her become successful. Finally, the planning process strengthens the person's alliances, clarifies individual interests and needs, and energizes new demands on the system and community (Smull, 1997).

REFERENCES

Butterworth, J., & Strauch, J. (1994). The relationship between social competence and success in the competitive work place for persons with mental retardation. *Education and Training in Mental Retardation, 29,* 118–133.

Condon, C., Fichera, K., & Dreilinger, D. (2003). More than just a job: Person-centered career planning. *The Institute Brief, 12*(1), 1–6.

Forest, M., & Lusthaus, E. (1989). Promoting educational equality for all students: Circles and maps. In S. Stainback, W. Stainback,

& M. Forest (Eds.), *Educating all students in the mainstream of regular education* (pp. 43–57). Baltimore: Brookes.

Kincaid, D., & Fox, L. (2002). Person-centered planning and positive behavior support. In S. Holburn & P. Vietze (Eds.), *Person-centered planning: Research, practice, and future directions* (pp. 29–49). Baltimore: Brookes.

Lehr, D., & Brown, F. (1996). *People with disabilities who challenge the system.* Baltimore: Brookes.

Mount, B. (1997). More than just a meeting: Benefits and limitations of personal futures planning. In J. O'Brien & C. O'Brien (Eds.), *A little book about person centered planning* (pp. 55–68). Toronto, Ontario: Inclusion Press.

O'Brien, C., & O'Brien, J. (2000). *The origins of person-centered planning: A community of practice perspectives.* Retrieved from http://thechp.syr.edu/PCP_History.pdf

O'Brien, J. (2000). A guide to personal futures planning. In J. O'Brien & C. O'Brien (Eds.), *A little book about person centered planning* (pp. 133–150). Toronto, Ontario: Inclusion Press.

O'Brien, J., & Lovett, H. (1997). Finding a way toward everyday lives: The contribution of person-centered planning. In J. O'Brien & C. O'Brien (Eds.), *A little book about person-centered planning* (pp. 113–132). Toronto, Ontario: Inclusion Press.

O'Brien, J., & O'Brien, C. (1997). Learning to listen. In J. O'Brien & C. O'Brien (Eds.), *A little book about person centered planning* (pp. 15–18). Toronto, Ontario: Inclusion Press.

Pearpoint, J., & Forest, M. (1997). The ethics of MAPS and PATH. In J. O'Brien & C. O'Brien (Eds.), *A little book about person centered planning* (pp. 93–103). Toronto, Ontario: Inclusion Press.

Smull, M. (1997). After the plan. In J. O'Brien & C. O'Brien (Eds.), *A little book about person centered planning* (pp. 75–81). Toronto, Ontario: Inclusion Press.

Whitney-Thomas, J., & Timmons, J. (1998). Building authentic visions: How to support the focus person in person centered planning. *Research to Practice, 4*(3), 1–5.

JULIE A. ARMENTROUT
*University of Colorado at
Colorado Springs*

SELF-DETERMINATION

PERSON-FIRST LANGUAGE

Smart (2001) asserts that language is a mirror that reflects society's views toward certain groups, and the words that are used quite accurately reveal aspects of the social and cultural history of those groups. Many words exist that are demeaning, hurtful, and perpetuate negative stereotypes. The words traditionally used to describe individuals with disabilities have all too often been offensive and demeaning and used in a manner that has set these people apart from the broader society. Further, society's traditional use of language has lumped (Smart) all the people perceived to be in the group together regardless of individual differences. The labels used to describe people with disabilities

often describe only one aspect of an individual's identity (Rossides, 1990).

The language we use as a society can have tremendous influence in determining the level of access to, and participation in, job opportunities, educational opportunities, and social participation (Hahn, 1993). Before behavior and attitudes can be changed, language must be changed (Smart, 2001). The language used to describe disabilities and the people who experience disabilities has commonly communicated deficit and inferiority. However, with the passage of such legislation as the Americans with Disabilities Act of 1990 and the Individuals with Disabilities Education Act of 1997, the reductionist reference to people with cognitive, physical, and emotional challenges is beginning to fade (Bickford, 2004). In addition to innovative special education law, the inclusion movement has also sparked the onset of more proactive and positive perceptions of individuals with disabilities. The inclusion of students with disabilities has challenged teachers to embrace all students in a "person-first way" (Lieberman & Arndt, 2004). "Person-first" is a movement that advocates looking at individuals instead of differences. The language that is specific to this movement is referred to as "person-first language."

Person-First Language

Person-first language refers to the person first and the disability second. The guiding principle with this type of language is to speak in a manner that does not make people feel uncomfortable with disabilities (Garcia, 2003). The intent of person-first language is twofold: (1) to emphasize the person over his or her disability and (2) to promote individual abilities instead of disabilities. Many organizations and advocacy groups have demanded the use of person-first language (Lieberman & Arndt, 2004). In addition, the language is required in all publications of the American Psychological Association. The *Publication Manual of the American Psychological Association* (5th ed., 2001, p. 69) notes that "the guiding principles for 'nonhandicapping' language is to maintain the integrity of individuals and human beings. Avoid language that equates persons with their conditions."

General Guidelines for Disability Etiquette

In addition to following the practice of person-first language, research (Garcia, 2003; Lieberman & Arndt, 2004; Milington & Leierer, 1996; Student Council for Exceptional Children, 2001) suggests 10 common rules of etiquette that, when followed, enable individuals with disabilities to be treated with dignity, worth, and respect. First, when speaking or writing, remember that children and adults with disabilities are like everyone else, with the exception being that they have a disability. Emphasize the abilities of the individual rather than their limitations. Second, avoid patronizing individuals with disabilities and refrain from giving excessive praise or attention to an individual with disabilities. Third, encourage an individual with disabilities to speak for himself or herself as often as possible. Fourth, remember that a "disability" is a functional limitation that interferes with a person's ability to walk, hear, talk, and/or learn. The term "handicap" is often defined specifically as environmental obstacles imposed by society upon individuals, not as something intrinsic to the individual (Garcia, 2003). Fifth, use possessive language when referring to disabilities and assistive technology. Use the word "has" or "uses" instead of the word "is" or "confined" (e.g., Sally has autism, instead of Sally is autistic; Sam uses a wheelchair to navigate his environment, instead of Sam is confined to a wheelchair). However, individuals who are deaf, especially those in the Deaf Culture, prefer to be referred to as a "deaf person." This is based on the deaf's identity as a culture, as a group not unified by a disability, but rather, unified by shared experiences and a common language (Garcia). Sixth, be aware that special education is a service rather than a set of services. Special education is not a place. Seventh, always speak directly to the person with a disability, not to their companion, aide, or sign language interpreter. Eighth, keep the ramps clear and wheelchair-accessible doors unlocked. When talking to a person who uses a wheelchair, pull up a chair for yourself or stand at a slight distance so that they are not straining their neck to make eye contact with you. Ninth, people who are blind know how to orient themselves and get around. Identify yourself before a handshake and be sure to introduce them to others in the group so they are not excluded. If people who are blind or visually impaired regularly use your facility, inform them about any physical changes, such as rearranged furniture or equipment. Tenth, if the person has a guide dog, walk on the opposite side and remember not to make contact with the dog.

Table 1 provides a list of suggestions for the proper usage of person-first language.

Table 1

Say	In place of
Child with a disability	Disabled or handicapped child
Person with cerebral palsy	Palsied, CP, spastic
Person who has	Afflicted, suffers from, victim
Without speech, nonverbal	Mute, or dumb
Developmental delay	Slow
Emotional disorder or mental illness	Crazy or insane
Deaf or hearing impaired	Deaf and dumb
Uses a wheelchair	Confined to a wheelchair
Person with mental retardation; person with significant cognitive disabilities	Retarded
Has a learning disability	Is learning disabled
Nondisabled	Normal, healthy
Has a physical disability	Crippled
Congenital disability	Birth defect

Conclusion

Using person-first language is also an effective way to use communication as a tool for promoting self-determination in individuals with disabilities (Lynch, Thuli, & Groombridge, 1994; Smart, 2001). Person-first language is based on respect, dignity, and enabling individuals with disabilities to feel welcome. Finally, the words we use have the potential of fostering the full inclusion of individuals with disabilities throughout every fiber of their community. Language does, indeed, shape perceptions.

REFERENCES

American Psychological Association. (2001). *Publication manual of the American Psychological Association* (5th ed.). Washington, DC: Author.

Bickford, J. (2004). Preferences of individuals with visual impairments for the use of person-first language. *Re:view, 36,* 120–126.

Garcia, S. (2003). Treat people with disabilities like people. Retrieved from *The Pueblo Chieftain Online,* April 2003, at http://www.chieftain.com/print/sunday/lifestyle/articles/h10.htm

Hahn, H. (1993). The political implications of disability definitions and data. *Journal of Disability Policy Studies, 4,* 41–52.

Lieberman, L., & Arndt, K. (2004). Language to live and learn by. *Teaching Elementary Physical Education, 12,* 33–34.

Lynch, R., Thuli, K., & Groombridge, L. (1994). Person-first disability language: A pilot analysis of public perceptions. *Journal of Rehabilitation, 7,* 18–22.

Milington, M., & Leierer, S. (1996). A socially desirable response to the politically incorrect use of disability labels. *Rehabilitation Counseling Bulletin, 39,* 276–283.

Rossides, D. W. (1990). *Social stratification: The American class system in comparative perspective* (2nd ed.). Englewood Cliffs, NJ: Prentice Hall.

Smart, J. (2001). *Disability, society, and the individual.* Gaithersburg, MD: Aspen.

Student Council for Exceptional Children—University of Wisconsin (2001). *Person first language.* Retrieved from www.uwec.edu/sped/info/1stperson.pdf

JULIE A. ARMENTROUT
University of Colorado at Colorado Springs

DISABILITY ETIQUETTE

PERSONNEL PREPARATION FOR WORKING WITH DIVERSE INDIVIDUALS

In contrast to the increasing number of students from diverse cultural and linguistic backgrounds, the teaching force is predominantly white, monolingual, female and suburban (Zeichner, 1993). The culture clash resulting from this disparity between the characteristics of students and those of teachers is a contributing factor to the underachievement of culturally and linguistically diverse (CLD) students in both general and special education, with Hispanic/Latino, African American, and American Indian children and youth experiencing the most significant achievement difficulties. As a group, these students are disproportionately overrepresented in special education, underrepresented in gifted education, and have higher dropout rates when compared to their white counterparts (García & Dominguez, 1997).

Essential Knowledge and Skills Related to Diversity

Institutions of higher education must adopt training models that prepare special educators to be culturally and linguistically competent service providers. To effectively address the diverse backgrounds of the students in their classrooms, teachers must have both culture-general and culture-specific knowledge and skills. Culture-general knowledge emphasizes cultural phenomena that occur across cultures and that are widely applicable in a variety of settings (Brislin & Yoshida, 1994). This information provides the initial foundation for understanding cultural/linguistic factors in schooling and education. Culture-specific knowledge, on the other hand, provides an understanding of the customs, norms, traditions, and values of a specific racial/ethnic community and helps prepare teachers to better serve the communities in which they teach. In addition, there are several other essential components of culturally-responsive personnel preparation programs.

Cultural Self-Awareness

Cultural self-awareness serves as the foundation on which individuals build their knowledge and skills related to diversity (Brislin & Yoshida, 1994). Teachers of CLD students should have the opportunity to examine their own beliefs, attitudes, and assumptions related to individuals from culturally and linguistically diverse backgrounds. They must consider how current practices associated with labeling students (e.g., at-risk, disabled, low-performing) impact their own perceptions of, and expectations for, CLD students, and develop educationally valid perspectives that promote effective teaching practices (Cloud, 1993).

Cultural/Linguistic Knowledge

Educators must understand cultural/linguistic variables influencing the teaching-learning process at two levels. First, they must possess a foundation of culture-general knowledge such as cultural variations in childrearing practices, culturally-based learning and communication styles, acculturation, bilingualism, second language acquisition, and dialectal differences, as well as the influences of these on the teaching-learning process. Second, variations in these dimensions of human development and learning must be understood in relation to the specific ethnolinguistic com-

munities of their CLD students and families (Gay, 1993). Moreover, it is important for educators to know how to gather these culture-specific data in their school communities (Hollins, 1996), and to be able to incorporate what they have learned into their professional practice; i.e., design culturally/linguistically responsive curricula and instruction, conduct non-biased assessments, and communicate effectively with diverse families.

Culturally/Linguistically Responsive Practice

When students' background experiences are different from those expected by the school, it is important that educators design instructional programs that foster academic success as well as a positive, bicultural/bilingual identity (Cummins, 1986). Effective educational practices for CLD students include high expectations for all students, accepting and culturally pluralistic classroom and school environments, a culturally- and linguistically-inclusive curriculum, use of varied teaching and classroom management styles, teaching aimed at preventing academic failure, culturally-appropriate assessment procedures and materials, and support systems for teachers (Banks, 1990; Ortiz & Wilkinson, 1991). Special educators who serve CLD students with disabilities must also be able to design and implement individualized educational plans that are culturally and linguistically responsive (e.g., Franklin, 1992; García & Malkin, 1993). This includes the ability to provide special education services in the student's native language and/or English-as-a-second-language (ESL) instruction for students with disabilities who are also still in the process of acquiring English (Yates & Ortiz, 1998). Similarly, students who are nonstandard speakers of English need services that are responsive to their dialectal differences as well as which provide opportunities to acquire standard English. To do this effectively, professionals must be able to modify assessment, instruction, and related services to accommodate the intrapersonal interactions between culture, language, and disability (Cloud, 1993).

Collaboration

An integral aspect of a multicultural, pluralistic school is the development of collaborative partnerships between schools and families. Recognizing that schools and professionals have often interacted with families in ways that effectively discourage their participation (Harry, Allen, & McLaughlin, 1995), teacher education programs should foster pluralistic models of family involvement. Professionals must understand cultural variations in family structures and in views about disability, and the impact of these different perspectives on how families and individuals with disabilities interact with the educational system. They must be able to work with family members to build on their strengths and available resources (Ford, 1995; Harry, 1992).

Special educators must also be able to work collaboratively with bilingual education teachers, ESL teachers, general education teachers, paraprofessionals, assessment and related services personnel, and others involved in implementing the student's intervention plan. It is likely that CLD students with disabilities will be served simultaneously by special education and a variety of other programs, resulting in the need to coordinate selection and implementation of goals and objectives, including responsibility for meeting these goals, language(s) of instruction, as well as instructional materials and procedures used across programs.

Reflection and Problem-Solving

The process of designing culturally- and linguistically-responsive programs and services implies that teachers can evaluate available materials and resources, adapt them to be sensitive to individual students' educational needs, and determine when and whether modifications are required (Kennedy, as cited in Burstein, Cabello, & Hamann, 1993). This is achieved by developing teachers' self-reflection and problem-solving skills through field experiences, reflective logs, structured and guided discussions, and activities designed to apply classroom-based theoretical knowledge in field-based settings (Burstein, Cabello, & Hamann, 1993). Without such guided reflection, the educational value of practica and other field-based assignments may be minimal or detrimental (Zeichner, 1993).

Cultural Brokers and Change Agents

Finally, teachers must also be capable of functioning as change agents and as cultural brokers (Gay, 1993). They must take a leadership role in helping educational systems shift from a traditional deficit view of CLD students and communities to one which reflects acceptance of cultural and linguistic differences as assets (Obiakor & Utley, 1997). That is, they must have developed a sociopolitical or critical consciousness (Ladson-Billings, 1995) which promotes and supports changes at the institutional level (Gay, 1993). According to Gay, teachers must thus be reflective practitioners, adept at critically examining the nature of schooling, the culture of the dominant society, cultural similarities and differences, and potential sources of conflict or dissonance. They must understand the organizational culture of schooling and be able to employ effective strategies to foster student success, and to initiate and support change. Finally, they must have the requisite cross-cultural communication and counseling skills to be effective cultural brokers and change agents.

To achieve institutional change in practices affecting CLD learners, general and special educators must additionally (a) understand the historical and contemporary factors which have led to disproportionate representation of CLD students in special and gifted education; (b) develop problem solving processes to systematically eliminate school-related factors which have contributed to the underachievement

of CLD students (García & Ortiz, 1988); and (c) critically examine assessment and identification procedures (Cummins, 1986) as well as programs and services to ensure that they are effectively meeting the educational needs of CLD students.

Related Issues

Many special education programs which serve CLD students are staffed by professionals who are not adequately trained and who are acquiring their expertise on the job. While efforts are underway to increase the number of CLD teachers who enter and remain in the profession, experience suggests that these efforts will not be sufficient to meet the needs of a growing CLD student population (Hill, Carjuzza, Aramburo, & Baca, 1993). Competencies must be identified and programs developed at the preservice and inservice levels to prepare all teachers to better serve the needs of culturally and linguistically diverse learners to reduce or eliminate the continuing cultural clashes resulting from the discontinuities between teachers' and students' backgrounds. In addition, institutions of higher education as well as school systems must continue to explore alternative approaches for recruitment and retention of professionals committed to working with CLD populations.

Contributing to the shortage of special education teachers with skills and competencies to serve CLD students is the serious shortage of university faculty who themselves have expertise related to CLD students with disabilities. This is a critical issue in that higher education faculty play a central role in the creation of new knowledge relative to the education of language minority students. Of particular concern, then, is the serious shortage of researchers from CLD backgrounds. Attention must be given to the retooling of university faculty to participate in the preparation of teachers for an increasingly pluralistic society. The special education literature on the preparation of teachers and other professionals to serve CLD populations is quite limited (Tulbert, Sindelar, Correa, & LaPorte, 1996), and studies of effective practices or program designs for diversity training in special education are even more scarce (Artiles & Trent, 1997). Several issues surround the question of how best to prepare professionals in general and special education to meet the needs of an increasingly diverse student population. Questions which must be addressed by future research in teacher education include:

What competencies are needed by all educators who serve CLD exceptional learners?

What is the role of bilingual/multicultural special education specialists in services for CLD exceptional children and youth?

What are essential professional competencies related to diversity that produced high student outcomes for CLD exceptional learners?

What is the most effective program design for multicultural/bilingual special education?

How does program philosophy and design (e.g., inclusion vs. specialized courses) influence the quality of the teachers' learning?

Professional Standards

There are several efforts underway aimed at identifying essential knowledge and skills of novice and exemplary teachers. For example, the Council for Exceptional Children has developed professional standards for the preparation of special educators (Council for Exceptional Children, 1996) and is currently collaborating with its Division for Culturally and Linguistically Diverse Exceptional Learners to identify entry-level knowledge and skills associated with teaching CLD students. Similarly, the National Board for Professional Teaching Standards is preparing standards for what accomplished special education teachers should know and be able to do, and has designed a system for recognizing exemplary teachers of special needs students. All Board certificates include equity, fairness, and diversity standards which underscore the importance of respecting and responding to individual and group differences and of ensuring that all students have access to academically challenging curricula and opportunities to learn.

REFERENCES

Artiles, A., & Trent, S. (1997). Forging a research program on multicultural preservice teacher education in special education: A proposed analytic scheme. In J. W. Lloyd, E. J. Kameenui, & D. Chard (Eds.), *Issues in educating students with disabilities* (pp. 275–304). Hillsdale, NJ: Erlbaum.

Banks, J. A. (1990). *Preparing teachers and administrators in a multicultural society*. Austin, TX: Southwest Educational Development Laboratory.

Brislin, R., & Yoshida, T. (1994). *Intercultural communication training: An introduction*. Thousand Oaks, CA: Sage.

Burstein, N., Cabello, B., & Hamann, J. (1993). Teacher preparation for culturally diverse urban students: Infusing competencies across the curriculum. *Teacher Education and Special Education, 16*(1), 1–13.

Cloud, N. (1993). Language, culture and disability: Implications for instruction and teacher preparation. *Teacher Education and Special Education, 16*, 60–72.

Council for Exceptional Children. (1996). *What every special educator must know: The international standards for the preparation and certification of special education teachers* (2nd ed.). Reston, VA: Author.

Cummins, J. (1986). Empowering language minority students. *Harvard Educational Review, 56*, 18–36.

Ford, B. A. (1995). African American community involvement processes and special education: Essential networks for effective education. In B. A. Ford, F. E. Obiakor, & J. M. Patton (Eds.), *Effective education for African American exceptional learners* (pp. 235–272). Austin, TX: PRO-ED.

Franklin, M. (1992). Culturally sensitive instructional practices for African-American learners with disabilities. *Exceptional Children, 59*, 115–122.

García, S. B., & Dominguez, L. (1997). Cultural contexts that influence learning and academic performance. *Child and Adolescent Psychiatric Clinics of North America, 6*, 621–655.

García, S. B., & Malkin, D. H. (1993). Toward defining programs and services for culturally and linguistically diverse learners in special education. *Teaching Exceptional Children, 26*(1), 52–58.

García, S. B., & Ortiz, A. A. (1988). *Preventing inappropriate referrals of Hispanic students to special education*. New Focus Series No. 3. Washington, DC: National Clearinghouse for Bilingual Education.

Gay, G. (1993). Building cultural bridges: A bold proposal for teacher education. *Education and Urban Society, 25*(3), 285–299.

Harry, B. (1992). Making sense of disability: Low-income, Puerto Rican parents' theories of the problem. *Exceptional Children, 59*, 27–40.

Harry, B., Allen, N., & McLaughlin, M. (1995). Communication versus compliance: African-American parents' involvement in special education. *Exceptional Children, 61*, 354–377.

Hill, R., Carjuzza, J., Aramburo, D., & Baca, L. (1993). Culturally and linguistically diverse teachers in special education: Repairing or redesigning the leaky pipeline. *Teacher Education and Special Education, 16*, 258–269.

Hollins, E. (1996). *Culture in school learning: Revealing the deep meaning*. Mahwah, NJ: Erlbaum.

Ladson-Billings, G. (1995). Toward a theory of culturally relevant pedagogy. *American Educational Research Journal, 32*, 465–491.

Obiakor, F. E., & Utley, C. A. (1997). Rethinking preservice preparation for teachers in the learning disabilities field: Workable multicultural strategies. *Learning Disabilities Research and Practice, 12*, 110–116.

Ortiz, A. A., & Wilkinson, C. Y. (1991). Assessment and Intervention Model for the Bilingual Exceptional Student (AIM for the BEST). *Teacher Education and Special Education, 14*, 37–42.

Tulbert, B., Sindelar, P. T., Correa, V. I., & La Porte, M. A. (1996). Looking in the rear view mirror: A content analysis of *Teacher Education and Special Education*. *Teacher Education and Special Education, 19*, 248–261.

Yates, J. R., & Ortiz, A. A. (1998). Developing individualized education programs for exceptional language minority students. In L. M. Baca & H. T. Cervantes (Eds.), *The bilingual special education interface* (3rd ed., pp. 188–210). Upper Saddle River, NJ: Merrill/Prentice Hall.

Zeichner, K. M. (1993). *Educating teachers for cultural diversity*. NCRTL Special Report. East Lansing: Michigan State University, National Center for Research on Teacher Learning.

SHERNAZ B. GARCÍA
ALBA A. ORTIZ
University of Texas

PERSONNEL TRAINING IN SPECIAL EDUCATION

See SPECIAL EDUCATION, TEACHER TRAINING IN.

PERU, SPECIAL EDUCATION IN

Special education services became established within the Ministry of Education following the passage of Educational Reform in 1971 (Legislative Decree No. 19326). These services currently are supported under the General Law of Education No. 23384, and the Regulation of Special Education D.S. No. 02-83-ED. Various special education programs are offered to students ages 0 through 20, including early intervention, elementary education, special primary education, and vocational education. Special education offers services principally to students with hearing and visual impairment, mental retardation, and those who are highly gifted. Services for those with impairments typically include language or physical therapy, promotion of psychomotor or social skills, and meetings/workshops to train parents of students with these disabilities (Benites, 2003).

Students with special educational needs who are integrated into regular schools are supported by Educational Centers through the Diversity Service Offices (*Servicio de Atención a la Diversidad*), which provide specialized resource to families, regular schools, and the community. Special education services are based on the key principles of inclusion, normalization, individualization, community integration, and provision of services in regional sectors (Ministry of Education, 2005).

In 2000, there were 397 special education centers in Peru, 92 percent of which were located in urban areas (Ministry of Education, 2000). These centers served 28,369 students (accounting for 0.4 percent of the Peruvian school population), 45 percent of whom live in Lima. They mainly served the needs of students with mental retardation (81 percent), those who were deaf or hard of hearing (10 percent), who were physically impaired (4 percent), were blind or visually impaired (4 percent), had a language disorder (1 percent), or displayed a behavior problem (1 percent; Ministry of Education, 2004). Practitioners serving these children include teachers, (56 percent), auxiliary employees (15 percent), specialists in mental retardation (9 percent), psychologists (6 percent), hearing and language specialists (4 percent), specialists for the visually impaired (2 percent), social assistants (3 percent), and physical therapists (2 percent). Thirty-eight percent of the centers have language therapy classrooms, 35 percent have physical therapy classrooms, 33 percent have early stimulation classrooms, and 17 percent have rooms for psychological services.

Both inclusive public and private schools are located in the various Local Educational Management Units throughout Peru. There are 120 inclusive schools in Lima, and 13 in Callao (Benites, 2003). Current priorities include improving special education services. In addition, efforts are needed to inform classmates and other peers as well as parents and other adults of characteristics of exceptional students, with the goal to promote understanding and prevent discrimination and, even more, to prevent physical and psychological mistreatment (Ministerio de Educación de Perú y Organización de Estados Iberoamericanos, 1994).

REFERENCES

Benites, L. (2003). *Atención a la Diversidad. Guía Psicoeducativa para Padres y Familiares de Niños y Jóvenes con necesidades educativas especiales.* Lima: Universidad de San Martín de Porres.

Defensoría del Pueblo. (2001). *Situación de la Educación Especial en el Perú: Hacia una educación de calidad.* Lima: Defensoría del Pueblo.

Ministry of Education. (2000). *Estadística Básica 2000.* Unidad de Estadística del Ministerio de Educación.

Ministry of Education. (2004). *Estadística Básica 2004.* Unidad de Estadística Educativa del Ministerio de Educación.

Ministry of Education. (2005). Unidad de Educación Especial—Ministerio de Educación. Acceso el 19/9/2005. En línea en http://www.huascaran.edu.pe/estudiantes/educacion_especial/tecno_edu_especial.htm

Ministerio de Educación de Perú y Organización de Estados Iberoamericanos. (1994). Sistema Educativo Nacional del Perú: 1994. Madrid: Organización de Estados Iberoamericanos para la Educación, la Ciencia y la Cultura (OEI). Documento en línea en http://www.campus-oei.org/quipu/peru/index.html

Rios, C., & Amaya, F. (1986). *Priorización de problemas y necesidades para establecer demandas en educación.* Lima: INIDE.

Tapia, V. (1975). La psicología educacional como profesión en el Perú. En R. Alarcón y otros (Eds.), *La investigación psicológica en el Perú* (pp. 285–291.) Lima: Sociedad Peruana de Psicología.

CESAR MERINO SOTO
University Privada San Juan Bautista, Lima, Peru

LUIS BENITES MORALES
Universidad San Martin de Porres, Lima, Peru

PESTALOZZI, JOHANN HEINRICH (1746–1827)

Johann Heinrich Pestalozzi, a Swiss educator, greatly influenced education in Europe and the United States. Believing that ideas have meaning only as related to concrete things and that learning must therefore proceed from the concrete to the abstract, he developed a system of education through object lessons that were designed to help the child develop abstract concepts from concrete experience.

Pestalozzi operated a number of orphanages and schools, the most notable being his boarding school at Yverdon, founded in 1805. His school demonstrated concepts such as readiness, individual differences, ability grouping, and group instruction, and contributed to the inclusion in the curriculum of the practical subjects of geography, nature, art, music, and manual training. Large numbers of educators visited Yverdon and hundreds of Pestalozzian schools were established in Europe. Pestalozzi's object method was first used in the United States in the schools of Oswego, New York; the Oswego Normal School trained teachers in Pestalozzi's methods. Of his numerous publications, Pestalozzi's *How Gertrude Teaches Her Children* best sets forth his educational principles.

REFERENCES

Pestalozzi, J. H. (1978). *How Gertrude teaches her children.* New York: Gordon.

Silber, K. (1973). *Pestalozzi: The man and his work.* New York: Schocken.

PAUL IRVINE
Katonah, New York

PETS IN SPECIAL EDUCATION

Animals have long been used in classrooms throughout the world (Hulme, 1995). The classic goldfish and gerbils have been used to teach basic animal facts. Teachers have also used pets to foster responsibility in their students. Animals can provide valuable classroom or instructional assistance far beyond the traditional expectations. Sustenance instruction, responsible behavior training, and abstract concepts development can be enhanced by involving special education students with animals. These animals may be provided in the classroom or they may be pets from home.

Any pet (fish, dog, cat, bird, etc.) may be used for sustenance instruction. Special education students can better learn the basic needs of animals through active participation in the pet's care. The students identify the need for food, water, shelter, and love. Instruction may include concepts such as appropriate food for different species, appropriate quantities of food and water, how climate affects the need for shelter, and how animals exhibit and respond to affection.

Teaching responsibility is a multifaceted, often difficult task. Whenever special education students have the responsibility for pets in the classroom or at home, the teacher should be attempting to develop various components of responsible behavior. Students should learn to create feeding, watering, bathing, walking, etc., schedules. In creating schedules for their pets, students may learn to develop schedules for their own lives. Caring for pets also aids in developing task commitment, as well as relationship commitment. Another facet of responsibility, self-initiation, is readily taught when students must care, without reminders from the teacher, for classroom animals.

Students may also develop observation skills through involvement with pets. Because pets are basically nonverbal, students must watch for changes in the animals' appearance or mannerisms to detect illness or injury.

Many special education students have difficulty in understanding abstract concepts such as life, death, and love. The birth or death of a classroom pet may be used to teach the rudiments and sentiments of such abstract concepts. The emotions of love, caring, and affection may be developed or more objectively understood by special education students when pets are used.

REFERENCE

Hulme, P. (1995). *Historical overview of nonstandard treatments.* (ERIC Clearinghouse No. EC303986)

JONI J. GLEASON
University of West Florida

EQUINE THERAPY
RECREATION, THERAPEUTIC

PEVZNER, MARIA SEMENOVNA (1901–1986)

As a physician-psychiatrist and doctor of pedagogical sciences, Maria Pevzner is known for her work on oligophrenia (mental deficiency). Her research was concentrated in the areas of child psychopathology and clinical assessment of atypical children. She suggested classification of oligophrenics into five groups: (1) with diffuse maldevelopment of the cortical hemispheres without serious neurological implications; (2) with cortical deficits and impaired perceptual abilities; (3) with various sensory, perceptual, and motor deficits; (4) with psychopathological behavior; and (5) with maldevelopment of the frontal lobes (Pevzner, 1970). Pevzner has extensively studied the criteria and clinical aspects necessary for a diagnosis of oligophrenia in school-age children (Mastyukova, Pevzner, & Peresleni, 1986), and she and her colleagues also investigated the intellectual development of children with cerebral palsy, finding considerable variation in intellectual disorders, thus suggesting the benefit of comprehensive examination for these children (Mastyukova, Pevzner, & Peresleni, 1987, 1988). Well-known publications of Pevzner are *Children Psychopaths* (1941), *Developmental Assessment and Education of Oligophrenic Children* (1963), and *Children with Atypical Development* (1966).

REFERENCES

Mastyukova, E. M., Peresleni, L. I., & Pevzner, M. S. (1988). A study of intellectual structure impairment in children with cerebral palsy. *Defektologiya, 4,* 12–17.

Mastyukova, E. M., Pevzner, M. S., & Peresleni, L. I. (1986). The diagnosis and clinical picture of oligophrenia in school children with cerebral palsy. *Zhurnal Neuropatologii I Psikhiatrii Imeni S-S-Korsakova, 86*(3), 386–389.

Mastyukova, E. M., Pevzner, M. S., & Peresleni, L. I. (1987). Diagnostic and clinical aspects of congenital mental retardation in pupils with cerebral palsy. *Soviet Neurology and Psychiatry, 20*(3), 36–43.

Pevzner, M. S. (1970). Etiopathogenesis and classification of oligophrenia (G. Malashko, Trans.). *Szkola Specjalna* (4), 289–293.

IVAN Z. HOLOWINSKY
Rutgers University
First edition

TAMARA J. MARTIN
*The University of Texas of the
Permian Basin*
Second edition

PHENOBARBITAL

Of the many available anticonvulsant medications, phenobarbital is the least expensive, most effective, best known, and most widely used barbiturate. It is the drug of choice for tonic-clonic (grand mal) epilepsy, neonatal fits, and febrile convulsions (Maheshwari, 1981), and may be viewed as the drug of choice for childhood epilepsy except in cases of absence (petit mal) attacks (Swanson, 1979). It even may be used as an effective agent in pure petit mal epilepsy as a measure against the development of grand mal epilepsy (Livingston, Pruce, & Pauli, 1979).

All anticonvulsant medications have side effects and the extent and severity of such side effects often influence medication choice. Unlike many anticonvulsant drugs, phenobarbital has few somatic side effects; however, it appears to have more pronounced effects on mental or cognitive functions in children (National Institutes of Health, 1980). Sedation or drowsiness is the chief side effect of phenobarbital in children. This initial effect of mental slowing is most pronounced when the drug is first administered. The effect generally declines within several weeks (Livingston, Pauli, Pruce, & Kramer, 1980; Schain, 1979) and appears to be dose related (Livingston et al., 1980; Livingston, Pruce, Pauli, & Livingston, 1979; Swanson, 1979; Wolf, 1979). Common behavioral side effects include hyperactivity, extreme irritability, and aggression (Fishman, 1979; Livingston et al., 1980; Nelson, 1983; Wilensky, Ojemann, Temkin, Troupin, & Dodrill, 1981). Other side effects involving cognitive or higher cortical functions include impaired attention, short-term memory deficits, defects in general comprehension, dysarthria, ataxia, and, in some cases, poor language development (Levenstein, 1984; Shinnar & Kang, 1994).

Fortunately, the side effects do not appear to be permanent, and withdrawal or replacement with other medications often produces significant amelioration of these deficits. For example, withdrawal may lead to dramatic improvements in personality patterns and learning skills (Schain, 1979). Continuous monitoring of possible side effects and appropriate adjustment of anticonvulsant medication is therefore of the utmost importance in effective management of seizure disorders.

REFERENCES

Fishman, M. A. (1979). Febrile seizures: One treatment controversy. *Journal of Pediatrics, 94,* 177–184.

Levenstein, D. (1984). Phenobarbital side effects: Hyperactivity with speech delay. *Pediatrics, 74,* 1133.

Livingston, S., Pauli, L. L., Pruce, I., & Kramer, I. I. (1980). Phenobarbital vs. phenytoin for grand mal epilepsy. *American Family Physician, 22,* 123–127.

Livingston, S., Pruce, I., & Pauli, L. L. (1979). The medical treatment of epilepsy: Initiation of drug therapy. *Pediatrics Annals, 8,* 213–231.

Livingston, S., Pruce, I., Pauli, L. L., & Livingston, H. L. (1979). The medical treatment of epilepsy: Managing side effects of antiepileptic drugs. *Pediatrics Annals, 8,* 261–266.

Maheshwari, M. C. (1981). Choice of anticonvulsants in epilepsy. *Indian Pediatrics, 18,* 331–346.

National Institutes of Health. (1980). Febrile seizures: Long-term management of children with fever-associated seizures. *British Medical Journal, 281,* 277–279.

Nelson, K. B. (1983). The natural history of febrile seizures. *Annual Review of Medicine, 34,* 453–471.

Schain, R. J. (1979). Problems with the use of conventional anticonvulsant drugs in mentally retarded individuals. *Brain & Development, 1,* 77–82.

Shinner, S., & Kang, H. (1994). Idiosyncratic phenobarbital toxicity mimicking a neurogenerative disorder. *Journal of Epilepsy, 7*(1), 34–37.

Swanson, P. D. (1979). Anticonvulsant therapy: Approaches to some common clinical problems. *Postgraduate Medicine, 65,* 147–154.

Wilensky, A. J., Ojemann, L. M., Temkin, N. R., Troupin, A. S., & Dodrill, C. B. (1981). Clorazepate and phenobarbital as antiepileptic drugs: A double-blind study. *Neurology, 31,* 1271–1276.

Wolf, H. S. (1979). Controversies in the treatment for febrile convulsion. *Neurology, 29,* 287–290.

CHARLES J. LONG
Memphis State University

ABSENCE SEIZURES
ANTICONVULSANTS
MEDICAL MANAGEMENT
SEIZURE DISORDERS

PHENOTHIAZINES

Phenothiazine is the class of drugs that historically was most often prescribed in the treatment of psychotic disorders, until the late 1990s and the advent of new atypical antipsychotics such as Rispudal and Sinequan. This class of medications, which provides symptomatic relief from many of the disturbing symptoms of disorders like schizophrenia and borderline personality disorder in males (Andrulonis, 1991), replaced the more radical methods of symptom control (e.g., psychosurgery). In addition, the significant behavioral changes that occur when medication regimens are optimally effective allow patients to be treated in outpatient clinics rather than be chronically hospitalized. There are three major classes of phenothiazines that are relatively similar in their overall actions but different in their dose/response ratios and the overall amount of sedation produced (Bassuk & Schoonover, 1977). The subgroups include

Aliphatic
Chlorpromazine (Thorazine)
Promazine (Sparine)

Piperidine
Thioridazine (Mellaril)
Piperacetazine (Quide)
Mesoridazine (Serentil)

Piperazine
Trifluoperazine (Stelazine)
Perphenazine (Trilafon)
Fluphenazine (Prolixin)

The major criticisms of phenothiazines revolve around the exclusive, long-term use of these drugs to control observable symptoms without an attempt to deal with etiology or overall adaptiveness (Marholin & Phillips, 1976). Crane (1973) provides an additional criticism indicating that phenothiazines also have been used within long-term treatment centers to control reactions to institutionalization and enforced restrictions: i.e., punitively.

Phenothiazines produce side effects that may be grouped into four classes: involuntary muscular contractions, especially in the area of the face; motor restlessness; parkinsonlike symptoms such as rigidity, motor slowing, excess salivation, slurred speech, flat facial expression, and gait disturbance; and tardive dyskinesia, a syndrome that consists of stereotyped, repetitive involuntary movements

and persists even after medication is discontinued (Bassuk & Schoonover, 1977). Side effects in children are similar to those of adults; however, parents additionally should be aware of sun sensitivity, when children are outside for extended periods of time, and learning/concentration difficulties, especially during onset of treatment (Bassuk & Schoonover).

REFERENCES

Andrulonis, P. A. (1991). Disruptive behavior disorders in boys and borderline personality disorder in men. *Annals of Clinical Psychiatry, 3*(1), 23–26.

Bassuk, E. L., & Schoonover, S. C. (1977). *The practitioner's guide to psychoactive drugs.* New York: Plenum Medical.

Crane, G. (1973). Clinical pharmacology in its 20th year. *Science, 181,* 124–128.

Marholin, D., & Phillips, D. (1976). Methodological issues in psychopharmacological research: Chlorpromazine–a case in point. *American Journal of Orthopsychiatry, 46,* 477–495.

ROBERT F. SAWICKI
*Lake Erie Institute of
Rehabilitation*

MELLARIL
THORAZINE
TRANQUILIZERS

PHENYLKETONURIA

Phenylketonuria (PKU) was one of the earliest biochemical irregularities associated with mental retardation. Folling noted in 1934 that a few institutionalized retardates had urine with a peculiar "mousy" odor, which was found to arise from the excretion of phenylacetic acid. Classic PKU results from the absence of the enzyme phenylalanine hydroxylase, which normally converts phenylalanine, an essential amino acid common to most proteins and many other foods, into tyrosine and its constituent components. The resulting high levels of phenylalanine damage developing brain tissue. Since brain damage is irreversible, permanent and severe retardation is a predictable outcome, as are seizures, tremors, and hypopigmentation of skin (Smith, 1985).

An autosomal recessive inborn error of amino-acid metabolism, PKU is expressed only in those homozygotic for the defective gene. Incidence is about 1 in 10,000 births in Whites and Asians, but much lower in Blacks. Heterozygotes typically produce enough enzymes for normal metabolism. Affected homozygotes are usually normal at birth since prenatally they received already metabolized nutrients through the umbilical cord. If the disorder is undiagnosed and untreated, progressive brain damage begins. Until the

1950s, prognosis was poor; most affected individuals had IQs of about 30 and were institutionalized.

Neonatal screening is now universal. Although a urine test was originally used, diagnosis is now through the Guthrie test, which reveals excess phenylalanine through a blood test 24 to 48 hours after birth. If PKU is diagnosed, the infant is placed on a low phenylalanine diet, which is synthetic because of the ubiquitous presence of phenylalanine in protein. Dietary treatment must begin within a few days of birth for maximal effectiveness. Adult IQ of early treated PKU individuals is about 90; IQ becomes lower with delay of treatment so that by about 3 years of age, maximal damage has occurred. The diet is the sole nutrient fed in infancy. Some (e.g., Berkow, 1977) suggest that thereafter low-protein foods such as fruits and vegetables may be tolerated, whereas others (e.g., Smith, 1985) recommend strict adherence to the diet. The taste of the diet is aversive, and maintaining the child on it while the rest of the family eats regular food can be an increasingly serious problem as the child grows.

Since phenylalanine is toxic only to developing brain tissue, treatment can cease or be relaxed when brain development is complete. Authorities disagree on when the diet can be terminated, but common practice has been to return the child to normal food at about age eight. However, research suggests that longer dietary treatment may be advisable. Dietary treatment for PKU is a classic example of genetic-environmental interaction. On a normal diet, individuals with PKU genotype will develop phenotypic IQ of about 30; dietary intervention alters the predicted developmental pathway, resulting in nearly normal phenotypic IQ (Brown, 1986).

However, treated PKU children may show specific deficits in perceptual motor functioning and arithmetic achievements that are more serious than would be expected on the basis of their slightly below average IQs. They appear to have neuropsychological deficits similar to those of brain-damaged children (Brunner, Jordon, & Berry, 1983; Pennington, von Doorninck, McCabe, & McCabe, 1985), and have particular deficits in visuospatial and conceptual skills, which may partially account for their problems with mathematics. Pennington et al. (1985) suggest that the deficits may occur because the children are taken off of the diet before the completion of relevant brain development. Although the number of subjects in these studies was small and the findings need confirmation, those working with treated PKU children should be aware that such children may have some specific learning deficits.

The effectiveness of the diet has had one tragic and unexpected effect. In the late 1960s, it became clear that children born to PKU women who had eaten normal food during pregnancy suffered prenatal growth retardation, microcephaly, and brain damage, even though the children did not have the PKU genotype. Although the effects were variable, many of the children died early or became severely retarded. The problems may have been more serious than in untreated PKU itself (Lenke & Levy, 1980). The pregnant women had transmitted unmetabolized phenylalanine to their embryos and fetuses at the prenatal critical period for adverse influences on brain development. A common recommendation now is for PKU women to return to the diet throughout the time they may become pregnant. But regulation of optimal phenylalanine levels is difficult, and no dietary program is completely effective. The safest recommendation is for PKU women not to have children. Thus treated women have an additional responsibility during childbearing years, and some who are at a marginal level of functioning may need some social service assistance (Brown, 1986).

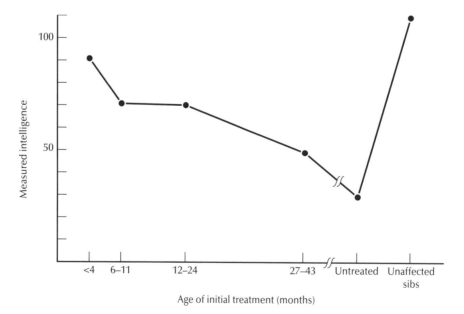

Mean IQ of PKU children as a function of the age at which dietary treatment

Recent research has changed previous recommendations that children with PKU could discontinue the special diet at about 8 years. Early-treated children who stop the diet actually show deterioration in functioning (IQ, reading and spelling, social behavior). Further, children on the diet show deficits in short-term memory and "executive functioning" relative to nondisabled children. Some studies suggest that children with PKU who are on the diet still have higher levels of phenylalanine relative to tyrosine in their brains than do normal children. Tyrosine is a precursor to dopamine, a main neurotransmitter in frontal lobe functioning, and some of the problems shown by children with PKU who are on the diet resemble those associated with frontal-lobe syndrome. Thus, life-long dietary treatment is now recommended, and even then, some specific deficits in functioning are likely. Some of this information can be found in Batshaw (1997).

REFERENCES

Batshaw, M. L. (1997). PKU and other inborn errors of metabolism. In M. L. Batshaw (Ed.), *Children with disabilities* (4th ed., pp. 389–404). Baltimore: Brookes.

Berkow, R. (Ed.). (1977). *The Merck manual* (13th ed.). Rahway, NJ: Merck, Sharpe, & Dohme.

Brown, R. T. (1986). Etiology and development of exceptionality. In R. T. Brown & C. R. Reynolds (Eds.), *Psychological perspectives on childhood exceptionality* (pp. 181–229). New York: Wiley.

Brunner, R. L., Jordon, M. K., & Berry, H. K. (1983). Early treated PKU: Neuropsychologic consequences. *Journal of Pediatrics, 102*, 381–385.

Lenke, R. R., & Levy, H. (1980). Maternal phenylketonuria and hyperphenylalaninia: An international survey of untreated and treated pregnancies. *New England Journal of Medicine, 303*, 1202–1208.

Pennington, B. F., von Doorninck, W. J., McCabe, L. L., & McCabe, E. R. B. (1985). Neuropsychological deficits in early treated phenylketonuric children. *American Journal of Mental Deficiency, 89*, 467–474.

Smith, L. H., Jr. (1985). The hyperphenylalaninemias. In J. B. Wyngaarden & L. H. Smith, Jr. (Eds.), *Cecil textbook of medicine* (17th ed., pp. 1126–1128). Philadelphia: Saunders.

ROBERT T. BROWN
University of North Carolina at Wilmington

BIOCHEMICAL IRREGULARITIES
INBORN ERRORS OF METABOLISM

PHILLIPS, BEEMAN N. (1927–   )

A mathematics and physics major, Beeman N. Phillips completed his BA degree at Evansville College in 1949. He pursued graduate training at Indiana University, earning both

Beeman N. Phillips

his MS, in 1950, and EdD, in 1954, in educational psychology. Immediately following the completion of his doctoral degree, Phillips served as director of the Division of Research of the Indiana State Department of Public Instruction. In 1956 Phillips joined the faculty of the Department of Educational Psychology at the University of Texas, Austin, where he has remained.

At the University of Texas, Austin, Phillips founded one of the first doctoral training programs in school psychology, a program considered by many in the field to be the leading program in the country. Though its focus has changed in recent years, the program was particularly successful in pioneering and promoting consultation models for indirect service delivery in the provision of school psychological services. As the director and only continuous faculty member of the program, Phillips has been a key element in the development of the profession of school psychology. Among other professional leadership roles, Phillips has served as president of the Division of School Psychology of the American Psychological Association and was the editor of the *Journal of School Psychology* from 1972 to 1980. In 1978 Phillips was given the Division of School Psychology Distinguished Service Award. He was also the recipient of the 1991 Outstanding Education Alumnus Award from the School of Education, Indiana University (Bloomington), and in 1992 received the first annual Dean's Distinguished Faculty Award in the College of Education from the University of Texas at Austin. In June, 1998 he became professor emeritus.

Applied educational and psychological research has been the consistent focus of Phillips' research program. He has also been concerned with developing conceptual and methodological rigor in school psychological research, the latter perhaps best exemplified in his chapters in the *Handbook of School Psychology*. As a major research interest, Phillips has studied school stress and its relationship to school adjustment and learning. His work as a whole reflects a strong educational orientation to psychological research coupled with a concern for theoretical relevance and practical applications of research. He has emphasized the need for a better interface between psychology and schooling as well as the means for achieving it. Phillips's books include *School Psychology at a Turning Point: Ensuring a Bright Future for the Profession* (1990) and *Educational and Psychological Perspectives on Stress in Students, Teachers, and Parents* (1993).

REFERENCES

Phillips, B. N. (1978). *School stress and anxiety: Theory, research, and intervention.* New York: Human Sciences.

Phillips, B. N. (1982). Reading and evaluating research in school psychology. In C. R. Reynolds & T. B. Gutkin (Eds.), *The handbook of school psychology.* New York: Wiley.

Phillips, B. N. (1990). Reading, evaluating, and applying research in school psychology. In T. B. Gutkin & C. R. Reynolds (Eds.), *The handbook of school psychology* (2nd ed.). New York: Wiley.

Phillips, B. N. (1990). *School psychology at a turning point: Ensuring a bright future for the profession.* San Francisco: Jossey-Bass.

Phillips, B. N. (1993). *Educational and psychological perspectives on stress in students, teachers, and parents.* Brandon, VT: Clinical Psychology.

Phillips, B. N. (1999). Strengthening the links between science and practice: Reading, evaluating, and applying research in school psychology. In C. R. Reynolds & T. B. Gutkin (Eds.), *The handbook of school psychology* (3rd ed.). New York: Wiley.

Cecil R. Reynolds
Texas A&M University
First edition

Tamara J. Martin
The University of Texas of the Permian Basin
Second edition

JOURNAL OF SCHOOL PSYCHOLOGY

PHILOSOPHY OF EDUCATION FOR INDIVIDUALS WITH DISABILITIES

The philosophical beliefs and values that underlie special education are diverse, dynamic, and interrelated. They reflect broad social issues such as attitudes toward individuals with disabilities as well as specific educational concerns. Three key issues are access to education, placement, and instruction.

Issues of access to education involve questions relating to which children have a right to education and whether all children can benefit from instruction. Questions of access and educability were first raised with respect to individuals with severe and obvious disabilities—the blind, deaf, mentally retarded, and seriously emotionally disturbed. Concern for these individuals prompted the earliest intervention efforts, beginning in the United States as early as 1817. The achievements of educators such as Edouard Seguin gave rise to optimism that education could cure or ameliorate severe handicapping conditions and resulted in an expansion in the number of available treatment programs for these populations (Kauffman, 1981).

The enactment of compulsory school attendance laws in the early twentieth century brought a wider range of students to the public schools. As a result, the special educational needs of students became apparent. Special classes were instituted, providing these students with some measure of access to education, but few programs were designed to deliver the type of instructional program necessary to ensure that these students could profit from their schooling. (See Kauffman, 1981, Reynolds & Birch, 1982, for a detailed chronology of major historical influences in special education.)

The beginnings of the civil rights movement in the 1950s set the stage for further changes in philosophies of educational access. Equal educational opportunity became a focus for the efforts of increasingly active parent groups and professionals in special education. A body of case law, beginning with the *Brown* v. *Board of Education* decision, eventually developed and affirmed the principle of children with disabilities' right to education.

The question of what organizational setting, or placement, is most appropriate for students with disabilities has been answered differently through the history of special education. Beginning with residential institutions, the range of placement options has gradually increased to include special schools, special classes within public schools, and, finally, integration into regular public school classes (mainstreaming) and inclusion. IDEA requires that students with disabilities be placed, to the maximum extent appropriate, in regular educational environments with their nondisabled peers. This mandate is known as placement in the least restrictive environment. Inclusion and least restrictive placement are outgrowths of the broader philosophical concept of normalization—the belief that persons with disabilities should, to the greatest extent possible, be integrated into society.

Without appropriate instructional strategies, any inclusive or least restrictive placement efforts are unlikely to succeed. Individualized instruction, first advocated by nineteenth-century educators such as Itard and Seguin, has been formalized through IDEA's requirement that an individualized education program be developed and its execution monitored for each child placed in special education.

The philosophical issues that have shaped special education have evolved and changed significantly over the past two centuries. A contemporary philosophy of education for the individuals with disabilities incorporates a diversity of complex issues that include those related to access to education, educability, placement, and instruction.

REFERENCES

Hallahan, D. P., & Kauffman, J. M. (1982). *Exceptional children: Introduction to special education.* Englewood Cliffs, NJ: Prentice Hall.

Kauffman, J. M. (1981). Historical trends and contemporary issues in special education in the United States. In J. M. Kauffman & D. P. Hallahan (Eds.), *Handbook of special education* (pp. 3–24). Englewood Cliffs, NJ: Prentice Hall.

Paul, J. L. (1981). Service delivery models for special education. In J. M. Kauffman & D. P. Hallahan (Eds.), *Handbook of special education* (pp. 291–310). Englewood Cliffs, NJ: Prentice Hall.

Reynolds, M. C., & Birch, J. W. (1982). *Teaching exceptional children in all America's schools.* Reston, VA: Council for Exceptional Children.

MARY LOUISE LENNON
RANDY ELLIOT BENNETT
Educational Testing Service

INDIVIDUALS WITH DISABILITIES EDUCATION IMPROVEMENT ACT OF 2004 (IDEIA)

PHOBIAS AND FEARS

Fear in children and youths is a very strong emotion and is associated with behavioral, cognitive, and physiological indicators of anxiety. When a child or youth with disabilities experiences fear that is not age-related in a setting where there is no obvious external danger, the fear is irrational, and the person is said to have a phobia. When the person begins to avoid the nondangerous feared situation, even while maintaining that such action is foolish, the phobia is commonly referred to as a phobic reaction (Morris & Kratochwill, 1983). Fear, on the other hand, is an integral part of normal child development. Many children's fears are transitory, appear in children of similar age, and generally do not interfere with everyday functioning. In fact, some fears that occur during development provide children with a means of adapting to various life stressors.

Those fears observed in infancy typically occur as a reaction to something taking place in the child's environment (e.g., the presence of strangers or loud noises). As the child grows into the toddler and preschool years, the fears broaden and involve the dark, ghosts and other supernatural figures, parent separation, and fears of particular events, objects, or persons. With growth in to the early to middle school years, developmental fears continue to broaden and include such stimuli as animals, thunder and lightning, the dark, parent separation, bodily injury, and sleeping alone. As the child enters preadolescence and adolescence, the normative fears turn more toward school performance, physical appearance, bodily injury, peer acceptance, death, and imaginary figures (Morris & Kratochwill, 1983).

Separating the meaning of fear from the meaning of phobia has been discussed by Marks (1969). He suggests that phobia is a subcategory of fear that "(1) is out of proportion to the demands of the situation, (2) cannot be explained or reasoned away, (3) is beyond voluntary control, and (4) leads to avoidance of the feared situations" (p. 3). In addition, Miller, Barrett, and Hampe (1974) have stated that a phobia "persists over an extended period of time . . . is unadaptive . . . [and] is not age or stage specific" (p. 90).

Although a fair amount of research has been conducted on the incidence and prevalence of children's fears, less research has been published on children's phobias. Miller et al. (1974), for example, report that the incidence of intense fears (phobias) was about 5 percent of their sample of 7- to 12-year-old children. Similarly, Marks (1969) reported that the percentage of children having phobias who were referred to a British clinic was only 4 percent. Other studies estimated the prevalence of phobias among children to be less than 8 percent of the number of child referrals to a clinic or in the general child population.

With respect to developmental or normative fears, studies have shown that young children, 24 to 71 months of age, experience on the average 4.6 fears (Jersild & Holmes, 1935). Forty-three percent of children who are 6 to 12 years of age experience at least seven or more fears (Lapouse & Monk, 1959). In preadolescent and adolescent youths, 66 percent of those sampled reported fears of violence (Orton, 1982). Although girls tend to be more fearful than boys in the early years, this difference does not seem to appear on a regular basis in pre- and early adolescence. No literature exists on the incidence or prevalence of phobias and fears in children and youths with disabilities.

Numerous studies have been published over the past several years on intervention approaches for reducing fears and phobias. The assumptions underlying these approaches have generally followed a behavioral orientation. There are five major behavior therapy approaches for fear or phobia reduction in children and youths: systematic desensitization (including variations of this procedure); flooding-related therapies; contingency management procedures; modeling; and self-control procedures. Of these methods, the one that has been used primarily in research is systematic desensitization or variations of this method. Although there are many studies on fears and phobias available for study, with regard to children and youths with disabilities, few research studies have been published on the treatment of fears and phobias; however, of those studies that have been published, the majority have used a procedure that is based on systematic desensitization.

REFERENCES

Jersild, A. T., & Holmes, F. B. (1935). Methods of overcoming children's fears. *Journal of Psychology, 1,* 75–104.

Lapouse, R., & Monk, M. A. (1959). Fears and worries in a representative sample of children. *American Journal of Orthopsychiatry, 29,* 803–818.

Marks, I. M. (1969). *Fears and phobias.* New York: Academic.

Miller, L. C., Barrett, C. L., & Hampe, E. (1974). Phobias in childhood in a prescientific era. In A. Davis (Ed.), *Child personality and psychopathology: Current topics* (pp. 84–120). New York: Wiley.

Morris, R. J., & Kratochwill, T. R. (1983). *Treating children's fears and phobias: A behavioral approach.* New York: Pergamon.

Orton, G. L. (1982). A comparative study of children's worries. *Journal of Psychology, 110,* 153–162.

RICHARD J. MORRIS
University of Arizona

THOMAS R. KRATOCHWILL
*University of Wisconsin at
Madison*

**ANXIETY DISORDERS
EMOTIONAL DISORDERS**

PHONOLOGICAL AWARENESS TEST

The Phonological Awareness Test (PAT) is an extension of the Phonological Awareness Profile, which was first published in 1995. The profile proved useful in planning instruction; however, users of the profile hoped for a standardized version of the assessment. Thus, the authors developed the PAT. This test was designed to assess students' awareness of the oral language segments that make up words. It comprises four sections:

1. *Rhyming:* Discrimination—identify rhyming words presented in pairs; Production—provide a rhyming word given a stimulus word.

2. *Deletion:* Compounds and syllables—say a word and say it again deleting a root word or syllable; Phonemes—say a word and say it again deleting a phoneme.

3. *Substitution:* With Manipulatives—using colored blocks, isolate a phoneme, then change it to another phoneme to form a new word; Without Manipulatives—isolate a sound in a word, then change it to another sound to form a new word.

4. *Isolation:* Final—identifies final phoneme in a word; Medial—identifies medial phoneme in a word.

The PAT provides opportunities for analysis of student performance on each subtest. Performance can be classified according to four developmental levels: word, syllable, phoneme, and grapheme. Depending on student performance on the PAT, sample activities for instruction are presented to increase students' sound awareness. The manual recommends beginning instruction at the earliest level in which the student demonstrates difficulty. The Phonological Awareness Kit and the Phonological Awareness Kit—Intermediate provide a program of activities for each level of phonological awareness and phoneme-grapheme correspondence. The manual specifies that this test should be administered by a professional trained in analyzing the phonological structure of speech. It further indicates that it is unlikely that support personnel or paraprofessionals can adequately administer, interpret, and score the test.

The PAT was standardized from September to November 1996 on a sample of 1,235 students from five U.S. states.

RON DUMONT
Fairleigh Dickinson University

JOHN O. WILLIS
Rivier College

PHONOLOGY

Phonology is a study of the rule-based system underlying phoneme development and speech production. The focus is not on the emergence of specific phonemes but rather on sound classes such as stridency and nasality. The organizational schemata for the formation and use of the phoneme system is the focus of attention.

The need to convey meaning drives this system. At first, children may have only gross classifications like consonant versus vowel as tools to communicate. To get their needs met, they learn that words need beginnings and ends and that there are classes of sounds like stops and front sounds. They acquire the global classes and gradually refine within those classes to ultimately differentiate between a /t/ and a /k/. Children's productions, at any point in time, may be transcribed, analyzed and the rules written to describe the strategies they are using to articulate.

Phonological maturation information exists, but it relates to phonological process usage, the rule-bound simplification and (at times) complication strategies children use to produce speech. In contrast to articulation, the developmental data for phonological maturation is not when sound classes emerge but rather when the processes cease to operate. As children's oral motor, sensory, and discrimination skills develop and their knowledge about combining phonemes into words and larger units of speech increases, process usage decreases. Eighteen-month-old children are likely to know that words need a beginning sound but they are unlikely to use word final consonants. Thus, they exhibit the process *final consonant deletion.* This process typically drops out by the time a child is three. Higher level processes such as stopping and stridency deletion drop out much later in normal developing children (Grunwell, 1987).

Children with phonological disorders have difficulty abstracting the rules for articulation from the input they hear from others. Their speech is generally unintelligible. The number of phonemes in error will be in excess of 10, and the errors will have a rule-based pattern. Children with phonological disorders generally use the same processes that younger, normal-developing children use, but they have more processes functioning and tend to maintain them longer (Ingram, 1976). In evaluating the severity of the disorder, two considerations are the age of the child and the number of processes being used. In addition, if there are vowel errors, a more complex disorder is signaled because vowels emerge very early in speech production. Similarly, if a child has truly been taught to self-evaluate and does not do so after a reasonable amount of time, it may be the first indicator of an accompanying auditory processing difficulty. Most children with phonological process disorders are normal developing children with intact systems who for no known reason are having trouble with the organizational structure of speech production. The prognosis for this latter group is very good. Children with auditory processing deficits and those with motor/neurological involvement also benefit from phonological process treatment but progress more slowly.

Prior to treatment, an extensive speech analysis is needed to determine the rules being applied and the extent of process usage. Treatment focuses on providing children with information that assists them in revising the rules they are using for speech production. For example, they are taught that most words must have endings and that any consonantal ending is acceptable. They are reinforced for putting on any end. Once endings emerge, refinement of the process may begin. They may be then told that for these particular words, a ending is still needed but it has to be a stop. As the child progresses, finer and finer distinctions are made. Treatment moves from global to specific. Geirut, Elbert, and Dinnsen (1987) report that the more children are taught what they do not know, the quicker generalization will occur throughout the sound system. Gierut advocates the use of maximal oppositions in treatment; contrasting two phonemes representing processes the child does not know (Gierut, 1989). Sound classes are taught on a cognitive level by modeling and labeling, having the youngster produce exemplars representative of the class, and then having them self-evaluate whether they produced, for example, a strident.

Phonological processes are most frequently discussed relative to developing rule systems, typically that of children. Older individuals with mental retardation or neurological involvement which presents as apraxia and/or dysarthria also benefit from process-based treatment. The person with retardation may not have mastered the rule-based system for speech. Focus on low level processes like ends-on-words, syllableness, front and back sounds, and others produces gains in intelligibility. Adults with dysarthria and apraxia have previously learned the rules for speech production but due to neurological insult, now have difficulty executing or planning movements. Broader-based treatment which organizes speech by category, assists these persons in improving their speech. For example, if a patient is substituting one sound for another, in-class substitutions will produce greater intelligibility than those which are out-of-class. Thus, the applicability of phonological process treatment is broad and not limited solely to young children.

REFERENCES

Gierut, J. (1989). Maximal opposition approach to phonological treatment. *Journal of Speech and Hearing Disorders, 54,* 9–19.

Geirut, J., Elbert, M., & Dinnsen, D. (1987). A functional analysis of phonological knowledge and generalization learning in misarticulating children. *Journal of Speech and Hearing Research, 30,* 462–479.

Grunwell, P. (1987). *Clinical phonology* (2nd ed.). Baltimore: Williams and Wilkins.

Ingram, D. (1976). *Phonological disability in children.* New York: Elsevier.

SUSANN DOWLING
University of Houston

LINGUISTIC READERS
READING DISORDERS
READING REMEDIATION

PHOTO ARTICULATION TEST–THIRD EDITION

The Photo Articulation Test–Third Edition (PAT-3; Lippke, Dickey, Selmar, & Soder, 1997) is a completely revised edition of the Photo Articulation Test. It a standardized way to document the presence of articulation errors. The PAT-3 enables the clinician to rapidly and accurately assess and interpret articulation errors. The test consists of 72 color photographs (9 photos on each of eight sheets). The first 69 photos test consonants and all but one vowel and one diphthong. The remaining 3 pictures measure connected speech and the remaining vowel and diphthong. Consonant sounds are differentiated into the initial, medial, and final positions within the stimulus words. A deck of the same 72 color photographs, each on a separate card, is provided for further diagnosis and may be used in speech-language remediation.

The PAT-3 was standardized in a 23-state sample of more than 800 public and private school students in pre-kindergarten through grade 4. The students have the same characteristics as those reported in the 1990 Statistical Abstract of the United States. Percentiles, standard scores (mean = 100, SD = 15), and age equivalents are provided. Internal consistency, test-retest, and interscorer reliability coefficients approximate .80 at most ages, and many are in the .90s. Information is provided for content, criterion-related, and construct validity.

Earlier editions of the PAT were reviewed; references for the newest edition of the instrument are unavailable because of its recent publication date. Shriberg (1978) reviewed the PAT and reported that the one feature that distinguished the PAT from other commercially available three-position tests is that children do respond readily to the photographs.

REFERENCES

Lippke, B. A., Dickey, S. E., Selmar, J. W., & Soder, A. L. (1997). *Photo Articulation Test–Third Edition.* Austin, TX: PRO-ED.

Shriberg, L. D. (1978). Review of the Photo Articulation Test. In O. K. Buros (Ed.), *The eighth mental measurements yearbook* (pp. 1506–1508). Lincoln, NE: Buros Institute of Mental Measurements.

TADDY MADDOX
PRO-ED, Inc.

PHYSICAL ANOMALIES

A physical anomaly is any bodily attribute that deviates significantly from normal variation. Technically, physical anomalies need not be disabling or handicapping though, as will be noted, they often occur concomitant to a variety of handicapping conditions. For instance, prematurely gray-haired individuals exhibit a physical anomaly, yet, the anomaly is unlikely to be viewed as an impairment (i.e., a disability). It is also unlikely to serve as a disadvantage that makes achievement in particular circumstances exceptionally difficult (i.e., a handicap).

Special educators are most directly concerned with physical anomalies that limit an individual's success in typical life activities (e.g., occupational, familial, and social activities). Such physical anomalies may be found in virtually all of the traditional exceptionalities. However, they are most clearly apparent in the following categories: visual, hearing, and physical handicaps, health problems, and mental retardation.

Physical anomalies can impose handicaps in one or many important domains (e.g., cognition, affect, and motor). Functionally, the individual may have difficulty in academic achievement (e.g., reading, mathematics), in social/emotional adjustment (e.g., making and sustaining friendships, attaining a positive self-concept), and in physical activities (e.g., locomotion, orientation).

Visual anomalies, depending on the age at onset, may be classified as congenital (present at birth) or adventitious acquired sometime after birth). Generally, the impairment concerns visual acuity, field of vision, ocular motility, accommodation, color vision, or corneal opacity.

Like visual anomalies, hearing problems may be classified in different ways. For instance, classification may depend on age of onset (congenital vs. adventitious). Distinctions are also based on the degree of hearing loss (i.e., deaf or hard of hearing). Finally, hearing problems may be conductive or sensorineural in nature. A conductive hearing loss results from interference with the physical transmission of sound waves from the outer ear to the inner ear. On the other hand, a sensorineural hearing loss, as suggested by the name, is caused by neurological damage to nerve tissue in the inner ear. Sound may be grossly distorted to the listener or may not be transmitted at all. In general, sensorineural hearing losses have the more pessimistic prognosis.

Physical handicaps are varied but are commonly categorized as neurological or orthopedic in origin. The former results from injuries, congenital defects, or the progressive deterioration of portions of the central nervous system (CNS). Because most human functions are heavily dependent on an intact CNS, neurological disorders may present particular difficulty for the child and the educator. For instance, it is often difficult to determine a child's true intellectual ability because a motoric handicap may prevent the child from exhibiting it. Cerebral palsy, spina bifida, convulsive disorders, and poliomyelitis are common neurological disorders.

Orthopedic, or musculoskeletal, disorders may be congenital or adventitious. They affect the bones (including joints) and muscles. Accidents, diseases, and hereditary anomalies cause most of the orthopedic disorders. Some of the more common of these conditions are muscular dystrophy, amputations, osteogenesis imperfecta, scoliosis, arthritis, and Legg-Perthes disease.

Other children have conditions in which physical health is poor either permanently of intermittently. Although their conditions are frequently less visually apparent than neurological or orthopedic disorders, they may well face handicapping circumstances in many functional areas (e.g., academic performance, social acceptance). Among the most common of these conditions are epilepsy, cystic fibrosis, juvenile diabetes mellitus, sickle cell anemia, and hemophilia.

The physical anomalies that exist among the mentally retarded population are extensive. Over 250 have been classified so far. Even so, these represent no more than about 25 percent of the diagnosed cases of mental retardation in the United States. The American Association on Mental Deficiency (now American Association on Mental Retardation; Grossman, 1973) classified the known causal agents of mental retardation as follows: (1) infections and intoxication; (2) trauma and physical agents; (3) metabolism and nutrition; (4) gross brain disease; (5) prenatal influence; (6) chromosomal abnormality; (7) gestational disorders; (8) psychiatric disorders. As with other physical anomalies individuals with mental retardation suffer from a wide array of affective and motor problems. However, it is their difficulty in cognition and adaptive behavior that best characterizes these children.

Physical anomaly is a term also used to describe a variety of physical aberrations that accompany a host of medical syndromes that typically require special education. Many of these syndromes are genetic disorders that are diagnosed by the specific constellation of physical anomalies apparent to the trained eye. In cases where only one or two minor physical anomalies are present (e.g., hair whorls and a palmar crease), they are often considered to be "soft signs" indicative of neurological problems. Observable minor physical anomalies are often related to neurological problems through coincidental development. The same initial tissue that develops during the embryonic stage into the central nervous system (the neural tube) also forms the epidermis, the outer covering of the body. Also, human chromosomes control more than one aspect of physical development and where one abnormality occurs, others are likely to be present.

Minor physical anomalies occur in many forms and in conjunction with a host of disorders. In Down syndrome (trisomy 21) one finds a broad flat face, pronounced epicanthal folds, a small palate, and malformed ears. Trisomy 13 will result in microcephaly, physical cardiac defects, polydactyly, cleft lip and palate, and malformation of the eyes and ears. Both of these syndromes frequently result in mental retardation ranging from mild to profound. Marfan's syndrome, most often associated with learning disabilities, though occasionally resulting in mild retardation, occurs with elongated arms and legs, arachnodactyly (long, spider-like fingers), and malformations of the eyes and heart.

REFERENCES

Abuelo, D. N. (1983). Genetic disorders. In J. L. Matson & J. A. Mulick (Eds.), *Handbook of mental retardation.* New York: Pergamon.

Brown, R. T. (1986). Etiology and development of exceptionality. In R. T. Brown & C. R. Reynolds (Eds.), *Psychological perspectives on childhood exceptionality: A handbook.* New York: Wiley-Interscience.

Grossman, H. J. (Ed.). (1973). *Manual on terminology and classification in mental retardation.* Washington, DC: American Association on Mental Deficiency.

RONALD C. EAVES
Auburn University

CECIL R. REYNOLDS
Texas A&M University

DOWN SYNDROME
GENETIC FACTORS AND BEHAVIOR
MENTAL RETARDATION
MINOR PHYSICAL ANOMALIES

PHYSICAL EDUCATION FOR STUDENTS WITH DISABILITIES

Physical education is a means of developing motor and sports skills and physical fitness with disabled populations. Physical education programs for individuals with disabilities have been ongoing throughout the United States in residential, private, and public educational institutions (American Association of Health, Physical Education and Recreation, 1981).

The federal government's concern for disabled veterans during and after World War II and its provisions to mainstream and rehabilitate them played a seminal role in the development of adapted physical education. Adapted physical education is the commonly accepted term to designate physical education instruction to persons with disabilities in a public or private school setting. Veterans Administration hospitals use corrective, occupational, and physical therapists to help the veterans get back into the mainstream of society and to lead productive lives. Also, innovations developed through federally supported research have found their way in adapted physical education programs across the country (Sherrill, 1985).

From 1950, owing to a variety of political and legal means used by advocacy groups, programs for other disabled populations began to grow as the rights of disabled persons with congenital disorders advanced across a broad front. Evidence from numerous research studies began to indicate the positive value of sports participation for all disabled populations. Programs such as wheelchair sports and the Special Olympics focused on promoting athletic participation among disabled populations. From 1952 to 1979 the American Association for Health, Physical Education and Recreation (AAHPER) published a series of monographs on curriculum training of staff and guidelines for adapted physical education for schools (Adams, 1981).

It was not until the late 1960s and early 1970s that the federal government began to play a vital role in spurring the growth of adapted physical education programs in the public schools. Large sums of money were allocated for staff training of adapted physical education teachers, and for research and demonstration projects (Adams, 1981). The focus of these federally supported projects was to place more adapted physical education teachers in the field and to use special demonstration centers as models for others looking to upgrade their programs.

During the mid-1970s the federal government enacted

the Rehabilitation Act of 1973 (PL 93-112) and the Education for All Handicapped Children Act of 1975 (PL 94-142). The most far-reaching part of PL 93-112 was section 504. It stated that "no qualified person . . . shall be excluded from participation or denied the benefits . . . under any program receiving federal assistance" (Sherrill, 1985). This nondiscriminatory clause indicated physical education was an important concern.

Until the enactment of PL 94-142, there were very few physical education programs in the public schools for children with disabilities. The new law, however, stated that education for children with disabilities shall include instruction in physical education. Also, the regulations called for equal opportunities to intramural and interscholastic sports competition. As a result, all children with disabilities were accorded rights to physical education instruction to the same extent as the nondisabled (Auxter & Pyer, 1985).

Since 1975 more and more persons with disabilities are being identified and placed in adapted physical education programs. About 12 percent of the school-age population is disabled and receiving appropriate instruction. According to IDEA, children with disabilities must be placed in the least restricted school environment with an individualized educational program prepared by the appropriate personnel. This law provided the impetus for the use of individualized education plans (IEP) in physical education and the opportunity for children with disabilities to participate with nondisabled children in actual physical activity.

Because of the need to collaborate with other professionals regarding each disabled student's activity needs and educational goals, adapted physical educators may serve as part of a multidisciplinary team with occupational and physical therapists and the special education teacher.

Many terms have been applied to programs of physical activity for individuals with disabilities. Each of these terms represents a specific approach to improving motor and physical performance. Terms such as corrective, developmental, modified, therapeutic, or special physical education are representative of aspects of adapted physical education.

Corrective physical education is a means of remediating structural and functional dysfunctions through physical exercise or motor activities. The dysfunctions, although impairing, are generally correctable. Developmental physical education focuses on improving delayed motor and physical development through exercise and motor skill activities. Modified physical education has activities that are adapted to learning levels regardless of individual differences. Therapeutic physical education denotes the use of physical education activities under the prescription of a medical doctor. Special physical education is a selected program of developmental activities designed to meet the limitations of those who cannot participate in unrestricted and regular physical education. This term has not gained nationwide acceptance owing to its controversial connotation.

Adapted physical education is a "diversified program of developmental activities, games, sports, and rhythms suited to the interests, capacities, and limitations of students with disabilities who may not safely and successfully engage in unrestricted participation in vigorous activities of the general physical education program" (AAHPER, 1952).

By definition, adapted physical education includes activities:

Planned for persons with learning problems owed to motor, mental, or emotional impairment, disability, or dysfunction.

Planned for the purpose of rehabilitation, remediation, prevention, or physical development.

Modified so the impaired, disabled, or handicapped can participate.

Designed for modifying movement capabilities.

Planned to promote optimum motor development.

Occurring in a school setting or within a clinic, hospital, residence facility, daycare center or other locale where the primary intent is to influence learning and movement potential through motor activity.

Adapted physical education differs from regular physical education in that it has a federally mandated base and a multidisciplinary approach to individual program planning, covers an age spectrum from early childhood to adulthood, has educational accountability through the IEP, and emphasizes cooperative service among the school, community, and home to enhance a disabled person's capabilities (Sherrill, 1985).

The aim of physical education for individuals with disabilities is to aid in achieving physical, social, and emotional growth commensurate with their potential. Objectives of adapted physical education programs vary from program to program depending on population characteristics, instructional expertise, facilities, and equipment. Some of the commonly accepted objectives of most programs are

To help students correct physical conditions that can be improved.

To help students protect themselves from any conditions that would be aggravated through physical activity.

To provide students with opportunities to learn about and participate in a number of appropriate recreational leisure time sports and activities.

To help students to become self-sufficient in the community.

To help students to understand their physical and mental limitations.

To help students to understand and appreciate a variety of sports that they can enjoy as spectators.

Prior to participation in a physical education program conducted by a public school, the student with disabilities must have a thorough physical examination. Abnormalities are identified by the physician and suggestions for management are made to school personnel. The physician's suggestions usually include follow-through procedures to ensure proper class placement and appropriate educational placement based on the extent of physical activity needs and limitations. The adapted physical education teacher must be aware of the physician's guidelines and interpret them into an appropriate physical activity program.

Often, identification of the student needing special help is made by teacher observation in the regular physical education class or in the student's regular classroom. Sometimes the student is not making adequate progress or is frustrated by his or her present involvement in games and sports. The student may not be classified as needing special help because he or she passed the medical examination by the physician. In this case, the physical education program is adapted to suit the capabilities of the student.

Students with disabilities are required to take a battery of motor, physical fitness, and perceptual-motor tests for the making of the yearly IEP (AAHPER, 1981). Short- and long-term goals for the academic year are developed from the test results along with the specific activities recommended for each goal.

After being identified as needing special help, a handicapped student, depending on the size of the school, may be assigned to different types of programming classes. The first is a segregated program in which all of the students are in need of adapted physical education. The student receives individual attention, is accepted, and is protected from unlimited competition. The disadvantage of a segregated program is that the class fosters isolation and nonacceptance from peers. In the second type, a student may be placed in an integrated class participating with able-bodied students in the least restricted environment in terms of physical activity. Studies indicate that inclusive practices in physical education do not necessarily lead to peer acceptance for students with physical disabilities (Toon & Gench, 1990; Tripp, French & Sherrill, 1995).

A third type of physical education program for the student with disabilities is the dual class, in which the student is placed one day in the segregated class and one day in the integrated class. With this approach, individual attention may be given for special needs. At the same time, the student is able to interact with peers in the regular physical education class. Again, there is no guarantee that inclusion will work; therefore consistent evaluations must be made and kept ongoing.

Once a pupil with disabilities is given an appropriate physical education class placement, it is the role of the physical education instructor to provide a program of physical activity throughout the school year. In addition to planning and implementing the IEP, the physical education instructor acts as a counselor to aid the student in:

Setting reasonable physical activity goals

Transferring class skills and habits to other environments

Promoting healthful practices

Coordinating program goals with the student's family and related services within the school and community

Providing a framework that fosters socialization skills in the least restrictive environment

Recording progress and continually evaluating needs and interests through physical activity

The aim of a physical education curriculum for individuals with disabilities is to develop physical fitness and motor skills through exercise and sports. For effective learning to take place, it is necessary to know the different levels of functioning in motor learning that affect a student's performance in class. There are three levels of functioning in motor skill acquisition: (1) input functions, (2) abilities, and (3) motor skill.

Basic input functions include the equilibrium reflexes, the vestibular system, vision, audition, and tactile and the kinesthetic senses. Their role is to provide sensory information to the central nervous system. If all systems are intact, the person will have a coordinated sense of movement and motion. If one or more are not intact, as is the case in many handicaps, it is important for the instructor to adapt activities that either develop or compensate for that input function.

The second level of functioning includes abilities that are perceptual-motor and physical in nature. Perceptual-motor abilities include balance, laterality, directionality, body image, spatial awareness and cross-lateral integration. Physical fitness parameters consist of strength, muscle and cardiovascular endurance, and flexibility. Motor fitness includes speed, power, agility, and motor coordination. If the sensory input functions are intact, the abilities develop through developmental motor and fitness experiences. If all of the abilities are intact, their use and development provide the groundwork for learning motor and sports skills.

The highest level of functioning is motor and sport skill acquisition. Motor skills are fundamental movement patterns of daily activity such as walking, running, hopping, etc. Sports skills are motor in nature but are specific to learning a particular sport. Examples of sports skills are throwing a ball, doing the crawl stroke, and riding a bike. If the input systems and the abilities are intact, then skill acquisition occurs through movement and sports experiences. This means instruction, practice, and instructional feedback in sport and movement activities.

Activities to develop motor, sports, and physical fitness are classified according to the number of participants and the level of skill acquisition. Individual activities include swimming, self-defense, tennis, bowling, dancing, weight training, and karate. Team sports include such activities as wheelchair basketball, soccer, frisbee, and softball. The third type are activities that enhance physical and motor development such as aerobics, dance, and weight training. In many schools, classes may be subdivided according to skill levels within the particular activity. In swimming, for instance, there may be classes or subdivisions within a class for beginners, intermediates, and advanced swimmers.

For the student with disabilities to meaningfully participate in a sport, it is often necessary to modify some aspect of the sport to suit the capabilities of the student. For instance, wheelchair basketball is an adaptation of regular basketball in which the participants wheel around and pass the ball as opposed to dribbling and running. General guidelines followed by most instructors who teach adapted physical education state that the activity must be adaptable for effective learning to occur. This means that equipment, rules, or the manner of play may need to be modified for the participants. For instance, to accommodate the limited motor capabilities of a developmentally delayed group, the soccer field could be smaller and the ball could be lighter for it to be kicked farther and more accurately. In addition, activities could be designed to suit the students' abilities and not their disabilities. For example, a student with spina bifida is capable of learning how to swim because of intact upper body coordination. Finally, the instructor should be able to sequence and time learning experiences according to the students' capabilities.

REFERENCES

Adams, R. C. (1981). Adapted physical education. In J. Kauffman & D. Hallahan (Eds.), *Handbook of special education* (pp. 1–27). Englewood Cliffs, NJ: Prentice Hall.

American Association of Health, Physical Education and Recreation (AAHPER). (1981). *Resource guide in adapted physical education.* Reston, VA: Author.

Auxter, D., & Pyer, J. (1985). *Adapted physical education.* St. Louis, MO: Mosby.

Guiding principles for adapted physical education. (1952). *Journal of Health, Physical Education & Recreation, 35,* 15–16.

Sherrill, C. (1985). *Adapted physical education and recreation* (3rd ed.). Dubuque, IA: Brown.

Toon, C. J., & Gench, B. E. (1990). Attitudes of handicapped and nonhandicapped high school students towards physical education. *Perceptual and Motor Skills, 70*(3), 1328–1330.

Tripp, A., French, R., & Sherrill, C. (1995). Contact theory and attitudes of children in physical education programs towards peers with disabilities. *Adapted Physical Activity Quarterly, 12*(4), 323–332.

THOMAS R. BURKE
*Hunter College, City University
of New York*

ADAPTIVE BEHAVIOR
OLYMPICS, SPECIAL
RECREATION FOR INDIVIDUALS WITH DISABILITIES

PHYSICAL DISABILITIES

A variety of interchangeable terms have been used to describe persons with physical handicaps. For example, these individuals will often be categorized as physically disabled, physically impaired, crippled, orthopedically impaired, other health impaired, or multiply handicapped. The legal definition for orthopedically impaired is a severe orthopedic impairment that adversely affects a child's education performance (IDEA). The term includes impairments caused by a congenital anomaly (e.g., clubfoot, absence of some member, etc.), impairments caused by disease (e.g., poliomyelitis, bone tuberculosis, etc.), and impairments from other causes (e.g., cerebral palsy, amputations, and fractures or burns that cause contractures). The legal definition for other health impaired is having a condition that is manifested by severe communication and other developmental and educational problems; or having limited strength, vitality, or alertness because of chronic or acute health problems (e.g., a heart condition, tuberculosis, rheumatic fever, nephritis, asthma, sickle cell anemia, hemophilia, epilepsy, lead poisoning, leukemia, or diabetes) that adversely affect a child's educational performance (IDEA).

The range of disability varies from mild to profound physical impairment. Nonetheless, it is current practice to categorize students with physical handicaps as having average to above average intelligence, and physically handicapped/multiply handicapped students as having additional impairments such as mental retardation, blindness, or deafness. Additionally, mild to moderate learning disabilities often are found with students whose only handicapping condition is physical.

It is estimated that the incidence of physical disabilities is 2 percent (Smith, 1984). In the school year 1984–1985, 73,292 multihandicapped, 58,924 orthopedically impaired, and 69,688 other health-impaired students received special education services (Office of Special Education and Rehabilitation, 1985). The most common physical impairments found in schools are cerebral palsy, myelomeningocele (spina bifida), and muscular dystrophy. Although children with communicable diseases such as cytomegalovirus, herpes, hepatitis, and acquired immune deficiency syndrome (AIDS) are being denied entry into some schools (Dykes, 1984–1985), the incidence of these diseases is on the rise and will have to be addressed within the public school system.

Most physically disabled and health-impaired students are served in a combination of regular and special programs (Walker & Jacobs, 1984). Nevertheless, Dykes

(1984–1985) suggests that 85 percent of health-impaired and 35 percent of orthopedically impaired children should be served solely in regular classrooms. Physically and multiply handicapped students are usually served in special education classrooms, separate facilities, or hospital/homebound programs if their conditions do not permit inclusive programming.

The educational needs of physically disabled students vary as widely as the definitions, etiologies, and educational placements. For most physically handicapped students, the regular academic curriculum is most appropriate. In addition, an emphasis is placed on helping the students to gain independent living skills such as grooming, dressing, and food preparation. Perhaps the greatest needs of these students are in the areas of adaptive equipment (Campbell, 1983) and technology (Vanderheiden & Walstead, 1982). Often physically disabled students require wheelchairs, crutches, head pointers, arm and leg braces, etc. It is common for the physically disabled child to use a nonverbal/augmentative communication system (e.g., Zygo 100, Tetra-Scan II, Omni) or use computers for a variety of instructional purposes (Rushakoff & Lombardino, 1983). Technological advances have narrowed the gap in providing adequate educational instruction to students who cannot speak, move, or use their hands.

Another major area for intervention with physically disabled students is in social and self-concept development. Often the physically impaired student is characterized as passive, less persistent, having a shorter attention span, engaging in less exploration, and displaying less motivation (Jennings et al., 1985) and less self-esteem (Lawrence, 1991). Additionally, physically disabled students are found to be more dependent on adults and to interact less with their peers. Programs serving these students must consider socialization and independence. Parents as well as teachers need to find ways to facilitate independence and build self-esteem.

The education of physically disabled students requires a transdisciplinary team effort. Because the students have a variety of medical needs, educational program planning often will include pediatricians, neurologists, physical therapists, occupational therapists, speech clinicians, nurses, orthopedic surgeons, vision specialists, and most important, the families of these students. Often, families of physically disabled children must be the central focus of the educational process. It is with their support that programs in daily living and social skills training can actually work. Likewise, it is team support that enables families to more easily adjust to the demands of raising a child with physical or other health impairments.

REFERENCES

Campbell, P. (1983). Basic considerations in programming for students with movement difficulties. In M. Snell (Ed.), *Systematic instruction of the moderately and severely handicapped* (2nd ed., pp. 168–102). Columbus, OH: Merrill.

Dykes, M. K. (1984–1985). Assessment of students who are physically or health impaired. *Diagnostique, 10,* 128–143.

Jennings, K., Connors, R., Stegman, C., Sankaranarayan, P., & Mendelson, S. (1985). Mastery motivation in young preschoolers: Effect of a physical handicap and implications for educational programming. *Journal of the Division for Early Childhood, 9,* 162–169.

Lawrence, B. (1991). Self-concept formation and physical handicap: Some educational implications for integration. *Disability, Handicap & Society, 6*(2), 139–146.

Office of Special Education and Rehabilitation. (1985). *School year 1984–85 report of services by category.* Washington, DC: U.S. Department of Education.

Rushakoff, G., & Lombardino, L. (1983). Comprehensive microcomputer applications for severely physically handicapped children. *Teaching Exceptional Children, 16,* 18–22.

Smith, O. S. (1984). Severely and profoundly physically handicapped students. In P. Valletutti & B. Sims-Tucker (Eds.), *Severely and profoundly handicapped students: Their nature and needs* (pp. 85–152). Baltimore: Brookes.

Vanderheiden, G., & Walstead, L. (1982). *Trace Center internationally software / hardware registry.* Madison: University of Wisconsin, Trace Center.

Walker, D. K., & Jacobs, F. H. (1984). Chronically ill children in school. *Peabody Journal of Education, 61*(2), 28–74.

VIVIAN I. CORREA
University of Florida

ACCESSIBILITY OF BUILDINGS
MULTIPLE HANDICAPPING CONDITIONS
OTHER HEALTH IMPAIRED

PHYSICAL RESTRAINT

A punishment procedure that involves the immobilization of limbs or the entire body is referred to as physical restraint. The intent of physical restraint is to decrease or eliminate the unacceptable behavior immediately preceding the onset of the physical restraint procedure. Physical restraint should be employed only after ample documentation is obtained that lesser intrusive interventions were ineffective.

Immobilization methods vary and may range from holding a student's hands by the side of the body to applying a mechanical arm restraint at the elbows to prevent self-injurious blows to the face. Several recommendations have been offered for implementing physical restraint procedures. Bitgood, Peters, Jones, and Hathorn (1982) recommend that the teacher be positioned behind the student and firmly grasp the student's shoulders to hold them against the back of the seat. A second method of physical restraint involves holding the shoulders while the student is in a bent-over position in a chair (Reid, Tombaugh, & Heuvel, 1981). A third method is holding both of the student's hands behind the back of a chair (Rapoff, Altman, & Christopherson, 1980). The exact method of restraint will vary along several lines, including the size of the student; the size of the teacher; the alternative activity to be taught to the student to replace previously observed unacceptable behaviors; and the position of the student relative to the activity being taught.

In addition to actively immobilizing parts of a student's body, mechanical restraints can be employed. These restraints can restrict the student's movements to strike parts of the body, or materials (e.g., elbow pads, helmets, face masks) can be worn over injured areas to prevent future injuries.

The duration of time during which each instance of physical restraint is employed has varied from 3 seconds to 15 minutes, with most reported studies containing recommendations of 10 seconds to 1 minute. That is, following the occurrence of an unacceptable behavior, the teacher would employ a restraint procedure for a pre-established time interval. If the student is calm, nonaggressive and willing to verbally process the incident (Rich, 1997) at the end of the time interval, the restraint is removed. However, if the student continues to struggle as the time expires, an additional duration of time must elapse during which the student is calm prior to removing the physical restraint.

Applying physical restraint as a behavioral intervention should not automatically be associated with punishment. Researchers have observed that physical restraint may act as a reinforcer for continued maladaptive behaviors. Favell, McGimsey, and Jones (1978) evaluated situations in which physical restraint actually resulted in increased frequencies of aggressive behaviors. Similarly, Singh, Winton, and Ball (1984) documented an increase in out-of-seat behavior when followed by contingent physical restraint. Finally, Foxx and Dufrense (1984) evaluated the reinforcing effects of hinged metal splints on the self-injurious behavior of a mentally retarded resident within a large residential facility. Interestingly, the authors were able to fade a self-restraint of a preferred object (large plastic glass) to a socially accepted form of self-restraint in the form of a wristwatch and eyeglasses.

Reasons cited for the reinforcing properties of physical restraint include a relaxing feeling of being immobile and resultant drowsiness; physical contact from a reinforcing adult i.e. attachment (Bath, 1994); reduction in demands placed on the student who escapes from disliked activities by engaging in unacceptable behaviors resulting in physical restraint procedures.

When physical restraint results in a decrease or elimination of unacceptable behavior, several potential advantages may occur: undue physical strength or endurance by the teacher may not be required; little staff training is required; no verbal instruction is necessary, although some teachers include a verbalization of the unacceptable behavior prior to the physical restraint; minimum level of discomfort is afforded the student; the student cannot engage in unacceptable behaviors while being restrained; long-lasting effects are observed; and few side effects are noted.

Potential disadvantages that need to be considered prior to the implementation of a physical restraint procedure include an inability of small-frame teachers to restrain physically stronger students; the association of restraint with close physical contact and attention from the teacher; time lost from educational activities while the student is restrained; restraint itself may be reinforcing for the student; procedures have the potential to be highly aversive and intrusive; the student's physical strength may be increased through isometric type of exercising while resisting the restraint; an inexperienced teacher may use physical restraint in an arbitrary, capricious manner; physical restraint has the potential for injury.

Guidelines have been offered for the judicious application of physical restraint procedures, and teachers need to safeguard the rights of each student by adhering to at least the following:

1. Obtain informed consent from the student's guardian

2. Closely monitor the procedure to prevent intentional or unintentional abuse

3. Positively reinforce appropriate behaviors

4. Consider less restrictive alternatives prior to physical restraint

5. Use minimum physical force

6. Document length of time and frequency of instances of physical restraint

7. Administer physical restraint only in a contingent manner

8. Train all individuals in all environments frequented by the student

9. Maintain a resource file of successful documentations of the use of physical restraint to guide the development of the parameters for a targeted student

10. Fade the intensity of restraint materials to socially acceptable, nondebilitating materials (Foxx & Dufrense, 1984)

11. Identify functional, life skill activities to replace self-injurious or stereotypic behaviors when decreasing unacceptable behaviors via physical restraint

REFERENCES

Bath, H. (1994). The physical restraint of children: Is it therapeutic? *American Journal of Orthopsychiatry, 64*(1), 40–49.

Bitgood, S. C., Peters, R. D., Jones, M. L., & Hathorn, N. (1982). Reducing out-of-seat behaviors in developmentally disabled children through brief immobilization. *Education & Treatment of Children, 5,* 249–260.

Favell, J. E., McGimsey, J. F., & Jones, M. L. (1978). The use of physical restraint in the treatment of self-injury and as positive reinforcement. *Journal of Applied Behavior Analysis, 11,* 225–241.

Foxx, R. M. (1982). *Decreasing behaviors of severely retarded and autistic persons* (pp. 51–60). Champaign, IL: Research Press.

Foxx, R. M., & Dufrense, D. (1984). "Harry": The use of physical restraint as a reinforcer, timeout from restraint, and fading restraint in treating a self-injurious man. *Analysis & Intervention in Developmental Disabilities, 4,* 1–13.

LaGraw, S. J., & Repp, A. C. (1984). Stereotypic responding: A review of intervention research. *American Journal of Mental Deficiency, 88,* 595–609.

Rapoff, M. A., Altman, K., & Christophersen, R. (1980). Elimination of a retarded blind child's self-hitting by response-contingent brief restraint. *Education & Treatment of Children, 3,* 231–237.

Reid, J. G., Tombaugh, T. N., & Heuvel, K. V. (1981). Application of contingent physical restraint to suppress stereotyped body rocking of profoundly mentally retarded persons. *American Journal of Mental Deficiency, 86,* 78–85.

Rich, C. R. (1997). The use of physical restraint in residential treatment. *Residential Treatment for Children Youth, 14*(3), 1–12.

Shapiro, E. S., Barrett, R. P., & Ollendick, T. H. (1980). A comparison of physical restraint and positive practice overcorrection in treating stereotypic behaviors. *Behavior Therapy, 11,* 227–233.

Singh, N. N., Winton, A. S. W., & Ball, P. M. (1984). Effects of physical restraint on the behavior of hyperactive mentally retarded persons. *American Journal of Mental Deficiency, 89,* 16–22.

Waddell, P. A., Singh, N. N., & Beale, I. L. (1984). Conditioned punishment of self-injurious behavior. In S. E. Breuning, J. L. Matson, & R. P. Barrett (Eds.), *Advances in mental retardation and developmental disabilities* (pp. 85–134). Greenwich, CT: JAI.

Ernest L. Pancsofar
University of Connecticut

PHYSICAL THERAPY

Physical therapists are responsible for physical restoration. Employing a variety of equipment, they use massage and regulated exercise to improve coordination and balance, reeducate muscles, restore joint motion, and increase the patient's tolerance for activity.

A physical therapist employs mechanical and muscle strengthening exercises to assist students who will benefit from these activities to improve their quality of life. Physical therapists are frequently members of interdisciplinary teams, where they contribute to the overall management of the patient. The goal of most client service is to obtain entry into independent living and competitive employment. An example of services might include deep heat, paraffin baths, hydrotherapy, mild stretching, or strengthening exercises for a person with a crippling arthritis; strengthening and coordinating exercises for a person with a cerebral palsy; development, frequently in concert with an occupational therapist, of exercises for mobility through walking, leg braces, a wheelchair, or some combination; and the appropriate use of any prosthetic devices. Braces, wheelchairs, and other appliances require instruction in their use and care. Physical therapists generally teach these skills. They also join with occupational, speech, hearing, or other therapists in assisting the patient in the use of the prosthetic device to accomplish independent living or vocational skills.

Physical therapy, then, is the act of teaching motor strengthening, motor control, balance, and other skills to persons with disabilities. It combines these motoric trainings with prosthetic devices to help the patient to accomplish needed goals by reducing the effects of disability. Physical therapy is one aspect of the total training needed to reduce the effects of disability to enable the person with a disability to profit from residual (normal) bodily functions. Frequently, both the general public and the person with a disability, particularly the newly disabled person, become overwhelmed at the presence of a handicapping condition. What frequently is not seen is the amount of usable function that remains. The principle involved is to provide the person with a disability with training of muscle groups, motor control, balance, etc., to promote the use of the residual, nondisabled functions.

A few of the categories and types of skills taught in physical therapy as they apply to special education are listed.

1. Health (severity of problem health behaviors)
2. Attendance and promptness (degree of presence in school and time-telling behaviors)
3. Feeding/eating (degree of competency in eating skills)
4. Drinking (degree of competency in drinking skills)
5. Toileting (degree of competency in toilet skills)
6. Grooming (degree of competency in washing, showering, and personal hygiene skills)
7. Dressing (degree of competency in independent dressing skills)
8. Undressing (degree of competency in independent undressing skills)
9. Nasal hygiene (degree of competency in maintaining hygienic and socially acceptable conditions of the nose)

10. Oral hygiene (degree of competency in toothbrushing behavior)

11. Self-identification (degree of competency in pointing to body parts, knowing family members, and information about self)

12. Sensory perception (degree of competency in discriminating among stimuli on the basis of touch, taste, smell)

13. Auditory perception (degree of competency in discriminating among stimuli on the basis of auditory cues)

14. Visual Motor I (degree of competency in interpreting simple fine-visual motor skills)

15. Visual Motor II (degree of competency in integrating complex visual motor skills)

16. Gross Motor I (degree of competency in demonstrating simple mobility, eye-hand coordination, and gross motor skills)

17. Gross Motor II (degree of competency in demonstrating complex gross motor skills, motor sports)

18. Prearticulation (degree of competency in controlling mouth parts)

19. Articulation (degree of competency in making vowel and consonant sounds)

20. Language comprehension (degree of competency in understanding communication)

21. Language development (degree of competency in using gestures, sounds, and words to communicate)

22. Listening (degree of competency in attending and reacting to verbal communication)

23. Adaptive behaviors (degree of competency involving exploratory play and problem-solving skills)

24. Impulse control (degree of competency in controlling disruptive behaviors and accepting criticism)

25. Interpersonal relations (degree of competency in cooperating and interacting with others in social situations)

26. Responsible behaviors (degree of competency in accepting rules, obeying authorities, and demonstrating socially approved behaviors)

27. Personal welfare (degree of competency in demonstrating safe behaviors in hazardous conditions)

DAVID A. SABATINO
*West Virginia College of
Graduate Studies*

OCCUPATIONAL THERAPY
PHYSICAL DISABILITY

PHYSICIAN'S DESK REFERENCE

The *Physicians' Desk Reference,* known popularly as the *PDR,* is an annual publication of Medical Economics Company. It reports information on more than 2500 drugs. The information is supplied entirely by the drug's manufacturer but is edited and approved by medical personnel employed by the publisher. The *PDR* contains descriptions of drugs (with pictures in many cases of the most common form), indications for use, recommendations regarding dosage levels, and antidotes for some drugs. Management information for overdosage developed by the Institute for Clinical Toxicology is also presented. The *PDR* is intended primarily for use by physicians and was developed to make readily available essential information on major pharmaceutical products. The *PDR* is useful to allied health professionals and to special educational personnel. It is particularly useful to the latter because of the high incidence of medication usage by children with disabilities. The *PDR* is likely to be available in the reference library of any special education program.

CECIL R. REYNOLDS
Texas A&M University

PHYSIOTHERAPY

Physiotherapy or physiatry is the treatment of disease with the aid of physical agents such as light, heat, cold, water, and electricity, or with mechanical apparatus. The person responsible for physiotherapy is a physiatrist: a physician who specializes in physiotherapeutics or physiotherapy. Physical therapy, or the application of physiotherapy as practiced by physical therapists or occupational therapists, is supervised by the physiatrist responsible for the physical therapy unit.

The primary purpose of physiotherapy is to provide for the controlled movement of the extremities and for the other muscle and joint articulation necessary for the activities of daily living or competitive employment. Muscles are strengthened, coordination exercises are offered, and mechanical (nonchemical) applications to increase the range of motion and strength for each joint are provided.

The range of patients includes those suffering from damage to either the central or peripheral nervous systems; those suffering from any disease or mechanical injury; and those afflicted with a birth defect affecting muscle and bone. Two primary systems treated are the skeletal and nervous systems. Some of the more common conditions treated are strokes (cerebral vascular accidents), cerebral palsy, head trauma, spinal cord injuries, arthritis, polio, and a number of inherited and acquired bone, joint, or muscle problems.

Educators have traditionally used the term physically handicapped to categorize those children and youths who, because of bodily disability, require specialized education. Under such a rubric, physical handicap equates with bodily disability; therefore, practically all handicapping conditions are physical (e.g., vision and hearing impairments, forms of mental retardation, and brain injury).

Generally, a physical handicap can contain four characteristics: (1) a neuromuscular disability resulting from damage to the central nervous system; (2) a disability related to a lower common neural pathway (nerves and muscles outside of the central nervous system); (3) a disability resulting from an injury or disease that destroys nerves, muscles, or bone peripheral to the central nervous system; or (4) a health impairment that reduces vitality and thereby results in a weakened physical condition.

Diagnostically the two major groups are orthopedically handicapped and other health impaired. The orthopedically handicapped constitute the group that is neuromuscularly handicapped as a result of insult or trauma to the central nervous system or as a result of lower common neural-muscular-orthopedic (skeleton system) damage peripheral to the central nervous system. Other health-impaired conditions have numerous etiologies but have in common a condition that so weakens the individual that he or she must limit or modify the activities and therefore participate in physiotherapy to obtain relief.

DAVID A. SABATINO
*West Virginia College of
Graduate Studies*

ORTHOPEDIC IMPAIRMENTS
OTHER HEALTH IMPAIRED

PIAGETIAN APPROACH TO SPECIAL EDUCATION

Jean Piaget (1950, 1952, 1977), Switzerland's noted genetic epistemologist, proposed a developmental and constructivist model of human cognition from birth to adolescence based on biological processes. Although his theory has been applied to regular education for several decades, fewer efforts have been made to apply his work to exceptional populations (Gallagher & Reid, 1981; Reid, 1981; Wachs & Furth, 1980). One reason for this apparent lack of interest is Piaget's derivation of theoretical principles from observations of essentially normal children, with the consequent assumption of lack of applicability to handicapped individuals. A second obstacle has been an assumed lack of fit between more holistic and social/linguistic (Beilin, 1996) instructional goals and strategies compatible with Piagetian theory and the specific, step-by-step goals and methods typically prescribed for handicapped learners. Nevertheless, Piaget's cognitive-

development theory provides a useful means of understanding and teaching children with exceptional needs.

Concepts integral to Piaget's theory include structures, adaptation, stages of development, conservation, equilibration, and egocentrism. According to his theory, cognitive development consists of progression through an invariant sequence of stages, with the child incorporating the structures (organized patterns for dealing with the environment) acquired at each stage into qualitatively different, higher order structures at each succeeding stage. The child's progression from stage to stage results from adaptation, which describes the process of interaction between the child's current maturational level and environmental stimuli. Two complementary processes constitute adaptation: assimilation and accommodation. Assimilation refers to the child's incorporation of features of the environment into his or her existing structures. Accommodation is the modifying of one's structures in response to environmental demands. To illustrate, when an infant desires to touch a new mobile dangling from the crib, the infant must accommodate his or her vision and movements to the distance. Simultaneously, the infant assimilates the mobile into already existing patterns of behavior: structures for reaching and grasping.

As a result of adaptation, the developing child continually creates new structures out of previously acquired structures to better interact with the environment. Piaget describes the development of these structures in terms of a series of stages: sensorimotor, preoperational, concrete operational, and formal operational. The sensorimotor stage (birth to 1½ years) describes the infant and prelinguistic child. The infant manifests cognition through actions on objects, such as jiggling the crib to set a mobile in motion. The preoperational stage (1½ to 7 years) is characterized by use of language, symbolic behavior, and lack of conversational logic. The 2-year-old child demonstrates symbolic behavior by pretending that a broom is a horse and "riding" it. The preoperational child has not yet acquired the structures necessary for conservation: the ability to recognize that matter is conserved despite superficial changes in shape or form. For example, when a 3 year old is presented with two identical balls of clay, one of which is subsequently rolled into a cigar shape, the child perceives the remaining ball and the cigar as being unequal in size. When asked which is larger (or "has more"), the child may attend only to length and select the cigar, or only to width, and choose the ball. The child does not consider the two dimensions simultaneously.

Children in the stage of concrete operations (7 to 12 years) have acquired the rules of conservation as well as an understanding of relational concepts. The fourth state, formal operations (12 and above) describes children who can use abstract rules in problem solving and conceptualize in hypothetical terms.

Piaget's theory postulates that although children vary in the age at which they reach a given stage, all follow the same sequence. Progression from stage to stage occurs through equilibration, or the reorganization of structures through assimilation and accommodation, resulting in higher order structures. Disequilibrium, or a state of conflict, occurs when the child's current structures are applied (assimilation) and found insufficient to the task. According to Piaget, the child is inherently motivated toward equilibrium and therefore toward resolving the conflict. For example, the child entering the stage of concrete operations recognizes that the cigar-shaped clay is longer than the ball and yet was an equivalent ball in its original form. To resolve the conflict, the child reorganizes (accommodates) his or her structures; new structures for the simultaneous consideration of the two dimensions of length and width and for conservation result. The child thus reaches a new state of equilibrium.

Piaget's constructivist model has been used to explain social cognition, or children's logical understanding of themselves and other individuals in interaction. Children's development of social cognition parallels their intellectual development, progressing through a sequence of stages from egocentric to sociocentric thought. The infant is egocentric, or centered around the self. As children mature and gain experience with the environment, they become decentered; they learn that the self is separate from other people, that other people have thoughts and feelings, and that other people's thoughts and feelings may differ from their own. Development of social cognition in several areas parallels stages of cognitive development. These areas include referential communication, role taking, moral judgment, and rule implementation.

Referential communication refers to one's ability to describe a stimulus such that the listener can correctly locate the same stimulus out of an array of similar items, and is examined using speaker-listener pairs or dyads. Young children's referential communication is often termed egocentric in that they usually fail to consider the listener's perspective. For example, a 2 year old requesting a favorite cup may ask a listener to bring the "cup Grandpa gave me," not recognizing that the listener is not privy to Grandpa's gift. Role or perspective taking refers to the ability to consider other people's point of view: their thoughts, feelings, or, literally, what is in their range of vision. Children progress from a lack of separation between self and environment (early infancy) to simultaneous consideration of multiple perspectives.

Three stages characterize children's development of moral judgment: objective morality, subjective morality, and interpretation of the act (Piaget, 1932). Children in the stage of objective morality base their judgments of good and bad behavior on objective criteria such as the amount of damage incurred, for example, when someone breaks a lamp while trying to clean the table. In subjective morality, good or bad intentions become a prime criterion for judging behavior. At the highest level, children simultaneously consider intent and outcome and develop a sense of moral responsibility for the own actions.

Children's play and use of rules in play follow a similar developmental pattern. In parallel play, young children share materials and physical proximity but act independently, without a common set of rules. At a later stage (incipient cooperation), they know the rules and attempt to win at games. Finally, children together develop and elaborate rules appropriate for the situation (genuine cooperation).

Much of the research on Piaget's theory has addressed the invariance of the sequence of stages: the impact of specific training on development, especially on acquisition of conservation; the relationship of social cognition to cognitive development; and the relationship between social cognition and social behavior. For a more comprehensive discussion of the research, the reader is referred to Flavell (1971, 1972) on invariant sequence, Klein and Safford (1977) on training, and Shantz (1975) on social cognition.

In general, the research in all four areas has produced somewhat inconsistent results interpretable in a variety of ways depending on the researcher's theoretical orientation. Moreover, attempts to measure level of cognitive development have been criticized as producing merely another assessment of general intelligence. Studies of cognitive development in young children have questioned preschoolers' apparent egocentricity and inability to conserve as artifacts of task difficulty (Gelman, 1979). On the other hand, inconsistent findings regarding stage invariance, training of conservation concepts, and correlation between stages of cognitive and social cognitive development may be interpreted within a Piagetian framework as reflective of the fact that a given child may simultaneously be at different stages of development for different concepts (e.g., conservation of quantity, conservation of mass, role taking, moral judgment). Inconsistencies may result from investigators' use of different measures to assess levels of cognitive development. In addition, procedures may fail to discriminate between children who have already attained a given stage and children who are in transition between stages.

Because cognitive development results from an interaction between child structures and environmental stimuli, differences in quantity and quality of experience may affect acquisition of concepts. For example, a mentally disabled child with a chronological age of 10 and a mental age of 7 might be expected to perform at approximately the same level as an intellectually average child with a chronological and mental age of 7 and a gifted child with a chronological age of 5 and a mental age of 7. However, differences among these children in years of experience would impact on acquisition of cognitive concepts. In short, although more definitive research is needed, Piaget's theory of cognitive development has contributed significantly to thinking about the learning process.

Piaget himself made little reference to the application of his theory to educational practice. However, psychologists and educators have derived from Piaget's work several principles for instruction appropriate for both academic and social learning. Piaget's theory, applied to special populations, assumes that all children, disabled and nondisabled, proceed through the same invariant sequence of stages using the same processes of assimilation, accommodation, and equilibration. Thus, while the rate of development may differ for exceptional learners, the instructional principles continue to be applicable. Experimental attempts to propel children (exceptional and nonexceptional) to a higher level of development through training generally have been unsuccessful (Gallagher & Reid, 1981), theoretically because children's stage progression depends on maturation as well as environment. The instructional principles that follow are directed at the teaching of concepts, generalizations, and thinking processes rather than at increasing the level of cognitive development.

1. Because children's thinking is qualitatively different at the various stages of development, teaching objectives should be matched to children's level of development.

2. Learning is the acquisition of higher order structures transformed from and built on previous structures. Thus, learning involves the acquisition of broad, general rules or frameworks rather than particular, isolated facts. As such, learning proceeds through understanding rather than through incorporation of rote responses.

3. Children are internally motivated by a desire for achieving equilibrium. Thus, learning is facilitated by the presentation of optimally challenging tasks and discrepant events that predispose the child to disequilibrium.

4. Children learn best through interacting with and manipulating environmental stimuli.

5. Group interactions may present children with ideas that challenge their own, leading to disequilibrium, reorganization, and new structures.

These principles have been translated into more specific guidelines for teaching learning-disabled students (Moses, 1981). These guidelines are appropriate for other special needs children:

1. Begin with an encountering stage that permits children to interact with the materials before a problem is posed. Present concrete materials that permit children to experience and impose many kinds of change.

2. Allow children to set goals before they deal with transformations.

3. Present problems that involve puzzling transformations. Create situations that stimulate children to infer and reason spontaneously.

4. Permit children's creation and use of alternative methods of problem solving.

5. Accept children's methods of problem solving, even if they lead to failure.

6. Create a nonthreatening, nonexternally evaluating atmosphere. Avoid praise, criticism, or other announcements that label children's responses, since external evaluation reinforces dependence on the environment.

7. Require children to anticipate or predict the results of their actions, observe outcomes, and compare their hypothesized outcomes with results.

8. Be responsive to the children: listen, accept all responses, and respond with appropriate feedback.

Teaching methods consistent with these principles and guidelines include cooperative learning, hypothesis testing, discovery learning, inquiry, and other approaches that encourage inductive thinking. Cooperative learning is an instructional strategy whereby students work together in small groups to complete academic tasks. Potential benefits include gains in academic content, basic skill development, problem solving, and socialization. More research is needed on the efficacy of cooperative learning with exceptional students (Pullis & Smith, 1981). Gallagher and Reid (1981) describe hypothesis testing approaches for teaching exceptional students as another method consonant with Piagetian theory.

The inductive approaches developed by Taba and her colleagues (Taba et al., 1971), and Suchman's problem-solving methods (Kitano & Kirby, 1986), provide step-by-step information for developing teaching activities consistent with Piagetian theory and applicable to mildly handicapped and gifted students. Taba's inductive approaches include methods for developing concepts, attaining concepts, applying generalizations, exploring feelings, and solving interpersonal problems. For example, a concept attainment strategy for the concept "square" requires teacher presentation of examples and nonexamples of squares and children's induction of a definition for square. Teachers may use the developing concepts strategy for assessing children's current ideas about a subject and for encouraging classification of concepts related to the subject. Suchman's problem-solving approach provides a concrete method for children's attainment of such objectives as letter, numeral, color, and shape names, vocabulary, sight words, and arithmetic facts.

A federally funded research project (Kitano et al., 1982) provides preliminary data supporting the use of inductive methods based on Suchman's problem-solving approach with mildly mentally retarded and learning-disabled elementary-age students. Results indicated that learning-disabled children who received instruction in language arts using inductive methods showed gains similar to those achieved by learning-disabled controls who received instruction with traditional didactic and behavioral approaches. As a group, the educable mentally handicapped children demonstrated greater achievement in language arts objectives with inductive approaches than matched peers in the control condition. These results suggest that inductive methods may constitute a viable addition to traditional approaches to instruction with mildly handicapped learners. While more research is needed to validate the efficacy of such approaches for special populations, the approaches have theoretical merit and provide alternatives to traditional deductive methods.

Piaget's theory of cognitive development has had specific application to mild and severe/profound mental retardation, learning disabilities, gifted, and other categories.

Mental Retardation

Although Piaget's writings reflect little interest in individual differences, his ideas have been used to interpret the cognitive behavior of exceptional individuals. For example, Inhelder (1968) noted that the level of cognitive development ultimately achieved by mentally retarded individuals depended on their degree of impairment, with the severe-profound fixated at the sensorimotor level, the moderately retarded at the preoperational stage, and the mildly retarded rarely advancing beyond the level of concrete operations.

During the 1960s and 1970s, Piaget's theory sparked a new view on the field of mental retardation. The developmental approach to mild, familial mental retardation provided a positive alternative to deficit approaches, which assume that mentally handicapped individuals by definition possess deficits (e.g., in processes such as attention, memory, organization, or in neurological structures) that require remediation. The developmental view, articulated by Zigler (1967; Zigler & Balla, 1982) and Iano (1971), suggests instead that the familial educable mentally retarded constitute the lower end of the normal curve and differ from the intellectually average only in terms of rate of development and final level achieved. Mental age serves as an indicator of current developmental level.

In general, proponents of developmental theory as applied to the mildly mentally retarded suggest that this approach enables teachers to view retarded children in terms of normal stages achieved at a slower rate. Klein and Safford (1977) concluded from their review of research literature that stages of development in the mentally retarded population parallel those described by Piaget for nonhandicapped children, but appear at later chronological periods. Hence, the mildly retarded can be expected to perform according to their mental ages. The implication for educators is that methods applied to normal children can be used effectively with mildly retarded students of similar mental age. Thus, these individuals can profit from many regular instructional techniques and a broader curriculum appropriate to normally achieving children. Iano (1971) noted that edu-

cators too often assume that the mentally retarded have deficiencies in learning rate, retention, and the ability to generalize and abstract. As a result, teachers emphasize great amounts of repetition, structure, concrete presentation, and slow, step-by-step introduction of new material. He asks whether the retarded child's failure to reason and problem solve is due to an inability to understand or to an emphasis in teaching on the rote and mechanical.

Although the developmental approach as applied to mental retardation has received serious criticism (e.g., Spitz, 1983), research has neither disproved the developmental approach nor proved the deficit position, and probably never will (Spitz, 1983). In the meantime, the application of Piagetian instructional methods with the mildly retarded merits serious investigation and offers an exciting alternative to teachers wishing to broaden their instructional repertoire. Most important, application of Piagetian approaches to instruction may provide variety and challenge to the children themselves.

Piaget's descriptions of the sensorimotor stage, normally covering birth to 18 months, have served as a basis for interpreting the behavior of the severely/profoundly handicapped, assessing their level of cognitive development, and developing appropriate curricula. The six substages of the sensorimotor period can be summarized as follows (Stephens, 1977), together with sample instructional tasks appropriate to each.

Reflexive (Birth–1 Month)

This phase is initially characterized by reflex actions (e.g., hand waving, kicking, crying, sucking, grasping) and visual tracking of objects. These actions become more coordinated and generalized. Sample task: To encourage visual tracking, hold a bright moving object 10 inches from the subject's eyes and move the object slowly across the subject's field of vision. If visual tracking fails to occur spontaneously, physically turn the subject's head to follow the object.

Primary Circular Reactions (1–4.5 Months)

Reflexive behavior becomes elaborated and coordinated. The infant becomes interested in movement itself, as in observing his or her own hand waving. Repeated as ends in themselves, these actions are "circular" responses. Sample task: Move a colorful, sound-producing object from side to side and up and down to encourage coordination of visual tracking and touching of the object with the hand. If visual tracking coordinated with touching the object does not occur spontaneously, physically guide the behavior.

Secondary Circular Reactions (4.5–9 Months)

The infant intentionally repeats chance movements that produce a desirable effect (e.g., shaking a rattle to produce a sound). Sample task: Demonstrate a squeeze toy and hand it to the subject. Guide the squeezing behavior to elicit the sound if the behavior does not occur spontaneously.

Coordination of Secondary Schema (9–12 Months)

The infant begins to discriminate between self and environment, to imitate speech sounds and movements of others, and to differentiate means and ends. Sample task: Demonstrate and guide a means-ends activity such as dropping an object into water to create a splash.

Tertiary Circular Reactions (12–18 Months)

The infant actively experiments and discovers new means to ends, such as pulling a blanket to reach a toy that is resting on it. Sample task: Provide opportunities for (and guidance as necessary) discovering a means-ends activity such as obtaining an unreachable object using a stick.

Invention of New Means Through Mental Combinations (18–24 Months)

The infant considers alternatives, solves problems, and completes development of object permanence. Sample task: Demonstrate and permit experimentation with fitting objects of different sizes and shapes into slots of various size and shape.

Based on her earlier work with severely retarded individuals, Woodward (1963) concluded that many of the seemingly inappropriate behaviors of this population are explainable within a Piagetian framework. Given that profoundly handicapped individuals operate at a sensorimotor level, mannerisms such as hand flapping in front of the eyes can be interpreted as sensorimotor patterns developed in the course of coordinating vision and grasping, as in the subphase of primary circular reactions.

Uzgiris and Hunt (1975) developed an assessment procedure for charting infant development founded on major areas of cognitive functioning during the sensorimotor period. Such an assessment procedure can be adapted for use with severely/profoundly handicapped individuals of various chronological ages. Areas of functioning assessed by Uzgiris and Hunt include visual pursuit and object permanence; means for achieving desired environmental events; gestural and vocal imitation; operational causality; object relations in space; and development of schemas in relation to objects.

Because severely/profoundly handicapped individuals generally do not proceed beyond the preoperational stage, curricula can be derived for this population based on the sensorimotor subphases and adapted according to chronological age. Development of appropriate curricula of a Piagetian nature for the severely/profoundly handicapped requires matching objectives to the individual's present level of development; active involvement of the individual; opportunity for the individual to proceed at his or her own pace; opportunities for exploration and manipulation; opportunities for repetition and practice; and adaptation for any associated sensory or motor impairments.

Learning Disabilities

By most definitions, learning-disabled students possess average to superior intellectual potential but manifest academic and social achievement at levels significantly lower than this potential would predict. Delays in cognitive and social-cognitive development have been explored through research as possible factors in explaining the discrepancy between potential and achievement in academic and social areas. Suggestions for teaching interventions based on Piagetian theory have also been offered in the literature.

Research

In general, the research suggests that learning-disabled (LD) children demonstrate performance inferior to that of nondisabled (NLD) children on tasks designed to measure cognitive development and social cognition. Speece, McKinney, and Appelbaum (1986) found a developmental delay in LD children's attainment of concrete operations compared with nondisabled (NLD) controls over a 3-year-period. However, their results also suggested that when the LD children attained the concrete operational stage, they acquired specific concepts in the same sequence and at the same rate as did NLD children. Moreover, for the LD but not the NLD group, Piagetian measures of cognitive development (conservation scores) and age better predicted academic achievement than did verbal intelligence. Most important was the finding that while the LD children as a group improved over the 3-year period, they failed to catch up with their NLD peers. Speece et al. (1986) concluded that delayed cognitive development may constitute an important explanatory factor for continued academic underachievement experienced by LD children despite intervention.

Dickstein and Warren (1980) reported similar delays in LD children's role-taking ability compared with NLD children in cognitive, affective, and perceptual tasks. Their analysis of the performance of children from 5 to 10 years of age suggested that larger differences in scores occurred in the younger age groups and that performance among LD children improved little between ages 8 and 10. Horowitz (1981) also found lower performance for LD children on an interpersonal role-taking task, but no significant differences between the two groups on a perceptual role-taking measure. However, as indicated by Horowitz, results were confounded by differences between the two groups in intelligence. Wong and Wong (1980) found significant differences between LD and NLD children in role taking, with LD girls demonstrating much poorer skills than LD boys.

Finally, investigations of LD children's referential communication skills corroborate the findings on role taking that LD children possess deficits in social cognition relative to their NLD peers. Noel (1980) found LD students less effective in providing descriptive information about objects than NLD controls because of the LD children's tendency to describe objects by shape rather than by label or name. Spekman (1981) further reported that LD speakers tended to give more unproductive, irrelevant, or repetitious messages than did NLD children on communication tasks. These findings suggest that LD children communicate less effectively than do NLD children.

As a whole, results of investigations on role taking and communication suggest that deficits in these skills may be one source of social problems evidenced by some LD children. Having difficulty in anticipating other people's views and accommodating their messages to others' needs reduces LD children's chances for successful social interactions.

Teaching

The literature has suggested Piagetian-derived instructional strategies for LD students both as tools for presenting academic content and for remediating deficits in social-cognitive skills. Gallagher and Quandt (1981) presented questioning strategies consistent with Piagetian theory for improving reading comprehension of LD students. They suggest, for example, the use of inference questions that require students go beyond the information given. Such questioning strategies present puzzling problems that stimulate equilibration. Moses (1981) offers examples of arithmetic instruction to illustrate the use of Piagetian guidelines for teaching LD students. Role-taking training through each child's sequential adoption of the various roles in a story also has been suggested (Chandler, 1971) as a vehicle for improving role-taking skills and social behavior.

Gifted

As with other areas of exceptionality, Piaget's theory as applied to the gifted has implications for research and practice.

Research

Piaget's theory would predict that the intellectually gifted, like the intellectually handicapped, follow the same sequence of stages as average children but differ in rate of progression. Carter and Ormrod (1982) found through their review of research that mentally retarded, average, and gifted children follow the same sequence of stages, supporting Piaget's view of sequence invariance. However, studies investigating differences between gifted and nongifted learners in rate of progression have yielded conflicting results. Carter and Ormrod suggest that discrepant findings

might be due in part to differences in age groups studied. For example, young gifted children may not show superiority over average children in rate of cognitive development because such development, according to Piaget, is limited by maturity and experience, which may not differ significantly in quantity or quality in the early years.

There is some evidence to suggest that gifted children progress more rapidly than average children within a stage but achieve transitions to concrete and formal operations at approximately the same age as their peers. However, research by Carter (1985) and Carter and Ormrod (1982) indicates that gifted children both progress more rapidly than average children within a stage and demonstrate earlier transition to succeeding stages. In a study of 125 gifted and 98 average children aged 10 through 15, Carter and Ormrod (1982) found that the gifted outperformed controls at each age level and achieved formal operations at earlier ages. Specifically, the gifted students appeared to enter formal operations by age 12 or 13, while the average students, including 15 year olds, had not yet attained formal operations. Carter (1985) compared the cognitive development of 180 intellectually gifted, 325 bright average, and 168 average children ages 10 to 16. Major findings were that the gifted children outperformed intellectually average children at all age levels and outperformed bright average children at the lower age levels (10 to 14). Data were interpreted as indicating that gifted children establish their cognitive advantage as early as age 10. These studies suggest that intellectually gifted children may achieve higher stages of cognitive development at earlier ages than their average peers.

Despite common observations that gifted children express earlier concerns about morals and values, research on gifted children's social-cognitive development does not provide clear evidence that gifted children are advanced in this area relative to their average peers. Moral reasoning has some relationship to verbal intelligence. However, while some intellectually gifted students demonstrate advanced levels of moral judgment development, this is not true of all gifted students.

Teaching

Gifted children who are advanced in cognitive development compared with their intellectually average peers may require special interventions to prevent boredom and accompanying frustration. However, educators should not assume that all gifted children function at an advanced stage of cognitive development relative to their chronological age. Rather, every child should be assessed to determine level of cognitive development.

The process of concept acquisition through equilibration described by Piaget has relevance to instruction for the gifted. Guidelines for instruction consistent with Piaget's theory, described earlier, appear highly appropriate for gifted students because of their consistency with goals for the gifted, including optimum use of intellectual abilities, development of self-direction, and practice in higher level thinking skills (e.g., analysis, synthesis, evaluation). Kitano and Kirby (1986) describe specific methods for teaching the gifted consistent with Piagetian guidelines.

Other Categories

A few investigators have examined the application of Piagetian principles to children with other types of exceptionalities: cerebral palsy, hearing handicaps, visual impairments, and emotional disturbance. A review of these studies by Gallagher and Reid (1981) suggests that (1) intellectually normal children who have cerebral palsy progress at approximately the same rate as nonhandicapped children, although the former are slower to perform on tasks requiring manipulation, need more trials and encouragement, and have a lower frustration tolerance; (2) deaf children and blind children display minor or no delays in attainment of conservation compared with normal peers when accommodations are made for language and sensory differences and subjects are carefully matched; and (3) seriously emotionally disturbed children show deviations from normal developmental patterns.

In conclusion, the available research on cognitive development of exceptional learners suggests, for the most part, that exceptional individuals progress through the same sequence of stages described by Piaget for normal children, although they vary in rate of development and level ultimately attained. Application of Piagetian theory to practice suggests use of strategies that engage children in active problem solving appropriate to their current level of development. Additional research is required to demonstrate the efficacy of Piagetian-derived instructional strategies for handicapped and gifted learners. Such strategies have potential as additions to the instructional repertoire of special education teachers.

REFERENCES

Beilin, H. (1996). Mind and meaning: Piaget and Vygotsky on causal explanation. *Human Development, 39*(5), 277–286.

Carter, K. R. (1985). Cognitive development of intellectually gifted: A Piagetian perspective. *Roeper Review, 7*(3), 180–184.

Carter, K. R., & Ormrod, J. E. (1982). Acquisition of formal operations by intellectually gifted children. *Gifted Child Quarterly, 26*(3), 110–115.

Chandler, M. J. (1973). Egocentrism and antisocial behavior: The assessment and training of social perspective-taking skills. *Developmental Psychology, 9*(3), 326–332.

Dickstein, E. B., & Warren, D. R. (1980). Role-taking deficits in learning disabled children. *Journal of Learning Disabilities, 13*(7), 378–382.

Flavell, J. (1971). Stage-related properties of cognitive development. *Cognitive Psychology, 2,* 421–453.

Flavell, J. (1972). An analysis of cognitive developmental sequences. *Genetic Psychology Monographs, 86,* 279–350.

Gallagher, J. M., & Quandt, I. J. (1981). Piaget's theory of cognitive development and reading comprehension: A new look at questioning. *Topics in Learning & Learning Disabilities, 1*(1), 21–30.

Gallagher, J. M., & Reid, D. K. (1981). *The learning theory of Piaget and Inhelder.* Austin, TX: PRO-ED.

Gelman, R. (1979). Preschool thought. *American Psychologist, 34*(10), 900–905.

Horowitz, E. C. (1981). Popularity, decentering ability, and role-taking skills in learning disabled and normal children. *Learning Disability Quarterly, 4*(1), 23–30.

Iano, R. P. (1971). Learning deficiency versus developmental conceptions of mental retardation. *Exceptional Children, 58,* 301–311.

Inhelder, B. (1968). *The diagnosis of reasoning in the mentally retarded.* New York: John Day.

Kitano, M. K., Julian, N., Shoji, C., Trujillo, R., & Padilla, E. (1982). *Heuristic methods for the mildly handicapped: Research report and manual for teaching language arts and reading.* Las Cruces, NM: New Mexico State University.

Kitano, M. K., & Kirby, D. F. (1986). *Gifted education: A comprehensive view.* Boston: Little, Brown.

Klein, N. K., & Safford, P. L. (1977). Application of Piaget's theory to the study of thinking of the mentally retarded: A review of research. *Journal of Special Education, 11*(2), 201–216.

Moses, N. (1981). Using Piaget principles to guide instruction of the learning disabled. *Topics in Learning and Learning Disabilities, 1*(1), 11–19.

Noel, M. M. (1980). Referential communication abilities of learning disabled children. *Learning Disability Quarterly, 3*(3), 70–75.

Piaget, J. (1932). *The moral judgment of the child* (M. Gabain, Trans.). New York: Harcourt, Brace & World.

Piaget, J. (1950). *The psychology of intelligence* (M. Percy & D. E. Berlyne, Trans.). London: Routledge & Kegan Paul.

Piaget, J. (1952). *The origins of intelligence in children* (M. Cook, Trans.). New York: International University.

Piaget, J. (1977). *The development of thoughts: Equilibration of cognitive structures.* New York: Viking.

Pullis, M., & Smith, D. C. (1981). Social cognitive development of learning disabled children: Implications of Piaget's theory for research and intervention. *Topics in Learning & Learning Disabilities, 1*(1), 43–55.

Reid, D. K. (Ed.). (1981). Piaget learning and learning disabilities. *Topics in Learning & Learning Disabilities, 1*(1).

Shantz, C. U. (1975). The development of social cognition. In E. M. Heatherington (Ed.), *Review of child development research* (Vol. 5, pp. 257–323). Chicago: University of Chicago Press.

Speece, D. L., McKinney, J. D., & Appelbaum, M. I. (1986). Longitudinal development of conservation skills in learning disabled children. *Journal of Learning Disabilities, 19*(5), 302–307.

Spekman, N. J. (1981). Dyadic verbal communication abilities of learning disabled and normally achieving fourth- and fifth-grade boys. *Learning Disability Quarterly, 4*(2), 139–151.

Spitz, H. H. (1983). Critique of the developmental position in mental-retardation research. *Journal of Special Education, 17*(3), 261–294.

Stephens, B. (1977). A Piagetian approach to curriculum development for the severely, profoundly, and multiply handicapped. In E. Sontag (Ed.), *Educational programming for the severely and profoundly handicapped* (pp. 237–249). Reston, VA: Council for Exceptional Children, Division on Mental Retardation.

Taba, H., Durkin, M. C., Fraenkel, J. R., & McNaughton, A. H. (1971). *A teacher's handbook to elementary social studies. An inductive approach* (2nd ed.). Menlo Park, CA: Addison-Wesley.

Uzgiris, I. C., & Hunt, J. M. (1975). *Assessment in infancy ordinal scales of psychological development.* Urbana: University of Illinois Press.

Wachs, H., & Furth, H. (1980). Piaget's theory and special education. In B. K. Keogh (Ed.), *Advances in special education* (Vol. 2, pp. 51–78). Greenwich, CT: JAI.

Wong, B. Y. L., & Wong, R. (1980). Role-taking skills in normal achieving and learning disabled children. *Learning Disability Quarterly, 3*(2), 11–18.

Woodward, M. (1963). The application of Piaget's theory to research in mental deficiency. In N. Ellis (Ed.), *Handbook of mental deficiency: Psychological theory and research.* New York: McGraw-Hill.

Zigler, E. (1967). Familial mental retardation: A continuing dilemma. *Science, 155,* 292–298.

Zigler, E., & Balla, D. (Eds.). (1982). *Mental retardation: The developmental-difference controversy.* Hillsdale, NJ: Erlbaum.

MARGIE K. KITANO
New Mexico State University

COGNITIVE DEVELOPMENT
DIRECT INSTRUCTION
INDIVIDUALIZATION OF INSTRUCTION
INTELLIGENCE
PIAGET, JEAN

PIAGET, JEAN (1896–1980)

Jean Piaget was a Swiss psychologist whose explorations of the cognitive development of children helped to revolutionize education in the twentieth century. He described the sequence of mental development in three phases: (1) the sensory-motor phase, from birth to about age 2, during which children obtain a basic knowledge of objects; (2) the phase of concrete operations, from about 2 to 11, characterized by concrete thinking and the development of simple concepts; and (3) the formal operations phase, from about age 11, emphasizing abstract thinking, reasoning, and logical thought. Piaget's theories and descriptions of developmental sequences have encouraged teaching methods that emphasize the child's discovery of knowledge through the presentation of developmentally appropriate problems to be solved.

Born in Neuchatel, Switzerland, Piaget was educated at the university there, was director of the Jean Jacques Rousseau Institute in Geneva, and professor at the University of Geneva. In 1955 he established in Geneva the International Center of Genetic Epistomology, where he and his associates published voluminously on child development.

REFERENCES

Furth, H. G. (1969). *Piaget and knowledge.* Englewood Cliffs, Prentice Hall.

Piaget, J. (1926). *The language and thought of the child.* New York: Humanities.

PAUL IRVINE
Katonah, New York

PIC

See PERSONALITY INVENTORY FOR CHILDREN.

PICA

The word "pica" originates from the Latin word for magpie, a bird known for ingesting a wide variety of food and nonfood items (Danford & Huber, 1982). Pica is seen in various species, including birds, fish, apes, and humans (Diamond & Stermer, 1998). Pica as a disorder is characterized by habitual ingestion of inedible substances (Kerwin & Berkowitz, 1996). It is frequently associated with mental retardation (Danford & Huber, 1982), but also occurs in normal young children (less than age 3) and pregnant women within certain cultural groups. As many as 90 percent of children with elevated levels of blood-lead may show pica behavior. Pica sometimes continues into adolescence and adulthood (Diamond & Stermer, 1998). In infancy and early childhood, children often chew on their cribs, wood, sand, and grass as a method of early exploration (Erickson, 1998).

According to *DSM-IV,* pica is defined as "persistent eating of nonnutritive substances for a period of at least 1 month" that is "inappropriate to the developmental level" or "not part of a culturally sanctioned practice." *DSM-IV* also states that if pica behavior occurs in conjunction with another mental disorder (e.g., mental retardation, pervasive developmental disorder, or schizophrenia), it should be sufficiently severe to warrant independent clinical attention for a separate diagnosis to be given (APA, 1994, p. 96). Pica may be both underdiagnosed and undertreated (Katsiyannis, Torrey, & Bond, 1998).

Paint chips, dirt and sand, paper, fabric, feces, cigarette stubs, and bugs are among the substances commonly consumed by those with pica. Pica is a prevalent cause of lead poisoning, especially in children, due to lead-based paint that is common in cribs, other wooden objects, and some dirt. Dirt near houses may particularly contain lead in paint that has flaked off outside walls. Pica can also lead to severe nutritional deficits, intestinal obstruction or perforation, parasitic infections such as toxoplasmosis (through eating of cat feces), and even death (Katsiyannis et al., 1998; Kerwin & Berkowitz, 1996; Wiley, Henretig, & Selbst, 1992). Intestinal blockage may necessitate surgery to remove the obstruction.

Although pica is generally associated with adverse consequences, eating dirt or clay under some conditions may have benefits. The practice of eating soil is termed "geophagy." Geophagy may relieve hunger, provide grit for grinding food, provide nutritional value, cure diarrhea, buffer stomach contents, or protect against toxins (Diamond & Stermer, 1998). In the southeastern United States, pregnant women may eat clay and/or laundry starch owing to a superstitious belief that the practice prevents fetal curses and reduces the side effects of pregnancy (Nelson-Wicks & Israel, 1997). In one area of China, where geophagy is common, some people consume soil in a belief that it provides valuable nutrients. Indeed, a soil sample from the area contained iron, calcium, and manganese. In Zimbabwe, where people eat soil to soothe upset stomachs, one sample contained kaolinire, an ingredient that pharmaceutical companies use to treat diarrhea (Current Science, 1998). South American Indians reportedly regularly eat toxic potatoes mixed with an alkaloid-containing clay. The clay neutralizes the potatoes' toxicity (Diamond & Stermer, 1998).

Pica is a learned behavior, but its maintenance may owe to a number of factors. Since one of those factors may relate to a nutritional inadequacy, medical and nutritional analyses should precede any treatment program (Katsiyannis et al., 1998). If it is associated with some nutritional inadequacy, pica may be successfully treated with some dietary changes or mineral supplements targeted at the particular deficiency. In cases where no nutritional problem is found, a functional analysis of behavior should be conducted. Several types of behavioral interventions have been used successfully, ranging from less intrusive (e.g., differential reinforcement for non-pica behavior) to more aversive (e.g., overcorrection or brief physical restraint contingent upon pica). Obviously, any treatment program should begin with the least restrictive interventions unless the child's behavior presents an immediate risk. One interesting treatment uses a "pica box." A pica box is a small box containing edible items for a child. When a child attempts to eat a nonedible item, he or she is stopped, and after a brief time-out, is reinforced by being allowed to get a treat out of the pica box. This method has been especially useful in working with mildly retarded and autistic children (Hirsch & Myles, 1996). A particular

source for those in special education is Katsiyannis et al. (1998), who not only describe several programs in detail but provide useful case studies.

REFERENCES

American Psychiatric Association. (1994). *Diagnostic and statistical manual of mental disorders* (4th ed.). Washington, DC: Author.

Danford, D., & Huber, A. (1982). Pica among mentally retarded adults. *American Journal of Mental Deficiency, 87,* 141–146.

Diamond, J., & Stermer, D. (1998). Eat dirt. *Discover, 19*(2), 70–76.

Erickson, M. T. (1998). *Behavior disorders of children and adolescents.* Upper Saddle River, NJ: Prentice Hall.

Hirsch, N., & Myles, B. (1996). The use of a pica box in reducing pica behavior in a student with autism. *Focus on Autism and Other Developmental Disabilities, 11,* 222.

How would you like a dirt sandwich? (1998). *Current Science, 16,* 12–15.

Katsiyannis, A., Torrey, G., & Bond, V. (1998). Current considerations in treating pica. *Teaching Exceptional Children, 30*(4), 50–53.

Kerwin, M. E., & Berkowitz, R. I. (1996). Feeding and eating disorders: Ingestive problems of infancy, childhood, and adolescence. *School Psychology Review, 25,* 316–329.

Wicks-Nelson, R., Israel, A. C. (1997). *Behavior disorders of childhood.* Upper Saddle River, NJ: Prentice Hall.

LAUREN M. WEBSTER
ROBERT T. BROWN
University of North Carolina at Wilmington

ANOREXIA NERVOSA
EATING DISORDERS
LEAD POISONING
OBESITY

PICTORIAL TEST OF INTELLIGENCE–SECOND EDITION

The Pictorial Test of Intelligence–Second Edition (PTI-2; French, 2001) is an individually administered measure of intelligence designed for use with children with and without disabilities. Its multiple choice format and lack of time constraints make it useful for children with motor or speech delays or both. No vocalization is required on the part of examinees; they need only point to the correct response. Motorically impaired children can respond by fixing their eyes on the correct response, since the stimulus cards and the space between the choices are large enough to allow this accommodation.

PTI-2 is composed of three subtests. Verbal Abstractions measures the child's ability to demonstrate word knowledge, verbal comprehension, and verbal reasoning using pictorial stimuli. Form Discrimination measures the child's ability to match forms, differentiate between similar shapes, and reason about abstract shapes and patterns. Quantitative Concepts measures the child's ability to perceive and recognize size and number symbols, count, and solve simple arithmetic problems.

Scores on these three subtests (M = 10, SD = 3), are combined to yield a composite score (M = 100, SD = 15) referred to as a Pictorial Intelligence Quotient (PIQ). The choice of the abbreviation PIQ may lead to some confusion with Wechsler's PIQ (Performance IQ).

Directions for subtests are provided both on the examiner's side of the easel and in the record book. Basal and ceiling rules, as well as starting and stopping points, are simple to understand. The manual provides raw score to standard score and percentile conversions. Age equivalents are also supplied, but the author discourages users from reporting them.

The PTI-2 was standardized on 970 children from 15 states who were selected to correspond to the 1997 census report. Stratification variables included age, gender, race, ethnicity, residence (urban and rural), disability status, family income, and parental education. The average number of children tested at each age level was 162, with the smallest numbers at ages 3 (N = 136) and 8 (N = 144). While the school age norms approximate the U.S. population, the demographic characteristics of the preschool sample are not described.

Split-half, test-retest, and interscorer reliability statistics presented in the manual reflect excellent internal consistency and stability as well as agreement between raters. Internal consistency was addressed through split-half procedures for the entire normative sample. Coefficient alphas for PIQ exceed .90 at every age, with an average reliability of .94. The reliabilities for the three subtests exceed .80 at every age. Stability data is limited to a study of 27 Wyoming children between the ages of 5 and 8. Evidence for criterion-related validity is limited to one study examining the correlation between the PTI-2 PIQ, the Cognitive Abilities Scale–Second Edition (CAS-2; Bradley-Johnson & Johnson, 2001) and the Wechsler Preschool and Primary Scale of Intelligence–Revised (WPPSI-R; Wechsler, 1989) in a small group (N = 32) of 8-year-olds.

The PTI-2 is an objective and quickly administered measure of general cognitive ability. The manual is clear, thorough, and well organized. Overall, the psychometric properties of the PTI-2 are very good, though the standardization sample could be better defined. Additional validation studies with other, larger, and more representative samples are needed.

REFERENCES

Reviewed in Plake, B. S., Impara, J. C., & Spies, R. A. (Eds.). (2003). *The fifteenth mental measurements yearbook*. Lincoln, NE: Buros Institute of Mental Measurements.

Bradley-Johnson, S., & Johnson, C. M. (2001). *Cognitive Abilities Scale–Second Edition*. Austin, TX: PRO-ED.

Stavrou, E. (2002). Test Review: Pictorial Test of Intelligence–Second Edition (PTI-2). *Communiqué, 31*, 8.

Wechsler, D. (1989). *Wechsler Preschool and Primary Scale of Intelligence–Revised*. San Antonio, TX: Psychological Corporation.

RON DUMONT
Fairleigh Dickinson University

JOHN O. WILLIS
Rivier College

PICTURE EXCHANGE COMMUNICATION SYSTEM

The importance of communication and social competence among school-age children is undisputed. Children with communication disorders may have difficulty communicating verbally, resulting in frustration and inappropriate externalizing behaviors. The Picture Exchange Communication System (PECS) teaches children to communicate through an exchange of pictures and symbols, thus avoiding the need to verbalize (Bondy & Frost, 1994). This direct behavioral intervention is divided into a series of phases that become increasingly more complex, eventually leading to independent communication through the use of picture cards.

Research on PECS is limited. However, some evidence suggests its use increases verbal speech, social-communicative behavior, spontaneous language, and appropriate social interactions, and decreases problem behaviors (Charlop-Christy, LeCarpenter, LeBlanc, & Kelley, 2002). Preschoolers with severe communication delays and disorders can effectively and quickly learn to use PECS and are able to generalize these skills across numerous settings (Schwartz, Garfinkle, & Bauer, 1998).

Actions directed to the environment that lead to rewarding outcomes may not constitute communication. Communication must involve actions directed toward other individuals (Frost & Bondy, 2002). For example, a child may cry and point to a toy that is difficult to reach, resulting in an adult getting the toy for the child. Another child may approach an adult and ask for the toy. Although both examples have the same result, the first is not an example of communication. This rationale provides the theory behind the use of PECS.

Parents and teachers of nonverbal children initiate communication through questions (e.g., What do you want? Are you hungry? Do you want the ball?) However, PECS emphasizes initiation of communication by the child rather than through questions from an adult. Children are taught strategies to appropriately and independently obtain the attention of an adult; only then will the adult acknowledge the child and accept the picture card exchange.

PECS recognizes the importance of communication and attempts to promote it. Typically, developing children learn to persist when trying to initiate communication by using repetition, raising their voice, or tapping on another's shoulder continually until the person responds. They understand the importance of persistence in communication. PECS attempts to promote persistent communication patterns in children with communication disorders who otherwise may not exhibit such persistence as a result of many unsuccessful attempts that cause the child to quit or revert to inappropriate behaviors.

REFERENCES

Bondy, A., & Frost, L. (1994). PECS: The picture exchange communication system. *Focus on Autistic Behavior, 9,* 1–9.

Charlop-Christy, M. H., LeCarpenter, M. L., LeBlanc, L., & Kelley, K. (2002). Using the Picture Exchange Communication System (PECS) with children with autism: Assessment of PECS acquisition, speech, social-communicative behavior, and problem behaviors. *Journal of Applied Behavior Analysis, 35,* 213–231.

Frost, L. A., and Bondy, A. S. (2002). *PECS: The Picture Exchange Communication System training manual* (2nd ed.). Newark, DE: Pyramid Educational Consultants.

Schwartz, I. S., Garfinkle, A. N., & Bauer, J. (1998). The picture exchange communication system: Communication outcomes for young children with disabilities. *Topics in Early Childhood Special Education, 18,* 144–159.

Eric Rossen
University of Florida

ASPERGER SYNDROME
AUTISM

PIERRE-ROBIN SYNDROME

Hypoplasia of the mandible, prior to 9 weeks of intrauterine development, results in a posteriorly located tongue which, in turn, impairs closure of the posterior or soft palate. Children born with the syndrome of micrognathia (small lower jaw) are at risk for airway obstruction which may be present at birth or develop over the first month of life, requiring endotracheal tube or tracheostomy. Lack of oxygen can lead to damage to the heart and brain during this critical period. Most infants are otherwise normal and mandibular growth catches up, the long-term prognosis is good both for appearance and function. This anomaly is, however, also seen as part of other multiple malformation syndromes that may include mental retardation.

REFERENCES

Dennison, W. M. (1965). The Pierre-Robin syndrome. *Pediatrics, 36,* 336–341.

Jones, K. J. (1997). *Robin sequence: Smith's recognizable patterns of human malformation* (5th ed., pp. 234–235). Philadelphia: W. B. Saunders.

Patricia L. Hartlage
Medical College of Georgia

PIERS-HARRIS CHILDREN'S SELF-CONCEPT SCALE–SECOND EDITION

The Piers-Harris Children's Self-Concept Scale–Second Edition (PHCSCS-2; Piers, Harris, & Herzberg, 2003) is an individually or group administered paper and pencil, self-rating scale that assesses an individual's perception regarding self-esteem, self-concept, and personal regard. The PHCSCS-2 may be used as a screening instrument for children and adolescents age 7 through 18 to determine the need for additional assessment, treatment, and to aid in the determination of emotional difficulties in youth when accompanied by other psychological measures. It is often used in collaboration with other psychological batteries of assessment in both clinical and school settings as a means of gaining first-hand evidence of a youngster's views about him- or herself as well as to further support other personality and projective measures. The scale is frequently included in research endeavors and can also be used as a means to monitor an individual's level of self-concept over time.

The scale consists of 60 items reflecting descriptive statements that require the individual to select a "yes" or "no" response based on his or her personal perceptions about how the statement reflects his or her character. A second grade reading level is required for individuals completing the scale. The scale consists of the following domains:

Total Score (TOT): A measure of global self-concept and level of self-esteem based on 60 items.

Behavioral Adjustment (BEH): Consists of 14 items and reveals acceptance or denial of problematic behaviors within the home and school environment.

Intellectual and School Status (INT): Includes 16 items reflecting the individual's views regarding one's own intellectual and academic abilities.

Physical Appearance and Attributes (PHY): Consists of 11 items that measures the individual's assessment of his or her physical appearance, leadership skills, level of assertiveness, and ability to express oneself effectively.

Freedom From Anxiety (FRE): Consists of 14 items that elicit information pertaining to level of anxiety and dysphoric/depressed mood. This particular domain taps into the individual's perception of one's emotional experiences, such as sadness, fears, nervousness, and related areas.

Popularity (POP): Consists of 12 items that address the individual's level of socialization skills, participation in age-related activities, and one's ability to make friends.

Happiness and Satisfaction (HAP): Consists of 10 items reflecting the individual's level of personal satisfaction with life.

The instrument also includes two validity scales to identify inconsistencies in responses from the individual and specific tendencies toward responding in a consistent manner (i.e., responses geared in a direction to appear positive or negative). This aspect of the scale allows the examiner to determine if the individual completing the scale attempted to exaggerate or distort responses to gain an outcome, obtain attention, or appear in a socially desired manner.

The scoring system for the PHCSCS-2 consists of normalized *t*-scores and percentile scores. Qualitative descriptors accompany scores for specific ranges. Raw scores are converted into *t*-scores that have a mean of 50 and a standardized deviation of 10. Percentile scores represent the percentage of individuals from the normative sample whose scores were less than the individual being evaluated. The interpretive labels consist of Very Low, Low, Low Average, Average, High Average, High, Very High for the Total Score, and Very Low, Low, Low Average, Average and Above Average for the domain scales.

The PHCSCS-2 was standardized on a nationally represented normative sample that included 1,387 students from the United States between the ages of 7 through 18 years old. Individuals were recruited from elementary, middle, junior, and high school. The sample was based on a demographically diverse standardization sample including consideration of aspects such as age, sex, ethnicity, socioeconomic status, and representation from various geographic regions of the United States.

The internal consistency coefficients for each domain ranges from .74 though .91, indicating good internal consistency throughout the cluster scales. Test-retest reliability data were not yet available for the PHCSCS-2 as the instrument was recently revised; however, based on the original PHCSCS, which consisted of 80 items, coefficients were cited as .77 for both 2- and 4-month intervals between testing, indicating the potential for stability across testing. (Note that the 60 items contained on the revised PHCSCS-2 remained fairly consistent to the original 80 items on the PHCSCS.) Reviews of the PHCSCS-2 are pending for the upcoming *Sixteenth Mental Measurements*.

REFERENCES

Demetrios, A., & Foudoulaki, E. (2002). Construct validity of the Piers-Harris Self-Concept Scale. *Psychological Reports, 91,* 827–838.

Gans, A., Maureen, C., & Ghany, D. (2003). Comparing the self-concept of students with and without learning disabilities. *Journal of Learning Disabilities, 36,* 285–293.

Linyan, S., Luo, X., Zhang, J., Xie, G., & Liu, Y. (2002). Norms of the Piers-Harris Children's Self-Concept Scale in Chinese urban children. *Chinese Mental Health Journal, 16,* 31–34.

Piers, E., & Herzberg, D. (2003). *Piers-Harris Children's Self-Concept Scale–2nd Edition.* Los Angeles: Western Psychological Services.

RON DUMONT
Fairleigh Dickinson University

JOHN O. WILLIS
Rivier College

PINEL, PHILIPPE (1745–1826)

Phillipe Pinel, French physician and pioneer in the humane treatment of the mentally ill, served as chief physician at two famous mental hospitals in France, the Bicêtre and the Salpêtrière. Convinced that mental illness was not a result of demoniacal possession, as was commonly believed, but of brain dysfunction, Pinel released his patients from the chains that were used to restrain them and replaced deleterious remedies such as bleeding and purging with psychological treatment by physicians.

Through publications in which he set forth his methods for the care and treatment of the mentally ill, Pinel's ideas gained wide acceptance throughout the western world. France, through Pinel's efforts, became the first country to attempt the provision of adequate care for the mentally ill.

REFERENCE

Pinel, P. (1801). *Traité médico-philosophique sur l'aliénation mentale.* Paris: Richard, Caille & Revier.

PAUL IRVINE
Katonah, New York

PITUITARY GLAND

The pituitary is a small gland located at the base of the brain immediately beneath the hypothalamus, above the roof of the mouth, and behind the optic chiasma. The pituitary lies in a bony depression called the sella turcia. The pituitary is also sometimes referred to as the hypothysis.

The pituitary regulates the secretions of a number of other endocrine glands and often is referred to as the master gland. However, its function is closely linked to the hypothalamus, and the pituitary and hypothalamus must be thought of as a system rather than independent entities. The hypothalamus and the pituitary are connected by a rich supply of nerves called the infundibulum.

Morphologically, the pituitary is a small gland. It weighs less than a gram and is only about a centimeter in diameter. It consists of two major lobes, the anterior pituitary (adenohypophysis) and the posterior pituitary (neurohypophysis). These two lobes are connected by a much smaller pars intermedia. The anterior pituitary manufactures a number of hormones that serve to trigger the release of still others. The hormones directly secreted by the anterior pituitary include growth hormone, thyroid-stimulating hormone (TSH), adrenocorticotrophic hormone (ACTH), and gonadotrophic hormones such as follicle-stimulating hormone (FSH), luteinizing hormone (LH), and lactogenic hormone (prolactin).

Adrenocorticotrophic hormone (ACTH) is intimately involved in stress reactions. Release of this hormone by the pituitary causes the adrenal cortex to produce cortisol and other steroid hormones that help prepare the body for fight or flight. Gonadotrophic hormones (e.g., follicle-stimulating hormone and luteinizing hormone) activate the ovaries and testes so that estrogen and testosterone, respectively, are produced.

Prolactin is a hormone that affects the mammary glands and that appears to be involved in the regulation of maternal behavior in vertebrates. Somatotropin (STH or growth hormone) is a hormone necessary for normal growth. Excesses of somatotropin result in the clinical condition of acromegaly.

It is useful to view the pituitary as a link in a complex chain of events that tie the hypothalamus to other glands. However, the hypothalamus lacks direct neural connection with the anterior pituitary, and instead influence is exerted by release factors transported through a complex system of blood vessels called the hypothalamic-hypophyseal portal system.

The posterior pituitary (neurohypophysis) secretes antidiuretic hormone (ADH) and oxytocin. Release of these hormones is triggered by complex connections with other parts of the nervous system. The cells of the posterior pituitary do not produce hormones themselves but instead serve as storage sites for hormones produced by the anterior hypothalamus. When blood pressure falls, the secretion of ADH stimulates the kidneys to reduce their excretion of water into the urine. Lack of ADH can produce diabetes insipidus. Oxytocin plays an important role in inducing contractions during labor, and it is necessary for the contraction of the smooth muscles of the mammary glands, which are needed to produce milk in response to sucking.

It has been found that individuals with anorexia and bulimia have some pituitary atrophy due to nutritional and/or endocrine alterations (Doraiswamy, Krishnan, Figiel, & Husain, 1990).

REFERENCES

Asterita, M. F. (1985). *The physiology of stress.* New York: Human Sciences.

Doraiswamy, P., Krishnan, K., Figiel, G. S., & Husain, M. (1990). A brain magnetic resonance imaging study of pituitary gland morphology in anorexia nervosa and bulimia. *Biological Psychiatry, 28*(2), 110–116.

Groves, P., & Schlesinger, K. (1979). *Biological psychology.* Dubuque, IA: Brown.

DANNY WEDDING
Marshall University

ANOREXIA NERVOSA
BULIMIA NERVOSA
DIABETES
EATING DISORDERS

PKU

See PHENYLKETONURIA.

PLACEBOS

Placebos are substances or therapeutic interventions that produce their effects as a result of the expectations of the recipient and the therapist. As originally applied in medicine, placebo therapies improved patients' conditions despite the fact that the placebos had no direct physiological action. Placebos, therefore, became an aid to physicians who lacked a specific therapy and a nuisance variable to researchers studying therapeutic effectiveness.

The placebo effect is most powerful in social situations where an experimental approach produces high hopes for success (Orne, 1969). To differentiate between placebo and direct therapeutic physiological effects, it has become commonplace in drug research to use a double-blind procedure. In such a design, both the person administering the therapy and the subject are unaware (blind) as to whether a given dose contains the experimental substance or a physiologically inert placebo. If the placebo and treatment interventions result in similar effects, the value of the new therapy is called into question. Practical or ethical considerations often limit the applicability of double-blind studies, and the existence of potential placebo effects remains a problem in a variety of areas of research.

Although placebos may be physiologically inert, recent research has indicated that they may have a biological effect. For example, Levine, Gordon, and Fields (1978) have provided some evidence that placebos that were supposedly analgesics activated the endorphins that are the body's internal painkillers.

There has been great controversy concerning the use of the placebo concept in understanding behavioral change interventions. Simeon & Willins (1993) suggest that there has not been enough research done in the use of placebos with children. Critelli and Neumann (1984) have argued that the placebo effect is more than a nuisance variable and the display of empathy, nonpossessive warmth, etc., that may occur in a placebo intervention may be an important part of the therapy. In the classroom, the expectations of teachers and students about the probabilities of high student performance during an educational intervention may play a significant role in its effectiveness (Zanna, Sheras, Cooper, & Shaw, 1975).

Thus both the special education researcher and classroom teacher may need to take placebos into account. The researcher may wish to provide a placebo control group where subjects receive a treatment that is irrelevant to the planned intervention. Such a treatment allows control subjects to experience the attention that goes to those undergoing the treatment of interest (Cook & Campbell, 1979). The classroom teacher should be aware of the combination of placebo and direct effect of interventions and, therefore, foster expectations of success.

REFERENCES

Cook, T., & Campbell, D. (1979). *Quasi-experimentation: Design and analysis issues in field settings.* Boston: Houghton Mifflin.

Critelli, J., & Neumann, K. N. (1984). The placebo: Conceptual analysis of a construct in transition. *American Psychologist, 39,* 32–39.

Levine, J., Gordon, N., & Fields, H. (1978). The mechanism of placebo analgesia, *Lancet, 2,* 654–657.

Orne, M. (1969). Demand characteristics and the concept of quasi-controls. In R. Rosenthal & R. Rosnow (Eds.), *Artifact in behavioral research* (pp. 147–181). New York: Academic.

Simeon, J. G., & Wiggins, D. M. (1993). The placebo problem in children and adolescent psychiatry. *International Journal of Child and Adolescent Psychiatry, 56*(2), 119–122.

Zanna, M., Sheras, P., Cooper, J., & Shaw, C. (1975). Pygmalion and Galatea: The interactive effect of teacher and student expectancies. *Journal of Experimental Social Psychology, 11,* 279–287.

LEE ANDERSON JACKSON, JR.
University of North Carolina at Wilmington

DOUBLE-BLIND DESIGN
TEACHER EXPECTANCIES

PLACENTA

The placenta (Latin for "cake") transfers life-sustaining supplies from the mother to the prenate, disposes of the prenate's wastes, and protects the prenate from some harmful substances. It begins to form during the germinal period and becomes differentiated as a separate disk-shaped organ during the embryonic phase (Annis, 1978). The umbilical cord extends from the center of the smooth fetal surface. The maternal surface is composed of many convoluted branches, creating a surface area of about 13 m^2, which provides maximum exposure to blood vessels in the uterine lining. At term the placenta is about 18 cm in diameter and weighs about 570 g.

The placenta includes two completely separate sets of blood vessels—one fetal and one maternal. Only small, light molecules may pass through the placental barrier; maternal and fetal blood never mix. Although the exact mechanisms of transfer of nutrients and wastes between the two systems are not completely understood, transfer of gases and water is accomplished by simple diffusion (Hytten & Leitch, 1964). The placenta protects the prenate from overexposure to elements in the mother's blood (e.g., hormones and cholesterol) by reducing their concentration in the fetal blood; it also prevents some teratogens from reaching the fetus.

In a small percentage of pregnancies, impairments involving the placenta create serious consequences. In about 10 percent of pregnancies the placenta fails to produce progesterone in the early weeks, resulting in spontaneous abortion. Infrequently, the placenta is small or malformed, causing retarded fetal growth or possibly stillbirth. When the placenta partially or entirely covers the cervical opening (placenta previa), the membranes usually rupture early in the third trimester, leading to a premature delivery.

Even during normal functioning, the placenta is an imperfect filter. As the fetus matures, placental blood vessels enlarge and stretch the placental barrier more thinly, thus decreasing its ability to filter larger molecules. Many harmful agents (e.g., bacteria) are kept out during the early prenatal stages, when teratogens are potentially most dangerous. For example, syphilis cannot cross until after the twentieth week. Viruses (including rubella), because they are so small, are able to pass through during this critical period. Many chemicals that the mother ingests that are potentially harmful (e.g., alcohol, caffeine, and carbon monoxide) pass through in ever-increasing dose levels as the placental barrier thins.

REFERENCES

Annis, L. F. (1978). *The child before birth.* Ithaca, NY: Cornell University Press.

Assali, N. S., Ditts, P. V., Jr., Plentl, A. A., Kirschbaum, T. H., & Gross, S. J. (1968). Physiology of the placenta. In N. S. Assali (Ed.), *Biology of gestation.* New York: Academic.

Hytten, F. E., & Leitch, I. (1964). *The physiology of human pregnancy.* Oxford, England: Blackwell.

PAULINE F. APPLEFIELD
University of North Carolina at Wilmington

CONGENITAL DISORDERS
PREMATURITY

PLANTAR REFLEX

The word plantar means "of, pertaining to, or occurring on the sole of the foot" (Rothenberg & Chapman, 1994). The plantar reflex is observed when the sole of the foot is scratched or stroked with a dull object and the toes bunch or curl downwards. The plantar response is a reflex that involves all the muscles that shorten the leg and the toes and is present in normal children (after the age of one year), adolescents, and adults.

Abnormal response to the plantar stimulation is usually in the form of the big toe extending upward toward the head, the toes fanning out, and withdrawal of the leg. This response is known as the Babinski reflex or sign and is indicative of neurological damage.

REFERENCES

Bassetti, C. (1995). Babinski and Babinski sign. *Spine, 20*(23), 2591–4.

Rothenberg, M. A., & Chapman, C. F. (1994). *Dictionary of medical terms* (3rd ed.). Hauppauge, NY: Barron's.

van Gijn, J. (1995). The Babinski reflex. *Postgraduate Medical Journal, 71*(841), 645–8.

ELAINE FLETCHER-JANZEN
University of Colorado at Colorado Springs

APGAR RATING SCALE
BABINSKI REFLEX
DEVELOPMENTAL MILESTONES

PLASTICITY

Plasticity in the human sciences is the absence in an individual of predetermined developmental characteristics and a concomitant modifiability by organismic or environmental influences. The concept is not limited to the capacity to change in accord with outside pressure. It includes the power to learn from experience and modify behavior while retaining predisposing genetic inheritance (Kolb & Whishaw, 1998). Educator John Dewey (1916) emphasized the characteristic plasticity of the immature child as a specific adaptability for growth. Basic to this concept is a person's power to modify actions on the basis of the results of prior experiences. In addition, plasticity implies the development of definite dispositions or habits. Habits, Dewey wrote, give control over the environment and power to use it for human purposes.

As a feature of the young child, plasticity is often most evident in exceptional children where deviation from the norm is significant. It has been seen frequently in gifted children, in schizophrenic children, and in some children with organic brain disorders (Bender, 1952). Many such children show prodigious accomplishments or become late bloomers and manage to make up for what they might have missed in earlier years both in educational and social development.

A study by Chess, Korn, and Fernandez (1971) of 235 victims of a 1964 worldwide rubella epidemic began when the youngsters were 2 years old. Development showed an overall delay during the first years of life, with characteristic impairment in language and motor sensorimotor functions. One-third of the children were diagnosed as showing varying degrees of mental retardation during the preschool period, while only one-fourth showed evidence of mental retardation at ages eight and nine. The IQs of the nonretarded children also showed progressive increases as they entered the school-age period. Detailed case studies of a number of the children who showed such improvement demonstrated that they came through a diverse and roundabout pattern to normal school functioning. Often they pioneered new territory in the acquisition of language, social development, and learning—thereby affirming the inherent plasticity of human brain function in the young child.

Similar individual-specific roads to cognitive language and social functioning have been demonstrated for children with congenital heart disease who had corrective surgery, children who contracted polio before the days of the Salk vaccine, children with rheumatic fever, and children with chronic kidney disease. Studies of blind children have demonstrated similar plasticity (Fraiberg, 1977) and Attention-Deficit/Hyperactivity Disorder (Jensen et al., 1997).

Plasticity takes on a negative connotation as applied by Bender (1953) to the concept of childhood schizophrenia. According to Bender, a physiological crisis may interfere with the maturation of the child in every area of functioning. The disturbance has a plastic quality that gives a primitive pattern to all behavior and renders the child incapable of satisfactorily dealing with autonomic responses, motility perceptions, symbol formation, language, ideation, and interpersonal relationships. This causes anxiety and elicits defense mechanisms. Because of the plastic quality of the disorder, any function or area of behavior can be retarded, regressed, fixated, or accelerated. In *Principles of Education,* Bolton (1910) stated, "Where there is evolution, there is plasticity" (p. 8). Biological plasticity underlies the adaptive physiological process primary to organic evolution. Psychological plasticity underlies the adaptive behavior process primary to education and social evolution.

REFERENCES

Bender, L. (1952). *Child psychiatric techniques.* Springfield, IL: Thomas.

Bender, L. (1953). *Aggression, hostility and anxiety in children.* Springfield, IL: Thomas.

Bolton, F. E. (1910). *Principles of education.* New York: Scribner.

Chess, S., Korn, S., & Fernandez, P. (1971). *Psychiatric disorders of children with congenital rubella.* New York: Brunner/Mazel.

Dewey, J. (1916). *Democracy and education.* New York: Macmillan.

Fraiberg, S. (1977). *Insights from the blind.* New York: International Universities Press.

Jensen, P. S., Mrazek, D., Knapp, P. K., Steinberg, L., Pfeffer, C., Schowalter, J., & Shapiro, T. (1997). Evolution and revolution in child psychiatry: ADHD as a disorder of adoption. *Journal of American Academy of Child & Adolescent Psychiatry, 36*(12), 1672–1681.

Kolb, B., & Whishaw, I. Q. (1998). Brain plasticity and behavior. *Annual Review of Psychology, 49,* 43–64.

Warner H. Britton
Auburn University

INTELLIGENCE
ZONE OF PROXIMAL DEVELOPMENT

PLATO AND THE GIFTED

Plato was among the earliest philosophers to formulate a classification of students within three levels of public education. Plato wanted to separate "men with hearts and intellects of gold" to train and educate them for the highest functions of the state as kings, rulers, or executives. Without proper nurture, the brightest student would not be likely to be willing to serve the state's citizens (Burt, 1975).

Plato's three levels of public education included common elementary school, secondary school with selective admission, and a state university with admission still more selective. On the elementary level, the curriculum covered literature, music, and civics. On the secondary level, students were prepared for future military and civil service posts by studying in the curriculum areas of mathematics, arithmetic, plane and solid geometry, astronomy, and harmonics. In higher education there were 5 years of "dialectic" learning followed by 15 years of practical experience for those chosen to be the leaders of the ideal state (Brumbaugh, 1962).

These rulers or guardians were trained and later employed for external warfare and internal police work. The 15 years of rigorous intellectual training prepared the select few for lives as philosophers. Plato's ideal state depended on its kings being philosophers or its philosophers being kings (Plato, 1973/393BC).

The republic of Plato required education for both men and women. This was thought to be revolutionary at the time. Women received the same educational opportunities and training for the mind and body; they were also instructed in the art of war. If a woman possessed the right natural gifts, she shared the highest of public duties equally with men. Every occupation was open to her, but it understood that she was physically weaker. A man's nature was thought to be suited for majesty and valor and a woman's for orderliness and temperance (Morrow, 1960).

The idea of gifted students within the educational system was especially evident in the republic during the open discussions on mathematics. Plato believed that all students should be introduced to mathematics and discussed how this subject had an effect on the mental powers of a student; he believed it sharpened a student's wits and helped to fix attention. The skills of higher mathematics were seen as needed by the chosen few future rulers. These gifted students would study with systematic thoroughness and exactness (Morrow, 1960). Students were chosen for this advanced curriculum if they demonstrated that they understood the general connection of the various curriculum areas. If a student successfully grasped both a practical and theoretical connection, at the age of 30 the student would be admitted to the highest and most complete of all possible studies—philosophy.

REFERENCES

Bosanquet, B. (1908). *The education of the young in the republic of Plato.* Cambridge, England: Cambridge University Press.

Brumbaugh, R. S. (1962). *Plato for the modern age.* New York: Crowell-Collier.

Burt, C. (1975). *The gifted child.* New York: Wiley.

Morrow, G. R. (1960). *Plato's Cretan city: A historical interpretation of the laws.* Princeton, NJ: Princeton University Press.

Plato. (1972). *The republic of Plato* (F. M. Cornford, Trans.). New York: Oxford University Press. (Original work published 370 BC)

Plato. (1973). *Plato: Laches and charmides* (R. E. Sprague, Trans.). Indianapolis: Bobbs-Merrill. (Original work published 393 BC)

Deborah A. Shanley
Medgar Evers College, City University of New York

GIFTED CHILDREN
HISTORY OF SPECIAL EDUCATION

PLAY

Play among humans can be described as an attitude rather than a category of behaviors (Damon, 1983). Play is often regarded as the opposite of work in so far as attitude is concerned. A child who is having fun with an activity (as evidenced by laughing and smiling) is playing. Conversely, a child who is practicing his game skills to perfection is working. In fact, it has been suggested that the word play is most effectively used as an adverb, as in "the child stacked the blocks playfully" (Miller, 1968).

Regardless of its seemingly nonserious origins, play is a critical developmental activity. Many aspects of our social, motor, and cognitive lives have their origins in childhood play. The famous Russian psychologist Lev Vygotsky argued throughout his short, albeit brilliant career, that play creates the conditions for the child's acquisition of new competence in imaginative, social, and intellectual skills. Recently, computers and the internet have provided a new form of play for many children and adolescents (Griffiths & Hunt, 1995).

One method of classifying children's play is based on interactions with other children. Five categories of play can be distinguished (Parten, 1932). The first type, solitary play, involves no interaction at all with other children. In onlooker play, the second type, the child simply observes other children at play. This is thought to be the first phase of a preschooler's interaction with other children.

When children begin to engage in the same activity side by side without taking much notice of each other, parallel play is said to occur. Associative play, the fourth type, occurs in older preschoolers; in this type, play becomes much more interactive. During this phase, two or more children partake in the same activity doing basically the same thing; however, there is no attempt to organize the activity or take turns.

Cooperative play, an organized activity in which individual children cooperate to achieve some sort of group goal, usually does not appear until age 3. At this stage children become more able and eager to participate in social forms of play. Solitary play does not ever disappear. Most children are capable of playing alone if a companion is not available. Onlooker behavior persists even into adulthood.

The symbolic nature of play is vital to the development of the child; it performs several functions in that development. First, children can use their symbolic skills, like language, in new and different ways, in a sense testing the limits of those skills. Second, children can, through play, do and say things that are normally difficult to express or taboo. Third, as children exit infancy they can use play in a cooperative, social fashion. "Make believe" allows children to explore social roles, work in cooperation with others, and experiment with social roles and rules (Damon, 1983).

Children who are handicapped may be less able to use play effectively and therefore may lose out on some of the important outcomes of play. For example, a child with a physical disability may not be able to engage in normal social play with other children. Hence, that child needs special arrangements or interventions to make sure that he or she has access to normal opportunities for play (Cattanach, 1995).

REFERENCES

Cattanach, A. (1995). Drama and play therapy with young children. *Arts in Psychotherapy, 22*(3), 223–228.

Damon, W. (1983). *Social and personality development: Infancy through adolescence.* New York: Norton.

Griffiths, M. D., & Hunt, N. Computer game playing in adolescence: Prevalence and demographic indicators. *Journal of Community & Applied Social Psychology, 5*(3), 189–193.

Miller, S. (1968). *The psychology of play.* Middlesex, England: Penguin.

Parten, M. B. (1932). Social participation among preschool children. *Journal of Abnormal & Social Psychology, 27,* 243–269.

MICHAEL J. ASH
JOSE LUIS TORRES
Texas A&M University

CONCEPT OF ACTIVITY
VYGOTSKY, LEV S.
ZONE OF PROXIMAL DEVELOPMENT

PLAYTEST

The PLAYTEST procedure is recognized as one possible approach to screening and direct assessment of an infant's auditory functioning (Butterfield, 1982). The PLAYTEST system was originally developed by B. Z. Friedlander as a research tool for measuring infants' selective listening and receptive voice discrimination abilities within the home environment (Friedlander, 1968).

The system consists of a simple, portable, automated toy apparatus that attaches to the infant's crib or playpen. An audio or video-audio recorder and response recorder complete the equipment. The apparatii are attached at different locations on the crib or playpen. When the infant attends to either device, the responses activate the accompanying stereophonic tape recorder. The tape recorder is fitted with an endless loop audio tape. Certain systems are equipped to provide video-audio feedback instead of just audio feedback. Separate channels on the device carry different prerecorded sound samples.

The infant's frequency and duration of response to the various sources of auditory stimuli are used to infer the current level of auditory discrimination and selective listening abilities. Both the audio and the video-audio PLAYTEST systems use a response recorder to register the infant's differential response to the various auditory stimuli.

The PLAYTEST system has proven a valuable research tool in the investigation of auditory functioning in infants (Friedlander, 1968, 1970, 1971, 1975). One interesting finding is that very young infants show a clear preference for the mother's voice as opposed to a simple musical score.

It appears that the PLAYTEST system also provides an invaluable means of identifying infants at high risk for developing significant language disorders later in life (Butterfield, 1982; Friedlander, 1975). Butterfield (1982) envisions the PLAYTEST procedure as an instrumental screening and assessment procedure in the very early detection of auditory processing and/or discrimination problems in infants. He has described modifications of the existing system that would enable professionals to assess infants less than 6 months of age for possible auditory dysfunctions (Butterfield, 1982).

REFERENCES

Butterfield, E. C. (1982). Behavioral assessment of infants' hearing. In M. Lewis & L. T. Taft (Eds.), *Developmental disabilities: Theory, assessment, and intervention.* New York: SP Medical & Scientific.

Friedlander, B. Z. (1968). The effect of speaker identity, voice inflection, vocabulary, and message redundancy on infants' selection of vocal reinforcement. *Journal of Experimental Child Psychology, 6,* 443–459.

Friedlander, B. Z. (1970). Receptive language development in infancy: Issues and problems. *Merrill Quarterly of Behavior & Development, 16,* 7–51.

Friedlander, B. Z. (1971). Listening, language, and the auditory environment: Automated evaluation and intervention. In J. Hellmuth (Ed.), *The exceptional infant* (Vol. 2). New York: Brunner/Mazel.

Friedlander, B. Z. (1975). Automated evaluation of selective listening in language impaired and normal infants and young children. In B. Z. Friedlander, G. M. Sterritt, & G. E. Kirk (Eds.), *The exceptional infant* (Vol. 3). New York: Brunner/Mazel.

JULIA A. HICKMAN
*Bastrop Mental Health
Association*

AUDITORY DISCRIMINATION
DEAF
LANGUAGE DISORDERS

PLAY THERAPY

Play therapy is a therapeutic technique used with children that emphasizes the medium of play as a substitute for the traditional verbal interchange between therapists and adult clients. The roots of play therapy can be traced back to the psychoanalytic work of Sigmund Freud (1909), and

Small furniture, a pleasant atmosphere, and a caring therapist, all prerequisite to successful play therapy

the classic case of Little Hans, in which Freud directed the child's father in techniques used to treat the child's severe phobia. Direct work with a child was first initiated by Hug-Hellmuth (Gumaer, 1984), who applied Freudian analysis to children under age 7. It soon became apparent that children lacked the verbal ability, interest, and patience to talk with a therapist for an extended period of time. Thus in the late 1920s, both Melanie Klein and Anna Freud developed therapeutic methods that used play as the child's primary mode of expression (see Figure). Anna Freud stressed the importance of play in building the therapeutic relationship, deemphasizing the need for interpretation. Klein, however, approached play therapy much like traditional adult psychoanalytic work, with free play becoming a direct substitution for free associations, and insights and interpretation retaining primary importance.

In the following decade, Otto Rank was an important contributor with his notion of relationship therapy. Rank stressed the importance of the emotional attachment between the child and the therapist, focusing mainly on present feelings and actions of the child. In the 1940s and 1950s, Carl Rogers' client-centered therapy was modified by Virginia Axline (1947) into a nondirective play therapy. Axline's work, which has remained one of the cornerstones of current play therapy, is predicated on the belief that the child has within himself or herself the ability to solve emotional conflicts. According to Axline, it is the job of the play therapist to provide the optimal conditions under which the child's natural growth and development will occur. The basic rules of Axline's approach have become the standard for nondirective play therapy. They include the development of a warm relationship, acceptance, permissiveness with a minimum of limits, reflection of feelings, and giving the child responsibility for directing the sessions, making choices, and implementing change.

The effectiveness of play therapy has been attributed

to its direct relevance to the child's developmental level and abilities. Woltmann (1964) stresses that play allows the child to act out situations that are disturbing, conflicting, and confusing and, in so doing, to clarify his or her own position in relation to the world around. Inherent to the success of play therapy is the make-believe element. Through fantasy and play, children are able to master tasks (drive a car, fly a spaceship), reverse roles (become parent or teacher), or express overt hostility without being punished. Woltmann believes that play therapy allows the child to "eliminate guilt and become victorious over forces otherwise above his reach and capabilities." Caplan and Caplan (1974) provide a further rationale for the effectiveness of play therapy. They contend that the voluntary nature of play makes it intrinsically interesting to the child and reduces the occurrence of resistance. The child is free to express himself or herself without fear of evaluation or retaliation. Through fantasy, the child can gain a sense of control over the environment without direct competition from others. Finally, play therapy is seen as developing both the child's physical and mental abilities.

The selection of the play media is an important part of the therapy. Gumaer (1984) notes that toys should be durable, inexpensive, and safe. They should be versatile (e.g., clay, paints) so that children may use them in a number of ways. Toys should encourage communication between the child and therapist (e.g., telephones, puppets). Some toys should be selected for their ability to elicit aggression such as a toy gun or a soldier doll. Finally, toys should be relatively unstructured; items such as board games or books leave little room for creativity. In addition to the toys already mentioned, Axline (1947) commonly employs a set of family dolls, a nursing bottle, trucks and cars, and, if possible, a sandbox and water.

Play therapy has expanded to include a number of settings, participants, and techniques (Phillips & Landreth, 1995). Ginott (1961) developed a method that provides a specific rationale for toy selection and that emphasizes the importance of limit setting. Dreikurs and Soltz (1964) use play therapy that emphasizes the natural and logical consequences of a child's behavior. Myrick and Haldin (1971) describe a play process that is therapist directed and shorter in duration than Axlinian therapy, thus making it more practical for use in school settings. For further study, the reader is directed to *The Handbook of Play Therapy* (Schaefer & O'Conner, 1983), which describes specific techniques such as family play and art therapy, as well as play therapy directly tailored to such childhood disturbances as abuse and neglect, divorced parents, aggression, learning disability, and mental retardation.

REFERENCES

Axline, Virginia (1947). *Play therapy*. Boston: Houghton Mifflin.

Caplan, F., & Caplan, T. (1974). *The power of play*. New York: Anchor.

Dreikurs, R., & Soltz, V. (1964). *Children: The challenge*. New York: Hawthorne.

Freud, S. (1909). Analysis of a phobia in a five-year-old boy. In *Standard edition* (Vol. 10). London: Hogarth.

Ginott, H. (1961). *Group psychotherapy with children*. New York: McGraw-Hill.

Gumaer, J. (1984). *Counseling and therapy for children*. New York: Free Press.

Myrick, R., & Haldin, W. (1971). A study of play process in counseling. *Elementary School Guidance and Counseling, 5*(4), 256–263.

Phillips, R. D., & Landreth, G. L. (1995). Play therapists on play therapy: A report of methods, demographics and professional practices. *International Journal of Play Therapy, 4*(1), 1–26.

Schaefer, C., & O'Conner, K. (1983). *The handbook of play therapy*. New York: Wiley.

Woltmann, A. (1964). Concepts of play therapy techniques. In M. Haworth (Ed.), *Child psychotherapy* (pp. 20–31). New York: Basic Books.

FRANCES F. WORCHEL
Texas A&M University

FAMILY THERAPY
PLAY
PSYCHOTHERAPY WITH INDIVIDUALS WITH
  DISABILITIES

PLURALISM, CULTURAL

Cultural pluralism is a sociological concept that refers to the dual enterprise of acceptance and mobility within the mainstream, majority culture while preserving the minority cultural heritage. Cultural pluralism is seen by many as the most desirable cultural milieu and has been promoted in a variety of settings, including education and employment.

The term is recognized in special education in relation to the work of Mercer et al. (Mercer & Lewis, 1979) in the assessment of mental retardation. Mercer has argued that past efforts in assessment and placement in special education programs for mildly mentally retarded children have failed to recognize the pluralistic nature of American society. In addition to the mainstream Anglo cultural, Mercer has proposed that Black, Hispanic, and other cultures need to be recognized and their norms and mores accepted as equivalent to Anglo norms and mores. Mercer attempts to equate these groups' performance on intelligence tests by developing pluralistic norms. According to Mercer (Mercer & Lewis, 1979), traditional intelligence tests developed and normed on the White majority only measure the degree of Anglocentrism (i.e., relative adherence to White middleclass values) in the home when used with minorities. To accommodate other cultures, principally Black and Hispanic, Mercer developed a set of regression equations to equate the IQ distributions of each ethnic group. Mercer hopes to promote cultural pluralism in special education by equating the relative proportions of each ethnic group in special education programs. Mercer believes that by equating these distributions, the stigma associated with special education placement will be evenly distributed, leading to greater tolerance and acceptance of alternative cultures.

The cultural competence movement in teacher education has grown considerably in recent years in terms of legislative support (IDEA, Part H in particular) and with the development of instruments such as the Pluralism and Diversity Attitude Assessment (PADAA) instrument, which assesses preservice attitudes of educators (Stanley, 1997). Cultural competence is becoming a good for special and regular education.

REFERENCES

Mercer, J. R., & Lewis, J. (1979). *System of multicultural pluralistic assessment.* New York: Psychological Association.

Stanley, L. S. (1997). Preservice educator's attitudes toward cultural pluralism: A preliminary analysis. *Journal of Teaching in Physical Education, 16*(2), 241–249.

STAFF

CULTURAL BIAS IN TESTING
CULTURAL/LINGUISTICALLY DIVERSE STUDENTS
DISPROPORTIONALITY
SYSTEM OF MULTICULTURAL PLURALISTIC ASSESSMENT

POLAND, SPECIAL EDUCATION IN

Special education in Poland has a long history. In 1817, the Institute of Deaf-Mute and Blind was established in Warsaw. In 1922 Maria Grzegorzewska (1888–1967) established the Institute of Special Education, which conducted research and trained teachers. In 1924 a special education section of the Polish Teachers Association was established (Kirejczyk, 1975). In 1976 the National Institute of Special Education was reorganized into the Graduate School of Special Education.

In the 1950s programs for the mentally retarded were segregated into 120 self-contained schools. In the 1960s there were 331 special classes within elementary schools with an enrollment of over 5000 youngsters. By the 1970s the number of such classes increased to 698, with an enrollment of nearly 11,000. Currently, there are over 250 special schools in Poland, in addition to a considerable number of special classes within public schools.

Handicapped pupils in Poland are educated in special preschool facilities, special elementary schools, special vocational schools, residential boarding schools, and rehabilitation and therapeutic facilities; they also receive home instruction (Belcerek, 1977). Various levels of interaction of exceptional children within the mainstream of education are also provided (Hulek, 1979), e.g., regular programs with some supplemental instruction, special classes within regular schools (there are presently over 1100 such classes for the mildly handicapped within the Polish public schools and 57 within the vocational schools), selected activities within regular schools, and special schools in the vicinity of regular schools, with cooperative programs.

The intellectually subnormal population in Poland has been estimated to range from 1.3 to 1.87 percent of the general population. Polish psychologists are using IQs in their classification of the mentally retarded. The ranges of the levels of classification are similar to the AAMD classification system. In addition to health examinations, psychological and social-developmental examinations are also given. An evaluation for the purpose of special class placement consists of a detailed classroom observation, educational evaluation, and psychological and medical evaluation. Structural classroom observation usually lasts 1 school year. Additionally, a detailed anecdotal record of the child's activities is maintained. The record includes a description of the role of the parents and the extent of their cooperation with the school. Detailed records with samples of the child's performance are sent to the child study team as additional information. Slow learners and children who do not show good educational progress are directed to prevocational classes at 14 or 15 years of age. Curriculum in Polish special schools consists of the study of the Polish language, geography, music, history, and nature.

Special educators in Poland prefer the term therapeutic pedagogy, or special pedagogy, rather than defectology, a term widely used in Russia. The mildly retarded attend 8 years of basic special school, followed by 3 years of specialized vocational training. A new 10-year curriculum for the mentally retarded recommends the following areas of training and education: adaptation and social living, language stimulation, arithmetic, visual-motor tasks, music, physical exercise, technical-practical activities, and prevocational training. Training goals and objectives for the severely handicapped include physical development and acquisition of manual skills, development of self-help and everyday activity skills, development of basic information, appropriate interpersonal relationships, and prevocational training.

Elska (1985) reported that vocational curriculum for the mildly handicapped consists of two periods per week in grades 1 through 4, four periods in grade 4, and six periods in grades 5 through 8.

Within the system of special education exist numerous vocational schools, e.g., 248 schools with a 3-year curriculum, 5 with a 4-year, and 6 with a 5-year.

Special education teachers in Poland are prepared at 4-year teacher's training institutions, which they enter after graduation from high school. Some experienced teachers of subjects enter universities that have a special education teachers' training program. Since 1973, in addition to the

National Institute of Special Education, special education teachers are also prepared at 11 universities (Belcerek, 1977). In 1977 the Polish Ministry of Education opened post-graduate studies in special education at the Graduate School of Special Education in Warsaw. The areas of study at the school include diagnosis and assessment of exceptionalities and the study of deaf, hard-of-hearing, chronically ill, and socially maladaptive children. Special educators are also trained at the Graduate School of Education in Krakow.

Guidelines for the training of special educators have been developed by the special education team of the Pedagogical Science Committee of the Polish Academy of Sciences (Hulek, 1978). Guidelines recommend that a student in special education become familiar with teaching non-handicapped and subsequently handicapped children; teachers should cooperate with various agencies and institutions outside the school; and teachers should continuously be upgrading their education after graduation by attending in-service classes.

Special education studies in Poland are published in *Informator Szkolnictwa Specjalnego* (Bulletin of Special Education), *Nowa Szkola* (New School), *Szkola Specjalna* (Special School), and *Educacja* (Education; formerly *Badania Os'wiatowe,* Educational Research).

REFERENCES

Belcerek, M. (1977). Organization of special education in Poland. In A. Hulek (Ed.), *Therapeutic pedagogy.* Warsaw: State Scientific Publication.

Elska, V. (1985). Organization of vocational training of abnormal children in special schools in Polish Peoples Republic. *Defectologia* (Defectology), *1,* 62.

Holowinsky, I. Z. (1980). Special education in Poland and the Soviet Union: Current developments. In L. Mann & D. Sabatino (Eds.), *The fourth review of special education.* New York: Grune & Stratton.

Hulek, A. (1978, June). *Personnel preparation: International comparison.* Paper presented at the First World Congress on Future Special Education, Sterling, Scotland.

Hulek, A. (1979). Basic assumptions of mainstreaming exceptional children and youth. *Badania Oswiatowe* (Educational Research), *3*(15), 99–112.

Kirejczyk, K. (1975). Half-century of activity of the Special Education Section of the Polish Teachers Association. *Szkola Specjalna* (Special School), *1,* 7–18.

IVAN Z. HOLOWINSKY
Rutgers University

POLITICS AND SPECIAL EDUCATION

Through the middle of the twentieth century, the politics surrounding special education can be characterized as the politics of exclusion. The primary decision makers were school officials who excluded from the public schools students with special needs requiring services not provided to the majority of students (Copeland, 1983). The grounds for exclusion tended to be observably inappropriate or disruptive behavior, rather than rigorous identification of the nature of students' needs or impediments to learning. Parents typically acquiesced in such decisions without questioning the denial of public school resources to their children.

A minority of the excluded students were kept at home, while the majority were referred to publicly or charitably supported residential institutions, often at some distance from their homes. There is little evidence to suggest that either local government authorities or school officials sought to establish locally situated residential institutions. Presumably, they sought to avoid the tax burden that might be incurred owing to the high costs of providing for severely impaired students.

By the beginning of the twentieth century, state-supported systems of residential institutions had emerged, with annual budgets and bureaucracies to administer them and ensure implementation of state regulations (Lynn, 1983). The institutions tended to specialize in one particular type of handicap. Funding formulas varied according to labeled disabilities. Children and youths with special needs were often improperly classified and placed because of inadequate evaluation and subjective if not prejudicial stereotypes (Kirp & Yudof, 1974). Few students with disabilities transferred from one institution to another, and few permanently exited the institutions of initial placement to enter public schools. There was little coordination among different institutions. Many were, in fact, in competition with each other for scarce state resources.

Organized advocacy groups tended to lobby state legislatures individually on behalf of their particular clients (Lynn, 1983). Public policies were differentiated by type of handicap and servicing institution, advocates and clients, and implementing bureaucracies. They also varied from state to state. The overall pattern, however, was for the major portion of special needs students, funds, and service delivery systems to be located outside the public school systems.

Around the turn of the century forces began to emerge that would contribute toward the inclusion rather than the exclusion of special needs students from public school systems (Sarason & Doris, 1979). Refinements in evaluation technology facilitated the identification of the special needs of students with disabilities and suggested management and instructional methods appropriate to them. As a result, there was a widespread increase in the number of special classes within public schools (though outside the mainstream of regular students). State and federal legislative bodies enacted programs and provided funds for such classes. Parent advocacy groups and associations of special educators pressed for increased outlays to meet the needs of specific categories of children and youths with disabilities.

Since services for different disabilities incurred different costs, there are indications that various funding formulas may have had a significant effect on local school policies and practices (Lynn, 1983). The proportion of students labeled as having particular disabilities varied from district to district and among states, often in relation to variations in the amounts of funds that could be obtained for specific handicaps. It also varied in relation to the type of diagnostic instruments used, the type of specialists in the school, and the type of specialized services already provided. The politics of inclusion were thus influenced by local practices and political configurations and maneuverings of special education interest groups, legislators, and bureaucracies.

Although emerging special education policies, funds, programs, and practices may not have always matched the needs of special education students, their legitimacy was increasingly accepted, and they provided the leverage for progressively including special needs students within the public schools. By 1975 mandatory legislation that provided for the education of special needs students had been passed in all but two states. By that time, the states' financial contribution had risen to more than half the total revenues allocated to special education. By 1979 approximately 140 different federal programs serving the handicapped had been enacted. By the early 1980s, localities and special districts were contributing a total of $5.8 billion; states $3.4 billion; and the federal government a total of $804 million (Lynn, 1983).

However, it became clear as support for special education advanced, that two separate systems had developed: one outside the public schools, the other inside. Parent advocates now moved to expand the one that had been established within the public schools by pressing for geographic, social, and educational inclusion of special needs students within the system. These efforts contributed to the exodus of the majority of special education students from state-run residential institutions into the public schools, and to considerable cost shifting from the former to the latter.

The legal basis for this shift came from landmark court decisions establishing the rights of special education students to free and appropriate public schooling (*Watt* v. *Stickney,* 1970; *Diana* v. *State Board of Education,* 1970 and 1973; *PARC* v. *Pennsylvania,* 1972). The Fourteenth Amendment guarantees of due process and equal protection were invoked to affirm the rights of special needs children to the free public schooling offered to other children. The U.S. Constitution was applied to protect these students from discriminatory public school practices in the same manner in which it had been applied to protect minority group students in such decisions as *Brown* v. *Board of Education* in 1954.

While court action gave significant impetus to recognition of the rights of access of students with special needs to public schools, it did so by declaring prior school policies and practices unconstitutional. Yet such determinations tended not to specify what was or would be judged constitutional.

Rather, the courts began to act as umpires, ordering plaintiffs and defendants to negotiate compromises that would be acceptable to both and not unconstitutional (Kirp, 1981). Their role was to set up a structured, adversarial process within state and local school systems in which the courts would act as mediators rather than law-givers. The process would thus be open-ended in terms of its duration, given the lengthiness of legal proceedings, and unpredictable in terms of its possible outcomes.

The debates and conflicts as to placement of students with disabilities, as well as services to be provided them, spread to the federal arena as well, where advocates sought to apply the inclusionary principles of court decisions to congressional enactments. These advocates rode on the coattails of the civil rights movement and the Civil Rights Act of 1964. They encountered countervailing forces similar to those that hampered civil rights activists in their efforts to obtain federal enactments and implement them through the federal system. The movement and the act and its numerous amendments sought to eliminate discriminatory practices by public schools that had denied students geographic, social, and educational inclusion because of their ethnicity, national origin, sex, or impoverishment (Bordier, 1983).

They provided the U.S. Congress with a model for a major legislative enactment designed to protect the rights of special needs students. Passed in 1975, the Education for All Handicapped Children Act, PL 94-142, affirmed their right to a free, appropriate public education in the least restrictive environment; required the identification, evaluation, and placement of students with special needs according to an individual educational plan (IEP); and guaranteed parental rights of participation in educational decisions concerning their children.

Under PL 94-142, the federal government was to pay a graduated percentage of average per pupil expenditures by public elementary and secondary schools, starting with 5 percent in 1979 and culminating in 40 percent by 1982. Implementation of the legislature was nominally nonmandatory. However, most school districts followed suit, presumably because they would have been hard pressed by the parents of special needs students if they did not seek to obtain available federal funds. Furthermore, an earlier law, Section 504 of the Vocational Rehabilitation Act of 1973; forbade discrimination against handicapped students in programs receiving federal financial assistance. Under 504, school districts were routinely required to sign compliance statements affirming that they did not discriminate against students on the basis of race, national origin, sex, or handicap. Since the law was initially interpreted to mean that failure to sign compliance statements could jeopardize receipt of federal financial assistance, compliance (at least on paper) via these statements became the norm.

Program guidelines and regulations of federal implementing agencies such as the Department of Health, Education, and Welfare reflected court decisions and congressional enactments and established compliance machinery within the department (later the Department of Education) and the Justice Department. The Office of Civil Rights was established to coordinate the compliance activities of the federal agencies involved. While this machinery has not been shown to have had a significant impact on educational practices, it provided an institutional and legal context for the politics of inclusion at state and local levels.

By the middle 1980s, at the end of the first Reagan presidency and at the beginning of the second term, funding for implementation of PL 94-142 was curtailed. The law and its regulations were weakened by congressional interventions and Department of Education actions designed to lessen the federal role in education and to devolve social sector responsibilities (including education in general and special education in particular) to the states.

However, because PL 94-142 had assigned significant responsibilities and funds for implementation to state authorities, by the early 1980s, the latter had already adopted laws and regulations reflective of the principles and the delivery system the federal government had mandated earlier. Such legal frameworks, created at state levels, remained in force even after the federal law itself was weakened in the 1980s. Furthermore, state and local authorities had voted to increase expenditures in order to comply with PL 94-142.

When cutbacks in funding occurred at the federal level, and signs of backlash against rapidly increasing expenditures for previously underserved groups appeared at local and state levels, advocates seeking to protect the rights of special needs students used these policies and funding allocations as precedents to justify continuing aid to special education. The role and responsibilities of state and local authorities became established independent of federal laws and regulations. Local school systems followed suit, and the progressive inclusion of special education students proceeded, geographically, socially, and educationally, in more depth than ever anticipated (Brantlinger, 1997).

The enrollment of special needs students increased significantly. Schools formalized their identification, evaluation, and referral procedures, and included new participants in the process. These included committees on the handicapped, appointed by local school boards; parents and their counsels; new categories of special educators and clinicians; "regular" teachers, administrators, and ancillary personnel who had not previously had responsibility for special needs students; and multidisciplinary evaluation teams. The earlier politics of inclusion that affected the federal court system and the federal government had thus significantly increased the number of participants in the politics of inclusion at the local level. Their participation was focused on the legally specified, formalized procedures that court decisions and legislative enactments had established to improve educational services provided to students with special needs.

In the meantime, the signs of a new movement in the field of special education appeared; this would engender new policy approaches designed to integrate a whole spectrum of institutions providing services to students with disabilities, including but not limited to school systems (Copeland, 1983). The needs of special education students for services beyond those provided by public schools had became increasingly apparent, and new service providers outside the schools had emerged. The institutions that provided these services, and the funding sources on which they drew, were separate from the public schools.

Interinstitutional cooperation and coordination was needed, but it would require the development of policies, regulations, and funding formulas that were complementary. For example, agencies dealing with public welfare (e.g., social services, aid for dependent children, foster care, Medicaid), health (e.g., maternal and child health), mental health/retardation/developmental disabilities, vocational rehabilitation, and corrections needed to work more closely. As the public schools incorporated the major portion of the children and youths who had previously been assigned to residential institutions, it became clear that the schools could not provide all the collateral services that these students would require.

Linking these services required interagency cooperation (as mandated by IDEA) and the development of coalitions of advocacy groups to formulate legislation and programs to link their budgets, staffs, and services into an integrated delivery system of which the public schools would be a part. It also required intricate planning that would continue to promote the inclusion of special needs students within the educational mainstream while at the same time requiring the differentiation of these students according to their needs for external services. This blueprint for the 1990s and beyond would require interagency policy making; programming, and budgeting. It would provide an ambitious and complex political agenda for the advocates of special and general education, as well as external social services for children and youths.

REFERENCES

Bordier, J. (1983). Governance and management of special education. *The Forum, 4*(3), 4–13.

Brantlinger, E. (1997). Using ideology: Cases of non recognition of the politics of research and practice in education. *Review of Educational Research, 67*(4), 425–459.

Copeland, W. C. (1983, January). Strategies for special education in the 1980s. *Policy Studies Review, 2* (Special Issue 1), 242–260.

Kirp, D. (1981). The bounded politics of school desegregation litigation. *Harvard Educational Review, 51*(3), 395–414.

Kirp, D., & Yudof, M. (1974). *Education and the law.* Berkeley, CA: McCutchan.

Lynn, L., Jr. (1983). The emerging system for educating handicapped children [Special issue]. *Policy Studies Review, 2,* 21–58.

Sarason, S., & Doris, J. (1979). *Educational handicap, public policy, and social history*. New York: Free Press.

NANCY BORDIER
*Hunter College, City University
of New York*

HISTORY OF SPECIAL EDUCATION
INCLUSION
INDIVIDUALS WITH DISABILITIES EDUCATION ACT OF 2004 (IDEIA)
MAINSTREAMING

POLYDIPSIA

Polydipsia is excessive drinking of water. It is often associated with water intoxication and polyuria (excessive urination). It is essential to distinguish polydipsia that is biologically based from psychogenic polydipsia (Singh, Padi, Bullard, & Freeman, 1985). Most cases of polydipsia are not due to psychogenic factors (Wright, Schaefer, & Solomons, 1979). Psychogenic polydipsia involves the consumption of excessive quantities of water over a brief time period that is often associated with water intoxication. Water intoxication symptoms include headache, excessive perspiration, and vomiting, as well as more severe symptoms such as convulsions and even death (Blum, Tempey, & Lynch, 1983). Psychogenic polydipsia in children is reported to be rare and there is a lack of epidemiological studies available reporting reliable incidence. Among psychiatric patients, the incident is reported to range from 6.6 to 17.5 percent (Singh et al., 1985).

Biological determinants of abnormal thirst and polydipsia include diabetes, hypercalcemia, congestive heart failure, intracranial disease, potassium deficiency associated with renal disease, and meningitis (Chevalier, 1984). Another physical form of polydipsia during infancy occurs when infants are fed on demand with an overly diluted formula (Horev & Cohen, 1994; Wright et al., 1979).

Psychogenic polydipsia is associated with a wide spectrum of psychopathology ranging from mild personality disorders to severe psychosis (Singh et al., 1985). Various explanations for psychogenic polydipsia have been provided including the psychodynamic concept of an oral personality (Singh et al., 1985) or an obsessive-compulsive personality (Wright et al., 1979). It may also result from a behavioral condition such as a conditioned response (Linshaw, Hipp, & Gruskin, 1974).

There is presently no single treatment recommended in the literature for psychogenic polydipsia. The treatment would depend on the aspects of the aspects of the condition relative to a particular case. Polydipsic children with central nervous system (CNS) involvement would be at risk for learning disorders and possibly special education services. Those with more severe psychological disorders may be in need of special programs for behavioral handicaps.

REFERENCES

Blum, A., Tempey, F. W., & Lynch, W. J. (1983). Somatic findings in patients with psychogenic polydipsia. *Journal of Clinical Psychiatry, 44,* 55–56.

Chevalier, R. L. (1984). Polydipsia and enuresis in childhood renin-dependent hypertension. *Journal of Pediatrics, 104,* 591–593.

Horev, Z., & Cohen, H. H. (1994). Compulsive water drinking in infants and young children. *Clinical Pediatrics, 33*(4), 209–213.

Linshaw, M. A., Hipp, T., & Gruskin, A. (1974). Infantile psychogenic water drinking. *Journal of Pediatrics, 85,* 520–522.

Singh, S., Padi, M. H., Bullard, H., & Freeman, H. (1985). Water intoxication in psychiatric patients. *British Journal of Psychiatry, 146,* 127–131.

Wright, L., Schaefer, A. B., Solomons, G. (1979). *Encyclopedia of pediatric psychology*. Baltimore: University Park Press.

JOSEPH D. PERRY
Kent State University

MEDICAL HISTORY
MEDICAL MANAGEMENT

PONCE DE LEON, PEDRO DE (1520–1584)

Pedro de Ponce de Leon, a Spanish Benedictine monk, is credited with creating the art of teaching the deaf. His method, as described by early historians, consisted of teaching the student to write the names of objects and then drilling the student in the production of the corresponding sounds. Whether lip reading was taught is not known, nor from the surviving accounts of his work can it be ascertained whether Ponce de Leon used any signs in teaching his students. It is known that his methods were successful with a number of children.

After Ponce de Leon's death in 1584, no one continued his work, but it is probable that his success, which received much publicity, influenced the development of methods to educate the deaf in Spain in the early seventeenth century.

REFERENCE

Bender, R. E. (1970). *The conquest of deafness*. Cleveland, OH: Case Western Reserve University Press.

PAUL IRVINE
Katonah, New York

PORCH INDEX OF COMMUNICATIVE ABILITIES

The Porch Index of Communicative Ability (PICA) is designed to assess and quantify gestural, verbal, and graphic abilities of aphasic patients. Asia reliable standardized instrument, the PICA provides quantitative information about a patient's change in communicative function and enables the examiner to make predictive judgments relative to amount of recovery (Porch, 1971).

The PICA is a battery of 18 subtests; 4 verbal subtests ranging from object naming to sentence completion; 8 gestural ranging from demonstrating object function to matching identical objects; and 6 graphic on a continuum from writing complete sentences to copying geometric forms. For consistency, 10 common objects are used within each subtest (e.g., toothbrush, cigarette, fork, pencil). A multidimensional binary choice 16-point scoring system is used to determine the degrees of correctness of a patient's response. The scoring system judges responses according to their accuracy, responsiveness, completeness, promptness, and efficiency. Administration time is variable, usually averaging approximately 60 minutes.

Prior to administering the PICA, participation in a 40-hour workshop for test administration, scoring, and interpretation is required. Examiners must complete a rigid testing protocol to insure a high degree of reliability. The PICA is a valuable clinical tool for providing valid and accountable descriptions of an aphasic patient's current and future level of communicative performance.

REFERENCE

Porch, B. (1971). *Porch Index of Communicative Ability. Vol. 2. Administration, scoring, and interpretation* (Rev. ed.). Palo Alto, CA: Consulting Psychologists.

SUSAN MAHANNA-BODEN
TRACY CALPIN CASTLE
Eastern Kentucky University

APHASIA
DEVELOPMENTAL APHASIA

PORTAGE PROJECT

The Portage project was first funded in 1969 as a model home-based program by the Bureau of Education for the Handicapped under the Handicapped Children's Early Education Program (HCEEP). In rural Portage, Wisconsin, the project's staff traveled to the homes of children to help parents learn how to work with children in a home setting (Lerner, 1985). The experimental edition of the Portage project was developed during the first 3 years of the project

and was published by McGraw-Hill in 1972. The revised edition (1976) was developed by Susan Bluma, Marsha Shearer, Alma Froham, and Jean Hillard (Bailey & Worley, 1984; Bluma, et al., 1976; Thurman & Widerstrom, 1985). The project was a developmental, criterion-referenced, behavioral model that employs precision teaching to evaluate a child's developmental level and to plan an educational program for children from birth to 6 years of age. The complete guide came in three parts: a checklist of behaviors on which to record an individual child's developmental progress; a file card listing possible methods of teaching these behaviors; and a manual of directions for use of the checklists, card files, and various methods of remediation. The assessment procedure was administered in 20 to 40 minutes. The behavioral checklist consisted of a 25-page color coded booklet that contains 580 developmentally sequenced behaviors.

Ages were listed at 1-year intervals. The first 45 items were grouped under infant stimulation. Many of the items in this development area were activities that a parent or teacher performed with a child. These behaviors served as a guide for teaching infants up to 4 months. The area of socialization evaluated the young child's interactions with other people. A systematic pattern of language development that focuses on content and the form that was used to express that content was outlined in the checklist. The self-help category defined those behaviors that enabled the child to care for himself or herself in feeding, dressing, and toileting. The motor area was primarily concerned with the coordinated movements of the large muscles of the body. For each of the 580 items, there were curriculum cards that provide teaching suggestions. These cards were in a card file and were color coded to match corresponding sections in the checklist.

For a home-based program, children were assigned to a home teacher who spent about an hour and a half a week with each child assigned. Instruction during the remainder of the week was the responsibility of the parent. Prescriptions were modified according to each child's individual progress from week to week. Three new behavior targets were identified each week, and it became the parents' responsibility to provide instruction on these behaviors between the home teacher's visits. The home teacher collected data before and after instruction and helped parents with their teaching skills by modeling techniques and allowing parents to try the skills each week.

The success of the Portage model was seen in its wide dissemination and replication. Over 30 replications across the United States have been reported as well as international recognition (Mittler, 1990). The project staff provided training and technical assistance to the replicated sites while the sites provided input regarding changes and additions. (Bluma et al., 1976; Southworth, Burr, & Cox, 1980; Thurman & Widerstrom, 1981).

REFERENCES

Bailey, D., & Worley, M. (1984). *Teaching infants and preschoolers with handicaps.* Columbus, OH: Merrill.

Bluma, S., Shearer, M., Froham, A., & Hilliard, J. (1976). *The Portage project: Portage guide to early education manual* (Rev. ed.). Portage, WI: Cooperative Educational Services Agency.

Lerner, J. (1985). *Learning disabilities: Theories, diagnosis, and educational strategies* (4th ed.). Boston: Houghton Mifflin.

Mittler, P. (1990). Prospects for disabled children and their families: An international perspective. *Disability, Handicap, & Society,* 5(1), 53–64.

Southworth, L., Burr, R., & Cox, A. (1980). *Screening and evaluating the young child: A handbook of instruments to use from infancy to six years.* Springfield, IL: Thomas.

Thurman, K. S., & Widerstrom, H. A. (1985). *Young children with special needs: A developmental and ecological approach.* Boston: Allyn & Bacon.

FRANCES T. HARRINGTON
Radford University

HOMEBOUND INSTRUCTION
PARENT EDUCATION

POSITIVE BEHAVIORAL SUPPORT

Positive behavioral support (PBS) is a dynamic and collaborative process for implementing environmental and lifestyle changes as part of a comprehensive plan of behavioral support for individuals with chronic or persistent problem behavior. Behavior support plans are based on data from functional assessments that result in environmental modifications and instructional procedures that the person of concern, teachers, family, and support personnel can implement in order to increase positive alternative behaviors, decrease problem behaviors, and increase attributions of self-determination, inclusion, and independence for the person of concern (Carr et al., 2002; De Pry, 2006; Field, Martin, Miller, Ward, & Wehmeyer, 1998; O'Neill et al., 1997; Sugai & Horner, 1994; Turnbull, & Turnbull, 1990). In other words, "*positive behavior* includes all those skills that increase the likelihood of success and personal satisfaction in normative academic, work, social, recreational, community, and family settings. Support encompasses all those educational methods that can be used to teach, strengthen, and expand positive behavior and all those systems change methods that can increase opportunities for the display of positive behavior" (Carr et al., pp. 4–5).

Behavioral support planning is an evidenced-based and nonaversive approach for reducing challenging behaviors that utilizes systems-level change and individual skill development (Horner, et al., 1990; Sugai & Horner, 1994;

Turnbull, Turnbull, Shank, & Leal, 1999). O'Neill et al. (1997, p. 8) writes that the outcome of behavioral support is "not just to define and eliminate undesirable behavior but to understand the structure and function of those behaviors in order to teach and promote effective alternatives." Positive behavioral support focuses on strategies that are designed to promote and sustain durable and generalizable change that positively affects an individual's access to the general education curriculum, community settings, preferred activities, and preferred persons within and across environments (Horner et al., 1990).

Carr et al. (2002) notes that the application of positive behavioral support has several critical features, including: (1) the development of a comprehensive plan that specifically focuses on the person of concern's quality of life; (2) consideration is given to a life span perspective that is taking into account long-term and comprehensive change plans, procedures, and supports; (3) application of scientific principles to real-life situations; (4) active involvement of the consumer and critical stakeholders as part of a collaborative process of providing positive behavioral support; (5) increased emphasis on use of socially valid methods; (6) application of strategies that promote systems-level change; (7) a focus on the use of proactive and preventative strategies, instead of using reactive and aversive methods to address chronic and persistent problem behavior; (8) incorporation of multiple data collection methods for both evaluation and practice; and (9) incorporation of multiple perspectives and paradigms into plans of behavioral support. These features include research and practice grounded in applied behavior analysis (Baer, Wolf, & Risley, 1968; Sulzer-Azaroff & Mayer, 1991), principles from the normalization and inclusion movements (Wolfensberger, 1983), and strategies associated with person-centered planning and self-determination (Kincaid, 1996; Martin, Marshall, & De Pry, 2005).

Positive behavioral support planning is predicated on an accurate functional assessment. Functional assessment is a term that describes a process for gathering information about the factors that predict and/or maintain chronic or persistent problem behavior. Data from indirect and direct functional assessments are used to develop and implement comprehensive behavior support plans, including data of any setting events, immediate antecedents or triggers, and consequent events that are hypothesized to maintain the problem behavior. Summary statements are developed from this data and are organized into a competing behavior path analysis (see O'Neill et al., 1997). A behavior support plan is then collaboratively developed that delineates environmental modifications, curricular adaptations, and instructional strategies for teaching replacement responses that serve the same function of the problem behavior, but are more socially acceptable given the individual's home, school, and work environments. O'Neill et al. concludes that the ultimate purpose of the functional assessment is to "increase the effectiveness and efficiency of behavior support plans" (p. 65).

Because schools are dynamic and complex social systems, policies and procedures need to be in place that promote positive behavioral support across settings, faculty, staff, and students in our schools (Sugai & Horner, 1994). This method, often referred to as schoolwide positive behavior support, provides a continuum of behavioral support for all learners, with additional support being available for students with targeted needs and intensive/individualized behavior support needs (Sugai et al., 2000). Sugai (1996) has identified four major schoolwide positive behavior support systems that should be considered when addressing the behavioral support needs of all learners in schools. These systems include schoolwide behavioral support systems (all students, all staff, and all settings), specific setting behavioral support systems (hallways, bathrooms, cafeteria, playground, parking lot), classroom-specific behavioral support systems (instructional classroom management), and individual student behavioral support systems (targeted and function-based support). Each of these systems incorporate (1) procedures for teaching expected behaviors to all students, (2) procedures for monitoring and evaluating student progress using both formative and summative assessments, and (3) procedures for accessing local behavioral expertise (e.g., behavior support team or school-based PBS leadership team) so that teachers can receive assistance and support in the implementation of the schoolwide program, including functional behavioral assessment and individualized behavioral support planning (Colvin, Kame'enui, & Sugai, 1993; Sugai & Horner, 1994).

Positive behavioral support has also received increased attention in the area of family-based behavioral support (Lucyshyn, Dunlap, & Albin, 2002). Specific strategies and methods for providing ongoing behavioral support have been implemented for persons with autism, developmental disabilities, and emotional and behavioral disorders (Dunlap & Fox, 1996; Lucyshyn, Horner, Dunlap, Albin, & Ben, 2002; Whaley, 2002) across a variety of home, school, and community settings. Application of function-based support in home environments has been shown to be an effective strategy for addressing chronic and persistent problem behavior (Lucyshyn, Kayser, Irvin, & Blumberg, 2002; Wacker, Peck, Derby, Berg, & Harding, 1996). In addition, an increased interest in collaborative family support strategies and collaborative research practices has been documented in the extant literature (Turnbull & Turnbull, 1996).

O'Neill et al. (1997) offers four considerations for building effective behavioral support plans, including (1) behavioral support plans should describe *our* behavior, that is, the changes that teachers, family, and support personnel will make within and across environments to support the person of concern; (2) behavior support plans should always build upon the results of comprehensive functional assessments; that is, the behavior support team should always incorpo-

rate both indirect and direct functional assessment data as a means to understand the purpose or function that the problem behavior serves for the individual; (3) behavior support plans should be technically sound and include strategies that make the problem behavior irrelevant, ineffective, and inefficient by implementing empirically validated behavioral principles across settings, persons, and time; and (4) behavior support plans should fit the setting where they will be implemented by taking into account the values, time, and resources of those that will be asked to implement the procedures, including the person of concern.

In conclusion, positive behavioral support is a process for creating responsive environments that take into account the preferences, strengths, and needs of the person of concern by promoting systems-level change across environments and by using instructional strategies that teach the individual effective alternatives to the behaviors of concern (Sugai & Horner, 1994; Turnbull et al., 1999). These strategies are based on an extensive literature found in the study of applied behavior analysis, strategies associated with functional behavioral assessment and individualized behavior support planning, practices associated with the normalization and inclusion movements, and values found in both person-centered planning and self-determination movements (Carr et al., 2002). Positive behavioral support has specific applications for individuals with chronic or persistent problem behavior (O'Neill et al., 1997), as well as systems-level change and evidence-based strategies that are used in school environments (Sugai et al., 2000) and in home and community settings (Koegel, Koegel, & Dunlap, 1996; Lucyshyn, Dunlap, & Albin, 2002).

REFERENCES

Baer, D. M., Wolf, M. N., & Risley, T. R. (1968). Some current dimensions of applied behavior analysis. *Journal of Applied Behavior Analysis, 1,* 91–97.

Carr, E. G., Dunlap, G., Horner, R. H., Koegel, R. L., Turnbull, A. P., Sailor, W., et al. (2002). Positive behavior support: Evolution of an applied science. *Journal of Positive Behavior Interventions, 4,* 4–16, 20.

Colvin, G., Kame'enui, E. J., & Sugai, G. (1993). Reconceptualizing behavior management and school-wide discipline in general education. *Education and Treatment of Children, 16,* 361–381.

De Pry, R. L. (2006). Positive behavioral support. In E. Fletcher-Janzen & C. R. Reynolds (Eds.), *The special education almanac* (pp. 363–367). Hoboken, NJ: Wiley.

Dunlap, G., & Fox, L. (1996). Early intervention and serious problem behaviors: A comprehensive approach. In L. K. Koegel, R. L. Koegel, & G. Dunlap (Eds.), *Positive behavioral support: Including people with difficult behavior in the community* (pp. 31–50). Baltimore: Brookes.

Field, S., Martin, J., Miller, R., Ward, M., & Wehmeyer, M. (1998). *A practical guide for teaching self-determination.* Reston, VA: Council for Exceptional Children.

Horner, R. H., Dunlap, G., Koegel, R. L., Carr, E. G., Sailor, W., Anderson, J., Albin, R. W., & O'Neill, R. E. (1990). Toward a technology of "nonaversive" behavioral support. *The Journal of the Association for Persons with Severe Handicaps, 15*, 125–132.

Kincaid, D. (1996). Person-centered planning. In L. K. Koegel, R. L. Koegel, & G. Dunlap (Eds.), *Positive behavioral support: Including people with difficult behavior in the community* (pp. 439–465). Baltimore: Brookes.

Koegel, L. K., Koegel, R. L., & Dunlap, G. (1996). *Positive behavioral support: Including people with difficult behavior in the community.* Baltimore: Brookes.

Lucyshyn, J. M., Dunlap, G., & Albin, R. W. (2002). *Families and positive behavior support: Addressing problem behavior in family contexts.* Baltimore: Brookes.

Lucyshyn, J. M., Horner, R. H., Dunlap, G., Albin, R. W., & Ben, K. R. (2002). Positive behavior support with families. In J. M. Lucyshyn, G. Dunlap, & R. W. Albin (Eds.), *Families and positive behavior support: Addressing problem behavior in family contexts* (pp. 3–43). Baltimore: Brookes.

Lucyshyn, J. M., Kayser, A. T., Irvin, L. K., & Blumberg, E. R. (2002). Functional assessment and positive behavior support at home with families: Designing effective and contextually appropriate behavior support plans. In J. M. Lucyshyn, G. Dunlap, & R. W. Albin (Eds.), *Families and positive behavior support: Addressing problem behavior in family contexts* (pp. 97–132). Baltimore: Brookes.

Martin, J. E., Marshall, L. H., & DePry, R. L. (2005). Participatory decision-making: Innovative practices that increase student self-determination. In R. W. Flexer, T. J. Simmons, P. Luft, & R. M. Baer (Eds.), *Transition planning for secondary students with disabilities* (2nd ed., pp. 304–332). Columbus, OH: Merrill Prentice Hall.

O'Neill, R. E., Horner, R. H., Albin, R. W., Sprague, J. R., Storey, K., & Newton, J. S. (1997). *Functional assessment and program development for problem behavior: A practical handbook* (2nd ed.). Pacific Grove, CA: Brooks/Cole.

Sugai, G. (1996). Providing effective behavioral support to all students: Procedures and processes. *SAIL, 11* (1), 1–4.

Sugai, G., & Horner, R. (1994). Including students with severe behavior problems in general education settings: Assumptions, challenges, and solutions. In J. Marr, G. Sugai, & G. Tindal (Eds.), *The Oregon conference monograph* (pp. 102–120). Eugene: University of Oregon.

Sugai, G., Horner, R. H., Dunlap, G., Hieneman, M., Lewis, T. J., Nelson, C. M., et al. (2000). Applying positive behavior support and functional behavioral assessment in schools. *Journal of Positive Behavior Interventions, 2*, 131–143.

Sulzer-Azaroff, B., & Mayer, G. R. (1991). *Behavior analysis for lasting change.* Fort Worth, TX: Harcourt Brace College Publishers.

Turnbull, A. P., & Turnbull, H. R., III. (1990). A tale about lifestyle changes: Comments on "toward a technology of 'nonaversive' behavioral support." *Journal of the Association for Persons with Severe Handicaps, 15*, 142–144.

Turnbull, A. P., & Turnbull, H. R., III. (1996). Group action planning as a strategy for providing comprehensive family support. In L. K. Koegel, R. L. Koegel, & G. Dunlap (Eds.), *Positive behav-ioral support: Including people with difficult behavior in the community* (pp. 99–114). Baltimore: Brookes.

Turnbull, A. P., Turnbull, H. R., III, Shank, M., & Leal, D. (1999). *Exceptional lives: Special education in today's schools* (2nd ed.). Upper Saddle River, NJ: Merrill.

Wacker, D. P., Peck, S., Derby, K. M., Berg, W., & Harding, J. (1996). Developing long-term reciprocal interactions between parents and their young children with problematic behavior. In L. K. Koegel, R. L. Koegel, & G. Dunlap (Eds.), *Positive behavioral support: Including people with difficult behavior in the community* (pp. 51–80). Baltimore: Brookes.

Whaley, R. M. (2002). Finding positive behavior support one piece at a time: Living and growing with David. In J. M. Lucyshyn, G. Dunlap, & R. W. Albin (Eds.), *Families and positive behavior support: Addressing problem behavior in family contexts* (pp. 45–55). Baltimore: Brookes.

Wolfensberger, W. (1983). Social role valorization: A proposed new term for the principle of normalization. *Mental Retardation, 21*, 234–239.

RANDALL L. DE PRY
*University of Colorado at
Colorado Springs*

POSITIVE BEHAVIORAL SUPPORT, SCHOOLWIDE

POSITIVE BEHAVIORAL SUPPORT, SCHOOLWIDE

Schoolwide Positive Behavior Support (SWPBS) is a systems approach for establishing the social, culture and behavioral supports needed for schools to be effective learning environments for all students. Based on principles of behavioral theory and applied behavior analysis, SWPBS focuses on the school as the "unit of analysis" by considering how resources, activities, and initiatives are organized, implemented, and evaluated. Because the accurate adoption and sustained use of evidence-based practices are considered essential in effective schools, SWPBS emphasizes systems factors, like team-based coordination and action planning, data-based decision making, active administrator participation, and ongoing and long-term professional development. The Office of Special Education Programs (OSEP) Center on Positive Behavioral Interventions and Supports has indicated that "Positive behavioral support is not a new intervention package, nor a new theory of behavior, but an application of a behaviorally-based systems approach to enhancing the capacity of schools, families, and communities to design effective environments that improve the fit or link between research-validated practices and the environments in which teaching and learning occurs" (1999, p. 7). Positive behavior support (PBS) is the outcome of the systematic integration of behavioral science, practical interventions, social values, and a systems perspective (Carr et al. 2002; Sugai et al. 2000).

Features

School adoption of SWPBS is associated with a number of characteristics. First, implementers of SWPBS use four important criteria to guide their decision making. Attention is focused on the careful selection, definition, and acknowledgment of *outcomes* that are valued by significant stakeholders (e.g., students, families, community members), described in measurable terms, based on local data and input, and used to guide intervention selection and measure progress. Priority is given to the identification, adoption, adaptation, and sustained use of evidence-based *practices* that are linked to achieving desired outcomes. Information or *data* systems are established to define outcomes and guide evaluation of implementation efforts and practices (e.g., discipline referrals, specialized support requests, academic achievement patterns). Before any practice is put in place, *systems* for supporting users and implementers of the practice must be established (e.g., professional development, resources, coaching, coordination). Together these elements serve as the core operating features of SWPBS (see Figure 1; Sugai & Horner, 2002).

Second, the SWPBS approach is based on a prevention logic that has been adopted from the public health literature (Larson, 1994; Moffitt, 1994). A three-tiered continuum of positive behavior support is emphasized for all students (see Figure 2; Colvin, Kame'enui, & Sugai, 1993; Sugai & Horner, 2002; Walker et al., 1996). At the primary level, all students and all school staff members across all school settings are involved in a universal prevention strategy that consists of (1) clear purpose statement for the importance of maintaining classroom and school climates, (2) small number of positively stated behavioral expectations, (3) formal yearlong process for teaching and practicing the behavioral expectations, (4) continuum of ongoing procedures for en-

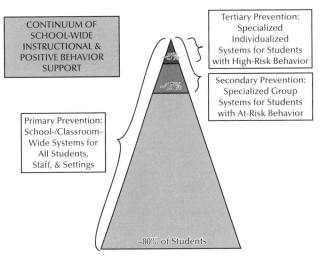

Figure 2 Continuum of PBS

couraging student use of these behavioral expectations, (5) continuum of clearly defined consequences for discouraging rule-violations, and (6) regular routines and procedures for monitoring student behavior and intervention effectiveness. At the secondary prevention level, more intensive strategies are put in place for those students who do not benefit from primary prevention strategies. These strategies are applied similarly across these students and focus on increasing teacher monitoring and reinforcement and teaching and fostering self-management skills. At the tertiary level, specially designed, function-based, and individually implemented and monitored interventions are emphasized (e.g., special education, alternative programming).

Third, although procedures for responding to rule violation and problem behaviors are considered necessary, SWPBS emphasizes the teaching of prosocial skills at the individual, classroom, and schoolwide levels. The teaching of social skills is similar to the procedures for teaching academic skills: (1) define, tell, show, and/or explain; (2) arrange regular opportunities to practice to fluency; (3) monitor continuously and acknowledge regularly; and (4) modify and adapt based on student performance (Colvin & Sugai, 1988). Similarly, student learning of social skills is evaluated along the same phases of academic learning; that is, acquisition, fluency, maintenance, generalization, and adaptation (White & Haring, 1980).

Finally, implementation of SWPBS is guided by a systemic or organizational approach (Colvin et al., 1993; Lewis & Sugai, 1999). Before any practice is adopted and implemented, a schoolwide leadership team with representation from within and outside the school is established to coordinate accurate and sustained implementation. The team uses local data from students, family members, and staff to guide the development of a contextually relevant action plan that has clear and measurable outcomes and evidence-based interventions that are linked to achieving those outcomes. After the plan is developed and approved,

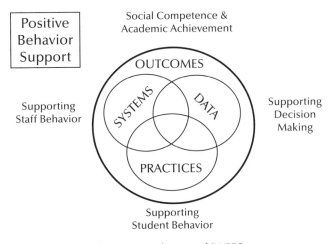

Figure 1 Four elements of SWPBS

the team prepares the staff for the implementation of the action plan interventions. Throughout the process, the team monitors information on the effects of intervention on student behavioral and academic performance, and the extent to which staff are consistently, accurately, and comprehensively using interventions. From the results of these evaluations, the team makes adaptation to the action plan to improve the effectiveness, efficiency, and relevance of the interventions.

Implementation Indicators and Outcomes

Depending on the focus of the action plan, the implementation of SWPBS can be associated with a range of outcomes; for example, improvements in discipline referral and suspension patterns, increased opportunities for student learning and teaching instruction, improvements in classroom and school climate, and increases in the proportion of students meeting state academic standards when combined with effective instruction (Sugai & Horner, 2002).

In addition, the successful implementation of SWPBS interventions is associated with other indicators. For example, more than 80 percent of a random sample of students can name the schoolwide positive expectations and give a behavioral example of what that expectation looks like in a typical school setting, and indicate that an adult has acknowledged them for a display of a behavioral expectation in the last week. Similarly, more than 80 percent of the school staff can state the schoolwide expectations and have taught the skills to the students. The SWPBS leadership team has met at least monthly to review their data and evaluate the implementation of their action plan. When these teams meet, the school administrator is an active participant. For additional information on SWPBS go to the OSEP Technical Assistance Center on Positive Behavior Interventions and Supports web site at http://www.PBIS.org.

REFERENCES

Carr, E. G., Dunlap, G., Horner, R. H., Koegel, R. L., Turnbull, A. P., & Sailor, W. (2002). Positive behavior support: Evolution of an applied science. *Journal of Positive Behavior Interventions, 4,* 4–16.

Colvin, G., Kame'enui, E. J., & Sugai, G. (1993). School-wide and classroom management: Reconceptualizing the integration and management of students with behavior problems in general education. *Education and Treatment of Children, 16,* 361–381.

Colvin, G., & Sugai, G. M. (1988). Proactive strategies for managing social behavior problems: An instructional approach. *Education and Treatment of Children, 11*(4), 341–348.

Horner, R. H., & Sugai, G. (2005). School-wide positive behavior support: An alternative approach to discipline in schools. In L. Bambara & L. Kern (Eds.), *Individualized supports for students with problem behaviors: Designing positive behavior plans* (pp. 359–390). New York: Guilford.

Larson, J. (1994). Violence prevention in the schools: A review of selected programs and procedures. *School Psychology Review, 23*(2), 151–164.

Lewis, T. J., & Sugai, G. (1999). Effective behavior support: A systems approach to proactive school-wide management. *Focus on Exceptional Children, 31*(6), 1–24.

Moffitt, T. (1994). Adolescence-limited and life-course-persistent antisocial behavior: A developmental taxonomy. *Psychological Review, 100,* 674–701.

Safran, S. P., & Oswald, K. (2003). Positive behavior supports: Can schools reshape disciplinary practices. *Exceptional Children, 69,* 361–373.

Sugai, G., & Horner, R. H. (2002). The evolution of discipline practices: School-wide positive behavior supports. *Child and Family Behavior Therapy, 24,* 23–50.

Sugai, G., Horner, R. H., Dunlap, G., Hieneman, M., Lewis, T. J., Nelson, C. M., Scott, T., Liaupsin, C., Sailor, W., Turnbull, A. P., Turnbull, H. R., III, Wickham, D., Reuf, M., & Wilcox, B. (2000). Applying positive behavioral support and functional behavioral assessment in schools. *Journal of Positive Behavioral Interventions, 2,* 131–143.

Walker, H. M., Horner, R. H., Sugai, G., Bullis, M., Sprague, J. R., Bricker, D., & Kaufman, M. J. (1996). Integrated approaches to preventing antisocial behavior patterns among school-age children and youth. *Journal of Emotional and Behavioral Disorders, 4,* 194–209.

White, O. R., & Haring, N. G. (1980). *Exceptional teaching* (2nd ed.). Columbus, OH: Merrill.

George Sugai
University of Connecticut

Robert H. Horner
University of Oregon

POSITIVE BEHAVIORAL SUPPORT

POSITIVE PRACTICE

Positive practice is a behavior change technique whereby a misbehaving individual is required to practice correct or appropriate behaviors repeatedly. The term positive practice is frequently used as a synonym for overcorrection, a punishment technique (MacKenzie-Keating & McDonald, 1990). In fact, positive practice is actually a subcomponent of overcorrection. With overcorrection, a misbehaving individual is required to overcorrect the environmental effects of his or her inappropriate act and/or repeatedly practice correct forms of relevant behavior in situations where the misbehavior commonly occurs (Foxx & Bechtel, 1982a). The first part of the overcorrection procedure outlined is commonly referred to as restitution and the latter portion of the procedure is often labeled positive practice. Foxx and Bechtel (1982a) have recommended the terms restitution and positive practice be dropped and replaced by overcorrection for purposes of conceptual clarity and communication.

The concept of positive practice has been the central feature of numerous intervention techniques such as theft reversal (Azrin & Wesolowski, 1974), cleanliness training (Azrin & Foxx, 1971), and social apology training (Carey & Bucher, 1981). Two common misconceptions about positive practice, however, exist. The first is that positive reinforcement is part of positive practice. This is probably owed to the fact that many people associate the performance of appropriate behaviors solely with the delivery of positive reinforcers. In overcorrection, the performance of appropriate behaviors is elicited by graduated guidance (verbal and physical) from a therapist, not positive reinforcement (Carr, 1997). The second misconception is that positive practice is similar to negative practice (Dunlap, 1930), a procedure whereby an individual repeatedly practices an inappropriate behavior. Clearly, positive practice is conceptually and pragmatically antithetical to negative practice.

By design, positive practice is a consequence to be used as an aversive stimuli following the occurrence of an inappropriate behavior. Therefore, when the presentation of positive practice results in the reduction of a response in the future, it functions as a punishment procedure. The research literature documents that positive practice, or more accurately overcorrection, can produce large, fairly enduring reductions in inappropriate behavior. Overcorrection procedures have been used with several response classes of behaviors (e.g., aggressive-disruptive behaviors, self-stimulating behaviors, self-injurious behaviors, personal hygiene, social interactions), populations (e.g., mentally handicapped, behaviorally disordered, undersocialized children and adults), and settings (e.g., schools, homes, and institutions). Foxx and Bechtel (1982b) provide an extensive review of the outcomes and side effects of overcorrection, and detailed guidelines for the use of overcorrection.

REFERENCES

Azrin, N. H., & Foxx, R. M. (1971). A rapid method of toilet training the institutionalized retarded. *Journal of Applied Behavior Analysis, 4,* 89–99.

Azrin, N. H., & Wesolowski, M. D. (1974). Theft reversal: An overcorrection procedure for eliminating stealing by retarded persons. *Journal of Applied Behavior Analysis, 7,* 577–581.

Carey, R. G., & Bucher, B. (1981). Identifying the educative and suppressive effects of positive practice and restitutional overcorrection. *Journal of Applied Behavior Analysis, 14,* 71–80.

Carr, A. (1997). Positive practice in family therapy. *Journal of Marital & Family Therapy, 23*(3), 271–293.

Dunlap, K. (1930). Repetition in the breaking of habits. *Scientific Monthly, 30,* 66–70.

Foxx, R. M., & Bechtel, D. R. (1982a). Overcorrection. In M. Hersen, R. M. Eisler, & P. M. Miller (Eds.), *Progress in behavior modification* (pp. 227–288). New York: Academic.

Foxx, R. M., & Bechtel, D. R. (1982b). Overcorrection: A review and analysis. In S. Axelrod & J. Apsche (Eds.), *The effects of punishment on human behavior* (pp. 133–220). New York: Academic.

MacKenzie-Keating, S. E., & McDonald, L. (1990). Overcorrection reviewed, revisited, and revised. *Behavior Analyst, 13*(1), 39–48.

STEPHEN N. ELLIOTT
University of Wisconsin at Madison

APPLIED BEHAVIOR ANALYSIS
BEHAVIOR MODIFICATION
NEGATIVE PUNISHMENT
OVERCORRECTION

POSITIVE REINFORCEMENT

Behavioral psychology, in particular operant conditioning theory, is based on the supposition that behavior is maintained by its consequences. A consequence that leads to an increase in the frequency of a behavior is called a reinforcer. Conversely, a consequence that results in a decrease in the frequency of a behavior is called punishment.

The principle of positive reinforcement has two parts: (1) if in a given situation a person's behavior is followed close in time by a consequence, then (2) that person is more likely to exhibit the same behavior when he or she is in a similar situation at a later time. This consequence is referred to as a positive reinforcer and is roughly synonomous with the concept of reward.

The person credited with first experimentally investigating the effects of rewards on learning is E. L. Thorndike. In 1898 he began seminal work with hungry cats who learned to escape from a cage to acquire food. After many investigations, Thorndike (1911) conceptualized the law of effect, which in part stated that if a stimulus was followed by a response and then a satisfier, the stimulus-response connection would be strengthened. Skinner (1938, 1953) followed up on Thorndike's work and chose the term positive reinforcer in place of satisfier because he felt satisfier was clumsy and not appropriate for a scientific system of behavior. With the work of Skinner and others such as Premack (1959), the principle of positive reinforcement has become the cornerstone of behavior theory and technology.

The application of positive reinforcement is deceptively simple. Two important components in the successful application of positive reinforcement are the selection of a reinforcer and the schedule for delivering the reinforcer. Some stimuli are positive reinforcers for virtually everyone. For example, food is a reinforcer for almost anyone who has not eaten in several hours; money also is generally reinforcing. It is very important, however, to understand that one can actually determine if a stimulus is reinforcing only after it has been administered contingent on the appearance of a desired behavior. In other words, a stimulus is defined as a reinforcer only by its effect on behavior. Failure to select a stimulus that is reinforcing is one of the most common errors in implementing a behavior change program.

The relationship between a behavior and its consequence is called a contingency. Contingencies can operate continuously (i.e., the consequence follows every occurrence of the target behavior) or intermittently (i.e., the consequence follows only a portion of the occurrences of the target behavior). Most contingencies operate on intermittent schedules (e.g., variable ratio, variable interval, fixed ratio, fixed interval). Each reinforcement schedule has been demonstrated to have a different effect on behavior. In general, continuous schedules are used effectively to develop a new behavior, whereas intermittent schedules are used effectively to increase and maintain a behavior already in a person's repertoire. Ratio schedules generally produce high rates of response, and interval schedules produce lower rates of response. In summary, the selection of a stimulus that is reinforcing and the schedule by which it is administered will determine the strength of the positive reinforcement.

REFERENCES

Premack, D. (1959). Toward empirical behavioral laws. I. Positive reinforcement. *Psychological Review, 66,* 219–233.

Skinner, B. F. (1938). *The behavior of organisms.* New York: Appleton-Century-Crofts.

Skinner, B. F. (1953). *Science and human behavior.* New York: Macmillan.

Thorndike, E. L. (1898). Animal intelligence: An experimental study of associative processes in animals. *Psychological Review, Monograph Supplement, 2,* 8–7, 28–31.

Thorndike, E. L. (1911). *Animal intelligence.* New York: Macmillan.

STEPHEN N. ELLIOTT
Louisiana State University

APPLIED BEHAVIOR ANALYSIS
BEHAVIOR MODIFICATION

POSITRON EMISSION TOMOGRAPHY

Positron Emission Tomography, also referred to as PET imaging or a PET scan, is a diagnostic process that involves the acquisition of physiologic images based on the detection of radiation from the emission positrons. Positrons are tiny particles omitted from a radioactive substance administered to the patient. The subsequent images of the human body developed with this technique are used to evaluate a variety of diseases. The PET scanner is a large machine that looks like a donut. Within the machine are multiple rings of detectors that record the emission of energy from the radioactive substance injected into the individual and permit an image of the body to be obtained. While lying on an examination table, the individual is moved through the hole of the machine. The images are displayed on a computer monitor. Before the examination begins a radioactive substance is produced in a machine called a cyclotron, then attached to a natural body compound, usually glucose but sometimes water or ammonia. Once this substance is administered to the individual, the radioactivity localizes in the appropriate areas of the body and is detected by the PET scanner. A radioactive substance is usually administered through an existing intravenous line or an inhaled gas. It takes approximately 30 to 90 minutes for the substance to travel through the body and accumulate in the tissue under study. Different colors or degrees of brightness on a PET image represent different levels of tissue or organ function. For example, healthy tissue uses glucose for energy. It then accumulates some of the tagged glucose which shows up on the PET images. However, cancerous tissue uses more glucose than normal tissue and therefore it accumulates more of the substance and appears brighter than normal tissue on a PET image.

PET scans are particularly useful in detecting cancer and examining the effects of cancer therapy by characterizing biochemical changes in the cancer. The scans can be performed on the whole body or specific parts of the body. PET scans of the heart can be used to determine blood flow to the heart muscle and help evaluate signs of coronary artery disease. PET scans can also be used to determine if areas of the heart that showed decrease function are alive rather than scarred as the result of a prior heart attack. Combined with other studies, PET scans allow differentiation of nonfunctioning heart muscle from heart muscle that would benefit from corrective procedures. PET scans of the brain are used to evaluate individuals with memory disorders of an undetermined cause, suspected or proven brain tumors, or seizure disorders that are not responsive to medical therapy and therefore candidates for surgery. Because the probe is very short lived, radiation exposure is low. The substance amount is so small that it does not affect the normal processes of the body.

SAM GOLDSTEIN
University of Utah

DIFFUSION TENSOR IMAGING
MAGNETIC RESONANCE IMAGING
SPECT

POST-INSTITUTIONALIZED CHILD PROJECT

One of the most devastating examples of early childhood neglect and deprivation can be seen in the experiences of children living in some foreign orphanages. It is known that maternal deprivation, neglect, and severe malnutrition in the early lives of children put them at greater risk for growth failure and developmental delays in the early years. Little is known, however, about long-term growth and development of these children. More and more of these children are being adopted by families within the United States. Individual reports suggest that these children may experience long-term growth failure, continued developmental delays and abnormalities related to the onset of puberty. Definitive data are not yet available.

Physicians from Emory University School of Medicine, The Marcus Institute for Development and Learning, and The Hughes Spalding International Adoption Evaluation Center are researching the potential problems that children adopted from international orphanages who are exposed to severe deprivation and/or neglect may struggle with as they grow. Currently, the research is focusing on children adopted from Romania. Efforts to expand this research may be taken.

Families who have experience with a child adopted from an orphanage or institution from any country and who are interested in assisting with the development of knowledge in the field are encouraged to contact the project.

Further information can be obtained on the Internet at http://www.emory.edu/PEDS/ENDO/orphan/ or http://www.adopt@oz.ped.emory.edu

PATRICK MASON
KRISTA BIERNATH
*The Hughes Spalding
International Adoption
Evaluation Center*

POST-INSTITUTIONALIZED CHILDREN

A wide variation of scenarios are envisioned when a child is described as neglected. Tangible resources that are considered primary needs of a child such as food, shelter, and clothing may not be provided by caretakers. Services such as appropriate medical care or education may be withheld. In addition, less tangible neglect may occur in the form of lack of emotional interaction with caregivers and/or lack of developmental or intellectual stimulation.

This emotional neglect, which is a product of social, developmental, and intellectual understimulation, may result from a variety of early environmental situations. The parent who is too busy or too overwhelmed by his or her own issues may not take the time to provide stimulation and attention that the child needs. Likewise, a child who has been moved from one overcrowded foster care home to another may also be exposed to such neglect. One of the most devastating examples of neglect and deprivation can be seen in the experiences of children living in some foreign orphanages.

After the fall of the Romanian communist regime in 1989, a disturbing system of state-run child care was discovered. The government was housing up to 300,000 children in an orphanage system. These orphanages became a dumping ground for either the country's most severely diseased and damaged children or for those that were without a home or family. Children were often placed into orphanages that provided minimal amounts of clothing and food, and little medical attention. The orphanages were also generally devoid of personal contact, with ratios of children to caregivers often as high as 60 to 1. Children were left unattended, with contact only for adding food to the bottle suspended above the crib and occasional diaper changes.

Children raised in such understimulating, neglectful, and even abusive environments may suffer a host of adverse consequences. The following discussion will focus on the severely neglected and sometimes abused children; in particular, children with a history of institutionalization. The discussion will address the neurobiological and physiological effects of such neglect, the stress on family systems, and recommendations for educational modifications.

In the 1940s, scientists such as Rene Spitz, William Goldfarb, and John Bowlby described the effects of deprivation, severe neglect, and institutionalization on the well-being of children. At this early time, emotional attachment between the caregiver and infant or young child was already described as important for the child's future development. In the 1960s and early 1970s, definitive work was done to show that the effects of institutionalization on a child was linked to social impairment in the development of that child. This work was carried out by Drs. Sally Province and Rose Lipton. In addition, animal studies at this time demonstrated the effects of sensory deprivation on the animal's well-being. The famous experiments with monkeys performed by Dr. Harry Harlow are an example of such important work.

As these research findings became more widely credited, the orphanage system in the United States became less accepted in favor of the currently used foster care system. Other countries, however, continued to place unwanted children in institutions. Many families in the United States are now adopting these post-institutionalized children from countries within Eastern Europe, China, Korea, and elsewhere. Many of these children are suffering from numerous psychological and developmental disorders.

Studies suggest that approximately 80 percent of children adopted from foreign institutions show some developmental delay at the time of entry into the United States (Johnson et al., 1992). Long-term studies of these children are few due to the relatively short time that the majority of these children have been in the United States. One study demonstrated that after approximately 3 years in the United States, 30 percent of the children continued to demonstrate language delays, 28 percent demonstrated delayed fine motor skills, and 25 percent demonstrated delayed social skills (Groze & Ileana, 1996).

The exact mechanism in the brain for the cause or etiology of these developmental problems is usually unknown. Children in an orphanage system are at risk for factors before birth, at the time of birth, and after birth that may contribute to the injury of the brain causing developmental difficulties.

Alcohol use is prominent in many of the countries, especially in Eastern European countries. This substance can have a profound negative impact on the developing neurologic system of the developing fetus.

Fetal alcohol syndrome (FAS) is a combination of clinical characteristics including growth retardation, abnormal facial features, and neurocognitive or neurobehavioral effects. But alcohol may also have a partial effect on the fetus. The child may then have only one or two of the above characteristics in a pattern that has been labeled partial fetal alcohol effects (PFAE).

Stress may also have a negative effect on the developing brain. The exact mechanism for this is unknown. Some postulated theories suggest negative effects are due to excess cortisol on the developing brain (Carlson, 1997). The brain's limbic system may also be involved. It is thought that even young infants, when exposed to severe environmental deprivation, neglect, or abuse can manifest negative developmental and psychological consequences (Frank, 1996).

Whatever the cause may be, some of the diagnoses these children may have include symptoms that include Post-Traumatic Stress Disorder (PTSD), attachment disorders, functional mental retardation, learning disabilities, sensory integration abnormalities, depression, anxiety, behavioral disturbances, personality disorders, FAS, PFAE, Attention-Deficit Hyperactivity Disorder (ADHD) and others. Children may also be diagnosed with Pervasive Developmental Disorder (PDD) and/or autism. Dr. Ronald Federici, a developmental neuropsychologist who specializes in the care of post-institutionalized children, proposes a unique type of autism sometimes seen in these children. He terms this autism: an acquired syndrome.

Unique medical problems can also be seen in these children. These may include infectious diseases, gastrointestinal problems, and heart conditions. A common medical problem that may be related to the negative effects on the brain is growth retardation. Some research has also pointed to an increased risk of early puberty onset (Proos et al., 1991).

It is very important that a child adopted from such an institution be followed by medical specialists who have experience and expertise in some of the medical, developmental, and psychiatric issues that these children and their families face. A primary pediatrician who is willing to work with subspecialists, educators and service providers is valuable. Other specialists who may be needed include a pediatric infectious disease specialist, a developmental pediatrician, a pediatric gastroenterologist (stomach doctor), a pediatric endocrinologist (hormone doctor), and a pediatric psychiatrist, among many others. The primary pediatrician, however, can coordinate appropriate referrals as needed.

The adoptive parents and siblings may have difficulty integrating the child into the family. Unfortunately, some agencies organizing such adoptions may promise a perfect child who just needs a little TLC. Families may become very frustrated if the child continues to demonstrate delays or behavioral difficulties.

Likewise, the child may have great difficulty adapting to his or her new environment. Culture shock is common. A modestly decorated home in the United States may be as stimulating as a crowded, colorful amusement park to a post-institutionalized child. Some things that we take for granted may be threatening or scary to the child who has been deprived. These things may include new foods; the introduction to warm and hot water at bath time; car rides; being outside; hugs, kisses, and other forms of physical affection. Professional assistance from individuals such as pediatric psychologists and/or pediatric and family counselors who are familiar with foreign adoption issues may be of great benefit to such families and children.

As for educational recommendations, Debra Schell-Frank, special education consultant for the Parent Network for the Post-Institutionalized Child, strongly recommends that initially these children be considered as special needs children. Parents, educators, and physicians must work together to evaluate the child's strengths and weaknesses and to offer appropriate intervention services early with close monitoring in order to help the child develop to his or her maximum potential.

Resources

The Parent Network for the Post-Institutionalized Child (PNPIC)
Tel: (724) 222-1766
Fax: (770) 979-3140
E-mail: PNPIC@aol.com

The Hughes Spalding International Adoption Evaluation Center
Tel: (404) 616-0650
Fax: (404) 616-1982
E-mail: adopt@oz.ped.emory.edu

Help for the Hopeless Child: A Guide for Families, by Dr. Ronald S. Federici.

Children with Backgrounds of Deprivation: Educational Issues for Children Adopted from Institutions, by Dr. Debra Schell-Frank.

The above two books may be obtained through the PNPIC.

REFERENCES

Carlson, M., & Earls, F. (1997). Psychological and neuroendocrinological sequelae of early social deprivation in institutionalized children in Romania. *Annals of New York Academy of Sciences, 807,* 419–428.

Federici, R. (1998). *Help for the hopeless child: A guide for families.* Alexandria, Virginia: Dr. Ronald S. Federici and Associates.

Fischer, K., & Lazerson, A. (1984). *Human development: From conception through adolescence.* New York, Oxford: W. H. Freeman.

Frank, D., Klass, P., Earls, F., & Elsenberg, L. (1996). Infants and young children in orphanages: One view from pediatrics and child psychiatry. *Pediatrics, 97,* 569–578.

Groze, V., & Ileana, D. (1996). A follow-up study of adopted children from Romania. *Child and Adolescent Social Work Journal, 13,* 541–565.

Johnson, D., Miller, L., Iverson, S., Thomas, W., Franchino, B., Dole, K., Kieman, M., Georgieff, M., & Hostetter, M. (1992). The health of children adopted from Romania. *JAMA, 268,* 3446–3451.

Proos, L., Hofvander, Y., & Tuveno, T. Menarcheal age and growth pattern of Indian girls adopted in Sweden. *Acta Paediatrica Scandinavia, 80,* 852–8.

Schell-Frank, D. (1996). *Children with backgrounds of deprivation: Educational issues for children adopted from institutions.* (ERIC Clearinghouse No: EC 302143)

Spitz, R. (1945). Hospitalism: An inquiry into the genesis of psychiatric conditions in early childhood. *Psychoanalytic Study of the Child, 1,* 53–74.

KRISTA R. BIERNATH
*The Hughes Spalding
International Adoption
Evaluation Center*

POSTLINGUAL DEAFNESS

Postlingual deafness is a general term for profound hearing loss that occurs after the normal acquisition of language and speech. It is also called acquired or adventitious deafness. Those who sustain this type of hearing loss are referred to as deafened rather than deaf.

Postlingual deafness is differentiated from prelingual deafness. The latter interferes with the normal acquisition of language and speech, and frequently affects educational achievement to such an extent that deaf students leaving special schools at the age of 18 are often 7 or 8 years behind their hearing peers (Thomas, 1984). A postlingually deafened child has learned to speak before losing his or her hearing. The child has the memory of the sound and rhythm of speech and has acquired vocabulary and grammar normally. If the child had normal hearing, even for a short time, the outlook is improved (Webster & Elwood, 1985) however not necessarily predictive of cerebral symmetry (Szelag, 1996). The education of postlingually deaf children should encourage creative thinking and verbal expression, and include vocabulary enrichment, aural rehabilitation, and the opportunity for speech refinement and maintenance (Northcott, 1984).

The etiology of acquired or adventitious hearing loss may be familial, noise-induced, by accident or illness, or, in the case of adults, the result of old age (presbycusis). The onset of a hearing loss is sometimes so gradual that it may go unnoticed for a long time. However, any hearing loss, whether acquired gradually or suddenly, that is extensive enough to interfere with the normal communication process creates a myriad of problems so complex that coping with the hearing world becomes difficult (Giolas, 1982). Formal speech-reading lessons are required in most instances. Sometimes individual hearing aids and cochlear implants (Langereis, Bosman, van Olphen, & Smoorenburg, (1997) can supplement residual hearing to facilitate communication.

Children who lose their hearing between the ages of 3 and 12 sometimes complete their education in programs for the deaf and later become the leaders and spokespeople of the deaf community. Children who lose their hearing at ages older than 12 are more likely to remain with their former hearing friends and not join the community of deaf adults (Jacobs, 1980). Modern technological devices such as hearing aids, auditory trainers, TDDs (telecommunication devices), and television decoders that display captions, are of great assistance in the education of deaf and deafened children.

REFERENCES

Giolas, T. (1982). *Hearing-handicapped adults.* Englewood Cliffs, NJ: Prentice Hall.

Jacobs, L. (1980). *A deaf adult speaks out.* Washington, DC: Gallaudet College Press.

Langereis, M. C., Bosman, A. J., van Olphen, A. F., & Smoorenburg, G. F. (1997). Changes in vowel quality in post-lingually deafened cochlear implant users. *Audiology, 36*(5), 279–297.

Northcott, W. (1984). *Oral interpreting: Principles and practices.* Baltimore: University Park Press.

Szelag, E. The effect of auditory experience on hemispheric asymmetry in a post-lingually deaf child. *Cortex, 32*(4), 647–661.

Thomas, A. (1984). *Acquired hearing loss: Psychological and psychosocial implications.* Orlando, FL: Academic.

Webster, A., & Ellwood, J. (1985). *The hearing-impaired child in the ordinary school.* Dover, NH: Croom Helm.

ROSEMARY GAFFNEY
*Hunter College, City University
of New York*

DEAF
DEAF EDUCATION

POVERTY, RELATIONSHIP TO SPECIAL EDUCATION

Poverty alone does not cause learning and behavior problems. However, poverty is associated with a variety of environmental variables that could result in the manifestation of learning and behavior problems in children. Mental retardation, learning disabilities, and emotional disturbances have all been linked to environmental circumstances associated with poverty. The vast majority of individuals with mental retardation fall into the mild category, and the majority of these children come from lower socioeconomic status families (MacMillan, 1982). Although difficult to confirm, poverty has also been linked to learning disabilities (Reid & Hresko, 1981). There is evidence that supports the lower socioeconomic environment's contribution to learning problems. Furthermore, many of these same environmental circumstances have also been linked with emotional disturbance and social maladjustment (Smith, Price, & Marsh, 1985).

Although the connection between poverty and special education is easy to establish, it is difficult to separate the many variables and determine which is the most critical to the child. This is because many of the variables are interwoven at points in the child's development. Malnutrition, poor maternal health, inadequate prenatal care, a child's poor health, homelessness (Masten, 1992) and general environmental deprivation demonstrate complex interrelationships that make it difficult to isolate a single and specific causal agent. Nevertheless, all of these factors associated with poverty have been shown to have an influence on an individual's cognitive and behavioral development.

A lower socioeconomic environment harbors many potential hazards for a developing child (Robinson & Robinson, 1976). For instance, children from these environments are exposed to greater health risks, and their health care is generally inferior to that of children from higher socioeconomic families; nutritional deficiencies are more common in poor families owing to a lack of food or adequate nutritional intake; and the use of standard English in this environment is generally poorer than it is in more affluent families.

Child rearing also takes a somewhat different form in many poor families than in middle-class families. Low-income families tend to have more children and fewer adults. Discipline in lower-income families tends to rely on punishment, especially physical punishment; middle-class families tend to rely more on reasoning, isolation, and appeals to guilt. Poor families also tend to delay training their children for independence until they are able to learn rapidly, which provides few opportunities for learning how to make mistakes without disgrace.

Another negative aspect of this environment is a restricted range of sensory stimulation. Low-income families are usually associated with restricted developmental stimulation because there are fewer objects for the child to react to (Smith, Neisworth, & Hunt, 1983). This restricted range of sensory stimulation will hinder a child's interaction with physical and social environments by providing fewer behavioral cues.

An inadequate home environment that fails to interest children and promote learning is still another environmental factor associated with poverty. It is common to find less value placed on education in lower income homes. Parents existing at the poverty level may have experienced poor academic progress themselves and dropped out of school early. They may not see education as a vehicle for their child's escape from a similar situation. After all, education did not help them escape poverty. In addition, the parents may be more concerned with day-to-day survival than the perceived value of education. Consequently, when their children ask questions; they may fail to respond or regard that behavior as an interruption.

The environmental factors mentioned are not meant to be inclusive. There are many other factors associated with poverty that also influence learning and behavior. But these factors do point out that poverty is an underlying cause for many of the negative environmental variables associated with handicapping conditions. In some cases (e.g., poor maternal nutrition and health care), these factors can affect the child's development prenatally, resulting in an organic origin for the disability (e.g., damage to brain cells). In other cases, poor environmental circumstances cause children to be ill-prepared to start school. These children lack the experiences that are common to children of higher income families and can be overcome by preservice intervention programs (Barnett, 1998; Evans, Okifuji, Engler & Bromley, 1993).

Even though these poverty factors underlie many of the negative variables associated with handicapping conditions, it must be remembered that these learning and behavior problems apply to only a small number of children. The large majority of children living in poor environments will show normal development. While these factors can cause cognitive and behavioral problems in some children, they produce no ill effects in others.

REFERENCES

Barnett, S. W. (1998). Long-term cognitive and academic effects of early childhood education of children in poverty. *Preventative Medicine, 27*(2), 204–207.

Evans, I. M., Okifuji, A., Engler, L., & Bromley, K. (1993). Home-school communication in the treatment of childhood behavior problems. *Child & Family Behavior Therapy, 15*(2), 37–60.

MacMillan, D. L. (1982). *Mental retardation in school and society* (2nd ed.). Boston: Little, Brown.

Masten, A. S. (1992). Homeless children in the United States: Math of a nation. *Current Directions in Psychological Science, 1*(12), 41–44.

Reid, D. K., & Hresko, W. P. (1981). *A cognitive approach to learning disabilities.* New York: McGraw-Hill.

Robinson, N. M., & Robinson, H. B. (1976). *The mentally retarded child* (2nd ed.). New York: McGraw-Hill.

Smith, R. M., Neisworth, J. T., & Hunt, F. M. (1983). *The exceptional child: A functional approach* (2nd ed.). New York: McGraw-Hill.

Smith, T. E. C., Price, B. J., & Marsh, G. E. (1985). *Mildly handicapped children and adults.* St. Paul, MN: West.

LARRY J. WHEELER
*Southwest Texas State
University*

**CULTURAL DEPRIVATION
CULTURAL-FAMILIAL RETARDATION
SOCIOECONOMIC IMPACT OF DISABILITIES
SOCIOECONOMIC STATUS**

POWER AND RESEARCH IN SPECIAL EDUCATION

The scientific method has evolved in such a way as to allow researchers to observe phenomena, question, formulate hypotheses, conduct experiments, and develop theories. In hypotheses testing, one compares scientific theories in the form of a statistical hypothesis (H^1) versus a null hypothesis (H^0). According to Kirk (1984), the "statistical hypothesis is a statement about one or more parameters of a population distribution that requires verification" (p. 236). An example is

$$H^1 : m > 80,$$

where the mean score of a population of children is hypothesized to be greater than 80 after participating in a remedial reading program. The statistical hypothesis is thus based on the researcher's deductions from the appropriate theory and on prior research. The null hypothesis involves formulating a hypothesis that is mutually exclusive of the statistical hypothesis. In other words, if the researcher believes that children's mean reading scores will be greater than 80 after participating in a reading program, a mutually exclusive hypothesis by which to test the researcher's premise is given by

$$H^0 : < 80.$$

If the null hypothesis is rejected, by default the statistical or alternative hypothesis is assumed to be true but not proven; it is retained as the most likely truth.

In hypothesis testing, rejection or nonrejection of the null hypothesis is based on probability. Incorrect decisions can occur in two ways. If the null hypothesis is rejected when it is in reality true, this is defined as a Type I error. Should the null hypothesis fail to be rejected when it is in fact false, a Type II error is said to have occurred. The following Table displays the possible decision outcomes.

Power is a basic statistical concept that should be taken into consideration in the design of any research study that samples data for inferential purposes. Rejecting the null hypothesis is dependent on whether the test statistic falls within a specified critical region at a particular level of significance, or alpha level (a). The probability of committing a Type I error depends on the alpha level specified. The alpha level also determines the probability of correctly accepting the true null hypothesis (1 – a). The probability of committing a Type II error is labeled b; the probability of a correct rejection is based on 1 – b, or the power level. Figure 1 illustrates the relationship among the four outcomes a, 1 – a, b, and 1 – b, or power. b and power are affected by (1) the size of the sample; (2) the level of significance (a); (3) the size of the difference between m1 and m0; (4) the size of the population; and (5) whether a one- or two-tailed test is used. One method of increasing the power of a statistical test is to increase the sample size. Figure 2 demonstrates this relationship in a correlational study.

Using power in an a priori fashion enables the researcher to compute the sample size necessary for testing the null

Decision Outcomes for Hypothesis Testing

		True State	
		H_0 True	H_0 False
Decision	Fail to reject H_0	Correct acceptance	Incorrect acceptance (Type II error)
	Reject H_0	Incorrect rejection (Type I error)	Correct rejection

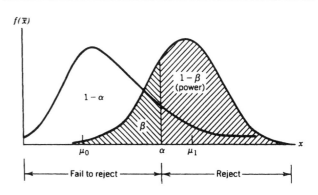

Figure 1 Relationship among power, alpha, one minus alpha, and beta

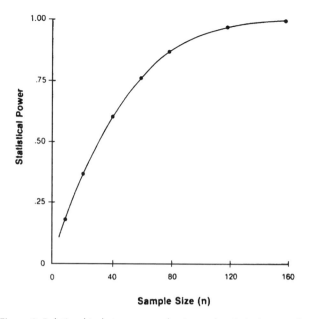

Figure 2 Relationship between sample size and statistical power for detecting a correlation of approximately .30 when $p < .05$

hypothesis, given a level of power and alpha. Often, a researcher is faced with a restricted or small sample size on which he or she wishes to determine the power level. Furthermore, in many research situations, as in evaluating special education programs, assessing the impact of a new teaching technique, or exploring the effectiveness of new medication compared with existing therapies, power allows the experimenter to consider, while in the planning stages, what effect size is needed to detect a significant difference. Similarly, the use of two-tailed tests, greater alpha levels, and small population standard deviations contribute to studies with more powerful results. However, it is worthy to note that the cost of committing a Type I error can be as damaging as committing a Type II error. Adopting a new diet program for the treatment of attention deficit children by falsely deciding that the diet is more effective than behavior therapies and medications is as serious as denying the new diet plan any effectiveness as a springboard for future research. Although power is of central consideration in research design and planning, its contribution must be weighted with other important statistical, methodological, and practical facets of the study.

REFERENCE

Kirk, R. E. (1984). *Elementary statistics* (2nd ed.). Monterey, CA: Brooks/Cole.

Mary Leon Peery
Texas A&M University

RESEARCH

PRACTICAL INTELLIGENCE

See INTELLIGENCE, PRACTICAL

PRADER-WILLI SYNDROME

First described in 1956 by Swiss physicians A. Prader, A. Labhart, and H. Willi, Prader-Willi syndrome (PWS) is a complex disorder and a rare birth defect. Common characteristics include hypotonia in early infancy, hypogonadism, short stature, and, after age 2, excessive weight gain and obesity (Cassidy, 1984). Perhaps the most outstanding characteristic of PWS is the individual's constant preoccupation with food and the compulsion to be eating all the time (Otto, Sulzbacher, & Worthington-Roberts, 1982; Pipes, 1978). This voracious craving for food finds PWS victims often exhibiting unselective and bizarre food behaviors such as eating spoiled meat, rotten vegetables, and/or cat food as well as foraging, stealing, or gorging food (Bottel, 1977; Clarren & Smith, 1977; Dykens & Cassidy, 1996; Otto et al., 1982).

The excessive appetite of PWS victims is not the only factor contributing to their obesity. They seem to require fewer calories than the average person of comparable age to maintain weight (Nardella, Sulzbacher, & Worthington-Roberts, 1983; Neason, 1978). In order to lose weight, further reduction in caloric intake is necessary, sometimes restricting the person to a 1000-calorie or less daily diet plan (Cassidy, 1984; Nardella et al., 1983).

Characteristics of PWS individuals usually include erratic and unpredictable behavior such as stubbornness, outbursts of temper, depression (Watanabe & Ohmori, 1997), and even rage (Otto et al., 1982). Personality problems, behavioral disorders, and emotional problems are frequent though not consistent findings in people with PWS (Cassidy, 1984). Many of the more aggressive behaviors escalate out of anger or desire for food.

Current research indicates that an aberration in a portion of chromosome 15 may be the cause of PWS (Nardella et al., 1983). However, PWS is not a high-risk condition and is most likely a noninherited chromosome defect (Neason, 1978). Another prevailing theory is that PWS is due to a defect within the hypothalamus and thus PWS victims never reach a sense of satiety (Clarren & Smith, 1977).

Mental retardation, particularly in the borderline to moderate range, has been considered to be an integral part of the syndrome (Cassidy, 1984; Neason, 1978). However, recent reports by Holm (1981) indicate that for many of these people, cognitive functioning is more typical of learning disabilities. That is, the child has strengths in several areas and weaknesses in others, unlike a retarded child, who tends to be developmentally delayed across skill areas. Academic weaknesses are commonly found in arithmetic, particularly in the understanding of time and the handling of money, and in writing. Reading and language commonly are mentioned as academic strengths. Holm (1981) sees the intellectual functioning of the PWS individual as a central nervous system disorder.

Because of its rarity, insufficient evidence exists on the social and emotional consequences of having PWS. However, there is no question that those afflicted with the disorder have sufficient intelligence to recognize the social stigma obesity has in our society (Cassidy, 1984). At the present time there is no known cure or treatment for PWS. The critical component of any program, however, is the constant monitoring of caloric intake. If the weight of the individual with PWS is not kept under control, death may occur at an early age from complications associated with extreme obesity.

Educational intervention for individuals with PWS should begin in early childhood with a program that assists and supports parents and children in managing eating behaviors. Food and nutrition management must be the first and foremost objective of any school program. Deliberate and calculated attempts by the teacher must be made to rid the classroom of any and all food, including pet food. Alternate reward and reinforcement systems other than food reinforcers such as candy must also be instituted. All school personnel who come in contact with the child (particularly lunchroom aides) must be made aware of the child's condition and the consequences of additional caloric intake. The child should be encouraged to stay away from food at all cost.

Physical activity designed to enhance body awareness and activities that encourage social interaction should be stressed and deliberately planned in any class with a PWS child. Academic weaknesses should be addressed as well, and particular attention should be paid to eliminating or modifying temper tantrums or extreme stubbornness by using a behavior-modification approach (Cassidy, 1984). Secondary-level students should be prepared in independent living skills such as math in daily living and vocational/occupational skills, with an emphasis on increasing the child's responsibility for weight control. Competitive employment is rare and most adults are employed in noncompetitive structured workshops and centers. At all times, in any school or workshop program, students with PWS must be watched to prevent their consuming other people's leftovers and food items.

REFERENCES

Bottel, H. (1977, May). The eating disease. *Good Housekeeping*, 176–177.

Cassidy, S. B. (1984). Prader-Willi syndrome. *Current Problems in Pediatrics, 14*(1), 18.

Clarren, S. K., & Smith, D. W. (1977). Prader-Willi syndrome: Variable severity and recurrence risk. *American Journal of Diseases in Children, 131,* 798–800.

Dykens, E. M., & Cassidy, S. B. (1996). Prader-Willi syndrome: Genetic, behavioral, and treatment issues. *Child & Adolescent Psychiatric Clinics of North America, 5*(4), 913–927.

Hom, V. A. (1981). The diagnosis of Prader-Willi syndrome. In V. A. Holm, S. Sulzbacher, & P. L. Pipes (Eds.), *Prader-Willi syndrome*. Baltimore: University Park Press.

Nardella, M. T., Sulzbacher, S. I., Worthington-Roberts, B. S. (1983). Activity levels of persons with Prader-Willi syndrome. *American Journal of Mental Deficiency, 89,* 498–505.

Neason, S. (1978). *Prader-Willi syndrome: A handbook for parents.* Longlake, MN: Prader-Willi Syndrome Association.

Otto, P. L., Sulzbacher, S. I., Worthington-Roberts, B. S. (1982). Sucrose-induced behavior changes of persons with Prader-Willi syndrome. *American Journal of Mental Deficiency, 86,* 335–341.

Pipes, P. L. (1978). Weight control. In S. Neason (Ed.), *Prader-Willi syndrome: A handbook for parents.* Longlake, MN: Prader-Willi Syndrome Association.

Watanabe, H., & Ohmori, A. K. (1997). Recurrent brief depression in Prader-Willi syndrome: A case report. *Psychiatric Genetics, 7*(1), 41–44.

Marsha H. Lupi
Hunter College, City University of New York

CHROMOSOMES, HUMAN ANOMALIES, AND CYTOGENETIC ABNORMALITIES

PRAGMATICS AND PRAGMATIC COMMUNICATION DISORDERS

Pragmatics is the study of language use independent of language structure, rules, and principles which relate the structure of language to its use (Duchan, 1995; Duchan, Hewitt, & Sonnenmeier, 1994). The rules and principles of pragmatics define who can communicate (talking, writing, signing) what, to whom, how, when, where, and why. Pragmatics includes verbal and nonverbal dimensions of communication and the rules are often implicit and dynamic. Competence in pragmatics includes the development of scripts (the stereotypical knowledge structures that people have for common routines) and schemas (hierarchical cognitive categories of synthesized scripts; Hedberg & Westby, 1993; Nelson, 1998). Social, academic, and employment schemas and scripts are important in development. The social scripts of eating at different fast-food restaurants and eating at a full-service restaurant contribute to the schema of "eating out." The academic scripts of studying for a multiple choice test, studying for an essay exam, and making a diorama contribute to the schema "doing homework." The employment scripts of knowing and following the "rules" of a job setting and knowing and using the "politics" of a job setting contribute to the schema of "employment success."

Communication registers, or codes, occur as people adapt to the social and communication demands of situations (Lane & Molyneaux, 1992). Registers are differences observable within speakers, across situations. The different registers allow speakers to convey their social position relative to that of their listeners while simultaneously communicating a message. Registers range from "frozen," which is the most distant, noninteractive form of communication code, to "intimate," a form that excludes public information. Restricted codes are the context-dependent modes of communication used with close friends and coworkers when details are unnecessary. Precise, detailed, context-independent statements that anyone can understand are elaborated codes.

Pragmatic theory suggests that every communication act has three aspects: (1) the illocutionary intent of the sender to accomplish some goal, such as to inform, request, persuade, or promise; (b) the locutionary dimension, i.e., the actual words and sentence structure of the communication act; (c) the perlocutionary effect that the act has on the receiver (e.g., did the receiver comply with the request, understand the information?; Haynes & Shulman, 1998; Hulit & Howard, 1997; Lane & Molyneaux, 1992; McLaughlin, 1998; Nelson, 1998; Owens, 1996; Paul, 1995; Wallach & Butler, 1994).

Communication style is a type of language variation that distinguishes individual speakers in different contexts. A formal, grammatically correct style, acrolect, would be appropriate for academic or some employment situations; a conversational, everyday style, mesolect, would be appropriate for conversations and some types of employment; and basolect (vulgarity) may be used by some individuals in certain situations (Muma, 1978).

Pragmatic communication disorders include violating the verbal, nonverbal, oral, and written rules of communication styles, codes, or scripts. They can interfere with social and academic aspects of the communication-learning process. Pragmatic communication disorders are seen frequently in persons with developmental or acquired disorders such as autism, blindness, deafness, language-learning disorders, mental retardation, and emotional-behavioral disorders (Duchan, 1995; Duchan et al., 1994). Individuals who are gifted and talented may also manifest pragmatic communication problems. Pragmatics of communication varies from culture to culture and should not be confused with a pragmatic language disorder.

REFERENCES

Duchan, J. F. (1995). *Supporting language learning in everyday life.* San Diego: Singular.

Duchan, J. F., Hewitt, L. E., & Sonnenmeier, R. M. (Eds.). (1994). *Pragmatics: From theory to practice.* Englewood Cliffs, NJ: Prentice Hall.

Haynes, W. O., & Shulman, B. B. (1998). *Communication development: Foundations, processes, and clinical applications.* Baltimore: Williams & Wilkins.

Hedberg, N. L., & Westby, C. E. (1993). *Analyzing storytelling skills: Theory to practice.* Tucson, AZ: Communication Skill Builders.

Hulit, L. M., & Howard, M. R. (1997). *Born to talk: An introduction to speech and language development.* Boston: Allyn & Bacon.

Lane, V. W., & Molyneaux, D. (1992). *The dynamics of communicative development.* Englewood Cliffs, NJ: Prentice Hall.

McLaughlin, S. (1998). *Introduction to language development.* San Diego: Singular Publishing Group.

Muma, J. R. (1978). *Language handbook: Concepts, assessment, intervention.* Englewood Cliffs, NJ: Prentice Hall.

Nelson, N. W. (1998). *Childhood language disorders in context: Infancy through adolescence* (2nd ed.). Boston: Allyn & Bacon.

Owens, R. E. (1996). *Language development: An introduction* (4th ed.). Boston: Allyn & Bacon.

Paul, R. (1995). *Language disorders from infancy through adolescence: Assessment and intervention.* St. Louis, MO: Mosby.

Wallach, G. P., & Butler, K. G. (1994). *Language learning disabilities in school-age children and adolescents: Some principles and applications* (2nd ed.). New York: Merrill/Macmillan College Publishing.

STEPHEN S. FARMER
New Mexico State University

PRECISION TEACHING

Precision teaching, a measurement system developed by Ogden R. Lindsley at the University of Kansas in the mid-1960s (McGreevy, 1984; Potts, Eshleman, & Cooper, 1993), involves daily measurement and graphing of student performance for the purpose of formative evaluation. Frequency of behavior (the number of occurrences divided by minutes of observation) is charted on the Standard Behavior Chart, a graph designed to highlight changes in frequency. Data are evaluated daily to determine if changes in curriculum are necessary to promote learning and progress toward performance goals (or, in the language of precision teaching, aims).

There are four steps in precision teaching. First, a precisely stated behavior or pinpoint is selected. An example of a pinpoint statement is "see word/say word." Next, frequencies of correct and incorrect responses are obtained and charted on the Standard Behavior Chart. Third, curricular events are modified to change performance in the desired direction. Finally, the graph is evaluated and instructional decisions are made according to trends in the data. Of course, these final two steps are repeated as necessary until progress allows for the attainment of aims.

The Standard Behavior Chart is a semilogarthmic or equal-ratio graph. Frequency is represented along its vertical axis as Movements/minute (M/m). Equal changes in the frequency of behavior are represented by equal distances along this Y-axis. Thus, the distance between 10 and 20 M/m is identical to the distance between 50 and 100 M/m since both represent a 2 × (times 2) change. In fact, any 2 × change, regardless of where along the Y-axis it occurs, will appear as the same distance on the Standard Behavior Chart. Behaviors ranging in frequency from 1 to 1000 minutes (.001 M/m) to 1000 in 1 minute (1000 M/m) can be represented on the Standard Behavior Chart. The unit along the X or horizontal axis is actual calendar days.

Data are obtained directly through observations of student behavior. For example, word recognition could be measured each day by counting the number of words said correctly and incorrectly per minute of reading. Also, in precision teaching, data are recorded continuously. Once recording starts, behavior is monitored without interruption until the recording period stops.

One of the principal measures used in precision teaching is celeration (Pennypacker, Koenig, & Lindsley, 1972). Celerations are standard straight line measures describing the trend of graphed data. For example, an upward trend or acceleration in correct responses and a downward trend or deceleration in incorrect responses, describe a desirable pattern. Precision teaching suggests that certain teaching decisions be based on a minimum acceptable celeration toward a performance aim. In practice, if the teacher sees the student's performance drop below acceptable minimums, then decisions are made to change some aspect of the curriculum (White & Haring, 1980). The changes are evaluated to see if restoration of student progress is obtained. Various adjustments are tried until acceptable celerations and progress toward aims are achieved.

The Figure shows examples of correct (•) and incorrect

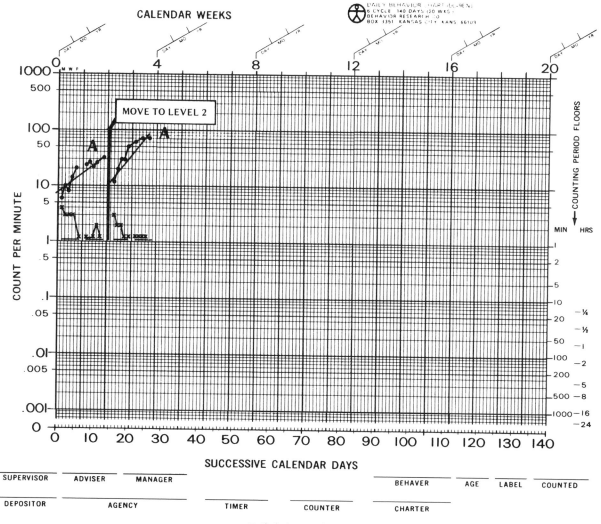

Daily behavior chart

(x) data points on a standard behavior chart. The lines drawn through the data represent celerations. Various changes in the teaching procedures are indicated by notations on the chart. The correct data are accelerating to the previously chosen performance aim the symbol "A" on the chart. Incorrect responses are decelerating. This pattern is a desirable one showing learning and growth in both accuracy and fluency (Binder, 1996) of performance. If the data change in an undesirable manner—e.g., if frequency correct decelerates and frequency wrong accelerates—then teachers must select a program adjustment and try again (Lindsley, 1971).

Thus the process of precision teaching is an optimistic one. Once responses are precisely defined, observed, and recorded, the elements of a self-correcting instructional system are in place. Teachers may not interpret failure to maintain adequate progress toward an aim as a limitation of the student. Rather, such failure signals a limitation of the existing instructional program. Their ability to solve even the most difficult instructional problems of handicapped learners is limited only by their creativity in developing program adjustments.

The *Journal of Precision Teaching* is dedicated to dissemination of data-based information about human performance and is an excellent resource. The journal is available through Louisiana State University, Special Education, 201 Peabody Hall, Baton Rouge, Louisiana 70803.

REFERENCES

Binder, C. (1996). Behavioral fluency: Evaluation of a new paradigm. *Behavior Analyst, 19*(2), 163–197.

Lindsley, O. R. (1971). From Skinner to precision teaching: The child knows best. In J. B. Jordan & L. S. Robbins (Eds.), *Let's try doing something else kind of thing* (pp. 1–11). Arlington, VA: Council for Exceptional Children.

McGreevy, P. (1984). Frequency and the standard celeration chart: Necessary components of precision teaching. *Journal of Precision Teaching, 5*(2), 28–36.

Pennypacker, H. S., Koenig, C. H., & Lindsley, O. R. (1972). *Handbook of the standard behavior chart.* Kansas City, KS: Precision Media.

Potts, L., & Eshleman, J. W., & Cooper, J. O. (1993). Ogden R. Lindsley and the historical development of precision teaching. *Behavior Analyst, 16*(2), 177–189.

White, O. R., & Haring, N. G. (1980). *Exceptional children* (2nd ed.). Columbus, OH: Merrill.

MARK A. KOORLAND
PAUL T. SINDELAR
Florida State University

DIRECT INSTRUCTION
DATA-BASED INSTRUCTION
TEST-TEACH-TEST PARADIGM

PREHM, HERBERT J. (1937–1986)

A native of Aurora, Illinois, Herbert J. Prehm obtained his BS (1959) in elementary education and psychology from Concordia Teacher's College, River Forest, Illinois, later earning both his MS in 1962 and PhD in 1964 in education and psychology from the University of Wisconsin, Madison.

Trained as an elementary school teacher and experienced as a reading consultant for children with dyslexia, Prehm maintained an interest in the learning problems of children throughout his distinguished career. As a professor of education at various universities for some 20 years, his work primarily concerned the effective teaching of mentally retarded children (Hersh & Prehm, 1977; Prehm, 1967; Prehm & Stinnett, 1970). Prehm's publications regarding the elements necessary for preparation of students in the special education field at the doctoral level was a result of this experience as a teacher and advisor of those entering the profession (Prehm, 1980).

Prehm's later work included instructional strategies for individuals with severe disabilities, with this research resulting in the development of a model allowing for controlled formal investigation of relevant variables, including handicapping condition, race, and age (Zucker & Prehm, 1984). This model was an important tool utilized in studying teaching methods via the use of results of previous investigations.

Among his numerous contributions, Prehm served as assistant executive director of the Department of Professional Development of the Council for Exceptional Children and president of the Teacher Education Division of the Council for Exceptional Children. Additionally, he was a fellow of the American Association on Mental Deficiency (now AAMR) and recipient of the TED-Merril Award for Excellence in Teacher Education. The book he coauthored with Kathleen McCoy, *Teaching Mainstreamed Students* (1987), was published only a short time after his death in 1986.

Herbert J. Prehm

REFERENCES

Hersh, R., & Prehm, H. J. (Eds.). (1977). Issues in teacher preparation. *Teacher Education & Special Education, 1*(1), 320–349.

McCoy, K. M., & Prehm, H. J. (1987). *Teaching mainstreamed students: Methods and techniques.* Denver, CO: Love.

Prehm, H. J. (1967). Rote learning and memory in the retarded: Some implications for the teacher-learning process. *Journal of Special Education, 1,* 397–399.

Prehm, H. J. (1980). Research training and experience in special education doctoral programs. *Teacher Education and Special Education, 3*(4), 3–9.

Prehm, H. J., & Stinnett, R. D. (1970). Effects of learning method on learning stage in retarded and normal adolescents. *American Journal of Mental Deficiency, 75,* 319–322.

Zucker, S. H., & Prehm, H. J. (1984). *Parameters of cumulative programming with severely / profoundly handicapped pupils.* Tempe: Arizona State University.

E. Valerie Hewitt
Texas A&M University
First edition

Tamara J. Martin
The University of Texas of the Permian Basin
Second edition

PRELINGUAL DEAFNESS

Prelingual deafness refers to profound hearing loss sustained before language has been acquired. Age at onset of profound hearing loss is a major factor because of its implications for language development. The critical age at onset of profound hearing loss is about 2 years (Quigley & Kretschmer, 1982). Children born deaf, or deafened before the age of 2 years, are prelingually deaf. Deafness is a profound degree of hearing impairment, a bilateral loss of 90 dB or greater on the audiometric scale of −10 to 110 dB (Quigley & Paul, 1984).

Prelingually deaf children rely on vision as their primary channel of communication and language acquisition. Since language plays such a important role in thinking and in conceptual growth (Webster & Ellwood, 1985), prelingually deaf children require special educational programs with emphasis on all the skills related to language and communication.

Prelingual deafness is more than the inability to hear sound. It is a pervasive handicap that, because of its effects on language and communication, has an impact on almost all aspects of child development.

REFERENCES

Forecki, M. C. (1985). *Speak to me.* Washington, DC: Gallaudet College Press.

Quigley, S., & Kretschmer, R. (1982). *The education of deaf children: Issues, theory and practice.* Baltimore: University Park Press.

Quigley, S., & Paul, P. (1984). *Language and deafness.* San Diego, CA: College-Hill.

Webster, A., & Ellwood, J. (1985). *The hearing-impaired child in the ordinary school.* Dover, NH: Croom Helm.

Rosemary Gaffney
Hunter College, City University of New York

DEAF
DEAF EDUCATION
SPEECH, ABSENCE OF

PREMACK PRINCIPLE

The original definition of reinforcement (Skinner, 1938; Spence, 1956) was circular. A stimulus could not be identified as a reinforcer until it had been tested and shown to increase the probability of a response. This left behavior modifiers with no a priori method of choosing effective reinforcers. However, Premack (1965) solved this problem of circularity by devising an independent means of determining the reinforcing power of different consequences. Premack found that under certain circumstances, an organism's own behavior can function as a reinforcer. More specifically, a less probable behavior within a person's repertoire can be strengthened by making the occurrence of a more probable behavior contingent on it.

This principle was first demonstrated in an intensive set of experiments in which Premack shifted the probability of animals drinking or running by alternately depriving them of water or activity. When drinking was made a high-probability behavior by depriving the animals of water, drinking reinforced the low-probability behavior of running. Similarly, when running was made a high-probability behavior by depriving the animals of activity, running served as a reinforcer for drinking. In both situations, low-probability behavior was increased by following it with high-probability behavior.

Moving from the animal laboratory to the applied setting is always a difficult transition. Identifying reinforcers by the Premack principle requires assessing the relative probabilities of the reinforcing behavior and the behavior to be changed by counting their rate of occurrence in a free environment. This arduous task seriously limits the usefulness of the Premack principle in applied settings. Fortunately, behavior modifiers have found it adequate to identify high-probability behaviors by asking a person about preferred activities or by casually observing the person to determine the activities from which he or she derives overt pleasure (Danaher, 1974). Once the preferred behavior is identified, the behavior modifier will allow the person to engage in that behavior only after performing the targeted low-probability or less preferred behavior. Because of this formulation, the Premack principle is sometimes referred to as "Grandma's rule" (Becker, 1971; Homme, 1971) or "you do what I want you to do before you get to do what you want to do."

Preferred activities have been frequently used in special education to reinforce or increase the rate of less preferred activities as demonstrated in the following three examples. First, in a deaf education class, Osborne (1969) allowed students to earn 5 minutes of free time, the preferred activity, for every 15 minutes they remained in their seats, the less preferred activity. Second, Hart and Risley (1968) gave economically disadvantaged children access to recreational materials contingent on the appropriate use of adjectives in spontaneous speech. Third, Kane and Gantzer (1977) showed that in a special class, academically preferred activities could be used to increase the amount of time spent in less desirable academic activities. The Premack principle has been particularly successful in the treatment of feeding disorders and diet maintenance (Amari, Grace & Fisher, 1995; O'Brien, Repp, Williams & Christophersen, 1991).

REFERENCES

Amari, A., Grace, N. C., & Fisher, W. W. (1995). Achieving and maintaining compliance with the ketogenic diet. *Journal of Applied Behavior Analysis 28*(3), 341–342.

Becker, W. C. (1971). *Parents are teachers*. Champaign, IL: Research.

Danaher, B. G. (1974). Theoretical foundations and clinical applications of the Premack principle: Review and critique. *Behavior Therapy, 5,* 307–324.

Hart, B. M., & Risley, T. R. (1968). Establishing use of descriptive adjectives in the spontaneous speech of disadvantaged preschool children. *Journal of Applied Behavior Analysis, 1,* 109–120.

Homme, L. (1971). *How to use contingency contracting in the classroom*. Champaign, IL: Research.

Kane, G., & Gantzer, S. (1977). Preferred lessons as reinforcers in a special class: An investigation of the Premack principle. *Zeitschrift fur Entwicklungspsychologie and Padagogische Psychologie, 9,* 79–89.

O'Brien, S., Repp, A. C., Williams, G. E., & Christophersen, E. R. (1991). Pediatric Feeding disorders. *Behavior Modification, 15*(3), 394–418.

Osborne, J. G. (1969). Free time as a reinforcer in the management of classroom behavior. *Journal of Applied Behavior Analysis, 2,* 113–118.

Premack, D. (1965). Reinforcement theory. In D. Levine (Ed.), *Nebraska symposium on motivation*. Lincoln: University of Nebraska Press.

Skinner, B. F. (1938). *The behavior of organisms*. New York: Appleton-Century-Crofts.

Spence, K. (1956). *Behavior theory and conditioning*. New Haven, CT: Yale University Press.

JOHN O'NEILL
*Hunter College, City University
of New York*

BEHAVIOR MODIFICATION
OPERANT CONDITIONING
POSITIVE REINFORCEMENT

PREMATURITY

Prematurity or preterm refers to infants born prior to completion of 37 weeks gestation. Although the overall survival rate of premature infants has steadily increased with advances in perinatal and neonatal care, the incidence of prematurity has not significantly changed in the past 20 years and remains at about 10 percent of all live births (Spitzer, 1996).

The exact cause of the majority of premature births remains unknown. The cause is hypothesized to be a combination of maternal, paternal, fetal, and environmental factors. Maternal risk factors for prematurity include pregnancy-induced hypertension, antepartum hemorrhage, infection, and premature rupture of membranes. Maternal social factors often contributing to prematurity are low socioeconomic status, age less than 16 or greater than 40 years, history of premature births, history of repeated abortions, non-white race, maternal substance abuse (including cigarettes and alcohol), lack of prenatal care, and poor nutritional status (Spitzer, 1996). Paternal factors include genetic makeup and older age. Fetal factors related to prematurity include presence of congenital anomalies, fetal disease, and multiple gestation. Environmental factors include stress, injury, and exposure to teratogens (Johnson, 1986). The cause of prematurity continues to be elusive, making prediction of premature births difficult.

Gestational maturity is determined by both neurological and physical characteristics (Dubowitz & Dubowitz, 1977). The premature infant's head generally appears large for its small body and the skin is bright pink, wrinkled, and translucent. The eyes remain fused until about 22–25 weeks gestation and after opening appear large for the face. The abdomen looks distended, and genitalia are not fully developed (Merenstein & Gardner, 1998). The fingernails are thin and the body is covered with fine downy hair and a layer of sebaceous skin covering. The preterm infant's arms and legs are thin and muscle tone is poor, causing it to lie in an extended position unless supported against gravity. Reflex movements are only partially developed, and breathing and crying are often spasmodic and weak (Schuster & Ashburn, 1986).

Preterm infants have physiologically immature organ systems that cause many clinical problems. These problems include immature lungs, apnea, hemorrhaging into the brain, infections of the gastrointestinal tract, poor weight gain, inability to maintain body temperature, and infection (Merenstein and Gardner, 1998).

The clinical problems often require intensive management involving a team of healthcare professionals providing multisystem support. This support may include the use of incubators, ventilators, intravenous fluids, and physiologic monitoring. Survival rates are improving, with reports of 61 percent survival of infants born between 23–26 weeks gestation. Of those infants, 6 to 36 percent survived intact without long-term handicapping conditions. The more immature the infant, the greater the incidence and severity of long-term complications. Survival rates improve and incidence of complications diminish rapidly after 26 weeks gestation (Goldsen, 1996).

The long-range sequelae of prematurity are closely associated with both prenatal and postnatal complications and the disruption of the parent-infant attachment process. Long-term sequelae include breathing disorders, retinopathy of prematurity, increased incidence of SIDS, and neurologic impairment leading to sensorimotor and developmental delays (Merenstein & Gardner, 1998).

Preterm infants may develop breathing disorders such as apnea, in which breathing is not regular and rhythmical, or bronchopulmonary dysplasia (BPD), in which the lungs are damaged and infants require supplemental oxygen and breathing support. Another potential complication is impaired vision or blindness associated with retinopathy of prematurity (ROP). Once believed to be caused solely by excess oxygen, ROP is now known to owe to many contributing factors, including the degree of prematurity, nutritional status, and exposure to light (Spitzer, 1996). Serious and sometimes devastating complications arise from intracranial hemorrhage and other forms of hypoxic brain damage. Intracranial bleeding into the ventricular system in the brain is graded in severity from I–IV (I the least damaging, IV meaning bleeding has progressed into the brain tissue itself).

Other potential long-range effects of preterm birth include lack of parent-infant attachment and delays in growth and development. Lack of attachment can be caused by separation, guilt, fear, and poor parenting skills. Attachment can be strengthened by encouraging and supporting early parent-infant interaction and involving parents in the care of their hospitalized child. Teaching parents developmentally appropriate interactions, helping them to understand their infant's cues, and encouraging skin to skin contact all help in the attachment process (Merenstein & Gardner, 1998).

Preterm infants often experience a lag in growth and development. Improved infant formulas and the increased sup-

port of breastfeeding greatly contribute to improved nutrition and growth. Environmental control of light and noise, positioning that provides containment and support, and intervention strategies that avoid overstimulation encourage normal growth and development. Early and regular developmental assessment to detect delays is important to allow for early intervention and improved outcomes for these infants.

REFERENCES

Dubowitz, L. M. S., & Dubowitz, V. (1977). *Gestational age of the newborn.* Menlo Park, CA: Addison-Wesley.

Goldsen, E. (1996). The micropremie: Infants with birthweights less than 800 grams. *Infants and Young Children, 8*(3), 1–10.

Johnson, S. H. (1986). *Nursing assessment and strategies for the family at risk: High risk parenting* (2nd ed.). Philadelphia: Lippincott.

Merenstein, G. B., & Gardner, S. L. (1998). *Handbook of Neonatal Care* (4th ed.). St. Louis, MO: Mosby.

Shuster, C. S., & Ashburn, S. S. (1986). *The process of human development. A holistic lifespan approach* (2nd ed.). Boston: Little, Brown.

Spitzer, A. R. (Ed.). (1996). *Intensive care of the fetus and neonate.* St. Louis, MO: Mosby.

ELIZABETH R. BAUERSCHMIDT
*University of North Carolina at
Wilmington*
First edition

BRENDA MELVIN
*New Hanover Regional Medical
Center*
Second edition

AMNIOCENTESIS
APGAR RATING SCALE
BABY DOE
BIRTH INJURIES
LOW BIRTH WEIGHT INFANTS

PREREFERRAL INTERVENTION

Graden, Casey, and Christenson (1985) state that the goal of a prereferral intervention model "is to implement systematically intervention strategies in the regular classroom and to evaluate the effectiveness of these strategies before a student is formally referred for consideration for special education placement" (p. 378). The prereferral intervention model is intended to prevent unnecessary referrals for psychoeducational testing for purposes of determining eligibility for special education programs. The prereferral intervention model is an indirect, consultative service, and has several advantages as an alternative to the traditional process of teacher referral, psychoeducational testing, determination of eligibility, and special education placement. It has also paralleled the movement towards inclusion (Wilson, Gutkin, Hugen, & Oats, 1998).

First, while traditional psychoeducational testing assumes the child's problem resides in the child (e.g., a learning disability, low intelligence, or a personality disorder), the prereferral intervention model assumes that the child's problems are a result of the interaction of the child's characteristics with setting and task variables. When those setting and task variables that result in improved child performance are identified through careful observation and problem-solving efforts, modifications can be implemented in the classroom without removing the child from the regular class. Second, in the traditional testing approach, if the child is found ineligible for special education services, a great deal of resources are allocated to the child, but the child does not necessarily benefit from these resources. Third, because some testing does not use instructional data, the recommendations may not have instructional ramifications. Contributing to the problem of the relevance of recommendations is the fact that the problem for which the child is referred often does not show up in the testing situation. For example, a child who is fidgety and has trouble concentrating in the classroom may demonstrate excellent concentration in the one-on-one testing relationship. In this example, the testing results and recommendations would not address the referral problem. Fourth, when special education services are the only assistance available to children with problems, teachers will refer children whose needs could be met in the less restrictive environment of the regular classroom. If consultative help were available to the teacher, the child's needs could be served through an indirect model. Fifth, indirect services serve preventive goals. If teachers can request consultation from a school psychologist or special education teacher-consultant soon after a child's problem becomes evident, more severe problems can be avoided. In the traditional testing model, children who do not qualify tend to get referred again and again by teachers until the problems are severe enough to qualify these children for special education programs. Finally, the teacher develops new knowledge and skills in consultation that will assist in providing for the needs of other children.

Because 73 percent of referred children are placed in special education (Algozzine, Christenson, & Ysseldyke, 1982), referral for testing is a critical point in the referral-testing-determination-placement process. The preferral interventions model is aimed at increasing the probability that a child referred for testing has needs that cannot be met by modifications in the regular classroom. Graden et al. (1985a) delineate four steps in the preferral intervention model. These steps occur prior to a formal referral for special education testing. First, the teacher requests consultation from the school psychologist or special education teacher-

consultant. This step may be a requirement or an option for the teacher. Second, the consultant and teacher engage in a problem-solving process that involves specifying the problem, generating alternative interventions, and evaluating the intervention. This step may be repeated. Third, if the interventions tried out during the first consultation are unsuccessful, the consultant and teacher collect additional observational data. The data include an analysis of antecedents and consequences of the child's behavior. These more detailed observations are used to plan interventions that are then implemented and evaluated. If these interventions are unsuccessful, the teacher and consultant refer the child to a child review team that reviews the problem and the data collected. This team may recommend additional data to collect or additional interventions, or it may formally refer the child for psychoeducational testing for purposes of determining eligibility for special education. If the child is referred for testing, the data collected in the prereferral phases are used to select an assessment strategy and to plan for the child's instructional needs.

The prereferral model is a consultative model. The consultant must possess the consultation skills necessary to engage the teacher in a collaborative, problem-solving process to create an open and trusting relationship with the consultee and to guide the teacher in a problem-solving sequence.

Although there have been many studies evaluating the effectiveness of consultation, few of these have evaluated consultation as a systematic strategy for reducing inappropriate referrals for special education testing. An exception is the case study by Graden, Casey, and Bonstrom (1985), they found that four out of six schools that implemented the prereferral model experienced a decrease in referrals for testing and special education placements. The authors suggest that the model was not successful in the other two schools because there was a lack of system support and the model was not fully implemented.

REFERENCES

Algozzine, B., Christenson, S., & Ysseldyke, J. E. (1982). Probabilities associated with the referral to placement process. *Teacher Education and Special Education, 5,* 19–23.

Graden, J., Casey, A., & Bonstrom. (1985). Implementing a prereferral intervention system: Part II. The Data. *Exceptional Children, 51,* 487–496.

Graden, J., Casey, A., & Christenson, S. (1985). Implementing a prereferral intervention system: Part I. The Model. *Exceptional Children, 51,* 377–384.

Wilson, C. P., Gutkin, T. B., Hagen, K. M., & Oats, R. G. (1998). General education teacher's knowledge and self-reported use of classroom interventions: Implications for consultation prereferral intervention and inclusive services. *School Psychology Quarterly, 13*(1), 45–62.

JAN N. HUGHES
Texas A&M University

PRESCHOOL SCREENING CONSULTATION
PREVENTION, PRIMARY

PRESCHOOL-AGE GIFTED CHILDREN

Services for gifted children below kindergarten age have received increased attention as a means of encouraging development of the child's potential, stimulating interest in learning, and providing support for parents. Several authors (Fox, 1971; Isaacs, 1963; Whitmore, 1979, 1980) have pointed to lack of support and intellectual challenge in the early years as one source of later underachievement among the gifted. Programs for young gifted children facilitate early interaction between parents and educators that can promote supportive parenting practices and parent advocacy (Karnes, Shwedel, & Linnemeyer, 1982). Early identification and parent training are particularly critical for gifted children from economically disadvantaged backgrounds.

Despite the need, few programs exist that are specifically designed for preschool 3- to 4-year-old children (Roedell, Jackson, & Robinson, 1980). Several factors account for the sparsity of such programs. First, lacking state and federal incentives for providing appropriate education to preschool-age gifted and talented children, few systematic procedures have been implemented for early identification and service delivery. Second, critics have questioned the reliability and validity of currently available measures for identifying giftedness in 3- and 4-year-old children. Third, parents of young gifted children frequently have little access to information about referral characteristics, available services, and need for advocacy in initiating services.

A review of current literature on gifted education, however, reveals growing recognition of the special needs of gifted and talented children in the early years (Karnes, 1983; Whitmore, 1986). Significant topics include identification procedures, characteristics, programs, and cultural issues (Sandel, McCallister, & Nash, 1993).

As indicated, one of the major obstacles to large-scale development of preschool programs for the gifted has been the concern that current measures lack reliability and validity in discriminating among children who are truly precocious, children of average ability who are early developers, and children of average ability whose high performance stems from an enriched environment. Another concern has been the efficacy of such measures in identifying gifted children who are "late bloomers." However, it has recently been argued that standardized intelligence measures truly differentiate between advanced and normal development at the preschool level (Silverman, 1986), and that giftedness should be conceptualized as significantly advanced development at the time of testing rather than as potential for adult achievement. Moreover, the imperfection of currently available measures should not preclude the delivery of services to children.

Because of concerns about reliability and validity of standardized measures when employed with young children, there is general consensus that multiple sources of data, formal and informal, should be used to identify gifted preschool-age children.

Karnes and Johnson (1986) list a number of formal instruments that have been used to assess the potential and current functioning of young gifted and talented children in intellectual, perceptual-motor, social, creative, self-concept, and musical areas. Commonly used formal measures for identifying gifted preschool-age children are the Stanford-Binet and Draw-a-Man for intelligence; the Peabody Individual Achievement Test and Woodcock-Johnson Psychoeducational Battery, Part II, for achievement; and Thinking Creatively in Action and Movement (Torrance, 1981) and the Structure of Intellect Learning Ability Tests, Primary Form (Meeker, 1984) for creativity and divergent thinking.

Informal data sources include parent and community nominations, teacher checklists, and child products (Karnes & Johnson, 1986). The Seattle Child Development Preschool Comprehensive Parent Questionnaire (Roedell, Jackson, & Robinson, 1980) provides an excellent source of data based on both parent perception and parent assessment of child performance. Pediatricians, artists, religious instructors, and other community members who are familiar with the child constitute valuable referral sources. Teacher checklists (Karnes et al., 1978a, 1978b) have been developed to assess young children's performance in a variety of talent areas. Finally, collections developed by the child as well as artistic, scientific, and other creative products provide useful assessment data.

Formal and informal data collected for each child being assessed may be reviewed by an identification/selection committee composed of professionals in gifted education, diagnostic specialists, parents, and community members. While not always possible or desirable, use of identification criteria consistent with criteria used by local school districts can facilitate children's transition to programs after preschool age.

Characteristics of young gifted children are most readily observable in comparison with other children of the same age, sex, and cultural group. Cognitively, young gifted children often display advanced vocabulary and general information, early interest in books and numbers, long attention spans, persistence and creativity in solving problems, vivid imaginations, broad or intense interests, metacognition (Moss & Strayer, 1990) unusual memory for detail, and an intense desire to know "why."

Many young gifted children also possess social-emotional characteristics such as preference for associating with older children, capacity for intense emotions, and a high level of empathy, traits that render them vulnerable to stress. Additionally, young gifted children may become frustrated by their uneven development, e.g., when their advanced thinking but average fine-motor coordination results in products that fail to meet their goals. Kitano (1985a) found characteristics of competitiveness and perfectionism in some children attending a preschool for the gifted. These socio-emotional vulnerabilities (Roedell, 1986) may become manifested in withdrawn, shy, aggressive, or attention-getting behaviors.

Program goals for gifted children in preschool settings derive from these children's cognitive, socio-emotional, and developmental characteristics and from the rationale underlying early identification: the need to provide challenge and stimulation. Goals include (1) developing a positive attitude toward oneself and toward learning; (2) developing positive social values and interaction skills, including prosocial attitudes, independence, responsibility, task commitment, and risk taking; (3) developing and using creative and higher level thinking skills; and (4) developing competency in basic skills (language, readiness, motor) and in general knowledge.

Many of the models employed in programs for elementary-age gifted children have been successfully applied to preschool-level programs. For example, programs at the University of Illinois, Champaign-Urbana (Karnes & Bertschi, 1978; Karnes et al., 1982) have incorporated Structure-of-Intellect and open classroom models. The Hunter College (Camp, 1963) and New Mexico State University (Kitano & Kirby, 1986a, 1986b) programs involve children in unit-based curricula and independent projects. The Astor program (Ehrlich, 1980) focuses on the higher level skills of Bloom's (1956) taxonomy as well as on academic skills and creative investigation. Taylor's (1968) multiple talent approach and Renzulli's (1977) enrichment triad model have also been applied to programs for preschool-level gifted children.

Experience with gifted preschool-age children over the last several years raises a number of issues that must be considered in serving this population (Kitano, 1985b). Evaluation studies of individual preschool programs for the gifted (Karnes, Shwedel, & Lewis, 1983a, 1983b; Vantassel-Baska, Schuler, & Lipschutz, 1982) indicate that young gifted children make academic, social, and affective gains if given services designed to meet their needs. However, several questions pertinent to preschool programs for the gifted have yet to be answered: Should gifted children acquire skills at an early age just because they are able to? What are the long-term effects of early identification and early education for the gifted? Does early identification as gifted alter parent expectations for the child as well as the child's self-expectations? Does enriched preschool programming render later regular education experiences redundant?

Many gifted children enter preschool programs with academic skills and knowledge well above their chronological age expectancy levels. A major focus for these children might well be the encouragement of humanistic values and prosocial motivation. Some gifted children lose their previously acquired status as top achievers when they enter homogeneously grouped preschools for the gifted. Further research might explore the effects of early identification and early education on self-concept. Finally, it is clear that many gifted preschool-age children acquire new knowledge and skills at a rapid rate. Without stimulation and challenge, some will find their first school experiences to be alienating. It is critical that preschools for the gifted facilitate the continuation of enrichment programs beyond the preschool level.

REFERENCES

Bloom, B. S. (1956). *Taxonomy of educational objectives, the classification of educational goals—Handbook I: Cognitive domain.* New York: McKay.

Camp, L. T. (1963). Purposeful preschool education. *Gifted Child Quarterly, 7,* 106–107.

Ehrlich, V. Z. (1980). The Astor program for gifted children. In *Educating the preschool / primary gifted and talented* (pp. 248–250). Ventura, CA: Office of the Ventura County Superintendent of Schools.

Fox, A. E. (1971). Kindergarten: Forgotten year for the gifted? *Gifted Child Quarterly, 15,* 42–48.

Isaacs, A. F. (1963). Should the gifted preschool child be taught to read? *Gifted Child Quarterly, 7,* 72–77.

Karnes, M. B. (Ed.). (1983). *The underserved: Our young gifted children.* Reston, VA: Council for Exceptional Children.

Karnes, M. B. et al. (1978a). *Preschool talent checklists manual.* Urbana: Institute for Child Development and Behavior, University of Illinois.

Karnes, M. B. et al. (1978b). *Preschool talent checklists record booklet.* Urbana: Institute for Child Behavior and Development, University of Illinois.

Karnes, M. B., & Bertschi, J. D. (1978). Teaching the young gifted handicapped child. *Teaching Exceptional Children, 10*(4), 114–119.

Karnes, M. B., & Johnson, L. J. (1986). Identification and assessment of the gifted/talented handicapped and nonhandicapped children in early childhood. In J. R. Whitmore (Ed.), *Intellectual giftedness in young children: Recognition and development.* New York: Haworth.

Karnes, M. B., Shwedel, A. M., & Lewis, G. F. (1983a). Long-term effects of early programming for the gifted/talented handicapped. *Journal for the Education of the Gifted, 6*(4), 266–278.

Karnes, M. B., Shwedel, A. M., & Lewis, G. F. (1983b). Short-term effects of early programming for the young gifted handicapped child. *Exceptional Children, 50*(2), 103–109.

Karnes, M. B., Shwedel, A. M., & Linnemeyer, S. A. (1982). The young gifted/talented child: Programs at the University of Illinois. *Elementary School Journal, 82*(3), 195–213.

Kitano, M. K. (1985a). Ethnography of a preschool for the gifted: What gifted young children actually do. *Gifted Child Quarterly, 29*(2), 67–71.

Kitano, M. K. (1985b). Issues and problems in establishing preschool programs for the gifted. *Roeper Review, 7*(4), 212–213.

Kitano, M. K., & Kirby, D. F. (1986a). *Gifted education: A comprehensive view.* Boston: Little, Brown.

Kitano, M. K., & Kirby, D. F. (1986b). The unit approach to curriculum planning for the gifted. *G / C / T, 9*(2), 27–31.

Meeker, M. (1984). *The structure of intellect: Its interpretation and uses.* Los Angeles: Western Psychological Services.

Moss, E., & Strayer, F. F. (1990). Interactive problem-solving of gifted and non-gifted preschoolers with their mothers. *International Journal of Behavioral Development, 13*(2), 177–197.

Renzulli, J. S. (1977). *The enrichment triad model: A guide for developing defensible programs for the gifted and talented.* Wethersfield, CT: Creative Learning.

Roedell, W. C. (1986). Socioemotional vulnerabilities of young gifted children. In J. R. Whitmore (Ed.), *Intellectual giftedness in young children: Recognition and development.* New York: Haworth.

Roedell, W. C., Jackson, N. E., & Robinson, H. B. (1980). *Gifted young children.* New York: Teachers College Press.

Sandel, A., McCallister, C., & Nash, W. R. (1993). Child search and screening activities for preschool gifted children. *Roeper Review, 16*(2), 98–102.

Silverman, L. K. (1986). What happens to the gifted girl? In C. J. Maker (Ed.), *Critical issues in gifted education.* Rockville, MD: Aspen.

Taylor, C. W. (1968). Multiple talent approach. *The Instructor, 77*(8), 27, 142, 144, 146.

Torrance, E. P. (1981). *Thinking creatively in action and movement.* Bensenville, IL: Scholastic Testing Service.

Vantassel-Baska, J., Schuler, A., & Lipschutz, J. (1982). An experimental program for gifted four year olds. *Journal for the Education of the Gifted, 5*(1), 45–55.

Whitmore, J. R. (1979). The etiology of underachievement in highly gifted young children. *Journal for the Education of the Gifted, 3*(1), 38–51.

Whitmore, J. R. (1980). *Giftedness, conflict, and underachievement.* Boston: Allyn & Bacon.

Whitmore, J. R. (Ed.). (1986). *Intellectual giftedness in young children: Recognition and development.* New York: Haworth.

MARGIE K. KITANO
New Mexico State University

GIFTED CHILDREN
GIFTED AND TALENTED, UNDERACHIEVEMENT IN THE

PRESCHOOL ASSESSMENT

See SPECIFIC TEST OR ASSESSMENT

PRESCHOOL SCREENING

Preschool screening is the evaluation of large groups of children 3 to 5 years of age with brief, low-cost procedures to identify those who may be at risk for later problems. It is based on the assumptions that early intervention should produce a significant positive effect on development, that children with developmental problems must be identified accurately as their problems are developing, and that early identification and intervention programs should be implemented without prohibitively high costs (Holland & Merrell, 1998; Lichtenstein & Ireton, 1984). While also used frequently in the field of medicine, screening in special education and related fields refers to the early identification of risk factors associated with later school achievement and social adjustment. Because of the complexity of outcomes from many early childhood health problems such as otitis media (Mandell & Johnson, 1984), screening approaches that draw from several disciplines are considered the most comprehensive (Elder & Magrab, 1980).

Historically, several movements and philosophies from various disciplines have been associated with preschool screening and have defined its methods and purposes. These movements include the early enrichment and compensatory education programs (e.g., Head Start), the Early and Periodic Screening, Diagnosis, and Treatment (EPSDT) program designed to focus on medically oriented services for children with developmental disabilities or neurological impairment, and the Education for All Handicapped Children Act (PL 94-142), and its successor legislation, the Individuals with Disabilities Education Act (IDEA) which includes "child find" provisions and mandates a broad range of special educational and related services for children with disabilities in schools.

Preschool screening can be seen as a continuum of opportunities available at any time in a child's early development. Within this larger conceptual context, procedures can be initiated before the child's birth, with the identification of mothers who possess characteristics linked with developmental or learning problems (e.g., genetic defects, maternal illness, high maternal age, exposure to drugs, toxins, and radiation, poor maternal health or nutrition during pregnancy). Factors occurring at birth or shortly thereafter can also impact a child's later development. These include anoxia, birth injury, low birth weight, and physical or sensory defects. Because some infants with known risk factors show no early signs of disability, have mild impairments, or exhibit developmental delay falling within the boundaries of normal functioning, the establishment of registries for periodic rescreening has been suggested as a strategy for identifying and monitoring the progress of these hard-to-detect children (Lloyd, 1976).

Screening activities constitute the first stage of a longer assessment process. Other stages include readiness, diagnosis, instructional-related assessment, evaluation of the results of instruction, and program evaluation (Boehm & Sandberg, 1982). Screening is sometimes confused with readiness, which focuses on a child's preparedness to benefit from a specific academic program (Meisels, 1980). All stages of the assessment process comprise a sequence proceeding from general to specific, culminating with individualized programming and ongoing monitoring of the child's progress within the intervention program (Bagnato & Neisworth, 1981). As the first stage of this process, screening does not comprise diagnostic procedures leading to recommendations about instructional programming. Rather, it involves general decision making that differentiates children in need of further assessment. This must be done with the knowledge that most screening instruments do not meet the requirements of the IDEA for educational placement. When done with proper understanding of its major purpose and the limitations of screening instruments, screening can enhance a school's or district's ability to identify and serve preschoolers with disabilities. If used to substitute for comprehensive individual examinations, it can lead to major errors in identification and educational programming (Reynolds & Clark, 1983).

Screening can be conceptualized as a process consisting of two components (Lichtenstein & Ireton, 1984). The first component, outreach, involves initial contact with parents, professionals, preschool centers, and community agencies to inform them about the services offered and to arrange for children to participate in the screening program. Other terms used to refer to this initial location of children are "child find" (Harbin, Danaher, & Derrick, 1994; Meisels, 1980), from the provisions of the IDEA (20 U.S.C. § 1412), and "case finding" (Barnes, 1982; Harrington, 1984). The major goals are to locate a target population and to maximize attendance at the actual screenings. To these ends, it has been recommended (Zehrback, 1975) that outreach procedures emphasize the growth-related needs of all children instead of developmental impairments. Thus strong case finding and publicity efforts are essential so that services will be rendered to all families rather than only to those families who have the sophistication to find out about them. (Crocker & Cushna, 1976).

An approach designed to maximize correct identification within the target population is mass screening. This refers to a program that has the goal of screening every child in the target population—a goal emphasized by the most recent iteration of the IDEA, passed in 2004, which expressly adds homeless children with disabilities to a state's obligation to identify and locate all children with disabilities (20 U.S.C. § 1412[a][3]). Such a program serves an entire preschool population; hence, there is little stigma associated with parents' positive response to the offer of screening services. Selective screening, a variation of mass screening, provides services to particular demographic subgroups or geographic areas that have a large number of unidentified children with special needs.

The second component of the screening process consists of the assessment of those children found eligible, the synthesis of information, and the determination of need for further assessment. Generally, the structure of this component is based on: (1) the kinds of questions that need to be answered; (2) the types and severity of handicapping conditions to be assessed; (3) the ages of the children; and (4) the psychometric properties of available instruments (Harrington, 1984; Scott & Hogan, 1982). Specifically, screening activities should answer whether the child is delayed enough in one or more domains (cognitive, sensory, motor, social/emotional, speech, language) to be considered at risk and in need of further diagnosis. If so, the screening should provide direction regarding what types of diagnostic assessments are needed to confirm or refute the screening impressions (Horowitz, 1982). The handicapping conditions should have a prevalence rate high enough to justify screening large numbers of children but not so high that every child must receive a diagnostic evaluation. Also, instruments should be chosen that have been normed on the ages of children represented in the target population and that have good reliability and validity. The precision of screening instruments is not as crucial as that of diagnostic instruments because of the general nature of the decisions made from them. It should be realized that individual administration maximizes the validity of test results with preschool-age children (Reynolds & Clark, 1983).

With respect to the psychometric properties of screening instruments, reliability and validity are often reported in correlational terms. These correlations provide only an approximation of a measure's accuracy in assigning individuals for further assessment (Lichtenstein, 1981). Thus a more strongly recommended method of determining a screening instrument's psychometric adequacy is in terms of classificational outcomes. In this way, validity is measured by comparing the screening decision (whether to refer a child for further evaluation) with the child's actual status as determined by a criterion measure. This is called the *hit rate* method (Lichtenstein & Ireton, 1984); it provides a direct indication of the suitability of decisions from screening. The validity of an entire screening system rests on correct understanding of the problem to be identified (the base rate), the rate of referrals for further assessment (the referral rate), and the hit rate (the percentage of children identified as needing services).

Generally, screening outcomes can be organized into screening positives (children regarded as high risk and referred for further assessment) and screening negatives (children regarded as low risk and not referred). For each child screened, four results are possible, based on the accuracy of the screening decision and the child's actual performance on criterion measures during a diagnostic evaluation. A child may be found to be in need of special services and referred by the screening procedures, or a child may be found to not need additional help. Given the possibility of error in screening decisions, however, a child may be referred by the screening procedure but not need special services (a false positive or overreferral error), or not referred but be in need of services (a false negative or underreferral error). To evaluate the consequences of using a given screening system, then, it must be determined whether children are referred at the rate intended, whether the right children are referred, and whether alternative procedures might accomplish the task more successfully. Other relevant issues are the appropriateness of the criterion measures used, the possibility of bias in the screening process (Reynolds & Clark, 1983), and strategies for maximizing parent involvement.

Given the long-held recognition that parents are vitally important in meeting the educational needs of their children, they should be involved in every phase of screening (Lichtenstein & Ireton, 1984). Not only is parent involvement mandated by IDEA, but parents also constitute a rich source of information about specific aspects of their child's development that may be unavailable elsewhere. Parents can also make sure that the assessment of their child is culturally competent. The screening of environmental influences from home and classroom settings is a rapidly growing area of research and clinical attention (Adelman, 1982).

REFERENCES

Adelman, H. S. (1982). Identifying learning problems at an early age: A critical appraisal. *Journal of Clinical Child Psychology, 11,* 255–261.

Bagnato, S. J., & Neisworth, J. T. (1981). *Linking developmental assessment and curricula.* Rockville, MD: Aspen Systems.

Barnes, K. E. (1982). *Preschool screening: The measurement and prediction of children at-risk.* Springfield, IL: Thomas.

Boehm, A., & Sandberg, B. (1982). Assessment of the preschool child. In C. R. Reynolds & T. B. Gutkin (Eds.), *Handbook of school psychology* (pp. 82–120). New York: Wiley.

Coons, C. E., Gay, E. C., Fandal, A. W., Ker, C., & Frankenburg, W. K. (1981). *The home screening questionnaire.* Denver, CO: Ladoca.

Crocker, H. C., & Cushna, B. (1976). Ethical considerations and attitudes in the field of developmental disorders. In R. B. Johnson & P. R. Magrab (Eds.), *Developmental disorders.* Baltimore: University Park Press.

Elder, J. O., & Magrab, P. R. (1980). *Coordinating services to handicapped children.* Baltimore: Brookes.

Frankenburg, W. K., van Doornick, W. J., Liddell, R. N., & Dick, N. P. (1976). The Denver Prescreening Developmental Questionnaire. *Pediatrics, 57,* 744–753.

Harbin, G., Danaher, J., & Derrick, T. (1994). Comparison of eligibility policies for infant/toddler programs and preschool special education programs. *Topics in Early Childhood Special Education, 14,* 455–471.

Harrington, R. (1984). Preschool screening: The school psychologist's perspective. *School Psychology Review, 13,* 363–374.

Holland, M. L., & Merrell, K. W. (1998). Social emotional characteristics of preschool-aged children referred for child find screening and assessment: A comparative study. *Research in Developmental Disabilities, 19,* 167–179.

Horowitz, F. D. (1982). Methods of assessment for high risk and handicapped infants. In C. T. Ramey & P. L. Trohanis (Eds.), *Finding and educating high risk and handicapped infants.* Baltimore: University Park Press.

Lichtenstein, R. (1981). Comparative validity of two preschool screening tests: Correlational and classificational approaches. *Journal of Learning Disabilities, 14,* 68–73.

Lichtenstein, R., & Ireton, H. (1984). *Preschool screening.* Orlando, FL: Grune & Stratton.

Lloyd, L. L. (1976). Discussant's comments: Language and communication aspects. In T. D. Tjossem (Ed.), *Intervention strategies for high risk infants and children* (pp. 199–212). Baltimore: University Park Press.

Mandell, C. J., & Johnson, R. A. (1984). Screening for otitis media: Issues and procedural recommendations. *Journal of the Division of Early Childhood, 8,* 86–93.

Meisels, S. J. (1980). *Developmental screening in early childhood: A guide.* Washington, DC: National Association for the Education of Young Children.

Reynolds, C. R., & Clark, J. (1983). Assessment of cognitive abilities. In K. D. Paget & B. A. Bracken (Eds.), *The psychoeducational assessment of preschool children* (pp. 163–189). New York: Grune & Stratton.

Scott, G., & Hogan, A. E. (1982). Methods for the identification of high-risk and handicapped infants. In C. T. Ramey & P. L. Trohanis (Eds.), *Finding and educating high-risk and handicapped infants.* Baltimore: University Park Press.

Zehrback, R. R. (1975). Determining a preschool handicapped population. *Exceptional Children, 42,* 76–83.

KATHLEEN D. PAGET
J. MICHAEL COXE
University of South Carolina
First and Second editions

KIMBERLY F. APPLEQUIST
*University of Colorado at
Colorado Springs*
Third edition

HEAD START
PRESCHOOL ASSESSMENT
PRESCHOOL SPECIAL EDUCATION

PRESCHOOL SPECIAL EDUCATION

Preschool special education is the delivery of therapeutic and educational services to handicapped infants and children from birth to age 6. These services are designed to provide optimum learning experiences during the crucial early childhood developmental period for children with a wide variety of handicapping conditions. The importance of the preschool years to future success has been documented by many child development authorities, who emphasize that the first 5 or 6 years of a child's life are the periods of highest potential growth in physical, perceptual, linguistic, cognitive, and affective areas (Lerner, Mardell-Czudnowski, & Goldenberg, 1981). These early periods of development are particularly important to the handicapped child, since the earlier that these children are identified and education begun, the greater the chances of lessening the impact of the handicapping condition on the child and society. A recent report by the House Select Committee on Children, Youth, and Families (1985) stated that for every dollar invested in preschool special education programs, there is a $3 reduction in special education cost later.

In 1968 Congress recognized the need for services and models of effective preschool special education programs, and the Handicapped Children's Early Education Assistance Programs (HCEEP; PL 90-583) was enacted. This act, sometimes known as the First Chance program, provided monies for the development and implementation of experimental projects for young handicapped children and their families. These projects developed effective programs for children, but they also were required to include parents in the activities, operate in-service training, evaluate the progress of both the children and the programs, coordinate their activities with the public schools and other agencies, and disseminate information on the projects (DeWeerd, 1977). Legislative support continues with IDEA Part H and Part B.

The Head Start movement, which began in 1964 as part of the War on Poverty and was funded by the Office of Economic Opportunity, was another reason for the growth of preschool special education programs. The goal of the Head Start program was to offer preschool children from economically deprived homes a comprehensive program to compensate for their deprivation. These programs involved medical care, nutrition, parent involvement, socialization, and educational intervention.

A further influence on preschool special education was the passage and implementation of PL 94-142, the Education for All Handicapped Children Act of 1975, which mandated services for all handicapped children from 3 to 5 years of age unless such a mandate conflicted with state law. This legislation provided the following two sources of funds for handicapped preschool children: state entitlement money, which depends on the number of handicapped children counted by the state in its child-find activities; and incentive grants, available to states with approved state plans that offer services for 3- to 5-year-old handicapped children (Lerner et al., 1981). Current issues of service provision under IDEA focus on eligibility continuity for children moving from early intervention programs under Part H to preschool special education programs under Part B of IDEA (Harbin, Danaher, & Derrick, 1994).

One of the important areas in preschool special education is the early identification of children with handicapping conditions. Attempts are being made to locate children who will need additional or special assistance in order to succeed in school because of physical, social, intellectual, emotional, or communications problems. The federal child-find program, which mandates states to actively seek out handicapped children, is one way to locate children who can benefit from early intervention services. Identifying children who should receive special services is a complex task because of the wide variety of needs and characteristics of the children (Lerner et al., 1981). Children with severe handicapping conditions are often identified at birth or shortly thereafter; however, many children with milder or less obvious handicaps are not so easily identified. Tjossem (1976) has presented three categories of high-risk infants. First, there are those at established risk; they have diagnosed medical disorders that are known to result in developmental delays. The early medical, social, and educational interventions used with these children are designed to help them function at the higher end of potential for those with their disorders. Second, children at biological risk have a history that suggests biological insults to their developing central nervous system. While early diagnosis is often inconclusive for these children, close monitoring and modified care are important during the developmental years. Third, children at environmental risk are those who are biologically sound, but who have early life experiences, that, without intervention, have high probability for resulting in delayed development. These early experiences could include problems with maternal and family care, health care, and opportunities for expression and stimulation. These three categories are not mutually exclusive, and when they interact, they increase the probability of abnormal development.

Being identified and placed into preschool intervention programs is a difficult process for many handicapped young children. However, for early intervention to be effective, provisions must be made for early identification and rapid entrance into community preschool special education programs (Tjossem, 1976). This identification process begins with both medical and educational screening to locate children at high risk for developmental and learning problems. Three comprehensive screening tests used in this process are the Denver Developmental Screening Test, Developmental Indicators for the Assessment of Learning, and the Developmental Screening Inventory. Once these children have been identified, the next step, a comprehensive diagnostic assessment, can be done to pinpoint a child's particular skills and deficits. The purpose of this assessment should be to prepare appropriate intervention programs. It is critical to match the assessment techniques to the needs of the individual child (Hayden & Edgar, 1977). Two criterion referenced tests that can be used for diagnosis and program planning for many children with handicaps, in many curriculum areas, are the Brigance Diagnostic Inventory of Early Development and the Learning Accomplishment Profile Diagnostic Assessment Kit. Detailed descriptions of screening instruments and diagnostic tests can be found in Lerner et al. (1981), Fallen and McGovern (1978), Safford (1978), and Salvia and Ysseldyke (1985). This assessment of handicapped children requires the expertise of many professionals and needs to be a team effort.

Identifying, screening, and assessing handicapped preschool children are meaningless tasks unless appropriate services are then provided to them (Hobbs, 1975). Once the child has been identified and diagnostic information is complete, then an appropriate program plan and curriculum must be developed. There are many different program delivery models that can be used, as well as a wide variety of philosophical bases for the programs.

Preschool special education programs have evolved from many varied theoretical positions, ranging from a child development model to precision teaching and systematic instruction. These approaches may be used with different populations, or in different environments, but they have all been shown to be beneficial. The child development model is mainly an enrichment model that provides multiple activity centers such as often found in many regular preschool programs. This is the model that many Head Start programs follow, and it is most successful with children with mild handicapping conditions. The sensory-cognitive model is based on the work of Maria Montessori. It emphasizes materials designed for the child's developmental level; these materials are presented in a carefully constructed environment. Other programs are based on the verbal-cognitive model, which draws heavily from the developmental theory of Piaget and stresses structured teacher-child interactions. A more formal approach was proposed by Bereiter and Englemann in their verbal-didactic model; this approach attempts to raise each child to the essential level for success in first grade by frequent repetition of teacher-child responses accompanied by the principles of reinforcement (Ackerman & Moore, 1976). Severely handicapped children often benefit from highly structured systematic instruction programs that rely on detailed task analysis and behavioral theory.

Other factors to be considered include the type of handicapping condition, the age of the child, and the geographical area to be served. Some programs are noncategorical and serve children from a wide variety of handicapping conditions; the Portage Project and the Rutland Center are examples. Other programs specialize in serving children from limited categories or even subcategories of handicapping conditions. One of the best known programs of this type is the Seattle Model Preschool Center for children with Down's syndrome.

The age of the child often affects where the educational services are delivered; since it is difficult to transport infants for long distances, many of the programs for younger children are home-based, with the teacher traveling to the students. As the child becomes older, programs may be center-based, with the child attending a school program or a combination of home and school program. Another factor that affects where programs are delivered is the geographic region. Sparsely populated rural regions may not have suf-

ficient numbers of children within a reasonable distance of a school; therefore, they may rely on more home-based services than might be found in large urban areas. Examples of home-based projects are the Portage project, the Marshalltown project, and Project SKI*HI; the Precise Early Education of Children with Handicaps (PEECH) project, the Chapel Hill project, and the Magnolia Preschool are all combined home- and center-based programs. Center-based programs include the Rutland Center, the Seattle Model Preschool Center, and the UNISTAPS project. These programs were all originally supported by HCEEP funding and are representative of many programs across the United States (Karnes & Zehrbach, 1977).

The actual curriculum content in preschool special education programs varies depending on the needs of the children; however, in most cases, the programs are based on one or more of the following approaches. Some preschool special education curricula are organized around an amelioration of deficits approach, which builds the curriculum based on an assessment of a child's problems; the content areas are directed toward correcting identified deficits. Other programs use a basic skills area approach. In this, curricula are organized around skills or processes such as attention, language, sensory motor processes, social skills, perception, auditory processes, gross and fine motor skills, self-help skills, and memory. The developmental tasks approach uses sequences of normal development to derive the curricula. The content areas in this approach are broad categories of child development that are task analyzed and sequenced. Finally, the educational content approach begins with areas of academic content; it defines areas of learning on the basis of preacademic or academic content. The most often included areas are prereading, numbers, music, art, dance, play, storytelling, social studies, and nature. In many cases these various approaches are combined to develop appropriate educational programs (Wood & Hurley, 1977).

A crucial component to any preschool special education program is parent involvement. As stated by Shearer & Shearer (1977), there are several reasons to involve parents in their child's education. The parents are the consumers and often want to participate in the education of their children. When parents are taught how to teach their children, they can help transfer what is being learned in school to the home environment. These teaching skills can also be used in new situations, and with the handicapped child's siblings, making the parents better teachers of all their children. Research has shown that significant gains made by children are often lost when the school programs end. A key factor in preventing this is the effective involvement of parents. In addition, if parents are knowledgeable about their child's program, they can be advocates for the services that the child needs; this skill can be used all through the child's life.

Recent research studies have demonstrated the effectiveness of preschool special education programs for handicapped young children. Karnes et al. (1981) presented a review of many studies that examined the efficacy of preschool special education. While there are some methodological questions about early studies by Skeels and Dye, the research, in general, has shown that early stimulation and preschool attendance make a significant difference in the rate of growth of children, and that these gains are maintained over time. It has been shown that diverse curriculum models can be equally effective in promoting school success if high standards of quality are maintained (Schweinhart & Weikart, 1981). In addition, inclusive programming for there children is being heavily supported (Cavallaro, Ballard-Rosa, & Lynch, 1998; Holland, Guitierrez, Morgan, Brennan, & Zercher, 1997).

A longitudinal study of the Perry Preschool Program (Schweinhart & Weikart, 1981) has provided a strong argument for preschool special education programs. This study followed 123 children from age three through the school years. It found that those children who attended preschool had consistently higher school achievement, higher motivation, fewer placements in special education programs, and less delinquent behavior. An economic benefit-cost effectiveness analysis of the Perry Preschool Program was conducted; it found that there was a 248 percent return on the original investment when savings from lowered costs for education, benefits from increases in projected earnings, and value of mothers' time released when the child attended preschool were considered.

There are many reports of successful preschool special education programs. While many of these programs differ greatly in the populations they serve, their theoretical bases, and their curriculum content, their effectiveness has been demonstrated. It is essential that these benefits be recognized, and that programs for all handicapped preschool children be supported.

REFERENCES

Ackerman, P., & Moore, M. (1976). Delivery of educational services to preschool handicapped children. In T. Tjossem (Ed.), *Intervention strategies for high risk infants and young children* (pp. 669–689). Baltimore: University Park Press.

Cavallaro, C. C., Ballard-Rosa, & Lynch, E. W. (1998). A preliminary study of inclusive special education services for infants, toddlers, and pre-school children in California. *Topics in Early Childhood Special Education, 18*(3), 169–182.

DeWeerd, J. (1977). Introduction. In J. Jordan, A. Hayden, M. Karnes, & M. Wood (Eds.), *Early childhood education for exceptional children* (pp. 2–7). Reston, VA: Council for Exceptional Children.

Fallen, N., & McGovern, J. (1978). *Young children with special needs.* Columbus, OH: Merrill.

Hanson, M. J., Gutierrez, S., Morgan, M., Brennan, E. L., & Zercher, C. (1997). Language, culture, & disability: Preschool inclusion. *Topics in Early Childhood Special Education, 17*(3), 307–336.

Hayden, A. (1979). Handicapped children, birth to age three. *Exceptional Children, 45,* 510–517.

Hayden, A., & Edgar, E. (1977). Identification, screening, and assessment. In J. Jordan, A. Hayden, M. Karnes, & M. Wood (Eds.), *Early childhood education for exceptional children* (pp. 66–93). Reston, VA: Council for Exceptional Children.

Hayden, A., & Gotts, E. (1977). Multiple staffing patterns. In J. Jordan, A. Hayden, M. Karnes, & M. Wood (Eds.), *Early childhood education for exceptional children* (pp. 236–253). Reston, VA: Council for Exceptional Children.

Harbin, G., Danaher, J., & Derrick, T. (1994). Comparison of eligibility policies for infant/toddler programs and preschool special education programs. *Topics in Early Childhood Special Education, 14*(4), 455–471.

Hobbs, N. (1975). *The futures of children.* San Francisco: Jossey-Bass.

Karnes, M., Schwedel, A., Lewis, G., & Esry, D. (1981). Impact of early programming for the handicapped: A follow-up study into the elementary school. *Journal of the Division for Early Childhood, 4,* 62–79.

Karnes, M., & Zehrbach, R. (1977). Alternative models for delivering services to young handicapped children. In J. Jordan, A. Hayden, M. Karnes, & M. Wood (Eds.), *Early childhood education for exceptional children* (pp. 20–65). Reston, VA: Council for Exceptional Children.

Lerner, J., Mardell-Czudnowski, C., & Goldenberg, D. (1981). *Special education for the early childhood years.* Englewood Cliffs, NJ: Prentice Hall.

Safford, P. (1978). *Teaching young children with special needs.* St. Louis, MO: Mosby.

Salvia, J., & Ysseldyke, J. (1985). *Assessment in special and remedial education* (3rd ed.). Boston: Houghton Mifflin.

Schweinhart, L., & Weikart, D. (1981). Effects of the Perry Preschool Program on youths through age 15. *Journal of the Division for Early Childhood, 4,* 29–39.

Select Committee on Children, Youth, and Families. (1985). *Opportunities for success: Cost effective programs for children.* Washington, DC: U.S. Government Printing Office.

Shearer, M., & Shearer, D. (1977). Parent involvement. In J. Jordan, A. Hayden, M. Karnes, & M. Wood (Eds.), *Early childhood education for exceptional children* (pp. 208–235). Reston, VA: Council for Exceptional Children.

Swan, W. (1981). Efficacy studies in early childhood special education: An overview. *Journal of the Division for Early Childhood, 4,* 1–4.

Tjossem, T. (1976). Early intervention: Issues and approaches. In T. Tjossem (Ed.), *Intervention strategies for high risk infants and young children* (pp. 3–33). Baltimore: University Park Press.

Wood, M., & Hurley, O. (1977). Curriculum and instruction. In J. Jordan, A. Hayden, M. Karnes, & M. Wood (Eds.), *Early childhood education for exceptional children* (pp. 132–157). Reston: VA: Council for Exceptional Children.

DEBORAH C. MAY
State University of New York at Albany

PRESCHOOL ASSESSMENT
PRESCHOOL SCREENING

RACHEL TOPLIS
Falcon School District 49,
Colorado Springs, Colorado

MENTAL RETARDATION

PRESIDENT'S COMMITTEE FOR PEOPLE WITH INTELLECTUAL DISABILITIES

President's Committee for People with Intellectual Disabilities changed its name from President's Committee on Mental Retardation in July 2003, through an executive order signed by President George W. Bush. As stated on the PCPID website (2006), PCPID is a federal advisory committee, established by presidential executive order to advise the President of the United States and the Secretary of the Department of Health and Human Services on issues concerning citizens with intellectual disabilities, coordinate activities between different federal agencies, and assess the impact of their policies upon the lives of citizens with intellectual disabilities and their families. PCPID was initially organized as a blue-ribbon panel by President John F. Kennedy in 1961 and formally established as a committee by President Lyndon B. Johnson in 1966 under an executive order. Eight years later, in 1974, new goals for the committee, focusing on deinstitutionalization, prevention, and legal rights were established by President Nixon. In 1996, a new set of goals for the committee encouraging full community inclusion and citizens' rights were created by President William J. Clinton.

The committee produces an annual report to the President which is the product of members of the committee resulting from a variety of committee conferences. All committee activities include input from self-advocates (consumers), family members, professionals, researchers, service providers, state agency leaders, and direct support professionals. The members of the President's Committee for People with Intellectual Disabilities have taken the New Freedom Initiative introduced by President George W. Bush in February 2001 and built their work around the same basic categories: expanding educational opportunities, increasing access to technology, improving individual and family support, increasing employment and economic independence, and promoting access and integration into community life. PCPID offices are located at Aerospace Center, Suite 701, 370 L'Enfant Promenade, SW Washington DC 20447.

REFERENCE

President's Committee for People with Intellectual Disabilities (PCPID). (2006). http://www.acf.hhs.gov/programs/pcpid/pcpid_about.html

TAMARA J. MARTIN
The University of Texas of the
Permian Basin

PREVENTION, PRIMARY

This term refers to efforts made to reduce the incidence or prevalence of handicapping conditions through the establishment of medical and social programs that attempt to change those conditions responsible for their development. During the past 30 years, several approaches have been emphasized that have resulted in significant progress in the prevention of handicapping conditions.

A number of programs have been developed to provide neonatal care for those children delivered at risk. Some of these programs have been effective in reducing various postnatal factors that result in retardation. For example, infant stimulation programs have been established in hospitals to facilitate the development of low-birth-weight or high-risk infants (Brown & Hepler, 1976). These programs use such measures as involving mothers in infant stimulation techniques, making infants in incubators more attractive to staff who interact with them by placing ribbons on them, and providing intensive follow-up services to both mothers and infants. These programs have been brief and the results somewhat time-limited, but they have resulted in increased attention to opportunities for preventive intervention models.

It is widely recognized that a small proportion of children are mentally retarded because of organic causes; the majority are retarded because of environmental and cultural deficiencies, poverty, and inadequate child-rearing approaches (Grossman, 1983). Massive social changes that address these causes must occur to achieve comprehensive prevention of mental retardation and other handicapping conditions.

The President's Committee on Mental Retardation set a goal of preventing the occurrence of 50 percent of all cases of mental retardation by the year 2000 (President's Committee on Mental Retardation, 1976). As a result, research has been done on virtually all known causes of mental retardation. Patton, Payne, and Beirne-Smith (1986) indicate that for each cause, a specific preventive measure has been found. The most fruitful approaches to prevention include carrier detection, prenatal monitoring, and newborn screening. Combinations of these approaches appear to be more successful in preventing various handicapping conditions than the use of individual techniques (Sells & Bennett, 1977). Prevention is often approached within the framework of determining cause. The major causes appear to result from infections and intoxications, trauma or physical agents, disorders of metabolism and nutrition, gross brain disease, unknown prenatal influence, and chromosomal abnormalities (Grossman, 1983).

Preventive measures implemented during the preconception period can significantly reduce hereditary, innate, congenital, and other constitutional disorders. Adequate prenatal care and analysis for possible genetic disorders are two general approaches to prevention usually associated with the gestational period. Yet one out of every four women who gives birth in a hospital has never received prenatal care from a physician during her pregnancy (Koch & Koch, 1976). Anticipating potential problems that may occur at delivery can avert problems during the perinatal period. For example, anoxia (lack of oxygen to the brain that may cause mental retardation and other learning problems) is a condition that can be prevented (Kirk & Gallagher, 1979).

Environmental intervention, adequate nutrition, and avoidance of hazards constitute the bulk of preventive measures during the childhood period. For example, a high correlation between ingestion of lead in drinking water and mental retardation has been reported (Gearheart, 1980; Needleman, 1994).

Blood-screening techniques can be used to identify some conditions (e.g., Tay-Sachs disease) transmitted through autosomal recessive genes or x-linked genes. Using several screening procedures, Thoene et al. (1981) identified seven metabolic disorders caused by an enzyme deficiency. Because of the low incidence rate of most conditions, carriers are so rare that general screening procedures would have to involve massive numbers of people to be effective (Westling, 1986). Thus genetic screening is most often used by those who have already had one child with a disorder or who are aware that the condition exists in their family.

Monitoring the fetus prior to birth has resulted in the identification of over 100 inherited disorders (Sells & Bennett, 1977). Amniocentesis (drawing some of the amniotic fluid surrounding the fetus for cellular examination) is used to detect three types of problems: those identified through the chromosomal structure, those identified through enzyme deficiencies, and neural tube defects. Milunsky (1976) indicated that women who are over 35, couples in which one parent is a balanced carrier of translocation, and couples who have already had one Down's syndrome child are the three groups that most frequently seek chromosomal analysis through amniocentesis. The use of fetoscopy permits the physician to insert a small tube through the mother's abdominal wall to examine parts of the fetus. This permits the determination of physical characteristics that may be useful in determining whether a disorder exists. Senography consists of the use of ultrasound waves to outline the fetus and identify structures indicative of handicapping conditions (e.g., spina bifada, microcephaly) through different densities. Rh incompatibility may be prevented through Rh gloubulin injections for the Rh-negative mother after the birth of her first Rh-positive child or after a miscarriage.

Newborn screening tests permit the identification of many infants with inborn errors of metabolism (e.g., galactosemia, phenylketonuria). In some cases, mental retardation may be prevented by altering the diet (Carpenter, 1975). Hypothyroidism can also be detected through birth screening using the same blood samples used with phenylketonuria (Dussualt et al., 1975). Since some diagnostic indicators develop slowly during the first 6 months, the newborn screening should be followed with additional testing during later infant examinations.

Avoidance of certain substances (e.g., drugs, alcohol, X-rays) is the only current source of prevention for some disorders. Avoidance behavior can sometimes be the only method of prevention, as in the case of HIV/AIDS (Kelly, Murphy, Sikkema, & Kalichman, 1993). Preconceptual vaccinations can fight some bacterial infections (e.g., rubella, syphilis). Yet it has been estimated that 25 percent of children, older girls, and young women in the United States are not protected against rubella (Gearheart, 1980). A Caesarean-section birth may be used with women who have a herpes virus at the time of delivery. Postnatal causes that can often be prevented include direct trauma to the head, cerebral hemorrhage, lesions on the brain, infections that cause conditions such as encephalitis and meningitis, and electric shock. Although controversy still surrounds the role that chronic malnutrition plays in mental development, there is evidence that it can result in a greater risk of infection and increased likelihood of disease from other agents (Westling, 1986).

REFERENCES

Brown, J., & Hepler, R. (1976). Care of the critically ill newborn. *American Journal of Nursing, 76,* 578–581.

Carpenter, D. G. (1975). Metabolic and transport anomalies. In C. H. Carter (Ed.), *Handbook of mental retardation syndromes* (3rd ed.). Springfield, IL: Thomas.

Dussault, H. H., Coulombe, P., Laberge, C., Letarte, J., Guyda, H., Khoury, K. (1975). Preliminary report on a mass screening program for neonatal hypothyroidism. *Journal of Pediatrics, 86,* 670–674.

Gearheart, B. R. (1980). *Special education for the 80s.* St. Louis, MO: Mosby.

Grossman, H. J. (1983). *Classification in mental retardation.* Washington, DC: American Association on Mental Deficiency.

Kelly, J. A., Murphy, D. A., Sikkema, K. J., & Kalichman, S. C., (1993). Psychological interventions to prevent HIV infection: New priorities for behavioral research in the second decade of AIDS. *American Psychologist, 48*(10), 1023–1034.

Kirk, S. A., & Gallagher, J. J. (1979). *Educating exceptional children* (3rd ed.). Dallas: Houghton Mifflin.

Koch, R., & Koch, J. H. (1976). We can do more to prevent the tragedy of retarded children. *Psychology Today, 107,* 88–93.

Milunsky, A. (1976). A prenatal diagnosis of genetic disorders. *New England Journal of Medicine, 295,* 377–380.

Needleman, H. L. (1994). Preventing childhood lead poisoning. *Preventative Medicine, 23*(5), 634–637.

Patton, J. R., Payne, J. S., & Beirne-Smith, M. (1986). *Mental retardation* (2nd ed.). London: Merrill.

President's Committee on Mental Retardation. (1976). *Mental retardation: The known and the unknown.* Washington, DC: U.S. Government Printing Office.

Sells, C. J., & Bennett, F. C. (1977). Prevention of mental retardation: The role of medicine. *American Journal of Mental Deficiency, 82,* 117–129.

Thoene, J., Higgins, J., Krieger, I., Schmickel, R., & Weiss, L. (1981). Genetic screening for mental retardation in Michigan. *American Journal of Mental Deficiency, 85,* 335–340.

Westling, D. L. (1986). *Introduction to mental retardation.* Englewood Cliffs, NJ: Prentice Hall.

LONNY W. MORROW
*Northeast Missouri State
University*

SUE ANN MORROW
EDGE, Inc.

GENETIC COUNSELING
INBORN ERRORS OF METABOLISM
PHENYLKETONURIA
PREMATURITY

PREVOCATIONAL SKILLS

Secondary handicapped students may have difficulty in learning vocational concepts because they have not mastered prerequisite basic skills that serve as the foundation for many vocational activities. Three areas closely related to vocational skills are reading skills such as vocabulary, comprehension, and the use of a glossary; mathematic skills such as time, measurement, and application of algorithms; communication skills, including listening, speaking, and writing.

Essential to learning vocational skills is a set of hands-on exploratory experiences that will help each individual to answer self-awareness questions and develop work values. Examples of hands-on experiences include setting up a printing press, practicing laboratory safety, and following directions. These prevocational hands-on activities help students to identify materials, tools, and processes, discover physical properties of materials, measure sizes and quantities, compute costs, and develop social skills (Phelps & Lutz, 1977).

A student's success in a vocational program is influenced by his or her readiness to participate. Readiness skills are often identified as prevocational knowledge and attitudes. Brolin and Kokaska (1979) identified three curriculum areas with 22 major competencies. The areas and skills are (1) daily living (i.e., managing family finances, caring for personal needs, and engaging in civic activities); (2) personal-social abilities (i.e., interpersonal relationships, problem solving, independence); (3) occupational guidance and preparation (i.e., knowing and exploring occupational possibilities, work habits, and behaviors; being able to seek, secure, and maintain satisfactory employment).

Several factors can be considered predictors of vocational development for handicapped individuals. These include achievement of basic academic skills, adaptive behavior, verbal manners and communication skills, performance on vocational checklists, and actual samples of work behavior (Forness, 1982). A closer look at these predictors indicates that assessing a handicapped individual's vocational potential by evaluating his or her academic and social skills within the context of a work-related situation is valuable. Skills learned in a classroom setting may not generalize when applied to work settings. One step toward achieving generalization of academic skills is to develop a technique to assess applied academic and social skills. Neff (1966) suggested four approaches to the evaluation of the work potential of handicapped individuals. They are the mental testing approach, the job analysis approach, the work sample approach, and the situational assessment approach.

REFERENCES

Brolin, D. E., & Kokaska, C. J. (1979). *Career education for handicapped children and youth.* Columbus, OH: Merrill.

Forness, S. R. (1982). Prevocational academic assessment of children and youth with learning and behavior problems. In K. P. Lynch, W. E. Kiernan, & J. A. Stark (Eds.), *Prevocational and vocational education for special needs youth.* Baltimore: Brooks.

Neff, W. S. (1966). Problems of work evaluation. *Personnel and Guidance Journal of Mental Deficiency, 44,* 682–688.

Phelps, A. L., & Lutz, R. J. (1977). *Career exploration and preparation for the special needs learner.* Boston: Allyn & Bacon.

KAREN L. HARRELL
University of Georgia

VOCATIONAL EVALUATION
VOCATIONAL REHABILITATION COUNSELING
VOCATIONAL EDUCATION

PRIMARY IMMUNODEFICIENCY DISORDERS

This classification of health-related disorders encompasses over fifty distinct, genetically determined illnesses and does not include HIV, AIDS, or secondary causes such as chemotherapy. The incidence of these disorders range from 1 in 500 to 1 in 1,000,000, with approximately 25,000 patients identified in the United States at the time of this submission. As the title suggests, these disorders affect the immune system, and though most are congenital (patients are born with them), symptoms may not become apparent until adulthood.

Perhaps the most famous case of primary immunodeficiency disorders involved David, "the bubble boy" in Houston, Texas. His particular type of disorder involved several different parts of his immune system, causing severe susceptibility to infections from all viruses and bacteria. David lived 12 courageous years inside a sterile environment. Though the immune system disorders were first recognized in the mid 1950s, David's ordeal advanced our understanding of immune deficiencies, autoimmune disorders, cancer, and infection process in general.

As with David, children and adults with primary immunodeficiency disorders are susceptible to infectious diseases. Some experience chronic, recurrent, unusual, invasive, or severe infections, and have multiple concurrent conditions before the immune system is evaluated. Some of these disorders are treatable by replacing the portions of the immune system that is missing. An example would be intravenous gamma globulin (IVIG; a product containing antibodies from pooled human plasma donations) for patients with X-linked aggamaglobulinanemia or Common Variable Immunodeficiency. Patients with one particular disorder were the first to undergo "gene therapy," in which affected cells were removed and DNA containing the normal genes was inserted. When these cells were reintroduced to the patient, the symptoms of their disorder were relieved, allowing a decrease in reliance on costly, complicated medical therapies. Similar to David's story, these patients have contributed to a very promising new field of study that may help most genetically determined illnesses (i.e., cystic fibrosis, sickle cell anemia, and so on).

Due to the chronic nature of these disorders and their sequelae, many of those affected alter their lifestyle to preserve their health. Most patients and family members quickly become experts in their particular disease and must be accepted as such in order to create the most "normal" lifestyle possible. The most common obstacles to overcome are those associated with absences from work or school. Absences may frequently occur due to illnesses or the need for doctor visits and therapy. Anticipation of this need allows for unique, innovative solutions. Homebound programs and dual enrollment options provide the flexibility needed to adapt to this unusual situation. As always, open communication between school officials, families, physicians, and students is required. Often, the school setting provides the opportunity for affected children to become more responsible for their own health care. Public education, though it results in increased infection exposure, is usually well tolerated by patients whose immune systems are being reconstituted. Outbreak of any infectious diseases (such as measles, chicken pox, hepatitis A, or influenza) should result in immediate notification of patients so that physicians can decide on the appropriate course of action.

Other special needs may be required on an individual basis, not as a direct result of the immune disorders but due to the sequelae of repeated infections. Some examples include special diets, frequent meals or special restroom privileges due to intestinal malabsorption, hall passes or scheduled nursing visits for medication administration, or assignment of classes to minimize absences.

Physicians, patients, and families should be flexible to work within the school system when possible, scheduling routine care around important times and dates; however, they must also rely on the patience, compassion, and understanding of others in their lives to reach the goals set by the patients themselves. Further information and support can be obtained from the Immune Deficiency Foundation at 25 West Chesapeake Avenue, Suite 206, Towson, MD, 21204.

REFERENCE

Immune Deficiency Foundation. (1998). *Informational brochure.* Towson, MD: Author.

STEPHEN E. MILES
SUSIE WHITMAN
Immune Deficiency Foundation

AIDS DYSMORPHIC SYNDROME
CHRONIC ILLNESS IN CHILDREN
NATIONAL ORGANIZATION FOR RARE DISORDERS
OFFICE OF RARE DISEASES, NATIONAL INSTITUTES OF HEALTH
OTHER HEALTH IMPAIRED

PRIMARY MENTAL ABILITIES TEST

The Primary Mental Abilities Test (PMA; Thurstone & Thurstone, 1965) is a group-administered measure of both general intelligence and specific intellectual factors that the authors call primary mental abilities. In earlier versions of the PMA, six to eight primary mental abilities were identified. Subsequently, this number was reduced to the current five factors. There are six levels of the test (K–1, 2–4, 4–6, 6–9, 9–12, and adult). The adult test is identical to that for grades 9–12. No attempt was made to prepare adult norms, and no additional psychometric characteristics at the adult level are included in the documentation.

A description of the behaviors sampled by the five subtests of the PMA is provided by Salvia and Ysseldyke (1978). Verbal meaning assesses one's ability to derive meaning from words. Number facility assesses one's ability to work with numbers, to handle simple quantitative problems rapidly and accurately, and to understand and recognize quantitative differences. Reasoning requires a person to solve problems logically. Perceptual speed assesses quick and accurate recognition of similarities and differences in pictured objects or symbols. Spatial relationships assesses ability to visualize how parts of objects or figures fit together, what their relationships are, and what they look like when rotated in space. The presence of and emphasis given to each of the specific intellectual factors within the various levels reflect the judgment of the authors as to their relative importance within each grade level. Only one level (grades 4–6) includes all five factors; perceptual speed is omitted from levels 6–9 and 9–12 and reasoning is omitted from K–1 and 2–4.

The test has several technical limitations. Standardization of the scale was based only on geographic, age, and grade stratification; reliabilities of the subtests are not included for K–1 and are relatively low for the other levels (Salvia & Ysseldyke, 1978). The test-retest reliability estimates for total scores range between .83 and .95 and may be deemed satisfactory, while the reliability estimates for the levels vary considerably from one grade to another and frequently are too low to be used with confidence (Quereshi, 1972). As expected, the total score is superior to any of the subtest factor scores in predicting grades in separate school subject areas (Milholland, 1965). The PMA was developed using techniques to demonstrate that there are several factors involved in intelligence and learning. Yet, the total score is superior to single factors in predicting achievement in any one subject area. This contradicts the theoretical underpinnings of the test itself.

Historically, the PMA occupied a prominent position in the development of cognitive tests. The original series, published between 1938 and 1941, was based on extensive factor analytic work and represented a major contribution to test construction. The high aspirations held for the PMA battery reflected in early reviews were never realized (Schutz, 1972). While the Thurstones continued to contribute to both multifactor science and technology after the PMA was commercially available, very little of this new knowledge and technology found its way back into subsequent PMA revisions. Thus the PMA soon became outstripped by competing tests in terms of technical quality and functional utility. Because of the technical superiority of other instruments assessing similar abilities, reviewers have questioned the continued use of the PMA (Quereshi, 1972; Schutz, 1972).

REFERENCES

Milholland, J. E. (1965). SRA Primary Mental Abilities, Revised. In O. K. Buros (Ed.), *The sixth mental measurements yearbook* (pp. 1048–1050). Highland Park, NJ: Gryphon.

Quereshi, M. Y. (1972). SRA Primary Mental Abilities (1962 ed.). In O. K. Buros (Ed.), *The seventh mental measurements yearbook* (pp. 1064–1066). Highland Park, NJ: Gryphon.

Salvia, J., & Ysseldyke, J. E. (1978). *Assessment in special and remedial education* (pp. 293–295). Boston: Houghton Mifflin.

Schutz, R. E. (1972). SRA Primary Mental Abilities (1962 ed.). In O. K. Buros (Ed.), *The seventh mental measurements yearbook* (pp. 1066–1068). Highland Park, NJ: Gryphon.

Thurstone, L., & Thurstone, T. (1965). *Primary Mental Abilities Test.* Chicago: Science Research.

JEFF LAURENT
THOMAS OAKLAND
University of Texas

PRIVATE SCHOOLS AND SPECIAL EDUCATION

Prior to the passage of the Education for All Handicapped Children Act of 1975 (PL 94-142), private schools that existed to provide services to disabled children were mainly tuition-based, profit-making institutions that held the parents responsible for costs. With the passage of PL 94-142, it became the local education agency's responsibility to provide a free, appropriate, public education to all children regardless of severity of disability.

Until 1977, handicapped children, especially those with severe handicapping conditions, had fewer, consistent options for receiving educational services. Although many school districts had developed programs, especially for the less severely disabled, there were still areas of the United States where children remained at home without an education, were institutionalized without an education, or received private education at the parents' expense (Bajan & Susser, 1982).

After 1977, local education agencies began to quickly develop or expand their own programs to meet this new responsibility. There still remained those few students for whom appropriate services could not be provided, either because of the severity of their disability or because of a lack of appropriate numbers of a specific handicapping condition within the local education agency. These are the students who were typically enrolled in private schools as of 1985. Public Law 94-142 and subsequent amendments also mandated that it was the local education agency's (LEA) responsibility to provide the tuition for those students that the LEA placed in private schools (McQuain, 1982). Although it is clear that the LEA must be responsible for paying the tuition for students who are in private placement as a result of LEA placement, it is unclear as to the responsibility for payment for those students who are in church-related or other private schools at the request of the parent or a social agency (Wylie, 1981). For example, if a child's handicapping condition necessitates placement in a residential school to provide education, the placement, including nonmedical care and room and board, becomes the responsibility of the LEA. If placement is for noneducational concerns, home or community problems, then the LEA is responsible only for the educational costs. It sometimes becomes extremely difficult to separate education from other needs (McQuain, 1982).

Some decisions have been made by the courts related to placement issues. A program must be state approved to receive tuition payments from the LEA (Grumet & Inkpen, 1982). If an appropriate program exists within the LEA for a child, the LEA will not be responsible for private tuition (McQuain, 1982). Parents are not entitled to reimbursement for tuition as a result of voluntary placement in nonapproved schools (Grumet & Inkpen, 1982), unless a clear case can be made that the program was appropriate and the LEA failed to take timely and appropriate action in evaluation or placement. The decision as to whether a child should attend a private school should involve the availability of an appropriate program in the LEA, the proximity of the program to home, the severity of the handicapping condition, and the provision of related services (Guarino, 1982). The LEA must ensure that all children in private placement receive the same rights and procedures that they would receive if in public placement (Grumet & Inkpen, 1982). Therefore, the LEA, in conjunction with the state education agency, has the responsibility to monitor the programs in the private sector.

Within the continuum of services concept, a private placement is seen as most restrictive because of the inability to mainstream. Therefore, being placed in a residential setting, a child must first receive the full benefit of opportunities provided within the LEA (Grumet & Inkpen, 1982).

A recent Supreme Court decision has lifted restrictions on on-site instruction, and the 1997 IDEA amendments helped to clarify an LEA's obligation to provide services to parochial school students (Osborne, DiMattia, & Russo, 1998).

Audette (1982) described additional areas in which concerns must be addressed in the future. These include transportation, coordination of individual education plans, artificiality of environment of private placement, rising costs of placement, unanticipated placements, and due process issues. The questions about whether parochial school students with disabilities must have the same level of service as their peers, and on-site services remain and need to be satisfied (Osborne et al., 1998).

REFERENCES

Audette, D. (1982). Private school placement: A local director's perspective. *Exceptional Children, 49*(3), 214–219.

Bajan, J. W., & Susser, P. L. (1982). Getting on with the education of handicapped children: A policy of partnership. *Exceptional Children, 49*(3), 208–212.

Grumet, L., & Inkpen, T. (1982). The education of children in private schools: A state agency's perspective. *Exceptional Children, 49*(3), 100–106.

Guarino, R. L. (1982). The education of handicapped children in private schools. *Exceptional Children, 49*(3), 198–199.

McQuain, S. (1982). Special education private placements: Financial responsibility under the law. *Journal of Educational Finance, 7*(4), 425–435.

Osborne, A. G., DiMattia, P., & Russo, C. J. (1998). Legal considerations improving special education services in parochial schools. *Exceptional Children, 64*(3), 385–394.

Wylie, R. J. (1981). The handicapped child and private education. *Journal of Adventist Education, 8*(9), 35–36.

SUSANNE BLOUGH ABBOTT
*Bedford Central School District,
Mt. Kisco, New York*

**INDIVIDUALS WITH DISABILITIES EDUCATION IMPROVEMENT ACT OF 2004 (IDEIA)
MAGNET SCHOOLS
MAINSTREAMING**

PRIVILEGED COMMUNICATION

Privileged communication is a legal concept which protects the communications within certain professional relationships from disclosure in a court of law without the client's consent. Privileged relationships have historically included the attorney-client and spousal privileges, which are based in common law traditions, and clergy-communicant and physician-patient relationships, which have been established by statute in all fifty states and U.S. territories. All fifty states have also enacted privileged communication laws covering licensed psychiatrists and psychologists and their patients. Only a few states, however, have included other counselors and psychotherapists, licensed or unlicensed, under their privilege statutes.

Privileged communication laws are an exception to most rules of evidence for court proceedings, which generally work to promote the discovery of any relevant information. Privilege exists in response to society's acknowledgement that the effectiveness of certain relationships depends upon allowing clients to speak freely within the professional relationship, with the assurance that what is said within that relationship will remain private and will not later be used against the person's interests. All groups that have received privileged status have done so because they made the successful argument that their ability to help their clients would be seriously impaired or even destroyed if they were forced to reveal confidential information against the client's wishes.

Legal privilege must be distinguished from confidentiality; though they are related in the sense that both address conditions in which professional communications may or may not be disclosed, they originate from different sources and provide different levels of protection from unwanted disclosure. Confidentiality is a professional duty to refrain from disclosing client information gained during the course of the professional interaction with a client, and is based upon the ethical standards and rules of the various professions. In addition, confidentiality requirements have been incorporated into legislation and the licensure laws of every state, prohibiting certain professionals from revealing client information without client consent, and specifying the conditions under which confidentiality may or must be broken (Knapp & Vandecreek, 1996). Confidentiality is not, however, protected when the professional is required to testify in court.

In contrast, privilege "is an exception to the general rule that the public has a right to relevant evidence in a court proceeding . . . " (Smith-Bell & Winslade, 1994, p. 184), and is based in privileged communication laws enacted by state legislatures and Congress. Thus, privilege is strictly a legal principle, applies only in legal situations, and is the only legally permissible basis for a professional's refusal to disclose client information in a legal court. The distinction between confidentiality and privilege is, most simply, that confidentiality *restricts* what the professional can reveal without the client's consent, whereas privilege *relieves* the professional from revealing client information in court.

However, there are a number of statutory limitations to both confidential and privileged communications. The most common exceptions to privilege require the professional to disclose privileged information when (a) there is reason to believe the client may be a danger to him or herself or others (b) child abuse is suspected, (c) the client puts his or her own mental state at issue, and (d) various other conditions are present, as specified by individual state statutes, such as elder abuse, sexual abuse by a psychotherapist, in malpractice suits against one's therapist, among others.

A recent Supreme Court case has established new and important precedent regarding the psychotherapist-patient privilege. In the case of *Jaffe* v. *Redmond* (1996), the Court held "the confidential communications between a licensed psychotherapist and the psychotherapist's patient in the course of diagnosis or treatment are protected from compelled disclosure under Rule 501 of the Federal Rules of Evidence" (p. 338). This finding addressed two major problems in the privileged communication arena: it effectively established a federal psychotherapist-patient privilege for the first time, and it extended the privilege to licensed "psychotherapists," thus acknowledging the many professionals, other than physicians and psychologists, who provide mental health services that warrant privileged status. Although the Court's finding is binding only in federal courts, it delivers clear guidance to state courts and legislatures through its message about the importance the nation's highest Court gives to therapeutic relationships.

Privileged communication laws are not, however, applicable to most educational settings, including special education contexts. Educators have not been included in the groups whose communications with clients have been afforded privileged status, with the possible exception of doctoral-level, licensed school psychologists. The *Jaffe* v. *Redmond* case discussed above did extend privilege to a master's

level therapist, but did not address whether privilege would apply to any educational setting. It is possible that school counselors, if they are licensed, could make a case for the need for privileged communication in certain circumstances, but this has not happened to date. Thus, communications with school counselors and other education professionals must be disclosed in court when required.

In summary, privileged communication is a legal concept that protects the communications between certain groups of professionals and their clients from disclosure in court. Most education professionals are not currently covered under these statutes, however, and thus their communications with students and parents are not protected from disclosure in legal proceedings. Legal views of privilege are continuing to evolve on both state and federal levels, and new statutes and interpretations are most likely to appear in the future.

REFERENCES

Jaffe v. *Redmond,* 135 L.Ed.2d 337 (S. Ct. 1996).

Knapp, S., & VandeCreek, L. (1997). *Jaffe* v. *Redmond:* The Supreme Court recognizes a psychotherapist-patient privilege in federal courts. *Professional Psychology: Research and Practice, 28,* 567–572.

Smith-Bell, M., & Winslade, W. J. (1994). Privacy, confidentiality, and privilege in psychotherapeutic relationships. *American Journal of Orthopsychiatry, 64,* 180–193.

KAY E. KETZENBERGER
*The University of Texas of the
Permian Basin*

CONFIDENTIALITY OF INFORMATION

PROBLEM SOLVING, CREATIVE

See CREATIVE PROBLEM SOLVING.

PROCEDURAL SAFEGUARDS

See DUE PROCESS.

PROCESS ASSESSMENT OF THE LEARNER–TEST BATTERY FOR READING AND WRITING

The Process Assessment of the Learner–Test Battery for Reading and Writing (PAL-RW; Berninger, 2001), uses a variety of tasks to assess children's development of reading and writing processes. According to the author, the PAL-RW can be used to screen by identifying students at risk for reading or writing problems, monitor by tracking student progress in early intervention and prevention programs, and diagnose by evaluating the nature of reading, or writing-related processing problems.

The PAL-RW includes the following subtests (with examples given):

Alphabet Writing (speed of writing lowercase letters of the alphabet from memory in 15 seconds)

Receptive Coding

> Task A: student is shown a word (AT) for 1 second, then shown IT. Are the words the same?
>
> Task B: student is shown a word (BAT) for 1 second, then shown C. Is the letter in the word?
>
> Task C: student is shown a word (ATE) for 1 second, then shown ET. Are the two letters in the word in the correct order?
>
> Task D: student is shown a word (MOTHER) for 1 second, then shown L. Is the letter in the word?
>
> Task E: student is shown a word (SOCIETY) for 1 second, then shown EI. Are the two letters in the word in the correct order?

Expressive Coding

> Task A: student is shown a word (QAST) for 1 second, and then must write the word.
>
> Task B: student is shown a word (LADFUST) for 1 second, and then must write the third letter.
>
> Task C: student is shown a word (POGDUS) for 1 second, and then must write the last three letters.

Rapid Automatic Naming (RAN)

> Rapid Letter Naming: student names letters as fast as he or she can. (Item 1: m t g k b h r a n; Item 2: fi ps er ou.)
>
> Rapid Word Naming: student names words as fast as he or she can. (dog eat of sit over.)
>
> Rapid Digit Naming: student names numbers as fast as he or she can. (Item 1: 3 7 8 1 9 6 2; Item 2: 67 89 45 73.)
>
> Rapid Word and Digit Naming: student names Words and Digits as fast as he or she can. (tea eat 56 of 89 over.)

Note-Taking Task A: Listen to a story and take notes as it is read.

Rhyming

> Task A: Listen to three words and tell which one does not have the same sound. (ball call help.)
>
> Task B: (The word is PIG. Tell me all the real words you can that rhyme with PIG.)

Syllables: Hear a word (both real and made-up), say the word, and now say it with a sound left out. (PUTTING. Say PUTTING. Now say it without the PUT.)

Phonemes: Hear a word (both real and made up), say the word, then say it with a sound left out, and then say what sound was left out. (SIT. Say SIT. Now say IT. What sound is missing?)

Rimes: Say a word (real or made up) with a sound left out. (Say BIKE without /b/.)

Word Choice: Student is shown three words, indicate the one which is spelled correctly. (PIG PAG PIZE.)

Pseudoword Decoding: Read some words that are not real words. (DRIY HAFFE STROC.)

Story Retell: After being read a short story, student answers questions and then retells story in his or her own words.

Finger Sense

> Repetition (1 and 2): Touch thumb to index finger 20 times (right and left hands); scored for completion time).
>
> Succession (1 and 2): Touch thumb to each finger five complete times (right and left hands; scored for completion time).
>
> Localization: After having one finger touched out of sight, tell which finger was touched.
>
> Recognition: Each finger is assigned a number. After having one finger touched out of sight, tell what number of the finger was touched.
>
> Fingertip Writing: After having a letter "written" onto a fingertip, tell which letter was written.

Sentence Sense: Read three sentences and tell which one makes sense.

> I ATE THE CAKE.
>
> I EIGHT THE CAKE.
>
> I ATE THE CAPE.

Copying: Here is a sentence (or paragraph). Copy it as fast as you can.

> Task A: THE LAZY BOY JUMPED OVER A BALL.
>
> Task B: paragraph

Note-Taking Task B: Take the notes created earlier (Note-Taking Task A) and write a paragraph based on the notes.

The PAL-RW was normed in 1999–2000 on 868 individuals in grades K–6 from around the United States and was stratified for sex, race/ethnicity, parental education, and geographic region. Normative sampling is adequate (>100 at each grade, ranging from 105 in grade 6 to 142 in grade 1). All scores are based upon the grade of the child tested, not the chronological age.

Test-retest comparisons based on 86 children in grades 1, 3, and 5 tested a second time 14 to 49 days later show reliabilities that ranged from .61 to .92. Five measures had reliabilities below .70. Of the 14 tests, seven had lower scores on retest.

RON DUMONT
Farleigh Dickenson University

JOHN O. WILLIS
Rivier College

PROCESS TRAINING

See ABILITY TRAINING.

PRODUCTION DEFICIENCY

Production deficiency is closely tied to mediation theory (Flavell, 1970). Mediation refers to the intervention of some process between the initial stimulating event and the final response (Reese & Lipsitt, 1970). Special education students are often unable to "mediate" or use other task-appropriate strategies as intermediate steps in the learning process (Torgersen, 1977). Such inability may be due to special education students being inactive learners lacking goal-directed motivation (Torgerson, 1977), or the learning environment not stimulating mediational interventions with the learner (Kozulin, & Falik, 1995).

Additional research in this area has resulted in an alternative explanation to those previously mentioned; special education students' poor academic performance may reflect a production deficiency (Naron, 1978; Wong, 1980). A production deficiency suggests that a student may have the ability to use the mediation strategy or another strategy but fails to spontaneously and appropriately produce it (Wong, 1980). For these children, prompting and training in metacognition and related processes might prove helpful.

REFERENCES

Flavell, J. H. (1970). Developmental studies in mediated memory. In H. W. Reese & L. P. Lipsitt (Eds.), *Advances in child development and behavior.* New York: Academic.

Kozulin, A., & Falik, L. (1995). Dynamic cognitive assessment of the child. *Current Directions in Psychological Science, 4*(6), 192–196.

Naron, N. K. (1978). Developmental changes in word attribute utilization for organization and retrieval in free recall. *Journal of Experimental Child Psychology, 25,* 279–297.

Reese, H. W., & Lipsitt, L. P. (1970). *Experimental child psychology.* New York: Academic.

Torgersen, J. K. (1977). The role of nonspecific factors in the task performance of learning disabled children: A theoretical assessment. *Journal of Learning Disabilities, 10,* 27–34.

Wong, B. Y. L. (1980). Activating the inactive learner: Use of questions/prompts to enhance comprehension and retention of implied information in learning disabled children. *Learning Disability Quarterly, 3,* 29–37.

JOHN R. BEATTIE
University of North Carolina at Charlotte

MEDIATIONAL DEFICIENCY

PRO-ED, INCORPORATED

PRO-ED is a publishing company that deals exclusively in the disability area (i.e., special education, counseling, rehabilitation, psychology, and speech/language pathology). The product line focuses on assessment measures, remedial and therapy materials, professional books, and periodicals. Among the latter are the following journals: *Journal of Learning Disabilities, Journal of Special Education, Remedial and Special Education, Intervention in School and Clinic, Reclaiming Children and Youth, Focus on Autism and other Developmental Disabilities, Topics in Early Childhood Special Education, Journal of Emotional and Behavioral Disorders.* PRO-ED is a privately held corporation founded in 1977. Its current address is 8700 Shoal Creek Blvd, Austin, Texas, 78757-6897, www.proedinc.com.

DONALD D. HAMMILL
PRO-ED, Inc.

RASE
TECSE

PROFESSIONAL COMPETENCIES FOR WORKING WITH CULTURALLY AND LINGUISTICALLY DIVERSE STUDENTS

Students in public schools today look, sound, learn, and live in ways that differ from past populations. Of the 45 million students enrolled in public and private elementary and secondary schools, over 30 percent are from groups designated as racial/ethnic minorities (Gonzalez, Brusca-Vega & Yawkey, 1997). In addition, many students are at risk for school failure because they live in poverty, live in a single-parent family, or have a poorly educated mother (Pallas, Natriello, & McDill, 1989). Therefore, culture, as used in this article, refers to differences in race and ethnicity as well as socioeconomic status, beliefs, values, modes of expression, ways of thinking, and ways of resolving problems. The competencies listed below represent minimal competencies that teachers working with culturally and linguistically diverse students with exceptionalities (CLDE) should have.

Culture

All educators working with CLDE students should (1) understand culture in relation to child-rearing practices, socialization systems, and differences in attitudes toward education and motivation; (2) understand cross-cultural patterns, practices, and attitudes and their effect on learning and behavior; (3) understand diversity in behavior and learning styles; and (4) understand the historical origins of local communities (Baca & Almanza, 1991).

Language

As there is considerable research to suggest that inclusion of minority students' language and culture into the school program is a significant predictor of academic success, all educators working with CLDE students should (1) understand the basic concepts regarding the nature of language; (2) understand the theories of first and second language acquisition; (3) identify and understand regional, social, and developmental varieties in language use; and (4) encourage parents to provide appropriate language models for their children, whether that be English or another language (Baca & Almanza, 1991). Educators should be able to use functional language and purposeful conversational interactions (Tharp, 1994). If educators are not fluent in the student's native language, they will need to work in collaboration with their bilingual and ESL colleagues.

Consultation and Collaboration

The basic collaboration abilities needed by educators working with CLDE students have been identified by Harris (1991, 1996). The first is "to understand one's own perspective." Educators should be able to understand their own cultures and their relationship to other cultures. Educators also need to understand their own beliefs and expectations, especially regarding the abilities of students from various cultures.

The second collaborative ability is "the effective use of interpersonal, communication, and problem-solving skills." Educators must be caring, respectful, empathetic, congruent, and open in collaborative interactions. They must be able to communicate clearly and effectively in oral and written form. For effective cross-cultural communication, educators must be aware of cultural differences in communication and relationships and, when necessary, use interpreters appropriately. Educators should be familiar with the kinds of information that can be easily interpreted and conduct pre- and post-sessions with interpreters so that the language and intent of communications are clearly expressed. Educators must be able to grasp and validate overt as well as covert meanings and affects in communication. They also must be able to interview effectively to elicit information, explore problems, and set goals and objectives for the collaboration (Harris, 1991, 1996).

The third ability is "to understand the roles of collaborators." In a multicultural society, educators should be able to facilitate problem-solving sessions with individuals with different values and problem-solving styles and collaborate with culturally diverse personnel (Harris, 1996). Therefore,

educators working with CLDE students need to be familiar with familial and institutional objectives relevant to CLDE students, and understand the resources that can be provided by other personnel such as bilingual educators, ESL educators, parents, and paraprofessionals (Harris, 1991).

Working with Families and Communities

According to Baca and Almanza (1991), educators who work with CLDE students should be able to plan and provide for the direct participation of parents and families of CLDE students in the instructional program and related activities. They should also know local community resources for CLDE students.

Assessment

Alternative assessment models have been present over the last two decades in response to inconsistencies found with students from culturally and linguistically diverse backgrounds (Mercer & Rueda, 1991). Therefore, it is of critical importance for educators to be able to use a wide variety of alternative assessments with CLDE students. Because language assessment is key to documenting the difference between language difference and language disability, educators working with CLDE students should know existing assessment procedures and instruments in language proficiency, language dominance, and language development, as well as cognitive/intellectual development, social-emotional behavior, adaptive behavior, and achievement. They should also be able to adapt evaluation procedures to compensate for potential cultural and linguistic biases of the assessment process (Baca & Almanza, 1991).

Curriculum

Educators working with CLDE students should know and understand the philosophies and content of general education, bilingual education, special education, bilingual special education, multicultural education, and ESL (Baca & Almanza, 1991), because these programs may represent the least restrictive environment for CLDE students.

Instructional Planning

Educators working with CLDE students should be able to use data from language and achievement assessment to plan instructional programs and determine appropriate instructional goals and objectives. They should be able to monitor the effectiveness of instructional programs and modify them when needed to meet the unique needs of CLDE students (Baca & Almanza, 1991). Educators also need to plan for the instructional roles of other adults, e.g., paraprofessionals, bilingual educators, and ESL educators.

Instruction

All educators should be able to adapt instruction, use ESL strategies, and use appropriate behavior management strategies. Educators should have, as a primary objective, the establishment of a classroom climate that fosters successful experiences for *all* students (Baca & Almanza, 1991).

Materials

Educators working with CLDE students should know sources for materials appropriate for students from various cultural and linguistic backgrounds and should be able to evaluate materials in terms of their quality, availability, and appropriateness. The materials educators use should stimulate active, meaningful, and purposeful involvement of students (Baca & Almanza, 1991).

REFERENCES

Baca, L. M., & Almanza, E. (1991). *Language minority students with disabilities.* Reston, VA: Council for Exceptional Children.

Gonzalez, V., Brusca-Vega, R., & Yawkey, R. (1997). *Assessment and instruction of culturally and linguistically diverse students with or at-risk of learning problems: From research to practice.* Boston: Allyn & Bacon.

Harris, K. C. (1991). An expanded view on consultation competencies for educators serving culturally and linguistically diverse exceptional students. *Teacher Education and Special Education, 14*(1), 25–29.

Harris, K. C. (1996). Collaboration within a multicultural society: Issues for consideration. *Remedial and Special Education, 17*(6), 355–362, 376.

Mercer, J. R., & Rueda, R. (1991, November). *The impact of changing paradigms of disabilities on assessment for special education.* Paper presented at The Council for Exceptional Children Topical Conference on At-Risk Children and Youth, New Orleans, LA.

Pallas, A. M., Natriello, G., & McDill, E. L. (1989). The changing nature of the disadvantaged population: Current dimensions and future trends. *Educational Researcher, 18,* 16–22.

Tharp, R. G. (1994, June). *Cultural compatibility and the multicultural classroom: Oxymoron or opportunity.* Paper presented at the Training and Development Improvement Quarterly Meeting, Albuquerque, NM.

KATHLEEN C. HARRIS
Arizona State University

PROFESSIONAL SCHOOL PSYCHOLOGY

Professional School Psychology is the official journal of Division 16 of the American Psychological Association. *Professional School Psychology* in intended as a forum to promote and maintain high standard of preparation for professional school psychologists and effective delivery of school psychological services. The journal publishes empirically and theoretically based papers intended to reflect a cross-section of school psychology and suitable for a broad readership. Papers that analyze, synthesize, reformulate, or offer an empirical or conceptual perspective to issues involving the underpinnings of the profession, the delivery and evaluation of services, ethical and legal aspects, and approaches to education and training are encouraged. Of special interest are articles that outline innovative professional procedures with rigorous, theoretical, and empirical support.

The type of manuscripts published in *Professional School Psychology* includes theoretical pieces, literature reviews, models of professional practice, policy examinations, ethical/legal manuscripts, major addresses, interviews, proceedings from national or international conferences or symposiums, miniseries devoted to special topics in the field of school psychology, and reviews of books and materials. *Professional School Psychology* is published quarterly by Lawrence Erlbaum Associates.

THOMAS R. KRATOCHWILL
University of Wisconsin at Madison

PROFESSIONAL STANDARDS FOR SPECIAL EDUCATORS

Professional standards for special educators are rules and guidelines governing the conduct of persons who work in special education. The development of competency standards is an attempt to increase the overall quality of service in the field and to strive for excellence in the profession. In 1966 the Council for Exceptional Children developed Professional Standards for Personnel in the Education of Exceptional Children. In 1979 the council approved Guidelines for Personnel in the Education of Exceptional Children. These standards did not include formal definable criteria for determining whether a teacher had acquired the necessary competencies. The most recent set of standards published by the council (*Exceptional Children*, 1983) consists of three policy statements focusing on common requirements for the practice of special education: Code of Ethics, Professional Practice, and Standards for the Preparation of Special Education Personnel. These statements describe the philosophical position of special education professionals, the skills the specialists should exhibit in their jobs, and how training organizations should best prepare future special educators.

The development of competency standards for special educators is important for a variety of reasons. One is to increase the consistency and quality of service across the special education field. Another is to require excellence so that it may translate into greater academic and social achievements for the students with disabilities being served. Standards also serve as a way to measure the quality of performance of special educators. They help protect the profession from embracing techniques or skills that are based more on subjectivity than on empirical data. Heller (1983) suggested that if professionals in special education do not oversee themselves, someone else will.

Standards of professional competence for special educators describe expectations in two general categories of duties: those that are necessary for successful and ethical treatment of persons labeled with special needs, and those that are necessary for the growth and stature of the field of special education. The specific details can be found in *Exceptional Children* (1983). Professionals have several obligations, including the use of their training to help those with special needs. Their methods must be appropriate and effective. Special educators must also use techniques to manage behavior that are ethical, humane, and consistent with existing rules and regulations. Aversive techniques may not be used except as a last resort. Professionals also serve the parents of exceptional children by communicating clearly and by soliciting and using their advice and information. Parents should be informed of all matters related to their particular situations and of the rights afforded them by law. Special educators should serve as advocates for the exceptional person in a variety of ways—changing government policy, monitoring adequacy of available resources, and protecting the individual rights of the special needs person. Special educators also have the responsibility of keeping abreast of new developments and findings in special education.

Professional standards exist to guide the conduct of special education professionals. One way to ensure that special educators are influenced by these standards is for all institutions that prepare special education teachers and professionals to provide for their students the most current standards and to incorporate those standards into the educational process (Standards for the Preparation of Special Education Personnel, 1983). At the state and national levels, any licensing or accreditation requirements in existence could be compared with the profession's standards and adjusted accordingly.

Once the development and implementation of the standards are completed, professionals in the field need to concentrate their efforts in three areas. First, the development of continuing or in-service education must address the competencies needed by professionals already in the field (Stedman, Smith, & Baucom, 1981). Second, as mentioned by Gersten (1985), efforts should focus on which teacher competencies actually make a difference to people with special needs (Englert, 1983). Interviewing experts to develop professional competencies (Zane, Sulzer-Azaroff, Handen,

& Fox, 1982) is useful in developing a large number of skills and standards that seem logical, but such a strategy is insufficient in that it does not provide for a determination of whether such skills are functionally related to student improvement. Third, updating and changing of the standards must continue (Standards for the Preparation of Special Education Personnel, 1983). The validation process is one way that new skills and competencies will become known and incorporated into the standards as the nature of the field changes and the needs of the developmentally disabled shift over time. By validating them, updating as needed, and incorporating them into institutions that train special educators, the standards will become an integral part of the training of special educators and will achieve the original purpose for their development—producing qualified professionals and providing maximum improvement of persons with special needs.

REFERENCES

Englert, C. S. (1983). Measuring special education teacher effectiveness. *Exceptional Children, 50,* 247–254.

Gersten, R. (1985). Direct instruction with special education students: A review of evaluation research. *Journal of Special Education, 19,* 41–58.

Heller, H. H. (1983). Special education professional standards: Need, value, and use. *Exceptional Children, 50,* 199–204.

Standards for the preparation of special education personnel. (1983). *Exceptional Children, 50,* 210–218.

Stedman, D. J., Smith, R. R., & Baucom, L. D. (1981). Toward quality in special education programs. In D. Stedman & J. Paul (Eds.), *New directions for exceptional children: Professional preparation for teachers of exceptional children* (No. 8). San Francisco: Jossey-Bass.

Zane, T., Sulzer-Azaroff, B., Handen, B. L., & Fox, C. J. (1982). Validation of a competency-based training program in developmental disabilities. *Journal of the Severely Handicapped, 7,* 21–31.

THOMAS ZANE
Johns Hopkins University

ETHICS
TEACHER EFFECTIVENESS

PROFILE VARIABILITY

Profile variability is an index of test scatter (individual variation in test scores between or within various psychological and educational tests) first defined by Plake, Reynolds, and Gutkin (1981). It is used as a diagnostic aid in determining the degree of intratest variability in an individual's performance on the subtests of any multiscale assessment device. A large degree of within test scatter has long been held to be an indicator of the presence of a learning disability (Chalfant & Scheffelin, 1969).

Test scatter has typically been determined by range (the highest minus the lowest score for an individual on a common family of tests), or by the number of test scores deviating at a statistically significant level from the individual's mean score on all tests administered (the latter sometimes is referred to as the number of deviant signs, or NDS). Profile variability is similar in some respects to range, but it is more accurate, more stable, and more powerful than older indexes of scatter. Profile variability encompasses data from all tests or subtests administered to an individual. It is not limited to the two most extreme scores as is the range.

Calculation of the index of profile variability is straightforward because it is the variance of a set of scores for one person on more than one measure, hence, the name profile variability. Profile variability for each member of a group or population can be estimated to be (Plake et al., 1981):

$$S^2 = \sum_{j=1}^{k} \frac{(x_{ij-\bar{x}_i})}{k-1}$$

where S^2 = the index of profile variability

x_{ij} = the score of person i on test or subtest j

$\bar{x}_j$ = the mean score for person i on all tests (k) administered

k = the number of tests administered

The resulting value can then be compared with data taken from the standardization sample of a test or some other group to determine whether the variance of the individual's profile is an unusual or a common occurrence. In a research setting, it may also be of interest to know if the mean S^2 for one group differs at a statistically significant level from the mean S^2 for another group. A statistical test of the significance of the difference has been developed and is detailed in Plake et al. (1981).

Relatively little research on the clinical utility of S^2 has been completed as yet. However, of the various scatter indexes, profile variability is the most stable and the most mathematically sound.

REFERENCES

Chalfant, J. C., & Scheffelin, M. A. (1969). *Central processing dysfunctions in children.* (NINDS Monograph No. 9). Bethesda MD: U.S. Department of Health, Education, and Welfare.

Plake, B., Reynolds, C. R., & Gutkin, T. B. (1981). A technique for the comparison of profile variability between independent groups. *Journal of Clinical Psychology, 37,* 142–146.

CECIL R. REYNOLDS
Texas A&M University

PROFOUNDLY RETARDED

See MENTAL RETARDATION.

PROGRAM EVALUATION

Program evaluation in elementary school and secondary school education has been an area of considerable activity during the past 20 years. Program evaluation has been such an active area largely because of public concern about program accountability as well as a desire by school professionals to provide quality programs, and outcomes services, (Cronbach, 1982). Although no universal definition exists, program evaluation can be characterized by two essential activities: systematic, purposeful data collection relative to one or more important evaluation questions; and the use of evaluation information to judge whether a program is worthwhile (Rossi, Freeman, & Wright, 1985).

Numerous educational program evaluations have been conducted in school settings, with many of the evaluations focused on federally funded programs and projects such as Head Start, Follow-Through, and Chapter I programs. Essentially, these program evaluations have been summative in nature, whereby large numbers of students who received the program were compared with large groups of students with similar characteristics who did not receive the program or who received another program. The primary intent of these evaluations has been to determine program effectiveness and to decide whether the outcome justifies disseminating the program to other sites and students as part of public policy initiatives.

Large-scale educational program evaluation has been proven beneficial to federal and state policy makers in terms of aggregate data for decision-making purposes. Additionally, issues and methods have been clarified in important ways for those interested in evaluation design and measurement. Despite these gains in understanding, what does not seem to have been readily established is the direct and practical relevance of program evaluation to local level programs, especially small-size school districts. More specifically, local school professionals have voiced concern over how they can use program evaluation to help them develop and improve local offerings (Dunst, 1979; Kennedy, 1982).

In special education, program evaluation has become an area of avid interest and increasing activity at local school district levels nationwide, with collaborative efforts being undertaken among administrators, staff, and outside consultants. An important impetus to this avid interest and increasing activity at the local level was a two-day national conference on special education program evaluation held in St. Louis during December 1983 (Council of Administrators of Special Education, 1984). At that conference, which was jointly sponsored by the Council of Administrators of Special Education and the Office of Special Education and Rehabilitation Services, four proven models of local-level special education program evaluation were presented by their proponents. The invited audience of over 100 special education directors and supervisors from throughout the nation took part in workshops to learn about these practical approaches. Subsequent to the conference, local school district applicants were reviewed and the various models were field tested during 1984 at about 20 local sites (Associate Consultants, 1985).

Case study results of these field tests, along with empirical results from additional evaluations of local special education programs that occurred during 1985 and 1986 through state department initiatives, coupled with professional publications on special education program evaluation, have all coalesced to delineate and propose several important features and characteristics of this rapidly developing area. These features and characteristics are reflected in terms of the process of special education program evaluation, the foci of evaluation efforts, the methods, procedures, and instruments for conducting evaluations of special programs, and the enhancement of the use of evaluation information for program planning.

The process of special education program evaluation is best considered in the generic sense, i.e., as the systematic gathering of data about a program or service to answer one or more clearly articulated evaluation questions. For special education programs, the following evaluation questions usually have been raised by local level practitioners when planning an evaluation: (1) What were the characteristics of the students who were provided the program? (2) How was the program actually implemented? (3) Were program goals attained? (4) How did various individuals—teachers, parents, students—react to the program and its outcomes? (5) Was the program responsible for the outcome results? (6) Was the program worth the investment? Although it is not possible for all of these questions to be addressed in a particular evaluation, the questions are important in that the evaluation information gathered in response to them can lead to particular program planning actions.

The foci of special education program evaluation can be numerous, since a special education services delivery system includes a range of programs and services (Maher & Bennett, 1984). For instance, various instructional programs serving special needs learners can be the foci of evaluation efforts including programs such as resources rooms, self-contained classrooms, supplemental instructional programs, regular class mainstreaming programs and, of course, individualized education programs (IEPs). In the area of related services, a district's student counseling program, for example, can be the object of an evaluation as can other programs such as parent education programs or physical therapy services. Similarly, a special education program evaluation can focus on a staff development course or on an important, yet often neglected type of program, e.g., an assessment program such as preplacement evaluation. In deciding the evaluation questions to be addressed in relation to special education programs and services, a local-level team or committee approach has been found to be useful in selecting the most appropriate questions and in facilitating the involvement of staff in the evaluation endeavor (Maher & Illback, 1984).

Since diverse evaluation questions can be addressed in relation to various special programs and services, it is not surprising that a plan for special education program evaluation lists many kinds of methods, procedures, and instruments. At the local level, special education program evaluation plans seem to reflect not comparative group evaluation designs, as has been typical in regular education special evaluation, but special education evaluation plans characterized by a single case approach, where the program (e.g., resource room) is compared with itself over time (e.g., over a 2- to 3-year period) to determine whether it is effective (Tawney & Gast, 1984). Usually, evaluations include use of instruments and procedures that rely on teacher or staff retrospective judgment, especially through use of behavioral checklists and rating scales and parent and teacher interviews. Additionally, criterion-referenced testing and review of IEP goal attainment data have been commonly employed to answer important evaluation questions. Hence, both qualitative and quantitative data gathering approaches appear to be necessary to the conduct of practical and meaningful special education program evaluation.

An emphasis on the use of special education program evaluation information seems to have been a positive outgrowth of practitioners' desires to act on the information for program planning purposes. In this regard, it has been found important that written evaluation reports be kept brief, that they be written in the nontechnical language of the school audience for which it is intended, and that the narrative be augmented with clearly developed tables, graphs, figures, and other illustrations to emphasize important points. Most important, recommendations for program planning should be specific as to how to take the next steps and clear as to how the steps were derived. To facilitate use of the information, it has been found useful to hold group meetings or forums between evaluation personnel and target audiences.

REFERENCES

Associate Consultants. (1985). *Results of the field tests of the special education program evaluation models.* Washington, DC: Author.

Council of Administrators of Special Education. (1984). *Proceedings of the national conference on special education program evaluation.* Indianapolis, IN: Author.

Cronbach, L. J. (1982). *Designing evaluations of educational and social programs.* San Francisco: Jossey-Bass.

Dunst, C. J. (1979). Program evaluation and the Education for All Handicapped Children Act. *Exceptional Children, 46,* 26–31.

Kennedy, M. M. (1982). *Recommendations of the Division H Task Force on Special Education Program Evaluation.* Washington, DC: American Educational Research Association.

Maher, C. A., & Bennett, R. E. (1984). *Planning and evaluating special education services.* Englewood Cliffs, NJ: Prentice Hall.

Maher, C. A., & Illback, R. J. (1984). A team approach to evaluating special services. In C. A. Maher, R. J. Illback, & J. E. Zins (Eds.), *Organizational psychology in the schools.* Springfield, IL: Thomas.

Rossi, P., Freeman, H., & Wright, L. (1985). *Evaluation: A systematic approach.* Beverly Hills, CA: Sage.

Tawney, J. W., & Gast, D. L. (1984). *Single subject research in special education.* Columbus, OH: Merrill.

CHARLES A. MAHER
Rutgers University

LOUIS J. KRUGER
Tufts University

NATIONAL CENTER ON EDUCATIONAL OUTCOMES

SCHOOL EFFECTIVENESS

SUPERVISION IN SPECIAL EDUCATION

PROGRAMMED INSTRUCTION

Programmed instruction is a unique educational method based on principles emphasized by B. F. Skinner (1954, 1958). First, the use of positive reinforcement is preferable to punishment or lack of feedback. Second, positive reinforcement is more effective in producing behavioral changes if given frequently and immediately after each response. Last, there is value in presenting students with small chunks of information to learn that will eventually result in desired behaviors. Skinner sought to apply these principles through programmed learning and the use of teaching machines.

The development of an automated teaching machine by Pressley in the 1920s anticipated Skinner's work. Pressley's machine required students to read questions and then press buttons to answer (in multiple-choice format). The machine presented the next question in a sequence only after the student made the correct choice. Pressley's concept and technology were not readily accepted or widely used. Skinner (1958) attributed the limited use of Pressley's teaching machine to "cultural inertia" and the incomplete or inappropriate application of learning principles. Skinner developed another teaching machine that not only provided frequent and immediate feedback, but also presented the information to be learned in small, easily acquired segments that the student had to master before moving on to new material.

The small steps increased the chances of a student's making a correct response, provided positive reinforcement and student motivation, and ensured student success at each step as well as at the final goal.

Programmed learning has been hailed as allowing truly individualized instruction permitting students to progress at their own pace. In many cases, it seems to be highly motivating to the student because of the immediacy of results, high density of reinforcement, and enjoyment from manipulating the machine (when a teaching machine is used). It has also been instrumental in showing how to teach complex tasks by breaking them down into small, teachable segments. In addition, when using teaching machines, teachers are freer to use their time in more productive ways than presenting information to students.

While the early application of programmed instruction used machines to present learning programs, programmed texts and workbooks soon followed. The increasing use of computers in special education has been revitalizing interest in variations of programmed instruction. An impressive characteristic of modern computers is the great degree of individualized instruction now possible for each student because of the development of branching programs (Rubin & Weisgerber, 1985; Schackenberg & Sullivan, 1997). Students diagnosed as learning disabled and mentally retarded (mild to profound) have learned a variety of skills on computers, such as addition, subtraction, word recognition, matching to sample (Richmond, 1983).

However, it is the application of learning principles and not the use of a computer that is the important issue. A computer does not automatically incorporate programmed instruction principles; in fact, much of the educational software in use today is to a large extent based on the traditional trial-and-error procedures that may result in academic failure in many children (LeBlanc, Hoko, Aangeenbrug, & Etzel, 1985). Integrating instructional principles of programmed learning into the development of educational methodologies, whether in software, textbooks, or other forms, is a way to maximize the chances for learning in special education students.

REFERENCES

LeBlanc, J. M., Hoko, J. A., Aangeenbrug, M. H., & Etzel, B. C. (1985). Microcomputers and stimulus control: From the laboratory to the classroom. *Journal of Special Education Technology, 7,* 23–30.

Richmond, G. (1983). Comparison of automated and human instruction for developmentally retarded preschool children. *Journal of the Association for the Severely Handicapped, 8,* 78–84.

Rubin, D. P., & Weisgerber, R. A. (1985). The center for research and evaluation in the application of technology to education. *Technological Horizons in Education, 12,* 83–87.

Schackenberg, H. L., & Sullivan, H. J. (1997, February 14–18). *Learner ability and learner control in computer assisted instructional programs.* Paper presented at the National Convention of the Association for Educational Communications and Technology, Albuquerque, New Mexico.

Skinner, B. F. (1954). The science of learning and the art of teaching. *Harvard Educational Review, 24,* 86–97.

Skinner, B. F. (1958). Teaching machines. *Science, 128,* 969–977.

THOMAS ZANE
Johns Hopkins University

COMPUTER MANAGED INSTRUCTION
COMPUTER USE WITH STUDENTS WITH DISABILITIES
DIRECT INSTRUCTION
OPERANT CONDITIONING

PROJECTIVE TECHNIQUES

See PERSONALITY ASSESSMENT.

PROJECT ON CLASSIFICATION OF EXCEPTIONAL CHILDREN

In the early 1970s, Nicholas Hobbs was asked to direct a systematic review of the classification and labeling practices for exceptional children. Sponsored by 10 federal agencies and organized by Elliot Richardson, then secretary of health, education, and welfare, this review had several objectives.

The first objective was to increase public understanding of the issues associated with labeling and classifying handicapped individuals. The second objective was to formulate a statement of rationale for public policy, including suggestions for regulatory guidelines. The third objective was to educate professionals who were ultimately responsible for the provision of services to the population of exceptional children (Hobbs, 1975a).

The results of this review, known as the Project on Classification of Exceptional Children, were reported in the publication *The Futures of Children* (Hobbs, 1975b). Included in this report was a list of recommendations that detail actions to be taken as well as who should be responsible for the implementation, the cost of service, and the length of time required to accomplish the project objectives.

Hobbs, a distinguished psychologist and educator, was generally opposed to the practice of labeling individuals. His major argument against labeling was that it is very limited in value. Hobbs pointed out that while the original intent of classification was to provide equal access and opportunity for the handicapped population, the process usually resulted in the transfer of the label or classification to a negative condition or description of the child. For example, a child

who was classified within the category of mental retardation became known as a mental retardate.

Hobbs (1975b), citing the current practices of the time, warned:

> categories and labels are powerful instruments for social regulation and control, and they are often employed for obscure, covert, or hurtful purposes: to degrade people, to deny them access to opportunity, to exclude "undesirables" whose presence in some way offends disturbs familiar custom, or demands extraordinary effort. (p. 11)

One of the seven major recommendations to emerge from the project was the call to improve the classification system. Specifically, the project report suggested five ways to improve the existing process. The suggestions included (1) revision of the classification process; (2) constraints in the use of psychological testing; (3) improvements in early identification procedures; (4) safeguards in the handling of confidential records; and (5) provision of due process in identification and placement.

One finding of the project was that the current classification systems were inadequate. Citing arbitrary and outmoded conceptual guidelines, the members called for a comprehensive classification system that would be based on the needs of exceptional children. According to the general recommendations, the classification system should reflect the full range of conditions of children who need special services. Under this model, classification would emphasize the services required rather than the types of children served.

The specific recommendations of the project members included the formation of a national advisory committee for the purpose of establishing a comprehensive classification system. As a result of such a system, there would be increased understanding of the complexities of the characteristics and etiology of handicapping conditions. The changes proposed in the classification system were not regarded as an end product but rather as a vehicle for improving service and programming for handicapped individuals and their families.

Historically, there has been a great deal of controversy associated with the classification systems for handicapped populations. Since the introduction of the first special education textbook in the early 1920s, there has been a demand for more accurate classification systems Kaufman & Hallahan, 1981).

Currently, there is little evidence in relevant literature that the recommendations resulting from the Project on Classification of Exceptional Children have been implemented on a national level. Individual agencies have made progress in several areas identified by the project report (e.g., improvement of diagnostic procedures, increases in services for the families of handicapped individuals, reclassification of mental retardation based on structural support needed [Gresham, MacMillan, & Siperstein, 1995] and protection of individual's right to due process). However, the major recommendation calling for a national advisory panel that would help to establish policy and direct relevant research has yet to be realized.

REFERENCES

Gresham, F. M., MacMillan, D. L., Siperstein, G. N. (1995). Critical analysis of the 1992 AAMR definition: Implication for school psychology. *School Psychology Quarterly, 10*(1), 1–19.

Hobbs, N. (Ed.). (1975a). *Issues in the classification of children* (Vols. 1, 2). San Francisco: Jossey-Bass.

Hobbs, N. (1975b). *The futures of children.* San Francisco: Jossey Bass.

Kaufman, J. M., & Hallahan, D. P. (Eds.). (1981). *Handbook of special education.* Englewood Cliffs, NJ: Prentice Hall.

FRANCINE TOMPKINS
University of Cincinnati

AAMR CLASSIFICATION SYSTEM
LABELING

PROJECT RE-ED

The project on the Re-Education of Emotionally Disturbed Children (Project Re-ED) evolved after a 1953 study of mental health needs by the Southern Regional Education Board. The study indicated that there was great need for child mental health programs with demonstrated effectiveness, reasonable cost, access to a large talent pool of trained personnel, and potential for transfer of techniques to public schools. In 1956 the federal government sponsored a study of mental health programs in France and Scotland, where mental health services were provided by French *educateurs* and Scottish "educational psychologists" to children with desperate needs because of the effects of evacuation and other traumas resulting from World War II. The National Institute for Mental Health (NIMH) study group recommended a pilot project using trained personnel in the United States (Hobbs, 1983).

In 1961 a NIMH grant of $2 million was awarded to George Peabody College for Teachers (now part of Vanderbilt University) and the states of Tennessee and North Carolina. Nicholas Hobbs was the primary developer of the 8-year pilot project for moderately to severely disturbed children (ages 6 to 12) in residential centers in Nashville, Tennessee, and Durham, North Carolina. Centers were in residential areas and provided services to groups of 24 and 40, subdivided into groups of eight. Program planning emphasis was on health rather than illness, teaching rather than therapy, the present rather than the past, and the operation of a total social system of which the child is a part rather than intrapsychic processes alone. Initial planning was pragmatic rather than theoretical; the theory developed with project research and experience. Hobbs (1978) later commented that one of the important ideas in the planning and development of Project Re-ED was that there should be no orthodoxy or dogma, but a "colleagueship" of discovery guiding the activities of professional individuals working together closely.

Basic ideas underlying program development included (1) insight is a possible consequence but not a cause of behavioral change; (2) health and happiness must grow out of life as it is lived, not as talked about in the context of personality theory; and (3) emotional disturbance in children is not something within the child, but a symptom of a malfunctioning ecosystem. Teacher-counselors and liaison teachers were carefully selected and provided with condensed, highly functional training (master's level) and a dependable system of day-to-day consultation by highly trained and skilled professional personnel. Teachers were not expected to solve complex problems intuitively, but were trained in understanding psychodynamics of individual development and families. Training also included child development, remedial instruction, management of behavior, recreational skills, and use of consultants.

Hobbs believed that trust between children and adults is basic to reeducation and that training of the children should be designed to encourage development of self-confidence by ensuring success. Symptoms were treated directly (controlled) without emphasis on causality. Family and school contacts were maintained while children were in residence. By 1970 the age range was expanded to include adolescents and preschool children.

Follow-up studies of Project Re-ED children (Weinstein, 1974) indicated that although the reeducation program did not change the students into "normal" children, they were better adjusted than disturbed children who were not in the project. Since the average length of stay in centers was about 7 months (contrasted to several years in some other types of residential centers), it appears that the project met its goal, which was not to cure children, but to restore to effective operation the small social system of which the child is an integral part. Hobbs thought that Project Re-ED would be most likely to pay off when its concepts were applied in public schools. By 1983 about two dozen reeducation centers were established in nine states and several others were being planned. Professional consensus now is the Project Re-ED is a viable means of providing effective services to disturbed children.

REFERENCES

Hobbs, N. (1975). *The future of children.* San Francisco: Jossey-Bass.

Hobbs, N. (1978). Perspectives on re-education. *Behavior Disorders,* *3*(2), 65–66.

Hobbs, N. (1983). Project Re-Education: From demonstration project to nationwide program. *Peabody Journal of Education,* *60*(3), 8–24.

Weinstein, L. (1974). *Evaluation of a program for re-educating disturbed children: A follow-up comparison with untreated children* (ERIC Document Reproduction Service No. ED-141-966). Washington, DC: U.S. Department of Health Education, and Welfare.

SUE ALLEN WARREN
Boston University

LIFE SPACE INTERVIEWING
RESIDENTIAL FACILITIES

PROJECT SUCCESS

Project Success (PS) is an academic and social remediation program for the college-bound specific language-handicapped or dyslexic student. The intent of the program is for the language-handicapped student to become language-independent as well as socially and psychologically adjusted to the new environment.

Becoming language-independent means that the dyslexic individual learns how to read and spell any word by relying on his or her own integrated knowledge of the phonemic structure of the American-English language. Students in PS acquire this knowledge initially by memorizing how the 50 phonemes and 26 letters can be employed to identify 271 sound symbol assignments for reading and 245 sound symbols assignments for spelling.

This total number of assignments for both reading and spelling are taught using a multisensory approach. The instructional methodology used is Nash's (1984) adaptation of the original Orton Gillingham, Tri-Modal, Simultaneous Multi-Sensory Instructional Procedure (OG, TM, SMSIP). This procedure trains the learner to use the senses simultaneously to memorize and to integrate up to 84 percent of all American-English words. In addition to reading and spelling remediation, the program remediates math and writing deficits. There is also a social habilitation program.

The written expression program concentrates on teaching the writing of sentences as outlined by Langan (1983). The social habilitation/remediation component of PS was developed to give students an opportunity to give back to fellow students what they have received in a therapeutic, personal, and productive way. As students go through the PS social component, they learn about the secondary characteristics associated with dyslexia. In addition, students have the opportunity to enhance their sense of self-awareness and to be more sensitive to the psychosocial implications of being dyslexic.

The project's arithmetic remediation component assumes that the carrying out of math functions is an exercise in decoding. Thus students who are deficient in math skills are taught to analyze a math problem into a sequence of sentences; each sentence is representative of a particular step or procedure associated with the solving of a particular math problem.

REFERENCES

Langan, J. (1983). *Sentence skills* (3rd ed.). New York: Holt, Rinehart, & Winston.

Nash, R. (1984). *Manual for remediating the reading and spelling deficits of elementary, secondary, and postsecondary students.* Oshkosh, WI: Robert T. Nash Language Training School.

ROBERT T. NASH
*University of Wisconsin at
Oshkosh*

READING DISORDERS

PROJECT TALENT

Project Talent was conceived in the late 1950s as an ambitious survey of American youth. A two-day battery of specially designed tests and inventories was administered to a 5 percent sample of high-school students from across the United States. The intention was to follow-up those tested at regular intervals, and through this process develop an information base about the processes by which men and women develop and use their abilities. The goals of Project Talent were to develop a national inventory of human resources; to achieve a better understanding of how young people choose and develop their careers; and to identify the educational and life experiences that are most important in preparing individuals for their life work (Flanagan et al., 1962).

The group tested included over 400,000 students, constituting a 5 percent probability sample of all students in grades 9, 10, 11, and 12 in public and nonpublic secondary schools in the United States in the spring of 1960. In addition, several supplemental samples were tested in 1960 to address special questions. These included a probability sample of all 15 year olds, whether or not they happened to be in the grade 9 to 12 range or, for that matter, in school. Also included were all high-school students in Knox County (Knoxville), Tennessee. Finally, over 10,000 students from 100 schools originally tested as ninth graders in 1960 were retested for two days as twelfth graders in 1963.

The Project Talent battery included a wide variety of aptitude and achievement tests, sample information in academic and nonacademic areas, and a questionnaire on vocational interests. There was also a personality inventory and a biographical questionnaire containing nearly 400 questions about school life, out-of-school activities, general health, plans, aspirations, home, and family. In addition, each of the more than 1000 participating junior and senior high schools provided information on its instructional and guidance programs, facilities, staffing, and student/community characteristics.

The original plan for Project Talent called for follow-up of those tested 1, 5, 10, and 20 years following the expected graduation of each class. There were subsequent modifications with follow-up surveys 1, 5, and 11 years following the year of class graduation. For example, the original twelfth-, eleventh-, tenth-, and ninth-grade students were surveyed in 1961 through 1963, respectively, when students in each sample were at the model age of 19 years. Surveys were by mail, with a random sample of nonrespondents intensively pursued (by questionnaire or, if necessary, interview) to allow the development of accurate population statistics.

Each of the follow-up surveys sought information on postsecondary education, career choices, work experiences, and family plans, and were timed to occur at key points in individuals' personal and career development. The first- and fifth-year follow-ups focused on the years in which the participants began to put their career choices into action, either through education, training, or direct job experience. Most individuals had completed their formal education had entered the labor force, and had started their families at the time of the 11-year follow-up. The most recent survey focused on each individual's satisfaction with educational preparation, careers, and general quality of life.

Another more limited line of research involved the follow-back design. This approach was based on the fact that approximately 5 percent of those entering medical school in the mid 1960s, for example, were part of the Project Talent sample. It is possible to check names of those enrolling in medical school against the Project Talent files, and as a result have valuable precollege data on a random sample of those entering medical school.

The results of Project Talent are far more extensive than can be covered in this report. The body of knowledge includes technical reports and published articles by the Project Talent staff between 1962 and the present, as well as articles by researchers accessing the information through the Project Talent Data Bank. Many of these reports are in university libraries; others can be obtained through Publications Service, American Institutes for Research, P.O. Box 1113, Palo Alto, California 94302.

The initial report of results from the Project Talent staff was in 1964; it described the inventory of talent in the United States (Flanagan et al., 1964). One highlight from the one-year, follow-up surveys was the tremendous amount of change in career plans. For example, those tested in 1960 were asked to indicate career plans. One year after high school graduation, more than half of those electing each of the career alternatives as high school seniors had changed their plans (Flanagan et al., 1966). Percentages were even lower for those graduating in 1961 to 1963. Of interest was the fact that changes were toward career choices more in line with abilities and interests.

Results of the fifth- (Flanagan et al., 1971) and the eleventh-year (Wilson & Wise, 1975; Wise, McLaughlin, & Gilmartin, 1977) follow-up studies have also been reported. An important finding from the eleventh-year follow-up was that nearly 25 percent of the men and women at age 29 still planned to obtain further education toward various degrees (Wise et al., 1977).

The data collected in conjunction with Project Talent are available to scientists, stripped of identifying information and on a cost-recovery basis. The most comprehensive study done by an outside investigator using this data was that published by Christopher Jencks and his colleagues in the book *Inequality: A Reassessment of the Effect of Family and Schooling in America* (1972).

REFERENCES

Flanagan, J. C., Cooley, W. W., Lohnes, P. R., Schoenfeldt, L. F., Holdeman, R. W., Combs, J., & Becker, S. (1966). *Project Talent one-year follow-up studies*. Pittsburgh: Project Talent.

Flanagan, J. C., Dailey, J. T., Shaycoft, M. F., Gorham, W. A., Orr, D. B., & Goldberg, I. (1962). *Design for a study of American youth*. Boston: Houghton Mifflin.

Flanagan, J. C., Davis, F. B., Dailey, J. T., Shaycoft, M. F., Orr, D. B., Goldberg, I., & Neyman, C. A., Jr. (1964). *The American high school student*. Pittsburgh: American Institutes for Research.

Flanagan, J. C., Shaycoft, M. F., Richards, J. M., Jr., & Claudy, J. G. (1971). *Five years after high school*. Palo Alto, CA: American Institutes for Research.

Jencks, C., Smith, M., Acland, H., Bane, M. J., Cohen, D., Gintis, H., Heyns, B., & Michelson, S. (1972). *Inequality: A reassessment of the effect of family and schooling in America*. New York: Basic Books.

Wilson, S. R., & Wise, L. L. (1975). *The American citizen: 11 years after high school* (Vol. 1). Palo Alto, CA: American Institutes for Research.

Wise, L. L., McLaughlin, D. H., & Gilmartin, K. J. (1977). *The American citizen: 11 years after high school* (Vol. 2). Palo Alto, CA: American Institutes for Research.

LYLE F. SCHOENFELDT
Texas A&M University

PROSOPAGNOSIA

Prosopagnosia is a rare acquired defect in facial recognition that is a consequence of focal brain damage. Visual acuity remains intact. Individuals that develop prosopagnosia are unable to recognize faces as familiar and so do not know whose specific face they are seeing. This is true despite adequate ability to recognize the generic face. For example, a young patient who developed prosopagnosia was puzzled as to why all the actors on a favorite television program had been changed. The faces no longer looked familiar to her, nor could she recognize particular characters by sight. Similarly, she was unable to recognize pictures of members of her own family. This deficit in visual recognition of familiar faces occurs independently of any defect in language or cognition.

Prosopagnosia is often accompanied by other specific kinds of visual disturbances. Individuals with prosopagnosia usually have either a unilateral or bilateral visual field defect. That is, they are unable to see one portion of what ordinarily can be seen when the eyes are held fixed at mid position. This defect is secondary to brain damage or damage to the optic nerve radiations, not to eye damage. In addition, prosopagnosia frequently is accompanied by central achromatopsia, the acquired inability to perceive color as a consequence of central nervous system disease despite adequate retinal function. Visual agnosia also is often present. Visual agnosia is normal ability to see and perceive without the ability to give meaning to what one sees Normal visual acuity, visual scanning, and visual perception must be demonstrable in an individual diagnosed with visual agnosia. Despite the adequacy of visual skills, the individual is unable to recognize what is seen. Difficulty in identification is not a consequence of deficits in language or cognition. Indeed, many of these patients can recognize objects once they touch them, or once their function is described to them.

Historically, there has been substantial contention about the localization of the brain lesion producing prosopagnosia. Initially, most authors identified the necessary lesion as restricted to the right hemisphere (Hecaen & Albert, 1978), as many of the individuals who had prosopagnosia had left-sided visual field defects indicative of right hemisphere pathology. Recent studies using both radiologic and autopsy findings suggest that prosopagnosia requires bilateral damage to the mesial and inferior visual association cortex (Damasio & Damasio, 1983; Damasio, Damasio, & Van Hoesen, 1982).

REFERENCES

Damasio, A. R., & Damasio, H. (1983). Localization of lesions in achromotopsia and prosopagnosia. In A. Kertesz (Ed.), *Localization in neuropsychology* (pp. 331–341). New York: Academic.

Damasio, A. R., Damasio, H., & VanHoesen, G. W. (1982). Prosopagnosia: Anatomic basis and behavioral mechanisms. *Neurology, 32,* 331–341.

Hecaen, H., & Albert, N. L. (1978). *Human neuropsychology.* New York: Wiley.

GRETA N. WILKENING
Children's Hospital

VISUAL IMPAIRMENT
VISUAL PERCEPTION AND DISCRIMINATION
VISUAL TRAINING

PROTECTION AND ADVOCACY SYSTEM—DEVELOPMENTALLY DISABLED

The protection and advocacy system (P&A) was established under federal legislation for the developmentally disabled (Section 113, PL 94-103). Each state or territory receiving funding from the Administration on Developmental Disabilities is required to have a P&A agency. The P&A agencies must be independent of any other state agency or governmental unit to ensure their ability to freely protect and advocate the rights of developmentally disabled (DD) individuals.

Activities of P&A staff may involve negotiation, administrative or legal remedies on behalf of clients seeking programs, services, or protection of clients' rights as DD citizens. The agency's staff is also responsible for information dissemination concerning the rights of DD clients. Activities include presentations and workshops for lay and professional groups on the rights of the disabled. Areas such as education, employment, transportation, housing, architectural barriers, and legal aid are concerns of a P&A agency. The P&A office for each state or territory may be located through the Office of the Governor or by contacting Commissioner, Administration on Developmental Disabilities, OHDS/HHS, Washington, DC 20201.

PHILIP R. JONES
*Virginia Polytechnic Institute
and State University*

PRUNE BELLY SYNDROME

See NATIONAL ORGANIZATION OF RARE DISORDERS.

PSYCHOANALYSIS AND SPECIAL EDUCATION

Until the beginning of the twentieth century, mental illness was believed to be the result of biological and organic factors residing within the individual. Sigmund Freud, who was a practicing physician and neurologist at the turn of the century, began to doubt that the hysterical reactions he was treating in his patients had solely an organic basis. Freud formulated an alternative theory to the development of personality that has subsequently had a profound effect on the way the behavior of an individual is explained. From Freud's psychoanalytic point of view, the psychological processes are the primary determinants of emotionally disturbed behavior. Psychological processes include all mental operations, thoughts, emotions, desires, needs, and perceptions.

Psychoanalysis is a specialized technique in which the individual verbalizes all of his or her thoughts and feelings without censorship (Finch, 1960). Freud's theory holds that individuals are only minimally aware of the causes of their behavior. Behavior is propelled by unconscious forces that are too threatening to be part of the conscious. In treatment, patients are taught to free associate to understand the meaning of their behavior and become better acquainted with the unconscious. Eventually, basic conflicts emerge and are understood and dealt with by the individual. Psychoanalysis is a long, tedious, and complex process that has had limited use in the schools (Finch, 1960). It is based on a medical or disability model where the pathology is believed to reside within the individual. To educators who do not have extensive training in psychology or, more specifically, psychoanalysis, the process seems complex and mysterious. Teachers prefer to refer students with emotional problems to outside agencies or self-contained special education classes rather than to risk making a serious mistake that would do further damage to the student.

Newcomer (1980) discusses both the positive and negative contributions of psychoanalysis to special education. There is the notion in psychoanalytic theory that personality characteristics are determined by childhood events; thus, pathology would develop before a child arrives in school. The problems in school are caused by disorders that are within the child. Therefore the strategies for remediation focus on the child and the family rather than the school. This may result in the school having a passive role in resolution of the conflict.

In addition, because of the psychoanalytic belief that abnormal behaviors are symptoms of unconscious conflicts and that resolution lies in open expression, educators are encouraged to treat disturbed children carefully to avoid repressing their behavior. A nonrepressive environment often provides little structure, and the expectations for normal behavior are reduced. Teachers are encouraged to stop teaching content material until the child's behavior is stable (Newcomer, 1980). It is not clear that this is the most effective way to deal with abnormal behavior. However, there has been a longstanding close association between special education and psychoanalysis in terms of understanding and providing for the needs of students (Pajak, 1981). Psychoanalytic theory has promoted the idea that children do not always consciously plan and cannot always control their disruptive behaviors, but they do respond to internal conflicts (Newcomer, 1980). These beliefs have resulted in more understanding and less primitive treatment of children with emotional disturbance.

Significant contributions to psychoanalysis and special education have been made by Bruno Bettleheim and Fritz Redl (Haring & Phillips, 1962). Their approaches have been primarily permissive in nature, and school work is often used as a vehicle to assist the child in bringing the unconscious conflict to a conscious level of awareness. In general, special education programs have moved from child-directed, psychoanalytic models to more teacher-directed behavioral models where emphasis is primarily on academics and behavior control. IDEA mandates teaching students in the least restrictive environment. Therefore, the emphasis in special education is on teaching children appropriate and acceptable behavior in school, which is in conflict with the free and open expression advocated by Freud and his followers.

REFERENCES

Finch, S. M. (1960). *Fundamentals of child psychiatry.* New York: Norton.

Haring, N. G., & Phillips, E. L. (1962). *Educating emotionally disturbed children.* New York: McGraw-Hill.

Mendelsohn, S. R., Jennings, K. D., Kerr, M. M., Marsh, J., May, K., & Strain, P. S. (1985). Psychiatric input as part of a comprehensive evaluation program for socially and emotionally disturbed children. *Behavioral Disorders, 10*(4), 257–267.

Newcomer, P. L. (1980). *Understanding and teaching emotionally disturbed children.* Boston: Allyn & Bacon.

Pajak, E. F. (1981, Nov.). Teaching and the psychology of the self. *American Journal of Education,* 1–13.

Rezmierski, V., & Kotre, J. (1977). A limited literature review of theory of the psychodynamic model. In W. C. Rhodes & M. L. Tracy (Eds.), *A study of child variance: Vol. 1. Conceptual models* (pp. 181–258). Ann Arbor, MI: University Press.

NANCY J. KAUFMAN
University of Wisconsin at Stevens Point

CHILD PSYCHIATRY
PSYCHODRAMA
PSYCHOTHERAPY WITH INDIVIDUALS WITH
  DISABILITIES

PSYCHODRAMA

Psychodrama is a method of group psychotherapy devised and developed by Moreno (1946). Psychodrama requires a well-trained therapist, preferably one with special certification as a psychodramatist. Psychodrama consists of using dramatic techniques with clients who act out real-life situations, past, present, or projected, in an attempt to gain insight into their behavior and emotions. Psychodrama also provides the opportunity to practice specific behaviors in a supportive group atmosphere. The method of psychodrama integrates insight and cognitions with experiential, participatory involvement, taking advantage of the group therapy setting and using physical movement to bring non-verbal cues to the client's attention. This component of psychodrama can be crucial in therapy with individuals who have limited verbal skills, particularly children and delinquent adolescents (Blatner, 1973). Another significant advantage of psychodrama is its ability to convert the child or adolescent's urge to act out into a more constructive form of "acting in," with guided role playing.

Many production techniques have been devised since psychodrama was introduced, including the auxiliary ego, the double, and the soliloquy. Important to the success of psychodrama is a time for warm-up at the beginning of each session. Participants must also know that the dramatic qualities of the production are not being evaluated, nor are they crucial to the success of therapy. Trust and support of the group are far more important. The role of the director (the psychodramatist) is primarily one of keeping the action moving and helping to lead the participants toward a resolution of the problem situation presented. Keeping the audience (the remainder of the group) involved is also an important role for the director. Three phases will typically constitute a psychodrama, the warm-up phase, the action phase, and the discussion phase.

Psychodrama can be a particularly useful form of psychotherapy with children and adolescents with a variety of behavior disorders. It offers an opportunity for understanding and gaining insight, but it also offers a setting for the development of alternative behaviors and an opportunity for rehearsal in a realistic and supportive setting.

REFERENCES

Blatner, H. A. (1973). *Acting-in: Practical application of psycho-dramatic methods.* New York: Springer.

Moreno, J. L. (1946). *Psychodrama* (Vol. 1). New York: Beacon House.

CECIL R. REYNOLDS
Texas A&M University

SOCIODRAMA

PSYCHOGENIC MODELS

Psychogenic models present causes of human behavior in terms of the psychological functioning of the individual. The cognitive and emotional aspects of personality are central to explaining behavior. The psychogenic approach emphasizes emotional distress as the root of deviant behavior (Bootzin, 1984). The model stands in contrast to the biogenic approach in placing little emphasis on the physiological factors underlying behavior.

Psychogenic models, however, emphasize factors internal to the individual as mechanisms of behavior. For example, personality integration is the central construct of psychological definitions of mental health (Freeman & Giovannoni, 1969). The effects of the ecology of the family or school are mediated by psychological factors, and changes in behavior result from improvements in psychological functioning. The psychogenic model may share with the biogenic model a tendency to blame the victim.

Balow (1979) noted that psychological models are compatible with special education practice because most educational interventions are based on psychological principles. The models, techniques, and measurements of special education used to be expressed typically in terms of psychological function of individual students. The current focus in special education has moved away from the psychogenic model and is much more based in outcome assessments and are more focused on outcome.

REFERENCES

Balow, B. (1979). Biological defects and special education: An empiricist's view. *Journal of Special Education, 13,* 35–40.

Bootzin, R. (1984). *Abnormal psychology: Current perspectives* (4th ed.). New York: Random House.

Freeman, H., & Giovannoni, J. (1969). Social psychology and mental health. In G. Lindzey & E. Aronson (Eds.), *The handbook of social psychology.* (Vol. 5, 2nd ed., pp. 660–719). Reading, MA: Addison-Wesley.

LEE ANDERSON JACKSON, JR.
University of North Carolina at Wilmington

BIOGENIC MODEL OF BEHAVIOR ETIOLOGY

PSYCHOLINGUISTICS

Psycholinguistics refers to the study of language and how individuals acquire, use, and understand language in their daily lives. Initial investigation and study in psycholinguistics was based in philosophy and anthropology; with the work of people like van Humboldt, Wundt, and others, psychology added to what is known about the acquisition of language (Lahey, 1988). Despite the theoretical basis to the initial joint interest in language development, psycholinguistics has become a field of interest for professionals in a multitude of fields, including psychiatry, education, and cognitive psychology.

In the field of education, the interest in psycholinguistics is related to the understanding and increased awareness that atypical language development may underlie many learning, behavior, and psychiatric disorders (Carroll & Snowling, 2004; Clegg, Hollis, Mawhood, & Rutter, 2005; Tallal, 2004). Atypical language development sufficient to warrant identification as speech-language impairment (SLI) occurs in approximately 3 to 15 percent of children ranging in age from 3 to 21 years (American Psychiatric Association, 2000; Riccio & Hynd, 1993). In a large scale epidemiological study, 7.4 percent of kindergarten children were identified as delayed in language areas (Tomblin et al., 1997). Thus, disorders of language are among the most common disorders of higher cerebral function in children. Further, the prognosis for these children, based on retrospective data, is relatively guarded, with a direct relationship between prognosis and the severity of the language impairment (Aram, Ekelman, & Nation, 1987; Lahey, 1988).

Children with SLI typically exhibit limited vocabulary knowledge, underdeveloped or unusual syntax, and impaired grammatical morphology (Bishop, 1992). These language deficits hinder a child's ability to acquire new vocabulary, leading to deficits in global language learning and academic difficulties. Given the relative frequency of SLI in children, it is important for those professionals who work with these children (e.g., teachers, speech-language pathologists, school psychologists) to have some understanding of the cognitive, academic, and behavioral characteristics associated with differing subtypes of SLI in order to most effectively meet the needs of these children. It has been argued that language impairment and learning disabilities are often only distinguished by the age of the child at the time of diagnosis (Carroll & Snowling, 2004; Kamhi & Catts, 1986). Where the SLI is less severe, language problems may not be recognized until school entry. With elementary school children, the problem lies in the presentation of SLI as a learning disability. Language disorders can often be quite subtle and may manifest as a learning disorder rather than language impairment because these language problems surface in the child's difficulty in learning to read, difficulty keeping up with peers, difficulty attending to group lessons, and difficulty with organization (Tallal, 2004).

One of the more difficult tasks facing clinicians is that of differential diagnosis of SLI as opposed to hearing impairment, global intellectual disability, and Pervasive Developmental Disorder/Autistic Spectrum Disorder. This is particularly true of Pervasive Developmental Disorder, where the chief complaint of parents is frequently that of language disorder. Early diagnosis of SLI is often further hampered because the child may appear to be intellectually disabled. Further, it has been found that preschool children with SLI frequently demonstrate behavior problems (e.g., hyperactivity, inattention, social withdrawal, immaturity, dependency). It has been suggested that these behavioral problems may be secondary to the SLI (Clegg et al., 2005).

Given the high frequency of children, youth, and adults affected by language deficits, and the potential impact on educational outcome as well as psychosocial adjustment (Clegg et al., 2005; Tallal, 2004), there is much additional research to be done concerning the best means for prevention,

identification, and intervention of language disorders. It is generally agreed that multiple factors (e.g., biological factors, environmental factors, psychological factors) all contribute to language development (e.g., Lahey, 1988); the interaction of these factors suggests that the area of psycholinguistics will continue to be one of interest across fields with increased research collaboration in the years to come.

REFERENCES

American Psychiatric Association. (2000). *Diagnostic and statistical manual of mental disorders* (4th ed., text revision). Washington, DC: Author.

Aram, D. M., Ekelman, B., & Nation, J. (1987). Preschoolers with language disorders: 10 years later. *Journal of Speech and Hearing Research, 27,* 232–245.

Bishop, D. V. M. (1992). The underlying nature of specific language impairment. *Journal of Child Psychology and Psychiatry, 33,* 1–64.

Carroll, J. M., & Snowling, M. J. (2004). Language and phonological skills in children at high risk of reading difficulties. *Journal of Child Psychology and Psychiatry, 45,* 631–640.

Clegg, J., Hollis, C., Mawhood, L., & Rutter, M. (2005). Developmental language disorders—a follow-up in later adult life. Cognitive, language, and psychosocial outcomes. *Journal of Child Psychology and Psychiatry, 46,* 128–149.

Kamhi, A. G., & Catts, H. W. (1986). Toward an understanding of developmental language and reading disorders. *Journal of Speech and Hearing Disorders, 51,* 337–347.

Lahey, M. (1988). *Language disorders and language development.* New York: Macmillan.

Riccio, C. A., & Hynd, G. W. (1993). Developmental language disorders in children: Relationship with learning disability and attention deficit hyperactivity disorder. *School Psychology Review, 22*(4), 696–708.

Tallal, P. (2004). Improving language and literacy is a matter of time. *Nature Reviews Neuroscience, 5,* 721–728.

Tomblin, J. B., Records, N. L., Buckwalter, P., Zhang, X., Smith, E., & O'Brien, M. (1997). Prevalence of specific language impairment in kindergarten children. *Journal of Speech, Language, and Hearing Research, 40,* 1245–1260.

CYNTHIA A. RICCIO
Texas A&M University

DYSLEXIA
EMOTIONAL DISORDERS
LANGUAGE DISORDERS

PSYCHOLOGICAL ABSTRACTS

Psychological Abstracts (PA) provides nonevaluative summaries of the world's literature in psychology and related disciplines. Over 950 journals, technical reports, monographs, and other scientific documents provide material for coverage in PA. *Psychological Abstracts* includes bibliographic citations or annotations that are used to cover books, secondary sources, articles peripherally relevant to psychology, or articles that can be represented adequately in approximately 30 to 50 words. Since 1967 the abstracts have been entered into machine-readable tapes that now provide the basis for the automated search and retrieval service known as Psychological Abstracts Information Service (PsychINFO).

As psychology has multiple roots in the older disciplines of philosophy, medicine, education, and physics, the vocabulary of psychological literature is characterized by considerable diversity. Each new generation of psychologists added to the vocabulary in attempting to describe their research and perceptions of behavioral processes. As a result, the American Psychological Association standardized the vocabulary by designing a Thesaurus of Psychological Index Terms in 1974, a few years after establishing the computerized version of PA. By 1967 there were over 800 terms that indexed psychological research and writing. In 1974, when the first *Thesaurus* was published, the index and terms were based on the frequency of the occurrence of single words in titles or abstracts in PA over the preceding years. The *Thesaurus* was revised in 1977 and 1982. Each entry in the *Abstracts* and the PsychINFO system is indexed for retrieval by one or more *Thesaurus* index terms, which reflect broader, narrower, and related terms that may describe content in the article. In addition, each article is identified as belonging to one of 16 major content categories and 64 subcategories.

Using these index and content classification terms enables the user to locate articles of interest for hand searchers of PA issues or for computerized retrieval from the PsychINFO system.

Further information about PA or the PsychINFO system can be obtained from the American Psychological Association, 750 First St., N.E., Washington, DC 20002-4242, or by telephone at (202)336-5568.

NADINE M. LAMBERT
University of California, Berkeley
First edition

MARIE ALMOND
The University of Texas of the Permian Basin
Second edition

PSYCHOLOGICAL CLINICS

University psychological clinics are generally student training facilities that have a cooperative relationship with the surrounding community. The clinics provide undergraduate and graduate students in disciplines such as education, counseling, and psychology with an opportunity to apply their theoretical and technical knowledge in working with a variety of clients in a closely supervised practicum. Individuals from the communities surrounding the university psychological clinics are able to receive innovative, state-of-the-art evaluations and treatments at reasonable fees from professionals in training. Each clinic usually has a director who is responsible for the coordination and overall functioning of the clinic and each student's activities are generally scrutinized by one or more qualified supervisors (i.e., licensed psychologists, speech pathologists, or special educators). A number of types of services are usually offered in the psychological clinics, including: child assessment and treatment; parent training; family counseling; teacher consultation; program evaluation; and organizational consultation. Therefore, the clinic provides clients with a wide array of psychological services and the students in training with exposure to a number of different approaches to a particular problem.

TIMOTHY L. TURCO
STEPHEN N. ELLIOTT
Louisiana State University

**CHILD GUIDANCE CLINIC
COLLEGE PROGRAMS FOR DISABLED COLLEGE
   STUDENTS**

PSYCHOLOGICAL CORPORATION

The Psychological Corporation was the world's oldest and largest commercial test publisher. It was founded in New York City in 1921 by three noted professors from Teachers College of Columbia University: James M. Cattell, Edward L. Thorndike, and Robert S. Woodworth. Over its 65-year history, the corporation's primary mission has been the application of principles of psychology and measurement to the solution of educational, clinical, industrial, and social problems. On the eve of its fiftieth anniversary, the Psychological Corporation merged with the test department of Harcourt, Brace, & World, and in 1975 it became a subsidiary of Harcourt Brace Jovanovich. Growth in development programs, services, and professional staff required the corporation to move from New York to Cleveland, Ohio, in 1983. The corporation continued to expand rapidly, employing over 200 people, including 50 psychologists specializing in measurement, child development, and education, by 1985. In 1986 the corporation relocated to permanent headquarters at 555 Academic Court, San Antonio, Texas 78204, with field offices in New York, Chicago, Atlanta, San Diego, Orlando, and Toronto.

The corporation is well known for high-quality educational and psychological tests. Names such as the Wechsler Intelligence Scales for Children–Revised, Children's Memory Scales, McCarthy Scales of Children's Abilities, Baley Scales of Infant Development, and Stanford Diagnostic Reading and Mathematics Tests are familiar to scholars throughout the world. The corporation also provides tests and services to many of the nation's largest companies, government agencies, and health care institutions, and holds contracts for large-scale assessment programs in English- and non-English-speaking countries worldwide. The corporation now publishes over 200 tests and has a computer software development program. In the late 1990s, the company was acquired by Elsevier Science and in 2004 was renamed Harcourt Assessment.

PAUL A. MCDERMOTT
University of Pennsylvania

PSYCHOLOGICAL REPORTS

Psychological Reports is published bimonthly, two volumes a year, the first with issues in February, April, and June and the second with issues in August, October, and December. Between 2000 and 3000 pages are published annually. Approximately one-third of the articles come from outside the United States. The purpose of this journal is to encourage scientific originality and creativity in the field of general psychology for the person who is first a psychologist and then a specialist. It carries experimental, theoretical, and speculative articles; comments; special reviews; and a listing of new books and other materials received. Controversial material of scientific merit is welcomed. Multiple referees examine submissions. Critical editing is balanced by specific suggestions as to changes required to meet standards (Ammons & Ammons, 1962a).

The complete publication process requires as little as 8 to 12 weeks. Distribution of the journal is international. Abstracts appear in standard outlets (e.g., *Psychological Abstracts*), in numerous on-line services for special interest areas, and in journals with particular emphases. A survey made in 1985 (the thirty-first year of publication) showed that *Psychological Reports* appeared in the top 5 percent of psychology journals for number of citations of articles and number of refereed, selected archival articles published, and that it had held that position for the preceding decade. The journal has consistently maintained for 30 years a policy of being highly experimental, open to all defensible points of view, encouraging of new and often unpopular ways of looking at problems, and protective of authors by careful but open-minded refereeing and editing (Ammons & Ammons, 1962b).

REFERENCES

Ammons, R. B., & Ammons, C. H. (1962a). Permanent or temporary journals: Are PR and PMS stable? *Perceptual & Motor Skills, 14,* 281.

Ammons, C. H., & Ammons, R. B. (1962b). Permanent or temporary journals: PR and PMS become stable. *Psychological Reports, 10,* 537.

C. H. AMMONS
*Psychological Reports /
Perceptual and Motor Skills*

PSYCHOLOGY IN THE SCHOOLS

Psychology in the Schools began in 1964 with William Hunt serving as editor. He was followed briefly by B. Claude Mathis and then in 1970 by Gerald B. Fuller of Central Michigan University, who remains as editor. In an attempt to meet the practical needs of professionals in the field, this journal emphasizes an applied orientation. It addresses practicing school and clinical psychologists, guidance personnel, teachers, educators, and university faculty. Articles of preference clearly describe the relevancy of the research for these practitioners. However, occasionally important experimental and theoretical papers may be included.

The major areas of focus include (1) theoretical papers and interpretive reviews of literature when these relate to some aspect of school psychology; (2) opinions that are well formulated and presented; (3) treatment and remediation approaches; (4) evaluation of treatment and remediation or other program evaluations; (5) deviant or atypical features of the behavior of school children; (6) social or group effects on adjustment and development; (7) educational, intellectual, and personality assessments; (8) etiology and diagnosis; and (9) case studies. These areas are grouped into four categories within the journal: evaluation and assessment; educational practices and problems; strategies for intervention; and general topics.

GERALD B. FULLER
Central Michigan University

PSYCHOMETRICS

See MEASUREMENT.

PSYCHOMOTOR SEIZURES

The term psychomotor was introduced in 1938 by Gibbs and Lennox (Lennox & Lennox, 1960) to describe epileptic manifestations composed of various multiple psychic or motor activities. These manifestations are associated with spikes, sharp or slow waves on the electroencephalogram over the anterior area of the temporal lobe; therefore, the manifestations are also called temporal lobe seizures. According to the classification of the International League Against Epilepsy (1981), the seizures are partial, as they begin locally, and also complex, as they are associated with "a clouding of consciousness and complete or partial amnesia for the event" (Livingston, 1972). They may be followed by generalized tonic-clonic seizures.

Psychomotor seizures are more frequent in older children, adolescents, and young adults (Currie et al., 1971; Gastaut, 1953; Livingston, 1972). However, Holowach et al. (1961) and Chao et al. (1962) reported this kind of seizure in 11 and 15.7 percent of children with all types of epilepsy up to 15 years of age. The onset occurred before the age of 6 years in more than 50 percent and before the age of 3 years in almost 30 percent.

As in every partial seizure, the temporal lobe epilepsy may start with an aura that is the first subjective and remembered symptom of the seizure. This aura is indicative of the starting point of the fit, and sometimes of its spreading. In psychomotor epilepsy, the wide variety of symptoms, sensory, motor, or mental, are due to the structures encountered in the temporal lobe area, such as the temporal convolutions, the cortex in the fissure of Sylvius, the insula, the amygdaloid nucleus, the uncus, and the hippocampal zone. The International League Against Epilepsy (1985) proposes to classify the multiple clinical pictures into four subtypes: hippocampal (mesiobasal limbic or primary rhinencephalic psychomotor), amygdalar (anterior polaramygdalar), lateral posterior temporal, and opercular (insular) epilepsies. The symptoms may be motor, sensory, or psychic, appearing simultaneously or consecutively, but they present some clinical patterns (Chao et al., 1962; Gastaut, 1953; Holowach et al., 1961; Livingston, 1972).

Young children may, as an aura, run to their mother with fear or complain of gastric discomfort or unpleasant smell or taste before the loss of consciousness. The symptoms often start with an arrest of motion, with eye staring eventually followed by simple and/or complex automatisms such as repetitive oral movements (e.g., lip smacking, chewing, and swallowing; Ebner, Noachter, Dinner, & Lueders, 1996; Serafetinides, 1996). The motor activities, like rubbing the face, fumbling with buttons of clothing, or wandering around the room, appear purposive but inappropriate at the time. Speech may become incoherent or mumbled. Autonomic disturbances such as urination, vomiting, salivation, or flushing of the face may be present. Awareness is impaired and amnesia of the attack is a fairly constant finding. The episodes are not very frequent (from one to five per day to one to five per month) and usually brief, 2 to 3 minutes, but the return to consciousness is often gradual. Mental or psychic seizures are variable, but visual or auditory hallucinations are frequent and owed to connections with the vicinity.

Affective manifestations such as fear or aggressiveness are frequently present. The attack may terminate in a grand mal seizure. The symptomatology is often associated with mental retardation, cerebral palsy, and hyperkinetic syndrome (as with any organic brain disorder of childhood).

In children the etiology is most often the result of a chronic, nonprogressive neurologic disease. The seizures may be due to previous insult to the brain in the neonatal period as in hypoxia, infection, trauma, or congenital malformations, but also to severe or prolonged seizures in early life or to febrile convulsions. Tumors are rare. Often, no definite cause can be established (Gomez & Klass, 1983). The most common abnormality is mesial temporal sclerosis (incisural sclerosis). The prognosis is better than previously thought (Lindsay et al., 1979; Staff, 1980), and treatment is mainly medical through drug therapy.

REFERENCES

Chao, D., Sexton, J. A., & Santos Pardo, L. S. (1962). Temporal lobe epilepsy in children. *Journal of Pediatrics, 60,* 686–693.

Currie, S., Heathfield, K. W. G., Henson, R. A., & Scott, D. F. (1971). Clinical course and prognosis of temporal lobe epilepsy: A survey of 666 patients. *Brain, 94,* 173–190.

Ebner, A., Noachter, S., Dinner, D., & Lueders, H. (1996). Automatisms with preserved responsiveness: A lateralizing sign in psychomotor seizures: Commentary Reply. *Neurology, 46*(4), 1189.

Gastaut, H. (1953). So called "psychomotor" and "temporal" epilepsy—A critical review. *Epilepsia, 2,* 59–99.

Gomez, M. R., & Klass, D. W. (1983). Epilepsies of infancy and childhood. *Annals of Neurology, 13,* 113–124.

Holowach, J., Renda, Y. A., & Wapner, J. (1961). Psychomotor seizures in childhood. A clinical study of 120 cases. *Journal of Pediatrics, 59,* 339–346.

International League Against Epilepsy. (1981). Proposal for revised clinical and electroencephalographic classification of epileptic seizures. *Epilepsia, 22,* 489–501.

International League Against Epilepsy. (1985). Proposal for classification of epilepsies and epileptic syndromes. *Epilepsia, 26,* 268–278.

Lennox, W. G., & Lennox, M. A. (1960). *Epilepsy and related disorders.* Boston: Little, Brown.

Lindsay, J., Ounsted, C., & Richards, P. (1979). Long-term outcome in children with temporal lobe seizures. *Developmental Medicine and Child Neurology, 21,* 285–636.

Livingston, S. (1972). *Comprehensive management of epilepsy in infancy, childhood, and adolescence.* Springfield, IL: Thomas.

Serafetinides, E. A. (1996). Automatisms with preserved responsiveness: A lateralizing sign in psychomotor seizures: Comment. *Neurology, 46*(4), 1189.

Staff. (1980). Prognosis of temporal lobe epilepsy in childhood. *British Medical Journal, 280,* 812–813.

HENRI B. SZLIWOWSKI
Hôpital Erasme, Université
Libre de Bruxelles, Belgium

ABSENCE SEIZURES
SEIZURE DISORDERS

PSYCHOMOTRICITY

An independent science firmly established in France, psychomotricity is based on the interdependence of physical, affective, and intellectual functions and thus covers a wide field that encompasses neurology, pedagogy, and psychoanalysis.

Numerous scientific ideas from various disciplines have contributed for more than a century to the elaboration of the concept of psychomotricity. Near the end of the nineteenth century, scientific achievements made it necessary to abandon Cartesian dualism, which separated body and mind and led to a mechanistic approach to the body. Instead, the integrative action of the nervous system and its role in the regulation of the organism interacting with its environment were stressed. Neurophysiologists started to examine the bases of tonus and movement (gamma loop and Renshaw recurrent circuit, cerebellum, subcortical nuclei, neocortex, etc.). Penfield's center-encephalic theory of motor adjustment (counter to traditional associationism) underscored the importance of the basal centers and their integrating role, and of the vertical cortical-subcortical relationships.

Dupré, a neuropsychiatrist, described the syndrome of motor deficiency in relation to mental deficiency and compared it with the immature state of newborn babies (limb hypertonicity, enuresis, etc.). For the first time, motricity and intelligence were linked.

In *La naissance de l'intelligence chez l'enfant* (1936), Piaget stated that the first stage in the development of intelligence is the coordination of sensorimotor schemas (i.e., feeling and movement systems such as suction, sight, prehension, etc.) leading to adaptations and assimilations that enable the individual to reach a higher (preoperative) type of intelligence. Piaget's ideas were developed further. De Ajuriaguerra showed that the tonic state is used by the newborn baby as a mode of relation (e.g., crying hypertonicity, contentment hypotonicity). A structuring dialogue actually takes place between mother and child. Wallon studied the relationship between motricity and character (*L'enfant turbulent,* 1925). He described the body image as a progressive construction involving all our perceptive, motor, and affective experiences. Phenomenology, too, played a role in the coming about of psychomotricity. It gave birth to the gestalt theory, in which every physical or psychological phenomenon is seen as an indivisible whole known as the form. This theory helped shape the notions of body schema, behavior, and movement. According to Merleau-Ponty and Buytendijk, the different types of behavior are modalities of the *in-der-Welt-sein,* that is, of mind and body as they interact continuously in the flow of life. Thus, in the phenomenal world body and mind were no longer separated and psychomotricity could enter the field.

Psychoanalysis also contributed to the elaboration of the concept. The body was defined as a scene of pleasure, and psychic development was divided into organic stages: oral, anal, phallic, and genital. Moreover, it was contended that an organic or perceptual-motor function could be used effectively only if it had been effectively invested. An emotional disorder can easily bring about physical dysfunctions such as conversion hysteria or organic neurosis. Reich stated that the social-emotional state of a person influences his or her tonic state (tension rings). The ethology of the child also played a role. Montagner gave a minute description of the child's behavior in the nursery and highlighted socio-affective correlations.

In France, psychomotricity was recognized as a discipline in the early 1960s. The first French Psychomotricity Charter (de Ajuriaguerra-Soubiran) was promulgated and a curriculum was created. A trade union and various publications came about.

As far as practice is concerned, a distinction is usually made between education, remedial work, and therapy. Education aims at stimulating the healthy child's psychomotor functions. This concept is slowly spreading in nursery schools. Remedial exercises aim at improving psychomotor symptomatology through a reprogramming of the neuromotor sphere. Model lessons by the well-known team of the Henri-Rousselle Hospital in Paris are available. Therapy aims at deblocking and developing the disturbed child's psychic structures through bodily and relational interaction with the therapist and mediatory objects. According to Aucouturier, technicity consists of working out sensorimotor pleasure and treatment of aggressive and fantasmatic productions. These various approaches are used primarily with children up to 7 years of age when symbolizing processes enable them to dissociate themselves from their bodily experiences. However, the concept of psychomotricity applies in theory to every stage of life.

REFERENCES

Piaget, J. (1936). *Le naissance de l'intelligence chez l'enfant.* Neuchatel: Delachaux et Niestlé

Wallon, H. (1925). *L'enfant turbulent.* Paris: Alcan.

DANIELLE MICHAUX
Vrije Universiteit Brussel

PSYCHONEUROTIC DISORDERS

The term psychoneurotic as a description of childhood emotional disorders is associated with the psychoanalytic tradition of Sigmund Freud. It is a general term that has been applied to specific clinical syndromes, including phobias, anxiety reactions, obsessive-compulsive behavioral patterns, and hysterical or conversion disorders. Anxiety is postulated by all authorities as being the prime causal process in these clinical syndromes. Some authorities also include childhood and adolescent depressive reactions under the conceptual rubric of psychoneurotic disorders.

Obsessive-compulsive neurosis is characterized by recurrent thoughts or actions that the child feels he or she must think about or perform. To the objective outside observer, these appear to be irrational ideas and unnecessary or ridiculous behaviors. The obsessive child is seen as a highly anxious child whose obsessional thoughts and compulsive behaviors are a way to defend against intense anxiety. Unfortunately for the child, this cognitive and behavioral style never totally alleviates the anxiety and often leads to new problems in adapting to the social environment.

Virtually all people have occasional obsessive thoughts. A highly valued activity may lead to recurrent thoughts and excitement, or a catchy tune may roll over and over in one's head. Clinicians also observe a degree of compulsiveness in anxious children that, while of a significant proportion, does not occur with enough frequency or intensity to warrant the diagnosis of an obsessive-compulsive syndrome. For example, a 9-year-old boy was seen for an evaluation. Psychological tests revealed a clear compulsive style in executing a variety of cognitive and educational tasks. He was a slow worker with perfectionistic tendencies who functioned at a fairly high level academically and socially. His role in the family was that of a "pleaser." His sister had recently been discharged from a psychiatric hospital after a suicide attempt, and there was an inordinate amount of external stress on the family. It was clear that this child was developing a compulsive behavioral style in defense against the insecurity he felt as a member of this family system.

When the obsessive compulsiveness reaches a high degree, the child can become extremely dysfunctional. Obsessive compulsive children are haunted by extreme irrational thinking and ritualistic behavioral patterns. Kesler (1972) classifies obsessional fears experienced by such children into two types. The first is precautionary fear, which includes worries about one's health, safety, or cleanliness. The second is repugnant fears such as concern that one might engage in sexual abnormalities or some type of conspicuously taboo behavior. Kesler also suggests that compulsive acts can be dichotomized into those that are precautionary such as washing one's hands repeatedly to rid oneself of germs, and those that act as self-punishment such as compulsive counting or bed making.

It should be stressed that the diagnosis of this disorder is made only when the pattern leads to dysfunctional behavior and that a certain degree of compulsive traits are functional. Attention to cleanliness and detail can be very helpful in participation in the family and performing well in school. A bedtime ritual such as reading stories before bed is a beneficial quieting behavior at the end of the day. Few teachers complain about elementary school children who have their desks neatly organized each school day. Most authorities agree that the incidence of obsessive-compulsive disorders is extremely rare (Achenbach, 1974). It appears to be roughly equally distributed among both sexes (Templer, 1972).

Conversion reaction also is described as hysteria. It is most closely associated with the psychoanalytic tradition. Anxiety is presumed to be converted into physical complaints and illnesses. A hysterical syndrome can be contrasted with a psychosomatic disorder in that the former has no medical basis and may be totally contradicted by medical findings. The types of physical symptoms that may represent conversion reactions are almost limitless. Sometimes they mimic known physical diseases and specific organic dysfunctions such as blindness.

A clinical case demonstrates the unique form that conversion reactions can take. A 14-year-old girl was seen for the presenting complaint of a sudden onset of the inability to read normally. She was, in fact, reading backward in mirror-image form. Examinations by a neurologist and an ophthalmologist suggested there was no organic basis for the problem. The case was treated as a conversion reaction. Individual psychotherapy revealed a highly stressful family environment. The father suffered from a terminal illness. Emerging adolescent sexuality also was an issue. The girl was very afraid of growing up and was treated like a young child by the family. The inability to read was treated as a manipulation to avoid these developmental issues. Both the patient and her family denied that this was a psychologically caused symptom. Denial is common among hysterical syndromes. An unorthodox paradoxical treatment approach was employed whereby the girl was not allowed to read and was given the message by the parents that she needed to be more independent and grown up. After much hostility and acting out behavior by the patient, she did begin to read again. It is noteworthy that when stress again peaked several months later, the same symptoms resurfaced. They again remitted with treatment.

Most approaches to the study of psychoneurotic abnormalities follow either a psychoanalytic theory or a learning-behavioral approach. Each theoretical orientation has a substantial following and, at this point, there is no basis for rejecting or accepting the superiority of one approach over the other for the treatment of psychoneurotic dysfunction. Each of these two general theoretical frameworks also have application to the explanation and treatment of a wide range of abnormal behaviors.

The psychoanalytic approach is primarily based on Freud's theory of neurosis. According to this approach, psychoneurotic manifestations result from the individual's response to unconscious conflicts involving sexual and aggressive impulses. At the center of Freud's theory is his emphasis on defense mechanisms, particularly repression.

In hysterical behavior, the affective arousal (presumed to be sexual in origin) is pushed out of consciousness and converted into somatic complaints. According to Freud, the obsessive-compulsive child, in contrast, is unable to convert anxiety into physical symptoms so repression is used to destroy the emotional link between an unacceptable idea and the feelings about it. The obsessive can be aware of the unacceptable idea, but manages to keep from thinking about it.

The sexual conflict that leads to neurotic symptoms was postulated by Freud to involve a conflict between the ego, or the child's emerging personality structure, and the libido, the unconscious psychological energy. Symptoms reflect this conflict between the ego and unacceptable ideas. Freud's theory, often labeled the libido theory, proposes that the effect of excitation can be displaced, discharged, or converted into other forms such as bodily or compulsive behaviors. For more complete descriptions of the psychoanalytic theory of neurosis, including Freud's revision of his theory in 1923, see Kesler (1972) or Achenbach (1974).

A learning theory approach discounts the importance of internal unconscious impulses or a personality structure. The learning theorist traces the cause of anxiety to specific environmental circumstances. The operant conditioning paradigm focuses on environmental or behavioral contingencies that reinforce symptomatic behavior (e.g., make it more likely to be repeated). Psychoneurotic symptoms emerge as a way of reducing the aversive effects of feeling anxious; in this way they reinforce the hysterical or obsessive-compulsive behaviors. The reinforced behavior can be generalized to different but similar situations. Thus the learning theory approach discusses complex associations that are learned as the child attempts to cope with anxiety.

Conversion reactions and obsessive-compulsive disorders have traditionally been treated with individual psychotherapy from a psychoanalytic approach. Behavioral approaches have been more frequently applied to the anxiety disorders such as phobias where their efficacy is well established. Noticeably fewer applications of behavioral therapy to obsessive-compulsive and conversion reactions have been reported. Psychodynamic individual therapy with children with these disorders is based on the intensity of the relationship between the child and the therapist. This approach attempts to examine the intrapsychic conflicts that produce the anxiety and then the psychoneurotic disorder. Play therapy is often used for younger children as part of the therapeutic process so that the child can express his or her conflicts through play. The Freudian approach emphasizes that the symptom must be removed by resolving the basic conflict. Otherwise, it is postulated that symptom substitution will occur where the intrapsychic conflict that is left unresolved will resurface in the form of a different pattern of abnormal behavior.

In contrast, behavior therapists reject the notion of symptom substitution and directly attack the symptom or problem behavior. Reinforcement contingencies may be set up by the therapist and implemented by the significant adults in the child's life. The problem behaviors would no longer be positively reinforced and may be negatively reinforced; more appropriate ways of responding would be positively reinforced with the goal that the child would learn new ways of coping with anxiety. For example, in the classroom setting, the teacher, after consultation with the therapist, would implement responses to compulsive behavior by the child that would encourage the child to be less perfectionistic and work at a greater rate of speed. The case of the 14-year-old with conversion reaction discussed at the beginning of this entry illustrates a behavioral intervention following a psychodynamic formulation. The secondary gain from the conversion reaction behavior (i.e., failing to read) was eliminated. The child was not allowed to read and did not receive special tutoring at school. Emphasis was placed on normal social behavior involved with growing up and focus was shifted away from the symptom.

Family therapy is usually a valuable, if not necessary, adjunct to individual therapy for psychoneurotic children. Recent trends are highlighting short-term dynamic psychotherapy, probably as a response to managed care as well as progression in theory (Davanloo, 1995). The traditional psychoanalytic point of view would assign a separate therapist to work with the parents while the individual psychotherapist worked with the child. More often today, the same therapist works individually with the child and consults with the parents. Family therapy sessions may also be held. The behavior therapist often consults with the parents on specific behavioral interventions that they could make at home. In this way, the parents become collateral therapists. School consultation is frequently a valuable adjunct to effective intervention. The therapist can educate the teacher on the nature of the problem and give suggestions for appropriate responses. These teacher behaviors might include being more patient, as in the case of a conversion reaction or excessive compulsivity; specific behavioral interventions by the teacher can play an important role in changing behavior. Drug therapy is generally inappropriate for these disorders, as there is little evidence of biological causes. An exception would be if a parallel disorder, such as depression in an older adolescent, called for antidepressant medication.

REFERENCES

Achenbach, T. M. (1974). *Developmental psychopathology.* New York: Ronald.

Davanloo, H. (1995). Intensive short-term dynamic psychotherapy: Spectrum of psychoneurotic disorders. *International Journal of Short-Term Psychotherapy, 10*(3), 121–155.

Kesler, J. W. (1972). Neurosis in childhood. In B. B. Wolman (Ed.), *Manual of child psychopathology* (pp. 387–435). New York: McGraw-Hill.

Templer, D. (1972). The obsessive-compulsive neurosis: Review of research findings. *Comprehensive Psychiatry, 13,* 375–398.

WILLIAM G. AUSTIN
Cape Fear Psychological Services

ANXIETY DISORDERS
CHILDHOOD PSYCHOSIS
DEPRESSION, CHILDHOOD AND ADOLESCENT
EMOTIONAL DISORDERS
SERIOUSLY EMOTIONALLY DISTURBED

PSYCHOPATHY

See SOCIOPATHY.

PSYCHOSIS, AMPHETAMINE

See AMPHETAMINE PSYCHOSIS.

PSYCHOSOCIAL ADJUSTMENT

Psychosocial adjustment refers to social and emotional functioning: the way a person relates to and interacts with other people in his or her environment. It is one noticeable area of difference between special needs students and those labeled normal. While problems in psychosocial development and intrafamily relations may contribute to later psychosocial difficulties (Erickson, 1963), a behavioral analysis position (Bryant & Budd, 1984) emphasizes the importance of environmental stimuli in reinforcing and maintaining appropriate social skills.

A number of remedial techniques have been used when an exceptional child exhibits psychosocial problems. Often parents can be taught to provide a more positive family environment and to more effectively communicate with their child. In school and during play, specific appropriate social behaviors, such as approaching other children, sharing, and playing social games, can be targeted for training and shaping using reinforcement techniques (Davies & Rogers, 1985). A high density of positive reinforcement for correct approximations of social contact may also be used to strengthen appropriate social relationships.

REFERENCES

Bryant, L. E., & Budd, K. S. (1984). Teaching behaviorally handicapped preschool children to share. *Journal of Applied Behavior Analysis, 17,* 45–56.

Davies, R. R., & Rogers, E. S. (1985). Social skills with persons who are mentally retarded. *Mental Retardation, 23,* 186–196.

Erickson, E. H. (1963). *Childhood and society* (2nd ed.). New York: Norton.

THOMAS ZANE
Johns Hopkins University

EMOTIONAL DISORDERS
FAMILY COUNSELING
FUNCTIONAL ASSESSMENT
SOCIAL SKILLS INSTRUCTION

PSYCHOSOMATIC DISORDERS

The somatic expression of anguish is a frequent phenomenon in childhood and adolescence. More than 90 percent of children between the ages of 3 and 18 years have established a psychological relationship with the surrounding world and expressed a confusion in a psychosomatic form at some time during their development. Somatic expression in childhood is always bound with anxiety either in reaction to a situation objectively traumatic or in relation to the perceptive distortion of an objectively nontraumatic situation. Somatic expression in the child in regard to the adult is specific and evolutionary in relation to the maturational stage of the child (affective and neurological). It is associated with a quantitative or qualitative deficiency in the parent/child relationship, most often with the mother.

Somatizations are frequent in the everyday life of a family, and are expressed through abdominal pain, headaches, fatigue, syncopal tendencies, and breathing difficulties without any objective clinical manifestation. The causes are multiple and often related to situational stress, e.g., divorce of the parents, death, academic examinations, personal crises, and approaching adolescence. Through somatic symptoms, the child frequently aims to provoke a modification in the family system by focusing the tension on himself or herself. Sometimes the child preserves the equilibrium of parents who are ready to break down. There is always a message in somatization; it is chosen consciously or unconsciously by the child in families where only this type of expression is tolerated. The underlying personality is not specific but is generally strong. The somatization is a means of expression limited in time and related to a difficult situation experienced by the child that could regress through verbal exchanges and dramatization. At times, somatization presents itself in a family context called psychosomatic and is characterized through a systematic avoidance of conflicts, enmeshment of roles, pseudomutuality, and functional rigidity. The treatment will then be systemic (familial). The somatization cannot be underestimated even if physical examination is normal; the symptoms are real. It is not a simulation, and the symptoms must be seriously taken into account and the context carefully analyzed.

Psychosomatic diseases of children differ from those of adults and result from the conjunction of various factors. A calendar of psychosomatic diseases exists: colic at 3 months, vomiting at 6 months, eczema between 8 and 12 months, breath-holding spells at 2 years, abdominal pain at 3 years, asthma at 5 years, headaches at 6 years, and Crohn's disease at adolescence. The development of a psychosomatic syndrome is associated with (1) a genetically fragile somatic background (repetitive infections); (2) a precocious inappropriate parent–child relationship (rejection, overprotection, aggression, anxiety); (3) physical stress (allergene) or psychological reactivation of a previous problem of anguish until compensated; and (4) a familial functioning of the psychosomatic type. According to age, the prevalent etiology, and the therapeutic possibilities, the treatment will be made along an organistic or psychological point of view, individually or familial, and symptomatic or global.

Every serious somatic disease is stressful for the child, the family, and those surrounding the child (teachers, grandparents, etc.). The factors of adaptation are related to the nature of the disease itself, to the child (age and personality), and to the possibilities of modification in the functioning of the family facing a distressing situation, e.g., new context of life, hospital, family doctor. Frequently the child uses the physical symptoms to express feelings of discomfort. The diabetic child cheats with treatment, the hemophiliac tempts the danger of bleeding, and the child with cystic fibrosis refuses treatment. The use of an organic symptom that does not have objective reality (e.g., pain in the appendicular region after appendectomy) is frequent and testifies to the nonrecognition of an underlying message by the family of the child: the organ is removed but the psychic suffering persists.

The psychosomatic symptomatology of the child is the borderline of the physical and the psychical, of the inborn and the acquired, of the personal and the relational, and of the conscious and the unconscious. The approach to such a symptomatology needs a great deal of empathy, tact, and comprehension of the global context of the child, the family, and the society surrounding the child. Special educators are in an optimal situation to assist in the diagnosis of these disorders because of the consistent daily observations made by all teachers. School clinicians can refer to the *Diagnostic and Statistical Manual of Mental Disorders,* fourth edition (*DSM-IV*) for diagnostic criteria (American Psychiatric Association, 1994). If physical complaints over a period of time alert the teacher to suspect a somatic disorder, the school psychologist and parents should be made aware of the situation. Referrals to support professionals in the community should be on hand to assist the family in diagnosis and treatment.

REFERENCES

American Psychiatric Association. (1994). *Diagnostic and statistical manual of mental disorders* (4th ed.). Washington, DC: Author.

Ajuriaguerra, J. de (1984). *Psychopathologie de l'enfant* (2nd ed.). Paris: Masson.

Kreisler, L. (1981). *L'enfant du désordre psychosomatique.* Toulouse: Privat Editeur.

Kreisler, L., Fain, M., & Soule, M. (1974). *L'enfant et son corps.* Paris: Presses Universitaires de France.

J. Appelboom-Fondu
Université Libre de Bruxelles, Belgium

Henri B. Szliwowski
Hôpital Erasme, Université Libre de Bruxelles, Belgium

EMOTIONAL DISORDERS
FAMILY COUNSELING
PHYSICAL DISABILITIES
SCHOOL PHOBIA

PSYCHOSURGERY

Psychosurgery is not an intervention that responds to a specific mental disorder. Instead, it is a neurosurgical procedure that was derived from observations made in animal aggression research (Fulton, 1949; Jacobsen, 1935) and applied to humans to control more violent psychiatric and neurological symptoms. Psychosurgical techniques were employed in the United States starting in the 1940s (Freeman & Watts, 1950). A variety of techniques that proceeded from gross frontal destruction by means of injections of alcohol into the frontal white matter (Kalinowsky, 1975) to sophisticated stereotaxic, electrically produced, ablative procedures (Kelly, Richardson, & Mitchell-Heggs, 1973) have been used. The location of lesions also has become more sophisticated. Initially, the goal of practitioners appeared to be to destroy enough anterior brain matter to create the desired effect, which was pacification of the patient. Contemporary techniques focus on greater localization of a lesion, hence avoiding large-scale brain destruction. Sites include parts of the limbic system, the anterior cingulum, and the posteromedial hypothalamus (Sano, Sekino, & Mayanagi, 1972).

The effectiveness of psychosurgery is straightforward. The issue is not one of vitiating the disorder but of limiting an individual's responsiveness to frightening and disturbing mental symptoms (Kalinowsky, 1975). Thus an individual is still likely to perceive threatening voices, but not react to them. Much like patients suffering the residuals of an accidental traumatic brain injury, leucotomized patients often were perceived by others as generally less spontaneous, more socially withdrawn, and more interpersonally distant. Psychosurgery has been used for schizophrenic conditions, obsessive compulsive neuroses, and affective disorders. As may be expected, given the more general effects of the lesions, psychosurgery with affective disorders produces the least favorable outcome. With the prevalence of psychotropic medications, the use of psychosurgery for behavioral management has diminished significantly.

Recent applications of neurosurgical procedures have noted success in dealing with pain (Culliton, 1976), obsessive-compulsive disorder (Rappaport, 1992) and uncontrolled seizures (Spiers, Schomer, Blume, & Mesulam, 1985). The latter approach is the best example of what psychosurgery was intended to do; that is, to remove a brain area that is intimately involved in producing a disorder. The goal of surgical intervention with an uncontrolled epileptic disorder is to remove the brain tissue that is producing a seizure focus. Thus, the techniques used to identify that focus are as important as the surgical procedure itself. This last point draws the most clear distinction between earlier psychosurgical procedures and current methods. When performed to alleviate behavioral dysfunction, psychosurgery was essentially an approach to limit reactivity without affecting the underlying disorder; in contrast, when surgery is performed to alleviate uncontrolled seizures, the underlying cause is removed with changes in behavior following.

REFERENCES

Culliton, B. J. (1976). In R. N. De Jong & O. Sugar (Eds.), *The yearbook of neurology and neurosurgery: 1978.* Chicago: Year Book Medical.

Freeman, W., & Watts, J. W. (1950). *Psychosurgery.* Springfield, IL: Thomas.

Fulton, J. F. (1949). *Functional localization in the frontal lobes and cerebellum.* Oxford, England: Oxford University Press.

Jacobsen, C. F. (1935). Functions of frontal association areas in primates. *Archives of Neurology and Psychiatry, 33,* 558.

Kalinowsky, L. (1975). Psychosurgery. In A. M. Freedman, H. I. Kaplan, & B. J. Sadock (Eds.), *Comprehensive textbook of psychiatry–II* (pp. 1979–1982). Baltimore: Williams & Wilkins.

Kelly, D., Richardson, A., & Mitchell-Heggs, N. (1973). Techniques and assessment of limbic leucotomy. In L. V. Laitinen & K. E. Livingston (Eds.), *Surgical approaches in psychiatry* (p. 201). Lancaster, England: Medical & Technical.

Rappaport, Z. H. (1992). Psychosurgery in the modern era: Therapeutic and ethical aspects. *Medicine & Law, 11*(5), 449–453.

Sano, K., Sekino, H., & Mayanagi, Y. (1972). Results of stimulation and destruction of the posterior hypothalamus in cases with violent, aggressive, or restless behavior. In E. Hitchcock, L. Laitinen, & K. Vaernet (Eds.), *Psychosurgery* (p. 203). Springfield, IL: Thomas.

Spiers, P. A., Schomer, D. L., Blume, H. W., & Mesulam, M. (1985). Temperolimbic epilepsy and behavior. In M. Mesulam (Ed.), *Principles of behavioral neurology* (pp. 289–326). Philadelphia: Davis.

ROBERT F. SAWICKI
*Lake Erie Institute of
Rehabilitation*

NEUROPSYCHOLOGY

PSYCHOTHERAPY WITH INDIVIDUALS WITH DISABILITIES

Psychotherapy is defined as the application of psychological theories and principles to the treatment of problems of abnormal behavior, emotions, and thinking. The three major schools of psychotherapy are psychodynamic therapies, behavior therapies, and humanistic therapies.

The goal of psychodynamic, or insight, therapies is to help the client gain a sound understanding of his or her problems. Psychodynamic therapies are rooted in Freud's personality theory. Current behavioral and emotional problems are assumed to be the result of unconscious, intrapsychic conflicts and the unconscious mechanisms (i.e., defense mechanisms) employed to deal with them. It is a major goal of insight therapies to help bring this unconscious material into consciousness and thereby allow the client to exercise conscious, rational control over his or her actions. Hostile and sexual impulses as well as other motives or needs not acceptable to the individual's conscious sense of morality exert an influence on behavior through the unconscious. Techniques used in classical psychoanalysis to accomplish the goal of insight include free association, interpretation, and transference. Through free association, the client is encouraged to say whatever comes into his or her mind, no matter how trivial, embarrassing, or illogical. The analyst minimizes his or her influence on the client's verbal associations by responding minimally and nondirectively. At critical times during the free association, the analyst provides interpretations of the verbalizations in an attempt to help the client gain insight.

Transference refers to the expected tendency on the part of the client to experience the therapist-client relationship as similar to the parent-child relationship. Because the origin of the client's problems is assumed to reside in early parent-child interactions, transference permits the client to resolve problems from the past in the context of a new relationship. It is hoped that in the process, the client will discover insight into his or her behavior. When the patient sees a replaying of the old role of helpless child, he or she realizes the possibility of assuming adult roles in relationships with significant others rather than being driven by old, unresolved feelings experienced in the original parent-child relationship. Psychoanalysis is a complex and time-consuming process (50 minutes per day for months or years). Scientific evidence of its effectiveness is inadequate compared with that on more recent behavior therapies. Contemporary psychodynamic therapists retain an appreciation for unconscious influences on behavior but use more direct and focused techniques to help the client gain insight and exercise more rational control. The goal is to help clients find more realistic and effective ways to cope with their emotional needs. The client is helped to accept emotional needs and to find ways to meet them within the demands of external reality.

Behavior therapies differ from psychodynamic therapies in several ways. First, the presenting problem is viewed as the appropriate focus for the treatment rather than assumed underlying causes in the client's intrapsychic life. Second, principles of learning derived from experimental psychology studies are applied to modifying maladaptive behaviors and cognitions. Maladaptive behaviors and cognitions are assumed to be learned, and they can be modified through the application of learning principles. Behavior therapists focus on the here and now rather than on the historical causes of a problem. Behavior therapy is a broad term encompassing a wide variety of therapeutic techniques. A basic tenet of behavior therapy is that different problems require different treatments. Furthermore, the selection of treatment procedures are based on empirical studies of the effectiveness of different procedures with similar problems.

Humanistic therapies also incorporate a wide range of techniques. Therapies with a humanistic orientation share a belief that each client is a unique individual striving for personal growth, or self-actualization. Carl Rogers' (1951) client-centered therapy is the best known example of the humanistic therapies. Key therapy techniques include the therapist's positive regard for the client and empathic, or reflective, listening. In reflective listening, the therapist is nondirective, serving as a mirror for the client, helping the client to sort out thoughts, attitudes, and feelings. It is assumed that the patient has the personal resources for solving his or her problem but needs the support of the therapist and an opportunity to see the problems more clearly.

The rationale for providing psychotherapy to pupils with disabilities is that persons with disabilities have the same or greater need for improved psychological functioning as nondisabled persons. Some pupils may not be able to focus their mental energies on learning because they are experiencing psychological stress and emotional confusion. When a child's emotional and behavioral problems interfere with his or her learning and social behavior, educational interventions need to be supplemented by interventions that focus on the interfering emotional and behavioral problems.

REFERENCE

Rogers, C. (1951). *Client-centered therapy: Its current practice, implications, and theory.* Boston: Houghton-Mifflin.

JAN N. HUGHES
Texas A&M University

ADJUSTMENT OF INDIVIDUALS WITH DISABILITIES
FAMILY COUNSELING
FAMILY THERAPY

PSYCHOTROPIC DRUGS

The majority of drugs classified as psychotropic affect brain processes and thus indirectly produce behavioral changes. Their chemicals work by either increasing or decreasing the availability of specific neurotransmitters. The major classifications include hypnotics, major tranquilizers (antipsychotic agents), minor tranquilizers (antianxiety agents), stimulants, opiates, and psychedelics (hallucinogens). In most cases, these drugs increase or decrease activity level by producing effects on an individual's level of arousal. Potent psychedelic drugs add perceptual distortions to the more general effects.

Hypnotics are intended to produce drowsiness, enhance the onset of sleep, and maintain the sleep state (Katzung, 1982). These drugs produce a more profound depression on the central nervous system. They typically are referred to as barbiturates. Examples of this class of drugs are pentobarbital (Nembutal); secobarbital (Seconal); amobarbital (Amytal); and glutethimide (Doriden, Tuinal).

Barbiturates often are called "downers" because of their soporific action. Intoxication from barbiturates produces effects similar to those noted with alcohol. (For a complete review of barbiturate effects, see Blum, 1984, pp. 165–210.) Of particular concern in the use of barbiturates is the tendency to produce physical dependence over time. Additionally, unless withdrawal is performed in graded steps under medical supervision, there is the possibility of mortality during sudden withdrawal.

Barbiturates are the drugs most involved in suicides, including accidental suicides (automatisms). The latter refers to a state of confusion during which an individual who habitually uses sedatives is unsure whether a pill has been ingested and proceeds to take additional pills (Ray, 1972).

Tranquilizers are intended to diminish the discomfort associated with anxiety states. Stimulants are intended to combat fatigue and have been used with children to limit hyperactivity. Moderate doses of stimulants (amphetamines) have been prescribed as adjuncts to weight reduction programs. Examples of these drugs are amphetamines (Benzedrine), caffeine (coffee, cola), cocaine, dextroamphetamine (Dexedrine), methamphetamine (Methedrine), methylphenidate (Ritalin), and nicotine (tobacco).

Stimulants may be drunk (coffee), smoked (tobacco), inhaled (cocaine), ingested (amphetamines of various types), or injected (amphetamines). Though the following effects are seen most often in amphetamine abuse, they also are evident in relative degrees with the abuse of any of the stimulants. After use, the individual experiences a mild flush, which in the case of injectable amphetamines is compared to sexual orgasm. Feelings of euphoria, invulnerability, absence of boredom, and unlimited energy follow. Since abusers are likely to build up a tolerance for a specific drug, increased dosages or drug mixtures are used to create the "high." Continued abuse of a stimulant appears related both to the wish to recreate the high and to the desire to avoid the fatigue and depression that occur during withdrawal.

Negative side effects of chronic abuse include malnutrition, insomnia, impulsiveness, defective reasoning, delusional thinking, hallucinations, and paranoia (Blum, 1984). Owing to the affective lability of abusers, the associated hyperactivity, and the significant paranoia, abuse of amphetamines tends to set up conditions in which violence may occur.

Opiates are intended to provide relief from pain and appear to mimic natural analgesics (endorphins). Historically, morphine was used not only to provide relief from extreme pain, but also for diarrhea, cough, anxiety, and insomnia (Katzung, 1982). Examples of drugs in this class include opium, morphine, codeine, heroin, dihydromorphine (Dilaudid), and meperidine (Demerol).

Of particular concern with this class of drug is that, along with tolerance for a specific drug, physical dependence also occurs. Though central nervous system depressants, opiates produce feelings of euphoria in persons who are experiencing either physical or emotional pain (Leavitt, 1982). Persons appear to start abusing opiates secondary to situational stress, unenlightened treatment for severe pain, and comradeship (Blum, 1984). Chronic abuse produces periods of nausea, vomiting, constipation, respiratory inefficiency, and limited pain awareness. The latter produces additional effects since abusers are unaware of physical distress (Leavitt). Mortality rates among heroine addicts under 30 are approximately 8 times that of nonaddicts (Leavitt).

Psychedelics have been used in various research programs, from perceptual research to brainwashing techniques (Leavitt, 1982). They have no consistent, specified therapeutic value. Some, like peyote, have been used in religious ceremonies because they bring on visions (hallucinations). It is this hallucinogenic property that makes these drugs attractive to abusers.

REFERENCES

Blum, K. B. (1984). *Handbook of abusable drugs.* New York: Gardner.

Katzung, B. G. (1982). *Basic & clinical pharmacology.* Los Altos, CA: Lange Medical.

Leavitt, F. (1982). *Drugs and behavior.* New York: Wiley.

Ray, O. S. (1972). *Drugs, society and human behavior.* St. Louis, MO: Mosby.

ROBERT F. SAWICKI
*Lake Erie Institute of
Rehabilitation*

DRUG ABUSE
DRUG THERAPY
HALLUCINOGENS
TRANQUILIZERS

PSYC SCAN

During the past decade, a vast amount of information, traditionally available only in print, has been placed into computer-readable and retrievable form. Consequently, psychologists, special educators, and researchers have at their disposal a wealth of knowledge that has been classified, summarized, and stored for easy, quick, inexpensive retrieval by computer. Psyc SCAN is a service of Psyc INFO, which is part of the Psychological Abstract Information Services Department of the American Psychological Association.

Psyc SCAN provides computer-readable information and publications in various areas that are important to professionals involved in special education: applied, clinical, and developmental psychology, learning/communication disorders (LD) and mental retardation (MR). On a quarterly basis, Psyc SCAN offers subscribers an effective and efficient way of keeping up to date on practice and research in their fields by providing citations and abstracts from recently published journal articles.

Abstracts in the applied, clinical, and developmental psychology sections of Psyc SCAN are derived from a set of core journals. When a publication is selected for one of these three areas, all relevant articles are summarized and listed by journal title along with complete citation, abstract, and index terms.

Abstracts in the LD/MR section of Psyc SCAN likewise are published quarterly and offer a practical way of keeping abreast of clinical and educational literature in the field. For this section, however, material is taken from all of the approximately 13,000 serial publications covered by the Psyc INFO Data Base. As such, each issue is arranged by three broad areas: learning disorders, communication disorders, and mental retardation; they are further subdivided into theories, research, and assessment and educational issues. All entries in this section contain full bibliographic citations, index terms, and abstracts.

Additional information about Psyc SCAN and related services can be obtained from Psych INFO Services, American Psychological Association, 750 First St., N.E., Washington, DC 20002-4242.

CHARLES A. MAHER
Rutgers University

LOUIS J. KRUGER
Tufts University
First edition

MARIE ALMOND
*The University of Texas of the
Permian Basin*
Second edition

COMPUTER-ASSISTED INSTRUCTION
SPECIAL NET

KIMBERLY F. APPLEQUIST
*University of Colorado at
Colorado Springs*
Third edition

PUBLIC LAW 108-446

See INDIVIDUALS WITH DISABILITIES EDUCATION IMPROVEMENT ACT OF 2004 (IDEIA).

PUBLIC LAW 95-561

The Gifted and Talented Children's Education Act of 1978 was added, by PL 95-561, as Part A of Title IX of the Elementary and Secondary Education Act. The statute and its companion regulations describe gifted and talented children as individuals from birth through 18 years of age who require special educational services or activities because they possess demonstrated or potential abilities that give evidence of high performance capability in areas such as intellectual, creative, specific academic, or leadership ability, or in the performing and visual arts.

Financial assistance was provided under the Gifted and Talented Children's Education Program through two types of awards. Each state educational agency was eligible for a grant to plan, develop, operate, and improve programs for gifted and talented children. Eligible public or private organizations, agencies, or institutions also could compete for awards to conduct personnel training, model projects, information dissemination, or research.

On August 13, 1981, this funding program was consolidated into a block grant under Chapter 2 of the Education and Consolidation Improvement Act of 1981. States and localities may use the block grant funds, as appropriate, for continued services to gifted and talented children. Although recent years have seen the introduction of numerous bills designed to provide additional support for the education of gifted and talented students (e.g., the Gifted and Talented Students Education Act of 2001 and the Gifted and Talented Students Education Act of 2003), such measures have met with limited success, often folded into other education measures with reduced funding. Notable successors to PL 95-561 include the Javitz Gifted and Talented Students Education Act, which provided funding of demonstration grants and the National Research Center on the Gifted and Talented, and the No Child Left Behind Act of 2001, which authorized competitive grants to states to allow them to expand their capacity to meet the needs of gifted and talented children.

SHIRLEY A. JONES
*Virginia Polytechnic Institute
and State University*
Second edition

PUERTO RICO, SPECIAL EDUCATION IN

Special education services in Puerto Rico are administered under the legislative provisions of IDEA, which are reflected in territorial law concerning the handicapped. Before IDEA and PL 94-142, there were few services. Since the legislation there has been greater consistency and continuity of services, improvement and expansion of personnel preparation, reduction of negative attitudes, and increasing movement of children toward the mainstream (Smith-Davis, Burke, & Noel, 1984).

Until a few years ago, the handicapped population in Puerto Rico was generally served in self-contained classes at the elementary level. Since 1979 programming has shifted to the mild and moderately handicapped, to mainstreaming, and to programs at intermediate and secondary levels. Prevocational and vocational centers for the handicapped have also been established (Smith-Davis et al., 1984).

Teacher certification policies in Puerto Rico are primarily noncategorical, with categorical certification reserved for those serving low-incidence populations. Smith-Davis et al. (1984) report that the University of Puerto Rico, which has had a special education program since 1965, and the Inter-American University, both offer undergraduate and graduate programs in special education. The University of the Sacred Heart and the Catholic University of Puerto Rico offer primarily undergraduate programs. In addition, two American universities, Fordham University–Puerto Rico Campus, and New York University's extension program offer graduate training at campuses on the island. All of these institutions offer adequate programs on learning disabilities, mental retardation, emotional disorders, and behavioral disorders. However, formal programs on the severely retarded and multiply handicapped are inadequate although some course work is available. The Department of Education carries on a vigorous in-service program at both local and regional levels and employs tuition assistance and other means to retrain and recertify practitioners.

Special education practices in Puerto Rico must be interpreted in light of the school system, which is highly centralized. It is organized into a central office responsible for all administrative and policy decisions, and six educational regions, each under a director appointed by the secretary of education (who is appointed by the governor at cabinet level). Each region is subdivided into districts run by superintendents. Within this structure, special education is largely centralized. It is directed by a special education director and is divided into four units: administrative, curricular, academic, and vocational. Regional special education supervisors are appointed to each region. Thus there are six plus two supervisors, one each for prevocational and vocational programs (Brown, 1977).

Unlike the United States, where Puerto Ricans are a linguistic minority, in Puerto Rico they are the majority. Consequently, all services and instructional aids and materials for special education are in Spanish. It is important that U.S. special educators be aware that Puerto Rico, through the governor's office and other agencies, is ready to offer technical assistance in these areas to anyone who requests it (Cruz, 1979).

REFERENCES

Brown, F. M. (1977, August). *Southeast Area Learning Resource Center: Final technical report, Sept. 1, 1974 through May 31, 1977.* Washington, DC: Bureau of Education for the Handicapped.

Cruz, D. (1979, June). Outreach problems in Puerto Rico. In G. Dixon & D. Bridges (Eds.), *On being Hispanic and disabled: The special challenge of an underserved population.* Chicago: Illinois State Board of Vocational Education and Rehabilitation.

Olizares, G. (1979, June). Hispanic and disabled. In G. Dixon & D. Bridges (Eds.), *On being Hispanic and disabled: The special challenge of an underserved population.* Chicago: Illinois State Board of Vocational Education and Rehabilitation.

Smith-Davis, J., Burke, P. J., & Noel, M. M. (1984). *Personnel to educate the handicapped in America: Supply and demand from a programmatic viewpoint.* College Park: Maryland University College of Education.

H. ROBERTA ARRIGO
*Hunter College, City University
of New York*

MEXICO, SPECIAL EDUCATION IN

PUNISHMENT

Punishment, defined functionally, occurs when the presentation of an aversive consequence contingent on the emission of a behavior reduces the subsequent rate of that behavior. It is a commonly employed operant conditioning procedure. As Alberto and Troutman (1986) state, "Any stimulus can be labeled a punisher if its contingent application results in a reduction of the target behavior. A punisher, like a reinforcer, can be identified only by its effect on behavior—not on the nature of the consequent stimulus" (p. 245). Thus the mere application of an aversive stimulus (such as a spanking) or removal of a positive stimulus (such as a token or money) cannot be termed a punishment procedure unless a reductive effect on the target behavior occurs. Unfortunately, this reductive effect on behavior by a consequent stimulus is seldom evaluated in everyday use, thus resulting in inappropriate and ineffective use of the punishment procedure.

Although punishment may involve the removal of a positive stimulus, it is most commonly applied by parents and teachers as the application of an aversive stimulus contingent on a behavior in order to reduce that behavior (Walker & Shea, 1984). A common example of this form would be physical or corporal punishment. Although the application of aversive stimuli has been documented as an effective procedure in reducing self-injurious behaviors (Dorsey et al., 1980; Sajwaj, Libet, & Agras, 1974) and severe aggressive behaviors toward others (Ludwig et al., 1969), its use in the form of physical punishment is not generally advocated by most professionals in the field of behavior management as the preferred means of reducing inappropriate behaviors. Besides legal, humane, and ethical concerns, there are a multitude of other disadvantages associated with the use of punishment:

> In the long run, it could cause people to punish more often and to harm themselves and their victims by injuring them, if the punishment is physical, or by impairing social relationships and promoting aggression or escape, self-blame, imitative aggression, and other harmful side-effects. (Sulzer-Azaroff, & Mayer, 1986, p. 146)

REFERENCES

Alberto, P. A., & Troutman, A. C. (1986). *Applied behavior analysis for teachers* (2nd ed.). Columbus, OH: Merrill.

Dorsey, M. F., Iwata, B. A., Ong, P., & McSween, T. E. (1980). Treatment of self-injurious behavior using a water mist: Initial response suppression and generalization. *Journal of Applied Behavior Analysis, 13,* 324–333.

Kerr, M. M., & Nelson, M. N. (1983). *Strategies for managing behavior problems in the classroom.* Columbus, OH: Merrill.

Ludwig, A. M., Marx, A. J., Hill, P. A., & Browning, R. M. (1969). The control of violent behavior through faradic shock. *Journal of Nervous & Mental Disease, 148,* 624–637.

Sajwaj, T., Libet, J., & Agras, S. (1974). Lemon juice therapy: The control of life-threatening rumination in a six-month old infant. *Journal of Applied Behavior Analysis, 7,* 557–563.

Sulzer-Azaroff, B., & Mayer, G. R. (1986). *Achieving educational excellence using behavioral strategies.* New York: Holt, Rinehart, & Winston.

Walker, J. E., & Shea, T. M. (1984). *Behavior management: A practical approach for educators* (3rd ed.). St. Louis, MO: Mosby.

LOUIS J. LANUNZIATA
*University of North Carolina at
Wilmington*

APPLIED BEHAVIOR ANALYSIS
AVERSIVE STIMULUS
NEGATIVE PUNISHMENT
PUNISHMENT, POSITIVE

PUNISHMENT, POSITIVE

Punishment is a procedure in which the presentation of a stimulus contingent on a behavior reduces the rate of emission of the behavior (Azrin & Holz, 1966). Punishment, like reinforcement, is defined by its effect on behavior. Numerous behavior change techniques used by psychologists and educators can be classified as punishment techniques (e.g., timeout, response cost, overcorrection, verbal reprimands, and electric shock; Axelrod & Apsche, 1983).

The use of adjectives such as "positive" and "negative" are most frequently associated with reinforcement techniques, but occasionally have been employed to further define punishment techniques. Behaviorists use these adjectives to describe the contingent presentation of a stimulus (positive) or the contingent removal of a stimulus (negative). These terms should *not* be interpreted as value judgments synonymous with "good" and "bad." Therefore, *positive punishment* is the contingent presentation of an aversive stimuli for a misbehavior or rule violation. Spanking a child for fighting with a peer is a classic example of positive punishment. Socially more acceptable examples of positive punishment include undertaking a noxious task such as cleaning a restroom (i.e., the aversive stimulus) contingent on messing it up. *Negative punishment* is the contingent removal of a positive stimulus. Common examples of negative punishment techniques include response cost or timeout.

REFERENCES

Axelrod, S., & Apsche, J. (1983). *The effects of punishment on human behavior.* New York: Academic.

Azrin, N. H., & Holz, W. C. (1966). Punishment. In W. A. Honig (Ed.), *Operant Behavior: Areas of research and application* (pp. 380–447). New York: Appleton.

STEPHEN N. ELLIOTT
University of Wisconsin at Madison

PUNISHMENT

PURDUE PERCEPTUAL-MOTOR SURVEY

The Purdue Perceptual-Motor Survey (PPMS; Roach & Kephart, 1966) was developed to enable qualitative observations of problem areas of perceptual-motor development. Subtests include walking board, jumping, identification of body parts, imitation of movements (following the examiner's arm movements), obstacle course, Kraus Weber (requiring the child to raise first the upper and then the lower torso while prone), angels in the snow (differentiation of arms and legs in various patterns), chalkboard (e.g., drawing simple to complex patterns), ocular pursuits (visual tracking), and visual achievement forms (a paper and pencil copying task).

The theoretical and practical implications of the scale were described in Kephart (1971). The major assumptions that were controversial (Hammill, 1982) were that higher levels of learning are dependent on a motor base of achievement, and that perceptual-motor interventions are important for the remediation of academic deficits.

The norms were based on data from 200 children in grades one through four. Means and standard deviations were provided by grade. Test-retest reliability was .95 ($n = 30$, one-week interval). A validation study compared the performance of a sample of 97 nonachieving children with the normative sample (children with mental retardation were excluded). With one exception, items differentiated between groups.

REFERENCES

Hammill, D. D. (1982). Assessing and training perceptual-motor skills. In D. D. Hammill & N. R. Bartel, *Teaching children with learning and behavior problems* (3rd ed., pp. 379–408). Boston: Allyn & Bacon.

Kephart, N. C. (1971). *The slow learner in the classroom* (2nd ed.). Columbus, OH: Merrill.

Roach, E. G., & Kephart, N. C. (1966). *The Purdue Perceptual-Motor Survey.* Columbus, OH: Merrill.

DAVID W. BARNETT
University of Cincinnati

PERCEPTUAL AND MOTOR SKILLS

PUTAMEN

The putamen is the largest nucleus of the basal ganglia (caudate nucleus, putamen, globus pallidus, claustrum and amygdala) that function in background motor control via the extrapyramidal motor system (Carpenter & Sutin, 1983). The putamen also houses receptor sites for the dopamine containing neurons projecting from the substantia nigra. (The nigrastriatal system with the striatum is the putamen and candate nucleus.) The putamen is located lateral to the thalamus and internal capsule but medial to the external capsule and inner aspect of the Sylvian fissure (see Figure 1 under CAT scan in this encyclopedia for depictions of its location). Since dopamine is an essential neurotransmitter for both normal motor and mental functioning, damage to the putamen may result in a wide spectrum of neurobehavioral changes. The prototype disorder of the basal ganglia that best exemplifies these motor and mental changes is Huntington's chorea. In Huntington's chorea there are specific motor deficits characterized by uncontrolled choreic movements as well as progressive dementia (Heilman &

Valenstein, 1985). The disruption of any part of the nigra-striatal system will affect dopamine production and will have significant neurobehavioral effects. These are discussed in the section on the substantia nigra. Recent research has also implicated a greater role of the basal ganglia in language function than had been suspected (Segalowitz, 1983).

REFERENCES

Carpenter, M. B., & Sutin, J. (1983). *Human neuroanatomy* (8th ed.). Baltimore: Williams & Wilkins.

Heilman, K. M., & Valenstein, E. (1985). *Clinical neuropsychology.* New York: Oxford University Press.

Segalowitz, S. J. (1983). *Language functions and brain organization.* New York: Academic.

ERIN D. BIGLER
Brigham Young University

HUNTINGTON'S CHOREA
SUBSTANTIA, NIGRA

Q

Q-SORT

The Q-sort is a technique used to implement Q-methodology, a set of philosophical, psychological, statistical, and psychometric ideas propounded by William Stephenson (1953). The Q-sort was developed as a research tool, in particular a tool for exploring and testing theoretical formulations (e.g., about the existence of different educational philosophies). However, its use has been extended to both clinical assessment and to program evaluation.

The Q-sort is a way of rank-ordering objects. The objects ranked usually take the form of statements written on cards (though real objects, such as works of art, have been subjected to the Q-sort also). The sorter is given a set of cards—usually between 60 and 120—and instructed to distribute them into a fixed number of piles arranged along some continuum (e.g., approval to disapproval). The sorter is required to put a specified number of cards in each pile, resulting in a normal or quasi-normal distribution. This distribution permits the use of conventional statistical techniques, including correlation, analysis of variance, and factor analysis, in analyzing the results.

The results of the Q-sort typically are used to draw inferences about people (not the objects they are ranking) for theoretical, clinical, or program evaluation purposes. For example, a preliminary theory about the existence of two opposing educational philosophies can be tested by creating a set of statements reflecting each philosophy, having the combined set sorted on an "approval-disapproval" continuum, and analyzing the results to determine if there are groups of people who rank-order the statements in the same way. In the clinical setting, the patient's sort can be compared with those associated with known pathological syndromes. Finally, in program evaluation, sorts made before and after a program can be compared with one another or with a criterion sort meant to represent the desired outcome of the program.

Q-methodology is not universally accepted in the research community (Kerlinger, 1973). Criticisms of Q are based primarily on the fact that it cannot be used easily with large samples and on its violation of the statistical assumption of independence (i.e., the response to one item should not be affected by the response to any other). However, even with these liabilities, Q is regarded by many as a useful tool for particular research and applied purposes.

REFERENCES

Kerlinger, F. N. (1973). *Foundations of behavioral research* (2nd ed.). New York: Holt, Rinehart, & Winston.

Stephenson, W. (1953). *The study of behavior.* Chicago: University of Chicago Press.

RANDY ELLIOT BENNETT
MARY LOUISE LENNON
Educational Testing Service

FACTOR ANALYSIS
MEASUREMENT
PHILOSOPHY OF EDUCATION FOR INDIVIDUALS WITH DISABILITIES
RESEARCH IN SPECIAL EDUCATION

QUADRIPLEGIA

Quadriplegia is often referred to as paralysis from the neck down. Although this definition may be accurate for certain conditions, it is also misleading. A more accurate description of quadriplegia is a nonspecific paralysis or loss of normal function in all four limbs of the body. The condition most often affects motor skills but also may affect sensory awareness. Quadriplegia may result from damage to or dysfunction of the brain (e.g., cerebral palsy, stroke, traumatic head injury), spinal cord (e.g., spinal cord injury, amyotrophic lateral sclerosis), or peripheral structures (e.g., muscular dystrophy, multiple sclerosis). The condition also may occur as a result of tumor, toxic chemicals, congenital abnormalities, or infection. The term sometimes includes quadriparesis, which is considered a weakness or incomplete paralysis of the four extremities. Quadriplegia is not generally associated with the head or neck, but it may involve these structures in some conditions (e.g., cerebral palsy).

The specific skills or functions that are lost or impaired for persons with quadriplegia may vary considerably and depend largely on the individual's primary impairment. For example, a person who experiences quadriplegia as a result of a spinal cord injury experiences a loss of sensation and movement below the level of the injury. When the injury occurs at the level of the third cervical vertebra (C3), the person has essentially no sensation or functional use of the body below the neck. On the other hand, a person with a C5 injury has some active movement available at the elbow (flexion and supination) and shoulder (abduction and external rotation), but most other movements are lost. In the latter stages of the Duchenne's form of muscular dystrophy, a person may be able to use the fingers to write, type, or manipulate other small objects. Because of progressive weakness in the large muscles of the body, people with this type of quadriplegia are unable to move their arms at the shoulder or wrist. Unlike quadriplegia from spinal cord injury, sensation in this type of impairment remains intact. Children with quadriplegia owed to cerebral palsy are almost always able to move the joints in their upper extremities. They usually experience normal tactile sensation, but they may have abnormal kinesthetic sensation. Because of abnormal changes in muscle tone in various groups of muscles, movements are either very rigid and stiff, uncoordinated, or limp and flaccid. Children with quadriplegic cerebral palsy also may experience abnormal muscle tone and movement patterns in their neck or facial muscles in addition to involvement in all four extremities.

The specific treatment, education, or other intervention for persons with quadriplegia also is dependent on the impairment that causes this condition. A team approach using multidisciplinary, transdisciplinary, or interdisciplinary models is essential in the care and management of an individual with quadriplegia. Team members may include physicians, nurses, teachers, physical therapists, occupational therapists, speech pathologists, rehabilitation engineers, family members, attendants, and, as often as possible, the affected individual. Sometimes individuals with quadriplegia need considerable assistance for even the most routine activities (e.g., eating a meal), while others are able to live independently, pursue a career, and raise a family.

Although quadriplegia usually results in extensive disability, a variety of electronic and nonelectronic devices may be used to facilitate more normal experiences or abilities. Electrically powered wheelchairs, specially designed passenger vans, adapted eating utensils, augmentative communication systems, and personal hygiene and grooming devices are only a few examples that may be used to compensate for impaired skills. These technologic advances have fostered a more independent lifestyle for many people with quadriplegia, but some advocates for people with disabilities would argue that social changes also are needed to permit the greatest level of independence. Elimination of environmental and attitudinal barriers and affirmative action for employment often are identified as essential components of a productive and satisfying life. References illuminating etiology, definition, and management are cited below for further reading.

REFERENCES

Bobath, B. (1985). *Abnormal postural reflex activity caused by brain lesions* (3rd ed.). Rockville, MD: Aspen Systems.

Bobath, B., & Bobath, K. (1975). *Motor development in the different types of cerebral palsy.* London: Heinemann Medical Books.

Ford, J., & Duckworth, B. (1974). *Physical management for the quadriplegic patient.* Philadelphia: Davis.

Miller, B., & Keane, C. (1983). *Encyclopedia and dictionary of medical nursing and allied health* (3rd ed.). Philadelphia: Saunders.

Nagel, D. A. (1975). Traumatic paraplegia and quadriplegia. In E. E. Bleck & D. A. Nagel (Eds.), *Physically handicapped children—A medical atlas for teachers* (pp. 209–214). New York: Grune & Stratton.

Trombly, C. A. (1983). Spinal cord injury. In C. A. Trombly (Ed.), *Occupational therapy for physical dysfunction* (2nd ed., pp. 385–398). Baltimore: Williams & Wilkins.

DANIEL D. LIPKA
*Lincoln Way Special Education
Regional Resources Center*

ACCESSIBILITY OF BUILDINGS

QUANTITATIVE NEUROIMAGING

Contemporary neuroimaging began with the introduction of computerized tomography (CT) in the 1970s and magnetic resonance imaging (MRI) in the 1980s. Initially, scans were interpreted solely on a clinical basis by appearance of an abnormality, but now because of the excellent image resolution and structural detail of gross brain anatomy, any identifiable brain structure can be quantified. For example, Figure 1 is an MRI from a child who suffered a severe traumatic brain injury, resulting in hippocampal atrophy. While the reduction in the hippocampus is obvious on visual inspection, quantitative analysis actually demonstrates that it was less than 35 percent of normal. Since the hippocampus is a critical structure in short-term memory processing, knowing about its structural integrity, through quantitative analysis, helps the clinician understand the type and extent of cognitive deficits exhibited by a child like this. Computer programs are now available that permit rapid and automated quantitative analyses of the brain integrated with functional neuroimaging techniques that will likely yield powerful clinical tools in understanding the influences

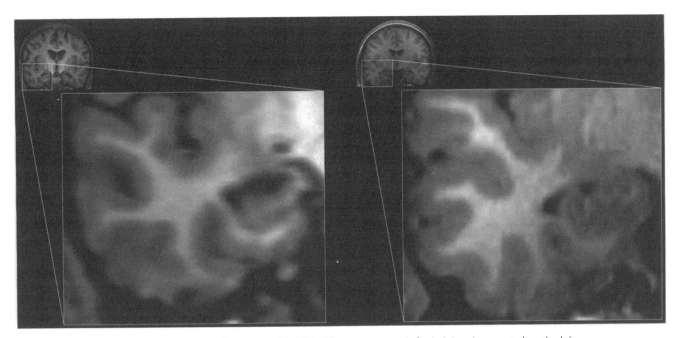

Figure 1 A coronal MRI of a 12-year-old child with severe traumatic brain injury is presented on the left, with the right temporal area blown-up in the inset, showing severe hippocampal atrophy, as compared to an age-matched control subject on the right. Quantitative analysis indicated the hippocampus to be 2.0 cm³ in the child with a brain injury, whereas the control child had a value consistent with the control mean for this age, which is 6.1 cm³. Presence of severe hippocampal atrophy is associated with cognitive problems, particularly with memory.

of brain damage and dysfunction in special education (see Kesler et al., 2006).

REFERENCE

Kesler, S. R., Vohr, B., Schneider, K. C., Katz, K. H., Makuch, R. W., Reiss, A. L., & Ment, L. R. (2006). Increased temporal lobe gyrification in preterm children. *Neuropsychologia, 44,* 445–453.

ERIN D. BIGLER
Brigham Young University

DIFFUSION TENSOR IMAGING
MAGNETIC RESONANCE IMAGING

QUAY, HERBERT C. (1927–   )

Born in Portland, Maine, Herbert C. Quay received his BS (1951) and MS (1952) in psychology from Florida State University. He later earned his PhD (1958) in clinical psychology from the University of Illinois. During his distinguished career as a teacher and researcher, Quay was chairman of the department of psychology, director of the program in applied sciences, and professor of psychology and pediatrics at the University of Miami. He is currently retired.

Quay questioned the traditional classification system of special education categories, and in 1971 he discovered that the number, rather than type, of behavior symptoms was more effective in identifying psychopathology in a child. This finding acknowledges that most children exhibit most behaviors labeled pathologic at some point in their development without becoming pathological themselves (Werry & Quay, 1971). He also found that an assessor's theory of development and pathology was a factor in how that assessor diagnosed a child (Quay, 1973). That is, if an assessor believed in a theory of process dysfunctions, there would be a different diagnosis than from an assessor who believed in experiential deficits.

His work in the area of psychopathology in children includes the development of the Behavior Problem Checklist, a three-point scale devised using factor analysis to rate traits of problem behaviors in children and adolescents. Quay advocated the checklist to differentiate dimensions of deviance, select treatment programs, and determine systematic differences among children with divergent patterns of deviance (Quay, 1977). Revised procedures for assessment using this tool are delineated in the *Manual for the Revised Behavior Problem Checklist* (1996).

Since the early 1980s, the vast majority of Quay's work has been in the field of child clinical psychology, including *Handbook of Juvenile Delinquency* (1987), part of a Wiley series on personality processes, and *Disruptive Behavior Disorders in Childhood* (1994), a compilation of papers prepared in honor of his retirement (H. C. Quay, pers. comm., May 21, 1998). Quay has been recognized in *Who's Who in the World*, *Who's Who in America*, *American Men of Science*, and *Leaders in Education*.

REFERENCES

Quay, H. C. (1973). Special education: Assumptions, techniques, and evaluative criteria. *Exceptional Children, 40,* 165–170.

Quay, H. C. (1977). Measuring dimensions of deviant behavior: The Problem Behavior Checklist. *Journal of Abnormal Child Psychology, 5,* 277–287.

Quay, H. C. (1987). *Handbook of juvenile delinquency.* New York: Wiley.

Quay, H. C., & Peterson, D. R. (1987). *Manual for the Revised Behavior Problem Checklist.* Coral Gables, FL: University of Miami.

Quay, H. C., & Routh, D. K. (1994). *Disruptive behavior disorders in childhood.* New York: Plenum.

Werry, J. S., & Quay, H. C. (1971). The prevalence of behavior symptoms in younger elementary children. *American Journal of Orthopsychiatry, 41,* 136–143.

E. Valerie Hewitt
Texas A&M University
First edition

Tamara J. Martin
The University of Texas of the Permian Basin
Second edition

QUESTIONNAIRES IN SPECIAL EDUCATION

Questionnaires are often used for gathering research data in special education. They are relatively inexpensive, can assure anonymity, and can be used with relative ease by novice researchers as well as seasoned professionals.

Pride (1979) has observed that the mail questionnaire in particular is useful in obtaining data from distant populations. It reaches subjects too busy to be interviewed, enables targeting subgroups of respondents, and is conducive in format to framing responses in a manner suitable for statistical analysis. The mail questionnaire can also "eliminate interviewer bias to questions that are sensitive or embarrassing when posed by an interviewer" (Pride, 1979, p. 59).

As popular survey research tools questionnaires (whether mailed, completed by telephone, or administered in person) require careful design. The design process includes separate decisions about (1) the kind of information sought (e.g., attitudinal, behavioral), (2) the question structure (e.g., open-ended, close-ended with ordered categories), and (3) the actual choice of words (Dillman, 1978, pp. 79–80). Every investigation presents special requirements and different

problems. Oppenheim (1966), Dillman (1978), and Sudman and Bradburn (1982) provide thorough discussions about the many factors to be considered when designing questionnaires and detailed recommendations for writing and presenting questions.

Despite the fact that the mail survey is, in many cases, the most feasible approach for retrieving data from large, widely dispersed samples, many researchers have expressed concern about its methodological rigor and adequacy. This concern is based largely on the grounds of seriously deficient response rates. "The most common flaw is nonresponse of a size or nature which makes the answers nonrepresentative of the total sample and thus the total universe" (Erdos, 1970, p. 142). Returns of less than 40 or 50 percent are common. Additionally, there are limitations on the nature of data that may be obtained and the quality of responses to many mail questionnaires.

Kanuk and Berenson (1975) confirmed that, despite the proliferation of research studies (well over 200) reporting techniques to reduce nonresponse bias, "there is no strong empirical evidence favoring any techniques other than follow-up and the use of monetary incentives" (p. 451). Research on the topic generally has been narrowly focused, poorly integrated, and contradictory. Erdos (1970) and Dillman (1978) represent the few attempts to improve response rates to mail questionnaires from the perspective of addressing the entire mail survey process.

Dillman's recommendations offer a fully integrated, planned sequence of procedures and techniques that are designed to increase response rates and that are fully adaptable to research problems in special education. His total design method (TDM) attempts to present mail surveys in such a way that respondents develop proprietary attitudes toward the research project in which they are being asked to participate. Based on the tenets of motivational psychology, Dillman has postulated that the process of designing and sending a questionnaire, and getting respondents to complete it in an honest manner and return it, is a special kind of social exchange. His highly prescribed method and related strategies are designed to minimize the costs for responding, maximize the rewards for doing so, and establish trust that those rewards will be delivered. Readily adaptable in its present form, the TDM also provides a useful frame of reference against which the design aspects of each mail survey research problem may be considered.

REFERENCES

Dillman, D. (1978). *Mail and telephone surveys: The total design method.* New York: Wiley.

Erdos, P. L. (1970). *Professional mail surveys.* New York: McGraw-Hill.

Kanuk, L., & Berenson, C. (1975). Mail survey and response rates: A literature review. *Journal of Marketing Research, 12,* 440–453.

Oppenheim, A. N. (1966). *Questionnaire design and attitudes measurement.* New York: Basic Books.

Pride, C. (1979). Building response to a mail survey. *New Directions for Institutional Advancement, 6,* 59–69.

Sudman, S., & Bradburn, N. M. (1982). *Asking questions.* San Francisco: Jossey-Bass.

LAWRENCE S. COTE
Pennsylvania State University

RESEARCH IN SPECIAL EDUCATION

QUIGLEY, STEPHEN P. (1927–   )

Born in Belfast, Northern Ireland, Stephen P. Quigley obtained his BA in 1953 in psychology from the University of Denver. He went on to earn both his MA in 1954 in speech and hearing disorders and PhD in 1957 in speech science and psychology at the University of Illinois. Prior to his retirement. Quigley was professor of education, speech, and hearing at the University of Illinois, Urbana-Champaign.

Quigley is best known for his work in the area of communication, language, and the improvement of education for children with hearing impairments (McAnally, Rose, & Quigley, 1999; Paul & Quigley, 1994; Quigley, 1992). His investigations of Noam Chomsky's theory that careful manipulation of stimulus-response could produce more effective insights into language acquisition led to his development of the Test of Syntactical Abilities (Quigley, Steinkamp, Power, & Jones, 1978), a standardized test for the diagnosis and assessment of the syntactical abilities of deaf children.

Quigley has noted the absence of a well-developed first language for deaf children entering school and the manner in which this deficit prevents the examination of language development. He has thus conducted important research on the instructional use of American Sign Language and English (Quigley & Paul, 1984a, 1984b). Findings of these investigations suggest the benefits of teaching children with deafness American Sign Language and, as a second language, providing instruction in English.

In addition to his work involving language development, Quigley advocates reading materials for deaf children that recognize their needs while avoiding overspecialization (Quigley, 1982). Among his numerous publications, he has written several books on the topic of reading, including *Reading Practices With Deaf Learners* (McAnally et al., 1999) and *Reading Milestones* (Quigley, 1992).

REFERENCES

McAnally, P. L., Rose, S., & Quigley, S. P. (1999). *Reading practices with deaf learners.* Austin, TX: PRO-ED.

Paul, P. V., & Quigley, S. P. (1994). *Language and deafness.* San Diego, CA: Singular.

Quigley, S. P. (1982). Reading achievement and special reading materials. *Volta Review, 84*(5), 95–106.

Quigley, S. P. (1992). *Reading milestones. Level 6. The orange books.* England: Dormac.

Quigley, S. P., & Paul, P. V. (1984a). ASL and ESL? *Topics in Early Childhood Education, 3*(4), 17–26.

Quigley, S. P., & Paul, P. V. (1984b). *Language and deafness.* San Diego, CA: College Hill.

Quigley, S. P., Steinkamp, M., Power, D., & Jones, B. (1978). *Test of Syntactical Abilities.* Beaverton, OR: Dormac.

E. VALERIE HEWITT
Texas A&M University
First edition

TAMARA J. MARTIN
*The University of Texas of the
Permian Basin*
Second edition

R

RACIAL BIAS IN TESTING

See CULTURAL BIAS IN TESTING.

RACIAL DISCRIMINATION IN SPECIAL EDUCATION

The right to education, nondiscriminatory treatment, equal protection, and due process protection for all children with disabilities was first established by Congress with the Education Amendments of 1974 and the Education for All Handicapped Children Act of 1975 (PL 94-142) and continued in the more recent Individuals with Disabilities Education Act (IDEA). Prior to this national policy, more than 36 court cases throughout the country brought convincing documentation that racially and culturally discriminatory practices existed in special education. Racially and culturally diverse school children continue to be disproportionately represented in special education programs while local and state education officials attempt to improve testing and classification procedures.

Racially and culturally biased identification and placement procedures in special education were initially disputed in *Hobson* v. *Hansen* (1967). Judge J. Skelly Wright found that the ability-grouping track system in the public schools of the District of Columbia deprived African American disadvantaged students and students with disabilities of "their right to equal educational opportunity with white and more affluent public school children" (p. 401). Relying on factual findings of discrimination, the court ordered the track system abolished in 1969. Subsequently, seven African American exceptional children labeled as either behavior problems, mentally retarded, emotionally disturbed, or hyperactive sued the District of Columbia Public Schools for failing to provide them with special education while providing such education to other children (*Mills* v. *Board of Education, District of Columbia,* 1972). Holding "that Constitutional rights must be afforded citizens despite the greater expense involved" (p. 876), the court's decree established (1) standards and procedures for an "appropriate educational program," (2) a required "comprehensive plan" for identification and notification of exceptional students and their parents, and (3) in the absence of an "alternative program of education, placement in a regular public school class with appropriate ancillary services [, which] is preferable to placement in a special class" (p. 880).

In California, nine Mexican American students in *Diana* v. *State Board of Education* (1970) and six African American students in *Larry P.* v. *Riles* (1972) alleged that they were being misplaced in special classes for the educable mentally retarded on the basis of inappropriate tests and testing procedures that ignored their cultural and racial learning experiences. Both cases were brought to the Northern California Federal District Court and documented the statistically significant overrepresentation statewide of minorities in special education. *Diana*'s stipulated settlement agreement (1973) established testing procedures in the student's primary language, retesting of Mexican American and Chinese American students currently in classes for the mentally retarded, and a mandate for a state-developed and appropriate standardized intelligence test.

Judge Peckham in *Larry P.* cited California's historical racial discriminatory use of intelligence quotient (IQ) tests against African Americans and issued a preliminary injunction in 1972 against the San Francisco Unified School District. The injunction prevented the use of intelligence tests for placement purposes and ordered the elimination of the disproportionate placement of African American children in special classes for the educable mentally retarded. Similarly, a statewide order by the court on December 13, 1974, and a state-imposed moratorium in January 1975 stopped all IQ testing of the educable mentally retarded for the purposes of placement (1979, p. 931, n.4). The decision was affirmed in 1984.

Mattie T. v. *Holladay* was a class action suit filed in 1975 on behalf of 26 students with disabilities from seven local school districts in Mississippi against state and local school officials. The suit challenged the policies and practices in special education. The plaintiffs in *Mattie T.* claimed that the schools used racially and culturally discriminatory procedures in the identification, evaluation, and education placement of children with disabilities. Evidence showed that 3 times as many African American children as Anglo-American children were placed in educable retarded classes, and, conversely, twice as many Anglo-American children as African American children were placed in higher-cost and more integrated specific learning disability classes. The court ordered in a consent decree on January 26, 1979, requiring the state to substantially reduce the racial disparity by 1982 by establishing new identification practices and monitoring and enforcement procedures.

Lora v. *Board of Education of the City of New York* was filed in June 1975 on behalf of all African American and Hispanic students assigned to special day schools for the emotionally disturbed in New York City. Citing statistically significant disparities between minorities and Anglo-American students with the same problems, the plaintiffs alleged discriminatory testing and claimed that "the special day schools are intentionally segregated dumping grounds for minorities forced into inadequate facilities without due process" (1978, p. 1214). Following lengthy proceedings, appeals, and recommendations of a national "Lora Advisory Panel," a conciliatory agreement produced nondiscriminatory standards and procedures in 1984.

REFERENCES

Diana v. *Board of Education,* No. C-70-37 RFP (N.D. Cal. Jan. 7, 1970, June 18, 1973, and Order of May 27, 1974).

Hobson v. *Hansen,* 269 F. Supp. 401 (D.D.C. 1967), *Smuck* v. *Hobson,* 408 F.2d. 175 (D.C. Cir. 1969).

Larry P. v. *Riles,* 343 F. Supp. 1306 (N.D. Cal. 1972), 502 F.2d. 963 (9th Cir. 1974), 495 F. Supp. 926 (N.D. Cal. 1979), aff'd. 9th Cir., Jan. 23, 1984 (EHLR 555:304, Feb. 3, 1984).

Lora v. *Board of Educ. of City of New York,* 456 F. Supp. 1211 (E.D.N.Y. 1978), 623 F.2d. 248 (2d Cir. 1980), 587 F. Supp. 1572 (E.D.N.Y. 1984).

Mattie T. v. *Holladay,* 522 F. Supp. 72 (N.D. Mississippi, 1981).

Mills v. *Board of Education of District of Columbia,* 348 F. Supp. 866 (D.D.C. 1972).

LOUIS SCHWARTZ
Florida State University
First and Second editions

KIMBERLY APPLEQUIST
*University of Colorado at
Colorado Springs*
Third edition

DIANA v. BOARD OF EDUCATION
INDIVIDUALS WITH DISABILITIES EDUCATION IMPROVEMENT ACT OF 2004 (IDEIA)
LARRY P.
SPECIAL EDUCATION, LEGAL REGULATIONS OF
MATTIE T. v. HOLLADAY
MILLS v. BOARD OF EDUCATION
PASE v. HANNON

RARE DISEASES

See NATIONAL ORGANIZATION OF RARE DISEASES.

RASE

See REMEDIAL AND SPECIAL EDUCATION.

RATIO IQ

A ratio intelligence quotient or ratio IQ is a score from a test of intelligence (or cognitive or mental ability). Now obsolete as a statistical term, it is still a useful concept for interpreting current levels of mental functioning and, to a limited extent, for predicting future mental development. The ratio IQ has been replaced by most authors of mental ability tests with a standard score such as a deviation IQ.

At the turn of the twentieth century, and for the next several decades, tests of mental ability were administered to children of several different chronological ages. The average number of items answered correctly at each age level was recorded. Then the number of items answered correctly by a given child could be compared with the average performance of children of various ages. Such scores were known as a mental age (MA) or age equivalent (AE). Such scores made it possible to say that a particular child of a given age performed on the test as a typical 4-year-old, or another as a typical 6-year-old, or another as an 8-year-old, and so on, but MAs describe only present status.

The concept of a mental quotient to indicate the rate of cognitive development was introduced by William Stern in a paper to the German Congress of Psychology in Berlin in April 1912. With the Stanford Revision and Extension of the Binet-Simon Intelligence Scale in 1916, Lewis Terman introduced the term *intelligence quotient* and its abbreviation, IQ, as a prediction of the rate of future mental development (based on the rate of previous accomplishment). Early IQs were simply the ratio of the mental age to the chronological age, multiplied by 100 to eliminate the decimals (i.e., $IQ = MA/CA \times 100$). However, mental ages represent ordinal, not interval, data, and therefore the distance between two ages (e.g., 4 and 6) is not necessarily the same as between two other ages (e.g., 12 and 14). Also, test authors have not been able to construct tests with equal variability at each age level. As a result, the standard deviation of scores is not the same at each age, and therefore the same ratio IQ obtained at different age levels may not be equal to the same percentile rank. (A ratio IQ that equals or exceeds 3 percent of the population might be 75 at one age, 68 at another, and 60 at another.) Whereas the statistical properties of a ratio IQ present too many difficulties for its use to be continued except as a concept for interpretation, the simplicity of the concept is still helpful in explaining performance to many consumers. One can say that a 10-year-old child with an IQ of 65 is functioning mentally much like most 6- to 7-year-olds and is exhibiting about two-thirds of a year of mental growth each year. The concept of ratio IQ and mental age seem almost nonsensical when applied to adults. Since ratio IQs represent only ordinal scaling, they can be neither multiplied, divided, added, nor subtracted across ages and are obsolete for most needs in diagnostic settings.

JOSEPH L. FRENCH
Pennsylvania State University

DEVIATION IQ
INTELLIGENCE QUOTIENT

RATIO SCHEDULES

When teaching new behaviors to children, parents and instructors often begin with a goal of generating high response rates. During house cleaning, for example, chores should be selected, tools assembled, and tasks begun rapidly so that time will be available for more interesting activities when the work is done. In the classroom, hands should be raised so that the teacher can call on many students and rapidly assess what the group has learned and what skills individuals in the group still need to acquire. At work, rapid completion of a set of tasks enables an employee to take a quick break or have an extra few minutes at lunch. Generating such high performance rates from learners involves scheduling reinforcement that can be easily sustained by the instructor or shifted to less intensive schedules as learners' skills become fluent. Effective contingency management requires a basic knowledge of the schedules of reinforcement that make acquiring high rates of desired behavior attainable and sustainable.

Schedules of reinforcement are the conditions under which reinforcers are delivered (Ferster & Skinner, 1957). Under time schedules, reinforcement is provided independent of responses. Interval schedules reinforce on the basis of responses that occur after a given period of time. Ratio schedules are in effect when reinforcement is contingent upon a specified number of responses. Each of these broader schedule categories may be encountered with either fixed or variable requirements. Interval schedules promote lower response rates, whereas ratio schedules encourage higher rates of behavior. Time-based schedules may be useful in reducing unwanted behaviors that have been maintained previously on either of the other schedules.

Fixed-ratio (FR) schedules require a specific number of responses. Factory work involving piecework that pays by the number of products assembled is a good example. When the number of responses required varies at an average rate, reinforcement is said to occur on a variable-ratio (VR) schedule. A teacher assesses that her students on average can complete between 6 and 12 math problems at a time depending on their difficulty level, so she develops a series of work sheets that are completed on a VR 9 schedule, meaning that a student completes each assignment after attempting nine problems on the average.

Three notable characteristics of ratio schedules have been identified through empirical analysis. Studies on both simple and complex ratio schedules with human participants have indicated that ratio schedules promote high response rates (Bijou & Orlando, 1961; Hutchinson & Azrin, 1961). A child permitted extra time at recess upon completion of three classroom cleanup details will hurry to satisfy this requirement. Truckers may rest upon arrival at their destination, so they hasten to deliver their wares as rapidly as possible. If the ratio requirements are abruptly set too high, the worker may give up and not perform on schedule. Individuals who have given up in this manner may become aggressive. This is the result of ratio strain (Hutchinson, Azrin, & Hunt, 1968), which may be remedied by gradually increasing the work load using a progressive ratio schedule. If the rate of responding begins to deteriorate, the instructor may temporarily reduce the response requirement and build back to the previous level more gradually.

A second characteristic of ratio schedules is the probability that after his behavior has been reinforced, an individual will pause before resuming work. Post-reinforcement pause (Reynolds, 1968) is mostly associated with FR schedules; the higher the ratio, the longer the pause. After finishing a lengthy geography exam, William skips his afternoon class and goes to play ball with his friends. Less pronounced pausing is generated on VR schedules and may be seen in the gradually increasing response-rate patterns of fixed interval schedules. Since the longest pauses are generated by FR schedules, VR schedules are preferred when the goal is high and consistent performance.

The third characteristic of ratio responses is their durability under extinction. Typically, after termination of an FR schedule, a burst of responding is seen. After discontinuing their inadvertent FR reinforcement of Elizabeth's hand-mouthing, staff noted that for a few weeks she initiated hand-mouthing more than ever. VR schedules may be exceptionally persistent under extinction. Tina used to receive phone calls from Jed once every three or four days. Although Jed has not called in over a month, Tina still races home to sit beside the telephone. In most cases, responding will decrease in frequency over time if the extinction is executed consistently. If a behavior is intermittently reinforced, however, it will resume its previous rate. Tina had begun staying after school to participate in activities and meet new people, but one night Jed called for an assignment; afterward, Tina began racing home again to sit by the phone. Instructors wishing to maintain a behavior over time should consider thinning the schedule of reinforcement as much as possible. Conversely, when the goal is to extinguish a response, great care should be taken to avoid intermittently reinforcing the behavior.

Ratio schedules produce desirable high rates of response. However, because they also promote intense resistance to extinction, it may be beneficial to consider shifting from ratio to interval schedules once a new behavior has been learned in order to thin reinforcement schedules without engendering the kind of emotional responses discussed previously. Fortunately, many studies have demonstrated that the high rates of responding generated under FR schedules can be maintained by VR reinforcement and then continued under interval schedules (Weiner, 1964a, 1964b). Recently, investigators have thinned reinforcement schedules developed when using functional communication training (FCT) to reduce problem behavior by using multiple schedules (Hanley, Iwata, & Thompson, 2001). In this arrangement, three individuals with profound mental retardation who learned alternatives to self-injurious behavior (SIB) for gaining access to food under FR 1 reinforcement were taught to discriminate between periods when reinforcement was and was not available by pairing discriminative stimuli with reinforcement or extinction respectively. Red and white cards distinguished periods when reinforcement was and was not available and succeeded in lowering rates of SIB, maintaining a contingency between the learned behavior and reinforcement, maintaining low levels of alternative responding when reinforcement was unavailable, and decreasing the overall amount of reinforcement that was necessary to maintain the desired behavior.

Another recent investigation has demonstrated the potential efficacy of using fixed-time (FT) and variable-time (VT) schedules to reduce behaviors previously maintained on VR reinforcement schedules. When an otherwise desirable behavior has been inadvertently shaped up to the point of being maladaptive with ratio-scheduled reinforcement, it may be very difficult to decrease because of the resistance to extinction generated under ratio schedules. Carr, Kellum, and Chong (2001) found that both FT and VT schedules effectively reduced excessive responding to acceptable levels and suggested that this may be useful since it is likely to be easier for caregivers to reinforce behavior at regularly scheduled times. Additionally, the study demonstrated that noncontingent reinforcement could produce durable results even when the time that reinforcement is delivered inadvertently becomes variable.

In summary, ratio schedules are valuable for generating new behaviors at high performance rates. FR schedules may be used when initially training a response; VR schedules are more practical in natural settings. Although ratio schedules support high rates of responding, ratio strain may occur and may be accompanied by emotional behaviors if schedule requirements are increased abruptly. Using an adjusting schedule can remedy the effects of temporary ratio strain. Post-reinforcement pause is a by-product of FR schedules that is often accompanied by unproductive adjunctive behaviors. Ratio schedules produce behaviors that are intensely resistant to extinction. To reduce staff time and costs, it is possible to thin reinforcement rates on a ratio schedule. Care should be taken to avoid intermittently

reinforcing unwanted behaviors that have been maintained on ratio schedules. In order to reduce behaviors maintained under ratio schedules, one can consider switching to interval schedules, multiple schedules, or time-based schedules.

REFERENCES

Bijou, S. W., & Orlando, R. (1961). Rapid development of multiple-schedule performances with retarded children. *Journal of the Experimental Analysis of Behavior, 4,* 7–16.

Carr, J. E., Kellum, K. K., & Chong, I. M. (2001). The reductive effects of noncontingent reinforcement: Fixed-time versus variable-time schedules. *Journal of Applied Behavior Analysis, 34,* 505–509.

Ferster, C. B., & Skinner, B. F. (1957). *Schedules of reinforcement.* New York: Appleton.

Hanley, G. P., Iwata, B. A., & Thompson, R. H. (2001). Reinforcement schedule thinning following treatment with functional communication training. *Journal of Applied Behavior Analysis, 34,* 17–38.

Hutchinson, R. R., & Azrin, N. H. (1961). Conditioning of mental hospital patients to fixed-ratio schedules of reinforcement. *Journal of the Experimental Analysis of Behavior, 4,* 87–95.

Hutchinson, R. R., Azrin, N. H., & Hunt, G. M. (1968). Attack produced by intermittent reinforcement of a concurrent operant response. *Journal of the Experimental Analysis of Behavior, 11,* 489–495.

Reynolds, G. S. (1968). *A primer of operant conditioning.* Glenview, IL: Scott, Foresman.

Weiner, H. (1964a). Conditioning history and fixed-interval performance. *Journal of the Experimental Analysis of Behavior, 7,* 383–385.

Weiner, H. (1964b). Response cost effects during extinction following fixed-interval reinforcement with humans. *Journal of the Experimental Analysis of Behavior, 7,* 333–335.

Thomas G. Szabo
Western Michigan University

BEHAVIOR ASSESSMENT
INTERVAL RECORDING
INTERVAL SCHEDULES

RAVEN'S MATRICES

The Standard Progressive Matrices and the Colored Progressive Matrices (Raven, 1938–1983) are a collection of figures that resemble swatches removed from a wallpaper pattern. The test requires the examinee to locate the swatch that best fits the removed pattern. The test is purportedly an excellent measure of *g* factor intelligence (general intellectual ability; Marshalek, Lohman, & Snow, 1983). The matrices have received wide use around the world because of their easy administration, nonverbal format, and high correlations with traditional measures of intelligence and achievement. The progressive matrices have been used in hundreds of psychological studies internationally.

Since the progressive matrices (developed in the United Kingdom) originated in a psychometric era known for providing examiners with minimal information on standardized sample characteristics, technical adequacy, item construction and use, rationale and theory, and potential uses and misuses of instruments, the progressive matrices manuals provide little information in these areas. Additionally, Levy and Goldstein (1984), editors of *Tests in Education,* the British equivalent of the *Buros Mental Measurements Yearbook,* note that the British have lagged behind the Americans in the care that psychologists have used in the development of psychoeducational assessment measures. However, the large number of studies compiled on the progressive matrices attest to the instruments' use and value.

The matrices are appropriate for individuals ages 5 through adult and are printed in both color (ages 5 to 11) and standard black-and-white versions (ages 6 and over). The test provides only percentile ranks as an individual's reported score, but even these are not complete; the manual reports performance level only at the 5, 10, 25, 50, 75, 90, and 95th percentiles. Thus, the test only approximates levels of performance. For this reason, the matrices are useful for the rough assessment of the nonverbal reasoning abilities of individuals 5 years and above. Because of the many deficiencies in the test's manuals and standardized samples, it is best used as an assessment tool for research purposes and those occasional clinical instances in which an estimate of an individual's intellectual abilities is needed.

REFERENCES

Levy, P., & Goldstein, H. (Eds.). (1984). *Tests in education: A book of critical reviews.* London: Academic.

Marshalek, B., Lohman, D. F., & Snow, R. (1983). The complexity continuum in the radex and hierarchical models of intelligence. *Intelligence, 7,* 107–127.

BRUCE A. BRACKEN
University of Memphis

LINDSAY S. GROSS
University of Wisconsin

"g" FACTOR THEORY
INTELLIGENCE
INTELLIGENCE TESTING

RAY ADAPTATION OF THE RAY WECHSLER INTELLIGENCE SCALE FOR CHILDREN–REVISED

Ray (1979) adapted the Wechsler Intelligence Scale for Children–Revised (WISC-R) performance scales for an intelligence test designed especially for the hearing impaired. He introduced a set of simplified verbal instructions and added more practice items in an attempt to provide standardized test administration techniques to increase a deaf child's comprehension and performance. Therapists who are unskilled in American Sign Language are able to administer the test. In addition to Ray's version of instructions, several different techniques exist for nonverbal administration (Sullivan, 1982). Seven scores are yielded in the adaptation: Picture Completion, Picture Arrangement, Block Design, Object Assembly, Coding, Mazes, and Total. Administration time averages about 45 minutes.

The adaptation was normed on 127 hearing-impaired children from 6 to 16 years old. The sample used was not representative of the deaf school-age population, including no low-verbal deaf children and no multiply handicapped children (Sullivan, 1985). Norms provided in Ray's test should be regarded with caution, and thought should be given to other deaf norms developed. The WISC-R performance scales can be a suitable alternative to the Hiskey-Nebraska if the Anderson and Sisco norms are used with a total communication approach for administration (Phelps & Enson, 1986). Genshaft (1985) thinks that the most useful improvement in the adaptation would be separate, representative norms for deaf children.

REFERENCES

Genshaft, J. L. (1985). Review of the WISC-R: For the deaf. In J. V. Mitchell, Jr. (Ed.), *The ninth mental measurements yearbook* (Vol. 2). Lincoln: University of Nebraska.

Phelps, L., & Enson, A. (1986). Concurrent validity of the WISC-R using deaf norms and the Hiskey-Nebraska. *Psychology in the Schools, 23,* 138–141.

Ray, S. (1979). *An adaptation of the Wechsler Intelligence Scale for Children–Revised for the deaf.* Natchitoches: Northwestern State University of Louisiana.

Sullivan, R. M. (1982). Modified instructions for administering the WISC-R performance scale subtests to deaf children (Appendix B). In J. M. Sattler (Ed.), *Assessment of children's intelligence and special abilities* (2nd ed.). Boston: Allyn & Bacon.

Sullivan, P. M. (1985). Review of the WISC-R: For the deaf. In J. V. Mitchell, Jr. (Ed.), *The ninth mental measurements yearbook* (Vol. 2). Lincoln: University of Nebraska.

LISA J. SAMPSON
Eastern Kentucky University

DEAF
WECHSLER INTELLIGENCE SCALE FOR CHILDREN–
FOURTH EDITION

REACTION TIME

Reaction time (RT) tasks are designed to measure the amount of time it takes from presentation of a stimulus to the execution of a designated response. In the classical psychophysics experiment, the examinee is supposed to press a response when a light or auditory signal is presented. The examiner triggers the activation of a timer when presenting the visual or auditory signal (Spreen & Strauss, 1998). Studies have consistently indicated that psychomotor speed accounted for the differences between groups of individuals with brain damage, emotional disorders, and normal controls regardless of modality or hand used in responding. RT tasks have been used to investigate various interactions with cognitive ability (e.g., Deary & Der, 2005; Deary, Der, & Ford, 2001) as well as to measure effects of environmental factors such as sleep deprivation or medication treatment (e.g., Babkoff, Kelly, & Naitoh, 2001).

Simple RT tasks are those tasks that require the individual to respond to each and every stimulus in the same way. In contrast, choice RT tasks require the individual to make choices. For example, the directions may be that if the light is red, the examinee should press the right lever or other specific response, but if the light is blue, the examinee should press the left lever or other specific response. With advances in technology, the study of RT has transitioned to computer-administered tasks with set or random intervals between stimuli and multiple paradigms, including continuous-performance tests (CPTs; see Riccio, Reynolds, & Lowe, 2001 for review).

REFERENCES

Babkoff, H., Kelly, T. L., & Naitoh, P. (2001). Trial to trial variance in choice reaction time as a measure of the effect of stimulants during sleep deprivation. *Military Psychology, 13,* 1–16.

Deary, I. J., & Der, G. (2005). Reaction time explains IQ's association with death. *Psychological Science, 16,* 64–69.

Deary, I. J., Der, G., & Ford, G. (2001). Reaction times and intelligence differences: A population-based cohort study. *Intelligence, 29,* 389–399.

Luciano, M., Wright, M. J., Geffen, G. M., Geffen, L. B., Smith, G. A., et al. (2004). A genetic investigation of the covariation among inspection time, choice reaction time, and IQ subtest scores. *Behavior Genetics, 34,* 41–50.

Riccio, C. A., Reynolds, C. R., & Lowe, P. A. (2001). *Clinical applications of continuous performance tests.* New York: Wiley.

Spreen, O., & Strauss, E. (1998). *A compendium of neuropsychological tests* (2nd ed.). Oxford: Oxford University Press.

CYNTHIA A. RICCIO
Texas A&M University

INTELLIGENCE

REACTIVE ATTACHMENT DISORDER

See ATTACHMENT DISORDER.

READABILITY FORMULAS

Readability formulas are used to measure the difficulty of a text passage. They are intended to help match readers with ideal texts. They may be calculated by hand or by computer and may rely on such characteristics as word length, sentence length, and vocabulary level.

Controversy About and Evolution of Readability Formulas

The first readability formula was published in 1923 (Lively & Pressey), but long before that there were "leveled" readers, like the McGuffy readers, which were developed in 1836 and sold millions of copies before the beginning of the twentieth century. After reading formulas came into being, it became possible to "level" any book so instructors would not have to rely on pre-leveled books. The use of readability formulas has not been without controversy, however. Over the years, researchers have criticized readability formulas for imprecision, inconsistency, and inaccuracy (Britton & Lumpkin, 1977; Fuchs, Fuchs, & Deno, 1984). Some argue for a separation of "readability" from "comprehensibility," because comprehension is more contextual. In the early 1990s another "leveling" movement began, which is not entirely quantitative and takes into account some of the factors that have seemed to be missing in past formulas, such as use of illustrations, required prior knowledge, and topic appropriateness. Newer readability formulas include some of these aspects.

Specific Formulas

There are dozens of readability formulas, some more popular than others. Currently, some of the most prominent are the following.

Fry Readability Graph

The Fry readability graph (Fry, 2002) allows the user to plot the difficulty of a passage based on sentence length and the average number of syllables per word. Because the graph is not under copyright protection, it is available in many publications and at many sites on the Internet (e.g., http://www.csudh.edu/soe/dcc/readability.htm).

Bormuth Formula

The Bormuth (1969) formula is calculated according to average number of letters per word, the average number of words per sentence, and the number of words in the passage that are not on the Dale list. The Dale list is a roster of 3,000 words familiar to 80 percent of fourth graders.

Flesch Reading Ease Score and Flesch-Kinkaid Grade Level Score

These computer-calculated formulas are included in Microsoft Office applications and can be used to calculate the readability of any passage that can be opened in Microsoft Word. The reading ease score and the grade level score are both computed based on average sentence length (ASL) and average syllables per word (ASW).

$$\text{Ease score: } 206.835 - (1.015 \times \text{ASL}) - (84.6 \times \text{ASW})$$
$$\text{Level: } (.39 \times \text{ASL}) + (11.8 \times \text{ASW}) - 15.59$$

New Dale-Chall Readability Formula

The latest revision to the instructions for using the Dale-Chall formula (Chall & Dale, 1995) contains work sheets for assessing necessary prior knowledge, vocabulary and concepts, overall organization, use of headings, questions, illustrations, and physical features, in addition to the standard work sheet for sentence and word length indicators. Scores are given as Cloze scores or grade equivalents. This formula is specifically meant for texts at above the third grade reading level.

The Lexile Framework

The lexile framework is a two-factor computerized formula that is based on word frequency and sentence length. The range of scores (called lexiles) is from 200 to 1200 and is equated on a table to grade levels 1–12. Lexiles are growing in popularity, partially due to the fact that a database of lexiles for more than 30,000 books is available at www.lexile.com, which allows the user to enter a lexile level and get a list of appropriate books.

This is a very incomplete list of readability formulas. Further examples can be found in journal articles devoted to describing or critiquing them (Gunning, 2003; Kotula, 2003).

Despite the practical usefulness of readability formulas, it is always important to interpret the scores cautiously. A single passage can have widely varying scores on the differing scales, and formulas alone cannot take into account the meaning and context of a passage.

REFERENCES

Bormuth, J. R. (1969). *Development of readability analysis.* Chicago: University of Chicago Press.

Britton, G. E., & Lumpkin, M. C. (1977). Computerized readability verification of textbook reading levels. *Reading Improvement, 14,* 193–199.

Chall, J. S., & Dale, E. (1995). Readability revisited: *The new Dale-Chall readability formula.* Cambridge, MA: Brookline Books.

Fry, E. (2002). Readability versus leveling. *The Reading Teacher, 56,* 286–291.

Fuchs, L. S., Fuchs, D., & Deno, S. L. (1984). Inaccuracy among readability formulas: Implications for the measurement of reading proficiency and selection of instructional material. *Diagnostique, 9,* 86–97.

Gunning, T. G. (2003). The role of readability in today's classrooms. *Topics in Language Disorders, 23,* 175–189.

Kotula, A. W. (2003). Matching readers to instructional materials: The use of classic readability measures for students with language learning disabilities and dyslexia. *Topics in Language Disorders, 23,* 190–203.

Lively, B. A., & Pressey, S. L. (1923). A method for measuring vocabulary burden of textbooks. *Educational Administration and Supervision, 9,* 389–398.

MICHELE W. POTTER
University of California, Riverside

READING

Reading is the process of deriving meaning from print. While people have been reading as long as language has been written, interest in reading, from both a research and a practical standpoint, has grown markedly in recent years, as evidenced by the demand for such publications as the National Research Council report (Snow, Burns, & Griffin, 1998) on preventing reading disabilities in young children, the National Reading Panel (2000) on research-proven methods for teaching children to read, the RAND Reading Study Group (2002) on reading comprehension, and the Carnegie Corporation (Biancarosa & Snow, 2004) on middle school and high school literacy. In the past 25 years, there has been a concerted effort to understand how the reading process occurs and to translate that knowledge into materials and strategies that more effectively teach reading. Reading educators, long concerned with reading research and its implementation, now work alongside cognitive, educational, and developmental psychologists, linguists, and sociolinguists in the attempt to unravel the mysteries of reading. The stakes in this endeavor have become higher with the recent implementation of the No Child Left Behind Act (NCLB; 2002), which mandates that all students reach proficiency in reading (and other academic subjects) as evidenced by performance on state-administered assessments by the year 2014. Bringing all students to proficiency in reading will require that educators and researchers develop greater understanding both of how the reading process unfolds and of how all students can learn to participate in that process skillfully.

What does it mean to be a proficient reader? Readers can interact with print in a variety of ways; presumably a proficient reader is one who consistently performs these interactions effectively and successfully, carrying out their intended purpose in reading. There are four typical general purposes for reading, corresponding to four basic types of reading. The four types of reading to be discussed are developmental reading, studying, functional reading, and recreational reading.

Developmental reading can be described as the activity undertaken for the purpose of learning how to read. During the colonial period, the *Bible,* the *psalter,* and other religious materials were used to teach children to read. A century later, the McGuffey readers were published. These readers were the forerunners of the graded readers often used today, and their appearance paralleled the development of graded schools. Several decades ago, children learned to read with the assistance of the "Dick and Jane" books. With such familiar phrases as "See Dick" and "See Jane," school-aged children across the United States entered the world of formal reading instruction. Today, much of the formal reading instruction in the early elementary grades is still devoted to developmental reading, although children may now encounter in their reading classrooms both commercially produced reading materials created for the purpose of reading instruction and trade books intended for the general public. The appropriate role of each of these types of instructional materials in furthering development in reading remains an issue for reading educators and researchers (Hiebert & Martin, 2004; Morrow & Gambrell, 2000).

As students progress through elementary school, developmental reading remains an integral part of their schooling, with the goal of increasing reading proficiency. Although developmental reading was confined to elementary grades in past years, it has become increasingly common to find developmental reading courses being offered even at the college level. The rationale for this upward trend in developmental reading is the persistent presence of large numbers of college students who have not reached proficiency in reading and who still require some instruction in learning how to read effectively.

In the upper elementary grades and throughout formal schooling, developmental reading is joined by another type of reading: studying. According to Anderson (1979), studying is a special form of reading that is concerned with the accomplishment of some instructional goal. The type of reading engaged in during studying is special for a number of reasons.

While the material used for developmental reading tends to be narrative text (i.e., storylike text), the kind of text students most often study is expository in nature. In its demands on comprehension and recall, expository text appears to possess certain disadvantages compared to narrative text, in that it has no identifiable elements such as plot, character, and setting. In addition, expository text is frequently less colorful, contains more technical language, and can vary in structure. Therefore, the task of studying may be more difficult than other forms of reading because expository text, particularly as presented in textbooks, may be more

difficult and less motivational to read. Not only is the text used in studying potentially more difficult to process, but when students study expository texts it is often with the unpleasant expectation of being tested on its content; both of these factors may make studying a less enjoyable reading experience for students.

Because of its nature, studying requires individuals to employ specialized learning and study skills. In addition to the well-known SQ3R method (Robinson, 1970), there are such cognitive strategies as note taking, outlining, paraphrasing, imaging, and rereading that enhance student performance. Some of the other study strategies that have been looked at by researchers in recent years include annotation (Hynd, Simpson, & Chase, 1990), self-testing (Stone, 2000), and graphic organizers (Robinson & Kiewra, 1995).

While developmental reading and studying are the forms of reading most directly associated with school, there is another form of reading that arises from real-world needs. This form of reading is called functional reading. When we read road signs, find our way on a map, follow a recipe, or order from a menu, we are employing functional reading. Simply stated, functional reading is the reading that is required to accomplish some personal or social as opposed to instructional goal.

It is disheartening to note that there are still many adults in the United States who cannot even read well enough to make sense of the critical print around them. They cannot read the road signs along the road, follow a recipe, fill out a job application, or read the dosage on a medicine bottle. Individuals who lack even this limited reading proficiency are called functionally illiterate. According to government estimates, they number in the tens of millions in the United States.

The final form of reading, recreational, is internally motivated. This form of reading is sometimes described as reading for enjoyment. Recreational reading aims primarily at the reader's entertainment. When you read the comics, a novel, or poetry for pleasure, then you are engaging in recreational reading. There appears to be a strong relation between the amount of recreational reading individuals engage in and their performance on other types of reading tasks such as studying. Because of this relation, programs such as Sustained Silent Reading (SSR), Drop Everything And Read (DEAR), and Accelerated Reader (AR) were developed to encourage children to read more often. The hope of such programs is that students will begin to read more often and, ultimately, more effectively. However, research has not established that encouragement to read does, in fact, improve children's reading achievement or fluency in reading (National Reading Panel, 2000).

Whether developmental, study-oriented, functional, or recreational, reading remains a complex and much-investigated cognitive process. Although most reading researchers and educators would agree that reading is an extremely complex activity involving written language, there is much debate as to which elements of the reading process to foreground in research and instruction. A consensus seems to have been achieved in recent years that some form of balanced instruction is most beneficial for the majority of developmental readers, meaning that they should receive phonics-based instruction aimed at improving their decoding skills, as well as comprehension instruction aimed at improving their grasp of reading as meaning making. The degree of emphasis that each type of instruction should receive for learners at different stages of learning to read and at different levels of proficiency remains controversial, however.

An area of emphasis in the last decade has been a focus on early reading and reading readiness, with the rationale that once children get started on reading successfully, their career as proficient readers is secured. Although attention to the early stages of developmental reading may prevent some reading problems, it appears clear that giving children access to print via decoding is not sufficient for them to develop into proficient readers. Just as learning to read words does not tend to occur naturally without the benefit of targeted instruction, so, too, comprehension of texts, particularly expository or instructional texts, is not a natural by-product of development for many students. Children who can decode competently may still find themselves struggling with comprehension of texts in the higher grade levels, or may experience decreasing motivation to read as they move into adolescence (Guthrie & Alao, 1997). Declining motivation to read in adolescence and adolescents' declining levels of reading achievement have recently moved into the foreground as issues for reading educators, and they will become increasingly important as the provisions of NCLB calling for reading proficiency for all high school students take effect.

Thus, there is growing awareness that a fully developmental model of reading is called for, one that follows the reading process from the earliest stages of gaining access to print all the way through the independent reading of the proficient adult. In aiming at the goal of bringing all students up to proficiency in reading, a full understanding of what the development of proficiency in all types of reading means is warranted. Such an understanding will need to consider the multiple levels and complex interactions involved in reading development, including the delineation of the roles of such varied elements as facilitative reading skills, reading strategies, readers' knowledge and metacognition, and motivation (Alexander, 2002).

Further, it is not enough to consider the internal processing of an individual reader without considering also their reading environment; the importance of understanding situational and contextual aspects of reading is gaining increased recognition. The RAND Reading Study Group (2002) identified three critical elements in reading comprehension: the reader, the text, and the activity, all of which are embedded in a larger sociocultural context. As noted earlier, an individual's purpose for reading is directly linked to the type of reading undertaken (i.e., developmental, for study, functional, or recreational) and influences the nature of the reading process that occurs and also what it means to be a proficient reader in that situation.

Research and instruction in reading are beginning to take these interactive factors into account, but much theoretical and practical groundwork remains to be established. Regardless of the type or view of reading, one fact remains clear: In an information-processing age, the ability to read well is an essential life skill. Further, the investigation of the reading process and of the development of reading ability will continue to reveal new aspects of reading, a complex, dynamic, and fascinating human activity.

REFERENCES

Alexander, P. A. (2002, December). *Profiling the developing reader: The interplay of knowledge, interest, and strategic processing.* The Oscar Causey Research Award Presentation to the National Reading Conference, Miami, FL.

Anderson, T. H. (1979). Study skills and learning strategies. In H. F. O'Neil & C. D. Spielberger (Eds.), *Cognitive and affective learning strategies* (pp. 77–98). New York: Academic.

Biancarosa, G., & Snow, C. E. (2004). *Reading next—A vision for action and research in middle and high school literacy: A report to the Carnegie Corporation of New York.* Washington, DC: Alliance for Excellent Education.

Guthrie, J. T., & Alao, S. (1997). Engagement in reading for young adolescents. *Journal of Adolescent & Adult Literacy, 40*(6), 438–447.

Hiebert, E. H., & Martin, L. A. (2004). The texts of beginning reading instruction. In R. B. Ruddell & N. J. Unrau (Eds.), *Theoretical models and processes of reading* (5th ed., pp. 390–411). Newark, DE: International Reading Association.

Hynd, C. R., Simpson, M. L., & Chase, N. D. (1990). Studying narrative text: The effects of annotating vs. journal writing on test performance. *Reading Research & Instruction, 29*(2), 44–54.

Morrow, L. M., & Gambrell, L. B. (2000). Literature-based reading instruction. In M. L. Kamil, P. B. Mosenthal, P. D. Pearson, & R. Barr (Eds.), *Handbook of reading research, Vol. III* (pp. 563–586). Mahwah, NJ: Erlbaum.

National Reading Panel. (2000). *Teaching children to read: An evidence-based assessment of the scientific research literature on reading and its implications for reading success.* Washington, DC: National Institutes of Child Health and Human Development.

No Child Left Behind Act of 2001. (2002). Public Law No. 107-110, Paragraph 115, Stat. 1425.

RAND Reading Study Group. (2002). *Reading for understanding: Toward an R&D program in reading comprehension.* Santa Monica, CA: Science & Technology Policy Institute, RAND Education.

Robinson, D. H., & Kiewra, K. A. (1995). Visual argument: Graphic organizers are superior to outlines in improving learning from text. *Journal of Educational Psychology, 87,* 455–467.

Robinson, E. P. (1970). *Effective study* (2nd ed.). New York: Harper & Row.

Snow, C. E., Burns, M. S., & Griffin, P. (Eds.). (1998). *Preventing reading difficulties in young children.* Washington, DC: National Academy Press.

Stone, N. J. (2000). Exploring the relationship between calibration and self-regulated learning. *Educational Psychology Review, 12*(4), 437–475.

PATRICIA A. ALEXANDER
University of Michigan

EMILY FOX
University of Maryland

REFERENCES

Rayner, K. (1985). The role of eye movements in learning to read and reading disability. *Remedial & Special Education, 6,* 53–59.

Reichle, E. D., Rayner, K., & Pollatsek, A. (2003). The E-Z Reader model of eye-movement control in reading: Comparison to other models. *Behavioral and Brain Sciences, 26,* 445–526.

Starr, M. S., & Rayner, K. (2001). Eye movements during reading: Some current controversies. *Trends in Cognitive Sciences, 5,* 156–164.

OLGA JERMAN
*University of California,
Riverside*

READING AND EYE MOVEMENTS

Eye-movement research is used to understand the underlying cognitive processes involved in reading. Although it seems as if the eyes move continuously along the text except for some places, in reality it is not so. The eyes make series of stops and jumps. The periods when the eyes come to rest are called fixations. Visual information is processed only during the fixations. Between the fixations are the periods when eyes move rapidly. These eye movements are called saccades after the French word for *jump*. During the saccade the vision is blurred and processing is hindered. When we read our eyes usually move 6 to 9 character spaces with each saccade. While most saccades in reading move forward, about 10 to 15 percent move backward, and these are called regressive saccades or regressions. When the eyes move from near the end of one line to near the beginning of the next, this movement is called return sweep.

Recently a number of debates emerged with regard to eye movements. Starr and Rayner (2001) examine three main controversies that exist in the eye-movement research. The first is the extent to which eye-movement behavior is affected by low-level oculomotor factors versus higher-level cognitive processes. The second has to do with the amount of information that can be extracted from the right of fixation. The last one is the question of whether readers process information serially or in parallel.

There are various models of eye-movement control in reading (e.g., Morrison model, EMMA, attention-shift model, SWIFT, minimal control model, and many others). The E-Z Reader model (Reichle, Rayner, & Pollatsek, 2003) is one of the most popular. This model provides a theoretical framework for understanding how word identification, visual processing, attention, and oculomotor control jointly determine where and when the eyes move during reading.

A good reader is expected to have regular, fewer, and shorter fixations, as well as fewer regressions. Examining eye movements is part of studying reading deficits. However, some researchers concluded that eye movements are not the cause of reading disabilities but rather the reflection of them (Rayner, 1985; Starr & Rayner, 2001).

READING DISORDERS

It is an understatement to say that the process of reading is complex. The variety of models of the reading process that have been created serves as evidence of this complexity. However, it is also true that most individuals will master the demanding skill of reading without much difficulty and in spite of the instructional methods by which they are taught. For many, the acquisition of reading appears to be more or less second nature; yet there are those for whom learning to read is anything but second nature. For these individuals, attempts to acquire even rudimentary reading skills seem destined to fail. Rather than being "reading-able," these individuals are the reading disabled. It is the purpose of this discussion to look more closely at this reading-disabled population and to consider potential sources of their reading difficulties.

Before we deal specifically with sources of reading difficulties, it is important that this examination of reading disorders be placed into a historical framework. By dealing briefly with the historical perspective, the reader may come to understand some of the issues underlying present thinking in the area of reading disorders.

References to reading difficulties can be traced as far back as the early seventeenth century. The earliest published studies of reading disorders, appearing around the turn of the twentieth century, were undertaken by people in the medical profession. In 1896, W. Pringle Morgan, a British ophthalmologist, published what is credited as the first report of a reading disorder. In this report, Morgan presented a detailed account of a young man who could not read despite seemingly adequate intelligence. Morgan speculated that the youth suffered from "congenital word blindness." The explanation of reading problems articulated by Morgan was followed by a series of clinical studies published by Hinshelwood (1917). In his internationally recognized book, Hinshelwood, a Scottish eye surgeon, investigated the role of the brain in congenital word blindness.

The research of British medical professionals like Morgan and Hinshelwood, although generally stimulating little interest among most educators and psychologists at home and abroad, did influence the work of others. Notable among this work were Orton's (1925) studies of hemispheric imbalance. Orton, a neurologist, felt that the principal symptom of reading disorders was strephosymbolia, or severe reversals of language symbols. He felt that this condition was attributable to the lack of cerebral dominance. This pattern of letter reversal, which is often associated with the condition of dyslexia, remains a popular but poor indicator of reading problems.

Two important outcomes of the early medical writings on reading disabilities were rare. First, a medical perspective on reading disorders became evident. As a consequence of this perspective, which is still evident in certain educational circles today, the causes of reading problems were primarily sought among neurological factors. In other words, the focus of reading disorders was believed to lie within the reader (Lipson & Wixson, 1997): a neurological deficit that prevented the reader from successfully completing the reading act.

Even today, those who do not embrace the strongly neurological or psychoneurological view of reading problems (e.g., Spear-Swerdling, 2004) cannot dismiss the lasting impression made by early medical research on the identification and treatment of reading disorders. To illustrate, we need only look at the language of reading remediation. In a clinical setting, in order to provide remediation (improvement) of reading difficulties, the client (reader) is diagnosed (tested), and an instructional treatment (program) is prescribed (developed).

The second outcome of the early medical influence in reading disorders was the development of scientific instruments to isolate the source of reading problems. For example, in 1914, Thorndike developed a group test of reading ability, and in 1915, Gray followed with an oral reading test. As the number of such assessments grew, so did the concern for the improvement of the identified disorder, or remediation. Diagnostic instruments became components of early clinical programs, which were established most often in conjunction with medical schools for the purpose of determining the cause of reading problems (etiology).

Initially, the diagnosis of reading disorders consisted of an extensive battery of physical, neurological, and language assessments that often entailed the individual's admission into a hospital. Today, while these more extensive diagnostic screenings are still administered, particularly in medically related clinics, briefer, more educationally related screenings have become far more prevalent. These school-based assessments focus heavily on reading achievement and aptitude measures and less on the physical characteristics of the reader, such as auditory discrimination and acuity, and even less on potential neurological factors.

Further, at the school level, most initial decisions about students' reading abilities or disabilities are made on the basis of group testing administered by classroom teachers, not by individual tests administered by trained specialists, as is the case in clinical programs. These variations in tests and testing procedures between school-based and medically based reading programs are indicative of fundamental differences between such programs with regard to reading disorders. As noted, the neurological view of reading disorders focuses on functional deficits within the reader. Alternative perspectives in reading disorders center attention elsewhere.

Even from the beginning, with the work of Morgan and others, some preferred to look outside the reader for factors contributing to reading difficulties. Some have sought to blame reading problems on the instruction these readers achieved (Judd, 1918; Uhl, 1916). For example, Judd (1918) contended that the emphasis on phonics instruction in education led to confusion in the reader's eye fixations, thus producing reader disability. C. T. Gray (1922) also put the burden for reading difficulties outside the reader and inside the educational system. Like those holding strongly to neurological views of reading disorders, those holding as strongly to instructional explanations for reading problems, like Judd and Gray, found only limited support.

In contrast to either view, the predominant current approach to reading disorders is an interaction of the two positions, reflecting a position somewhere between the two extremes. Within this more moderate perspective, serious reading problems can be a consequence not only of neurological deficits or misguided instruction but of multiple factors that include physical, emotional, and social conditions. For the remainder of this discussion, we will examine each of these potential contributors to reading failure.

Reading is a complex mental activity that involves the acquisition, manipulation, and retrieval of language symbols by the reader. As discussed, when a failure to read successfully exists, there is the tendency to examine that situation's etiology or cause. Terms such as brain injury, damage, dysfunction, and neuropsychological disorder reflect a neurological etiology. Harris and Sipay (1980) summarized potential indicators of reading-related neurological problems as encompassing (a) a history of a difficult birth, perhaps involving prolonged labor, an instrumental delivery, or deformity of the head; (b) premature birth; (c) poor balance or general awkwardness; (d) marked language delay; (e) attention deficit; or (f) a history of seizures or brief lapses in consciousness.

There has been a resurgence in emphasis on neurological factors in recent decades (e.g., Shaywitz et al., 2000). This resurgence may be accounted for, in part, by the increased awareness of the brain and brain functioning provided by expanded imaging technology. Among the most common neurologically related reading disorders are alexia (partial or total loss of reading ability), dyslexia, deficit language production, and learning disability. Because of the widespread application of the labels of dyslexia and learning disability, we will consider these conditions in more depth.

Dyslexia is certainly one of the most widely applied and perhaps one of the most misused labels for reading problems; the term *dyslexia* has come to be seen as virtually synonymous for reading disability (Lipson & Wixson, 1997). References to dyslexic conditions, which can be traced all the way back to Morgan's writings on congenital word blindness and Orton's research on strephosymbolia, have continued to appear with regularity in the literature. Although many definitions of dyslexia do exist, the root of the word relates to word distortion, and it is frequently and mistakenly associated with letter or word reversals. Dyslexia tends to be considered to be neurological in origin, and thus it is viewed as inherent in the affected individual and not susceptible to cure. A number of typologies of dyslexia have been proposed, with one of the most prominent being the distinction of "deep" and "surface" dyslexia (Balajthy & Lipa-Wade, 2003). "Deep" dyslexia involves decoding difficulties originating in deficient phonological processing, while children with "surface" dyslexia have adequate phonological processing but have difficulties in recognizing words for other reasons.

Despite the popularity of the term, many, principally in the educational community, do not find it useful to label reading-related learning difficulties as dyslexia (Gunning, 2002). While it seems likely that the word *dyslexia* is too easily and invalidly applied by the general populace, it is equally difficult to discount the number of individuals who display an inability to encode or to manipulate written language; problems in decoding language in written form are central to most current definitions of dyslexia (e.g., Reid, 1998).

Some of the same characteristics that apply to the condition of dyslexia apply as well to the condition of learning disability (LD). According to the Individuals with Disabilities Education Act (IDEA), a specific learning disability is "a disorder in one or more of the basic psychological processes" required to understand language. "The term includes such conditions as perceptual handicaps, brain injury, minimal brain dysfunction, dyslexia, and developmental aphasia" (p. 65083, 1997).

Beyond this legal definition, however, there is ample disagreement about the nature, identification, and treatment procedures for learning disabilities. What is most interesting about LD is that in many ways the condition is primarily an educational problem. What frequently unites the vast numbers of students labeled LD is that there is a significant gap between perceived potential and demonstrated academic performance. In addition, there is no apparent cause for this gap. It may be related to a combination of affective and cognitive factors, and it may be reflected both in learning and behavioral problems within the learner. Often, teachers and specialists struggle to bring the LD student's performance up to potential through the application of medical and educational treatments.

While important, neurological factors such as those discussed here account for relatively few of the reading problems encountered in classrooms (Gunning, 2002; Reid, 1998). Other factors, such as physical ones, may also contribute to reading difficulties.

Although reading is a cognitive activity, it also relies heavily on visual and auditory stimuli. There are several sensory deficits that can have an immediate and significant effect on an individual's acquisition and maintenance of reading proficiency. Several of these deficits will be examined in this section.

Although the terms *sight* and *vision* are frequently used interchangeably, there are semantic differences in these terms that become important in a discussion of reading disorders. Basically, the word *sight* refers to the eye's response to light. By comparison, the word *vision* implies that there is some interpretation of the information transmitted by the eye to the brain. In reading disability research, the term *visual acuity* is employed to represent the state of having good sight. Visual discrimination refers to the individual's ability to detect minute differences between and among visual stimuli. During reading, the learner's eyes must not only see and discriminate among single stimuli but also make saccadic movements or smooth left-to-right progressions and sweeps from line to line of text. The eyes are also required to pause and focus periodically in the reading process. These periodic pauses are called fixations.

Without a doubt, clear and appropriate visual access to the printed page facilitates the individual's ability to process written language. When visual acuity is impaired, the process of reading is diminished, at best, or made extremely difficult, at worst. What precisely is the effect of various visual defects on reading performance? Reviews of the research present inconclusive evidence on the relationship of visual defects to reading performance (Harris & Sipay, 1980), and remediation based on visual training does not appear to be effective (American Academy of Pediatrics, 1998). Several factors that can account for the inconsistent findings of this research include (a) variations in what supposedly similar tests are actually measuring; (b) the brief and unreliable nature of visual tests; (c) the lack of comparability in the ages and visual development of learners; and (d) the adaptability of learners.

There are many visual problems that can impede the learning process. Among the most common visual deficiencies are nearsightedness (myopia), farsightedness (hyperopia), and astigmatism; all are refractive errors or abnormalities in eye shape. When functioning during the reading process, the eyes must make several critical adjustments, and difficulties in performing these adjustments can interfere with the reading process. For example, the muscles of the eye must operated together in a coordinated fashion, focusing and centering on the visual target in such a way as to produce a single, clear image. At times, there can be a muscular imbalance preventing the eyes from operating in a coordinated way. In certain cases, one eye may assume dominance over the other eye and suppress the vision in the weaker eye, a condition commonly referred to as lazy eye (amblyopia). For the most part, readers with milder cases of muscular imbalance can accommodate well, except when they experience fatigue, tension, or headaches.

While successful reading depends on auditory skills, few severe reading problems can be directly linked to auditory factors. However, in our discussion of reading disorders, several auditory classifications should be considered. These categories are auditory acuity, auditory discrimination, and auditory memory. Auditory acuity refers to the state of having good hearing. Auditory discrimination involves the recognition of minute differences in speech sounds. Phonological awareness, which has been identified as a potential risk factor for the development of reading disability (Blachman, 2000; Snow, Burns, & Griffin, 1998), originates in this ability to discriminate the sounds in spoken words. Students' appropriate production of speech sounds is dependent on their ability to hear such differences as well. Most early reading programs include phonic analysis, which requires students to recognize and reproduce the common sound-symbol patterns in language. Consequently, deficits in auditory acuity or discrimination would place the child at a disadvantage in these early stages of reading acquisition.

Auditory memory comes into play in learning when students encode the sounds in a word to store that word in working memory. Certain students appear to have difficulty in encoding phonological or verbal information completely and accurately, which tends to have negative effects on their comprehension and also on their formation of stable associations between sounds and letters (Torgeson & Hecht, 1996). Also of importance in the reception of auditory stimuli is the individual's ability to mask or eliminate extraneous noises in the environment. As most of us know, the classroom, where so much information is transmitted auditorily, is anything but noise-proof. Focusing on important information in the classroom demands that the learner mask out sounds that would otherwise interfere with the acquisition of salient information.

Beyond the visual and auditory factors presented, there are other physical conditions that may contribute to reading problems. Among these conditions are illness, general awkwardness, glandular problems, and poor nutrition. It must be noted, however, that there is little direct evidence that such conditions significantly affect reading performance. For example, illnesses tend to come into play in reading problems when students suffer from prolonged or chronic ailments. Yet, in most instances, prolonged illnesses prevent the learner from attending school, and it is this lack of school attendance that contributes most to reading difficulties. General awkwardness is not, in itself, a factor in reading problems, but it is of importance in that it is frequently a symptom of minimal brain dysfunction. Further, while glandular abnormalities can result in such physical abnormalities as dwarfism or obesity, there is limited understanding of the effects of endocrine treatments on reading disorders. The effect of malnutrition on reading disorders is also difficult to pinpoint since this condition is also closely tied to socioeconomic status.

To this point, we have been discussing neurological and physical factors that influence reading performance. There are also less easily measured factors within the individual that may influence the reading process. Among these less measurable factors are psychosocial characteristics of the reader. Even from the beginning of work in the area of reading disorders, writers such as Orton (1925) and C. T. Gray (1922) have contended that successful readers are socially and emotionally different from struggling readers. Successful readers have been seen as not only good at reading skills but also psychosocially adjusted. By comparison, disabled readers have been categorized as restless, withdrawn, or introverted (Robinson, 1953).

That certain psychosocial behaviors have been frequently related to poor reading performance is widely accepted. However, the significance of emotional and social factors in causing reading disorders is unclear. Do certain psychosocial behaviors result in reading failure? Does the presence of reading problems have particular emotional or social effects on the reader? Do certain emotional or social behaviors and reading problems develop simultaneously? These questions remain unanswered by the existing literature.

In part, we know little about the relation of psychosocial conditions and reading disorders because the techniques for gathering data in these areas are somewhat unreliable. For example, teacher observation, which may be employed to gather information on a learner's emotional or social behavior, can be biased. Further, teachers generally conduct observations without the benefit of training. Interviews may also be used to collect data on these factors. Yet, even when these interviews are performed by trained specialists, there is little assurance that what the learner says is an accurate reflection of the internal state. Personality measures are another tool for assessing an individual's emotional and social condition. While such measures may provide a better understanding of the condition of the learner than observation and interviews, however, the reliability of these measures is still a point of contention.

Although failing to discern consistent differences on these factors between disabled and able readers, research (Harris, 1971; Harris & Sipay, 1980), has identified various aspects of psychosocial behavior that may contribute to reading problems. For example, Harris and Sipay (1980) delineate the following characteristics as related to reading problems:

Conscious refusal to learn
Overt hostility
Negative conditioning to reading
Displacement of hostility
Resistance to pressure

Clinging to dependency

Quick discouragement

Conviction that success is dangerous

Extreme distractibility or restlessness

Absorption in a private world

Harris and Sipay's characteristic of extreme distractibility and restlessness as indicative of reading problems relates to the work on attention deficit disorders in the literature on reading disabilities. In particular, attention deficit may be associated specifically with greater risk for a reading disorder (Willcutt & Pennington, 2000). Since the research of Bandura (1969) and Gibson (1969), the importance of attention to learning has been widely accepted. It would appear that LD students, for whom there is a gap between potential and academic performance, may suffer from a developmental lag with regard to attention (Reid, 1998; Ross, 1976). Often, LD students are unable to sustain attention to task, and the effect is decreased learning. An important element in assisting LD students in improving reading performance may be to structure instructional activities to minimize the need for extended attention and to highlight explicitly the features to which students should attend.

Several of the psychosocial characteristics listed by Harris and Sipay (e.g., quick discouragement and negative conditioning) are taken up also in the literature on motivation and engagement (Guthrie & Wigfield, 2000; Wigfield & Eccles, 2000). Byrnes (2001) describes the importance of engagement to learning as follows:

> A child who is engaged in a classroom activity is an active, attentive, curious, and willing participant. The opposite would be a disengaged, inattentive, and even resistant student. For obvious reasons, most teachers would love to have a classroom full of engaged students. (p. 94)

According to Guthrie and Wigfield (2000), enjoyment of reading for its own sake (intrinsic motivation) and focus on learning goals spur increased engagement in reading, and the resulting enhanced sense of competence, in turn, increases motivation for further learning. On the other hand, students who are motivated by a desire to appear successful or to receive recognition or reward (extrinsic motivation), although they may work at reading, tend to engage less deeply and, as a result, to read less effectively. They are more likely to become discouraged and give up on a task easily when frustrated.

There are also those in reading classes who have simply given up any chance of increased competence, for whom learning represents little more than an unbroken chain of failure and frustration. These individuals suffer from a condition called learned helplessness (Seligman, 1975). Because the learned helpless expect failure to occur, they seem unwilling to exert the effort that may be required to succeed in the reading classroom. Indeed, they are so conditioned to failure that they may be uncomfortable with successful learning experiences. Observations in remedial reading classrooms reveal many who attribute their reading problems to personal failure and who have chosen to abandon any attempts to gain competence in reading. Such motivational conditions are apt to make improvements in reading performance unlikely.

Two important points need to be made with regard to psychosocial behaviors and reading disorders. First, reading, as it occurs in the context of school, remains a social activity. The reader must not only process text to achieve personal ends but also demonstrate understanding of text for teachers and peers in a way that is seen as appropriate. Therefore, whether or not social and emotional factors are significant in a causal way, they will continue to be related to reading performance. Second, schools tend to see themselves as being in the business of teaching reading skills, not of treating emotional or social problems. With the advent of the No Child Left Behind Act (2002), scores on reading assessments have become the bottom line, the goal toward which reading instruction aims. This focus on skills and scores means that the emotional and social needs of the struggling reader are not likely to be given serious attention in classrooms or clinics. It would seem that those working with problem readers often feel that the emotional and social conditions of these readers will be taken care of when the specific reading problems are dealt with and acceptable reading scores achieved. Others, however, would argue that to treat only the reading problem without treating the concomitant emotional and social concerns would result in only partial and temporary gains in learner performance. Continued research in the area of psychosocial factors is necessary if we are to understand how best to improve the performance of disabled readers.

REFERENCES

American Academy of Pediatrics. (1998). Learning disabilities, dyslexia, and vision: A subject review. *Pediatrics, 102,* 1217–1219.

Balajthy, E., & Lipa-Wade, S. (2003). *Struggling readers: Assessment and instruction in grades K-6.* New York: Guilford Press.

Bandura, A. (1969). *Principles of behavior modification.* New York: Holt, Rinehart, & Winston.

Blachman, B. A. (2000). Phonological awareness. In M. L. Kamil, P. B. Mosenthal, P. D. Pearson, & R. Barr (Eds.), *Handbook of reading research* (Vol. 3, pp. 483–501). Mahwah, NJ: Erlbaum.

Byrnes, J. P. (2001). *Cognitive development and learning in instructional contexts* (2nd ed.). Boston: Allyn & Bacon.

Gibson, E. J. (1969). *Principles of perceptual learning and development.* Englewood Cliffs, NJ: Prentice Hall.

Gray, C. T. (1922). *Deficiencies in reading ability: Their diagnosis and remedies.* Boston: Heath.

Gray, W. S. (1915) *Oral reading paragraph test.* Bloomington, IN: Public School.

Gunning, T. G. (2002). *Assessing and correcting reading and writing difficulties* (2nd ed.). Boston: Allyn & Bacon.

Guthrie, J. T., & Wigfield, A. (2000). Engagement and motivation in reading. In M. L. Kamil, P. B. Mosenthal, P. D. Pearson, & R. Barr (Eds.), *Handbook of reading research* (Vol. 3, pp. 403–422). Mahwah, NJ: Erlbaum.

Harris, A. J. (1971). Psychological and motivational problems. In D. K. Bracken & E. Malmquist (Eds.), *Improving reading ability around the world* (pp. 97–103). Newark, DE: International Reading Association.

Harris, A. J., & Sipay, E. R. (1980). *How to increase reading ability* (7th ed.). New York: Longman.

Hinshelwood, J. (1917). *Congenital word-blindness.* London: Lewis.

Judd, C. H. (1918). *Reading: Its nature and development.* [Educational Monograph No. 10]. Chicago: University of Chicago.

Lipson, M. Y., & Wixson, K. K. (1997). *Assessment and instruction of reading and writing disability: An interactive approach* (2nd ed.). New York: Longman.

Morgan, W. P. (1896). A case of congenital word-blindness. *British Medical Journal, 2,* 1612–1614.

No Child Left Behind Act of 2001. (2002). Public Law No. 107-110, Paragraph 115, Stat. 1425.

Orton, S. T. (1925). Word-blindness in school children. *Archives of Neurology & Psychiatry, 14,* 582–615.

Reid, G. (1998). *Dyslexia: A practitioner's handbook* (2nd ed.). New York: Wiley.

Robinson, H. M. (1953). Personality and reading. In A. E. Traxler (Ed.), *Modern educational problems* (pp. 87–99). Washington, DC: American Council on Education.

Ross, A. O. (1976). *Psychological aspects of learning disabilities and reading disorders.* New York: McGraw-Hill.

Seligman, M. E. P. (1975). *Helplessness.* San Francisco: Freeman.

Shaywitz, B. A., Pugh, K. R., Jenner, A. R., Fulbright, R. K., Fletcher, J. M., Gore, J. C., et al. (2000). The neurobiology of reading and reading disability (dyslexia). In M. L. Kamil, P. B. Mosenthal, P. D. Pearson, & R. Barr (Eds.), *Handbook of reading research* (Vol. 3, pp. 229–249). Mahwah, NJ: Erlbaum.

Snow, C. E., Burns, M. S., & Griffin, P. (Eds.). (1998). *Preventing reading difficulties in young children.* Washington, DC: National Academy Press.

Spear-Swerdling, L. (2004). A road map for understanding reading disability and other reading problems: Origins, prevention, and intervention. In R. B. Ruddell & N. J. Unrau (Eds.), *Theoretical models and processes of reading* (5th ed., pp. 517–573). Newark, DE: International Reading Association.

Torgeson, J. K., & Hecht, S. A. (1996). Preventing and remediating reading disabilities. In M. F. Graves, P. van den Broek, & B. M. Taylor (Eds.), *The first R: Every child's right to read* (pp. 160–188). Newark, DE: International Reading Association.

Uhl, W. L. (1916). The use of the results of reading tests as bases for planning remedial work. *Elementary School Journal, 17,* 266–275.

Wigfield, A., & Eccles, J. S. (2001). The development of competence beliefs, expectancies for success, and achievement values from childhood through adolescence. In A. Wigfield & J. S. Eccles (Eds.), *Development of achievement motivation* (pp. 92–120). San Diego, CA: Academic Press.

Willcutt, E. G., & Pennington, B. F. (2000). Comorbidity of reading disability and attention-deficit hyperactivity disorder: Differences by gender and subtype. *Journal of Reading Disabilities, 33,* 179–191.

PATRICIA A. ALEXANDER
University of Michigan

EMILY FOX
University of Maryland

READING IN THE CONTENT AREAS

For over at least half a century, reading and curriculum specialists have claimed that every teacher is a teacher of reading. Many books, articles, and research reports have been published during this period, and courses in teaching reading in the content areas are offered in many colleges of education. Despite these efforts, content teachers have typically maintained that they are teachers of subject matter and not teachers of reading. In a comprehensive and critical review of the research in reading in the content areas, Dupois (1984) concludes that content teachers know too little about reading in general and reading in their subjects in particular. She further reports that teachers feel "helplessness and frustration in the face of students who cannot read classroom materials" (p. 1).

This frustration is further amplified when students are labeled as special or disabled. Teachers feel especially helpless in their attempts to deal with the reading needs of the special student, assuming they lack some vital prerequisite training or technique. Yet what has been repeatedly revealed in research studies is the need for good holistic language teaching for students of all ability levels, rather than separate programs for special populations.

Specialists have a vital role to play in the field of special education, but it is not in the creation of separate programs focused on subskills of language; these programs often are less of a solution than a perpetuation of a problem with a child's reading. One major role of the special education specialist is that of collaborator and consultant to the content teacher in mainstream classrooms. The purpose of this relationship is to strengthen the regular classroom teacher as he or she plans to more fully involve special children in the intellectual and social life of the classroom.

In 1981, 27 national organizations of teachers, supervisors, administrators, and lay groups endorsed a statement called "The Essentials Approach: Rethinking the Curriculum for the 80's" (Mercier, 1981), which proclaims the interdependence of skills and content as well as interdependence of knowledge in the several content areas. Interdependence of skills and content refers to the learner's use of reading, writing, talking, and thinking in learning literature, social studies, science, and math. The "Essentials" consortium argued that teachers will teach their subjects more effectively if they teach students the special reading, writing, and study strategies for acquiring and critically responding to knowledge in their disciplines. Ultimately, such a concerted effort will prepare students for a lifetime of learning, helping to make them independent learners. Clearly, the direction proposed is not limited to the relationship between reading and learning but rather extends to writing, studying, talking, and thinking.

The "Essentials" consortium warned against two related practices in many schools that stand in the way of fostering the interdependence principle. The first faulty practice defines basic skills by what can be measured at a time when tests are severely limited in what they can measure. Related to this is the practice of teaching the skills identified by such tests in isolation from significant content (i.e., from texts that look like the tests rather than real content texts). In short, reading skill has been fragmented away from the content areas and further fragmented into discrete subskills. Goodlad (1983) documented this state of the schools, which he characterized as being preoccupied with lower intellectual processes and boredom of epidemic proportions. The problem is exacerbated in special and mainstream classrooms for special educational populations, where it has been erroneously believed that there needs to be more emphasis on isolated subskills to remediate the poor reading skills of these students.

In 1985, the Commission on Reading of the National Academy of Education published *Becoming a Nation of Readers* (Anderson et al., 1985), which synthesized current sociopsycholinguistic theory and research on learning to read and reading to learn. This document provides a theoretical rationale for teachers who would implement the "Essentials" approach.

Reading is not defined as a product or as a set of subskills to be tested but rather as "a process for constructing meaning from written texts . . . a complex skill requiring the coordination of a number of interrelated sources of information" (p. 7). Those sources lie in the reader, in the text, in fellow students, and in the teacher. Readers bring to the reading task knowledge of the world, of language, of strategies for reading various texts, and of their teachers' purposes and expectations. They also bring their own interests and purposes. Texts present world knowledge in special ways; for example, literary texts have different conventions and structures from informational texts. They vary in purpose, content, and style. Fellow students constitute a community of comprehenders. Through interaction they can share relevant prior knowledge, text knowledge, and reading strategies.

The role of teachers is to orchestrate these interrelated sources, developing productive transactions among readers and texts that lead to more efficient strategies for information processing by students. Information processing involves such active mental searches as drawing on prior knowledge, predicting, questioning, elaborating, transforming, structuring, restating, summarizing, synthesizing, reflecting, and critically evaluating. In practical terms, content teachers can teach reading and study by modeling strategies that incorporate one or more of these searches by having students practice strategies in pairs and in small groups as well as on their own and by having students reflect on and share their experiences with each other in using the strategies.

Two lists of such strategies follow. They were developed by Botel (1984) at the University of Pennsylvania for preparing teachers and reading specialists. The first list includes strategies for reading and comprehending literary texts; the second includes strategies for reading and comprehending expository texts. These strategies are no less vital for the special education student than the regular student. It will be noted that these strategies enable students to experience reading at their own levels.

Strategies for Reading, Writing, and Studying Library Texts

Before Reading
Brainstorming
> What questions, ideas, or experiences were suggested by the title and opening paragraph(s) or verse?

Write or Talk and Write
> Write nonstop about what comes to mind as you think about the title.
> Write whatever questions come to mind as you think about the title.
> Recall a related remembered experience; share it; write it.
> Take notes on the way of life of a character from another culture (categories: family relationships, sources of food, beliefs about nature, housing, community, recreation, education).

While Reading
> If you do not understand something, put a mark in the margin and go on.
> Picture in your mind's eye what happens in the story.

After Reading
Personal Responding
> What stands out for you in the selection?

Retelling
> Retell history from the point of view of different characters.
> Tell the story to someone in the family, to a friend, to a younger person, etc.

Vocabulary Development

Write key words or expressions and define them in context.

Write words the writer uses to describe a character; then write a brief paragraph about the character using these words.

Write synonyms for key words.

Writing

Prepare questions you would ask if you could interview a character.

Write a journal entry about an important event as if you were the character who experienced it.

Write notes as if you were one of the characters.

Write an eyewitness or reporter's account of a scene as it might appear in a newspaper.

Making Tests

Prepare tests on content studied using the same form found in standardized and other tests.

Illustrating

Draw a floor plan of a major setting.

Illustrate a scene.

Make a map or graphic diagram of a key concept or relationship.

Illustrate key words and expressions.

Show the story or episode in a four-frame cartoon.

Dramatizing

Plan a "Reader's Theater."

Plan a panel discussion as if you were characters in the story.

Plan an informal dramatization.

Plan a debate.

Compare similarities and differences between your culture and that of a character.

Strategies for Reading, Writing, and Studying Expository Texts

Before Reading

Brainstorming

List words and phrases you associate with the title; see if your items can be grouped or chunked.

What questions are suggested by the title or opening paragraphs?

What questions would you hope would be answered by the selection?

Previewing

Read the headings and first and last paragraphs; then say or recite briefly what they suggest about the text.

Based on your review, what are the main questions that the author probably set out to answer in the selection?

Making Tests

Prepare tests on content studied using the same form found in standardized and criterion-referenced tests.

While and After Reading

Personal Responding

What stands out for you in the selection?

Taking Notes

Turn headings into questions and answer them.

Underline one or two key words in each paragraph.

Write a question for each paragraph or section.

Make marginal notes.

Make a map or graphic diagram of a key concept or relationship.

Develop Vocabulary

Write key words and expressions and define them in context.

Reread and Recite

Reread only the key words and write them from memory.

Reread only the key words and write a summary.

As noted earlier, Dupois reported that content teachers know little about teaching reading of their subject. Adaptation of the two lists of strategies in teaching subject matter should correct that problem. That leaves the problem of students who cannot read texts on their own. These students would benefit greatly from having the material read to them while others in the class read silently. But they can also benefit from involvement with classmates in the learning of the strategies, in particular when they are practiced and reflected on collaboratively.

Beyond the learning of strategies for comprehending texts, students in the content areas should be reading a variety of periodicals and library books independently to broaden their perspectives, deepen their knowledge, and excite their interest in the content. Self-selected independent reading provides another way of accommodating the varying reading levels in a classroom (Anderson et al., 1985; Botel, 1981). Librarians and professional associations of content teachers are excellent sources for such reading. In social studies, the Children's Book Council (1984) produces an excellent list. Earle (1976) prepared a list of high-interest materials for the math classroom.

It is clear that reading in the content areas today deals with how teachers can organize and plan for instruction so as to relate the basic academic competencies (language processes of not only reading but also writing, listening, and speaking) to learning the basic academic subjects. That is true for all students, including special education students in mainstream classrooms as well as in learning centers.

In summary, from the point of view of special education, the proposed ways of teaching content reading would have the effect of providing for more learning and less isolation and fragmentation, less stigmatization and separation from peers, less isolation of teachers, and less fragmentation of language.

REFERENCES

Anderson, R. C., Hiebert, E. H., Scott, J. A., & Wilkinson, I. A. G. (1985). *Becoming a nation of readers: The report of the Commission on Reading.* Washington, DC: National Institute of Education.

Botel, M. (1981). *A Pennsylvania comprehensive reading/communication arts plan.* Harrisburg: Pennsylvania Department of Education.

Botel, M. (1984). *Comprehending texts: Subskills or strategies.* Philadelphia: Graduate School of Education, University of Pennsylvania.

Children's Book Council. *Notable children's trade books in the field of social studies.* New York: Author.

Dupois, M. M. (Ed.). (1984). *Reading in the content areas: Research for teachers.* Newark, DE: International Reading Association.

Earle, R. A. (1976). *Teaching reading and math.* Newark, DE: International Reading Association.

Goodlad, J. I. (1983). What some schools and classrooms teach. *Educational Leadership, 40*(7), 8–19.

Mercier, L. Y. (Ed.). (1981). *The essentials approach: Rethinking the curriculum for the 80's.* Washington, DC: U.S. Department of Education, Basic Skills Improvement Program.

MORTON BOTEL
University of Pennsylvania

READING DISORDERS
READING REMEDIATION

READING MILESTONES–THIRD EDITION

Reading Milestones, a basal reading series developed by Quigley and King (1991) with McAnally, Rose, and Quigley (1999), was designed specifically for individuals with hearing impairment and was originally published in the early 1980s by Dormac, Inc. The series was then acquired by PRO-ED, Inc., in 1995.

Reading Milestones is the most popular reading program of its kind. It is an example of a special text that is recent, extensive, and research based (Power & Leigh, 2000). This successful alternative, language-controlled program is designed to take readers to approximately a fifth-grade reading level. It is especially effective for students with hearing impairments and language delays and is also widely used with others who have special language and reading needs, including individuals with learning disabilities and students learning English as a second language (ESL).

The *Reading Milestones* program includes student readers, student workbooks, spelling books, teachers' guides, and placement tests at each of the six levels. There are 10 student readers included in each level of the program with six stories per book. The stories are representative of the culture of the students using the program. A student workbook accompanies each student reader and includes tasks that emphasize the development of comprehension through the use of procedures such as semantic, story, and word maps; word analogies; and semantic feature analyses. Each level of the program consists of one spelling book that covers books one through five and one spelling book that covers books six through ten, using a number of spelling tasks consisting of words that appear in the story. The teachers' guides provide detailed instructional suggestions that allow educators to create a self-contained program from the reading series (PRO-ED, Inc.). The *Reading Bridge* series includes extension materials for students reading at grade levels 4–5. Additional resources that adhere to the structured approach presented in *Reading Milestones* include the *Simple Language Fairy Tales, Simple English Classics,* and *Most Loved Classics* series.

Extensive revisions were made in the third edition of the program based on recent research, new practices in reading, and feedback from users of the series. Because most students with hearing impairments and/or other special needs lack a basic knowledge base in oral/aural aspects of language, there can be a resulting gap between their language experience and the assumptions inherent in the materials they are given to read. *Reading Milestones* was designed to minimize this gap by beginning with the simplest possible language to ensure initial success in reading and by increasing language acquisition. Students are guided to progress in small increments, accompanied by constant reinforcement and review of concepts, vocabulary, and language constructions, to ensure continuing success and motivation.

REFERENCES

Brockmiller, P., & Coley, J. (1981). A survey of methods, materials, and teacher preparation among teachers of reading to the hearing-impaired. *The Reading Teacher, 34,* 526–529.

King, C., & Quigley, S. (1985). *Reading and deafness.* Austin, TX: PRO-ED.

Lasso, C. (1987). Survey of reading instruction for hearing-impaired students in the United States. *The Volta Review, 89,* 85–98.

Lasso, C. J., & Mobley, R. T. (1997). National survey of reading instruction for deaf or hard-of-hearing students in the U.S. *The Volta Review, 99,* 31–58.

McAnally, P., Rose, S., & Quigley, S. (1999). *Reading practices with deaf learners.* Austin, TX: PRO-ED.

Power, D., & Leigh, G. R. (2000). Principles and practices of literacy development for deaf learners: A historical overview. *Journal of Deaf Studies and Deaf Education, 5,* 3–8.

PRO-ED, Inc. (n.d.). *Reading milestones: An alternative reading program* (3rd ed.). Retrieved May 30, 2005, from http://www.proedinc.com

Quigley, S., & King, C. (Eds.). (1991). *Reading milestones* (2nd ed.). Austin, TX: PRO-ED.

PEGGY KIPPING
PRO-ED, Inc.
First and Second editions

ROSE FAIRBANKS
Temecula, California
Third edition

READING REMEDIATION

Reading can be described as a highly complex cognitive activity. As a cognitive task, the reading act requires the successful completion of many simple and complex linguistic skills (Perfetti, 1983). As an illustration, consider the task of reading aloud the word *dog*. To accomplish this seemingly simple task, a reader must know the letters of the alphabet, must have internalized the sound/symbol patterns common to the English language, and must be able to decode or sound out the word accurately. Decoding alone can be a troublesome venture in the English language, where exceptions appear to outnumber phonetic rules. Further, if an understanding of *dog* is also required, then the reader must relate the abstract symbols and sounds to the concept of *dog* stored in long-term memory.

If many skills are required to read and understand a single word, then the skills necessary to make sense of the previous paragraph are far more extensive. It is therefore not surprising that some individuals never acquire reading proficiency. Those individuals who consistently experience difficulties in processing print are part of a population of learners who require special instruction. This special instruction is referred to as reading remediation.

Reading remediation is a branch of language instruction that is concerned with the identification and treatment of reading problems, particularly for students for whom the regular classroom instruction does not prove effective. The successful remediation of reading problems has become of particular importance in recent years due to the enactment of the No Child Left Behind Act (NCLB; 2002), with its requirement that all students be proficient in reading by the year 2014 and its goal of adequate yearly progress toward that goal for students in subgroups, including students in special education and English language learners.

The following text will examine factors that contribute to reading difficulties, consider how the cycle of remediation occurs, discuss levels of reading diagnosis, survey principles that should guide effective diagnosis, and review profiles of readers who may require additional attention in reading instruction.

Even before an individual begins learning to read, there are personal factors that are likely to enhance or inhibit reading performance. Rupley and Blair (1983) identify two broad categories of variables that relate to reading performance: functional and facilitative factors. Functional factors are those personal variables that actually pertain to reading. Sight vocabulary, reading rate, and oral language development are examples of functional factors. In many ways, however, these functional variables are the outcome of other variables that are not directly part of the reading performance but contribute to it. These variables are called facilitative factors, and they are of particular importance in reading remediation. Facilitative factors fall under broad headings such as physical, cognitive, and emotional characteristics. Within each of these broad areas there are conditions that can significantly influence reading performance.

For example, among physical characteristics, we know that gender, visual and auditory ability, and general health influence reading performance; neurological development may have a role as well. Whether owing to genetic or environmental factors, or a combination of both, females have long been thought to have an advantage over males in language acquisition and early language proficiency. Although doubt has been raised as to the existence of such a gender difference in language acquisition and proficiency (Byrnes, 2001), boys do tend to outnumber girls consistently in remedial reading classes.

It is also clear that individuals who suffer from visual or auditory impairments will have more difficulty in acquiring proficiency in written language. Adequate sight and hearing are basic to reading. Among young children, many suspected reading problems can be traced to visual or auditory impairments, many of which are correctable. Once the vision or hearing problem has been corrected, many young children go on to acquire reading proficiency. Consequently, analysis of reading problems frequently begins with vision and hearing screening. In these screenings, visual and auditory acuity and discrimination are tested.

Variations in neurological development or neurological damage during development may be involved in some cases of reading disability. Differences in how the brain is organized and in which areas are active during reading and language processing may result in impaired reading ability, by interfering with the phonological processing involved in learning to read or by more general language processing disturbances (Shaywitz et al., 2000).

Cognitive factors also contribute significantly to the reading process. As we will see in the discussion of reader profiles, the cognitive ability an individual brings to the reading act is a major determinant of the level of proficiency expected. While there is no one-to-one correspondence between intelligence and reading ability, the relationship between the two is strong indeed. Other cognitive factors involved in successful reading performance include memory, attention, and the ability to learn by forming associations. Cognitive factors may be assessed by means of achievement or intelligence test data, or school performance records.

Similarly, an individual's emotional well-being can positively or negatively affect the ability to read. The significant influence of affective factors on learning should not be ignored in the evaluation of reading problems (Gunning, 2002; Richek, Caldwell, Jennings, & Lerner, 1996). Learners who have the cognitive potential may lack the desire or commitment required to do well in reading. Parent/student interviews and self-concept and personality tests may be used to gather information on the emotional condition of a reader.

When a reading problem is suspected, it is prudent to determine whether existing physical, cognitive, and emotional, as well as socioeconomic, cultural, or educational, factors are potential sources of the problem. The systematic assessment of functional and facilitative factors is part of reading diagnosis, which, in turn, is a major component in the remediation cycle.

Much of the language of reading remediation is borrowed from medical science. The medical influence is particularly apparent in the cycle of reading remediation, which comprises three phases: diagnosis, prescription, and treatment.

The diagnosis or data-collection phase of the remediation cycle is devoted to the systematic assessment of existing conditions: a search for evidence that might indicate the source of a reader's problems. It is in this phase that information about the reader and reading performance is gathered and analyzed. Knowledge about the reader may be collected in a spontaneous fashion within the classroom, or it may be amassed through a formal and extensive procedure.

On the basis of careful diagnosis, the second phase of the cycle, the prescription or program-specific phase, is put into place. Prescription is the delineation of the appropriate instructional treatment to be administered. As with the diagnostic procedure, the instructional plan may be informal or formal in nature. An informal prescription might entail little more than the teacher's specification of instructional objectives that seem appropriate for a given reader. A formal prescription, by comparison, may be an elaborate instructional program to be administered by a specialist within a clinic or resource room.

Finally, there is the treatment or program-implementation phase of the cycle. In this phase, the prescribed instructional treatment is carried out and its effectiveness evaluated. From the knowledge gained during instruction and evaluation, additional information gained about the reader and reading performance is gathered. Based on these new data, a revised diagnosis may be rendered, and the remediation cycle begins anew. This remediation cycle forms the basis of reading instruction, whether it occurs in the regular classroom or in the resource room (Barr, Blachowicz, Katz, & Kaufman, 2002).

Diagnosis can take place at several levels of complexity. Those levels, in order of increasing formality, are informal, classroom, and clinical diagnosis (Wilson & Cleland, 1985). In the previous section, the data gathering was apt to be part of the more extensive form of clinical reading diagnosis. Meeting the needs of most readers does not often require that diagnosis reach such a formal level, however. Rather, clinical diagnosis should be the last stage in the diagnostic procedure. For the most part, serving the needs of the reader entails only the first two levels in the sequence of diagnosis, informal and classroom diagnosis.

Informal diagnosis is an ongoing process that takes place continuously in the regular reading classroom. This stage of diagnosis encompasses the teacher's monitoring of reading instruction to determine whether that instruction is appropriate for the learner. If found inappropriate or ineffective, the instruction should be adjusted in some fashion to suit the learner's needs and capabilities more adequately.

If the teacher's minor adjustments in reading instruction are not successful in improving the situation, the teacher moves to the second stage of diagnosis, conducting some testing within the classroom in an attempt to identify the nature of the reading problem. Classroom diagnosis may involve the use of teacher-made or commercial tests that can be administered and interpreted by teachers who have no specialized knowledge of reading or assessment.

Should the classroom teacher's attempts to identify or remediate the reading problem fail, then it is probably time to call in a specialist. It is at this point in the diagnostic sequence that a clinical assessment of the reading problem may be conducted. Following the assessment of facilitative factors, a battery of reading tests may be given. Among the reading skills frequently tested in a clinical diagnosis are sight vocabulary, oral reading, silent reading, listening comprehension, rapid naming, and word analysis skills. The information amassed in diagnosis permits the clinical specialist to prescribe a remediation program for the learner that should improve reading performance. This remediation program may be implemented by the classroom teacher or may require the supplementary services of a reading specialist or resource teacher, which may be provided either in a pull-out program in the resource room or, increasingly in recent years, in the regular classroom, following the mainstreaming or inclusion model of remediation and special education (Gunning, 2002).

The remedial services available for the learner depend on the nature and severity of the diagnosed reading difficulty. School districts vary in the definition of reading difficulty that they use to determine eligibility for remedial reading services, but the most common definitions are based on either functional impairment or discrepancy between assessed ability and achievement. Students with functional impairment fail to meet certain standards of reading achievement and thus are hampered in their functioning in the academic environment. Title 1 and Reading Recovery are programs that use a functional definition of eligibility for the supplemental reading assistance they provide. A discrepancy definition of reading difficulty compares students' assessed level of cognitive ability, typically from an IQ test, with their assessed level of reading achievement. Many states use this standard for eligibility for programs intended to remediate serious reading disabilities (Snow, Burns, & Griffin, 1998). One problem with the use of the discrepancy definition is the likelihood that students with poor reading ability will, for a variety of reasons, perform poorly also on tests of cognitive ability, minimizing the apparent discrepancy and thus rendering them ineligible for additional supportive services.

Because of the major role that diagnosis plays in the remediation cycle, it is imperative that the assessment provide valid and reliable information. Bond and Tinker (1973) outlined some guiding principles for clinical diagnosis that should result in the more effective remediation of reading problems. Many of these principles can still be applied to informal and classroom diagnosis.

1. Diagnosis should be directed toward formulating methods of improvement.
2. Diagnosis should involve more than an appraisal of reading skills and abilities.
3. Diagnosis should be efficient and effective.
4. Diagnosis should be continuous.
5. Diagnosis should seek to identify patterns of behavior.

According to the first of these principles, it is important to remember that diagnosis is not an end in itself. It is conducted to provide accurate information from which effective remediation can be developed. Without the other components of prescription and treatment, diagnosis would be an isolated and meaningless undertaking. Further, for diagnosis to be effective, it must go beyond the assessment of reading alone and examine the learner in a more holistic and multidimensional fashion. That is, the physical, cognitive, emotional, socioeconomic, and educational characteristics of the learner must also be part of the decision-making process.

Another pragmatic concern in the diagnostic procedure is that the amount of testing and the instrumentation be appropriate for the individual case under question. For example, if a physical condition is suspected as the primary cause for existing reading problems, and if visual/auditory screening confirms that hypothesis, then further testing may prove unwarranted. Likewise, it is essential to employ effective (i.e., valid and reliable) measures to test for physical or other factors, and to have those measures administered and evaluated by qualified individuals.

Diagnosis should generally be an ongoing process. Once information has been gathered and an instructional pro-

gram prescribed, the effects of the prescribed program should be assessed. Even as it pertains to clinical diagnosis, no diagnosis is final, and the treatment prescribed on the basis of formal assessment should be periodically reviewed and revised. It is important to remember that converging evidence is essential for an effective diagnosis. One piece of information is, under most circumstances, insufficient for building a remediation program that will lead to improvement for the learner. Patterns of scores are more likely to convey a more accurate view of the reader's strengths and needs.

Not only do scores produce certain patterns, but the diagnostic data across readers also tend to fall into certain patterns. It is on the basis of these diagnostic patterns that several commonly encountered reader profiles have been generated (Bond & Tinker, 1973; Harris & Sipay, 1980).

Gifted readers are individuals who manifest normal or above normal intelligence and who possess reading skills that are markedly above grade level, where a significant difference is performance at least two years above grade level. It is important to note that the gifted reader may or may not be gifted in other domains; that is, the learner may be advanced in reading skills but average in mathematics or science. Correspondingly, a gifted reader may have intelligence only slightly above average, despite having reading skills that are significantly above grade level. For example, Ruth is a fourth grader with a measured IQ of 125. According to diagnosis, Ruth's sight vocabulary was 6-8 (grade equivalent of sixth grade, eighth month), oral reading 6-3, silent reading 7-1, and listening comprehension 7-5. As these scores indicate, Ruth's overall reading performance is well above the fourth-grade level. We would say that Ruth appears to be a gifted reader.

The needs of the gifted reader may be served within the context of the regular reading class or within a specific gifted program. However, it is expected that these proficient readers will be provided with reading materials and instruction that are commensurate with their demonstrated abilities, whether mainstreamed in the regular reading classroom or grouped with other advanced readers for separate instruction.

Underachievers are similar to gifted learners in that they demonstrate exceptional cognitive potential. However, they may fail to demonstrate reading skills that approach their potential. Dave, for example, is Ruth's fourth-grade classmate. Dave's IQ is estimated to be 140, yet he is performing barely at grade level in reading class. His sight vocabulary is 4-6, silent reading and listening comprehension 4-1, and oral reading 3-8. While Dave's reading scores are not significantly below his grade level, they are significantly below his potential. Although further diagnosis would be appropriate in this case, Dave would be classified as an underachieving reader.

The underachieving reader is often the most difficult case to identify. Primarily because this student's reading performance is near grade level, many classrooms do not recognize or attend to the gap between the underachiever's potential and performance. Further, prescribing and treating the underachiever is a complex undertaking; reading problems may be tied to any number of emotional, physical, neurological, social, or cultural factors that cannot be easily detected or treated.

Sometimes there are learners who do fairly well in reading but who have a problem in one or two skill areas. This type of reader possesses a specific skill deficiency, the most common problem-reader profile. For the most part, these skill-deficient readers remain in the regular classroom with help provided by their classroom reading teacher.

When reading assistance is given in the classroom and is administered by the classroom teacher, it is labeled a corrective reading program. Jake's situation is a case in point. Jake is also in Ruth's fourth-grade class. Although he usually does well in reading, Jake has problems with listening comprehension. As part of his corrective reading program, Jake's teacher works with him on a weekly basis to improve his listening skills. In this way, it is hoped that Jake's listening skills can be brought in line with his other reading skills.

Some readers' problems are not as limited or as easily treated as Jake's. There are those cases in which a learner with normal intelligence performs well below grade level on the majority of reading skills. For example, another fourth grader, Betsy, has an IQ of 101, but her reading grade equivalency scores are as follows: sight vocabulary 1-5; oral reading, preprimer, silent reading, 1-3; listening comprehension 3-5. Betsy exhibits "unexpected" poor reading (Spear-Swerdling, 2004) and fits into the traditional conception of reading disability as involving a particular difficulty with reading in the absence of other obvious cognitive or sensory impairments. The remediation program required to meet the needs of this type of problem reader is referred to as a remedial reading program. Because of the serious nature of the reading problems being treated, remedial reading programs become the responsibility of a reading specialist or resource teacher. Regular classroom teachers rarely have the training to deal effectively with remedial readers, nor can they provide these individuals the highly individualized attention they need to remediate their reading problems.

The determination to place a learner in a remedial reading program is often the result of a group decision-making process similar to that followed for other categories of special learners. While the primary responsibility for reading remediation falls to the reading specialist, the remediation program can and should involve parents, outside specialists, content-area teachers, and school administrators. Both long- and short-term goals are established for the reader, focusing on cognitive, metacognitive, and affective needs. Progress toward these goals is carefully documented, so that accurate evaluation of the program and the learner is possible.

The last reader profile is that of the garden-variety poor reader. Like the remedial reader, this student demonstrates reading skills that are far below grade level. However, unlike the remedial reader, the garden-variety poor reader's below-average reading performance is not unexpected. Children with garden-variety poor reading exhibit problems with language comprehension in general along with their difficulties with word recognition, hindering their acquisition of reading (Spear-Swerdling, 2004). Victor, who is also in Ruth's class, has reading scores similar to Betsy's. However, his listening comprehension is also well below grade level. Victor's reading scores appear to correspond to his level of language development and cognitive ability. By a discrepancy definition of reading disability, then, he would not be eligible for formal reading remediation. Because of the specialized treatment they require, however, it is often appropriate for garden-variety poor readers to be assigned to a reading specialist or resource teacher for remediation.

In addition to addressing the individual needs and capabilities of students falling under all of these learner profiles, remedial or corrective reading programs must now strive as well toward the goal of having all students score at a proficient level in reading by the year 2014, under NCLB (2002). Increasing awareness of risk factors for reading difficulties and the increasing implementation of effective preventive interventions may reduce the number of students who develop problems in processing print. However, as long as there is the complex process of reading, there will be learners who encounter difficulties and who will require special reading instruction. It is the purpose of effective reading remediation programs to provide appropriate instruction to those learners for whom proficient reading is a goal yet to be achieved.

REFERENCES

Barr, R., Blachowicz, C. L. Z., Katz, C., & Kaufman, B. (2002). *Reading diagnosis for teachers: An instructional approach* (4th ed.). Boston: Allyn & Bacon.

Bond, G. L., & Tinker, M. A. (1973). *Reading difficulties: Their diagnosis and correction* (3rd ed.). Englewood Cliffs, NJ: Prentice Hall.

Byrnes, J. P. (2001). *Cognitive development and learning in instructional contexts* (2nd ed.). Boston: Allyn & Bacon.

Gunning, T. G. (2002). *Assessing and correcting reading and writing difficulties* (2nd ed.). Boston: Allyn & Bacon.

Harris, A. J., & Sipay, E. R. (1980). *How to increase reading ability* (7th ed.). New York: Longman.

No Child Left Behind Act of 2001. (2002). Public Law No. 107-110, Paragraph 115, Stat. 1425.

Perfetti, C. A. (1983). Individual differences in verbal processes. In R. F. Dillon & R. R. Schmeck (Eds.), *Individual differences in cognition* (Vol. 1, pp. 65–104). New York: Amsterdam.

Richek, M. A., Caldwell, J. S., Jennings, J. H., & Lerner, J. W. (1996). *Reading problems: Assessment and teaching strategies.* Boston: Allyn & Bacon.

Rupley, W. H., & Blair, T. R. (1983). *Reading diagnosis and remediation: Classroom and clinic* (2nd ed.). Boston: Houghton Mifflin.

Shaywitz, B. A., Pugh, K. R., Jenner, A. R., Fulbright, R. K., Fletcher, J. M., Gore, J. C., et al. (2000). The neurobiology of reading and reading disability (dyslexia). In M. L. Kamil, P. B. Mosenthal, P. D. Pearson, & R. Barr (Eds.), *Handbook of reading research* (Vol. 3, pp. 229–249). Mahwah, NJ: Erlbaum.

Snow, C. E., Burns, M. S., & Griffin, P. (Eds.). (1998). *Preventing reading difficulties in young children.* Washington, DC: National Academy Press.

Spear-Swerdling, L. (2004). A road map for understanding reading disability and other reading problems: Origins, prevention, and intervention. In R. B. Ruddell & N. J. Unrau (Eds.), *Theoretical models and processes of reading* (5th ed., pp. 517–573). Newark, DE: International Reading Association.

Wilson, R. M., & Cleland, C. S. (1985). *Diagnostic and remedial reading for classroom and clinic* (5th ed.). Columbus, OH: Merrill.

PATRICIA A. ALEXANDER
University of Michigan

EMILY FOX
University of Maryland

REALITY THERAPY

Reality therapy is a recently developed method of psychotherapy that stresses the importance of clients' learning more useful behaviors to deal with their current situations. Reality therapy stresses internal motivation, behavior change, and development of the "success identity." In terms of philosophical or theoretical stance, reality therapy can be described as strongly cognitive or rational in its approach, appealing to the client's reason and emphasizing the possibility of meaningful change, not just in feelings, but in behavior. The therapist takes an active, directive role as teacher, but remains supportive and non-punitive.

William Glasser, a physician, developed the theory of reality therapy over a period of years beginning with his psychiatric training. Both Glasser's reaction against traditional psychoanalytic psychotherapy and his experiences in working with delinquent youths at a California school for girls probably played major roles in the development of reality therapy (Belkin, 1975).

Glasser (1965) sees the individual as motivated internally by need to belong, to be loved, and to be a successful, worthwhile person. Control is seen as a major element in the human system: the individual works to control the environment so that internal, personal needs can be met. The individual's interface with the reality of his or her current life situation is the arena of action. Therefore, reality therapy stresses personal commitment, change in behavior, responsibility, and the here and now. The individual's past history is not seen as particularly significant, and the medical model or orthodox concept of mental illness has no place in this approach (Corey, 1986).

The therapist is viewed as a coach or instructor who provides clients with assistance and encouragement in evaluating the usefulness of their current behavior in satisfying their needs. Where the appropriateness of change is recognized, the therapist assists in the development and execution of plans for remediation. Development of the client's strengths and feelings of self-worth leading to a success identity is a key responsibility of the therapist.

Reality therapy is basically a didactic activity, by which the client develops an understanding of reality and learns to act responsibly and effectively in accordance with that reality. A summary of the techniques and procedures of reality therapy is provided by Corey (1986), based on his adaptation and integration of material from several sources. Corey discusses eight steps in therapy: Create a relationship, focus on current behavior, invite clients to evaluate their behavior, help clients develop an action plan, get commitment, refuse to accept excuses, refuse to use punishment, and refuse to give up.

Glasser has promoted the acceptance of his approach by numerous presentations and publications. In *Reality Therapy: A New Approach to Psychiatry* (1965), *Stations of the Mind* (1981), and *Take Effective Control of Your Life* (1984), Glasser develops his theoretical approach to psychotherapy and demonstrates its application to clinical cases. Glasser's *Schools Without Failure* (1969) applies the concepts of reality therapy to the school setting. *Positive Addiction* (1976) treats a different, but related, theme; it also has met with wide public acceptance.

Reality therapy has grown in popularity and influence. It is particularly well received in schools and the criminal justice system, and with counselors who work to rehabilitate handicapped individuals. This psychotherapeutic approach lends itself to short-term, direct, and active therapy.

REFERENCES

Belkin, G. S. (1975). *Practical counseling in the schools.* Dubuque, IA: Brown.

Corey, G. (1986). *Theory and practice of counseling and psychotherapy* (3rd ed.). Monterey, CA: Brooks/Cole.

Glasser, W. (1965). *Reality therapy: A new approach to psychiatry.* New York: Harper & Row.

Glasser, W. (1969). *Schools without failure.* New York: Harper & Row.

Glasser, W. (1976). *Positive addiction.* New York: Harper & Row.

Glasser, W. (1981). *Stations of the mind.* New York: Harper & Row.

Glasser, W. (1984). *Take effective control of your life.* New York: Harper & Row.

ROBERT R. REILLEY
Texas A&M University

PSYCHOSOCIAL ADJUSTMENT

PSYCHOTHERAPY WITH INDIVIDUALS WITH DISABILITIES

RECEPTIVE-EXPRESSIVE EMERGENT LANGUAGE TEST–SECOND EDITION

The Receptive-Expressive Emergent Language Test–Second Edition (REEL-2; Bzoch & League, 1991) is a multidimensional analysis of emergent language. The REEL-2 is specifically designed for use with a broad range of infants and toddlers up to age 3 who are at risk. The instrument is a system of measurement and intervention planning based on neurolinguistic development to identify young children who have specific language problems based on specific language behaviors. Results are obtained from a parent interview and are given in terms of an Expressive Language Age, a Receptive Language Age, and a Combined Language Age.

Bachman (1995) reviewed the instrument and summarized that the REEL-2 covers a wide range of behaviors and could be used with direct observation to elicit information for developing a qualitative description of a child's early language development. Bliss (1995) reported that the advantages of the REEL-2 are in its easy administration and scoring.

REFERENCES

Bachman, L. F. (1995). Review of the Receptive-Expressive Emergent Language Test, Second Edition. In J. C. Conoley & J. C. Impara (Eds.), *The twelfth mental measurements yearbook* (pp. 843–845). Lincoln: University of Nebraska Press.

Bliss, L. S. (1995). Review of the Receptive-Expressive Emergent Language Test, Second Edition. In J. C. Conoley & J. C. Impara (Eds.), *The twelfth mental measurements yearbook* (pp. 845–846). Lincoln: University of Nebraska Press.

Bzoch, K. R., & League, R. (1991). *Receptive-Expressive Emergent Language Scale–Second Edition.* Austin, TX: PRO-ED.

TADDY MADDOX
PRO-ED, Inc.

RECEPTIVE LANGUAGE DISORDERS

A language disorder in which there is a severe loss or impairment in the understanding or use of language owing to brain injury or dysfunction is known as aphasia. This disorder may be dichotomized into expressive or motor aphasia, in which the ability to form speech is impaired, and receptive or sensory aphasia, in which the ability to comprehend the spoken word is affected. In adults, aphasia is acquired through brain damage and results in cessation or regression from a prior ability to use language. In children, language disorders may be acquired as a result of brain injury, or they may be developmental in nature. That is, because of abnormal development or injury to the language centers of the central nervous system prenatally, perinatally, or postnatally during the first year, the child has difficulty in developing normal understanding and use of language (Gaddes, 1980). This condition is also known as a primary or congenital language disorder (Deuel, 1983). When the dysfunction in the language centers of the brain is mild, it may be referred to as a learning disability.

Although many parts of the brain are active and interrelated in language and speech, certain areas are of greater importance to specific language functions (Benson, 1983). In 1874, Carl Wernicke, a German neurologist, identified the superior lateral surface of the left temporal lobe as the cortical area for decoding oral speech. Geschwind (1972) stressed the importance of subcortical bundles of neural fibers that connect distant cortical areas. However, the precise boundaries of important cortical areas remain vague owing to considerable interindividual variation and the fact that most brain lesions are not highly localized (Benson, 1983; Gaddes, 1980). Although the left hemisphere is dominant for language in most right-handed individuals, those who are left-handed or ambidextrous may have right hemisphere or bilateral language functions (Lezak, 1983). Some experts believe that comprehension of spoken language is more likely to have bilateral representation than other language functions (Benson et al., 1973).

Receptive language disorders may be classified in several ways. Johnson and Myklebust (1967) discuss a generalized deficit in auditory learning in which a child hears but does not interpret. Other children, less affected, can interpret nonverbal, social sounds, but cannot relate the spoken word to an appropriate unit of experience. In cases of less severe receptive language deficits, the inability to comprehend may be limited to abstract language or to specific parts of speech. Benson (1983) cites four clinically distinguishable comprehension disturbances and suggests a neuroanatomical locus of pathology for each. These are (1) receptive disturbances, involving comprehension and repetition of spoken language; (2) perceptive disturbances (also known as Wernicke's aphasia), in which comprehension of written and spoken language is involved; (3) semantic disturbances, characterized by an inability to understand the meaning of spoken and written language despite relatively normal ability to repeat spoken language; and (4) syntactic disturbances; involving difficulties with syntactical structures and sequencing. Benson emphasizes that there is much overlap among these comprehension problems, and they are rarely found in isolation.

Receptive language disorders frequently are observed in conjunction with other disabilities. In the developmental hierarchy of language outlined by Myklebust (1954), expressive language follows and is dependent on inner and receptive language. In a similar way, reading and written language are dependent on the acquisition of earlier levels of language. Therefore, it is not surprising that reading, writing, and the problem-solving areas of arithmetic may be affected by receptive language disorders. Johnson and Myklebust (1967) suggest that auditory cognitive skills, including discrimination, rhyming, and blending, often are correlates of receptive language disorders. Such skills are prerequisite to the success of an auditory-phonetic reading program and indicate the need for a global language approach to instruction.

To remediate receptive language disorders, it is necessary to create a match between the auditory symbol and a meaningful unit of experience. Although Myklebust (1971) stresses the importance of comprehensive diagnostic testing to determine a profile of strengths and weaknesses on which highly individualized remediation may be based, he acknowledges certain similarities common to all instructional programs. Johnson and Myklebust (1967) list several of these principles to be incorporated into successful remediation. The first is that training should begin early. Benson (1983) suggests the presence of residual language competency in the nondominant hemisphere that slowly decreases with age. The plasticity of a young brain may allow language function to be taken over by the nondominant hemisphere or be shared bilaterally. Other principles of remediation suggested by Johnson and Myklebust include (1) input precedes output (comprehension precedes expression); (2) auditory symbol and unit of experience are simultaneous; (3) repetition is used; and (4) vocabulary is carefully selected. Myklebust (1971) cautions against the indiscriminate use of a multisensory motor approach. In some cases, such a remedial approach may result in overloading and have a negative effect on attention, orientation, and motivation. McGinnis (1963) gives a detailed description of additional remedial procedures.

REFERENCES

Benson, D. F. (1983). The neural basis of spoken and written language. In H. R. Myklebust (Ed.), *Progress in learning disabilities* (Vol. 5, pp. 3–25). New York: Grune & Stratton.

Benson, D. F., Sheremata, W. A., Buchard, R., Segarra, J., Price, D., & Geschwind, N. (1973). Conduction aphasia. *Archives of Neurology, 28,* 339–346.

Deuel, R. K. (1983). Aphasia in childhood. In H. R. Myklebust (Ed.), *Progress in learning disabilities* (Vol. 5, pp. 29–43). New York: Grune & Stratton.

Gaddes, W. H. (1980). *Learning disabilities and brain function: A neuropsychological approach* (2nd ed.). New York: Springer-Verlag.

Geschwind, N. (1972). Language and the brain. *Scientific American, 226*(4), 76–83.

Johnson, D. J., & Myklebust, H. R. (1967). *Learning disabilities: Educational principles and practices.* New York: Grune & Stratton.

Lezak, M. D. (1983). *Neuropsychological assessment* (2nd ed.). New York: Oxford University Press.

McGinnis, M. A. (1963). *Aphasic children: Identification and education by the association method.* Washington, DC: Alexander Graham Bell Association for the Deaf.

Myklebust, H. R. (1954). *Auditory disorders in children: A manual for differential diagnosis.* New York: Grune & Stratton.

Myklebust, H. R. (1971). Childhood aphasia: Identification, diagnosis, remediation. In L. E. Travis (Ed.), *Handbook of speech pathology and audiology* (pp. 1203–1217). New York: Appleton-Century-Crofts.

Barbara S. Speer
Shaker Heights City School District, Shaker Heights, Ohio

APHASIA
AUDITORY DISCRIMINATION
AUDITORY PERCEPTION
DEVELOPMENTAL APHASIA

RECIPROCAL DETERMINISM

Reciprocal determinism refers to the interaction between cognition, environmental factors, and behavior, such that behavior is a function of the interaction of the individual with the environment (Bandura, 1986). It is a key component to social learning theory (Bandura) and has been used to explain various maladaptive behaviors exhibited by children and adolescents (e.g., aggression, substance use). It is most consistent with an ecological model in that, when a child is having difficulty in school, the focus is not just on the child but also takes into consideration contextual (i.e., ecological) factors that may be contributing to the child's difficulty. At the same time, reciprocity of interaction is considered in that the child's difficulty in an academic area may affect the feedback he/she is receiving and the teacher's frequency of interaction. In educational domains, this may include assessment of the academic ecology or learning environment. For example, a first grader who is having difficulty in early reading skills may become frustrated because of the lack of success. As a result, the student may exhibit inattention during reading tasks and become reluctant to engage in these tasks. The teacher's response may be to assume that the problem is due to lack of effort, as this is the most obvious behavior. Only by taking into consideration all information and the potential interactions of task demands, teacher response, and child behavior does it become evident that the child's initial difficulties led to the decreased effort, which in turn is furthering the difficulty and potentially leading to negative relations with the teacher, as well as low academic self-efficacy and decreased effort. Providing both academic supports and positive reinforcement for effort and progress can be implemented to effect change in both the learning and the behavior of the child.

In behavioral domains, this may include functional behavior assessment. By identifying the antecedents and consequences to the behaviors of question, cognitive, behavioral, and environmental factors can be identified. More important, the interactions between these components can be determined so as to effectively bring about change in cognition or behavior by altering the environment. Recent interventions for bullying and aggression have focused on antecedents (e.g., Mattaini et al., 1996). Alternatively, one could impact cognitive processes and behavior in the form of reinforcement or positive behavioral supports (i.e., consequences; Tapper & Boulton, 2005). In this way, understanding of the interaction provides a comprehensive base for case conceptualization and intervention planning.

REFERENCES

Bandura, A. (1986). *Social foundations of thought and action: A social cognitive theory.* Englewood Cliffs, NJ: Prentice Hall.

Mattaini, M. A., Twyman, J. S., Chin, W., & Nam Lee, R. (1996). Youth violence. In M. A. Mattaini & B. A. Thier (Eds.), *Finding solutions to social problems: Behavioral strategies for change* (pp. 75–111). Washington, DC: American Psychological Association.

Tapper, K., & Boulton, M. J. (2005). Victim and peer group responses to different forms of aggression among primary school children. *Aggressive Behavior, 31,* 238–253.

CYNTHIA A. RICCIO
Texas A&M University

BANDURA, ALBERT
BEHAVIORAL MODIFICATION
ECOLOGICAL ASSESSMENT
FUNCTIONAL BEHAVIOR ASSESSMENT
SOCIAL LEARNING THEORY

RECLAIMING CHILDREN AND YOUTH: JOURNAL OF EMOTIONAL AND BEHAVIORAL PROBLEMS

Reclaiming Children and Youth: Journal of Emotional and Behavioral Problems is a quarterly journal publishing practical, research-validated strategies for professionals and policy leaders concerned with young people in conflict within school, family, or community. Each issue is topical. The journal was first published in 1992 under the title of *Journal of Emotional and Behavioral Problems.* In 1995, the title was changed to the present title to better reflect the journal's emphasis on a positive, reclaiming environment in which changes are made to meet the needs of both youth and society. The journal is owned by Journal of Emotional and Behavioral Problems, Inc. and is published by PRO-ED, Inc.

JUDITH K. VORESS
PRO-ED, Inc.

RECORDING FOR THE BLIND

Recording for the Blind (RFB) is an organization that was founded in 1951 for the purpose of recording textbooks at no charge for persons unable to use ordinary print, whether because of visual, perceptual, or physical conditions. Kirchner and Simon (1984), in a study conducted in 1982–1983, stated that RFB serves over 7,300 students in higher education; 57 percent of the students served are visually impaired.

Recording programs such as RFB are invaluable to the education of visually impaired learners. Other service organizations provide audio-formatted materials for this population (Ferrell, 1985). The Talking Book Program, sponsored by the American Printing House for the Blind, is a source of materials for parents and teachers serving visually impaired students. American Printing House also distributes the variable speech control cassette recorder to be used with their audio cassettes. The National Library Service for the Blind and Physically Handicapped, of the Library of Congress, offers free library services to visually impaired persons. The Library of Congress also lends special talking book record and cassette players to applicants. Many of the materials available from these organizations are popular leisure books, magazines, religious materials, and newspapers.

Addresses for these organizations follow.

American Printing House for the Blind
1839 Frankfort Avenue
Louisville, KY 40206

National Library Service for the Blind and
Physically Handicapped
Library of Congress
Washington, DC 20542

Recording for the Blind, Inc.
545 5th Avenue
1005
New York, NY 10017

REFERENCES

Ferrell, K. (1985). *Reach out and teach: Meeting the training needs of parents of visually and multiply handicapped young children.* New York: American Foundation for the Blind.

Kirchner, C., & Simon, Z. (1984). Blind and visually handicapped college students—Part I: Estimated numbers. *Journal of Visual Impairment & Blindness, 78,* 78–81.

VIVIAN I. CORREA
University of Florida

BLIND
VERSABRAILLE

RECREATION, THERAPEUTIC

Therapeutic recreation is a form of play or physical activity that is used to improve a variety of behaviors that may occur in the cognitive, emotional, social, and physical domains. These activities include games, dancing, horseback riding, and a wide range of other individual and group games and sports.

The intellectual domain may be influenced through gross and fine motor movement activities. There are many theories of cognitive development occurring in sequential order in which motor abilities are the basis for higher thought processes (Kephart, 1960; Piaget, 1950). Theoretically, motor skills help to develop higher skill levels in persons with disabilities by increasing memory, language, and problem solving (Major & Walsh, 1977). Forms of recreation may be used as an alternate to more traditional teaching methods. Humphrey (1976) used games and dancing to aid in reversal difficulties, sequencing difficulties, left and right directionality, and improvement in following direction skills. Physical movement helped to present concepts and skills in a more concrete form. Through imitation and role playing, children were able to use intellectual concepts they had already learned and developed (Yawkey, 1979).

Other forms of learning may be influenced by physical activities and games that have the objective of increasing motivation and attention span. Naville and Blom (1968) stressed educational achievements of concentration, willpower, and self-control through movement.

Emotions can be influenced through recreational activities, which may help individuals improve self-concepts and self-confidence. Being aware of one's body and feeling good about oneself can be associated with the pleasure of recreation. Socially, organized group activities may offer social skill learning through structured interpersonal play. Individuals have opportunities to work together, follow leaders, engage in appropriate behaviors, and develop various forms of self-expression. Recreation can be used not only as a medium for communication but also to help integrate individuals with disabilities with nondisabled individuals and teach activities to decrease isolation.

Physically, recreational activities have endless limits. Movement may help individuals increase coordination and range of motion of body movement. For example, water sports, swimming, or water therapy can be extremely valuable to a variety of children and youths with disabilities, as can free motion activities such as creative dance. These activities can increase physical strength and flexibility; having a strong, attractive body correlates with a positive self-image.

Specific programs such as bowling, folk dancing, and even competitive sports have incorporated recreational activities as therapy for different populations; a good example of one of these programs is the Special Olympics for various groups of students with disabilities. Jacques-Dalcroze (1930) first developed eurhythmics for the blind to increase self-confidence and expression through music and rhythm. Gollnitz (1970) developed a rhythmic-psychomotor therapy that combined movement, music, and rhythm for individuals with psychic and developmental disorders. Lefco (1974) followed the idea of the integration of the body and mind when she used dance therapy to promote mental and physical well-being. The Cove Schools in Racine, Wisconsin, and Evanston, Illinois, were designed for brain-injured students to provide play experiences that may have been missed because of slow rates of development. The Halliwick method deals with the swimming ability of the physically disabled. Norway has a horseback riding school for individuals with disabilities. Mann, Berger, and Proger (1974) offer a comprehensive review of the research on the influence of physical education on the cognitive, physical, affective, and social domains in which movement was significant in helping individuals with disabilities with different variables in these areas.

In summary, therapeutic recreation includes structured physical and social activities that are designed to have as objectives the enjoyment of leisure time, improved movement, and development of physical strength and social skills. Recreation, adaptive physical education, and physical activities increase or improve social, physical, and mental abilities.

REFERENCES

Gollnitz, G. (1970). Fundamentals of rhythmic-psychomotor music therapy: An objective-oriented therapy for children and adolescents with developmental disturbances. *Acta Paedopsychiatrica: International Journal of Child Psychiatry, 37,* 130–134.

Humphrey, J. H. (1976). *Improving learning ability through compensatory physical education.* Springfield, IL: Thomas.

Jacques-Dalcroze, E. (1930). *Eurhythmics: Art and education.* London: Chatto & Windum.

Kephart, N. (1960). *The slower learner in the classroom.* Columbus, OH: Merrill.

Lefco, H. (1974). *Dance therapy.* Chicago: Nelson-Hall.

Major, S., & Walsh, M. (1977). *Learning activities for the learning disabled.* Belmont, CA: Fearon-Pitman.

Mann, L., Berger, R., & Proger, B. (1974). Physical education intervention with the exceptional child. In L. Mann & D. A. Sabatino (Eds.), *The second review of special education.* New York: Grune & Stratton.

Naville, S., & Blom, G. E. (1968). *Psychomotor education: Theory and practice.* Denver: University of Colorado Medical Center.

Piaget, J. (1950). *Psychology of intelligence.* New York: Harcourt & Brace.

Yawkey, T. D. (1979). More in play as intelligence in children. *Journal of Creative Behavior, 13,* 247–256.

DONNA FILIPS
Steger, Illinois

EQUINE THERAPY
RECREATIONAL THERAPY

RECREATIONAL READING FOR INDIVIDUALS WITH DISABILITIES

According to most dictionaries, recreation is an agreeable art, a pastime, or a diversion that affords relaxation and enjoyment. However, most students with disabilities would not link recreation with reading because books symbolize failure and emotional distress (Schanzer, 1973). Therefore, the goal of education should be to encourage students to be independent readers who regularly choose to read. For this to occur, it is necessary for teachers, librarians, and parents to become involved.

Teachers are likely to be the only reading models for many students (Smith, Smith, & Mikulecky, 1978). Therefore, they should be active reading models, talking about what they have been reading and allowing students to see them carrying personal books or magazines. In the classroom, free reading time, when everyone reads without the threat of book reports or lengthy comprehension checks, should be scheduled (Smith et al.). Teachers should be sure to have large classroom libraries of recreational reading materials. However, standard off-the-shelf novels or biographies present frustrating hurdles such as reading level, subject matter, and length (Hallenbeck, 1983). Therefore, such books should be didactic, with important words repeated several times. The themes should relate closely to the lives of the students, and the sentences should be short with simple verb tenses. In addition, pronouns should be placed near the nouns that they modify, and characters should be human beings, not abstract things or ideas. Finally, the style of writing should be conversational (Slick, 1969). This will help to eliminate the selection of reading material that is too difficult.

To halt deterioration of positive reading attitudes, teachers should talk to students about their reading habits and interests, observe what they read, and get to know their interests so appropriate suggestions can be made (Smith et al., 1978). In addition, reading-attitude measures and interest inventories are desirable since there is much intrinsic motivation in reading about something relevant and familiar. When vocabulary and concepts are known, rate may increase with excitement, and the likelihood of a successful, pleasurable experience is high (Smith et al.). When reading material is matched to interests, students tend to comprehend from one to two grade levels above tested reading levels (Estes & Vaughn, 1973, cited in Smith et al.). Matching students with reading materials dealing with life interests helps to initiate lifelong reading habits (Smith et al.). To encourage students to read past the school experience, reading must be motivated outside the classroom by curiosity, pleasure and excitement at the new, practicality, prestige and social status with peers, escape and vicarious experiences, expansion and reinforcement of present attitudes and interests, and reflection of personal situations and dilemmas (Smith et al.). Teachers can create this desire to read by conferencing with students about what they have read, by allowing students to conference with one another, and by engaging in motivational activities such as brief oral readings to students and games and gimmicks such as book auctions (Smith et al.).

Librarians can also be helpful in encouraging recreational reading among students with disabilities because they come in contact with all students in an average school week. The librarian should remove all stumbling blocks so that special education students feel free to use the library. For example, the borrowing period may have to be adjusted because these students may need more time to complete a book. In addition, it is important to eliminate the frustration of book selection by establishing a one-to-one relationship with the student and having enough high-interest low-reading-level books available. As special education students begin to frequent the library, praise and commendation should be given. In addition, individual guidance and personal service are needed. It would also be helpful for the librarian to supply the special education class with a list of the new books in the library so that students can request a particular book when visiting the library. Finally, it is helpful to have students act as library aides to assure them that they are needed, are helpful, and are appreciated (Slick, 1969).

For many students, reading takes place at school or not at all. If reading is to become an enjoyable and lifelong experience, it is necessary for reading to occur at home. However, pressure from the parents to read is not the answer since pressure violates the spirit of free reading (Haimowitz, 1977). As early as the 1940s in Japan, there were two home reading programs. One was a 20-minute mother-child reading process in which parents and children sat for 20 minutes a day and the children read to the mothers. The second was scheduled reading hours once a week in which everyone in the family read (Smith et al., 1978). Programs such as these and others initiated by PTA groups and community groups can be helpful in encouraging recreational reading among students with disabilities.

REFERENCES

Haimowitz, B. (1977, December). Motivating reluctant readers in inner-city classes. *Journal of Reading, 21,* 227–230.

Hallenbeck, M. J. (1983, March). A free reading journal for secondary LD students. *Academic Therapy, 18,* 479–485.

Schanzer, S. S. (1973, Fall). Independent reading for children with learning disabilities. *Academic Therapy, 9,* 109–114.

Slick, M. H. (1969, April 10). *Recreational reading materials for special education students.* Pittsburgh: University of Pittsburgh, School of Library Science. (ERIC Document Reproduction Service No. ED 046 173)

Smith, C. B., Smith, S. L., & Mikulecky, L. (1978). *Teaching reading in secondary school content subjects: A book-thinking process.* New York: Holt, Rinehart, & Winston.

CAROLINE D'IPPOLITO
*Eastern Pennsylvania Special
Education Resources Center*

HIGH INTEREST–LOW VOCABULARY
LIBRARY SERVICES FOR INDIVIDUALS WITH DISABILITIES
READING

RECREATIONAL THERAPY

Recreational activities are necessary for the total well-being of any individual. They provide an important source of pleasure and relaxation. Most individuals learn how to use recreational activities from a lifetime of learning how to play. But as with other skill areas, the disabled often experience difficulties in using free time appropriately. They may have been sheltered during much of their developmental period, or their disability may have prohibited them from acquiring the skills necessary for participation in recreational activities. Consequently, many disabled individuals will require intentional and systematic instruction if they are to acquire those skills. In that regard, recreational therapy is a planned intervention process developed to promote the growth and development of recreational skills and leisure-time activities.

Recreational therapy attempts to eliminate or minimize an individual's disability. It uses recreation to assist individuals with disabilities in changing certain physical, emotional, or social characteristics so they may pursue leisure activities and live as independently as possible (National Recreation and Park Association, 1978). Recreational therapy is also concerned with helping individuals with disabilities participate in activities with the nondisabled as much as possible. This integration allows individuals with disabilities to move into the recreational mainstream and become more involved in community recreational activities. In addition to helping individuals with disabilities to engage in recreational activities, recreational therapy also provides other benefits. A second advantage of the program is that appropriate recreational and leisure-time skills can lead to increased physical development, socialization skills, and even cognitive and language development (Schulz & Turnbull, 1984). Therefore, recreational therapy may be recommended to help individuals with disabilities maintain their physical skills, interact socially, and increase academic progress.

REFERENCES

National Recreation and Park Association. (1978). *The therapeutic recreator.* In W. L. Heward & M. D. Orlansky (1980), *Exceptional children.* Columbus, OH: Merrill.

Schulz, J. B., & Turnbull, A. P. (1984). *Mainstreaming handicapped students: A guide for classroom teachers* (2nd ed.). Boston: Allyn & Bacon.

LARRY J. WHEELER
*Southwest Texas State
University*

EQUINE THERAPY
OCCUPATIONAL THERAPY

RECREATION FOR INDIVIDUALS
WITH DISABILITIES

Recreation for individuals with disabilities includes individual and group programs of outdoor, social, sports, or educational activities conducted during leisure time. Such programs conducted in medically supervised institutions are identified as therapeutic recreation while those conducted in schools and the community are called community programs (Pomeroy, 1983). The overall goal of recreation programs is to enable each disabled person to participate at the lowest effective care level as independently as abilities and disabilities permit (Stein, 1985).

Recreation services for individuals with disabilities should be distinguished from therapeutic recreation. The latter is a means of intervention to bring about desired changes. In schools, therapeutic recreation is medically prescribed and programmed by recreational therapists. In contrast, the purpose of recreation programs for individuals with disabilities is to provide these students with opportunities to realize their leisure and recreational needs whether on an individual or group basis. Recreation programs in schools or communities for students with disabilities are voluntary in nature and programmed by recreational leaders.

Prior to 1960, most recreation programs for individuals

with disabilities were segregated or held in institutions (Robinson & Skinner, 1985). Since 1960 legislative forces and concerned professional organizations have sought to deinstitutionalize and desegregate such programs. With the enactment of PL 94-142, recreation came to be considered as a related service in the schools. During the late 1970s the federal government provided grants to colleges and universities to set up training programs for recreation therapists and adapted physical education teachers and for the development of regional information and resource centers (Robinson & Skinner). Private organizations such as Wheelchair Sports and the Association for the Help of Retarded Children have also been active in promoting recreational programs in schools and communities.

Although only 5 to 10 percent of all persons with disabilities are being reached by existing park and recreation service providers, the prognosis for the future appears to be positive. Statutes to promote barrier design, and the changing attitudes of service providers and participants, seem to indicate a trend toward more people with disabilities availing themselves of school or community recreation programs.

Delineated on the basis of the degree of supervision required, there are four types of recreation programs for individuals with disabilities. First, there are special programs limited to persons with specific disabilities (e.g. blind, deaf, or physically disabled persons). These programs often revolve around a single activity for the purposes of fun, socialization, and skill development. Second, there are semiintegregated services that allow individuals with disabilities to mix with the nondisabled in activities that lend themselves to integration. Third, some communities have a buddy system where persons with disabilities participate with nondisabled persons in the same activities and programs; scouts and Camp Fire Girls have used the buddy system extensively in their programs. The fourth type of program is one that provides opportunities for total integration in all activities, as is the case in many national parks and recreation areas.

The major categories listed by Russell (1983) of recreational activities for individuals with disabilities are sports and games, hobbies, music, outdoor recreation, mental and literary recreation, arts and crafts, dance, and drama.

Disability programs at the national and international levels are usually of a competitive nature. Examples of these include the Para-olympics, which meets every 4 years in a different part of the world and has four disability groups: deaf, amputee, cerebral palsy, and paraplegic competition. Wheelchair Sports, sponsored by the National Wheelchair Athletic Association, provides competition in track, basketball, and weightlifting. The National Handicapped Sports and Recreation Association promotes sports and recreational activities through 29 regional offices across the United States.

Most state and regional programs are part of national structures such as the Special Olympics program. Some state programs are resident or day camps or outdoor activity centers. There are very few recreation centers that exclusively serve individuals with disabilities. The majority are in large urban areas (e.g., the Anchor Program in New York City and the Recreation Center for the Handicapped in San Francisco).

Many schools, colleges, and communities sponsor local recreational programs for individuals with disabilities. Community swim programs seem to be the most popular and widespread. Hunter College in New York City conducts a recreation program for mentally retarded and physically disabled teenagers from the city, most of whom are minorities.

REFERENCES

Pomeroy, J. (1983). Community recreation for persons with disabilities. In E. Pan, T. Backer, & C. Vosh (Eds.), *Annual review of rehabilitation* (pp. 241–291). St. Louis, MO: Mosby.

Robinson, F., & Skinner, S. (1985). *Community recreation for the handicapped.* Springfield, IL: Thomas.

Russell, R. (1983). *Planning programs in recreation.* St. Louis, MO: Mosby.

Stein, J. (1985). Mainstreaming in recreational settings. *Journal of Physical Education, Recreation & Dance, 5*(56), 25–27.

THOMAS R. BURKE
Hunter College, City University of New York

EQUINE THERAPY
MUSIC THERAPY
OLYMPICS, SPECIAL

REDL, FRITZ (1902–1988)

Fritz Redl was born and educated in Austria and obtained a PhD in philosophy and psychology in 1925 from the University of Vienna. From 1925 to 1936, he trained as an analyst at the Wiener Psychoanalysis Institute, and was strongly influenced by the founders of child analytic work, particularly Anna Freud and August Aichhorn.

Redl maintained an interest in group psychology throughout his career. After coming to the United States in 1936, he accepted a teaching position at the University of Michigan and helped establish a guidance program at the Cranbook School, later moving to a position as professor of group work at Wayne State University, where he remained for 12 years. Redl's service to children and the field of mental health included his positions as clinical director of the University of Michigan Fresh Air Camp, chief of the Child Research Branch of the National Institute of Mental Health (1953–1959), and president of the American Orthopsychiatric Association.

Redl's work focused on the exploration of children's behavioral controls, their defenses, and how to prevent or

Fritz Redl

REFERRAL PROCESS

Referral is the process by which students' potential disabilities or gifts are identified for comprehensive individual evaluation by school officials. The identification of students for evaluation is a federally mandated activity for which all school districts and state education departments must have specific policies and procedures (U.S. Office of Education, 1977, sections 121a.128 and 121a.220). The law holds districts and state departments responsible for identifying all children with disabilities within their jurisdictions who require special education or related services, including those in the care of other public and private agencies.

It is reported that some 3 to 5 percent of the school-age population are referred each year (Algozzine, Christenson, & Ysseldyke, 1982). Of those referred, about three fourths are placed in special education. While these averages may characterize the nation as a whole, individual districts may vary widely in the percentage of students referred, evaluated, and placed.

Students can be referred in one of two major ways (Heller, Holtzman, & Messick, 1982). The first is through the systematic efforts of school districts, community agencies, or government institutions. For example, districts may use very low or very high performance on annually administered achievement tests to refer students. Similarly, hospitals may screen newborns for referral to early intervention programs. Finally, state education departments may conduct print and electronic media campaigns and establish toll-free hotlines aimed at encouraging the referral of students with disabilities or gifts currently not receiving services.

The second major referral mechanism involves the efforts of individuals who know the child. Such individuals include the child's teachers, parents, and physician. Of these individuals, the large majority of referrals appear to emanate from teachers (Heller et al., 1982). The advent of PL 94-142 increased the involvement of others both in and outside the school (Bickel, 1982).

Referrals made by teachers (and other individuals) are generally personal decisions based on subjective criteria. As such, these decisions are open to a variety of influences. The specific factors that influence teacher referrals are difficult to identify with any certainty (Bickel, 1982). However, research suggests that teachers are influenced by several considerations. One consideration is program availability; if no program exists to meet the student's needs, or if no room is available in an existing program, referral is unlikely. Second, teachers seem hesitant to refer if there is a large backlog in assessment. Such backlogs cause teachers to consider referral a meaningless action. Third, parents may influence the process. Teachers may hesitate to refer

treat the disorganization that results when the behavioral control system is maladaptive (Redl, 1966, 1975). His development of the "life space interview," providing strategies and techniques for immediately dealing with crises in the lives of children, showed his keen awareness of the effects of temporal and spatial arrangements (e.g., the stress of transition) on children's behaviors. Redl also saw how studying the behavior of severely disturbed children helped to illuminate techniques used by the normal child. As an outgrowth of his studies, group work, camp experience, and involvement with social agencies, he established Pioneer House, a residential program for the study and treatment of delinquent children, and the Detroit Group Project, providing clinical group work with children and a summer camp for children from low-income families. Redl's Pioneer House work is summarized in his book *The Aggressive Child* (Redl & Wineman, 1957).

A renowned lecturer and consultant worldwide, Redl was a Pinkerton guest professor in the School of Criminal Justice of New York State University and a visiting professor in the Department of Child Psychiatry of the University of Utrecht in Holland. He died in 1988 in North Adams, Massachusetts, where he had retired in 1973.

REFERENCES

Redl, F. (1966). *When we deal with children: Selected writings.* New York: Free Press.

Redl, F. (1975). Disruptive behavior in the classroom. *School Review, 83*(4), 569–594.

Redl, F., & Wineman, D. (1957). *The aggressive child.* New York: Free Press.

E. VALERIE HEWITT
Texas A&M University
First edition

TAMARA J. MARTIN
*The University of Texas of the
Permian Basin*
Second edition

children whose parents would be likely to react in a hostile manner, or be quick to refer those whose parents exert positive pressure. Finally, eligibility criteria affect the decision. For example, some states and districts require that teachers refer students for placement in a specific program such as one for educable mentally retarded pupils. Hence, teachers may be encouraged to refer only children with particular characteristics.

In addition to these factors, other influences on referral undoubtedly exist (Ysseldyke & Algozzine, 1984). Teachers' decisions likely are affected by their own beliefs about what constitutes normal child development and proper behavior, and by the extent to which a given child violates those assumptions. The referral decision is also governed by the teacher's skills in dealing with deviations; those who are less adept in handling learning or behavioral differences may be more likely to refer.

It should be clear, then, that a great amount of personal discretion exists in the referral process (Bickel, 1982). Such discretion allows substantial variation in referral practice within and across districts, suggesting that referral often depends as much on what class or school a child attends as on actual learning capabilities and performance. Because of this personal discretion, there is a tendency to refer children who disrupt school routines and those with more severe, easily verifiable problems.

The subjectivity inherent in the referral process has social and ethical implications. First, there is the possibility that substantial numbers of children are being referred inappropriately. Inappropriate referral is problematic because it wastes valuable resources; creates backlogs in assessment, thereby denying services to those truly in need; and subjects children to the potential stigma of special education placement and to education in an environment that may not meet their needs.

Second, inappropriate referral may disproportionately affect particular social groups. For many years, disproportionate placements of minority children and of males in programs for educable mentally retarded (EMR) students have been documented (Heller et al., 1982). The reasons for these disproportionate placements are many and complex. While these placements are not necessarily inappropriate, their existence raises the question of whether teacher referrals, too, are disproportionate.

Relatively little research has been conducted on the topic of disproportionate referral. Those studies that do exist have used two basic methodologies. Some investigators have analyzed existing referral data to determine whether disproportionate numbers of students from particular groups are referred. Other researchers have presented different groups of teachers with simulated data describing a student and have asked them to make referral decisions. The data received by the groups differed only in the social group membership assigned to the student. While no definitive conclusions can be drawn, the studies have shown a ten-dency toward higher rates of referral for minorities even though these students presented problems that appeared little different from those of their majority peers (Bickel, 1982).

Concern regarding both the possibility that children are being inappropriately referred and disproportionate placement of minority students in special education has led many school districts to refine their referral processes. These refinements have primarily occurred with respect to teacher referrals. Such referrals were originally passed directly through to the pupil evaluation team. Most refinements have focused on inserting checks and balances into this teacher-to-evaluation team pathway.

The most immediately useful refinement probably has been the introduction of consultation (Zins & Curtis, 1984). Consultation may be provided by a resource teacher, school psychologist, or other specialist. The aim of consultation is to help the teacher deal with the student in the regular classroom. The consultant may work with the teacher to develop, apply, and evaluate the effects of alternative instructional or behavior management strategies (Bennett, 1981).

A second type of referral refinement requires the provision of extensive evidence to support the need for referral. The aim of this evidence is to rule out deficiencies in the learning environment as explanations for failure. Failures of the educational system should be discounted first, lest they be interpreted erroneously as failures of the child (Messick, 1984).

Reporting the findings of the National Research Council Panel on Selection and Placement of Students in Programs for the Mentally Retarded, Messick (1984) suggests the provision of four kinds of evidence. First, evidence should be offered that the school is using effective programs and curricula. This evidence should support the effectiveness of those programs and curricula not just for students in general, but for the ethnic, linguistic, or socioeconomic group from which the referred students actually come. Second, evidence should be presented that the student in question has been adequately exposed to the curriculum. It should be documented that the student was not absent regularly from school and that the teacher implemented the curriculum effectively. Third, objective evidence should be offered that the child has not learned what was taught (e.g., through criterion-referenced tests, systematic behavioral recordings, student work samples). Finally, documentation should be provided to show that systematic efforts were made to correct the problem such as introducing remedial approaches, changing the curriculum materials, or trying a new teacher.

A third refinement is the review of referral requests. Review seems to be conducted most often at the building level. In this system, teacher referrals are reviewed by the principal—or by a committee consisting of the principal, guidance counselor, or other building staff—before being forwarded to the pupil evaluation team. The review is designed to encourage teachers and principals to make greater attempts to deal with problem situations within the regular classroom and local school, and, as a result, to limit the occurrence of inappropriate referrals.

The three refinements described—consultation, evidence, and review—are the major elements of a prereferral intervention model. While many variations on this model exist, prereferral intervention has become an important component in the referral process, helping to ensure that those students referred are truly the ones most in need of special education services.

REFERENCES

Algozzine, B., Christenson, S., & Ysseldyke, J. (1982). Probabilities associated with the referral to placement process. *Teacher Education & Special Education, 5,* 19–23.

Bennett, R. E. (1981). Assessment of exceptional children: Guidelines for practice. *Diagnostique, 7,* 5–13.

Bickel, W. E. (1982). Classifying mentally retarded students: A review of placement practices in special education. In K. A. Heller, W. H. Holtzman, & S. Messick (Eds.), *Placing children in special education: A strategy for equity.* Washington, DC: National Academy.

Heller, K. A., Holtzman, W. H., & Messick, S (Eds.). (1982). *Placing children in special education: A strategy for equity.* Washington, DC: National Academy.

Messick, S. (1984). Placing children in special education: Findings of the National Academy of Sciences Panel. *Educational Researcher, 13*(3), 3–8.

U.S. Office of Education. (1977). Education of handicapped children: Implementation of Part B of the Education of the Handicapped Act. *Federal Register, 42*(163), 42474–42518.

Ysseldyke, J. E., & Algozzine, B. (1984). *Introduction to special education.* Boston: Houghton Mifflin.

Zins, J. E., & Curtis, M. (1984). Building consultation into the educational service delivery system. In C. A. Maher, R. J. Illback, & J. E. Zins (Eds.), *Organizational psychology in the schools: A handbook for professionals.* Springfield, IL: Thomas.

RANDY ELLIOT BENNETT
MARY LOUISE LENNON
Educational Testing Service

INDIVIDUALS WITH DISABILITIES EDUCATION
IMPROVEMENT ACT OF 2004 (IDEIA)
PREREFERRAL INTERVENTION
RESPONSE TO INTERVENTION
THREE-TIER MODEL

REFLEX

A reflex is an automatic connection between a stimulus and a response. One example is the knee-jerk reflex. Another is the reflexive constriction of the pupil in response to light.

Historically, the concept of the reflex has captured the imagination of many theorists who wished to emphasize the mechanical nature of behavior. René Descartes proposed a hydraulic model to account for the behavior of nonhuman animals. The Russian physiologist Ivan Sechenov (1863/1965) argued that all behavior, including that of humans, is reflexive (meaning that it is determined). Ivan Pavlov and other theorists of learning have used such terms as *conditioned reflex* to imply that even learned behaviors are mechanically determined and that they can be described as stimulus-response connections.

Certain human reflexes can be observed only in infancy (Peiper, 1963). For example, infants reflexively grasp any object placed firmly in the palm of the hand. Newborns grasp an elevated bar tightly enough to support their own weight, at least briefly. If someone strokes the sole of an infant's foot, the infant extends the big toe and fans the others (this is known as the Babinski reflex). If someone touches an infant's cheek, an infant who is awake will often, but not always, turn toward the stroked cheek and begin to suck.

Infant reflexes are suppressed in older children and adults, but the connections responsible for the reflexes are not destroyed. The infant reflexes may return as a result of brain damage, especially damage to the frontal lobes of the cerebral cortex. Neurologists often test for the presence of the Babinski reflex or the grasp reflex as a means of detecting possible dysfunction of the frontal lobes. The infant reflexes may also return temporarily as a result of interference with cerebral activity, such as that caused by an epileptic seizure, excessive levels of carbon dioxide, or certain drugs (Paterson & Richter, 1933).

REFERENCES

Paterson, A. S., & Richter, C. P. (1933). Action of scopolamine and carbon dioxide on catalepsy produced by bulbocapnine. *Archives of Neurology & Psychiatry, 29,* 231–240.

Peiper, A. (1963). *Cerebral function in infancy and childhood.* New York: Consultants Bureau.

Sechenov, I. (1863/1965). *Reflexes of the brain.* Cambridge, MA: MIT Press.

JAMES W. KALAT
North Carolina State University

BEHAVIORISM
BEHAVIOR MODIFICATION
DEVELOPMENTAL MILESTONES

REGIONAL MEDIA CENTERS FOR THE DEAF

In 1959 the U.S. Office of Education implemented a program, under PL 85-905, to provide captioned films and related media to assist in bringing deaf persons into the mainstream of American life. The program featured the development and dissemination of highly specialized media services and products through four regional media centers. In the 1960s, 13 special education instructional media centers were established in addition to the four regional centers for the deaf. By the end of that decade, those 17 centers had been consolidated into four area learning resource centers (ALRCs). The ALRCs conducted activities related to educational media and technology for all handicapped persons, but specialized centers within the ALRC structure provided educational media and technology services for deaf persons. In 1972 the National Center on Education Media and Materials for the Handicapped replaced the ALRCs.

SHIRLEY A. JONES
*Virginia Polytechnic Institute
and State University*

REGIONAL RESOURCE CENTERS

The Regional Resource Centers (RRCs) were created by the Elementary and Secondary Education Act, Title 6, of 1965. They were intended to assist state educational agencies (SEAs) in the implementation of special education services at a time when special education was just beginning to be recognized as a national concern. The RRCs were intended to help SEAs and local educational agencies (LEAs) in the development of special education services and resources by serving as agents in planning, programming, service delivery, training, and the creation of instructional materials.

The actual operations of the RRCs proceeded through a variety of agencies, including state educational departments, universities, and LEAs. The funding was not as generous as originally intended because the federal government envisioned RRCs as a nationwide enterprise. In the first funding cycle (1970–1974), Pennsylvania established an RRC whose services were directed statewide. Other RRCs, however, had multistate service areas (e.g., the Southwest Regional Resource Center served Arizona, Colorado, Nevada, New Mexico, and the Bureau of Indian Affairs). In multistate agencies, the major modes of service were information, consultation, and in-service training. In state-limited programs such as that of Pennsylvania, it was easier to focus services on specified state needs. For example, Pennsylvania used its funds to create diagnostic-prescriptive programs and to help fund classes to validate them (National Association of State Directors of Special Education, 1976).

A later round of funding of RRCs (1974–1977) resulted in some states being refunded and others funded for the first time. While some states, such as New York and Pennsylvania, maintained statewide services, efforts were being made to move to multistate and regional operations. Thus, the Southeastern Regional Resource Center at Auburn University, in Montgomery, Alabama, was given the responsibility for Alabama, Florida, Georgia, Louisiana, Mississippi, Puerto Rico, South Carolina, and the U.S. Virgin Islands. Separate agencies were split off from the RRCs to assist in the provision of instructional resources to special educators. These were the Area Learning Resource Centers. By 1983, with legislative amendments to the Education of the Handicapped Act, the RRCs became a matter of discretionary support and funding on the part of states. They were adopted in various forms by state educational agencies or subsumed by the SEAs into other entities.

REFERENCE

National Association of State Directors of Special Education. (1976). *A survey of opinions of state directors of special education on Regional Resource Centers: Report*. Washington, DC: Bureau of Education for the Handicapped.

DON BRASWELL
*Research Foundation, City
University of New York*

SPECIAL EDUCATION, FEDERAL IMPACT ON SPECIAL EDUCATION PROGRAMS

REGRESSION (STATISTICAL)

Regression is a term widely used in behavioral research. It represents both a statistical technique and a statistical phenomenon. Regression as statistical phenomenon or artifact is addressed here. Simply, it is the effect of imperfect correlation between a predictor and outcome on the mean of the outcome.

The origin of the term dates to Sir Francis Galton's investigations into correlations among human physical characteristics. Galton's (1886) focus was the relationship between the height of adult children and their "midparent" (the average of the mother's height times 1.08 and the father's height), and he collected data on 928 offspring of 205 parents. Galton observed that if a parent grew to be taller than average, the adult offspring's height would tend to be closer to the mean of adult children, and hence smaller than the parent (DiNardo & Tobias, 2001). If one started with the children the same result was found for the parents. Galton used the term *regression* for this finding. He actually observed what occurs when a linear relationship is created for two variables. When both variables are standardized to have a mean of zero and variance of 1.0, the correlation represents the slope of the line representing the linear relationship. As one variable—say, the predictor—increases, the slope shows the increase of the average of the outcome at each predictor score value. Since correlation is in general less than 1.0, this slope predicts that the outcome average score will be less extreme than the predictor. In other words, for an increase of 1 unit of the predictor, the outcome will increase the value of the correlation. If the correlation is .5, then a 1 unit increase in predictor will be associated with an increase of .5 units of outcome, thus the "regression to the mean." If the predictor and outcome are reversed, the same phenomenon is seen.

The importance for special education, gifted education, and other disciplines that routinely deal with populations whose characteristics may often include extreme values is that regression effects occur commonly when another measurement is made and compared to a standard or perhaps to the original characteristics. Assume that students are selected because they are all 2 standard deviations below the mean on a standardized test. Any other measurement made on the students, whether contemporaneous or later, will exhibit a regression effect in that students will be expected to be less extreme on the new variable than the 2 standard deviation below mean that was the basis for their selection. If the new variable correlates .7 with the selection variable, and all the students are exactly 2 standard deviations below the mean on the selection test, they will on average be 1.4 standard deviations ($-2 \times .7$) below average on the new variable. If the group was given a particular treatment, inexperienced researchers might confuse the improvement in the outcome due to regression with a treatment effect.

Hopkins (1968) demonstrated various problems related to special education research following from regression effects. In particular he showed how nonrandom matching creates regression differences in groups that do not have identical population means and standard deviations. Since matched control group designs are common, the problem of misinterpreting regression effects as treatment effects is widespread. He noted that randomization of students into treatment and control groups is the only method that generates comparable regression effects and thus allows estimation of treatment effects without the confounding. In the absence of randomization it is possible under some circumstances to estimate the regression effect and subtract it from outcome scores to obtain an estimate of treatment effect. At best this is a poor substitute for better randomized studies, however.

Another example of the confusion about regression effects occurs with the use of intelligence tests to determine giftedness. Some states define giftedness as high performance on a standardized individual intelligence test, such as 1.25 standard deviations above the mean. When a new test is introduced, some researchers have given the new test to a previously identified gifted group, demonstrated that the mean of the new test is lower than that of the current standard, and concluded that the new test does not select gifted students with equal validity. It is fairly simple to demonstrate that the observed lower mean on the new test corresponds to the regressed estimate.

REFERENCES

DiNardo, J., & Tobias, J. L. (2001). Nonparametric density and regression estimation. *Journal of Economic Perspectives, 15,* 11–28.

Hopkins, K. D. (1968). Regression and the matching fallacy in quasi-experimental research. *Journal of Special Education, 3,* 329–336.

VICTOR L. WILLSON
Texas A&M University

REGULAR CLASS PLACEMENT

See INCLUSION.

REHABILITATION

The term *rehabilitation* refers to any process, procedure, or program that enables a disabled individual to function at a more independent and personally satisfying level. This functioning should include all aspects—physical, mental, emotional, social, educational, and vocational—of the individual's life. A disabled person may be defined as one who has any chronic mental or physical incapacity caused by injury, disease, or congenital defect that interferes with his or her independence, productivity, or goal attainment. The range of disabilities is wide and varied, including such conditions as autism, mental retardation, muscular dystrophy, and a variety of neurological and orthopedic disorders. These disparate conditions may appear singly or in concert. Clearly, the process that is designed to assist persons in obtaining an optimal level of functioning is a complex one.

The complexity of the rehabilitation process necessitates a team approach that involves a range of professionals almost as broad and varied as the types of conditions addressed. Goldenson, Dunham, and Dunham (1978) discuss no fewer than 39 rehabilitation specialists in their handbook. Their list includes such diverse professions as orientation and mobility training, genetic counseling, biomedical engineering, and orthotics and prosthetics, in addition to numerous medical, mental health, therapeutic, and special education fields. In view of the potential involvement of such an array of professionals, it becomes particularly important to remember that the rehabilitation process is not one that is done to or for disabled persons, but rather one that is done with disabled persons and often their families as well. If a person is to become as fully functional as his or her abilities will allow, a process that fosters dependence is a self-defeating one.

It is necessary for the professionals involved in the rehabilitation process to function as a team rather than as separate individuals. McInerney and Karan (1981) have pointed out that without information sharing and cooperative integration, the rehabilitation process will not fit the needs of the client. The client should not be expected to fit the needs of the service delivery system. As rehabilitation is a process, not an isolated treatment, a continuum of services must be provided to give the disabled person assistance in all aspects of life. A program that is cohesive in approach, regardless of the number of professionals involved, is essential. In addition, these services must alter to meet the client's changing needs.

REFERENCES

Goldenson, R. M., Dunham, J. R., & Dunham, C. S. (Eds.). (1978). *Disability and rehabilitation handbook.* New York: McGraw-Hill.

McInerney, M., & Karan, O. C. (1981). Federal legislation and the integration of special education and vocational rehabilitation. *Mental Retardation, 19,* 21–24.

LAURA KINZIE BRUTTING
*University of Wisconsin at
Madison*

REHABILITATION
VOCATIONAL EDUCATION

REHABILITATION ACT OF 1973

The Rehabilitation Act of 1973 authorizes comprehensive vocational rehabilitation services designed to help individuals with physical or mental disabilities become employable. The act also authorizes service projects for persons with special rehabilitation needs. For persons with severe disabilities without apparent employment potential, the act authorizes services to promote independent living. Training programs are provided to help ensure a supply of skilled persons to rehabilitate individuals with disabilities. The act also authorizes a research program, a national council to review federal policy regarding individuals with disabilities, and a compliance board to help enforce accessibility standards for those with disabilities.

The act authorizes state grants for comprehensive services designed to enable individuals with disabilities to become employable. Each state receives an allotment of federal funding that must be matched on a 20 percent state to 80 percent federal ratio. Federal funds are allotted on the basis of population and per capita income, with the lower per capita income states receiving a relatively higher allotment on a per capita basis.

Funds are authorized for various service projects for individuals with disabilities. These projects include programs to serve the severely handicapped, migrant workers, Native Americans, and other groups with special needs. Support is provided for training of rehabilitation personnel. State grants and discretionary funds are authorized for independent living services. A client assistance program is required in each state to help clients and applicants obtain services funded under the act.

The National Council on Disability is composed of 15 members appointed by the president. The council establishes general policies for the National Institute on Disability and Rehabilitation Research, advises the president and Congress on the development of programs carried out under the Rehabilitation Act, and reviews and evaluates federal policy regarding programs for individuals with disabilities.

The Architectural and Transportation Barriers Compliance Board was authorized to ensure compliance with the Architectural Barriers Act of 1968 and to promote accessibility for individuals with disabilities. The board is composed of 11 members from the general public (5 of whom must be individuals with disabilities) and 11 representatives of federal agencies.

The National Institute on Disability and Rehabilitation Research administers funds for the rehabilitation research programs. The institute, through a federal interagency committee, is responsible for the coordination of all major federal research related to individuals with disabilities.

JAMES BUTTON
*United States Department of
Education*
First and Second editions

KIMBERLY F. APPLEQUIST
*University of Colorado at
Colorado Springs*
Third edition

REHABILITATION ACT OF 1973, SECTION 504

Section 504 of what is commonly called the Rehabilitation Act is frequently cited as an important precursor to the passage of the Education of All Handicapped Children Act of 1975 (PL 94-142), itself a precursor to the Individuals with Disabilities Education Act. Section 504, among other things, protects the rights of children with disabilities and precludes discrimination in employment and education. The stipulations of the Rehabilitation Act apply to the programs receiving federal financial assistance.

The Rehabilitation Act was cited in the noted *Larry P.* v.

Riles decision by Judge Peckham in 1979. This decision cited the state as being in noncompliance with Section 504 in its use of intelligence tests for making placement decisions in special education. Certainly, the Rehabilitation Act of 1973 has had an important impact on special education practice by encouraging more sophisticated and humane treatment of children with disabilities.

REFERENCE

Bersoff, D. N. (1982). The legal regulation of school psychology. In C. R. Reynolds & T. B. Gutkin (Eds.), *The handbook of school psychology*. New York: Wiley.

RANDY W. KAMPHAUS
University of Georgia
First and Second editions

KIMBERLY F. APPLEQUIST
*University of Colorado at
Colorado Springs*
Third edition

LARRY P.

REHABILITATION LITERATURE

Rehabilitation Literature is a bimonthly journal published by the National Easter Seal Society. It is principally an educational service journal that abstracts articles published elsewhere and reviews books, journals, films, treatment programs, and so on dealing with the rehabilitation of all types of human disabilities. At least one original feature article appears in each issue. It is written at a level for professional personnel and students training to become professional service providers in all disciplines concerned with the rehabilitation of persons with handicapping conditions.

This abstracting and review journal receives wide circulation among rehabilitation workers and is well regarded in the field. It has been in continuous publication since January 1940; it was taken over by the National Easter Seal Society in 1959. *Rehabilitation Literature* has taken the position that, as an educational service of a large charitable organization, up to 100 reproductions of articles may be made without permission provided they are for free distribution within an organization or classroom. Other rights of reproduction have been reserved. Frequent topics of interest to special educators appear in nearly every issue, bridging such broad areas as stuttering, learning disabilities, aphasias, spina bifida, reading, and general techniques in special education.

CECIL R. REYNOLDS
Texas A&M University

REINFORCEMENT, DIFFERENTIAL

Differential reinforcement procedures follow a schedule of reinforcement wherein one response from a response class receives reinforcement and all other responses do not (Alberto & Troutman, 2006; Kazdin, 1980). Four basic types of differential reinforcement exist (Magg, 2004): differential reinforcement of incompatible behavior (DRI), differential reinforcement of alternative behavior (DRA), differential reinforcement of low rates (DRL), and differential reinforcement of other behavior (DRO). These procedures represent positive methods to increase the frequency of a desired behavior or decrease unwanted behavior. Each procedure requires (a) identification of a target behavior, (b) development of a reinforcement schedule that will provide sufficient opportunities for students to receive rewards, and (c) providing the student a reward contingent upon the target behavior and the set schedule, by the teacher either giving the reward or teaching the student to self-reinforce contingent upon the target behavior and schedule. Two of the differential reinforcement strategies (DRI and DRA) enable educators to focus on the wanted or positive behavior rather than the unwanted or negative behavior. The other two differential reinforcement strategies (DRL and DRO) decrease the occurrence of unwanted behaviors by specifically focusing on the rate or occurrence of the unwanted behavior.

Differential Reinforcement of Incompatible Behavior (DRI)

The teacher and/or student select a behavior that is incompatible with the problematic target behavior. The selected replacement behavior must be topographically incompatible with the unwanted behavior. If students are out of their seat to the point of causing disruption or interrupting learning, for example, sitting in their seat represents an incompatible behavior. Occurrence of the incompatible behavior results in students being rewarded.

Differential Reinforcement of Alternative Behavior (DRA)

Rather than rewarding only actions incompatible to the unwanted behavior, as does DRI, DRA rewards the contingent occurrence of *any* specified functional alternative behavior. Like DRI, DRA procedures reward alternative behavior to replace the function that the unwanted behavior served. If students call out in class consistently without giving others the opportunity to respond, DRA will reward writing answers on response boards and holding the boards up in the air when the teacher asks all students to do this. When implementing DRA teachers either ignore unwanted behavior and reward the performance of the alternative behavior, or interrupt and redirect the unwanted behavior so that the desired alternative behavior occurs, which they then reward.

Differential Reinforcement of Low Rates (DRL)

This procedure gradually decreases the rate of occurrence of unwanted behaviors from an unacceptable level to a rate that can be tolerated. Students receive rewards for scheduled reductions in performance of the target behavior. Rewards can be delivered by the teacher or self-reinforced for either the reduction in the overall occurrence or an increase in the amount of time that occurs between responses. A student, for example, talks 33 times an hour to classmates during lecture or quiet independent work. With the DRL procedure, the student receives a reward for talking 30 times or less for two consecutive days, then 27 times or less or two consecutive days, and so on until the behavior has decreased to only 1 or 2 times per day and maintains at that level. Graphing progress using a changing criterion design provides an excellent means to show progress to students, parents, and educators. The inverse of this procedure, differential reinforcement of higher rates of behavior, can be used in the same way as DRL to increase the occurrence of wanted behavior.

Differential Reinforcement of Other Behavior (DRO)

This procedure delivers a reward, usually after an interval of time, for not engaging in the targeted unwanted behavior. At the end of the time interval whatever the student did, as long as it wasn't the target behavior, receives a reward. If the student has any occurrence of the behavior during the interval, a reward is not delivered. Once the occurrence of the unwanted behavior begins to decrease, the time interval gradually increases. Students, for example, who talk, lightly punch others, or pass papers to classmates during independent seat work an average of four times every 10 minutes may decrease the occurrence of these behaviors when the teacher uses DRO. When students do not talk, punch, or pass papers to classmates during independent seatwork for 3 minutes, they will receive a reward. When this happens for 2 consecutive days, the interval length may be increased to 5 minutes, then 8, and so on until the students do not perform these behaviors during independent seatwork times.

Differential reinforcement procedures provide useful tools to increase the occurrence of desired behaviors or decrease unwanted behaviors. Their effectiveness depends upon selecting a meaningful primary (e.g., candy), tangible (e.g., chance to pull school spirit or supply item from a reward bag), or social (e.g., lunch with teacher) reward. The delivery of the rewards can occur using a fixed schedule (specific number of times or minutes) or a variable schedule (the number changes from one instance to the next but always in the desired direction and close to a specific average value). Fortunately for teachers, variable schedules generally obtain the best results and facilitate maintenance better than fixed schedules, and these are also the easiest to implement.

REFERENCES

Alberto, P. A., & Troutman, A. C. (2006). *Applied behavior analysis for teachers* (7th ed.). Upper Saddle River, NJ: Pearson Merrill Prentice Hall.

Kazdin, A. E. (1980). *Behavior modification in applied settings.* Homewood, IL: Dorsey Press.

Magg, J. W. (2004). *Behavior management from theoretical implications to practical applications* (2nd ed.). Belmont, CA: Wadsworth/Thomson Learning.

JAMES E. MARTIN
University of Oklahoma

NEGATIVE REINFORCEMENT
POSITIVE REINFORCEMENT

REINFORCEMENT, NEGATIVE

See NEGATIVE REINFORCEMENT.

REINFORCEMENT, POSITIVE

See POSITIVE REINFORCEMENT.

REISMAN, FREDRICKA KAUFFMAN (1930–)

Fredricka Kauffman Reisman obtained her BA (1952) in psychology, her MS in 1963 in education, and her PhD in 1968 in math education from Syracuse University. Formerly a professor of mathematics education and special education at the University of Georgia in Athens (1979–1983), Reis-

Fredricka Kauffman Reisman

man began teaching at Drexel University in Philadelphia in 1985, where she became director of the Division of Instruction and Programs and head of teacher preparation in 1991. She currently holds the position of Director of the School of Education at Drexel. Her primary fields of interest include mathematics education, the integration of computing into the assessment and instruction of mathematics, teacher preparation, and diagnostic teaching. Her work has emphasized the prevention of learning difficulties rather than prescription or remediation. Reisman advocates teacher awareness of learner and content characteristics as well as the design of instructional environments that use modern technology.

Reisman has been recognized in *Who's Who in the East* and *Who's Who in America* (1997). Her major publications include *A Guide to the Diagnostic Teaching of Arithmetic* (1982), *Sequential Assessment in Mathematics Inventories* (1986), and *Becoming a Teacher: Grades K–8* (1987).

REFERENCES

Reisman, F. K. (1982). *A guide to the diagnostic teaching of arithmetic* (3rd ed.). Columbus, OH: Merrill.

Reisman, F. K. (1986). *Sequential assessment in mathematics inventories: K–8.* San Antonio, TX: Psychological Corporation.

Reisman, F. K. (1987). *Becoming a teacher: Grades K–8.* Columbus, OH: Merrill.

E. Valerie Hewitt
Texas A&M University
First edition

Tamara J. Martin
The University of Texas of the Permian Basin
Second and Third editions

REITAN-INDIANA NEUROPSYCHOLOGICAL TEST BATTERY FOR CHILDREN

The Reitan-Indiana Neuropsychological Test Battery for Children (RINTBC; ages 5 through 8), the Halstead Neuropsychological Test Battery for Children (ages 9 through 14), and the Halstead Neuropsychological Test Battery for Adults (ages 15 and older) constitute a global battery commonly referred to as the Halstead-Reitan Neuropsychological Test Battery. Each of these three batteries was devised as a tool for the assessment of brain-behavior relationships. The RINTBC was developed after it became apparent that many of the items on the battery for older children were too difficult for children below the age of 9 (Reitan, 1979).

The developmental research for the RINTBC, conducted at the Neuropsychology Laboratory of the Indiana University Medical Center, began in the mid-1950s. R. M. Reitan,

a student of W. C. Halstead, modified several of the tests from Halstead's original adult battery (Halstead, 1947) and also created six new tests to complete this battery for young children. The modified tests include children's versions of the Category Test, Tactual Performance Test, Sensory-Perceptual Disturbances Tests, Finger Oscillation Test, and Aphasia Screening Test. New tests include the Color Form Test, Progressive Figures Test, and Matching Picture Tests; these were designed to measure cognitive flexibility and concept formation. The Target Test and the Individual Performance Test assess reception and expression of visuospatial relationships, while the Marching Test measures gross motor coordination (Reitan, 1979). The RINTBC customarily is supplemented by the Reitan-Klove Lateral Dominance Examination, the Reitan-Klove Sensory-Perceptual Examination, Strength of Grip, the Wechsler Preschool and Primary Scale of Intelligence, and the Wide Range Achievement Test (Reitan, 1974).

Reitan and Davison (1974) present a review of research that has demonstrated that the RINTBC effectively differentiates brain-damaged from normal-functioning children, provided the test is administered and interpreted properly by trained professionals. An interpretive guide is available from Reitan (1987).

REFERENCES

Halstead, W. C. (1947). *Brain and intelligence.* Chicago: University of Chicago Press.

Reitan, R. M. (1974). Psychological effects of cerebral lesions in children of early school age. In R. M. Reitan & L. A. Davison (Eds.), *Clinical neuropsychology: Current status and applications* (pp. 53–89). New York: Hemisphere.

Reitan, R. M. (1979). *Manual for the administration of neuropsychological test batteries for adults and children.* Tucson, AZ: Reitan Neuropsychology Laboratories.

Reitan, R. M. (1987). *Neuropsychological evaluation of children.* Tucson, AZ: Reitan Neuropsychology Laboratories.

Reitan, R. M., & Davison, L. A. (1974). *Clinical neuropsychology.* New York: Hemisphere.

Gale A. Harr
*Maple Heights City Schools,
Maple Heights, Ohio*

HALSTEAD-REITAN NEUROPSYCHOLOGICAL TEST BATTERY
NEUROPSYCHOLOGY

RELATED SERVICES

The Education for All Handicapped Children Act of 1975 (PL 94-142) was the first federal law to hold education agencies responsible not only for the provision of special education services, but for the delivery of related services as well. Related services are defined as "transportation, and such developmental, corrective, and other supportive services . . . as may be required to assist a handicapped child to benefit from special education" (Section 4a). Subsequent versions of IDEA advance nearly identical language.

Among the services specifically included within the related services definition are speech pathology and audiology, psychological services, medical services (for diagnostic and evaluation purposes only), physical and occupational therapy, recreation, and counseling. However, because the phrase "other supportive services . . . as may be required" is included in the law, the precise definition of related services remains the subject of debate.

Disputes regarding the type and extent of related services required under PL 94-142 have been the focus of a series of court cases, including the first Supreme Court decision on federal special education law. Litigation has involved questions of eligibility, definition, and financial responsibility. All three issues were addressed in *Hendrick Hudson Board of Education* v. *Rowley.* In this case, the Supreme Court ruled that a high-achieving deaf student need not be provided a sign language interpreter at the school district's expense, given her demonstrated ability to benefit from the educational program already provided. While the court's decision focused on the narrow issue of one student's right to a particular related service, it suggested that the term "related services" need not be interpreted broadly to mean any service that would improve the quality of a handicapped child's education.

In the subsequent case of *Irving Independent School District* v. *Tatro,* definition was again at issue, with the focus on medical services required by the law. Medical services are defined in the law as those services provided by a physician for diagnostic and evaluation purposes. The school district argued that catheterizing a student (inserting a tube to drain the bladder) several times daily constituted a nondiagnostic medical service and therefore was not a related service for which the district was responsible. However, the Supreme Court ruled that catheterization is included within the related services definition because it is a simple nonmedical procedure that can be administered by a school nurse. As such, the court felt, catheterization was representative of the other supportive services needed to provide "the meaningful access to education that Congress envisioned" ("Court Backs Catheterization," 1984).

A major issue underlying both Supreme Court cases is financial responsibility. Related services are expensive to provide, and school districts are struggling to define the limits of their fiscal responsibility. Interpreting the *Rowley* decision, U.S. District Judge John A. Nordberg said, "the Court recognized the unfairness of imposing large financial burdens on states on the basis of broad interpretation of ambiguous language in funding statutes" ("Students Have," 1983). Even with a conservative interpretation of what constitutes related services, state and local education agencies often find themselves in a difficult financial position.

Dealing with the financial ramifications of providing related services is a continuing challenge. In its *Seventh Annual Report to Congress* (1984), the United States Department of Education described effective policies developed to provide related services in cost-efficient ways. One strategy has been to pool resources among local education agencies to make a range of related-service specialists available to students. Another has been to seek third-party funding from public and private insurance providers. A third approach involves establishing joint funding and cooperative programming arrangements among education and human service agencies. For example, a school district and local mental health agency might agree that the mental health agency will provide and assume the related-services costs for the district's seriously emotionally disturbed children (Maher & Bennett, 1984). Each of these arrangements exemplifies efforts to share financial responsibility and work cooperatively to improve the quality of related services available to handicapped children.

REFERENCES

Court backs catheterization; limits fees in handicap cases. (1984). *Education of the Handicapped, 10*(14), 1–3.

Maher, C. A., & Bennett, R. E. (1984). *Planning and evaluating special education services.* Englewood Cliffs, NJ: Prentice Hall.

Students have no right to free psychiatric care, court rules. (1983, Aug. 24). *Education of the Handicapped, 9*(17), 7–8.

U.S. Department of Education. (1984). *Seventh annual report to Congress on the implementation of the Education of the Handicapped Act.* Washington, DC: U.S. Government Printing Office.

MARY LOUISE LENNON
RANDY ELLIOT BENNETT
Educational Testing Service

DIAGNOSIS IN SPECIAL EDUCATION
INDIVIDUALS WITH DISABILITIES EDUCATION
    IMPROVEMENT ACT OF 2004 (IDEIA)
INTERPRETERS FOR THE DEAF
SPEECH-LANGUAGE SERVICES

RELIABILITY

Reliability is a core measurement concept in education and the social sciences and is associated with the development and use of psychoeducational tests and direct observation tools. Whether for the purpose of diagnosis or prognosis, reliability provides an index of how much we can depend on an instrument to predictably measure physical, psychological, or educational outcomes of interest. The more dependable an achievement test or observation instrument is, the more confident we are that accurate decisions will be made in special education. The need for measurement confidence is especially important in public education, where educators routinely use test or assessment data to help guide their instructional programming decisions for students. While few measurement tools are perfectly reliable, selecting a commercially available test with a known reputation for being erratic and inconsistent would simply be unethical and unprofessional (American Educational Research Association, American Psychological Association, & National Council on Measurement in Education, 1999).

Reliability is not an all-or-nothing concept; rather, it can be thought of as a sliding scale that ranges from minimal accuracy of measurement to highly dependable measurement of some variable of interest (Gregory, 2004). The degree of a test's reliability is often affected by the number and selected type of items for the test that, in reality, represent a limited and often indirect sampling of the behavioral or cognitive processes of concern. Compounding the issue is that such sampling of human processes is conducted at only one point in time and often in an artificial context. Because of this, test scores can and should be treated only as gross and approximate *indicators* of the construct being measured. For example, when a teacher rates a student on a measure of social competence as having average cooperation skills, the score does not, in itself, tell us all there is to know about the student's true cooperation skills. In this case, it tells us only what the teacher's perception is, as assessed by that instrument and the items responded to. Reliability, in relation to the aforementioned problems of test construction and restricted sampling of complex processes or total content knowledge, should press educators to ask what generalizations are reasonable and appropriate to make from such test or assessment results so that important decisions or conclusions can be made with confidence (Salvia & Ysseldyke, 2004; Thorndike, 2001). When reliability is considered, test scores themselves should be of little inherent interest to educators; educators should ask whether such scores generalize or are reliable over time, whether test items generalize to or are reliable with other test items within the test or assessment instrument itself, and whether there is interscorer generalization, which informs users about the level of scoring agreement between two (or more) examiners. The reliability or generalizability of a test or assessment tool is really about its ability to predict *itself*, thereby demonstrating a high degree of internal quality and structure, which will be needed before external utility (validity) can be expected (Thorndike, 2001).

Perfect internal and time-based consistency is highly desirable in a test or assessment tool, but subtle inconsistencies will inevitably occur in the course of measuring individual or between-group performance. This inconsistency, or variance, in obtained scores is referred to as measurement error and impacts reliability. Charles Spearman (1904) described this problematic issue in relation to measuring human intelligence, thereby laying the foundation for *classical test theory* in the social sciences. Two cornerstone assumptions of this theory are that (a) each person has a stable attribute to measure as captured by the true score on the test, and (b) in the process of measuring such human attributes, measurement error will occur, contributing to the inconsistency or unreliability of an instrument (Gregory, 2004; Kerlinger, 1986). A "true score" is a convenient fiction, because in actuality we can never obtain a pure measure of a person's true traits or abilities on a test. Nevertheless, the theoretical assumption is that a person's underlying true score is stable across successive test administrations (Kaplan, 1964; Thorndike, 2001). In essence, one's true score of a hypothetical trait or skill on a test is the expected value or average score one would receive on an infinite number of repeated measurements of that attribute by the test in use (Lord & Novick, 1968). While an index of reliability contains a hypothetical true score component, it also contains a measurement error component, which consists of random deviations from the true score. In light of this, reliability is defined through error, where the greater the measurement error, the greater the unreliability; less error means greater reliability (Kerlinger, 1986). In the statistical pursuit of estimating the amount of error present between measurement systems and with a person's obtained score on a test, one needs a reliability coefficient and the standard error of measurement (SEM; Salvia & Ysseldyke, 2004). Reliability coefficients are correlations (represented by r) that describe the magnitude or strength of relationship between scores obtained on successive test administrations. Correlations range from 0.0 to +1.0 (the theoretical upper limit) and provide us with information about how stable or accurate measurements are between those successive test administrations (Gregory, 2004). Acceptable magnitudes of reliability range from .70 to more robust correlations of .90 or higher. An acceptable reliability level will depend on what the actual test is being used for (Gregory, 2004). The reliability coefficient helps mathematically explain the proportion or percentage of error variance that exists between the obtained scores of two test administrations. If, for example, the reliability coefficient between two independently obtained IQ scores is $r = .80$, and is then squared, it tells us that 64 percent of the variance of the true IQ score can be accounted for or explained between the two test administrations; conversely, 36 percent of the total test variance is due to error from uncontrolled factors affecting the true measurement of IQ (Kerlinger, 1986; Salvia & Ysseldyke, 2004). There are many good descriptions of what types of variance might occur to affect reliability (i.e., the magnitude of the reliability coefficient; see Cronbach, Gleser, Nanda, & Rajaratnam, 1971; Thorndike, 2001), but generally they come from factors associated with test length, test-retest intervals, constriction or extension of ability range, guessing, and variation within the testing situation (Isaac & Michael, 1981; Salvia & Ysseldyke, 2004).

The other procedure of accounting for reliability error, SEM, is useful for interpreting an *individual's* score on a test and becomes vital in special education when determining eligibility, assessing present level of educational performance, or making appropriate placement decisions. Test administration guides (should) provide SEM data to help users gauge just how much score fluctuation to expect if the test were administered to the individual again. Inextricably linked to SEM is the confidence interval, which conveys the degree of accuracy with which the test identified the underlying true score in relation to the person's obtained score. For example, if a person obtains a full-scale IQ standard score of 100 and that full-scale score is reported to be 90 percent accurate within a SEM of +/– 10 points, then the examiner would report that, with 90 percent certainty, the person's *true* IQ is found somewhere between the scores of 90 and 110. If one wants a greater degree of confidence of where that true score falls in relation to the obtained score (e.g., at the 95 percent level), then the confidence interval will necessarily increase in width to account for more error (Salvia & Ysseldyke, 2004). Again, test manuals or guides should report such information to the consumer.

The purpose of the reliability coefficient, then, is to describe the strength of the test's internal item structure or the stability of test scores over an interval of time. To this end, several reliability methods exist to help achieve this goal (see Gregory, 2004; Isaac & Michael, 1981; Salvia & Ysseldyke, 2004; Thorndike, 2001). In the test-retest reliability method, one test is administered twice to the same group of heterogeneous and representative subjects. Scores are then correlated to see if the second obtained score can be predicted from the first obtained score. The reliability coefficient that is obtained provides an index of temporal stability, which helps us know whether the traits and characteristics being measured between the two time points change a great deal. Shorter time periods between the test-retest points generally produce higher reliability coefficients because there is less chance that true scores have changed. Alternate form (or equivalent form) reliability estimates the extent to which two (or more) different forms of a test are temporally stable from one administration point to the next. For example, if a test developer wants a Form A and a Form B version of an academic achievement test, he or she will have to generate reliability coefficients based on test-retest methodology that informs the user of stability of comparable items over time. In this approach, subjects are not tested twice with identical test items from one test, but with a set of items from Form A at time one and then a set of items from Form B at time two. Fewer and fewer alternate or parallel forms of tests are sold today because it is generally more expensive and difficult to identify equally appropriate and representative items for two forms of a test, and it potentially introduces more error variance from

improper content-sampling procedures. Split-half reliability is a substitute for alternate forms whereby items from an existing test are divided into halves. There may be many possible divisible permutations for a test depending on its total item content, but one practical way would be to use an odd-even division of those items. Once properly divided, the two halves are then correlated with each other to estimate the test's internal consistency reliability. This procedure, however, does not provide the best precision for estimating internal consistency. In order to avoid having to correlate all possible divisible permutations to find the best statistical balance between the halves, test developers can now use the coefficient alpha method, which quickly and efficiently indexes the average split-half correlations on all possible divisions of a test into two equally correlated halves. Finally, interscorer reliability supplements the test-retest method, but it is still important because it tells us how much consistency there is in the results when two or more examiners score the same test.

The importance of interscorer or interobserver reliability cannot be understated for applied behavior analysis (ABA) in special education. Although ABA does use correlational methodology, indexing the reliability of instruments is more often accomplished by calculating the percentage of agreement between raters or observers of human behavior. Depending on the recording technique, reliability agreement can be indexed as simple agreement, point-to-point agreement, agreement for occurrence, or kappa index of agreement.

Promoting reliable decisions about special education treatment effectiveness is essential in ABA because of effects such as observer drift, where observer accuracy in recording behavior decays over time; reactivity by those who are aware that they are being observed; observer bias, where assessment errors occur because of observers' expectancies and prejudices; and observer cheating, where in rare cases, observers may purposefully exaggerate reliability agreements (Hartmann, 1984). To enhance proper decisions about treatment effectiveness in ABA, thereby improving an assessment instrument's reliability, Hartmann (1984) suggests that observers should (a) be given enough time to acclimate to the observational setting before reliability data are taken; (b) be separated and made unaware of the purpose of the study as well as when quality control reliability assessment sessions are scheduled; and (c) be reminded about the importance of accuracy and be regularly retrained on observation instruments. It is critically important in ABA that reliability checks be conducted throughout treatment investigation and be calculated by the investigator, not by the observers (Hartmann, 1982).

Reliability is an important measurement concept and standard to consider in special education, especially when numerous commercially available tests or assessment instruments are poorly constructed or possess little or no reliability data attesting to their stability and accuracy.

When special educators maintain high standards in their choice of reliable measurement systems, it advertises to the community at large that the profession is concerned about using only the most dependable and accurate decision tools with students with disabilities.

REFERENCES

American Educational Research Association, American Psychological Association, & National Council on Measurement in Education. (1999). *Standards for educational and psychological testing* (2nd ed.). Washington, DC: American Psychological Association.

Cronbach, L. J., Gleser, G. C., Nanda, H., & Rajaratnam, N. (1971). *The dependability of behavioral measurements*. New York: Wiley.

Gregory, R. J. (2004). *Psychological testing: History, principles, and applications* (4th ed.). Wheaton, IL: Allyn & Bacon.

Hartmann, D. P. (1982). Assessing the dependability of observational data. In D. P. Hartmann (Ed.), *Using observers to study behavior: New directions for methodology of social and behavioral science* (pp. 51–65). San Francisco: Jossey-Bass.

Hartmann, D. P. (1984). Assessment strategies. In D. H. Barlow & M. Hersen (Eds.), *Single case experimental designs: Strategies for studying behavior change* (2nd ed., pp. 107–139). Elmsford, NY: Pergamon Press.

Isaac, S., & Michael, W. B. (1981). *Handbook in research and evaluation for education and the behavioral sciences* (2nd ed.). San Diego, CA: EdITS.

Kaplan, A. (1964). *The conduct of inquiry*. San Francisco: Chandler.

Kerlinger, F. N. (1986). *Foundations of behavioral research* (3rd ed.). Orlando, FL: Holt, Rinehart & Winston.

Lord, F., & Novick, M. (1968). *Statistical theories of mental test scores*. Reading, MA: Addison-Wesley.

Salvia, J., & Ysseldyke, J. E. (2004). *Assessment in special and inclusive education* (9th ed.). Boston: Houghton Mifflin.

Spearman, C. (1904). "General intelligence," objectively determined and measured. *American Journal of Psychology, 15*, 201–293.

Thorndike, R. M. (2001). Reliability. In B. F. Bolton (Ed.), *Handbook of measurement and evaluation in rehabilitation* (3rd ed., pp. 29–48). Gaithersburg, MD: Aspen.

ROLLEN C. FOWLER
*Eugene 4J School District,
Eugene, Oregon*

RESEARCH IN SPECIAL EDUCATION

REMEDIAL AND SPECIAL EDUCATION

In 1982, PRO-ED, Inc., purchased the journal *Exceptional Education Quarterly* from Aspen Systems Corporation. In 1984, the name of the journal was changed to *Remedial and Special Education* (RASE), and the journal became a bimonthly. That same year, PRO-ED acquired two additional journals, *Topics in Learning and Learning Disabilities* (from Aspen Press) and *The Journal for Special Educators* (from the American Association of Special Educators); these were also merged into RASE. This journal is devoted to topics involving the education of persons for whom typical instruction is not effective. Emphasis is on the interpretation of research literature and recommendations for the practice of remedial and special education. RASE thus is alternative to practitioner-oriented teacher journals and pure research journals within the field. All published articles have been peer reviewed.

JUDITH K. VORESS
PRO-ED, Inc.

REMEDIAL INSTRUCTION

The term *remediation* is derived from the word *remedy*, meaning a correction, repair, or cure of something that is awry. Medicines are medical remedies. Remedies in education are called remediations (Ysseldyke & Algozzine, 1984).

Remedial teaching has been distinguished from developmental teaching and from corrective teaching. As usually construed, developmental teaching is the type of instruction given to the majority of students attending regular classes (Otto & McMenemy, 1966; Rupley & Blair, 1983).

Developmental instruction in the modern classroom is likely to be guided by clearly defined instructional objectives. Thus, developmental reading instruction has been described as "a systematic guided series of steps, procedures or actions intended to result in learning or in the reaching of a desired goal" (Harris & Hodges, 1981, p. 157).

Corrective and remedial instruction are both forms of academic assistance provided to students who need special help in various areas of instruction. When that assistance is offered by the classroom teacher within a regular classroom setting to students who are deficient in some particular skills or not achieving up to expectations in particular subject matters, help is identified as corrective instruction. Corrective instruction is given when the type of learning problem, or its degree, is not judged as severe enough to require specific types of remediation. Remedial instruction is usually given to students with more severe or persistent academic difficulties. Usually it is provided by a specialist in a particular skill or content area and in circumstances apart from the child's regular classroom. Remedial instruction often suggests a learning disability; indeed, remedial instructors often act as learning disability specialists.

Arbitrary standards are often set for eligibility for corrective or remedial services: Within 2 years of grade expectation the child may be given corrective instruction, but beyond 2 years the child will receive remedial instruction. Such criteria are often insensitive to growth curves and normal developmental changes and make little sense.

While developmental and corrective as well as remedial instruction attempt to individualize according to students' needs, remedial instruction is most likely to address a student and his or her problems diagnostically and to offer intensive interventions (Reisman, 1982). Thus, remedial instruction is likely to be provided to students whose academic deficiencies or disabilities appear so severe or specialized as to require more precise, intense, or individualized assistance.

In remedial instruction the distinction may be made between skill remediation and ability or process remediation. The first attempt to correct or strengthen particular academic skills, such as decoding in reading, carrying in two-column addition, and not writing out silent sounds in spelling. In the second, efforts are made to correct presumed deficits in cognitive processes such as perception, memory, and attention. A popular current process approach is that of teaching learning-disabled children to more effectively use cognitive strategies in learning and school performance.

Since special education is based on individualized intensive interventions addressed to students who, because of their handicapping conditions, may not be able to keep up with their nondisabled peers, the notion of remediation, from a special educator's point of view, may be redundant. Indeed, the special education resource room, whether in regular or special education, is likely to be a place where remedial education is offered. Cawley (1984) believes that carefully controlled curricular approaches to the problems of learning-disabled students are likely to be more effective than the traditional diagnostic-prescriptive remedial methods so often emphasized in remediation.

Remedial reading is the most frequently offered form of remedial or corrective help provided in grade school, both elementary and secondary. Remedial mathematics, writing, and so on also go on in regular education settings, but they are less likely to be carried out by remedial specialists. Remedial instruction is often provided at the college level as well as during the lower grades. It is most often required by students who, because of poor earlier preparation, problems in managing English, or specific cognitive deficits, require specialized help to succeed in higher education. Many colleges and other institutions of higher learning provide remedial writing.

REFERENCES

Cawley, J. F. (1984). Preface. In J. F. Cawley (Ed.), *Developmental teaching of mathematics for the learning disabled*. Rockville, MD: Aspen.

Harris, T. L., & Hodges, R. E. (Eds.). (1981). *A dictionary of reading and related terms*. Newark, DE: International Reading Association.

Otto, W., & McMenemy, R. A. (1966). *Corrective and remedial reading*. Boston: Houghton Mifflin.

Reisman, F. (1982). *A guide to the diagnostic teaching of arithmetic*. Columbus, OH: Merrill.

Rupley, W. H., & Blair, T. R. (1983). *Reading diagnosis and remediation: Class & clinic*. Boston: Houghton Mifflin.

Ysseldyke, J. E., & Algozzine, B. (1984). *Introduction to special education*. Boston: Houghton Mifflin.

LESTER MANN
*Hunter College, City University
of New York*

**DIAGNOSTIC PRESCRIPTIVE TEACHING
DIRECT INSTRUCTION
REMEDIAL READING**

REMEDIAL READING

According to Smith (1965), the term *remedial reading* first appeared in the professional literature in a 1916 journal article by W. H. Uhl; however, like so many of the terms in the field of reading, the term *remedial reading* has no universally agreed on operational definition. The amount of confusion that exists with respect to the term was expressed well some years ago by Goldberg and Schiffman (1972), who noted:

> Some educators refer to the problem category as remedial, strephosymbolia, associative learning disability, specific reading or language disability, congenital word blindness, primary reading retardation, or developmental dyslexia. One school district may refer to all retarded readers as remedial; another agency, in the same community, may use the term remedial for a small group of children with specific learning disabilities. (pp. 156–157)

Goldberg and Schiffman go on to point out that, because of the widely varying definitions, estimates of the percent of students requiring remedial reading instruction vary from as low as 1 percent to as high as 20 percent.

A Dictionary of Reading and Related Terms (T. L. Harris & Hodges, 1981) provides a realistic, though somewhat vague, definition of the term *remedial reading*:

> Any specialized reading instruction adjusted to the needs of a student who does not perform satisfactorily with regular reading instruction.
>
> Intensive specialized reading instruction for students reading considerably below expectancy.

Before examining this definition, it might be helpful to quickly introduce two reading terms that are frequently contrasted with the term *remedial reading:* developmental reading and corrective reading. Developmental reading refers to instruction that is designed for and offered to the average child who is acquiring reading skills at an average rate. Group instruction, centering around the use of basal readers, is the typical approach to developmental reading instruction.

Corrective reading is a term usually applied to instruction that is offered to children who are essentially average intellectually but who are slower than average in the rate at which they are acquiring reading skills; however, the disparity between where they are expected to be reading, usually based on age, grade placement, and intelligence, is not large. The difficulties that they are encountering are mild enough that, with some adjustments, the responsibility for their reading instruction can be assumed by a regular classroom teacher.

While it seems fairly easy to separate developmental reading from remedial reading, the distinction between corrective and remedial reading is not so clear. The first definition offered by Harris and Hodges would make the two indistinguishable; however, even the second definition offers no clear criteria for separating the two. A. J. Harris and Sipay (1985) list four characteristics that distinguish corrective from remedial programs. The first characteristic is where the treatment takes place. Remedial reading usually takes place in a special classroom or even in a special clinic. The second characteristic is who provides the treatment. Corrective instruction is usually offered by a classroom teacher, while remedial instruction is within the province of a reading or learning disabilities specialist. Third is the number of children treated in a session. Group size is smaller for remedial instruction or is on a one-to-one basis. The final characteristic is the severity of the problem. Otto and McMenemy (1966) sum up this definitional problem when they write

> In terms of diagnostic and instructional techniques, the distinction between actual corrective and remedial instruction is often one of degree rather than kind. Strictly remedial techniques tend to be more intensive and more highly individualized but usually not intrinsically different from corrective techniques. (pp. 38–39)

Some authors have tried to bring objectivity to the definition of remedial reading by defining it as referring to children who are reading 2 or more years below grade level. Unfortunately, this simple approach is fraught with problems. To begin with, years with regard to reading skill development are not equal interval units. Reading skills tend to develop rapidly during grades 1 through 3 and to develop at a negatively accelerating rate thereafter. A child

who at the end of grade 2 has acquired no reading skills (hence is 2 years behind) is very different from a grade 8 student who has acquired grade 6 skills. Even Otto and McMenemy (1966), who are among the few professionals who attempt to justify the adoption of a 2-year criterion for defining a remedial reader, are quick to point out that it is "clearly unrealistic" in the early grades and that "slavish application of such an arbitrary criterion would be unfortunate" (p. 37).

A second major problem in adopting a 2-year disparity criterion lies in the method for calculating that disparity. In most cases, the disparity is based on a difference between actual, measured reading achievement of a student and the level he or she should have attained based on some measure of capacity to learn, usually an intelligence test. Unfortunately, there is no agreed-on method for calculating the amount of disparity between expectancy and achievement. Stauffer, Abrams, and Pikulski (1978) have shown that widely different results will be achieved depending on the formula used to calculate the expected level of reading achievement. In addition, tests of intelligence and of reading can yield widely differing results depending on the tests used.

Yet another problem in defining remedial reading lies in the enormous overlap between the concepts of learning disabilities and remedial reading. Given our present level of diagnostic sophistication, distinguishing between these two classifications appears to depend almost totally on arbitrary local definitions or regulations or on funding considerations. Lewis (1983) presents an excellent summary of some of the major considerations that need to be taken into account in providing instruction for the student who is severely disabled in reading, regardless of whether that student is labeled as a remedial reader or as a child with a learning disability. The article is also excellent in providing evidence that challenges some widely held misconceptions about students who have severe reading problems.

The confused situation relative to the use of the term *remedial reading* and related terms, described by Goldberg and Schiffman earlier, continues to exist today; in fact, the confusion may be exacerbated by the introduction of even more terms.

While there are apparently no clear-cut ways to diagnostically differentiate among remedial readers, the learning disabled, corrective readers, dyslexics, and so on, one might wonder if there are any instructional methods or materials that are unique to remedial reading. Textbooks dealing with this topic imply that there are. For example, Bond et al. (1984) indicate that there are four important elements of remedial instruction: It is individualized, it encourages the reader, it uses effective teaching procedures, and it enlists cooperative efforts. While these elements are important to remedial reading, they are also important to all reading instruction. These authors go on to suggest that basal readers, the hallmark of developmental reading instruction, are a primary source of materials for remedial reading.

A careful reading of discussions of remedial reading suggests that the principles of teaching reading are the same regardless of whether we are concerned with remedial or developmental readers. The basic consideration is that remedial reading be based on a careful assessment of what the reader knows and needs to learn in terms of reading skills and that instruction then be at an appropriate level of challenge. Many of the techniques are similar to those used for teaching reading to achieving readers. For example, Rude and Oehlkers (1984) describe how a language experience approach to teaching reading, which centers around the use of reading materials that are dictated by the reader and written by the teacher, can be used for remedial reading; the language experience approach is also a major developmental technique for teaching reading. Nevertheless, there are three approaches that might be considered specifically designed for use in remedial reading.

The first approach is the use of high interest–low vocabulary materials. These materials are books, usually designed as a series, that are specifically written to appeal to the interests of older children but that use a limited vocabulary. A. J. Harris and Sipay (1985) include a list of over 90 such series.

The Fernald V-A-K-T approach (V-A-K-T stands for visual, auditory, kinesthetic, and tactile) was devised by Grace Fernald (1943) to treat children with learning problems. In this approach, children learn to read by using all four senses; they see words written by a teacher, they pronounce and hear those same words, and they trace the written copy of the words so as to receive tactile and kinesthetic stimulation. The technique, which is highly prescribed, forces the learner to pay full attention to the word learning process. See Johnson (1966) and Stauffer et al. (1978) for descriptions of this approach.

The Orton-Gillingham approach stresses the importance of learning phonics as the major reading skill. Students learn sounds for letters and are taught to blend the sounds to make words. This, too, is a highly structured and prescribed approach. It also uses multiple sensory stimuli. It is based on the work of an influential neurologist, Samuel T. Orton. The technique is fully described by Orton (1966) and Gillingham and Stillman (1966).

REFERENCES

Bond, G. L., Tinker, M. A., Wasson, B. B., & Wasson, J. B. (1984). *Reading difficulties: Their diagnosis and correction* (5th ed.). Englewood Cliffs, NJ: Prentice Hall.

Fernald, G. M. (1943). *Remedial techniques in basic school subjects.* New York: McGraw-Hill.

Gillingham, A., & Stillman, B. W. (1966). *Remedial training for children with specific difficulty in reading, spelling, and penmanship* (7th ed.). Cambridge, MA: Educators Publishing Service.

Goldberg, H. K., & Schiffman, G. B. (1972). *Dyslexia: Problems of reading disabilities.* New York: Grune & Stratton.

Harris, A. J., & Sipay, E. R. (1985). *How to increase reading ability* (5th ed.). White Plains, NY: Longman.

Harris, T. L., & Hodges, R. E. (Eds.). (1981). *A dictionary of reading and related terms.* Newark, DE: International Reading Association.

Johnson, M. S. (1966). Tracing and kinesthetic techniques. In J. Money (Ed.), *The disabled reader.* Baltimore: Johns Hopkins University Press.

Lewis, R. B. (1983). Learning disabilities and reading: Instructional recommendations from current research. *Exceptional Children, 50*(3), 230–240.

Orton, J. L. (1966). The Orton-Gillingham approach. In J. Money (Ed.), *The disabled reader.* Baltimore: Johns Hopkins University Press.

Otto, W., & McMenemy, R. A. (1966). *Corrective and remedial reading: Principles and practices.* Boston: Houghton Mifflin.

Rude, R. T., & Oehlkers, W. J. (1984). *Helping students with reading problems.* Englewood Cliffs, NJ: Prentice Hall.

Smith, N. B. (1965). *American reading instruction.* Newark, DE: International Reading Association.

Stauffer, R. G., Abrams, J. C., & Pikulski, J. J. (1978). *Diagnosis, correction and prevention of reading disabilities.* New York: Harper & Row.

JOHN J. PIKULSKI
University of Delaware

BASAL READERS
FERNALD METHOD
HIGH INTEREST–LOW VOCABULARY
ORTON-GILLINGHAM METHOD
READING
READING DISORDERS

REMEDIATION, DEFICIT-CENTERED MODELS OF

Deficit-centered models for the remediation of children's learning problems have been the predominant model, though certainly not the only model, of special education worldwide throughout the twentieth century. Deficit-centered remediation focuses on the identification of underlying process deficiencies on the part of the child; it then directs any subsequent intervention at the remediation of these process deficiencies. The assumption of such programs is that once the underlying deficit has been remediated (fixed, removed, or cured), academic learning will occur at a more or less normal pace. Deficit-centered remediation has undergone numerous facelifts since the 1930s, although the strong influence of Samuel T. Orton is felt in most of these programs even today.

One of the most notable examples of deficit-centered

remediation is the Illinois Test of Psycholinguistic Abilities (ITPA; Kirk, McCarthy, & Kirk, 1971) and its accompanying curriculum, interventions, and training materials. (Perhaps a more popularly known deficit-centered program, and also one of the most heavily refuted and ineffective, is the Doman and Delacato program at the Institute for the Achievement of Human Potential. This is the approach that calls on the concept of neurological organization and treatment through patterning among other activities.) The ITPA focuses on the identification and assessment of basic psycholinguistic processes such as auditory reception, auditory sequential memory, visual sequential memory, auditory association, and so on. If a deficit appears in one or more of these areas, a remedial program is then prescribed (Kirk & Kirk, 1971). For example, if a child is referred for a reading program and found to have an auditory reception deficit (determined on the ITPA by the child's inability to respond correctly at an age-appropriate level to such questions as Do bananas fly? Do barometers congratulate? Do chairs sit?), exercises might be prescribed for the child aimed at practicing the hearing and discrimination of similar sounds (e.g., noting the differences between pin and pen, pet and let, then and tin, dot and spot). The child also might be given practice in the following of instructions. Once these activities are mastered, the deficit-centered model argues, learning to read would proceed more or less normally since the cognitive processing (or central process) dysfunction that was the stumbling block to reading has been removed.

Many other assessment techniques and programs exist to identify weaknesses or deficits in cognitive processes for subsequent intervention. Some of the approaches that emphasize treating the child's greatest area of weakness in cognitive processing include those of Ayres (1974), Bannatyne (1980), Ferinden and Jacobson (1969), Frostig and Horne (1964), Kephart (1963), and Vallett (1967). The efficacy of deficit-centered models has been the subject of considerable scrutiny by researchers in psychology and special education for some time. Unfortunately, support for the effectiveness of deficit-centered remediation programs for the remediation of academic deficits is nil, particularly when reading and math are the academic problem areas (Glass & Robbins, 1967; Mann, 1979; Reynolds, 1981a, 1981b; Ysseldyke & Mirkin, 1982). Perceptual and visual-motor functioning can be improved by deficit-centered remediation programs (Myers & Hammill, 1976), but there is, as yet, no documentable generalization for the remediation of the learning problems that trigger the referral.

Other, related areas of research have repeatedly noted potentially major limiting factors in the application of deficit-centered models. Findings from the fields of neurology, genetics, and related areas demonstrate neurological (Adams & Victor, 1977; L. C. Hartlage, 1975; P. L. Hartlage & Givens, 1982; Kolb & Whishaw, 1980; Levine, Brooks, & Shonkoff, 1980) or genetic bases (Adams & Victor, 1977; P. L. Hartlage & Hartlage 1973a, 1973b) for many learning problems in which deficit-centered models or remediation had been thought to be appropriate as the primary method of intervention. From the point of view of many contemporary neuropsychological models, the deficit-centered process approach to remediation is doomed to failure because it takes damaged, dysfunctional, or undeveloped areas of the brain and focuses training specifically on those areas. Not only does our existing knowledge of neurology predict failure for such efforts, but the efforts will not withstand empirical scrutiny.

L. C. Hartlage and Reynolds (1981) have criticized deficit-centered models of remediation as potentially harmful to children. The emotional trauma that may accompany the treatment approach of Doman and Delacato has been widely discussed, and the method has been condemned (Levine et al., 1980). While it is unlikely that other deficit-centered models are as emotionally damaging, it is likely (though unproven) that making children work and practice for lengthy periods (in some cases, years) process skills in which they are deficient without noticeable academic gains is emotionally damaging, particularly to the child's self-esteem, motivation, and likelihood of continuing in school. Glass (1981), in a meta-analysis of the effectiveness of what were deficit-centered models of remediation, reported that a significant number had net negative effects on academic skills—that is, many deficit-centered remediation programs resulted in less academic gains than no special education program at all. In some instances, then, doing nothing is superior to a deficit-centered approach to remediation, when only academic skills are considered.

Recently, cognitive psychologists have become interested in children's information-processing strategies and have made great strides in understanding how children organize, store, and manipulate stimuli. Concomitant with the revival of interest in cognitivism have been attempts to assess "new" cognitive deficits and provide remedial strategies. Haywood and Switzky (1986), among others, propose that through such techniques as Feuerstein's (1979) Learning Potential Assessment Device (known popularly as the LPAD), deficiencies in children's cognitive processes can be identified and targeted for remediation. Conceptually, this new "cognitive science" approach is no different from the approaches of the past—only the names of the processes thought to be deficient are new. The new deficit-centered models have been the subject of debate (Gresham, 1986; Haywood & Switzky, 1986; Reynolds, 1986), and there is evidence that, through the use of a like set of materials, children's scores on tests such as Raven's Matrices (a nonverbal test of intelligence) improve.

However, many of the specific abilities included in the cognitive science models of deficit-centered remediation are covered overtly in prior models and implicitly in many training programs. The cognitive science models do give us some new abilities to train, notably thinking skills and strategies such as metacognition, regrouping, rehearsal, and various methods of classification, but merely leave us with new labels for others. The intelligence test score improvement reported by Feuerstein, Haywood, and others (Haywood & Switzky, 1986) likely is due to teaching the test, and generalizability to other tests or to academic skills is not in evidence. As with deficit-centered remediation programs throughout the twentieth century, the new cognitive science model is narrow and highly task-specific in its effects. While improvements in these characteristics of children's thinking are desirable, they are not desirable at the neglect of the academic deficiencies that trigger the referral.

There is no evidence that deficit-centered remediation programs aid in such real-world tasks as learning to read, write, or cipher. They remain popular largely on the basis of rational, intuitive appeal and personal testimony or anecdotal data. However, occasional children do improve without treatment and the same percentage or less improve under deficit-centered remediation. As Mann (e.g., 1979) periodically reminds us, we are better off training or teaching for the task at hand, not for the latest process. In assessing the new cognitive science approach to remediation, we are forced to conclude, as has Mann (1979) in his review of process training, "The new scientific pedagogy was going to revitalize education, provide individual prescriptive correctives for learning problems, reclaim the cognitively impaired. Down with models of general intellectual incompetency! Down with medical models of noneducational etiology! . . . The promised land was at hand. Alas, neither Moses nor we ever crossed to the other side" (Mann, 1979, pp. 529, 538, 539). Process is not a useless variable, however. It is crucial to consider in the diagnosis of learning disabilities as well as certain other disorders; efforts to use process approaches to remediate academic problems seem better built on strength models of remediation than on deficit-centered models.

Strength Models of Remediation

Strength models of remediation also invoke the concept of cognitive or intellectual processes and often measure them in the same way. The resulting approach and techniques differ greatly, however. Strength models argue that the best remedial approach for a child who cannot read is to teach the child reading, not metacognition, rehearsal strategies, auditory reception, or grouping and classification.

In strength models of remediation, direct instruction is encouraged in the area(s) of academic or behavioral difficulty. However, instruction is formatted around the child's best-developed processes, taking advantage of the child's best intellectual abilities and avoiding those processes that are poorly developed, dysfunctional, or inept in this function. As Reynolds (1981b) describes this method, "The strength model is based on processes that are sufficiently intact so as to subserve the successful accomplishment of the steps in the educational program, so that the interface

between cognitive strengths [determined from the assessment process] . . . and the intervention is the cornerstone of meaningfulness for the entire diagnostic-intervention process" (p. 344). In Lurian terminology, this would denote the need for locating a complex functional system within the brain that operates well enough to be capable of taking control and moderating the learning process necessary to acquire the academic skills in question.

This view is hardly new, though it remains largely untested. Woodrow (1919) suggested teaching to cognitive strengths on the basis of scientific psychology and the interpretation of "laws" of factor analysis, while attempting to reconcile the views of Spearman and of Thurstone (Mann, 1979). Woodrow (1919) observed that "sometimes a high order of intelligence is accompanied by defects which make it imperative to use . . . the stronger faculties" (p. 293). More directly and in reference to the mildly mentally retarded, Woodrow (1919) argued that since "Their most valuable asset is rote memory . . . its training should . . . form a conspicuous part in their education" (pp. 285–286). Today we hope to use the stronger faculties in developing instructional strategies, as Woodrow also proposed, rather than in training the stronger processes to become even stronger; the latter is not an unlikely side effect of strength models of remediation, however.

Strength models do not tell us specifically what to teach children, as do deficit-centered models, which tell us to teach the specific process that has been found to be deficient. In strength models, the specifics of what to teach come from a detailed task analysis or a diagnostic achievement test that delineates precisely what academic skills are problematic for the child. The strength model of remediation tells us how to teach: how the material best can be organized and presented so that learning has the best opportunity to occur (Reynolds, 1985). The specific techniques of strength models of remediation have been elaborated in a variety of sources, as has validity evidence for the approach (Gunnison & Kaufman, 1982; L. C. Hartlage & Reynolds, 1981; Reynolds, 1981a, 1981b, 1985). Building on strengths has intuitive appeal as well. Deficit models focus on the child's weakest, least developed areas of cognitive processing, the areas in which failures have been experienced most frequently. The stress, anxiety, and self-denigration that may be fostered can be intolerable for many children. Using the child's strengths as building blocks for the acquisition of academic skills or even the remediation of behavioral disorders increases the probability of more positive and successful experiences, reducing stress and alleviating anxiety. Strength models of remediation may have other emotional benefits for children as well.

A strength model of remediation also can serve as a meeting ground for a variety of divergent theoretical models in use in the remediation of a child's problems. One can easily blend cognitive, behavioral, neuropsychological, and psychoeducational models in a strength approach. Behavioral and psychoeducational models that focus on academic skill delineation through task analysis or diagnostic achievement testing are needed to tell us specifically what to teach; cognitive and neuropsychological models that focus on how the child best thinks and processes information tell us how to organize, present, and teach the content and behaviors; behavioral models, particularly positive reinforcement programs using operant techniques, are best at giving the child reason, purpose, and motivation, the why of learning. Of the various processing theories from which to build the how, to implement strength models of remediation, the neuropsychological model seems the most promising (Reynolds, 1981b, 1985), and a blending of this model with others has been proposed on several occasions.

An Illustrative Example

Some authors have advocated the use of behavioral principles in conjunction with neuropsychological techniques for the remediation of academic problems (Horton, 1981; Reynolds, 1981a, 1985). Others have presented exemplary case studies that recommend inclusion of behavior management techniques based on the unique patterns of cognitive strengths within a given child (L. C. Hartlage, 1981; L. C. Hartlage & Telzrow, 1983). The focus in all cases is on assessing as accurately as possible the various dysfunctional or intact neuropsychological processing systems for the child using a variety of assessment devices integrated with data from numerous other sources (e.g., teachers, parents, physicians). The goal is then to design a behavior management program (usually in conjunction with an academic remediation program) that emphasizes the child's particular strengths.

Although this approach seems almost matter of fact in terms of face validity, what actually occurs in schools is usually quite contrary to this model. The following hypothetical case can illustrate how a remediation program might be designed for a given child, based first on a deficit-centered model and second on a strength model.

Tina is an 8-year-old female who is experiencing problems learning to read. The teacher describes her as immature, distractible, and unable to follow classroom instruction. Results of a complete evaluation reveal that Tina possesses average to above average intellectual abilities with significant weakness in her auditory and visual sequencing abilities. She seems to exhibit above average visuo-spatial skills. A classroom observation reveals that she appears to be daydreaming when the teacher gives the morning's assignments and she is frequently reprimanded for talking while she attempts to get information from her peers. Achievement data indicate that she is functioning significantly below her ability in reading, exhibiting almost no

knowledge of grapheme-phoneme relationships. Auditory comprehension of material is excellent.

The resultant educational plan based on a traditional deficit-centered model might proceed as follows: Tina would go to a resource room for 45 minutes, 3 days a week, for drill in phonics. This is in addition to the 30 minutes she spends each day in her regular reading program, where phonics is also heavily emphasized. In addition, once a week Tina is provided with training in auditory sequencing skills. A behavior management system is designed whereby she stays in from recess when she has not completed assignments as instructed by the teacher. If this fails, she also stays after school to complete assignments.

On adoption of a strength model perspective, a radically different plan would be designed for Tina. Based on the identical assessment information, the emphasis would shift to capitalizing on Tina's strong visuo-spatial skills while bypassing her weaknesses in auditory sequencing to the maximum extent possible. Therefore, Tina may still benefit from additional reading instruction with a resource teacher, but the emphasis of the techniques would be quite different. It is probable that for a child with deficient auditory sequencing abilities, a strong phonics program to teach reading would prove futile and subsequently frustrating to the child and the teacher. Under the strength model, one would incorporate techniques into the reading program that would allow Tina to use her stronger visuo-spatial abilities. Look-say, rebus, and language experience stories with pictures are all reading programs that have techniques to emphasize visuo-spatial skills and deemphasize sequencing skills. Context would be emphasized. Strength models demand an emphasis on one system not to the exclusion of the other, but rather in preference to it.

Another obvious recommendation would be to have Tina sit as close to the teacher as possible and for the teacher to provide additional visual cues whenever giving oral directions to the class. Writing the directions on the board and having Tina copy them and then illustrate them might be helpful in maintaining her attention. Tina also might benefit from direct instruction in the use of visual imagery for remembering sight words, following direction, and so on.

As for the appropriate behavior management technique, it is possible that simply changing the classroom environment and the demands of the activities would result in an increase in work completed and a reduction in the time spent off task. Strategies that emphasize verbal understanding or memory of specific rules should be avoided. Techniques that provide Tina with visual representation of her behavioral progress (e.g., charting amount of tasks completed) might be the most effective for her. These recommendations may be more difficult to implement only in that they require more creative teachers and support staff. There are, as yet, no purely canned programs or specific techniques for strength models of remediation, since the approach is relatively new and requires great individualization of instruction. It does appear to be worth the effort. Student characteristics should affect the choice of an instructional method. As obvious as this seems, given the tremendous differences observed among children in the depth and breadth of their learning when exposed to a common method, this is clearly not the case in regular or special education at present (Hayes & Jenkins, 1986). Convenience and the needs of administrators all too often dictate the choice of curriculum and methods in special education instruction. Allowing students' characteristics to drive this process under a strength approach to implementing differential instruction offers far greater promise than current practice.

REFERENCES

Adams, R. D., & Victor, M. (1977). *Principles of neurology.* New York: McGraw-Hill.

Ayres, A. J. (1974). *Sensory integration and learning disorders.* Los Angeles: Western Psychological Services.

Bannatyne, A. (1980, September). *Neuropsychological remediation of learning disorders.* Paper presented at the NATO/ASI International Conference on Neuropsychology and Cognition, Augusta, GA.

Ferinden, W. E., & Jacobson, S. (1969). *Educational interpretation of the Wechsler Intelligence Scale for Children (WISC).* Linden, NJ: Remediation Associates.

Feuerstein, R. (1979). *The dynamic assessment of retarded performers: The learning potential assessment device, theory, instruments and techniques.* Baltimore: University Park Press.

Frostig, M., & Horne, D. (1964). *The Frostig program for the development of visual perception.* Chicago: Follett.

Glass, G. V. (1981, September). *Effectiveness of special education.* Paper presented at the Working Conference of Social Policy and Educational Leaders to Develop Strategies for Special Education in the 1980s, Wingspread, Racine, WI.

Glass, G. V., & Robbins, M. P. (1967). A critique of experiments on the role of neurological organization in reading performance. *Reading Research Quarterly, 3,* 5–52.

Gresham, F. (1986). On the malleability of intelligence: Unnecessary assumptions, reifications, and occlusion. *School Psychology Review, 15,* 261–262.

Gunnison, J., & Kaufman, N. L. (1982, August). Cognitive processing styles: Assessment and intervention. In *Assessment and diagnostic—prescriptive intervention: Diversity and perspective.* Symposium conducted at the annual meeting of the American Psychological Association, Washington, DC.

Hartlage, L. C. (1975). Neuropsychological approaches to predicting outcome of remedial educational strategies for learning disabled children. *Pediatric Psychology, 3,* 23–28.

Hartlage, L. C. (1981). Clinical application of neuropsychological test data: A case study. *School Psychology Review, 10,* 362–366.

Hartlage, L. C., & Reynolds, C. R. (1981). Neuropsychological assessment and the individualization of instruction. In G. W. Hynd & J. E. Obrzut (Eds.), *Neuropsychological assessment of the school-aged child: Issues and procedures.* New York: Grune & Stratton.

Hartlage, L. C., & Telzrow, C. F. (1983). Neuropsychological assessment. In K. D. Paget & B. A. Bracken (Eds.), *The psychoeducational assessment of preschool children.* New York: Grune & Stratton.

Hartlage, P. L., & Givens, T. S. (1982). Common neurological problems of school age children. In C. R. Reynolds & T. B. Gutkin (Eds.), *The handbook of school psychology.* New York: Wiley.

Hartlage, P. L., & Hartlage, L. C. (1973a). Comparison of hyperlexic and dyslexic children. *Neurology, 23,* 436–437.

Hartlage, P. L., & Hartlage, L. C. (1973b). *Dermatoglyphic markers in dyslexia.* Paper presented at the annual meeting of the Child Neurology Society, Atlanta, GA.

Hayes, M. C., & Jenkins, J. R. (1986). Reading instruction in special education resource rooms. *American Educational Research Journal, 23,* 161–190.

Haywood, H. C., & Switzky, H. N. (1986). The malleability of intelligence: Cognitive processes as a function of polygenic experiential interaction. *School Psychology Review, 15*(2), 245–255.

Horton, A. M. (1981). Behavioral neuropsychology in the schools. *School Psychology Review, 10,* 367–373.

Kephart, N. C. (1963). *The brain injured child in the classroom.* Chicago: National Society for Crippled Children and Adults.

Kirk, S. A., & Kirk, W. D. (1971). *Psycholinguistic learning disabilities: Diagnosis and remediation.* Urbana: University of Illinois Press.

Kirk, S. A., McCarthy, J., & Kirk, W. D. (1971). *Illinois Test of Psycholinguistic Abilities.* Urbana: University of Illinois Press.

Kolb, B., & Whishaw, I. Q. (1980). *Fundamentals of human neuropsychology.* San Francisco: Freeman.

Levine, M. D., Brooks, R., & Shonkoff, J. P. (1980). *A pediatric approach to learning disorders.* New York: Wiley.

Mann, L. (1979). *On the trail of process.* New York: Grune & Stratton.

Myers, P., & Hammill, D. (1976). *Methods of learning disorders* (2nd ed.). New York: Wiley.

Reynolds, C. R. (1981a). The neuropsychological basis of intelligence. In G. Hynd & J. Obrzut (Eds.), *Neuropsychological assessment of the school aged child: Issues and procedure.* New York: Grune & Stratton.

Reynolds, C. R. (1981b). Neuropsychological assessment and the habilitation of learning: Considerations in the search for the aptitude × treatment interaction. *School Psychology Review, 10,* 343–349.

Reynolds, C. R. (1985, August). *Putting the individual into the ATI.* Paper presented at the annual meeting of the American Psychological Association, Los Angeles.

Reynolds, C. R. (1986). Transactional models of intellectual development, yes. Deficit models of process remediation, no. *School Psychology Review, 15,* 256–260.

Vallett, R. E. (1967). *The remediation of learning disabilities: A handbook of psychoeducational resource programs.* Palo Alto, CA: Fearon.

Woodrow, H. (1919). *Brightness and dullness in children.* Philadelphia: Lippincott.

Ysseldyke, J., & Mirkin, P. K. (1982). The use of assessment information to plan instructional intervention: A review of research. In C. R. Reynolds & T. B. Gutkin (Eds.), *The handbook of school psychology.* New York: Wiley.

CECIL R. REYNOLDS
Texas A&M University

JULIA A. HICKMAN
*Bastrop Mental Health
Association*

FROSTIG, MARIANNE
ILLINOIS TEST OF PSYCHOLINGUISTIC ABILITIES
INFORMATION PROCESSING
KAUFMAN ASSESSMENT BATTERY FOR CHILDREN–II
LEARNING POTENTIAL ASSESSMENT DEVICE
NEUROLOGICAL ORGANIZATION
ORTON, SAMUEL T.
PERCEPTUAL TRAINING
SEQUENTIAL AND SIMULTANEOUS COGNITIVE
  PROCESSING

REMEDIATION, STRENGTH MODELS OF

See REMEDIATION, DEFICIT-CENTERED MODELS OF.

RENZULLI, JOSEPH S. (1936–   )

Joseph S. Renzulli received his BS in 1958 from Glassboro State College, his MEd in 1962 from Rutgers University, and his EdD in 1966 in educational psychology from the University of Virginia. He is currently the Neag Professor of Gifted Education and Talent Development at the University of Connecticut, where he also serves as the director of the National Research Center on the Gifted and Talented.

Renzulli's research has focused on identification and programming models for both gifted education and general school improvement. In this area, he has developed means of identifying high potential in individuals and creating educational models to maximize giftedness. Developed in the early 1970s, his Three Ring Conception of Giftedness (1978) is considered by many to be the foundation of a more flexible approach to identifying and developing high levels of potential in young people. The Enrichment Triad Model (Renzulli, 1984), a widely used approach for special programs for the gifted and talented, includes general exploratory activities, group training activities, and individual and small-group investigators of real problems. Renzulli is also credited with devising the Revolving Door Identification Model (Renzulli, Reis, & Smith, 1981), a flexible approach to identifying high potential in young people, and the Schoolwide Enrichment Model (Renzulli & Reis, 1997), a plan for general schoolwide enrichment that applies practices developed for the gifted and talented to a system that serves the highly able as well as providing all students a general upgrade of the curriculum.

Renzulli has contributed numerous books and articles to professional literature. His two most recent books are *Enriching Curriculum for All Students* (Renzulli & Gardner, 2000) and *Identification of Students for Gifted and Talented Programs* (Renzulli & Reis, 2004).

Joseph S. Renzulli

REFERENCES

Renzulli, J. S. (1978). What makes giftedness? Re-examining a definition. *Phi Delta Kappan, 60,* 180–184.

Renzulli, J. S. (1984). The triad/revolving door system: A research based approach to identification and programming for the gifted and talented. *Gifted Child Quarterly, 28,* 163–171.

Renzulli, J. S. (1994). *Schools for talent development: A practical plan for total school improvement.* Mansfield Center, CT: Creative Learning.

Renzulli, J. S., & Gardner, H. (2000). *Enriching curriculum for all students.* Thousand Oaks, CA: Sage.

Renzulli, J. S., & Reis, S. M. (1997). *The schoolwide enrichment model: A how-to guide for educational excellence.* Mansfield Center, CT: Creative Learning.

Renzulli, J. S., & Reis, S. M. (2004). *Identification of students for gifted and talented programs.* Thousand Oaks, CA: Sage.

Renzulli, J. S., Reis, S. M., & Smith, L. H. (1981). *The revolving door identification model.* Mansfield Center, CT: Creative Learning.

TAMARA J. MARTIN
*The University of Texas of the
  Permian Basin*

C. WILLIAMS
*Falcon School District 49,
  Colorado Springs, Colorado*
Third edition

REPEATED READING

Repeated reading is a remedial reading technique designed to improve fluency and indirectly increase comprehension. The method is based largely on the teaching implications of automatic information processing theory in reading (La-Berge & Samuels, 1974). In automaticity theory, fluent readers are assumed to decode text automatically; attention is therefore free for comprehension. Nonfluent, word-by-word readers, on the other hand, must focus excessive amounts of attention on decoding, making comprehension difficult. The purpose of repeated reading is to make decoding of connected discourse automatic; thus fluency is increased and the reader is able to concentrate on comprehension.

The method involves multiple oral rereadings of connected discourse until a prescribed level of fluency is attained. Samuels's (1979) method, intended as a supplement to developmental reading programs, consists of multiple rereadings of a short passage of from 50 to 200 words, depending on the skill of the student. Reading speed and number of word recognition errors are recorded for each repetition. When the fluency criterion is reached, the student moves on to a new passage.

Chomsky (1976) proposes a similar method. In this variation, students listen to a tape recording of a storybook while following the text. Students read and listen repeatedly to the text until oral reading fluency is achieved. In addition to reported gains in fluency and comprehension, the method of repeated reading is said to promote more positive attitudes toward reading in that it virtually ensures a successful reading experience (Kann, 1983).

Moyer (1982) offers a theoretical rationale for the potential effectiveness of the method with disabled readers. She suggests that for some poor readers the amount of repetition/redundancy offered by traditional reading programs is insufficient to permit the acquisition of reading. Repeated reading of entire passages, however, maximizes redundancy at all levels of written expression. Thus readers are given much practice in using syntactic and semantic cues, as well as in acquiring knowledge of graphophonemic word structure.

REFERENCES

Chomsky, C. (1976). After decoding: What? *Language Arts, 53,* 288–296.

Kann, R. (1983). The method of repeated readings: Expanding the neurological impress method for use with disabled readers. *Journal of Learning Disabilities, 16,* 90–92.

LaBerge, D., & Samuels, S. J. (1974). Toward a theory of automatic information processing in reading. *Cognitive Psychology, 6,* 293–323.

Moyer, S. B. (1982). Repeated reading. *Journal of Learning Disabilities, 15,* 619–623.

Samuels, S. J. (1979). The method of repeated readings. *Reading Teacher, 32,* 403–408.

TIMOTHY D. LACKAYE
*Hunter College, City University
of New York*

READING
READING REMEDIATION

RESEARCH IN SPECIAL EDUCATION

Research in special education is the means through which knowledge and methods of treatment are acquired and verified for application to persons exhibiting special needs. Such research encompasses a wide range of methodologies, subjects, issues, and data collection and analysis techniques. Although all special education research contributes to the ever-increasing knowledge base of the field, all types are different to some extent. Research ranges from case studies to single subject and group designs. Each method differs from the others in terms of ease of use, confidence and validity of results obtained, and generality of findings.

Through the process of research, advances are made in what is known about disabilities and how to prevent and treat them through education and training. The importance of research methodology in validating the findings of research must be emphasized. Many hypotheses related to developmental disabilities are advanced in the form of anecdotal reporting and logical analyses. But these hypotheses are speculative, and before being applied to the special education field they must be subjected to verification through research. Only by careful study through controlled research designs can research findings be considered useful and be applied to persons other than those involved in the research study.

Special education research is usually applied research; in other words, it is conducted primarily in the places where handicapped persons live, work, and attend school. For example, research has been conducted in group homes, sheltered workshops, resource rooms, and the community. Although less rigorous than research in the experimental laboratory, special education research has the advantage of being relevant to and practical for the subjects involved; that is, the issues studied are usually of high priority for the well-being of the people involved because of their functional relevance. Through rigorously applied research programs, professionals in special education can confirm observations by testing hypotheses on persons with special needs and verifying known effects with different populations. In the long view, research provides a solid foundation of knowledge from which to increase and maintain the intellectual vitality of special education (Drew, Preator, & Buchanan, 1982).

Observation of phenomena is inherent in all research and particularly in special education research. Naturalistic observation is one way to collect information about subjects. With this technique, the researcher observes a person (or group of people) and makes extensive records of the subject's behaviors. The purpose is to be as descriptive as possible to provide a post hoc analysis of possible mediating factors. For example, Currin and Rowland (1985) assessed the communication ability of persons who were labeled profoundly handicapped. These researchers videotaped interactions among adult teachers and 15 nonverbal youths and then divided the communication behaviors exhibited by the subjects into eight categories. The researchers provided no training or other intervention. Such a naturalistic account is important because it can provide an accurate description of specific skills in a certain population. This description can, in turn, later be used as a base from which to provide more precise analyses or from which to guide subsequent interventions. Authors of the majority of articles published from 1983 to 1985 in four major special education research journals used naturalistic observation for collecting and reporting their respective information.

Another important characteristic of research is that of systematically manipulating variables and observing the effects of such manipulations on other variables. Typically, a researcher wants to measure accurately how the dependent variable (e.g., subject behaviors targeted for change) is affected when the subject is exposed to the independent variable (one or more factors manipulated by the researcher). Some examples of dependent variables in special education research are number of words read, frequency of correct expressive signs made, number of problems solved, percentage of inappropriate social behaviors exhibited, and frequency of interruptions. Some examples of independent variables in research are teacher praise, repetition of task, removal of child from activity, use of a particular prompting strategy, and administration of drugs.

A third characteristic of most research is use of an experimental method to determine the extent to which independent variables are functionally related to changes in dependent variables. Researchers carefully design how and when their subjects are exposed to independent variables. Experimental designs minimize the possibility that uncontrolled, extraneous factors play a part in changing dependent variables. Research that is not adequately designed to decrease the impact of extraneous factors must be viewed with caution (Sidman, 1960).

A final characteristic of research is analysis of findings. Typically, researchers have used statistical methods to determine whether their results demonstrate a strong (significant) change. Whether the research compares a pre- and postintervention difference, or whether the results obtained from one subject exposed to an independent variable are compared with those of another subject who is not exposed, the intent of the analysis is to assess the degree of difference and make a statement as to whether such a difference could be expected by chance. Statistical methods used in special education research include t-tests, analysis of variance, analysis of covariance, and regression analysis. Numerous authors have addressed the role of statistics and research (e.g., Edwards, 1985; Galfo, 1983). In addition, researchers can determine whether their work has caused an observable practical change in their subjects. This determination is termed functional or clinical significance. For example, assume that a researcher is testing a new method for teaching handicapped students to tell time. For those subjects who learn to use a clock during their daily routine, a definite functional skill has been learned regardless of whether a statistical test indicates statistical significance.

A research design describes the manner in which subjects are exposed to independent variables. Researchers must structure their designs to meet basic criteria that permit confidence in results obtained by the research. All researchers must control for extraneous variables entering into and possibly affecting the research outcome. In other words, the dependent variables measured by the researcher must be affected only by variables manipulated by the researcher. Campbell and Stanley (1963) proposed eight factors that may cause changes in dependent measures regardless of the effect of the independent variables studied. These eight threats to the validity of research follow.

1. *History:* experiences (in addition to the independent variable) of the subjects. For example, assume that a student is a subject in a research project focusing on peer tutoring to increase appropriate social skills. If the peer tutor becomes ill and misses 3 days of the study, causing the subject to be in training for a fewer number of sessions than the other subjects, this will threaten the validity of the results.

2. *Maturation:* uncontrolled changes in subjects. For example, handicapped infants may become fatigued and lose attentiveness over a few hours or late in the day. Behavior changes owed to weariness, hunger, or aging illustrate a maturation threat.

3. *Testing:* the effect of taking a first test on subsequent tests. For example, students who repeatedly take a test improve their test scores over time.

4. *Instrumentation:* changes in the devices measuring behavior of subjects. For example, mechanical items such as a video camera or cumulative recorder may fail to operate properly. Human observers may become bored or fatigued and as a result unknowingly alter their scoring.

5. *Statistical regression:* subjects selected for inclusion in a study because of extreme scores on some test or mea-

sure. For example, assume some learning-disabled students are selected for a research study on improving reading. These particular students are selected because of their low scores on a reading achievement test given as a pretest measure. The experimental treatment is applied, and then a posttest is given (the same reading achievement assessment). Any increases in posttest scores cannot be assumed to be related to the experimental manipulation because there is a tendency for low scores on a test to rise on subsequent testing.

6. *Selection:* subjects for experimental and control groups. If a project involves the comparison of two subject groups, the research results may be a function of the subjects' being different initially rather than a function of the experimental manipulation. For example, assume that a school district receives financial support to hire extra vocational counselors and trainers to work with handicapped students for a year in vocational training. At the end of the year, the superintendent of the district decides to assess whether the extra staff made a positive impact on the vocational success of the students. The administrator arranges for a standard vocational assessment to be given to all of the vocational students who received the assistance and to students in another district who did not. Differences in the assessment scores may be due to a basic difference between the students of the two districts.

7. *Experimental mortality:* losing subjects from a research study. For example, researchers frequently group subjects along relevant variables such as age, sex, and handicapping condition. If several subjects in one group drop out of the study for any reason, any results of the research showing a difference between the two groups may be due to the loss of the subjects rather than an effect of the independent variable.

8. *Selection-maturation interaction, etc:* a combination of any of the previous factors.

According to Campbell and Stanley, if a researcher arranges the experimental design to minimize the possibility of the mentioned potential alternative explanations, then any changes in the dependent measures can be confidently assumed to be due to the experimental intervention.

A second criterion for all research designs concerns the extent to which results can generalize (be applied directly) to other subjects or conditions. In special education particularly, the results of research need to be relevant to persons similar to those involved in the particular research project. Campbell and Stanley recognized four factors that reduce confidence in generalizing the results of a research study to special needs persons not participating in that study or in settings other than the experimental one:

1. *Effect of testing:* subjects who are tested may be affected by testing and thus react differently than an untested population. For example, assume that handicapped students are enlisted as subjects in a research project testing the impact of an innovative procedure for increasing spelling accuracy. The subjects are given a preintervention spelling test followed by treatment. Finally, the subjects complete a posttest. The subjects may do better than other students simply because they were given a spelling test before the intervention.

2. *Effect of selection of subjects and experimental variable:* subjects may be more or less sensitive to the experimental intervention than other students. For instance, a special education classroom may be used extensively by special education researchers for research purposes. If the students in such a classroom are frequently involved as research subjects, and if there are constant visitors and observers in the classroom, then these students may be more or less sensitive to any experimental manipulations than students in other special education classes.

3. *Effect of experimental arrangements:* conditions of the research itself may affect subjects in a special way. This threat exists, for example, when students from several classes are randomly selected to be in an experimental group and are taken to a new classroom for the study. Subjects who are in an unfamiliar environment with unfamiliar people may react differently to experimental procedures than those in their familiar surroundings.

4. *Multiple treatment / interference of previous treatments:* previous treatments may have effects on subjects that are unknown, and when working with humans as subjects, locating experimentally naive individuals can be extremely difficult. For example, some researchers study the effect of different variations of a prompting strategy known as stimulus-delay on academic skills. If they were to use the same subjects repeatedly in different experiments, over time these subjects might become familiar with the stimulus-delay method and do better or worse than subjects not initially exposed.

It is important to note that to the greatest extent possible, research in special education must meet these concerns of generalization. The importance of educational research lies with both the improvement of the particular subjects in a research project and the belief that the results and knowledge gained from the research can be applied to other persons with special needs.

All research projects involve either one or more subjects. Single-subject and group designs are labels that describe the primary categories used in special education. The majority of articles published between 1983 and 1985 in four journals devoted exclusively to research on special needs incorporated a group experimental design, either random or matched. A variety of single-subject designs were used as well.

Typically, a single-subject design involves one subject being exposed to all of the experimental conditions involved in the research. One unique characteristic of such designs is that an individual is compared with his or her own performance only. The measurement of behavior takes place before and repeatedly during the intervention. This permits a comparison of an individual's performance at regular points in time. Such within-subject analyses (Sulzer-Azaroff & Mayer, 1977) potentially yield richer information on the performance of individuals than the traditional experimental and control group designs that stress comparing average scores of large groups of subjects. Single-subject designs are particularly useful with both mildly and severely handicapped persons.

The single-subject designs are withdrawal of treatment, alternating treatment, and multiple baseline. Each is relatively easy to use in a classroom, has strong validity, and has been proven useful in many classroom situations. These designs are adaptable for use when targeting academic and social behavior, when attempting to increase or decrease a response, or when working with a single student or group.

The withdrawal-of-treatment evaluation technique typically involves four distinct phases. First, the researcher measures the subject's performance on the target skill prior to a formal attempt at changing the instructional method (baseline). In some cases, the baseline consists of a previous intervention or teaching method other than the intervention of interest. Once this phase is completed, the experimenter intervenes with the independent variable(s) selected. There is frequent measurement of subject performance, usually either per lesson or daily. After the subject's performance stabilizes, the experimenter terminates the intervention and continues to measure the subject's behavior during this second baseline phase. Finally, the researcher reinstates the instruction and continues to measure performance.

Correa, Poulson, and Salzberg (1984) used this design to test the effects of a graduated prompting procedure on the behavior of toy grasping in a 2-year-old visually impaired and mentally retarded youngster. The general procedure involved the presentation of a noise-making toy in front of the child and the opportunity for the child to grasp it with no assistance. If the child did so within 10 seconds, he was given praise and the opportunity to manipulate the toy. The experimenters first conducted a series of baseline trials and found that the child touched the toy only when assisted. During the first treatment condition, unassisted touching of the toy increased to a mean of 7 percent of the trials. Although the following return-to-baseline phase resulted in no unassisted touching of the toy, the subsequent treatment condition increased touching once again to a mean of approximately 18 percent.

The rationale and strength of this design are apparent. If there is improvement in performance during the times in which the intervention is in effect, and deterioration in performance during the baseline conditions, then the researcher can have confidence that the teaching is the factor resulting in the learning. Such a research design demonstrates experimental control of behavior (Hersen & Barlow, 1976) and minimizes the possibility that uncontrolled factors are responsible for the changes in the subject's performance. On the other hand, there are times when a withdrawal-of-treatment design is not used (Tawney & Gast, 1984). Ethical concerns may contraindicate withdrawing an intervention if the target behavior is very important (e.g., aggression toward peers) or if a clear, clinically significant change in behavior occurs in the first intervention phase. Methodological concerns may also argue against the use of this design when the target behavior is one that, once learned, is not likely to return to preintervention levels (e.g., learning addition).

The alternating-treatments design involves the exposure of the subject to two or more different treatment strategies for the same behaviors. The treatments are alternated over time. Although obtaining a baseline measure of the behavior is desirable, the researcher need not do this because the primary variable of interest is observed changes in the behavior with respect to the different treatments.

An important characteristic of this design is the use of teacher instructions or cues to signal the student as to which intervention is in effect. Typically, the design is used as follows. The researcher first develops the different strategies and selects a means for notifying the subject of each. The researcher also determines a schedule of when each treatment is to be used. The schedule must allow for each treatment to be used an equal number of times in random order. Once the research begins, the experimenter alternates the conditions, measures the subject's behavior, and records it separately for each treatment.

Barrera and Sulzer-Azaroff (1983) used such a design to compare two different language training programs (oral and total communication) in an attempt to improve expressive labeling of three autistic children. Each day, subjects were exposed to both training programs, but the sequence in which they were used alternated randomly. The experimenter signaled which treatment was in use by providing either vocal cues only (oral communication training) or vocal and gestural cues (total communication).

With this design, a teacher can immediately start to remediate a behavior rather than waiting for the rate of behavior to stabilize during a baseline period. In addition, this design can be used with behaviors irreversible once learned. However, this design is unusual in that it does not reflect the "natural" form of classroom instruction whereby one treatment strategy is used consistently over a period of time. There is also the possibility that the subject might be affected by the sequence of the various treatments. Last, a behavior that changes slowly will not be discovered with this design owing to the frequent switching of independent variables.

The multiple-baseline design involves measurement of multiple target behaviors, subjects, or situations. The targeted responses, for example, may be from one subject, different behaviors of several subjects, or one behavior exhibited by a subject in different situations. After obtaining baseline measures, the researcher applies the intervention to just one behavior while continuing to collect baseline data on the others. The intervention is subsequently applied to the remaining targets in a successive fashion. This design objectively demonstrates the success of intervention if a target response changes only when the intervention is applied to it.

The multiple-baseline design can be used in a variety of different situations. First, it is excellent for use when teaching a student similar behaviors. For example, Haring (1985) used such a design when teaching students labeled moderately/severely handicapped to play with different toys. Haring first noted that the children exhibited no appropriate play with any of four different toys. He then trained the children to play correctly with one toy while noting whether spontaneous play occurred with any of the other three toys. Although the children learned to play correctly with the trained toy, there was no generalized play to the other three toys. The children played correctly only after receiving direct training with the other toys.

Such a design is used across individuals and situations in the same manner as with behaviors. Foxx, McMorrow, and Mennemeier (1984) trained two groups of three adults labeled mildly and moderately retarded to exhibit appropriate social skills such as being polite and responding to criticism. After obtaining a preintervention assessment on all subjects, they taught one group while assessing the other. After several sessions, the subjects in the second group received the training. A multiple baseline across settings is used in a similar fashion. Instead of targeting different behaviors or students, the teacher assesses one behavior of a single student in different situations (e.g., at recess, at lunch, in reading class) and applies the intervention in one setting at a time.

There are limitations associated with the multiple-baseline design (Tawney & Gast, 1984). One concerns repeated testing during the baseline conditions; this could potentially continue for many sessions, especially for the third or fourth behavior (or setting or person). Such a lengthy assessment period precludes training and increases the potential for student frustration. However, this problem is minimized by either providing some type of treatment during baseline—so that the student receives some intervention, albeit not the one of interest—or by collecting baseline assessment infrequently. For example, although a minimum of three assessments is recommended, they could be done at random points throughout the baseline phase. Another disadvantage concerns measuring several behaviors or the behaviors of several different subjects, possibly even in different settings. Such a demanding requirement could be time-consuming and impractical in some situations.

There are several research methodologies incorporating a group design approach, such as random group, matched group, counterbalanced, and norm referenced.

In the random-group design, subjects are randomly selected from a defined population and assigned to two groups. Both groups are given the same pretest. One group is then given the experimental treatment while the other group is given either no treatment or a treatment that will be compared with the experimental treatment. Finally, both groups are given the same posttest. Wang and Birch (1984) used the random-group design when comparing the instructional effectiveness of two different remedial programs for handicapped students. A total of 179 children were randomly assigned to either a part-day resource room or a full-day class representing an adaptive learning environments model (ALEM). Dependent measures consisted of scores from standardized achievement tests, student attitude surveys, and classroom processes. The results indicated that on the average, students in the ALEM class progressed more than students in the part-day resource room.

Another design, matched group, involves matching subjects in both groups as closely as possible with each other. The matching can occur on variables such as age, sex, learning histories, or intelligence. The variables along which the matching will occur depend on the purposes of the research. For example, Jago, Jago, and Hart (1984) matched subjects in the experimental and control groups along the dimensions of age and etiology of disability. Pretesting, experimental manipulation, and posttesting are done in a manner similar to that in the random-group design.

Counterbalanced design involves exposing subjects to identical experimental interventions but in a different sequence. For example, Carr and Durand (1985) assessed the rate of disruptive behavior exhibited by four developmentally disabled children in four conditions: (1) an easy task with constant teacher attention, (2) a difficult task with constant teacher attention, (3) an easy task with limited teacher attention, and (4) a difficult task with limited teacher attention. Each child was observed in each of these four situations, but in a varying sequential order. For example, one child was exposed to easy task/limited attention, easy task/constant attention, and difficult task/constant attention. A second child was observed in the order of difficult task/constant attention, easy task/constant attention, and easy task/limited attention.

With the norm-referenced design, only one group of subjects is exposed to the experimental intervention, and standardized tests are used for pretest and posttest assessments. The results are then compared with results obtained by the standardization for that particular test; in other words, the standardization sample serves as the control group. For example, Gersten and Maggs (1982) assessed cognitive and academic changes in a group of moderately retarded children and adolescents over a 5-year period. The dependent measure was the score of the Stanford-Binet Intelligence Test. The independent measure was the DISTAR Language Program. After almost 5 years of language training, the subjects were given the Stanford-Binet, and postexperimental scores were compared with preexperimental scores on the same test. The researchers found that the subjects were gaining points on their IQ scores faster than the population of children used to standardize the test. The norm-referenced design has serious problems, since seldom will the research sample match a test's standardization sample or all key variables. Standardization samples of tests are just not good control groups.

Group designs are particularly useful when testing the effectiveness of a treatment package or when addressing questions concerning the magnitude of an effect in terms of the number of people positively or negatively affected. They are the design of choice when testing for a general effect. However, giving treatment to one group of subjects and withholding treatment from another group can be ethically questionable. This is a particular concern in the context of educational treatment, but it can be minimized by offering the control group a treatment different from the experimental intervention, or perhaps the treatment in use prior to the experimental intervention. Another limitation concerns the practical difficulty of finding a sufficient number of matched subjects. Special needs people have unique strengths and disabilities, and finding truly matched subjects may be difficult to achieve.

One other disadvantage with some group designs concerns the portrayal of results in statistical means (averages). One can determine a general outcome when experimental and control group averages are compared, but any analysis of the effect the experimental intervention has on individuals is difficult. Reporting averages ignores the number of subjects positively affected, negatively affected, or not affected at all.

A unique problem with a norm-referenced design is that virtually all of the standardized tests developed to date have used nondisabled persons for standardization. Using the results of such a group to assess disabled subjects is questionable. However, tests (e.g., the American Association of Mental Deficiency Adaptive Behavior Scales) are being developed using a developmentally disabled population for standardization purposes. This could make the use of norm-referenced designs more valid.

Meta-analysis is a research approach providing a quantitative analysis of multiple studies, allowing one to address specific research questions across many studies. Kavale and Furness (1999) provide multiple examples of how meta-analysis can be useful in special education, especially in the evaluation of intervention programs.

Research conducted in special education has increased knowledge in the field and at the same time has raised new questions. One important concern is the ethical conduct of the special educator while doing research. Experimenters who use humans as subjects have the responsibility of providing stringent safeguards to protect the health and well-being of their subjects. Professionals in special education must be particularly sensitive to these concerns in that developmentally disabled subjects may not be capable of understanding the issues involved in the research and thus may not be able to give truly informed consent.

Research safeguards to protect subject rights do exist, and professionals must abide by them. Kelty (1981) summarized several key guidelines for researchers to consider when planning studies using humans. Generally, these involve informed consent on the part of the subject so that the subject truly understands the purpose of the study, any risks or benefits to the subject, and the option to volunteer or to withdraw so that there is maximum possibility for benefit with minimum possibility of harm.

A standard component of research studies is a description of reliability procedures to verify that the primary data collector is accurate in recording the responses of the subjects. Unfortunately, few researchers present a similar case verifying that an experimental treatment is actually applied as proposed. This issue has been termed integrity of treatment (Salend, 1984) and is crucial for confidence in research results. For example, if an experimenter inadvertently implements a different intervention than the one planned, relating the proposed experimental method to the results would be erroneous. Integrity of treatment may be verified with little extra effort on the part of the research designers. As reported in Zane, Handen, Mason, and Geffin (1984), the integrity check can be made part of the traditional reliability check. The reliability scorer notes whether the person implementing the experimental program uses the correct intervention and scores the subject response correctly. By presenting both sets of data, readers can judge to what extent the proposed intervention is actually implemented.

What are some recognized areas of special education in which more research could profitably be done? One area is diagnosis. Techniques that accurately assess the etiology of a person's deficits and discovery of the youngest age at which a true diagnosis can be achieved for various handicapping conditions would have a significant impact. Another area concerns the success of mainstreaming. Ideally, a solid research base should exist to support mainstreaming as well as to delineate ways of making it more successful. Several important questions can be addressed. What is the optimal class ratio of children labeled normal and developmentally disabled? How does mainstreaming affect the individual student in terms of academic and social success? What effect is there, if any, on the students labeled normal? Answers to these questions obtained from systematic research will shed light on the future direction of mainstreaming and lead to even further improvements for disabled people.

One final research area to pursue is the extent to which practitioners in the field actually apply the findings from special education research (Englert, 1983). The purpose of research is to provide information that can be used to improve the lives of special needs persons. To what extent do the techniques and knowledge of special education professionals reflect the most recent research findings? If research findings are not being used by teachers and other special education professionals, the reasons must be sought and corrected. Such a discrepancy may be due to limited access to sources of research findings, a possible lack of skills training, or research that is not useful to practitioners. Whatever the reason(s), research findings must make their way to the people who can use them to enhance the lives of special needs people.

REFERENCES

Barrera, R. D., & Sulzer-Azaroff, B. (1983). An alternating treatment comparison of oral and total communication training programs with echolalic autistic children. *Journal of Applied Behavior Analysis, 16,* 379–394.

Campbell, D. T., & Stanley, J. C. (1963). *Experimental and quasi-experimental designs for research.* Chicago: Rand McNally College.

Carr, E. G., & Durand, V. M. (1985). Reducing behavior problems through functional communication training. *Journal of Applied Behavior Analysis, 18,* 111–126.

Correa, V. I., Poulson, C. L., & Salzberg, C. L. (1984). Training and generalization of reach-grasp behavior in blind, retarded young children. *Journal of Applied Behavior Analysis, 17,* 57–69.

Currin, F. M., & Rowland, C. M. (1985). Communicative assessment of nonverbal youths with severe/profound mental retardation. *Mental Retardation, 2,* 52–62.

Drew, C. J., Preator, K., & Buchanan, M. L. (1982). Research and researchers in special education. *Exceptional Education Quarterly, 2,* 47–56.

Edwards, A. L. (1985). *Multiple regression and the analysis of variance and covariance.* New York: Freeman.

Englert, C. S. (1983). Measuring special education teacher effectiveness. *Exceptional Children, 50,* 247–254.

Foxx, R. M., McMorrow, M. J., & Mennemeier, M. (1984). Teaching social/vocational skills to retarded adults with a modified table game: An analysis of generalization. *Journal of Applied Behavior Analysis, 17,* 343–352.

Galfo, A. J. (1983). *Educational research design and data analysis.* New York: University Press of America.

Gersten, R. M., & Maggs, A. (1982). Teaching the general case to moderately retarded children: Evaluation of a five-year project. *Analysis & Intervention in Developmental Disabilities, 2,* 329–334.

Haring, T. G. (1985). Teaching between class generalization of toy play behavior to handicapped children. *Journal of Applied Behavior Analysis, 18,* 127–139.

Hersen, M., & Barlow, D. H. (1976). *Single-case experimental designs: Strategies for studying behavior change.* New York: Pergamon.

Jago, J. L., Jago, A. G., & Hart, M. (1984). An evaluation of the total communication approach for teaching language skills to developmentally delayed preschool children. *Education & Training of the Mentally Retarded, 19,* 175–182.

Kavale, K., & Furness, S. (1999). Effectiveness of special education. In C. R. Reynolds & T. B. Gutkin (Eds.), *The handbook of school psychology* (3rd ed.). New York: Wiley.

Kelty, M. F. (1981). Protection of persons who participate in applied research. In G. T. Hannah, W. P. Christian, & H. B. Clark (Eds.), *Preservation of client rights: A handbook for practitioners providing therapeutic, educational, and rehabilitative services.* New York: Free Press.

Salend, S. J. (1984). Integrity of treatment in special education research. *Mental Retardation, 6,* 309–315.

Sidman, M. (1960). *Tactics of scientific research.* New York: Basic Books.

Sulzer-Azaroff, B., & Mayer, G. R. (1977). *Applying behavior-analysis procedures with children and youth.* New York: Holt, Rinehart, & Winston.

Tawney, J. W., & Gast, D. L. (1984). *Single subject research in special education.* Columbus, OH: Merrill.

Wang, M. C., & Birch, J. W. (1984). Comparison of a full-time mainstreaming program and a resource room approach. *Exceptional Children, 51,* 33–40.

Zane, T., Handen, B. L., Mason, S. A., & Geffin, C. (1984). Teaching symbol identification: A comparison between standard prompting and intervening response procedures. *Analysis & Intervention in Developmental Disabilities, 4,* 367–377.

THOMAS ZANE
Johns Hopkins University

MEASUREMENT
MULTIPLE BASELINE DESIGN
MULTIPLE REGRESSION
REGRESSION (STATISTICAL)

RESIDENTIAL FACILITIES

Residential facilities in America have been provided a variety of labels, including school, hospital, colony, prison, and asylum. Both the roles and the labels that institutions for the disabled have taken on have been reflective of the social and cultural climate of the time (Wolfensberger, 1975). The periods that had major influence on residential institutions have been characterized as follows: early optimism, 1800–1860; disillusionment, 1860–1900; reconsideration, 1920–1920; ebb and flow, 1930–1950; new reconsideration, 1950–1960; and enthusiasm, 1960–1970 (Cegelka & Prehm, 1982).

In the United States no public provisions were made for

residential placement and care for the disabled until the 1800s. Prior to that time individuals with disabilities were placed in a variety of settings. These ranged from poorhouses to charitable centers. Such institutions provided no systematic attempts at rehabilitation or training of individuals with disabilities. Rather, they served as facilities that stored and maintained individuals with and without disabilities. It has been estimated that as late as 1850, 60 percent of the inhabitants of all institutions in the United States were deaf, blind, insane, or mentally retarded (National Advisory Committee for the Handicapped, 1976).

The first residential institution designed for individuals with disabilities was established in 1817. That year the American Asylum for the Education and Institution of the Deaf was established in Hartford, Connecticut. In 1819 a second school, for the blind, was established in Watertown, Massachusetts; it was named the New England Asylum for the Blind. During this period and continuing until the Civil War, a number of eastern states established residential schools for the deaf, blind, orphaned, and mentally retarded (National Advisory Committee for the Handicapped, 1976).

The development of residential institutions for the mentally retarded in the United States began in the 1840s. The growth of such institutions was strongly influenced by the work of Johann Guggenbuhl in Switzerland. In 1848 Samuel Howe convinced the Massachusetts legislature to allocate funds for the establishment of the first public setting for individuals with retardation. That same year Harvey Wilbur founded the first private institution for treating retarded persons. These institutions were designed to provide education and training to mildly, and occasionally to moderately, handicapped children and adolescents. After the Civil War, residential institutions fell into disfavor. However, the latter portion of the century was marked by continued growth, in both numbers of facilities and numbers of individuals within those facilities. As the nineteenth century came to a close, it became clear that institutions were not accomplishing training that would lead to the reintegration of individuals with disabilities into the community. By 1900, 7,000 individuals with disabilities were housed in institutions. During this time, the role of residential institutions changed significantly. Their emphasis shifted from training to prevention of retardation through systematic segregation of the mentally retarded from society (Wolfensberger, 1975).

The view of institutions held by state legislatures and the general public fluctuated until after World War II. By this time institutions were overcrowded and understaffed. The effects of the baby boom in the late 1940s and the early 1950s placed further pressures on these settings. After World War II, a growing acknowledgment of the existence and needs of the exceptional person was experienced by the nation. This awareness was fostered by parental pressures, returning servicemen's needs, professional enthusiasm, and the availability of public and private funding. These factors led to a reevaluation of procedures, research, and a new understanding of individuals with disabilities and the role of institutions in their treatment, care, and training. By 1969, 190,000 individuals with disabilities were housed in institutions (Cegelka & Prehm, 1982).

By the 1970s a new view of the dangers and inadequacies of institutions was recognized. The courts played a major role in bringing this realization to the fore. *Watt v. Stickney* (1972) affirmed mentally retarded persons' right to treatment. *Lessard v. Schmidt* (1972) ensured due process for institutionalized individuals. *Souder v. Brennan* (1973) outlawed involuntary servitude of institutionalized persons. The federal government also caused major reforms with the passage of Title XIX (Medicaid) provisions in 1971. These provisions brought institutions under the same controls and review processes as other service providers for individuals with disabilities. A nationwide push to return disabled individuals to the community was experienced. Deinstitutionalization became a social, fiscal, and moral goal within each of the states. Between the late 1960s and the early 1980s, the number of disabled persons being served by public residential institutions declined by over 50,000. At the same time, staff-to-client ratios improved along with the physical quality of many institutions. During the 1980s and 1990s, nearly half of state-operated residential facilities for persons with mental retardation were closed in favor of movement to group homes and other less restrictive environments.

To facilitate the deinstitutionalization process, community-based alternatives were developed and expanded during the 1970s and 1980s. During the same period, a number of small institutions (less than 100 residents) were built. Small group homes, foster placements, semi-independent residences, and nursing homes were heavily relied on to handle individuals leaving institutional placements and as alternatives to initial placement in large residential institutions. Contrary to expectation, few of the older large institutions were closed, and many of the disabled stayed within those larger institutions. Changes in the nation's economic stability during the late 1970s and early 1980s also led to many difficulties in realizing the successful integration of the majority of disabled persons into the community (Cegelka & Prehmn, 1982).

Current data concerning residential institutions for individuals with mental retardation reveal a clear picture of institutions in general throughout the United States. In summary, facilities with 15 or fewer residents increased over 500 percent from 1977 to 1982; they are continuing to increase. Each year in the recent past, 17 percent of residential facilities have closed or moved, displacing approximately 2.7 percent of all retarded individuals. The large institutions are far more stable. Within these institutions (generally exceeding 300 clients), the profoundly retarded make up the largest portion of residents. In public institutions, staff-to-client ratio is approximately 1.6 to 1. In these facilities, the direct-care staff ratio is .82 to 1 and the clinical staff ratio is .32 to 1. On the other hand, in community-based residential facilities, the functioning level of the individuals served is notably higher while staff ratios are notably lower (Hill et al., 1985; Eplle, Jacobson, & Janicki, 1985).

From these data, general conclusions may be drawn concerning the future of residential institutions. First, large residential facilities will continue to provide services for individuals with disabilities. These institutions will serve increasingly involved persons. This will be done at an increased actual dollar cost per resident. Community-based residential programs will grow as alternative residential settings for disabled individuals. These community-based programs will provide services to the majority of previously unserved individuals. Such settings will provide financially and morally appropriate residential services to a large percent of all individuals with disabilities, thus reducing, but not eliminating, the need for the large residential institutions.

REFERENCES

Cegelka, P. T., & Prehm, H. J. (1982). *Mental retardation*. Columbus, OH: Merrill.

Eplle, W. A., Jacobson, J. W., & Janicki, M. R. (1985). Staffing ratios in public institutions for persons with mental retardation. *Mental Retardation, 23,* 115–124.

Giffth, R. G. (1985). Symposium: Residential institutions. *Mental Retardation, 23,* 105–106.

Hill, B. K., Bruininks, R. H., Lakin, K. C., Hauber, F. A., & McGuire, S. P. (1985). Stability of residential facilities for people who are mentally retarded 1977–1982. *Mental Retardation, 23,* 108–114.

National Advisory Committee for the Handicapped. (1976). *The unfinished revolution: Education for the handicapped, 1976 annual report*. Washington, DC: U.S. Government Printing Office.

Wolfensberger, W. (1975). *The origin and nature of our institutional models*. Syracuse, NY: Human Policy.

ALAN HILTON
Seattle University

HISTORY OF SPECIAL EDUCATION
PHILOSOPHY OF EDUCATION FOR INDIVIDUALS WITH
  DISABILITIES

RESISTANT BEHAVIOR, MANAGEMENT OF

One of the most vexing problems facing educators is managing students' resistance. Serious noncompliant behavior is the most frequent reason young children are referred for psychiatric services (Kuczynski, Kochanska, Radke-Yarrow, & Girnius-Brown, 1987). The comorbidity between emotional/behavioral disorders and defiance has been especially high

(Cullinan, 2002). However, students with learning disabilities and those at risk also display serious noncompliant behaviors (McWhirter, McWhirter, McWhirter, & McWhirter, 1998; Smith, 1998).

Walker, Ramsey, and Gresham (2004) state that noncompliance serves as a "gateway behavior" for children developing serious antisocial behavior. It can lead to tantrums, uncooperativeness, aggression, and stealing, and ultimately culminate with delinquency. Walker and colleagues also believe that, in some instances, effectively dealing with noncompliance can prevent children from developing more serious antisocial behavior. The most common approaches for treating noncompliance involve a combination of providing highly contingent positive and negative consequences; providing clear, direct, and specific commands; and having children self-monitor and self-evaluate their behavior (Rhode, Morgan, & Young, 1983; Walker et al., 2004; Zirpoli & Melloy, 1997).

Dimensions of Resistance

Compliance typically has been conceptualized as obedience to adult directives and prohibitions, cooperation with requests and suggestions, or the willingness to accept suggestions in teaching situations (Rocissano, Slade, & Lynch, 1987). From this definition, Zirpoli and Melloy (1997) inferred that noncompliance involves disobedience to directives, uncooperativeness with requests and suggestions, and unwillingness to accept suggestions. Schoen (1986) defined noncompliance in a child as responding to an adult request by refusing to comply, providing no response, or engaging in some unrequested behavior.

Oppositional Defiant Disorder

Severe oppositional behaviors have become so pervasive that they were classified as a psychiatric disorder over 20 years ago in the third edition of the *Diagnostic and Statistical Manual of Mental Disorders* (*DSM-III;* American Psychiatric Association [APA], 1980). However, the term *Oppositional Defiant Disorder* first appeared in the revised version of the third edition (*DSM-III-R*). The current diagnostic criteria, which can be found in the fourth edition (*DSM-IV-TR*), require a pattern of negativistic, hostile, and defiant behavior lasting 6 months in which at least four of the following eight symptoms are present: temper outbursts, arguing with adults, refusing to follow adult requests, deliberately annoying people, blaming others for own mistakes, touchy or easily annoyed by others, angry and resentful, and spiteful or vindictive.

Although the inclusion of oppositional defiant disorder in the *DSM* nosology has been questioned (Kazdin, 1989; McMahon & Forehand, 1988), noncompliance represents a practical problem for parents, teachers, and clinicians. As a psychiatric disorder, it is believed to occur in between 2 percent and 16 percent of children, depending on the nature of the population sample and methods of estimation (APA, 2000). These estimates should not come as a surprise, because children typically disobey about 20 percent to 40 percent of parental requests and commands (Forehand, 1977).

Targets for Intervention

The literature on noncompliance typically has focused on modifying children's behaviors because they are often seen as the source of the problem. However, Walker et al. (2004) insightfully noted that "whether or not a child complies with an adult directive has as much to do with how the command is framed and delivered as it does with the consequences, or lack thereof, that follow the delivery" (p. 309). Walker et al. went on to describe the difference between *alpha* and *beta* commands. Alpha commands are given in a clear, direct, and specific manner, with few verbalizations, and they allow a reasonable time for compliance to occur. Beta commands are vague, overly wordy, and often contain multiple instructions to engage in a behavior. The implication of their discussion is that students' noncompliance may be exacerbated by educators' behaviors.

The modification of educators' behavior has generally focused on maximizing the use of alpha commands (e.g., Forehand & McMahon, 1981; Morgan & Jenson, 1988; Walker & Walker, 1991). However, what is sometimes lost in this discussion is that a plethora of other adult factors can spawn noncompliance in children. In fact, Cormier and Cormier (1985) stated that resistance can arise from any behavior, regardless of the source, that interferes with the likelihood of a successful outcome. This definition provides the impetus for using the term *resistance* instead of the more common words *noncompliance, oppositional,* or *defiant. Resistance* is a more inclusive term because it focuses on the interaction between children's and adults' behaviors. On the other hand, the terms *noncompliance* and *oppositional* suggest that the locus of the problem resides within a child. Consequently, solutions to the problems of noncompliance or opposition will focus solely on changing children's behaviors to the exclusion of also modifying adults' behaviors to obtain a desired outcome.

The Role of Functional Assessment

Functional assessment consists of five processes: (1) describing the problem behavior; (2) identifying events, situations, and times that predict when it will and will not occur; (3) identifying consequences that maintain it; (4) developing hypotheses that describe the behavior, when it occurs, and what reinforcers maintain it; and (5) collecting direct observation data that support the hypotheses (O'Neill et al., 1997). There are two core functions of problem behavior: (1) to obtain something desirable, such as attention from others, tangible objects, or activities (positive reinforcement); and (2) to escape or avoid something aversive, such as a difficult or boring task (negative reinforcement).

This conclusion may be expected because human behavior is complex and subtle. For example, literature from the field of social psychology highlights the influence power/control has on human functioning and interaction. Although power/control does not fit as well into an applied behavior analysis (ABA) paradigm as do attention and escape/avoidance, it nevertheless may be an equally valid function of maladaptive behaviors displayed by some students. Furthermore, it can be functionally analyzed using ABA methodology similar to that used for attention and escape/avoidance (Maag & Kemp, 2003).

Power and Human Functioning

Over 40 years ago, Cartwright (1959), a noted researcher and theorist of group dynamics, believed that few social interactions advance very far before elements of power come into play. Buckley (1967) defined power as "control or influence over the actions of others to promote one's goals without their consent, against their will, or without their knowledge or understanding" (p. 186). In a general sense, power is defined as behaviors producing social influence. It involves one person causing another person to perform a behavior that is contrary to the latter's desire (French & Raven, 1959).

Falbo (1977) described two dimensions of power tactics: (1) rationality versus nonrationality and (2) directness versus indirectness. Rational modes of influence include bargaining techniques. A student who tries to make a deal with the teacher by saying that he will begin his work if he first can finish drawing is an example of direct power behaviors. Nonrational tactics are present in students who try to evade an issue or deceive those who disagree with them. An example of this type of power would be a student who tries to goad a teacher into an argument by saying that she completed her homework but it was taken by a classmate. An example of a direct approach would be ignoring a teacher's direction and continuing to perform the current behavior. Indirect tactics would include hinting or ingratiating oneself. The classic example of this is the "teacher's pet," the student who tries to gain more of the teacher's favor than is given to other students and thus gain more power in the classroom.

Power and Resistance

Many students who show resistance in school do so to obtain power that is absent in other aspects of their lives (Maag, 2001). Being homeless, having parents with mental illnesses, and coming from a family where physical or sexual abuse occurs all contribute to feelings of helplessness (McWhirter et al., 1998). Some children who are depressed often display noncompliant behaviors as a way to combat helplessness, which is characteristic of this disorder (Maag & Forness, 1991). Perceived lack of personal power has resulted in parental discipline styles' contributing to children's delinquency and learning difficulties (Hagan, Simpson, & Gillis, 1987; Leiber & Wacker, 1997; Plax, Kearney, McCroskey, & Richmond, 1986).

Some level of resistance is normal and even desirable. As toddlers and when entering adolescence, children behave in ways to obtain power as a way to assert independence (Richardson, 2000). There is a fine line between refusing to comply with a teacher's request and refusing to yield to peer pressure to take drugs. Nevertheless, to manage students' resistance effectively, teachers must determine if the function of the inappropriate behavior is power/control.

Tactics for Managing Resistance

The process of managing resistance begins by educators ruling out escape/avoidance and attention as the functions of misbehavior (Maag & Kemp, 2003). For example, a student may make animal noises during class. An escape function may be ruled out (or confirmed) by replacing the assigned task with a high-interest activity. If the student makes animal noises to escape a difficult or boring task, then there would be no reason for him to misbehave when given a desirable task because he would not want to escape it. If the student continues to make animal noises when given a high-interest activity, then attention may be tested. An A-B-C analysis would be conducted to determine the antecedents and consequences prompting and maintaining the behavior that, in turn, would be manipulated. The teacher and peers may ignore the student when he makes animal noises, or the student may be removed from class. If animal noises do not decrease, then power may be tested using the techniques described by Maag and Kemp (2003). The following techniques—which are described in greater detail elsewhere (e.g., Maag, 1999; Maag & Kemp, 2005)—are based on the premise that power is the function of a student's misbehavior and focus on changing the context surrounding a behavior.

Changing context can have a profound impact upon reducing resistance. It is based on the assumptions that (a) behaviors derive meaning from context and (b) context serves as a cue that elicits certain behaviors. Therefore, it is axiomatic that when the context surrounding a behavior changes, the meaning, purpose, and desire to engage in the behavior also change (Maag, 1999).

Creating Ordeals

Creating ordeals in order to change context was first described in a systematic way by Haley (1984). The approach is straightforward: A teacher imposes an ordeal appropriate to a student's problem that causes equal or greater distress than the problem. Ordeal therapy shares some similarities with negative practice except that in ordeal therapy the task is something to which the student cannot legitimately object.

Maag (1997) describes a situation in which a teacher who was confronted with a boy who refused to complete his math assignment and instead wrote the name of his school followed by the word "sucks" on the paper. The teacher nonchalantly said that she was sorry his school "sucked" but that he was not being very creative in his writing of the words. She enthusiastically suggested that the boy turn over the paper and write the words repeatedly in various print styles and sizes. The boy, who began in earnest, quickly lost interest and began working on the math assignment.

There are several important qualities in the ordeal described above. First, the teacher did not present the ordeal as a punitive consequence for misbehaving. Instead, she appeared apologetic that the student did not like the school but also pleased that he had the opportunity to practice writing more creatively. Her reaction automatically changed the context: She was not confrontational and consequently was able to avoid a power struggle. Second, the student performed the ordeal because it was congruent with what he wanted to do—write that his school sucked. Third, complying with the teacher's direction to write that his school sucked no longer meant that he was defying a teacher's request and consequently became a bother.

Scrambling Routine

The performance of a series of behaviors can be conceptualized in terms of a stimulus-response chain (Malott, Whaley, & Malott, 1997). A stimulus elicits a response, which in turn becomes a cue to perform another behavior. This approach is sometimes referred to as "sequence confusion" (Lankton, 1985). For example, preparing to take a math quiz may be a cue for a student to feel anxious. Anxiety then becomes a cue for the student to begin crying. Crying, in turn, becomes a cue for the student to run out of the room, and so forth. However, instructing the student to "feel anxious" 15 minutes prior to taking a math quiz scrambles the stimulus-response chain, and the student can no longer perform the behavior as it was performed previously. This example is paradoxical (Simon & Vetter-Zemitzsch, 1985) because if the student brings on anxiety, then he has proof that anxiety is under his control; if he refuses to bring on anxiety, he also has proof that anxiety is under his control because he was able to avoid experiencing it.

Embedding Instructions

Embedding instructions is a technique in which a teacher directs a student to do what she is already doing while interspersing a request for the desired behavior (Maag, 1999). For example, a teacher may embed the following instruction:

"Mary, as you shuffle your papers, open your math book to page 18 while talking to Susie." In this situation, Mary is engaging in two undesirable behaviors: shuffling her papers and talking to Susie. This instruction embeds three separate tasks—two of which Mary is already performing. The part of the instruction with which her teacher is trying to get compliance is opening the math book to page 18. If the instructions were separated, Mary could easily refuse one or all of them. But a refusal when the tasks are combined into a single instruction means what? That Mary will not shuffle her papers? That she will not open her book? That she will not talk to Susie? The effort required to identify what one is refusing in itself is a deterrent to refusal (Bandler & Grinder, 1975). Nor can a refusal of the entire instruction be offered comfortably. To the single tasks she can easily say no. But to the combined task she cannot say no because, if she is shuffling her papers, she must "immediately" open her book and talk to Susie. Hence, Mary may prefer to perform the combined tasks unwillingly rather than put forth the effort to analyze the instruction minutely.

Conclusion

Managing resistance may at first seem to be a massive job because resistant students often do not respond to traditional interventions. However, understanding that adult behavior should be examined and modified as well as the student's is a good first step. The use of functional assessment will help educators determine if noncompliance serves the function of attention, escape, or power. Behaviors controlled by the desire for attention or escape are not truly indicative of resistance, but they are modifiable using traditional ABA techniques, in which most special educators have received training. Techniques for managing resistance are based on the impact of context on behavior. These techniques include, but are not limited to, creating ordeals, scrambling routine, reframing, and embedding instructions. These techniques share the commonality of changing context as a way to facilitate a change in the meaning, purpose, and desire for a student to engage in resistant behaviors.

REFERENCES

American Psychiatric Association (APA). (1980). *Diagnostic and statistical manual of mental disorders* (3rd ed.). Washington, DC: Author.

American Psychiatric Association (APA). (1987). *Diagnostic and statistical manual of mental disorders* (3rd ed., rev.). Washington, DC: Author.

American Psychiatric Association (APA). (2000). *Diagnostic and statistical manual of mental disorders* (4th ed., text rev.). Washington, DC: Author.

Bandler, R., & Grinder, J. (1975). *Patterns of the hypnotic techniques of Milton H. Erickson, M.D.* Capitola, CA: Meta.

Buckley, W. (1967). *Sociology and modern systems theory.* Englewood Cliffs, NJ: Prentice Hall.

Cartwright, D. (1959). A field theoretical conception of power. In D. Cartwright (Ed.), *Studies in social power* (pp. 183–220). Ann Arbor, MI: Institute for Social Research.

Cormier, W. H., & Cormier, L. S. (1985). *Interviewing strategies for helpers: Fundamental skills and cognitive behavioral interventions* (2nd ed.). Monterey, CA: Brooks/Cole.

Cullinan, D. (2002). *Students with emotional and behavior disorders.* Upper Saddle River, NJ: Merrill Prentice Hall.

Falbo, T. (1977). Power strategies in intimate relationships. *Journal of Personality and Social Psychology, 35,* 537–548.

Forehand, R. (1977). Child noncompliance to parental requests: Behavioral analysis and treatment. In M. Hersen, R. M. Eisler, & P. M. Miller (Eds.), *Progress in behavior modification* (Vol. 5, pp. 111–147). New York: Academic Press.

Forehand, R., & McMahon, R. (1981). *Helping the noncompliant child.* New York: Guilford.

French, J. R. P., Jr., & Raven, B. (1959). The bases of social power. In D. Cartwright (Ed.), *Studies in social power* (pp. 118–149). Ann Arbor, MI: Institute for Social Research.

Hagan, J., Simpson, J., & Gillis, A. R. (1987). Class in the household: A power-control theory of gender and delinquency. *American Journal of Sociology, 92,* 788–816.

Haley, J. (1984). *Ordeal therapy.* San Francisco: Jossey-Bass.

Kazdin, A. E. (1989). Conduct and oppositional disorders. In C. G. Last & M. Hersen (Eds.), *Handbook of child psychiatric diagnosis* (pp. 129–155). New York: Wiley.

Kuczynski, L., Kochanska, G., Radke-Yarrow, M., & Girnius-Brown, O. (1987). A developmental interpretation of young children's noncompliance. *Developmental Psychology, 23,* 779–806.

Lankton, C. H. (1985). Generative change: Beyond symptomatic relief. In J. K. Zeig (Ed.), *Ericksonian psychotherapy* (Vol. 1, pp. 137–170). New York: Brunner/Mazel.

Leiber, M. J., & Wacker, M. E. (1997). A theoretical and empirical assessment of power-control theory and single-mother families. *Youth and Society, 28,* 317–350.

Maag, J. W. (1997). Managing resistance: Looking beyond the child and into the mirror. In P. Zionts (Ed.), *Inclusion strategies for students with learning and behavior problems* (pp. 229–271). Austin, TX: PRO-ED.

Maag, J. W. (2001). *Powerful struggles: Managing resistance, building rapport.* Longmont, CO: Sopris West.

Maag, J. W., & Forness, S. R. (1991). Depression in children and adolescents: Identification, assessment, and treatment. *Focus on Exceptional Children, 24*(1), 1–19.

Maag, J. W., & Kemp, S. E. (2003). Behavioral intent of power and affiliation: Implications for functional analysis. *Remedial and Special Education, 24,* 57–64.

Maag, J. W., & Kemp, S. E. (2005). I can't make you: Attitude shifts and techniques for managing resistance. In P. Zionts (Ed.), *Inclusion strategies for students with learning and behavior problems* (2nd ed., pp. 247–281). Austin, TX: PRO-ED.

Malott, R. W., Whaley, D. L., & Malott, M. E. (1997). *Elementary principles of behavior* (3rd ed.). Upper Saddle River, NJ: Prentice Hall.

McMahon, R. J., & Forehand, R. (1988). Conduct disorders. In E. J. Mash & L. G. Terdal (Eds.), *Behavioral assessment of childhood disorders* (2nd ed., pp. 105–153). New York: Guilford.

McWhirter, J. J., McWhirter, B. T., McWhirter, A. M., & McWhirter, E. H. (1998). *At-risk youth: A comprehensive response* (2nd ed.). Pacific Grove, CA: Brooks/Cole.

Morgan, D. P., & Jenson, W. R. (1988). *Teaching behaviorally disordered students: Preferred practices.* Columbus, OH: Merrill.

Plax, T. G., Kearney, P., McCroskey, J. C., & Richmond, V. P. (1986). Power in the classroom VI: Verbal control strategies, nonverbal immediacy and affective learning. *Communication Education, 35,* 43–55.

Rhode, G., Morgan, D. P., & Young, K. R. (1983). Generalization and maintenance of treatment gains of behaviorally handicapped students from resource rooms to regular classrooms using self-evaluation procedures. *Journal of Applied Behavior Analysis, 16,* 171–188.

Richardson, K. (2000). *Developmental psychology: How nature and nurture interact.* Basingstoke, England: Macmillan.

Rocissano, L., Slade, A., & Lynch, V. (1987). Dyadic synchrony and toddler compliance. *Developmental Psychology, 23,* 698–704.

Schoen, S. (1986). Decreasing noncompliance in a severely multihandicapped child. *Psychology in the Schools, 23,* 88–94.

Simon, D. J., & Vetter-Zemitzsch, A. (1985). Paradoxical interventions: Strategies for the resistant adolescent. In M. K. Zabel (Ed.), *Teaching: Behaviorally disordered youth* (Vol. 1, pp. 17–22). Reston, VA: Council for Children with Behavioral Disorders.

Smith, C. R. (1998). *Learning disabilities: The interaction of learner, task, and setting* (4th ed.). Boston: Allyn and Bacon.

Walker, H. M., & Walker, J. E. (1991). *Coping with noncompliance in the classroom: A positive approach for teachers.* Austin, TX: PRO-ED.

Walker, H. M., Ramsey, E., & Gresham, F. M. (2004). *Antisocial behavior in school: Evidence-based practices* (2nd ed.). Belmont, CA: Wadsworth/Thomson Learning.

Zirpoli, T. J., & Melloy, K. J. (1997). *Behavior management: Applications for teachers and parents* (2nd ed.). Upper Saddle River, NJ: Prentice Hall.

JOHN W. MAAG
University of Nebraska–Lincoln

BEHAVIOR MODIFICATION
CLASSROOM MANAGEMENT

RESOURCE ROOM

The resource room concept gained popularity following the *Hobsen v. Hansen* litigation, which declared tracking systems illegal and required reevaluation on a regular basis. This litigation was a forerunner for mainstreaming and the concept of least restrictive alternative (environment). This model of service delivery allows the handicapped child to remain in the educational mainstream as much as possible. With the passage of PL 94-142 and further emphasis on the least restrictive alternative, the resource room gained even further popularity. There are over 100,000 resource room teachers in the United States today. Professional special educators have consistently cited the importance of the resource room concept and have noted its viability as a promising alternative to placement in self-contained classes or regular classes without support services (Cartwright, Cartwright, & Ward, 1995; Fimian, Zaback, & D'Alonzo, 1983; Kasik, 1983; Learner, 1985; Marsh, Price, & Smith, 1983; Meyen, 1982; Reger, 1973; Sabatino, 1972; Sindelar & Deno, 1978; Wiederholt, 1974).

Usually, students attending resource rooms are identified as mildly handicapped (4 to 6 percent of the total school population). Resource rooms are a widespread means of service delivery for the mildly handicapped, and are gaining acceptance for use with gifted exceptional children.

There are voluminous data available on the definition of resource rooms (Chaffin, 1974; Deno; 1973; Fox et al. 1972; Hammill & Wiederholdt, 1972; Kasik, 1983; Lilly, 1971; Reger, 1972, 1973; Sabatino, 1972; Wiederholt, 1974). According to Kasik (1983), a resource room is a place special education students attend for less than 50 percent of their school day for support services. The student remains in the regular classroom for the majority of the academic instruction. The resource room is staffed by a resource room teacher. Attendance in the resource room is determined by a multidisciplinary staff according to the student's individual needs. Students are scheduled into specific time slots to attend the resource room, where they receive remedial instruction from a trained specialist in their deficit areas. A resource room should be well equipped with a wide variety of instructional materials. Individualized instruction may include perceptual training, language development, motor training, social and emotional development, and academic skills development. Resource room class size should be small. A recommended caseload per teacher would be no more than 20 students at any one time. Class sessions are either individual or in small groups of up to five students per session. They are a minimum of 20 minutes and a maximum of 45 minutes in length. The resource room should have the same comfortable characteristics of a regular classroom, such as dimensions of at least 150 square feet, adequate lighting, ventilation, and temperature control. The resource room should be easily accessible to teachers and students and should possess adequate storage space for folders and materials. In general, the resource room should provide a positive learning environment.

Placement in the resource room is intended to be of short duration (Kasik, 1983). As students progress toward specified goals, they are returned to full-time placement in the regular classroom. Return to the regular classroom should progress through a gradual phasing out of support services. The resource room is to be considered as one type of service delivery within the continuum of services available.

REFERENCES

Cartwright, P., Cartwright, C., & Ward, M. (1995). *Educating special learners* (4th ed.). Boston: Wadsworth.

Chaffin, J. D. (1974). Will the real mainstreaming program please stand up! *Focus on Exceptional Children, 5*(6), 1–18.

D'Alonzo, B. (1983). *Educating adolescents with learning and behavior problems.* Rockville, MD: Aspen Systems.

Deno, E. (1973). *Instructional alternatives for exceptional children.* Reston, VA: Council For Exceptional Children.

Fox, W. L., Egnar, A. N., Polucci, P. E., Perelman, P. F., & McKenzie, H. S. (1972). An introduction to regular classroom approaches to special education. In E. Deno (Ed.), *Instructional alternatives for exceptional children.* Reston, VA: Council for Exceptional Children.

Hammill, D. D., & Wiederholdt, L. (1972). *The resource room: Rationale and implementation.* Ft. Washington, PA: Journal of Special Education Press.

Kasik, M. M. (1983). Analysis of the professional preparation of the resource room teacher. *Dissertation Abstracts International.* (University Microfilms International No. DAO 56766)

Learner, J. (1985). *Learning disabilities: Theories, diagnosis, and teaching strategies* (4th ed.). Boston: Houghton Mifflin.

Lilly, M. S. (1971). A training based model for special education. *Exceptional Children, 37,* 747–749.

Marsh, G. E., Price, B. J., & Smith, T. E. C. (1983). *Teaching mildly handicapped children: Methods and materials: A generic approach to comprehensive teaching.* St. Louis, MO: Mosby.

McLaughlin, J. A., & Kelly, D. (1982). Issues facing the resource teacher. *Learning Disability Quarterly, 5,* 58–64.

Meyen, E. L. (1982). *Exceptional children and youth* (2nd ed.). Chicago: Love.

Reger, R. (1972). Resource rooms: Change agents or guardians of the status quo? *Journal of Special Education, 6,* 355–360.

Reger, R. (1973). What is a resource room program? *Journal of Learning Disabilities, 6,* 609–614.

Sabatino, D. A. (1972). Resource rooms: The renaissance in special education. *Journal of Special Education, 6,* 235–348.

Sindelar, P. T., & Deno, E. (1978). The effectiveness of resource room programming. *Journal of Special Education, 12,* 17–28.

Wiederholdt, J. L. (1974). Planning resource rooms for the mildly handicapped. *Focus on Exceptional Children, 5*(8), 1–10.

MARIBETH MONTGOMERY KASIK
Governors State University

CASCADE MODEL OF SPECIAL EDUCATION SERVICES
INCLUSION
LEAST RESTRICTIVE ENVIRONMENT
RESOURCE TEACHER
SELF-CONTAINED CLASS

RESOURCE TEACHER

Much of the research literature calls for resource rooms to be staffed by highly trained special educators who are personable, demonstrate good human interactional skills, and are prepared professionally in the diagnosis and remediation of single or multiple groups of disabled children. Wallace and McLoughlin (1979) identify the resource teacher's main role as including assessment, instructional planning, teacher evaluation, and liaison-consultant duties. Learner (1985) describes the resource teacher as a highly trained professional who is capable of diagnosing the child, planning and implementing the teaching program, assisting the classroom teacher, providing continuous evaluation of the student, and conducting in-service sessions with other educators and the community. Sabatino (1981) states that the role of the resource teacher includes direct service to individuals and small groups of children, consultant services to classroom teachers, and responsibility for assessment and delivery of individualized programs. Kasik (1983) states that the resource teacher needs to be well organized, flexible, self-directed, and effective in time management. Paroz, Siegenthaler, and Tatum (1977) suggest that the resource teacher be actively involved with the total school community, including students and staff members. They add that the "teacher's role is open ended and limited only by time, talent, and acceptance of the teacher by the school administration and staff" (p. 15). The resource teacher is a trained specialist who works with, and acts as a consultant to, other teachers, providing materials and methods to help children who are having difficulties within the regular classroom. Usually, the resource teacher works with the mildly disabled population in a centralized resource room where appropriate materials are housed.

Some of the most common responsibilities a resource teacher will probably be asked to undertake have been identified by Sabatino (1982). The resource teacher will conduct and participate in screening for children with learning disabilities, determine the nature of their learning, and prepare final reports for each referral. Instruction will be provided individually or in small groups. The resource teacher will prepare lessons for use when a child cannot function within the framework of the regular lesson. Students will participate in the resource room until they are integrated full time or until successful transition is complete. Schedules should include six or seven sessions daily, except on Fridays, when the session should be half a day. This allows the teacher to complete reports, observations, parent meetings, consultations, and so on. Consultation with classroom teachers and other pupil services personnel should be consistent. The resource teacher should serve as a resource person and provide supportive assistance for all classroom teachers. Observation in the regular classroom and conferences with regular class teachers and parents about pupil progress should be continuous. In addition to meeting with teachers, the resource teacher may be required to prepare in-service materials and supervise the work of paraprofessionals and volunteers. Despite these suggestions, there is no consistency within the field regarding actual practice.

There are four different types of resource room teachers: (1) categorical, (2) noncategorical, (3) itinerant (or mobile), and (4) teacher-consultant. Categorical programs serve one specific population; noncategorical programs may serve one or more populations. The itinerant resource room teacher travels from one building to another and usually does not have an assigned room from which to work. The teacher-consultant resource room teacher provides consultation to regular class teachers, parents, and other service delivery personnel. Cartwright, Cartwright, and Ward (1995) provide a description of a typical day in the life of a resource teacher in today's schools.

REFERENCES

Cartwright, P., Cartwright, C., & Ward, M. (1995). *Educating special learners* (4th ed.). Boston: Wadsworth.

Kasik, M. M. (1983). Analysis of the professional preparation of the special education resource room teacher. *Dissertation Abstracts International.* (University Microfilms International No. DAO 56766)

Learner, J. (1985). *Learning disabilities: Theories, diagnosis, and teaching strategies* (4th ed.). Boston: Houghton Mifflin.

Paroz, J., Siegenthaler, L., & Tatum, V. (1977). A model for a middle school resource room. *Journal of Learning Disabilities, 8,* 7–15.

Sabatino, D. A. (1981). Overview for the practitioner in learning disabilities. In D. A. Sabatino, T. L. Miller, & C. R. Schmidt (Eds.), *Learning disabilities: Systemizing teaching and service delivery.* Rockville, MD: Aspen.

Sabatino, D. A. (1982). An educational program guide for secondary schools. In D. A. Sabatino & L. Mann (Eds.), *A handbook of diagnostic and prescriptive teaching.* Rockville, MD: Aspen.

Wallace, G., & McLoughlin, J. A. (1979). *Learning disabilities: Concepts and characteristics* (2nd ed.). Columbus, OH: Merrill.

MARIBETH MONTGOMERY KASIK
Governors State University

DIAGNOSTIC PRESCRIPTIVE TEACHING
RESOURCE ROOM

RESPITE CARE

Respite care complements special education in providing support to families of children with disabilities. Respite care may be defined as temporary care given to a disabled or otherwise dependent individual for the purpose of providing relief to the primary caregiver (Cohen & Warren, 1985). The concept of respite care is generally associated with intermittent services, although this term is also sometimes used to refer to regularly scheduled services occurring once or twice a week.

Respite care programs first appeared in the mid-1970s in response to the deinstitutionalization movement. Deinstitutionalization meant that many families who would probably have placed their disabled children in institutions, either out of choice or as a result of professional advice, no longer had the option to do so. In addition, some children who had been placed in institutions in earlier years were being returned to their families. Thus a substantial number of parents now had to cope with the care needs of their severely disabled children each day. The natural breaks that parents of nondisabled children experience when their children sleep at a friend's home, visit with relatives, or go to camp were usually not available. It was virtually impossible to obtain paid babysitters, and even relatives were reluctant to assume this responsibility. The primary caregiver, usually the mother, found it impossible to engage in normal activities such as shopping, caring for medical and dental needs, or seeing friends. Parents rarely had time for each other or for their other children. Families experienced severe problems in coping.

Some parents' cries for help were heard by professionals. Other parents, receiving no help from the service field, organized themselves and initiated respite care programs while continuing to bring their plight to the attention of service agencies. It was not until the late 1970s that professionals recognized the importance of respite care services. Parents were the primary advocates for these services prior to that time.

Respite care is a family-support service, designed to improve family functioning and help normalize families of the disabled. This service is of particular importance to families with weak natural support systems, poor coping skills, or strenuous care demands. Difficulty in care provision may reflect the severity of the behavioral problems or the extensiveness of the physical and health care needs of the disabled person. Primary caregivers use the relief provided through respite care services to rest, meet their own medical needs, improve relationships with other family members, and engage in some of the common personal or social activities that other adults are able to enjoy (e.g., visiting with a friend, taking a vacation, going shopping).

Models of respite care may vary along several dimensions, such as where the service is provided, what the content/nature of the care is, who provides the care, how the service is administered, and how much time is allotted. The most important variation in models is whether services are provided in the home or in some other setting. In-home services are preferred by a majority of families. In-home services are economical and minimize the adjustments that must be made by the disabled individual and the family. These services may be of short duration, as when the parents go to a movie, or for a period of a week or two when parents take a vacation. In-home services may be provided by a sitter with only a few hours of training or by a homemaker/home health aide with substantial training.

About 40 percent of families experience a strong need to have their disabled members temporarily out of the home (Cohen & Warren, 1985). Out-of-home services may be provided on evenings, weekends, and holidays, or for continuous periods up to 30 days. These services may be provided in a respite care facility, in a residential facility that reserves some beds for temporary care, or in the home of the respite care provider. Services based on the home of the provider are personalized and economical. They can help expand the social/community experiences of the disabled child, and they allow for the development of an ongoing relationship between the provider family and the disabled child.

Babysitting and companionship are the major ingredients of respite care services that are of brief duration. Personal care and nursing care may be required when the client has severe physical or health problems. Social/recreational programming is usually a major component of longer respite care episodes.

Respite care services are often funded through state mental retardation/developmental disabilities agencies, with families obtaining services either directly through local offices of these agencies or through community programs supported by funds from these state sources. The provision of respite care services is uneven from state to state and from region to region within states. States that have made strong efforts to provide sufficient respite care services of good quality include Massachusetts, California, Washington, and, most recently, Ohio. Funding problems remain the greatest impediment to the provision of adequate respite care services. In light of funding limitations, parent co-ops and volunteer models of respite care have become popular. Such programs are low in cost and are congruent with the zeitgeist of the 1980s that emphasized self-help and alternatives to government provision.

REFERENCE

Cohen, S., & Warren, R. D. (1985). *Respite care: Principles, programs, and policies.* Austin, TX: PRO-ED.

SHIRLEY COHEN
*Hunter College, City University
of New York*

DEINSTITUTIONALIZATION

RESPONSE GENERALIZATION

Often after someone learns a particular behavior, new, untaught responses will emerge in the learner's repertoire. These new behaviors have operant functions similar to the previously learned behavior, but they differ in form or topography and are said to be the result of response generalization. This entry will provide examples that illustrate response generalization, a brief review of the research literature on generalization, and some notes on application.

Examples

Nelson was taught to say "Hello" to his friends in the morning. Subsequent to training, he began saying "Good morning," "What's up?" and "How're you doing?" Similarly, Paula was trained while walking to look both ways before crossing the street. Recently on her walks, Paula has begun to stop at intersections before crossing.

Problems may ensue if novel responses do not emerge to meet environmental demands. Jasmine has learned to check her pockets for her mittens before leaving for school, but if the mittens are not in her pockets, she does not ask for help and will leave without protection for her hands. Wayne was taught to raise his hand to speak in class. Recently, he began standing and jumping to be called on by his teacher.

Each of these examples illustrates response generalization. The first two scenarios reflect socially relevant results of training that have generalized to new behaviors that are members of the same response class or category as the response initially taught. The third example illustrates a well-learned skill that did not properly shift into a novel behavior with similar behavioral function when warranted. The last scene depicts a learned response that has overgeneralized to a new form that is inappropriate for the setting. As important skills are taught, learners may fail to generate a full repertoire of behaviors to meet the challenges of situations that occur in natural settings. Inversely, a learner may modify strategies to an extent that is inappropriate. An understanding of the process of response generalization is an important tool to assist learners in tasks ranging from developmentally appropriate behaviors to scholastics.

Research

Generalization research began in the early twentieth century and focused on continued responding in the presence of novel stimuli. In an early textbook on behavior theory, Clark Hull (1943) hypothesized that behavioral variability occurred after response requirements were altered and previous responses were no longer reinforced. He termed the emergence of novel responses in this manner response generalization, but little empirical research on this behavioral process ensued.

Twenty-five years later, Baer, Wolf, and Risley (1968) encouraged behavior analysts to turn their attention from explorations of basic processes that govern behavior to the development of empirically validated approaches to solving socially relevant problems. These researchers distinguished two predominantly overlooked categories of generalization for applied empirical research, maintenance and response generalization, but again response generalization received little empirical attention.

In recent years, noting the paucity of research in this area, some investigators have asked whether it may be appropriate to soften the criteria for attributing an event to response generalization, which had been defined in the experimental literature as the emergence of novel responses that were neither (a) reinforced during the teaching process nor (b) coached by rules implied during training (Stokes & Baer, 1977). To this end, Ludwig and Geller (1997, 2000) documented the spread of effect of a driving safety training program in which drivers emitted novel desired safe driving responses that had not been trained during the intervention. Even though the untaught safe behaviors may have occurred and been reinforced during the teaching procedure, Ludwig and Geller attributed these novel behaviors to response generalization.

The behavior analytic community has not yet reached consensus over what to include in the classification of response generalization. Some researchers caution that the data have not supported the view that all extensions of a previously taught behavior constitute response generalization (Houchins & Boyce, 2001). Houchins and Boyce (2001) suggest that overgeneralizing in applying the construct of response generalization may cause us to overlook other processes that more accurately account for learning in a specific context. Precise identification of how a response has been brought under stimulus control will highlight the features necessary for subsequent interventions to be successful. For a teacher in the field, the take-home point is that knowing the exact process involved in a learning task makes training the associated behaviors an empirically driven craft, efficient, predictable, and replicable.

Application

Promoting response generalization initially requires using techniques that increase behavioral variability. Instead of reinforcing precisely repeated behaviors, teachers should reinforce a broad spectrum of responses. This loose training prevents the development of overselected response dimensions and fosters creativity (Sulzer-Azaroff & Mayer, 1991).

When seeking to encourage a learner to expand a repertoire of behaviors, use differential reinforcement and extinction. Offering reinforcement for new forms, shapes, or topographies of a previously taught behavior, while withholding reinforcement for the first taught form of the response, aids in the development of novel characteristics of behavior (Cooper, Heron, & Heward, 1987).

To prevent overgeneralization from occurring, discrimination training should accompany training for response generalization. That is, a learner should be taught to distinguish the boundaries of each addition to a class of responses. Teaching learners to mediate their own responses by watching videos of others, watching videos of themselves, removing pictures from icon books, or checking off items on a self-monitoring checklist enables learners to effectively discriminate the limits of acceptability while trying out novel responses across environments (Sulzer-Azaroff & Mayer, 1991).

Conclusions

Generalization is a fundamental behavioral process that often occurs without direct training but should not be expected to occur without instruction. Laboratory experiments with humans and nonhumans have identified several processes associated with generalized responding: stimulus generalization, maintenance, and response generalization. Applied research has emerged in the last 40 years bringing the understanding of basic processes to bear on matters of social importance. The precise, technical definition of response generalization may have put constraints on research development that have impeded empirical investigation. Further dialogue and research are needed to identify the exact process involved in the development of novel behaviors. This knowledge is vital for constructing sound, empirically validated intervention strategies. Specific strategies such as loose training and differential instruction with extinction have been identified and empirically verified in the teaching and remediation of generalized responding. Such socially relevant outcomes have been the direct result of behavior analytic investigations.

REFERENCES

Baer, D. M., Wolf, M. M., & Risley, T. R. (1968). Some current dimensions of applied behavior analysis. *Journal of Applied Behavior Analysis, 1*, 91–97.

Cooper, J. O., Heron, T. E., & Heward, W. L. (1987). *Applied behavior analysis.* Columbus, OH: Merrill.

Houchins, N., & Boyce, T. E. (2001). Response generalization in behavioral safety: Fact or fiction? *Journal of Organizational Behavior Management, 21*(4), 3–11.

Hull, C. L. (1943). *Principles of behavior: An introduction to behavior theory.* Oxford, England: Appleton-Century.

Ludwig, T. D., & Geller, E. S. (1997). Managing injury control among professional pizza deliverers: Effects of goal setting and response generalization. *Journal of Applied Psychology, 82*, 253–261.

Ludwig, T. D., & Geller, E. S. (2000). Intervening to improve the safety of occupational driving: A behavior-change model and review of empirical evidence [Special issue]. *Journal of Organizational Behavior Management, 19*(4).

Stokes, T. F., & Baer, D. M. (1977). An implicit technology of generalization. *Journal of Applied Behavior Analysis, 10*, 349–367.

Sulzer-Azaroff, B., & Mayer, G. R. (1991). *Behavior analysis for lasting change.* Orlando, FL: Holt, Rinehart, & Winston.

THOMAS G. SZABO
PAIGE B. RAETZ
BRITT L. WINTER
Western Michigan University

BEHAVIOR MODIFICATION
GENERALIZATION

RESPONSE TO INTERVENTION

The Individuals with Disabilities Education Improvement Act (IDEIA) of November 2004 included the option of using the Response to Intervention Model (RTI) as a means of identifying children with specific learning disabilities. Previous methods of identifying students with specific learning disabilities have raised concerns regarding their efficacy, accuracy, timeliness, equity, and feasibility. Critics of the discrepancy model, for example, described it as a "wait-to-fail" approach, because in order for interventions to be implemented, students had to "qualify" by exhibiting a severe enough discrepancy between their cognitive and intelligence measures. If the discrepancy was not severe enough, then the student could not receive any additional services or benefit from any interventions. What is unique to RTI is that students do not have to wait for formal identification of a learning disability but instead can begin receiving targeted interventions immediately (Education Evolving R&D Alert, 2005). RTI is an individual, comprehensive, student-centered assessment and intervention approach (National Resource Center on Learning Disabilities, 2003) that "use[s] the quality of student responses to research-based interventions as the basis for decisions about needed services" (Barnett, Daly, Jones, & Lentz, 2004, p. 67).

Some elements common to RTI models include "providing meaningful services prior to special education, employing systematic decision making, and demonstrating that special education would be necessary for further progress" (Barnett et al., 2004, p. 68). A key component to RTI is utilizing research-based instructional interventions and obtaining data-driven evidence of the impact of these interventions on students' performance (Education Evolving R&D Alert, 2005). Continued difficulty after implementation of research-based interventions indicates the presence of a legitimate learning disability and not just the need for additional instruction.

The core features of RTI are the following (Mellard, 2004; National Joint Committee on Learning Disabilities, 2005):

1. Students should receive high-quality classroom instruction in their general education setting.
2. The general education instruction and practices utilized should be research based. This eliminates the possibility that student difficulty is a result of inadequate classroom instruction.
3. General education instructors and staff should assume an active role in assessing students' performance, including designing and completing student

assessments and not relying on standard, externally developed testing materials.

4. Universal screening of academics and behavior should be conducted, emphasizing specific criteria for assessing learning and achievement in order to identify students who may require closer monitoring or intervention.
5. Students' classroom progress should be monitored continuously so staff may be capable of easily identifying students with limited educational gains or students who may not be meeting expected standards.
6. When results indicate the necessity for an intervention to address student difficulty, the interventions implemented should be research based. These interventions should not be a simple adaptation to the current curriculum but rather an 8- to 12-week program designed to increase the intensity of the learner's instructional experience.
7. After the intervention is implemented, progress should be monitored to determine the effectiveness of the interventions or identify the need for modifications. Data should be collected on a regular basis, even daily, to provide a cumulative representation of the response to the intervention.
8. Systematic assessment of the fidelity or integrity with which the intervention is implemented helps ensure interventions were implemented as intended.

RTI models can be implemented in many different ways or forms. However, most RTI models have some attributes in common. First of all, most models operate in tiers of increasingly intense student interventions (Mellard, 2004). RTI models also offer the option of a different curriculum should the standard one be ineffective (Mellard, 2004). Interventions also should vary in frequency, duration, and time of intervention (Mellard, 2004). RTI models can be distinguished according to whether interventions are individualized. Students' deficits can be addressed either by implementing a research-based intervention program that specifically addresses one student's needs or by grouping students with similar difficulties and utilizing a research-based intervention that has been standardized and proven effective with students who exhibit similar difficulties (National Resource Center on Learning Disabilities, 2003).

REFERENCES

Barnett, D. W., Daly, E. J., III, Jones, K. M., & Lentz, F. E., Jr. (2004). Response to intervention: Empirically based special service decisions from single-case designs of increasing and decreasing intensity. *Journal of Special Education, 38*(2), 66–79.

Education Evolving R&D Alert. (2005, July). *Response to intervention: An alternative to traditional eligibility criteria for students with disabilities.* Retrieved August 31, 2005, from http://www.educationevolving.org/pdf/Response_to_Intervention.pdf

James, F. (2004, December 5). *Response to intervention in the Individuals with Disabilities Education Act (IDEA), 2004.* Retrieved August 31, 2005, from http://www.reading.org/downloads/resources/IDEA_RTI_report.pdf

Mellard, D. (2004, September 15). *Understanding responsiveness to intervention in learning disabilities determination.* Retrieved August 31, 2005, from http://www.nrcld.org/publications/papers/mellard.pdf

National Joint Committee on Learning Disabilities. (2005, July). *Responsiveness to intervention and learning disabilities.* Retrieved August 31, 2005 from http://www.dldcec.org/pdf/rti_final.pdf

National Resource Center on Learning Disabilities. (2003, July 3). *Information sheet for regional resource centers, response to intervention models, identify, evaluate, & scale.* Retrieved August 31, 2005, from http://nrcld.org/research/rti/RTIinfo.pdf

Ready, K. (2004). *R&D alert: A promising alternative for identifying students with learning disabilities.* Retrieved August 31, 2005, from http://www.wested.org/online_pubs/RD-04-01.pdf

TANYA Y. BANDA
Texas A&M University

EMPIRICALLY SUPPORTED TREATMENT
LEARNING DISABILITIES
LEARNING DISABILITIES, PROBLEMS IN DEFINITION OF

RESTRAINT

See PHYSICAL RESTRAINT.

RETARDATION

See CULTURAL-FAMILIAL RETARDATION; MENTAL RETARDATION.

RETENTION IN GRADE

Retention in grade is the practice of having a child stay in or repeat an entire grade after he/she has already completed an entire school year at that grade level (Jackson, 1975). The practice of retention as an intervention for improving skills is controversial. A current increase in retention practice may in part be attributable to both President Clinton, whose educational goals included the ending of social promotion (i.e., promoting children to the next grade who have not met grade-level requirements; Clinton, 1999), and the No Child Left Behind Act (2002), which emphasizes accountability and standards in school.

Many studies have been conducted on retained children and have been compiled in several meta-analyses (Holmes, 1989; Holmes & Matthews, 1984; Jimerson, 2001). Overall, these meta-analyses showed that nonretained students performed around one third of a standard deviation unit better than retained students in both academic and behavioral measures. Because Jimerson's (2001) is the most current meta-analysis, including the most recent studies on retention, his results are further reviewed.

Jimerson's (2001) meta-analysis shows that promotion leads to better outcomes than does retention. Although some effect sizes showed retained students to have more favorable outcomes the year after they had been retained, most of the longitudinal effect sizes showed better outcomes for those students who had been promoted. More specifically, students who had been retained were on average .3 standard deviation units below students who had been promoted in both academic and socioemotional outcomes. Attendance rates were also significantly greater for promoted students (Jimerson). It has also been found that retained students are more likely to drop out of high school and to have lower-paying jobs as adults than students who had been promoted.

It can be concluded that the evidence is in favor of promoting students over retaining students. Promoted students have better long-term outcomes than their matched retained counterparts.

REFERENCES

Clinton, W. J. (1999, January 19). *State of the union.* Retrieved June 28, 2005, from http://www.cnn.com/ALLPOLITICS/stories/1999/01/19/sotu.transcript/

Holmes, C. T. (1989). Grade-level retention effects: A meta-analysis of research studies. In L. A. Shepard & M. L. Smith (Eds.), *Flunking grades: Research and policies on retention* (pp. 16–32). London: Falmer.

Holmes, C. T., & Matthews, K. M. (1984). The effects of nonpromotion in elementary and junior high school pupils: A meta-analysis. *Review of Educational Research, 54,* 225–236.

Jackson, G. B. (1975). The research evidence in the effect of grade retention. *Review of Educational Research, 45,* 438–460.

Jimerson, S. R. (2001). Meta-analysis of grade retention research: Implications for practice in the 21st century. *School Psychology Review, 30,* 420–437.

No Child Left Behind Act of 2001. (2002). Public Law No. 107-110, Paragraph 115, Stat. 1425.

KRISTA D. HEALY
*University of California,
Riverside*

RETICULAR ACTIVATING SYSTEM

The reticular activating system is the mass of cells in the brain stem associated with arousal, wakefulness, attention, and habituation. Its dysfunction may be associated with the hyperactivity and attention deficits often observed in brain-damaged children.

The major function of the reticular system is to provide for cortical activation via its connections through the diffuse thalamic projection system. If the reticular system is significantly impaired, as in severe head trauma, coma results. However, even with less severe impairment, wakefulness, perception (Livingston, 1967), or cognitive functions are attenuated. The second major function is through the posterior hypothalamus, an area that provides a similar activating influence on the limbic system (Feldman & Waller, 1962; Iwamura & Kawamura, 1962; Routtenberg, 1968).

Specific investigations of the dual arousal systems have revealed different functions of each. Damage to the reticular system attenuates its cortical activation effects but does not impair behavioral arousal. In contrast, damage to the posterior hypothalamus impairs arousal, but cortical activation remains (Feldman & Waller, 1962; Kawamura, Nakamura, & Tokizane, 1961; Kawamura & Oshima, 1962). Because of their anatomical proximity and the neuronal interconnections between the posterior hypothalamus and the reticular system, it is likely that both systems will become impaired by injury or disease, although one system may be affected to a greater extent. This may account for some of the variability observed in brain-impaired children.

REFERENCES

Feldman, S., & Waller, H. (1962). Dissociation of electrocortical activation and behavioral arousal. *Nature, 196,* 1320.

Iwamura, G., & Kawamura, H. (1962). Activation pattern in lower level in the neo-, paleo-, archicortices. *Japanese Journal of Physiology, 11,* 494–505.

Kawamura, H., Nakamura, Y., & Tokizane, T. (1961). Effect of acute brain stem lesions on the electrical activities of the limbic system and neocortex. *Japanese Journal of Physiology, 11,* 564–575.

Kawamura, H., & Oshima, K. (1962). Effect of adrenaline on the hypothalamic activating system. *Japanese Journal of Physiology, 12,* 225–233.

Livingston, R. (1967). Brain in circuitry relating to complex behavior. In G. Quarton, T. Melnechuk, & Schmitt, F. (Eds.), *The neurosciences: A study program.* New York: Rockefeller University Press.

Routtenberg, A. (1968). The two arousal hypothesis: Reticular formation and limbic system. *Psychological Review, 75,* 51–80.

CHARLES J. LONG
Memphis State University

GERI R. ALVIS
University of Tennessee

ATTENTION-DEFICIT/HYPERACTIVITY DISORDER
BRAIN DAMAGE/INJURY
HYPERKINESIS

RETINITIS PIGMENTOSA

Retinitis pigmentosa (RP), "more appropriately named rod-cone generalized dystrophy, is a varied group of disorders characterized by . . . [progressive] retinal rod and cone degeneration" (Reynolds, 2001, p. 1). No single classification system has been generally accepted; one version is the following: "1) Congenital RP or Leber's Congenital Amaurosis. 2) Autosomal Recessive RP. 3) Autosomal Dominant RP. 4) X-linked or Sex-linked Recessive RP. 5) Sporadic RP. 6) RP Associated with Systemic Diseases" (Reynolds, 2001, p. 1). Types 1 and 6 are rare; Type 5 is not familial. About 22 percent and 9 percent of RP cases are autosomal dominant and sex-linked, respectively. Most of the remaining cases appear to have an autosomal recessive basis, but RP cases do not always follow Mendelian patterns of inheritance, leading to uncertainty about their genetic basis (Baumgartner, 2000). Overall incidence is about 1 in 4,000. Generally, rods are affected first and more severely, leading initially to loss of night and peripheral vision, although cones may become involved in advanced cases (MedlinePlus Health Information, 2001).

The type of RP influences severity, time of onset, speed of progression, and order of appearance of symptoms. Congenital RP is present at birth and associated with persistent visual loss. Recessive RP (Types 2 and 4) usually have childhood or early adolescent onset and poor prognosis. Dominant RP (Type 3) tends to be milder. Sporadic RP has variable outcome. The systemic illnesses with which Type 6 is associated are rare and often fatal; severe RP symptoms often occur early and involve central vision loss (Reynolds, 2001).

Characteristics might include:

1. Night blindness
2. Tunnel vision
3. Vision loss
4. Splotchy pigmentation on the retina

Frequently, RP is not diagnosed until an affected individual begins to lose night or peripheral vision. An ophthalmologist's exam will show splotchy pigmentation on the retina. Vision continues to decline, although total blindness is rare. Because RP is associated with a number of other conditions and disorders, differential diagnosis is important (Beauchamp, 2000).

The symptoms of RP are progressive and often follow a predictable course in which the first symptom is night blindness. Some RP patients may not realize that they have night blindness, although they have noticed difficulty seeing at dusk or nighttime. The next symptom of RP is tunnel vision: The RP patient loses peripheral vision, but central vision is still intact. When RP is in the advanced stages, central vision is compromised and blindness is a possibility. Rate of progression is highly variable from patient to patient and may be correlated with type of RP (Baumgartner, 2000).

No effective treatment to stop the progression of RP is available. Sunglasses may help preserve sight by protecting the retina from ultraviolet light. Some recent but controversial studies suggest that treatment with antioxidant agents such as vitamin A palmitate may delay progression. Treatment consists of vision aids such as corrective glasses or contact lenses, although prescriptions need to be updated in order to keep up with the disorder's progression. More sophisticated aids to vision may be needed depending on the disorder's progression. Counseling is also recommended to help the patient deal with the psychological aspects of vision loss, and a low-vision specialist may help to maintain patient independence (MedlinePlus Health Information, 2001).

REFERENCES

Baumgartner, W. (2000). Etiology, pathogenesis, and experimental treatment of retinitis pigmentosa. *Medical Hypotheses, 54,* 814–824.

Beauchamp, G. R. (2000). Retinitis pigmentosa (RP). In C. R. Reynolds & E. Fletcher-Janzen (Eds.), *Encyclopedia of special education* (2nd ed., Vol. 3, pp. 1546–1547). New York: Wiley.

MedlinePlus Health Information. (2001). *Retinitis pigmentosa.* Retrieved from http://www.nlm.nih.gov/medlineplus/ency/article/001029.htm

Reynolds, J. D. (2001). *Retinitis pigmentosa: Med Help International.* Retrieved from http://medhlp.netusa.net/lib/retinit.htm

Melanie Moore
Robert T. Brown
University of North Carolina at Wilmington

RETINOBLASTOMA

Retinoblastoma is a rare form of childhood cancer in which malignant tumor(s) originate in the retina of the eye. The majority (75 percent) of cases are unilateral retinoblastoma, in which tumors develop in one eye. Tumors that are found in both eyes are referred to as bilateral retinoblastoma (Abramson & Servodidio, 1997).

Retinoblastoma affects one in every 15,000–30,000 children who are born in the United States (Abramson & Servodidio, 1997). There are approximately 300 newly diagnosed cases each year in this country (Abramson & Servodidio, 1997; Demirci, Finger, Cocker, & McCormick 1999). It affects children of both genders and of all races equally (Abramson & Servodidio, 1997; Margo, Harman, & Mulla, 1998).

Although there are still many unanswered questions as to why retinoblastoma occurs, it is known that in all cases there is an abnormality in Chromosome 13, the chromosome responsible for controlling retinal cell division. In retinoblastoma, a piece of the chromosome is either deleted or mutated, causing retinal cell division to proceed and the tumor(s) to develop (Abramson & Servodidio, 1997; Finger, 2000; Margo et al., 1998). Most patients (90 percent) have no family history of the disease. However, when it is inherited, the prevalence rate of retinoblastoma is more common in children whose parents have the bilateral form of the disease (45 percent) than in children whose parents have the unilateral form (7–15 percent; Abramson & Servodidio, 1997).

Characteristics include:

1. Initial signs of retinoblastoma usually include pupils that have an abnormal white appearance (leukocoria) or crossed eyes (strabismus).
2. Possible redness in eye, pain, poor vision, or inflammation of tissue surrounding the eye.
3. Small tumors appear as translucent, off-white patches, or well-defined nodular lesions of retinal vessels.
4. Large tumors often produce retinal detachment; some portions of the detached retina appear creamy-white, with newly formed blood vessels extending over the surface and dividing into the substance of a tumor.
5. Other indications include failure to thrive (trouble eating or drinking), extra fingers or toes, malformed ears, or mental retardation.

Retinoblastoma can be diagnosed through retinal dilation. An ultrasound examination and a CAT scan may also be performed. Treatment of retinoblastoma varies according to the extent of the disease within and outside of the eye. The current methods for treating retinoblastoma include enucleation, external beam radiation, radioactive plaques, laser therapy, cryotherapy, and chemoreduction. Enucleation involves the surgical removal of the eye and fitting the socket with a synthetic implant at the time of surgery (Abramson & Servodidio, 1997).

Retinoblastoma is a progressive disease. Therefore, most children have vision through at least their 1st year of life (Warren, 1994). In fact, the majority of children retain vision in at least one eye (Abramson & Servodidio, 1997). Because children with this disorder usually are able to adapt quite well, they are able to lead a normal life and to attend a regular education classroom (Heller, Alberto, Forney, & Schwartzman, 1996). However, it is very important that they wear protective eyewear when engaging in sports and other hazardous activities. There are some instances in which normal vision is impaired sufficiently to necessitate the assistance of visual aids and support systems in order for these children to attend mainstream classes. Some educational components might include using assistive technology, adapting written material, coordinating orientation and mobility services, fostering the development of appropriate play with toys, and promoting peer interactions (Heller et al., 1996). In cases of more serious loss of vision, it may be necessary for some children to attend programs for individuals who are visually impaired or blind (Rosser & Kingston, 1997). There also seems to be a bimodal distribution of intelligence scores among children with retinoblastoma: Some children's performance falls in the low-average range, whereas other children perform in the well-above-average range (Warren, 1994).

Prognosis is generally successful, especially if the diagnosis occurs early. However, children who inherit retinoblastoma from a parent who has had the bilateral form of the disease may also be at risk for developing other cancers, such as bone tumors (osteogenic sarcoma), skin cancers (cutaneous melanoma), muscle and connective tissue tumors (soft tissue sarcoma), and brain tumors (pineoblastomas; Finger, 2000). Thus, those with a genetic form of the disorder have a less favorable prognosis (Margo et al., 1998). Current research is focused on genetic testing as well as on combating secondary cancers (Rosser & Kingston, 1997).

REFERENCES

Abramson, D. H., & Servodidio, C. (1997). *A parent's guide to understanding retinoblastoma*. Retrieved from http://www.retinoblastoma.com/guide

Demirci, H., Finger, P. T., Cocker, R., & McCormick, S. A. (1999). Interactive case challenge: A 7-week-old female with a "White Pupil" in the left eye. *Medscape Oncology, 2*(5).

Finger, P. T. (2000). *Retinoblastoma*. Retrieved from http://www.eyecancer.com/conditions/Retinal percent20Tumors/retino.html

Heller, K. W., Alberto, P. A., Forney, P. E., & Schwartzman, M. N. (1996). *Understanding physical, sensory, and health impairments: Characteristics and educational implications*. Pacific Grove, CA: Brooks/Cole.

Margo, C. E., Harman, L. E., & Mulla, Z. D. (1998). Retinoblastoma. *Cancer Control: Journal of the Moffitt Cancer Center, 5*(4), 310–316.

Rosser, E., & Kingston, J. (1997). *Retinoblastoma: Fighting eye cancer in children*. Retrieved from http://ds.dial.pipex.com/rbinfo/information.html

Warren, D. H. (1994). *Blindness and children: An individual differences approach*. New York: Cambridge University Press.

MICHELLE PERFECT
University of Texas at Austin

RETINOPATHY OF PREMATURITY

Retinopathy of prematurity (ROP) is the most common cause of retinal damage in infancy. Incidence has recently been stable, but prevalence is increasing because of the increased survival of infants with very low birth weight—about 67 percent of infants who weigh less than 3 pounds (1,251 g) and about 80 percent of infants who weigh less than 2.2 pounds (1,000 g) at birth will manifest some degree of ROP (Menacker & Batshaw, 1997; Merck Manual of Diagnosis and Therapy [Merck], 2001). Exposure to excessive or prolonged oxygen is the major risk for ROP, but presence of other medical complications also increases risk. Unfortunately, threshold safe levels or durations of oxygen are not known (Merck, 2001).

Characteristics might include:

1. Abnormal proliferation of blood vessels in the retina.
2. Progressively, the vascular tissue invades the vitreous and sometimes engorges the entire vasculature of the eye.
3. Abnormal vessels stop growing and may subside spontaneously.
4. In severe cases, scarring from abnormal vessels contract, leading to retinal detachments and vision loss in early infancy.

Development of the inner retinal blood vessels occurs across the second half of pregnancy. Thus, their growth is incomplete in premature infants. If they continue growth abnormally, ROP results. Incidence and severity of ROP vary with the proportion of retina that is avascular at birth (Merck, 2001).

Vision loss ranges from myopia (correctible with glasses) to strabismus, glaucoma, and blindness (Menacker & Batshaw, 1997). Children with moderate, healed ROP but who have cicatrices (dragged retina or retinal folds) have increased risk for retinal detachments later in life.

Diagnosis is through ophthalmological examination by a specialist in examination of premature infants. Premature infants should have regular examinations over the first year of life because early detection can often lead to effective treatment. ROP is defined by both the stage or degree of the disorder and the area in which it occurs. The American Academy of Pediatrics Section on Ophthalmology (2001) has recently provided detailed recommendations for screening for and intervening in cases of ROP. Appropriately managed premature infants with birth weights of more than 1,500 grams (3 lb 5 oz) rarely develop ROP, so differential diagnosis of other disorders such as familial exudative retinopathy or Norrie disease should be considered.

Prevention of premature birth when possible is the best approach to avoiding ROP (Menacker & Batshaw, 1997; Merck, 2001). Where prematurity does occur, levels of oxygen should be at the lowest safe levels, and surfactant should be provided to reduce respiratory distress. Recent developments in treatment of ROP with cryotherapy and laser therapy have reduced the incidence of posterior retinal traction folds or detachments by more than 40 percent and of blindness by about 24 percent (American Academy of Pediatrics Section on Ophthalmology, 2001). Affected individuals with residual scarring should be examined at least annually for life. Later retinal detachments resulting from such scarring can often be treated effectively if they are detected early. For cases with residual visual loss, special education and adaptive technology may be needed.

REFERENCES

American Academy of Pediatrics Section on Ophthalmology. (2001). Screening examination of premature infants for retinopathy of prematurity. *Pediatrics, 108,* 809–811.

Menacker, S. J., & Batshaw, M. L. (1997). Vision: Our window to the world. In M. L. Batshaw (Ed.), *Children with disabilities* (4th ed., pp. 211–239). Baltimore: Brookes.

Merck Manual of Diagnosis and Therapy. (2001). *Retinopathy of prematurity (retrolental fibroplasia).* Retrieved from http://www.merck.com/pubs/mmanual/section19/chapter260/2601.htm

ROBERT T. BROWN
University of North Carolina at Wilmington

BRENDA MELVIN
New Hanover Regional Medical Center

RETROLENTAL FIBROPLASIA

Retrolental fibroplasia (RLF) was first recognized in the early 1940s, with the first literature description published in 1942. Over the ensuing decade, many unrelated and sometimes conflicting etiologies for the disease were considered. Among these were water miscible vitamins, iron, oxygen, cow's milk, and abnormal electrolytes, all of which have been shown in positive association to the incidence of RLF. Experimental evidence implicated vitamin E deficiency as a possible cause. Other factors that have been associated with RLF are viral infections, hormonal imbalances, premature exposure of infant eyes to light, and vitamin A deficiency in the mother. The observation that the incidence of the disease increases in direct relation to the duration and exposure of premature infants to oxygen was reported first in 1952. A controlled study was completed in 1954; it established oxygen as the most likely etiologic agent for the condition. The rise of this disease, called by some an epidemic, closely parallels the development of the ability to effectively concentrate oxygen administration to infants in incubators (Silverman, 1980).

The importance of oxygen concentration monitoring became apparent as experimental evidence of the early 1950s accumulated. Ambient oxygen levels were limited whenever possible to 40 percent, and measurements of oxygen concentration in the blood were made. This did not entirely resolve the issue for several reasons: The disease occurred in the absence of supplemental oxygen therapy; it occurred when 40 percent oxygen was administered "appropriately"; and this level of supplemental oxygen often was not sufficient to relieve the respiratory distress syndrome that often accompanies prematurity. The important relationship between arterial blood oxygen (PO^2), the respiratory distress syndrome, and retrolental fibroplasia is now well established. However, numerous attempts to monitor and control arterial blood oxygen (PO^2) have been fraught with great difficulties, both technical and physiologic.

Approximately 10 percent of infants under 2,500 g birth weight are afflicted with the respiratory distress syndrome, accounting for approximately 40,000 infants per year in the United States; the incidence of RLF blindness following oxygen administration is a small percentage of the group, perhaps 2 percent. Recognizing this, many authors now designate this disease retinopathy of prematurity (ROP).

An appreciation of the clinical stages of the disease accompanied experimental evidence concerning its pathophysiology. Evidence suggests that high arterial oxygen levels cause vasospastic constriction of developing peripheral retinal vasculature, inciting the elaboration of vasoproliferative factors. New vessels grow in a moundlike elevation, typically in the temporal peripheral retina (Tasman, 1971). Such neovascularization either may proceed or spontaneously regress. With resolution of the active process, cicatrization (scarring) occurs, which on contraction may drag the retina temporally. If traction is sufficient, peripheral retinal detachment occurs. When the entire retina becomes detached and drawn into a fibrous cicatrix (scar) behind the lens, the disease has reached its most advanced stage, representing the clinical picture for which the disease was named. Additional ocular sequelae include myopia; vitreous opacification; and a variety of retinal changes, including chorioretinal atrophy, pigmentary retinopathy, and retinal folds. Based on these observations, clinical characterization of the disease recently has been reviewed and a proposed international classification published.

The relationship of oxygen therapy to neurological outcome also was studied. In general, neurologic outcome is inversely related to ocular outcome; that is, spastic diplegia incidence falls and retrolental fibroplasia rises with increased duration of oxygen treatment. Thus, there is a desire to prevent neurologic events following cyanotic attacks (secondary to cardiorespiratory insufficiency) by extending treatment with oxygen; this then increases the risk of RLF.

The full spectrum of consequences of RLF blindness to the child, family, social agencies, school, and community is beginning to be fully considered. Affected individuals tend not to see loss of sight as a major burden. Preconceptions, paternalism, and insensitivity of authorities in the visually oriented world often constrict the lives of those who wish to see this same world nonvisually. A number of factors—medical, legal, and societal—tend to perpetuate the stereotype that the blind wish to shed in their desire to move toward independence. Thus, the complexity of this disease at several levels—visual, neurological, personal, and social—is only now being appreciated.

The visually disabling forms of RLF may affect school performance by limiting sensory input; the degree of disability reflects the severity of disease. Teachers may observe "blindness" where disability is severe. When bilateral retinal blindness is present, braille instruction is required. The educator should be aware of the complexity of problems for individuals with this condition.

REFERENCES

Silverman, W. A. (1980). *Retrolental fibroplasia: A modern parable.* New York: Grune & Stratton.

Tasman, W. (Ed.). (1971). *Retinal diseases in children.* New York: Harper & Row.

GEORGE R. BEAUCHAMP
Cleveland Clinic Foundation

RETT SYNDROME

Rett syndrome (RS) is a disorder that initially appears as a deterioration from apparently normal development in infancy or early childhood. It involves a slowdown in normal development, deceleration of head growth, uninterest in the environment, deterioration of motor functioning, loss of hand use and subsequently locomotion, hand stereotypies (typically hand wringing or clapping), loss of expressive language, autistic and self-abusive behavior, and eventual severe/profound mental retardation. Prevalence estimates vary. Hagberg (1995b) revised the estimate of prevalence of classic RS from 1:10,000 females to closer to 1:15,000. Cases have been reported in all parts of the world and in all ethnic groups (e.g., Moser & Naidu, 1991; Naidu, 1997). First described by Andreas Rett (1966), it initially came to the world's attention largely through the work of Hagberg and his associates (Hagberg, Aicardi, Dias, & Ramos, 1983).

Unique to RS is apparently normal initial development followed by rapid mental and physical deterioration followed by stabilization or even reduction in some symptoms (e.g., Budden, 1997; Hagberg, 1995b). RS is also unusual in that it (a) apparently affects only women, whereas most gender-specific disorders affect only men; (b) is manifested in part through loss of acquired function, but is apparently neurodevelopmental and not neurogenerative (e.g., Glaze, 1995); (c) presents in a fairly striking set of behavioral symptoms that have consistent developmental trends; and (d) is almost undoubtedly genetically based, but no marker has been identified. Although the subject of hundreds of articles, it is still relatively unknown in comparison to many other developmental disorders of comparable prevalence. As

would be expected, research on the genetic basis focuses on an X-chromosome abnormality. RS is associated with numerous neuroanatomical and neurochemical disturbances, summaries of which can be found in Brown and Hoadley (1999), Budden (1997), Hagberg, (1996), or Percy (1996).

Diagnostic Symptoms: Classic RS and RS Variant

Necessary for diagnosis of Classic RS is apparently normal pre-, peri-, and early postnatal development followed in infancy or early childhood by sudden deceleration of head growth and loss of acquired skills, including hand use and language (Rett Syndrome Diagnostic Criteria Work Group, 1988). Also required is evidence of mental retardation and the appearance of intense and persistent hand stereotypies: "The almost continuous repetitive wringing, twisting or clapping hand automatisms during wakefulness constitute the hallmark of the condition" (Hagberg, 1995b, p. 973). Girls who had developed walking must show gait abnormalities; some never develop walking. EEG abnormalities, seizure disorder, spasticity, marked scoliosis, and overall growth retardation are also typical. A number of other behaviors may also be shown, including episodic hyperventilation and breath holding, bloating owing to air swallowing, bruxism, hypoplastic cold red-blue feet, scoliosis, and night laughing (Hagberg, 1995a).

The RS variant model was developed owing to the realization that females with RS are much more heterogeneous than originally thought (Hagberg, 1995a, 1995b). Diagnosis of RS variant should be made only in girls of 10 years or older age when a subset of the symptoms for Classic RS has been met. These behaviors may appear throughout childhood. Typically, girls who meet the criteria for RS variant show less severe symptoms than those associated with classic RS. Both gross and fine motor control may be spared, and mental retardation is less severe. RS variant girls may retain some language, although it tends to be abnormal and telegraphic. Those with language tend to have had a later and milder regression period.

For both parents and therapists, diagnosis should be made as early as possible. Some physicians may be reluctant to diagnose RS early owing to the eventual severity of the disorder, but many parents are frustrated by the lack of a diagnosis that fits their children's behaviors or has implications for treatment and care (Brown & Hoadley, 1999). For that reason, the term *potential RS* (Hagberg, 1995b) has been suggested for use with young cases. RS may be confused with a number of other disorders, particularly autism, so careful diagnosis is necessary.

Developmental Trend

Most girls with classic RS develop through a fairly reliable four-stage sequence of behavioral and physical changes first described by Hagberg and Witt-Engerström (1986). Age of onset, duration of transition from one stage to another, and duration of each is highly variable, however. Except as specifically referenced, information in this section comes from Budden (1997), Hagberg (1995b), Hagberg and Witt-Engerström (1986), and Naidu (1997).

Pre-Stage 1: Early Development

Much pre-Stage 1 development appears normal until at least 5–6 months of age. Early motor skills appear, including reaching for objects. Self-feeding commonly develops, with infants weaning onto solid foods. Many children develop walking, but often with an unusual gait. However, appearance of many infant developmental milestones is delayed or absent. Some slowing of brain growth may be seen in unusually low occipito-frontal circumference as early as 2 months of age. Many girls develop single-word communication, and a few use short phrases.

Stage 1: Early Onset Stagnation

The first stage begins at from 6 to 18 months of age and may last from weeks to months. In many ways the infant appears to hit a developmental wall. Many aspects of cognitive development cease. A deceleration of head growth leads to head circumference generally below average by the end of the second year of life. Hypotonia, uninterest in play and the environment, loss of acquired hand functions, and random hand movements are typical. No obvious pattern of abnormalities is apparent, however.

Stage 2: Rapid Developmental Regression

At between 1 and 3 or 4 years of age, functioning begins to deteriorate so generally and rapidly that the onset may be taken for a toxic or encephalitic state (Hagberg & Witt-Engerström, 1986). Further, Budden (1997, p. 2) reports that the onset "may be so acute that parents can sometimes give a specific date after which their child was no longer 'normal.'" General cognitive functioning, purposeful hand use, and expressive language deteriorate. The classic hand stereotypies, including hand wringing, washing, and mouthing, typically appear and may be continuous during waking hours. Walking may deteriorate or not develop. Gait abnormalities, particularly a spread-legged stance, are generally evident in girls who can walk. Hyperventilation and breath holding are common, as are behaviors characteristic of autism. Seizures and vacant spells resembling seizures may occur, and virtually all RS girls have abnormal EEGs.

Stage 3: Pseudostationary

Stage 3 has a highly variable age of onset, occurring at the end of the rapid deterioration, and lasts until about 10 years of age. Hand stereotypies continue, and mobility may

further deteriorate. Mental retardation in the severe/profound range is characteristic. On the other hand, autistic symptoms may diminish, and social interactions, hand use, communication, alertness, and self-initiated behavior may increase. Tremulousness, ataxia, teeth grinding (bruxism), hyperventilation or breath holding, and seizures are common. Overall rigidity is likely to increase and scoliosis to appear. Nonverbal communication through eye pointing may improve.

Stage 4: Late Motor Deterioration

After about age 10 years, motor function decreases further, with increased rigidity, scoliosis, and muscle wasting. Mobility continues to decrease; many girls will be wheelchair-bound. Hands may be held in mouth for long periods. Expressive language, if previously present, generally disappears, and receptive language is decreased. Eye pointing as communication may continue. Chewing and swallowing may be lost, necessitating artificial feeding. However, the final phenotypic characteristics of classic RS cases vary widely. Life span varies, but overall longevity is shorter than normal (Naidu, 1997).

Overall Intellectual Characteristics

Formal assessments indicate that RS girls function at a severe/profound level of mental retardation, but their actual cognitive functioning may be difficult to assess owing to motor and language impairments. For a group of RS girls with a mean age of 9.4 years, Perry, Sarlo-McGarvey, and Haddad (1991) reported these Vineland Adaptive Behavior Scale (VABS) scores, based on potentially biased interviews with parents: Communication, mean 17.4 months; Daily living skills, mean 16.9; and Socialization, mean 25.9 months. Mean mental age on the Cattell Infant Intelligence was 3.0 months. Most girls attended to visual and auditory stimuli, were interested in toys, and anticipated being fed. Only one appeared to have object permanence, and none succeeded on items requiring language or fine motor skills. The girls attended when spoken to and showed some understanding, but most did not speak or have any other communication system. Most could feed themselves, some with their fingers, and some could use a cup. Most were in diapers and did not perform other self-care tasks. They showed some interest in other people and could discriminate among them, but they showed virtually no play behaviors.

Overall Emotional Characteristics

RS girls show a variety of emotional and behavioral problems. The following information is from a survey of parents by Sansom, Krishnan, Corbett, and Kerr (1993) when the girls' mean age was 10.6 years. Over 75 percent showed anxiety, particularly in response to external situations.

Most episodes were brief and consisted of screaming, hyperventilation, self-injury, frightened expression, and general distress. Precipitating events included novel situations and people, sudden noises, some music, change of routine, and high activity by others close to the child. Low mood, reflected partly in crying, occurred in 70 percent, but for extended periods in only a few. Almost 50 percent showed self-injurious behaviors (SIBs). Most were relatively mild, such as biting fingers or hands, but more serious chewing of fingers, head banging, and hair pulling also occurred. Epilepsy was reported in 63 percent. Although most slept well, early wakening and nighttime laughing, crying, and screaming were common.

Treatment and Management

No completely effective treatment regime is available, and the symptoms appear to follow an inexorable course. However, active intervention may delay the appearance of some symptoms and alleviate others (Glaze, 1995). RS girls typically have very long latencies to respond to directions, an important consideration in all aspects of therapy. Delay to respond may be as long as a minute. Accurate diagnosis is important both to ensure appropriate treatment and to avoid ineffective treatment. For example, three RS girls who had initially been diagnosed with autism were inadvertent participants in Lovaas's intensive behavior modification program, which has been demonstrably effective with autistic children (Smith, Klevstrand, & Lovaas, 1995.). Overall, the girls showed few if any changes that might not have occurred without treatment. Individual differences in the degree of various impairments and responsiveness to, as well as tolerance of, various interventions necessitate individualized treatment programs (e.g., Van Acker, 1991). Owing to the multiplicity and diversity of problems associated with RS, a team approach is indicated.

Specialized behavior modification programs have been successful on a variety of behaviors in RS girls of different ages. Techniques such as shaping, graduated guidance, and hand regulation have increased self-feeding and ambulation in RS girls (e.g., Bat-Haee, 1994). Use of mechanical and computer-based adaptive devices may also modify RS girls' behavior, enabling them to communicate and discriminate between such things as favored and nonfavored foods (e.g., Van Acker & Grant, 1995). One caution must be expressed, however, about the routine implementation of some of these programs, particularly by parents. Much effort, persistence, and tolerance for frustration are required, since improvement can be slow and even difficult to see. Indeed, Piazza et al. (1993) suggest that parents be warned about the effort involved and the need to keep careful response records in order to see progress.

As apraxia is one of the main effects of RS, physical therapy is critical. It helps RS girls to maintain or reacquire ambulation and to develop or maintain transitional behaviors needed to stand up from sitting or lying positions. The stereotypic hand movements are involuntary, so behavior modification techniques designed to reduce them not only will likely be ineffective but may actually increase the movements by increasing anxiety. Several techniques, including restraints that prevent hand-to-mouth movements or simply holding the girl's hand, may be effective. Generally, whirlpool baths may be helpful. Some of the stereotyped hand clasping and other movements may be reduced by allowing the girl to hold a favored toy (Hanks, 1990).

Most RS girls begin to develop scoliosis before age eight, and many also show kyphosis (hunchback; Huang, Lubicky, & Hammerberg, 1994). The disorders are basically neurogenic but are exacerbated by other factors such as loss of transitional motor skills and spatial perceptual orientation, postural misalignment, and rigidity (Budden, 1997). Physical therapy and careful positioning in seated positions may help slow the development of scoliosis, but corrective surgery is often required.

Although showing strong appetites, most RS girls show serious growth retardation to the point of meeting criteria for moderate to severe malnutrition. Chewing and swallowing problems, as well as gastroesophageal reflux and digestive problems, contribute to the retardation. Speech therapy may be helpful not so much for retaining language as for facilitating chewing and swallowing. Supplementary tube feedings may be necessary to help increase growth (Glaze & Schultz, 1997). Further complicating feeding issues, constipation is common in RS. Although it is generally controllable through diet, laxatives or enemas may be necessary in some cases.

Seizures occur in most RS girls, and their control "is perhaps the most common problem facing the primary care provider or the treating neurologist" (Budden, 1997, p. 7). Seizures occur most commonly in Stage 3 (Glaze & Schultz, 1997). Most seizures can be controlled with antiseizure medication, most frequently carbamazepine and/or valproic acid. Occasionally, in otherwise intractable cases, the ketogenic diet may be used (Budden, 1997), although it presents its own management problems.

Agitation, screaming, and tantrums are frequently reported. The rapid neurologic and physical changes associated with the onset of the disease may understandably provoke emotional outbursts. RS girls frequently respond negatively to stimulus or routine change, so transitions from one setting or pattern to another should be gradual and accompanied by a parent if possible. Agitation or screaming may also reflect pain or irritation from a physical condition that in the absence of language or gestures RS individuals may have no other way to signal. Since the girls go through puberty, caretakers need to be sensitive to their menstrual cycles. Some agitation in older individuals may reflect menstrual discomfort or some other gynecologic disorder that may be easily treatable (Budden, 1997). A variety of treatment approaches have been used; behavior modification may be helpful.

Owing to the lifelong impact of the disorder on parents

and other family members, ranging from home care issues to decisions about educational and other placement, counseling for the family will be particularly important (Lieb-Lundell, 1988). Training of the parents in behavior modification may be helpful in managing some aspects of their RS daughter's behavior, including tantrums. Of importance, given the degree of care that RS adults may require and their relative longevity, parents will eventually need to face the issue of lifelong care and make financial arrangements for care of the woman after their death.

REFERENCES

Bat-Haee, M. A. (1994). Behavioral training of a young woman with Rett syndrome. *Perceptual and Motor Skills, 78,* 314.

Brown, R. T., & Hoadley, S. L. (1999). Rett syndrome. In S. Goldstein & C. R. Reynolds (Eds.), *Handbook of neurodevelopmental and genetic disorders of children* (pp. 459–477). New York: Guilford.

Budden, S. S. (1997). Understanding, recognizing, and treating Rett syndrome. *Medscape Women's Health, 2*(3), 1–11. http://www .medscape.com/Medscape/WomensHealth/journal/1997/v2.n03/ w3185.budden.html

Glaze, D. G., & Schultz, R. J. (1997). Rett syndrome: Meeting the challenge of this gender-specific neurodevelopmental disorder. *Medscape Women's Health, 2*(1), 1–9. http://www.medscape .com/Medscape/WomensHealth/journal/1997/v2.n01/w223 .glaze.html

Hagberg, B. (1995a). Clinical delineation of Rett syndrome variants. *Neuropediatrics, 26,* 62.

Hagberg, B. (1995b). Rett syndrome: Clinical peculiarities and biological mysteries. *Acta Paediatrica, 84,* 971–976.

Hagberg, B. (1996). Rett syndrome: Recent clinical and biological aspects. In A. Arzimanoglou & F. Goutières (Eds.), *Trends in child neurology* (pp. 143–146). Paris: John Libby Eurotext.

Hagberg, B., Aicardi, J., Dias, K., & Ramos, O. (1983). A progressive syndrome of autism, dementia, ataxia, and loss of purposeful hand use in girls: Rett's syndrome: Report of 35 cases. *Annals of Neurology, 14,* 471–479.

Hagberg, B., & Witt-Engerström, I. (1986). Rett syndrome: A suggested staging system for describing impairment profile with increasing age toward adolescence. *American Journal of Medical Genetics, 24*(Suppl. 1), 47–59.

Hanks, S. (1990). Motor disabilities in the Rett syndrome and physical therapy strategies. *Brain and Development, 12,* 157–161.

Huang, T. J., Lubicky, J. P., & Hammerberg, K. W. (1994). Scoliosis in Rett syndrome. *Orthopaedic Review, 23,* 931–937.

Lieb-Lundell, C. (1988). The therapist's role in the management of girls with Rett syndrome. *Journal of Child Neurology, 3*(Suppl.), S31–S34.

Moser, H. W., & Naidu, S. (1991). The discovery and study of Rett syndrome. In A. J. Capute & P. J. Accardo (Eds.), *Developmental disabilities in infancy and childhood* (pp. 325–333). Baltimore: Brookes.

Naidu, S. (1997). Rett syndrome: A disorder affecting early brain growth. *Annals of Neurology, 42,* 3–10.

Percy, A. K. (1996). Rett syndrome: The evolving picture of a disorder of brain development. *Developmental Brain Dysfunction, 9,* 180–196.

Perry, A. K., Sarlo-McGarvey, & Haddad, C. (1991). Brief reports: Cognitive and adaptive functioning in 28 girls with Rett syndrome. *Journal of Autism and Developmental Disabilities, 21,* 551–556.

Piazza, C. C., Anderson, C., & Fisher, W. (1993). Teaching self-feeding skills to patients with Rett syndrome. *Developmental Medicine and Child Neurology, 35,* 991–996.

Rett, A. (1966). Uber ein eigenartiges Hirnatrophisches Syndrom bei Hyperammonamie im Kindes alter. [On an unusual brain atropic syndrome with hyperammonia in childhood] *Wiener Medizinische Wochenschrift, 116,* 425–428. (As cited in Moser & Naidu, 1991, and Rett Syndrome Diagnostic Criteria Work Group, 1988.)

Rett Syndrome Diagnostic Criteria Work Group. (1988). Diagnostic criteria for Rett syndrome. *Annals of Neurology, 23,* 425–428.

Sansom, D., Krishnan, V. H. R., Corbett, J., & Kerr, A. (1993). Emotional and behavioural aspects of Rett syndrome. *Developmental Medicine and Child Neurology, 35,* 340–345.

Smith, T., Klevstrand, M., & Lovaas, O. I. (1995). Behavioral treatment of Rett's disorder: Ineffectiveness in three cases. *American Journal of Mental Retardation, 100,* 317–322.

Van Acker, R. (1991). Rett syndrome: A review of current knowledge. *Journal of Autism and Developmental Disabilities, 21,* 381–406.

Van Acker, R., & Grant, S. H. (1995). An effective computer-based requesting system for persons with Rett syndrome. *Journal of Childhood Communication Disorders, 16,* 31–38.

ROBERT T. BROWN
University of North Carolina at Wilmington

REVERSALS IN READING AND WRITING

The term *reversals* is usually associated with reading or writing disabilities. Reversals are difficulties characterized in either reading or writing by reversing letters, numbers, words, or phrases (e.g., *saw* for *was, p* for *q*), or what some have referred to as mirror reading or writing.

In Orton's first theoretical papers on reading disabilities (1925, 1928), he suggested that such reversal problems were due to poorly established hemispheric dominance. Orton (1928) cited the following examples of strephosymbolia (literally, "twisted symbols"): (1) difficulty discriminating *b* and *d;* (2) confusion with words like *ton* and *not;* (3) ability to read from mirror images; and (4) facility at writing mirrorlike images. Orton further stipulated that these reversal problems were not caused by mental retardation. Other investigators have since promoted the concept of developmental lag in perceptual abilities as causally related to reading disorders (Bender, 1957; Fernald, 1943).

As a result of this initial work, a variety of programs were developed that attempted to remediate reading disabilities by treating perceptual problems (Forness, 1981). For example, Kephart (1960) focused on the use of motor activities for developing perceptual skills. Additionally, programs such as Barsch's (1965) movigenic curriculum and Delacato's (1966) patterning techniques promoted the evolutionary progression that was seen as a necessary prerequisite for complete perceptual development. Frostig and Horne (1964) developed a visual perceptual program to remediate these difficulties, while Gillingham and Stillman (1960) prescribed the language triangle approach of combining the visual, auditory, and kinesthetic modes for teaching reading and writing.

Empirical support that reversals are due to perceptual deficits has been equivocal. It has been seen that many beginning readers reverse letters and words (Gibson & Levin, 1980). In fact, more than one half of all kindergarten students typically reverse letters (Gibson & Levin, 1980). This is considered a part of the normal component of discrimination learning when children first acquire reading skills. Gibson and Levin (1980) cite research that indicates that normal children continue to make reversal errors until the age of eight or nine. It was also found that single-letter reversals account for only a small percent of total reading errors exhibited by poor readers. In addition, it has been questioned whether such reversals in learning-disabled students indicate underlying perceptual problems rather than, for example, linguistic problems (Gupta, Ceci, & Slater, 1978).

Remedial programs based on visual motor perceptual training generally have not resulted in reading improvement (Keogh, 1974). Later research efforts have suggested that reversal problems can be remediated with the use of behavioral techniques. Hasazi and Hasazi (1972) reported an instance in which digit reversals (e.g., 12 for 21) of an 8-year-old boy were remediated by means of contingent teacher attention. With respect to letter reversals, Carnine (1981) provided evidence that discriminations that reflect differences in spatial orientation only (e.g., *b, d*) are best taught singly. In other words, a student should be taught to discriminate *b* from nonreversible letters first, followed by the separate introduction of the letter *d*. Some specific instructional techniques are provided by Hallahan, Kauffman, and Lloyd (1985).

REFERENCES

Barsch, R. H. (1965). *A movigenic curriculum* (Publication No. 25). Madison, WI: Wisconsin State Department of Instruction.

Bender, L. A. (1957). Specific reading disability as a maturational lag. *Bulletin of the Orton Society, 7,* 9–18.

Carnine, D. W. (1981). Reducing training problems associated with visually and auditorily similar correspondences. *Journal of Learning Disabilities, 14,* 276–279.

Delacato, C. H. (1966). *Neurological organization and reading.* Springfield, IL: Thomas.

Fernald, G. (1943). *Remedial techniques in basic school subjects.* New York: McGraw-Hill.

Forness, S. R. (1981). *Recent concepts in dyslexia: Implications for diagnosis and remediation.* Reston, VA: Council for Exceptional Children.

Frostig, M., & Horne, D. (1964). *The Frostig program for the development of visual perception: Teacher's guide.* Chicago: Follett.

Gibson, E. J., & Levin, H. (1980). *The psychology of reading.* Cambridge, MA: MIT Press.

Gillingham, A., & Stillman, B. W. (1960). *Remedial training for children with specific disability in reading, spelling, and penmanship.* Cambridge, MA: Educator's.

Gupta, R., Ceci, S. J., & Slater, A. M. (1978). Visual discrimination in good and poor readers. *Journal of Special Education, 12,* 409–416.

Hallahan, D. P., Kauffman, J. M., & Lloyd, J. W. (1985). *Introduction to learning disabilities* (2nd ed.). Englewood Cliffs, NJ: Prentice Hall.

Hasazi, J. E., & Hasazi, S. E. (1972). Effects of teacher attention on digit-reversal behavior in an elementary school child. *Journal of Applied Behavior Analysis, 5,* 157–162.

Keogh, B. K. (1974). Optometric vision training programs for children with learning disabilities: Review of issues and research. *Journal of Learning Disabilities, 7,* 219–231.

Kephart, N. C. (1960). *The slow learner in the classroom.* Columbus, OH: Merrill.

Orton, S. T. (1925). Word-blindness in school children. *Archives of Neurology and Psychiatry, 14,* 581–615.

Orton, S. T. (1928). Specific reading disability—strephosymbolia. *Journal of the American Medical Association, 90,* 1095–1099.

THOMAS E. SCRUGGS
MARGO A. MASTROPIERI
Purdue University

AGRAPHIA
DYSGRAPHIA
HANDWRITING
REMEDIATION, DEFICIT-CENTERED MODELS OF

REVERSE MAINSTREAMING

Reverse mainstreaming is a procedure that introduces nondisabled students into special classrooms to work with students with severe disabilities. The purpose is to maximize integration of severely disabled and nondisabled students. Mainstreaming, a more familiar concept, refers to the integration of individuals with disabilities into the nondisabled classroom to enable each individual to participate in patterns of everyday life that are close to the mainstream. Reverse mainstreaming is, as the name suggests, a procedure carried out in reverse of mainstreaming but striving for the same goals. Reverse mainstreaming can be used with all severe disabilities.

The primary use of reverse mainstreaming has been with the severely and profoundly mentally disabled and the autistic. Until the early 1970s these severely disabled students were educated in segregated environments that had only disabled individuals. These environments included institutions and special education schools. Mildly mentally disabled students, on the other hand, were more likely to be educated in closer proximity to nondisabled peers.

There has been widespread acceptance in the past 25 years of the philosophy of normalization. This philosophy holds that individuals with disabilities should be able to live as similarly as possible to the nondisabled. Public Law 94-142, adopted in 1978, required that the disabled be educated as similarly as possible to the nondisabled. For the mildly mentally disabled, this has resulted in considerable integration into nondisabled classrooms. For the severely mentally disabled, this has meant placement in buildings occupied by the nondisabled. It is frequently unrealistic to expect individuals with severe mental disabilities to participate in regular classrooms because of their low functioning levels and special needs. In these cases, in order to maximize interactions, special educators arrange for nondisabled students to participate in the classrooms of the disabled as volunteers, or "peers"; hence, mainstreaming in reverse.

The implementation of reverse mainstreaming requires cooperation and communication between teachers. They must work together to prepare the nondisabled peers who will participate. Poorman (1980), who started Project Special Friend in a central Pennsylvania community, recommends using slides of children with disabilities followed by discussions about their characteristics and behaviors and about the role of the peers. Topics include communication skills, handicaps, realistic expectations, and dealing with inappropriate behaviors. Opportunities should be provided for the nondisabled students to interact in a social way with their special friends.

Poorman (1980) outlines a sequential program, moving from introductions through free play activities to instructional activities in the reverse mainstreaming setting. Almond, Rodgers, and Krug (1979) provide a detailed presentation of techniques for training peer volunteers to work with severely disabled autistic students. The volunteers initiate individualized educational programs on a one-to-one basis under the supervision of special educators. They participate in the classroom of the severely disabled on a weekly schedule. Donder and Nietupski (1981) describe how reverse mainstreaming can be implemented to maximize social integration on the playground.

In all these instances, nondisabled students are introduced into the classroom and playground environment of the severely disabled in order to maximize interactions

between the disabled and the nondisabled. This procedure has been shown to lead to increased learning of preacademic skills and socially appropriate behavior by individuals with disabilities. It also contributes to greater acceptance by their nondisabled peers. While sharing goals and accomplishments with mainstreaming, the procedure is still mainstreaming in reverse—bringing the mainstream into the classrooms and the lives of individuals with severe disabilities.

REFERENCES

Almond, P., Rodgers, S., & Krug, D. (1979). A model for including elementary students in the severely handicapped classroom. *Teaching Exceptional Children, 11,* 135–139.

Donder, D., & Nietupski, J. (1981). Nonhandicapped adolescents teaching playground skills to their mentally retarded peers: Toward a less restrictive middle school environment. *Education & Training of the Mentally Retarded, 16,* 270–276.

Poorman, C. (1980). Mainstreaming in reverse with a special friend. *Teaching Exceptional Children, 12,* 136–142.

NANCY L. HUTCHINSON
BERNICE Y. L. WONG
Simon Fraser University

INCLUSION
LEAST RESTRICTIVE ENVIRONMENT
MAINSTREAMING
PEER RELATIONSHIPS

REVISED CHILDREN'S MANIFEST ANXIETY SCALE

See CHILDREN'S MANIFEST ANXIETY SCALE.

REVISUALIZATION

Revisualization has been defined as the active recall of the visual image of words, letters, and numbers (Johnson & Myklebust, 1967). Deficiencies in revisualization prevent students from picturing the visual form of printed material, and are related to difficulty in spelling and writing. By contrast, good spellers are able to compare their productions against an auditory or visual image when checking their spelling.

In terms of memory functioning, recall tends to be the area most substantially impaired for children with revisualization deficits, while recognition is somewhat less affected. Therefore, activities such as dictated spelling tests, number sequencing, and drawing from memory are often extremely difficult for students with revisualization deficits. Such deficits will be less apparent when matching and multiple-choice activities are employed.

Johnson and Myklebust (1967) have listed closure and visual sequential memory as two component subprocesses that are deficient in children who cannot revisualize printed material. Closure is the extrapolation of a whole from an incomplete gestalt. Children who have problems with closure are unable to supply missing details and thus are less able to code visual information for later retrieval. Deficiencies in visual sequential memory, the recall of images in order, impairs children's ability to remember the order and position of letters within words and words within sentences.

Instructional materials and techniques have been designed to help children compensate for deficits in closure and sequencing by capitalizing on their intact perceptual processes (Johnson & Myklebust, 1967). Training materials that use well-formed, heavily outlined letters have been recommended for circumventing closure problems. Sequencing deficits have been remediated by using different print sizes or colors. Multisensory techniques have also been suggested for remediating revisualization deficits. Other methods specify the use of initial-consonant cues, verbal labels, verbal mediators, and categorization strategies (Peters & Cripps, 1980).

McIntyre (1982), reporting on research with learning-disabled children, criticizes the reliance on visual memory in Johnson and Myklebust's approach and contends that reading is a verbal skill. On the other hand, Dodd (1980) has reported that deaf children, relying strictly on visual coding, are able to recognize regular spelling patterns. Peters and Cripps (1980), consolidating the two positions, state that words that have regular sound-letter associations can be coded verbally but that irregular words must be revisualized.

REFERENCES

Dodd, B. (1980). The spelling abilities of profoundly prelingually deaf children. In U. Firth (Ed.), *Cognitive processes in spelling*. London: Academic.

Johnson, D. J., & Myklebust, H. R. (1967). *Learning disabilities*. New York: Grune & Stratton.

McIntyre, T. C. (1982). *Dyslexia: The effects of visual memory and serial recall*. (ERIC Document Reproduction Service No. ED 227 603)

Peters, M. L., & Cripps, C. (1980). *Catchwords: Ideas for teaching spelling*. New South Wales, Australia: Harcourt Brace Jovanovich.

GARY BERKOWITZ
Temple University

IMAGERY
VISUAL TRAINING

REYE SYNDROME

Reye syndrome is an acute, frequently fatal disease of childhood. It is given the name of the Australian pathologist, R. D. K. Reye, who described the characteristics of this syndrome in the early 1960s. It is a rare condition with a reported risk of 1 to 2 per 100,000 children per year (Kolata, 1985). The onset of Reye syndrome frequently follows an upper respiratory or gastrointestinal viral infection, such as may be associated with influenza B or chicken pox (*Mosby's*, 1983; Silberberg, 1979). Recovery from these relatively mild symptoms may appear to be under way when the life-threatening symptoms of Reye syndrome ensue. These symptoms include persistent vomiting, fever, disturbances of consciousness progressing to coma, and convulsions. A characteristic posture (flexed elbows, clenched hands, extended legs) may be identified in some patients (Magalini, 1971). Deep, irregular respiration may occur, sometimes leading to respiratory arrest. The pathology associated with Reye syndrome includes massive edema (swelling) of the brain and fatty infiltration of the liver and kidneys (Magalini, 1971; Silberberg, 1979).

The etiology of Reye syndrome is unknown. A number of findings, including increased incidence following influenza B outbreaks and the localization of a virus in some Reye patients, suggest a viral infection as the precipitating factor (Silberberg, 1979). Some studies have reported a link between aspirin given as a therapeutic agent during influenza or chicken pox and the subsequent development of Reye syndrome. A study of 29 children with Reye syndrome and 143 controls reported that "children with chicken pox or flu who take aspirin may be 25 times more likely to get Reye's syndrome than those who do not" (Kolata, 1985, p. 391). In January 1985, Margaret Heckler, secretary of the U.S. Department of Health and Human Services, requested that manufacturers of aspirin include warning labels on aspirin products (Kolata, 1985). Further studies of the link between aspirin and Reye syndrome are being conducted.

The course of Reye syndrome is variable (Gillberg, 1995). A high percentage of afflicted children die. Estimates of mortality range from 25 to 50 percent, although more recent figures are consistent with the lower figure, probably as a result of enhanced medical management (Kolata, 1985; Silberberg, 1979). Survivors of Reye syndrome frequently display significant neurologic sequelae, including mental retardation, seizures, hemiplegia, or behavior problems including hyperactivity and distractibility (Culbertson et al., 1985; Silberberg, 1979). There is evidence of an age effect on outcome for survivors of Reye syndrome, with younger children exhibiting more severe impairment (Culbertson et al., 1985; Hartlage, Stovall, & Hartlage, 1980).

Although Reye syndrome is an extremely rare condition, it is of relevance for educators since it afflicts children exclusively and is associated with sometimes devastating impairment. Because of the suspicion of an association between aspirin and Reye syndrome, school officials should exercise caution in the use of aspirin with children. Survivors of Reye syndrome may require special education or related services, which should be determined following a multifactored evaluation.

REFERENCES

Culbertson, J. L., Elbert, J. C., Gerrity, K., & Rennert, O. M. (1985, February). *Neuropsychologic and academic sequelae of Reye's syndrome.* Paper presented to the International Neuropsychological Society, San Diego.

Gillberg, C. (1995). *Clinical child neuropsychiatry.* Cambridge: Cambridge University Press.

Hartlage, L. C., Stovall, K. W., & Hartlage, P. L. (1980). Age related neuropsychological sequelae of Reye's syndrome. *Clinical Neuropsychology, 21,* 83–86.

Kolata, G. (1985). Study of Reye's-aspirin link raises concerns. *Science, 227,* 391–392.

Magalini, S. (1971). *Dictionary of medical syndromes.* Philadelphia: Lippincott.

Mosby's medical and nursing dictionary. (1983). St. Louis, MO: Mosby.

Silberberg, D. (1979). Encephalitic complications of viral infections and vaccines. In P. B. Beeson, W. McDermott, & J. B. Wyngaarden (Eds.), *Cecil textbook of medicine* (pp. 836–839). Philadelphia: Saunders.

CATHY F. TELZROW
Kent State University

ENCEPHALITIS

REYNOLDS, CECIL R. (1952–   )

Before receiving his BA in psychology in 1975 from the University of North Carolina at Wilmington, Cecil Reynolds was a professional baseball player with the New York Mets organization for five years. He received his MEd in psychometrics in 1976, his EdS in school psychology in 1977, and his PhD in educational psychology in 1978, all from the University of Georgia. There his mentors were Alan S. Kaufman and E. Paul Torrance, both of whom have continued to strongly influence Reynolds.

Reynolds became assistant professor at the University of Nebraska in 1978 and remained there until 1981. During that time, he was acting director and subsequently associate director of the Buros Institute of Mental Measurement, and was responsible for moving the Buros Institute to Nebraska. Reynolds was the first director to succeed the institute's founder, Oscar K. Buros, who served as director from 1928 until his death in 1978. In 1981, Reynolds went to Texas A&M University as an associate professor and later became

Cecil R. Reynolds

director of the Doctoral School Psychology Training Program, which he led to American Psychological Association accreditation in 1985. He achieved the rank of professor in that year. He is currently a professor of educational psychology, professor of neuroscience, and a distinguished research scholar at Texas A&M University.

Reynolds's primary interests are in the subject of measurement, particularly as related to the practical problems of individual assessment and diagnosis. He has also worked in the area of childhood emotional disturbance, and is the author of the Revised Children's Manifest Anxiety Scale (Reynolds & Richmond, 1985), the Behavior Assessment System for Children (Reynolds & Kamphaus, 1992), and the Test of Memory and Learning (Reynolds & Bigler, 1994), along with six other tests of affect and intelligence. He is best known in school psychology for his work in the area of the cultural test bias hypothesis (Reynolds, 1983) and as progenitor of *The Handbook of School Psychology.*

He is a member of the editorial board of more than 13 journals, including *Learning Disabilities Quarterly, Journal of School Psychology, Journal of Learning Disabilities,* and the *Journal of Forensic Neuropsychology.* With more than 300 scholarly and professional papers to his credit, he is the author or editor of 27 books. In addition, he is senior editor (with Terry Gutkin) of *The Handbook of School Psychology* (3rd ed.) and is editor of the Plenum book series *Perspectives on Individual Differences* and Plenum's *Critical Issues in Neuropsychology.* He is currently in his second term as editor-in-chief of the *Archives of Clinical Neuropsychology,* the official journal of the National Academy of Neuropsychology.

In 1983, Reynolds chaired the Special Education Programs Work Group on Critical Measurement Issues in Learning Disabilities of the U.S. Department of Education. The report of this task force and several related works (Reynolds, 1981, 1984) have been instrumental in developing practical, psychometrically sound models of severe discrepancy analysis in learning disabilities diagnosis.

He is the youngest recipient of the American Psychological Association (APA) Division of School Psychology's (16) Lightner Witmer Award, and has also received early career awards from the Division of Educational Psychology (15) and the Division of Evaluation, Measurement, and Statistics (5) of the APA. In 1995, he received the Robert Chin Award from the Society for the Psychological Study of Social Issues for his contributions to the scientific study of social issues. In 1997, he received the President's Medal for service to the National Academy of Neuropsychology and, in 1998, the Razor Walker Award for service to the youth of America from the University of North Carolina at Wilmington. In November of 1998, he received the American Board of Professional Neuropsychology's Distinguished Contributions Award in the areas of both science and service. He is the 1999 recipient of the APA Division of School Psychology Senior Scientist Award. In 2000, he received the National Academy of Neuropsychology Distinguished Clinical Neuropsychologist Award.

Reynolds has also been politically active, serving a 3-year term on the executive board of the National Association of School Psychologists and as vice-president of the Division of School Psychology of the APA. In 1986, he was elected to a 2-year term as president of the National Academy of Neuropsychology, and he has served as president of the American Psychological Association Division (5) of Evaluation, Measurement, and Statistics (1997–1998) and the Division (40) of Clinical Neuropsychology (1998–1999). He is a diplomate and past president of the American Board of Professional Neuropsychology, a diplomate in school psychology of the American Board of Professional Psychology, and a fellow of the American Psychological Association (Divisions 1, 5, 15, 16, and 40), the National Academy of Neuropsychology, and the American Psychological Society.

Among his most recent books are *The Handbook of Cross-Cultural Neuropsychology* (Fletcher-Janzen, Reynolds, & Strickland, 2000) and *The Handbook of Psychological and Educational Assessment of Children: Intelligence, Aptitude, and Achievement* (2nd edition; Reynolds & Kamphaus, 2003).

REFERENCES

Fletcher-Janzen, E., Reynolds, C. R., & Strickland, T. L. (2000). *The handbook of cross-cultural neuropsychology.* Boston: Kluwer Academic/Plenum.

Reynolds, C. R. (1981). The fallacy of "two years below grade level for age" as a diagnostic criterion for reading disorders. *Journal of School Psychology, 19,* 250–258.

Reynolds, C. R. (1983). Test bias: In God we trust, all others must have data. *Journal of Special Education, 17,* 214–268.

Reynolds, C. R. (1984). Critical measurement issues in learning disabilities. *Journal of Special Education, 18,* 451–476.

Reynolds, C. R., & Bigler, E. D. (1994). *Test of memory and learning.* Austin, TX: PRO-ED.

Reynolds, C. R., & Kamphaus, R. W. (1992). *Behavior assessment system for children.* Circle Pines, MN: American Guidance Service.

Reynolds, C. R., & Kamphaus, R. W. (2003). *The handbook of psychological and educational assessment of children: Intelligence, aptitude, and achievement* (2nd ed.). New York: Guilford.

Reynolds, C. R., & Richmond, B. O. (1985). *Revised Children's Manifest Anxiety Scale.* Los Angeles: Western Psychological Services.

RAND B. EVANS
Texas A&M University
First edition

TAMARA J. MARTIN
The University of Texas of the Permian Basin
Second edition

C. WILLIAMS
Falcon School District 49, Colorado Springs, Colorado
Third edition

BUROS MENTAL MEASUREMENT YEARBOOK
KAUFMAN, ALAN S.
LEARNING DISABILITIES, SEVERE DISCREPANCY ANALYSIS
REVISED CHILDREN'S MANIFEST ANXIETY SCALE
TEST OF MEMORY AND LEARNING
TORRANCE, E. PAUL

REYNOLDS INTELLECTUAL ASSESSMENT SCALE

The Reynolds Intellectual Assessment Scales (RIAS) is an individually administered test of intelligence assessing two primary components of intelligence, verbal (crystallized) and nonverbal (fluid). Verbal intelligence is assessed with two tasks (Guess What and Verbal Reasoning) involving verbal problem solving and verbal reasoning. On the Guess What (GWH) subtest, the examinee attempts to identify an object or concept from verbal clues (e.g., "What is made of wood, plastic, or metal and makes graphite marks on paper?" or "What is circular or semicircular, is marked with degrees, and is used to measure angles?" or "Who discovered the moons of Jupiter, discovered laws of motion, and was imprisoned for one of his publications?"). On the Verbal Reasoning (VRZ) subtest the examinee completes spoken analogies (e.g., "*Stroll* is to *slow* as *sprint* is to _____" or "*Circumnavigate* is to *perimeter* as *traverse* is to _____"). Nonverbal intelligence is assessed by subtests (Odd-Item Out and What's Missing) that utilize visual and spatial ability tasks. On the Odd-Item Out (OIO) subtest the examinee is given 20 seconds to determine which of six objects or abstract designs does not belong with the others. If the examinee chooses incorrectly, there is a second, 10-second chance to earn partial credit. On the What's Missing (WHM) subtest the examinee is given 20 seconds to tell what part has been removed from a drawing. If the examinee chooses incorrectly, there is a second, 10-second chance to earn partial credit. These two scales combine to produce a Composite Intelligence Index (CIX). In contrast to many existing measures of intelligence, the RIAS eliminates dependence on motor coordination, visual-motor speed, and reading skills.

A Composite Memory Index (CMX) can be derived from two supplementary subtests (Verbal Memory and Nonverbal Memory) that assess verbal and nonverbal memory. However, these memory measures do not contain delayed recall components.

The Verbal Memory (VRM) subtest provides a basic, overall measure of short-term memory skills (e.g., working memory, short-term memory, learning) and measures recall in the verbal domain. The examinee attempts to repeat as precisely as possible several sentences or two short stories that have been read aloud by the examiner. The Nonverbal Memory (NVM) subtest measures the ability to recall pictorial stimuli in both concrete and abstract dimensions. The examinee is given 20 seconds to choose one of six pictures that matches a model that was exposed for 5 seconds and removed. If the examinee chooses incorrectly, there is a second, 10-second chance to earn partial credit. These short-term memory assessments require approximately 10 minutes of additional testing time.

The makeup of the battery also allows for the completion of the Reynolds Intellectual Screening Test (RIST). The RIST consists of only two RIAS subtests (one verbal and one nonverbal) that were selected on the basis of theoretical, empirical, and practical considerations. The RIST index is highly correlated with the full-scale IQs of both the WISC-III and the WAIS-III. The RIST was designed to be used as a measure for reevaluations or in situations where the full RIAS may not be warranted.

A variety of scores, including T-scores, Z-scores, normal curve equivalents (NCE), stanines, and age-equivalent (age 3 to 14 only) scores, are provided.

The RIAS was standardized on a normative data sample of 2,438 individuals, from 41 states, aged 3 to 94 years. The normative sample was matched to the 2001 U.S. Census on age, ethnicity, gender, educational attainment, and geographical region. During standardization an additional 507 individuals, in 15 different clinical groups, were administered the RIAS to supplement validation of RIAS.

Mean reliability coefficients ranged from .94 to .96 for the four RIAS indexes and from .90 to .95 for the six RIAS subtests. Test-retest reliability of the four index scores ranged from .83 to .91.

The RIAS manual reports high correlations with the Wechsler Intelligence Scale for Children (WISC-III; r = .76), Wechsler Adult Intelligence Scale (WAIS-III; r = .79), and Wechsler Individual Achievement Test (WIAT; r = .69 for total achievement).

The manual is impressive in its organization and breadth and depth of content and is written in a style that makes it appropriate for psychologists. Reviews of this test are pending for *The Sixteenth Mental Measurements Yearbook*.

RON DUMONT
Fairleigh Dickinson University

JOHN O. WILLIS
Rivier College

REYNOLDS, MAYNARD C. (1922–   )

A native of Doyan, North Dakota, Maynard Reynolds received his BS in education from Moorhead State University in 1942. He obtained his graduate degrees in educational psychology at the University of Minnesota after World War II, receiving his MA in 1947 and his PhD in 1950. After brief teaching assignments at the University of Northern Iowa and Long Beach State University, he returned to the University of Minnesota first as the director of the Psychoeducational Clinic, then as the chairman of the Department of Special Education, and, more recently, as professor of educational psychology and special education.

In the 1950s Reynolds became involved in the development of programs for exceptional students and issues concerning the diagnosis of such children. In the 1960s Reynolds became the international president of the Council of Exceptional Children (CEC). Later, as the first chair of CEC's Policy Commission, he was increasingly active in

Maynard C. Reynolds

advancing the concept that every child has a right to an education. Since the passage of PL 94-142, the Education for All the Handicapped Children Act, Reynolds has led national programs in technical assistance systems relating to changes in special education programs. From 1978 to 1984, with James Ysseldyke and Richard Weinberg, Reynolds also helped in Network, a technical assistance effort in the field of school psychology. He has also worked closely with organizations concerned with general and special education teacher preparation, editing a volume entitled *Knowledge Base for the Beginning Teacher* (1989) for the American Association of Colleges for Teacher Education.

Since his retirement from the University of Minnesota in 1989, Reynolds has served in endowed professorships at California State University, Los Angeles and the University of San Diego. He also worked part-time, over a period of seven years, at the Research and Development Center on Inner City Education headed by Margaret Wang at Temple University. With Wang and Herbert Walberg, he edited a five-volume compendium on research and practice in special education.

Reynolds has been included in *Who's Who in America* and *American Men and Women of Science*. He has been given the J. E. Wallace Wallin Award by the CEC for service to handicapped children and the Mildred Thomson Award by the American Association on Mental Deficiencies.

Some of his principal publications include a text, *Teaching Exceptional Children in All America's Schools,* and several articles, including "Categories and Variables in Special Education" (1972), "A Framework for Considering Some Issues in Special Education" (1962), and "A Strategy for Research" (1963).

REFERENCES

Reynolds, M. C. (1962). A framework for considering some issues in special education. *Exceptional Children, 28,* 367–370.

Reynolds, M. C. (1963). A strategy for research. *Exceptional Children, 29*(5), 213–219.

Reynolds, M. C., & Balow, B. (1972). Categories and variables in special education. *Exceptional Children, 38*(5), 357–366.

Reynolds, M. C., & Birch, J. W. (1982). *Teaching exceptional children in all America's schools* (2nd ed.). Reston, VA: Council for Exceptional Children.

Wang, M. C., Reynolds, M. C., & Walberg, H. J. (Eds.). (1987–92). *Handbook of special education: Research and practice* (Vols. 1–5). Oxford: Pergamon Press.

E. VALERIE HEWITT
Texas A&M University
First edition

TAMARA J. MARTIN
The University of Texas of the Permian Basin
Second edition

Rh FACTOR INCOMPATIBILITY

Rh factor incompatibility (erythroblastosis fetalis) results from an antigen-antibody reaction with destruction of the fetal red blood cells (Sherwen, Scoloveno, & Weingarten, 1999). The most lethal form of Rh factor incompatibility is erythroblastosis fetalis. Generally defined, erythroblastosis fetalis is a type of hemolytic disorder found in newborns that results from maternal-fetal blood group incompatibility of the Rh factor and blood group (Anderson, 1998). When an Rh-positive fetus begins to grow inside an Rh-negative mother, it is as though the mother's body is being invaded by a foreign agent or antigen (Pillitteri, 1995). The mother's body reacts to this invasion by forming antibodies that cross the placenta and cause hemolysis of fetal red blood cells. The fetus becomes deficient in red blood cells that transport oxygen and develops anemia; enlarged heart, spleen, and liver; and a cardiovascular system that easily decompensates (Lowdermilk, Perry, & Boback, 1997). Without prompt treatment, hypoxia, cardiac failure, respiratory distress, and death may result (Anderson, 1998).

Prenatal diagnosis of erythroblastosis fetalis is confirmed through amniocentesis and analysis of bilirubin levels within the amniotic fluid (Anderson, 1998). The treatment regime may include intrauterine transfusions to combat red blood cell destruction or immediate transfusions after birth (Pillitteri, 1995). Preterm labor may also be induced to remove the fetus from the destructive maternal environment.

In Rh factor incompatibility, the hemolytic reactions take place only when the mother is Rh-negative and the infant is Rh-positive (Sherwen et al., 1999). This isoimmunization process rarely occurs in the first pregnancy, but risk is great in subsequent pregnancies. A simple injection of a high-titer Rho(D) immune-globulin preparation after delivery or abortion of the Rh-positive fetus can prevent maternal sensitization to the Rh factor (Anderson, 1998).

Hemolytic diseases of the fetus or newborn are on the decline and occur in only 1.5 percent of all pregnancies (Sherwen et al., 1999). Since the availability of Rho(D) immune globulin (RhoGAM), the incidence of Rh factor incompatibilities has drastically decreased (Sherwen et al., 1999). Caucasian newborns remain most at risk (15 percent) for erythroblastosis fetalis; African American newborns have a 6 percent occurrence rate (Medical College of Wisconsin Physicians and Clinics, 1999).

REFERENCES

Anderson, K. N. (1998). *Mosby's medical, nursing, and allied health dictionary* (5th ed.). St. Louis, MO: Mosby-Year Book.

Lowdermilk, D., Perry, S., & Bobak, I. (1997). *Maternity and women's health care* (6th ed.). St. Louis, MO: Mosby-Year Book.

Medical College of Wisconsin Physicians and Clinics. (1999). *Erythroblastosis fetalis.* Retrieved from http://chorus.rad.mcw.edu/doc/00889.html

Pillitteri, A. (1995). *Maternal and child health nursing: Care of the childbearing and childrearing family* (2nd ed.). Philadelphia: J. B. Lippincott Company.

Sherwen, L., Scoloveno, M., & Weingarten, C. (1999). *Maternity nursing: Care of the childbearing family* (3rd ed.). Stamford, CT: Appleton & Lange.

KARI ANDERSON
University of North Carolina at Wilmington

RIGHT-HANDEDNESS

Right-handedness is a species-specific characteristic of humans (Hicks & Kinsbourne, 1978). Additionally, right-handedness, also called dextrality, can be considered universal in that 90 percent of the human population is right-handed (Corballis & Beale, 1983). Since the majority of individuals prefer using their right hands and are also more skilled with their right hands, more positive properties and values have come to be associated with the right than with the left. For example, throughout history the right has represented the side of the gods, strength, life, goodness, light, the state of rest, the limited, the odd, the square, and the singular. The left has been signified by the polar opposites of these characteristics. Maleness also has been traditionally associated with the right, providing symbolic expression of the universality of male dominance (Needham, 1974).

Although people classify themselves as right-handed or left-handed, handedness more accurately spans a continuous range from extreme right-handedness through mixed-handedness or ambidexterity to extreme left-handedness (Corballis & Beale, 1976). Investigators always have been curious about the abundance of right-handedness and the rarity of the various degrees of nonright-handedness. However, studies of historical records and artifacts have revealed enough inconsistencies in incidence to preclude any simple choice between culture or biology to explain the origin of handedness. Consequently, combinations of these various nature and nurture explanations have been invoked. Harris (1980) provides an interesting and detailed account of these various theories.

Corballis and Beale (1983), in an extensive study of the neuropsychology of right and left, have argued that right-handedness is biologically rather than culturally determined. They cite the fact that right-handedness has always has been universal across diverse and seemingly unrelated cultures; moreover, although right-handedness itself is not manifest until late in the first year of life, it is correlated with other asymmetries that are evident at or before birth. They acknowledge that there are environmental pressures to be right-handed and that some naturally left-handed individuals may be compelled to use their right hands for certain tasks, but suggest that these very pressures have their origins in the fundamental right-handedness of most human beings.

Today the relationship between right-handedness and the unilateral representation of language in the left cerebral hemisphere is well documented. Case studies linking the side of brain damage and the incidence of aphasia, or language impairment, have revealed that approximately 98 percent of right-handers use the left hemisphere of their brain for language. A similar conclusion has been drawn from studies in which linguistic functioning has been impaired in 95 percent of the right-handers whose left cerebral hemispheres were injected with sodium amobarbitol, a momentarily incapacitating drug.

The hemisphere of the brain used for language in left-handers is more variable. Two-thirds of left-handers have demonstrated the use of their left hemisphere. Almost half of the remaining left-handers use their right hemispheres for speech, while the remainder have some capacity for speech in both hemispheres (Rasmussen & Milner, 1975). In view of these data, many investigators suggest that both right-handedness and left cerebral dominance for language are genetically controlled expressions of some underlying biological gradient. This relationship further reveals the significance of right-handedness in the unique cognitive functioning of the human species.

REFERENCES

Corballis, M. C., & Beale, I. L. (1976). *The psychology of left and right.* Hillsdale, NJ: Erlbaum.

Corballis, M. C., & Beale, I. L. (1983). *The ambivalent mind.* Chicago: Nelson-Hall.

Harris, L. J. (1980). Left-handedness: Early theories, facts, and fancies. In J. Herron (Ed.), *Neuropsychology of left-handedness* (pp. 3–78). New York: Academic.

Hicks, R. E., & Kinsbourne, M. (1978). Human handedness. In M. Kinsbourne (Ed.), *Asymmetrical function of the brain* (pp. 267–273). New York: Cambridge University Press.

Needham, R. (Ed.). (1974). *Right and left: Essays on dual symbolic classification.* Chicago: University of Chicago Press.

Rasmussen, T., & Milner, B. (1975). Clinical and surgical studies of the cerebral speech areas in man. In K. J. Zulch, O. Creutzfeldt, & G. Galbraith (Eds.), *Otfried Foerster symposium on cerebral localization.* Heidelberg: Springer-Verlag.

GALE A. HARR
*Maple Heights City Schools,
Maple Heights, Ohio*

CEREBRAL DOMINANCE
HANDEDNESS
LEFT BRAIN/RIGHT BRAIN

RIGHT HEMISPHERE SYNDROME (LINGUISTIC, EXTRALINGUISTIC, AND NON-LINGUISTIC)

The role of the right hemisphere in communication was largely unknown 30 years ago (Meyers, 1997). Since then an extensive body of research has determined that the right hemisphere handles holistic, gestalt-like stimuli and visual-spatial information, and has identified a wide range of communication impairments that can occur subsequent to right hemisphere damage. Three types of right hemisphere syndrome (RHS) deficits are *extralinguistic* (discourse), *nonlinguistic* (perceptual and attentional), and, to a lesser degree, *linguistic* deficits (phonological, semantic, syntactical, and morphological; Hegde, 1998; Myers, 1997; Payne, 1997).

Extralinguistic Deficits

Discourse is the aspect of communication that transcends individual phonemes, words, or sentences. It links "the bits and pieces of language to create representations of events, objects, beliefs, personalities, and experiences" (Brownell & Joanette, 1993, p. vii). Discourse competence is context driven, and context includes a variety of cues—not only words and sentences, but tone of voice, gestures, body positions, facial expressions of the speaker, and the overall purpose and relative formality of the communicative event. Discourse also involves organization, sequencing, and the generation of projections, predictions, and inferences so that sentences are not taken as independent units, but as part of a larger whole (macrostructure) in which central ideas are emphasized and supported. Four major areas make up extralinguistic deficits associated with RHS (Hegde, 1998; Myers, 1997; Payne, 1997).

Macrostructure—reduced number and accuracy of core concepts and inferences, reduced specificity or explicitness of information, and reduced efficiency of listening, speaking, reading, writing, and thinking

Impaired nonliteral language—reduced sensitivity to and use of figurative language (similes, metaphors, idioms, proverbs), humor (cartoons, jokes, riddles, puns), teasing, advertisements, slang, verbal aggression, ambiguity, multiple meanings, deception (irony, sarcasm), and capacity to revise original interpretations

Rhetorical sensitivity/affective components—reduced sensitivity to communicative purposes, shared knowledge, emotional tone, partner's communicative state, turn-taking, topic maintenance, gaze; increased impulsivity, excessive talking, shallow responses, and monotonal speech

Impaired prosody—reduced sensitivity to affective prosody (comprehension of others' emotions as reflected in the voice) and use of prosodic features (production of personal emotional states)

Nonlinguistic Deficits

Nonlinguistic deficits associated with RHS include visual perceptual problems, left-side neglect, attentional deficits, and denial of deficits.

Visual perceptual deficits include reduced ability to recognize faces (prosopagnosia) and to construct or reproduce block designs, two-dimensional stick figures, or geometric designs.

Left-side neglect is reduced sensitivity to respond to information on the left, despite the motor and sensory capacity to do so. The definition of *left* may vary according to the type of neglect and the environment. In body-centered neglect, *left* may refer to the left of the body midline. In environment-centered neglect, *left* may refer to the left side of a group of stimuli, regardless of their spatial location, or to the left side of fixed environmental coordinates, such as the left side of a room or book. In other cases, neglect may occur on the left side of a given object, even if that object is located in the right visual field. Thus, neglect may occur in the left or right visual field, depending on the stimulus environment; left may, therefore, be considered relative. Left-side neglect can occur in all modalities (auditory, visual, tactile, smell, taste) but is most often noted and tested in the visual modality. In addition to ignoring the left, individuals with neglect also may demonstrate an orienting bias toward the right: That is, right-sided stimuli "capture" the person's attention.

Attentional deficits include reduced arousal (alertness), vigilance (focusing on relevant pieces of information), and maintained attention to stimuli; selective attention.

Linguistic Deficits

Unlike the communication deficits that occur with left-hemisphere impairment, linguistic deficits are less problematic in RHS. Word retrieval deficits (semantics) occur frequently. Defining categories (e.g., apple, peach, cherry are *fruit*) and identifying collective and single nouns through confrontation naming are characteristic linguistic impairments. Phonological, syntactic, and morphological errors do not characterize the communication patterns of RHS (Hegde, 1998).

Right hemisphere syndrome is associated with strokes, tumors, head trauma, and various neurological diseases in all ethnic groups (Payne, 1997). The syndrome can have significant effects on social and academic aspects of communication-learning.

REFERENCES

Brownell, H. H., & Joanette, Y. (Eds.). (1993). *Narrative discourse in neurologically impaired and normal aging adults*. San Diego, CA: Singular.

Hegde, M. N. (1998). *A coursebook on aphasia and other neurogenic language disorders* (2nd ed.). San Diego, CA: Singular.

Myers, P. E. (1997). Right hemisphere syndrome. In L. L. LaPointe (Ed.), *Aphasia and related neurogenic language disorders* (2nd ed.). New York: Thieme.

Payne, J. C. (1997). *Adult neurogenic language disorders: Assessment and treatment—A comprehensive ethnobiological approach.* San Diego, CA: Singular.

STEPHEN S. FARMER
New Mexico State University

NONVERBAL LANGUAGE

PRAGMATICS AND PRAGMATIC COMMUNICATION DISORDERS

RIGHT TO EDUCATION

The right to education refers to the legal concept that justifies a school-aged person's freedom to receive educational services. The conceptual and legal development of this right has occurred in conjunction with an increasing societal concern for individuals who exhibit exceptional educational needs. These changing social attitudes have been reflected in judicial decisions and legislative efforts that have substantiated the right of all school-aged children and youths to receive educational services.

The U.S. Constitution, although not explicit in its guarantee of the right to education, has been cited as the fundamental justification for the provision of educational services. Specifically, the right to education has been implied from the Fourteenth Amendment, which states in its equal protection clause, "No State shall . . . deny to any person within its jurisdiction the equal protection of the laws." Thus, this amendment requires that, where educational services are available, such services must be available to all on an equivalent basis.

Early court cases that addressed the right of the exceptional needs learner to receive educational services did not reflect this interpretation. Generally, litigation in this area prior to the 1950s resulted in exclusionary educational policies (e.g., *Watson v. Cambridge,* 1883; *Beattie v. State Board of Education of Wisconsin,* 1919). However, with the onset of increasing civil rights awareness in the early 1950s, right-to-education court cases evidenced a more positive trend. Some of the more influential court cases that have related to the development of the right-to-education concept for the exceptional needs learner include *Brown v. Board of Education of Topeka* (1954), *Pennsylvania Association for Retarded Citizens v. the Commonwealth of Pennsylvania* (1971), and *Mills v. Board of Education of the District of Columbia* (1972).

The *Brown* case dealt with the rights of a class of citizens (African Americans in the South) to attend public schools in their community on a nonsegregated basis. The major issues in this case were suspect classification (i.e., classification by race) and equal protection. In a unanimous decision for the plaintiff, the Supreme Court emphasized the social importance of education and also ruled that education must be made available on equal terms to all.

The *Pennsylvania Association for Retarded Citizens (PARC)* case dealt more specifically with the educational rights of exceptional needs learners. Citing the Fourteenth Amendment rights to due process and equal protection, the judge in this case ruled that Pennsylvania statutes permitting denial or postponement of entry to public schools by mentally retarded children were unconstitutional. The terms of the settlement reached in this case included provision of due process rights to the plaintiffs and identification and placement in public school programs of all previously excluded children.

More general in its plaintiff class, the *Mills* case challenged the exclusion of mentally retarded, epileptic, brain-damaged, hyperactive, and behavior-disordered children from public schools. Finding for the plaintiffs, the court required the defendants to provide full public education or "adequate alternatives." These alternatives could only be provided after notice and a reasonable opportunity to challenge the services that had been given. The progression from *Brown* (1954) to *PARC* (1971) to *Mills* (1972) reflects an increasing sophistication in the awareness of the educational needs of individuals with exceptional learning characteristics. This more complete view of the educational needs and rights of exceptional individuals is also apparent in recent legislation.

Two major legislative efforts that have addressed the educational rights of exceptional needs learners are Section 504 of the Rehabilitation Act of 1973, the Education for All Handicapped Children Act of 1975 (PL 94-142), and its successor, the Individuals with Disabilities Education Act (IDEA). Section 504 of the Rehabilitation Act of 1973 is particularly important because it deals with all programs that receive federal funds. This legislation mandates nondiscrimination on the basis of handicapping conditions if these funds are to continue.

Public Law 94-142 and the IDEA embody the intent of all litigation and legislation that they follow in their highly specific delineation of the educational rights of exceptional needs learners. The law requires that all individuals, regardless of disability or its degree, be offered a free, appropriate education at public expense. The law further specifies that these services must be delivered in the least restrictive environment appropriate for the individual child.

The right to education for children and youths with exceptional learning characteristics has resulted from changing societal views of the needs and rights of these individuals. These attitudes have been reflected in increased litigation questioning the adequacy, availability, and appropriateness of the educational services offered this group. The outcome of these cases has established a legal basis for a right to education. This litigation has in turn led to legislation developed to ensure that right. For a comprehensive discussion of the right to education for the exceptional needs learner see Wortis (1978) and Sales, Krauss, Sacken, and Overcast (1999).

REFERENCES

Sales, B. D., Krauss, D., Sacken, D., & Overcast, B. (1999). The legal rights of students. In C. R. Reynolds & T. B. Gutkin (Eds.), *The handbook of school psychology* (3rd ed.). New York: Wiley.

Wortis, J. (Ed.). (1978). *Mental retardation and developmental disabilities.* New York: Brunner/Mazel.

J. Todd Stephens
University of Wisconsin at Madison
First and Second editions

Kimberly F. Applequist
University of Colorado at Colorado Springs
Third edition

BROWN v. BOARD OF EDUCATION
INDIVIDUALS WITH DISABILITIES EDUCATION IMPROVEMENT ACT OF 2004 (IDEIA)
MILLS v. BOARD OF EDUCATION
PENNSYLVANIA ASSOCIATION FOR RETARDED CITIZENS v. PENNSYLVANIA

RIGHT TO TREATMENT

The term *right to treatment* refers to the legal concept that justifies an individual's freedom to receive therapeutic and/or curative services. Although it was initially developed as an extension of litigation that targeted the availability of medically oriented services for institutionalized individuals, recent legal interpretations of this right have been broadened to include the right to habilitation and the right to education.

The development of the right to treatment reflects a trend of change in societal attitudes about providing services for individuals with exceptional learning or behavioral characteristics. As attitudes have changed, concerned individuals have organized systematic efforts to ensure the availability of these services. These changes have resulted in litigative and legislative efforts that have addressed both the availability and the adequacy of treatment for institutionalized people.

The three major court cases that shaped the legal interpretation of the right to treatment are *Rouse v. Cameron* (1968); *Wyatt v. Stickney* (1970), a class action suit; and

New York Association for Retarded Citizens v. Rockefeller (1972). In these cases constitutional amendments and state laws were interpreted as requiring treatment services for institutionalized persons. The first court case that dealt with the right of an institutionalized person to receive treatment was *Rouse v. Cameron* (1968). In this case, a man was institutionalized for 4 years after having been found not guilty, by reason of insanity, of a misdemeanor. While institutionalized, Rouse did not receive treatment. Citing constitutional rights (due process, equal protection, freedom from cruel and unusual punishment) and basing the decision on state law, the court ruled that confinement for treatment purposes when treatment was not made available was equivalent to imprisonment. Rouse was subsequently freed.

The *Wyatt v. Stickney* case (1970) was a class action suit filed on behalf of the residents of three residential facilities in Alabama. The case was exhaustive in its pursuit of information and remedies. In the final ruling, standards were delineated with regard to treatment, habilitation, freedom from restraint, and a host of other treatment considerations. The court-ordered remedies included development of appropriate staff ratios, individual habilitation plans, and the delineation of specific procedures for treatment. Thus, according to the rulings of *Wyatt* (1970), treatment must not only be available but also be supported by sufficient staff and planning. Following the initial hearing of *Wyatt,* the New York Association for Retarded Citizens (NYARC) filed a petition against the then governor of the state, Nelson Rockefeller (*NYARC v. Rockefeller,* 1972), requesting relief from the overcrowded and inhumane conditions at the Willowbrook state institution. Citing the constitutional right to due process, the judge in this case ruled for immediate reduction of the resident population and appropriate development of community-based programs. Thus, the *NYARC* case indicated that in addition to having the right to receive adequate services in humane conditions, residents must also be considered as members of a society to which they should be allowed reasonable access.

Each of these cases represents a litigative response to either a complete lack of treatment availability, ineffective delivery of treatment, or use of inappropriate treatment. The decisions in these cases reflect an expanding awareness of the legal right of institutionalized individuals not only to receive treatment but to be allowed access to systematically planned programming that meets the varied needs of the resident.

J. Todd Stephens
University of Wisconsin at Madison
First and Second editions

Kimberly F. Applequist
University of Colorado at Colorado Springs
Third edition

RIGHT TO EDUCATION
WYATT v. STICKNEY

RILEY-DAY SYNDROME

Riley-Day syndrome, also referred to as Familial Dysautonomia (FD), is a rare, autosomal (non-sex-related chromosome) recessive, genetic disease primarily afflicting Jewish children of Ashkenazi or Eastern European heritage. First described in 1949 by Drs. Riley, Day, Greeley, and Langford, Riley-Day syndrome/FD is a malfunction of the autonomic nervous system and poses severe physical, emotional, and social problems for the afflicted patients.

Individuals affected with FD are incapable of producing overflow tears with emotional crying. Frequent manifestations of FD include inappropriate perception of heat, pain, and taste, as well as labile blood pressures and gastrointestinal difficulties. Other problems experienced by individuals with FD include dysphagia (difficulty in swallowing), vomiting, aspiration and frequent pneumonia, speech and motor incoordination, poor growth, and scoliosis. Other frequent signs are delayed developmental milestones; unsteady gait; corneal anesthesia; marked sweating with excitement, eating, or the first stage of sleep; breath-holding episodes; spinal curvature (in 90 percent by age 13); red puffy hands; and an absence of fungiform papillae (taste buds) on the tongue (New York University Health System, 1999).

FD is transmitted by a recessive gene provided by both the mother and the father. Although the gene has been localized to the long arm of chromosome 9 (9q31) with flanking markers, FD carrier detection can only be offered to a family that already has an affected child (McKusick, 1999). Both males and females are equally affected. As yet, there is no screening test for the general population. It is estimated that one in 30 Jews of Eastern European (Ashkenazi) extraction are carriers of the FD gene, with an estimated prevalence of 1 out of every 10,000–20,000 of Ashkenazi heritage. The prognosis of FD is poor, with most patients dying in childhood of chronic pulmonary failure or aspiration (Gandy, 1999), although FD individuals can survive into their 20s and 30s.

There is no cure for FD, but many of the symptoms can be treated through a variety of interventions and medication. Affected individuals usually are of normal intelligence, and FD patients can be expected to function independently if treatment is begun early and major disabilities avoided. Special education services may be provided under the category of Noncategorical Early Childhood or Other Health Impaired. Early identification and intervention is extremely important for FD children to address developmental delays, gross motor and walking delays, and failure to thrive due to feeding difficulties and excessive vomiting. Upon entering school, speech, physical, and occupational therapies may be beneficial. Specialized feeding techniques may need to be taught. Adapted physical education may be needed to prevent injuries due to insensitivity to pain, and to monitor difficulties with the inability to control body temperature. Individuals affected with FD are prone to depression, anxieties, and even phobias. Families of FD affected children may need psychological support to assist with the emotional demands of caring for a child with a debilitating disease. For additional information contact the Dysautonomia Foundation Inc., 20 East 46th Street, New York, N.Y., 10017 or call (212) 949-6644.

REFERENCES

Gandy, A. (1999). *Pediatric database* (PEDBASE). Retrieved from http://www.icondata.com/health/pedbase/files/LAURENCE.HTM

McKusick, V. A. (1999). *OMIM™, Online Mendelian Inheritance in Man.* National Center for Biotechnology Information (NCBI). Retrieved from http://www3.ncbi.nlm.nih.gov:80/Omim/

New York University Health System. (1999). http://www.med.nyu.edu/fd/fdcenter.html

KIM RYAN ARREDONDO
Texas A&M University

RIMLAND, BERNARD (1928–   )

Bernard Rimland earned his BA in 1950 and MA in 1951 at San Diego State University and his PhD in experimental psychology in 1954 from Pennsylvania State University. Upon the diagnosis of his eldest son as autistic, Rimland began extensive research that led to his neural theory of infantile autism. He later founded the National Society for Autistic Children, which later became the Autism Society of America, and established the Autism Research Institute

Bernard Rimland

in San Diego in 1967. He currently serves as director of the Autism Research Institute, a nonprofit organization providing parents and professionals worldwide with information on the etiology and treatment of severe behavior disorders in children.

Rimland was an early advocate of the use of behavior modification and a pioneering researcher on the effects of nutrition on behavior and mental health. In his massive review of the literature on autism in the early 1960s, Rimland found no scientific support for the widely held psychoanalytic theories that blamed supposedly unloving families for the child's severe disorder. Discarding the psychoanalytic explanation, Rimland advocated a neurophysiological cause of autism involving, in part, a possible dysfunction of the brain stem reticular formation. The reticular formation is known to play an important role in perception, and children with autism appear to have a perceptual malfunction that results in difficulty distinguishing boundaries between themselves and their surrounding world. Rimland's treatments of choice for the disorder are behavior modification and megavitamin therapy. His research and that of others have shown promising results for megavitamin therapy for treatment of autism and other childhood disorders.

Rimland's major publication is *Infantile Autism: The Syndrome and Its Implications for a Neural Theory of Behavior*, which won him the Appleton-Century-Crofts Award for the 1963 Distinguished Contribution to Psychology. He has published and contributed to more than 100 journal articles, and served as coeditor of *Modern Therapies*.

In addition to being an honorary board member and founder of the Autism Society of America, Rimland also serves on 32 advisory boards for publications, research organizations, and schools for children with severe behavior disorders. He has also been vice president of the Academy of Orthomolecular Psychiatry and the Orthomolecular Medical Society, and served as the chief technical advisor on autism for the popular film *Rain Man*.

MARY LEON PEERY
Texas A&M University
First edition

TAMARA J. MARTIN
*The University of Texas of the
Permian Basin*
Second edition

RISK MANAGEMENT IN SPECIAL EDUCATION

Many times educational settings are unaware of the relationship between school practices and legal liability. Risk management is a proactive stance that attempts to identify potential areas of liability, evaluate current policy and standards, and provide workable strategies in an attempt to prevent injury and minimize liability (Phillips, 1990). In addition, risk management allows for consistent practices among school personnel covering a wide range of situations and circumstances.

Common risk management strategies in educational settings include appropriate documentation when altering a child's instructional curriculum, specified protocol when a student has expressed suicidal feelings, adherence to state regulations and guidelines in diagnostic assessments, informed consent procedures for parents and children regarding school counseling, and maintaining adequate liability coverage (Wood, 1988). Risk management strategies for school personnel include knowing and following ethical guidelines, and keeping current with professional development and standards of practice (Phillips, 1990).

REFERENCES

Phillips, B. N. (1990). Law, psychology, and education. In T. R. Kratochwill (Ed.), *Advances in school psychology* (Vol. 7, pp. 79–130). Hillsdale, NJ: Erlbaum.

Wood, R. H. (1988). *Fifty ways to avoid malpractice*. Sarasota, FL: Professional Resource Exchange.

LINDA M. MONTGOMERY
*The University of Texas of the
Permian Basin*

RITALIN

Ritalin, the trade name for methylphenidate, is a central nervous system stimulant commonly prescribed for children with an abnormally high level of activity or with Attention-Deficit/Hyperactivity Disorder (ADHD). Ritalin is also occasionally prescribed for individuals with narcolepsy, mild depression, or withdrawn senile behavior (Shannon, Wilson, & Stang, 1995).

Although all the intricacies of Ritalin are not fully understood, it increases the attention span in ADHD children (Deglin & Vallerand, 1999). Ritalin stimulates the central nervous system with effects similar to weak amphetamines or very strong coffee. Its effects include (a) increasing attention and reducing activity in hyperactive children, apparently by stimulating inhibitory centers (NIDAInfofax, 1998); (b) diminishing fatigue in individuals with narcolepsy; and (c) increasing motor activity and mental alertness in individuals exhibiting withdrawn senile behavior (Shannon et al., 1995).

All individuals need to be advised to take sustained released Ritalin as a whole tablet and never to crush or chew the pill. Ritalin should be taken at regular intervals during the day and only by the individual for whom it is prescribed (Deglin & Vallerand, 1999). As a stimulant medication, Ritalin may cause sleep disorders if taken late in the day (Skidmore-Roth & McKenry, 1997). To minimize insomnia, the last dose of Ritalin should be taken before 6:00 PM. Weight loss is another potential side effect of this medication, and individuals should be advised to weigh themselves at least twice weekly (Deglin & Vallerand, 1999). Because of the combined effects of multiple stimulants, all individuals should be informed that they should refrain from drinking any caffeine-containing beverages such as cola or coffee (Skidmore-Roth & McKenry, 1997). As with any continuous medication regime, school personnel should be notified of the medication and any other health-related concerns (Wong, 1995).

Stimulant medications such as Ritalin have strong potential for abuse, and the United States Drug Enforcement Administration (DEA) has placed numerous stringent controls on Ritalin's manufacture, distribution, and prescription. Ritalin is documented to be a strong, effective, and safe medication, but the potential risks in long-term usage need further investigation (NIDAInfofax, 1998).

REFERENCES

Deglin, J., & Vallerand, A. (1999). *Davis's drug guide for nurses* (6th ed.). Philadelphia: F. A. Davis.

NIDAInfofax. (1998, February 27). Retrieved from http://www.nida.nih.gov/Infofax/ritalin.html

Shannon, M., Wilson, B., & Stang, C. (1995). *Govoni & Hayes drugs and nursing implications* (8th ed.). Norwalk, CT: Appleton & Lange.

Skidmore-Roth, L., & McKenry, L. (1997). *Mosby's drug guide for nurses* (2nd ed.). St. Louise, MO: Mosby-Year Book.

Wong, D. (1995). *Whaley & Wong's nursing care of infants and children* (5th ed.). St. Louis, MO: Mosby-Year Book.

KARI ANDERSON
University of North Carolina at Wilmington

ATTENTION-DEFICIT/HYPERACTIVITY DISORDER
MEDICAL MANAGEMENT

ROBERTS APPERCEPTION TEST FOR CHILDREN

The Roberts Apperception Test for Children (RATC) is a personality assessment technique designed for children ages 6 to 15. The RATC is an attempt to combine the flexibility of a projective technique with the objectivity of a standardized scoring system. Similar to the Thematic Apperception Test and the Children's Apperception Test, the RATC consists of a set of drawings designed to elicit thematic stories. The test consists of 27 cards, 11 of which are parallel forms for males and females. Thus 16 cards are administered during testing, which takes 20 to 30 minutes.

The RATC is said to have significant benefits over similar project measures (McArthur & Roberts, 1982). The test manual is well designed and includes substantial information on psychometric properties of the test, administration, and scoring, as well as several case studies. The picture drawings were designed specifically for children and young adolescents and depict scenes designed to elicit common concerns. For example, specific cards portray parent/child relationships, sibling relationships, aggression, mastery, parental disagreement and affection, observation of nudity, school, and peer relationships. The test has a standardized scoring system, with scores converted to normalized *T*-scores based on data from a sample of 200 well-adjusted children. The following information may be obtained from the RATC:

1. *Adaptive Scales.* Reliance on others, support for others, support for the child, limit setting, problem identification, resolution.

2. *Clinical scales.* Anxiety, aggression, depression, rejection, lack of resolution.

3. *Critical Indicators.* Atypical response, maladaptive outcome, refusal.

4. *Supplementary Measures.* Ego functioning, aggression, levels of projection.

A review of the RATC in the *Ninth Mental Measurements Yearbook* (Sines, 1985) describes four unpublished validity studies and concludes that the psychometric properties of the test are unimpressive. In perhaps the most substantial of these studies, 200 well-adjusted children were compared with 200 children evaluated at guidance clinics. The normal children scored higher than the children at clinics on all eight adaptive scales; however, the two groups could not be reliably differentiated on the clinical scales for anxiety, aggression, and depression.

Overall, the RATC appears to be a well-designed projective technique for children and young adolescents. The standardized scoring system, while lacking in evidence compared with purely objective measures of personality, appears to be relatively satisfactory compared with similar projective techniques.

REFERENCES

McArthur, D., & Roberts, G. (1982). *Roberts Apperception Test for Children: Test manual.* Los Angeles: Western Psychological Services.

Sines, J. (1985). The Roberts Apperception Test for Children. In J. Mitchell (Ed.), *The ninth mental measurements yearbook.* Lincoln, NE: Buros Institute.

FRANCES F. WORCHEL
Texas A&M University

CHILD PSYCHOLOGY
PERSONALITY ASSESSMENT

ROBINOW SYNDROME

See NATIONAL ORGANIZATION OF RARE DISORDERS.

ROBINSON, HALBERT B. (1925–1981) AND ROBINSON, NANCY M. (1930–)

Nancy and Hal Robinson performed extensive work in the areas of children with mental retardation, early child care, and gifted children. They coauthored *The Mentally Retarded Child: A Psychological Approach* (1976), an influential text defining the field of mental retardation and emphasizing its research base, and coedited the *International Monograph Series on Early Child Care* (Robinson, Robinson, Wolins, Bronfenbrenner, & Richmond, 1974), which offers descriptions of early child care options of nine nations, including the United States.

In 1966, with Ann Peters, Hal Robinson founded the Frank Porter Graham Child Development Center at the University of North Carolina (Robinson & Robinson, 1971), and in 1969 he accepted a position at the University of Washington, Seattle (UW) as a professor of psychology. While at UW, Hal also served as the principal investigator of the Child Development Research Group (CDRG, now the Halbert Robinson Center for the Study of Capable Youth). Child Development Preschool, formerly a CDRG program (later independent of UW), focused on the identification and development of curriculum for children with advanced intellectual and academic skills (Roedell, Jackson, & Robinson, 1980), while the UW Early Entrance Program admitted middle school-age students to the University, depending on their readiness, prior to entering high school (Robinson & Robinson).

Of their many honors, the Robinsons received the Education Award of the American Association on Mental Deficiency in 1982. Additionally, Nancy has served as editor of the *American Journal of Mental Deficiency,* and after Hal's death in 1981, she assumed the directorship of the Hal Robinson Center for the Study of Capable Youth, a position she holds today. She is also a professor of psychiatry and behavioral science at UW, and has continued to publish on important topics including the counseling of highly gifted children and mathematically gifted children (Robinson, 1996; Robinson, Abbot, Berninger, Busse, & Mukhopadhyay, 1997).

REFERENCES

Robinson, H. B., & Robinson, N. M. (1971). Longitudinal development of very young children in a comprehensive day care program: The first two years. *Child Development, 42,* 1673–1683.

Robinson, H. B., Robinson, N. M., Wolins, M., Bronfenbrenner, U., & Richmond, J. B. (1974). Early child care in the United States. In H. B. Robinson & N. M. Robinson (Eds.), *International monograph series on early child care*. London: Gordon, Breach.

Robinson, N. M. (1996). Counseling agendas for gifted young people: A commentary. *Journal for the Education of the Gifted, 20*(2), 128–137.

Robinson, N. M., Abbot, R. D., Berninger, V. W., Busse, J., & Mukhopadhyay, S. (1997). Developmental changes in mathematically precocious young children: Longitudinal and gender effects. *Gifted Child Quarterly, 41*(4), 145–158.

Robinson, N. M., & Robinson, H. B. (1976). *The mentally retarded child: A psychological approach* (2nd ed.). New York: McGraw-Hill.

Robinson, N. M., & Robinson, H. B. (1982). The optimal match: Devising the best compromise for the highly gifted student. In D. H. Feldman (Ed.), *Developmental approaches to giftedness and creativity*. San Francisco: Jossey-Bass.

Roedell, W. C., Jackson, N. E., & Robinson, H. B. (1980). *Gifted young children*. New York: Columbia University.

ANN E. LUPKOWSKI
Texas A&M University
First edition

TAMARA J. MARTIN
The University of Texas of the Permian Basin
Second edition

ROBOTICS

A robot is a programmable multifunctional device that is capable of performing a variety of tasks, manipulations, and locomotions. Robots come in one of four configurations: rectangular, cylindrical, spherical, and anthropomorphic articulated (Yin & Moore, 1984). These electronic devices have five characteristics that set them apart from other devices: mobility, dexterity, payload capacity, intelligence, and sensory capability. The characteristics are found singly or in combination; however, at present there is no single system that integrates all of the characteristics.

Industrial robots are known for their payload capacity. For example, the large electronic arms used on the automotive assembly lines in Japan are capable of lifting enormous weights and performing the same routines tirelessly. Other robots are recognized for their sensory capability (e.g., to sense temperature or to recognize patterns). Educational robots usually have mobility and dexterity. For example, the Health Company's robot Hero can be told to go forward, backward, left, or right. Hero's arm and hand can manipulate objects. The arm's five axes allow him to wave, gesticulate, lift objects, and drop them. Hero also speaks 64 phonemes, which means the robot can be programmed to speak almost any language. Hero can also respond to light, sound, and objects (Slesnick, 1984).

Turtle Tot is a small robot that can be programmed by young children to count, draw pictures, and move at various angles. A machine that has greater dexterity but less mobility is the Rhino XR II, which is used in college-level engineering classes. The arm is a five-axis manipulator that has a hip, shoulder, elbow, and hand. The hand is capable of pitch, roll, and grip (Shahinpoor & Singer, 1985).

In special education, robots offer the potential to perform two basic functions. First, they can serve as an extension of the teacher by interacting with students and providing instruction in a fascinating area of technology. Second, robots can be controlled by students to meet their personal needs and objectives. For individuals with disabilities, robotics can help alleviate many of the restrictions imposed by limited mobility and dexterity. For the orthopedically disabled in particular, robotics may compensate for missing or impaired human functions (Kimbler, 1984). In the future, robotics may help compensate for visual and auditory disabilities. Scientists are working on robots that will respond to voice commands and have computerized vision.

REFERENCES

Kimbler, D. L. (1984, June). *Robots and special education: The robot as extension of self.* Paper presented at Special Education Technology Research and Development Symposium, Washington, DC.

Shahinpoor, M., & Singer, N. (1985). A new instructional laboratory. *T.H.E. Journal, 13,* 54–56.

Slesnick, T. (1984). Robots and kids. *Classroom Computer Learning, 4,* 54–59.

Yin, R. K., & Moore, G. B. (1984). *Robotics, artificial intelligence, computer simulation: Future applications in special education.* (Contract No. 300-84-0135). Washington, DC: U.S. Department of Education.

ELIZABETH MCCLELLAN
Council for Exceptional Children

COMPUTER-ASSISTED INSTRUCTION
COMPUTER USE WITH INDIVIDUALS WITH DISABILITIES

ROBOTICS IN SPECIAL EDUCATION

Robotics in special education serves two potential functions. First, robotics can operate as an auxiliary to education by providing novel instruction to students, increasing motivation, and acting as an extension of the teacher in an instructional role. These auxiliary educational functions can be found in robots and robotic educational systems available today. They have been put to productive, albeit limited, use in special education. Little research has been conducted to test the efficacy of such uses.

A second, and perhaps potentially more dramatic, use of robotics for the handicapped concerns the robot as an extension of self. The robot is controlled by the individual to meet his or her personal needs and objectives and to control the environment. These functions demand a robot capable of a high level of sophistication in its logic and actions, a level not currently available in a single robotics unit (Kimbler, 1984). Nevertheless, the potential of the robot as an extension of the handicapped individual has prompted speculation concerning relevant applications and preliminary work on requisite performance characteristics.

Speculation on the usefulness of robotics has focused on handicapped conditions that limit mobility, dexterity, and interaction with the environment (Kimbler, 1984). The robot has been conceptualized as providing missing or impaired human functions under the direction of the disabled individual. Remote control devices have been used in this manner to some extent, and individual robots have been employed in restricted environments to perform limited functions such as serving meals. However, these applications have required modification of the environment. Ideally, the capacity of the robot would be more generalized; it would perform its functions by interacting with existing environments. A second major type of disability for which robotics applications have been conceptualized is sensory impairments, including visual and auditory disabilities. In these cases, the robot would provide sensory interaction as a mobile, dextrous adaptive device, permitting individuals to perceive the environment and then to operate on the setting directly or to control the robot to interact for them.

To support these functions, certain performance characteristics are necessary. For example, mobility under internal control to accomplish external demands is required. This movement needs to be smooth, to vary in speed from very slow to quick, and to react to novel environments through sensory systems. Robotics for these purposes require both payload, or strength and manipulation for that which needs to be carried, and dexterity dimensions to support varied and precise functions. The intelligence of the robot must allow reception and transmission of information through sensory apparatus, coordination of basic motion with its command and sensory input, communication in a conversational mode, and adaptation to new settings and uses. Finally, the robot must combine these characteristics with reasonable size; for acceptable and practical use, the robot must approximate the size of an average adult but maintain adequate bulk, stability, and power.

The robot that meets these requirements is complex and beyond current capabilities. Nevertheless, research on machine intelligence, performance characteristics, and integration proceeds. Work on artificial intelligence, expert systems, real-time computing, sensing capabilities, environmental mapping, conversational input and output, and power sources continues. The present state of technology in each of these areas supports feasibility of the robotic extension but requires packaging into a single working unit

(Kimbler, 1984). Additionally, philosophical issues related to the cost of such technology must be addressed before applications of robotics to improve the ability of individuals with disabilities to function in uncontrolled environments can be realized (Blaschke, 1984).

REFERENCES

Blaschke, C. (1984). *Market profile report: Technology and special education*. Falls Church, VA: Project Tech Mark, Education TURNKEY Systems.

Kimbler, D. L. (1984). Robots and special education: The robot as extension of self. *Peabody Journal of Education, 62,* 67–76.

LYNN S. FUCHS
Peabody College, Vanderbilt University

Moores, D. (1982). *Educating the deaf: Psychology, principles and practices.* Boston: Houghton Mifflin.

Quigley, S., & Paul, P. (1984). *Language and deafness.* San Diego, CA: College-Hill.

Quigley, S., & Young, J. (Eds.). (1965). *Interpreting for deaf people.* Washington, DC: U.S. Department of Health, Education, and Welfare.

ROSEMARY GAFFNEY
Hunter College, City University of New York

DEAF
SIGN LANGUAGE
TOTAL COMMUNICATION

ROCHESTER METHOD

The Rochester method is an oral, multisensory procedure for instructing deaf children in which speech reading is simultaneously supplemented by finger spelling and auditory amplification. The language of signs is wholly excluded from this procedure of instruction (Quigley & Young, 1965).

The Rochester method was established by Zenos Westervelt at the Rochester School for the Deaf, in Rochester, New York, in 1878. Westervelt was convinced that finger spelling was the best means of teaching deaf children grammatically correct language. He believed that the easy visibility of finger spelling could help in lip reading as well as in speech instruction (Levine, 1981). The Rochester method is directly related to the method used by Juan Pablo Bonet of Spain. He advocated the use of a combination of a one-handed alphabet and speech in his book *The Simplification of Sounds and the Art of Teaching Mutes to Speak,* published in 1620. This method had a resurgence in the Soviet Union in the 1950s under the name neo-oralism, and in the United States in the 1960s (Moores, 1982).

Various studies have assessed the effectiveness of the Rochester method as an educational tool. Reviewing these, Quigley and Paul (1984) reported that, in general, researchers concluded that deaf children exposed to the Rochester method performed better than comparison groups in finger spelling, speech reading, written language, and reading. They also found that, when good oral techniques are used in conjunction with finger spelling, there are no detrimental effects to the acquisition of oral skills.

REFERENCES

Levine, E. (1981). *The ecology of early deafness.* New York: Columbia University Press.

ROEPER REVIEW

The *Roeper Review,* published since 1977 by the Roeper Institute, is a journal on the education of gifted students. It originated as an information periodical for parents whose children attended the Roeper School. The journal has three purposes: (1) presenting philosophical, moral, and academic issues that are related to the lives and experiences of gifted and talented persons; (2) presenting various views on those issues; and (3) translating theory into practice for use at school, at home, and in the general community.

The audience and authors for *Roeper Review* include practicing teachers and administrators, teacher-educators, psychologists, and scientists. They are served by in-depth coverage of important topics in each issue. Some examples of issues discussed in past editions are teacher education for gifted education, social studies education for the gifted, special subpopulations among gifted students, and perceptions of gifted students and their education. The mailing address is *Roeper Review,* 41190 Woodward Avenue, Bloomfield Hills, MI 48304-5020.

ANN E. LUPKOWSKI
Texas A&M University

ROGER, HARRIET B. (1834–1919)

Harriet B. Roger began the first oral school for the instruction of the deaf in the United States in 1863 when she accepted a deaf child as a private pupil in her home. With published accounts of the instruction of the deaf in Germany to guide her, she taught herself how to instruct the child. Her success in this undertaking led to the admission of other deaf children. One of these was Mabel Hubbard, who became Mrs. Alexander Graham Bell and whose father, a prominent lawyer, obtained legislation for the creation of an oral school for the deaf in Massachusetts. Hubbard formed this school by moving Roger's school to Northampton, where, in 1867, they established the Clarke School for the Deaf, the second purely oral school for the deaf in the United States (the Lexington School for the Deaf having opened in New York City earlier that year). Roger, the first teacher and the instructional leader of the Clarke School, remained there until her retirement in 1886.

REFERENCE

Lane, H. (1984). *When the mind hears.* New York: Random House.

PAUL IRVINE
Katonah, New York

ROOS, PHILIP (1930–　　)

Born in Brussels, Belgium, Philip Roos obtained his BS in 1949 in biology and psychology with highest distinction from Stanford University, and from 1950 to 1951 did postgraduate work there in statistics and clinical and child psychology. He then earned his PhD in 1955 in clinical psychology at the University of Texas, Austin. Roos is currently President of Roos & Associates in Hurst, Texas, a consulting firm providing training to business and industry, and he maintains a private clinical psychology practice as well.

Roos advocates the early use of behavior modification with institutionalized individuals with severe and profound retardation and adolescents with mild retardation who exhibit behavior disorders (Roos & Oliver, 1970). He is the orig-

Philip Roos

inator of the Developmental Model, used for programming persons with mental retardation, emphasizing the potency of expectations in working with individuals with handicaps, and evaluating the impact of the interpersonal environment in shaping individual development. Roos' model has been the basis for many programs for those with mental retardation and a component of numerous national accreditation standards of agencies working with this population.

Roos has been an active advocate on behalf of children with disabilities and their families, assisting them in dealing with both emotional and practical frustrations, helping to individualize services, and aiding in the establishment of their rights (Roos, 1983). His service to the profession has included the positions of associate commissioner in the Division of Mental Retardation of the New York State Department of Mental Hygiene (1967–1968); national executive director of both the Association of Retarded Citizens (1969–1983) and Mothers Against Drunk Driving (1983–1984); and a member of the board of directors of the Sunny Von Bulow Victim Advocacy Center (1986–1994). Roos has also been recognized in *Who's Who in America, Who's Who in the South and Southwest,* and *Who's Who in Medicine and Healthcare.*

REFERENCES

Roos, P. (1983). Advocate groups of the mentally retarded. In J. L. Matson & J. Mulick (Eds.), *Comprehensive handbook of mental retardation.* New York: Pergamon.

Roos, P., & Oliver, M. (1970). Evaluation of operant conditioning with institutionalized retarded children. *American Journal of Mental Deficiency, 74,* 325–330.

E. VALERIE HEWITT
Texas A&M University
First edition

TAMARA J. MARTIN
The University of Texas of the Permian Basin
Second edition

RORSCHACH

The Rorschach, developed by Hermann Rorschach in 1921, is generally regarded as the most widely used projective personality assessment technique (Lubin, Wallis, & Paine, 1971). Five distinct scoring systems developed following Rorschach's death in 1922. Exner's Comprehensive Rorschach System (Exner, 1974, 1978; Exner & Weiner, 1982) has provided the fragmented Rorschach community with a common methodology, language, and literature; it is one of the most frequently used systems.

The Rorschach test stimuli consist of 10 inkblots, half achromatic and half with different degrees of color. Cards are presented individually to subjects, who are allowed to give as many responses as they wish describing "what the cards might be." Determinants that are scored include location, form, color, shading, movement, and quality and quantity of responses. Information obtained from the scored protocol includes personality state and trait characteristics, coping style, extent and quality of self-focus, quality of reality testing, likelihood of suicidal ideation or schizophrenia, depression, maturity, and complexity of psychological operations. Scoring and interpretation of the Rorschach, which is time-consuming and detailed, requires that the examiner be thoroughly trained in Rorschach assessment.

Criticisms of the Rorschach include the length of the time needed for administration, scoring and interpretation, and the fact that accurate usage is highly dependent on the clinical skills of the administrator. When used to gather descriptive clinical information, the Rorschach is considered to be an empirically valid instrument (Maloney & Glasser, 1982; Parker, 1983). Gittelman-Klein (1978) has presented an in-depth review of the validity of projective techniques, with positive results.

REFERENCES

Exner, J. E. (1974). *The Rorschach: A comprehensive system. Vol. 1: Basic foundations.* New York: Wiley.

Exner, J. E. (1978). *The Rorschach: A comprehensive system. Vol. 2: Current research and advanced interpretation.* New York: Wiley.

Exner, J. E., & Weiner, I. B. (1982). *The Rorschach: A comprehensive system. Vol. 3: Assessment of children and adolescents.* New York: Wiley.

Gittelman-Klein, R. (1978). Validity of projective tests for psychodiagnosis in children. In R. L. Spitzer & D. F. Klein (Eds.), *Critical issues in psychiatric diagnosis.* New York: Raven.

Lubin, B., Wallis, R. R., & Paine, C. (1971). Patterns of psychological test usage in the United States: 1935–1969. *Professional Psychology, 2,* 70–74.

Maloney, M. P., & Glasser, A. (1982). An evaluation of the clinical utility of the Draw-A-Person test. *Journal of Clinical Psychology, 38,* 183–190.

Parker, K. A. (1983). A meta-analysis of the reliability and validity of the Rorschach. *Journal of Personality Assessment, 47,* 227–231.

CONSTANCE Y. CELAYA
Irving, Texas

FRANCES F. WORCHEL
Texas A&M University

RORSCHACH INKBLOT TEST

The Rorschach inkblot test is a widely used projective personality assessment technique. The test is administered in a nondirective fashion (Exner, 1995). Respondents are asked to describe what they can see in a series of 10 inkblots. Administration time with children is approximately 30 minutes, with interpretation taking 30 to 45 minutes. Examiners transcribe the respondent's words and identify the visual percepts, which are then coded and tabulated through an extensively researched, empirically based system. Considerable examiner training is necessary to accomplish the administration, coding, and interpretation tasks.

The Comprehensive System (Exner, 1993) approach makes the Rorschach an objective multiscale performance and personality test. Its administration and coding standards, normative data, and accumulated research provide a sturdy empirical basis to the test. Test-retest reliability for children is as expected given developmental considerations: Some variables demonstrate relatively strong test-retest reliability for a year or two during the primary grade school years (Exner, Thomas, & Mason, 1985; Exner & Weiner, 1995). Test-retest reliability increases gradually, so that almost all measures of trait variables are relatively stable by age 18.

The test yields a large number of variables related to the domains of cognition, affect, interpersonal perception, self-perception, and coping styles, and also various characteristics related to diagnostic categories. Personality, coping, and problem-solving interpretations can be synthesized, along with observations about social, school, family, and problem behaviors, into a description of the psychological functioning of the child.

Criticism of the test has been a popular rallying cry, but empirical reports indicate adequate validity and utility, particularly for issues that are not readily accessible through self-report, brief interview, or observation (Exner, 1993; Viglione, 1999). The fact that all responses are formulated by the subject without prefabrication from test developers allows the test to access personally meaningful information. For example, the Rorschach can shed light on issues that the respondent may be unwilling or unable to express. No other instrument yields such an efficient, yet comprehensive, empirically based understanding of the individual. Criticism about the test may result from a misunderstanding of its so-called projective components. This is not a test of imagination, and it goes far beyond projective processes, despite unfortunate and inaccurate characterizations (e.g., Dawes, 1994).

Rorschach variables have demonstrated concurrent and predictive validity for both academic achievement test scores and classroom performance by young children, even after the effects of intelligence were statistically removed (e.g., Russ, 1980, 1981; Wulach, 1977). These results support the belief that the Rorschach addresses cognitive motivational trends and real-life application of abilities.

As far as the special education evaluation goals of truly understanding a child, the Rorschach can help to identify the psychological factors associated with the expression of observed strengths and weaknesses. For example, the test can help to identify and to understand emotional and psychological disturbances that impede learning, difficulties with peer and authority relationships, inappropriate behaviors that interfere with school performance and socialization, and problem-solving styles that result in poor performance despite intellectual abilities. However, the use of the Rorschach remains controversial, and an opposing view of its reliability and validity is available in Sechrest, Stickle, and Stewart (1998).

REFERENCES

Dawes, R. M. (1994). *House of cards: Psychology and psychotherapy built on myth.* New York: Free Press.

Exner, J. E. (1993). *The Rorschach: A comprehensive system. Vol. 1: Basic foundations* (3rd ed.). New York: Wiley.

Exner, J. E. (1995). *A Rorschach workbook for the comprehensive system* (4th ed.). Asheville, NC: Rorschach Workshops.

Exner, J. E., Thomas, E. A., & Mason, B. J. (1985). Children's Rorschachs: Description and prediction. *Journal of Personality Assessment, 49,* 13–20.

Exner, J. E., & Weiner, I. B. (1995). *The Rorschach: A comprehensive system. Vol. 3: Assessment of children and adolescents* (2nd ed.). New York: Wiley.

Russ, S. W. (1980). Primary process integration on the Rorschach and achievement in children. *Journal of Personality Assessment, 44,* 338–344.

Russ, S. W. (1981). Primary process integration on the Rorschach and achievement in children: A follow-up study. *Journal of Personality Assessment, 45,* 473–477.

Sechrest, L., Stickle, T., & Stewart, M. (1998). The role of assessment in clinical psychology. In C. R. Reynolds (Ed.), *Assessment,* Vol. 4 of A. Bellack & M. Hersen (Eds.), *Comprehensive clinical psychology* (pp. 1–32). Oxford: Elsevier Science.

Viglione, D. J. (1999). A review of recent research addressing the utility of the Rorschach. *Psychological Assessment, 11,* 251–265.

Wulach, J. S. (1977). Piagetian cognitive development and primary process thinking in children. *Journal of Personality Assessment, 41,* 230–237.

Donald J. Viglione
*California School of
Professional Psychology*

ROSS INFORMATION PROCESSING ASSESSMENTS

The Ross Information Processing Assessment–Second Edition (RIPA-2) provides quantifiable data for profiling 10 key areas basic to communicative and cognitive functioning: Immediate Memory, Recent Memory, Temporal Orienta-

tion (Recent and Remote Memory), Spatial Orientation, Orientation to Environment, Recall of General Information, Problem Solving and Abstract Reasoning, Organization, and Auditory Processing and Retention. The RIPA-2 enables the examiner to quantify cognitive–linguistic deficits, determine severity levels for specific skill areas, and develop rehabilitation goals and objectives.

The study sample included 126 individuals with traumatic brain injury in 17 states and was representative of TBI demographics for gender, ethnicity, and socioeconomic status. Raw scores are converted to standard scores. Reliability and validity studies performed on individuals with traumatic brain injury (TBI) are reported. Internal consistency reliability was investigated, and the mean reliability coefficient for RIPA-2 subtests was .85, with a range of .67 to .91. Content, construct, and criterion-related validity are reported in the manual.

The earlier edition of RIPA-2 was reviewed in *Eleventh Mental Measurements Yearbook* and *Test Critiques;* references for the newest edition of the instrument are unavailable because of its recent publication date. Franzen (1988) reported that the RIPA appeared to be a good beginning toward producing an instrument capable of profiling the different areas of information processing that might be affected by diffuse or right-hemisphere injury. Ehrlich (1992) felt that the instrument measured selected verbally mediated aspects and could be a useful tool in a clinical setting.

The Ross Information Processing Assessment–Geriatric (RIPA-G) is an adaptation that is designed for residents in skilled nursing facilities (SNFs), hospitals, and clinics. In addition to standard questions and stimulus items used for assessing cognitive-linguistic deficits, the RIPA-G incorporates questions from the Minimum Data Set used by nursing staffs in SNFs. These questions provide correlational data with nursing staff's assessments of patients' cognitive-linguistic abilities. Percentile ranks, standard scores, and composite quotients are provided for individual subtests, skill areas, and overall cognitive-linguistic functioning. Periodic retesting provides objective data to assess treatment efficacy and documents progress often required for Medicare and third-party payment. Internal consistency reliability coefficients of the RIPA-G were found to be .80 or greater.

The Ross Information Processing Assessment–Primary is designed for children ages 5 through 12 who have had a traumatic brain injury, experienced other neuropathologies such as seizure disorders or anoxia, or exhibit learning disabilities or weaknesses that interfere with learning acquisition. The eight subtests measure immediate and recent memory, spatial orientation, temporal orientation, organization, problem solving, abstract reasoning, and recall of general information.

The RIPA-P was standardized on 115 individuals ages 5 through 12. Reliability coefficients were found to be .81 or above, and more than a third of them were over .90. Validity studies show that the test discriminates between "normal" and LD or neurological problems. Item discrimination coefficients for the RIPA-P range from .39 to .94. Norms include children who have learning disabilities.

REFERENCES

Ehrlich, J. (1992). Review of the Ross Information Processing Assessment. In J. J. Kramer & J. C. Conoley (Eds.), *The eleventh mental measurements yearbook* (pp. 775–776). Lincoln: Buros Institute of Mental Measurements, University of Nebraska Press.

Franzen, M. D. (1988). Review of the Ross Information Processing Assessment. In D. J. Keyser & R. C. Sweetland (Eds.), *Test critiques–Volume VII* (pp. 496–498). Austin, TX: PRO-ED.

Ross-Swain, D. (1996). *Ross Information Processing Assessment–Second edition.* Austin, TX: PRO-ED.

Ross-Swain, D. (1999). *Ross Information Processing Assessment–Primary.* Austin, TX: PRO-ED.

Ross-Swain, D., & Fogle, P. (1996). *Ross Information Processing Assessment–Geriatric.* Austin, TX: PRO-ED.

TADDY MADDOX
PRO-ED, Inc.

ROSWELL-CHALL DIAGNOSTIC READING TEST OF WORD ANALYSIS SKILLS, REVISED AND EXTENDED

The Roswell-Chall Diagnostic Reading Test was developed to evaluate the word analysis and word recognition skills of pupils reading at the first- through fourth-grade levels. It may also be used with pupils who are reading at higher levels where there is a suspicion of decoding and word recognition difficulties or for research and program evaluation.

Two comparable forms of the test are available. Each is individually administered. The test has 10 main subtests and four extended evaluation subtests. All of the subtests or only those deemed appropriate may be given. The following skills are measured: high-frequency words, single consonant sounds, consonant diagrams, consonant blends, short vowel words, short and long vowel sounds, rule of silent e's, vowel diagrams, common diphthongs and vowels controlled by *r,* and syllabication (and compound words). The extended evaluation subtests include naming capital letters, naming lower-case letters, encoding single consonants, and encoding phonetically regular words.

The test takes approximately 10 minutes to administer, score, and interpret. Score interpretations are provided in the manual. The test has good reliability and validity. Users should be concerned about the size and somewhat limited nature of the norm sample; therefore, the administrator should be knowledgeable in the kinds of skills needed in

most individual testing situations and, in order to interpret the test accurately, be a relatively skilled reading clinician.

REFERENCE

Manual of instructions: Roswell-Chall Diagnostic Reading Test of Word Analysis Skills, Revised and Extended. (1978). LaJolla, CA: Essay.

RONALD V. SCHMELZER
Eastern Kentucky University

ROTHMUND-THOMPSON SYNDROME

See NATIONAL ORGANIZATION OF RARE DISORDERS.

ROUSSEAU, JEAN J. (1712–1778)

Jean Jacques Rousseau, French-Swiss philosopher and moralist, revolutionized child-rearing and educational practices with the publication, in 1762, of *Emile,* a treatise on education in the form of a novel. Rousseau contended that childhood is not merely a period of preparation for adulthood to be endured, but a developmental stage to be cherished and enjoyed. He enjoined parents and educators to be guided by the interests and capacities of the child, and was the first writer to propose that the study of the child should be the basis for the child's education. Probably every major educational reform since the eighteenth century can be traced in some way to Rousseau, and indebtedness to him is clear in the works of Pestalozzi, Froebel, Montessori, and Dewey. An eloquent writer, Rousseau's works on man's relationship with nature, as well as his writings on social, political,

Jean J. Rousseau

and educational matters, were major contributions to the literature of his day.

REFERENCES

Boyd, W. (1963). *The educational theory of Jean Jacques Rousseau.* New York: Russell & Russell.

Rousseau, J. J. (1969). *Emile.* New York: Dutton.

PAUL IRVINE
Katonah, New York

RUBELLA

Postnatal rubella (German measles) is a relatively mild viral infection that is generally inconsequential. It was first differentiated from measles and scarlet fever by German workers in the latter part of the eighteenth century. German scientists termed the disease *Roethelm.* According to *Black's Medical Dictionary,* the term *German measles* has no geographical reference but rather comes from the word germane, meaning akin to. Rubella comes from the Latin word *rubellus* meaning red (*Black's,* 1984).

The postnatal rubella virus is transmitted through contact with blood, bodily waste excretions, nasopharyngeal secretions of infected persons, and, possibly, contact with contaminated clothing (*Professional Guide to Diseases,* 1984). Humans are the only known host for the rubella virus and the period of communicability lasts from about 10 days before the rash appears until about 5 days after it appears. When acquired postnatally, rubella is a self-limited viral infection. It appears most frequently in the late winter or spring, particularly in large urban communities. Rubella is distributed worldwide. Although major epidemics occur in intervals ranging from 10 to 30 years, sizable epidemics may occur every 6 to 9 years (Alford, 1976). The factors responsible for the continuation of the epidemics is unknown.

It is believed that the rubella virus enters the body through the upper respiratory tract, is transmitted to the blood system, and results in low levels of viral production from 9 to 11 days. After this time, virimic seeding results in viral excretion from the nasopharynx, urine, cervix, and feces. After the incubation period of 14 to 21 days, a red rash erupts. Enlargement of the lymph nodes, most easily identified on the face or the neck, is a hallmark of a rubella infection. The rash, which typically begins on the face, rapidly spreads to the trunk and other parts of the body. The rash may be accompanied by a low-grade fever (99° to rarely higher than 104°). In adults, the rash may also be accompanied by headaches, joint pains, and conjunctivitis.

Because of the mild nature of rubella acquired postnatally, there is little concern for active treatment. The rash rarely requires topical ointments but aspirin may be taken to ease the discomfort associated with fever and body pains. Children or adults with postnatal rubella should be isolated owing to the threat of infecting newly pregnant mothers.

Congenital rubella is a concern because of the 20 to 30 percent chance of damage to the fetus when a mother contracts the infection during the first trimester of pregnancy (Bonwick, 1972). Catastrophic damaging effects were first reported by Sir Norman Gregg, an Australian ophthalmologist, in 1941. The classic congenital rubella syndrome as described by Gregg consists of fetal anomalies, ocular defects, and hearing impairment. Mental retardation was also shown to be a common result of early damage to the fetus.

Shortly after the rubella virus was isolated in 1961, the first epidemic since 1940, and the last major epidemic to date, struck the United States. The results of the epidemic are reported by Rudolph and Desmond (1972):

> Some 30,000 pregnancies ended in miscarriage or stillbirth, and between 20,000 to 30,000 infants suffered from various defects . . . 8,000 cases of deafness, 3,600 cases of deafness and blindness, 1,800 cases of mental retardation, and 6,600 other malformations . . . 5,000 therapeutic abortions and 2,000 excess neonatal deaths. (p. 4)

It appears that circulation of the virus in the blood of the infected mother during the incubation period of her postnatal infection is the initial step in contraction of congenital rubella by the fetus. The virus is transferred from the mother's bloodstream to the placenta and then often to the fetal bloodstream. Although the exact reasons for this are not known, it is apparent that the earlier in the pregnancy the mother contracts the viral infection, the more pervasive the damage to the fetus. It is also apparent that congenital rubella is very different from postnatal rubella in that the former is widely disseminated throughout the body of the fetus.

Extensive investigations during the last 20 years have characterized congenital rubella as having pathologic potential much greater than was first assumed by Gregg. For instance, it is now hypothesized that congenital rubella, in addition to being responsible for the anomalies previously reported, may also be responsible for numerous abnormalities that appear later in life. These include dental problems, anemia, encephalitis, giant cell hepatitis, dermatitis, and diabetes.

Active prevention seems the key to reducing the impact of congenital rubella, as once the damage has been done in utero there appears to be little hope of reversing the effects. Of course, corrective surgery can be performed in cases where the fetus suffers cardiac damage or has cataracts, and hearing aids can be given to the hearing-impaired child, but the damage is not reversible.

Passive immunization procedures such as large doses of gamma globulin have been shown to be ineffective in preventing damage to the fetus once the mother has contracted the virus. Chemotherapeutic procedures also have proven inadequate as protection against the devastating effects of congenital rubella (Alford, 1976).

An active immunization program seems to hold the best promise to date to reducing the spread of rubella to pregnant females. Immunization with live virus vaccine RA27/3 is used in the United States. This preventive program is aimed at vaccinating large numbers of infants and young children in the hopes of reducing circulation of the virus in the general population and thus protecting females in the childbearing years. Some have advocated that all young girls between 11 and 14 years should be vaccinated if they have not had the disease. It is also advocated now that all young women of childbearing age who have not had the disease and who are not pregnant be vaccinated. In Europe immunization programs are directed toward young married women. This approach is not without its risks and questions (Alford, 1976). Certain guidelines for administering the vaccine are available (*Professional Guide to Diseases,* 1984).

Often the psychological impact of giving birth to a disabled child can be as damaging as the virus itself. Parents of children with congenital rubella can obtain help and advice from the National Association for Deaf, Blind and Rubella Handicapped, 12 A Rosebery Avenue, London, England ECIR 4TD.

REFERENCES

Alford, C. A. (1976). Rubella. In J. S. Remington, & J. O. Klein (Eds.), *Infectious diseases of the fetus and newborn infant.* Philadelphia: Saunders.

Black's medical dictionary. (1984). Totowa, NJ: Barnes & Noble.

Bonwick, M. (1972). *Rubella and other intraocular viral diseases in infancy.* Boston: Little, Brown.

Professional guide to diseases. (1984). (pp. 384–386). Springhouse, PA: Springhouse.

Rudolph, A. J., & Desmond, M. M. (1972). Clinical manifestations of the congenital rubella syndrome. In M. Bonwick (Ed.), *Rubella and other intraocular viral diseases in infancy.* Boston: Little, Brown.

JULIA A. HICKMAN
*Bastrop Mental Health
Association*

CATARACTS
CONGENITAL DISORDERS
MENTAL RETARDATION

RUBENSTEIN-TAYBI SYNDROME

See NATIONAL ORGANIZATION OF RARE DISORDERS.

RURAL SPECIAL EDUCATION

Approximately 67 percent of the 16,000 public school districts in the United States are classified as rural because of sparse population or geographic location (Sher, 1978). According to Helge (1984), educational characteristics of rural areas are distinctly different from those of urban areas. Rural areas have higher poverty levels and serve greater percentages of children with disabilities. Populations in rural areas are increasing; however, their tax bases are not. Education costs more in rural areas than in nonrural areas because of transportation requirements and scarce professional resources.

Because of the remoteness of the areas, assessing the effectiveness of special education services to disabled and gifted children has been difficult. One reason for this, according to the director of the National Rural Research Project (Helge, 1984) has been the absence of a consistently applied definition of the term rural among federal agencies, educators, and professional organizations. The definition that is most commonly used is the one developed for the 1978 to 1983 research projects funded by the U.S. Office of Special Education Programs and conducted by the National Rural Research and Personnel Preparation Project. This definition reads:

> A district is considered rural when the number of inhabitants is fewer than 150 per square mile or when located in counties with 60 percent or more of the population living in communities not larger than 5,000 inhabitants. Districts with more than 10,000 students and those within a Standard Metropolitan Statistical Area (SMSA), as determined by the U.S. Census Bureau, are not considered rural. (p. 296)

The National Rural Research and Personnel Preparation Project was funded (to be conducted in four phases from 1978 to 1981)

> to investigate state and local educational agencies nationwide in order to determine problems and effective strategies for implementing Public Law 94-142; and to develop profiles of effective special education delivery systems and strategies, given specific rural community and district subcultural characteristics. (p. 296)

Phase I, conducted during 1978 and 1979, focused on identifying facilitating and hindering factors that operate to determine the success or failure of rural local educational agency compliance with PL 94-142. Results of this phase showed that problems identified by state educational agencies were grouped in three categories: (1) staffing problems (recruiting and retaining qualified staff); (2) attitudinal variables (resistance to change, suspicions of outside interference, and long distances between schools); and (3) problems based on rural geography (fiscal problems, difficult terrain and economic conditions). Phase II, conducted during 1979 and

1980, was designed to develop profiles interrelating community characteristics and school district characteristics with service delivery options proven viable in other local education agencies with similar characteristics. Phase III (1980) involved using Phase I and II data to develop interdisciplinary models of personnel preparation for effective service delivery to rural subcultures. Phase IV, conducted in 1980 and 1981, was designed to field test and disseminate the modules for use in preservice and in-service training programs (Helge, 1981).

A series of in-service training modules have been developed with topics that range from stress reduction to alternate rural service delivery systems. In addition, several preservice modules are presently being field tested in universities across the country. Topics of the modules include alternate instructional arrangements and delivery systems for low-incidence students with disabilities in rural America; Warren Springs, Mesa: a rural preservice simulation; solving rural parent-professional related dilemmas; working with parents of rural students with disabilities; involving citizens and agencies of rural communities in cooperative programming for students with disabilities; working with peer professionals in rural environments; creative resource identification for providing services to rural students with disabilities; solving educational dilemmas related to school administration; and personal development skills and strategies for effective survival as a rural special educator. These modules are available through the American Council on Rural Special Education.

In a report on the state of the art of rural special education (Helge, 1984), it was noted that major service delivery problems remained basically the same as in the initial study done in 1979. These problems were associated with funding inadequacies, difficulties in recruiting and retaining qualified staff, transportation inadequacies, problems with providing services to low-incidence disabled populations, and inadequacies of preservice training. In addition, many of these inadequacies were seen as future problems.

In an effort to focus on rural special education and the identified service delivery problems, the American Council on Rural Special Education was founded in 1981. This nonprofit national membership organization is an outgrowth of the National Rural Development Institute, headquartered at Western Washington University in Bellingham. The organization is composed of approximately 1,000 rural special educators and administrators, parents of students with disabilities, and university and state department personnel. The specific purposes of the organization are to enhance direct services to rural individuals and agencies serving exceptional students; to increase educational opportunities for rural disabled and gifted students; and to develop a system for forecasting the future for rural special education and planning creative service delivery alternatives.

The American Council on Rural Special Education (ACRES) serves as an advocate for rural special education at the federal, state, regional, and local levels; provides professional development opportunities, and disseminates information on the current needs of rural special education. The ACRES has established a nationwide system to link educators and administrators needing jobs with agencies having vacancies. The ACRES Rural Bulletin Board communicates to interested agencies information regarding rural special education issues and promising practices through SpecialNet, the electronic communication system operated by the National Association of State Directors of Special Education. ACRES publishes a quarterly newsletter and a journal, the *Rural Special Education Quarterly*. These publications include up-to-date information on issues facing students with disabilities in rural America, problem-solving strategies, pertinent legislation and conferences, and articles on rural preservice and in-service strategies. The ACRES also holds a conference each year in the spring, usually at the institute's headquarters. The conferences feature presentation to enhance services to rural disabled and gifted children, media displays of curriculum materials, and hardware and software exhibits.

REFERENCES

Helge, D. I. (1981). Problems in implementing comprehensive special education programming in rural areas. *Exceptional Children, 47,* 514–524.

Helge, D. I. (1984). The state of the art of rural special education. *Exceptional Children, 50,* 294–305.

Sher, J. P. (1978). A proposal to end federal neglect of rural schools. *Phi Delta Kappan, 60,* 280–282.

CECELIA STEPPE-JONES
*North Carolina Central
University*

RUSH, BENJAMIN (1745–1813)

Benjamin Rush, physician, teacher, reformer, and patriot, began medical practice in Philadelphia in 1769. He taught chemistry at the College of Philadelphia, and published the first American textbook on that subject. During the Revolutionary War, he served as surgeon-general of the Army and published a textbook on military medicine that was still in use at the time of the Civil War. Following his military service, Rush returned to the practice of medicine in Philadelphia, where he established the first free dispensary in the United States. He is believed to be the first physician to relate smoking to cancer and to advocate temperance and exercise to promote good health. An outspoken advocate of humane treatment for the mentally ill, in 1812 Rush published a work that would influence medical education for generations to come, *Medical Inquiries and Observations Upon the Diseases of the Mind.*

Despite his accomplishments as a physician, political and social issues were Rush's major interests. He was a member of the Continental Congress and a signer of the Declaration of Independence. He was active in the movement to abolish slavery, and was influential in the ratification of the federal Constitution in Pennsylvania. He involved himself in a number of educational causes, advocating improved education for girls and proposing a comprehensive system of public schools that would offer science and practical subjects as well as traditional academics.

REFERENCES

Hawke, D. (1971). *Benjamin Rush*. New York: Bobbs-Merrill.

Rush, B. (1962). *Medical inquiries and observations upon the diseases of the mind*. New York: Hafner.

PAUL IRVINE
Katonah, New York

RUSSELL-SILVER SYNDROME

See NATIONAL ORGANIZATION OF RARE DISORDERS.

RUSSIA, SPECIAL EDUCATION IN

Special education in Russia first developed from the then-progressive ideas of Vygotsky, Luria, Boskis, Pevzner, Levina, Rau and other behavioral researchers. They approached the education of a child with special needs while considering his or her complex psychophysiological development, with the most complete possible social rehabilitation of a child as a goal. During the Communist regime these ideas were replaced by a pedagogy that was less child-centered, isolating a child with special needs from society, and establishing several boarding institutions (van Rijswijk et al., 1996).

Recently, Russia has entered a new phase in its thinking and attitudes about special education. A return to the individual child-focus has been augmented by the ideal for full participation or integration in society. Social rehabilitation continues to be valued, but social participation is also highly valued.

The modern phase into which special education has recently entered was necessary because of the absence of protective legislation for the civil rights of children with handicaps or with other special needs. This modern phase of special education in Russia places new emphases on preschool interventions and on staff training of teachers, psychologists, social workers, and others.

Legal Bases for Special Education

During the Soviet period in the republics of the former USSR, the rights of the child (as indicated in the UNO Convention, the UNO Declaration on the rights of the invalids and the rights of the mentally handicapped people) were not well-observed. Within the last decade, Russia's central government has taken firm steps toward ratification and realization of these international documents. Nevertheless, still there is inadequate legislation for special education, although there is some progress in this direction (Aksenova, 1997). The new phase for special education was signaled in part by a landmark Law on Education (1992), which was considered one of the most democratic in the history of Russia. This law was followed four years later by several further insertions and improvements to "About the Education"; these went into effect January 5th, 1996.

The Law on Education significantly improves the state guarantee of a free, appropriate public education to people with disabilities. Particularly, Article 50, Point 10 of the Law foresees the establishment of the special (correctional) educational institutions for children and adolescents with special needs, where they can have treatment, upbringing, education, social adaptation, and integration into society. Note that social rehabilitation is emphasized more than social participation.

A second new law that marks the modern phase of special education in Russia is "On Social Care of Invalids," which went into effect on January 1st, 1996. Article 18 of this Law is dedicated to the upbringing and education of child invalids. According to the law, the educational institutions together with social and health care organizations must provide upbringing and education of children with disabilities, from preschool through secondary school, both within classrooms and outside, according to an individually defined program of rehabilitation. In both mainstream schools and special educational institutions, this education is free.

Another change in the modern phase is that the subjects of the Russian Federation (RF) have received the right to make legislation for solving their local problems, including the field of help and care of children and their families. This is appropriate because the financing of education, health, and other social services is carried out mainly at the expense of local budgets (which also brings about regional differences in type and quality of services). These legislative changes have encouraged public organizations to play a significant role in the improvement of children with special needs. In addition, public interest groups are beginning to attempt to influence regional decision making in the field of special education. Newly active public organizations are representing the interests of children with disabilities and their families. However, the national networking and sharing of information is still minimal. For example, there is not a uniform data bank on children with disabilities and programs in operation, let alone data on program effectiveness.

Although the recent Russian legislation for the children with special needs is a major step forward, it touches only some aspects of special education. Now Russia must develop a new law specifically for special education; in fact, a draft has been worked out and is under consideration by the State Duma.

Structure of Special Education

In Russia, several ministries are responsible for children with special needs, which causes a number of difficulties. The interdepartmental barriers interfere with creation of an integrated, harmonious, and effective system of social care and support. There is a whole complex of problems: social, scientific, practical. The largest obstacle to progress is the absence of high-grade statistical information about such children; in the Russian Federation there is no uniform state system to account for them.

The system of special education in Russia is based on five age designations and the specific type of disability.

Age Structure

The vertical structure consists of five levels:

1. early childhood (from 0 to 3 years old);
2. preschool period (from 3 to 7);
3. compulsory education (from 7 to 16);
4. comprehensive education and vocational training (from 15 to 18 and up to 21 for the blind, deaf, and physically handicapped);
5. adults-invalid training.

During the period of early childhood (from the birth to 3) children are trained and brought up in home conditions, in establishments for infants, and in homes for children if the child is an orphan. Developmental and remedial work with children with developmental problems is carried out in various centers of early intervention and rehabilitation, in special groups and at psychological-medical-pedagogical consulting centers.

For children of preschool age there are the following establishments:

- special kindergartens with day and day-night stay
- remedial homes for children
- special groups in regular kindergartens
- special rehabilitation centers
- preschool groups in special schools (for children with visual, hearing, emotional, and mental disorders).

Special (remedial) educational establishments for children with developmental problems offer programs of el-

ementary regular education, general regular education, and general comprehensive regular education. These establishments must meet special state educational standards. They focus on special remedial work, education, treatment, social adaptation, and integration into the society.

Special education is offered within a variety of administrative structures:

- special (remedial) school (daily or evening)
- special boarding school
- rehabilitation centers
- special class at a regular educational establishment
- individually in a regular educational establishment
- home education
- external education
- education in a stationary medical establishment.

Persons with developmental problems may receive both a regular education and vocational training in:

- special average schools
- special industrial workshops
- centers of social-labor rehabilitation
- special vocational schools.

Disability Type (Horizontal) Structure

The horizontal structure of special education in Russia is by eight types of disability:

I. for the deaf (classes for mentally retarded children)
II. for the hard of hearing (classes for mentally retarded children)
III. for the blind (classes for mentally retarded children)
IV. for visually impaired (classes for mentally retarded children)
V. with severe speech and language disorders
VI. with emotional disabilities (classes for mentally retarded children)
VII. with learning disabilities
VIII. for mentally retarded (special classes for children with severe mental retardation, classes for children with multiple and complex disorders).

For children and teenagers with deviant behavior there exist three kinds of special educational establishments in Russia:

- special educational school
- special vocational technical school

- special (remedial) comprehensive school and special (remedial) professional technical school for children and teenagers with problems in development (learning disabilities, light forms of mental retardation) who commit socially dangerous actions.

In Russia, statistics on children with special needs were not available during most of the Communist era. But beginning from 1993 according to the Russian Governmental Decree N 848 (23.08.93), "About the Realization of the UNO Convention on the Rights of a Child" and "International Declaration about the Providing of the Surviving, Care and Development of Children," a governmental statistical report is published every year. Entitled "About the Situation of Children in the Russian Federation," it contains statistics related to demographic and legal mandates for service in Russia as a whole and specific Russian regions.

The number of special schools for children with developmental problems (see table) is annually increasing. Special (remedial) classes in the mainstream schools have also grown.

In Russia, there are no special schools for children with emotional and behavioral problems. Concerning the education of children with early infant autism, there was no specific approach until recently, when individual groups in special kindergartens and primary schools began to be created for such children. Children with moderate and severe mental retardation usually live in state-financed boarding schools or with families, where education is partial or nonexistent. Until recently such children were labeled incapable of studying. Improvements in the education of these children is slow, but there are increasing numbers of special developmental classes in the schools for the children with mild mental retardation.

Russia is still marked by the existence of large numbers of separate special education boarding schools, where the majority of children get psychological, medical, and pedagogical help. Such boarding schools became popular for two reasons. First, because of Russia's large territory, in rural areas the school is usually situated so far from home that daily attendance is impossible. Second, many of these children do not have parents, have been given up for adoption, or have been refused by their parents, becoming wards of the state.

In Russia, approximately 1 to 2 percent of children from 6 to 16 years old attend special schools (and, more recently, special classes). Until recently in the Russian Federation, a significant number of children who needed special education could not get it because of the scarcity of special schools and personnel, especially in the regions of the far North, Siberia, and rural districts. In remote areas, many children with disabilities received no help.

Integrated Education for Children with Special Needs

In the latter part of this decade, special education in Russia has been improving in two main ways. First, there has been improvement in the existing network of special education programs and their expansion. The second improvement has been in the integrated education of these children (Shipitsina, 1996). The first improvement in the type and extent of special services is noted in the table. Note that the number of special schools has increased gradually or has been static. On the other hand, the number of special classes within regular public schools is expanding rapidly (see table).

Undoubtedly, not all children with problems in development can be integrated into a regular school, but many more can than are presently doing so. The difficult problem is identifying those particular children with developmental problems who can be integrated and when is the best time to start their integrative education.

Generally, in Russia, there are few statistics about the number of children with visual, hearing, and other impairments educated in mainstream schools. We do know that the majority of such children do not get any special help in ordinary schools. In recent years in Moscow, Saint Petersburg, and some other big cities of Russia, research began on the practical psychological and pedagogical guidance of children with sensory and moving problems in the mainstream school.

So far in Russia, the attitude to integrative education is restrained. Parents of children with impairments are commonly advised to place their child in a special boarding home from his or her very early life. The justification is usually that mainstream schools do not have the special staff and that the children cannot receive necessary support in mainstream classes in these schools. Unfortunately, this argument is partly true, as regular schools lack resources, expertise, and philosophies of integration. Usually the nature of integration is not questioned; the majority agree that it is good in the abstract, but that the practical obstacles are too great. Where attitudes are the problem, they usually come from the teachers in the mainstream schools (Makhortova, 1996).

Inclusive Education in the Regular Classroom

Children with different disabilities are included differentially in general education classrooms in Russia. Children with hearing impairments have only recently been included. Today the process of integration of such children into mainstream establishments is steadily expanding (Shmatko, 1996). The integrated education of children with sight impairments in the mainstream school is a rare phenomenon, and most mainstream schools are not yet ready for it. Some of the hesitation is due to concern for the adjustment of the child with disabilities. Some contend that full integration may increase personal problems (Makhortova, 1996).

Special Classes in the Mainstream School

Today in Russia, one of the fastest growing models of integrative education is the organization of special classes in the mainstream school. They are organized:

Schools for children with mental and physical disorders in the Russian Federation (beginning of educational year)*

Types of establishments for	Number of schools				Number of students (in thousands)			
	1990	1992	1994	1996	1990	1992	1994	1996
Children with mental or physical handicaps—Total	1817	1835	1848	1889	312.1	277.4	267.6	277.2
Mentally retarded	1452	1459	1443	1440	251.6	217.9	203.9	205.5
The blind	20	19	18	20	3.7	3.3	2.9	3.4
Visually impaired	51	52	56	61	7.8	7.4	8.0	8.5
The deaf (and mute)	82	81	85	84	12.5	11.9	12.0	11.3
The hard of hearing	70	73	73	77	11.2	10.8	10.6	11.0
Children with consequences of poliomyelitis and cerebral palsy	40	40	43	52	6.5	6.0	6.1	6.7
Severe speech and language problems	61	61	61	62	10.8	11.0	11.5	11.9
Learning disabilities	41	50	65	71	8.0	9.1	12.1	13.4
Children with mental or physical disorders set up in regular schools					53.0	119.7	155.5	192.0
Mentally retarded in regular					7.1	10.7	10.6	14.7
Learning disabled in regular schools					44.9	103.2	141.9	175.9

*Data of the State Statistical Committee of Russian Federation.

- for children with intellectual impairments (where there are not any special schools for this category of the children nearby); their number is rather small
- for children with learning difficulties; classes with special educational support or remedial classes
- for children of "risk groups" (with learning difficulties, behavior problems, weak health); classes of compensative education, special educational support, adaptation, and recreation.

In rare cases, due to the large distance from the special schools and unwillingness of the parents to refer their children to receive the education in the boarding schools, special classes, or groups for children with sight, hearing, and speech impairments are organized in the mainstream kindergartens and schools.

Despite the positive results of the work of special classes in mainstream schools, serious problems are still not solved.

- Students depend upon the existence of specialists (psychologists, speech therapists, special teachers), which are too few to service the children.
- Frequently, teachers refuse to work in special classes because of difficulties and lack of necessary knowledge about children with problems in development.

- Special classes often have a stigma attached, leading to aggressive social behavior and negative attitudes among peers.
- These classes promote the process of separating out children from the mainstream, permitting general educators to escape from their full responsibilities. Thus, the methods of selecting children for the special classed may be suspect.
- Mainstream education lacks the vocational training that many students with disabilities need in the secondary grades.

Despite all the problems and difficulties, it should be understood that in Russia the process of integration of the children with special needs into the mainstream schools is accelerating. Throughout the country, diverse models and forms of interaction between special and mainstream schools are developing; special schools are being deemphasized; and conditions for both social adaptation and personal development are being more closely approached than ever before.

REFERENCES

Aksenova, L. I. (1997). Legal bases of special education and social care of children with problems in development. *Journal of Defectology, 1*, 3.

Makhortova, G. H. (1996). Problems of psychological adaptation of children with visual impairments in the mainstream schools. *Journal of Defectology, 4,* 45–50.

Shipitsina, L. M. (1996). The topical aspects of integrative education of children with problems in development in Russia. *Integrative Education: Problems and Prospects.*

Shmatko, N. D. (1996). Integrative approach to education of children with hearing impairments in Russia. *Integrative Education: Problems and Prospects.*

State Report about the Situation of Children in Russian Federation—1996. (1997). Moscow.

van Rijswijk, K., Foreman, N., & Shipitsina, L. M. (Eds.). (1996). *Special education on the move.* Acco Leuven/Amersfoort.

Vygotsky, L. S. (1983). Principles of education of children with problems in physical development. *Complete works. Volume 5: Bases of defectology* (T. Vlasova, Ed.). Moscow.

LUDMILLA SHIPITSINA
RAOUL WALLENBERG
*International University for
Family and Child*

**LURIA, A. R.
VYGOTSKY, LEV S.**

RUTTER, MICHAEL (1933–   )

On completing his basic medical training at the University of Birmingham, England in 1955, Michael Rutter took residencies in internal medicine, neurology, and pediatrics. His training in general and child psychiatry was done at Maudsley Hospital. Away on fellowship study for a year (1961–1962), Rutter returned to work in the Medical Re-

Michael Rutter

search Council Special Psychiatry Research Unit. From 1965 to 1994, Rutter served as professor and head of the Department of Child and Adolescent Psychiatry at the University of London's Institute of Psychiatry. His distinguished appointments include honorary director of the Medical Research Council Child Psychiatry Unit (1984–1998); honorary director of the Social, Genetic and Developmental Psychiatry Research Centre (1994–1998); honorary consultant psychiatrist, Bethlehem and Maudsley Hospitals Trust; and research professor at the Institute of Psychiatry in 1998.

Rutter's major fields of interest indicate a strong interdisciplinary approach, include schools as social institutions, and stress resilience in relation to developmental links between childhood and adult life, psychiatric genetics, neuropsychiatry, psychiatric epidemiology, and infantile autism. As a teacher and researcher, his work centers on building bridges between the areas of child development and clinical child psychiatry.

Rutter's major published contributions include *Child and Adolescent Psychiatry: Modern Approaches* (3rd ed.), *Depression in Young People: Developmental and Clinical Perspectives* (1986), *Antisocial Behavior By Young People* (1998), *Fifteen Thousand Hours: Secondary Schools and Their Effects On Children* (1994), and *Psychosocial Disorders in Young People* (1995). To date, he has written 36 books, 138 chapters, and 300 research articles and associated works.

In 1979 Rutter served as a fellow at the Center for Advanced Study in the Behavioral Sciences at Stanford. He is a Fellow of The Royal Society (FRS), London; Foreign Associate Member of the Institute of Medicine of the National Academy of Sciences, United States; Foreign Honorary Member of the American Academy of Arts and Sciences; Foreign Associate Member of the US National Academy of Education; Founding Member of Academia Europaea; and Fellow of the Academy of Medical Sciences. In addition, he has been a trustee of the Nuffield Foundation since 1992, and became governor of the Wellcome Trust in 1996.

The numerous honorary degrees bestowed upon Rutter include the University of Birmingham in 1990, University of Edinburgh in 1990, University of Chicago in 1991, University of Ghent in 1994, and University of Jyvaskyla, Finland in 1996. He was knighted in January of 1992, and has received many prestigious awards, the most recent being the John P. Hill Award for Excellence in Theory Development and Research on Adolescence from the Society for Research on Adolescence in 1992; the American Psychological Association Distinguished Scientists Award in 1995; the Castilla del Pino Prize for Achievement in Psychiatry, Cordoba, Spain in 1995; and the Helmut Horten Award for research in autism that has made a difference to clinical practice in 1997. He is a member of the editorial boards of some 20 journals.

Rutter is currently Professor of Developmental Psychopathology at the Institute of Psychiatry, Kings College, Lon-

S

SABATINO, DAVID A. (1938–   )

David A. Sabatino obtained his BA in 1960, MA in 1961, and PhD in 1966 from Ohio State University. He is currently a professor in the department of human development and learning at East Tennessee State University, Johnson City.

Sabatino's interests have focused on gifted children and adolescents, children with disabilities, and psychological assessment (Fuller & Sabatino, 1998; Sabatino, Miller, & Schmidt, 1981; Sabatino, Spangler, & Vance, 1995; Spangler & Sabatino, 1995). He views learning disabilities as complex problems associated with difficulty in information processing. As a complicated problem, Sabatino contends that no one professional, from any single discipline, can meet the needs of all children. Instead, he advocates input from any service provider that can assist a particular child with a disability (Sabatino et al., 1981).

In his work, Sabatino noted that increasing numbers of children with disabilities were being neglected and secondary schools were ill-equipped to handle the influx, frequently stressing subject mastery rather than individual growth and learning. Thus, he advocated functional teaching, or teaching the necessary information in order for a child to function at a basic academic level. Teaching a child to read, if he or she does not know how to read, is preferable to labeling that child, according to Sabatino (Sabatino & Lanning-Ventura, 1982).

Sabatino continues his work involving programming for school-age children, investigating demographic and personality characteristics of at-risk high school students. This study indicated a prevalence of six factors, including defensiveness-hopelessness, attention seeking, and family relationship problems, as well as the predominant characteristics of absence of extra-curricular activities, a negative attitude toward school, and truancy. This research has important implications for programming at-risk students (Fuller & Sabatino, 1996).

REFERENCES

Fuller, C. G., & Sabatino, D. A. (1996). Who attends alternative high school? *High School Journal, 79,* 293–297.

Fuller, C. G., & Sabatino, D. A. (1998). Diagnosis and treatment considerations with comorbid developmentally disabled populations. *Journal of Clinical Psychology, 54,* 1–10.

Sabatino, D. A., & Lanning-Ventura, S. (1982). Functional teaching, survival skills and teaching. In D. A. Sabatino & L. Mann (Eds.), *A handbook of diagnostic and prescriptive teaching.* Rockville, MD: Aspen.

Sabatino, D. A., Miller, T. L., & Schmidt, C. R. (1981). *Learning disabilities: Systemizing teaching and service delivery.* Rockville, MD: Aspen.

Sabatino, D. A., Spangler, R. S., & Vance, H. B. (1995). The relationship between the Wechsler Intelligence Scale for Children–Revised and the Wechsler Intelligence Scale for Children–III scales and subtests with gifted children. *Psychology in the Schools, 32,* 18–23.

Spangler, R. S., & Sabatino, D. A. (1995). Temporal stability of gifted children's intelligence. *Roeper Review, 17,* 207–210.

E. Valerie Hewitt
Texas A&M University
First edition

Tamara J. Martin
The University of Texas of the Permian Basin
Second edition

SAFETY ISSUES IN SPECIAL EDUCATION

Accountability, malpractice, due process, and liability insurance are all terms familiar to special educators. For teachers to gain protection from legal situations it is critical that children's safety become a high priority. In particular, physically impaired and severely disabled children are more prone to accidents, medical emergencies, and injuries. Therefore, teachers must take certain precautions to protect students and staff from unnecessary risks. Specifically, educators must consider many facets of the classroom program in order to create safe environments for children. Four major areas related to safety must be considered: (1) basic first aid skills, (2) emergency weather and fire drill procedures, (3) safe classroom environments, and (4) parent consent and involvement in classroom activities.

Many states require teachers to obtain certification in first-aid procedures before they are eligible to obtain a teaching certificate. In particular, teachers should be trained in cardiopulmonary resuscitation (CPR) and anti-choking procedures such as the Heimlich maneuver. For teachers working with children who have seizures, a clear understanding of first-aid procedures for managing seizures is critical. Furthermore, basic instruction on poison management, eye injuries, and contusions must be included in first-aid programs. In the same context, children on medication such as Ritalin, Phenobarbital, and Dilantin, must be carefully monitored for signs of over or under dosage. Teachers should never be left solely responsible for dispensing any medications to children without the assistance of a physician or school nurse.

Emergency weather and fire drill procedures should be clearly posted in all classrooms. For teachers in certain areas of the country, where tornados and hurricanes are likely, extra efforts must be taken to understand the civil defense procedures for the school. For teachers of the physically disabled, visually impaired, and nonambulatory severely impaired, procedures should be established with the school principal for added assistance during civil defense drills and fire drills.

Much has been written on designing school facilities and classroom environments for students with disabilities (Abend, Bednor, Froehlinger, & Stenzler, 1979; Birch & Johnstone, 1975; Forness, Gutherie, & MacMillan, 1982; Hutchins & Renzaglia, 1983; Zentall, 1983). Environmental designing of classrooms also involves a safety aspect for children in special education. For example, many classrooms for physically disabled or visually impaired students should have adequate storage space for bulky equipment (e.g., wheelchairs, walkers) and materials (e.g., braillers, books, canes). A classroom that is organized and neat ensures safety for children. Cabinets within the classroom holding harmful materials should be inaccessible to students. Rossol (1982) discusses the possible hazards to students in special education using art materials.

Many of the activities developed for disabled students involve out-of-school visits such as field trips, community-based training, and recreation/leisure trips. Parental consent would be critical if liability issues arose from one of these activities. Additionally, behavioral intervention programs that might appear intrusive (e.g., time-out, physical restraint, withholding food) must be discussed by the educational team and parents prior to implementation of any such procedures. Each school or district should have policies regarding corporal punishment. Those policies must be understood by all special education teachers and all parents.

In conclusion, safety in special education is a topic that is rarely found in the literature, yet it has enormous implications for teachers working with children with disabilities. Although much of what has been discussed is commonsense, it is important to remind teachers of the many safety aspects in special education.

REFERENCES

Abend, A., Bednor, M., Froehlinger, V., & Stenzler, Y. (1979). *Facilities for special education services.* Reston, VA: Council for Exceptional Children.

Birch, J., & Johnstone, B. (1975). *Designing schools and schooling for the handicapped.* Springfield, IL: Thomas.

Forness, S., Guthrie, D., & MacMillan, D. (1982). Classroom environments as they relate to mentally retarded children's observable behavior. *American Journal of Mental Deficiency, 3,* 259–265.

Hutchins, M., & Renzaglia, A. (1983). Environmental considerations for severely handicapped individuals: The needs and the questions. *Exceptional Education Quarterly, 4,* 67–71.

Rossol, M. (1982). *Teaching art to high risk groups.* (ERIC Document Reproduction Service No. ED 224 182)

Zentall, S. (1983). Learning environments: A review of physical and temporal factors. *Exceptional Education Quarterly, 4,* 90–115.

VIVIAN I. CORREA
University of Florida

ACCESSIBILITY OF PROGRAMS
LIABILITY OF TEACHERS IN SPECIAL EDUCATION
MEDICALLY FRAGILE STUDENT
RITALIN

SALVIA, JOHN (1941–   )

John Salvia was born in St. Louis, Missouri. He obtained his BA in 1963 in education and MEd in 1964 in history from the University of Arizona, later earning his EdD in 1968 in special education (with a minor in educational psychology) from Pennsylvania State University. Salvia is currently a professor of special education at Pennsylvania State University.

Early in his professional career, Salvia was a teacher of the educable mentally retarded. His interests have included color blindness in children with mental retardation and assessment in special education (Salvia, 1969; Salvia & Ysseldyke, 1978). His book, coauthored with Ysseldyke, *Assessment in Special and Remedial Education,* provided basic information regarding the assessment process and its resulting data to those who use and need the information but are not involved in the assessment process. His work in this area has also included assessment bias, comparison of test profiles of students with and without disabilities, and assessment strategies for use in instructional decisions (Salvia, 1988, 1990; Salvia & Meisel, 1980).

Salvia has been involved in a children's television workshop and a visiting professor at the University of Victoria, British Columbia, Canada. He was a Fulbright fellow at the University of São Paulo, Brazil, and has been recognized in *Leaders in Education.*

REFERENCES

Salvia, J. (1969). Four tests of color vision: A study of diagnostic accuracy with the mentally retarded. *American Journal of Mental Deficiency, 74*(3), 421–427.

Salvia, J. (1988). A comparison of WAIS-R profiles of nondisabled college freshmen and college students with learning disabilities. *Journal of Learning Disabilities, 21*(10), 632–636.

Salvia, J. (1990). Some criteria for evaluating assessment strategies. *Diagnostique, 16*(1), 61–64.

Salvia, J., & Meisel, C. J. (1980). Observer bias: A methodological consideration in special education research. *Journal of Special Education, 14*(2), 261–270.

Salvia, J., & Ysseldyke, J. E. (1978). *Assessment in special and remedial education.* Boston: Houghton Mifflin.

E. Valerie Hewitt
Texas A&M University
First edition

Tamara J. Martin
*The University of Texas of the
Permian Basin*
Second edition

SAPIR, SELMA GUSTIN (1916–   )

Born in New York City, Selma Gustin Sapir obtained her BS in 1935 in education and psychology from New York University and her MA in 1956 in psychology from Sarah Lawrence College. She went on to earn her EdD in 1984 in applied clinical psychology from Teachers College, Columbia University. Sapir organized and directed the Learning Disability Laboratory at Bank Street College, New York, a child demonstration center and interdisciplinary training project.

Sapir is the author of the Sapir Dimensions of Learning (1980), Sapir Learning Lab Language Scale (1979), and Sapir Self-Concept Scale, as well as other educational treatment methods combining psychological theory and practices with educational models for children with learning disabilities. Based on child development research, these models emphasize the continual nature of the development process, noting that when a change occurs in one dimension (e.g., social, emotional, or cognitive), growth in other areas takes place as well. Therefore, according to Sapir, recognizing and understanding the norms of development is crucial in this respect (Sapir, 1985).

Sapir advocates a broad theoretical understanding of individual differences, proposes generic training programs, and emphasizes training implications of interdisciplinary collaboration for personnel who work with children with learning disabilities (Sapir, 1986). Additionally, she has examined the concept of "reverse mainstreaming," with nondisabled children, their parents, and teachers visiting the classes of children with disabilities and emphasizing social and physical integration of those with disabilities (Sapir, 1990). This experimental program increased the probability of successful mainstreaming as well as providing parents and students opportunities for mutual acceptance and perceptions based on experience.

Sapir has made numerous contributions to the field of special education, including the development of graduate programs in learning disabilities and special education in Mayaguez, Puerto Rico and Mons, Belgium. Her service to professional organizations includes United Nations delegate in 1982; member of the board of directors from 1985–1987 and president-elect in 1996 of the International Council of Psychologists; and past president of the Multidisciplinary Academy of Educators.

Selma Gustin Sapir

REFERENCES

Sapir, S. G. (1985). *The clinical teaching model: Clinical insights and strategies for the learning disabled child.* New York: Brunner Mazel.

Sapir, S. G. (1986). Training the helpers. *Journal of Learning Disabilities, 19*(8), 473–476.

Sapir, S. G. (1990). Facilitating mainstreaming: A case study. *Journal of Reading, Writing, & Learning Disabilities International, 6*(4), 413–418.

E. Valerie Hewitt
Texas A&M University
First edition

Tamara J. Martin
*The University of Texas of the
Permian Basin*
Second edition

SARASON, SEYMOUR B. (1919–   )

Seymour B. Sarason was born in Brooklyn, New York. He received his BA in 1939 from the University of Newark (now the Newark campus of Rutgers, The State University of New Jersey), later earning both his MA in 1940 and PhD in 1942 in psychology from Clark University. Sarason began his professional career in Connecticut as chief psychologist at the Southbury Training School for the Mentally Retarded and later joined the faculty at Yale University, where he retired in 1989 after two decades of directing the clinical training program.

As one of the first to argue social and cultural influences in the etiology of mental retardation, Sarason is regarded as a major figure in the field (Cherniss, 1991). His advocacy role included broadening society's conceptualization of the needs of those with mental retardation and emphasizing the ability to understand an individual from observation in noncontrived, naturally occurring situations as opposed to test scores obtained in an artificial setting.

As an author and guest lecturer, Sarason continues to be a leader in the field of psychology, writing extensively on school change and school governance (Sarason, 1996, 1997, 1998). A prevailing theme throughout his work is his view that the primary problem confronting our educational system is that schools are uninteresting places for both teachers and children (Cherniss, 1991). Charging the current educational system as incapable of reform, Sarason proposes a system in which adults, both teachers and parents, are responsible for the education of children.

Sarason is the recipient of the Gold Medal Award for Life Contribution by a Psychologist in the Public Interest in 1996 awarded by the American Psychological Foundation. His major publications include *Psychological Problems in Mental Deficiency* (1969) and *Revisiting the Culture of School and the Problem of Change* (1996).

REFERENCES

Cherniss, C. (1991). Biography of Seymour Sarason. *Journal of Applied Behavioral Science, 27*(4), 407–408.

Sarason, S. B. (1969). *Psychological problems in mental deficiency* (4th ed.). New York: Harper, Row.

Sarason, S. B. (1996). *Revisiting the culture and the problem of change.* New York: Teachers College.

Sarason, S. B. (1997). *How schools might be governed and why.* New York: Teachers College.

Sarason, S. B. (1998). *Political leadership and educational failure. The Jossey-Bass education series.* San Francisco: Jossey-Bass.

E. Valerie Hewitt
Texas A&M University
First edition

Tamara J. Martin
The University of Texas of the Permian Basin
Second edition

SATTLER, JEROME M. (1931–   )

Born in New York City, Jerome M. Sattler received his BA from the City College of New York in 1952. He went on to the University of Kansas and earned his MA in psychology in 1953 and PhD in psychology in 1959. As a professor of psychology at San Diego State University, Sattler's research led him to become an authority in the areas of intelligence testing, interviewing, child maltreatment, racial experimenter effects, ethnic minority testing, and racial factors in counseling and psychotherapy. His introductory text, *Assessment of Children* (Third Edition), is a standard textbook used in the field of school psychology and clinical psychology, and it remains a classic reference text in the field of special education. He published another assessment text, *Clinical and Forensic Interviewing of Children and Families: Guidelines for the Education, Pediatric, and Child Maltreatment Fields,* in 1988.

Sattler was an expert witness and consultant to the California Attorney General's Office for the case of *Larry P.* v. *Riles* from September 1977 to April 1978; this was a landmark case in the area of cultural bias in assessment. In addition, he is a coauthor with R. E. Thorndike and E. Hagen of the *Stanford-Binet Intelligence Scale,* Fourth Edition, published in 1986.

Sattler was a Fulbright lecturer at the University of Kebangsaan, Malaysia, from 1972 to 1973, and an exchange

Jerome M. Sattler

professor at the Katholicke Universiteit, Instituut voor Orthopedagogiek, Nijmegen, Netherlands, from 1983 to 1984. He also was an exchange professor at University College Cork, in Cork, Ireland, from 1989 to 1990. In 1979 he was elected a fellow of the American Psychological Association. Sattler has published over 99 articles in the field of psychology and has been a special reviewer for over 70 books, articles, and grant proposals, as well as an editor for such journals as the *Journal of Consulting and Clinical Psychology, Psychology in the Schools, the Journal of Psychoeducational Assessment,* and *Psychological Reports.*

Recently, Jerome Sattler, professor emeritus of psychology was honored by the American Psychological Association's Foundation with its 2005 Gold Medal Award for life achievement in the application of psychology.

REFERENCES

Sattler, J. M. (1992). *Assessment of children* (3rd ed.). San Diego, CA: Sattler.

Sattler, J. M. (1998). *Clinical and forensic interviewing of children and families: Guidelines for the education, pediatric, and child maltreatment fields.* San Diego, CA: Sattler.

L. WILLIAMS
Falcon School District 49,
Colorado Springs, Colorado

SAVANT SYNDROME

Savant syndrome is the nomenclature applied to individuals who exhibit an incredible ability (or abilities) in stark contrast to their overall cognitive span. The term "idiot savant" used to describe these individuals is no longer in widespread use due to its negative connotations. Historically, probably the earliest depiction of an individual with savant syndrome appeared in an essay by T. Holliday in 1751 (Treffert, 1988) where Jedediah Buxton is described as having the ability to rapidly multiply nine digit by nine digit integers. Then in 1887, J. Langdon Down, thought to be the first person to use the appellation "idiot savant," relayed detailed information on 10 patients exhibiting this dichotomous skill set seen during his 30-year tenure as superintendent of the Earlswood Asylum in England (Treffert, 1999). Recent research has yielded findings that indicate most people with savant syndrome fall into the moderate to mild cognitive range, with IQs from 40 to 70 (Miller, 1998; Treffert, 1988). While not as common, savants are also found with normal, or greater, IQs (Treffert & Wallace, 2004). Many show language impairments (with and without autism), have extremely narrow areas of interest, and are extremely rule-bound, with little flexibility for creative or cognitive processes (Treffert, 1999). Almost all possess stupendous memory skills (Treffert & Wallace, 2004).

Another common thread with savant syndrome is the consistency of abilities in five areas: music, art, mathematic calculation, mechanical or spatial skills, and calendrical calculation (Miller, 1998; O'Conner & Hermelin, 1989; Treffert, 1988). Of interest is the repeated combination of blindness, autism, and musical genius (Treffert, 1988; Treffert & Wallace, 2004). Rare abilities in multilingual (polyglot) acquisition, exact time sense, visual measurement, memorization of maps, and writing and composition from memory have been documented (Snyder & Mitchell, 1999). Splinter skills, talented savants, and prodigious savants reflect different skill levels displayed. Individuals with splinter skills (or skill) exhibit intense focus on, and memorization of, extremely narrow areas of personal interest: historical facts, sports trivia, maps, and even vacuum cleaner sounds may be the target of concentration by these individuals (Treffert, 1999, 2001; Treffert & Wallace, 2004). A talented savant's abilities are generally more extensive and polished (Treffert, 2001). The majority of people with savant syndrome are contained within these two categories. Prodigious savants are exceedingly rare; in fact, Treffert (2001) expressed the likelihood that fewer than 50 individuals with this level of ability are alive today. Extraordinary in any sense, prodigious savant talents would be astonishing in anyone (Treffert, 2001; Treffert & Wallace, 2004).

Savant syndrome, in and of itself, is uncommon. Approximately 10 percent of those with an autism diagnosis and 1 percent of individuals considered mentally retarded, or who have other central nervous system (CNS) disease or injury, exhibit savant syndrome (Miller, 1998; Treffert, 1988, 1999, 2001). Interestingly, the savant population divides equally into autistic persons and those with other types of CNS deficits. Considering estimates that 50 out of any 10,000 people have autism (classic autism, Asperger, and pervasive developmental disorders, inclusively; Jacobson, 2005), autistic individuals are diagnosed with savant syndrome far more frequently than any other population. Another peculiarity is the four to six times likelihood of being a male with savant syndrome (Treffert, 1988, 1999, 2001, 2004). The condition manifests via two pathways. Congenital defect or CNS damage arising genetically or from prenatal, perinatal, or postnatal injury (Treffert, 2001) account for almost all cases of savant syndrome and are seen in early childhood. The other road to savant syndrome is acquired due to disease or illness of the CNS, which can arise at any point in the life span (Treffert, 2001).

Many theories have been put forth to explain this intriguing syndrome, including eidetic imagery, inherited skills, sensory deprivation with accompanying social isolation, compensation, and reinforcement (Treffert, 1988). While each of these ideas has merit, none can wholly account for the entire sphere of issues surrounding savant syndrome.

However, two other, interlocking areas—unconscious mental processes and cerebral lateralization—have undergone either research or review. Snyder and Mitchell (1999) profess that all humans have tremendous mathematical calculating abilities. According to them, the majority of human beings cannot access the low-level, unconscious mental processes where raw data is used first. Spitz (1995) discusses automaticity in relation to his research with a nonsavant graduate student trained in calendrical calculation. Ultimately, the student was able to perform calculations with the same speed as George, one of the celebrated calendar-calculating twins (Spitz). At this point, the student was no longer easily able to discuss the mental processes he performed. His knowledge in this area had become implicit, with the resultant automaticity equivalent to the cognitive processes of those with savant syndrome (Spitz). O'Connor and Hermelin (1989) investigated the memory structure in autistic savants and found very organized, highly structured memory, with verbal memory ability seemingly independent of verbal IQ level.

Next, investigations into left brain/right brain lateralization of cognitive functions have elicited fascinating data. In this area, the left hemisphere, considered the seat of symbolism, logic, conceptual and verbal processes, contrasts with the nonsymbolic, concrete, and visual right hemisphere. Much of the research performed with those with savant syndrome implicates left temporal lobe dysfunction. Snyder et al (2003) conducted studies where suppression of the left frontotemporal lobes of nonsavants resulted in dramatic changes in the artistry for four of the eleven participants. Koshino et al. (2005) used functional magnetic resonance imaging (fMRI) of working memory tasks performed by high-functioning autistics and age/IQ matched controls and found significant differences between the groups' left/right hemisphere prefrontal and parietal temporal regions, both in activity as well as in functional connectivity. While the overall configurations of functional connectivity were similar for the two groups, those with autism evidenced more right prefrontal and parietal temporal activity. The control group's patterns were reversed. Also significant was the higher activation of the right hemisphere (and posterior regions-of-interest) in the autistic group compared to that of the controls. Considering the high percentage of autistic savants, this evidence is extremely relevant. Furthermore, all the preceding research begins to paint a more comprehensive picture of why people with savant syndrome are the way they are. With the advent of sophisticated research techniques like fMRIs and the increased use of standardized testing, far more information is available today regarding savant syndrome. As more data is unearthed, it is probable that these rare individuals may be the keys used to unlock everyone's access to unconscious mental processes and a deeper understanding of the mind/brain system.

REFERENCES

Jacobson, J. W. (2005). Is autism on the rise? *Science in Autism Treatment.* Retrieved July 28, 2005, from http://www.asatonline.org/resources/library/autism_rise.html

Koshino, H., Carpenter, P. A., Minshew, N. J., Cherkassky, V. L., Keller, T. A., & Just, M. A. (2005). Functional connectivity in an fMRI working memory task in high-functioning autism. *NeuroImage, 24*(3), 810–821.

Miller, L. K. (1998). Defining the savant syndrome. *Journal of Developmental and Physical Disabilities, 10*(1), 73–85.

O'Conner, N., & Hermelin, B. (1989). The memory structure of autistic idiot-savant mnemonists. *British Journal of Psychology, 80*(1), 97–111.

Snyder, A. W., & Mitchell, D. J. (1999). Is integer arithmetic fundamental to mental processing? The mind's secret arithmetic. *Proceedings of the Royal Society: Biological Sciences, 266*(1419), 587–592.

Snyder, A. W., Mulcahy, E., Taylor, J. L., Mitchell, D. J., Sachdev, P., & Gandevia, S. C. (2003). Savant-like skills exposed in normal people by suppressing the left frontotemporal lobe. *Journal of Integrative Neuroscience, 2*(2), 149–158.

Spitz, H. H. (1995). Calendar calculating idiot savants and the smart unconscious. *New Ideas in Psychology, 13*(2), 167–182.

Treffert, D. A. (1988). The idiot savant: A review of the syndrome. *American Journal of Psychiatry, 145*(5), 563–572.

Treffert, D. A. (1999). The savant syndrome and autistic disorder. *CNS Spectrums, 4*(12), 57–60.

Treffert, D. A. (2001). Savant syndrome: 'Special faculties' extraordinaire. *Psychiatric Times, 18*(10).

Treffert, D. A., & Wallace, G. L. (2004). Islands of genius. *Scientific American,* January Special Edition, 14(1), 14–23.

SUZANNE M. GRUNDY
*California State University, San
Bernardino*

SAVE THE CHILDREN FUND AND CHILDREN WITH DISABILITIES

Save the Children began when Eglantyne Jebb, the organization's founder, drew up the *Charter On the Rights of the Child* in 1919. Special mention was made of the disabled child, and this charter has now been enshrined in the U.N. Convention on the Rights of the Child. Disabled children are children first, and all articles in the convention that refer to children include disabled children.

Save the Children's current policy and practice on disabled children and education has developed from ongoing analytical reflection on a strong body of practical experience in a wide range of countries (in Asia, Africa, the Middle East, and Europe). Disabled children are defined as children with impairments (physical, mental, visual, hearing, speech, or multiple impairments) who are excluded or discriminated against in their local context and culture (Stubbs, 1997).

Beginning in 1960, for 30 years Save the Children supported a pioneering residential school for physically disabled children in Morocco. This was a residential institution that enabled a small group of academically able children to gain access to a high-quality education; many students went on to universities. However, this strategy did nothing for the majority of disabled children, who were still unable to access mainstream education; it did nothing to support parents or to change the negative attitudes of the majority; and it was also unsustainable financially. This concept of "special" and segregated education, while sometimes (not always) providing a quality education to a few, had many limitations.

Learning lessons from this experience, in 1987 Save the Children adopted a clear policy to promote the basic rights of the majority of disabled children, in the context of their family and community, rather than offering a privileged education to a few. Community-based rehabilitation (CBR) was promoted as a strategy to support the disabled child within his or her family and community, and CBR workers would work with the family, the child, and the local school to integrate the disabled child. For more severely disabled children, the focus was on providing daycare, support to parents, and education on activities of daily living in the home. This strategy of integrated education was sustainable, low-cost, and enabled children with disabilities to stay within their families and community. However, the strategy was very dependent on the goodwill of the local school and teachers, and relied largely on changing the child to fit a rigid system (which was not always possible) rather than changing the system to accommodate a variety of children.

In 1990, the Jomtien Conference promoted Education for All. It was followed by the Salamanca Conference in 1994, which drew attention to problems in the school system (methodology, curriculum, teacher skills, attitudes, environment, and so on) that resulted in the exclusion of large numbers of children: disabled children, street children, ethnic minorities, and girls. This was the concept of inclusive education, which differs from special or integrated education in that it places the responsibility on the system, not the child, and is based on a strong belief that children should receive appropriate and relevant education together with their peers in their own communities.

Save the Children's current policy and strategy is "towards inclusion," acknowledging that inclusion is an ideal, and that the vast majority of education systems are difficult to change. Interestingly, the increasing number of successful examples of progress towards inclusion are in developing countries in Asia and Africa (Holdsworth & Thepphavongsa, 1996).

In a poor province in China with 56 million people, Save the Children supported a pilot project that integrated two children with mild to moderate mental disabilities into each class. This was achieved through training teachers in child-focused approaches, introducing flexible methodology such as team-teaching and group work, large scale awareness-raising, promoting parental involvement, and transforming the system from teacher-centered to child-centered. This project is extremely successful in that it not only allowed disabled children access to essential early childhood education, but also improved the system for all children. It has now been scaled up throughout the province with existing resources, as schools support each other.

In Lesotho, Save the Children supported a national inclusive education program, aiming to include all types of disabled children in existing primary schools. The project was piloted in one school in each district by providing in-service training to all teachers in each school, working with the national Disabled People's Organizations to develop knowledge and skills in braille and sign language, and by involving parents and the community. Now it is possible to visit schools where the class sizes are over 100 and to see children signing, visually impaired children sitting next to buddies who offer support, and children with learning difficulties in the front row where the teacher can give them extra support (Stubbs, 1995).

Many of the Western industrialized countries have a legacy of segregated special education provision and professional special educators. In many economically poorer countries, there is more expertise on managing sparse resources, more community solidarity, and a strong tradition and experience of self-reliance. It is Save the Children's experience that pioneers in inclusive education are increasingly found in developing countries, and that there are many "lessons from the south" that can inform the international community (Holdsworth & Kay, 1996; Stubbs, 1997).

REFERENCES

Holdsworth, J., & Kay, J. (Eds.). (1996). *Toward inclusion: SCF UK's experience in integrated education.* Discussion paper, N.I. SEAPRO Documentation Series. Save the Children Fund.

Holdsworth, J., & Thepphavongsa, P. (Eds.). (1996). *Don't use mature wood if you want to bend it: Don't pick old mushrooms if you want to eat them. Experiences of the Lao People's Republic in provision for children with disabilities using the kindergarten sector.* Washington, DC: Save the Children Fund.

Stubbs, S. (1995). *The Lesotho National Integrated Education Programme: A case study on implementation.* Master's thesis, University of Cambridge, England.

Stubbs, S. (1997). *Education and geopolitical change.* Presented at the Oxford International Conference on Education and Development, Great Britain.

SUE STUBBS
Save the Children Fund

SCALE FOR ASSESSING EMOTIONAL DISTURBANCE

The Scale for Assessing Emotional Disturbance (SAED; Epstein & Sharma) is an individually administered, 52-item measure of emotional and/or behavioral disturbance in children ages 5 through 18. The four-page response form can be completed in approximately 10 minutes by caregivers, counselors, teachers, or other persons knowledgeable about the child. The scale has three sections. The first is Student Competence Characteristics, in which the adult rater compares this child to other students of the same age on a scale of 0 to 4 (0 = far below average, 4 = far above average) in categories such as family support, level of academic achievement, and motivation. The second section is Student Emotional and Behavioral Problems, in which the rater reads a statement (e.g., "makes threats to others") and chooses the number on a scale from 0 to 3 (0 = not at all like the child, 3 = very much like the child) that best represents the child's emotions and behaviors in the past 2 months. The final section is Adversely Affects Education Performance, in which the rater judges the extent to which the student's educational performance is affected by emotional and behavioral problems on a scale of 0 to 5 (0 = not adversely affected, 5 = affected to an extreme extent). The SAED also includes eight open-ended questions that address the child's situational and personal resiliencies and protective factors (e.g., "In what school subject[s] does the child do best?" or "What job[s] or responsibilities has this student held in the community or in the home?"). The scale provides an overall emotional and behavioral functioning SAED Quotient and percentile rank, and seven subscale scores measuring Inability to Learn, Relationship Problems, Inappropriate Behavior, Unhappiness or Depression, Physical Symptoms or Fears, Social Maladjusted, and Overall Competence. Information obtained from the SAED is useful in identifying children with emotional disturbance; in developing Individualized Education Programs (IEPs), treatment, or intervention planning; and in evaluation of a program or treatment plan.

The SAED was normed on students between the ages of 5:0 and 18:11 using data collected from January 1996 to May 1997. Separate norms were produced for 2,266 students without disabilities and 1,371 students with emotional and behavioral disorders. (No explanation whatsoever is given about how these 1,371 children came to be classified as emotionally disturbed.) The manual reports demographics of this standardization sample based on age, gender, geographic location, race, ethnicity, and socioeconomic status.

Scores on the seven subtests are presented in standard scores with a mean of 10 and standard deviation of 3. The overall SAED quotient score has a mean of 100 and a standard deviation of 15.

The interrater reliability of the SAED was tested on six pairs of teachers who were asked to complete the SAED on 44 students previously diagnosed with emotional or behavioral disorders. Correlations between the two raters on the seven subscales and overall SAED scores were around .80. Content sampling revealed that items on the SAED correlate above .75, making it a highly reliable scale. The test-retest reliability was determined by SAED scores for special education children whose teachers rated them twice with about 2 weeks between each rating. Correlations between the two sets of ratings on the seven subscales and overall SAED quotient were between .84 and .94. The SAED was deemed to have criterion validity based on the positive relationships between the SAED and the Teacher Report Form (Achenbach, 1991) and the SAED and the Revised Behavior Problem Checklist (Quay & Peterson, 1996). Construct validity was confirmed through statistically significant differences between the mean scores of the nondisordered and disordered children used to norm the scale.

REFERENCES

Achenbach, T. M. (1991). *Manual for the Teacher Reports Form and 1991 profile*. Burlington, VT: University of Vermont, Department of Psychiatry.

Cullinan, D., Evans, C., & Epstein, M. H. (2003). Characteristics of emotional disturbance of elementary school students. *Behavioral Disorders, 28,* 94–110.

Dumont, R., & Rauch, M. (2000). Test review: Scale for Assessing Emotional Disturbance by M. Epstein & D. Cullinan (PRO-ED, 1998). *NASP Communiqué, 28,* article 8. Retrieved May 22, 2004, from http://www.nasponline.org/publications/cq288SAED.html

Epstein, M. H., Cullinan, D., & Ryser, G. (2002). Development of a scale to assess emotional disturbance. *Behavioral Disorders, 28,* 5–22.

Epstein, M. H., & Cullinan, D. (1998). *The Scale for Assessing Emotional Disturbance*. Austin, TX: PRO-ED.

Floyd, R. G., & Bose, J. E. (2003) Behavior rating scales for assessment of emotional disturbance: A critical review of measurement characteristics. *Journal of Psychoeducational Assessment, 21,* 43–78.

Quay, H., & Peterson, D. R. (1996). *Revised Behavior Problem Checklist: Professional manual*. Odessa, FL: Psychological Assessment Resources.

RON DUMONT
Fairleigh Dickinson University

JOHN O. WILLIS
Rivier College

SCALES OF INDEPENDENT BEHAVIOR–REVISED

The Scales of Independent Behavior–Revised (SIB-R; Bruininks, Woodcock, Weatherman, & Hill, 1996) is used to assess adaptive behavior and problem behavior. It includes three forms—a Full Scale, Short Form, and Early Development

Form. A Short Form for the Visually Impaired is also available. Administration time ranges from 15 to 20 minutes for either the Short Form or Early Development Form to 45 to 60 minutes for the Full Scale. The SIB-R is norm-referenced and nationally standardized on 2,182 individuals. It is appropriate for use with individuals from birth to 80+ years.

The SIB-R is easier to administer than its predecessor, the original SIB. In addition to the structured interview procedure, a checklist procedure is now available. It is also easier to score. Age-equivalent scoring tables are included in the response booklets for each subscale. A significant feature is the addition of a Support Score, which predicts the level of support a person will require based on the impact of maladaptive behaviors and adaptive functioning. Another unique feature of the SIB-R is the functional limitations index, which can be used to define the presence and severity of functional limitations in adaptive behaviors.

The test manual contains internal consistency reliabilities (mid to high .90s), test-retest reliabilities for the adaptive behavior scales (.83–.97) and the maladaptive behavior indexes (.69–.90), and interrater reliabilities (most correlations in the .80s). Extensive validity studies reported in the Comprehensive Manual support the developmental nature of the SIB-R adaptive behavior scales. The SIB-R is strongly related to other adaptive behavior measures and highly predictive of placements in different types of service settings.

There is very little independent research on the SIB-R. This is unfortunate, because the comprehensiveness, usefulness, and psychometric qualities of this instrument are truly outstanding.

REFERENCE

Bruininks, R. K., Woodcock, R. W., Weatherman, R. F., & Hill, B. (1996). *Scales of Independent Behavior–Revised* (SIB-R). Itasca, IL: Riverside.

FREDERICK A. SCHRANK
Olympia, Washington

ADAPTIVE BEHAVIOR

SCALES OF ORDINAL DOMINANCE

See ORDINAL SCALES OF PSYCHOLOGICAL DEVELOPMENT.

SCANDINAVIA, SPECIAL EDUCATION IN

Since the publication of the first edition of the *Encyclopedia of Special Education* (Braswell, 1987), Scandinavian perspectives on special education have changed in some respects. It is true that, in the terms of Braswell, Scandinavian countries "have been in the vanguard with respect to their concern for the social welfare for their citizens" (p. 1381), including those with disabilities. But it is also true that much social policy has been difficult to implement in practice, especially since 1986.

In all Scandinavian countries, special education reform has been dependent on reforms in regular education systems and schools. As part of ongoing globalization patterns, higher priority has been given to values such as competition and education for excellence. These values have been embraced in general education. The guiding perspective of special education policy is an inclusive one, with special education support as much as possible integrated into regular education frameworks. Sweden and Denmark have traditionally been considered leaders in inclusion, and Norway and Finland were seen as following behind (Tuunainen, 1994). This is no longer the case, at least regarding Norway. Decisions on school laws and curricula during the 1990s by Norway's Parliament are more radically inclusive than in the other Scandinavian countries.

As in Sweden, a few general societal policy conditions greatly influence special education. There is ongoing decentralization of decision power and responsibilities from the national level to local municipalities (less evident in Finland). This process happened concurrent with the effects of an economic recession during most of the 1990s (less evident in Norway). In combination, these two circumstances meant that responsibilities and decision-making power were moved from national and/or central bodies to local municipalities and schools. In Sweden, Denmark, and Norway, there are little or no resources earmarked specifically for special education any longer. School laws and other official guidelines stress that schools shall give high priority to the fulfillment of students' special needs. These resource allocation decisions, made on local levels of the system, had to be made at the same time as severe budget cuts during most of the 1990s. These matters raised sincere questions about what is possible to spend on students with special needs, especially compared to other school and student needs. This is most evident in Sweden and Denmark and, to a lesser extent, in Norway. Norway still has some stipulations for resource allocation for guaranteed support to students with certain severe disabilities. This is a small proportion (only around 2 percent) of all students, though, and is also a small fraction of all students given special education support in the schools. According to results from an evaluation study (Skårbrevik, 1995), the support given in this way to students with severe disabilities also covers only 20 percent to 30 percent of their weekly hours in school. In Sweden and Denmark, this support has to be financed within the frameworks of regular school budgets.

The process of closing down special schools and institutions has continued, and very few special schools are now in use. Most of those are for students who are deaf or hard of hearing, or who have intellectual or multiple disabilities. Again, this closing is going on at a slower rate in Finland than in the other three countries. Many of the former institutions and special schools are in the process of developing into resource centers. Their responsibilities are firsthand competence development and consultant support to schools attended by students with severe disabilities. They also often give shorter, intensive training courses for students, family members, and school teachers. They are still financed by government money, which is seen as necessary in order to guarantee qualified support to children with the greatest need, regardless of where they live or go to school. In most respects these resource centers and their consultant responsibilities are organized on a basis. At the national level, Sweden has a National Swedish Agency for Special Education, a separate administrative body parallel to the National Agency for Schools. In Norway, the same national administrative body monitors both regular and special education, as well as education for those with more severe disabilities.

In all countries, there is concern about the availability of qualified support given from resource centers to schools, and measures are continuously taken to satisfy necessary competence development. Especially in Norway, where special schools for students with intellectual disabilities have been closed, many resource centers will have to deal with new disability areas, and therefore develop broader and deeper competence. This is a need also in the other Scandinavian countries. In Sweden, this is a responsibility for the National Swedish Agency for Special Education and is financed within regular government budget framework. In Norway, where there is no such monitoring body between the national government ministry and resource centers, the ministry has used some of the financial resources saved by closing institutions toward competence development. A five-year research and development program (1993–98) and a three-year program of resource center development initiatives were both implemented. In comparison to the other Scandinavian countries, this was a massive national government input for increasing the level of competence needed to guarantee the meeting of severe disability special needs, independent of geographic location. The research and development program in special education also meant broadening the competence area through involvement of more academic disciplines and university departments. Over the last twenty to twenty-five years, it has been important to see special education as a more comprehensive domain than simply medical disability knowledge.

An inclusive education policy means demands on teacher education programs for both special educators and regular education professionals. In all Scandinavian countries, special education objectives are included in regular teaching training programs. This has proven difficult in all the countries, and too little has really been included. This prevents new teachers from being as well prepared as they should be for a job in an inclusive environment. These matters are of current concern, especially in Sweden and Denmark, where preparatory work for teacher training reforms is ongoing. Teacher training is clearly a field of many controversies, and it is not evident that inclusive education needs will be a part of the guidelines for future reforms training for regular education teachers. The continuous changes of special education teacher programs have been more successfully implemented, but this has caused increasing differences between programs at different universities, within Scandinavian countries and within the region of Scandinavia itself. This may be less the case in Finland, where special education programs are still more centralized, and where there are still specific programs for teaching in special classes or special schools.

Decreasing proportions of students attend special schools or special classes, usually less than 2 or 3 percent a year. It must be taken into account, though, that such proportion figures do not always give the full picture. This has to do with the decentralized and goal-based educational systems. Partly, this means that differences between local municipalities and schools are increasing, even affecting definitions for special education. There are some statistics from evaluation study reports on what could be a trend toward increasing proportions of students referred to special groups or schools again. For instance, clustering of special education resources sometimes means organization of special classes and schools turning up again on local or regional levels. This is the case in Sweden, according to special schools for students with intellectual disabilities, but corresponding trends are clearly seen in Denmark and, lately, Norway. One factor behind such trends is a lack of sufficient resources, which is related to elite and competitive values and priorities. Also, school officials hear parent worries and complaints that their disabled children are not being adequately supported in the integrated settings. Both circumstances lead to more segregated solutions.

Compulsory schooling is nine years in all countries, and in some special schools it may be extended to ten. But today there is generally a need for further education in order to meet the demands of employment and society. An increasing number of students have had to continue their educations and go on to upper secondary schools, and the current proportion of each age group doing so is between 95 to 98 percent in all of the Scandinavian countries. Although this schooling is officially voluntary, from the student point of view it has become obligatory. This is also the case for students with disabilities and learning difficulties. Consequently, special needs have also become important issues in these schools.

Adult education has a long tradition in the Scandinavian countries, and so has special education support within this education area. In Scandinavia, as elsewhere, lifelong learning has become a more commonly used concept in education policy and planning, especially during the 1990s. This meant an expansion of adult education in many respects. Expansion of adult education has also been one of the most important measures taken toward increasing unemployment, especially in Sweden. Special education support within regular programs, as well as special courses for those with disabilities, have a long tradition. In colleges, universities, and the adult education system at large, support to meet special needs has been further developed in the past twenty years.

From having been nearly culturally homogeneous until the 1960s, Scandinavia has become increasingly multicultural through immigration. During the first decades immigration was mostly a result of labor; more recently, immigrants have moved to Scandinavian countries as refugees for different reasons. This is so especially in Denmark, Sweden, and Norway, while Finland still has a comparatively small immigration rate. In many Danish and Swedish municipalities, the proportion of inhabitants with immigrant background reaches 30 percent or more, and there are schools in these places where the proportion of immigrant background students are up to 80 to 85 percent. This multicultural situation creates challenges for special education.

Scandinavian countries are still in the vanguard of special education development in inclusive education. However, there are many conflicting trends and widening gaps between more privileged students and those who are less well off. The welfare state model, often thought of as guaranteed, has become at risk of being dismantled during the last two decades. These trends also have great influence on education policies, and especially on special education policy and practice. Therefore, Scandinavia will continue to be a very interesting focus for studies of special education.

REFERENCES

Braswell, D. (1987). Scandinavia, special education in. In C. R. Reynolds & L. Mann (Eds.), *Encyclopedia of special education.* New York: Wiley.

Haug, P. (1997). *Integration and special education research in Norway.* Paper presented at the AERA 1997 Annual Conference, Chicago.

Skårbrevik, K. (1995). Spesialpedagogiske tiltak pa dagsorden. Evaluering av prosjektet "Omstrukturering av spesialundervisning." Volda: Høgskulen og Møreforsking, Forskingsrapport no. 14.

Tuunainen, K. (1994). Finland, Norway, and Sweden. In K. Mazurek & M. Winzer (Eds.), *Comparative studies in special education.* Washington, DC: Gallaudet University Press.

INGEMAR EMANUELSSON
Goteburg University

FRANCE, SPECIAL EDUCATION IN
WESTERN EUROPE, SPECIAL EDUCATION IN

SCAPEGOATING

A scapegoat is generally defined as a person or group that bears the blame for the mistakes of others. Typically, this is manifested as a group singling out an individual for unfair attack. In schools such systematic victimization of one child by a group of others can isolate the child from the social life of the class and cause the child to feel unworthy of inclusion in the peer group. At times children with disabilities may be scapegoats, particularly those with low self-esteem, which is usual with disabled children owing to academic, emotional, or physical problems (Gearheart, 1985).

Allan (1985) has reported that the scapegoating of one child by others is a common problem facing teachers and counselors. The scapegoats suffer from social isolation and poor self-concept. This type of environment can only have a negative effect on learning. This is especially true for children in classes for the disabled. However, the disruptiveness caused by scapegoating is not only destructive to the scapegoat, but also to children who fear that they may become the next victim. These children may develop coping strategies to avoid that possibility. Such strategies may include ingratiating themselves with class leaders, mistreating scapegoats to prove that they are not scapegoats themselves, and refusing to associate with former friends who are now scapegoats.

Nondisabled children require help with social skills as they interact with disabled peers in mainstreamed classrooms. One problem that may arise is the calling of names, which can be dealt with in a variety of ways. Salend and Schobel (1981) described one strategy that they implemented with a fourth-grade class. Discussion included the meaning of names, how names differ, and the positive and negative consequences of names. The last topic included a discussion of the negative effects of nicknames and the importance of considering another person's reaction to the nickname. It is obvious that educators must seriously consider the effects of scapegoating and must continue to develop strategies to counteract the negative effects of scapegoating on children with disabilities.

REFERENCES

Allan, C. L. (1985). Scapegoating: Help for the whole class. *Elementary School Guidance and Counseling, 18,* 147.

Gearheart, B. R. (1985). *Learning disabilities.* St. Louis, MO: Times Mirror/Mosby College.

Salend, S. J., & Schobel, J. (1981). Coping with namecalling in the mainstream setting. *Education Unlimited, 3*(2), 36–38.

JOSEPH M. RUSSO
*Hunter College, City University
of New York*

SELF-CONCEPT

SCATTER PLOT ASSESSMENT

Scatter plot assessment is an observational method used to identify temporal conditions and (in some formats) other stimulus conditions that may reliably predict the occurrence or absence of problem behavior. A scatter plot typically resembles a grid with a specified time interval represented by the ordinate axis and successive dates represented by the abscissa. Time intervals can be divided into hour, half-hour, quarter-hour, or smaller increments, depending on the frequency of the behavior, capabilities of the observer, and what information the observer would like to determine (Martella, Nelson, & Martella-Marchand, 2003). At the end of each time interval in the corresponding grid box, relative or absolute problem behavior occurrences are recorded. For example, an open box might indicate the absence of problem behavior, a slash through the box, between 1 and 5 occurrences of problem behavior, and a filled box, more than 5 occurrences of problem behavior (see Figure). Numbers may also be recorded in each box, indicating the exact number of occurrences of problem behavior (Axelrod, 1987). After collecting data (typically for several days), time-correlated patterns of problem behavior responding may emerge. These patterns can be further analyzed to determine environmental events that may evoke problem behavior occurrences (e.g., engaging in specific activities, caregivers present, or transitions).

The scatter plot has been used as a tool to measure multiple types of problem behaviors across multiple situations (Alberto & Troutman, 2003). Touchette, MacDonald, and Langer (1985) suggest that the scatter plot also provides more specific information than a line graph, which reflects response frequency but not temporal distribution. Additionally, scatter plots are said to be easy to use and require minimal training (Symons, McDonald, & Wehby, 1998). However, Axelrod (1987) states that scatter plots are insensitive to identifying noncyclical patterns of behavioral responding and do not specifically identify antecedent and consequent events that may be maintaining problem behavior. Kahng et al. (1998) state further that when analyzing scatter plot data, patterns of responding may not be discernable without the use of statistical analysis procedures. Despite some reservations about the use of scatter plots, they continue to be employed extensively by clinicians and practitioners (Desrochers, Hile, & Williams-Mosely, 1997).

Research

Though many empirical studies reference scatter plots (Durand & Kishi, 1987; Kennedy & Souza, 1995; Lalli, Browder, Mace, & Brown, 1993), the scatter plot itself has been the focus of relatively few empirical evaluations (Kahng et al., 1998). Touchette et al. (1985) published the first article regarding scatter plot assessment and demonstrated that frequency data collected during 30-min intervals successfully detected time periods and subsequently other stimulus conditions that reliably predicted problem behavior occurrences for two of three participants. Interventions were designed and implemented based on the scatter plot assessment data and were effective in reducing problem behavior to near-zero levels. However, Touchette and colleagues (1985) stated that one participant's scatter plot was

Name _____		Behavior _____		
Scoring	0 = leave blank	1 to 5 = slash in box	5 + = fill in box	

8:00–8:30					
8:30–9:00					
9:00–9:30					
9:30–10:00					
10:00–10:30					
10:30–11:00					
11:00–11:30					
11:30–12:00					
12:00–12:30					
12:30–1:00					
1:00–1:30					
1:30–2:00					
2:00–2:30					
Date	9/1	9/2	9/3	9/4	9/5

Figure 1 Scatter plot example

deemed "uninterpretable" (p. 349). An effective intervention was eventually developed for the third participant based on other collected data.

Kahng and others (1998) sought to replicate the study of Touchette et al. (1985) and collected scatter plot data continuously during 30-min intervals for 20 individuals living in residential facilities. They visually analyzed the data from 15 of the 20 scatter plots (the data for five participants were not used due to poor interobserver agreement), but could not discern any temporal patterns of significance. However, when the data were transformed using statistical process control procedures (SPC) into control charts, one or more 30-min intervals were identified in which problem behavior was more likely to occur for 12 of the 15 data sets. The authors conclude that use of statistical procedures (e.g., SPC) may more precisely and accurately identify temporal patterns of responding.

Guidelines for Practice

The usefulness of scatter plot data can be enhanced by considering a few suggestions. First, to set behavior frequency cutoffs or criteria for each time interval (e.g., 0, 1 to 4, >4), Symons and colleagues (1998) suggest determining the number of disruptive behavior events that may be tolerable to a teacher or caregiver during a given time interval and using that information to identify frequency criteria. Second, consider the frequency with which the problem behavior is occurring when choosing a time interval for observation. For example, high-frequency behavior may need to be recorded during shorter time intervals than low-frequency behavior (unless each behavior is discretely recorded), so as not to underestimate the frequency with which the behavior occurs.

Third, numbering each event in the appropriate grid box is a more precise data collection method and alleviates the need to set behavior frequency criteria. Because each event is recorded, selection of an observational time interval is less important, but it may be difficult to monitor accurately when engaging in simultaneous tasks. Fourth, Kahng et al. (1998, p. 602) recommend "that in some cases it may be necessary to assign a 1:1 staff-to-client ratio while scatter plot data are being collected" due to frequent interruptions that may preclude the observer from collecting reliable data. Last, because scatter plots are not conducive to identifying noncyclical patterns of behavior, making notes of antecedent and consequent events can help to identify functional response patterns, when temporal patterns are not observed. O'Neill et al. (1997) developed the Functional Assessment Observation Form (FAO), which incorporates features of a typical scatter plot but also provides columns in which an observer can denote what behavior occurred and possible predictors to and consequences of the behavior.

Though scatter plots are widely used, the research findings suggest that they may not always assist in identifying patterns of behavioral responding. Using scatter plots as part of a multiple method and multiple source assessment plan will help in developing a clearer understanding of the behavior of concern and conditions that affect the probability of its occurrence.

Case Examples

Example 1. "Virginia" frequently engaged in head hitting throughout the day. To determine possible temporal patterns to Virginia's responding, her caregivers collected scatter plot data. Every 30-min caregivers recorded whether 0, 1 to 10, or more than 10 head hits occur during an interval. After collecting data for 2 weeks, caregivers reviewed the data and identified that head-hitting occurrences were highly correlated with the presence of one of Virginia's caregivers and/or when Virginia was asked to practice dressing herself. The scatter plot assessment information then informed the development of a behavior intervention to reduce the number of head hits Virginia engaged in.

Example 2. "Jorge" interrupted his classmates and used profanities during the school day. An instructional assistant, Mrs. Montgomery, collected data regarding Jorge's verbal behavior using the Functional Assessment Observation Form (O'Neill et al., 1997). Mrs. Montgomery recorded the number of interruptions and profanities Jorge produced every 30-min and also recorded events that preceded and followed each behavior. After collecting data for 3 weeks, Mrs. Montgomery identified that interruptions and profanities were more likely to occur during whole-class instruction and were usually followed by peer laughter. The assessment information was then used to develop a behavior intervention aimed to reduce Jorge's inappropriate verbal behavior.

REFERENCES

Alberto, P. A., & Troutman, A. C. (2003). *Applied behavior analysis for teachers* (6th ed.). Upper Saddle River, NJ: Merrill Prentice Hall.

Axelrod, S. (1987). Functional and structural analyses of behavior: Approaches leading to reduced use of punishment procedures? *Research in Developmental Disabilities, 8,* 165–178.

Desrochers, M. N., Hile, M. G., & Williams-Mosely, T. L. (1997). Survey of functional assessment procedures used with individuals who display mental retardation and severe problem behaviors. *American Journal on Mental Retardation, 101,* 535–546.

Durand, V. M., & Kishi, G. (1987). Reducing severe behavior problems among persons with dual sensory impairments: An evaluation of a technical assistance model. *Journal of the Association for Persons with Severe Handicaps, 12,* 2–10.

Kahng, S., Iwata, B. A., Fischer, S. M., Page, T. J., Treadwell, K. R. H., Williams, D. E., & Smith, R. G. (1998). Temporal distributions of problem behavior based on scatter plot analysis. *Journal of Applied Behavior Analysis, 31,* 593–604.

Lalli, J. S., Browder, D. M., Mace, F. C., & Brown, D. K. (1993). Teacher use of descriptive analysis data to implement interventions to decrease students' problem behaviors. *Journal of Applied Behavior Analysis, 26,* 227–238.

Martella, R. C., Nelson, J. R., & Marchand-Martella, N. E. (2003). *Managing disruptive behavior in the schools: A schoolwide, classroom, and individualized social learning approach.* Boston: Allyn and Bacon.

O'Neill, R. E., Horner, R. H., Albin, R. W., Sprague, J. R., Storey, K., & Newton, J. S. (1997). *Functional assessment and program development for problem behavior: A practical handbook* (2nd ed.). Pacific Grove, CA: Brooks/Cole.

Symons, F., McDonald, L., & Wehby, J. (1998). Functional assessment and teacher collected data. *Education and Treatment of Children, 21,* 135–159.

Touchette, P., MacDonald, R., & Langer, S. (1985). A scatter plot for identifying stimulus control of problem behavior. *Journal of Applied Behavior Analysis, 18,* 343–351.

SARAH FAIRBANKS
University of Connecticut

REFERENCES

Schaefer, E. S. (1991). Goals for parent and future-parent education: Research on parental beliefs. *Elementary School Journal, 91*(3), 239–247.

Schaefer, E. S., & Bell, R. Q. (1958). Development of a parental attitude research instrument. *Child Development, 29,* 339–361.

Schaefer, E. S., & Burnett, C. K. (1987). Stability and predictability of women's marital relationships and demoralization. *Journal of Personality and Social Psychology, 53*(6), 1129–1136.

Schaefer, E. S., & Edgerton, M. (1985). Parent and child correlates of parental modernity. In E. Sigel (Ed.), *Parental belief systems.* Hillsdale, NJ: Erlbaum.

E. VALERIE HEWITT
Texas A&M University
First edition

TAMARA J. MARTIN
The University of Texas of the Permian Basin
Second edition

SCHAEFER, EARL S. (1926–   )

A native of Adyeville, Indiana, Earl S. Schaefer received his BA (1948) in psychology from Purdue University, and later earned both his MA (1951) and PhD (1954) in psychology at the Catholic University of America. He is currently a professor in the department of maternal and child health in the School of Public Health, University of North Carolina, Chapel Hill. He is also senior investigator at the Frank Porter Graham Child Development Center at the University.

Schaefer's early research began with studies of parent attitudes and behavior as related to child development, resulting in the development of the Parental Attitude Research Instrument and an infant education program (Schaefer & Bell, 1958). This research was later extended to parent-child relationships, child social-emotional development, husband-wife relationships, and mental health of parents and children (Schaefer, 1991; Schaefer & Burnett, 1987; Schaefer & Edgerton, 1985). In his investigations, Schaefer has shown correlations between parental beliefs/values and a child's intellectual development, correlations between a parent's behavior and the child's school development, and the effects of a perceived marital relationship on individual adjustment. This research has important implications for the development of parent education programs.

Among his many honors, Schaefer is the recipient of the Research Scientist Award of the National Institute of Mental Health (1975–1979), and has served as consulting editor of the *American Journal of Mental Deficiency* and *Child Development.*

SCHIEFELBUSCH, RICHARD L. (1918–   )

Richard Schiefelbusch received his BS (1940) from Kansas State Teachers College and his MA (1947) in speech pathology and psychology from the University of Kansas. He went on to earn his PhD (1951) in speech pathology at Northwestern University. Schiefelbusch was director of the Bureau of Child Research at the University of Kansas from 1955 to 1990, and since 1989 has held the distinction of professor emeritus at that university.

Schiefelbusch has spent his career helping persons with

Richard L. Schiefelbusch

disabilities. As director of the Bureau of Child Research, he conducted research related to language and communications programs for mentally retarded children and he was instrumental in discovering and developing effective applied behavior techniques for those with severe mental retardation. The studies conducted during his time there were designed to alter the range of educational and social activities of institutionalized children, demonstrating that children with no history of educational success could participate in productive instructional programs. This research was instrumental in the development of innovative treatment and training in language and social skills for children with severe and multiple handicaps. Schiefelbusch's work involving the language potential of people with severe mental retardation was a key element in the establishment of the constitutional right to education and the enactment of the Education of the Handicapped Act in 1966.

Among his numerous awards, Schiefelbusch is the recipient of the Distinguished Service award of the National Association for Retarded Citizens (1983) and the Distinguished Accomplishment award of the American Association of University Affiliated Programs (1987). His major publications include *Language Intervention Strategies* (1978) and *Communicative Competence* (1984).

REFERENCES

Schiefelbusch, R. L. (Ed.). *Language intervention strategies.* Baltimore: University Park Press.

Schiefelbusch, R. L., & Pickar, J. (Eds.). (1984). *Communicative competence: Acquisition and intervention.* Baltimore: University Park Press.

E. VALERIE HEWITT
Texas A&M University
First edition

TAMARA J. MARTIN
The University of Texas of the Permian Basin
Second edition

SCHIZENCEPHALY

Schizencephaly is a disorder of grossly abnormal neuronal migration patterns with onset during fetal development. It is characterized by clefts in the parasylvian region of the brain along with additional openings in the regions of the pre- and postcentral gyri. These anomalies may or may not be symmetrical (Baron, Fennell, & Voeller, 1995). Other regions of the brain may also be involved in ways that are not predictable solely on the basis of the diagnosis of schizencephaly. The disorder is diagnosable via fetal ultrasound but

CT and MRI studies after birth are necessary to view the extent of the abnormalities in brain structure.

Outcomes vary widely and may range from microcephaly and severe or profound levels of mental retardation to normal intelligence, although at least some neuropsychological impairment will always be present. Children with schizencephaly may have a variety of neurological problems including hydrocephalus, seizure disorders of various types, mental retardation, and coordination disorders of varying degrees of severity (Baron, Fennell, & Voeller, 1995). Special education programming will be necessary in virtually all cases, but only after careful assessment due to the highly variable expressivity of symptoms. As the child develops, the behavioral and mental symptom complex may change significantly and frequent, comprehensive neuropsychological examinations are recommended.

REFERENCE

Baron, I., Fennell, E., & Voeller, K. (1995). *Pediatric neuropsychology in the medical setting.* Oxford: Oxford University Press.

CECIL R. REYNOLDS
Texas A&M University

SCHIZOPHRENIA

See CHILDHOOD SCHIZOPHRENIA.

SCHOOL ATTENDANCE OF CHILDREN WITH DISABILITIES

School attendance of students with disabilities, and of all children, is affected by the following factors: motivational level, home and community problems, levels of stress, academic underachievement, rate of failure, negative self-concept, social difficulties, external directedness, improper school placement, inconsistent expectations by parents and teachers, employment outside of school, aversive elements in the school environment, and skill deficiencies (Grala & McCauley, 1976; Schloss, Kane, & Miller, 1981; Sing, 1998; Unger, Douds, & Pierce, 1978). Absenteeism is learned; as it becomes habitual, it increases and continues to reinforce itself (Stringer, 1973).

Since it is difficult to develop effective intervention strategies in academic, social, emotional, and vocational areas if children are not in school, attendance becomes a parallel goal to the successful completion of the disabled student's individual educational plan (IEP). Various authors (Bosker & Hofman, 1994; Jones, 1974; Schloss et al., 1981; Unger et al., 1978) have suggested programs for motivating or changing patterns of behavior of special education students to assist in increasing their school attendance.

Jones (1974) described the Diversified Satellite Occupations Program and Career Development, which allows the student to register in a less structured school setting from the one he or she normally attends, provides a curriculum with an emphasis on occupational guidance for all ages, and shortens the school day. The program was successful in decreasing truancy.

Schloss et al. (1981) evaluated factors related to adverse aspects of attending school and pleasant aspects of staying at home. An intervention program was individually developed to assist the student in increasing the amount of satisfaction received from going to school, decreasing the amount of satisfaction gained from staying home, and actively teaching skills that enhance the student's ability to benefit from going to school. Not only did school attendance improve, but test scores also increased. Unger et al. (1978) described a program that taught students the skills necessary to succeed in school. Each student's attendance pattern was examined, reasons for truancy evaluated, and individual lessons devised. Students' attendance and attitudes toward school both improved.

School attendance for disabled children is mandated by the Individuals with Disabilities Education Act (IDEA). It is extremely important that absenteeism be evaluated constantly by the local educational agency and that steps be undertaken to remediate the situation on an individual basis whenever possible.

REFERENCES

Bosker, R. J., & Hofman, W. H. A. (1994). School effects on dropout: A multi-level logistic approach to assessing school-level correlates of dropout of ethnic minorities. *Tijdschrift voor Onderwijsresearch, 19*(1), 50–64.

Grala, R., & McCauley, C. (1976). Counseling truants back to school: Motivation combined with a program for action. *Journal of Counseling Psychology, 23,* 166–169.

Jones, H. B. (1974). *Dropout prevention: Diversified Satellite Occupations Program and Career Development. Final report.* Washington, DC: Bureau of Adult, Vocational, and Technical Education.

Schloss, P. J., Kane, M. S., & Miller, S. (1981). Truancy intervention with behavior disordered adolescents. *Behavior Disorders, 6*(3), 175–179.

Sing, K. (1998). Part-time employment in high school and its effect on academic achievement. *Journal of Educational Research, 91*(3), 131–139.

Stringer, L. A. (1973). Children at risk 2. The teacher as change agent. *Elementary School Journal, 73*(8), 424–434.

Unger, K. V., Douds, A., & Pierce, R. M. (1978). A truancy prevention project. *Phi Delta Kappan, 60*(4), 317.

SUSANNE BLOUGH ABBOTT
*Bedford Central School District,
Mt. Kiseo, New York*

INDIVIDUALS WITH DISABILITIES EDUCATION IMPROVEMENT ACT OF 2004 (IDEIA)

SCHOOL EFFECTIVENESS

School effectiveness is a term adopted in the late 1970s to refer to a body of research on identifying effective schools and the means for creating more of them. The movement to research effective schools has been driven largely by three principal assumptions. According to Bickel (1983), these are that: (1) it is possible to identify schools that are particularly effective in teaching basic skills to poor and minority children; (2) effective schools exhibit identifiable characteristics that are correlated with the success of their students and these characteristics can be manipulated by educators; and (3) the salient characteristics of effective schools form a basis for the improvement of noneffective schools.

Bickel (1983) has traced the origins of the school effectiveness movement to three factors. The first is the backlash that developed in response to the Coleman studies (and like research) of the 1960s. These studies left the unfortunate impression that differences among schools were irrelevant in the education of poor and minority children. The second basis, according to Bickel, was the general psychological climate of the 1970s. Principals, teachers, parents, and others seemed ready for a more positive, hopeful message, one that said schools could make a difference and that effective schools did exist in the real world. The final factor described by Bickel is the readiness of the educational research community to accept the findings that to date include such intuitively appealing variables as strong instructional leadership, an orderly school climate, high expectations, an emphasis on basic skills, and frequent testing and monitoring of student progress.

MacKenzie (1983) has noted broad, rapid agreement on the dimensions and fundamental elements of what constitutes effective schools. Table 1, adapted from MacKenzie's (1983) excellent review, lists these various elements; however, as MacKenzie has discussed, the listing of attributes is truly misleading in this instance. The characteristics of effective schools are largely interactive, producing a circumstance that promotes learning that goes far beyond a summation of the parts. The effectiveness of a school cannot be predicted by determining the mere presence or absence of each of these factors—they must be assessed as they interact within the school under observation.

As can be seen from the elements of school effectiveness given in the table, making schools particularly good learning environments is a total system effort. Elements are listed that affect the district level, building level, and classroom level. It is difficult to point to any one level as being the most crucial, even though schools are hierarchically arranged; however, if there is one level that deserves more emphasis, it

Table 1 Dimensions of effective school research and corresponding elements of effective schools

Leadership dimensions

Core elements

1. Positive overall school and organizational climate
2. Activities focused toward clear, attainable, relevant, and objective goals
3. Teacher-directed classroom management
4. Teacher-directed decision making
5. In-service training designed to develop effective teaching

Facilitating elements

1. Consensus among teachers and administrators on goals and values
2. Long-range planning
3. Stability of key staff
4. District-level support for school improvement

Efficacy dimensions

Core elements

1. Expectations for high achievement
2. Consistent press for excellence
3. Visible rewards for academic excellence
4. Group interaction in the classroom
5. Autonomy and flexibility to implement adaptive practices
6. Total staff involvement in school improvement
7. Teacher empathy, rapport, and interaction with students

Facilitating elements

1. Emphasis on homework and study
2. Acceptance of responsibility for learning outcomes
3. Strategies to avoid nonpromotion of students
4. Deemphasis on ability grouping

Efficiency dimensions

Core elements

1. Amount and intensity of time engaged in learning
2. Orderly school and classroom environments
3. Continuous assessment, evaluation, and feedback
4. Well-structured classroom learning activities
5. Instruction driven by content
6. Schoolwide emphasis on basic and on higher order skills

Facilitating elements

1. Opportunities for individualized work
2. Number and variety of opportunities to learn
3. Reduced class size

Source: MacKenzie, 1983

is the classroom. The individual classroom is where instruction takes place; it will always be the key to the educational process. The classroom is affected by many elements that cannot be ignored. MacKenzie (1983) emphasizes:

> The classroom as a learning environment is nested in the larger environment of the school, which is embedded in a political-administrative structure through which it relates to the surrounding community. . . . It will be difficult if not impossible to provide effective classroom teaching in a disorderly, disorganized, and disoriented school environment, and it may be nearly as difficult to organize good schools in an atmosphere of political and managerial indifference. (p. 9) (Also see Purkey and Smith, 1982.)

Effective schools may have been thought, intuitively, by some to bring all students to some designated average level of performance. However, instead of causing students to cluster tightly about some central tendency, effective schools expand the differences among students rather than restrict them. Rich, facilitative environments enhance the results of ability differences, allowing the maximum possible levels of growth; deprived, restrictive environments slow and constrain growth. This does not mean that group differences will necessarily increase. If schools and instruction are particularly effective for all groups, as should be the case, then the overall level of achievement should increase for all groups along with the within group dispersion. This, at least in theory, is currently being attempted in terms of school accountability movement, in which expectations for schools now include test results of special education students (CISP, 1998).

As promising as the school effectiveness literature appears to be, and even with the consensus on the core elements of school effectiveness, a variety of valid criticisms have been offered. These have been summarized and reviewed by Rowan, Bossert, and Dwyer (1983). The technical properties of the research have been criticized as (1) using narrow, limited measures of effectiveness that focus only on instructional outcomes; (2) using design that allows an analysis of relational variables from which cause and effect cannot be inferred; and (3) making global comparisons on the basis of aggregate data, without assessing intraschool variations in organizational climate or outcomes across classes within schools. Rowan et al. (1983) also caution that the effect sizes present in this line of research are questionable. They have argued that the traditional methods of research in school effectiveness resemble "fishing expeditions" that spuriously inflate the probability of finding significant results. Despite these and other problems, the school effectiveness movement has rekindled optimism that schools can be organized and restructured to enhance student performance. As yet, the application of the methods and concepts of the school effectiveness literature have not been applied to special education programs. Special education programs are typically excluded from the data in such studies and desperately need to be assessed. It remains to be seen whether special education programs that can be identified as particularly effective in educating the handicapped are affected by the same variables and with the same form of interaction as are regular education programs. The time to apply the concepts and research methods of school effectiveness to special education is past due. It holds much promise for understanding what makes special education effective and how to effect such changes.

REFERENCES

Bickel, W. E. (1983). Effective schools: Knowledge, dissemination, inquiry. *Educational Researcher, 12,* 3–5.

Clark, T. A., & McCarthy, D. P. (1983). School improvement in New York City: The evolution of a project. *Educational Researcher, 12,* 17–24.

Consortium on Inclusive Schooling Practices. (1998). *Including students with disabilities in accountability systems.* Issue brief. Pittsburgh, PA: Allegheny University of Health Sciences.

MacKenzie, D. E. (1983). Research for school improvement: An appraisal of some recent trends. *Educational Researcher, 12,* 5–19.

Purkey, S. C., & Smith, M. S. (1982). Too soon to cheer? Synthesis of research on effective schools. *Educational Leadership, 40,* 64–69.

Rowan, B., Bossert, S. T., & Dwyer, D. C. (1983). Research on effective schools: A cautionary note. *Educational Researcher, 12,* 24–32.

CECIL R. REYNOLDS
Texas A&M University

SPECIAL EDUCATION PROGRAMS
TEACHER EFFECTIVENESS

SCHOOL FAILURE

There are many reasons why children fail in school. In some cases, failure may be due to circumstances within the child's environment. In other cases, school failure may be the result of a physical problem originating before, during, or after birth. This section identifies and discusses some of the chief causes of failure in school.

Failure in school often occurs when children come from environments characterized by economic hardship, deprivation, neglect, trauma, divorce, death, foster parenting, drug abuse, poor school attendance, or lack of adequate instruction. Indeed, dyspedagogia carries more of a role in school failure simply because of the theoretical paradigm in Western schools of individualism as opposed to social/interactive paradigms such as those favored in Russian schools for so many years. Some change may be noted in the teacher preparation and involvement in inner-city schools (Yeo, 1997).

Cultural differences also contribute to school failure. When a language other than English is used in the home and children are limited in English proficiency, they do poorly in school. The cultural values held by students also affect how they perceive their school, their teachers, and their peer group. For example, students' values determine how much they will be motivated in class, how they perceive and respond to authority, and whether they will be highly competitive or more responsive to a cooperative approach to learning. When values differ widely from one culture to another, what is valued in one culture may serve as a barrier to learning in another (Saville-Troike, 1978).

Children who exhibit behavior problems in the classroom also experience school failure. Some children have conduct disorders in which they disrupt the class, constantly irritate the teacher, do not follow directions, are easily distracted, are impulsive, or fail to attend. Other students who are fearful, anxious, withdrawn, or immature have difficulty in responding freely in the classroom and fail to learn to the limits of their abilities. Children whose self-esteem is so low that they believe they are of little worth often learn to be helpless. These children stop trying in school because they think they cannot learn. When children with behavior problems do not conform to the standards of the school environment, they may become socially aggressive, reject the values of the school and society, and come into conflict with authorities. A student may openly confront teachers and administrators, begin using drugs or alcohol, join gangs, break laws, steal, and eventually be expelled from or drop out of school (Knoblock, 1983; Long, Morse, & Newman, 1980; Quay & Werry, 1979).

Children who have difficulty in seeing and hearing often fail in school. Although 1 child in 10 enters school with some degree of visual impairment, most of these problems can be corrected and have no effect on educational development. One child out of a thousand, however, has visual impairments so severe they cannot be corrected. Children who are hard of hearing or deaf have difficulty in learning to understand language. This causes difficulty in learning to speak, read, and write the English language (Barraga, 1983).

Mental retardation results in school failure. Mental retardation may range in severity from mild to moderate to severe to profound. Delayed mental development can contribute to failure in language acquisition and use, achievement in academic subjects, social adjustment, and becoming a self-supporting adult (Mittler, 1981).

Specific learning disabilities can result in failure in school. A learning disability is a dysfunction in one or more of the psychological processes that are involved in learning to read, write, spell, compute arithmetic, etc. In some cases, a child may have an attention disability and may not be able to direct attention purposefully, failing to selectively focus attention on the relevant stimuli or responding to too many stimuli at once. A memory disability is the inability to remember what has been seen or heard. Perceptual disabilities cover a wide range of disorders in which a child who has normal vision, hearing, and feeling may experience difficulty in grasping the meaning of what is seen, heard, or touched. An example is a child who has difficulty in seeing the directional differences between a "d" and a "b," or who requires an excessive amount of time to look at a printed word, analyze the word, and say the word. Thinking disabilities involve problems in judgment, making comparisons, forming new concepts, critical thinking, problem solving, and decision making. A disability in oral language refers to difficulties in understanding and using oral language. All of these specific learning disabilities might cause difficulty in learning to read, write, spell, compute arithmetic, or adopt appropriate social-emotional behaviors (Kirk & Chalfant, 1984). Research cites the need for school-family partnerships (Poole, 1997) and intensive case management (Reid, Bailey-Dempsey, Cain, & Cook, 1994).

School failure is associated with poor physical and mental health outcomes in adulthood. It has long been recognized and documented as a significant pathway to downward social mobility, an effect exaggerated in children with disabilities (Reynolds, 2005).

REFERENCES

Barraga, N. (1983). *Visual handicaps and learning* (rev. ed.). Austin, TX: Exceptional Resources.

Kirk, S. A., & Chalfant, J. C. (1984). *Academic and developmental learning disabilities.* Denver: Love.

Knoblock, P. (1983). *Teaching emotionally disturbed children.* Boston: Houghton Mifflin.

Long, N., Morse, W., & Newman, R. (Eds.). (1980). *Conflict in the classroom: The education of emotionally disturbed children* (4th ed.). Belmont, CA: Wadsworth.

Mittler, P. (Ed.). (1981). *Frontiers of knowledge in mental retardation: Vol. 1. Social educational and behavioral aspects; Vol. 2. Biomedical aspects.* Baltimore: University Park Press.

Poole, D. L. The SAFE Project. *Health & Social Work, 22*(4), 282–289.

Quay, H., & Werry, J. (Eds.). (1979). *Psychopathological disorders of childhood* (2nd ed.). New York: Wiley.

Reid, W. J., Bailey-Dempsey, C. A., Cain, E., & Cook, T. V. (1994). Case incentives versus case management: Preventing school failure? *Social Work Research, 18*(4), 227–236.

Reynolds, C. R. (2005, August). *School failure and public health outcomes.* Presidential address to the Division of School Psychology at the annual convention of the American Psychological Association, Washington, DC.

Saville-Troike, M. (1978). *A guide to culture in the classroom.* Rosslyn, VA: National Clearinghouse for Bilingual Education.

Yeo, F. (1997). Teacher preparation and inner-city schools: Sustaining educational failure. *Urban Review, 29*(2), 127–143.

JAMES CHALFANT
University of Arizona

EMOTIONAL DISORDERS
LEARNED HELPLESSNESS
LEARNING DISABILITIES
MENTAL RETARDATION

SCHOOL PHOBIA

School phobia has been the subject of hundreds of research studies and dozens of literature reviews over the past several decades. The phenomenon was first described in 1932 when Broadwin distinguished a type of school refusal from truancy by an anxiety component. The term school phobia was coined in 1941 (Johnson, Falstein, Szurek, & Svendson, 1941). A common definition of school phobia cited in some literature includes the following characteristics:

Severe difficulty in attending school often amounting to prolonged absence.

Severe emotional upset shown by such symptoms as excessive fearfulness, undue temper, misery or complaints of feeling ill without obvious organic cause on being faced with the prospect of going to school.

Staying at home during school hours with the knowledge of the parents at some stage in the course of the disorder.

Absence of significant antisocial disorder, such as stealing, lying, wandering, destructiveness, or sexual misbehavior. (Berg, Nichols, & Pritchard, 1969, p. 123)

In contrast to school phobia, truancy is characterized by behaviors that are the opposite of the last two behaviors.

Contemporary writers who use the term school refusal generally describe it with the same set of characteristics that defines school phobia that lack intensity (Kearney, Eisen, & Silverman, 1995). An exception is the American Psychiatric Association's (1994) classification system (*DSM-IV*), which describes school refusal as one possible concomitant of separation anxiety disorder, while reserving the term school phobia for a fear of the school situation even when parents accompany the child.

The occurrence of school phobia is relatively rare when one considers the abundance of literature devoted to it. Estimates of the incidence of school phobia range from 3.2 to 17 per 1,000 schoolchildren (Kennedy, 1965; Yule, 1979). The wide discrepancy may be due in part to the age at which children are sampled. Prevalence is thought to peak at three different ages: 5 to 7, on entry or shortly after entry to school; 11, around the time children change schools; and 14, often concomitant with depression (Hersov, 1977). Many writers consider school phobia to occur in three girls for every two boys (Wright, Schaefer, & Solomons, 1979). However, this ratio has not appeared in several studies of school phobics reported in the literature (Baker, & Wills, 1978; Berg et al., 1969; Hersov, 1960; Kennedy, 1965).

The causes of school phobia have been couched in psychoanalytic, psychodynamic, and social learning theory terms. The psychoanalytic focus frames school phobia within a mutually dependent and hostile parent-child relationship. Some psychoanalysts believe that the unconscious conflict resulting from this relationship leads the child to want to protect the mother, and hence, not leave her. Other psychoanalysts indicate that the conflict surrounding the hostile-dependent relationship with mother is displaced onto the school situation, which becomes the manifest phobic object. In any case, both agree that separation anxiety plays a key role in school phobia (Atkinson, Quarrington, & Cyr, 1985; Kelly, 1973).

An alternative theory that was intended to explain the occurrence of school phobia at later ages was postulated by Leventhal and Sills (1964). Kelly (1973) labeled this theoretical approach, which focuses on the school phobic's unrealistic self-image, as "nonanalytic psychodynamic." According to Leventhal and Sills (1964):

> These children commonly overvalue themselves and their achievements and then try to hold onto their unrealistic self-image. When this is threatened in the school situation, they suffer anxiety and retreat to another situation where they can maintain their narcissistic self-image. This retreat may very well be a running to a close contact with mother. (p. 686)

Others have used the term fear of failure in referring to this theory (Atkinson et al., 1985).

Behavioral theories account for school phobia in terms of both classical and operant conditioning. The former model explains school phobia as a conditioned anxiety response elicited by the school situation or some other school-related event. For instance, an often cited case (Garvey & Hegrenes, 1966) involved a boy whose mother repeatedly told him as he was leaving for school that she might die while he was gone. Eventually, the thought of going to school led to fear of his mother's death. The operant model assumes that internal or environmental cues both trigger and maintain the school phobic behavior.

Atkinson et al. (1985) argued that the three perspectives differ more in focus than in substance because all can account for school phobia as a fear of separation, of the school situation, or of failures in school. For example, the child whose unrealistic self-image leads to a fear of failure in the school situation may be reinforced by parents for not attending school. Similarly, separation anxiety may be a component of school phobia triggered by a traumatic school event.

Coolidge, Hahn, and Peck (1957) were the first to describe subtypes of school phobia. Based on differences within a fairly small sample of 27 school phobics, they discussed neurotic and characterological types. The former were char-acterized by sudden onset after several years of normal school attendance while the latter were described as more severely disturbed, with the fear of school being only one fear among many in a generally fearful personality. Subsequent investigations by Kennedy (1965) and Hersov (1960) confirmed the general distinction between an acute form and a more pervasive disturbance. Kennedy (1965) elaborated 10 criteria that distinguished type 1 (neurotic) from type 2 (characterological) school phobics based on a sample of 50 children aged 4 to 16. Generally, the former was characterized by acute onset, a first episode, intact family relations, and occurrence in younger children. Type 2 was characterized as being chronic, often accompanied by a character disorder, unstable parental relationship, incipient onset, and a history of prior episodes.

Family relations have been investigated as a separate correlate of school phobia. Hersov (1960) described three patterns of parent-child relationships that characterized his sample of 50 school phobic children aged 7 to 16 years:

1. An overindulgent mother and an inadequate, passive father dominated at home by a willful, stubborn, and demanding child who is most often timid and inhibited in social situations.

2. A severe, controlling, and demanding mother who manages her children without much assistance from her passive husband; a timid and fearful child away from home and a passive and obedient child at home, but stubborn and rebellious at puberty.

3. A firm, controlling father who plays a large part in home management and an overindulgent mother closely bound to and dominated by a willful, stubborn, and demanding child, who is alert, friendly, and outgoing away from home. (p. 140)

The first two relationship types have been considered to be subtypes of characterological school phobia while the third seems more characteristic of the neurotic type (Atkinson et al., 1985). It should be noted that categorization based on a sample of 50 children needs further validation before conclusions are drawn about parent-child correlates. The same caution holds for Kennedy's classification system, particularly of type 2 school phobia, which was based on six children.

As Atkinson et al. (1985) noted in their review, the construct of school phobia is too heterogeneous to be described by a simple dichotomy. They examined five variables related to school phobia, some of which overlap more than others—extensiveness of disturbance, source of fear, mode of onset, age, and gender of the child. The extensiveness of fear can be conceptualized along a continuum with the dichotomies of neurotic/characterological or type 1/type 2 at the end points. Generally, acute or sudden onset is characteristic of type 1 and chronic or gradual onset is characteristic of type 2. When researchers have operationalized acute mode of onset as the occurrence of school phobia after 3 or more years of trouble-free attendance, other correlates emerge. For instance, chronic onset tended to be associated more than acute onset with poor premorbid adjustment, dependency on parents, low self-esteem, and a poor prognosis.

Similarly, source of fear, age, and gender do not bear a one-to-one correspondence with the dichotomous classifications. Generally, four sources of fear have been reported that correspond to the etiological approaches—fear of maternal separation, fear of something or someone at school, fear of failure, and a generally fearful disposition. Atkinson et al. (1985) conclude that the fear sources are not mutually exclusive, and that fears surrounding separation may coincide with more general fearfulness. They caution, however, that conclusions relating the extensiveness of disturbance to a specific fear source are premature based on current studies. In contrast, extent of disturbance and age appear to be related, with older children generally exhibiting more severe disturbance. While Kennedy differentiated type 1 from type 2 phobics in part on age differences, there is no consistent finding that type 1 or acute type is more typical of younger children.

Both psychological and pharmacotherapy have been employed for children experiencing school phobia. We focus here on psychological interventions only. The interested reader is referred to Gittelman and Koplewicz (1985) for an overview of pharmacotherapy of childhood anxiety disorders. Early treatments of school phobia stemmed from the psychoanalytic tradition and focused on resolving the mutual hostile-dependent relationship between the school phobic child and his or her parents. Typically, parallel treatment was carried out on mother and child, with one therapist using play therapy with the child and another therapist "treating" the mother. Johnson et al. (1941) describe treatment as "a collaborative dynamic approach . . . to relieve the guilt and tension in both patients" (p. 706). Treatment of eight cases reported in their seminal study of school phobia lasted from 5 months to over a year. There does not appear to be consensus among the psychoanalytic clinicians on whether gradual or immediate return is preferable.

The treatment that emerged from Leventhal and Sills' (1967) psychodynamic theory involves "outmaneuvering" the child. Unlike the psychoanalytic approach, rapid return rather than insight is the primary goal of treatment. Once parents are helped to see their complicity in maintaining school avoidance, the parent who is likely to stand firm is chosen to carry out the plan, which is essentially immediate, forced return to school. Kennedy (1965) also advocates forced return to school and described successful treatment of 50 cases of type 1 school phobia. He identified the following six components as essential to successful treatment: (1) good professional public relations; (2) avoidance of emphasis on somatic complaints; (3) forced school attendance; (4) structured interview with parents; (5) brief interview with child; and (6) follow-up (p. 287).

During the past 20 years a proliferation of behavioral treatments of school phobia have occurred. Yule (1979) and Trueman (1984) provide critical reviews of the behavioral treatment of school phobia. Trueman (1984) reviewed 19 case studies between 1960 and 1981 that used behavioral treatments based on classical, operant, or a combination of those techniques. Of the eight studies reviewed that used techniques based on classical conditioning, six used reciprocal, one used implosion, and one used emotive imagery. Six of the studies involved boys aged 10 to 17; two studies involved girls aged 8 and 9. Trueman noted considerable variation among the reciprocal inhibition treatments, making conclusions difficult concerning the most efficacious component. Additionally, he noted the difficulty in distinguishing between systematic densensitization and shaping.

Among the 10 case studies reviewed by Trueman that used operant procedures, five involved boys aged 7 to 12 and five involved girls aged 6 to 14. The change agents varied among studies as well as the specific techniques and the criteria for success. Thus comparisons between procedures are hard to make. The procedures included training parents in positive reinforcement methods, contingency contracting, prompting and shaping, and school-based contingencies. It is important that resolution is long-term for these cases, because longitudinal studies indicate lifelong outcomes (Flakierska, Lindstroem, & Gillberg, 1997). Home-school collaboration is essential (Jenni, 1997).

REFERENCES

American Psychiatric Association. (1980). *Diagnostic and statistical manual of mental disorders* (3rd ed.). Washington, DC: Author.

Atkinson, L., Quarrington, B., & Cyr, J. J. (1985). School refusal: The heterogeneity of a concept. *American Journal of Orthopsychiatry, 55,* 83–101.

Baker, H., & Wills, U. (1978). School phobia: Classification and treatment. *British Journal of Psychiatry, 132,* 492–499.

Berg, I., Nichols, K., & Pritchard, C. (1969). School phobia—Its classification and relationship to dependency. *Journal of Child Psychology & Psychiatry, 10,* 123–141.

Broadwin, I. T. (1932). A contribution to the study of truancy. *American Journal of Orthopsychiatry, 2,* 252–259.

Coolidge, J., Hahn, P., & Peck, A. (1957). School phobia: Neurotic crisis or way of life. *American Journal of Orthopsychiatry, 27,* 296–306.

Flakierska, P. N., Lindstroem, M., & Gillberg, C. (1997). School phobia with separation-anxiety disorder: A comparative 20 to 29-year follow-up study of 35 school refusers. *Comprehensive Psychiatry, 38,* 17–22.

Garvey, W. P., & Hegrenes, J. R. (1966). Desensitization techniques in the treatment of school phobia. *American Journal of Orthopsychiatry, 36,* 147–152.

Gittelman, R., & Koplewicz, M. S. (1985). Pharmacotherapy of childhood anxiety disorders. In R. Gittelman (Ed.), *Anxiety disorders in children.* New York: Guilford.

Hersov, L. A. (1960). Refusal to go to school. *Child Psychology & Psychiatry, 1,* 137–145.

Hersov, L. A. (1977). School refusal. In M. Rutter & L. Hersov (Eds.), *Child psychiatry: Modern approaches* (pp. 455–486). Oxford, England: Blackwell.

Jenni, C. B. (1997). School phobia: How home school collaboration can tame this dragon. *School Counselor, 44*(3), 206–217.

Johnson, A. M., Falstein, E. J., Szurek, S. A., & Svendsen, M. (1941). School phobia. *American Journal of Orthopsychiatry, 11,* 702–711.

Kearney, C. A., Eisen, A. R., & Silverman, W. K. (1995). The legend and myth of school phobia. *School Psychology Quarterly, 10*(1), 65–85.

Kelly, E. W. (1973). School phobia: A review of theory and treatment. *Psychology in the Schools, 10,* 33–42.

Kennedy, W. A. (1965). School phobia: Rapid treatment of fifty cases. *Journal of Abnormal Psychology, 70,* 285–289.

Leventhal, T., & Sills, M. (1964). Self-image in school phobia. *American Journal of Orthopsychiatry, 34,* 685–694.

Leventhal, T., Weinberger, G., Stander, R. J., & Stearns, R. P. (1967). Therapeutic strategies with school phobics. *American Journal of Orthopsychiatry, 37,* 64–70.

Trueman, D. (1984). The behavioral treatment of school phobia: A critical review. *Psychology in the Schools, 21,* 215–223.

Wright, L., Schaefer, A., & Solomons, G. (1979). *Encyclopedia of pediatric psychology.* Baltimore: University Park Press.

Yule, W. (1979). Behavioral approaches to the treatment and prevention of school refusal. *Behavioral Analysis & Modification, 3,* 55–68.

JANET A. LINDOW
THOMAS R. KRATOCHWILL
University of Wisconsin at Madison

RICHARD J. MORRIS
University of Arizona

CHILDHOOD NEUROSIS
PHOBIAS AND FEARS
SEPARATION ANXIETY DISORDER

SCHOOL PSYCHOLOGY

Psychology is devoted to the goals of describing and explaining human behavior and promoting conditions that foster human development and welfare. School psychologists generally share these goals and strive to apply psychological theories, concepts, and techniques to facilitate growth and development through education and schools. The birth of psychology occurred about 100 years ago in Germany. Psychologists began working in U.S. schools about 20 years later as child study departments and clinics began to form.

The number of school psychology programs and students has increased during the last two decades (Fagan, 1985). An estimated 2,200 students graduate yearly from more than 200 school psychology programs (Brown & Lindstrom, 1978). Students seeking a specialist's degree frequently take 2 years of graduate work plus a full-time, yearlong internship. Those seeking a doctoral degree frequently take 3 years of graduate work and devote 1 or more years each to an internship and a dissertation. Thus, with 3 to 5 years of graduate preparation, school psychologists tend to be the most highly educated behavioral scientists employed by the schools.

Some (Brown, 1982) view school psychology as a profession separate and independent from the professions of psychology and education; others (Bardon, 1982) view school psychology as a specialty within the profession of psychology. In fact, most school psychologists straddle the professions of psychology and education. They provide many services that are unique and drawn from psychology as well as education. A comprehensive study of the expertise of school psychologists (Rosenfeld, Shimberg, & Thornton, 1983) found the practice of school psychology to be similar to the practice of clinical and counseling psychology. In fact, school psychologists devote considerable attention to assessment and organizational issues.

School psychological services differ between communities. Their character is influenced by many conditions: federal and state laws and policies; local institutional traditions, policies, and practices; financial resources and practices governing allocation; availability of psychologists and the nature of their professional preparation; and national, state, and local professional standards. Furthermore, the services often differ for elementary and secondary grades. Although the nature of their services differ, many school psychologists are guided by a scientist-practitioner model (Cutts, 1955), which holds that applications of psychology should be supportable empirically or theoretically and derived from a body of literature that is held in high esteem. Professionals are expected to have good command of this literature discussing the theoretical, empirical, and technical components of their specialties. They are also expected to deliver culturally competent services (Rogers & Ponterotto, 1997).

A comprehensive review of the school psychology literature (Ysseldyke, Reynolds, & Weinberg, 1984) identified the following 16 domains as ones in which school psychology has expertise: classroom management, classroom organization and social structure, interpersonal communication and consultation, basic academic skills, basic life skills, affective/social skills, parent involvement, systems development and planning, personnel development, individual differences in development and learning, school-community relations, instruction, legal, ethical, and professional issues, assessment, multicultural concerns, and research and evaluation.

While school psychology is a dynamic specialty and one not easily categorized or described, its work in five broad areas is described briefly. School psychologists frequently conduct psychoeducational evaluations of pupils needing special attention. The evaluations typically consider a student's cognitive (i.e., intelligence and achievement), affective, social, emotional, and linguistic characteristics, and use behavioral, educational, and psychological (including psychoneurological (D'Amato, Hammons, Terminie, & Dean, 1992) and psychoanalytic) techniques.

School psychologists also participate in planning and evaluating services designed to promote cognitive, social, and affective development. Their services can include teaching, training, counseling, and therapy. While their principal focus frequently is on individual pupils, they also work individually with parents, teachers, principals, and other educators.

School psychologists also offer indirect services to pupils through educators, parents, and other adults. Their indirect services typically involve in-service programs for teachers, parent education programs, counseling, consultation, and collaboration. Their consultative and collaborative activities involve them with groups composed of students, teachers, parents, and others. Their work as members of the education staff enables them to effect important changes in organizations by working on broad and important issues that impact classrooms, school buildings, districts, communities, corporations, or a consortium of districts and agencies.

School psychologists' knowledge of quantitive methods commonly used in research and evaluation often surpasses that of other educational personnel. Thus they frequently are responsible for conceptualizing and designing studies, collecting and analyzing data, and integrating and disseminating findings.

School psychologists also may supervise pupil personnel and psychological services. In this capacity, they are responsible for conceptualizing and promoting a comprehensive plan for these services, for hiring and supervising personnel, for promoting their development, and for coordinating psychological services with other services in the district or community.

School psychology, like other professions, has developed and promulgated a number of standards that exemplify the profession's values and principles and that serve the needs of service providers, clients, educators, society, and legal bodies (Oakland, 1986).

Most school psychologists work in the schools or within other organizational structures (e.g., mental health clinics, juvenile courts, guidance centers, private and public residential care facilities). State certification is important for these school psychologists. Forty-nine states presently certify school psychologists—an increase of 42 since 1946. Many school psychologists also want the option to practice privately. Although those who have doctoral degrees typically can be licensed by their states as psychologists, those holding subdoctoral degrees typically have been denied a license to practice psychology independently and increasingly are seeking the right to be licensed and to practice privately.

Five professional journals are devoted to advancing the knowledge and practice of school psychology: *Journal of School Psychology, School Psychology Quarterly, Psychology in the Schools, School Psychology International,* and *School Psychology Review.* An additional 16 secondary and 26 tertiary journals add to the literature (Reynolds & Gutkin, 1990). Persons interested in further information about school psychology are encouraged to consult the professional journals, *The Handbook of School Psychology* (Reynolds & Gutkin, 1999), and the National Association of School Psychologists (www.nasponline.org) and American Psychological Association (www.apa.org) web sites. The APA web site contains links not only to the Division of School Psychology web site but to the official documents of APA that define school psychology as a distinct field of practice and describe the typical purview of practice for school psychologists.

REFERENCES

American Psychological Association. (1968). *Psychology as a profession.* Washington, DC: Author.

American Psychological Association. (1972). Guidelines for conditions of employment of psychologists. *American Psychologist, 27,* 331–334.

American Psychological Association. (1973). *Ethical principles in the conduct of research with human subjects.* Washington, DC: Author.

American Psychological Association. (1977). *Standards for providers of psychological services* (Rev. ed.). Washington, DC: Author.

American Psychological Association. (1980). *Criteria for accreditation of doctoral training programs and internships in professional psychology.* Washington, DC: Author.

American Psychological Association. (1981a). *Ethical principles of psychologists* (Rev. ed.). Washington, DC: Author.

American Psychological Association. (1981b). Specialty guidelines for the delivery of services by school psychologists. *American Psychologist, 36,* 639, 670–682.

American Psychological Association. (1985). *Standards for educational and psychological testing.* Washington, DC: Author.

Bardon, J. (1982). The psychology of school psychology. In C. R. Reynolds & T. B. Gutkin (Eds.), *The handbook of school psychology* (pp. 1–14). New York: Wiley.

Brown, D. (1982). Issues in the development of professional school psychology. In C. R. Reynolds & T. B. Gutkin (Eds.), *The handbook of school psychology* (pp. 14–23). New York: Wiley.

Brown, D. T., & Lindstrom, J. P. (1978). The training of school psychologists in the United States: An overview. *Psychology in the Schools, 15,* 37–45.

Cutts, N. E. (Ed.). (1955). *School psychology at mid-century.* Washington, DC: American Psychological Association.

D'Amato, R. C., Hammons, P. F., Terminie, T. J., & Dean, R. S. (1992). Neuropsychological training in American Psychological Association-accredited and non-accredited school psychology programs. *Journal of School Psychology, 30*(2), 175–183.

Fagan, T. (1985). Quantitative growth of school psychology in the United States. *School Psychology Review, 14,* 121–124.

National Association of School Psychologists. (1978). *Standards for credentialing in school psychology.* Washington, DC: Author.

National Association of School Psychologists. (1984a). *Principles for professional ethics.* Washington, DC: Author.

National Association of School Psychologists. (1984b). *Standards for the provision of school psychological services.* Washington, DC: Author.

National Association of School Psychologists. (1984c). *Standards for training and field placement programs in school psychology.* Washington, DC: Author.

Oakland, T. (1986). Professionalism within school psychology. *Professional School Psychology, 1,* 9–27.

Reynolds, C. R., & Gutkin, T. B. (1999). *The handbook of school psychology.* (3rd ed.). New York: Wiley.

Rogers, M. R., & Ponterotto, J. G. (1997). Development of the multicultural school psychology counseling competency scale. *Psychology in the Schools, 34,* 211–217.

Rosenfeld, M., Shimberg, B., & Thornton, R. (1983). *Job analysis of licensed psychologists in the United States and Canada.* Princeton, NJ: Educational Testing Service.

Stapp, J., & Fulcher, R. (1981). *Salaries in psychology.* Washington, DC: American Psychological Association.

THOMAS OAKLAND
University of Florida

EDUCATIONAL DIAGNOSTICIAN
PSYCHOLOGY IN THE SCHOOLS

SCHOOL PSYCHOLOGY DIGEST

See SCHOOL PSYCHOLOGY REVIEW.

SCHOOL PSYCHOLOGY REVIEW

School Psychology Review, first published in 1972 as *The School Psychology Digest,* is the official journal of the National Association of School Psychologists (NASP). In 1980, the name of the journal was changed to reflect the change from the publication of condensations of previously published articles to the publication of original research, reviews of theoretical and applied topics, case studies, and descriptions of intervention techniques useful to psychologists working in educational settings. Scholarly reviews of books, tests, and other psychological materials are also published occasionally. Portions of two or three issues each year are reserved for guest-edited miniseries on themes relevant to NASP membership, such as program evaluation, testing and measurement issues, psychological theories, and special education practices. These solicited theme issues differentiate the *Review* from other major school psychology journals.

The primary purpose of the *Review* is to impact the delivery of school psychological services by publishing scholarly advances in research, training, and practices. *School Psychology Review* is a quarterly publication with an editor and appointed editorial advisory board. The founding editor was John Guidubaldi of Kent State University, and the current editor is Thomas J. Power of the University of Pennsylvania.

A content analysis of the *Review* indicates that approximately 10 to 20 percent of the articles concern professional issues in school psychology, 30 to 40 percent relate to interventions for academic and behavior problems of children, and 30 to 35 percent involve testing and measurement issues. The remaining articles cover a wide array of topics, including program evaluation, psychological theories, and special education practices.

The *School Psychology Review* enjoys the largest circulation (over 20,000 subscribers) of any of the journals representing the field of school psychology, and is the second most widely distributed journal in the entire discipline of psychology. *School Psychology Review* is published by the National Association of School Psychologists and is a benefit of membership; it may also be purchased separately.

STEPHEN N. ELLIOTT
University of Wisconsin
First edition

DONNA WALLACE
The University of Texas of the Permian Basin
Second edition

SCHOOL RECORDS

See FERPA (FAMILY EDUCATION & PRIVACY RIGHTS ACT).

SCHOOL REFUSAL

School refusal, also incorrectly known as school phobia, refers to excessive absenteeism from school that arises from qualities internal to the child, not from external forces. School refusal often is accompanied by significant anxiety and feelings of distress.

The term *school phobia* has been utilized incorrectly

to refer to chronic refusal to attend school. However, this term is too narrow, because not all school refusers display characteristics of a phobia (i.e., an intense and debilitating fear causing significant life impairment). School refusal does not have its own diagnostic category in the *Diagnostic and Statistical Manual for Mental Disorders* (*DSM-IV-TR*). Moreover, school phobia is not listed among the specific phobias in the *DSM-IV-TR*.

School refusal behavior has four distinct components (Berg, Nichols, & Prichard, 1969): The child remains at home with parental knowledge. There is an absence of severe antisocial disorders (such as juvenile delinquency, disruptiveness, and sexual activity). The parent(s) have taken reasonable measures to solicit school attendance. The child displays unsuitable emotional behaviors at the prospect of attending school (e.g., may involve temper tantrums or hysterical crying). In addition to observable anxiety symptoms such as crying and sleeping difficulties, school-refusing students may also exhibit somatic symptoms as primary or secondary complaints. Gastrointestinal illness (e.g., stomachaches, nausea), autonomic illness (e.g., headaches, dizziness), and muscular symptoms (e.g., back and joint pain) are common indicators (Fremont, 2003).

School refusal is not a unitary syndrome. Students often refuse to attend school for one or more of the following reasons: to avoid school-based stimuli that provoke a general sense of negative affectivity (e.g., playgrounds, buses, bathrooms, fire alarms); to escape aversive school-based social and/or evaluative situations (e.g., interacting with teachers or peers, avoiding bullying, taking tests); to pursue attention from significant others (e.g., parents or primary caregivers); to pursue tangible reinforcers outside of the school setting (e.g., shopping trips, arcade games; Kearney & Silverman, 1990).

The first two conditions are maintained by negative reinforcement: school avoidance reduces unpleasant physical or emotional symptoms. The last two conditions are maintained by positive reinforcement: the behavior is sustained because the child or adolescent is receiving something enjoyable from it. However, children who are positively reinforced for their school refusal may also be experiencing a relatively high level of anxiety (Brandibas, Jeunier, Clanet, & Fouraste, 2004).

Each of these reasons appears to correspond to a particular causality. Children who avoid school-based stimuli that elicit negative affectivity may be displaying a specific phobia. Children who seek to avoid aversive social or evaluative situations at school may be exhibiting social phobia. Children who stay home from school to spend time with significant others may be displaying separation anxiety. Children who pursue tangible reinforcers outside of school are demonstrating truant behavior; this behavior may also be associated with conduct disorder. It is important to consider that school refusal can serve more than one function (Kearney, Lemos, & Silverman, 2004).

School refusal behavior is commonly linked with anxiety disorders. School refusal was thought to always be due to a separation anxiety disorder. However, separation anxiety is now known to account for a small percentage of school refusals. Children who refuse to attend school are most likely to be diagnosed as displaying social phobia, specific phobias, Separation Anxiety Disorder, or Major Depressive Disorder (Elliot, 1999). Chronic forms of school refusal are likely to occur in the presence of other psychopathology.

As noted, some scholars consider truancy to be one form of school refusal behavior. However, other scholars believe truancy should not be considered school refusal. They note that truancy is usually accompanied by antisocial behavior and occurs without the knowledge of the child's parents, thus violating two of the four components of school refusal created by Berg and colleagues and discussed earlier.

Truant behavior is typically seen as a behavioral disorder, while school refusal is typically viewed as an anxiety disorder. Those who want to exclude truancy from school refusal believe truants have self-control of their actions, while anxiety-based school refusers often have little self-control (Heyne, King, Tonge, & Cooper, 2001). Truants are not likely to be excessively fearful about school attendance. Instead, their absences probably reflect a lack of interest in schoolwork, an unwillingness to conform to the school's expectations and code of behavior, and a desire to engage in more attractive activities in lieu of school (Elliot, 1999).

Estimated prevalence rates for school refusal behavior range from 1 percent (Heyne et al., 2001) to an astonishing 28 percent (Kearney et al., 2004). Most studies place the prevalence rate somewhere between 1 percent and 5 percent. School refusal appears to occur equally as often among males and females and is not prominent in any racial/ethnic group (King & Bernstein 2001; Kearney et al., 2004). However, school refusal associated with Separation Anxiety Disorder may be more common in younger children (Elliot, 2001). Students who exhibit school refusal generally have normal intelligence, and learning disabilities are not overrepresented in the population of school refusers (Heyne et al., 2001; Evans, 2000).

Triggers of school refusal behavior include family conflict or separation, transitions, academic difficulties, illness, bullying and peer conflict, and traumatic experiences (Heyne et al., 2001; McShane, Walter, & Rey, 2001). School refusal is most likely to occur between the ages of 5 to 7, 10 to 11, and 14 to 16. These ages correspond with early schooling, change of school, and nearing the end of compulsory education, respectively (Heyne et al., 2001). The first peak is associated with separation anxiety, the second with social phobia, and the third with social and other phobias and other disorders such as depression (Csoti, 2003).

Biology also appears to play a role in the manifestation of school refusal behavior. Parents of anxiety-based school refusers have a high rate of anxiety and depressive disorders. Parents of school refusers with separation anxiety have a high rate of Panic Disorder and Separation Anxiety Disorder, and parents of phobic school refusers have higher rates of phobic disorders. These findings suggest that anxiety-based school refusal is heritable (Martin, Cabrol, Bouvard, Lepine, & Maouren-Simeoni, 1999).

School refusal behavior is associated with many negative outcomes. Long-term absence from school interferes with a student's educational development, resulting in lower grades, grade retention, and a decrease in future opportunities. The social impacts of chronic school refusal include poor self-esteem and family conflict. Costs to society include increased educational expenditures, lessened productivity, and increased social support (Evans, 2000). School refusers are at increased risk for employment difficulties and mental health illness later in life (Fremont, 2003). In particular, students with a later onset of school refusal may have more severe disorders and a poorer prognosis (Elliot, 1999). Because of these negative outcomes, an accurate recognition of the behavior and effective treatment programs are needed to ensure the best possible outlook for these students.

Treatment options for school refusal behavior include behavioral methods, cognitive-behavioral therapy, parent/teacher training, educational support therapy, and medication. Behavioral therapy is primarily based on exposure to stimuli that provoke negative affect and may use systematic desensitization, flooding, modeling, shaping, and contingency management. Cognitive-behavioral therapy typically incorporates techniques to help the child manage anxiety by teaching the child to identify inaccurate beliefs and replace them with more accurate statements. Parent/teacher training encompasses behavior management principles to help the adults adjust the reinforcement contingencies and promote school attendance. Educational support therapy combines information presentations and supportive psychotherapy (Fremont, 2003). Although there is mixed evidence for the effectiveness of pharmacological treatments for school refusal, a tricyclic antidepressant, imipramine, has been found to be effective in conjunction with cognitive-behavioral therapy (Bernstein et al., 2000). Selective seratonin reuptake inhibitors have been utilized in children with Separation Anxiety Disorder, social phobia, and Generalized Anxiety Disorder (Heyne et al., 2001), and may be effective for school refusal behavior. Pharmacologic treatment of school refusal should be used in conjunction with other interventions (Fremont, 2003).

REFERENCES

American Psychiatric Association. (2000). *Diagnostic and statistical manual of mental disorders* (4th ed., text revision). Arlington, VA: Author.

Berg, I., Nichols, K., & Prichard, C. (1969). School phobia, its classification and relationship to dependency. *Journal of Child Psychology and Psychiatry, 10,* 123–141.

Bernstein, G. A., Borchardt, C. M., Perwien, A. R., Crosby, R. D., Kushner, M. G., Thuras, P. D., & Last, C. G. (2000). Imipramine plus cognitive-behavioral therapy in the treatment of school refusal. *Journal of the American Academy of Child and Adolescent Psychiatry, 39,* 276–283.

Brandibas, G., Jeunier, B., Clanet, C., & Fouraste, R. (2004). Truancy, school refusal, and anxiety. *School Psychology International, 25*(1), 117–126.

Csoti, M. (2003). *School phobia, panic attacks, and anxiety in children.* New York: Jessica Kingsley.

Elliot, J. G. (1999). School refusal: Issues of conceptualization, assessment, and treatment. *Journal of Child Psychology and Psychiatry, 40,* 1001–1012.

Evans, L. D. (2000). Functional school refusal subtypes: Anxiety, avoidance, and malingering. *Psychology in the Schools, 37,* 183–191.

Fremont, W. P. (2003). School refusal in children and adolescents. *American Family Physician, 68,* 1555–1560.

Heyne, D., King, N. J., Tonge, B. J., & Cooper, H. (2001). School refusal: Epidemiology and management. *Paediatric Drugs, 3,* 719–732.

Kearney, C. A., Lemos, A., & Silverman, J. (2004). The functional assessment of school refusal behavior. *The Behavior Analyst Today, 5*(3), 275–283.

Kearney, C. A., & Silverman, W. K. (1990). A preliminary analysis of a functional model of assessment and treatment for school refusal behavior. *Behavior Modification, 14,* 340–366.

King, N. J., & Bernstein, G. A. (2001). School refusal in children and adolescents: A review of the past 10 years. *Journal of the American Academy of Child and Adolescent Psychiatry, 40,* 197–205.

Martin, C., Cabrol, S., Bouvard, M. P., Lepine, J. P., & Maouren-Simeoni, M. C. (1999). Anxiety and depressive disorders in fathers and mothers of anxious school-refusing children. *Journal of the American Academy of Child and Adolescent Psychiatry, 38,* 916–922.

McShane, G., Walter, G., & Rey, J. M. (2001). Characteristics of adolescents with school refusal. *Australian and New Zealand Journal of Psychiatry, 35,* 822–826.

MARNI R. FINBERG
University of Florida

CHILDHOOD NEUROSIS
PHOBIAS AND FEARS
SCHOOL PHOBIA
SEPARATION ANXIETY DISORDER

SCHOOL STRESS

Stress is the nonspecific response of the human body to a demand. It is not simply nervous tension but a physiological response of the body. Stress occurs in all living organisms and is with us all the time (Selye, 1976). Stress comes from mental, emotional, and physical activity.

School stress results from the impact of the school environment on children. Physical stress is accompanied by feelings of pain and discomfort, but physical stress is seldom a major factor in school stress. In schools the stressors are most often psychological and result in emotional reactions with accompanying physiological changes in the body. Exceptional children experience more stress, less peer support, and poorer adjustment than peers without disabilities (Wenz-Gross & Siperstein, 1998).

In school stress, the demands usually result from significant others in the school (i.e., teachers and peers), or those who are expectant about school activities (e.g., parents). School stress is dependent on cognitive processes that lead to emotional reactions and a form or style of coping behavior. The coping behavior may or may not be effective, or the coping behavior may only appear to be effective. When this is the case, the body has changed from a state of alarm and is in the resistance stage. When in the resistance stage, one's ability to deal effectively with other stressors is reduced. Resistance can be maintained only so long before physical or psychological problems occur (Selye, 1976). In the stage of resistance, the person is much more susceptible than when not defensive. In reacting to stress, individuals usually try harder with the coping skills they have or search for other techniques, but when stress is prolonged or is particularly frustrating, it may cause distress physically or mentally. If the stimuli continue to be perceived as stressful, the individual's reaction can be as debilitating as prolonged physical stress in other situations.

Some children are bothered much more than others by what appear to be the same stressors. The intensity of the demand as perceived by the individual and whether the individual is able to manage the stress are the most important factors. Teachers and principals often represent authority and generate the stress that goes with reacting to authority figures. They, and/or parents, often press children to achieve more (sometimes much more) than they are able to produce. School stress often comes from a lack of perceived success, but stress may come from any segment of the environment. Stress can come from those things that are novel, intense, rapidly changing, or challenging the limits of a child's tolerance. Some children pressure classmates to keep up (or to not work very hard regardless of what adults say), to speak as they do, to appear as they do, to disclose secret thoughts, etc. Sometimes stress comes from crowding, racial imbalance, the opposite sex, or facing separation from one or both parents or certain friends. Whether in school or out, many children are pressured to perform competitively. Some children thrive on pressure, others wilt and withdraw.

School stress can be prevented by intervening in the environment to eliminate or modify stress-producing situations before they have a chance to affect children; by intervening with children to protect them from the impact of stress-

ors by building up their resistance and personal strength (i.e., self-concept); by intervening with children to increase their tolerance for stress; and by putting children who are adversely affected by stress in an environment that minimizes stress (Phillips, 1978). There are many techniques and strategies that can be used with children suffering from school stress. Most involve a focus on learning and motivational processes.

REFERENCES

Phillips, B. (1978). *School stress and anxiety*. New York: Human Sciences.

Selye, H. (1976). *The stress of life*. New York: McGraw-Hill.

Wenz-Gross, M., & Siperstein, G. N. (1998). Students with learning problems at risk in middle school: Stress social support, and adjustment. *Exceptional Children, 65*(1), 91–100.

JOSEPH L. FRENCH
Pennsylvania State University

SCHOOL PHOBIA
STRESS AND INDIVIDUALS WITH DISABILITIES

SCHOOL VIOLENCE

During the past decade, a number of highly publicized incidents of school violence in West Paducah, Kentucky, Jonesboro, Arkansas, Springfield, Oregon, Littleton, Colorado, and Red Lake, Minnesota, occurred, in which guns have been brought into schools and students and teachers have been killed. These incidents have left many parents, teachers, and students feeling vulnerable and concerned about school safety. According to the Office of Juvenile Justice and Delinquency Prevention of the U.S. Department of Justice, 12 percent of students reported carrying weapons to school for protection, 28 percent sometimes or never felt safe while at school, and 11 percent have stayed home from school or cut classes because of the fear of violence (Yell & Rozalski, 2000). Concern about the danger of weapons on school campuses has resulted in establishing zero-tolerance disciplinary policies associated with bringing weapons to school and with acts of violence. These guidelines grew out of the drug enforcement policies of the 1980s (Morrison & D'Incau, 1997).

Critics of zero-tolerance policy recommend the use of a proactive approach to violence prevention instead of the current focus on punishment of offenders. Although advocates who propose the use of proactive approaches recognize a need for zero-tolerance policy for offenders who bring weapons into the schools, they stress the need to adopt other prevention programs simultaneously. Such prevention strategies may involve a three-tiered model (primary, secondary, and tertiary), with the intensity of prevention and intervention strategies increasing at each level (Dwyer, Osher, & Hoffman, 2000).

At the primary prevention level, efforts to decrease violence and aggression should target all students schoolwide and should be implemented beginning in early elementary school. One of the first steps in implementing a primary prevention program is to address the physical condition of the school building (Dwyer et al., 2000). Physical conditions associated with safety can be addressed by supervising access to the building and grounds, minimizing time in hallways, providing supervision during transition times, and working with local law enforcement to ensure that routes to and from school are safe (Dwyer et al., 2000). Effective instruction of academic material is another crucial component to any violence prevention program (Scott, Nelson, & Liaupsin, 2001). Adequate curriculum contributes to a decrease in physical, relational, and verbal aggression. For example, identification and interventions for students with learning difficulties decreases the likelihood that such students will engage in disruptive behaviors.

Teaching social skills to all members of a school community is another primary prevention effort. The creation of a sense of belonging in a school community decreases risks of violence and aggression (Perry, 1999). The creation of a sense of belonging requires teachers to be trained and encouraged to show warmth and support to students, and for students to display cooperation and prosocial values. In addition, teachers should be trained to supplement strategies that decrease disruptive behaviors in the classroom, so that such behaviors do not escalate into classroom and school crises (Skiba & Peterson, 2000). Students should be taught specific social skills that involve the inclusion of others, ethical values such as fairness, respect, caring, responsibility, and citizenship, as well as conflict resolution and peer mediation skills (Perry, 1999).

At the secondary level of violence prevention, programs should be targeted toward students who are at risk for violent and antisocial behavior. At-risk students are identified through the implementation of early screening measures. Multiple gating approaches (i.e., the use of multiple screening techniques to minimize false positives and negatives) may be used to identify at-risk students (Sprague & Walker, 2000). The three gates to be screened are: teacher nominations and referrals of students exhibiting antisocial behaviors; teacher ratings of student academic and behavior skills; and a search of school, public safety, and corrections records. All school faculty members should be taught the early warning signs for violent and antisocial behavior (Dwyer et al., 2000). Students who are troubled often exhibit multiple early warning signs that, if recognized early, can help school faculty

identify maladaptive behaviors and immediately design and implement interventions for them. Some warning signs include social withdrawal, low school interest and academic performance, expression of violence in writing and drawings, bullying, a history of discipline problems, and excessive anger. After a student has been identified as being at risk for violent and antisocial behavior, comprehensive early interventions that involve both school and family need to be immediately implemented. The display of potential antisocial behaviors warrants interventions designed to target them. Professionals need to be knowledgeable of empirically supported interventions for antisocial behavior.

Finally, adequate early response programs should involve a tertiary tier of interventions, which are implemented when students engage in violent and antisocial behavior. All schools should have a program in place that can be implemented quickly and effectively during a time of crisis (Dwyer et al., 2000). Tertiary levels of early response should also include a zero-tolerance policy, especially when violent behavior and the risk for student safety are unable to be prevented or controlled with the aforementioned methods.

REFERENCES

Dwyer, K. P., Osher, D., & Hoffman, C. C. (2000). Creating responsive schools: Contextualizing early warning, timely response. *Exceptional Children, 66,* 347–365.

Morrison, G., & D'Incau, B. (1997). The web of zero tolerance: Characteristics of students who are recommended for expulsion. *Education and Treatment of Children, 20,* 1–17.

Perry, C. M. (1999). Proactive thoughts on creating safe schools. *The School Community Journal, 9,* 9–16.

Scott, T. M., Nelson, C. M., & Liaupsin, C. J. (2001). Effective instruction: The forgotten component in preventing school violence. *Education and Treatment of Children, 24,* 309–322.

Skiba, R. J., & Peterson, R. L. (2000). School discipline at a crossroads: From zero tolerance to early response. *Exceptional Children, 66,* 335–347.

Sprague, J., & Walker, H. (2000). Early identification and intervention for youth with antisocial and violent behavior. *Exceptional Children, 66,* 367–379.

Yell, M., & Rozalski, M. E. (2000). Searching for safe schools: Legal issues in the prevention of school violence. *Journal of Emotional and Behavioral Disorders, 8,* 1–17.

ALLISON G. DEMPSEY
University of Florida

HADLEY MOORE
University of Massachusetts

CRIME AND INDIVIDUALS WITH DISABILITIES

JUVENILE DELINQUENCY

SCHOPLER, ERIC (1927–   )

Eric Schopler received his BA (1949) from the University of Chicago. He received an MA (1955) in psychiatric social work from the School of Social Service Administration, and his PhD (1964) in clinical child development from the Committee on Human Development, University of Chicago. He is currently a professor of psychology and psychiatry, and the founder and co-director of the Division for the Treatment and Education of Autistic and related Communication handicapped CHildren (TEACCH), University of North Carolina, Chapel Hill.

Early experiences helped convince Schopler that Freudian theories applied to autism were mistaken (Schopler, 1993) and that parents were not the cause but, along with their children, the victims of a neurobiological disorder (1971, 1994). Schopler (1997) and colleagues identified principles for optimum education for children in the autism spectrum based on parent collaboration and including the use of a visually structured education (Schopler, Mesibov, & Hearsey, 1995).

Schopler initiated an effective statewide program with unified parent-professional collaboration that focuses on family adaptation, school adjustment, and community relations (Schopler, 1986). TEACCH includes both strong research and professional training components. The organization's publications have been translated into many languages and the TEACCH program has served as a national and international model. In recognition of his contributions, Schopler has received the American Psychiatry Association (APA) Gold Achievement Award, the University of North Carolina's O. Max Gardner Award for Outstanding Contribution to Human Welfare (1985), the APA Award for Distinguished Public Service (1985), and the North Carolina

Eric Schopler

Award (1993), the highest honor awarded by the state for achievements in public leadership.

REFERENCES

Schopler, E. (1986). Relationship between university research and state policy: Division TEACCH—Treatment and Education of Autistic and related Communication handicapped CHildren. *Popular Government, 51*(4), 23–32.

Schopler, E. (1993). The anatomy of a negative role model. In G. Brannigan & M. Merrens (Eds.), *The undaunted psychologist* (pp. 172–186). Philadelphia: McGraw-Hill.

Schopler, E. (1994). Neurobiological correlates in the classification and study of autism. In S. Broman & J. Grafman (Eds.), *Atypical cognitive deficits in developmental disorders: Implication for brain function* (pp. 87–100). Hillsdale, NJ: Erlbaum.

Schopler, E. (1997), Implementation of the TEACCH philosophy. In D. J. Cohen & F. R. Volkmar (Eds.), *Handbook of autism and pervasive developmental disorders.* New York: Wiley.

Schopler, E., Mesibov, G. B., & Hearsey, K. (1995). Structured teaching in the TEACCH system. In E. Schopler & G. B. Mesibov (Eds.), *Learning and cognition in autism* (pp. 243–267). New York: Plenum.

STAFF

SCHWARTZ-JAMPEL SYNDROME

See NATIONAL ORGANIZATION OF RARE DISORDERS.

SCOLIOSIS

Scoliosis, a lateral curvature of the spine, is the most common type of spinal deformity. Functional scoliosis results from poor posture or a difference in length of the legs. It is not progressive and usually disappears with exercise. Structural scoliosis, however, is a more severe form, involving rotation of the spine and structural changes in the vertebrae (Ziai, 1984).

Most cases of structural scoliosis are idiopathic—of unknown cause (Benson, 1983). Idiopathic scoliosis occurs most frequently in adolescent females during the growth spurt, ages 12 to 16. If untreated, the condition progresses rapidly throughout the spinal growth period (ages 15 to 16 for girls and ages 18 to 19 for boys). Scoliosis can also accompany neuromuscular disorders such as cerebral palsy and muscular dystrophy, or can develop as a result of infection, trauma, or surgery.

Early diagnosis of scoliosis is essential to prevent progression of the curvature. Treatment varies with the type of scoliosis, the age of the child, and severity of deformity.

Mild curvatures require only observation, while more pronounced curvatures require bracing and exercise. In severe cases, surgery is required. Treatment approaches have also included electrostimulation (Benson, 1983) and use of biofeedback techniques (Birbaumer, Flor, Cevey & Dworkin, 1994; Ziai, 1984).

REFERENCES

Birbaumer, N., Flor, H., Cevey, B., & Dworkin, B. (1994). Behavioral treatment of scoliosis and kyphosis. *Journal of Psychosomatic Research, 38*(6), 623–628.

Benson, D. R. (1983). The spine and neck. In M. E. Gershwin & D. L. Robbins (Eds.), *Musculoskeletal diseases of children* (pp. 469–538). New York: Grune & Stratton.

James, J. I. P. (1976). *Scoliosis* (2nd ed.). Edinburgh, Scotland: Churchill Livingstone.

Ziai, M. (Ed.). (1984). *Pediatrics* (3rd ed.). Boston: Little, Brown.

CHRISTINE A. ESPIN
University of Minnesota

CEREBRAL PALSY
MUSCULAR DYSTROPHY

SCOPE AND SEQUENCE

Scope and sequence information play an important role in the special education of exceptional individuals. In academic areas where curriculum is not readily available, the use of scope and sequence information and task analysis provides the special educator with ways of determining a set of skills (Hargrave & Poteet, 1984).

To provide appropriate programs, special educators need a clear understanding, in the form of a sequence of skills, of what each of the academic domains include. This array of skills is referred to as scope and sequence information. Scope and sequence charts provide schemata of an instructional domain. Scope refers to those skills that are taught; sequence refers to the order in which they are taught. Sequences may be determined from the work of others or may be synthesized by the special educator from experience (Wehman & McLaughlin, 1981).

Scope and sequence charts vary in structure and format among special educators and programs. Scope and sequence information provide a link between assessment and the specification of instructional goals and objectives (Wehman & McLaughlin, 1981). It is essential in developing individual educational programs. Knowledge of the scope and sequence of skills provides the teacher with a clearer profile of those skills that the student has acquired and those that he or she still needs to acquire (Mercer & Mercer, 1985).

REFERENCES

Hargrave, L. J., & Poteet, J. A. (1984). *Assessment in special education.* Englewood Cliffs, NJ: Prentice Hall.

Mercer, C. D., & Mercer, A. R. (1985). *Teaching students with learning problems.* Columbus, OH: Merrill.

Wehman, P., & McLaughlin, P. J. (1981). *Program development in special education.* New York: McGraw-Hill.

ANNE M. BAUER
University of Cincinnati

SCOTLAND, SPECIAL EDUCATION IN

In the United Kingdom, special education services began to be offered in a systematic way from 1913, when Cyril Burt began using psychometrics to assess and categorize children. From the 1920s, Scotland developed multidisciplinary assessment within a child guidance system, leading to special school or program placement recommendations. Over time, category labels became more sensitive to the feelings of those categorized (e.g., *idiot* and *moron* became *severely learning disabled*).

In 1980, simplistic disability categories, the implicit underpinning medical model, and automatic placement implications were abandoned, replaced by a law that required individual statements or *records* of special educational needs for children and young people who had pronounced, specific, or complex chronic difficulties together with the specification of how these needs were to be met and progress evaluated. The term *special needs* meant needs not being met. Thus, *records* were context-dependent, rather than focused on labeling a child. The earlier focus on school-age children expanded to include ages 0 through 19. More recently, the government espoused a *presumption of mainstreaming for all children* to promote social inclusion and raise educational attainment (Scottish Executive, 2000). Additionally, the age range expanded further, to age 24.

Special educational provision includes home-visiting or center-based assessment and advisory services; mobile human and/or material resources within normal classes in regular mainstream schools; special units located within schools; special units located outside (but hopefully near) schools; day special schools; residential special schools; and adult training centers.

In Scotland, approximately 33,000 children and young people have identified special educational needs (i.e., 4 percent of the population of that age): 11,000 in primary (elementary) schools with various kinds of support, 14,500 in secondary (high) schools with various kinds of support, and 7,400 in special schools. More students are expected to be mainstreamed at all ages in the future.

The Beattie Report (Scottish Executive, 1999) reviewed

the needs of young people requiring additional support to make the transition to postschool education, training or employment. It recommended the development of a postschool service for ages 16 through 24 that would complement the assessment and advice provided by colleges and training providers, contribute to contextual assessment that was solution-focused and consistent with inclusiveness, support the transition process, contribute to strategic developments at regional or national level, and improve the understanding, skills, and effectiveness of service providers through consultation, training, and action research. This is now being taken forward.

The 2005 Education (Additional Support for Learning; Scotland) Act (Scottish Executive, 2004) had major implications for special education services in Scotland. The term *Additional Support Needs* replaced that of *Special Educational Needs*. Additional support needs, a broader term, referred to any child or young person who, for whatever reason, required additional support for learning. Possible barriers to learning included physical, social, emotional, family, and care circumstances. The Act imposed duties on education authorities (i.e., school districts) to establish systems to identify and meet the additional support needs of young people. It also imposed duties on other agencies (e.g., social work services and health boards) to work with education authorities. Every education authority also had a duty to provide a free independent mediation service for parents of children and young people with additional support needs.

The pattern of special education assessment and other service provision has changed over the decades. Child guidance clinics traditionally offered multidisciplinary assessment by psychiatrists, social workers, and educational psychologists (McKnight, 1978). Assessments of special educational need, program planning, and subsequent evaluation of progress now more usually involve core input from teachers, educational psychologists (similar to the term *school psychologist* as used in other countries), school medical officers, and of course parents and the individual young person, with other professions (e.g., social worker, speech therapist, pediatrician) contributing as relevant. The ideal is an interdisciplinary rather than multidisciplinary assessment, but educational recommendations remain within the purview of the educational specialists.

Medically related services (including speech therapy) are provided by central government (federally) funded Area Health Trusts, while educational and social work services are provided by local government authorities funded by a combination of federal grants and local tax raising. Unsurprisingly, coordination of services can present organizational challenges, and the principle of *integrated services* has been the subject of much recent rhetoric, in some cases connected to the development of *community* or *full-service* schools.

Special education in Scotland has developed significantly during the last 100 years and has long been nationally man-dated. However, patterns of service provision still show considerable local variation. Some of this represents strategic adaptation to local needs (as in rural vs. urban communities) and in other cases reflects historical accident or political choice which may or may not be currently functional, or temporal variations in the quality of practice in service at the point of delivery.

REFERENCES

McKnight, R. K. (1978). The development of child guidance services. In W. Dockrell, W. Dunn, & A. Milne (Eds.), *Special education in Scotland.* Edinburgh: Scottish Council for Research in Education (SCRE).

Scottish Executive (1999). *Implementing inclusiveness: Realising potential.* (The Beattie Report). Edinburgh: Scottish Executive.

Scottish Executive (2000). *Standards in Scotland's schools act.* Edinburgh: Scottish Executive.

Scottish Executive. (2004). *Education (additional support for learning) (Scotland) act.* Edinburgh: Author. Retrieved July 11, 2004, from http://www.opsi.gov.uk/legislation/scotland/acts2004/20040004.htm

KEITH J. TOPPING
E. S. SMITH
University of Dundee

ENGLAND, SPECIAL EDUCATION IN *INTERNATIONAL SCHOOL PSYCHOLOGY ASSOCIATION*

SCOTT CRANIODIGITAL SYNDROME WITH MENTAL RETARDATION

Scott craniodigital syndrome with mental retardation is a rare, X-linked recessive genetic disorder. Children with this syndrome have mental retardation and various craniofacial and extremity abnormalities. Craniofacial features include a small, wide head; small, narrow nose; excessively small jaw; and eyes set far apart. Other head and facial characteristics include an extended hairline, thick eyebrows, and long eyelashes. A startled expression on their face is found among some children (National Organization for Rare Disorders [NORD], 2005).

Extremity abnormalities have also been found among these children, including webbing of their hands and feet. The heels of these children's feet are turned inward as well. Excessive hair growth on different parts of their body have also been reported (NORD, 2005).

Mental retardation is present; therefore, it will be important for the child to enter an early childhood intervention program at age 3, with continued special education services as the child progresses through school.

REFERENCE

National Organization for Rare Disorders (NORD). (2005). *Singleton-Merton syndrome.* New Fairfield, CT: National Organization for Rare Disorders, Inc.

PATRICIA A. LOWE
University of Kansas

JOAN W. MAYFIELD
Baylor Pediatric Specialty Service

SCOUTING AND INDIVIDUALS WITH DISABILITIES

The scouting movement for boys and girls has made a significant effort to involve youths with disabilities. This was not always the case (Stevens, 1995) but currently in America, all levels of scouting have provisions to mainstream scouts in community units and to develop specialized troops for youngsters with severe disabilities or unusual needs. Scouting organizations catering to members with given disabilities are capable of designing adapted activities. For example, Stuckey and Barkus (1986) reported that the Boy Scout Troop of the Perkins School for the Blind went on a special camping trip at the Philmont Scout Ranch in New Mexico.

The national scout offices coordinate their efforts with a variety of organizations serving and advocating for the disabled. Leadership training materials that deal with issues in scouting for members with disabilities and guidelines on adapting scouting activities are available, as are materials such as taped scout handbooks. A number of adapted merit badge programs allow impaired scouts to earn an award while knowing that they have truly met the requirements for a badge.

Scouting offers youths many opportunities for developing motor, cognitive, and social skills, increasing self-esteem and a sense of achievement, and obtaining a feeling of enjoyment. Boy Scout and Girl Scout programs have worked toward making these benefits available to all youths. Many publications and other materials are available to interested persons from the national offices of Girl Scouts and Boy Scouts and from various local scout executives.

REFERENCES

Stevens, A. (1995). Changing attitudes to disabled people in the Scout Association in Britain (1908–62): A contribution to a history of disability. *Disability & Society, 10*(3), 281–293.

Stuckey, K., & Barkus, C. (1986). Visually impaired scouts meet the Philmont challenge. *Journal of Visual Impairment & Blindness, 80,* 750–151.

LEE ANDERSON JACKSON, JR.
University of North Carolina at Wilmington

SECKEL SYNDROME

Seckel syndrome, also known as nanocephaly, is a genetic disorder. The incidence of Seckel syndrome is higher in females than males and is due to an autosomal recessive gene (Thoene, 1992). The primary characteristics of the disorder include a very small head (microcephaly); intrauterine and postnatal growth failure, resulting in dwarfism; and sharp facial features with an underdeveloped chin (Rudolph, 1991). Prominence of the midface is typical in children with Seckel syndrome. Children with this disorder have a beak-like nose, large, malformed eyes, and low-set ears without lobes. They are short in stature, ranging in height from 3 to 3½ feet as an adult (Jones, 1988). Other physical abnormalities may include permanent fixation of the fifth finger in a bent position, malformation of the hips, and dislocation of the radial bone in the forearm (National Organization for Rare Disorders, 1998).

Children with Seckel syndrome have moderate to severe mental retardation (Jones). These children often exhibit hyperactive behavior and have attention and concentration difficulties (Jones, 1988). These children would benefit from a small group educational setting that provides one-on-one instruction and allows them to progress at their own speed. A structured, educational setting with expected rewards and consequences would be optimal. The standard treatment of Seckel syndrome is symptomatic and supportive. Parent training with a pediatric psychologist including behavioral management techniques may be beneficial. Genetic counseling may be helpful as well (Thoene, 1992).

REFERENCES

Jones, K. L. (Ed.). (1988). *Smith's recognizable patterns of human malformation* (4th ed.). Philadelphia: W. B. Saunders.

Rudolph, A. M. (1991). *Rudolph's pediatrics–19th edition.* Norwalk, CT: Appleton & Lange.

National Organization for Rare Disorders (NORD). (1998). *Seckel syndrome.* New Fairfield, CT: Author.

Thoene, J. G. (Ed.). (1992). *Physician's guide to rare diseases.* Montvale, NJ: Dowden Publishing.

JOAN W. MAYFIELD
Baylor Pediatric Specialty Service

PATRICIA A. LOWE
University of Kansas

SECOND LANGUAGE LEARNERS IN SPECIAL EDUCATION

Special education is a field addressing many challenges, one of them being working with second language learners. Today, many children across the United States come from countries and homes where English is not spoken or used as a language in which concepts are discussed. If, as projections suggest, 10 percent to 20 percent of any given population has some or several disabilities, then special education serves a number of these children. For many such students, English is their second language. This condition currently presents challenges to educators and service providers, impacting the outcomes of evaluations and interventions (Ortiz, 1997). Unlike a child brought up in an English-only environment, the learner of English as a second language shows developmental lags in articulation, vocabulary, insights on syntax, and comprehension of complex oral and printed texts. These conditions, coupled with limited understanding of the stages of second language acquisition, tends to promote overreferral to and placement in special education (National Coalition of Advocates for Schools, 1991). For example, Ochoa, Robles-Pina, Garcia, and Breunig's (1999) study across eight states with large populations of second language learners revealed that oral language-related factors (acquisition and/or delays) were the third most common reason for referral of second language learners. Further, Ochoa et al. (1999) state that 8 of the top 13 most commonly cited reasons for referral of these learners could be linked to language; in their study, language reasons accounted for 54 percent of all responses provided. Equally, limited awareness of conditions that suggest a disability promote patterns of underreferral of this population among general educators who consider the students' problems as typical patterns of second language learners (De León & Cole, 1994).

Until recently, special education in general invested modest efforts attending to the specific communication needs of second language learners and their families, and most support focused on attending to their conditions or disabilities. However, literature within the last twenty years reveals a change in this trend, the effects of which will be reviewed perhaps five years from now. Consequently, increasing research, training, and publication efforts raise awareness and educate professionals. For example, guidelines and recommendations based on best practices for children without disabilities are advocated for second language learners with disabilities (California Department of Education, 1997; Fernández, 1992; Gersten, Brengelman, & Jimenez, 1994). The literature reflects continuous appeals to special educators and speech clinicians to incorporate modified approaches like English as a second language (ESL) and/or Sheltered English into their practice (De León & Cole, 1994; Garcia & Malkin, 1993; Gersten, Brengelman, & Jimenez, 1994). However, the appropriateness and effectiveness of such practices are yet to be validated. The following sections address critical issues and challenges related to the education of second language learners with disabilities served in special education programs.

Heterogeneity

Diversity effectively describes the linguistic abilities of second language learners (SLLs) served in special education programs. Different disabilities, cultural and socioeconomic backgrounds, communicative abilities, and degrees of exposure to English are interacting variables that easily confound design and outcomes of many studies involving SLLs. Surveys and studies involving teachers and other categories of service providers working in programs serving SLLs reveal limited knowledge of the stages of second language acquisition through which learners advance naturally (De León & Cole, 1994; Ochoa, Rivera & Ford, 1997; Ortiz & Yates, 1988). Common practice approaches this challenge by educating second language learners as if they were native speakers of English, promoting very few, if any, modifications to interventions (Fernández, 1992). For example, use of ESL or equally meaningful approaches for the instruction of SLLs is recommended in literature but seldom is practiced (De León & Cole, 1994). Quite often, focusing on the child's disability excludes other needs the learner might have related to his or her condition of being a second language learner (such a child is usually expected to perform like a native speaker of English). Furthermore, generic prescriptions studied and validated for children without disabilities continue to be proposed (Fueyo, 1997; Gersten et al., 1994) for a population whose specific linguistic characteristics remain undefined.

Assessment

English language learners (ELLs)[1], as they are currently named, pose a challenge to those participating in the identification process. Unless their disability is obvious—orthopedic or visual impairment, or moderate to severe mental retardation—the question most evaluators encounter upon referral to assessment and possible placement is whether the learner has acquired English in all its linguistic and functional dimensions, or if the learner is advancing within the earlier stages of the long-term process of second language acquisition (Cummins & Sayers, 1995). Has the learner received appropriate instruction using methodology appropriate to the condition of learning English as a second language? Such information is critical to establish a distinction between poor performance due to ongoing development of linguistic competence, due to a disability, or a combination of both. Actually, Ochoa, Galarza, and Gonzalez (1996) found that only 6 percent of school psychologists conducting bilingual assessments of second language learners referred for special education actually implemented best practices that would enable them to obtain this critical information. Without establishing this distinction clearly, interpretation of current performance, prereferral strategies, assessment results, categorization, progress, and redesignation can be impacted negatively. Reports continue to emerge that question classification and disqualification for services and offer criticism on the interpretation of assessment data (Cheng, Ima, & Labovitz, 1994; Garcia & Malkin, 1993; Ochoa et al., 1996; Ochoa, Rivera, & Powell, 1997). These matters demand attention at policy, research, and practice levels given the increasing expectations that all children be educated to reach their potential, and barely anything is being done to monitor an appropriate, meaningful, and effective learning opportunity.

Access to the Curriculum

Reviews of policies and practices affecting second language learners in the United States reveals very limited focus on the specific instructional needs of ELLs with disabilities. Instead, most frequently, discussions on ELLs are embedded within references addressing diversity issues. Searches that include articles referring to culturally and linguistically diverse (CLD) learners with disabilities enables access to some of the scant literature on the pedagogy to educate second language learners in special education. Extracting information from reports is complex since, frequently, linguistic diversity is used to refer to second language learners, particularly Spanish speakers, when in reality linguistic diversity is larger than this subcategory. A plethora of articles focus on cross-cultural variations and culturally relevant interventions rather than on the study of the best, or most effective, instructional practices for children with disabilities requiring the support of instruction in English as their second language.

Comprehensible input facilitates access and consequently impacts learning (Fueyo, 1997). Methodologies designed to teach second language learners without disabilities offer a promising potential in facilitating access to the English curriculum for second language learners affected by one or several disabilities. Attending to the provision of comprehensible input is crucial. Instructional approaches such as English as a Second Language (ESL), the purpose of which is to promote effective early English language acquisition, and Sheltered English, which facilitates the development of higher levels of competence in English as a second language focusing on the development of reading and content-area skills (or academic courses) while strengthening emerging English skills, beg validation of their effectiveness for individuals with disabilities. Such approaches constitute common options recommended for linguistically appropriate individualized education programs (IEPs) for second language learners with limited English proficiency (California Department of Education, 1997; Gersten et al., 1994; Ortiz, 1997; Ortiz & Garcia, 1990; Ortiz & Yates, 1988).

Opportunities to learn through the first language promise a greater degree of comprehension of the instructional content, but the literature reflects a paucity of studies documenting best practices where this approach is implemented (Cloud, 1993; Willig & Swedo, 1987). Ortiz and Wilkinson (1989) found that in only 2 percent of the 203 IEPs of second language learners they reviewed was the child's first language specified as the language of instruction. Furthermore, research needs to document for which students this is an effective and valid option.

Professional Development

Most of the research efforts involving second language learners in special education throughout the last 20 years have been dedicated to documenting disparity in identification, access to the curriculum, and appropriate services. Documentation reveals that programs are not responding to the individual needs of second language learners and that the number of teachers familiar with pedagogy that supports second language acquisition is extremely reduced, and in most cases, bilingual paraprofessionals are the ones with direct responsibility for the instruction of these students. As appropriate and effective research-based interventions are validated and cross-referenced with each learner's linguistic profiles, a priority needs to be established to support extended and comprehensive professional development related to the education of students with disabilities for whom English is the second, and often weakest language.

Research and Policy Agenda

A research agenda for the future demands attention to the identification of linguistic abilities, matching instruction to developmental stage, and documentation of effective interventions, with particular emphasis on methodology and support mechanisms to enhance the learning opportunity. A research agenda including attention both to the needs of individuals with moderate to severe disabilities, and to the effects of introduction of the second language for non-speakers or non-comprehenders of English with disabilities is equally crucial. As more is learned about the effects of modulating instructional practices for SLLs in special education, policies and practices need to respond to these research-based interventions. Ultimately, the role of the researcher, teacher, and service provider is to advocate for the study of a pedagogy that encompasses the range of abilities and competence within any classroom where second language learners are present, particularly those with a disability.

Conclusion

Much needs to be learned about effective interventions for children with disabilities who are learning or who have learned English as their second language. A research agenda must evolve from this critical need so that a solid understanding of appropriateness and effectiveness of recommendations can be developed.

NOTE

[1]The term ELL replaces LEP which is the most common in the literature when it deals with students learning English as their second language. The new term is more inclusive of different levels of proficiency not just beginning levels.

REFERENCES

California Department of Education. (1997). *Guidelines for language, academic, and special education services required for limited-English-proficient students in California public schools, K–12*. Sacramento: Special Education Division.

Cheng, L., Ima, K., & Lobovitz, G. (1994). Assessment of Asian and Pacific Islander students for gifted programs. In S. B. Garcia (Ed.), *Addressing cultural and linguistic diversity in special education* (pp. 30–45). Reston, VA: Council for Exceptional Children.

Cloud, N. (1993). Language, culture and disability: Implications for instruction and teacher preparation. *Teacher Education and Special Education, 16,* 60–72.

Cummins, J., & Sayers, D. (1995). *Brave new schools: Challenging cultural illiteracy through global learning networks*. New York: St. Martin's Press.

De León, J., & Cole, J. (1994). Service delivery to culturally and linguistically diverse exceptional learners in rural school districts. *Rural Special Education Quarterly, 13,* 37–45.

Fernández, A. T. (1992). Legal support for bilingual education and language appropriate related services for limited English proficient students with disabilities. *Bilingual Research Journal, 16,* 117–140.

Fueyo, V. (1997). Below the tip of the iceberg: Teaching language-minority students. *Teaching Exceptional Children, 30,* 61–65.

Garcia, S. B., & Malkin, D. H. (1993). Toward defining programs and services for culturally and linguistically diverse learners in special education. *Teaching Exceptional Children, 26,* 52–58.

Gersten, R., Brengelman, S., & Jiménez, R. (1994). Effective instruction for culturally and linguistically diverse students: A reconceptualization. *Focus on Exceptional Children, 27,* 1–16.

Ochoa, S. H., Galarza, A., & Gonzalez, D. (1996). An investigation of school psychologists' assessment practices of language proficiency with bilingual and limited English proficient students. *Diagnostique, 21*(4), 17–36.

Ochoa, S. H., Rivera, B. D., & Ford, L. (1997). An investigation of school psychology training pertaining to bilingual psychoeducational assessment of primarily Hispanic students: Twenty-five years after *Diana* v. *California. Journal of School Psychology, 35,* 329–349.

Ochoa, S. H., Rivera, B. D., & Powell, M. P. (1997). Factors used to comply with the exclusionary clauses with bilingual and L.E.P. pupils: Initial guidelines. *Learning Disabilities Research and Practice, 12,* 161–167.

Ochoa, S. H., Robles-Pina, R., Garcia, S. B., & Breunig, N. (1999). School psychologists' perspectives on referrals of language minority students. *Journal of Multiple Voices for Ethnically Diverse Exceptional Learners, 3*(1), 1–14.

Ortiz, A. A. (1997). Learning disabilities occurring concomitantly with linguistic differences. *Journal of Learning Disabilities, 30,* 321–332.

Ortiz, A. A., & Garcia, S. B. (1990). Using language assessment data for language and instructional planning for exceptional bilingual students. In *Teaching the bilingual special education student* (pp. 25–47). Norwood, NJ: Ablex.

Ortiz, A. A., & Wilkinson, C. Y. (1989). Adapting IEP's for limited-English-proficient students. *Academic Therapy, 24*(5), 555–568.

Ortiz, A. A., & Yates, J. R. (1988). Characteristics of learning disabled, mentally retarded, and speech-language handicapped Hispanic students at initial evaluation and reevaluation. In A. A. Ortiz & B. R. Ramirez (Eds.), *Schools and the culturally diverse exceptional student: Promising practices and future directions* (pp. 51–62). Reston, VA: Council for Exceptional Children.

Willig, A. C., & Swedo, J. J. (1987, April). *Improving teaching strategies for exceptional Hispanic limited English proficient students: An exploratory study of task engagement and teaching strategies*. Paper presented at the annual meeting of the American Educational Research Association, Washington, DC.

ELBA MALDONADO-COLON
San Jose State University

SALVADOR HECTOR OCHOA
Texas A&M University

BILINGUAL SPECIAL EDUCATION
BILINGUAL SPEECH LANGUAGE PATHOLOGY

SECONDARY SPECIAL EDUCATION

Special education practice at the secondary level must account for different competencies and a different orientation than would be expected at the elementary level. The practitioner at the elementary level is able to communicate easily with regular classroom teachers because they share common training and a similar purpose in the instruction of basic language and math skills. The most common type of service delivery system in the elementary school seems to be the resource room. This arrangement is a natural extension of the regular classroom, with activities integrated with regular school curriculum. The result is a high degree of continuity from one area to another. Several problems are associated with using this approach at the secondary level. Teachers tend to be divided by areas of specialization and do not focus on individual differences of learners as readily as at the elementary level. This often results in the misinterpretation or misunderstanding of the value and nature of special education programming (Ysseldyke & Algozzine, 1984). This approach is not usually successful because it fails to involve many regular education classroom teachers and disregards the realities of the advanced secondary curriculum. The efforts of the special education practitioner should, therefore, be directed toward immediate problems of the learner and provide for close interaction with teachers and the specific course of study for each student.

Because few models for service delivery of secondary special education services exist, and university training programs have traditionally prepared teachers with an elementary emphasis, many secondary systems have relied on the elementary resource room as a model for service delivery. If the school adopts the philosophy of providing assistance only in the acquisition of basic skills in language and mathematics, then the traditional elementary model might be useful. If the school recognizes, however, the special demands and circumstances of the exceptional student as well as the unique problems associated with the onset of adolescence, then different programming is needed (Marsh, Gearheart, & Gearheart, 1978).

Lerner (1976) asserts that a secondary service delivery system in special education must account for several options in programming. For some students it may be desirable to offer a self-contained classroom, while for others a special resource room may be more beneficial because the teacher can act as a liaison between the regular education teacher, counselor, student, and parent. The school also may offer a variety of specially designed courses for students with learning problems. Lerner holds that resource room teachers in high school must be familiar with the entire curriculum of the school to be successful in remediating and programming for exceptional students. This familiarity would enable the teacher to assist the students in a variety of courses rather than in the remediation of specific academic skills. Remediation must be tied closely to what happens in the mainstream classroom.

Goodman and Mann proposed a different model in 1976. They theorized a basic education program at the secondary level that restricts the activities of the teacher to instruction of mathematics and language arts. Enrollment of students would be limited to those who lacked sixth-grade achievement. The goal for the secondary teacher in special education would be to remediate students to a sixth-grade level to allow for mainstreaming into regular education classes.

Program options, in fact, lie somewhere between the two extremes, with decisions regarding the thrust of programming often dictated by local custom and philosophy. The main objective should be to provide a system of instruction that reduces the complexity without sacrificing quality. A carefully balanced program should include the provision for specific remediation as well as assistance in addressing course work through the accommodation of individual needs. Equal opportunity should allow each student to ben-efit from academic training and career education to the fullest extent possible. Insufficiency in reading should not deny a student the opportunity to participate and learn in an academic class; nor should it limit the student to training that leads to entry-level skills in low-status jobs. The verbal bias evidenced in the instruction of many schools should not limit the pursuits of intelligent but inefficient learners.

REFERENCES

Goodman, L., & Mann, L. (1976). *Learning disabilities in the secondary school.* New York: Grune & Stratton.

Lerner, J. W. (1976). *Children with learning disabilities* (2nd ed.). Boston: Houghton Mifflin.

Marsh, G. E., Gearheart, C., & Gearheart, B. (1978). *The learning disabled adolescent.* St. Louis, MO: Mosby.

Scranton, T., & Downs, M. (1975). Elementary and secondary learning disabilities programs in the U.S.: A survey. *Journal of Learning Disabilities, 8*(6), 394–399.

Ysseldyke, J. E., & Algozzine, B. (1984). *Introduction to special education.* Boston: Houghton Mifflin.

CRAIG D. SMITH
Georgia College

RESOURCE ROOM
RESOURCE TEACHER

SECTION 504 OF THE 1973 REHABILITATION ACT

See REHABILITATION ACT OF 1973.

SEEING EYE DOGS

See ANIMALS FOR INDIVIDUALS WITH DISABILITIES; DOG GUIDES FOR THE BLIND.

SEGUIN, EDOUARD (1812–1880)

Edouard Seguin, who demonstrated to the world that mentally retarded individuals can be educated, studied medicine under Jean Marc Gaspard Itard in Paris, and applied the training methods of that famous physician and teacher to the education of the mentally retarded. In 1837 Seguin established the first school in France for the mentally retarded, with remarkable success. In 1848 he moved to the United States, where he practiced medicine, served as director of the Pennsylvania Training School, and acted as adviser to numerous state institutions. He was a founder and first president of the Association of Medical Officers of American Institutions for Idiotic and Feeble-Minded Persons, now the American Association on Mental Retardation.

Seguin's methods, which provided the foundation for the movement for the education of the mentally retarded in the United States, were based on a number of principles: that observation of the child is the foundation of the child's education; that education deals with the whole child; that the child learns best from real things; that perceptual training should precede training for concept development; and that even the most defective child has some capacity for learning. Seguin incorporated art, music, and gymnastics into the educational program, and emphasized the use of concrete materials in the classroom.

Seguin's influence on the early development of special education services can hardly be overstated. Samuel Gridley Howe, who was responsible for the formation of the first state school for mentally retarded children in the United States, obtained much of his methodology directly from Seguin. Maria Montessori gave credit to Seguin for the principles on which she based her system of education. Today, more than a century after his death. Seguin's influence is evident in the methods being used to instruct children with learning disabilities.

REFERENCES

Kanner, L. (1960). Itard, Seguin, Howe—Three pioneers in the education of retarded children. *American Journal of Mental Deficiency, 65*, 2–10.

Seguin, E. (1907). *Idiocy and its treatment by the physiological method.* New York: Teachers College.

Talbot, E. *Edouard Seguin: A study of an educational approach to the treatment of mentally defective children.* New York: Teachers College.

PAUL IRVINE
Katonah, New York

SEIZURE DISORDERS

Seizures are relatively common in children and are the most common basis for a referral to a pediatric neurologist (Haslam, 1996). A seizure is a "paroxysmal involuntary disturbance of brain function that may manifest in an impairment or loss of consciousness, abnormal motor activity, behavioral abnormalities, sensory disturbances, or autonomic dysfunction" (Haslam, 1996, p. 1686). In many cases, seizures can be directly related to head trauma resulting from brain injury or high fever. Approximately 8 percent of children can be expected to have at least one seizure before adolescence (Brown, 1997). Epilepsy may be diagnosed only in an individual who has a series of seizures. Although de-

scriptions of childhood seizures by parents and others may be very helpful in diagnosis, some different seizures (for example, absence and complex partial) may present almost identically in different individuals. Thus, EEG records are an important aspect of diagnosis (Haslam, 1996). Seizure disorders frequently occur in association with more severe degrees of mental retardation and cerebral palsy.

Classification of Seizures

The International Classification of Seizures divides seizures into two major categories: partial and generalized. Partial seizures begin in unilateral (focal or local) areas and may or may not spread bilaterally. Generalized seizures begin with immediate involvement of bilateral brain structures and are associated with either bilateral motor movements, changes in consciousness, or both.

Partial Seizures

Partial seizures are divided into: (1) simple partial attacks that arise from a local area and do not impair consciousness and (2) complex partial attacks that begin in a local area but spread bilaterally and therefore impair consciousness. They are the most common type of seizure disorder, accounting for 40–60 percent of all childhood seizures (Brown, 1997; Haslam, 1996). In simple partial types, consciousness is unimpaired; in complex partial types, degree of altered awareness or unresponsiveness is involved.

Simple partial seizures often exhibit primary neurologic symptoms that indicate the site of origin. Partial seizures involve motor activity from any portion of the body. They usually involve the limbs, face, or head, and sometimes cause speech arrest. Hallucinations and visual illusions may occur, depending on the site of the seizure. Partial seizures that progress with sequential involvement of parts of the body that are represented in contiguous cortical areas are termed Jacksonian. Benign rolandic epilepsy is common and may result in the child awakening from sleep and showing motor symptoms. Localized paralysis or weakness that may last for minutes or days sometimes occurs and indicates an underlying structural lesion. Partial motor seizures also can be continuous for extended periods of time.

Complex partial seizures, previously called psychomotor or temporal lobe seizures, are the most common shown in older children and adolescents and occur in over 50 percent of adults with seizure disorders. The seizures characteristically begin with emotional, psychic, illusory, hallucinatory, or special sensory symptoms. Sometimes, consciousness becomes impaired at the onset of the attack. After the aura, the individual becomes completely or partially unresponsive and may perform apparently purposeful activity. The seizure consists of involuntary motor movements such as eye blinking, lip smacking, facial grimaces, groaning, chewing and other automatisms, but more elaborate behavior can occur. In the state of depressed awareness, patients may actively resist efforts to restrain them. A complete attack usually lasts between 1 and 3 minutes; on recovery, there is complete amnesia for the attack except for the aura or partial motor onset. Complex partial seizures usually begin in the temporal lobe but may originate from the frontal, parietal, or occipital regions.

Generalized Seizures

Generalized seizures involve bilateral brain regions and begin with immediate involvement of both hemispheres. Five types are recognized; (1) absence seizures with associated 3-Hz (cycles per second) generalized spike-and-wave discharges in the electroencephalogram (EEG); (2) atypical absence seizures; (3) myoclonic seizures; (4) tonic-clonic seizures; and (5) atonic seizures.

Absence seizures are not as common as other types of seizures, and account for only 5 percent of all seizure disorders. These seizures are short interruptions of consciousness that last from 3 to 15 seconds each. They are not associated with auras or other evidence of focal onset. Absence seizures begin and end abruptly and recur from a few to several hundred times per day. Ongoing behavior stops. While otherwise immobile, the individual may show inconspicuous flickering of the eyelids or eyebrows about three times per second; there may be simple automatic movements, such as rubbing the nose, putting a hand to the face, or chewing and swallowing. Falling does not occur because of the ability to retain muscle tone. Immediately following the short interruption of awareness, the individual is again mentally clear and fully capable of continuing previous activity. Patients with absence seizures of this type show bilaterally synchronous 3 Hz spike-and-wave discharges, usually occurring against an otherwise normal background activity. The age of onset of these short absence seizures is almost always after age 2; they almost never occur for the first time after age 20. Individuals with short absence seizures rarely have other neurological problems, but 40 percent to 50 percent of the patients have infrequent, easily controlled, generalized tonic-clonic seizures. Photic sensitivity is present in some cases.

Generalized tonic-clonic seizures occur at some time in most patients with seizure disorder regardless of the individual's usual pattern. This type of seizure can be triggered by many various events (e.g., fever, CNS infection, brain abnormality, and hereditary tendency) and also is commonly seen in childhood seizure disorders. A tonic-clonic seizure is classified under generalized seizures if the attack itself, the neurological examination, and the EEG all indicate that bilateral cerebral structures are simultaneously involved at the onset. A tonic-clonic seizure is classified as a partial seizure evolving to a secondarily generalized one if the same criteria indicate that the attack began in one hemisphere and then spread to produce a major generalized attack. Tonic-clonic convulsions usually last 3 to 5 minutes, and are characterized by a complex loss of consciousness and falling. As the patient falls, the body stiffens because of generalized tonic contraction of the limb and axial muscles. The legs usually extend and the arms flex partially. After the tonic stage, which usually lasts less than 1 minute, jerking or clonic movements occur in all four limbs for about 1 minute. Next, a period of unconsciousness follows (about 1 minute) during which the patient appears more relaxed. Consciousness then is regained and the patient usually is confused, sleepy, and uncooperative for several minutes prior to full recovery.

Atypical absence seizures generally result in blank stares that can last longer than the typical absence seizure. Atypical absence seizures are often associated with various types of seizure patterns including tonic-clonic, myoclonic, and atonic seizures. Atonic seizures usually begin in childhood and are characterized by sudden loss of postural tone which can cause slumping, a head drop, and even sometimes resulting in abrupt drops to the floor. These episodes occur without warning, are extremely short, and frequently cause injury. Myoclonic seizures are involuntary contractions of the limb and truncal muscles that are sudden, brief, and recurrent. Slight bilateral symmetric myoclonic movements often occur in persons who have absence seizures, but rarely are severe bilaterally symmetric myoclonic jerks the predominant symptoms of individuals with absence seizures.

Treatment

Seizure disorders can typically be treated with antiepileptic drugs (AEDs). In treating seizures, it is initially important to identify and eliminate factors that potentially cause or precipitate the attacks. Different medications are used for various types of seizures. Medications are used until seizure control is achieved or until toxic side effects limit further increments. In more severe cases, when pharmacological treatments prove completely ineffective, surgery is often the only alternative. Removing lesions or tumors from the brain is often risky and later impairs cognitive functioning. The anterior portion of the temporal lobe is the most frequent site of surgical excision in individuals with medically intractable seizures.

General Concerns

People, particularly children, with seizure disorders frequently and understandably are often fearful and feel that they have relatively little control. In addition to medical management, parents and children may need counseling. Rarely are any special restrictions on activity needed except during swimming and bathing, and parents should be encouraged to allow their children to behave as normally as possible.

An excellent source for further information is the Epilepsy

Foundation of America, 4351 Garden City Drive, Landover, MD 20785; phone: (800) EFA-1000; email: webmaster@efa.org; and web site: http://www.efa.org/index.html.

REFERENCES

Brown, L. W. (1997). Seizure disorders. In M. L. Batshaw (Ed.), *Children with disabilities* (4th ed., pp. 553–593). Baltimore: Brookes.

Haslam, R. H. A. (1996). Seizures in childhood. In R. E. Behrman, R. M. Kliegman, & A. M. Arvin (Eds.), *Nelson textbook of pediatrics* (15th ed., pp. 1686–1699).

ROBERT T. BROWN
AIMEE R. HUNTER
University of North Carolina at Wilmington

ABSENCE SEIZURES
CHRONIC ILLNESS IN CHILDREN

SELECTIVE MUTISM

Selective mutism is a psychological disorder of childhood characterized by total and persistent lack of speech in at least one specific environment (such as the classroom), despite the presence of normal speech in other environments. The child is physically capable of producing normal speech and understands the language being spoken. Further criteria for a diagnosis of selective mutism according to the *Diagnostic and Statistical Manual of Mental Disorders,* fourth edition, text revision (*DSM-IV-TR;* American Psychiatric Association, 2000) are: the interference with social communication or with educational or occupational achievement; the persistence of the disturbance for at least 1 month, not limited to the first month of school; the ability of the child to comfortably understand and produce the language being spoken; and the exclusion of another communication disorder (such as poor articulation), which causes the child embarrassment in speaking, or the presence of a Pervasive Developmental Disorder, Schizophrenia, or other Psychotic Disorder.

In the late nineteenth century in Germany, Kussmaul coined the term *aphasia voluntaria* to describe a condition in which individuals refused to speak in certain situations, despite the ability to speak normally in others (Dow, Sonies, Scheib, Moss, & Leonard, 1995). Tramer named the disorder "elective mutism" in 1934, with the belief that the child was "electing" when and where to speak. The current term, "selective mutism," is a reflection of new theories of etiology that deemphasize oppositional behaviors (Dow et al., 1995) and emphasize that the behavior is selectively dependent on social context (Dummit et al., 1997). Selective mutism has been found in various countries throughout the world, including Israel, Great Britain, Switzerland, Canada, France,

Japan, and the United States (Barowsky, 1999). Selective mutism typically develops during the preschool years and can persist through adolescence, although it is usually more transient (Carlson, Kratochwill, & Johnston, 1994) and lasts only for several months (Kehle, Hintze, & DuPaul, 1997). The longer selective mutism persists, the more debilitating it can become (Kehle et al., 1997). It is more common among girls than boys, and is seen across all social strata (Steinhausen & Juzi, 1996) and intellectual ability levels (Kehle et al., 1997). This disorder is relatively rare, although estimates of prevalence have been inconclusive (Carlson et al., 1992; Haeberli & Kratochwill, 2005). Bergman, Piacentini, and McCracken (2002) found the prevalence to be .71 percent in a public school sample. In a comparison of native-born versus immigrant children, selective mutism was found in less than 1 per 1,000 native-born children and 7.9 per 1,000 immigrant children (Dummit et al., 1997).

The etiology of selective mutism is uncertain. A recent shift in speculation as to its etiology deemphasizes its precipitation by a traumatic event (such as sexual abuse or hospitalization) or its possible expression of oppositional behavior, and instead concentrates on familial history and the presence of an underlying anxiety disorder. Some researchers have suggested that selective mutism be considered a behavioral manifestation of a Social Anxiety Disorder (Black & Uhde, 1995; Dummit et al., 1997; Yeganeh, Beidel, Turner, Pina, & Silverman, 2003). Kristensen (1999) found that selective mutism is associated with developmental delay almost as frequently as with anxiety disorders, suggesting a neurobiological etiology for the disorder. In contrast, the learning-theory approach suggests that selective mutism is a learned behavior maintained by social reinforcement, whereas the psychoanalytic approach suggests that selective mutism functions to reduce a child's fear in anxiety-provoking situations through unresponsiveness (Kehle et al., 1997). The following factors have been found to elevate the risk of selective mutism: a background of migration; early developmental risk factors, including complications during pregnancy and delivery; delayed motor development and toilet training; premorbid speech and language disorders (most commonly articulation and expressive language disorders); behavioral abnormalities during infancy and preschool ages (such as relationship problems, separation anxiety, sleep disorders, and eating disorders); comorbid diagnoses (typically enuresis but also including sleeping and eating disorders); and a pattern of social interactions that include withdrawal, anxiety, depression, and schizoid type behaviors (Steinhausen & Juzi, 1996). In addition, a family history of selective mutism, extreme shyness, and/or anxiety disorders may put the child at risk (Dow et al., 1995).

In order to assess selective mutism, the clinician should conduct a comprehensive assessment in order to rule out other possible explanations for the mutism and to evaluate comorbid conditions. The assessment should include: a structured diagnostic interview with the parent(s) with a review of academic, familial, and medical history; a formal evaluation of speech and language ability; an interview with the child, in which the child has the opportunity to respond nonverbally; a medical examination; auditory testing; standardized psychological testing; and a recorded audiotape of the child speaking at home (Dow et al., 1995).

Possibly because of the low incidence of this disorder, successful treatment protocols have not been extensively studied. Selective mutism has been shown to be highly resistant to treatment (Kehle et al., 1997). Psychotherapy is the most common form of intervention, including cognitive and cognitive-behavioral approaches. However, behavioral approaches have been found to be the most effective strategies to use in the treatment of children with selective mutism (Kehle et al., 1997). Behavioral strategies shown to be effective with these children include contingency management programs, stimulus-fading, shaping, escape-avoidance techniques, and self-modeling (Kehle et al., 1997). Barowsky (1999) has described a systematic desensitization, or stimulus-fading, approach. It consists of four phases: Initially the parent engages the child in conversation within the school setting, with the assumption that the child is most comfortable in talking with the parent. In the second phase, the teacher is included as a passive participant who gradually and unobtrusively increases his or her proximity to the child and parent as they converse. Then, in the third phase, the teacher asks the child questions with the parent as intermediary. Finally, in the fourth phase, the teacher and child interact in the presence of a small number of children.

As selective mutism has been redefined as a biologically influenced social phobia, clinicians have increasingly employed medication to treat it. Selectively mute children have made significant improvement after a 12-week trial of fluoxetine in a placebo-controlled, parallel design study (Black & Uhde, 1994), lending support to the placement of selective mutism as a variant of social anxiety, which is also successfully treated with fluoxetine. A trial of medication should be considered if anxiety is a prominent feature and/or if other treatment attempts have failed. Medication alone or in combination with learning-theory approaches has been found to be effective in the treatment of selective mutism in children (Kehle et al., 1997).

Speech therapy has also been successfully used to treat selective mutism, with a focus on articulation and language training, rather than on the psychological aspects of the mutism (Dow et al., 1995). If a selective mute child is insecure about the sound of his or her voice or pronunciation skills, the speech language pathologist can help him or her perfect pronunciation, learn pragmatic skills, and increase comprehension.

The school psychologist can help implement an individualized, school-based multidisciplinary treatment plan by coordinating efforts of parents, clinicians, and teachers. The goal of such a plan is to decrease the anxiety associated with speaking in the school environment and increasing normal interaction and communication.

REFERENCES

American Psychiatric Association. (2000). *Diagnostic and statistical manual of mental disorders* (4th ed., text rev.). Washington, DC: Author.

Barowsky, E. I. (1999). Elective mutism. In C. R. Reynolds & T. B. Gutkin (Eds.), *Handbook of school psychology* (3rd ed., pp. 674–676). New York: Wiley.

Bergman, R. L., Piacentini, J., & McCracken, J. T. (2002). Prevalence and description of selective mutism in a school-based sample. *Journal of the American Academy of Child and Adolescent Psychiatry, 41,* 938–946.

Black, B., & Uhde, T. W. (1994). Treatment of elective mutism with fluoxetine: A double-blind, placebo-controlled study. *Journal of the American Academy of Child and Adolescent Psychiatry, 33,* 1000–1006.

Black, B., & Uhde, T. W. (1995). Psychiatric characteristics of children with selective mutism: A pilot study. *Journal of the American Academy of Child and Adolescent Psychiatry, 34,* 847–856.

Carlson, J. S., Kratochwill, T. R., & Johnston, H. (1994). Prevalence and treatment of selective mutism in clinical practice: A survey of child and adolescent psychiatrists. *Journal of Child and Adolescent Psychopharmacology, 4,* 281–291.

Dow, S. P., Sonies, B. C., Scheib, D., Moss, S. E., & Leonard, H. L. (1995). Practical guidelines for the assessment and treatment of selective mutism. *Journal of the American Academy of Child and Adolescent Psychiatry, 34,* 836–846.

Dummit, E. S., Klein, R. G., Tancer, N. K., Asche, B., Martin, J., & Fairbanks, J. A. (1997). Systematic assessment of 50 children with selective mutism. *Journal of the American Academy of Child and Adolescent Psychiatry, 36,* 653–660.

Haerberli, F., & Kratochwill, T. R. (2005). Selective mutism. In S. W. Lee & P. A. Lowe (Eds.), *Encyclopedia of school psychology* (pp. 489–490). Thousand Oaks, CA: Sage.

Kehle, T. J., Hintze, J. M., & DuPaul, G. J. (1997). Selective mutism. In G. G. Bear, K. M. Minke, & A. Thomas (Eds.), *Children's needs II: Development, problems and alternatives* (pp. 329–337). Washington, DC: National Association of School Psychologists.

Kristensen, H. (1999). Selective mutism and comorbidity with developmental disorder/delay, anxiety disorder, and elimination disorder. *Journal of the American Academy of Child and Adolescent Psychiatry, 39,* 249–256.

Steinhausen, H., & Juzi, C. (1996). Elective mutism: An analysis of 100 cases. *Journal of the American Academy of Child and Adolescent Psychiatry, 35,* 606–614.

Yeganeh, R., Beidel, D. C., Turner, S. M., Pina, A. A., & Silverman, W. K. (2003). Clinical distinctions between selective mutism and social phobia: An investigation of childhood psychopathology. *Journal of the American Academy of Child and Adolescent Psychiatry, 42,* 1069–1075.

SUSAN M. UNRUH
PATRICIA A. LOWE
University of Kansas

SELF-CARE SKILLS

See SELF-HELP TRAINING.

SELF-CONCEPT

Self-concept is an individual's evaluation of his or her own abilities and attributes. It includes all aspects of an individual's personality of which he or she is aware. Although some authors have drawn distinctions between self-concept and self-esteem (Damon & Hart, 1982), the terms are frequently used interchangeably. Several theoretical models of self-concept exist in the literature. For example, Coopersmith (1967) has suggested that four factors contribute to an individual's self-concept: significance (feeling of being loved and approved of by important others), competence (ability to perform tasks considered important), virtue (adherence to moral and ethical principles), and power (the degree to which an individual is able to exert control over self and others). Harter (1982) found that self-concept can be broken down into three specific components: cognitive, social, and physical competence, and a general self-worth factor.

Children with a positive self-concept are described as imaginative, confident in their own judgments and abilities, assertive, able to assume leadership roles, less preoccupied with themselves, and able to devote more time to others and to external activities. Children with a negative self-concept are described as quiet, unobtrusive, unoriginal, lacking in initiative, withdrawn, and doubtful about themselves (Coopersmith, 1967). School progress and academic achievement are influenced by self-concept, as is vocational choice. Unfortunately, much of the research on the effects of self-esteem has been subject to methodological and theoretical criticism (Damon & Hart, 1982; Wylie, 1979).

Self-concept begins to develop early in life, with children as young as 18 to 24 months able to discriminate between self and others (Lewis & Brooks-Gunn, 1979). As children's thought processes become less concrete and more abstract, there are corresponding changes in self-concept. Younger children (e.g., 9 year olds) tend to describe themselves in categorical terms (name, age, gender, physical attributes, etc.), while older children take an increasingly abstract view, describing their personal and interpersonal traits, attitudes, and beliefs (Montemayor & Eisen, 1977). There is not, however, any consistent evidence of age-related changes in the level of self-esteem (how positively or negatively one views oneself). The one exception to this is a temporary decline in self-esteem around the time children enter their teens (Simmons et al., 1979).

A number of factors influence an individual's self-concept. Parents appear to play a particularly important role (Cooper-smith, 1967). Children with high self-esteem tend to have parents who themselves have high self-esteem and who are warm, nurturing, and accepting of their children while setting high academic and behavioral standards. They set and enforce strict limits on their children and are fair, reasonable, and consistent in their use of discipline. Parents of low self-esteem children alternate unpredictably between excessive permissiveness and harsh punishment. A close relationship with the same-sex parent is typical among high self-esteem children. Findings of higher self-esteem in only children and first-born children suggest that parental attention is important. Other factors associated with high self-esteem include academic success, the presence of a close friendship, and the perceived opinions of others. Physical attractiveness and height are unrelated to self-esteem (Coopersmith, 1967). It is very important for educators to remember that different ethnic groups perceive self-concept and its measurement in different ways (Obiakor, 1992).

Historically instruments with a singular focus was used to measure self-concept: the Piers-Harris Children's Self-Concept Scale (Piers, 1969), the Coopersmith Self-Esteem Inventory (Coopersmith, 1967), the Perceived Competence Scale for Children (Harter, 1982), and the Preschool and Primary Self-Concept Scale (Stager & Young, 1982). Omnibus scales such as the Behavior Assessment System for Children, 2nd edition (Reynolds & Kamphaus, 2004) include scales designed to measure self-esteem in the larger context of personality and behavioral development.

REFERENCES

Coopersmith, S. (1967). *Antecedents of self-esteem*. San Francisco: Freeman.

Damon, W., & Hart, D. (1982). The development of self-understanding from infancy through adolescence. *Child Development, 53,* 841–864.

Harter, S. (1982). The perceived competence scale for children. *Child Development, 53,* 87–97.

Lewis, M., & Brooks-Gunn, J. (1979). *Social cognition and the acquisition of self.* New York: Plenum.

Montemayor, R., & Eisen, M. (1977). The development of self-conceptions from childhood to adolescence. *Developmental Psychology, 13,* 314–319.

Obiakor, F. E. (1992). Self-concept of African-American students: An operational model for special education. *Exceptional Children, 59*(2), 160–167.

Piers, E. V. (1969). *The Piers Harris Children's Self-Concept Scale.* Nashville, TN: Counselor Recordings and Tests.

Reynolds, C. R., & Kamphaus, R. W. (2004). *Behavior assessment system for children, 2nd ed.* Circle Pines, MN: American Guidance Service.

Simmons, R. G., Blyth, D. A., Van Cleave, E. F., & Bush, D. M. (1979). Entry into early adolescence: The impact of school structure, puberty, and early dating on self-esteem. *American Sociological Review, 44,* 948–967.

Stager, S., & Young, R. D. (1982). A self-concept measure for preschool and early primary grade children. *Journal of Personality Assessment, 46,* 536–543.

Wylie, R. C. (1979). *The self-concept: Theory and research on selected topics* (Vol. 2, Rev. ed.). Lincoln: University of Nebraska Press.

ROBERT G. BRUBAKER
Eastern Kentucky University

**DEPRESSION, CHILDHOOD AND ADOLESCENT
EMOTIONAL LABILITY
SELF-MANAGEMENT**

SELF-CONTAINED CLASS

The first self-contained special classes were established in the late 1800s and early 1900s as public school classes for the moderately retarded, deaf, hard of hearing, blind, emotionally disturbed, and physically disabled. Esten (1900) states that special classes for the mentally retarded were established to provide slow learners with more appropriate class placement. A self-contained classroom for students with disabilities can be defined as one that homogeneously segregates different children from nondisabled children. Children are usually segregated along categorical groupings. As a result of Dunn's (1968) article on the detrimental aspects of self-contained placements for the mildly disabled, students receiving special education in self-contained classes today are usually "low-incidence," exhibiting more severe problems. Dunn was later refuted by Walker and McLaughlin (1992). However, Kirk and Gallagher (1983) report gifted students are also grouped into special classes according to interests and abilities.

A self-contained class is a place where special education students spend more than 60 percent of their school day and receive most of their academic instruction. Typically, caseloads are small, ranging from 5 to 10 students in a class. A wide variety of instructional materials are available to the students. The self-contained class provides the opportunity for highly individualized, closely supervised, specialized instruction. The self-contained classroom is usually taught by one trained teacher who is certified according to the categories served. The self-contained classroom may be categorically specific (serving one population) or cross-categorically grouped (serving multicategorical populations).

Major purposes of a self-contained class as outlined by Sabatino, Miller, and Schmidt (1981) include providing the student with the social and personal adjustment skills necessary to promote school success, and maintaining a constant structure within the instructional environment to reduce distractibility, hyperactivity, restlessness, poor attention span, and control over the rate of information flowing to the learner. Additionally, the purposes include teaching the basic academic and social skills necessary for success in life and making cooperative arrangements based on adequate communication with parents (p. 321). It is possible that a student may be assigned to a self-contained classroom and receive additional resource room assistance or partake in inclusive programming. Placement depends on what is best for the students in terms of least restriction. Usually, students are mainstreamed into regular education for nonacademic subjects such as music, physical education, and art, or academic areas of proficiency. Federal special education laws, especially IDEIA, require that children with disabilities be educated in the least restrictive environment.

REFERENCES

Dunn, L. M. (1968). Special education for the mildly handicapped: Is much of it justifiable? *Exceptional Children, 35,* 5–22.

Esten, R. A. (1900). Backward children in the public schools. *Journal of Psychoaesthenics, 5,* 10–16.

Kirk, S. A., & Gallagher, J. J. (1983). *Educating exceptional children* (4th ed.). Boston: Houghton Mifflin.

Sabatino, D. A., Miller, T. L., & Schmidt, C. R. (1981). *Learning disabilities: Systemizing teaching and service delivery.* Rockville, MD: Aspen Systems.

Walker, J. G., & McLaughlin, T. F. (1992). Self-contained versus resource room classroom placement: A review. *Journal of Instructional Psychology, 19*(3), 214–225.

MARIBETH MONTGOMERY KASIK
Governors State University

**LEAST RESTRICTIVE ENVIRONMENT
RESOURCE ROOM
SPECIAL CLASS**

SELF-CONTROL CURRICULUM

The self-control curriculum was a product of the work of Fagen, Long, and Stevens (1975). They contended that emotional and cognitive development are closely related and therefore both need to be addressed simultaneously in the instructional process. They held that learning is impaired when learners have negative feelings about themselves. Fagen et al. believed that in many cases of behavior disorders there was an inability on the part of the individual to exert self-control. The self-control curriculum had as its goals the development of self-control and positive feelings.

There were eight enabling skills in the self-control model. Four of these were in the cognitive area and four in the affective area. The eight skills are:

1. *Selecting.* Paying attention to directions/instruction.

2. *Storing.* Remembering directions/instructions.

3. *Sequencing and ordering.* Organizing materials/work areas to perform work.

4. *Anticipating consequences.* Realizing that behavior has consequences and predicting those consequences.

5. *Appreciating feelings.* Expressing feelings by words and actions.

6. *Managing frustrations.* Behaviorally maintaining control in stressful situations.

7. *Inhibiting and delaying.* Delaying actions and reflecting on consequences of possible actions even when excited.

8. *Relaxing.* Consciously relieving bodily tension.

The curriculum has pupil activities and guidelines for teachers for developing more lessons in each unit. The activities involve games, discussions, and role-playing activities. The position taken in the curriculum was that self-control must be taught just as any other subject. General recommendations throughout the curriculum were to proceed from easy to difficult, to proceed in small steps, to use repetition and provide practice, to make activities enjoyable, reinforce efforts, and provide opportunities to practice skills in new situations and settings. Little research has been conducted in the past to validate the curriculum.

REFERENCE

Fagen, S. A., Long, N. J., & Stevens, D. (1975). *Teaching children self-control.* Columbus, OH: Merrill.

ROBERT A. SEDLAK
University of Wisconsin at Stout

SELF-MONITORING
SOCIAL BEHAVIOR OF INDIVIDUALS WITH DISABILITIES
SOCIAL SKILLS INSTRUCTION

SELF-DETERMINATION

The concept of self-determination has had a long history in political science, religion, philosophy, and more recently in psychology and special education. Mencius, a Confucian scholar in 371–289 BCE, believed that common people were equal to kings and that the state should express the will of the people (Simpkins & Simpkins, 2000). The philosopher John Locke believed that men direct their own lives (Locke, 1715). African slaves in America viewed self-determination as the control that people have over their own destiny (Franklin, 1984). Mithaug, Martin, and Agran (1987), with

their Adaptability Model, began the conversation about self-determination in special education. They suggested that students with disabilities learn self-regulatory skills to adjust to change as a means of being successful in school and to make a meaningful transition to life after graduation from school. Ward (1988) formalized the introduction of the term self-determination into special education when he claimed that self-determination is the ability for students with disabilities to choose and attain their own goals. This history produced today's macro and micro view of self-determination (Martin, Marshall, & De Pry, 2005). Macro self-determination involves groups of people joining together to self-govern rather than being dominated by a dictator or ruthless ruler. Micro self-determination refers to individuals learning to direct their own lives by choosing and attaining their goals. Special education focuses upon micro-level self-determination issues and instructional strategies.

Self-determined students define and achieve their goals from knowing and valuing themselves (Field & Hoffman, 1994). The Self-Determined Learning Model believes that once students choose a goal, self-determined students will use self-management strategies to help attain their goals, and make adjustments in their environment, strategies, or supports to attain their goals (Wehmeyer, Palmer, Agran, Mithaug, & Martin, 2000). Self-determined learning theory (Mithaug, Mithaug, Agran, Martin, & Wehmeyer, 2003) postulates that learning is adjustment, and that students learn when an impediment blocks their goal attainment attempts and they need to make adjustments to attain their goals. Martin and Marshall (1995) believe that self-determined students set goals for themselves based on an understanding of their interests, skills, and limits. They then develop a plan to accomplish their goals, implement the plan, self-evaluate their performance, and make needed adjustments to their goals, strategies, or support. To enable students to do this Martin and Marshall (1995) identified seven self-determination constructs that students need to learn: (1) self-awareness, (2) self-advocacy, (3) self-efficacy, (4) decision making, (5) independent performance, (6) self-evaluation, and (7) adjustment.

Wehmeyer and Palmer (2003) found that former high school students with higher levels of self-determination skills had more positive post-school outcomes. Martin et al. (2003) demonstrated that increased use of self-determination skills resulted in improved class behavior, goal attainment, and academic performance. Janzen (2005) discovered that college freshmen that returned to school after their first semester had significantly higher self-determination levels than those who dropped out.

Several self-determination research-based instructional programs and strategies provide teachers the tools needed to increase the opportunities for students to become more self-determined (Trainor, 2005). These include *Steps to Self-Determination* (Hoffman & Field, 2005), the ChoiceMaker lesson packages (Martin et al., 2005), which include the

Self-Directed IEP (Martin, Marshall, Maxson, & Jerman, 1996), and *Take Action: Making Goals Happen* (Marshall et al., 1999). The *Self-Directed IEP,* for example, increased student participation in their secondary IEP meetings and increased students' level of self-determination (Martin et al., in press). *Take Action* taught students the skills needed to attain their own goals (German, Martin, Marshall, & Sale, 2000). Self-determination contracts enable students with disabilities to attain academic goals (Martin et al., 2003; Mithaug & Mithaug, 2003), and improve vocational performance (Woods & Martin, 2004). Self-determined individuals will use a variety of self-directed instructional strategies to attain self-selected goals, including self-instruction and self-evaluation (Agran, King-Sears, Wehmeyer, & Copeland, 2003).

Students' cultural decision-making identity may impact the viability of self-determination practices such as student-directed transition planning (Trainor, 2005; Valenzuela & Martin, 2005). Student-directed planning and goal attainment that emphasizes individualization may negatively impact collaborative planning with students and their families who view decision making from a collectivist perspective. This issue seems especially relevant to students and families from culturally and linguistically diverse backgrounds, where student goal attainment may reflect family or community needs and interests. Educators need to understand student and family decision-making orientation to successfully collaborate with educational planning and student goal attainment (Valenzuela & Martin).

Since the introduction of the Adaptability Model in 1997, much progress has been made in understanding self-determination. Self-determination powers secondary transition models and practice (Field, Martin, Miller, Ward, & Wehmeyer, 1998); its influence is starting to impact instruction for younger students as well (Palmer & Wehmeyer, 2003), and recommendations for building-level reforms that promote self-determination are emerging (Field & Hoffman, 2002). Yet, much remains to be done to fully understand the effectiveness of self-determination methodology and how to reach widespread implementation.

REFERENCES

Agran, M., King-Sears, M. E., Wehmeyer, M. L., & Copeland, S. R. (2003). *Student-directed learning.* Baltimore. Brookes.

Field, S., & Hoffman, A. (1994). Development of a model for self-determination. *Career Development for Exceptional Individuals, 17,* 159–169.

Field, S., & Hoffman, A. (2002). Preparing youth to exercise self-determination: Quality indicators of school environments that promote acquisition of knowledge, skills, and beliefs related to self-determination. *Journal of Disability Policy Studies, 13,* 113–118.

Field, S. S., Martin, J. E., Miller, R. J., Ward, M., & Wehmeyer, M. (1998). Self-determination for persons with disabilities: A position statement of the Division on Career Development and Transition. *Career Development for Exceptional Individuals, 21,* 113–128.

Franklin, V. P. (1984). *Black self-determination a cultural history of the faith of the fathers.* Connecticut: Lawrence Hill.

German, S. L., Martin, J. E., Marshall, L., & Sale, R. P. (2000). Promoting self-determination: Using Take Action to teach goal attainment. *Career Development for Exceptional Individuals, 23,* 27–38.

Hoffman, A., & Field, S. (2005). *Steps to self-determination: A curriculum to help adolescents learn to achieve their goals* (2nd ed.). Austin, TX: PRO-ED.

Janzen, A. (2005). *The Relationship between Self-Determination and Retention of College Freshmen.* Unpublished master's thesis, University of Oklahoma, Norman.

Locke, J. (1715). *An essay concerning human understanding.* Retrieved September 27, 2005, from http://oregonstate.edu/instruct/phl302/texts/locke/locke1/Book4b.html

Marshall, L. H., Martin, J. E., Maxson, L. M., Miller, T. L., McGill, T., Hughes, W. M., & Jerman, P. A. (1999). *Take Action.* Longmont, CO: Sopris West.

Martin, J. E., & Marshall, L. H. (1995). ChoiceMaker: A comprehensive self-determination transition program. *Intervention in School and Clinic, 30,* 147–156.

Martin, J. E., Marshall, L. H., & DePry, R. L. (2005). Participatory decision-making: Innovative practices that increase student self-determination. In R. W. Flexer, T. J. Simmons, P. Luft, & R. M. Baer (Eds.), *Transition planning for secondary students with disabilities* (2nd ed., pp. 304–332). Columbus, OH: Merrill Prentice Hall.

Martin, J. E., Marshall, L. H., Maxson, L. M., & Jerman, P. L. (1996). *The Self-Directed IEP.* Longmont, CO: Sopris West.

Martin, J. E., Mithaug, D. E., Cox, P., Peterson, L. Y., Van Dycke, J. L., & Cash, M. E. (2003). Increasing self-determination: Teaching students to plan, work, evaluate, and adjust. *Exceptional Children, 69,* 431–447.

Martin, J. E., Van Dycke, J. L., Christensen, W. R., Greene, B. A., Gardner, J. E., & Lovett, D. L. (in press). Increasing student participation in their transition IEP meetings: Establishing the self-directed IEP as an evidenced-based practice. *Exceptional Children.*

Mithaug, D. E., Martin, J. E., & Agran, M. (1987). Adaptability instruction: The goal of transitional programs. *Exceptional Children, 53,* 500–505.

Mithaug, D. K., & Mithaug, D. E. (2003). The effects of choice opportunities and self-regulation training on the self-engagement and learning of young children with disabilities. In D. E. Mithaug, D. Mithaug, M. Agran, J. E. Martin, & M. Wehmeyer (Eds.), *Self-determined learning theory: Predictions, prescriptions, and practice* (pp. 141–157). Mahwah, NJ: Erlbaum.

Mithaug, D. E., Mithaug, D., Agran, M., Martin, J. E., & Wehmeyer, M. (2003). *Self-determined learning theory: Predictions, prescriptions, and practice.* Mahwah, NJ: Erlbaum.

Palmer, S. B., & Wehmeyer, M. L. (2003). Promoting self-determination in early elementary school. *Remedial and Special Education, 24,* 115–126.

Simpklins, C. R., & Simpklins, A. (2000). *Simple Confucianism: A guide to living virtuously.* Boston: Tuttle.

Trainor, A. A. (2005). Self-determination perceptions and behaviors of diverse students with LD during the transition planning process. *Journal of Learning Disabilities, 38*, 233–249.

Ward, M. J. (1988). The many facets of self-determination. *National Information Center for Children and Youth with Handicaps: Transition Summary, 5*, 2–3.

Valenzuela, R. L., & Martin, J. E. (2005). The Self-Directed IEP: Bridging values of diverse cultures and secondary education. *Career Development for Exceptional Individuals, 28*, 4–14.

Wehmeyer, M. L., & Palmer, S. B. (2003). Adult outcomes for students with cognitive disabilities three years after high school: The impact of self-determination. *Education and Training in Developmental Disabilities, 38*, 131–144.

Wehmeyer, M. L., Palmer, S. B., Agran, M., Mithaug, D. E., & Martin, J. E. (2000). Promoting casual agency: The self-determined learning model of instruction. *Exceptional Children, 66*, 439–453.

Woods, L. L., & Martin, J. E. (2004). Improving supervisor evaluation through the use of self-determination contracts. *Career Development for Exceptional Individuals, 27*, 207–220.

JAMES E. MARTIN
University of Oklahoma

ADAPTIVE BEHAVIOR
SELF-HELP TRAINING

SELF-FULFILLING PROPHECY

See PYGMALION EFFECT.

SELF-HELP TRAINING

The skill areas typically included under the domain of self-help are toileting, eating, dressing, and personal hygiene. An obvious reason for training the developmentally disabled in these skills is that there are widespread self-help skill deficits among this population. Another reason is that the acquisition of these skills represents a critical step in the developmental process and can increase self-esteem, promote positive social interaction, and maintain physical health and well-being (Kimm, Falvey, Bishop, & Rosenberg, 1995). Once the skills are acquired, the caregiver's time devoted to the routine maintenance of the developmentally disabled person is reduced. The acquisition of self-help skills can have meaningful social consequences. It can increase the possibility of gaining access to valued places and activities.

Probably the most significant development in the training of self-help skills is the application of behavior modification procedures. This has been referred to as one of the most influential factors in improving the care and training of the developmentally disabled in the last 30 years (Whitman, Sciback, & Reid, 1983).

Research in each of the self-help skill training areas has undergone a similar developmental sequence (Reid, Wilson, & Faw, 1980). Early research demonstrated that caregivers, after receiving in-service training, could train a number of developmentally disabled individuals in self-help skills. Even though this research lacked experimental rigor, it did show the usefulness of behavior modification and stimulated further research. Contemporary research has focused on individual skills and has been more methodologically rigorous. There has also been an effort by Azrin et al. (Azrin & Fox, 1971; Azrin & Armstrong, 1973; Azrin, Schaeffer, & Wesolowski, 1976) to develop an intensive training approach that is more comprehensive than previous approaches. Intensive training is intended to produce rapid learning that is resistant to extinction.

Each self-help skill area has some unique characteristics that have affected the direction of research and training in that particular area (Reid et al., 1980). Training in independent toileting has become more complex and focuses on a more naturally occurring sequence of toilet behaviors. Automatic devices are being used to signal trainers when a trainee is about to have a toileting accident or has eliminated into the toilet. Nighttime toileting skills have also been trained to reduce the frequency of enuresis (bed wetting).

It is believed that training independent eating through behavior modification procedures has been relatively successful because food is an inherent reinforcer. In addition to focusing on the acquisition of independent eating skills, researchers and practitioners have attempted to eliminate or reduce inappropriate mealtime behaviors (e.g., eating too quickly and stealing food).

As in training eating skills, dressing has focused on acquisition of appropriate skills and the reduction of inappropriate behaviors (e.g., public disrobing). The generalization of dressing skills to other contexts has been an issue when developing training programs because training typically occurs when dressing is not naturally required. Maintenance over time has also been an important training issue because dressing is less inherently reinforcing than toileting and eating.

It is unusual that little research has been conducted on personal hygiene skills considering their importance in improving independent functioning and helping the developmentally disabled to gain community acceptance. A development in training personal hygiene skills is a packaged approach called independence training (Matson, DiLorenzo, & Esveldt-Dawson, 1981). This approach expands on the typical behavioral training strategy by having trainees evaluate their own progress (self-monitor) and give each other feedback.

There are several areas of concern for future research and practice (Whitman et al., 1983). Often there is a discrepancy between the development of an effective training technology and its day-to-day application by caregivers. Consequently, it is important to understand what factors contribute to caregivers' willingness to carry out training. A component analysis of the multifaceted training strategies, like the intensive training package, could assist practitioners in selecting the most effective and efficient training. As increasing numbers of developmentally disabled people live and work in the community, it will be necessary to train more advanced and complex skills in community contexts. It will also be necessary to determine the social validity of certain self-help skills, particularly in the areas of dressing and personal hygiene. By assessing social validity, practitioners will know what to teach in order to bring a skill into a socially acceptable range. Finally, effective and practical self-help training procedures need to be developed for the physically disabled.

REFERENCES

Azrin, N. H., & Armstrong, P. M. (1973). The "mini-meal." A method for teaching eating skills to the profoundly retarded. *Mental Retardation, 11,* 9–13.

Azrin, N. H., & Fox, R. M. (1971). A rapid method of toilet training the institutionalized retarded. *Journal of Applied Behavior Analysis, 4,* 89–99.

Azrin, N. H., Schaeffer, R. M., & Wesolowski, M. D. (1976). A rapid method of teaching profoundly retarded persons to dress by a reinforcement guidance method. *Mental Retardation, 14,* 29–33.

Kimm, C. H., Falvey, M. A., Bishop, K. D., & Rosenberg, R. L. (1995). Motor and personal care skills. In M. A. Falvey (Ed.), *Inclusive and heterogeneous schooling: Assessment, curriculum, and instruction* (pp. 187–227). Baltimore: Paul H. Brookes.

Matson, J. L., DiLorenzo, T. M., & Esveldt-Dawson, K. (1981). Independence training as a method of enhancing self-help skills acquisition of the mentally retarded. *Behavior Research Therapy, 19,* 399–405.

Reid, D. H., Wilson, P. G., & Faw, G. D. (1980). Teaching self-help skills. In J. L. Matson & J. A. Mulick (Eds.), *Handbook of mental retardation* (pp. 429–442). New York: Pergamon.

Whitman, T. L., Sciback, J. W., & Reid, D. H. (1983). *Behavior modification with the severely and profoundly retarded: Research and application.* New York: Academic.

JOHN O'NEILL
*Hunter College, City University
of New York*

DAILY LIVING SKILLS
FUNCTIONAL SKILLS TRAINING
HABILITATION OF INDIVIDUALS WITH DISABILITIES
REHABILITATION

SELF-INJURIOUS BEHAVIOR

Self-injury is one of the most unusual and probably least understood form of aberrant behavior. It may take a variety of forms, including biting, head banging, face slapping, pinching, or slapping. Such behavior has been reported to affect approximately 4 to 5 percent of psychiatric populations. Approximately 9 to 17 percent of normal young children (9 to 36 months of age) also exhibit self-injurious behavior (Carr, 1977).

Carr (1977) has reviewed the hypothetical causes of self-injurious behavior. These include positive reinforcement (seeking of attention), negative reinforcement (attempting to escape), sensory input (gaining stimulation), and psychogenic (psychosis) and organic (genetic and biological) factors. Carr was able to support each of the hypotheses, except for the psychogenic and the organic, by retrospectively applying research to each of the causal explanations. Since then, Evans and Meyer (1985) have proposed one additional hypothesis, an absence of appropriate skills, which research appears to substantiate. Each of these hypotheses warrants examination because of the effect they have on the selection of interventions.

Prior to the mid-1960s, self-injurious behavior was thought to be a product of insane persons with deranged or psychotic minds (Lovaas, 1982). This thinking shaped the model mental health professionals used to intervene with persons who exhibited self-injurious behavior. This dictated the extensive reliance on psychotherapy, drugs, and physical restraint for control.

Through a series of unrelated, yet complementary, studies, researchers were able to demonstrate that self-injurious behavior is regulated by the same laws that affect other human behaviors. The data from these early studies clearly point to the validity of applying the learning theory model to the treatment of self-injurious behavior (Lovaas, 1982).

The etiology of self-injurious behavior has been in debate for some time. There appears to be an organic basis for some self-injurious behavior. There are data to support the contention that self-injurious behaviors are seen in the Lesch-Nyhan and de Langhe syndromes, which are both genetically caused. In Lesch-Nyhan syndrome, a rare form of X-linked cerebral palsy found in only males, there is repetitive biting of the tongue, lips, and fingers. It is thought that this behavior is biochemically related. Considerable research has gone into finding a chemical cure for these characteristics. In de Lange syndrome, which is also genetic in origin, a broad variety of self-injurious behaviors have been reported. A biochemical association has not been presented. Other organic origins of self-injurious behavior have been identified. These include elevated pain thresholds and painful and prolonged infections of the middle ear. The data on organic causes of self-injurious behavior are contradictory, and limited chemical and medical mediations have been found. Although there is limited substantiation of organic causes of self-injurious behavior, awareness that there is a possibility of such causal factors, even in a small percentage of the handicapped population, is important. Those who deal directly with disabled individuals should recognize that medical screening is necessary at the onset of any treatment program, and in some cases medical intervention may be appropriate (Carr, 1977; Evans & Meyer, 1985).

The positive reinforcement hypothesis can be easily explained as the individual seeking attention through the use of self-injurious behavior. The caregivers, in turn, reinforce such behavior and allow it to continue or progress in intensity. Under such conditions, behavioral interventions that remove reinforcement (e.g., extinction or time out) from the individual would possess a high probability of being successful (Carr, 1977).

The negative reinforcement hypothesis is explained by the use of self-injurious behavior to escape demands being placed on the individual. By exhibiting this form of aberrant behavior, the disabled person is often allowed by the caregiver or teacher to refrain from participating in a required activity. Appropriate treatment for self-injurious behavior exhibited under these conditions should include interventions that focus on continued demand. In so doing the individual is not allowed to escape the demand (Carr, 1977).

The sensory input hypothesis is based on finding behaviors that provide the disabled person with input into sensory receptors that under average conditions receive limited amounts of stimulation. An example might be found in a visually impaired student who eye gouges. Self-injurious behavior becomes self-reinforcing and in turn self-maintaining. Interventions for behavior motivated in this manner have taken several different directions, including limiting the input that the self-injurious behavior provides the individual. This is done by modifying the environment (e.g., by using padding or placing adaptive devices on the individual). Another intervention that has been successful is the provision of increased amounts of stimulation from other sources (e.g., a vibrator; Carr, 1977).

The absence of alternative skills hypothesis rests on the concept that the disabled person has extremely limited skills. Self-injurious behavior is part of a behavior system of an individual who lacks appropriate behavior to meet functional needs. This hypothesis is probably a subset of one or more of the preceding explanations of self-injurious behavior; however, it implies a somewhat different treatment. Part of the intervention strategy for self-injurious behavior caused by lack of skills would include teaching appropriate skills to replace the self-injurious ones (Evans & Meyer, 1985; Gerra, Dorfman, Plaue & Schlachman, 1995; LeBlanc, 1993).

Iwata et al. (1982) have provided the practitioner with a method for functionally analyzing self-injurious behavior. Using this method it is possible to identify the specific motivational factors causing self-injury in many persons with disabilities. Employing this approach requires observing the individual in four situations: under negative reinforcement, social attention, play, and alone. Mean levels of self-injurious behavior across each situation are determined. Specific patterns of behavior are manifested in a specific setting that often clearly reflects a specific motivational cause for the behavior.

As previously noted, medical interventions are occasionally appropriate and successful in reducing or eliminating self-injurious behavior. Psychotherapy and other psychological methods have also been used to treat self-injurious behavior. Clearly, the most successful and effective interventions have been behaviorally based. Such interventions should be selected on a least-restrictive model and monitored by systematic data collection procedures. Behaviorally based intervention strategies include the use of punishment. Punishment has been shown to be highly successful, at least on a short-term basis, for the treatment of self-injurious behavior. In cases of chronic self-injurious behavior, where life or irreversible damage is threatened, steps as drastic as electrical shock have been used (Lovaas, 1982). These procedures are generally used to suppress serious self-injurious behavior until other approaches can replace them.

Self-injurious behavior poses many problems to the practitioner in its treatment. Although often misunderstood, recent work has provided both a theoretical explanation and a new direction for finding practical, effective, treatment methods for self-injurious behavior (Symons, 1995).

REFERENCES

Carr, E. (1977). The motivation of self-injurious behavior: A review of some hypothesis. *Psychological Bulletin, 84,* 800–816.

Evans, I. M., & Meyer, L. H. (1985). *An educative approach to behavior problems.* Baltimore: Brooks.

Gerra, L. L., Dorfman, S., Plaue, E., & Schlachman, S. (1995). Functional communication as a means of decreasing self-injurious behavior. *Journal of Visual Impairment & Blindness, 89*(4), 343–348.

Iwata, B. A., Dorsey, M. F., Slifer, K. J., Bauman, K. E., & Richman, G. S. (1982). Toward a functional analysis of self-injury. *Analysis and Intervention in Developmental Disabilities, 2,* 3–20.

LeBlanc, R. (1993). Educational management of self-injurious behavior. *International Journal of Child & Adolescent Psychiatry, 56*(2), 91–98.

Lovaas, O. I. (1982). Comments on self-destructive behaviors. *Analysis and Intervention in Developmental Disabilities, 2,* 115–124.

Symons, F. J. (1997). Self-injurious behavior. *Developmental Disabilities Bulletin, 23*(1), 90–104.

ALAN HILTON
Seattle University

APPLIED BEHAVIOR ANALYSIS
SELF-STIMULATION
STEREOTYPIC BEHAVIORS

SELF-MANAGEMENT

Self-management, also termed self-control, self-regulation, and self-direction, refers to actions intended to influence one's own behavior. Individuals are taught techniques that can be used in a deliberate manner to change their thoughts, feelings, or actions. Students who engage in self-management may, for example, work longer, complete more problems, make fewer errors, engage in fewer aggressive outbursts, or behave appropriately when an adult is not present.

The traditional approach in education has emphasized external management of programming by the teacher. As noted by Lovitt (1973). "Self-management behaviors are not systematically programmed [in the schools] which appears to be an educational paradox, for one of the expressed objectives of the educational system is to create individuals who are self-reliant and independent" (p. 139). Although frequently effective, use of external management procedures has several potential disadvantages (Kazdin, 1980). Implementation of procedures may be inconsistent as teachers may miss instances of behavior, or there may be problems with communication between change agents in different settings. A teacher may become a cue for particular behaviors, resulting in limited generalization to other situations in which that teacher is not present. Other potential disadvantages of external procedures include limited maintenance of behavior change, excessive time demands placed on educators, and the philosophic concern that the student has minimal involvement in the behavior change process.

Self-management procedures offset the concerns associated with external control and offer the possibility of improved maintenance and generalization of behavior change. The focus of self-management in special education is on teaching students to become effective modifiers of their own behaviors through use of such procedures as self-monitoring, self-evaluation, self-consequation, and self-instruction. Although each of these is discussed separately, in practice they frequently have been combined in self-management packages.

Self-monitoring refers to the observation, discrimination, and recording of one's own behavior. A child in the classroom, for example, may record on an index card each math problem completed. Self-monitoring has been demonstrated to have both assessment and therapeutic use with exceptional students who present a wide range of social and academic behaviors. Common problems associated with using self-monitoring as an assessment procedure include the inaccuracy and reactivity (spontaneous behavior change) of self-monitoring, both of which may result in a distorted picture of the initial levels of behavior. When self-monitoring is used as a treatment strategy, however, reactive effects are desired and inaccuracy may not interfere with obtaining this desired reactivity.

Self-evaluation, or self-assessment, is the comparison of one's own behavior against a preset standard to determine whether performance meets this criterion. Standards may be self-imposed or externally determined. In one study, special education students were asked to rate their behavior as "good," "okay," or "not good" when a timer rang at the end of 10-minute intervals. As is typical, self-evaluation was used as one component of a more comprehensive package; this resulted in reductions in disruptive behavior and increases in academic performance in these students (Robertson, Simon, Pachman, & Drabman, 1979).

Self-consequation refers to the self-delivery of positive consequences (self-reinforcement) or aversive consequences (self-punishment) following behavior. Self-reinforcement is preferred over self-punishment when possible and frequently is used in combination with other procedures. As an example, continued low levels of disruptive behavior or increased on-task behavior have been observed in special education students when self-reinforcement procedures were added to multicomponent programs (Shapiro & Klein, 1980).

Self-instruction is a process of talking to oneself to initiate, direct, or maintain one's own behavior. Children with attention deficit disorder, for example, may be taught specific coping self-statements that compete with such classroom problems as distractibility, overactivity, and off-task behavior. Typical training components include cognitive modeling, overt and covert rehearsal, graded practice on training tasks, and performance feedback (Meichenbaum, 1977).

Self-management training frequently combines these and other procedures in multicomponent self-management packages. In one example, disruptive developmentally disabled individuals were taught skills of self-monitoring, self-evaluation, self-consequation, and self-instruction that successfully reduced their chronic and severe conduct difficulties in a vocational training setting (Cole, Gardner, & Karan, 1985; Cole, Pflugrad, Gardner, & Karan, 1985).

Although total self-management is not possible for many special education students, most can be taught to be more self-reliant. Further, evidence suggests that self-management procedures are at least as effective as similar externally managed procedures in facilitating positive behavior change and in ensuring maintenance of this behavior change. Thus, in addition to its therapeutic effects, self-management offers economic, philosophic, legal, and professional benefits for use in special education.

REFERENCES

Cole, C. L., Gardner, W. I., & Karan, O. C. (1985). Self-management training of mentally retarded adults presenting severe conduct difficulties. *Applied Research in Mental Retardation, 6,* 337–347.

Cole, C. L., Pflugrad, D., Gardner, W. I., & Karan, O. C. (1985). *The self-management training program: Teaching developmentally disabled individuals to manage their disruptive behavior.* Champaign, IL: Research.

Kazdin, A. E. (1980). *Behavior modification in applied settings* (rev. ed.). Homewood, IL: Dorsey.

Lovitt, T. C. (1973). Self-management projects with children with behavioral disabilities. *Journal of Learning Disabilities, 6,* 15–28.

Meichenbaum, D. (1977). *Cognitive-behavior modification: An integrative approach.* New York: Plenum.

Robertson, S. J., Simon, S. J., Pachman, J. S., & Drabman, R. S. (1979). Self-control and generalization procedures in a classroom of disruptive retarded children. *Child Behavior Therapy, 1,* 347–362.

Shapiro, E. S., & Klein, R. D. (1980). Self-management of classroom behavior with retarded/disturbed children. *Behavior Modification, 4,* 83–97.

CHRISTINE L. COLE
University of Wisconsin at Madison

ATTENTION-DEFICIT/HYPERACTIVITY DISORDER
COGNITIVE BEHAVIOR THERAPY
SELF-CONTROL CURRICULUM
SELF-MONITORING

SELF-MONITORING

Self-monitoring is one component of a more general process variously known as self-management, self-regulation, or self-control. The process of self-monitoring first involves a person's recognizing that a need exists to regulate his or her behavior. To recognize this need, the person must be observing his or her behavior and comparing it with some preset standard. This self-observation and assessment then combines with recording the behavior to create the self-monitoring component (Shapiro, 1981). Other components in the self-management process can include self-reinforcement, standard setting, self-evaluation, and self-instruction. These components have been used in various combinations with self-monitoring to modify many different types of behaviors (e.g., overeating, temper outbursts, negative statements, attending to task) in the developmentally disabled (Cole, Gardner, & Karan, 1983; Marion, 1994).

It has been shown that many different types of developmentally disabled individuals are capable of self-monitoring a range of behaviors in various settings. However, at least some of these individuals, particularly the mentally retarded, need training to acquire self-monitoring skills (Litrownik, Freitas, & Franzini, 1978; Shapiro, McGonigle, & Ollendick, 1980).

Self-monitoring among nondevelopmentally disabled people has a reactive or therapeutic effect: those behaviors being monitored tend to change in a desirable direction (McFall, 1977; Nelson & Hayes, 1981). The studies that have assessed the use of self-monitoring in developmentally disabled populations have also found therapeutic effects. For example, mentally retarded individuals have shown increases in the percent of housekeeping chores completed (Bauman & Iwata, 1977), the frequency of appropriate classroom verbalizations (Nelson, Lipinski, & Boykin, 1978) and the productivity of work (Zohn & Bornstein, 1980). Therapeutic decreases have also occurred in face-picking, head-shaking (Zegiob, Klukas, & Junginger, 1978), and tongue-protrusion behaviors (Rudrud, Ziarnik, & Colman, 1984). However, some studies conducted with the developmentally disabled (Horner & Brigham, 1979; Shapiro & Ackerman, 1983) have found the desirable effects of self-monitoring to be short-term or nonexistent, which is consistent with some research conducted on the nondisabled (Kazdin, 1974).

The variable results obtained with self-monitoring are probably due to several intervening factors that can impact on the reactivity or therapeutic value of self-monitoring (Nelson, 1977). The following comments are only suggestive, because the empirical evidence is limited and most of the supporting research has been done with nondevelopmentally disabled people. First, a behavior's valence or a person's desire to change the behavior can affect reactivity. Positively valenced behaviors tend to increase and negatively valenced behaviors to decrease. Generally, reactivity is enhanced by the frequency of self-monitoring; however, there are situations where the act of monitoring can interfere with reactivity, particularly with positively valenced behaviors. Reactivity also tends to be augmented when the recording device is visible and apparent to the person doing the self-monitoring. In addition, if several behaviors are monitored concurrently, the likelihood of change in any of them is suppressed. Finally, training in self-monitoring seems to enhance reactivity, particularly if the behavior is negatively valenced.

REFERENCES

Bauman, K. E., & Iwata, B. A. (1977). Maintenance of independent housekeeping skills using scheduling plus self-recording procedures. *Behavior Therapy, 8,* 554–560.

Cole, C. L., Gardner, W. I., & Karan, O. C. (1983). *Self-management training of mentally retarded adults with chronic conduct difficulties.* Madison: University of Wisconsin, Rehabilitation Research and Training Center, Waisman Center on Mental Retardation and Human Development.

Horner, R. H., & Brigham, T. A. (1979). The effects of self-management procedures on the study behavior of two retarded children. *Education & Training of the Mentally Retarded, 14,* 18–24.

Kazdin, A. E. (1974). Self-monitoring and behavior change. In M. J. Mahoney & C. E. Thoresen (Eds.), *Self-control: Power to the person.* Monterey, CA: Brookes/Cole.

Litrownik, A. J., Freitas, J. L., & Franzini, L. R. (1978). Self-regulation in mentally retarded children: Assessment and training of self-monitoring skills. *American Journal of Mental Deficiency, 82,* 499–506.

Marion, M. (1994). Encouraging the development of responsible anger management in young children. *Early Child Development & Care, 97,* 155–163.

McFall, R. M. (1977). Parameters of self-monitoring. In R. B. Stuart (Ed.), *Behavioral self-management.* New York: Brunner/Mazel.

Nelson, R. O. (1977). Methodological issues in assessment via self-monitoring. In J. D. Cone & R. P. Hawkins (Eds.), *Behavioral assessment: New directions in clinical psychology.* New York: Brunner/Mazel.

Nelson, R. O., & Hayes, S. C. (1981). Theoretical explanations for reactivity in self-monitoring. *Behavior Modification, 5,* 3–14.

Nelson, R. O., Lipinski, D. P., & Boykin, R. A. (1978). The effects of self-recorders' training and the obtrusiveness of the self-recording device on the accuracy and reactivity of self-monitoring. *Behavior Therapy, 9,* 200–208.

Rudrud, E. H., Ziarnik, J. P., & Colman, G. (1984). Reduction of tongue protrusion of a 24-year-old woman with Down's syndrome through self-monitoring. *American Journal of Mental Deficiency, 88,* 647–652.

Shapiro, E. S. (1981). Self-control procedures with the mentally retarded. In M. Hersen, R. M. Eisler, & P. M. Miller (Eds.), *Progress in behavior modification.* New York: Academic.

Shapiro, E. S., & Ackerman, A. (1983). Increasing productivity rates in adult mentally retarded clients: The failure of self-monitoring. *Applied Research in Mental Retardation, 4,* 163–181.

Shapiro, E. S., McGonigle, J. J., & Ollendick, T. H. (1980). An analysis of self-assessment and self-reinforcement in a self-managed token economy with mentally retarded children. *Applied Research in Mental Retardation, 1,* 227–240.

Zegiob, L., Klukas, N., & Junginger, J. (1978). Reactivity of self-monitoring procedures with retarded adolescents. *American Journal of Mental Deficiency, 83,* 156–163.

Zohn, C. J., & Bornstein, P. H. (1980). Self-monitoring of work performance with mentally retarded adults: Effects upon work productivity, work quality, and on-task behavior. *Mental Retardation, 18,* 19–25.

JOHN O'NEILL
*Hunter College, City University
of New York*

IMPULSE CONTROL
SELF-CARE SKILLS
SELF-CONTROL CURRICULUM
SELF-MANAGEMENT

SELF-REINFORCEMENT

Self-reinforcement is a self-management strategy in which the performance of a certain behavior to a predetermined standard receives a self-chosen and self-administered reward

(Bandura, 1976; Marston, 1964; Shapiro, 1981; Wehman, 1975). With this strategy, individuals are taught to monitor their behavior and administer a reward to themselves rather than receiving it from their teachers (Kazdin, 1978). True self-reinforcement occurs in the absence of externally controlling influences, such as a teacher deciding the type of reward and when it should be given. In applied practice teachers typically provide a menu of rewards students can choose from and teachers establish the reinforcement schedule. Self-reinforcement is usually used in conjunction with self-monitoring or as an extension of self-evaluation (Browder & Shapiro, 1985; Agran, King-Sears, Wehmeyer, & Copeland, 2003). When individuals recognize that they have met a goal or completed a task, they give themselves a reward. Reliance on an external agent such as the teacher to administer the reward may result in missed reinforcement opportunities. With self-reinforcement, students administer the reward, which decreases the possibility of missing a reinforcement opportunity (Wehmeyer, Agran, & Hughes, 1998).

Self-reinforcement has been used to increase a wide variety of behaviors. Early studies demonstrated effectiveness of the strategy in increasing worker productivity (Helland, Paluck, & Klein, 1976), and social skills in the workplace (Matson & Andrasik, 1982). Self-reinforcement often accompanies a token economy system where tokens are distributed, collected, and redeemed at a predetermined time. For example, Novak and Hammond (1983) used self-reinforcement in a token economy to increase reading problem completion in a classroom setting. A meta-analysis of self-reinforcement research found that self-reinforcement had little to no effect on decreasing inappropriate behavior, had a small to moderate effect on increasing on-task behavior, and had a strong positive effect on academic accuracy and productivity (Reid, Trout, & Schartz, 2005).

REFERENCES

Agran, M., King-Sears, M. E., Wehmeyer, M. L., & Copeland, S. R. (2003). *Student-directed learning.* Baltimore: Brookes.

Agran, M., & Martin, J. E. (1987). Applying a technology of self-control in community environments for individuals who are mentally retarded. In M. Hersen, R. M. Eisler, & P. M. Miller (Eds.), *Progress in behavior modification* (Vol. 21). Newbury Park, CA: Sage.

Bandura, A. (1976). *Principles of behavior modification.* New York: Holt.

Browder, D. M., & Shapiro, E. S. (1985). Applications of self-management to individuals with severe handicaps: A review. *Journal of the Association for Persons with Severe Handicaps, 10,* 200–208.

Helland, C. D., Paluck, R. J., & Klein, M. (1976). A comparison of self and external reinforcement with the trainable mentally retarded. *Mental Retardation, 14,* 22–23.

Kazdin, A. E. (1978). *History of behavior modification.* Baltimore: University Park.

Marston, A. R. (1964). Variables affecting incidence of self-reinforcement. *Psychological Reports, 14,* 879–884.

Matson, J. L., & Andrasik, F. (1982). Training leisure-time social-interaction skills to mentally retarded adults. *American Journal of Mental Deficiency, 86,* 533–542.

Novak, G., & Hammond, J. M. (1983). Self-reinforcement and descriptive praise in maintaining token economy reading performance. *Journal of Educational Research, 76,* 186–189.

Reid, R., Trout, A. L., & Schartz, M. (2005). Self-regulation interventions for children with attention deficit/hyperactivity disorder. *Exceptional Children 71,* 361–377.

Shapiro, E. S. (1981). Self-control procedures with the mentally retarded. In M. Hersen, R. M. Eisler, & P. M. Miller (Eds.), *Progress in behavior modification* (Vol. 12). New York: Academic.

Wehman, P. (1975). Behavioral self-control with the mentally retarded. *Journal of Applied Rehabilitation Counseling, 6,* 27–34.

Wehmeyer, M. L., Agran, M., & Hughes, C. (1998). *Teaching self-determination to students with disabilities.* Baltimore: Brookes.

LEE L. WOODS
University of Oklahoma

BEHAVIOR MODIFICATION
METACOGNITION

SELF-SELECTION OF REINFORCEMENT

When the student involved in a contingency management program is permitted to choose a reinforcer or determine the cost of a reinforcer relative to a target behavior, the technique of self-selection of reinforcement is being used. It is one of several self-management methods. It may be used in isolation or in combination with self-recording or self-evaluation (Hughes & Ruhl, 1985). However, a recording and evaluation system (controlled by either the teacher or the student) must be in operation prior to implementing self-selection of reinforcement.

As with other self-management techniques, self-selection of reinforcement appears to be more effective with students previously exposed to a systematic, externally controlled reinforcement system. Consequently, it may function as a helpful transition step for students being weaned from externally controlled systems. Studies (Cosden, Gannon, & Haring, 1995; Dickerson & Creedon, 1981; Rosenbaum & Drabman, 1979) have indicated that student-selected reinforcers are more effective than those selected by the teacher. This may be true because students are more capable of identifying what is of value to them and what they are willing to work for.

According to Hughes and Ruhl (1985), the following considerations and steps are helpful when teaching students to use self-selection of reinforcement:

1. Begin with a system of externally controlled contingencies.
2. Verify student understanding of ongoing recording and evaluation procedures and directly reteach if student understanding is in doubt.
3. List available reinforcers and have the student identify one for which he or she is willing to work.
4. Determine stringent performance standards for obtaining reinforcement with the student.
5. Establish a time or signal for administration of the reinforcer.

Stringent performance standards for reinforcement (i.e., those requiring a high rating or frequency for all, or almost all, evaluation periods) are important because they result in significantly better performance results than do lax standards (Alberto & Troutman, 1982). Because students tend to set performance standards that are more lenient than those established by teachers (Flexibrod & O'Leary, 1973, 1974; Frederiksen & Frederiksen, 1975), students should be prompted to set vigorous criteria. Verbal prompts, providing examples and rationales and praising acceptable performance standards, will assist the student in determining appropriate criteria. Examples of criteria for reinforcement include obtaining a specified number of tokens or time intervals with low rates of occurrence of an inappropriate behavior.

Regardless of who is recording or evaluating the behavior, a method for communicating the time for reinforcement should be established. For example, the self-selected reinforcement might come at the end of an academic period, after reading five pages of a text, or at the end of the school day when the school bell rings.

REFERENCES

Alberto, P. A., & Troutman, A. C. (1982). *Applied behavior analysis for teachers: Influencing student performance.* Columbus, OH: Merrill.

Cosden, M., Gannon, G., & Haring, T. G. (1995). Teacher-control versus student-control over chance of task and reinforcement for students with severe behavior problems. *Journal of Behavioral Education, 5*(1), 11–27.

Dickerson, A. E., & Creedon, C. F. (1981). Self-selection of standards by children: The relative effectiveness of pupil-selected and teacher-selected standards of performance. *Journal of Applied Behavior Analysis, 141,* 425–433.

Flexibrod, J. J., & O'Leary, K. D. (1973). Effects of reinforcement on children's academic behavior as a function of self-determined and externally imposed contingencies. *Journal of Applied Behavior Analysis, 6,* 241–250.

Flexibrod, J. J., & O'Leary, K. D. (1974). Self-determination of academic standards by children: Toward freedom from external control. *Journal of Educational Psychology, 66,* 845–850.

Frederiksen, L. W., & Frederiksen, C. B. (1975). Teacher-determined and self-determined token reinforcement in a special education classroom. *Behavior Therapy, 6,* 310–314.

Hughes, C. A., & Ruhl, K. L. (1985). Learning activities for improving self-management skills. In B. Algozzine (Ed.), *Educators' resource manual for management of problem behaviors in students.* Rockville, MD: Aspen.

Rosenbaum, M. S., & Drabman, R. S. (1979). Self-control training in the classroom. *Journal of Behavior Analysis, 12,* 467–485.

KATHY L. RUHL
Pennsylvania State University

APPLIED BEHAVIOR ANALYSIS
BEHAVIOR MODIFICATION
CONTINGENCY CONTRACTING
POSITIVE REINFORCEMENT

SELF-STIMULATION

Self-stimulatory, or stereotypic, behaviors are highly consistent and repetitive motor behaviors in which the adaptive consequences are not immediately apparent (Smith & Van Houten, 1996). Examples include head weaving, light gazing, hand flapping, toe walking, laughing, rocking, twirling in circles, hand staring, spinning or banging objects, and masturbation (Dura, Mulick, & Rasnake as cited in Shabani, Flood, & Wilder, 2001). More subtle forms include rubbing hands along surfaces and sniffing.

Self-stimulatory behaviors are intrinsically motivating because they feel good. In addition, these behaviors tend to be environmentally reinforcing because they draw attention from others. This attention increases the likelihood that the behavior will be repeated in the future. It has also been suggested that self-stimulatory behaviors are acquired as a way of escaping a noxious stimulus. Thus a child, unwilling or unable to complete a difficult task, will engage in self-stimulation as a way of changing the focus of attention and escaping the task at hand.

Self-stimulatory behaviors occur more commonly in individuals with autism, mental retardation, and those with multiple disabilities. Thus, there are a greater number of self-stimulators in institutions and psychiatric settings. In settings and institutions with unpredictable routines and unstructured formats, self-stimulation can develop into self-injurious behavior, which refers to deliberate damage to one's own body without suicidal intent. Examples include cutting, scratching or pinching of one's skin, head banging, and face slapping. As with suicidal thoughts and behaviors, adolescence appears to be a period of increased risk for self-injurious behaviors. Studies suggest that 14 to 39 percent of adolescents in the community and 40 to 61 percent of adolescents in psychiatric inpatient settings display these behaviors (Nock & Prinstein, 2004).

Self-stimulatory and self-injurious behaviors interfere with learning, acquiring adaptive behaviors, and participating in social interactions or play (Brown & Middleton, 1998).

Because these behaviors constitute a significant proportion of an individual's repertoire, a major goal of those who educate and care for self-stimulators is eliminating or minimizing the frequency of self-stimulation (Shabani et al., 2001). As with most interventions, the earlier the intervention is applied, the better the outcome. Optimally, interventions should be unobtrusive and in the child's natural setting. Children should be ignored when self-stimulating, positively reinforced for engaging in appropriate behavior, and should lose privileges when engaging in the undesirable behavior (i.e., self-stimulation). Punishment should only be reserved for behaviors that are life threatening and resistant to less intrusive types of interventions. In situations where aversive consequences must be used, procedures must be carefully and continuously monitored and legal and ethical issues must be carefully considered.

REFERENCES

Ahearn, W., Clark, M., & Gardenier, N. C. (2003). Persistence of stereotypic behavior: Examining the effects of external reinforcers. *Journal of Applied Behavior Analysis, 36,* 439–448.

Berkson, G. (1998). Brief report: Control in highly focused top-spinning. *Journal of Autism and Developmental Disorders, 28,* 83–90.

Brown, G. W., & Middleton, H. (1998). Use of self-as-a-model to promote generalization and maintenance of the reduction of self-stimulation in a child with mental retardation. *Education and Training in Mental Retardation and Disabilities, 33,* 76–80.

Lee, S., & Odom, S. (1996). The relationship between stereotypic and peer social interaction for children with severe disabilities. *Journal of the Association for Persons with Severe Disabilities, 21,* 88–95.

Nock, M. K., & Prinstein, M. (2004). A functional approach to the assessment of self-mutilative behavior. *Journal of Consulting and Clinical Psychology, 72,* 885–890.

Shabani, D. B., Flood, W. A., & Wilder, D. A. (2001). Reducing stereotypic behavior through discrimination training, differential reinforcement of other behavior and self-monitoring. *Behavioral Interventions, 16,* 279–286.

Smith, E. A., & Van Houten, R. (1996). A comparison of the characteristics of self-stimulatory behaviors in "normal" children and children with developmental delays. *Research in Developmental Disabilities, 17,* 253–268.

ESMERELDA LÓPEZ
Texas A&M University

AUTISM
SELF-INJURIOUS BEHAVIOR
STEREOTYPIC BEHAVIORS

SEMMEL, MELVYN I. (1931–   )

Melvyn I. Semmel was born and educated in New York City, receiving his BS (1955) and MS (1957) in special education from City College, City University of New York. He later earned his EdD (1963) in special education with a minor in psychology from George Peabody College. He is currently a professor of special education and director of the Special Education Research Laboratory in the Graduate School of Education, University of California, Santa Barbara.

Semmel's early teacher training led to his involvement with teacher preparation and research on special education methods. In 1968, he pioneered the development of the Computer-Assisted Teacher Training System (CATTS), and later directed the Center for Innovation in Teaching the Handicapped (CITH), a research and development center for alternative teacher training methods and instructional materials. During his tenure at CITH, the center was recognized as the outstanding organization of the year by the National Society for Performance and Instruction. Semmel's research work at the University of California has focused on issues such as use of computers for learners with disabilities, development of new models for research teaching, and devising cognitively-oriented interventions for individuals with severe emotional disturbance. He and his colleagues have examined the effectiveness of special education for students with mild disabilities, finding that, based on student performance, no single factor (e.g., structure or organization of school environment) consistently indicated its relative effectiveness (Larrivee, Semmel, & Gerber, 1997).

Semmel has written over 100 books, research papers, articles, and chapters related to special education and educational psychology. He has been recognized in *Who's Who in American Education* and has been elected a life member and fellow of the American Association on Mental Retardation for 30 years of continuous service to the field.

REFERENCE

Larivee, B., Semmel, M. I., & Gerber, M. M. (1997). Case studies of six schools varying in effectiveness for students with learning disabilities. *Elementary School Journal, 98*(1), 27–50.

E. VALERIE HEWITT
Texas A&M University
First edition

TAMARA J. MARTIN
*The University of Texas of the
    Permian Basin*
Second edition

SENF, GERALD M. (1942–   )

Gerald M. Senf graduated with honors from Yale University with a BA (1964) in psychology. He went on to earn his MA (1966) in experimental psychology and his doctorate in 1968 in experimental and clinical psychology from the University of California, Los Angeles. During his career, Senf has held the positions of professor of psychology at University of Iowa, associate professor of psychology at University of Illinois, evaluation research director of the Leadership Training Institute in Learning Disabilities, and associate professor of special education at the University of Arizona.

Senf has written extensively on the topics of cognitive functioning and research methodology associated with the study of learning disabilities, with his principal focus on information-processing skills and memory of those with learning disabilities (Senf, 1969, 1972, 1976, 1981, 1986). He has continued to study in the area of cognitive functioning, investigating the comparison of electrical brain activity in normal individuals to individuals with various cognitive impairments to assist the clinician in diagnosing and treating the patient (Senf, 1988).

Senf is coauthor of a screening test, has coedited several books, and has devised computer programs to assist the learning disabled.

REFERENCES

Senf, G. M. (1969). Development of immediate memory for bisensory stimuli in normal children and children with learning disorders. *Developmental Psychology Monograph, 1* (Pt. 2).

Senf, G. M. (1972). An information integration theory and its application to normal reading acquisition and reading disability. In N. D. Bryant & C. E. Kass (Eds.), *Leadership Training Institute on Learning Disabilities* (Vol. 2). Tucson: University of Arizona Press.

Senf, G. M. (1976). Some methodological considerations in the study of abnormal conditions. In R. Walsh & W. T. Greenough (Eds.), *Environment as therapy for brain dysfunction*. New York: Plenum.

Senf, G. M. (1981). Issues surrounding the diagnosis of learning disabilities: Child handicap versus failure of the child-school interaction. In T. R. Kratochwill (Ed.), *Advances in school psychology* (Vol. 1, pp. 83–131). Hillsdale, NJ: Erlbaum.

Senf, G. M. (1986). LD research in sociological and scientific perspective. In J. K. Torgesen & B. Wong (Eds.), *Psychological and educational perspectives on learning disabilities*. San Diego, CA: Academic.

Senf, G. M. (1988). Neurometric brainmapping in the diagnosis and rehabilitation of cognitive dysfunction. *Cognitive Rehabilitation, 6*(6), 20–37.

ROBERTA C. STOKES
Texas A&M University
First edition

TAMARA J. MARTIN
*The University of Texas of the
    Permian Basin*
Second edition

SENSORINEURAL HEARING LOSS

A sensorineural hearing loss is a hearing impairment resulting from a pathological condition in the inner ear or along the auditory nerve (VIII cranial nerve) pathway from the inner ear to the brain stem. If the pathological condition or site of lesion is confined to the inner ear or cochlea, it is known as an inner ear or cochlea hearing loss. If the site of lesion is along the auditory nerve (as is the case with an acoustic nerve tumor), it is known as a retrocochlear hearing loss. Several audiological, medical, and radiological special tests have been developed to assist in the diagnosis of whether a sensorineural hearing loss is due to a cochlear or retrocochlear site of lesion.

An individual with a sensorineural hearing loss has reduced hearing sensitivity and lacks the ability to discriminate speech sounds, especially when listening in a noisy environment. Tinnitus is a common symptom of a sensorineural hearing loss. Tinnitus is any sensation of sound in the head heard in one or both ears. It may be described as a hissing, whistling, buzzing, roaring, or a high-pitched tone or noise. Dizziness is also a symptom of sensorineural hearing loss; it can range from light-headedness to a severe whirling sensation known as vertigo, that leads to nausea.

A sensorineural hearing loss can occur in varying degrees ranging from mild-moderate to severe-profound. The degree of sensorineural hearing loss is determined by averaging the decibel amount of hearing loss across the frequencies needed to hear and understand speech or the speech frequencies (500, 1000, and 2000 Hz). Individuals with a mild to severe hearing loss are usually classified as being hard of hearing, while individuals with a profound hearing impairment are classified as deaf. A sensorineural hearing loss can occur in just one ear (unilateral) or in each ear (bilateral). If the hearing loss occurs in each ear, one ear may be more affected than the other.

A sensorineural hearing loss can be caused by many factors, including genetic diseases (dominant, recessive, or sex-linked), diseases acquired during pre-, peri-, and post-natal periods, and childhood diseases. Adults can obtain sensorineural hearing loss from noise exposure, diseases, medication, and the aging process. Many sensorineural hearing losses are due to unknown etiology. A sensorineural hearing loss also may be part of a syndrome that affects the individual in other ways. A congenital sensorineural hearing loss is one that has existed or has an etiology from birth; an adventitious hearing loss is one that occurred after birth and in most cases is due to injury or disease. If the sensorineural hearing loss occurred prior to the development of speech and language skills, it is known as prelingual; if it occurred after the development of speech and language skills, it is known as postlingual. Standardized batteries of cognitive abilities and memory are being used to assess concurrent learning disabilities and skill strengths and weaknesses (Plapinger & Sikora, 1995; Sikora & Plapinger, 1994).

In children having sensorineural hearing losses, about half the cases are due to genetic causes and half to acquired causes. Meningitis and prematurity are the leading acquired causes of sensorineural hearing loss in children. For adults, the leading cause of sensorineural hearing loss is the aging process, known as presbyacusis, and excessive exposure to noise. Typically, the sensorineural hearing loss from presbyacusis or noise exposure is a progressive reduction of high frequency (1000 to 8000 Hz) hearing sensitivity that causes problems in understanding speech.

It is important that individuals with a sensorineural hearing loss have audiological and otological diagnosis and management. In almost all cases, there is no medical treatment for sensorineural hearing loss from a cochlear site of lesion. However, a retrocochlear lesion from a tumor, or some other growth along the auditory nerve may benefit from an operation. Cochlear implants are now available, but their use is controversial (Carver, 1997).

Children and adults with cochlear sensorineural hearing loss can benefit through the use of hearing aids. Most children are fitted with a hearing aid for each ear (binaural amplification) and require auditory and speech reading training, speech and language therapy, and academic tutoring. Adults are usually fitted with either a hearing aid on one ear (monaural) or with binaural amplification. Generally, adults do not need specialized training; however, many adults benefit from speech-reading therapy. References for in depth discussion of sensorineural hearing loss are cited below.

REFERENCES

Carver, R. (1997). *Questions parents should ask about cochlear implants.* British Columbia, Canada: DCSD.

Gerber, S. E., & Mencher, G. T. (1980). *Auditory dysfunction.* San Diego, CA: College-Hill.

Jerger, J. (1984). *Hearing disorders in adults.* San Diego, CA: College-Hill.

Plapinger, D. S., & Sikora, D. M. (1995). The use of standardized test batteries in assessing skill development of children with mild to moderate sensorineural hearing loss. *Language, Speech & Hearing in Schools, 26*(1), 39–44.

Schubert, E. D. (1980). *Hearing: Its function and dysfunction.* New York: Springer-Verlag.

Schuknecht, H. F. (1974). *Pathology of the ear.* Cambridge, MA: Harvard University Press.

Sikora, D. M., & Plapinger, D. S. (1994). Using standardized psychometric tests to identify learning disabilities in students with learning disabilities. *Journal of Learning Disabilities, 27*(6), 352–359.

Wolstenholmer, G. E. W., & Knight, J. (1970). *Sensorineural hearing loss*. London: J. & A. Churchill.

THOMAS A. FRANK
Pennsylvania State University

DEAF
DEAF EDUCATION

SENSORY EXTINCTION

Sensory extinction is a procedure developed by Rincover (1978) for reducing various pathological behaviors in developmentally disabled children. It has been used to suppress self-stimulation (Maag, Wolchik, Rutherford, & Parks, 1986; Rincover, 1978), compulsive behaviors (Rincover, Newsom, & Carr, 1979), and self-injury (Rincover & Devaney, 1981). In a sensory extinction paradigm, stereotypy is considered operant behavior maintained by its sensory consequences. For example, repetitive finger flapping might be conceptualized as being maintained by the specific proprioceptive feedback it produces, while persistent delayed echolalia may be maintained by auditory feedback.

Sensory extinction involves masking, changing, or removing certain sensory consequences of behavior. If the sensory reinforcement received is removed, the behavior will be extinguished. For example, if a child continuously spins a plate on a table, a piece of carpet could be placed on the table to remove the auditory feedback resulting from this behavior. Similarly, the stereotypic behavior of a child who ritualistically switches a light on and off could be extinguished by either removing the visual feedback (if seeing the light were reinforcing) or removing the auditory feedback (if hearing the light switch click were reinforcing).

When sensory extinction is used to suppress stereotypy, the preferred sensory consequences of the behavior can be used to teach appropriate behaviors. For example, the child who spins plates could be taught to spin a top instead, since this would provide the same sensory consequences as the maladaptive behavior. Rincover, Cook, Peoples, and Packard (1979) found that children preferred to play with toys that provided sensory reinforcement similar to the sensory reinforcement previously found in the stereotypy.

While sensory extinction is a procedure in which multiple components are altered at the same time (Maag et al., 1986), it remains unclear as to the extent to which stimulus modality is an important factor (Murphy, 1982). Maag et al. found that isolating the sensory consequences for some forms of behavior can be impractical and/or time-consuming. In addition, Maag et al. point out that a cumbersome apparatus is sometimes necessary to mask some types of sensory feedback. This apparatus may restrict the child's ability to participate in activities and also be socially stigmatizing.

Therefore, although sensory extinction may represent a viable set of procedures for reducing stereotypy, it should be assessed thoroughly to determine the appropriateness of this intervention for particular children.

REFERENCES

Maag, J. W., Wolchik, S. A., Rutherford, R. B., & Parks, B. T. (1986). Response covariation of self-stimulatory behaviors during sensory extinction procedures. *Journal of Autism & Developmental Disorders, 16,* 119–132.

Murphy, G. (1982). Sensory reinforcement in the mentally handicapped and autistic child: A review. *Journal of Autism & Developmental Disorders, 12,* 265–278.

Rincover, A. (1978). Sensory extinction: A procedure for eliminating self-stimulatory behavior in developmentally disabled children. *Journal of Abnormal Child Psychology, 6,* 299–310.

Rincover, A., Cook, R., Peoples, A., & Packard, D. (1979). Sensory extinction and sensory reinforcement principles for programming multiple adaptive behavior change. *Journal of Applied Behavior Analysis, 12,* 221–233.

Rincover, A., & Devaney, J. (1981). The application of sensory extinction principles to self-injury in developmentally disabled children. *Analysis & Intervention in Developmental Disabilities, 4,* 67–69.

Rincover, A., Newsom, C. D., & Carr, E. G. (1979). Using sensory extinction procedures in the treatment of compulsive-like behavior of developmentally disabled children. *Journal of Consulting and Clinical Psychology, 47,* 695–701.

ROBERT B. RUTHERFORD, JR.
Arizona State University

BEHAVIOR MODIFICATION
SELF-STIMULATION

SENSORY INTEGRATIVE DYSFUNCTION

Sensory Integrative Dysfunction (also known as Sensory Integration Disorder, or SID) is based on the theory of sensory integration developed by A. Jean Ayres. An occupational therapist by trade, Ayres also had training in neuroscience and educational psychology. She defined sensory integration as "the neurological process that organizes sensation from one's own body and from the environment and makes it possible to use the body effectively within the environment" (Ayres, 1972, p.11).

SID, then, occurs when there is a deficit or other problem with the neurological processes involved in the integration of sensory information. Specifically, SID can occur in one or more of three main areas: vestibular, tactile, or proprioceptive senses (Bundy, Lane, & Murray, 2002). According to the organization Sensory Integration International, this sensory deficit may manifest itself in a variety of symptoms. These include the following:

- Oversensitivity or under-reactivity to touch, movement, sights, or sounds
- High distractibility
- Social and/or emotional problems
- Unusually high or low activity level
- Physical clumsiness or seeming carelessness
- Impulsivity, or lack of self control
- Difficulty making transitions between situations
- Inability to "unwind" or soothe self
- Poor self-concept
- Delays in speech, language, or motor skills
- Delays in academic achievement

The most commonly used method of assessment for SID is the Sensory Integration and Praxis tests, a battery of assessments developed by Ayres specifically for this purpose (Bundy et al., 2002). Treatment for the disorder involves teaching children to successfully interpret and integrate sensory input, so that they can respond more appropriately to the demands of their environment (Sensory Integration International).

The theory of sensory integration exists primarily within the field of occupational therapy. Similarly, SID is a diagnosis given and treated almost exclusively by occupational therapists (Bundy et al., 2002). The diagnostic label is not found in the *Diagnostic and Statistical Manual of Mental Disorders* (*DSM-IV-TR;* American Psychiatric Association, 2000). Instead, symptoms associated with SID are included in the *DSM-IV-TR* under other diagnostic categories, such as pervasive developmental disorders (including autism spectrum disorders), Attention-Deficit/Hyperactivity Disorder, and various developmental and learning disabilities. SID is viewed by occupational therapists as a diagnosis separate from these other conditions, though they may share some symptoms (Bundy et al., 2002).

REFERENCES

American Psychiatric Association. (2000). *Diagnostic and statistical manual of mental disorders* (4th ed., text revision). Washington, DC: Author.

Ayres, A. J. (1972). *Sensory integration and learning disorders.* Los Angeles: Western Psychological Services.

Bundy, A. C., Lane, S. J., & Murray, E. A. (2002). *Sensory integration: Theory and practice.* Philadelphia: F. A. Davis.

Sensory Integration International. (n.d.). *Answers to frequently asked questions.* Retrieved August 29, 2005, from http://www.sensoryint/faq.html

LISA A. LOCKWOOD
Texas A&M University

ATTENTION-DEFICIT/HYPERACTIVITY DISORDER
AUTISM
DEVELOPMENTAL DISABILITIES
LEARNING DISABILITIES

SENSORY INTEGRATIVE THERAPY

Sensory integrative therapy is a technique for the remediation of sensory integrative dysfunction developed by A. Jean Ayres (Ayres, 1972). Sensory integrative dysfunction is believed by Ayres and others (Quiros, 1976; Silberzahn, 1982) to be at the root of many learning disorders. Ayres uses the term sensory integrative dysfunction to describe children whose learning problems are due to the failure of the lower levels of the brain (particularly the midbrain, brain stem, and vestibular system) to use and organize information effectively. The principal objective of sensory integrative therapy is to promote the development and the organization of subcortical brain mechanisms as a foundation for perception and learning. Treatment procedures consist of the use of gross motor activities and physical exercise to achieve this goal. Sensory integrative therapy has gained its greatest popularity among occupational therapists.

The five key features of sensory integrative dysfunction follow (Silberzahn, 1982):

1. *Developmental Apraxia.* This is a problem in motor planning and is part of a complex that includes deficits in tactile functions. According to Ayres (1972), the fundamental problem lies in the difficulty in recognizing the time and space aspects of sensation and the relationships among body parts that are necessary for cortical planning of events.

2. *Tactile Defensiveness.* This represents a defensive or hostile reaction to tactile stimuli and is part of a complex believed, in sensory integrative therapy, to include hyperactivity, distractibility, and discrimination problems in most major sensory modalities.

3. *Deficits in Interhemispheric Integration.* These deficits are manifest in problems integrating the two sides of the body. Ayres (1972) believes these deficits are common in children with reading problems and that they can be shown clinically as the child tends to use each side of the body independently and avoids crossing the midline.

4. *Visual and Space Perception Deficits.* These problems are typically associated with a more extensive problem that involves inadequate integration of vestibular, proprioceptive, tactile, and visual stimuli at the level of the brain stem. Developmental apraxia may also result.

5. *Auditory-Language Deficits.* These deficits are a result of problems in areas 3 and 4 and disrupt written and spoken language.

Sensory integrative therapy attempts to remediate these problems through the development of perception and learning via the enhancement of organizations and sensations at the brain stem level. Motor activities are the principal therapeutic media and center around activities that require the child to adapt and organize a variety of sensory motor experiences while taking an active role in each process. Coordinated use of the two sides of the body is promoted.

Carefully controlled studies of the outcome of sensory integrative therapy are lacking, particularly in regard to improvements in academic skills. The therapy is a deficit-centered approach to remediation, though not strictly a process approach. However, it seems unlikely that learning disabilities can be corrected through the use of gross motor activities and physical exercise.

REFERENCES

Ayres, A. J. (1972). *Sensory integration and learning disorders.* Los Angeles: Western Psychological Services.

Quiros, J. B. de. (1976). Diagnosis of vestibular disorders in the learning disabled. *Journal of Learning Disabilities, 9,* 39–47.

Silberzahn, M. (1982). Sensory integrative therapy. In C. R. Reynolds & T. B. Gutkin (Eds.), *The handbook of school psychology.* New York: Wiley.

CECIL R. REYNOLDS
Texas A&M University

AYRES, A. JEAN

REMEDIATION, DEFICIT-CENTERED MODELS OF

SENSORY MOTOR INTEGRATION

See SENSORY INTEGRATIVE THERAPY.

SEPARATION ANXIETY DISORDER

Separation Anxiety Disorder refers to excessive anxiety and fear in response to separation from the home or those with whom a child is attached. The anxiety is displayed before age 18, lasts for at least 4 weeks, and is greater than that normally displayed by others of the same age. Separation Anxiety Disorder results in significant distress or impairment in social, academic, or other important areas of functioning (American Psychiatric Association, 2000).

Separation anxiety is common in infants and young children. Its symptomology includes an acute and early onset and may occur following a major stressful event in a child's life (e.g., start of school, illness, or death of a parent, a move to a new home or city; American Psychiatric Association, 2000). Children with Separation Anxiety Disorder may display persistent and excessive worry about loss or danger occurring to a loved one, reluctance to go to school, impaired functioning in some areas (e.g., reluctant to engage in sports, clubs, or other social events), fear of being alone, reluctance to sleep alone, reoccurring nightmares, and somatic complaints (American Psychiatric Association, 2000).

Children who display anxious-resistant attachment, lack of social support, or diminished coping and problem-solving skills are at risk for this disorder. Risk factors for Separation Anxiety Disorder also include parent behaviors (e.g., depression, inhibition, anxiety, obsessive-compulsive, overprotective, or abnormal attachment to the child; Donavan & Spence, 2000; Kearney, Sims, Pursell, & Tillotson, 2003; Manicavasagar, Silove, Wagner, & Hadzi-Pavlovic, 1999). A genetic basis for separation anxiety has been identified (Donovan & Spence, 2000; Feigon, Waldman, Levy, & Hay, 2001). Intervention methods to help overcome Separation Anxiety Disorder may focus on the child, the family, or both. Child-focused interventions have found cognitive behavioral therapy generally provides the most effective treatment method (Barrett, Dadds, & Rapee, 1996). This treatment includes identifying anxious thoughts and replacing them with more adaptive coping self-statements, using small rewards, and promoting parental involvement (Kendall, 1994). Other treatment options include behavioral therapy that focuses strictly on the child's overt behavior, interventions designed to promote social and coping skills, and pharmacological treatments for anxiety (e.g., Fluoxetine and Fluvoxamine; Birmaher et al., 2003; Elliot, 1999; Pine, 2001; Shortt, Barrett, & Fox, 2001).

Family-focused interventions may include helping a parent replace excessive attachment with more healthy forms of attachment, promoting child-parent communication styles, assisting parents in providing social support, and promoting the child's independence (Donavan & Spence, 2000).

Many children display signs of separation anxiety without meeting the criteria for a separation anxiety disorder. For example, separation anxiety is somewhat common during early childhood at the start of school or if a parent must leave the home for a few days or weeks to attend to personal or business responsibilities. Under these conditions, the anxiety associated with separation is normal, often dissipates within a few days or weeks, and does not result in significant distress or impairment in life activities (Bernstein & Borchardt, 1991).

Separation Anxiety Disorder impacts many areas of a child's life, not only one (e.g., schooling). A diagnosis of school phobia, not Separation Anxiety Disorder, is suitable when the behaviors are limited to school resistance. Additionally, one needs to distinguish separation anxiety from other anxiety disorders, including Panic Disorder, Agoraphobia Generalized Anxiety Disorder, social phobia, specific phobia, Obsessive-Compulsive Disorder, Posttraumatic Stress Disorder, and Acute Stress Disorder. Anxiety is common in them and expressed through cognitive, physiological, and behavioral manifestations (Mash & Barkley, 2003).

Some cultures value childhood independence while others highly value interdependence. Young children in families that value and promote interdependence may be more inclined to display separation anxiety, given their fear to leave their loved ones. Thus, cultural influences should be considered when evaluating the causes of separation anxiety, forming a diagnosis, and planning treatment methods (American Psychiatric Association, 2000).

REFERENCES

American Psychiatric Association. (2000). *Diagnostic and statistical manual of mental disorders* (4th ed., text revision). Washington, DC: Author.

Barrett, P. M., Dadds, M. R., & Rapee, R. M. (1996). Family treatment of childhood anxiety: A controlled trial. *Journal of Consulting and Clinical Psychology, 64*(2), 333–342.

Bernstein, G. A., & Borchardt, C. M. (1991). Anxiety disorders of childhood and adolescence: A critical review. *Journal of the American Academy of Child and Adolescent Psychiatry, 30*, 519–532.

Birmaher, B., Axelson, D. A., Monk, K., Kalas, C., Clark, D. B., Ehmann, M., Bridge, J., Heo, J., & Brent, D. A. (2003). Fluoxetine for the treatment of childhood anxiety disorders. *Journal of the American Academy of Child and Adolescent Psychiatry, 42*(4), 415–423.

Donavon, C. L., & Spence, S. H. (2000). Prevention of childhood anxiety disorders. *Clinical Psychology Review, 20*(4) 509–531.

Elliott, J. G. (1999). Practitioner review: School refusal: Issues of conceptualization, assessment, and treatment. *Journal of Child Psychology and Psychiatry, 40*(7), 1001–1012.

Feigon, S. A., Waldman, I. D., Levy, F., & Hay, D. A. (2001). Genetic and environmental influences on separation anxiety disorder symptoms and their moderation by age and sex. *Behavior Genetics, 31*(5), 403–411.

Kearney, C. A., Sims, K. E., Pursell, C. R., & Tillotson, C. A. (2003). Separation anxiety disorder in young children: A longitudinal and family analysis. *Journal of Clinical Child and Adolescent Psychology, 32*(4), 593–598.

Kendall, P. C. (1994). Treating anxiety disorders in children: Results of a randomized clinical trial. *Journal of Consulting and Clinical Psychology, 62*(1), 100–110.

Manicavasagar, V., Silove, D., Wagner, R., & Hadzi-Pavlovic, D. (1999). Parental representations associated with adult separation anxiety and panic disorder-agoraphobia. *Australian and New Zealand Journal of Psychiatry, 33*, 422–428.

Mash, E. J., & Barkley, R. A. (2003). *Child psychopathology* (2nd ed.). New York: Guilford.

Pine, D. S. (2001). Fluvoxamine for the treatment of anxiety disorders in children and adolescents. *New England Journal of Medicine, 344*(17), 1279–1285.

Shortt, A. L., Barrett, P. M., & Fox, T. L. (2001). Evaluating the FRIENDS program: A cognitive-behavioral group treatment for anxious children and their parents. *Journal of Clinical Child Psychology, 30*(4), 525–535.

JULIE BELL
KELLY WINKELS
University of Florida

SEPTO-OPTIC DYSPLASIA

Septo-optic dysplasia, also known as De Morsier syndrome, is a rare disorder characterized by visual impairments and pituitary deficiencies. The etiology of Septo-optic dysplasia is not known; however, this birth defect is found in a higher percentage of infants who are the first-born children of young mothers. Both genders are affected equally by this rare disorder.

Visual impairments include dimness in sight, especially in one eye (often referred to as lazy eye), and dizziness. These symptoms result from small, not-fully-developed optic disks associated with the visual system. In this disorder, the pupil (the opening in the eyeball through which light enters) does not respond appropriately. Instead of a consistent response, the pupil's response to light of the same intensity varies from one occasion to another. Occasional field dependence has also been noted. Besides visual impairments, an underactive pituitary gland is present either at birth or later in development. If left untreated, a child's growth is stunted. Jaundice may also be present at birth.

Standard treatment for Septo-optic dysplasia is symptomatic and supportive. Hormone replacement therapy is used to treat the pituitary hormone deficiencies. Children with Septo-optic dysplasia are usually of normal intelligence; however, mental retardation or learning disabilities may occur (Thoene, 1992). Occasional sexual precocity has been reported (Jones, 1988).

If a child experiences learning problems or developmental delays, a comprehensive neuropsychological evaluation is recommended to determine cognitive strengths and weaknesses. Based on those results, recommendations can be made, and an individualized educational plan can be developed and implemented in the schools.

REFERENCES

Jones, K. L. (Ed.). (1988). *Smith's recognizable patterns of human malformation* (4th ed.). Philadelphia: W. B. Saunders.

Thoene, J. G. (Ed.). (1992). *Physician's guide to rare diseases*. Montvale, NJ: Dowden.

JOAN W. MAYFIELD
*Baylor Pediatric Specialty
Service*

PATRICIA A. LOWE
University of Kansas

SEQUENCED INVENTORY OF COMMUNICATION DEVELOPMENT, REVISED

The Sequenced Inventory of Communication Development, Revised Edition (SICD-R; Hendrick, Prather, & Tobin, 1984) is a diagnostic assessment tool to evaluate the communication abilities of normal and retarded children, ages 4 months to 4 years. The SICD-R utilizes both parental report and observation of communication behaviors. The inventory includes 100 items which are broken into Receptive and Expressive Scales. Responses may also be recorded on the Behavioral Profile that examines awareness, discrimination, understanding, imitation, initiation, response, motor, vocal, and verbal areas. There is also a Process Profile that examines semantics, syntax, pragmatics, perceptual, and phonological areas.

The normative data are from a sample of 252 children, all Caucasian from monolingual homes, who were believed to have normal hearing, language, physical, and mental development. Additional data from a field study in Detroit are also reported; however, Pearson (1989) notes that these additional data do not provide answers to questions about reliability or validity of the SICD-R. Only 10 subjects are reported as a sample providing test-retest data and the reliability value reported was .93. Interrater reliability (based on 21 children) was reported to be 96 percent agreement between two raters. The reliability data must be viewed with caution because of the small number of subjects in the reliability studies (Mardell-Czudnowski, 1989; Pearson, 1989). Validity data are not complete enough to warrant the SICD-R's use for determining delays (Pearson, 1989).

In 1989, a version of the SICD-R was developed for adults and adolescents who do not possess any speech skills or who have only minimal skills. This version is titled the Adapted Sequenced Inventory of Communication Development (A-SICD; McClennen, 1989). The A-SICD allows examinees to respond through gestures, signing, picture board communication, or voice communication. Like the SICD-R, the A-SICD has both a Receptive and Expressive Scale.

Validation studies for the A-SICD were conducted with 40 subjects between the ages of 16 and 55. Interrater reliability was reported ($N = 10$) to be 88 to 100 percent on the Receptive Scale and 90 to 100 percent on the Expressive Scale. Internal consistency was .78 for the Receptive Scale and .91 for the Expressive Scale. Because of the small sample size, the generalizability of these results is questionable. The A-SICD is not norm-referenced; thus, the examiner must use clinical judgement to interpret the inventory. Carey (1995) notes that much of the same information collected on the A-SICD could be obtained through structured observations of the examinee in educational, vocational, or home settings.

REFERENCES

Carey, K. T. (1995). Review of the Adapted Sequenced Inventory of Communication Development. In J. J. Kramer & J. C. Conoley (Eds.), *The twelfth mental measurements yearbook* (pp. 32–33). Lincoln, NE: Buros Institute of Mental Measurements.

Hendrick, D. L., Prather, E. M., & Tobin, A. R. (1984). *Sequenced Inventory of Communication Development.* Seattle: University of Washington Press.

Mardell-Czudnowksi, C. (1989). Review of the Sequenced Inventory of Communication Development. In J. J. Kramer & J. C. Conoley (Eds.), *The eleventh mental measurements yearbook* (pp. 740–742). Lincoln, NE: Buros Institute of Mental Measurements.

McClennen, S. E. (1989). *Adapted Sequenced Inventory of Communication Development.* Seattle: University of Washington Press.

Pearson, M. E. (1989). Review of the Sequenced Inventory of Communication Development. In J. J. Kramer & J. C. Conoley (Eds.), *The eleventh mental measurements yearbook* (pp. 742–744). Lincoln, NE: Buros Institute of Mental Measurements.

ELIZABETH O. LICHTENBERGER
The Salk Institute

VERBAL SCALE IQ

SEQUENTIAL AND SIMULTANEOUS COGNITIVE PROCESSING

Sequential and simultaneous are two of many labels used to denote two primary forms of information coding processes in the brain. These coding processes are the primary functions of Luria's (1973) Block II of the brain (the parietal, occipital, and temporal lobes, also known as the association areas of the brain). They have been proposed as fundamental integration processes in Das, Kirby, and Jarman's (1979) model of Luria's fundamental approach to human information processing. Other labels commonly used to distinguish these forms of processing include successive versus simultaneous (Das et al., 1979), propositional versus appositional (Bogen, 1969), serial versus multiple or parallel (Neisser, 1967), and analytic versus gestalt/holistic (Levy, 1972).

No matter what label is applied, the descriptions of the processes corresponding to each label appear to be defining similar processes though some minor distinctions may exist. Thus sequential processing is defined as the processing of information in a temporal or serial order. Using this coding process, analysis of information proceeds in successive steps in which each step provides cues for the processing of later steps. This type of processing is generally employed (e.g., when an individual repeats a series of numbers that have been orally presented). Each stage of processing is dependent on the completion of the immediately preceding stage.

Simultaneous coding processes are used when all the pieces of information or all the stimuli are surveyable at one time and are thus available for processing at one time;

Figure 1 An example of a task that might be used to assess an individual's simultaneous cognitive processing skills; what do you think is pictured here? (The answer is in the text)

that is, at the analysis of parts of information can take place without dependence on the parts' relationship to the whole. When an individual discerns the whole object with only parts of the picture available, this is usually accomplished using simultaneous processing. Figure 1 presents an example of a strongly simultaneous processing task. See if you can determine what is pictured. Even with many of the parts missing and the pictured figure only in silhouette form, most individuals beyond the age of 10 to 12 years will recognize the figure to be a man on horseback. Some will have great difficulty or take a long time to recognize the figure; this is true especially if one takes a step-by-step approach to determining the identity of the picture, looking at individual pieces and trying to add them as a simple sum of the separate parts. While not impossible, such an approach is more difficult.

In the literature, several assumptions regarding these two forms of processing are presented. First, sequential and simultaneous processing are not hierarchical. That is, one form of processing does not appear to be more complex than the other. Both appear to require the transformation of stimulus material before synthesis of the information can occur (Das et al., 1979).

Second, determining whether to process information sequentially or simultaneously is not solely dependent on the presentation mode of the stimuli to be processed (e.g., visual or auditory). Rather, the form of processing used appears to be more dependent on the cognitive demands of the task and the unique sociocultural history and genetic predisposition of the individual performing the task (Das et al., 1979; Kaufman & Kaufman, 1983). This may become habitual and individuals do develop preferred styles of information processing.

Third, sequential and simultaneous processing have been indirectly linked to various areas of the brain, but psychologists do not agree on the exact location of each of these functions. Some contend that processing abilities are best associated with the two hemispheres of the brain (Gazzaniga, 1975; Reynolds, 1981), with sequential processing being a left hemisphere function and simultaneous processing being a right hemisphere function. Luria (1973), on the other hand, located successive or sequential processing as a function of the frontal regions of the brain, with simultaneous processing carried out in the occipital-parietal or rear sections of the brain.

These forms of processing have traditionally been measured in nonbrain-damaged individuals with a battery of standardized tests, the components of which are certainly less than pure measures of process. Evidence of simultaneous processing abilities has been inferred from individuals' performance on such instruments as Raven's Progressive Matrices (Raven, 1956), Memory-for-Designs (Graham & Kendall, 1960), and Figure Copying (Ilg & Ames, 1964). Each of these tasks places a premium on visuo-spatial skills and the synthesis of information for successful performance.

Sequential processing abilities have typically been inferred from observing an individual's performance on such tasks as Digit Span (a purely auditory task), Visual Short-Term Memory, and Serial or Free Recall. It is apparent that it is not the mode of presentation but rather the cognitive demands of the task that are the major determining factors in what cognitive processing style is used.

In 1983, the Kaufman Assessment Battery for Children (K-ABC; Kaufman & Kaufman, 1983) was introduced into psychological and educational circles. This instrument was designed as an individually administered intelligence test for children ages 2½ and 12½; it is composed of several subtests that according to factor analytic data, measure sequential and simultaneous processing abilities. Focused on process rather than content as the major distinction of how children solve unfamiliar problems, this instrument has resulted in more controversy and discussion than any intelligence test in recent history (Reynolds, 1985).

Controversy has arisen over the Kaufmans' assertion that knowledge about a child's information-processing abilities, as measured on the K-ABC, in conjunction with other sources of data, can more easily translate into educational programming for children with learning or behavioral problems than traditionally had been possible from data gathered on other, content-based intelligence tests. Primarily employing an aptitude ¥ treatment interaction (ATI) paradigm (Cronbach, 1975) and the habilitation philosophy of neuropsychology (Reynolds, 1981), the Kaufmans propose using knowledge regarding a child's individual strengths in information processing (e.g., simultaneous processing) as the foundation for any remedial plans thus developed. The notion of a strength model of remediation is in direct contrast to the deficit-centered training models that have dominated special education remedial plans for years, but that have proven largely ineffective in improving academic abilities (Ysseldyke & Mirkin, 1982).

Although preliminary data seem encouraging regarding the efficacy of using knowledge of a child's individual processing style to remediate learning or behavioral difficulties (Gunnison, Kaufman, & Kaufman, 1983), the data are not sufficient to support this assumption unequivocably. Much research remains to be done in this area.

REFERENCES

Bogen, J. E. (1969). The other side of the brain: Parts I, II, & III. *Bulletin of the Los Angeles Neurological Society, 34,* 73–203.

Cronbach, L. J. (1975). Beyond the two disciplines of scientific psychology. *American Psychologist, 30,* 116–125.

Das, J. P., Kirby, J. R., & Jarman, R. F. (1979). *Simultaneous and successive cognitive processes.* New York: Academic.

Gazzaniga, M. S. (1975). Recent research on hemispheric lateralization of the human brain: Review of the split brain. *UCLA Educator, 17,* 9–12.

Graham, F. K., & Kendall, B. S. (1960). Memory-for-Designs Test: Revised general manual. *Perceptual & Motor Skills, 43,* 1051–1058.

Gunnison, J., Kaufman, N. L., & Kaufman, A. S. (1983). Reading remediation based on sequential and simultaneous processing. *Academic Therapy, 17,* 297–307.

Ilg, F. L., & Ames, L. B. (1964). *School readiness: Behavior tests used at the Gesell Institute.* New York: Harper & Row.

Kaufman, A. S., & Kaufman, N. (1983). *The Kaufman Assessment Battery for Children.* Circle Pines, MN: American Guidance Service.

Levy, J. (1972). Lateral specification of the human brain: Behavioral manifestations and possible evolutionary basis. In J. A. Kiger (Ed.), *Biology of behavior.* Cornallis: Oregon State University Press.

Luria, A. R. (1973). *The working brain: An introduction to neuropsychology.* London: Penguin.

Neisser, W. (1967). *Cognitive psychology.* New York: Appleton-Century-Crofts.

Raven, J. C. (1956). *Coloured progressive matrices: Sets A, Ab, B.* London: H. K. Lewis.

Reynolds, C. R. (1981). Neuropsychological assessment and the habilitation of learning: Considerations in the search for the aptitude ¥ treatment interaction. *School Psychology Review, 10,* 343–349.

Reynolds, C. R. (Ed.). (1985). K-ABC and controversy [Special issue]. *Journal of Special Education, 18*(3).

Ysseldyke, J., & Mirkin, P. (1982). The use of assessment information to plan instructional interventions: A review of the research. In C. R. Reynolds & T. B. Gutkin (Eds.), *The handbook of school psychology.* New York: Wiley.

Julia A. Hickman
Bastrop Mental Health Association

INFORMATION PROCESSING
KAUFMAN ASSESSMENT BATTERY FOR CHILDREN–SECOND EDITION

PERCEPTUAL TRAINING
REMEDIATION, DEFICIT-CENTERED MODELS OF

SEQUENTIAL ASSESSMENT OF MATHEMATICS INVENTORIES: STANDARDIZED INVENTORY

The Sequential Assessment of Mathematics Inventories: Standardized Inventory (SAMI; Reisman & Hutchinson, 1985) is designed to measure the achievement of specific mathematics content objectives and to compare students' performance to national norms. It may be used to assess children in kindergarten through the eighth grade.

The SAMI is presented to students in an easel format, with the questions read aloud by the examiner. Students respond by pointing, writing, or verbally responding. Nine scores are obtained on the SAMI: Mathematical Language (grades K–3 only), Ordinality (grades K–3 only), Number/Notation, Computation, Measurement, Geometric Concepts, Mathematical Applications (grades 4–8 only), Word Problems, and Total. Subtest standard scores have a mean of 10 and a standard deviation of 3.

The SAMI was normed on a sample of about 1,400 students in kindergarten through eighth grade. Test-retest reliability values over a 6-week interval ranged from .43 to .89 with a median of .66. However, five of the subtests have reliability values below .50. Internal consistency values range from .72 to .97 with a median of .93. Validity evidence is limited to one study comparing the SAMI and two standardized achievement tests, as well as the reported intercorrelation of subtests. Fleenor (1992) states that the SAMI has promise as a measure of mathematics performance, but needs more data supporting its reliability and validity.

REFERENCES

Fleenor, J. W. (1992). Review of the Sequential Assessment of Mathematics Inventories: Standardized Inventory. In J. J. Kramer & J. C. Conoley (Eds.), *The eleventh mental measurements yearbook* (pp. 817–819). Lincoln, NE: Buros Institute of Mental Measurements.

Reisman, F. K., & Hutchinson, T. A. (1985). *Sequential Assessment of Mathematics Inventories: Standardized Inventory*. San Antonio, TX: Psychological Corporation.

ELIZABETH O. LICHTENBERGER
The Salk Institute

MATHEMATICS, LEARNING DISABILITIES IN

SERIOUSLY EMOTIONALLY DISTURBED

The term seriously emotionally disturbed (SED) has been defined by federal legislation (IDEA) as a condition with one or more of the following characteristics occurring to a marked degree and over a long period of time: (1) inability to learn not explainable by health, intellectual, or sensory factors; (2) inability to develop or maintain appropriate interpersonal relationships with students and teachers; (3) inappropriate behaviors or feelings in normal circumstances; (4) a pervasive mood of depression; (5) a tendency to develop physical symptoms or fears in response to personal or school difficulties [Code of Federal Regulations, Title 34, Section 300. 7(b)(9)]. According to the legislative definition, the term specifically includes childhood schizophrenia but specifically excludes children who are socially maladjusted except when the maladjustment is accompanied by serious emotional disturbance. Although autism was originally included as a form of serious emotional disturbance, in the *Diagnostic and Statistical Manual of Mental Disorders* (DSM-III), autism was removed from classification as a psychosis and defined as a pervasive developmental disorder. This reclassification of autism was based on research that has established clear differences between autism and the childhood psychoses on a variety of dimensions, including symptomatology, age of onset, family history of psychopathology, language ability, intellectual functioning, and socioeconomic status.

The U.S. Department of Education (1997) reports that the incidence of emotional disturbance in children and youth served in the public schools for the 1995–96 school year was 438,217. The causes of emotional disturbance are varied and include factors such as genetics, trauma, diet, stress, social skills deficits, and family dysfunction. Children and youth exhibit psychiatric disorders in different ways than adults. Therefore, emotional disturbance may be seen in behaviors such as immaturity, hyperactivity, self-monitoring deficits, social skill deficits, learning difficulties and aggression or self-injurious behavior. Children with the most serious emotional disturbances may exhibit distorted thinking, extreme anxiety, abnormal mood swings, and other symptoms indicative of psychoses (NICHCY, 1998).

Children and youth with emotional disturbance are identified and referred to special education much in the same way as learning disabled or other exceptional students. Usually, the behaviors that are interfering with the student's ability to succeed in school have been longstanding and have not been responsive to preservice referral interventions by the teacher or school team. The student is assessed usually by the school psychologist who, through a process of inclusion and exclusion, assesses eligibility for services in special education. The assessment must have examined how the student is functioning across settings; have ruled out medical, neurological, and neuropsychological conditions; and have assessed the student across modalities and in an objective and comprehensive manner.

The entrance to special education for SED students has changed over the years to reflect the least restrictive environment (LRE) principle of IDEA and similar legislation. Placement of these students in psychiatric residential facilities has declined in recent years due to LRE and to financial constraints; however, the need for comprehensive treatment is still present. The inclusion movement has advocates that suggest that SED students are best served in the regular classroom with special education support. However, again, the least restrictive environment for SED students should be determined on a case-by-case method. What is least restrictive for one SED student may be a dangerous or nonadvantageous placement for another.

The difficulty of placement, treatment, and education for SED students has probably steered the field to look towards the identification of at-risk students and culturally competent intervention. Lago-Delello (1996) did a study of the differences between kindergarten and first-grade children identified as "at-risk" or "not-at-risk" for the development of severe emotional disturbance on selected factors of classroom dynamics. The comparison focused on teacher factors, classroom interactions, student factors, and instructional factors. Results indicated that at-risk students experienced a markedly different reality in the classroom than their not-at-risk peers. Four major-findings emerged: (1) At-risk students were generally rejected by their teachers and not-at-risk peers were not; (2) At-risk students received significantly more negative or neutral teacher feedback statements than not-at-risk peers; (3) At-risk students spent significantly less time academically engaged than not-at-risk peers; and (4) teachers made few accommodations for these students and were generally resistant to making adjustments in tasks, materials, or teaching methods to meet the individual needs of at-risk students. Others (e.g., McKinney, Montague, & Hocutt, 1998) are developing screening instruments and procedures to identify students at risk for emotional disturbance.

Ongoing teacher training for regular and special educators has been identified on many levels; and much of it has targeted multicultural competencies (Singh, 1997). The more that SED students are included in regular education, the more competencies are essential for all personnel involved in the regular education process.

Outcomes for SED students are not as good as they are for students with some other disabilities. Greenbaum (1996) has found that serious problems in these students tend to be present even seven years after the initial identification. These problems many times become lifelong adjustment issues and are highly correlated with adult high-risk behaviors in crime and substance abuse. The magnitude of the problem with the SED population is supported by data on these students concerning academic outcomes, graduation rates, school placement, school absenteeism, dropout rates, encounters with the juvenile justice system, and identification rates of students of varying socioeconomic backgrounds. Seven interdependent strategic targets have been identified by the Chesapeake Institution (1994) to address the future of policy, funding, and treatment of SED by federal, state, and local agencies: (1) expand positive learning opportunities

and results; (2) strengthen school and community capacity; (3) value and address diversity; (4) collaborate with families; (5) promote appropriate assessment; (6) provide ongoing skill development and support; and (7) create comprehensive collaborative systems. Three universal themes are also stressed: first, collaborative efforts must extend to initiatives that prevent emotional and behavioral problems from developing or escalating; second, services must be provided in a culturally sensitive and respectful manner; and third, services must empower all stakeholders and maintain a climate of possibility and accountability.

The federal government is revising the definition of SED (NICHCY, 1998). Hopefully, more emphasis will be placed on prevention. The identification of at-risk children is the key to preventing serious adjustment problems for many children and youth. The field is moving towards being able to identify, in an objective and a culturally competent manner, young students who are having problems meeting the demands of everyday living. Once identified, this population can receive sensitive programming that includes family participation. Together, the school and family can help those young children who have not yet developed serious emotional difficulties to adjust and to meet the demands of their age group. The alternative is the present situation, where hundreds of thousands of children and youth are already suffering and in serious jeopardy of losing their ability to receive the benefits of an appropriate education.

REFERENCES

American Psychiatric Association. (1980). *Diagnostic and statistical manual of mental disorders* (3rd ed.). Washington, DC: Author.

Chesapeake Institute. (1994). *National agenda for achieving better results for children and youth with serious emotional disturbance.* Washington, DC: Author.

Greenbaum, P. E. (1996). *National adolescent and child treatment study: Outcomes for children with serious emotional and behavioral disturbance.* (ERIC Clearinghouse No. EJ53063)

Lago-Delello, E. (1996, April 1–5). *Classroom dynamics and young children identified as at-risk for the development of serious emotional disturbance.* Paper presented at the Annual International Convention of the Council for Exceptional Children, Orlando, FL.

McKinney, J. D., Montague, M., & Hocutt, A. M. (1998, April 16). *A two year follow-up study of children at risk for developing SED: Implications for designing prevention programs.* Paper presented at the Annual Convention of the Council for Exceptional Children, Minneapolis, MN.

National Information Center for Children and Youth with Disabilities (NICHCY). (1998). *General information about emotional disturbance.* Fact Sheet Number 5 (FS5). Washington, DC: Author.

Singh, N. N. (1997). Value and address diversity. *Journal of Emotional & Behavioral Disorders, 5*(1), 24–35.

U.S. Department of Education. (1997). *Nineteenth annual report to Congress on the implementation of the Individuals with Disabilities Education Act*. Washington, DC: Author.

STAFF

CHILDHOOD PSYCHOSIS
CHILDHOOD SCHIZOPHRENIA
EMOTIONAL DISORDERS

SERVICE DELIVERY MODELS

Service delivery models are programs, processes, and safeguards established to ensure a free, appropriate public education for disabled children and youths. The models that have been developed for the delivery of services to school-aged children with disabilities generally reflect in their form and operation the influence of at least three factors: (1) the statutory requirements and congressional intent of Individuals with Disabilities Education Act (IDEA); (2) the nature of the particular state or local education agency providing the services in terms of physical size, population distribution, and, to some extent, the available fiscal and human resources; and (3) the specific needs of the children being served. IDEA requires that children with disabilities to the degree possible be educated with nondisabled children and that removal from the regular education environment occur "only when the nature or severity of the handicap is such that education in regular classes with the use of supplementary aids and services cannot be achieved satisfactorily" (U.S.C. 1412(5)(B)). The regulations for the Act elaborate on this condition and refer to a continuum of alternate placements that must include instruction in regular classes with access to resource room services or itinerant instruction if necessary, special classes, special schools, home instruction, and instruction in hospitals and institutions. The regulations also require assurance that the various alternative placements are available to the extent necessary to implement the individualized education program for each child with disabilities. The congressional intent clearly was to ensure the design of models for the delivery of services to meet the instructional needs of each child with disabilities rather than to allow assignment of a child with disabilities to whatever special education services happen to be available at the time, unless those services also happen to meet the needs of the particular child as detailed in that child's individual education plan (IEP).

The continuum of alternative placements as listed in the U.S. Department of Education regulations together with the language of IDEA suggest the basic models for the delivery of special education and related services. The number of children placed in different educational settings are reported every year as seen in Table 1 for the 1994–95 school year.

Reynolds (1962) originally laid out a chart showing various organizational patterns for instruction. His work was later modified by Deno and illustrates a cascade of services for disabled children (Reynolds & Birch, 1982). The placements as shown in Figure 1 can be classified according to the amount of direct intervention provided by someone other than the regular classroom teacher; the more direct services necessary, the more a child moves away from the first level placement, the regular classroom. As the triangular shape of the illustration might suggest more children with special needs should be found in regular classrooms with access to consultant or itinerant support or resource room assistance and fewer in the special classes, special schools, residential schools, or placements outside the school setting. The figure has been adapted to include collaborative/consultative teaching arrangements that allow the special education student to remain in the regular education classroom with direct instruction from the regular and special education teachers.

IDEA and its regulations intend for regular class placement to be the goal for students with disabilities. There will always be some students whose educational needs cannot be met in the regular class, however, without some adaptations, special equipment and/or materials, or extra help (Cartwright, Cartwright, & Ward, 1985). Because the regular class teacher may not be adequately trained to make those adaptations, secure the special equipment or materials, or provide the specialized instruction, full-time regular class placement for some children may be enhanced by the provision of consulting teachers who collaborate with regular class teachers and provide up to and including direct instruction.

Educators, parents, advocates, and others who promote appropriate inclusion of students with disabilities in general education classes believe that doing so will provide those students with greater access to the general education curriculum, appropriate education with their nondisabled peers, raise expectations for student performance, and improve coordination between regular and special educators. They also believe that greater inclusion will result in increased school-level accountability for educational results (U.S. Department of Education, 1998).

In 1994–1995, 2.2 million of the total 4.9 million students with disabilities ages 6 through 21 spent at least 80 percent of their school day in general education classes (see Table 1), and more than 95 percent of all students with disabilities attended regular schools. The environments in which students receive services vary according to the individual needs of the child. Although 87 percent of students with speech and language impairments were served in regular classes for 80 percent or more of the school day, only 9.7 percent of those with mental retardation were served in regular class placements. Students ages 6–11 were more likely to receive services in regular class placements than students ages 12–17 or 18–21 (U.S. Department of Education, 1998).

Table 1 Percentage of children ages 3–21 served in different educational environments under IDEA, Part B, during the 1994–95 school year

State	All disabilities (%)							
	Regular class	Resource room	Separ class	Public separ facil	Private separ facil	Public resid facil	Private resid facil	Home hosp envir
Alabama	44.36	37.73	15.28	1.23	0.17	0.61	0.20	0.41
Alaska	60.71	25.57	13.24	0.03	0.21	0.06	0.13	0.05
Arizona	40.67	36.35	19.82	1.64	0.92	0.19	0.21	0.20
Arkansas	41.13	38.84	14.19	0.29	2.90	0.01	1.11	1.52
California	51.54	19.40	25.09	1.38	1.58	0.20	0.31	0.50
Colorado	69.75	16.48	10.11	1.25	0.19	0.70	0.90	0.62
Connecticut	56.49	18.80	19.53	1.55	2.29	0.05	0.93	0.36
Delaware	26.93	60.21	7.66	4.58	0.01	0.05	0.09	0.47
District of Columbia	13.57	18.82	43.35	13.43	8.87	0.00	1.58	0.38
Florida	40.73	22.31	32.67	2.29	0.30	0.43	0.00	1.27
Georgia	42.38	31.03	25.46	0.67	0.14	0.01	0.10	0.20
Hawaii	43.49	32.24	22.97	0.38	0.06	0.04	0.10	0.72
Idaho	64.97	23.83	9.54	1.03	0.11	0.02	0.24	0.26
Illinois	27.46	33.96	31.17	4.18	2.00	0.42	0.30	0.51
Indiana	61.23	12.09	23.96	1.65	0.10	0.47	0.14	0.35
Iowa	60.77	26.01	10.14	1.65	—	0.90	0.19	0.33
Kansas	50.07	31.38	14.81	1.84	0.75	0.77	0.12	0.26
Kentucky	52.64	32.67	12.56	0.66	0.17	0.76	0.04	0.49
Louisiana	35.53	18.10	42.99	1.30	0.07	1.28	0.06	0.66
Maine	50.51	33.17	10.66	0.83	2.72	0.05	0.82	1.24
Maryland	49.09	19.40	24.36	3.77	1.93	0.65	0.42	0.38
Massachusetts	66.40	13.29	14.24	1.57	3.02	—	0.68	0.79
Michigan	45.10	24.89	22.36	5.50	—	0.20	0.10	1.86
Minnesota	60.06	22.75	10.30	4.70	0.39	0.83	0.26	0.72
Mississippi	34.39	37.25	25.81	0.88	0.18	0.67	0.05	0.76
Missouri	46.29	30.14	20.83	1.54	0.60	0.22	0.17	0.21
Montana	55.90	29.96	11.44	0.80	0.28	0.62	0.55	0.45
Nebraska	58.25	23.64	12.40	3.66	0.27	0.29	0.09	1.40
Nevada	42.18	36.88	17.39	3.28	0.00	0.00	0.03	0.25
New Hampshire	51.97	22.16	19.33	2.88	1.27	0.26	1.51	0.62
New Jersey	45.38	15.59	29.21	3.13	5.27	0.80	0.07	0.56
New Mexico	31.99	28.82	37.65	0.04	0.01	0.94	0.05	0.51
New York	38.82	14.62	35.02	7.42	2.18	0.64	0.52	0.80
North Carolina	58.63	20.75	17.45	1.55	0.46	0.67	0.01	0.47
North Dakota	75.10	12.56	8.98	1.78	0.22	0.52	0.46	0.38
Ohio	57.68	23.12	15.68	2.18	0.00	0.35	0.00	0.99
Oklahoma	49.39	32.96	15.60	0.93	0.09	0.53	0.09	0.40
Oregon	68.79	18.75	8.42	1.33	1.34	0.37	0.28	0.72
Pennsylvania	37.84	28.07	28.98	1.75	1.57	0.61	0.28	0.90
Puerto Rico	7.14	52.90	29.44	4.23	2.09	0.43	0.10	3.68
Rhode Island	51.03	18.76	24.63	0.79	2.67	0.00	1.38	0.73
South Carolina	36.80	36.47	24.26	1.59	0.04	0.48	0.03	0.34
South Dakota	60.81	23.70	11.67	0.58	0.76	0.69	1.63	0.15
Tennessee	49.70	28.79	17.75	0.93	0.80	0.47	0.43	1.13
Texas	27.40	46.78	23.88	0.52	0.03	0.13	0.01	1.26
Utah	40.20	34.98	20.04	2.79	0.00	1.67	—	0.34
Vermont	83.76	4.39	4.96	1.20	1.39	0.12	1.71	2.46
Virginia	38.36	31.14	26.65	1.10	0.73	0.67	0.25	1.09
Washington	50.14	29.22	18.57	1.03	0.32	0.20	0.01	0.51
West Virginia	9.98	70.10	18.32	0.43	0.08	0.57	0.03	0.49
Wisconsin	38.06	37.58	22.59	1.18	0.05	0.35	0.02	0.16
Wyoming	57.05	32.35	8.19	0.38	0.43	0.89	0.55	0.16
American Samoa	62.84	23.65	13.51	0.00	0.00	0.00	0.00	0.00
Guam	35.89	52.79	10.65	0.62	0.00	0.00	0.06	0.00
Northern Marianas	83.57	11.19	3.50	0.00	0.00	0.00	0.00	1.75
Palau	54.95	23.42	17.12	0.00	0.00	0.00	0.00	4.50
Virgin Islands	—	—	—	—	—	—	—	—
Bur. of Indian Affairs	24.49	58.75	14.90	0.22	0.24	0.90	0.40	0.09
U.S. and outlying areas	45.04	27.01	23.26	2.22	1.04	0.43	0.24	0.76
50 states, D.C., & P.R.	45.07	26.96	23.28	2.23	1.04	0.43	0.24	0.76

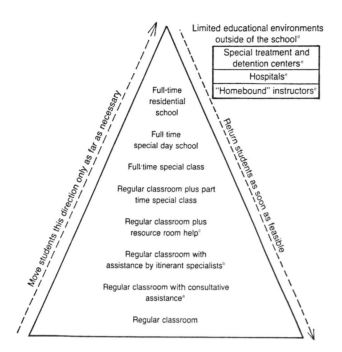

Figure 1 The original special education cascade. *Source:* Reynolds, M. C. and Birch, J. W. (1982). *Teaching exceptional children in all America's schools.* Reston, VA: Council for Exceptional Children. Adapted by E. Fletcher-Janzen.

[a]Consultative assistance might be offered, for example, by school psychologists, consulting teachers, resource room teachers, supervisors or others. The term *consultative* denotes only *indirect* services such as prereferral interventions and no *direct* service or instruction to the child by the consultant.

[b]Direct instruction is provided by the regular and special education teacher in a variety of collaborative or consultative arrangements.

[c]Itinerant specialists commonly include speech and hearing therapists and mobility instructors for the blind, for example. They offer some *direct* instruction to the students involved.

[d]A resource classroom is a special station in a school building that is manned by a resource teacher who usually offers some direct instruction to selected students but also usually offers consulting services to regular teachers. Sometimes resource teachers are categorical (such as resource teacher for the blind) but increasingly resource teachers are employed for a more generic, noncategorical role.

[e]This special set of environments is included here in set-aside fashion because usually students are placed in these settings for reasons other than educational. For example, they go to detention centers on court orders for reason of conviction for some criminal offense; or they go to hospitals or are held at home because of health problems. Special educators often work in these *limited* environments and some degree of specialization in education is required. But, in the main, there is strong preference, from an educational point of view, for return of the students to regular school environments as soon as feasible.

A resource room program can enable some children who need more intensive instruction in some or all of the basic skills, or whose behavior at times goes beyond what is appropriate or tolerable in the regular class, to remain in the regular class except for limited periods of time each day or week. The resource room model has been particularly popular for learning-disabled students, although students with other handicapping conditions also profit from additional help provided by resource room teachers. Some resource room programs are organized by disability area while others, particularly in more recent years, accommodate children with a variety of handicapping conditions but whose instructional needs are similar.

Placement in a special class for all or part of the school day is considered necessary for some children. Frequently, the deciding factors for inclusive programming, resource room, part-time special class, or full-time special class placement are the amount of time the disabled child can benefit from time in the regular class and the severity of the needs of that child. Interestingly, there seems to be considerable overlap in the types of students, the amount of time spent in the regular class, and the ways teachers actually use their time in resource room classes, self-contained special classes, and even residential classes, at least for emotionally disabled students (Peterson, Zabel, Smith, & White, 1983). This suggests some inconsistencies in determining appropriate placement for children and in defining responsibilities for special and regular education personnel.

Some children with disabilities are placed in special schools for their daily instructional programs. Such children, by the nature of their placement, have limited access to participation in social, academic, extracurricular, or spontaneous activities with nondisabled children. These children are, therefore, to be placed in special schools and residential settings only when the severity of their conditions warrants such placement and only for so long as that placement is necessary. The same holds true for those students in settings such as hospitals, treatment centers, and detention facilities that are outside the educational system.

The overriding principle in selecting appropriate placement for a child with disabilities who needs special education and related services is that of the least restrictive environment. No one placement or service delivery system described here can be cited as the best for all disabled children, and that includes the regular classroom, although some proponents of full inclusion would argue this point. Rather, selection must be made on the basis of what setting permits the implementation of the IEP designed for a given child and allows for meaningful involvement with nondisabled children, if possible in the same community where the disabled child would attend school if there were no handicapping condition necessitating a special education program.

While the service delivery models described represent the typical programs available for children with disabilities, or those that should be available by law and regulation, the specific character of any particular program will be determined in part by the nature of the geography, size, population distribution, and resources available in the child's district of residence. Rural areas have special challenges to face, among which are transportation, length of time en route to programs, recruitment and retention of qualified personnel to serve children with low-incidence disabilities, smaller tax base, and in some communities, the power of tradition (Helge, 1984). Urban areas face another set of challenges that typically include transportation in densely populated areas, desegregation issues, and the problems that develop when large numbers of people with little in common must interact under crowded conditions.

In addition to these special urban and rural factors, there is the impact that access to special education programs in private schools can have. The laws and regulations are clear that children with disabilities must be provided appropriate free public education in approved private day and residential schools only, and in accord with the principle of the least restrictive environment (Grumet & Inkpen, 1982; U.S. Office of Education, 1977). If parents wish their disabled child to attend a private school program and place their child in that program themselves, then except for special circumstances, the parents are responsible for the cost of their child's education. But if the private day or residential school placement is recommended as the appropriate one for the child by the child's local school district, then the education program must be provided at no cost to the parents. Already complex issues regarding private school placement become even more complicated when out-of-state private schools offer programs considered appropriate for children with certain types of needs as, for example, multihandicapped children or deaf-blind children.

In summary, the cascade of service delivery models emphasizes the place where children with special needs might be assigned for instruction. These models have collected criticism because of their focus on placement more than program content. Inherent in the instructional cascade is the goal of equipping the regular classroom to be a learning environment where the diverse needs of many children, including disabled, gifted, and disabled gifted learners, can be accommodated (Reynolds & Birch, 1982).

Service delivery models in the context of special education have changed over the years as laws, the inclusion movement, court decisions, local needs, parental pressures, fiscal and human resources, and community concerns have made their influence felt. Ysseldyke and Algozzine (1982) have suggested that change will continue but primarily in response to economic needs. More recently, Crowner (1985) has presented a taxonomy of special education finance and an analysis of funding bases, formulas and types and sources of funds for special education. The balance between congressional intent and legal necessity, local control, fiscal reality, and administrative expediency is delicate at best. For the benefit of all children currently in school and those to come, efforts must continue to be directed at designing and operating service delivery systems that meet the needs of all children, those who have conditions requiring special education and those who do not.

REFERENCES

Cartwright, G. P., Cartwright, C. A., & Ward, M. E. (1985). *Educating special learners* (2nd ed.). Belmont, CA: Wadsworth.

Crowner, T. T. (1985). A taxonomy of special education finance. *Exceptional Children, 51*(6), 503–508.

Fox, W. L., Egner, A. N., Paolucci, P. E., Perelman, P. F., McKenzie, H. S., & Garvin, J. S. (1973). An introduction to a regular classroom approach to special education. In E. Deno (Ed.), *Instructional alternatives for exceptional children*. Reston, VA: Council for Exceptional Children.

Grumet, L., & Inkpen, T. (1982). The education of children in private schools: A state agency's perspective. *Exceptional Children, 49*(3), 200–206.

Haight, S. L. (1984). Special education teacher consultant: Idealism versus realism. *Exceptional Children, 50*(6), 507–515.

Helge, D. (1984). The state of the art of rural special education. *Exceptional Children, 50*(4), 294–305.

Peterson, R. L., Zabel, R. H., Smith, C. R., & White, M. A. (1983). Cascade of services model and emotionally disabled students. *Exceptional Children, 49*(5), 404–408.

Reynolds, M. C., & Birch, J. W. (1992). *Teaching exceptional children in all America's schools*. Reston, VA: Council for Exceptional Children.

Salund, S. J. (1984). Factors contributing to the development of successful mainstreaming programs. *Exceptional Children, 50*(5), 409–416.

U.S. Office of Education. (1977, August 23). Education of handicapped children: Implementation of Part B of the Education of the Handicapped Act. *Federal Register, 42*(163), 42474–42518.

U.S. Department of Education. (1998). *Nineteenth Annual Report to Congress*. Washington, DC: Author.

Ysseldyke, J., & Algozzine, B. (1982). *Critical issues in special and remedial education*. Boston: Houghton Mifflin.

MARJORIE E. WARD
The Ohio State University

CASCADE MODEL OF SPECIAL EDUCATION SERVICES
INDIVIDUALS WITH DISABILITIES EDUCATION IMPROVEMENT ACT OF 2004 (IDEIA)
LEAST RESTRICTIVE ENVIRONMENT
RESOURCE ROOM
SELF-CONTAINED CLASSROOM

SETTING EVENT

Setting event is a term that is used to describe antecedent events, operations, or conditions that may influence student responding (Chandler & Dahlquist, 2006). The field of Applied Behavior Analysis also refers to setting events as establishing operations (Michael, 1993). Horner, Vaughn, Day, and Ard (1996) write that "the term *setting events* is used to indicate events that alter the likelihood of a behavior by momentarily altering the value of reinforcers or punishers" (p. 382). Generally, setting events are organized around three distinct contexts: (1) biological setting events, (2) environmental setting events, and (3) social or contextual setting events (Chandler & Dahlquist). Examples of setting events can include the presence or absence of medications, existing medical conditions or illnesses, unusual patterns of sleep, changes in diet, increases in classroom noise or other disruptions, difficult interactions with adults or peers, and alteration of an existing schedule (O'Neill, Horner, Albin, Sprague, Storey, & Newton, 1997).

Horner et al. (1996) emphasizes that setting events do not occasion a problem behavior; instead, they change the conditions that previously existed by altering what was reinforcing or punishing. For example, if a student comes to school and he or she did not have access to dinner the night before or breakfast that morning (biological setting event), the value of food and the desire to access it would be very different than if the student was satiated upon arriving at school. Additionally, if a student had a difficult interaction with a peer during passing period (social setting event), it might increase the likelihood that when presented with a request by the teacher to join a cooperative learning group that the student would refuse to follow that direction, even after prompting and encouragement was attempted, which had been a successful strategy in the past.

Setting events are best understood when examined as part of the three-term contingency (Maag, 1999). The three-term contingency allows teachers to look at behavior in relation to the antecedents that preceded the behavior and the consequences that followed the behavior. The three-term contingency uses the following notation: A–B–C, where A stands for "antecedent," B stands for "behavior," and C for "consequence." Using our definition, setting events are antecedent events, operations, or conditions that can be either proximal or distal to the actual behavior. Therefore, when added to the three-term contingency, you have the following notation: SE–A–B–C. In other words, when Maria misses her medications (setting event), and she is presented with a difficult academic task (antecedent), she runs out of the classroom (behavior), in order to escape or avoid the academic task (consequence).

As teachers and researchers learn to gather information on setting events and their relationship to changes in student behavior, positive behavior interventions and supports can be put in place that may diminish or eliminate the negative effect of the setting event for the person of concern and bring increasing understanding to the role that antecedents play in occasioning both appropriate and challenging behavior (Chandler & Dahlquist, 2006).

REFERENCES

Chandler, L. K., & Dahlquist, C. M. (2006). *Functional assessment: Strategies to prevent and remediate challenging behavior in school settings* (2nd ed.). Upper Saddle River, NJ: Pearson Merrill Prentice Hall.

Horner, R. H., Vaughn, B. J., Day, H. M., & Ard, W. R., Jr. (1996). The relationship between setting events and problem behavior: Expanding our understanding of behavioral support. In L. K.

Koegel, R. L. Koegel, & G. Dunlap (Eds.), *Positive behavioral support: Including people with difficult behavior in the community* (pp. 381–402). Baltimore: Brookes.

Maag, J. W. (1999). *Behavior management: From theoretical implications to practical applications.* San Diego, CA: Singular.

Michael, J. L. (1993). *Concepts and principles of behavior analysis.* Kalamazoo, MI: Association for Behavior Analysis.

O'Neill, R. E., Horner, R. H., Albin, R. W., Sprague, J. R., Storey, K., & Newton, J. S. (1997). *Functional assessment and program development for problem behavior: A practical handbook* (2nd ed.). Pacific Grove, CA: Brooks/Cole.

RANDALL L. DE PRY
University of Colorado at Colorado Springs

BEHAVIORAL ASSESSMENT

SEX DIFFERENCES IN LEARNING ABILITIES

Popular stereotypes and epidemiological research both suggest that boys have more learning and adjustment problems than girls. Boys are more readily referred for psychological services than girls with similar problems (Caplan, 1977). In addition, boys of all ages are more likely than girls to be evaluated or treated for learning problems (Eme, 1979). The reasons for apparent gender differences are widely debated. Some suggest that (1) boys are at some biological or developmental disadvantage that affects learning and adjustment (Ullian, 1981); (2) classrooms, teachers, or professionals are less tolerant of boys than girls (Pleck, 1981); and (3) the problems manifested by girls are perceived differently or considered to be less important. This debate leads one to question whether recognizable gender differences exist in children's learning abilities.

Many persons believe the cognitive abilities of boys and girls differ. The common notion is that boys have better developed quantitative abilities while girls are better in verbal areas. After reviewing literature on psychological gender differences, Maccoby and Jacklin (1974) conclude that three cognitive gender differences are well established: girls have greater verbal ability than boys, while boys have better visual-spatial and mathematical ability than girls. The authors further conclude that gender differences in verbal ability emerge after age 11, gender differences in quantitative (i.e., mathematical) abilities emerge at around 12, and gender differences in spatial ability emerge in adolescence.

Other investigations report gender differences in verbal and spatial abilities at earlier ages than those reported by Maccoby and Jacklin. A number of researchers have found that females as early as age 1 month and throughout the preschool years show some slight verbal advancement over males, an advancement that appears stronger and more reliable after age 10 or 11 (McGuinness & Pribram, 1979; Oetzel, 1966; Petersen & Wittig, 1979). While sex differences are seen more clearly during and after adolescence, male superiority in spatial performance may appear as early as age 6 (Harris, 1978; McGuinness & Pribram, 1979). The magnitude of differences between males and females depends in part on the type of spatial skill. Maccoby and Jacklin (1974) distinguish visual nonanalytic spatial skills (i.e., those solved without the use of verbal mediation) from visual analytic spatial skills (i.e., those solvable with verbal mediation). Postpubescent males score consistently higher than females on most spatial abilities, particularly nonanalytic visualization abilities (Maccoby & Jacklin, 1974; Petersen & Wittig, 1979).

Generalizations regarding gender differences in verbal, spatial, and quantitative areas do not go unchallenged. After reviewing the evidence on cognitive gender differences used by Maccoby and Jacklin, Sherman (1978) reported the magnitude of the gender differences to be very small. Hyde (1981) also concludes from a meta-analysis of the data used by Maccoby and Jacklin that the gender differences in verbal ability, quantitative ability, visual-spatial ability, and field articulation are small. Sex differences appear to account for no more than 5 percent of the population variance. In general, gender differences in verbal ability are smaller and gender differences in spatial ability are larger. Hyde questions whether statistically significant sex differences in cognitive abilities are practically significant. In other words, the common notion that girls are better at verbal tasks while boys excel in spatial or mathematical areas largely is meaningless in terms of educational implications. Moreover, a close review of literature examining gender differences is likely to lead readers to conclude that boys and girls exhibit similarities more frequently than differences.

Do sex differences exist in school achievement? The evidence is contradictory. Few gender differences in learning were found in a five-year longitudinal study of students ages 5 through 9 (Anastas & Reinherz, 1984). However, a review of the cross-national data on gender differences in achievement found that boys' mathematics achievement is higher than that of girls at both the elementary and secondary levels, that boys score higher in all areas of science, and that girls have higher achievement in verbal areas involving reading comprehension and literature (Fennema, 1982; McGuinness, 1993).

Assuming achievement is affected by opportunities to learn (e.g., participation in courses, amount of instruction), and that boys generally have more opportunities to learn mathematics and science than girls (Finn, Dulberg, & Reis, 1979), we may conclude that girls perform lower in math and science because of fewer opportunities in these areas rather than intrinsic factors. While research infrequently has considered the extent to which differences in socialization and educational experiences may account for differential performance and attainment, many social scientists believe most or even all sex differences in ability and achievement are due to differing cultural and social opportunities and expectations for boys and girls (Levine & Ornstein, 1983). Still, we know little about the origins of sex differences. When gender differences appear, we should be cautious in speculating about their etiologies.

REFERENCES

Anastas, J. W., & Reinherz, H. (1984). Gender differences in learning and adjustment problems in school: Results of a longitudinal study. *American Journal of Orthopsychiatry, 54,* 110–122.

Caplan, P. (1977). Sex, age, behavior and school subject as determinants of report of learning problems. *Journal of Learning Disabilities, 10,* 314–316.

Eme, R. (1979). Sex differences in childhood psychopathology. A review. *Psychological Bulletin, 86,* 574–593.

Fennema, E. (1982, March). *Overview of sex-related differences in mathematics.* Paper presented at the annual meeting of the American Educational Research Association, New York.

Finn, J. D., Dulberg, L., & Reis, J. (1979). Sex differences in educational attainment: A cross-national perspective. *Harvard Educational Review, 49,* 477–503.

Harris, L. J. (1978). Sex differences in spatial ability: Possible environmental, genetic, and neurological factors. In M. Kinsbourne (Ed.), *Asymmetrical function of the brain.* London: Cambridge University Press.

Hyde, J. S. (1981). How large are cognitive gender differences? A meta-analysis using w^2 and d. *American Psychologist, 36,* 892–901.

Levine, D. U., & Ornstein, A. C. (1983). Sex differences in ability and achievement. *Journal of Research & Development in Education, 16,* 66–72.

Maccoby, E. E., & Jacklin, C. N. (1974). *Psychology of sex differences.* Stanford, CA: Stanford University Press.

McGuinness, D., & Pribram, K. H. (1979). The origins of sensory bias in the development of gender differences in perception and cognition. In M. Bortner (Ed.), *Cognitive growth and development.* New York: Brunner/Mazel.

McGuinness, D. Gender differences in cognitive style: Implications for mathematics performance and achievement. In L. A. Penner & G. M. Batsche (Eds.), *The challenge in mathematics and science education. Psychology's response* (pp. 251–274). Washington, DC: APA.

Oetzel, R. (1966). Classified summary of research on sex differences. In E. E. Maccoby (Ed.), *The development of sex differences.* Stanford, CA: Stanford University Press.

Petersen, A. C., & Wittig, M. A. (1979). Sex differences in cognitive functioning: An overview. In M. A. Wittig & A. C. Petersen (Eds.), *Sex-related differences in cognitive functioning: Developmental issues.* New York: Academic.

Pleck, J. (1981). *The myth of masculinity.* Cambridge, MA: MIT Press.

Sherman, J. (1978). *Sex-related cognitive differences: An essay on theory and evidence.* Springfield, IL: Thomas.

Ullian, D. (1981). Why boys will be boys: A structural perspective. *American Journal of Orthopsychiatry, 51,* 493–501.

THOMAS OAKLAND
University of Florida

JEFF LAURENT
University of Texas

SEX EDUCATION OF INDIVIDUALS WITH DISABILITIES

Many professionals and parents believe the sexual needs of the disabled should be met (Craft & Craft, 1981; Fitz-Gerald & Fitz-Gerald, 1979; Love, 1983). The principle of normalization promoted in the United Nations Declaration of Rights of the Mentally Handicapped (United Nations, 1971) underscores this belief. The declaration states that people with disabilities have the same basic rights as other citizens of the same country and the same age. In the United States, normalization is espoused in the Rehabilitation Act of 1973 (PL 93-380) and the Individuals with Disabilities Act (IDEA), which provide for the individualized education of the disabled in accordance with the requirement of the least restrictive environment.

The advocacy of inclusion in school and the movement away from custodial institutional care and toward community living supply the impetus for focusing on the sexual rights of individuals with disabilities (Bass, 1974; Jacobs, 1978; Shindell, 1975; Thornton, 1979). In conjunction with the philosophy of protecting basic human rights, sex education is advocated to achieve the same ends for the disabled as for the nondisabled: to develop sexually fulfilled persons who understand themselves, their values, and resulting behaviors (Harris, 1974; Reich & Harshman, 1971). Moreover, many persons agree with Kempton (1977) that sex education is bound to the practical tasks of improving the social and sexual functions of the disabled. The need to moderate educational goals on the bases of age, gender, type of disability and severity of the disability is inherent in the nature of sex education of the disabled.

Alongside the demands for individualization of instruction is a humanistic approach that advocates meeting the needs of persons while deemphasizing labels (Johnson, 1981). In contradiction to the rationale given in the past, this outlook maintains that sex education should not only respond to critical sexual problems as they arise, or to conditioning that seeks to prevent all sexual experiences (Craft & Craft, 1978, 1980; Edmonson & Wish, 1975; Gordon, 1971a, 1971b; Kempton, 1977, 1978). Implied in the normalization philosophy is the goal of working for the good of all by securing individual freedom since, with teaching, training, and the availability of specific support services, individuals with disabilities are more likely to blend into society.

Notwithstanding the fact that the philosophy of normalization has impacted the literature, the topic of sex education for the disabled is fraught with controversy. Issues and concerns presently being raised include improvement of curricula and resources, training and preparation of teachers, assessment of the effects of teaching, and involvement of the parents in sex education.

Great strides have been made in the individualization of sex education (Johnson & Kempton, 1981). A wealth of curriculum guides exists that identifies programs to meet the varied needs of the disabled (see Edmonson, 1980, for a 30-reference list of programs and materials available for the blind, deaf, retarded, and emotionally impaired). Adapted sex education enables even the severely retarded to improve their sexual knowledge (Edmonson, 1980). However, outdated sex laws and repressive social attitudes often prevent the optimal development and employment of instructional resources (Sherwin, 1981). Teaching materials aimed at compensating for specific disabilities (e.g., genital models for use with the blind) can run afoul of obscenity laws. Also, few legal principles protect sex educators, counselors, or therapists (Sherwin, 1981). Audiotactual sex education programs for visually impaired children have been implemented successfully with the use of models, but touching the human body is seen as problematic (Knappett & Wagner, 1976; Tait & Kessler, 1976). Sex education programs for visually impaired children should take into account the sexual taboos of our culture (Torbett, 1974). Fortunately, according to Johnson (1981), this negativism is lifting somewhat as judged by a shift from a position of elimination regarding the acceptance of the sexuality of the disabled to a position of toleration. The evolution toward a more permissive attitude regarding sexual expression for recreational rather than procreational purposes has been conducive to this change. Still, sodomy laws in many states condemn all sexual activity as illegal except vaginal intercourse within marriage. These laws deny nonprocreative sex as a legitimate right. For a given disabled person, this form of sexual expression may be the only one possible. In light of such social taboos and legal restraints, the development of appropriate programming to suit the individual needs of the disabled is constrained.

Minimal attention is paid to sex education during the preparation of teachers for students with disabilities. A survey indicated that, while 61 percent of student teachers in special education courses received some preparation in sex education, this preparation was either an elective option or a few hours of coverage subsumed under a different topic such as methods of teaching (May, 1980). This is regrettable because sex education courses in special education could help teachers overcome their discomfort in dealing with this subject (Blom, 1971). Professionals can increase their comfort with sexual matters as well as improve attitude and knowledge levels as a result of systematic training in sexuality and disability (Chubon,

1981). Kempton (1978) has proposed training professionals to provide services, as well as develop policies, regarding the sexual rights of the disabled. She advises (1977) that successful programs be broadly conceived to prepare for skills for living in society.

A major obstacle to sex education of individuals with disabilities has been the denial of their sexuality by parents and teachers, who are concerned that education could trigger sexual experimentation and appetite (Craft, 1983). However, experts in this field (Gordon, 1975; Kempton, 1978) have argued that sex education results in improved social behavior, increased self-respect, more openness, and fewer guilt feelings. On the other hand, withholding information fails to deter sexual activity, causes confusion, needless fears, inappropriate behaviors, and unwanted consequences such as pregnancy.

In spite of this authoritative stance, advocates for sex education have provided little evidence that sex education has changed sexual behavior patterns or identified the valid expectations and limitations of their procedures (Balester, 1971). The literature that examines specific sex education programs for the disabled mainly presents theorizations rather than scientific data (Vockell & Mattick, 1972). Teaching the disabled is a complex task owing to such factors as low cognitive abilities and academic skill, short attention span, and secondary handicaps of a sensory, physical, emotional, or behavioral nature. Therefore, restraints in setting educational goals have been recommended (Watson & Rogers, 1980). However, programs that facilitate specific abilities (e.g., contraceptive use or knowledge of sexually transmitted diseases) seem to represent too modest a first step toward devising an educational technology of sexual instruction that will empirically appraise the limits of sexual development and social awareness in this diverse population.

While many parents are interested in sex education for their youngsters with disabilities, their sexual conservatism may severely limit the nature of the curriculum. For example, parents of sensorially impaired students give the highest rating to teaching less controversial topics such as cleanliness, knowledge of one's own body, venereal disease, dating, reproduction, pregnancy, marriage, and feelings about self and others. They frequently resist instruction regarding contraceptives, sexual intercourse, sexual deviancy, incest, divorce, masturbation, abortion, sterilization, and pornography (Love, 1983). Parental cooperation and support are crucial to program development and to the transfer of skills from school to home and community settings. Thus it remains essential to involve the parents in cooperative educational efforts by securing their agreement with expectations of instruction (Hamre-Nietupski & Ford, 1981; Kempton, 1975).

Normalization frequently entails the sexual development of individuals with disabilities to enable them to assume more normal lives. While there has been progress in designing and offering sex education program for the disabled, several areas of concern have hampered their acceptance. These include (1) constraints imposed on the design and implementation of curricula owing to legal and social restraints that pertain to sexual taboos; (2) neglect by teacher training institutes in the preparation of professionals in special education who are trained in sex education; (3) problems in assessing the effects of teaching because of the nature of affective instructional goals interacting with a diversity of abilities in this population; and (4) conservatism on the part of parents that tends to place limitations on expectations of instruction. These problems hinder but do not preclude change. Models for the successful institutionalization of sex education for the disabled exist elsewhere, as in Sweden (Grunewald & Linner, 1979). Public policy regarding sex education for the person with disabilities is desirable given the obvious needs in this area (Craft, 1983). The person with disabilities should understand their sexuality, should be safe from sexual exploitation, and should become responsible in their sexual behavior (Cole, 1993; Craft, 1983).

REFERENCES

Balester, R. J. (1971). Sex education: Fact and fancy. *Journal of Special Education, 5,* 355–357.

Bass, M. S. (1974). Sex education for the handicapped. *Family Coordinator, 23,* 27–33.

Blom, G. E. (1971). Some considerations about the neglect of sex education in special education. *Journal of Special Education, 5,* 359–361.

Chubon, R. A. (1981). Development and evaluation of a sexuality and disability course for the helping professions. *Sexuality & Disability, 4,* 3–14.

Cole, S. S., & Cole, T. M. (1993). Sexuality, disability, and reproductive issues through the lifespan. *Sexuality & Disability, 11*(3), 189–205.

Craft, A. (1983). Sexuality and mental retardation: A review of the literature. In A. Craft & M. Craft (Eds.), *Sex education and counseling for mentally handicapped people.* Baltimore: University Park Press.

Craft, A., & Craft, M. (1980). Sexuality and the mentally handicapped. In G. B. Simon (Ed.), *Modern management of mental handicap: A manual of practice.* Lancaster, England: MTP Press.

Craft, A., & Craft, M. (1981). Sexuality and mental handicap: A review. *British Journal of Psychiatry, 139,* 494–505.

Craft, M., & Craft, A. (1978). *Sex and the mentally handicapped.* London: Routledge & Kegan Paul.

Edmonson, B. (1980). Sociosexual education for the handicapped. *Exceptional Education Quarterly, 1,* 67–76.

Edmonson, B., & Wish, J. (1975). Sex knowledge and attitudes of moderately retarded males. *American Journal of Mental Deficiency, 80,* 172–179.

Fitz-Gerald, D., & Fitz-Gerald, M. (1979). Sexual implications of deaf-blindness. *Sexuality & Disability, 2*(3), 212–215.

Gordon, S. (1971a). Missing in special education. Sex. *Journal of Special Education, 5,* 351–354.

Gordon, S. (1971b). Okay, let's tell it like it is (instead of just making it look good). *Journal of Special Education, 5,* 379–381.

Gordon, S. (1975). Workshop: Sex education for the handicapped. In M. S. Bass & M. Gelof (Eds.), *Sexual rights and responsibilities of the mentally retarded.* Proceedings of the Conference of the American Association on Mental Deficiency, Washington, DC.

Grunewald, K., & Linner, B. (1979). Mentally-retarded: Sexuality and normalization. *Current Sweden,* 237–239.

Hamre-Nietupski, S., & Ford, A. (1981). Sex education and related skills: A series of programs implemented with severely handicapped students. *Sexuality & Disability, 4,* 179–193.

Harris, A. (1974). What does "sex education" mean? In R. Rogers (Ed.), *Sex education: Rationale and reaction.* Cambridge, England: Cambridge University Press.

Jacobs, J. H. (1978). The mentally retarded and their need for sexuality education. *Psychiatric Opinion, 15,* 32–34.

Johnson, W. R. (1981). Sex education for special populations. In L. Brown (Ed.), *Sex education in the eighties.* New York: Plenum.

Johnson, W. R., & Kempton, W. (1981). *Sex education and counseling of special groups.* Springfield, IL: Thomas.

Kempton, W. (1975). Sex education: A cooperative effort of parent and teacher. *Exceptional Children, 41,* 531–535.

Kempton, W. (1977). The mentally retarded person. In H. Gochros & J. Gochros (Eds.), *The sexually oppressed.* New York: Association.

Kempton, W. (1978). The rights of the mentally ill and mentally retarded: Are sexual rights included? *Devereux Forum, 13,* 45–49.

Knappett, K., & Wagner, N. N. (1976). Sex education and the blind. *Education of the Visually Handicapped, 8,* 1–5.

Love, E. (1983). Parental and staff attitudes toward instruction in human sexuality for sensorially impaired students at the Alabama Institute for Deaf and Blind. *American Annals of the Deaf, 128,* 45–47.

May, D. C. (1980). Survey of sex education coursework in special education programs. *Journal of Special Education, 14,* 107–112.

Reich, M., & Harshman, H. (1971). Sex education for the handicapped youngsters, reality or repression? *Journal of Special Education, 5,* 373–377.

Sherwin, R. (1981). Sex and the law on a collision course. In W. R. Johnson (Ed.), *Sex in life.* Dubuque, IA: Brown.

Shindell, P. E. (1975). Sex education programs and the mentally retarded. *Journal of School Health, 45,* 88–90.

Tait, P. E., & Kessler, C. (1976). The way we get babies: A tactual sex education program. *New Outlook for the Blind, 70,* 116–120.

Thornton, C. E. (1979). A nurse-educator in sex and disability. *Sexuality & Disability, 2,* 28–32.

Torbett, D. S. (1974). A humanistic and futuristic approach to sex education for blind children. *New Outlook for the Blind, 68,* 210–215.

United Nations. (1971). *Declaration of general and special rights of the mentally handicapped.* New York: U.N. Department of Social Affairs.

Vockell, E. L., & Mattick, P. (1972). Sex education for the mentally retarded: An analysis of problems, programs, and research. *Education & Training of the Mentally Retarded, 7,* 129–134.

Watson, G., & Rogers, R. S. (1980). Sexual instruction for the mildly retarded and normal adolescent. A comparison of educational approaches, parental expectations and pupil knowledge and attitude. *Health Education Journal, 39,* 88–95.

JACQUELINE CUNNINGHAM
University of Florida

THOMAS OAKLAND
University of Texas

PEDIATRIC AIDS
SOCIAL ISOLATION
SOCIAL SKILLS INSTRUCTION

SEX INFORMATION AND EDUCATION COUNCIL OF THE UNITED STATES

The Sex Information and Education Council of the United States (SIECUS) is a nonprofit, voluntary health organization dedicated to the establishment and exchange of information about human sexual behavior. The council is funded primarily by foundation grants and individual contributions. The SIECUS provides information and responds to requests for consultation from churches, communities, school boards, and any other national or international health or educational organizations interested in establishing or improving their sex education programs. As a part of this concern, SIECUS developed a policy and resource guide concerning sex education for the mentally retarded individual (SIECUS, 1971).

The guide begins by observing that the mentally retarded individual has sexual feelings similar to those of all humans, but that because of possible confusion and misunderstanding, the mentally retarded student may need sexual guidance and education to understand sex and his or her own sexuality. The SIECUS provides instructional, curricular, and counseling information in the guide that will be useful in helping the mentally retarded individual to achieve this understanding. Finally, information is provided regarding printed materials, films and filmstrips, tapes, and other teaching aids that may be useful in sex education for the mentally retarded individual.

REFERENCE

SIECUS. (1971). *A resource guide in sex education for the mentally retarded.* New York: Author.

JOHN R. BEATTIE
University of North Carolina at Charlotte

SEX RATIOS IN SPECIAL EDUCATION

As concern grows about sexual bias in society and its effect on children, attention is focusing on the classroom. Sex bias in education is of particular concern to the field of special education. Research indicates that more males than females are served in special education programs, and that the sex label has been recognized as having a profound impact on the education of children with disabilities. Gillespie and Fink (1974) report that the mere identification of exceptional children as either male or female results in arbitrary practice and discriminatory judgments, and in intervention decisions that limit opportunities for personal and vocational development of those children and youths.

There is a belief among educators that boys are more in need of special services than girls; consequently, more male students are provided with special education services. Boys are much more likely to be referred and treated in all the major areas of exceptionality; they are more likely to be identified as exhibiting reading problems, learning disabilities, and mental retardation (Gillespie & Fink, 1974). However, female students are shown to be more in need of special education assistance on the basis of standardized test data (Sadker, Sadker, & Thomas, 1981).

Caplan (1977) suggests that girls with learning disabilities are less likely than learning-disabled boys to be identified as learning disabled or to participate in special education programs. It is generally accepted among special educators that the male to female ratio in special education is about 3:1. Norman and Zigmond (1980) confirm that learning disabilities usually are identified as a male disorder; they find a ratio of 3.7:1. The authors report that the ratio is similar to the 3:1 ratio suggested by Kirk and Elkins (1975) and the 4.6:1 ratio reported by Lerner (1976). This has not been supported by research on reading disorders (Flynn & Rahbar, 1994).

Rubin and Balow (1971), in a longitudinal study of 967 kindergarten through third grade students, discovered that educationally defined behavior problems were exhibited by 41 percent of the children participating in their study. When results were reported by sex, the number of boys far exceeded the number of girls; boys were reported to have more attitude and behavior problems, to be receiving more special services, and to be repeating more grades. The authors suggested that teachers accept only a narrow range of behaviors, and that deviations outside this range are viewed as cause for intervention. This is supported by later research (Callahan, 1994).

Further evidence for the disproportionate number of males in special education comes from a study reported in Young, Algozzine, and Schmid. McCarthy and Paraskevopoulos (1969) examined behavior patterns of average, emotionally disturbed, and learning-disabled children, and found that boys outnumbered girls 8:1 in the emotionally disturbed sample and 9:1 in the learning-disabled sample.

Mirkin, Marston, and Deno (1982) investigated the referral-placement process and discovered that males were referred far in excess of females; however, this was true only for teacher judgment referrals. For referrals based on academic screening using curriculum-based tasks, no significant differences were found in the number of males versus females referred for special education. Furthermore, females who had been referred by teachers were rated as more problematic than the females referred by the screening tests.

A variety of theories have been proposed to account for the sex ratio discrepancy in special education. Caplan (1977) suggested that the boy/girl learning problem report ratio is aggravated by behavioral differences. Caplan and Kinsbourne (1974) discovered that girls who fail in school tend to behave in socially acceptable ways, but their male counterparts tend to react punitively and aggressively. On the basis of this discovery, the authors suggested that because teachers view aggression as the most disturbing type of behavior, they would be more likely to notice boys who are failing in school than their well-behaved, silent female counterparts. Consequently, boys would be more likely to be recognized as needing special attention, if only to get them out of the classroom.

Physiological explanations for the higher incidence of males in special education also have been offered; several categories of exceptionality such as that of learning disabilities have been explained on the basis of sex-linked genetic traits (Rossi, 1972). However, according to Singer and Osborn (1970), there are no known physiological causes to explain the higher number of males treated for mental retardation. Singer and Osborn explain the high ratio of males to females receiving treatment as stemming from sociocultural expectations such as behavior differences and less societal tolerance for boys with academic problems.

Whatever the cause of the unbalanced ratio of males to females in special education, it is apparent that a bias exists. Special educators must recognize this discrepancy, establish its causes, and make the delivery of special education services more equitable.

REFERENCES

Callahan, K. (1994). Causes and implications of the male dominated sex ratio in programs for students with emotional and behavioral disorders. *Education and Treatment of Children, 17*(3), 228–243.

Caplan, P. J. (1977). Sex, age, behavior and school subject as determinants of report of learning problems. *Journal of Learning Disabilities, 5,* 314–316.

Caplan, P. J., & Kinsbourne, M. (1974). Sex differences in response to school failure. *Journal of Learning Disabilities, 4,* 232–235.

Flynn, J. M., & Rahbar, M. H. (1994). Prevalence of reading failure in boys compared with girls. *Psychology in the Schools, 3, 1,* 66–71.

Gillespie, P. H., & Fink, A. H. (1974). The influence of sexism on the education of handicapped children. *Exceptional Children, 41,* 155–161.

Mirkin, P., Marston, D., & Deno, S. L. (1982). *Direct and repeated measurement of academic skills: An alternative to traditional screening, referral, and identification of learning disabled students* (Research Report No. 75). Minneapolis: University of Minnesota, Institute for Research on Learning Disabilities.

Norman, C. A., & Zigmond, N. (1980). Characteristics of children labeled and served as learning disabled in school systems affiliated with child service demonstration centers. *Journal of Learning Disabilities, 13*(9), 16–21.

Rossi, A. O. (1972). Genetics of learning disabilities. *Journal of Learning Disabilities, 5,* 489–496.

Rubin, R., & Balow, B. (1971). Learning and behavior disorders: A longitudinal study. *Exceptional Children, 38,* 293–299.

Sadker, D., Sadker, M., & Thomas, D. (1981). Sex equity and special education. *Pointer, 26*(1), 33–37.

Schlosser, L., & Algozzine, B. (1979). The disturbing child: He or she? *Alberta Journal of Educational Research, 25*(1), 30–36.

Singer, B. D., & Osborn, R. W. (1970). Special class and sex differences in admission patterns of the mentally retarded. *American Journal of Mental Deficiency, 75,* 162–190.

Young, S., Algozzine, B., & Schmid, R. (1979). The effects of assigned attributes and labels on children's peer accepted ratings. *Education & Training of the Mentally Retarded, 12,* 257–261.

KATHLEEN RODDEN-NORD
GERALD TINDAL
University of Oregon

PREREFERRAL INTERVENTION
SEX DIFFERENCES IN LEARNING ABILITIES

SEXUAL DISTURBANCES IN CHILDREN WITH DISABILITIES

Most of the research and study concerning sexual disturbances in individuals with disabilities has focused on those persons with physical disabilities and/or mental retardation in institutional settings. Sexual problems also exist in other special populations but they are less well documented.

Monat (1982) outlines a number of problems found in the mentally retarded population, including excessive and harmful masturbation, same-sex mutual masturbation, opposite-sex mutual masturbation, bestiality (especially in rural areas), sodomy, indecent exposure, child sexual abuse, lewd and lascivious behavior, and statutory rape. Undesired pregnancy is also a problem with the mentally retarded, though not necessarily a sexual disturbance.

The approaches recommended today for dealing with sexual disturbances in the mentally retarded ask that professionals who attempt to intervene be both knowledgeable about sex and sexuality and comfortable with this knowledge and their own sexuality. Recognition must be given to differing levels of cognitive ability with the mentally retarded population that lead to variable levels of conceptual understanding and to the likelihood of different sexual behaviors and problems at different levels of functioning. In the past, especially in residential facilities, excessive reliance on moralization, punishment, and sterilization (Haavik & Menninger, 1981) colored attempts to deal with sexual matters. Current approaches generally focus on staff training for desensitization, concrete sex education (including on birth control, marriage, and parenthood), the dispelling of sexual myths, the importance of personal choice and responsibility, the appropriateness of personal social behavior, and the concept of privacy. The staff needs to follow through and review to be certain learning has occurred and the information has been retained. Sex counseling, which is designed to deal with the values and feelings surrounding sexuality, is now more readily available to complement sex education (which is more concerned with the transfer of relevant information).

In examining sexual disturbances, the type of living environment involved is important. With the present preference for community living and independence for the disabled, greater emphasis must be placed on appropriate community behavior, the legality of different sexual behaviors, personal choices, and the acceptance of responsibility. The disabled adolescent or adult moving to a less restrictive setting must be aware of the dangers of venereal disease, acquired immune deficiency syndrome (AIDS), and prostitution (Monat, 1982). For some, especially those leaving certain residential facilities or protected home settings, community living arrangements, community-based training centers, or job sites of any type may offer the first true coeducational experiences. It has been shown that the knowledge of even noninstitutionalized mentally retarded young men and women is often severely limited (Brantlinger, 1985). West (1979) characterized the observed sexual behavior of institutionalized severely retarded adolescents and adults as essentially normal and appropriate, though sometimes socially improper. He noted that the residents' "sexual activity was very often the only spontaneous cooperative mutual behavior observed and the only interresident interaction apart from aggression."

Attitudes have always played a large part in viewing the sexuality of the disabled. Sexual disturbances or problems of physically disabled individuals, especially those with essentially normal intelligence whose physical disability resulted from postnatal accident, injury, or trauma, have been something of an exception among the general disabled population. Professionals, and probably society in general, seem more willing to recognize the sexual rights of this group and to provide the understanding, support, and even the aids or prostheses to help them regain normal sexuality (Thorn-Gray & Kern, 1983). This view is markedly different than that found when dealing with mentally retarded persons.

Where education has been unsuccessful in preventing sexual disturbances or counseling has been ineffective in eliminating inappropriate sexual behaviors, a variety of behavioral approaches have been found to be successful in individual cases. Hurley and Sovner (1983) describe case reports on the effective use of response cost procedures, aversive conditioning, overcorrection, in vivo desensitization, and positive reinforcement in dealing with problems such as exhibitionism, public masturbation, public disrobing, and fetishism. Assaultive and inappropriate interpersonal sexual behaviors were successfully eliminated in an adolescent male with Down syndrome through a combination of differential reinforcement of other behaviors and naturalistic social restitution. The control of this behavior was able to be generalized to the student's teachers (Polvinale & Lutzker, 1980).

Sexual problems noted in learning-disabled populations have often been attributed to conceptual difficulties, disinhibition, or inadequate impulse control. Insights into sex-related difficulties in blind and visually impaired persons can be found in Mangold and Mangold (1983) and in Welbourne et al. (1983). Information on sex deafness can be found in *Sexuality and Deafness* (Gallaudet College, 1979).

REFERENCES

Brantlinger, E. A. (1985). Mildly mentally retarded secondary students' information and attitudes toward sexuality and sex education. *Education & Training of the Mentally Retarded, 20,* 99–108.

Gallaudet College. (1979). *Sexuality and deafness.* Washington, DC: Outreach Services.

Haavik, S. F., & Menninger, K. A. (1981). *Sexuality, law, and the developmentally disabled person: Legal and clinical aspects of marriage, parenthood and sterilization.* Baltimore: Brookes.

Hurley, A. D., & Sovner, R. (1983). Treatment of sexual deviation in mentally retarded persons. *Psychiatric Aspects of Mental Retardation Newsletter, 2*(4), 13–16.

Mangold, S. S., & Mangold, P. N. (1983). The adolescent visually impaired female. *Journal of Blindness & Visual Impairment, 77*(6), 250–255.

Monat, R. K. (1982). *Sexuality and the mentally retarded.* San Diego, CA: College-Hill.

Polvinale, R. A., & Lutzker, J. R. (1980). Elimination of an inappropriate sexual behavior by reinforcement and social restitution. *Mental Retardation, 18*(1), 27–30.

Thorn-Gray, B. E., & Kern, L. H. (1983). Sexual dysfunction associated with physical disability: A treatment guide for the rehabilitation practitioner. *Rehabilitation Literature, 44*(5–6), 138–144.

Wellbourne, A., Lifschitz, S., Selvin, H., & Green, R. (1983). A comparison of the sexual learning experiences of visually impaired and sighted women. *Journal of Blindness & Visual Impairment, 77*(6), 256–261.

West, R. R. (1979). The sexual behaviour of the institutionalised severely retarded. *Australian Journal of Mental Retardation, 5,* II–L3.

JOHN D. WILSON
Elwyn Institutes

MASTURBATION, COMPULSIVE
MENTAL RETARDATION
SELF STIMULATION

SHELTERED WORKSHOPS

The concept of the sheltered workshop was introduced in the United States in 1838 by the Perkins Institute for the Blind. The early workshop programs that followed provided sheltered employment for those whose handicapping conditions precluded competitive employment.

Federal involvement with sheltered workshops came about 100 years later. In an effort to help sheltered workshops compete with other businesses for contracts, the 1938 amendments to the Vocational Rehabilitation Act (PL 75-497) allowed workshops to pay below-minimum wages to employees.

With the passage of the Vocational Rehabilitation Act of 1943 (PL 78-113), persons with mental retardation and mental illness were considered eligible for rehabilitation services. This initiated a change in rehabilitation programs in the United States. For the first time, there was recognition of persons who had never been employed.

The Vocational Rehabilitation Act amendments of 1965 (PL 89-333) expanded the definition of "gainful employment" to include not only competitive but also sheltered employment. There was an emphasis on the provision of services that would lead toward gainful sheltered employment for more severely disabled individuals. According to Snell (1983):

> Sheltered employment is when an individual is receiving subsidized wages or working for less than minimum wage, with handicapped co-workers at a job that provides limited advancement to competitive work settings and that is organized primarily for therapeutic habilitation or sheltered production. (p. 504)

The Rehabilitation Act of 1973 (PL 93-112) and the continuation amendments up to 1992 emphasized the provision of services that would lead toward gainful sheltered employment for persons with severe disabilities and the transition from school work.

Special education programs help prepare young adults with disabilities to work in sheltered workshops. According to Bigge (1982), the special education curriculum should include transition skills, work evaluation, work adjustment, work experience, vocational skills, and on-the-job training programs.

The sheltered workshop is the most widely used type of vocational training facility for adults with disabilities. Sheltered workshops can be classified into three general types: regular program workshops; work activities centers; and adult day programs. Regular program workshops (or transitional workshops) provide therapies and work intended to foster readiness for competitive employment. The Department of Labor requires that workers earn no less than 50 percent of minimum wages. Work activities centers (WACs) provide training, support, and extended employment in a sheltered environment to more severely disabled adults. A wage ceiling of 50 percent of minimum wage has been set for WACs clients. The Fair Labor Standards Act, as amended in 1966, defines regular program workshops and work activities centers. Both are monitored by the Department of Labor. Adult day programs, managed by state developmental disabilities agencies, provide nonvocational services such as socialization, communication skills, and basic work orientation. The primary goal of adult day programs is the acquisition of basic living skills, leading to a decrease in maladaptive behavior and movement toward more vocationally oriented programs.

A sheltered workshop operates as a business. It generally engages in one of three types of business activities: contracting, prime manufacturing, or reclamation. In contracting, there is an agreement that a sheltered workshop will complete a specified job within a specified time for a given price. Workshops bid competitively for each job. Prime manufacturing is the designing, producing, marketing, and shipping of a complete product. A reclamation operation is one in which a workshop purchases or collects salvageable material, performs a reclamation operation, and then sells the reclaimed product. Recently, sheltered workshops have been closing and competitive employment (supported employment, for example) has been substituted. The closure of some workshops has created a division of scholars as to what is the best interests of persons with disabilities' employment (Block, 1997).

REFERENCES

Bigge, J. L. (1982). *Teaching individuals with physical and multiple disabilities* (2nd ed.). Columbus, OH: Merrill.

Block, S. R. Closing the sheltered workshop. Toward competitive employment opportunities for persons with developmental disabilities. *Journal of Vocational Rehabilitation, 9*(3), 267–275.

Heward, W. L., & Orlansky, M. D. (1984). *Exceptional children.* (2nd ed.). Columbus, OH: Merrill.

Lynch, K. P., Kiernan, J. A., & Stark, J. A. (1982). *Prevocational and vocational education for special needs youth.* Baltimore: Brookes.

Mori, A. A., & Masters, L. F. (1983). *Teaching the severely mentally retarded.* Germantown, MD: Aspen.

Schreerenberger, R. C. (1983). *A history of mental retardation.* Baltimore: Brookes.

Snell, M. A. (1983). *Systematic instruction of the moderately and severely handicapped* (2nd ed.). Columbus, OH: Merrill.

CAROLE REITER GOTHELF
*Hunter College, City University
of New York*

**VOCATIONAL REHABILITATION COUNSELING
VOCATIONAL EDUCATION**

SIBLINGS OF INDIVIDUALS WITH DISABILITIES

Siblings of individuals with disabilities have received little research attention compared with the literature available on the effects of a disabled child on parents (Crnic, Friedrich, & Greenberg, 1983; Drew, Logan, & Hardman, 1984; Trevino, 1979). The available research, however, suggests that nondisabled siblings are a population at risk for behavioral problems, the degree to which is influenced by a number of variables and factors (Crnic et al., 1983; Gargiulo, 1984; Trevino, 1979). Specific factors that appear to interact and contribute to sibling adjustment include the number of normal siblings in the family (Powell & Ogle, 1985), the age and gender of siblings (Crnic et al., 1983; Grossman, 1972), and parental response and attitude toward the disabled child (Trevino, 1979). Trevino (1979) reports that prospects for normal siblings having difficulty in adjusting increase when (1) there are only two siblings in the family, one who is disabled and one who is not; (2) the nondisabled sibling is close in age to or younger than the disabled sibling or is the oldest female child; (3) the nondisabled child and the disabled child are the same sex; and (4) the parents are unable to accept the disability. Schwirian (1976), Farber (1959), and Cleveland and Miller (1977) found that the female sibling's role demanded more parent-surrogate duties as she was expected to help care for the disabled child when she was at home. In addition, sibling literature emphasizes healthy and honest parental attitudes and behaviors toward the child with disabilities as essential to the siblings positive growth and development.

Grossman (1972) found that socioeconomic status (SES) can also affect sibling responses to a disabled child. Middleclass families and those from higher SES families tended to be more financially secure and better prepared to use outside resources such as respite care services, thus lessening a youngster's responsibility of caring for a disabled sibling.

The emotional responses of siblings of the disabled have been reported to include hostility, guilt, fear, shame, embarrassment, and rejection. Crnic et al. (1983) found that the presence of a retarded child has a detrimental effect on a nonretarded sibling's (particularly a female's) individual functioning. This involves high degrees of anxiety, conflicts with parents, and problems in social and interpersonal relationships. On the other hand, Farber (1960) reported, after an extensive study, that many siblings adopted life goals toward dedication and sacrifice (Crnic et al., 1983).

Although the concerns of siblings vary according to the nature and degree of severity of their sibling's disability, key concerns, such as how to deal with parents, what to tell friends, and what kind of future they can expect for their disabled sibling, appear to be similar across types of impairments (Murphy, 1979). If the needs and concerns of siblings are not met, they may result in problems and negative feelings.

The psychological and behavioral problems that may result from having a sibling with diabilities is a reality that must be dealt with by parents and professionals. Siblings can benefit from the experience of having a sibling with disabilities if they are introduced to the situation in an understanding and compassionate way. Siblings and parents should seek support from family counselors, religious organizations, nonprofit agencies, and sibling support groups that focus on the individual needs, attitudes, concerns, and feelings of the nondisabled sibling. Teachers should be alerted to the child's family situation to provide additional support and information.

REFERENCES

Cleveland, D. W., & Miller, N. (1977). Attitudes and life commitments of older siblings of mentally retarded adults: An exploratory study. *Mental Retardation, 15,* 38–41.

Crnic, K. A., Friedrich, W. N., & Greenberg, M. T. (1983). Adaptation of families with mentally retarded children: A model of stress, coping and family ecology. *American Journal of Mental Deficiency, 88,* 125–139.

Drew, C. J., Logan, D. R., & Hardman, M. L. (Eds.). (1984). *Mental retardation: A life cycle approach* (3rd ed.). St. Louis, MO: Times/Mirror Mosby.

Farber, B. (1959). Effects of a severely mentally retarded child on family integration. *Monographs of the Society for Research in Child Development, 24* (whole No. 71).

Farber, B. (1960). Family organization and crisis: Maintenance of integration in families with a severely retarded child. *Monographs of the Society for Research in Child Development, 25,* 1–95.

Gargiulo, R. M. (1984). Understanding family dynamics. In R. M. Gargiulo (Ed.), *Working with parents of exceptional children* (pp. 41–64). Boston: Houghton Mifflin.

Grossman, F. K. (1972). *Brothers and sisters of retarded children: An exploratory study.* Syracuse, NY: Syracuse University Press.

Murphy, A. T. (1979). Members of the family: Sisters and brothers of the handicapped. *Volta Review, 81,* 352–354.

Powell, T. H., & Ogle, P. A. (1985). *Brothers and sisters in the family system.* Baltimore: Brookes.

Schwirian, P. M. (1976). Effects of the presence of a hearing impaired pre-school child in the family on behavior patterns of older "normal" siblings. *American Annals of the Deaf, 121,* 373–380.

Trevino, F. (1979). Siblings of handicapped children: Identifying those at risk. *Social Casework: Journal of Contemporary Social Work, 62,* 488–493.

MARSHA H. LUPI
Hunter College, City University of New York

FAMILY RESPONSE TO A CHILD WITH DISABILITIES
RESPITE CARE

SICARD, ABBÉ ROCHE AMBROISE CUCURRON (1742–1822)

Abbé Roche Ambroise Cucurron Sicard, educator of the deaf, studied with Abbé Epée at the National Institution for Deaf-Mutes in Paris and, in 1782, opened a school for the deaf at Bordeaux. Sicard succeeded Epée at the National Institution and, except for a few years during the French Revolution, served as its director until his death in 1822. Sicard made many improvements in Epée's educational methods. His most important publication was a dictionary of signs, a work begun by Epée.

The beginning of education for the deaf in the United States was greatly influenced by Sicard. He invited Thomas Gallaudet, who was planning the first school for the deaf in the United States, to observe the methods employed at the National Institute in Paris, with the result that Gallaudet became proficient in Sicard's methods. In addition, Sicard provided Gallaudet with his first teacher, Laurent Clerc.

REFERENCES

Bender, R. E. (1970). *The conquest of deafness.* Cleveland, OH: Case Western Reserve University Press.

Lane, H. (1984). *When the mind hears.* New York: Random House.

PAUL IRVINE
Katonah, New York

SICKLE-CELL DISEASE

Sickle-cell disease is an inherited blood disorder that occurs as two conditions, sickle-cell anemia (SCA) and sickle-cell trait (SCT). Sickle-cell anemia is the more serious of the two conditions; it can be defined as an abnormality of the hemoglobin molecule, the oxygen-carrying protein in the red blood cells. Oxygen-carrying red blood cells are usually round and flexible. Under certain conditions, the red blood cells of a person with sickle-cell anemia may change into a crescent or sickle cell. This unusual shape causes the cells to adhere in the spleen and other areas, leading to their destruction. This results in a shortage of red blood cells, which has serious consequences for the individual with SCA (Haslam & Valletutti, 1975; March of Dimes, 1985). These consequences include fever, abdominal discomfort, bone pain, damage to the brain, lungs, and kidneys, and, for some, death in childhood or early adulthood (Haslam & Valletutti, 1975; March of Dimes, 1985; National Association for Sickle Cell Disease [NASCD], (1978). Individuals with SCA will experience episodes of pain known as sickle-cell crisis. During these periods, the sickled cells become trapped in tiny blood vessels. This blocks other red blood cells behind them, which lose oxygen and become sickle-shaped, totally blocking the vessels. When the bone marrow inadequately produces red blood cells, the child experiences an aplastic crisis and requires blood transfusion (Weiner, 1973). These crises and their effects vary greatly from person to person. Most people with SCA enjoy reasonably good health much of the time (March of Dimes, 1985; NASCD, 1978).

Sickle-cell anemia occurs when a sickle-cell gene is inherited from each parent. A person with sickle-cell anemia has sickle cells in the bloodstream and has sickle-cell disease. The second condition, sickle-cell trait (SCT), occurs when a sickle-cell gene is inherited from one parent and a normal gene from the other. A person with sickle-cell trait does not have sickle cells in the bloodstream and does not have sickle-cell disease. Persons with SCT may pass the sickle-cell gene on to their offspring (March of Dimes, 1985; NASCD, 1978; Whitten, 1974). As an autosomal recessive disorder, children of parents who both carry the sickle-cell gene have a 50 percent chance of inheriting SCT, a 25 percent chance of being a carrier, and a 25 percent chance of having SCA (Whitten, 1974).

In the United States, sickle-cell disease occurs most frequently among blacks and Hispanics of Caribbean ancestry. About 1 in every 400 to 600 blacks and 1 in every 1,000 to 1,500 Hispanics inherit sickle-cell disease (March of Dimes, 1985). Approximately 1 in 12 black Americans carry a gene for sickle-cell trait (NASCD, 1978). Less commonly affected peoples include those whose ancestors lived in countries bordering on the Mediterranean Sea (Greeks, Maltese, Portuguese, Arabians; NASCD, 1978).

There is no known cure for sickle-cell anemia. However, a number of therapies for reducing the severity and frequency of crises are being tried (March of Dimes, 1985; Weiner, 1973). A blood test for sickle-cell anemia and its trait is readily available; it is called hemoglobin electrophoresis. There is also a prenatal test to determine whether the fetus will develop sickle anemia or be a carrier.

The child with SCA may need to be placed in an educational program that is geared to his or her physical capabilities. Services may assist the child and family in many areas such as adaptation to chronic illness and pain management (Conner-Warren, 1996). Since many individuals with SCA tire easily, children should be encouraged to participate in most school activities of other children their age with the understanding that they may rest more frequently. If communication between the child and family has been open and honest concerning SCA, then the child can develop healthy social attitudes and self-reliance (NASCD, 1978).

REFERENCES

Conner-Warren, R. L. (1996). Pain intensity and home pain management of children with sickle-cell disease. *Issues in Comprehensive Pediatric Nursing, 19*(3), 183–195.

Haslam, R. M. A., & Valletutti, P. J. (1975). *Medical problems in the classroom.* Baltimore: University Park Press.

March of Dimes. (1985). *Genetics series: Sickle cell anemia.* White Plains, NY: Author.

National Association for Sickle Cell Disease (NASCD). (1978). *Sickle cell disease: Tell the facts, quell the fables.* Los Angeles: Author.

Weiner, F. (1973). *Help for the handicapped child.* New York: McGraw-Hill.

Whitten, C. F. (1974). *Fact sheet on sickle cell trait and anemia.* Los Angeles: National Association for Sickle-Cell Disease.

MARSHA H. LUPI
Hunter College, City University of New York

SIDIS, WILLIAM JAMES (1898–1944)

William James Sidis was a famous child prodigy of the early twentieth century who came to a tragic end after leading a short, largely unfulfilled life. Sidis's history and early demise are often cited in early literature opposing acceleration and other aspects of special education for the intellectually gifted. Much of Sidis's life has been distorted in various informal accounts. Montour (1977) has characterized the use of Sidis's story to deny acceleration to intellectually advanced children as the Sidis fallacy. Simply stated, the Sidis fallacy denotes "early ripe, early rot."

In 1909, at the age of 11, Sidis entered Harvard College. A year later he lectured on higher mathematics at the Harvard Mathematical Club. Sidis had performed remarkably in intellectual endeavors throughout his life. By Montour's (1977) account, by the age of 3 he read fluently with good comprehension; he was writing with a pencil 6 months later. By age 4, Sidis was a fluent typist. When he was 6, Sidis could read English, Russian, French, German, and Hebrew; he learned Latin and Greek shortly thereafter. At the age of 8, Sidis passed the entrance exam at the Massachusetts Institute of Technology, developed a new table of logarithms employing base 12 instead of base 10, and passed the Harvard Medical School exam in anatomy. He was well qualified to enter Harvard at that time but was denied entrance based on his age. Sidis earned his BA in 1914, although it has been reported that he completed his work for the degree 2 years earlier. Sidis pursued some graduate study in several fields, including a year in law school, but never earned an advanced degree. He spurned academia after an unsuccessful year as a professor at Rice University at age 20. He became sullen, cynical, and withdrawn from society (Montour, 1977). Sidis chose to live as a loner, working at low-level clerical jobs until his death in 1944, at the age of 46, from a stroke.

Sidis's academic contributions were limited to two books. In 1926 he published *Notes on the Collection of Transfers.* A more serious volume, published in 1925 (but written in 1919 and 1920), *The Animate and Inanimate,* was devoted to a proof of James's theory of reserve energy.

Sidis's turn against academia and his choice to drop out of society seems related to his intellectual talent and precocity only in the most indirect fashion; it was certainly not a result of his academic acceleration. Montour (1977) argues credibly that it was the result of a rebellion against an overbearing, domineering, but emotionally barren father who rejected Sidis at the first sign of any weakness. Although the Sidis case is often cited in opposition to academic acceleration, there is little to support such a position on the basis of Sidis's history. In fact, far more cases of successful acceleration are present with outcomes strongly supportive of acceleration programs. Norbert Wiener (a classmate of Sidis), John Stuart Mill, Merrill Kenneth Wolf, David Noel Freedman, and John Raden Platt are but a few of many such successes (Montour, 1977). Indeed, educational acceleration will be the method of choice for the education of many intellectually precocious youths.

"It was not extreme educational acceleration that destroyed William James Sidis emotionally and mentally, but instead an interaction of paternal exploitation and emotional starvation" (Montour, 1977, p. 276). The events of Sidis's life are often exaggerated and misstated. The Sidis fallacy has restricted the education of the gifted and persists in some educational programs even today; it is yet another myth that afflicts programs for the gifted.

REFERENCES

Montour, K. (1977). William James Sidis, the broken twig. *American Psychologist, 32,* 265–279.

Sidis, W. J. (1925). *The animate and inanimate.* Boston: Badger.

Sidis, W. J. (1926). *Notes on the collection of transfer.* Philadelphia: Dorrance.

CECIL R. REYNOLDS
Texas A&M University

ACCELERATION OF GIFTED CHILDREN
STUDY OF MATHEMATICALLY PRECOCIOUS YOUTH

SIDIS FALLACY

See SIDIS, WILLIAM JAMES.

SIGHT-SAVING CLASSES

For much of the 20th century it was common to educate children with low vision in "sight-saving classes." This was done in public schools as well as in residential facilities. Such classes for partially sighted children were begun in public schools as far back as 1913 (Livingston, 1986).

The notion behind these sight-saving classes was that a low-vision child's residual vision would be damaged by overuse. The emphasis, thus, was on conserving the child's vision as far as possible. This meant that children whose vision was impaired but still usable were removed from presumably visually stressful situations by reducing visual demands made on them. Some were even educated in dark rooms or blindfolded. The situation today is dramatically altered. It is now believed that all children, including visually inpaired ones, benefit from using their visual abilities as much as possible.

REFERENCE

Livingston, R. (1986). Visual impairments. In N. G. Haring & L. McCormick (Eds.), *Exceptional children and youth* (4th ed., pp. 398–429). Columbus, OH: Merrill.

MARY MURRAY
Journal of Special Education

LOW VISION
PARTIALLY SIGHTED

SIGN LANGUAGE

Sign language is a general term that refers to any gestural/visual language that makes use of specific shapes and movements of the fingers, hands, and arms, as well as movements of the eyes, face, head, and body. There is no international system that is comprehensible to all deaf people. There exists a British Sign Language, a Spanish Sign Language, an Israeli Sign Language, and probably a sign language in every country where deaf people have needed to communicate among themselves rapidly, efficiently, and visually without the use of pad and pencil.

American Sign Language, sometimes called Ameslan or ASL, was created over the years by the deaf community in the United States. In ASL, one hand shape frequently denotes a concept. American Sign Language must be differentiated from finger spelling or dactylology, which is the use of hand configurations to denote the letters of the alphabet. In finger spelling, one hand shape stands for one letter. Sometimes finger spelling is used to spell out the English equivalent for a sign (especially proper nouns) when ASL is used. In ASL, interpreters frequently finger spell the word for a technical or uncommon sign the first time it is used during a conference. Finger spelling with speech and speech reading for additional acoustic and visual cues is called the Rochester method (Quigley & Paul, 1984).

Total communication is the use of signs, finger spelling, speech, speech reading, and, in reality, any and all modes of communication to ensure effective communication with hearing-impaired people. Although it is possible for ASL to be used as the manual component of total communication, the two terms are not synonymous.

Signed English, developed in the 1960s under the direction of Harry Bornstein of Gallaudet College, is a manually coded system of English used in conjunction with speech. It was devised to facilitate the acquisition of English by young deaf children. It incorporates special signs to indicate affixes (prefixes like un-, and suffixes like -s and -ment) and verb tense. Signed English is basically an educational tool used in some schools for deaf students. Its use of the specific tense and affix markers slows down the communication process considerably (Schlesinger & Namir, 1978).

Research into the linguistic nature of American Sign Language has shown that the grammar of ASL, like the grammar of all languages, consists of a finite set of rules with which an infinite number of sentences can be created or generated. Deaf children and hearing children of deaf parents who use ASL acquire these rules in much the same way that hearing children abstract linguistic rules from the spoken language to which they are exposed (Bellugi & Klima, 1985). Courses in sign language are offered in many colleges, schools for deaf students, centers for continuing education, and some public libraries. Courses in sign language for hearing learners may also enhance language acquisition because of the multimodal advantage (Daniels, 1994).

REFERENCES

Bellugi, U., & Klima, E. (1985). The acquisition of three morphological systems in American Sign Language. In F. Powell (Ed.), *Education of the hearing-impaired child.* San Diego, CA: College Hill.

Daniels, M. (1994). The effect of sign language on hearing children's language development. *Communication Education, 43*(4), 291–298.

Quigley, S., & Paul, P. (1984). *Language and deafness.* San Diego, CA: College Hill.

Schlesinger, I., & Namir, L. (1978). *Sign language of the deaf.* New York: Academic.

ROSEMARY GAFFNEY
Hunter College, City University of New York

LIPREADING/SPEECHREADING
ROCHESTER METHOD
TOTAL COMMUNICATION

SIMULTANEOUS COGNITIVE PROCESSING

See SEQUENTIAL AND SIMULTANEOUS COGNITIVE PROCESSING.

SINGLE-SUBJECT RESEARCH DESIGN

Increasingly, researchers are recognizing the importance of single-case investigations for the development of a knowledge base in psychology and education. Single-case time series designs involve observations before, during, and after interventions in order to describe changes in selected dependent variables. The development of time-series methodology, especially single-subject design, has been advantageous for researchers for several reasons. First, single-case research designs provide an important knowledge base that is unobtainable through traditional large-N between-group designs in clinical research. Single-subject designs are uniquely suited to evaluation of treatments involving a single client, a characteristic that is important given that it often is impossible to conduct group comparative outcome studies because of the limited number of subjects for a particular type of disorder or problem.

Another major advantage of single-case designs is that they provide an alternative to traditional large-N group designs about which various ethical and legal considerations are often raised (Hersen & Barlow, 1976). These concerns include the ethical objections of withholding treatment from clients in a no-treatment control group or randomly assigning clients to a particular treatment type.

Single-subject designs have been important in promoting the development of a measurement technology that can be used repeatedly throughout the intervention process. For example, various outcome measures such as direct observation, rating scales and checklists, self-monitoring, standardized tests, and psychophysiological recordings, can be used as ongoing measures of client functioning over the course of a research program. Such repeated measures taken over time allow for an analysis of individual variability as well as monitoring of potential response covariation within a single client. Perhaps the most important aspect of repeated measurement technology is its flexibility in the modification of treatment if the data indicate that this modification is necessary.

Single-case research strategies have also provided options for practitioners to be involved in research and evaluation of practice. There are differences of opinion, however, as to how feasible it is to implement well-controlled designs while providing clinical services. Carefully constructed single-case designs are usually difficult to implement (Kratochwill & Piersel, 1983). The use of a particular design may compromise the online clinical intuition of the therapist, yielding either a threat to internal validity of the evaluation or less appropriate treatment of the client. Finally, while clinicians may be concerned with the potential threats to being most responsive to patient needs, others may take the position that formal evaluation increases efficacy of the intervention itself (Barlow, Hayes, & Nelson, 1984). By implementing careful observation and measurement of behavior change, the therapist can measure type and degree of improvement and also know whether the treatment is responsible for change. The issues are readily subject to debate.

As single-subject strategies become more prevalent in the educational literature, it becomes important to discuss some design types. Three basic design types have been described in the literature (Barlow et al., 1984); they include within-, between-, and continued-series strategies.

In within-series designs, changes observed within a series of data points across time on a single measure or set of measures are analyzed. Each data point is analyzed in the context of those that immediately precede and follow it. Each consistent condition constitutes a phase in the series. Phases also are evaluated in the context of phases that pre-

cede and follow them. The researcher establishes internal validity in within-series designs by replicating effects of the independent variable across the phases.

One type of within-series design is the withdrawal procedure, that is used to assess whether responses are maintained under different conditions rather than to demonstrate the initial effects of an intervention in altering behavior (Kazdin, 1982). Typically, an A-B-A-B paradigm is used in which the intervention is introduced following a baseline, withdrawn for a phase, and then reintroduced. The withdrawal design seems best suited for evaluating the controlling effects of a reversible procedure, that is defined as one that would not produce a permanent change in the dependent variable. Withdrawal of the procedure would result in a return to baseline measures.

An example of the A-B-A-B withdrawal design is offered by Powers and Crowel (1985). They studied the effectiveness of a positive practice overcorrection procedure to decrease stereotypic vocal behavior produced by an 8-year-old autistic male. A baseline level of the child's percent of 10-second intervals of stereotypic vocalizations was obtained over 9 days. Treatment was then introduced and implemented for 7 days, withdrawn for 17 days, and reimplemented for 7 more days. Figure 1 illustrates the effects of the positive practice overcorrection procedure on the stereotypic vocalizations produced by the subject. During the initial baseline, the vocalizations averaged about 69 percent. During treatment, the percent of intervals of stereotypic vocalizations decreased to an average of about 17 percent. Withdrawal of the treatment resulted in a return to initial baseline levels of vocalizations, while reintroduction of the treatment resulted in another decrease in average levels of the stereotypic behavior.

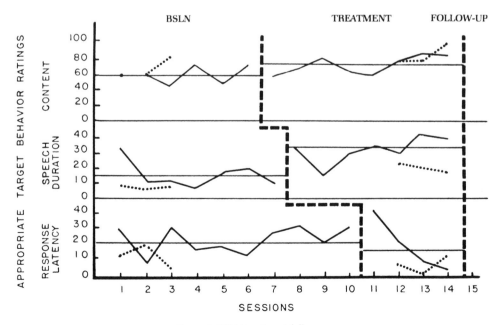

Figure 1 BSLN treatment follow-up

Since the A-B-A-B design is generally not appropriate for irreversible procedures (Hersen & Barlow, 1976), there are a number of considerations regarding its use. First, ethical decisions need to be made regarding withdrawal of treatment in any therapy program. Complicated decisions need to be made regarding the relative importance and overall advantages of obtaining reliable data about treatment efficacy as against withdrawing treatment from the client. Second, practical limitations may prevent one's choice of an A-B-A-B design. Often there is not enough time to institute two or more withdrawal phases. A third issue pertains to one's philosophy of intervention. In remediation of certain disorders, it might be argued that the client will not reverse to previous states once an intervention is introduced.

The withdrawal design might also be implemented in evaluating components of a treatment package. Specific aspects of a particular approach may be investigated by manipulating one variable at a time between adjacent phases in a withdrawal design. This type of strategy has been described in detail by several authors in their discussions of interaction designs (Barlow et al., 1984; Kratochwill, 1978; McReynolds & Kearns, 1983). Interaction designs examine the interactions of two or more variables over time in a basic within-series procedure. The purpose is to evaluate additive, subtractive, and interactive effects of individual components of a treatment.

If the researcher is interested in the effect of two independent variables but without evaluation of the individual contributions of B and C, the design would follow the classic A-B-A design, but it would specify the existence of the two variables. The design would be represented as A-BC-A-BC. However, if the investigator is interested in the relative contribution of B and C, and the interactive effects of both, each variable must be evaluated alone and in conjunction with the other. The design may be represented as A-B-BC-B-BC. In this format, the effect of B alone is tested as well as the effect of BC together.

It should be noted that only one variable is manipulated at a time and each variable to be evaluated must be adjacent to the rest. Unless the components are in adjacent phases (e.g., B-BC-B) the investigator cannot determine the effects of either component alone. For example, if one used an A-B-BC-A-B design, comparison of the behavior in B with the behavior in BC is confounded because of the intervening A phase. An A-B-A-B-BC design is often mistakenly interpreted as revealing interactive and relative effects. The final two phases (B-BC) form an uncontrolled A-B design and, therefore, are descriptive rather than experimental.

The interaction design may be time consuming since all the phases need to be completed. Also, there is a threat of sequence effects as one phase follows another. To control for order effects, the researcher would need to increase the number of subjects and implement counterbalancing and replication.

Other variations of the withdrawal design may be applicable. Maintenance of a behavior may be studied following a successful treatment package. A sequential withdrawal design might be implemented in which different components of the treatment package are gradually withdrawn while observations are made to see whether the behavior is maintained. A partial withdrawal design is another strategy that is used to evaluate maintenance. It consists of withdrawing a component of the treatment package from one of several different baselines, or from one of several subjects. This design would be readily applicable to many situations where one is interested in whether target behaviors measured during treatment are likely to be maintained if the treatment package or components are withdrawn.

Another within-series procedure is the changing criterion design. This design can be used to evaluate the effects of treatment on a single gradually acquired behavior. It is appropriate for studying the effectiveness of shaping behavior. The effect of the intervention is demonstrated by showing that behavior changes gradually over the course of treatment. Rather than withdrawing or withholding treatment, the design uses several subphases within the intervention phase. In each subphase a different criterion for performance is specified. When performance meets the criterion, more stringent criteria are set. This is done repeatedly over the course of the design.

During the baseline phase a single behavior is monitored until a stable response rate is achieved. Baseline data are used to establish an initial criterion level and treatment is initiated and continued until the target behavior stabilizes at that level. Both reinforcement schedules and criterion levels are then increased. The remainder of the phase progresses in a steplike manner, with each criterion adjustment more closely approximating a terminal level.

Many aspects and variations of the design are important in its use, including phase length, number and magnitude of criterion shifts, directionality of change, and potential data ambiguity. This design is most appropriate for behaviors acquired gradually; it does not require withdrawal or reversal of treatment. Only one behavior is selected for treatment, allowing inferences to be made about the efficacy of the treatment for that specific behavior. Possible confounding because of order effects and counterbalancing is also avoided in this design. This design is well suited for examining generalization across settings, subjects, and time.

Between-series designs allow comparisons of two or more treatments or conditions in order to examine relative effectiveness on a given behavior. There are two basic types of between-series designs: the alternating treatment design and the simultaneous treatment design (Barlow, Hayes & Nelson, 1984). The alternating treatment design involves the rapid alternation of two or more conditions. It exposes the subject to the separate treatment components for equal periods of time. The treatment may be alternated from one session to another or across two sessions each day, with sequence being determined randomly or through counterbalancing. Differences between the two treatments are examined rather than any differences over time within one condition. For example, an alternating treatment design was used to study the effects of teacher-directed versus student-directed instruction and cues versus no cues for improving spelling performance (Gettinger, 1985). Nine children received four alternating experimental treatments during a 16-week spelling program. The two cuing procedures (cues vs. no cues) were alternated weekly while the student-directed and teacher-directed components were alternated biweekly. Mean pretest, posttest, and retention scores were obtained for each treatment condition; they indicated improved spelling accuracy for all four conditions. The data also demonstrated that a student-directed procedure incorporating visual and verbal cues produces the highest posttest accuracy scores.

The simultaneous treatment design differs from the alternating treatment design in that the treatments (or conditions) are available simultaneously. The purpose of the design is to measure subject "preference" rather than the treatment efficacy (Barlow et al., 1984). For example, a simultaneous treatment design might be employed to determine which type of reinforcement is most preferred by a client. That particular reinforcement could then be incorporated into a remediation program.

Potential problems exist for the use of these designs in some areas of research. The interactive effects of two treatments or conditions would be difficult to ascertain, especially in patients exhibiting cognitive or language deficits. Carryover or generalization effects of one intervention may confound inferences that might be made with regard to the other treatment or condition. Both alternating treatment and simultaneous treatment designs depend on showing changes for a given behavior across sessions or time periods. The need for behavior to shift rapidly dictates both the type of interventions and the behaviors that can be studied in multiple treatment designs. Interventions suitable for these designs may need to show rapid effects initially and to have little or no carryover effects when terminated. If the effects of the first intervention linger after it is no longer presented, the intervention that follows would be confounded by the previous one.

In addition to alternating and simultaneous treatment designs, one other strategy has been employed when withdrawal and reversal designs are not feasible. These are multiple baseline designs that combine within and between series strategies with regard to inference.

The methodology for multiple baseline designs is relatively straightforward. Baseline data are collected on two or more units (e.g., subjects, settings, behaviors, or time). After performance is stable for all the units, treatment is applied to the first; measurements continue to be taken across all. The researcher's expectation is that changes will be seen quickly in the treated unit while the others remain stable at baseline levels. After performance again stabilizes across all the units, the treatment is applied to the second and continued on the first. Data continue to be taken across all units. This process is repeated until all units have been treated. The effect of the intervention is evaluated on whether the series remains stable at baseline levels until treatment, at which time a change is seen. Each time an intervention is introduced, a test is made between the level of performance during the intervention and the projected level of the previous baselines. A unique feature of this design is the testing of predictions across different units; these units serve as control conditions to evaluate what changes can be expected without the application of the treatment.

An example of the use of a multiple baseline design is offered in Figure 2, that illustrates the results of a study

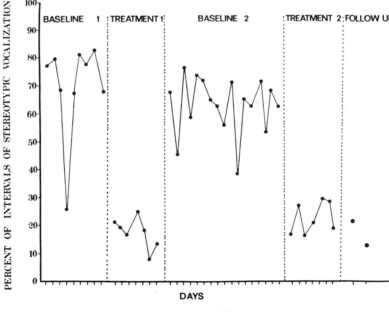

Figure 2 BSLN treatment follow-up 1 and 2

designed to test the effectiveness of social skills training for improving the social behaviors of a 17-year-old deaf female (Lemanek & Gresham, 1984). A multiple baseline design across behaviors was used to examine the effect of treatment on three dependent variables (duration of communications, response latency, and content).

Figure 2 illustrates the baseline measures across all three dependent variables, with treatment initiated on the first behavior (content) at session seven. Baseline measures continued to be taken on the second and third behaviors (speech duration and response latency). Treatment was then initiated on the second behavior, and at session 11, on the third behavior. Visual inspection of the data indicates a slight improvement in appropriate content during treatment. Speech duration increased significantly from baseline to treatment. Decreases in response latency occurred from baseline throughout treatment and follow-up.

Several variations of the multiple baseline design are often used, applying the strategy across subjects, or across situations, settings, and time (Kazdin, 1982). In the variation across subjects, baseline data are gathered for a specific behavior across two or more subjects. A selected treatment is then applied in sequence across the matched subjects, just as in the multiple baseline across behaviors. Preferably, the subjects are exposed to identical environmental conditions. In the variation across settings, a treatment variable is applied sequentially to the same behavior in the same subject across different and independent settings. The same procedures apply for introducing the treatment after the stabilization of behavior across each setting for each baseline.

Many issues that are important to the implementation of this design are beyond the scope of this presentation. However, among the more salient are that at least two baselines should be used and that more are preferable. Issues such as length of phase and counterbalancing are important in these designs as well, and should be taken into account. It also should be noted that the use of this design across subjects or behaviors could result in withholding treatment from a particular subject for a longer period of time than might be judged clinically appropriate.

In multiple baseline designs across behaviors, the assumption is that the targeted behaviors are independent from one another. In some disorders, it is reasonable to assume that targeted behaviors may covary. As a result, the controlling effects of the treatment variables are subject to question.

A particular problem with implementing many single-case time-series designs in applied settings is the amount of time required for appropriate baseline measures. Often the subject cannot handle a long treatment session, or is frustrated by repeated attempts at a difficult treatment. A balance must be reached between the amount of data needed to demonstrate experimental control and the practical aspects of working with the client. One design that has been offered to alleviate this problem is the multiple-probe design. This design is a combination of multiple baseline design and probe procedures.

A probe is defined as an intermittent assessment of selected target behaviors under nontreatment conditions. The nature of the probes depends on behaviors being investigated and practical considerations. There are three primary features of the multiple-probe design. First, there is an initial probe of every step in a chain or successive approximation. Second, a probe is conducted on each step in the treatment sequence after criterion is achieved on any one step. Third, a series of probes or real baselines are conducted immediately before the initiation of treatment on any given step in the sequence. Only probes following the completion of all prerequisite steps and immediately before intervention are considered a true measure of the subject's ability to perform a given step.

Experimental control can be shown despite less baseline data as long as the pretreated probe and true baseline data are stable and a consistent change with introduction of treatment is shown. Graphic representation of the data would resemble that of multiple baseline studies. Probes and true baselines along the abscissa can be examined to determine whether the behavior remained stable until intervention was initiated at each step in the training sequence.

In the multiple-probe design, similar but independent behavior must be chosen to maintain experimental control, as the design is not appropriate for studying steps that are truly interdependent. The multiple-probe design avoids problems of extinction, fatigue, and distraction that can occur as a result of continuous baseline testing. The design is a potentially efficient means of evaluating the effects of training on sequential steps in a treatment program for behaviors that are not totally interdependent.

Time-series designs, especially single-subject investigations, are increasingly recognized as important methodologies for the evaluation of the efficacy of treatment. Within-, between-, and combined-series designs each provide internally valid methods for answering questions regarding the effects of a particular treatment, or the relative effects of different treatments or conditions. The use of single-subject time-series designs offers the educational researcher a valid way of answering questions about the nature of the intervention offered clients.

REFERENCES

Barlow, D. H., Hayes, S. C., & Nelson, R. O. (1984). *The scientist practitioner: Research and accountability in clinical and educational settings.* New York: Pergamon.

Gettinger, M. (1985). Effects of teacher-directed versus student-directed instruction and cues versus no cues for improving spelling performance. *Journal of Applied Behavior Analysis, 18,* 167–171.

Hersen, N., & Barlow, D. H. (1976). *Single case experimental designs: Strategies for studying behavior change.* New York: Pergamon.

Kazdin, A. E. (1982). *Single-case research designs: Methods for clinical and applied settings.* New York: Oxford University Press.

Kratochwill, T. R. (Ed.) (1978). *Single-subject research: strategies for evaluating change.* New York: Academic.

Kratochwill, T. R., & Piersel, W. C. (1983). Time-series research: Contributions to empirical clinical practice. *Behavioral Assessment, 5,* 165–176.

Lemanek, K. L., & Gresham, P. M. (1984). Social skills training with a deaf adolescent. Implications for placement and programming. *School Psychology Review, 13,* 385–490.

McReynolds, L., & Kearns, K. (1983). *Single subject experimental designs in communicative disorders.* Baltimore: University Park Press.

Powers, M. D., & Crowel, R. L. (1985). The educative effects of positive practice overcorrection: Acquisition, generalization, and maintenance. *School Psychology Review, 14,* 360–372.

Edythe A. Strand
Thomas R. Kratochwill
*University of Wisconsin at
Madison*

APPLIED BEHAVIOR ANALYSIS RESEARCH IN SPECIAL EDUCATION

SINGLETON-MERTON SYNDROME

Singleton-Merton syndrome is a rare disorder of unknown etiology. The primary features of this syndrome include aortic calcification, dental abnormalities, and osteoporosis. Children with Singleton-Merton syndrome have abnormal accumulations of calcium deposits in their aorta, the major artery in the human body, and valves of their heart. Progressive calcification of the aorta and heart valves is life-threatening, as heart block or heart failure may result. In contrast, progressive loss of protein of the bones, resulting in osteoporosis, occurs in individuals with this disorder. Dental abnormalities in the form of poorly developed teeth and/or premature loss of primary teeth are seen in children with this syndrome as well (National Organization for Rare Disorders [NORD], 1997).

Other features of the disorder include generalized muscular weakness and hip and foot abnormalities. Motor delays are not uncommon. These children tend to be relatively short in stature due to growth retardation. Skin lesions, especially on their fingers, are also common among these children (Gay & Kuhn, 1976; NORD, 1997).

Physical therapy and occupational therapy may help motor development and increase muscle strength. Children may receive these support services through the school based on an Other Health Impaired diagnosis.

REFERENCES

Gay, B. B., Jr., & Kuhn, J. P. (1976). A syndrome of widened medullary cavities of bone, aortic calcification, abnormal dentition, and muscular weakness (the Singleton-Merton syndrome). *Radiology, 118*(2), 389–395.

National Organization for Rare Disorders (NORD). (1997). *Singleton-Merton syndrome.* New Fairfield, CT: Author.

Patricia A. Lowe
University of Kansas

Joan W. Mayfield
*Baylor Pediatric Specialty
Service*

SIX-HOUR RETARDED CHILD

The term *6-hour retardate* first appeared in the report of the Conference on Problems of Education of Children in the Inner City (President's Committee on Mental Retardation, 1969). The conference was charged with developing a new set of recommendations regarding the problems of mentally retarded children living within the ghettos of U.S. cities. After reviewing the papers of the 92 participants, 7 major recommendations were developed: (1) provide early childhood stimulation education as part of the public education program; (2) conduct a study of histories of successful inner-city families who have learned to cope effectively; (3) restructure education of teachers, administrators, and counselors; (4) reexamine present systems of intelligence testing and classification; (5) commit substantial additional funding for research and development in educational improvement for the disadvantaged; (6) delineate what constitutes accountability and hold the school accountable for providing quality education for all children; and (7) involve parents, citizens, citizen groups, students, and general and special educators in a total educational effort. However, one outcome overshadowed all of these recommendations. It was the conclusion that "we now have what may be called a 6-hour retarded child—retarded from 9 to 3, 5 days a week, solely on the basis of an IQ, without regard to his adaptive behavior, which may be exceptionally adaptive to the situation and community in which he lives."

The concept of the 6-hour retarded child survived into the mid-1980s. Today many psychologists and educators have accepted as a given that children identified as mildly retarded during the school-age years manifest retarded functioning only in the school setting, and that outside of school, during childhood and in their work lives as adults, they function successfully. Often their retardation is invisible to their employers, families, neighbors, and friends.

The conclusion of the conference participants was not

inconsistent with case studies and some published reports of the adult lives of the mildly retarded. Although observations of the mildly retarded as children led many to believe that as adults they would fail in community adaptation, many investigators observed a high proportion of the adult retarded who achieved satisfactory adjustment, even when a variety of criteria were used.

The results of these early conclusions were confounded by subsequent reports showing that success in adult adaptation was equivocal, at best. The challenge of a more definitive portrayal of the adult lives of the mildly retarded was undertaken by the Socio-Behavioral Research Group at UCLA, who produced several informative studies of mildly retarded children as adults. Edgerton (1984) and Koegel and Edgerton (1984) used a holistic natural approach rather than measures of discrete adult outcomes. They conducted extensive ethnographic participant research studies of several aspects of the adult behavior of individuals who had been mildly retarded as children.

One of their studies centered on the functioning of blacks who had been classified as educable mentally retarded (EMR) as children, an adult sample of those who were the object of concern in the 1969 Conference on Problems of Education of Children of the Inner City. They identified 45 residents in a black community who had attended EMR classes and who represented the broad range of competencies and lifestyles found among mildly retarded adults in the black community. The 12 subjects who were selected for their study satisfied one criterion: field researchers, during the course of their first visits, expressed serious doubt that they were, in fact, retarded. These 12 individuals, when compared with the remainder of the sample, clearly led more normal lives. They had mean IQ scores of 62, 33 percent were married, and 42 percent were competitively employed. For 1 year a staff of black ethnographic field researchers maintained regular contact with the 12 participants, visiting them for 1 to 4 hours a day on an average of 12 separate occasions. The visits took place in homes, at work sites, and schools, during leisure activities, shopping expeditions, and job searches. Both parents and subjects were interviewed regarding any limitations they perceived, as well as their experiences in various aspects of their adult lives.

Although the adult lives of the participants were varied, none of them had "disappeared" into his or her community as a normal person. All 12 were seen by others close to them as limited or impaired and most of the 12 participants acknowledged their own limitations. The participants continued to be troubled by the same problems that characterized them during their formal schooling—problems with reading, numerical concepts, and everyday tasks such as shopping, applying for jobs, travelling around the city, eating out in restaurants, making ends meet, etc.

Their problems transcended those associated with academic or intellectual pursuits. Their case histories included difficulties arising from poor judgment, vulnerability to exploitation and victimization, need for help in rearing their children, and an inability to comprehend satisfactorily their everyday experiences.

This study and several others of the adult lives of mildly retarded adults raise serious doubts regarding the efficacy and use of the concept of the 6-hour retarded child. The lives of these participants sometimes paralleled those of the nonretarded in the community, but never completely. Even though they were no longer receiving services as adults, they continued to face the same kinds of problems they did as children.

The contrast between the expectancies of the conference participants in 1969 and some of the recent studies such as the work by Edgerton et al. suggests that regular and special education programs should attend to preparing children with limited potential for the roles they will engage in as adults. Moreover, no one concerned about the future of the mildly retarded pupil can be content in the belief that their problems exist only in school, and that outside of this setting they function as capably as their age mates.

REFERENCES

Edgerton, R. B. (Ed.). (1984). *Lives in process: Mildly retarded adults in a large city.* Washington, DC: American Association on Mental Deficiency.

Koegel, P., & Edgerton, R. B. (1984). Black "six hour retarded" children as young adults. In R. B. Edgerton (Ed.), *Lives in process: Mildly retarded adults in a large city.* Washington, DC: American Association on Mental Deficiency.

President's Committee on Mental Retardation. (1969). *The six hour retarded child.* Washington, DC: Bureau of Education for the Handicapped, Office of Education, U.S. Department of Health, Education, and Welfare.

NADINE M. LAMBERT
University of California,
Berkeley

MENTAL RETARDATION

SKEELS, HAROLD M. (1901–1970)

Harold M. Skeels, pioneer researcher in the field of mental retardation, was responsible for a large number of studies of institutional populations during the 1930s and early 1940s. These studies showed that children placed in unstimulating institutional environments failed to develop normally, and that the longer they remained, the greater their deficits became. Skeels reached the conclusion that it is possible to improve intellectual functioning through early stimulation, and he advocated early adoption as an alternative to institutionalization. His findings set off a nature-nurture controversy, and Skeels and his associates were the targets of vehement attacks.

Harold M. Skeels

Following service in the armed forces during World War II, and subsequent employment with the U.S. Public Health Service and the National Institute of Mental Health, Skeels made a follow-up study of some of the subjects of his earlier research. The results showed dramatically the long-term effects of differences in childhood environments. By the time his report was published, many of Skeels's concepts from the 1930s had become common-place: adoption at an early age had become routine, institutional placements were decreasing, and a variety of early childhood services had been developed, including some programs, like Head Start, aimed specifically at early stimulation of disadvantaged and disabled children.

REFERENCES

Crissey, M. S. (1970). Harold Manville Skeels. *American Journal of Mental Deficiency, 75,* 1–3.

Skeels, H. M. (1966). Adult status of children with contrasting early life experiences. *Monograph of the Society for Research in Child Development, 33,* 1–65.

Skeels, H. M., & Dye, H. B. (1939). A study of the effects of differential stimulation. *Proceedings of the American Association on Mental Deficiency, 44,* 114–136.

PAUL IRVINE
Katona, New York

HEAD START
NATURE VS. NURTURE

SKILL TRAINING

The skill training model rests on the premise that assessment of a student's performance should focus on classroom tasks. Such assessment is usually tied to some hierarchy of skills. Instruction, then, follows directly from the results of the hierarchical assessment, and often uses direct instruction skills (Mercer, 1983).

Skill training is a commonly used approach in special education. It provides the teacher with an opportunity to evaluate specific skills, skills that are of immediate and direct concern to classroom instruction. The skill training process usually begins with the administration of a criterion-referenced or teacher-made assessment device. The analysis of the results of the assessment provides the teacher with additional information that is specifically related to classroom interventions. That is, the analysis, focusing on a hierarchy of skills, helps to pinpoint the specific error the student is making, allowing a more precise instructional decision to be made. This instructional decision will usually result in the teacher using some direct instructional technique, concentrating the teaching efforts on a specific academic skill (Gable & Warren, 1993). Pupil progress is continuously measured to ensure that instruction continues to focus on appropriate skills. On mastery of one skill, the teacher and student progress to the next hierarchical skill.

REFERENCES

Gable, R. A., & Warren, S. F. (Eds.). (1993). *Strategies for teaching students with mild to severe mental retardation.* Baltimore: Brookes.

Mercer, C. D. (1983). *Students with learning disabilities* (2nd ed.). Columbus, OH: Merrill.

JOHN R. BEATTIE
University of North Carolina at Charlotte

MASTERY LEARNING AND SPECIAL EDUCATION

SKINNER, BURRHUS FREDERICK (1904–1990)

B. F. Skinner was born in northeastern Pennsylvania in 1904. He continued to write and work until his death on August 18, 1990. Skinner studied English and classics at Hamilton College where he received his AB (1926) in literature. After his aspirations of becoming a writer were discouraged, he entered the graduate program in psychology at Harvard, earning his MA in 1930 and his PhD under E. G. Boring in 1931. Regarded as a classic, his dissertation reflected his theory that a reflex arc, a then widely-debated concept, was nothing more than the relationship between a stimulus and a response. He argued that all behavior, in fact, could be explained by looking at the stimuli that result in its occurrence. These themes were the root of his theoretical orientation throughout his distinguished and remarkable career.

Burrhus Frederick Skinner

Skinner completed several post-doctoral fellowships after leaving graduate school, subsequently accepting the position of assistant professor at the University of Minnesota (1936–1945). He was a Junior Fellow in the Society of Fellows of Harvard University from 1933 to 1936. After spending a short time at Indiana University as chairman of the department of psychology (1945–1947), he returned to Harvard as William James Lecturer, where he remained as professor and ultimately, professor emeritus of psychology until his death in 1990.

Skinner is considered by many to be the most important figure in 20th century psychology. In the field of education, he is perhaps best known for the development of programmed instruction and teaching machines as well as his behavior modification techniques. These areas allow the special educator to analyze and develop a systematic and situation-specific plan of instruction for learning or behavior. He denounced theoretical explanations of psychology, viewing the discipline as scientific and empirically driven, concerned with the observation of behaviors and the stimuli that bring them about. This Radical Behaviorism, as it has been termed, involves strict adherence to behavioral principles.

Skinner's concept of behaviorism, known as operant conditioning, as well as the results of numerous experiments, were outlined in his first major publication, *The Behavior of Organisms* (1938). The term *operant* refers to the identification of behavior which is traceable to reinforcing contingencies rather then to eliciting stimuli. Skinner believed speculation about what intervenes between stimulus and response or between response and reward to be superfluous.

The idea of creating a utopian community using his prin-ciples of conditioning, controlling all aspects of life using positive reinforcement, continued to interest him throughout his life. The notion of this ideal community was delineated in his 1948 novel, *Walden Two*. Another of his major books, *Science and Human Behavior* (1952), dealt with the application of behavioral principles to real-life situations including social issues, law, education, and psychotherapy. In this work, he postulated that the human organism is a machine like any other, thus behaving in lawful, predictable ways in response to external stimuli.

His notorious *Verbal Behavior* was published in 1957. This analysis of human language behavior was roundly criticized, most notably by linguist Noam Chomsky in a devastating review published in 1959. It is generally believed that neither Skinner nor his advocates ever responded successfully to the criticisms raised in this review, often noted as the beginning of the decline in influence of behavioral psychology.

Skinner advanced behaviorism by distinguishing between two types of behavior, respondent and operant, and showing how varying contingencies of reinforcement can be employed to modify or control any type of behavior. Controversy was raised once again by his publication of *Beyond Freedom and Dignity*, a 1971 book in which he dealt with the application of these principles. In this book, he interprets concepts of freedom, value, and dignity in objective terms, suggesting a society designed by shaping and controlling the behavior of citizens with a planned system of rewards (reinforcements). Among his numerous publications, *The Technology of Teaching* (1968) and his autobiographical trilogy (the last part, *A Matter of Consequence*, published in 1983) are of particular interest.

Skinner's contributions to psychology were recognized in 1958 by the American Psychological Association's (APA) Distinguished Scientific Award and again, just before his death, with a Lifetime Achievement Award. Other honors include the National Medal of Science (1968), the gold medal from the APA (1971), and his portrayal on the cover of *Time* magazine (1971).

In later years, Skinner extended his studies to psychotic behavior, instructional devices, and the analysis of cultures. Despite the criticisms and his unwavering position on a broad range of issues, his significant influence and impact on contemporary psychology assures him a place in its history.

REFERENCES

Skinner, B. F. (1938). *The behavior of organisms: An experimental analysis.* New York: Appleton-Century.

Skinner, B. F. (1948). *Walden two.* New York: Macmillan.

Skinner, B. F. (1953). *Science and human behavior.* New York: Macmillan.

Skinner, B. F. (1957). *Verbal behavior.* New York: Appleton-Century-Crofts.

Skinner, B. F. (1968). *The technology of teaching.* New York: Appleton-Century-Crofts.

Skinner, B. F. (1971). *Beyond freedom and dignity.* New York: Bantam.

Skinner, B. F. (1984). *A matter of consequences.* Washington Square, NY: New York University.

ELAINE FLETCHER-JANZEN
*University of Colorado at
Colorado Springs*
First edition

TAMARA J. MARTIN
*The University of Texas of the
Permian Basin*
Second edition

**BEHAVIOR MODIFICATION
OPERANT CONDITIONING**

setting and have been extremely successful in improving a variety of academic and social behaviors in diverse student populations (Kazdin, 1978).

REFERENCES

Kazdin, A. E. (1978). *History of behavior modification: Experimental foundations of contemporary research.* Baltimore: University Park Press.

Skinner, B. F. (1953). *Science and human behavior.* New York: Free Press.

Skinner, B. F. (1968). *The technology of teaching.* Englewood Cliffs, NJ: Prentice Hall.

CHRISTINE L. COLE
*University of Wisconsin at
Madison*

**BEHAVIOR MODIFICATION
CONDITIONING
OPERANT CONDITIONING
SKINNER, B. F.**

SKINNER'S FUNCTIONAL LEARNING MODEL

B. F. Skinner's functional learning model, known as operant conditioning, describes the relationship between behavior and the environmental events that influence it. The basic principles of operant conditioning include reinforcement, punishment, extinction, and stimulus control. These principles describe the functionality of events that precede or follow behavior. Reinforcement, for example, serves the function of increasing the strength of behavior. Skinner (1953) described two types of reinforcement. Positive reinforcement refers to the presentation of an event, commonly called a reward, following behavior. For example, a teacher smiles and says, "Good work" following completion of a child's assignment. Negative reinforcement refers to the removal of an event presumed to be unpleasant following behavior. For example, a child's aggressive behavior may cause a teacher to remove an unpleasant request. In both cases, the effect of reinforcement is the same—the child is more likely to engage in that behavior (assignment completion or aggressive behavior) under similar conditions in the future.

The application of operant conditioning to special education involves the arrangement of contingencies of reinforcement to ensure effective learning. Skinner (1968) noted that although students obviously learn outside the classroom without such systematic procedures, "teachers arrange special contingencies which expedite learning, hastening the appearance of behavior which would otherwise be acquired slowly or making sure of the appearance of behavior which might otherwise never occur" (p. 65). Operant techniques have been applied in classrooms more than in any other

SLINGERLAND SCREENING TESTS

The Slingerland screening tests are comprised of four forms with designated grade levels (Form A, grades 1 and 2; Form B, grades 2 and 3; Form C, grades 3 and 4; Form D, grades 5 and 6) (Slingerland & Ansara, 1974; Slingerland, 1974). There are eight subtests for Forms A, B, and C that may be either group or individually administered. These subtests require the students to copy letters and words from a board, copy from a page, perform visual matching exercises by selecting a stimulus word from an array of distractor words with various letter reversals, copy words presented in flashcard fashion, write dictated words, and detect initial and final sounds. For children that exhibit difficulties with portions of the eight subtests, there are individually administered auditory tests designed to assess auditory perception and memory. The student is asked to repeat individual words and phrases, to complete sentences with a missing word, and to retell a story. With the exception of additional subtests assessing personal orientation, Form D is comparable to the other three forms of the test. As noted by Fujiki (1985) and Sean and Keough (1993), the purpose of the Slingerland is not to identify linguistically disabled children, but to assess auditory, visual, and motor skills associated with learning to read and write.

Local norms are advocated to interpret the results of students' test performance. This recommendation is necessary because of the notable omission of adequate normative data. Also absent in the manuals is an adequate discussion of reliability stability, or validity.

REFERENCES

Fujiki, M. (1985). Review of Slingerland Screening Tests for identifying children with specific language disabilities. In J. V. Mitchell (Ed.), *The ninth mental measurements yearbook* (Vol. 2, pp. 1398–1399). Lincoln, NE: University of Nebraska Press.

Sean, S., & Keough, B. (1993). Predicting reading performance using the Slingerland procedures. *Annals of Dyslexia, 43,* 78–79.

Slingerland, B. H. (1974). *Teacher's manual to accompany Slingerland Screening Tests for Identifying Children with Specific Language Disability–Revised Edition* (Form D). Cambridge, MA: Educators.

Slingerland, B. H., & Ansara, A. S. (1974). *Teacher's manual to accompany Slingerland Screening Tests for Identifying Children with Specific Language Disability–Revised Edition* (Forms A, B, and C). Cambridge, MA: Educators.

JACK A. CUMMINGS
Indiana University

LANGUAGE DISORDERS

SLOSSON INTELLIGENCE TEST REVISED–THIRD EDITION FOR CHILDREN AND ADULTS

The Slosson Intelligence Test Revised–Third Edition for Children and Adults (SIT-R3; Slosson, 2002, with 1998 calibrated norms) provides a quick and reliable individual screening test of Crystallized Verbal Intelligence. This revision has adapted score sheets for scannable or electronic readers and offers a supplementary manual for the blind or visually impaired. The SIT-R3 has minimal performance items and features embossed materials, allowing for one of the only measures of intelligence for the visually challenged population of both children and adults.

The SIT-R3 test items are derived from the following subtests: Vocabulary (33 items), General Information (29 items), Similarities and Differences (30 items), Comprehension (33 items), Quantitative (34 items), and Auditory Memory (28 items).

The test has been nationally restandardized and developed with the American Psychological Association criteria clearly in mind. Multiple statistical procedures were used to assure that there is no significant gender or racial bias. Every item on the test was reevaluated using classical item analysis to choose good statistical items and new differential item functioning analysis to find and eliminate biased items. SIT-R3 users may continue to administer and score the SIT-R3 with the 1998 Calibrated Norms Tables as usual and just order the supplementary manual when testing persons with low visual acuity.

Administration time for the SIT-R3 is about 10–20 minutes. The SIT-R3 correlated .827 with the WISC-R Verbal Intelligence Quotient. The calibrated norms reflect a high .828 correlation between the SIT-R3 total standard score (TSS) and the WISC-III Full Scale Intelligence Quotient.

Computer Report aids educators in determining expected achievement and finding levels of ability or weakness. It scores and prints an individual three-page report using the TSS and computes the Severe Discrepancy Level to determine learning disabilities under federal guidelines. Computer Report is noncompliant with Windows XP. No reviews for the 2002 edition are anticipated by the Buros Institute of Mental Measurements—however, a review of earlier editions of the test is available (Conoley & Impara, 1995).

REFERENCE

Conoley, J. C., & Impara, J. C. (Eds.). (1995). *The twelfth mental measurements yearbook.* Lincoln, NE: Buros Institute of Mental Measurements.

RON DUMONT
Fairleigh Dickinson University

JOHN O. WILLIS
Rivier College

SLOW LEARNER

Historically, the slow learning child has been described in numerous ways. Ingram's (1960) book, the *Education of the Slow-Learning Child,* discussed the education of the educable mentally retarded child. Johnson (1963) noted that "slow learners compose the largest group of mentally retarded persons" (p. 9). Today, however, the term slow learner most accurately describes children and adolescents who learn or underachieve, in one or more academic areas, at a rate that is below average yet not at the level considered comparable to that of an educable mentally retarded student. Intellectually, slow learners score most often between a 75 and a 90 IQ—between the borderline and low-average classifications of intelligence.

It is unusual to find the slow learner discussed in the standard special education textbook. Indeed, slow learners are not special education students. There is no individuals with disabilities education act (IDEA) label or definition of slow learner, and these students are not eligible for any monies or services associated with that law. When slow learners receive additional supportive services, it is typically in the regular classroom or in remedial classes that may be supported by federal title funds or programs. These remedial classes are not conceptualized as alternative educational programs; they are used to reinforce regular classroom curricula and learning. Some slow learners are inappropriately labeled learning disabled to maintain the enrollment (and funding) of some special education classrooms, or because they would otherwise fail in the regular classroom, despite not having special education needs.

There is no consensus on a diagnostic or descriptive profile that characterizes the slow learner. Indeed, there is very little contemporary research with samples specifically labeled as slow learners. Many slow learners are now described by their specific academic weaknesses; research and/or remedial programs are applied to these academic areas—not to the slow learner labels. Because of this shift in emphasis, earlier research describing slow learners as being from low socioeconomic and minority family backgrounds, academically and socially frustrated, and devalued by teachers and peers, and as having low self-concepts, do not apply (Cawley, Goodstein, & Burrow, 1972).

REFERENCES

Cawley, J. F., Goodstein, H. A., & Burrow, W. H. (1972). *The slow learner and the reading problem.* Springfield, IL: Thomas.

Ingram, C. P. (1960). *Education of the slow-learning child* (3rd ed.). New York: Ronald.

Johnson, G. O. (1963). *Education for slow learners.* Englewood Cliffs, NJ: Prentice Hall.

HOWARD M. KNOFF
University of South Florida

**LEARNING DISABILITIES
RESPONSE TO INTERVENTION**

SMITH-LEMLI-OPITZ SYNDROME

Smith-Lemli-Opitz syndrome is a genetic disorder due to an autosomal recessive gene. A larger number of males are affected by the syndrome than females (Jones, 1988). Smith-Lemli-Opitz syndrome is characterized by facial, limb, and genital abnormalities. Children with Smith-Lemli-Opitz syndrome have small heads; long, narrow faces; slanted or low-set ears; heavy or thick upper eyelids; anteverted nostrils; and small jaws. Squinting of the eyes is also a common characteristic found among these children. These children tend to be short in stature as well. On the palms of their hands and soles of their feet, simian creases are present and webbing often appears between their toes (Jones, 1988; Thoene, 1992). Some children with Smith-Lemli-Opitz syndrome experience seizures, and have cardiac anomalies, abnormal EEGs, kidney defects, and cataracts (Jones, 1988).

There are two forms of Smith-Lemli-Opitz syndrome: types I and II. Type II, also known as Lowry-Miller-Maclean syndrome, is a more severe form of the disorder. Stillbirth is a common characteristic of the type II form. Those who do survive have a low birth weight and failure to thrive. A shrill cry, vomiting, and feeding problems are typical in early infancy.

Moderate to severe mental retardation is evident among these children (Thoene, 1992). Special education programs focusing on life-skill training would be beneficial.

REFERENCES

Jones, K. L. (Ed.). (1988). *Smith's recognizable patterns of human malformation* (4th ed.). Philadelphia: W. B. Saunders.

Rudolph, A. M. (1991). *Rudolph's pediatrics–19th edition.* Norwalk, CT: Appleton & Lange.

Thoene, J. G. (Ed.). (1992). *Physician's guide to rare diseases.* Montvale, NJ: Dowden.

JOAN W. MAYFIELD
*Baylor Pediatric Specialty
Service*

PATRICIA A. LOWE
University of Kansas

SNELLEN CHART

The Snellen chart is a measuring device used to determine an individual's central distance visual acuity. The chart contains eight rows of letters of the alphabet in graduated sizes. There is a version for young children and for people who cannot read that replaces the alphabet with the letter E in different orientations and sizes. The letter sizes on the chart correspond to the estimate of the ability of a typical person to read the material. It is constructed so that at a distance of 20 ft, a person reading the figures on the chart corresponding to what a normal eye sees at 20 ft is said to have 20/20 vision (Bryan & Bryan, 1979). A person with 20/20 vision and both eyes working in a coordinated fashion is considered to be normally sighted. When a person sees at 20 ft what a normal person sees at 70 ft or 200 ft, that person has 20/70 or 20/200 vision. Individuals who have low vision or who are visually limited may be legally blind (visual acuity of 20/200 or less), or partially sighted (visual acuity between 20/70 and 20/200; DeMott, 1982).

The Snellen chart is widely used as a screening device for detecting eye problems because of the ease and speed with which it can be administered, its low cost, and its wide range of applicability. When compared with the Orthorater vision tester, Johnson and Caccamise (1983) found the Snellen chart to be an "acceptable, less expensive alternative" (p. 406). It can be used with young children as well as adults. However, because the Snellen measures only central visual acuity, it should be combined with other procedures in screening. The Snellen chart gives no indication of near-point or peripheral vision, convergence ability, fusion ability, or muscular imbalance.

Bryan and Bryan (1979) list three shortcomings of the Snellen chart:

1. It is not a good predictor of competence in visual processing of objects and tasks.
2. It does not tell how a child uses vision in terms of discriminating light or darkness, estimating size, or determining spatial location.
3. The results are not translatable into educational programs. Children with the same visual acuity may respond differently to school tasks, and, therefore, require different programming.

However, DeMott (1982) holds that the most important initial screening device for detecting eye problems is one that measures central visual acuity. Combining results from the Snellen chart with other screening measures is important for early diagnosis and remediation of eye problems.

REFERENCES

Bryan, J. H., & Bryan, L. H. (1979). *Exceptional children.* Sherman Oaks, CA: Alfred.

Getman, G. N. (1985). A commentary on vision-training. *Journal of Learning Disabilities, 18*(9), 505–512.

DeMott, R. M. (1982). Visual impairments. In N. G. Haring (Ed.), *Exceptional children and youth.* Columbus, OH: Merrill.

Johnson, D. D., & Caccamise, F. (1983). Hearing impaired students: Options for visual acuity screening. *American Annals of the Deaf, 128*(3), 402–406.

Kirk, S. A. (1962). *Educating exceptional children.* Boston: Houghton Mifflin.

NANCY J. KAUFMAN
*University of Wisconsin at
Stevens Point*

VISUAL ACUITY
VISUAL IMPAIRMENT

SOCIAL BEHAVIOR OF INDIVIDUALS WITH DISABILITIES

Evidence from Lerner (1985) and Stephens, Hartman, and Lucas, (1983) has clearly documented that many exceptional children experience difficulty in the area of social skills. This difficulty could range from mild problems to severe disorders. Minskoff (1980) considers social perceptual difficulties as among the more serious problems of learning-disabled children. Drew, Logan, and Hardman (1984) indi-cate that retarded students often have a higher incidence of emotional problems than nonretarded students. Lerner (1985) identified six characteristics of social behavior that are common among disabled children and youths: (1) lack of judgment, (2) difficulties in perceiving others, (3) problems in making friends, (4) poor self-concept, (5) problems involving family relationships, and (6) social difficulties in the school setting.

In most instances, children who are receiving special education services have more than one problem and disabili-ties produce different behaviors in different children (Cart-wright, Cartwright, & Ward, 1984). Bloom (1956) proposes a system whereby all education-related activities would fall into three major domains—affective, psychomotor, and cog-nitive. Cartwright et al. (1984) define the affective domain as the social domain; this deals with an individual's social abilities, such as establishing and maintaining satisfactory interpersonal skills, displaying behavior within reasonable social expectations, and making personal adjustments. So-cial skills and the ability to get along with others are just as important to the disabled student as they are to the non-disabled student. In fact, these social skills are even more critical to the person who is disabled because the disabled are often compared with the norm and must compete for grades, social status, and employment.

Wallace and Kauffman (1986) indicate that social behav-ior development is inseparable from the student's acquisi-tion of academic skills and that "inappropriate behavior limits the student's chances for success in school: conversely, school failure often prompts undesirable behavior" (p. 165). Wallace and Kauffman (1986) strongly suggest that the remediation of students' social behavior problems is just as important as the remediation of their academic problems.

Social skills have been hard to define and even more dif-ficult to measure according to Wallace and Kauffman (1986), and Strain, Odom, and McConnell (1984). Direct observa-tion is perhaps one of the most reliable methods used in assessment of social skills problems. Other procedures used to assess competence in social behavior are self-reporting and screening instruments, clinical judgment, analysis of antecedent events, interviews, sociometric procedures, behavior and rating scales. However, when assessing an individual's social skills, one must be aware of the situa-tions and circumstances in which the behavior occurs. Social and emotional problems may not be the primary difficul-ties facing most exceptional children; nevertheless, except for behavior-disordered or seriously emotionally disturbed students, these problems are present.

Eleas and Maher (1983) suggest that well-adjusted chil-dren have certain social and academic skills that many mildly disabled students do not possess. Such skills as sen-sitivity to others' feelings, goal-setting persistence, and an adequate behavior repertoire are just a few mentioned. Many more social skills deficits that often plague students with disabilities such as poor self-concept, withdrawal, rejection, attention problems, compound the academic problems. School personnel need to address social skill problems of the student with disabilities. Mercer and Mercer (1985) indicate that teachers can "help foster the student's emotional development as well as the acquisition of social skills" (p. 132). Wallace and Kauffman (1986) and Mercer and Mercer (1985) believe that direct instruction may be the best method for remediating problems associated with social skills deficits. In addition to direct instruction, there are instructional materials and kits available commercially that are designed for teaching social skills. However, many of these kits have little validity data and vary widely in terms of the populations with which they have been used.

Perhaps social competence might be a better term to describe the skills necessary to get along with others. Schulman (1980) defines social competence as "getting along with people, communicating with them and coping with the frustrations of social living" (p. 285). Girls tend to achieve social competence more frequently than boys (Merrell, Merz, Johnson, & Ring, 1992). Nearly all of us need to feel accepted and socially competent. However, many students and adults with disabilities have difficulty, to some degree, in developing those skills necessary for adequate social acceptance.

REFERENCES

Bellach, A. S. (1983). Recurrent problems in the behavior assessment of social skills. *Behavior Research & Therapy, 21,* 29–41.

Bloom, B. (1956). *Taxonomy of educational objectives: The classification of educational goals.* New York: Longman.

Cartwright, C. P., Cartwright, C. A., & Ward, M. E. (1984). *Educating special learners.* Belmont, CA: Wadsworth.

Eleas, M. J., & Maher, C. A. (1983). Social and effective development of children: A programmatic perspective. *Exceptional Children, 4,* 339–346.

Drew, C. J., Logan, D. R., & Hardman, M. L. (1984). *Mental retardation: A life cycle approach* (3rd ed.). St. Louis, MO: Mosby.

Lerner, J. (1985). *Learning disabilities: Theories, diagnosis, and teaching strategies* (4th ed.). Boston: Houghton Mifflin.

Mercer, D. D., & Mercer, A. R. (1985). *Teaching students with learning problems* (2nd ed.). Columbus, OH: Merrill.

Merrell, K. W., Merz, J. M., Johnson, E. R., & Ring, E. N. Social competence of students with mild handicaps and low achievement: A comparative study. *School Psychology Review, 21*(1), 125–137.

Minskoff, E. H. (1980). Teaching approach for developing nonverbal communication skills in students with social perception deficits. *Journal of Learning Disabilities, 13,* 118–126.

Schulman, E. D. (1980). *Focus on retarded adults: Programs and services.* St. Louis, MO: Mosby.

Stephens, T. M., Hartman, A. C., & Lucas, V. H. (1983). *Teaching children basic skills: A curriculum handbook* (2nd ed.). Columbus, OH: Merrill.

Strain, P. S., Odom, S. L., & McConnell, S. (1984). Promoting social reciprocity of exceptional children: Identification, target behaviors selection, and intervention. *Remedial & Special Education, 1,* 21–28.

Wallace, G., & Kauffman, J. M. (1986). *Teaching students with learning and behavior problems* (3rd ed.). Columbus, OH: Merrill.

HUBERT B. VANCE
East Tennessee State University

ADAPTIVE BEHAVIOR
SOCIAL SKILLS INSTRUCTION
SOCIOGRAM

SOCIAL COMPETENCE

See ADAPTIVE BEHAVIOR.

SOCIAL DARWINISM

Social Darwinism, a social philosophy that was developed in the latter half of the nineteenth century, was based on the application of Darwin's principles of natural selection and survival of the fittest to the problems of society. Mental retardation, insanity, epilepsy, alcoholism, and other disorders were explained in terms of heredity, genetics, and Darwinian principles. Adams (1971) describes social Darwinism as follows: "the people of above average intelligence by previous standards become the norm in the next evolutionary phase, and the slow ones drop back to become the social casualties of the new order." Social Darwinism was also associated with attempts to interpret mental retardation as deviance rather than incompetence (Farber, 1968).

When Western Europe and North America became industrialized, environmental conditions that hindered the intellectual development of normal children resulted. Industrialization also led to health hazards that were responsible for the birth of biologically deficient children. At the same time, correlations were found between intellectual and social deficits that stimulated a variety of explanatory efforts. According to the principle of social Darwinism, human deficiencies were caused by evolutionary obstacles or the degeneration of genetic matter. The historical perspective of social Darwinism and its relation to the eugenics movement are central to understanding the treatment of disabled individuals from the 1850s to the 1950s.

In the 1850s, even before Darwin published his findings and theories, Morel speculated that all varieties of mental illnesses were related and were due to hereditary factors.

Noting an association between mental retardation and sterility, he further postulated that these illnesses became more profound with each succeeding generation, leading ultimately to, sterility and extinction. Morel suggested that mental illnesses were caused by physical diseases, alcoholism, and social environments, and called for more adequate food, housing, and working conditions as preventive measures. Concurrently, with evidence of a genetic inheritable component of intelligence mounting, mental health professionals were becoming convinced that institutional segregation of the disabled was necessary, thus abandoning their efforts to return individuals with disabilities to the community. Darwinism reached a height of popularity in England in the 14-year period from 1858 to 1872, but its effects were felt until the turn of the century. In the United States, Darwinian doctrine provided justification for the existing status structure prior to and during the Civil War. Darwinian proponents contended that foreigners and members of lower socioeconomic levels were distinct races that were inferior and might justifiably be subjugated. However, the North's victory strengthened the position of the anti-Darwinian proponents (Farber, 1968).

The optimism that characterized the treatment and care of the disabled in the early portion of the nineteenth century began to disappear in the latter half of the century. Institutions began moving away from treatment programs, replacing them with basic care and maintenance services. The emphasis on rehabilitation and education degenerated into support for terminal institutional placement (Hardman, Drew, & Egan, 1984). In the early portion of the twentieth century, with the introduction of mental tests, researchers found that a large proportion of prison inmates could be classified as feebleminded. Mentally retarded women were believed to be promiscuous, burdening society with many illegitimate offspring. It was estimated that criminals and unmarried mothers constituted 40 to 45 percent of the mentally retarded population. Furthermore, Tredgold and his followers contended that 90 percent of mental deficiency was due to hereditary factors. The feebleminded were regarded as unable to sustain gainful employment and a danger to the community and the "race." The solutions that were proposed most often were segregation and sterilization (Farber, 1968).

The "eugenic scare" of the early 1900s has been described as a shift in focus from the protection of the mentally handicapped from a cruel and exploitative society to the protection of society from contamination by inferior mental stock (Adams, 1971). With social Darwinism setting the stage, the eugenic movement was fed by the alarming increase in pauperism, vagrancy, alcoholism, and delinquency in society, and the association of low mentality and sociopathic behavior within identified families (e.g., the Jukes and the Kallikaks) whose genetic lines had been traced. The eugenic position was manifested in legislation for sterilization and

the proposal to extend custodial care to all the retarded in the United States during their childbearing years. The first sterilization law was passed in Indiana in 1907, followed by similar legislation in seven other states soon thereafter. (Adams, 1971).

By the 1920s, pessimistic forecasts appeared to have been vindicated in England, where the incidence of mental deficiency was sharply increasing. Although eugenicists strove to win the debate on mental deficiency during the period from 1900 to 1940, their efforts were hindered by their inability to identify the unfit, to prove causation, and to limit fertility (Macnicol, 1983). In reality, the concept of total social control over the retarded was never much more than an idea, and neither wholesale institutional commitment nor sterilization was implemented. Providing institutional care to segregate a large portion of society at public expense proved to be highly impractical. Nevertheless, by associating mental defects with genetic factors, the social forces that were causing pathological living conditions among the poor were neglected and the economic causes for social maladjustment were ignored (Adams, 1971). The negative side effects of involuntary sterilization of retarded persons have now been documented. Low self-esteem, feelings of failure, a sense of helplessness, and social isolation have all been associated with forced sterilization (Roos, 1975).

Social Darwinism and related social movements have had a profound impact on the treatment of the mentally retarded and other disabled individuals. However, not all of the effects of the social Darwinism movement were negative. Its popularity, along with the development of special educational services, has been credited with providing an impetus for the systematic study of the prevalence of mental retardation (Farber, 1968).

REFERENCES

Adams, M. (1971). *Mental retardation and its social dimensions.* New York: Columbia University Press.

Farber, B. (1968). *Mental retardation: Its social context and social consequences.* Boston: Houghton Mifflin.

Hardman, M. L., Drew, C. I., & Egan, M. W. (1984). *Human exceptionality: School, society, and family.* Boston: Allyn & Bacon.

Macnicol, J. (1983). Eugenics, medicine and mental deficiency: An introduction. *Oxford Review of Education, 3,* 177–180.

Roos, P. (1975). Psychological impact of sterilization on the individual. *Law & Psychology Review, 1,* 45–56.

GREG VALCANTE
University of Florida

EUGENICS
JUKES AND THE KALLIKAKS

SOCIAL INTEGRATION OF CHILDREN WITH DISABILITIES IN SCHOOL

See INCLUSION; MAINSTREAMING.

SOCIAL ISOLATION

Social isolation has been subsumed under the rubric of social skills or social competence. The problem of defining social isolation in children, specifically, is consonant with the problem of defining social skills or social competence in general. Children labeled as social isolates do not appear to constitute a homogeneous or clearly defined group, and several descriptors have been used in the literature as labels (e.g., shy, isolated, withdrawn, anxious-withdrawn). Social isolation is a behavior pattern that occurs across various categories of children such as autistic, mentally retarded, schizophrenic, severe visual impaired, (Gourgey, 1998) and normal.

There is a lack of agreement among investigators regarding the specific behaviors that need to be performed to indicate social skillfulness or competence, and the appropriate behaviors that are not performed, or the inappropriate behaviors that are performed, that indicate a lack of social skillfulness or competence. The contribution of several variables such as age, sex, social status, and situationally specific factors, in determining the presence or absence of social competence is poorly understood. Also, the criterion measures used to assess social isolation (behavioral observations, peer sociometric ratings, teacher ratings) may affect what is labeled as social isolate behavior (Conger & Keane, 1981). These criterion measures may not tap the same dimensions of behavior and may identify different subtypes of children (Gottman, 1977). The behaviors that have been selected as indicators of social isolate behavior have not been empirically determined. They have been chosen on the basis of the face validity of their relationship to the behavior pattern of social isolation, and single measures of social isolation typically have been employed (Conger & Keane, 1981). Additionally, little or no relationship has been found between the two main types of criterion measures used to assess social isolate behavior when they have been compared (i.e., global peer sociometric ratings of acceptance or rejection and behavioral observations of rate of discrete social interactions; Gottman, 1977).

The principal approaches in the conceptualization of social isolation in childhood have been in terms of withdrawal indicated by low rates of social interaction relative to other children and rejection or lack of acceptance by peers (Gottman, 1977). These two groups of social isolates may represent different populations; however, the infrequent use of both methods of assessment with the same groups of children does not allow for a determination of how well these measures agree on or discriminate among different subtypes of children. Also, given the lack of agreement on what behaviors or lack of behaviors are related to social isolation, it is unclear whether low rates of social interaction imply a lack of social skills or a lack of exhibiting social skills that the child possesses. In terms of peer acceptance or rejection, it is not clear whether this is based on a lack of social skills or on behaviors perceived as negative by peers such as aggressiveness. The grouping together of various behaviors within the category of social isolate behavior obscures assessment and intervention efforts and reduces the likelihood of heterogeneous grouping.

The development of positive social relationships with peers is an important developmental achievement. Typically, social interaction increases and relationships become more stable as children grow older (Asher, Oden, & Gottman, 1977). Thus social isolation may represent a significant deviation in social development. Gronlund (1959) reports that 6 percent of a sample of grades 3 to 6 had no classroom friends, and 12 percent had only one friend. A study of elementary age problem children identified 13.95 percent of the children referred by teachers for psychological services as withdrawn (Woods, 1964, as cited in Woods, 1969). Strain, Cook, and Apolloni (1977) estimate that 15 percent or more of children referred for psychological services exhibit social withdrawal as a major presenting symptom. Once a pattern of withdrawal behavior is established, it may persist through childhood and adolescence (Branson, 1968). The evidence for the carryover of social isolation into adulthood is beset with methodological problems and conflicting results that limit generalizations. It does appear, however, that adults with certain psychiatric disabilities were socially isolated as children, but that not all socially isolated children develop psychiatric disabilities as adults (Strain et al., 1977). Hops, Walker, and Greenwood (1979) note that children referred for psychological services because of social isolate behavior appear to lead quiet, retiring lives, with some restriction in social contacts.

Intervention approaches used with socially withdrawn children increasingly emphasize the training of social skills. Social learning procedures (Coombs & Slaby, 1977) have constituted major treatment methods for teaching social skills to socially isolated children (Conger & Keane, 1981; Hops, 1983). The use of instructional packages with multiple components appears to be the best method for teaching social skills. The packages may include a combination of shaping, modeling, coaching, and reinforcement. Cognitively oriented interpersonal problem-solving interventions have also been employed; they emphasize the training of cognitive processes to mediate performance across a range of situations rather than discrete behavioral responses to various situations (Urbain & Kendall, 1980). The cognitive-behavioral approach uses many of the same instructional methods as the social learning approach, but it focuses on teaching problem-solving strategies and verbally mediated self-control (e.g., self-instruction). Music therapy has also been used successfully (Gourgey, 1998).

The evidence to date suggests that interventions have demonstrated modest to moderate effects in teaching social skills to socially isolated children. Also, there are problems in establishing training effects that generalize beyond the treatment setting and maintain over time. Given the importance of positive social relationships with peers, efforts need to be continued to overcome conceptual, methodological, and assessment problems. Advances in these areas may further improve intervention efforts with children for whom peer relationships are problematic.

REFERENCES

Asher, S. R., Oden, S. C., & Gottman, J. M. (1977). Children's friendship in the school setting. In L. G. Katz (Ed.), *Current topics in early education* (Vol. 1). Norwood, NJ: Ablex.

Bronson, W. C. (1968). Stable patterns of behaviors: The significance of enduring orientations for personality development. In J. P. Hill (Ed.), *Minnesota symposia on child psychology* (Vol. 2). Minneapolis: University of Minnesota Press.

Conger, J. C., & Keane, P. (1981). Social skills intervention in the treatment of isolated or withdrawn children. *Psychological Bulletin, 90*(3), 478–495.

Coombs, M. L., & Slaby, D. (1977). Social skills training with children. In B. B. Lahey & A. E. Kazdin (Eds.), *Advances in clinical child psychology* (Vol. 1). New York: Academic.

Gottman, J. M. (1977). Toward a definition of social isolation in children. *Child Development, 48,* 513–517.

Gourgey, C. (1998). Music therapy in the treatment of social isolation in visually impaired children. *REView, 29*(4), 157–162.

Gronlund, N. E. (1959). *Sociometry in the classroom.* New York: Harper.

Hops, H. (1983). Social skills training for socially withdrawn/isolate children. In P. Karoly & J. J. Steffen (Eds.), *Improving children's competence.* Lexington, MA: Lexington.

Hops, H., Walker, H. M., & Greenwood, C. R. (1979). PEERS: A program for remediating withdrawal in school. In L. A. Hamerlynck (Ed.), *Behavioral systems for the developmentally disabled: In school and family environments.* New York: Brunner/Mazel.

Strain, P. S., Cooke, T. P., & Apolloni, T. (1976). *Teaching exceptional children: Assessing and modifying social behavior.* New York: Academic.

Urbain, E. S., & Kendall, P. C. (1980). Review of social-cognitive problem-solving interventions with children. *Psychological Bulletin, 88*(1), 109–143.

HAROLD HANSON
PAUL BATES
Southern Illinois University

SOCIAL BEHAVIOR OF INDIVIDUALS WITH DISABILITIES SOCIOGRAM

SOCIAL LEARNING THEORY

Social learning theory is one of the most well known and most influential models for understanding human behavior. In explaining this theory, it is helpful to describe what it is not, because social learning theory grew out of a reaction to other theoretical orientations. First, social learning theory does not view human behavior as purely a result of internal cognitive thoughts or feelings. Freud, for example, viewed human behavior as mediated by thoughts, wishes, self-concepts, impulses, etc. Neither does social learning theory view behavior as strictly a function of environmental events. Thus social learning theory is not a model of human behavior based strictly on the principles of operant conditioning developed by B. F. Skinner. Skinner and others believe that behavior is purely a function of environmental events.

Social learning theory does, however, provide an integration of previous theories such as Freud's and Skinner's. Although social learning theory is closely related to Skinner's principles of operant conditioning, the major difference is the incorporation of internal events as controlling stimuli. Social learning theorists recognize that an individual's thoughts and feelings have a significant impact on behavior.

Social learning theory is a term that has been applied to the views of a relatively wide range of theorists and researchers. Without question, the theorist who has done the most to conceptualize and advance the ideas of social learning theory is Albert Bandura of Stanford University. His more recent work has moved away from the early environmental determinism that characterized behavioristic social learning theory. His most comprehensive presentation is in his 1986 book in which he extensively details his social cognitive theory. No socialization theory has as much careful empirical support as social cognitive theory. Bandura has added significant arguments for why internal evaluative processes must be included in any behavioral theory. At the core of Bandura's theory is the concept of reciprocal determinism. Similar to but more limited than Bronfenbrenner's ecological model, reciprocal determinism conceptualizes behavior as a continuous reciprocal interaction between an individual's thoughts, behaviors, and environmental factors.

This triadic model views human functioning as a three-way interaction among behavior (B), cognitions and other internal events that affect perceptions and actions (P), and a person's external environment (E). An interesting aspect of this view is that each element of the triad affects the other two elements. Thus, not only do internal and environmental events affect behavior, but behavior also affects internal events and the environment in reciprocal fashion.

Bandura's (1986) emphasis on internal mediators can be seen in work on observational learning, enactive learning, predictive knowledge and forethought, interpretations of incentives, vicarious motivators, self-regulatory mechanisms, self-efficacy, and cognitive regulators. Bandura demonstrates how cognitive factors determine what we observe, how we evaluate our observations, and how we use this information in the future. For example when students take tests, they read the questions, answer according to their interpretations of what the teacher wants, receive feedback in the form of grades, and then adjust depending on how successfully they believe they answered the questions graded by the teacher. No behavior occurs in a vacuum without prior internal processes and external effects.

A key component in most social learning theories is observational learning, which is based on the process of modeling. Through modeling, children learn a wide array of complicated skills, such as language and social interaction. Moreover, these skills are learned without reinforcement. This is in stark contrast to radical behavioral theory, which posits that complex behaviors are learned through the reinforcement of gradual changes in molecular response patterns. Teachers make use of observational learning many times a day. For example, some teachers will verbally reinforce a child who is behaving appropriately just so other children will be encouraged to imitate the modeled behavior. Most socialization is the result of observational learning, because it is much more efficient and realistic than the step-by-step shaping advocated by radical behaviorists.

Another key component that has received considerable research attention is the concept of self-efficacy. Self-efficacy is a complex process in which persons assess the likelihood of successfully performing a task based upon their previous mastery (e.g., training), vicarious experience (e.g., modeling of others), verbal persuasion (e.g., encouragement), physiological condition (e.g., health), and affective state (e.g., happy). Persons high in self-efficacy will make realistic judgments of their abilities to perform tasks, will tend to seek appropriately difficult tasks, and will persist in them until completed (Bandura, 1997). Teachers with high teacher self-efficacy will be more likely to believe they can teach a classroom of difficult children. In special education classes, high teacher self-efficacy will result in greater progress and competence in the students.

Social learning theory has also emphasized the concept of internal dialogues. These dialogues, or internal speeches, are used by people to learn information (e.g., to rehearse a phone number), for self-instruction (e.g., "Now what do I do next?"), and for self-reinforcement (e.g., "Way to go!"). These internal dialogues fit in nicely with Vygotsky's developmental theory postulating a cognitive self-guidance system in which these dialogues eventually become silent or inner speech. Teaching internal dialogues to children with learning disabilities may help them become better problem solvers (Berk, 1992).

Because social learning theory has incorporated internal variables (e.g., thoughts and feelings) that are not directly observable, it has been criticized by radical behaviorists. Similarly, the emphasis within social learning theory on environmental factors and the lack of emphasis on cognitive development has caused it to be questioned by developmentalists. Freudian psychologists are dissatisfied with the lack of strong emotional components. Despite these detractors, social learning theory has enormous appeal to a wide variety of professionals. The reason for this appeal is the testability of the theory and the broad coverage of internal and external factors. Social learning theory is seen by many as being very comprehensive in its ability to handle a diverse range of human experiences and problems.

REFERENCES

Bandura, A. (1986). *Social foundations of thought and action: A social cognitive theory.* Englewood Cliffs, NJ: Prentice Hall.

Bandura, A. (1997). *Self-efficacy: The exercise of control.* New York: Freeman.

Berk, L. E. (1992). Children's private speech: An overview of theory and the status of research. In R. M. Diaz & L. E. Berk (Eds.), *Private speech: From social interaction to self-regulation.* Hillsdale, NJ: Erlbaum.

SPENCER THOMPSON
*The University of Texas of the
Permian Basin*

BANDURA, ALBERT
IMPULSE CONTROL
MEDIATIONAL DEFICIENCY
MEDIATION
OBSERVATIONAL LEARNING
RECIPROCAL DETERMINISM

SOCIAL MALADJUSTMENT

Social Maladjustment (SM) is, at best, a vaguely defined and intensely debated construct. It emerged approximately 30 years ago in an exclusionary clause to the federal definition of students with Emotional Disturbance (ED): "The term [ED] does not apply to children who are socially maladjusted, unless it is determined that they have an emotional disturbance" (34 CFR Part 300.7(c)(4); OSERS, 1997). Although the definition of ED was based on Eli Bower's research in the 1960s, the exclusionary clause for students considered SM seemed to appear with no basis in the empirical literature (Merrell & Walker, 2004). Since that time, researchers and practitioners have struggled to (a) define social maladjustment, (b) identify students who are SM and differentiate them from students who are ED, and (c) serve students who are SM.

Definition and Etiology

Attempts to define social maladjustment range from liberal, or inclusive, to more conservative, or exclusive, definitions. Each interpretation suggests a different etiology.

Liberal interpretation. Some researchers equate SM to a *DSM-IV-TR* (American Psychiatric Association, 2000) diagnosis of Conduct Disorder, Antisocial Personality Disorder, or Oppositional Defiant Disorder (e.g., Cullinan, 2004), which are assumed to be the product of a constellation of environmental and biological/dispositional risk factors (e.g., Frick, 2004). The range of students who meet criteria for one of the three diagnoses impedes the differentiation of students with SM from students with ED (Merrel & Walker, 2004), leading researchers and practitioners to employ more conservative criteria.

Conservative interpretations. Gacono and Hughes (2004) assert that the distinguishing factor of students with SM is psychopathy, which they describe as a "distinct personality syndrome" (p. 849). According to their definition, students with SM (a) demonstrate traits and behaviors considered "paranoid, borderline, narcissistic, histrionic, and antisocial" (p. 851), resulting from an interplay between physiological (e.g., biochemical abnormalities) and environmental (e.g., family dynamics) factors, and (b) present a greater risk for re-offending and violence.

Perhaps of more use to educators is a specific operational definition, based on an assumption that students with SM "engage in antisocial problem behavior in a willful manner, in the company of other antisocial youths, as a way to maintain or enhance their social status with in the antisocial subgroup, and in a manner that is unlawful" (Merrell & Walker, 2004, p. 902). Students with SM are defined as those who manifest "severe antisocial behavior" (Theodore, Akin-Little, & Little, 2004); that is, those who have been formally adjudicated for delinquent behavior that is purposeful in nature (Merrell & Walker, 2004).

A working definition. Merrell and Walker (2004) summarize that, regardless of interpretation, social maladjustment can best be described as "a pattern of engagement in purposive antisocial, destructive, and delinquent behavior" (p. 901).

Identification

Although a great deal of attention has been given to differentially diagnosing SM from ED, the focus has shifted to using assessment information to guide appropriate intervention (e.g., Hughes & Bray, 2004). Students with SM should be identified, as early as possible, through a comprehensive and intensive screening process in the context of a problem-solving model. Information should be gathered using multiple methods from multiple informants across settings and time.

Evidence-Based Strategies for Intervention

Walker, Ramsey, and Gresham (2004) summarize proven strategies for preventing, intervening with, and deescalating antisocial behavior. In general, students with SM benefit from assertive communication and function-based supports in a positive environment. Traditional forms of discipline, which may include punishment-based procedures (e.g., the "teacher look," verbal reprimand), typically result in power struggles that may escalate the situation. Because students with SM, by definition, may have a history of engaging in serious aggressive and unlawful behaviors, it is important to know a student's history; this understanding assists in determining the level at which outside support may be required.

A particularly promising approach to supporting students with SM emphasizes the determination of the function, or resulting consequences, of the emitted behavior, and the use of this information to develop behavior intervention plans (Crone & Horner, 2004). For example, one student who engages in intimidating stares may learn that this behavior successfully results in access to peer attention. Hypothesizing this function, an intervention might focus on teaching the student more prosocial behaviors that enable access to the same peer attention. In contrast, another student who engages in the same intimidating stares has learned that the same behavior effectively keeps peers away. The procedure that was used with the first student would be ineffective for this second student, who instead might need to learn how to disengage from peers in more socially acceptable ways (or how to engage peers in ways that are less aversive to him or her). The use of this type of function-based behavior intervention planning fits easily with the working definition of SM.

REFERENCES

American Psychiatric Association. (2000). *The diagnostic and statistical manual of mental disorders* (4th ed., text rev.). Washington, DC: Author.

Crone, D. A., & Horner, R. H. (2003). *Building positive behavior support systems in schools: Functional behavioral assessment.* New York: Guilford.

Cullinan, D. (2004). Classification and definition of emotional and behavioral disorders. In Rutherford, R. B., Quinn, M. M., & Mathur, S. R. (Eds), *Handbook of research in emotional and behavioral disorders.* New York: Guilford.

Frick, P. J. (2004). Developmental pathways to conduct disorder: Implications for serving youth who show severe aggressive and antisocial behavior. *Psychology in the Schools, 41,* 823–834.

Gacono, C. B., & Hughes, T. L. (2004). Differentiating emotional disturbance from social maladjustment: Assessing psychopathy in aggressive youth. *Psychology in the Schools, 41,* 849–860.

Hughes, T. L., & Bray, M. A. (2004). Differentiation of emotional disturbance and social maladjustment: Introduction to the special issue. *Psychology in the Schools, 41,* 819–821.

Merrell, K. W., & Walker, H. W. (2004). Deconstructing a definition: Social maladjustment versus emotional disturbance and moving the EBD field forward. *Psychology in the Schools, 41,* 899–910.

Office of Special Education and Rehabilitative Services (OSERS). (1997). IDEA '97 Final Regulations: 34 CFR Part 300, Assistance to States for the Education of Children with Disabilities: Part B of the Individuals with Disabilities Education Act. Retrieved from http://www.cec.sped.org/law_res/doc/law/regulations/index.php

Theodore, L. A., Akin-Little, A., & Little, S. G. (2004). Evaluating the differential treatment of emotional disturbance and social maladjustment. *Psychology in the Schools, 41,* 879–886.

BRANDI SIMONSEN
University of Connecticut

SOCIAL MATURITY

See ADAPTIVE BEHAVIOR.

SOCIAL SECURITY

Social Security is based on the concept of providing income and health maintenance programs for families in such instances as retirement, disability, poor health, or death. In general, to be eligible for Social Security a person must first pay into Social Security by working and allowing a certain amount of income to be deducted from earnings. Sixteen percent (over 3 million people) of the population in the United States receive Social Security checks. Individuals over 65 (about 25 million) are covered under health insurance called Medicare. In the category of disability, the number receiving benefits are about 3 million.

The Social Security Act of 1935 consisted of three broad areas: (1) Social Security insurance, which included old age, survivors, disability, and hospital insurance (DAS-DHI), unemployment insurance, workman's compensation, compulsory temporary disability insurance, and railroad retirement system and railroad unemployment and temporary disability insurance; (2) government sponsorship of government or farm workers under civil service retirement, national service life insurance, federal crop insurance, public assistance (which is based on need), and veterans benefits; and (3) social assistance (welfare), which includes public assistance, national assistance, old-age assistance, unemployment assistance, and social pension programs that provide cash payments and other benefits to individuals based on need. Owing to the many changes in our society since 1935 such as demographic shifts, changes in values and attitudes, and inflation the Social Security system has been revised.

To be considered disabled under Social Security law a person must have a physical or mental condition that prevents that person from doing any substantial gainful work. The condition must be expected to last for at least 12 months, or expected to result in death. Examples of such conditions include diseases of the heart, lungs, or blood vessels that have resulted in serious loss of heart or lung reserves or serious loss of function of the kidneys; diseases of the digestive system that result in severe malnutrition, weakness, and anemia; and damage to the brain that has resulted in severe loss of judgment, intellect, orientation, or memory. The World Health Organization revised the mental health aspects of the International Classification of Impairments, Disabilities, and Handicaps (ICIDH) in 1995 to assist in the planning of care. Children of individuals who are eligible disabled persons can receive benefits if they are under 18 or 19, still in high school full time, or disabled before age 22, unmarried, and living at home. If an individual is blind, there are special considerations such as a disability freeze on income averaging for retirement purposes. Work situations for all individuals must require skills and abilities that are comparable to those of the individual's previous work history. If, however, the person is disabled before 22 and the parents are paying into Social Security, they can receive disability benefits. In order to qualify, the person must be unable to work in gainful employment and the person under whose credits they are applying must be retired, disabled, deceased, or fully insured under Social Security.

Another federal program administered by the Social Security Administration for low-income individuals is Supplemental Security Income (SSI). Supplemental security income is not based on work credits. Eligibility is based on age (over 65), income guidelines, and disability at any age for persons who earn below a specific income. In general, individuals living in institutions are not eligible for SSI unless they are classified under the four exceptions listed by the Social Security Administration (1986):

1. A person who lives in a publicly operated community residence that serves no more than 16 people may be eligible for SSI payments.

2. A person who lives in a public institution primarily to attend approved educational or vocational training provided in the institution may be eligible if the training is designed to prepare the person for gainful employment.

3. If a person is in a public or private medical treatment facility and Medicaid is paying more than half the cost of his or her care, the person may be eligible, but the SSI payments limited to no more than $25 per month.

4. A person who is a resident of a public emergency shelter throughout a month can receive SSI payments for up to 3 months during any 12-month period. (pp. 9–10)

In the early 1990s the eligibility for SSI based on childhood disability was expanded because of a Supreme Court decision in *Zebley* v. *Sullivan* (Ford & Schwann, 1992).

To receive SSI under a disability option, the individual

must have a physical or mental disability that prevents him or her from gainful employment. The disability must be one that will last at least 12 months or be expected to end in death. For individuals under age 18, the decision is based on whether the disability would not allow the person to work if he or she were an adult.

REFERENCES

Ford, M. E., & Schwann, J. B. (1992). Expanding eligibility for SSI based on childhood disability: The Zebley decision. *Child Welfare, 71*(4), 307–318.

Uestuen, C., van Duuren-Kristen, S., & Kennedy, C. (1995). Revision of the ICIDH: Mental health aspects. *Disability & Rehabilitation: An International Multidisciplinary Journal, 17,* 3–4.

JANICE HARPER
North Carolina Central University

DISABILITY
REHABILITATION
SOCIOECONOMIC STATUS

SOCIAL SKILLS INSTRUCTION

Social skills instruction is a method for establishing important social behaviors in our schools. Research suggests that students with disabilities may have an increased likelihood of either exhibiting a social skills deficit (when the student does not know how to perform the targeted social skills) or a performance deficit (when the student does not perform the previously taught social skill at an acceptable level), thus supporting the need for the direct teaching of specific social skills as part of special education support and services (Fletcher-Janzen & De Pry, 2003). Social skills can be taught as part of a universal intervention or as a method of supporting students who need both targeted and intensive/individualized behavioral support (see Sugai et al., 2000). When taught as part of a universal intervention, social skills are also known as school wide behavioral expectations or character traits.

Social skills are "the individual skills and actions students must master . . . that allow them to initiate, sustain, adapt, alter, and discontinue interactions as conditions dictate" (Knapczyk & Rodes, 1996, p. 4). Social skills are specific behaviors (instead of feelings) that direct attention toward the development and maintenance of adult and peer relationships (Sugai & Lewis, 1996). Social competence, on the other hand, relates to the judgments that adults make about the student's use of targeted social skills within and across school environments (Fletcher-Janzen & De Pry, 2003). A student is said to be "socially competent" when she or he demonstrates fluency with a variety of socially

important skills and uses these skills as conditions dictate. Common social skills include listening to others, taking turns, greeting, joining activities or groups, expressing feelings appropriately, and helping peers.

Colvin and Sugai (1988) argued that in many educational settings academic instruction is approached very differently than social skills instruction. In the former, academic skills are directly *taught* to students with an emphasis on guided and independent practice, instructionally based error correction, and positive reinforcement. Colvin and Sugai noted that social skills instruction is often predicated on the faulty assumption that students already know how to perform socially important skills prior to entering our schools, that when social skills lessons are provided that strategic practice is not required, and that punishment-oriented approaches are typically used to try to shape social behavior. The central thesis of this research is that social skills instruction should be *taught* in a manner that is similar to how we teach academic content; that is, providing explicit social skills instruction with the provision of guided practice, independent practice, and positive reinforcement.

Several assumptions underlie the use of social skills instruction in our schools, including that most social skills are learned behaviors, most social skills problems are learning errors, that instructional methods for teaching social skills are similar to methods for teaching academic skills, and that a reciprocal relationship exists between academic and social competence (Sugai & Lewis, 1996). Social skills assessment should include formative strategies such as systematic direct observation methods (see Alberto & Troutman, 2006) and summative strategies that provide both identification and evaluation of social skills (see Gresham & Elliott, 1990; Walker & Mc Connell, 1988).

Lesson planning and implementation are often different dependent on whether the student has a performance deficit or a skill deficit. For a performance deficit, the teacher should take advantage of teachable moments, embedded instruction, antecedent-based approaches such as precorrection (see De Pry & Sugai, 2002) and adjusting the current schedule of reinforcement (Elliott & Gresham, 1991). For students who have a social skills deficit, a more direct or active form of instruction is needed (see Social Skills Lesson Plan Outline), including paying attention to three lesson planning features: before instruction, during instruction, and after instruction phases (Darch & Kame'enui, 2004). Before instruction planning includes defining the instructional goal, the learning objectives, and other features that need to be in place that will support the lesson; for example, materials, personnel, monitoring, and evaluation strategies. During instruction features include providing a review set, verbal presentation of the skill, and both guided and independent practice of the skill by the students. During this phase, students are asked to demonstrate the skill using role-plays or simulations (see Guidelines for Conducting Role Plays and Simulations) in the settings where the skill will be required, such as classroom, playground, or cafeteria (Stokes & Baer, 1977). After instruction strategies include the strategic use of teacher prompting to set the occasion for the use of the skill and positive reinforcement contingent upon the correct demonstration of the social skill. In addition, methods for evaluating the effect of the instruction as it relates to use of the skill over time and across settings is an important part of this phase.

In conclusion, students with disabilities may exhibit skill or performance deficits and may need ongoing support to learn and demonstrate socially important social skills in our schools. Social skills instruction is predicated on the belief that social skills are learned behaviors, social skills problems are learning errors, methods for teaching social skills are similar to academic instruction, and a reciprocal relationship exist between social competence and academic competence. As part of lesson planning, emphasis should be placed on before, during, and after instructional phases, as well as including multiple opportunities to practice the social skill in targeted settings. Specific social skills lesson planning features and guidelines for conducting role-plays and simulations are provided in the following (adapted from De Pry, 2005).

Social Skills Lesson Plan Outline

Skill Name _____

BEFORE THE LESSON

Lesson Planning
1. Establish Need through Assessment and Data Analysis

Goal:	Establish criteria for student mastery
Objectives:	Write instructional objectives across the following learning stages: acquisition, fluency, generalization, maintenance, and adaptation
Procedures:	Before the lesson review instructional strategies and prepare materials, personnel, room, and monitoring and evaluation procedures

DURING THE LESSON

Learning/Review Set
1. Create interest and motivation as you review prerequisite information and skills
2. Link previous lessons with current lesson
3. State instructional objective

Verbal Presentation of the Skill
1. Name the skill
2. Define the critical rule
3. Provide sufficient examples and nonexamples for students to reach 80 percent mastery

4. Provide multiple opportunities for student responding (4 to 6 responses per minute)
5. Provide immediate feedback and error correction

Doing the Skill—Guided Practice
1. Demonstrate the skill in the natural environment— MODEL
2. Practice the skill (teacher/student) using preplanned role-plays and simulations—LEAD
3. Evaluate role-plays
4. Provide immediate feedback and error correction
5. Initiate independent practice when at least 80 percent of the students reach mastery

Doing the Skill—Independent Practice
1. Provide students with clear instructions and expectations
2. Provide multiple practice opportunities using untrained role-plays and simulations—TEST
3. Actively monitor student progress and provide immediate feedback and error correction as needed
4. Assign homework that is school-based and/or home-based

AFTER THE LESSON

Prompting and Reinforcement
1. Provide student(s) with prompts prior to predictable errors in responding
2. Reinforce on a FR schedule during acquisition and VR schedule during maintenance and generalization

Evaluation
1. Collect and graph data on student progress over time and across settings
2. Evaluate student progress (formative and summative) and adjust teaching
3. Plan for additional teaching if needed

Guidelines for Conducting Role Plays and Simulations

- Have all materials ready before each role-play
- Remember, NEVER let participants practice nonexamples of the skill
- Conduct role-plays in target settings
- Pick students who are willing to participate
- Give each participant a script and/or background information of the situation they will role-play
- Remind each participant that it is very important that they try to do a good job
- Teach audience members expectations for watching and evaluating role-plays
- After each role-play (a) reinforce students for participating, (b) reinforce the audience for listening, and (c)

ask the audience and participants behavior-specific questions about the role-play; for example, *Was this an example of _____ (name of skill) _____? How do you know? What would you do differently to better show _____ (name of skill) _____?*

- Provide multiple opportunities to practice the skill to mastery and generalization
- Limit lessons to 15 to 20 minutes
- Have fun!

REFERENCES

Alberto, P. A., & Troutman, A. C. (2006). *Applied behavior analysis for teachers* (7th ed.). Upper Saddle River, NJ: Pearson Merrill Prentice Hall.

Colvin, G., & Sugai, G. (1988). Proactive strategies for managing social behavior problems: An instructional approach. *Education and Treatment of Children, 11,* 341–348.

Darch, C. B., & Kame'enui, E. J. (2004). *Instructional classroom management: A proactive approach to behavior management* (2nd ed.). Upper Saddle River, NJ: Pearson Merrill Prentice Hall.

De Pry, R. L. (2005). *Teaching social competence and character lesson plan template.* Unpublished manuscript.

De Pry, R. L., & Sugai, G. (2002). The effect of active supervision and precorrection on minor behavioral incidents in a sixth grade general education classroom. *Journal of Behavioral Education, 11,* 255–267.

Elliott, S. N., & Gresham, F. M. (1991). *Social skills intervention guide: Practical strategies for social skills training.* Circle Pines, MN: American Guidance Service.

Fletcher-Janzen, E., & De Pry, R. L. (2003). *Social competence and character: Developing IEP goals, objectives, and interventions.* Longmont, CO: Sopris West Educational Services.

Gresham, F. M., & Elliott, S. N. (1990). *Social skills rating system.* Circle Pines, MN: American Guidance Service.

Knapczyk, D. R., & Rodes, P. G. (1996). *Teaching social competence: A practical approach for improving social skills in students at-risk.* Pacific Grove, CA: Brooks/Cole.

Stokes, T. F., & Baer, D. M. (1977). An implicit technology of generalization. *Journal of Applied Behavior Analysis, 10,* 349–367.

Sugai, G., Horner, R. H., Dunlap, G. Hieneman, M., Lewis, T. J., Nelson, C. M., et al. (2000). Applying positive behavioral support and functional behavioral assessment in schools. *Journal of Positive Behavioral Interventions, 2,* 131–143.

Sugai, G., & Lewis, T. J. (1996). Preferred and promising practices for social skills instruction. *Focus on Exceptional Children, 29*(4), 1–16.

Walker, H. M., & McConnell, S. R., (1988). *The Walker-McConnell scale of social competence and school adjustment: A social skills rating scale for teachers.* Austin, TX: PRO-ED.

RANDALL L. DE PRY
*University of Colorado at
Colorado Springs*

SOCIAL SKILLS RATING SYSTEM

Social skills are socially acceptable learned behaviors that enable a person to interact effectively with others to avoid socially unacceptable responses (Gresham & Elliot, 1984). Social skills problems are persistent, related to low academic performance, and may result in social adjustment problems, even serious psychopathology. The Social Skills Rating System (SSRS) is a norm-referenced rating scale, the purpose of which is to assist professionals in screening and classifying children suspected of having significant social behavior problems and aid in the development of appropriate interventions for identified children (Gresham & Elliot, 1990). The SSRS is composed of separate rating forms for teachers, parents, and students, and is intended for use with preschool, elementary, and secondary students.

The SSRS samples behaviors in three domains: social skills, problem behaviors, and academic competence. The Social Skills Scale assesses cooperation, assertion, responsibility, empathy, and self-control. These qualities are rated by teachers, parents, and/or students using a three point Likert scale (*Never, Sometimes,* or *Very Often;* or *Not Important, Important,* or *Critical*). The Problem Behaviors domain assesses externalizing problems, internalizing problems, and hyperactivity. These qualities are rated by teachers and parents. Academic competence (i.e., reading, mathematics, motivation, parental support, and general cognitive functioning) assesses a student's performance as rated by a teacher using a five-point scale (1 = lowest 10 percent to 5 = highest 10 percent; Gresham & Elliot, 1990). The SSRS can be administered in about 20 minutes and provides standard scores, percentile ranks, confidence bands, and behavior levels (Demaray & Ruffalo, 1995).

The SSRS was standardized during 1988 on a national sample of 4,170 children using self ratings, 1,027 parent ratings, and 259 teacher ratings (Gresham & Elliot, 1990). The sample includes an equal number of girls and boys. Internal consistency coefficients range from .83 to .94 for social skills, from .73 to .88 for problem behaviors, and are .95 for academic competence. Thus, the scale displays a high degree of internal reliability. Test-retest reliability coefficients generally are in the .70s and .80s for the teacher and parent forms, indicating good stability. Coefficients for the student form are in the .50s and .60s. Although the test authors deem them adequate in view of other supporting evidence of their reliability, caution is needed when relying exclusively on them.

Content validity was demonstrated by the use of similar importance ratings for each skill and by previous research. The SSRS correlated significantly with other measures, including the Social Behavior Assessment, Harter Teacher Rating Scale, and various forms of the Child Behavior Checklist. Thus, criterion-related validity is demonstrated. Evidence supporting the construct validity of the SSRS was demonstrated through several studies evaluating developmental change, sex differences, internal consistency, correlations with other tests, factor analyses, convergent and discriminant correlation analyses, and comparisons of contrasted groups (Gresham & Elliot, 1990). International results show that for 7th to 9th grade students in Norway, teacher ratings consistently covaried with ratings of problem behaviors as well as academic competence and performance (Ogden, 2003). Also, students referred for services received significantly lower ratings than peers.

Thus, the SSRS is a reliable and valid instrument for assessing social skills in students. Strengths include ratings by multiple informants and the ability to inform interventions. The SSRS identifies specific skill deficits and contributes to an empirically validated method for designing, implementing, and evaluating a formal social skills intervention for elementary school students (Lane, Menzies, Barton-Arwood, Doukas, & Munton, 2005). Weaknesses include low reliability for the student form and a somewhat outdated standardization sample. Weaknesses of the standardization include an overrepresentation of Whites and Blacks, an underrepresentation of Hispanic Americans and other minorities, and limited numbers of students in the 11th ($N = 44$) and 12th ($N = 80$) grades (Demaray & Ruffalo, 1995). However, data obtained from the SSRS may be helpful when conducting a comprehensive assessment and engaging in intervention planning for students in the preschool through secondary grade levels.

REFERENCES

Demaray, M. K., & Ruffalo, S. L. (1995). Social skills assessment: A comparative evaluation of six published rating scales. *School Psychology Review, 24,* 648–671.

Gresham, F. M., & Elliot, S. N. (1984). Assessment and classification of children's social skills: A review of methods and issues. *School Psychology Review, 13,* 292–301.

Gresham, F. M., & Elliot, S. N. (1990). *Social Skills Rating System.* Circle Pines, MN: American Guidance Service.

Lane, K. L., Menzies, H. M., Barton-Arwood, S. M., Doukas, G. L., & Munton, S. M. (2005). Designing, implementing, and evaluating social skills interventions for elementary students: Step-by-step procedures based on actual school-based investigations. *Preventing School Failure, 49,* 18–26.

Ogden, T. (2003). The validity of teacher ratings of adolescents' social skills. *Scandinavian Journal of Educational Research, 47,* 63–76.

JEFFREY DITTERLINE
University of Florida

SOCIAL VALIDATION

In an educational context, social validation is the philosophy of providing psychological services that emphasize the importance of the student's or teacher's subjective opinions about intervention methods. Social validity differs from the statistical notion of validity in several aspects. Statistical validity refers to how well treatment results correlate with an objective set of criteria or other treatment methods. Social validity is concerned with the subjective opinions of teachers, parents, and/or students and how these subjective opinions affect the overall treatment outcomes. In social validity it is assumed "that if the participants don't like the treatment then they may avoid it, or run away, or complain loudly. And thus, society will be less likely to use our technology, no matter how potentially effective and efficient it might be" (Wolf, 1978, p. 206).

Social validity can be assessed on at least three levels (Wolf, 1978). First, we can evaluate the social significance of the treatment goals. Here we consider whether desired outcomes are of any real value to teachers, students, or society in general. The second level of assessment of social validity questions the social appropriateness of the treatment procedures. At this level, teachers and students are asked how acceptable the treatment methods are (i.e., whether the results of the treatment justify the methods used). "Judgements of acceptability include whether a treatment is appropriate for the problem, whether it is fair, reasonable, or intrusive, and whether it is consistent with conventional notions of what treatment should be" (Kazdin, 1980, p. 330). The treatment acceptability paradigm has been used with students and teachers in clinical settings (Kazdin, French, & Sherick, 1981); university settings (Kazdin, 1980); and primary and secondary school settings (Elliott, Witt, Galvin, & Moe, 1986; Turco, Witt, & Elliott, 1985). In the final level of social validation evaluation, teachers and students report their satisfaction with the methods used (i.e., How important are the effects of the treatment methods? Are the teachers and students satisfied with the results, even the unplanned ones?; Wolf, 1978).

Consumer satisfaction differs from treatment acceptability mainly in the timing of the measurements. Treatment acceptability requires teachers and students to judge treatments before they begin. Consumer satisfaction requires teachers and students to judge treatments during the treatment or after the treatment is over. In applied behavior analysis, it is believed that the outcomes of treatments are easily judged based on behavioral changes from baseline measurements. However, according to the social validity paradigm, the usefulness of school interventions can only be judged by the subjective evaluations of the teachers and students participating in the treatment program.

REFERENCES

Elliott, S. N., Witt, J. C., Galvin, G. A., & Moe, G. L. (1986). Children's involvement in intervention selection: Acceptability of interventions for misbehaving peers. *Professional Psychology: Research and Practice, 17*(3), 235–241.

Kazdin, A. E. (1980). Acceptability of alternative treatments for deviant child behavior. *Journal of Applied Behavior Analysis, 13,* 259–273.

Kazdin, A. E., French, N. H., & Sherick, R. B. (1981). Acceptability of alternative treatments for children: Evaluations by inpatient children, parents, and staff. *Journal of Consulting and Clinical Psychology, 49,* 900–907.

Turco, T. L., Witt, J. C., & Elliott, S. N. (1985). Factors influencing teachers' acceptability of classroom interventions for deviant student behavior. *Monograph on secondary behavioral disorders.* Reston, VA: Council for Exceptional Children.

Wolf, M. M. (1978). Social validity: The case for subjective measurement or how applied behavior analysis is finding its heart. *Journal of Applied Behavior Analysis, 11,* 203–214.

TIMOTHY L. TURCO
Louisiana State University

STEPHEN N. ELLIOTT
University of Wisconsin at Madison

APPLIED BEHAVIOR ANALYSIS
TEACHER EXPECTANCIES

SOCIAL WORK

Social work in special education traditionally falls within the realm of the school social worker. The functions performed by social workers within the school include individual and family casework, individual and group work with students, and community liaison services. School social workers have stated their goals as helping students to maximize their potential, developing relationships between the school and other agencies, and offering a perspective of social improvement in the education of students (Costin, 1981).

In 1975, PL 94-142 and subsequent amendments resulting in IDEA mandated free and appropriate education for all students; social work falls under the section providing for related services (Hancock, 1982). The school social worker often participates as a member of an interdisciplinary team, and in some states assumes a permanent position on a child study team. Local boards of education determine the specific roles of team members (Winters & Easton, 1983). As a team member, the social worker may be responsible for gathering family information, coordinating team meetings, developing individualized educational programs, and monitoring services.

The school social worker often participates in the evaluation of students who are being considered for special education. In this regard, the case history is an extremely important tool that the social worker uses to gain environmental, developmental, social, and economic information about the student.

To work effectively with a special population, the school social worker must have several basic competencies. Dick-

erson (1981) includes counseling, crisis intervention, knowledge of related services, and understanding of adapted curricula and techniques as required skills. To be effective, the school social worker must also hold the belief that special-needs children are entitled to the same rights and privileges as those afforded to their mainstreamed peers.

Often, family members of the children with disabilities need support from the social worker in their efforts to program for their impaired youngsters. The primary goal of the social worker in providing services to family members of individuals with disabilities is to help them face and accept the limiting condition (Dickerson, 1981). The family is encouraged to follow through on recommendations designed to enhance their child's functioning. The social worker helps the family to recognize that the problem is real and that it can be helped by the development of an accepting, positive attitude about the child.

The school social worker may provide a number of different services to the family. Hancock (1982) writes that one role for the school social worker is to support parents in their efforts to become more active participants in school decisions regarding their children. Social workers may contribute information regarding home versus institutional care for severely impaired children. The social worker may also provide direct counseling services to the family, or act as a link to other supportive services. For example, parents might be encouraged to find a support or advocacy group. Ensuring that families receive the financial support to which they are entitled is another important function.

Pupil services such as counseling, sex education, prevocational development, and child advocacy are often performed by the school social worker. As an advocate, the social worker attempts to create systemic changes that improve the quality of the impaired child's school life. The social worker may assume responsibility for shaping a school system's attitudes to reflect more adaptive, relevant, and socially responsible positions (Lee, 1983).

School social workers may be responsible for developing communication links within the school so that teachers, administrators, and other staff can exchange information necessary for student programming. They may also plan in-service workshops in areas related to student welfare. Future trends in special education social work will continue to expand the systems approach to service delivery. To this end, an increase in coordinator and liaison roles for special education social workers is predicted (Randolph, 1982), and mandated in inclusive programming (Pryor, Kent, McGunn, & LeRoy, 1996).

REFERENCES

Costin, L. B. (1981). School social work as specialized practice. *Social Work, 26,* 36–44.

Dickerson, M. O. (1981). *Social work practice and the mentally retarded.* New York: Free Press.

Hancock, B. L. (1982). *School social work*. Englewood Cliffs, NJ: Prentice Hall.

Lee, L. J. (1983). The social worker in the political environment of a school system. *Social Work, 28*(4), 302–307.

Pryor, C. B., Kent, C., McGunn, C., & LeRoy, B. (1996). Redesigning social work in inclusive schools. *Social Work, 41*(6), 668–676.

Randolph, J. L. (1982). School social work can foster educational growth for students. *Education, 102,* 260–265.

Winters, W. G., & Easton, F. (1983). *The practice of social work in the schools*. New York: Free Press.

GARY BERKOWITZ
Temple University

MULTIDISCIPLINARY TEAM
PERSONNEL TRAINING IN SPECIAL EDUCATION

SOCIODRAMA

Sociodrama is a group-therapy technique developed by J. L. Moreno (1946) as an extension of a group-therapy technique, also devised by Moreno, known as psychodrama. (Moreno is often credited with having initiated group therapy in Vienna just after the beginning of the twentieth century.) Though he developed the technique, Moreno did little with sociodrama, preferring to continue his efforts in the development and application of psychodrama. E. Paul Torrance, a psychodramatist who studied with Moreno, later reconceptualized and refined sociodrama as a group problem-solving technique based on Moreno's early work but also incorporating the creative problem-solving principles of Torrance (1970) and Osborn (1963). Sociodrama can be used with all ages from preschool through adulthood.

The primary uses of sociodrama, largely reflecting Torrance's interests and influence, have been in primary prevention of behavior problems with the disadvantaged and other high-risk populations. Sociodrama has also been used in specific treatment programs with adolescents who engage in socially deviant behaviors and with status offenders. Sociodrama seems particularly helpful in introducing and teaching new social behaviors as well as in improving the problem-solving skills of the youngsters involved, giving them more behavioral options.

During sociodrama, a problem or conflict situation that is likely to be common to the group is derived from group discussion. Members of the group are cast into roles, which they play as the situation is acted out. Many production techniques are brought into play to facilitate solution of the conflict; these include the double, the soliloquy, direct presentation, mirror, and role reversal.

The director's role is to keep the action moving in the direction of a resolution, or, preferably, multiple resolutions of the conflict. Each session should end with a series of potential resolutions that can be discussed by the group. Appropriate behaviors can also be practiced. By teaching participants to brainstorm alternative behaviors and to rehearse for real-life problem situations, sociodrama has proved a useful method for treatment and prevention of behavior problems in children and adolescents. Torrance (1982) provides a more detailed presentation of the techniques of sociodrama.

REFERENCES

Moreno, J. L. (1946). *Psychodrama*. Beacon, NY: Beacon House.

Osborn, A. F. (1963). *Applied imagination* (3rd ed.). New York: Scribner's.

Torrance, E. P. (1970). *Creative learning and teaching*. New York: Dodd, Mead.

Torrance, E. P. (1982). Sociodrama: Teaching creative problem-solving as a therapeutic technique. In C. R. Reynolds & T. B. Gutkin (Eds.), *The handbook of school psychology*. New York: Wiley.

CECIL R. REYNOLDS
Texas A&M University

GROUP THERAPY
PSYCHODRAMA

SOCIOECONOMIC IMPACT OF DISABILITIES

There is a well-established relationship between parents' socioeconomic status and children's school performance, (Barona, 1992). Caldwell (1970) reports that many of the children from lower socioeconomic classes live in restricted and nonstimulating environments. As a result, low socioeconomic profile is one factor that is significantly related to poor cognitive functioning. There are many more children from lower socioeconomic classes with poor cognitive functioning than from higher socioeconomic classes.

An investigation analyzing the extent to which parental social status influences the decisions made in reference to potentially disabled students was conducted by Ysseldyke et al. (1979). Individuals involved in decision making were given identical data on students referred for evaluation. All data were samples of normal or average performance. The decision makers were told in half of the cases that the child's father was a bank vice president and the mother a real estate agent. The other half were told that the child's father was a janitor at the bank and the mother a clerk at a local supermarket. As a result of knowledge of the parents' socioeconomic status, the decision makers made different placement and classification decisions for the children. This has been supported in later research (Podell & Scodlak, 1993).

There are many factors associated with socioeconomic status that are considered contributing factors to some disabilities. These include poor health care, inadequate pre- and postnatal care, improper diet, and lack of early stimulation. Zachau-Christiansen and Ross (1975) state that infants from lower socioeconomic families are at greater risk for experiencing or being exposed to conditions that may hinder development. These conditions include low birth weight, lead poisoning, malnutrition, and maternal infections during pregnancy. Kagan (1970) discusses other psychological differences between lower class and more privileged children. The differences are evident during the first 3 years of life and tend to remain stable over time. Variables include language, mental set, attachment, inhibition, sense of effectiveness, motivation, and expectancy of failure. All of the factors play a crucial role in influencing school performance. Deficits in any of these areas limits the child's ability in various cognitive skills. Young children raised in an environment lacking in stimulation and healthy interaction with adults will often be retarded in motor, language, cognitive, and social skills.

Lack of proper nutrition can negatively affect the maturation of the brain and central nervous system. Malnutrition affects brain weight and tends to have lasting effects on learning and behavior. It has a very damaging effect during the first 6 months of life owing to the rate of brain cell development during this period. In the area of mental retardation and learning disabilities, the majority of the students tend to be from lower socioeconomic status homes and racial and cultural minorities. In many cases, the poor achievement of the socioculturally different individual is related to lack of proper nutrition and medical care. Kavale (1980) reports that almost all complications of prenatal life, pregnancy, labor and delivery, and postnatal diseases that are potentially damaging to the infant's brain development are disproportionately high among low socioeconomic groups.

Many other correlates of low socioeconomic status are associated with poor school learning. Some of these correlates are delayed development of language; greater impulsivity; lower intelligence on standard intelligence tests that predict success in standard curricula; lower parental educational levels; families with over five children; poor home climate; lack of variety in sensory stimuli; minimal encouragement of scholastic success within the home; and less time spent on tasks in the classroom and on homework.

An area that is crucial to academic performance is language development. Jensen (1968) lists several factors associated with language development as sources of social class differences and intellectual achievement. In the lower classes, early vocalization by infants is less likely to be rewarded; the child is less likely to have a single mother-child relationship in the early years; there is less verbal interaction and verbal play in response to early vocalizations; and speech tends to be delayed. In the early stages of speech, there is less shaping of speech sounds, in which parents reinforce approximations of adult speech, and much vocal interaction with slightly older siblings whose own speech is only slightly more advanced and who do not systematically shape behavior.

According to MacMillian (1982), the physical environment of lower class homes tends to be related to cultural familial retardation. When compared with middle-class households, lower class households tend to have the father absent from the home, crowded living conditions, poor nutrition and medical care, large family size, dilapidated living environment, and high ratio of children to adults. These factors have a negative impact on the child and his or her social, emotional, and educational adjustment. In many instances, the lower classes are less likely to vote and participate in political or social activities.

MacMillian (1982) has emphasized the dangers of class stereotyping. Determining socioeconomic status and the relationship between the ratings and developmental outcomes can be misleading; there are some exceptions to every rule. It is very important that special education personnel are trained in cultural awareness programming that includes socioeconomic variables. The major concern should be placed on the overall impact of socioeconomic factors in preventing or enhancing the possibility of physical, social, emotional, and intellectual disabilities.

REFERENCES

Barona, A., & Faykus, S. P. (1992). Differential effects of sociocultural variables on special education eligibility categories. *Psychology in the Schools, 29*(4), 313–320.

Caldwell, B. (1970). The rationale for early intervention. *Exceptional Children, 36,* 717–727.

Jensen, A. R. (1968). Social class, race, and genetics: Implications for education. *American Educational Research Journal, 5,* 1–412.

Kagan, J. (1970). On class differences and early development. In V. Denenberg (Ed.), *Education of the infant and young child.* New York: Academic.

Kavale, K. A. (1980). Learning disability and cultural-economic disadvantage: The case for a relationship. *Learning Disability Quarterly, 3,* 97–112.

MacMillian D. L. (1982). *Mental retardation in school and society.* (2nd ed.). Boston: Little, Brown.

Podell, D. M., & Soodlak, L. C. (1993). Teacher efficacy and bias in special education referrals. *Journal of Educational Research, 86*(4), 247–253.

Ysseldyke, J. E., Algozzine, B., Regan, R., Potter, M., Richey, L., & Thurlow, M. L. (1979). *Psychoeducational assessment and decision making: A computer-simulated investigation* (Research Report No. 32). Minneapolis: University of Minnesota Institute for Research on Learning Disabilities.

Zachau-Christiansen, B., & Ross, E. M. (1979). *Babies: Human development during the first year.* Chichester, England: Wiley.

Zigler, E. (1970). Social class and the socialization process. *Review of Educational Research, 40*, 87–110.

JANICE HARPER
*North Carolina Central
University*

CULTURALLY/LINGUISTICALLY DIVERSE STUDENTS GIFTED AND TALENTED CHILDREN SOCIOECONOMIC STATUS

SOCIOECONOMIC STATUS

Davis (1986) defines socioeconomic status (SES) as a person's position in the community. There are many factors involved in determining SES. These factors include income, employment, location and cost of home, and social status of the family. Socioeconomic status influences various behavior patterns. For example, the number of children, the year and model of the family car, and the number of vacations per year will vary according to SES.

Society places a high value on wealth and material possessions. There is a tendency to rank individuals based on their wealth and power within the community. Wealth is highly correlated with education, income, and occupation. Studies of social classes in the United States report five or six classes. Hodges (1964) has developed a system of six social classes. The first is the upper-upper class, which represents 1 to 2 percent of the community. This group includes people with wealth, power, and a family name that is prominent. Individuals can only be born into this class, with the exception of a few marrying into it. The lower-upper class also represents 1 to 2 percent of the community. This class does not have a prominent family name and their money is fairly new. However, they have wealth and power. The upper-middle class represents 10 to 12 percent of the community. These people have college degrees, are usually professionals and successful merchants. The lower-middle class represents 33 percent of the community. These people are usually small business people, salespeople, clerks, and forepeople. They tend to have average income and education, with high value placed on family, religion, thrift, and hard work. The upper-lower class also represents 33 percent of the community. In many cases they are employees rather than employers. The lower-lower class represents 15 to 20 percent of the population. These people are unskilled workers. Many are not high-school graduates and may frequently be unemployed.

Socioeconomic status has a direct relationship to the length and quality of life. The lower-lower classes do not live as long as members of the upper class. The poor are more likely to suffer from chronic and infectious diseases and are less likely to see a physician or a dentist. This may be a result of lack of money to pay for medical expenses. However, it has also been found that minor illnesses such as fevers have a low priority in poverty-stricken homes. Other factors such as child-rearing practices are affected by socioeconomic status of the family. Middle-class parents tend to be more permissive, while lower class parents are more rigid (Bassis, Gelles, & Levine, 1980).

Kohn (1969) states that middle-class mothers value self-control, dependability, and consideration, while lower class mothers value obedience and the ability to defend oneself. The middle-class family raises the child in an environment where achievement and getting ahead are encouraged. The lower class family raises the child in an environment that emphasizes the immediate and the concrete. The child is taught to shy away from the new or unfamiliar. According to Boocock (1972), the family characteristic that is the most powerful predictor of school performance is socioeconomic status. More specifically, the higher the socioeconomic status of the family, the higher the child's academic achievement. Socioeconomic status also predicts the number and type of extracurricular activities the child will be involved in and social and emotional adjustment to school. Other areas highly correlated with socioeconomic status include grades, achievement test scores, retentions at grade level, course failures, truancy, suspensions from school, dropout rates, college plans, and total amount of schooling.

REFERENCES

Bassis, M. S., Gelles, R. J., & Levine, A. (1980). *Sociology: An introduction* (2nd ed.). New York: Random House.

Boocock, S. S. (1972). *An introduction to the sociology of learning.* Dallas: Houghton Mifflin.

Davis, W. E. (1986). *Resource guide to special education* (2nd ed.). Boston: Allyn & Bacon.

Hodges, H. M. (1964). *Social stratification.* Cambridge, MA: Schenkman.

Kohn, M. (1969). *Class and conformity.* Homewood, IL: Dorsey.

JANICE HARPER
*North Carolina Central
University*

SOCIOECONOMIC IMPACT OF DISABILITIES

SOCIOGRAM

A sociogram (Moreno, 1953) is a graphic display of interpersonal relationships within a group. It is considered one of the most common sociometric techniques used by teachers. In most instances, a sociometric test is administered to a group of children by asking each child who he or she would like to work with on a particular activity. The sociogram displays a diagram of students with whom other students prefer to study, play, or work. It also displays a diagram of students who are rejected and tend to be isolates. Each child is asked such questions as, With which three students would you prefer to study? Which three students do you like best? Which two students do you prefer to play with at recess? Which three students are your best friends? The students' responses to these types of questions are used to construct the sociogram.

There are two types of sociograms: the graphic and the target diagram. The graphic sociogram assigns initial letters of the alphabet (such as A, B, C) to the most popular students. These students appear in the center of the chart. The isolates are assigned middle letters (such as H, I, J), and appear on the edges of the diagram. Stanley and Hopkins (1972) listed the limitations of this chart as difficulty in reading with 30 or more students and requiring a great deal of practice to learn the most effective placement. The target diagram consist of circles, with the most popular students placed in the center and the isolated students placed on the outer edges. According to Stanley and Hopkins (1972), this diagram is more productive for teachers with large classrooms.

The information obtained from a sociogram can be used for assessing students who may be isolated, socially immature, unhappy, and who have disabilities (Conderman, 1995). Once this information has been obtained from the sociogram, the teacher may begin to ask questions to determine why some students are considered isolates and often rejected. This information can assist the teacher with assigning students to groups for class projects and making changes in classroom relationships. It may also alert the teacher to the possibility of an existing or potential handicapping condition. Almost 40 percent of all teachers use sociometric techniques (Vasa, Maag, Torrey, & Kramer, 1994).

REFERENCES

Conderman, G. (1995). Social status of sixth- and seventh-grade students with learning disabilities. *Learning Disability Quarterly, 18*(1), 13–24.

Moreno, J. L. (1953). *Who shall survive? Foundations of sociometry, group psychotherapy, and sociodrama* (2nd ed.). New York: Beacon House.

Stanley, J. C., & Hopkins, K. D. (1972). *Educational and psychological measurement and evaluation.* Englewood Cliffs, NJ: Prentice Hall.

Vasa, S. F., Maag, J. W., Torrey, G. K., & Kramer, J. J. (1994). Teachers' use of and perceptions of sociometric techniques. *Journal of Psychoeducational Assessment, 12*(2), 135–141.

JANICE HARPER
*North Carolina Central
University*

SOCIAL SKILLS INSTRUCTION

SOCIOMETRIC TECHNIQUES WITH INDIVIDUALS WITH DISABILITIES

Sociometric techniques originated by Moreno (1953) are a set of questions used to determine the social organization of a group. There are various types of sociometric techniques that are used with individuals with disabilities. The two most common forms are peer nomination and roster and rating methods. Most peer nomination techniques ask questions such as, With whom would you most like to study? Who would you most like to sit with at lunch? Who would you most enjoy working with on an art project? Who would you most enjoy being with during break? (Mercer & Mercer, 1981 p. 109).

Other forms of peer nomination techniques may ask students questions relating to attitudes and behavior: Which students are very popular? Which students does the teacher like most? Which students cause a lot of trouble? Which students are selfish? (Mercer & Mercer 1981, p. 110). The rating scales usually lists all students in the class along with the rating scale (e.g., 1 = low and 10 = high) and ask each student to rate each person in the class. A score is determined for each child based on the average of their ratings.

Another common sociometric technique is the use of the sociogram, which is a visual display of the interrelationships within a group. The sociogram clearly shows which child is popular and which child is isolated by their positions on a diagram. There are teacher-made sociometric techniques and commercially produced sociometric techniques. The commercially produced techniques include the Ohio Social Acceptance Scale, which is designed for children in grades three through six. There are six headings: (1) my very best friends; (2) my other friends; (3) not friends, but okay; (4) don't know them; (5) don't care for them; (6) dislike them. The children are asked to write the names of their classmates under each of the headings (Wallace & Larsen 1978).

Another commercial technique is the Peer Acceptance Scale, which is used to obtain social status scores of children. This test uses stick figures of two children playing ball together, which is labeled friend; two children at a blackboard, which is labeled all right; and two children with their backs to each other, which is labeled wouldn't like. The students are read a list of names of classmates they are familiar with and asked to circle the figure that best describes how they feel about the student (Goodman, Gottlieb, & Harrison, 1972). The information from these sociometric techniques may be helpful to the teacher for the following activities: (1) assigning instructional groups and peer tutors; (2) planning affective development activities; (3) identifying potential groups; (4) predicting interpersonal difficulties within the group; and (5) measuring change in social adjustment (Marsh, Price, & Smith, 1983, p. 51).

With disabled children social acceptance is considered

a very important aspect of school adjustment and educational achievement. Sociometric techniques may help the teacher determine whether the disabled child is accepted by his or her nondisabled peers (Conderman, 1995). If the child is not accepted, the next step is to decide which interventions will help to improve the child's social status.

REFERENCES

Conderman, G. (1995). Social status of sixth- and seventh-grade students with learning disabilities. *Learning Disability Quarterly, 18*(1), 13–24.

Goodman, H., Gottlieb, J., & Harrison, H. (1972). Social acceptance of EMRs integrated into a nongraded elementary school. *American Journal of Mental Deficiency, 76,* 412–417.

Marsh, G. E., Price, B. J., & Smith, T. E. (1983). *Teaching mildly handicapped children: Method and materials.* St. Louis, MO: Mosby.

Mercer, C. D., & Mercer, A. R. (1981). *Teaching students with learning problems.* Columbus, OH: Merrill.

Moreno, J. L. (1953). *Who shall survive? Foundations of sociometry, group psychotherapy and sociodrama* (2nd ed.). New York: Beacon House.

Wallace, G., & Larsen, S. (1978). *Educational assessment of learning problems: Testing for teaching.* Boston: Allyn & Bacon.

JANICE HARPER
North Carolina Central University

SOCIOGRAM

SOFT (NEUROLOGICAL) SIGNS

Neurological soft signs are defined by Shaffer, O'Connor, Shaffer, and Prupis (1983) as "non-normative performance on a motor or sensory test identical or akin to a test of the traditional neurological examination, but a performance that is elicited from an individual who shows none of the features of a fixed or transient localizable neurological disorder" (p. 145). Some sources (e.g., Buda, 1981; Gaddes, 1985) suggest soft signs have a strong age-related component, in that many of the behaviors judged to represent soft signs in children of a certain age would be considered within the range of normal behavior for chronologically younger children (Ardilla & Rosselli, 1996). The term is contrasted with hard neurological signs, which are medically documented symptoms of neurologic disease.

The concept of neurological soft signs developed during the 1960s in conjunction with the non-defunct description of the minimal brain dysfunction (MBD) syndrome (Spreen et al., 1984). Although there were behavioral differences observed in children described as having MBD syndrome, hard neurologic findings were not demonstrated in the population. The vague, inconsistent behaviors that were observed were called soft neurological signs. To be considered a soft sign, Shaffer et al. (1983) state there should be no association between the observed behavior and a positive history of neurologic disease or trauma. Furthermore, clusters of neurological soft signs should not be pathognomonic of neurologic disease or encephalopathy. Soft signs, by definition, are not indicative of specific central nervous system pathology. Soft signs are not additive in the traditional sense: "the presence of more than one soft sign does not make a hard sign" (Spreen et al., 1984, p. 246).

The generalizability of data from studies of neurological soft signs has been complicated by inconsistency across studies in the specific signs tested. Soft signs have been categorized into three different types: those that may suggest immaturity or developmental delay; those that are mild expressions of classic hard neurological signs, which are difficult to elicit and may be inconsistent; and behaviors that may be associated with nonneurologic causes (Spreen et al., 1984). Testing a population of children for soft signs of the type associated with the first category may identify a different subgroup than would testing for signs associated with the others.

Nearly 100 different neurological soft signs have been identified (Spreen et al., 1984). Such signs encompass a wide variety of behaviors, including impulsivity (Vitello, Stoff, Atkins, & Mahoney, 1990) attention, concentration, fine motor speed, activity level, and affect. Gaddes (1985) lists the following as among the most common neurologic soft signs: motor clumsiness, speech and language delays, left-right confusion, perceptual and perceptual-motor deficits, and deficient eye-hand coordination. Soft signs may occur in conjunction with hyperactivity and specific learning disabilities, but the presence should not be considered pathognomonic of these conditions (Gaddes, 1985).

The relationship between neurologic soft signs and learning and behavior disorders in children has been investigated widely. In a comprehensive review of studies of children conducted prior to 1983, Shaffer et al. (1983) reported these investigations demonstrated consistent relationships between neurological soft signs and IQ scores, as well as diagnosed psychiatric disturbances and behavior problems. The authors described a study of 456 children participating in the Collaborative Perinatal Project of the National Institute of Neurological and Communicative Disorders and Stroke (NINCDS). The subjects were examined for the presence or absence of 18 neurological soft signs at age 7. Specific signs included movement disorders (e.g., tics, tremors, mirror movements) and coordination difficulties (e.g., dysmetria, dysdiadochokinesia). Subjects were rated blind on 15 behaviors (e.g., fearfulness, verbal fluency, cooperativeness, attention span). As in previous studies, the authors reported increased incidence of cognitive dysfunction, learning problems, and behavior disorders in children who exhibited neurologic soft signs.

The etiology of neurological soft signs has not been delineated clearly, and it is likely there are multiple causes. Soft signs may constitute one end of a continuum of neurologic signs, and thus may be a result of mild central nervous system impairment. For other individuals, soft signs may represent a genetic variation (Shaffer et al., 1983). The high incidence of neurologic soft signs in the general population suggests that caution should be exercised when interpreting their significance.

REFERENCES

Ardilla, A., & Rosselli, M. (1996). Soft neurological signs in children: A normative study. *Developmental Neuropsychology, 12*(2), 181–200.

Buda, F. B. (1981). *The neurology of developmental disabilities.* Springfield, IL: Thomas.

Gaddes, W. H. (1985). *Learning disabilities and brain function: A neuropsychological approach* (2nd ed.). New York: Springer-Verlag.

Shaffer, D., O'Connor, P. A., Shafer, S. Q., & Prupis, S. (1983). Neurological "soft signs": Their origins and significance for behavior. In M. Rutter (Ed.), *Developmental neuropsychiatry* (pp. 144–163). New York: Guilford.

Spreen, O., Tupper, D., Risser, A., Tuokko, H., & Edgell, D. (1984). *Human developmental neuropsychology.* New York: Oxford University Press.

Vitello, B., Stoff, D., Atkins, M., & Mahoney, A. (1990). Soft neurological signs and impulsivity in children. *Journal of Developmental & Behavioral Pediatrics, 11*(3), 112–115.

CATHY F. TELZROW
Kent State University

NEUROPSYCHOLOGY
VISUAL-MOTOR AND VISUAL-PERCEPTUAL PROBLEMS

SOMPA

See SYSTEM OF MULTICULTURAL PLURALISTIC ASSESSMENT.

SONICGUIDE

The Sonicguide is a mobility aid and environmental sensor for the visually impaired. It operates on the principle of reflected high-frequency sound, which, when converted into audible stereophonic signals, provides the user with information about the distance, position, and surface characteristics of objects within the travel path and immediate environment. Users of all ages (Hill, Dodson-Burk, Hill, & Fox, 1995) learn to locate and identify objects up to a distance of approximately 5 meters.

A transmitter in the center of a spectacle frame radiates ultrasound (high-frequency sound inaudible to the human ear) in front of the wearer. When the ultrasound hits an obstruction such as a wall, a person, or a tree, it is reflected to the aid and received by two microphones below the transmitter. The microphones transform the reflected signals into electrical signals, which are shifted to a much lower range of frequency and converted into audible sounds by two small earphones in the arms of the spectacle frame. The sounds are then directed to each ear by small tubes. These tubes do not interfere with normal hearing and the user learns to integrate the sounds of the Sonicguide with natural sounds to enhance a concept of the environment. The microphones are deflected slightly outward so that sounds produced by objects to either side of the user will be louder in the ear nearer to the object. This process of sound localization occurs in normal hearing and therefore is a natural indication of direction. The pitch of the signal indicates the approximate distance of a reflecting object; it is highest at the maximum range of the aid and gradually reduces as the object comes closer. By interpreting the comparative loudness at each ear of the signal and its pitch and tonal characteristics, the user is able to judge the direction, distance, and surface qualities of reflecting objects.

The electronics of the aid are contained in a control box that is attached by a cable to the spectacle frame. The battery that powers the aid is attached under the control box and the complete unit can be carried in a pocket, at the belt, or on a shoulder strap. The aid's sensors are built into a spectacle frame to encourage the user to develop the same head movements and posture as a sighted person. When the skills of the aid are mastered, safer and more confident travel and a heightened awareness of the environment is assured. In outdoor situations, the device is to be used in conjunction with a long cane or guide dog, unless the area of travel is both familiar and free from hazards at ground level, which the Sonicguide may not detect.

REFERENCE

Hill, M. M., Dodson-Burk, B., Hill, E. W., & Fox, J. (1995). An infant sonicguide intervention program for a child with a visual disability. *Journal of Visual Impairments, 89*(4), 329–336.

MONIQUE BANTERS
*Centre d'Etude et de
Reclassement, Brussels,
Belgium*

BLIND
ELECTRONIC TRAVEL AIDS
VISUAL TRAINING

SOUTH AFRICA, SPECIAL EDUCATION IN

The history of education for pupils with disabilities dates back to the missionaries in South Africa. In 1863, three Dominican Sisters started a school for deaf children in the Cape under the guidance of the Roman Catholic Church (Schoeman, 2002). However, private institutions, individuals, and churches provided certain services in order to facilitate the education of pupils with disabilities (Cohen, 1935; Miles, 2001). In 1928, the South African government assumed responsibility for special education. The schools were supported by services (e.g., speech therapy) as depicted in the historical reviews by Marais (1973), Chubb (1932), Dunstan (1932), and Moll (1921). The historical review of speech therapy provides a case history of treatment and education of pupils with speech disabilities in 1927. In 1936, a speech clinic was opened at the University of Witwatersrand (Marais, 1973; Penn, 1978; and Salomon, 1942).

By 1948, with the introduction of apartheid, education was provided along racial lines. The result was an education system that was fragmented across 15 departments and unequal, with different special education budgets. In 1994, a single national department of education was established. The democratization process has been guided by a bill of rights and the constitution, which have laid the framework for a South African society based on human rights.

The constitution of South Africa (Act 108 of 1996) states in section 29(1) "that everyone has a right to a basic education including adult basic education." Section 9(3) stresses that the state may not unfairly discriminate directly or indirectly against anyone on one or more grounds, including race, gender, sex, disability, and age. The educational reform has been characterized by policy documents and legislation. The White Paper on Education and Training (Department of Education, 1995), the White Paper on an Integrated National Disability Strategy (Ministry in the Office of the Deputy President, 1997), and the South African Schools Act of 1996 stress the goals of educational reform for all South African citizens. The new goal of educational equity is aimed at redressing past inequalities, improving the quality and efficiency of education in South Africa, and practically realizing the right of all learners to equal access to educational opportunities. The National Education Policy Act 27 of 1997 states in section 4(d) that the Department of Education must endeavor to ensure that no person is denied the opportunity to receive an education to the maximum of his or her ability as a result of a physical disability. Two national commissions of inquiry reports in 1997 (Special Needs in Education and Training and Education Support Services) were used as a basis for a discussion document (Department of Education, 1999). This culminated in the White Paper on Special Needs Education published in 2001 (Department of Education, 2001).

The term *education for learners with special needs* refers to educational support services in public specialized, private specialized, and ordinary public schools in which pupils/learners experience severe learning difficulties and usually are placed in special or remedial classes. The majority of educational support services was earmarked for individual learners and includes support for learning difficulties and those pupils/learners regarded as being at risk due to medical, social, or emotional problems.

In the past, learners with special needs often were labeled in accord with a medical (deficiency-centered) model. Only 20 percent of children with disabilities were accommodated in specialized education (McClain, 2002). Many learners in mainstream schools have not been given any assistance.

Since 2001 there has been a philosophical shift from excluding learners from the mainstream because of a disability to an inclusive approach to assist all learners. This occurs within a systematic and developmental educational framework (Department of Education, 2001). Special needs include physical, mental, sensory, neurological, or developmental impairments; cognitive differences; and psychological disturbances. Inclusion respects differences and supports all learners to overcome personal and system-wide barriers, unlike a medical deficit model (Engelbrecht, 2004). The inclusive model attempts to change prior practices by creating space and possibilities for all learners.

The inclusive approach envisages that a learner's strengths are to be identified, utilized, and assisted in school-based support teams. The approach to inclusive education is through an organized, systematic, and manageable plan that initially focuses on 30 districts that offer service schools, support teams, and special schools or resource centers (Pandor, 2004).

In 2004, special education was assigned a budget of 1.6 billion rand. The immediate deficiencies in special education are being addressed, and access is being expanded to include the compulsory school age of 7 through 15 (Pandor, 2005).

Pandor (2004) emphasizes the need for early identification of learners (ages 0 through 9) who require personal and specialized support. Field tests adapted on curriculum, human, physical, and material resource development are being used to test strengths and limitations and decide on change and modifications of special schools. The 20-year time frame of the inclusive approach (Department of Education, 2001) is structured so that all barriers to learning will be removed, thereby accommodating special needs within an inclusive education system. Special schools for students with specific handicaps (e.g., students who are blind or deaf) would continue to cooperate with and assist mainstream schools. The inclusive approach encompasses a range of institutions including resource centers, special schools, public adult learning centers, and further and higher education institutions. Primary priorities of this approach include quality assurance, curricula improvements, and specialized training of teachers (Ashmal, 2001; Pandor, 2004).

Psychologists, medical practitioners, speech therapists,

and other support personnel are needed to play a vital role in making the inclusive approach a reality. At present the ratio of professionals in support services to students is 1:88, and the number of special schools is 380. Plans call for 500 of the 20,000 primary schools to be converted into schools serving learners with disabilities. During the last few years, the provision of special needs in education has grown significantly, including support services to at least 20 schools for the blind, 47 for the deaf, 54 for the physically disabled and cerebral palsied, 2 for the autistic, and a number for intellectually disabled (Schoeman, 2002).

REFERENCES

Ashmal, K. (2001). *Address by the minister of education, Professor Kader Ashmal, MP, at the official launch of the South African-Finnish Co-operation—Programme in Education sector.* Retrieved August 19, 2005, from http://www.info.gov.za/speeches/2001/0105141245p1006.htm

Chubb, E. M. (1932). Some statistics on mental deficiency. *South African Medical Journal, 6,* 649–652.

Cohen, M. J. (1935). The first South African institution for epileptics. *South African Medical Journal, 9,* 299–300.

Department of Education. (1995, March). *White Paper on Education and Training.* Pretoria, South Africa: Author.

Department of Education. (1996, November 6). *South African Schools Act.* Pretoria, South Africa: Author.

Department of Education. (1997). *Report of the National Commission on Special Needs in Education and Training (NCSNET) and the National Commission on Education Support Services (NCESS).* Pretoria, South Africa: Author.

Department of Education. (1999, August). *Consultative Paper No. 1 on Special Education: Building an Inclusive Education and Training System.* Pretoria, South Africa: Author.

Department of Education. (2001). *Education White Paper 6: Special needs education—Building an inclusive education and training system.* Pretoria, South Africa: Author.

Dominican Sisters. (1944). Schools for the deaf in South Africa. *Volta Review, 46,* 148–150.

Dunstan, J. T. (1932). The sterilization of the unfit. *South African Medical Journal, 6,* 112–117.

Engelbrecht, P. (2004). Changing roles for educational psychologists within inclusive education in South Africa. *School Psychology International, 25* (1).

Marais, M. J. (1973). An historical review of speech therapy services in the Transvaal, 1917–1973. *Education Bulletin, 17,* 77–86.

McClain, C. V. (2002). *Governance and legislation in South Africa: A contemporary overview.* Retrieved August 23, 2005, from http://www.disabilityworld.org/01-03_02/gov/southafrica.shtml

Miles, M. (2001). *History of educational and social responses to disability in anglophone eastern and southern Africa: Introduction and bibliography.* Retrieved August 19, 2005, from http://www.socsci.kun.nl/ped/whp/histeduc/mmiles/aesabib.html

Ministry in the Office of the Deputy President. (1997, November). The White Paper on an Integrated National Disability Strategy. Pretoria, South Africa: Office of the Deputy President.

Moll, J. M. (1921). *Report on the mentally-defective children in government schools, 1919–20.*

Pandor, N. (2004, August 12). *Address by the minister of education.* Retrieved August 16, 2005, from http://education.pwv.gov.za/mainMedia.asp?src=mvie&xsrc=667

Pandor, N. (2005, February 28). *Address by the minister of education.* Retrieved August 23, 2005, from http://education.pwv.gov.za/mainmedia.asp?src=mvie@xsrc=818

Penn, C. (1978). Speech pathology and audiology in South Africa: Past, present and future prospectives. In L. W. Lanham & K. P. Prinsloo (Eds.), *Language and communication studies in South Africa* (pp. 233–259).

Salomon, E. (1942). Speech disorders and their treatment. *South African Medical Journal, 16,* 215–218.

Schoeman, H. (2002). *South Africa: Moving from a centralized and segregated education system to a decentralized and inclusive education approach.* Retrieved August 19, 2005, from http://www.icevi.org/publications/ICEVI-WC2002/papers/01-topic/01-schoeman.htm

UNESCO. (1994). *The Salamanca World Conference on Special Needs Education: Access and quality.* UNESCO and the Ministry of Education, Spain. Paris: Author.

JENNIFER DAWN PRETORIUS
Vaal University of Technology

SOUTH AMERICA

See ARGENTINA, SPECIAL EDUCATION IN; MEXICO, SPECIAL EDUCATION IN; PERU, SPECIAL EDUCATION IN.

SOVIET EDUCATION

Soviet Education is a journal of English-language translations that started publication in 1959. It made Soviet education literature available through English-language translations for the first time. The founding editors of *Soviet Education* were Myron Sharpe, Murray Yanowitch, and Fred Ablin.

A topical journal, *Soviet Education* draws material from Russian-language books and works in teacher training texts, educational psychology, sociology, comparative education, and educational administration. The journal tends to focus on educational policy issues. It is published monthly.

ROBERTA C. STOKES
CECIL R. REYNOLDS
Texas A&M University

SPACHE DIAGNOSTIC READING SCALE

See DIAGNOSTIC READING SCALE.

SPAN OF APPREHENSION

See PERCEPTUAL SPAN.

SPASTICITY

Spasticity is a type of cerebral palsy involving a lack of muscle control. Spastic children make up the largest group of the cerebral palsied, constituting 40 to 60 percent of the total.

Another term that has been used to refer to spastic cerebral palsy is *pyramidal*. This term was coined because the nerves involved are shaped like pyramids. Spastic cerebral palsy is produced by damage sustained to the nerve cell that is found in the motor cortex. The motor cortex is the gray matter of the brain containing nerve cells that initiate motor impulses to the muscles. The nerve cells have tracts that extend from the neuron in the cortex to the spinal cord. These cells eventually connect with nerve tracts that innervate the limb so that muscle movement can be carried out. If these nerve cells or tracts are injured, spasticity results.

Because spasticity can affect one or all four extremities, it is subdivided into several types. Monoplegia involves one extremity only either an arm or leg. This type is extremely rare. Triplegia involves the impairment of three extremities; it is an unusual occurrence. Hemiplegia means that the abnormality is confined to half of the body, either the right or left side with the arm more involved than the leg. This is the most common locus of involvement. Bilateral hemiplegia or double hemiplegia involves weakness or paralysis of both sides of the body with the arms compromised more than the legs. Another type, quadriplegia, occurs in all four extremities with more disability of the legs than the arms. Diplegia means that all four limbs are affected, with minimal involvement of the arms. Paraplegia is neurologic dysfunction of the legs only. Spastic hemiplegias are the most common group, representing approximately 40 percent of the total cerebral palsied population, while spastic quadriplegias represent 19 percent of the total (Capute, 1978).

In mild cases, the spastic child has an awkward gait and may extend his or her arms for balance (Kerrigan & Annaswamy, 1997). In moderate cases, the child may bend the arms at the elbow and hold both arms close to the body with the hands bent toward the body. The legs may be rotated inwardly and flexed at the knees; this causes a "scissoring gait." In severe cases, the child may have poor body control and be unable to sit, stand, and walk without the support of braces, crutches, a walking frame, or other support (Kirk & Gallagher, 1979).

REFERENCES

Capute, A. (1978). Cerebral palsy and associated dysfunctions. In R. Haslam & P. Valletutti (Eds.), *Problems in the classroom* (pp. 149–163). Baltimore: University Park Press.

Kerrigan, D. C., & Annaswammy, T. M. (1997). The functional significance of spasticity as assessed by gait analysis. *Journal of Head Trauma Rehabilitation, 12*(6), 29–39.

Kirk, S., & Gallagher, J. (1979). *Educating exceptional children* (3rd ed.). Boston: Houghton Mifflin.

CECELIA STEPPE-JONES
*North Carolina Central
University*

CEREBRAL PALSY
PHYSICAL DISABILITIES

SPEARMAN, C. E. (1863–1945)

C. E. Spearman grew up in an English family of established status and some eminence; he became an officer in the regular army. He remained in the army until the age of 40, attaining the rank of major. He then obtained his PhD in Wundt's laboratory at Leipzig in 1908 at the age of 45. He was appointed to an academic position at University College, London, where he remained for the rest of his career.

Spearman is known for his theory of general intelligence and for a number of contributions to statistical methodology, including factor analysis, the Spearman rank correlation, and the Spearman-Brown prophecy formula. Spearman's primary interest was in the study of general intelligence, which he preferred to call g. His methodological innovations were directed toward the better definition and measurement of g.

Spearman conceived of intelligence as a general capability involved in the performance of almost all mental tasks, although he saw some tasks as more dependent on g than others. Thus the variance of any mental test may be divided into two parts: a part associated with individual differences in g and a part specific to the test in question. Since the correlation coefficient indicates the proportion of shared variation of two variables, Spearman was able to develop methods of analyzing a matrix of correlations among tests to determine the presence of a general factor and to calculate the g loading for a test, its correlation with the underlying general factor. The conception of intelligence as g provided an objective method of defining intelligence and of evaluating the adequacy of any proposed measure of intelligence.

Spearman's original two-factor theory (Spearman, 1904) included only g and a factor specific to each task. Subsequently, he expanded the theory to include group factors, which are factors common to a group of tasks independent of g. However, his major emphasis was always on g (Spearman, 1927). Subsequent development and mathematical refinement of factor analysis by Thurstone and others emphasized the group factors; g became obscured in the correlation among the primary factors. Today g is recognized as a second-order factor accounting for the correlations among the primaries. There is still disagreement concerning its importance.

REFERENCES

Spearman, C. E. (1904). "General intelligence" objectively determined and measured. *American Journal of Psychology, 15,* 201–293.

Spearman, C. E. (1927). *The abilities of man: Their nature and measurement.* London: Macmillan.

ROBERT C. NICHOLS
DIANE J. JARVIS
State University of New York at Buffalo

g FACTOR THEORY
INTELLIGENCE
REACTION TIME

SPEARMAN'S HYPOTHESIS

Charles E. Spearman (1863–1945), an early proponent of the use of factor analytic methods to examine the construct of intelligence, proposed a two-factor theory of intelligence, stating that a general factor (*g*) and one or more specific factors (*s*) account for performance on intelligence tests (Spearman, 1927). The *g* factor, an index of general intelligence, is involved in deductive operations. Tests with high *g* loadings involve complex mental operations, such as those needed for reasoning, comprehension, and hypothesis testing (Sattler, 2001). Tests with low *g* loadings require less complex thought processes and emphasize recognition, recall, speed, and visual-motor abilities.

In *The Abilities of Man* (1927), Spearman observed that the average standard score difference between samples of blacks and whites in the United States differed from one test to another, and the size of the difference is related to the size of the *g* loading of the tests. Jensen deemed this "Spearman's hypothesis." Formally stated, it posits that "the relative magnitudes of the standardized mean black-white differences on a wide variety of cognitive tests are related predominantly to the relative magnitudes of the tests' *g* loadings—the higher the test's *g* loading, the larger the mean black-white difference" (Jensen, 1992).

Jensen (1985) tested Spearman's hypothesis in 11 large-scale studies, each of which included tests of mental abilities that were administered to blacks and whites. The *g* factor correlated with measures of speed of information processing. In agreement with Spearman's hypothesis, the average differences between blacks and whites on mental tests could be interpreted as a difference in *g* rather than a difference in knowledge, skill, or type of test. Results suggested that black-white differences in the rate of information processing may account for some of the average difference between them on intelligence tests. An investigation of Spearman's hypothesis using test scores of blacks, whites, and Indians in

South Africa found strong support for black-white differences but not for Indian-white differences (Lynn & Owen, 2001).

In industrialized nations the statistical importance of Spearman's *g* is declining as individuals' IQs increase (Kane & Oakland, 2000). As IQs increase, variance from the average score decreases. This reflects Spearman's "law of diminishing returns," which states that *g* accounts for less variance in high-IQ groups than in low-IQ groups. High-IQ groups may have more specialized abilities and excel in certain areas over others. Meanwhile, low-IQ groups continue to reflect people with general intelligence, who may excel in areas not covered by current intelligence tests.

REFERENCES

Jensen, A. R. (1985). The nature of the black-white differences on various psychometric tests: Spearman's hypothesis. *Behavioral & Brain Sciences, 8,* 193–263.

Jensen, A. R. (1992). Spearman's hypothesis: Methodology and evidence. *Multivariate Behavioral Research, 27,* 225–233.

Lynn, R., & Owen, K. (2001). Spearman's hypothesis and test score differences between whites, Indians, and blacks in South Africa. *Journal of General Psychology, 121,* 27–36.

Sattler, J. M. (2001). *Assessment of children: Cognitive applications* (4th ed.). San Diego, CA: Jerome M. Sattler.

Spearman, C. (1927). *The abilities of man.* London: Macmillan.

JEFFREY DITTERLINE
University of Florida

INTELLIGENCE
g FACTOR THEORY

SPECIAL CLASS

The first special classes were established in the late 1800s and early 1900s as public school classes for the moderately retarded, deaf, hard of hearing, blind, emotionally disturbed, and physically disabled. Esten (1900) stated that special classes for mentally retarded were established to provide slow-learning children with more appropriate class placement.

A special classroom for the exceptional can be defined as one that homogeneously segregates different children from normal children. Children are usually segregated along categorical groupings. As a result of Dunn's (1968) article on the detrimental aspects of special class placements for the mildly handicapped, students receiving special education in self-contained special classes today are usually those with more severe problems. However, Kirk and Gallagher (1983) report that gifted exceptional students are also grouped into special classes according to interests and abilities. As low-incidence students demonstrate proficiency in specific skill areas, they are mainstreamed into regular classes.

Other types of service delivery for special education

students (e.g., resource rooms) do not fall under the label "special class." Resource rooms usually provide service for high-incidence populations. Special classes, on the other hand, usually service low-incidence populations. In addition, there are four different types of resource rooms: categorical, serving one population; noncategorical, serving more than one population; itinerant; and teacher-consultant. There is usually only one type of special class, self-contained.

REFERENCES

Dunn, L. M. (1968). Special education for the mildly handicapped: Is much of it justifiable? *Exceptional Children, 35,* 5–22.

Esten, R. A. (1900). Backward children in the public schools. *Journal of Psychoasthenics, 5,* 10–16.

MARIBETH MONTGOMERY KASIK
Governors State University

CASCADE MODEL OF SPECIAL EDUCATION SERVICES
INCLUSION
RESOURCE ROOM
SELF-CONTAINED CLASS
SERVICE DELIVERY MODELS

SPECIAL EDUCATION, EFFECTIVENESS OF

See EFFECTIVENESS OF SPECIAL EDUCATION.

SPECIAL EDUCATION, FEDERAL IMPACT ON

The impact of the federal government on special education occurs through two independent, but overlapping, functions: (1) the administration and development of programs, and (2) the compliance monitoring of state education agencies. The administration and development of programs involves the disbursement of discretionary grants and contracts as well as the disbursement of formula grant funds under Part B of the Individuals with Disabilities Education Act (IDEA) and under Part H of the Preschool Grant Program. Discretionary grants are awarded to individuals and organizations in states and territories on a competitive basis. Depending on the specific program for which awards are made, these funds are to be used for research, program/materials development, technical assistance, demonstration, or training. For the most part, these projects do not directly serve handicapped children and youths but rather are intended to support existing programs, demonstrate new or more effective ways of delivering services, train special education and related services personnel, or increase our knowledge of current or promising components of special education (i.e., research efforts). Table 1 is a list of state grant awards under IDEA Part B, Part H; and preschool grant programs.

Table 1 State grant awards under IDEA, Part B, preschool grant program and Part H

Appropriation year 1996
Allocation year 1996–1997

State	IDEA Part B	Preschool grant program	Part H
Alabama	40,895,889	5,640,150	4,483,470
Alaska	7,445,561	1,322,423	1,545,710
Arizona	30,926,630	5,149,246	5,306,409
Arkansas	21,767,818	4,947,109	2,549,297
California	228,622,421	36,022,407	41,438,233
Colorado	28,189,964	4,694,437	3,972,753
Connecticut	31,009,767	5,254,252	3,378,163
Delaware	6,415,559	1,273,857	1,545,710
District of Columbia	3,133,152	253,984	1,545,710
Florida	125,183,617	17,772,314	14,722,619
Georgia	54,500,058	8,737,835	8,226,009
Hawaii	6,468,961	857,114	1,569,551
Idaho	9,586,202	2,011,527	1,545,710
Illinois	103,277,776	16,385,574	13,785,909
Indiana	54,064,193	8,046,763	6,065,530
Iowa	26,735,870	3,830,760	2,712,211
Kansas	21,632,619	4,026,335	2,716,195
Kentucky	33,452,225	9,636,295	3,876,538
Louisiana	36,749,462	6,292,502	5,023,051
Maine	12,862,856	2,331,796	1,545,710
Maryland	40,707,760	6,228,185	6,148,806
Massachusetts	64,529,602	9,346,216	8,621,533
Michigan	76,182,721	11,971,373	10,071,913
Minnesota	39,676,213	7,075,455	4,873,116
Mississippi	26,960,663	4,336,103	3,120,649
Missouri	48,997,264	5,509,548	5,422,619
Montana	7,447,163	1,189,852	1,545,710
Nebraska	15,863,867	2,173,630	1,689,626
Nevada	11,381,723	2,077,812	1,783,636
New Hampshire	10,206,502	1,424,148	1,545,710
New Jersey	79,530,001	10,919,997	8,497,315
New Mexico	19,201,461	2,994,648	2,045,597
New York	159,349,369	31,853,656	20,119,188
North Carolina	59,357,530	10,940,998	7,582,020
North Dakota	5,044,365	767,202	1,545,710
Ohio	91,825,830	11,947,090	11,402,583
Oklahoma	29,633,498	3,486,209	3,381,056
Oregon	26,241,486	4,001,396	3,086,097
Pennsylvania	86,078,620	13,510,371	12,702,122
Puerto Rico	18,127,953	2,326,545	4,549,818
Rhode Island	10,118,522	1,531,123	1,568,805
South Carolina	34,921,251	6,775,530	3,852,059
South Dakota	6,432,855	1,428,085	1,545,710
Tennessee	51,036,950	6,661,992	5,414,050
Texas	178,197,295	21,173,206	23,718,333
Utah	21,172,943	3,190,222	2,768,788
Vermont	4,539,452	797,391	1,545,710
Virginia	57,509,947	8,676,144	6,930,714
Washington	43,138,514	8,246,275	5,664,434
West Virginia	18,358,789	3,177,753	1,798,698
Wisconsin	42,946,007	8,889,438	5,553,755
Wyoming	5,064,508	1,021,186	1,545,710
American Samoa	2,546,094	34,783	514,925
Guam	6,151,324	122,726	1,140,327
Northern Marianas	1,570,112	23,626	342,733
Palau	552,502	5,120	78,014
Virgin Islands	4,663,611	87,286	671,647
Bur. of Indian Affairs	28,408,765		3,864,276
U.S. and outlying areas	2,316,593,632	360,409,000	315,754,000
50 states, D.C., and P.R.	2,272,701,224	360,135,459	309,142,078

State grants awards are initial allocations for the 1996 appropriation. October 1, 1996.

Table 2 IDEA, Part B state grant program: Funds appropriated, 1977–1996

Appropriation year	IDEA, Part B state grants[a]	Per-child allocation[b]
1977	$ 251,770,000	$ 71
1978	566,030,000	156
1979	804,000,000	215
1980	874,190,000	227
1981	874,500,000	219
1982	931,008,000	230
1983	1,017,900,000	248
1984	1,068,875,000	258
1985	1,135,145,000	272
1986	1,163,282,000	279
1987	1,338,000,000	316
1988	1,431,737,000	332
1989	1,475,449,000	336
1990	1,542,610,000	343
1991	1,854,186,000	400
1992	1,976,095,000	410
1993	2,052,730,000	411
1994	2,149,686,000	413
1995	2,322,915,000[c]	418
1996	2,323,837,000	413[d]

Source: U.S. Department of Education, Office of Special Education Programs, Data Analysis System (DANS).

[a]The figures from 1977 through 1994 include amounts appropriated to the Federated States of Micronesia and the Republic of the Marshall Islands. In 1995, those entities received no appropriations.

[b]The per-child allocation excludes children and funds for the Outlying Areas and Bureau of Indian Affairs (BIA) and is based on the child count information available as of July 1 of the fiscal year.

[c]This amount includes $82,878,000 added to the Grants to States appropriation because of the elimination of the Chapter 1 Handicapped Program.

[d]This allocation was derived by dividing the total appropriations for the 50 States, District of Columbia, Outlying Areas, and BIA by the total number of children served in all of those areas.

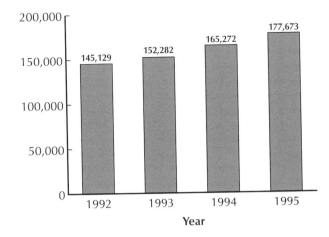

Figure 1 Number of infants and toddlers with disabilities served under IDEA, Part H.

Source: U.S. Department of Education, Office of Special Education Programs, Data Analysis System (DANS).

In addition to discretionary grant awards and contracts, states also receive annual funds based on the total number of handicapped children and youths receiving special education and related services. The history of funding for the Part B entitlement program under IDEA, state grant program from 1977 to 1996, is shown in Table 2.

Each state education agency (SEA) must distribute at least 75 percent of the total funds to local education agencies to be used directly for the education of disabled students. The remaining funds may be used by the SEA, with some portion going toward administrative costs. Thus, federal funds are used to offset some of the additional costs associated with educating students with disabilities.

Until 1994, children and youths with disabilities were also served under the Chapter 1 Handicapped Program. In October 1994, the Improving America's School Act (IASA) was enacted, which reauthorized the Elementary and Secondary Education Act of 1965 (ESEA). However, the Chapter 1 Handicapped Program was not reauthorized. Beginning

with the fiscal year (FY) 1995 appropriation, all children with disabilities were served under programs authorized by IDEA. The IASA included a number of amendments to IDEA to provide for a smooth transition to serving all children (U.S. Department of Education, 1997).

Part H of the Individuals with Disabilities Education Act (IDEA) was adopted by Congress in 1986. Part H was designed to address the needs of infants and toddlers with disabilities and their families through a "statewide system of coordinated, comprehensive, multidisciplinary, interagency programs providing appropriate early intervention services to all infants and toddlers with disabilities and their families" (20 U.S.C. §1476 (a)). Figure 1 shows the number of infants and toddlers with disabilities served under Part H from 1992 to 1995.

The increase in the number of infants and toddlers served under Part H since 1992 (22.4 percent) has been greater than the growth in the number of children served under Part B. The growth rate is, however, comparable to the number of 3- to 5-year-olds served under Part B (U.S. Department of Education, 1997).

Thus, one of the primary ways special education is impacted by the federal government is through a direct infusion of funds that assist state and local educational agencies in offering special education and related services, or through efforts that further state and local programs (discretionary grants and contracts).

The second major area in which the federal government impacts special education is through compliance monitoring. To accomplish this objective, special education programs engage in program administrative reviews that involve on-site and off-site reviews of information. Where deficiencies are found, corrective actions are requested from the SEA. The corrective actions report includes a description of the steps to be taken by the SEA, timelines for completion, and the documentation to be submitted verifying that deficiencies have been corrected. Should substantial noncompliance be noted, the U.S. Department of Education is authorized to withhold federal funds. Considerable leeway exists within the department's administration of its compliance monitoring efforts to ensure that each state receives funding. Nevertheless, the possibility that a state may not receive federal funds can be persuasive in altering special education programs in that state.

Audette and Algozzine (1997) have suggested that the dearth of legislation monitoring and regulations from the federal level have increased bureaucratic paperwork and procedures to the point of being a major hindrance, asserting that special education is "costly rather than free" (Audette & Algozzine, 1997).

REFERENCES

Audette, B., & Algozzine, B. (1997). Re-inventing government? Let's re-invent special education. *Journal of Learning Disabilities, 30*(4), 378–383.

U.S. Department of Education. (1997). *Nineteenth annual report to Congress on the implementation of the Individuals with Disabilities Education Act.* Washington, DC: Author.

MARTY ABRAMSON
University of Wisconsin at Stout

DEMOGRAPHY OF SPECIAL EDUCATION
POLITICS AND SPECIAL EDUCATION
SPECIAL EDUCATION PROGRAMS

SPECIAL EDUCATION, GENERIC

See GENERIC SPECIAL EDUCATION.

SPECIAL EDUCATION, HISTORY OF

See HISTORY OF SPECIAL EDUCATION.

SPECIAL EDUCATION, HUMANISTIC

See HUMANISTIC SPECIAL EDUCATION.

SPECIAL EDUCATION, PHILOSOPHERS' OPINIONS ABOUT

See PHILOSOPHY OF EDUCATION FOR INDIVIDUALS WITH DISABILITIES.

SPECIAL EDUCATION, PROFESSIONAL STANDARDS FOR

See PROFESSIONAL STANDARDS FOR SPECIAL EDUCATORS.

SPECIAL EDUCATION, RACIAL DISCRIMINATION IN

See RACIAL DISCRIMINATION IN SPECIAL EDUCATION.

SPECIAL EDUCATION, SUPERVISION IN

See SUPERVISION IN SPECIAL EDUCATION.

SPECIAL EDUCATION, TEACHER TRAINING IN

The training and practice of special educators have undergone rapid development and change over the past four decades. In recognition of the small number of individuals who were prepared to conduct research and train teachers to educate the retarded, PL 85-926 was passed in 1958. With the passage of this law, funds were allocated to establish doctoral-level university training programs in the area of mental retardation. These training programs, along with a robust postwar economy, resulted in a decade characterized by a proliferation of programs for exceptional children (Tawney & Gest, 1984). The need for trained individuals to run public and private school programs preceded a clear understanding of what and how to teach children with various handicapping conditions. The first special education curricula were watered-down or slowed-down adaptations of regular class programs; they underscored the absence of empirical data in the field. Training, for the most part, focused on how to control children's behavior. The hope was that a child controlled was a child ready to learn.

The 1970s saw a continuance of the optimism of the 1960s and a period of advocacy and activism. Public Law 94-142, a civil rights bill for the disabled, guaranteed a "free and appropriate" education for exceptional children. At the same time, it called on special educators to document, as precisely as possible, children's progress. For the first time in public education, teachers were called on to be accountable. Practically, concerns for accountability meant that the field moved to replace the generalized curricula of the 1960s with more individualized curricula focused on matching instructional strategies to individual learner characteristics. Tawney and Gest (1984) pointed out that "the cumulative effect of the developmental efforts of the 1970s, then, was to set the stage for a new era of intensive programming for handicapped students in the 1980s" (p. 5). Problems with a worsening economy in the late 1970s, however, shifted attention from the problems of the handicapped to more personal priorities.

The reality of the 1990s was essentially economic in character. Given the increase in the number of children being served and the fact that federal, state, and local budgets did not have unlimited resources, the 1990s became a period of retrenchment and uncertainty in special education. There was a clear and pressing need to increase the number of teachers qualified to work with children with disabilities, but at the same time newly trained teachers were being asked to do more with less. Teachers in special education were being called on to be more resourceful, more organized, and more precise in creating, planning, and executing instructional interventions and more directly involved in general or regular education.

In addition to these broad political and economic factors, the quantity and quality of research in human learning and development and pedagogy have had an impact on the preparation of teachers for pupils with disabilities. Out of the massive research and development efforts with disabled and nondisabled children that began in the 1960s, special educators have acquired a substantial base of knowledge concerning effective instructional practices. With this large and growing body of information and the complex roles that special education teachers are currently being asked to assume, effective training of special educators will require greater breadth and depth of preparation than ever before.

While there is a lack of agreement concerning specific knowledge and skills that teachers of individuals with disabilities should possess, there is a growing consensus among regular and special educators concerning the general characteristics of a professional teacher and the framework for teacher preparation programs. The general parameters include the following. First, teachers need a firm foundation in general literacy and in the basic disciplines of the humanities, liberal arts, and sciences as prerequisite to entering the teaching profession (Denemark & Nutter, 1980). Second, special education teachers must be well versed in general education requirements as well as those specific to special education; that is, they must be education generalists as well as education of the disabled specialists (Reynolds, 1979). Their training should include acquiring knowledge of school development; basic academic skill curricula; instructional methods, including the effective use of computer-assisted instruction; and instructional and behavioral management strategies. In return, the inclusion movement has mandated that general educators have the same training in special education. General education teacher license requirements in 22 states include a requirement that teachers have some coursework related to students with disabilities. Eleven states require some practical work with students as well as coursework (U.S. Department of Education, 1997).

Third, as a key to participation in inclusion efforts, special education teachers must function as team members and as consultants, providing interaction with the general education faculty on questions concerning handicapped pupils. Fourth, regardless of the nature and severity of a pupil's disability, all special education teachers must possess effective communication skills to work with parents of children with disabilities. These include a working knowledge of the motivational, cognitive, and social consequences associated with their pupils' handicapping conditions. Special educators should also be able to assess pupils' current levels of functioning, select and implement instructional strategies based on youngsters' learning characteristics, and evaluate the effectiveness of their instructional procedures.

Lastly, teacher training programs should provide extensive practical experience for their students. This practical experience should be initiated early in the students' training, with greater amounts of professional practice provided as students progress through the program (Scannell & Guenther, 1981). As researchers have recognized that the first year of teaching is critical for the maintenance and development of effective teaching skills, a year-long paid and supervised internship has been recommended as the culminating training experience of a preservice program. For student-teachers to gain the most from these practica, they should be closely monitored and effective models of teaching should be provided. Training that includes the previously noted components cannot be provided in an undergraduate teacher preparation program. The American Association of Colleges of Teacher Education Commission of Education for the Profession argues that the presently constituted teaching profession is, at best, a semiprofession (Howsam, Corrigan, Denemark, & Nash, 1976). The commission recommended a 5-year initial teacher preparation program combining the bachelor's and master's degrees, plus a 6th year of supervised internship to improve the quality of teacher education. Such an effort would enhance the profession of teaching and lead to outstanding pupil achievement. In view of these collective recommendations, it appears that preparation of special education teachers will require the extension of teacher education into graduate training.

Unfortunately, due to declining enrollments in teacher preparation programs and reductions in university budgets, few university faculties have decided to make their programs more rigorous by incorporating the recommendations of leaders in the area of teacher education and special education.

Attrition of special education teachers has been a major concern nationally. Moreover, lack of quality in preservice training has been related to teacher attrition rates. With the extensive and culturally competent (Miller, Miller, & Schroth, 1997) coursework, practica, and internship training required in new programs, graduates will be better prepared to meet the challenges and demands of special education instruction. As a consequence, they may continue to teach youngsters with disabilities for a longer period of time and in a more effective manner.

REFERENCES

Denemark, G., & Nutter, N. (1980). *The case for extended programs of initial teacher preparation.* Washington, DC: ERIC Clearinghouse on Teacher Education.

Howsam, R. B., Corrigan, D. C., Denemark, G. W., & Nash, R. J. (1976). *Education as a profession: Report of the Bicentennial Commission on Education for the Profession of Teaching of the American Association of Colleges for Teacher Education.* Washington, DC: American Association of Colleges for Teacher Education.

Keogh, B. K. (1985). *Learning disabilities: Diversity in search of order.* Paper prepared for the Pittsburgh Research Integration Project, University of Pittsburgh.

Miller, S., Miller, K. L., & Schroth, G. (1997). Teacher perceptions of multicultural training in preservice programs. *Journal of Instructional Psychology, 24*(4), 222–232.

Palmer, D. J., Anderson, C., Hall, R., Keuker, J., & Parrish, L. (1985). *Preparation of special educators: Extended generic special education training program* (Report to the U.S. Department of Education, Special Education Programs, Division of Personnel Preparation).

Reynolds, M. (1979). *A common body of practices for teachers: The challenge of Public Law 94-142 to teacher education.* Minneapolis, MN: The National Support System Project.

Scannell, D., & Guenther, J. E. (1981). The development of an extended program. *Journal of Teacher Education, 32,* 7–12.

Tawney, J. W., & Gest, D. L. (1984). *Single subject research in special education.* Columbus, OH: Merrill.

U.S. Department of Education. (1997). *Nineteenth annual report to Congress on the implementation of the Individuals with Disabilities Act* (IDEA). Washington, DC: Author.

DOUGLAS J. PALMER
ROBERT HALL
Texas A&M University

HUMAN RESOURCE DEVELOPMENT
TEACHER BURNOUT
TEACHER EFFECTIVENESS

SPECIAL EDUCATION, TELECOMMUNICATION SYSTEMS IN

See TELECOMMUNICATION SYSTEMS IN SPECIAL EDUCATION.

SPECIAL EDUCATION INSTRUCTIONAL MATERIALS CENTERS

More than a decade before the passage of the Education for All Handicapped Children Act, the U.S. Office of Education recognized that one of the main obstacles to education of quality for students with disabilities was the dearth of appropriate instructional materials and services both for the students and for those responsible for their education (Alonso, 1974). The federal government hoped to have established a network of service centers to address this problem by 1980.

The initiation of this effort began in 1963, when two projects were funded—one at the University of Southern California and the other at the University of Wisconsin—to serve as demonstration models for the development and dissemination of effective instructional materials and methods. From this modest beginning were to come 13 regional special education instructional materials centers (SEIMCs); four regional media centers for the deaf and hearing impaired (RMCs); a Clearinghouse on Handicapped and Gifted Children in the Educational Resources Information Center (ERIC) Network; an Instructional Materials Reference Center at the American Printing House for the Blind; and a National Center on Education Media and Materials for the Handicapped (NCEMMH).

The role of SEIMCs, some of which in various funding periods were also called regional resource centers (RRCs) and area learning resource centers (ALRCs), would change somewhat over the decade of their existence. During the experimental phase, which ran from 1964 to 1966, the two centers were expected to develop appropriate materials and methods for children with disabilities, transform them into workable curricula, and disseminate the results, along with other information, to the field. The early centers were also charged with the exploration of new technologies for instructional purposes as well as for information dissemination (Langstaff & Volkmor, 1974).

The official scope of the centers was not strictly defined by the government. It was acknowledged that needs varied widely from one service area to another, and each program was encouraged to respond to its local situation appropriately and to take full advantage of the special strengths of its staff. In general, however, the activities tended to break down into three categories. The first involved identifying, collecting, evaluating, circulating, and, when necessary, developing or stimulating the development of instructional materials. The second category consisted of field services of various sorts: the training of teachers in the choice, evaluation, and use of instructional media and materials; coordination activities that established or improved the delivery of services to special educators and their students; and technical assistance to state departments of education to ensure the institutionalization of ongoing support services within each state. Finally, the centers were all involved to some extent in the systematic dissemination of information regarding current research, methods, and materials for special education.

REFERENCES

Alonso, L. (1974). *Final technical report of the Great Lakes region special education instructional materials center.* Washington,

DC: Bureau of Education for the Handicapped. (ERIC Document Reproduction Service No. ED 094 507)

Langstaff, A. L., & Volkmor, C. B. (1974). *Instructional materials center for special education: Final technical report.* Washington, DC: Bureau of Education for the Handicapped. (ERIC Document Reproduction Service No. ED 107 086)

JANET S. BRAND
*Hunter College, City University
of New York*

ONLINE SPECIAL EDUCATION SPECIALNET

SPECIAL EDUCATION PROGRAMS

In 1982 Special Education Programs (SEP) succeeded the Office of Special Education as the primary federal agency responsible for overseeing federal initiatives in the education of individuals with disabilities. Although SEP's mission has basically remained the same since the creation of the Bureau of Education for the Handicapped in 1966, its organizational structure has changed. Special Education Programs is divided into five divisions.

The Division of Assistance to States (DAS) has four areas of responsibility. Its primary function is to monitor the extent to which states are implementing the requirements of PL 94-142 and PL 89-313 state-operated programs. The DAS is also SEP's liaison with the Office for Civil Rights when parent complaints are received. The DAS provides technical assistance to states either directly through its program officers or through a national network of regional resource centers. Finally, DAS oversees the awarding of grants to centers that serve the deaf-blind.

The Division of Innovation and Development (DID) carries out SEP's mission for generating new information to help individuals with disabilities. The DID administers several grant competitions. Field-initiated research allows any investigator to suggest a project and student projects are the most widely known. The DID has the U.S. Department of Education's responsibility for conducting the PL 94-142, Section 618, evaluation of the implementation of programs for individuals with disabilities whose results appear in the *Annual Reports to Congress* (U.S. Department of Education, 1986).

The Division of Personnel Preparation administers grant programs to prepare special educators and related services personnel, parents of children with disabilities, and doctoral-level professionals, among others, to serve the needs of students with disabilities.

The Division of Educational Services is responsible for grant projects that develop model programs in the areas of early childhood education, youth employment, services for the severely disabled, transitional services for students changing their least restrictive environment placement, and captioning of films for the hearing impaired.

The Division of Program Analysis and Planning has responsibility for managing the planning and budgetary processes within SEP. It also coordinates the efforts of other divisions when changes are proposed and made to regulations in the administration of PL 94-142, PL 89-313, and the various grant and contract programs.

The current address of SEP is U.S. Department of Education, Special Education Programs, 400 Maryland Avenue, SW, Washington, DC 20202.

REFERENCE

U.S. Department of Education. (1986). *Eighth annual report to Congress on the implementation of Public Law 94-142: The Education for All Handicapped Children Act.* Washington, DC: Author.

ROLAND K. YOSHIDA
Fordham University

OFFICE OF SPECIAL EDUCATION AND REHABILITATIVE SERVICES

SPECIALNET

SpecialNet, the largest education-oriented computer-based communication network in the United States, is operated by the National Association of State Directors of Special Education. SpecialNet makes it possible for its more than 2,000 subscriber agencies to use the system to send email (messages, forms, reports, questions, and answers) instantaneously to one or many participants. The system also contains electronic bulletin boards, which are topical displays of various information bases, administered by content experts around the country. Nearly 30 such bulletin boards are currently available; they include coverage of personnel development, early childhood education, computers and other technologies, program evaluation, promising practices, federal news, gifted education, parent programs, educational policy, vocational education, and many other topics.

SpecialNet can be accessed on any computer. Access through a local or toll-free 800 number is available nationwide via the GTE Telenet public data network, through which SpecialNet information is transmitted and stored. Access to SpecialNet is obtained through an annual subscription fee. Further charges accrue for online time spent accessing the system. SpecialNet may be contacted at LRP Publications, 747 Dresher Road, Suite 500, Horsham, PA, 19044; 1-800-341-7874, or http://www.lrp.com.

JUDY SMITH-DAVIS
*Counterpoint Communications
Company*

ONLINE SPECIAL EDUCATION
SPECIAL EDUCATION INSTRUCTIONAL MATERIALS
   CENTERS

SPECIAL SERVICES IN THE SCHOOLS

Published by Haworth Press (New York City), *Special Services in the Schools* (SSS) is a quarterly, refereed journal with an applied focus. It is now in its seventh volume. The *SSS* is intended to be read by multidisciplinary professional audiences who provide special services in schools and related educational settings, including school psychologists, guidance counselors, consulting teachers, social workers, and speech and language clinicians. It is the journal's policy to disseminate available information of direct relevance to these professionals. Thus, information published in *SSS* includes reviews of relevant research and literature, descriptions and evaluations of programs, viewpoints on latest trends in policy development, and guidelines for designing, implementing, and evaluating special service programs.

The issues of the journal are organized in a sequence whereby thematic and general issues alternate. Thematic issues have focused on topics such as computers and exceptional children, health promotion strategies, new directions in assessment of special learners, and international perspectives on facilitating cognitive development of children. Articles in general issues have included topics such as evaluation of programs of children of divorce, staff stress and burnout, curricula and programs for pregnant and parenting adolescents, and involving parents in the education of their children with disabilities.

Articles are aimed at being informative and instructive to special educators, psychologists, counselors, nurses, social workers, speech and language clinicians, physical and occupational therapists, and school supervisors and administrators. The material is intended to assist these professionals in performing a wide range of service delivery tasks. These include:

- Assessing individual pupils and groups to determine their special educational needs
- Designing individualized and group programs
- Assisting regular and special classroom teachers in fostering academic achievement and functional living for special students
- Enhancing the social and emotional development of pupils through preventive and remedial approaches
- Helping school administrators to develop smoothly functioning organizational systems
- Fostering the physical well-being of special students
- Involving parents and families in special programs

- Educating and training school staff to more effectively educate special needs students

Manuscripts that focus on the topical areas and service delivery tasks noted are routinely considered for publication. All manuscripts undergo blind review by editorial consultants.

CHARLES A. MAHER
Rutgers University

LOUIS J. KRUGER
Tufts University

SPECIFIC LEARNING DISABILITIES

See LEARNING DISABILITIES.

SPECT (SINGLE PHOTON EMISSION COMPUTED TOMOGRAPHY)

Brain SPECT imaging is a nuclear medicine procedure that directly measures relative cerebral blood flow and indirectly evaluates brain metabolism. It is a procedure similar to positron emission tomography (PET) scan. SPECT and PET scans are both nuclear medicine scans and have been conducted in research and clinical settings for the past 20 years. SPECT and PET technology offers unique opportunities to examine cerebral metabolism and physiology. New binding isotopes are also allowing researchers and clinicians to track specific neurotransmitters in the brain, including chemicals in the dopaminergic, opiate, benzodiazepine, serotonin, and cholinergic systems. SPECT and PET are considered noninvasive procedures. As nuclear medicine studies, they require the injection of a small amount of radioactive material. SPECT is about half the cost of PET, and both methods allow for specific in vitro measures not offered by other techniques. The isotopes find their way into the working brain, providing a picture of specific parts of the brain while it is engaged in specific tasks. The level of radiation for a single SPECT scan is considered safe. A normal SPECT study demonstrates full, even, symmetrical activity in the brain. Ongoing research continues to generate data defining patterns and meanings of abnormal SPECT studies for specific medical and developmental conditions.

The procedure guidelines of the Society of Nuclear Medicine list the evaluation of suspected brain trauma, dementia, presurgical location of seizures, and the detection and evaluation of cerebral vascular disease as common indications for brain SPECT. The guidelines also note that many additional indications for use of this imaging appear promising.

There is not yet consensus on the usefulness of SPECT in clinical practice in the field of psychiatry and special education. However, an increasing number of clinics around the world are using brain SPECT to evaluate individuals with complex neuropsychological illnesses, such as treatment-resistant depression and attention-deficit/hyperactivity disorder (ADHD) with significant comorbidity, violence, and psychosis. The procedure has yet to be used extensively for children with learning disabilities.

The following is a case example on the potential utility of brain SPECT. A 12-year-old child was admitted to the hospital for episodes of explosive rage. He had been treated for 7 years with six different medications, as well as receiving counseling for ADHD and depression, without benefit. A brain SPECT was ordered by his examining physician and was found to demonstrate marked decreased temporal lobe activity, a common finding in temporal lobe epilepsy. The child was placed on an anti-epileptic drug, carbomazepine, and responded well.

REFERENCES

Amen, D. (2001). Why don't psychiatrists look at the brain: The case for the greater use of SPECT imaging in neuropsychiatry. *Neuropsychiatry Reviews, 2*(1), 1, 19–21.

Brain perfusion single photon emission computed tomography (SPECT) using Tc-99m radiopharmaceuticals 2.0. Approved 1999. (2002). In *Society of Nuclear Medicine procedure guidelines manual.* Washington, DC: Society of Nuclear Medicine.

Devous, M. D. (2002). SPECT functional brain imaging. In *Brain mapping: The method* (513–533). San Diego, CA: Academic Press.

Holman, B. L., & Devous, M. D., Sr. (1992). Functional brain SPECT: The emergence of a powerful clinical method. *Journal of Nuclear Medicine, 33,* 1888–1904.

DANIEL G. AMEN
*University of California School
of Medicine*

SPEECH

In the context of special education, the word *speech* may have two different meanings. Sometimes, it is used to refer to the whole of linguistic skills. Such is the case in compounds such as *speech pathologist* and *speech therapy*. In other cases, the meaning is narrower, with the word referring to spoken language. The use of the word *speech* to denote the whole of verbal abilities is indicative of the cardinal importance of spoken language. Oral language is by far the most frequently used form of verbal communication. It is also the first linguistic ability to be acquired by the child.

Speech (i.e., spoken language) is produced by means of the speech organs. These organs make up parts of the respiratory system and the digestive tract. Usually, expiratory air is used to generate audible speech sounds. If air from the lungs activates the larynx, voiced sounds such as vowels or voiced consonants are produced. If the vocal cords are kept apart and consequently do not vibrate during exhalation, egressive air is turned into voiceless consonants (such as /s/ or /f/). Speech movements are rapid, complex, and finely timed sequences of gestures. Therefore, it takes the child several years to learn to perform them.

Since speech is ordinarily produced on exhalation, air is taken in just prior to starting to speak. Inspiration is caused by a contraction of the diaphragm and of the external intercostal muscles. When it contracts, the diaphragm flattens out and goes down. When the external intercostals contract, they lift up the rib cage. A membrane called parietal pleura is attached to both the diaphragm and the rib cage. When the diaphragm goes down and the rib cage goes up, the parietal membrane follows them. This enlarges the interpleural space, which is the closed space between the parietal membrane and the visceral membrane. The latter membrane enwraps each of the two lungs. Because the interpleural space becomes larger, the pressure in this space drops. Residual air (even after the most forcible expiration possible, some air remains in the lungs; this air is called residual) forces the expansible lungs to dilate so that the visceral pleura can follow the parietal pleura and annihilate the negative pressure in the interpleural space. In the expanded lungs the pressure is now negative, and external air flows in via the nose (or mouth), larynx, and trachea to annihilate it (Kaplan, 1971).

Once the diaphragm starts to relax, the lower part of the parietal pleura is sucked upward by the retractile lungs. Similarly, the upper part of the pleura is sucked downward once the external intercostals start to relax. The retraction of the lungs increases the air pressure in them and air escapes via the upper respiratory tract. If, at some point, the relaxation pressure becomes insufficient to produce audible speech, expiratory muscles, mainly the internal intercostals, are used to draw the rib cage further in (Perkins & Kent, 1985).

On its way out, egressive air passes the larynx. This organ comprises a vertical tube in which a V-shaped horizontal narrowing, called the glottis, is found. The sides of the glottis are formed by two ligaments, which together with the muscle fibers behind them constitute the vocal folds. If the vocal folds are approximated during expiration, the glottis is closed and the air can no longer flow out of the trachea. As a result, the air pressure in the trachea increases. At some point, the pressure is such that it blows the vocal folds apart. Some air escapes through the glottis. As a consequence, the pressure in the trachea diminishes. Moreover, a Bernoulli effect is created in the glottis. The Bernoulli effect is the negative pressure on the sides of a bottleneck when a gas or a liquid flows through it. The glottis forms a bottleneck between the trachea and the pharynx. As a consequence, when air escapes through the glottis, the vocal folds are sucked toward one another. The Bernoulli effect and the temporary decrease in tracheal air pressure enable the elastic vocal folds to come together again. Since the glottis is now closed again, pressure builds up in the trachea until it blows the vocal cords apart, and so on. In this way, the column of pulmonary air is divided into a quick succession of puffs that are fired into the supraglottal cavities (pharynx, mouth, and nasal cavity). The puffs of air hit the air mass present in the supraglottal cavities, causing it to vibrate. These vibrations, leaving the mouth of the speaker, propagate themselves in the air until they reach the ears of a listener, who perceives them as voice. The form of the individual vocal waves varies with the form of the supraglottal cavities (Zemlin, 1968). In this way, it is possible to produce vocal waves that sound like /a/, /u/, or any other vowel.

The puffs of air from the larynx not only hit the mass of air in the supraglottal cavities, but also move it forward. This forward movement can be used to form consonants. These consonants are voiced since their generation is synchronous with voice production. If, on the contrary, the vocal folds are kept in an abducted position and consequently do not vibrate, air from the lungs flows directly into the supraglottal cavities, where it can be molded into voiceless consonants. The shaping of the vocal waves and the molding of egressive air into speech sounds is performed by the articulators. The main articulators are the tongue and the velum. The latter moves upward and shuts off the nasal cavity from the oropharyngeal cavity during articulation of oral sounds. In English, most speech sounds are articulated with the velum in a raised position. Failure of the velum to occlude the passage of air to the nose results in hyper-rhinolalia (i.e., nasalized speech).

REFERENCES

Kaplan, H. (1971). *Anatomy and physiology of speech.* New York: McGraw-Hill.

Perkins, W., & Kent, R. (1985). *Textbook of functional anatomy of speech, language, and hearing.* Philadelphia: Taylor & Francis.

Zemlin, R. (1968). *Speech and hearing science: Anatomy and physiology.* Englewood Cliffs, NJ: Prentice Hall.

YVAN LEBRUN
*School of Medicine, Brussels,
Belgium*

**LANGUAGE DISORDERS
SPEECH DISORDERS**

SPEECH, ABSENCE OF

Many children use their first recognizable word at age 1 and by 2 are using some type of sentence. When a child has not started speaking by age 2, parents often become concerned about the child's development. However, it is not unusual for the normally developing child not to use his or her first word until some time after the second birthday. However, if a child has no speech by age 5, it is likely that a serious difficulty exists (Bloodstein, 1984).

The most common cause of a lack of speech is an intellectual disability. While many children exhibiting severe intellectual disabilities have the potential to develop some language, those with a profound disability are likely to have no speech throughout their lives (Robinson & Robinson, 1976). Intellectual disabilities may sometimes be due to genetic factors. In other instances, traumatic brain injuries are the known cause of intellectual difficulty. Children with intellectual disabilities who do develop language typically do so in much the same manner as normally developing children but more slowly (Naremore & Dever, 1975; Van Riper & Erickson, 1996). They do, however, tend to exhibit limitations in their vocabulary and syntax usage.

Congenital deafness is another possible cause of a child exhibiting no speech. When a child is born with a profound hearing loss, he or she does not generally develop speech without special intervention. A number of children are born with some degree of hearing loss, but the impairment is not so severe that they cannot use hearing for the development of speech and language. However, a child with profound deafness typically experiences severe problems in developing speech because they have no way of monitoring their own speech production. Surprisingly, a profoundly deaf child's difficulty with hearing is often not noticed until the child is about age 2 and has not spoken his or her first word. This is due in part to the fact that many children with hearing impairments appear to go through the babbling stage in much the same way that children with hearing do.

Once a hearing loss is identified, most children with hearing impairments are fitted with a hearing aid. If the child has more than a 90 dB loss, he or she will probably not learn speech and language through hearing alone. The speech and language training of some children begins with the oral method, where language instruction is carried out primarily by requiring the child to lip read and speak. During the last 30 to 35 years, however, language instruction for children who are deaf has changed. Now most children are exposed to a sign language system once they are identified as deaf. Of children who are born with a profound hearing loss, only a small percentage attain speech that is intelligible to a stranger. However, many do attain a fairly high level of intelligibility to those who are familiar with the speech patterns of individuals who are deaf. It is important to make a distinction between speech and language when referring to children with hearing impairments because many children with profound deafness acquire language without having usable speech.

Another cause of absence of speech is cerebral palsy (Cruickshank, 1976; Pausewang Gelfer, 1996). Cerebral palsy is caused by brain damage occurring at or near the time of birth. Cerebral palsy can be of the type and of such severity that the child will not have sufficient control of the speech mechanism to produce intelligible speech. Some children, as their speech mechanism matures, can learn to produce intelligible speech with the help of specialists. However, other children can communicate only through other means such as communication boards and computers. Because of the physical disability and difficulty in communicating, the intelligence of children with cerebral palsy is often considerably underestimated.

An additional problem that can cause an absence of speech is the presence of social/emotional disturbances, specifically childhood schizophrenia and early infantile autism (Van Riper & Erickson, 1996). Typically, a child with schizophrenia appears to develop normally for the first few years of life and then begins to regress, possibly losing all language and speech. Schizophrenia, characterized by periods of remission, has been found to be resistant to treatment. Unlike schizophrenia, autism seems to be present in a child from birth. Infants with autism often withdraw from social contact, not looking into the eyes of adults and not leaning on the person carrying them. As they grow, their behavior may be characterized by obsessive actions, with play appearing to be stereotyped. Many children with autism fail to develop language. Language usage that does develop can be quite deviant. Some children with autism have been known to speak fully formed sentences, but only once or twice in their lifetimes. Others develop what is known as echolalic speech, where they parrot back what is spoken to them. These utterances do not appear to be used meaningfully. Other children do use some sentences meaningfully, but these seem to be memorized strings of words and are often simple demands. A smaller percentage of children with autism eventually attain a fair degree of speech and language.

Social deprivation can also be a cause of language acquisition problems. However, deprivation must be extremely severe for the child to acquire no speech whatsoever. Human beings appear to have a strong predisposition for learning language. Only minimal conditions of exposure to language need be present for the child to learn to speak. However, there are a few isolated cases of children who apparently have had no exposure to language and therefore do not develop language (e.g., Fuller, 1975). In some cases where a child is consistently deprived of attention, severe language delay may occur. For example, some children who were institutionalized received no attention except for being fed and kept clean. In such situations, many children experienced severe delays in the acquisition of language.

Occasionally, a clinician will see a child who understands language but does not speak at all. No cause can be found. Previously, it was thought that these children were suffering from maternal overprotection: Because the mother anticipated the child's needs, the child did not learn to speak. Over time, however, clinicians expressed doubt about attributing the lack of language usage to the behavior of the mother. While it was true that the mother often responded to the nonverbal cues of the child, it was generally recognized that the mother did this to alleviate severe frustration on both their parts. The mother's behavior is now seen as a response rather than as a cause. Children exhibiting this disorder frequently develop normal language over a period of time.

In the past, many children who did not acquire speech were institutionalized, receiving little or no educational services. With the advent of PL 94-142, many of these children were able to live at home and were provided schooling on a regular basis. Continued refinement of public educational laws (e.g., Individual with Disabilities Education Act Revisions of 1997) and a broader base of services have resulted in marked improvement in the communication skills of a number of who have difficulty in this area.

REFERENCES

Bloodstein, O. (1984). *Speech pathology: An introduction*. Boston: Houghton Mifflin.

Cruickshank, W. M. (1976). *Cerebral palsy: A developmental disability* (3rd ed.). Syracuse, NY: Syracuse University Press.

Fuller, C. W. (1975). Maternal deprivation and developmental language disorders. *Speech & Hearing Review: A Journal of New York State Speech & Hearing Association, 7,* 9–23.

Naremore, R. C., & Dever, R. B. (1975). Language performance of educable mentally retarded and normal children at five age levels. *Journal of Speech & Hearing Research, 18,* 92.

Pausewang Gelfer, M. (1996). *Survey of communication disorders: A social and behavioral perspective.* New York: McGraw-Hill.

Robinson, N. M., & Robinson, H. B. (1976). *The mentally retarded child* (2nd ed.). New York: McGraw-Hill.

Van Riper, C., & Erickson, R. L. (1996). *Speech correction: An introduction to speech pathology and audiology* (9th ed.). Boston: Allyn & Bacon.

CAROLYN L. BULLARD
Lewis & Clark College
First edition

ROBERT L. RHODES
New Mexico State University
Second and Third editions

AUTISM
ELECTIVE MUTISM
MUTISM
SPEECH THERAPY

SPEECH AND LANGUAGE DISABILITIES

See COMMUNICATION DISORDERS; LANGUAGE DISORDERS.

SPEECH-LANGUAGE PATHOLOGIST

Speech-language pathologist is the recognized title of a professional who evaluates and treats persons with speech and/or language disorders. There is some confusion about this title because there are other equivalent titles for speech-language pathologist, including speech (-language) therapist, speech pathologist, and speech (-language) clinician. In addition, speech-language pathologists sometimes use the informal abbreviated title of SLP. Different titles are used depending on the preferences of speech-language pathologists as well as the particular work settings (schools vs. hospitals, etc.). Different titles do *not* necessarily reflect any differences in educational or skill levels.

Speech-language pathologist is the title officially recognized by the American Speech-Language-Hearing Association (ASHA), a professional organization whose members include speech-language pathologists and audiologists (Van Riper & Erickson, 1996). Although not all speech-language pathologists and audiologists are members of ASHA, many of its members earn ASHA's Certificate of Clinical Competence (CCC), given to persons who hold a master's degree in speech-language pathology.

Speech-language pathologists must also sometimes be licensed by individual jurisdictions (e.g., states or provinces) before being permitted to do speech or language therapy in those jurisdictions. Speech-language pathologists work in schools, universities, hospitals, rehabilitation centers, and other institutions that serve the communicatively disabled.

REFERENCE

Van Riper, C., & Erickson, R. L. (1996). *Speech correction: An introduction to speech pathology and audiology* (9th ed.). Boston: Allyn & Bacon.

EDWARD A. SHIRKEY
New Mexico State University

COMMUNICATION DISORDERS
SPEECH THERAPY

SPEECH-LANGUAGE SERVICES

The provision of services to children and adults who have speech and/or language disorders is a complex problem. According to Cleland and Swartz (1982), delivery of services includes such factors as funding, transportation, and consumer resistance, in addition to problems of keeping service providers up to date in the latest techniques and tools. Speech and language services are provided in a variety of settings (Van Riper & Erickson, 1996) but always by professionals trained as speech pathologists having appropriate certification or a state license. All clinically certified speech-language pathologists are capable of providing a complete range of services. Some choose to specialize, but all have knowledge across a variety of speech and language disorders. The greatest number of speech pathologists are employed in school settings, ranging from pre-school through high school. Services provided include screening for speech and hearing disorders, diagnosis, treatment, and referral for more complex disorders. Since children make up the caseload in public schools, the majority of disorders treated are those concerning speech, language, voice, and stuttering. Many hospitals provide speech and language services. Speech clinics are usually established in rehabilitation departments. Speech-language pathologists work with occupational and physical therapists to treat people with physical disorders. Sometimes hospitals also provide services for children, thus offering an alternative to the free services of public schools.

There are speech-language clinics in many large metropolitan areas. Some of these clinics are private; others are associated with hospitals or universities. These clinics usually provide a wide range of services while at the same time being used as a training base for future speech language professionals. Privately funded or publicly funded health service agencies may also provide speech-language services. These agencies provide speech-language services to people from less privileged socioeconomic backgrounds. Speech clinicians employed by these agencies usually are itinerant: They go to the home of the client to provide the speech-language service. Clinics run by these agencies also provide a wide range of clinical services. There is a trend for speech-language pathologists to establish their own speech-language services rather than work for a school, hospital, clinic, or public agency. These individuals set up offices and see clients there. Occasionally, they hire other speech pathologists and enlarge their caseloads to the point where they can call their practice a clinic. Again, services are provided across the full range of speech and hearing disorders. Occasionally, speech-language pathologists are employed by industry. In these settings, the pathologists usually serve a diagnostic function only. In summary, speech-language services cover a wide range of diagnostic and therapeutic treatments in a variety of settings. These settings include public schools, hospitals, private speech clinics, university speech clinics, health service agencies, and private practices.

REFERENCES

Cleland, C. C., & Swartz, J. E. (1982). *Exceptionalities through the lifespan.* New York: Macmillan.

Van Riper, C., & Erickson, R. L. (1996). *Speech correction: An introduction to speech pathology and audiology* (9th ed.). Boston: Allyn & Bacon.

EDWARD A. SHIRKEY
New Mexico State University

SPEECH-LANGUAGE PATHOLOGISTS
SPEECH THERAPY

SPEECH SYNTHESIZER

A speech synthesizer is an electronic device that attempts to duplicate the human voice. Essentially, it allows a machine to talk to a human being. Of course, a human being must program the synthesizer and tell it what to say.

There are two different techniques for producing speech output that account for almost all the current synthesizer designs. The first is called linear predictive coding (LPC), which attempts to make an electronic model of the human voice. It creates tones much like those of the human vocal folds. These tones are passed through a set of filters that shape the tones into sounds the way that the articulators (tongue, lips, teeth, etc.) shape tones into sounds. This is a popular technique because it requires only enough computer memory to store the filter configurations and therefore is relatively inexpensive to make. Sound quality is acceptable but not realistic because the modeling of the voice is not exact enough to duplicate all the subtle vocal characteristics of human speech. The result is a machinelike speech quality.

The second method of producing speech is referred to as digitized speech. Actually, digitized speech is not synthesized speech. In digitized speech, the sound waves of the speech signal rather than the throat positions are recorded. These waves are then digitized—converted to digital codes and played back when needed. The advantage to this method is that the speech quality is good, sounding like a high-quality tape recorder. Nonetheless, it still takes time for the average listener to adjust to and understand synthesized speech (Venkatagiri, 1994). The disadvantage is that great amounts of memory are required to store the speech waves.

Aside from the industrial application of speech synthesizers, the synthesizers are being used as communication devices for nonspeaking individuals with disabilities and to prompt individuals with disabilities using remediation software (Lundberg, 1995).

REFERENCES

Lundberg, I. (1995). The computer as a tool of remediation in the education of students with reading disabilities. *Learning Disability Quarterly, 18*(2), 89–99.

Venkatagiri, H. S. (1994). Effect of sentence length and exposure on the intelligibility of synthesized speech. *American Journal of Speech-Language Pathology, 4,* 4, 36–45.

FREDERICK F. WEINER
Pennsylvania State University

AUGMENTATIVE COMMUNICATION SYSTEMS
COMPUTER USE WITH INDIVIDUALS WITH DISABILITIES

SPEECH THERAPY

Speech therapy includes all efforts to ameliorate disordered speech. Treatment activities include attempts to improve the speech of persons who have never spoken normally (habilitation) as well as to improve the speech of persons who formerly had normal speech (rehabilitation). A variety of treatment approaches are used, depending on the speaker's age, speech disorder, and the professional training and experience of the speech pathologist. Speech therapy usually includes teaching a person with a speech disorder to speak differently. Concerning adults and older children, however, therapy may consist of play activities during which treatment is indirect.

Although many research investigations have been conducted into the nature and treatment of speech (and language) disorders, much remains unknown. Therapy remains, therefore, often more of an art than a science. The speech pathologist must often rely more on intuition and experience than on research results. Often, no attempt is made to determine the cause of the speech disorder because, in most cases, the cause(s) cannot be found (e.g., Van Riper & Erickson, 1996). Although some speech disorders can be completely cured so that no traces of the original behavior remain, some speech disorders cannot be completely eradicated. For instance, some children and adults who stutter will continue to have vestiges of stuttering despite successful speech therapy.

Clients receive therapy in group and/or individual sessions, and therapy may be short-term (a few sessions) or long-term (several years), depending on the nature and severity of the disorder. The length and frequency of therapy sessions also depend on a variety of factors. (The terms *client, patient,* and *student* are all variously used to refer to the person being treated for a speech disorder, depending on the treatment setting.)

Speech-language pathologists typically assess clients before therapy actually begins, although a period of diagnostic therapy may also be used to help determine the nature of the disorder. Sometimes clients are referred to other professionals by the speech-language pathologist (e.g., audiologists, dentists, physicians).

REFERENCE

Van Riper, C., & Erickson, R. L. (1996). *Speech correction: An introduction to speech pathology and audiology.* Boston: Allyn & Bacon.

EDWARD A. SHIRKEY
New Mexico State University

AUGMENTATIVE COMMUNICATION SYSTEMS
COMMUNICATION DISORDERS
SPEECH-LANGUAGE PATHOLOGIST

SPELLING DISABILITIES

Spelling is a traditional element of the elementary school curriculum and an integral part of the writing process. The primary goal of spelling instruction for both disabled and nondisabled students is to make the act of correctly spelling words so automatic that it requires only a minimal amount of conscious attention. If students master the ability to spell words with maximum efficiency and minimum effort, it is assumed that they will be able to devote more of their attention, and consequently more of their effort, to higher order writing processes such as purpose, content, and organization (Graham, 1982).

It is commonly believed that the majority of students who are labeled disabled exhibit spelling problems. This is particularly the case for disabled students with reading difficulties (Lennox & Siegal, 1993). For instance, MacArthur and Graham (1986) found that learning-disabled students made spelling errors in approximately 1 out of every 10 words that they used when writing a short story. Although similar spelling difficulties have been reported for other handicapping conditions (Graham & Miller, 1979), it is important to note that our present understanding of spelling difficulties and disabled students' development of spelling skills is incomplete.

One development of particular interest in the area of spelling disabilities is the formulation of various systems for classifying spelling problems. Poor spellers who are also poor readers have frequently been classified as dyslexic, while poor spellers who possess normal reading skills have been labeled dysgraphic. In addition, many of the classification schemes presently available represent an attempt to interpret various spelling errors and difficulties as evidence of neurological dysfunction.

Spelling instruction for the disabled has, in large part, been based on the use or modification of traditional spelling procedures and techniques. Although handicapped students may not progress as rapidly through the spelling curriculum or master all of the skills taught to normally achieving students, their spelling programs commonly emphasize the traditional skills of (1) mastering a basic spelling vocabulary; (2) determining the spelling of unknown words through the use of phonics and spelling rules; (3) developing a desire to spell words correctly; (4) identifying and correcting spelling errors; and (5) using the dictionary to locate the spelling of words. There is considerable controversy, however, surrounding the issue of which skills should receive primary emphasis. Some experts, for example, recommend that a basic spelling vocabulary should form the core of the spelling program, while others have argued that spelling instruction should take advantage of the systematic properties of English orthography and stress the application of phonics and spelling rules (Graham, 1983).

Although spelling instruction for students with disabilities has received little attention in the research literature, experts generally agree that these students should be taught a systematic procedure of studying unknown spelling words. Effective word study procedures usually emphasize careful pronunciation of the word, visual imagery, auditory and/or kinesthetic reinforcement, and systematic recall (Graham & Miller, 1979). Additional instructional procedures that are considered desirable for use with students with disabilities include using a pretest to determine which words a student should study; presenting and testing a few words on a daily basis; interspersing known and unknown words in each spelling test; requiring students to correct their spelling tests under the guidance of a teacher; periodically reviewing to determine whether spelling skills have been maintained; and using spelling games to promote interest and motivation.

A final point concerns the use of behavioral and cognitive procedures. Although the evidence is not yet conclusive, spelling procedures based on behavioral and/or cognitive principles appear to be particularly effective with disabled students. McLaughlin (1982) found, for example, that the spelling accuracy of students in a special class improved as a result of group contingencies. In terms of cognitive procedures, Harris, Graham, and Freeman (1986) found that strategy training improved learning disabled students' spelling performance and, in one study condition, improved their ability to predict how many words would be spelled correctly on a subsequent test. Others have found that computers assist in spelling skill acquisition in a meaningful way (Gordon, Vaughn, & Schumm, 1993; Van Daal & Van der Leij, 1992).

REFERENCES

Gordon, J., Vaughn, S., & Schumm, J. S. (1993). Spelling instruction: A review of literature and implications for instruction for student with learning disabilities. *Learning Disabilities Research and Practice, 8*(3), 175–181.

Graham, S. (1982). Composition research and practice: A unified approach. *Focus on Exceptional Children, 14,* 1–16.

Graham, S. (1983). Effective spelling instruction. *Elementary School Journal, 83,* 560–568.

Graham, S., & Miller, L. (1979). Spelling research and practice: A unified approach. *Focus on Exceptional Children, 12,* 1–16.

Harris, K., Graham, S., & Freeman, S. (1986). *The effects of strategy training and study conditions on metamemory and achievement.* Paper presented at the American Educational Research Association, San Francisco.

Lennox, C., & Siegal, L. S. (1993). Visual and phonological spelling errors in subtypes of children with learning disabilities. *Applied Psycholinguistics, 14*(4), 473–488.

MacArthur, C., & Graham, S. (1986). *LD students' writing under three conditions: Word processing, dictation, and handwriting.* Paper presented at the American Educational Research Association, San Francisco.

McLaughlin, T. (1982). A comparison of individual and group contingencies on spelling performance with special education students. *Child and Family Behavior Therapy, 4,* 1–10.

Van Daal, V. H., & Van der Leij, A. (1992). Computer-based reading and spelling practice for children with learning disabilities. *Journal of Learning Disabilities, 25*(3), 186–195.

STEVE GRAHAM
University of Maryland

WRITING REMEDIATION

SPERRY, ROGER W. (1913–1994)

Fifty years of systematic and ingenious research resulted in Roger Sperry's development of novel ideas about the nervous system and mind. Born to a middle-class family in Hartford, Connecticut on August 20, 1913, Sperry dedicated his professional life to understanding two basic questions in psychology: (1) what is consciousness? and (2) what roles do nature and nurture play in the regulation of behavior? Educated at Oberlin College in Ohio (BS in English and MS in psychology), Chicago (PhD in Zoology), and Harvard (postdoctoral fellowship in psychology), Sperry always went against the conventional wisdom of his day, tending to question established fact through simple but brilliant studies. Most of his important studies were completed as Hixson Professor of Psychobiology at the California Institute of Technology.

He indicated that his work could be divided into phases. The first phase, developed at Oberlin and continued through his Chicago years, focused on determining whether the nervous system was malleable or amenable to change through learning. After interchanging nerve fibers in rats, initially motor ones and later sensory ones also, he concluded that the nervous system was more hard-wired than we had previously thought. These experiments were later replicated in a variety of amphibians and mammals, using both motor and sensory fibers. It was during this time that he developed the theory of chemoaffinity of nerve fibers. He proposed that if nerve fibers were cut, they would grow back to their original site using chemically-induced growth.

During the 1950s, Sperry began to question whether this hard-wired concept was also found inside the brain (since he had previously worked with fibers in the peripheral nervous system). Initially working with cats and later with monkeys, Sperry began cutting the largest nerve tract in the brain, the corpus callosum. It had been previously thought that this fiber tract's role was essentially to hold the two sides of the brain together. His initial studies reflected that the two sides appeared to have different functions. However, he believed that humans could provide more accurate information regarding the perceived differences.

Together with surgeons Joseph Bogen and Phillip Voegl, Sperry designed a series of studies aimed at discovering the functions of the two sides of the brain and if the brain was as hard-wired as the peripheral nervous system. About a dozen patients with intractable epilepsy had their corpus callosum severed in what is now called "split-brain" preparation. Over numerous studies, some of which are still being carried out, it was discovered that the brain was indeed hard-wired, much like the peripheral nervous system. Further, it was found that the left hemisphere was primarily responsible for verbal information while the right hemisphere controlled visual information.

Additional studies revealed that the patients had two separate minds. Hence, their behavior was not integrated. After further study, Sperry concluded that consciousness was a function of the integration of both sides of the brain simultaneously. Also, he believed that the consciousness emerged from brain function and, in turn, had a downward control on the brain function from which it had been produced.

In his later years, Sperry became interested in the notion that specific value systems, as found in conscious thought, had an effect on the global situation. Specifically, he believed that appropriate values (reduction in overpopulation and pollution) were the solution to the modern problems facing society.

For his scientific work, Sperry shared the 1981 Nobel Prize in Medicine and received the highest awards in the disciplines he worked in, including psychology, neuroscience, and philosophy. With over 300 publications and close to 100 students doing research in nine different continents, Sperry's contributions extend far beyond his half century of research and modern-day psychology. He died at the age of

Roger W. Sperry

80 in Pasadena, California from complications of ALS. He is survived by his wife and two children.

REFERENCES

Puente, A. E. (1995). Roger Sperry (1913–1994). *American Psychologist.*

Sperry, R. W. (1952). Neurology and the mind-brain problem. *American Scientist, 40*, 291–312.

Sperry, R. W. (1982). Some effects of disconnecting the cerebral hemispheres. *Science, 217*, 1223–1226.

Antonio E. Puente
University of North Carolina at Wilmington

SPIELMEYER-VOGT DISEASE

See Juvenile cerebromacular degeneration.

SPINA BIFIDA

Spina bifida (myelomeningocele) is a congenital abnormality present at birth. The defect begins early in embryogenesis (the first 30 days of gestation), as the central nervous system is developing with a failure of the spinal cord to close over the lower end (Haslam & Valletutti, 1975). Without such closure, normal development of the spinal column cannot occur; the spinal cord and covering membranes bulge out and block further development.

It is a fairly common developmental anomaly, present in .2 to .4 per 1,000 live births (Haslam & Valletutti, 1975). The risks increase dramatically to 1/20 to 1/40 following the birth of one affected infant. It is possible to test for spina bifida through amniocentesis. The amniotic fluid is analyzed by testing for abnormally high alpha fetal protein and acetyl cholinesterase levels. Both are normally present in the fetal cerebrospinal fluid, which, in myelomeningocele, leaks into the amniotic fluid (Behrman & Vaugh, 1983).

Detection at birth is due to the presence of a large bulging lesion or swelling, with or without a skin covering, at the lower part of the back (lumbosacral region). It is the damage to or the defect of the spinal cord that results in a variety of handicapping conditions. Eighty percent of children with spina bifida have hydrocephalus, a condition caused by the accumulation of fluid in the ventricles of the brain (Haslam & Valletutti, 1975). If left untreated, hydrocephalus can result in severe mental retardation. Treatment consists of diverting the cerebrospinal fluid to some other area of the body, usually the atria of the heart or the abdominal cavity (Wolraich, 1983).

Paraplegia resulting from the disruption of the motor tracts from the brain to the muscles at the spinal cord level leads to weakness and paralysis of muscles. The degree of paralysis depends on the location and extent of spinal cord damage. Bladder and bowel control is often absent and may present one of the biggest obstacles to a child's participation in a regular school program.

Children with spina bifida will require extensive medical, orthopedic, and educational services. This is often expensive and time consuming, creating frustration and financial hardship for the family. Educational programming for these children must consider the need for personnel trained in toileting techniques and physical therapy. While some children with spina bifida may require a self-contained special education class setting, others who are less severely impaired cognitively may be able to perform successfully in a mainstream classroom with support services.

Incidence of spina bifida can be significantly reduced owing to the discovery of a strong link between neural tube defects in general and folic acid deficiency. Folic acid is now known to protect against such defects, although the mode of action is not clear. Women who have had one child with spina bifida who take folic acid supplements during subsequent pregnancies have a 70 percent reduction in recurrence. Further, folic acid supplements can reduce incidence of new cases of spina bifida by 50 percent. Thus, all women who may become pregnant are advised to take daily folic acid supplements both before and during the first 12 weeks of pregnancy. Such supplements are in common foods such as bread, flour, and rice (Liptak, 1997).

REFERENCES

Behrman, R. E., & Vaughn, V. C. (1983). Defects of closure tube. In W. B. Nelson (Ed.), *Nelson's textbook of pediatrics* (pp. 1560–1561). Philadelphia: Saunders.

Haslam, R. A., & Valletutti, P. J. (1975). *Medical problems in the classroom: The teacher's role in diagnosis and management.* Baltimore: University Park Press.

Liptak, G. S. (1997). Neural tube defects. In M. L. Batshaw (Ed.), *Children with disabilities* (4th ed., pp. 529–552). Baltimore: Brookes.

Wolraich, M. (1983). Myelomeningocele. In J. A. Blackman (Ed.), *Medical aspects of developmental disabilities in children birth to three: A resource for special service providers in the educational setting.* Iowa City: University of Iowa.

Marsha H. Lupi
Hunter College, City University of New York

HYDROCEPHALUS

SPINAL CORD INJURY

Damage to the spinal cord frequently, but not always, result in paralysis or paresis to the extremities. The specific impairment or dysfunction that occurs in the extremities depends on the corresponding spinal level and the severity of the injury. In some situations, the injury may be only temporary and the individual may not experience any permanent effects. More often, the injury results in permanent damage and loss of function in the involved extremities.

The most common causes of spinal cord injury are accidents in or about the home, falls, bullet wounds, sports injuries, or motor vehicle accidents. The injury is often associated with fractured bones of the spinal column but also may occur from dislocation of one or more of these bones on the other. When the spinal cord is damaged, the nervous pathways between the body and the brain are interrupted. All forms of sensation (e.g., proprioception, touch, temperature, pain) and muscular control are typically lost below the level of the damage. Although nerves outside the spinal cord may be repaired or heal spontaneously, damaged nerves within the spinal cord will not regenerate. If the injury is low on the spinal cord (usually below the first thoracic vertebra), only the lower extremities are involved. This type of injury is called paraplegia. If the injury is higher on the spinal cord (cervical level), all four extremities and the trunk may be involved; this condition is referred to as quadriplegia. Injury to the highest levels of the cervical spine may cause death because of the loss of innervation to the diaphragm. Occasionally, only one side of the cord is damaged. This type of condition is called Brown-Sequard syndrome. Loss of proprioception and motor paralysis occur on the same side as the injury, while loss of pain, temperature, and touch sensations occur on the opposite side.

Immediate treatment after a spinal injury or suspected injury is immobilization. Immobilization prevents further shearing of the spinal column, which may result in further or more permanent damage to the spinal cord. If there is any possibility of spinal cord injury, the injured person should not be moved until trained assistance arrives. Once the injured person has been transported to an appropriate medical facility, the course of treatment varies, depending on the nature of the injury.

During the initial stage of spinal cord trauma, autonomic and motor reflexes below the level of the injury are suppressed. This flaccid paralysis is called spinal shock and may last from several hours to 3 months. As the spinal shock recedes, spinal reflexes return in a hyperactive state. This spasticity or muscular hypertonicity may vary initially at different times of the day or in response to different stimuli, but it becomes more consistent within one year of the injury. The most common form of acute treatment is traction to the spinal column to bring about a realignment and healing of the fractured or displaced vertebrae. Special beds may be used to permit people in traction to be turned from their back to their abdomen, thereby reducing the chance of pressure sores (decubitus).

Artificial ventilation usually is necessary for persons with injuries at or above the level of the third cervical vertebra (C3). Decreased respiratory capacity is present in injuries from C4 through T7 (the seventh thoracic vertebra), making coughing difficult and often necessitating suctioning when the patient gets a respiratory infection. Dizziness or blackout may occur from pooling of blood in the abdomen and lower extremities when a person is first brought to an upright position following a period of immobilization. This is a normal reaction and is avoided through the aid of a reclining wheelchair or a tilt table that allows gradual adjustment to a full upright position. Numerous other secondary conditions or complications may occur for several months or years following a spinal cord injury. These include muscle contracture or shortening, loss of sexual functioning in males, impaired bowel or bladder control, kidney or urinary tract infections, or psychological reactions, to name but a few.

Rehabilitation procedures begin within a few days of the injury and usually continue for several weeks or months after the healing process is complete. The general goal of rehabilitation is to improve the physical capacities and develop adapted techniques to promote as independent a lifestyle as possible. Unfortunately, rehabilitation's goals all too often focus on participation rather than performance (Dudgeon, Massagli, & Ross, 1997). Educational performance for a person with a spinal cord injury is hampered only by the individual's physical limitations. However, the individual may have problems with self-image, coping strategies, accessibility support, and unresolved feelings, all of which may affect educational performance (Mulcahey, 1992). Persons with high-level injuries may require numerous assistive devices such as an electronic typewriter with mouthstick or mechanical page turner. Persons with low-level injuries may not require any specialized assistance to benefit from education. Counseling to help a person adjust to new physical impairments and to develop future vocational pursuits may also be in order.

REFERENCES

Dudgeon, B. J., Massagli, T. L., & Ross, B. W. (1997). Educational participation of children with spinal cord injury. *American Journal of Occupational Therapy, 51*(7), 553–561.

Hanak, M., & Scott, A. (1983). *Spinal cord injury: An illustrated guide for health care professionals.* New York: Springer-Verlag.

Long, C. (1971). Congenital and traumatic lesions of the spinal cord. In T. H. Krusen, F. H. Kottke, & P. M. Ellwood (Eds.), *Handbook of physical medicine and rehabilitation* (2nd ed., pp. 475–516). Philadelphia: Saunders.

Mulcahey, M. J. (1992). Returning to school after spinal cord injury: Perspectives from four adolescents. *American Journal of Occupational Therapy, 46*(4), 305–312.

Trombly, C. A. (1984). Spinal cord injury. In C. A. Trombly (Ed.), *Occupational therapy for physical dysfunction* (3rd ed.). Baltimore: Williams & Wilkins.

Wilson, D. J., McKenzie, M. W., Barber, L. M., & Watson, K. L. (1984). *Spinal cord injury: A treatment guide for occupational therapists.* Thorofare, NJ: Slack.

DANIEL D. LIPKA
*Lincoln Way Special Education
Regional Resources Center*

QUADRIPLEGIA

SPINOCEREBELLAR DEGENERATION

See FRIEDREICH'S ATAXIA.

SPITZ, HERMAN (1925–   )

Herman Spitz was born on March 2, 1925, in Paterson, New Jersey. He is a noted psychologist and researcher in the field of mental retardation. Spitz obtained his BA at Lafayette College (1948) and PhD at New York University (1955). He was an assistant psychologist (1951–1955) and chief psychologist (1955–1957) at Trenton State Hospital. From 1957 to 1989, Spitz was affiliated with the E. R. Johnstone Training and Research Center, initially as a research associate, and beginning in 1962, as the director of research.

As an author of over 90 publications, Spitz has written extensively on the subject of mental retardation, particularly as related to assessment, intervention (both cognitive and behavioral), and causes (Spitz, 1986a, 1986b, 1994). He has also shown an interest in the unconscious, and has authored a book on the topic, exploring how nonconscious movements can influence our expression of ideas, inner conflicts, and wishful thinking, and particularly serving to facilitate communication of individuals who are severely and profoundly retarded or autistic (Spitz, 1997).

Spitz has served as a consulting editor for several professional journals, including the *American Journal of Mental Deficiency* and *Memory and Cognition*. He is a fellow of the American Psychological Association and the American Psychological Society and member of the American Academy on Mental Retardation. In recognition of his research contributions, Spitz has served as an invited lecturer and consultant to numerous institutions, including Alabama University, Columbia University, George Peabody College for Teachers, and the Medical Research Council, London.

REFERENCES

American Men of Science. (1962). (10th edition). Tempe, AZ: Jaques Cattell.

Spitz, H. H. (1986a). Disparities in mentally retarded persons' IQ derived from different intelligence tests. *American Journal of Mental Deficiency, 90*(5), 588–591.

Spitz, H. H. (1986b). Preventing and curing mental retardation by behavioral intervention: An evaluation of some claims. *Intelligence, 10*(3), 197–207.

Spitz, H. H. (1994). Fragile X syndrome is not the second leading cause of mental retardation. *Mental Retardation, 32*(2), 156.

Spitz, H. H. (1997). *Nonconscious movement: From mystical messages to facilitated communication.* Mahwah, NJ: Erlbaum.

IVAN Z. HOLOWINSKY
Rutgers University
First edition

TAMARA J. MARTIN
*The University of Texas of the
Permian Basin*
Second and Third editions

SPITZ, RENE ARPAD (1887–1974)

Rene Arpad Spitz, educated in his native Hungary and in the United States, was a leading representative of psychoanalysis in the United States. He served on the faculty of the New York Psychoanalytic Institute, was professor of psychiatry at City College, City University of New York and the University of Colorado, and was clinical professor of psychiatry at Lenox Hill Hospital in New York City. The author of some 60 monographs and papers, Spitz is best known for his extensive studies of infant development.

REFERENCES

Spitz, R. A. (1962). *A genetic field theory of ego formation.* New York: International Universities Press.

Spitz, R. A., & Cobliner, W. G. (1966). *The first year of life.* New York: International Universities Press.

PAUL IRVINE
Katonah, New York

SPLINTER SKILL

See SAVANT SYNDROME.

SPLIT-BRAIN RESEARCH

The technique of cerebral commissurotomy (split-brain surgery) was first introduced by Van Wagenen in 1940 as a surgical solution for severe and intractible forms of epilepsy. Van Wagenen performed the operation on approximately 2 dozen cases, hoping to be able to restrict the abnormal electrical activation characteristic of epilepsy to a single hemisphere. Unfortunately, the early operations were not successful and the procedure was largely abandoned until the early 1960s, when it was taken up by Roger Sperry working in collaboration with Joseph Bogen and Philip Vogel (Beaumont, 1983). The refined operation proved to be effective in many cases and, more important from scientific perspective, the procedure allowed a unique opportunity to study cerebral organization. Sperry's work with split-brain patients was deemed so important that he shared the Nobel Prize in Medicine in 1984. This award appropriately reflects the tremendous advances that were made in the neurosciences following this seminal work.

The technique of cerebral commissurotomy involves the complete section of the corpus callosum, including the anterior and hippocampal commissures in the massa intermedia. This technique effectively isolates each half of the cortex and prevents transfer of information from one side of the brain to the other. Despite the operation's dramatic nature, postsurgical patients appear to function quite well. Fairly sophisticated testing procedures are necessary to isolate and identify the effects of surgery.

Detailed study of postsurgical split-brain patients reveals that, in fact, a number of problems do exist for these patients (Springer & Deutsch, 1981). The patients frequently report trouble with associating names and faces. This may be due to the differential loci for naming and facial recognition, with the assignment of names occurring in the left hemisphere and the recognition of faces more intimately linked to the right hemisphere. Patients also report difficulty with geometry, and many complain of memory loss. Finally, many postsurgical patients report cessation of dreaming; however, this has not been supported empirically, and these patients continue to show REM sleep postsurgically.

Sperry has consistently maintained that the operation produces two separate minds within one body, each with its own will, perception, and memories. This is supported by numerous anecdotes of conflict between the hemispheres or between the body parts controlled by the respective hemispheres. These reports, albeit fascinating, are largely anecdotal and appear to be somewhat exaggerated. In general, while early studies and writers emphasized the division and uniqueness of the two hemispheres, recent research has been devoted to how the brain works as a whole and how the hemispheres cooperate in transferring information back and forth. Zaidel (1979) has compared performance of each hemisphere operating singly with performance of the brain operating as a whole. He has found that much better results are evident when the brain is working as a whole with the hemispheres serving in tandem. In addition, it is important not to forget that both cortical structures are intimately linked to an integrated subcortical substrate with a number of linked bilateral structures (Corballis, 1998).

Eccles (1977) has reviewed the split-brain research and has argued that it suggests consciousness is intimately linked to speech and therefore must reside in the dominant left hemisphere. However, all such generalizations from split-brain research are limited by the fact that the brains studied are clearly pathological specimens and may not represent normal cognitive functioning.

One of the interesting findings that has emerged from split-brain research is that rudimentary language perception skills have been associated with the right cerebral hemisphere. Recognition of nouns by the right hemisphere appears to be easier than recognition of verbs (Gazzaniga, 1970). This difference is especially marked when a rapid response is required. If patients are given maximum time to respond, the noun-verb distinction is less apparent.

Levy and her colleagues have completed a number of studies with split-brain patients employing chimeric stimulae (Levy, Trevarthen, & Sperry, 1972). These are stimulus items that are composed by joining two half-stimuli. The stimuli are presented in such a way that each half goes to the isolated contralateral hemisphere. On the basis of these studies, Levy has argued that the left hemisphere is best described as analytic while the right is best described as holistic.

Split-brain patients make ideal subjects for dichotic listening experiments in which different stimuli are presented simultaneously in each ear. In addition, for those patients who receive a commissurotomy, divided visual field studies can be employed with less concern for saccadic eye movements. However, considerable experimental skill is necessary to avoid the phenomenon of cross-cuing. This occurs when a patient deliberately or inadvertently develops strategies for delivering information to both hemispheres simultaneously. For example, a subject who is palpating a comb may rub the teeth of the comb with the left hand. Although the tactile information will reach only the right hemisphere in the split-brain patient, the associated sound goes to both ears and may reach the left hemisphere and allow for linguistic identification.

Increasingly, neurosurgeons are performing partial commissurotomies with good success. These procedures allow still more detailed information about the localization of transference fibers in the corpus callosum. For example, it has become clear that somatosensory information is transmitted via the anterior corpus callosum while the rear portion, the splenium, transfers visual information. In addition, there is an indication that some perceptual judgements may be made sub-cortically (Corballis, 1994).

The work done to date on split-brain patients may offer important clues to help the teacher better understand and educate the child with special needs. Levy (1982) has used split-brain data to develop a model of handwriting posture; Obrzut and Hynd (1981) have applied these findings on cerebral lateralization to children with learning disabilities; and Hartlage (1975) has developed a plan for predicting the outcome of remedial educational strategies based on a model of cerebral lateralization. Perhaps it is only through understanding how each half of the brain works that we will ever approach an understanding of how it works as a whole—a concept supported fully by Sperry (Corballis, 1998).

REFERENCES

Beaumont, J. G. (1983). *Introduction to neuropsychology.* New York: Guilford.

Corballis, M. C. (1994). Split decisions: Problems in the interpretation of results from commissurotomized subjects. *Behavioral Brain Research, 64*(1), 163–172.

Corballis, M. C. (1998). Sperry and the age of Aquarius: Science values and the split brain. *Neuropsychologies, 36*(10), 1083–1087.

Eccles, J. C. (1977). *The understanding of the brain* (2nd ed.). New York: McGraw-Hill.

Gazzaniga, M. S. (1970). *The bisected brain.* Englewood Cliffs, NJ: Prentice Hall.

Hartlage, L. C. (1975). Neuropsychological approaches to predicting outcome of remedial educational strategies for learning disabled children. *Pediatric Psychology, 3,* 23–28.

Levy, J. (1982). Handwriting posture and cerebral organization: How are they related? *Psychological Bulletin, 91,* 589–608.

Levy, J., Trevarthen, C., & Sperry, R. W. (1972). Perception of bilateral chimeric figures following hemispheric disconnection. *Brain, 95,* 61–78.

Obrzut, J. E., & Hynd, G. W. (1981). Cognitive development and cerebral lateralization in children with learning disabilities. *International Journal of Neuroscience, 14,* 139–145.

Springer, S. P., & Deutsch, G. (1981). *Left brain, right brain.* San Francisco: Freeman.

Zaidel, E. (1979). Performance on the ITPA following cerebral commissurotomy and hemispherectomy. *Neuropsychologia, 17,* 259–280.

DANNY WEDDING
Marshall University

CEREBRAL DOMINANCE
LEFT BRAIN/RIGHT BRAIN

SPORTS FOR INDIVIDUALS WITH DISABILITIES

The origin of sports adapted to the needs of individuals with disabilities can be traced to the end of World War II, when thousands of physically disabled veterans joined already existing groups of people with congenital and traumatic disabilities. In 1948 Stoke Mandeville Hospital in Aylsburg, England, first introduced an organized wheelchair sports program for patients; the first international games were held there in 1952 (Wehman & Schleien, 1981). This use of sports in rehabilitation was the stimulus for the growth of the international sports for the disabled movement that is prevalent today (DePauw, 1984).

From the beginning it was apparent that adaptations of rules and equipment were going to be necessary for sports programs, and many of the adaptations were the result of the imaginative efforts of the participants themselves. In addition, the participants joined together with others who needed the same adaptations, and through their activities were able to participate within the wider community. For some disabled persons, a sports program means competition; in other situations, the aim of sports is to meet therapeutic needs; for others the objective of sports involvement is to fulfill leisure-time pursuits (R. C. Adams et al., 1982).

Currently, federal mandates regulate physical education services and sports opportunities for individuals with disabilities. IDEA requires a free appropriate public school education, which includes instruction in physical education, in the least restrictive environment. Section 504 of the Rehabilitation Act specifies nondiscrimination on the basis of handicap, and states that equal opportunity and equal access must be provided for handicapped persons, specifically including physical education services, intramurals, and athletics. The most direct mandate for sports opportunities is the Amateur Sports Act of 1978 (PL 95-606; DePauw, 1984).

As a result of this law, the U.S. Olympic Committee initiated a Handicapped in Sports Committee, which changed its name to the Committee on Sports for the Disabled (COSD) in 1983 (DePauw, 1984). Committee membership consists of two representatives from each major national organization in the United States offering sports opportunities for disabled individuals. At least 20 percent of COSD members must be, or must have been, actively participating disabled athletes.

There are seven organizations designated as members of COSD. The National Association of Sports for Cerebral Palsy is a program of United Cerebral Palsy providing competitive sports opportunities for individuals with cerebral palsy and similar physically disabling conditions (C. Adams, 1984). The American Association for the Deaf sanctions and promotes state, regional, and national basketball, softball, and volleyball tournaments, the World Games for the Deaf, the AAD Hall of Fame, and the Deaf Athlete of the Year (Ammons, 1984). The National Handicapped Sports and Recreation Association is unique in the world of sports groups in that its members possess a variety of physical and mental disabilities (Hernley, 1984). The National Wheelchair Athletic Association organizes and conducts competition in seven different Olympic sports, and also in wheelchair slalom, involving a race against time over a series of obstacles to challenge a competitor's wheelchair handling and speed skills (Fleming, 1984). The United States Amputee Athletic Association has grown from a small group of competitors in 1981 to a national organization which sponsors annual games (Bryant, 1984). The major purpose of the U.S. Association for Blind Athletes is to develop individual independence through athletic competition without unnecessary restrictions (Beaver, 1984).

Founded in 1968 by Eunice Kennedy Shriver, the first International Special Olympics was a single track and field event with about a thousand participants. Today over one million mentally impaired children and adults from around the world take part in Special Olympics; it is the biggest sports event in which children with disabilities are likely to be involved. Sports activities range from events in swimming, gymnastics, and bowling, to basketball, track and field, and soccer. Racewalking has been adopted as a new sport, and equestrian sporting events are now being offered as demonstration sports.

Sports activities for individuals with disabilities are sponsored by many nonschool groups, however, guarantees of equal opportunities for disabled students require that educators and psychologists give more attention to school-sponsored sports programs (Ashen, 1991). Unique and innovative approaches are needed so that these individuals can participate in sports within the schools. One possibility is to have special sections for the disabled as part of regular track, swimming, and gymnastic meets. It also may be possible to mix people with different handicapping conditions with able-bodied individuals in some sports programs. One promising program is the paralympic movement. The Paralympic Games is one of the largest sporting events in the world (Steadward, 1996).

REFERENCES

Adams, C. (1984). The National Association of Sports for Cerebral Palsy. *Journal of Physical Education, Recreation & Dance, 55,* 34–35.

Adams, R. C., David, A. N., McCubbin, J. A., & Rullman, L. (1982). *Games, sports and exercises for the physically handicapped* (3rd ed.). Philadelphia: Lea & Febiger.

Ammons, D. C. (1984). American Athletic Association for the Deaf. *Journal of Physical Education, Recreation & Dance, 55,* 36–37.

Ashen, M. J. (1991). The challenge of the physically challenged: Delivering sport psychology services to physically disabled athletes. *Sport Psychologist, 5*(4), 370–381.

Beaver, D. P. (1984). The United States Association for Blind Athletes. *Journal of Physical Education, Recreation & Dance, 55,* 40–41.

Bryant, D. C. (1984). United States Amputee Athletic Association. *Journal of Physical Education, Recreation & Dance, 55,* 40–41.

DePauw, K. P. (1984). Commitment and challenges, sport opportunities for athletes with disabilities. *Journal of Physical Education, Recreation & Dance, 55,* 34–35.

Fleming, A. (1984). The National Wheelchair Association. *Journal of Physical Education, Recreation & Dance, 55,* 38–39.

Hernley, R. (1984). National Handicapped Sports and Recreation Association. *Journal of Physical Education, Recreation & Dance, 55,* 38–39.

Steadward, R. D. (1996). Integration and sport in the paralympic movement. *Sport Science Review, 5*(1), 26–41.

Wehman, P., & Schleien, S. (1981). *Leisure programs for handicapped persons: Adaptations, techniques and curriculum.* Baltimore: University Park Press.

CATHERINE O. BRUCE
Hunter College, City University of New York

OLYMPICS, SPECIAL
RECREATIONAL THERAPY

STAFF DEVELOPMENT

Staff development represents the professional growth of persons toward observable and measurable objectives that benefit an organization and its members. Professional and personal growth are necessary if an organization is to maintain its performance standards, develop a feeling of pride, stimulate its membership, and generate a creative work environment, all of which contribute to personal and corporate well-being.

Staff development is necessary to improve the product of an organization by raising the skill level and awareness of the human resources of that organization. In public schools, the product is education. Teachers design and deliver the product; students consume; and the public evaluates the product based on their observations of its effects on the consumers (children). Education must be accepted as meaningful and pertinent to the children before they learn. The motivating and technical skills of teachers, as salespersons, are vital to the success of the enterprise. The delivery of the product—instruction—requires teacher performance, materials, physical plant, technology, and student motivation. These variables determine the amount of the product the consumers buy or, in some cases, refuse. The teachers' skills, as those of the producer and delivering agent, are the key input in the process. Because of the importance of those skills, development of the staff as a key resource should be continuous and planned, as with any of the other resources of an organization. Development must be perceived as required, meaningful, and attainable by the staff.

Initial planning may begin by determining the needs of the organization and its membership. Needs surveying instruments are designed for that purpose. A staff development plan will fulfill those preferred needs that have been identified. The staff may contribute by assembling a list of requirements that can be collectively prioritized with regard to an organization's needs. This allows for all staff to feel a part of the planning process. Communication of the results of the needs survey should follow.

Another component of basic staff development is the creation of a supportive environment. To establish this environment there are several desirable elements that an administrator should provide, including teaching assignments, scheduling, released time, and special instructional supplies. Administrators must also be sensitive to personal needs and personalities of the staff, supporting them with concern, sincerity, and other humanizing factors. Developing support groups among teachers, organizing functional committees, and being a public relations agent for the school are indicative of a supportive environment. Praising and supporting teachers in the community when adversarial situations are apparent is also important in providing a supportive environment.

The administration should develop a plan for the enhancement of the school's staff resource. The plan may encompass several areas: curriculum; instruction; personal skills; licensure; advanced education; stress management; work environment; administrative support; school, home, community relations; student management; and school organization. Once the needs of the organization have been identified, each staffer's part in the scheme is drawn up and agreed to. The individual's role is contracted for and evaluated in the routine teacher evaluation process. Methods for enhancing the skill level of the organization may include professional in-service training, team teaching, internships, remedial plans of development, individual guided education units, school visitations, outside instruction, and role modeling.

Once needs are identified, a positive environment established, and a plan designed and implemented, monitoring of the professional staff is recommended. Positive feedback to personnel regarding their teaching performance is essential for it identifies the organizational expectations. Monitoring/supervising can be the same activity. Being visible, asking curriculum-directed questions, acknowledging instructional changes, encouraging staff reviews and faculty support groups, organizing creative instructional changes, providing evaluative feedback, and holding teacher conferences are all supervisory techniques under the heading of monitoring. Classroom visitations are important to monitoring. These activities deliver a clear message of administrative interest. When these components are addressed, an environment of trust develops. The teaching staff becomes more accepting of staff development programs once positive staff development has occurred in the school among the staff.

Need identification, planning and implementation, support and monitoring are basic staff development and personal growth activities. Before the typical staff development plans are initiated, these components should be communicated to and experienced by the staff. Teaching personnel need to know their needs have been identified by the administra-

tion as part of the organization's requirements. They should realize that the administration wants to provide a supportive, positive, professional working environment and that a system of consistent, fair, sincere supervision/monitoring is in place. Before outside resources are brought to the organization, in-house staff development should be established on a continuing basis. Staff development strategies can fall on deaf ears unless teachers are in an accepting, creative, and productive atmosphere cultivated by involvement in the building's own program.

The administrator is the key person in preparing the staff for a resourceful plan, but only after the staff has been provided the opportunity for in-house planning and leadership. The assets of an organization, human and physical, must be known. A development system can allow for a committee of teachers to help decide in-service and other needs. As the human resources are assessed, staff should be placed in positions where personal/professional talents are best used. An extension of the effort can complete the plan for achievement of the overall objective of the organization.

ANN SABATINO
Hudson, Wisconsin

PERSONNEL TRAINING IN SPECIAL EDUCATION
SUPERVISION IN SPECIAL EDUCATION

STANDARD DEVIATION

The standard deviation is a measure of the dispersion of sample or population scores around the mean score. It is the most important and most widely used measure of dispersion for quantitative variables when the distribution is symmetric. We compute the standard deviation for a population of n scores by first averaging squared deviations of scores (X) from the mean population (m) using Equation 1:

$$\sigma^2 = \frac{\sum_{i=1}^{n}(X_i - \mu)^2}{n} \qquad (1)$$

This yields the variance of the scores, s^2. The square root of this value, s, is the population standard deviation. For a sample of n scores, the variance is computed using Equation 2:

$$s^2 = \frac{\sum_{i=1}^{n}(X_i - \overline{X})^2}{n-1}, \qquad (2)$$

where $\overline{X}$ is the mean sample score. Here we use ($n - 1$) as the divisor instead of n because this produces an unbiased sample estimate of σ^2. Dividing by n produces a biased estimate. The square root of this value, s, is the standard deviation of the scores in the sample (i.e., the average dispersion of the scores around the mean score).

This measure of dispersion is widely used in the behavioral sciences to describe the spread of scores around the mean score when the distribution of scores is normal. Then we can state the proportion of scores that fall above or below any given value or between any two values by first converting the value(s) to z-score units using

$$z_i = \frac{X_i - \overline{X}}{s} \text{ or } z_i = \frac{X_i - \mu}{\sigma} \qquad (3)$$

for a sample or population. For example, for a sample of scores with computed statistics $\overline{X} = 40$ and $s = 5$, the value $X_i = 50$ is two standard deviations above the mean. Thus, from a normal table, we find that 97.72 percent of the scores fall below 50 while 0.28 percent are larger than 50.

The size of the standard deviation also indicates the relative spread of two comparable distributions. For example, given that $s = 3$ for males and $s = 5$ for females on a given test, where the mean score, 15, is the same for either group, we can tell that the female scores span a wider range than the male scores, with 16 percent of the females scoring at least 20 while only 5 percent of the males obtain this score or higher.

In addition to describing a distribution of scores, the standard deviation is used widely in inferential statistics for describing the spread of the sampling distribution. For example, the standard deviation of the sampling distribution of the sample mean, $\overline{X}$, is given by $(\sigma/\sqrt{n})$ where s is defined in Equation 2. We may also obtain the standard deviation of the sample proportion, variance, correlation coefficient, or any other statistic. When so used, the standard deviation is called the standard error of estimate of the statistic. Further, in regression estimation procedures, the standard deviation of the errors of prediction is used to judge the precision of the predicted values. This measure is called the standard error of estimate of prediction. In measurement, we define the standard deviation of the errors of measurement, the standard error of measurement, and use it to infer the value of true scores (Hopkins & Stanley, 1981). Further information on the standard deviation is found in the following references.

REFERENCES

Glass, G. V., & Hopkins, K. D. (1984). *Statistical methods in education and psychology* (2nd ed.). Englewood Cliffs, NJ: Prentice Hall.

Hays, W. L. (1981). *Statistics* (3rd ed.). New York: Holt, Rinehart, & Winston.

Hopkins, K. D., & Stanley, J. C. (1981). *Educational and psychological measurement and evaluation* (6th ed.). Englewood Cliffs, NJ: Prentice Hall.

Kirk, R. E. (1984). *Elementary statistics* (2nd ed.). Monterey, CA: Brooks/Cole.

GWYNETH M. BOODOO
Texas A&M University

CENTRAL TENDENCY
NORMAL CURVE EQUIVALENT

STANDARDS FOR EDUCATIONAL AND PSYCHOLOGICAL TESTING

See CODE OF FAIR TESTING PRACTICES IN EDUCATION.

STANFORD-BINET INTELLIGENCE SCALE: FIFTH EDITION

The Stanford-Binet Intelligence Scale, Fifth Edition (SB5; Roid, 2003), is an individually administered test of cognitive abilities. The full scale IQ (FSIQ) is derived from the administration of 10 subtests (five verbal and five nonverbal). Subtests, including the two routing subtests, are designed to measure five factors: fluid reasoning, knowledge, quantitative reasoning, visual-spatial processing, and working memory. The first two subtests (contained in Item book 1) are routing subtests and are used to determine start points for the remaining nonverbal (Item book 2) and verbal (Item book 3) subtests. The two routing subtests contained in book 1 may also be used as a brief measure of intellectual ability. The SB5 also provides examiners the option of calculating change-sensitive scores (CSS)—a method of criteria-referenced rather than normative-referenced scoring—which avoids truncation at high and low ends, as well as an extended IQ (EXIQ)—a special-case application for evaluating subjects with extremely high (or low) IQs.

SB5 subtests are composed of testlets, brief mini-tests at each level (1 through 6) of difficulty. Testlets typically have either six items or a total of six points at each of the six ability levels for a given subtest.

The SB5 has a mean of 100 and a standard deviation of 15 (in contrast to the prior edition's standard deviation of 16). Individual subtests are now scaled with a mean of 10 and a standard deviation of 3.

The SB5 was standardized on a sample of 4,800 individuals. Each of the early years (ages 2 through 4) was divided into half-year groupings (doubling the sample size at that age period) to account for the instability and rapid cognitive change of the very youngest age group. Norm group individuals were stratified according to race/ethnicity, sex, parental education level, and geographic region.

The technical manual provides strong evidence for reliability and validity. Average internal consistency reliabilities were in the .90s for all scales and indexes, while the individual subtest reliabilities were all in the .80s. Concurrent validity evidence is strong.

The SB5 has an initially steep administration learning curve. While the materials at the lower levels are very child friendly, examiners may consider some difficult to manipulate and administer. Test administration sequence follows the examinee's ability level across all subtests. Testlets, starting at a particular ability level, are administered for individual subtests. If an examinee does not obtain a specified basal score for any subtest, the examiner immediately drops back one ability level and administers the specific testlet until a basal is reached.

Scoring of the SB5 test items is relatively easy and consistent with the scoring criteria of other standardized intelligence measures.

REFERENCE

SB5 Assessment Service Bulletin #3: Use of the Stanford-Binet Intelligence Scales, Fifth Edition in the Assessment of High Abilities. Chicago: Riverside Publishing.

RON DUMONT
Fairleigh Dickinson University

JOHN O. WILLIS
Rivier College

STANFORD DIAGNOSTIC MATHEMATICS TEST–FOURTH EDITION (SDMT4)

The Stanford Diagnostic Mathematics Test–Fourth Edition (SDMT4; 1996) is designed to measure which areas of mathematics are of specific difficulty to a student. The test is intended to be used for diagnostic purposes as well as to help create appropriate intervention. The test may be administered from grade 1 through community college. Two response formats are provided: multiple choice and free response. A group or individual format may be used in administration.

The content of the items varies across the various age levels. For example, for grades 6 and 7, numeration, graphs and tables, statistics and probability, and geometry are included in the Concepts section. For the Computation section at this level, addition and subtraction of whole numbers, multiplication facts and operations, and division facts and operations are included. Norm-referenced (scaled scores and percentile ranks) and criterion-referenced scores (cut scores) are provided.

The standardization sample of the SDMT4 involved over 40,000 students that were representative of the U.S. school population. Internal reliability coefficients were generally above .80, and interrater reliability for the free-response items is very good (above .95). Evidence for validity was provided by correlations with the Otis-Lennon School Ability test, with correlations among the two instruments in the .60s and .70s.

Generally, the SDMT4 has been favorably reviewed (e.g., Lehmann, 1998; Poteat, 1998). It provides much detail in terms of diagnostic information. The psychometric qualities are strong, and lead to obtained scores that are reliable and valid. The SDMT4 is not useful for simply obtaining achievement test norms. It also does not provide information about algebraic operations. It is best used for assessing students that are below average, rather than those that are at or above average functioning.

REFERENCES

Lehmann, I. J. (1998). Review of the Stanford Diagnostic Mathematics Test, Fourth Edition. In J. C. Impara & B. S. Plake (Eds.), *The thirteenth mental measurements yearbook* (pp. 932–936). Lincoln, NE: Buros Institute of Mental Measurements.

Poteat, G. M. (1998). Review of the Stanford Diagnostic Mathematics Test, Fourth Edition. In J. C. Impara & B. S. Plake (Eds.), *The thirteenth mental measurements yearbook* (pp. 937–938). Lincoln, NE: Buros Institute of Mental Measurements.

Stanford Diagnostic Mathematics Test–Fourth Edition. (1996). Cleveland, OH: Harcourt Brace Jovanovich.

ELIZABETH O. LICHTENBERGER
The Salk Institute

MATHEMATICS, LEARNING DISABILITIES AND

STANFORD DIAGNOSTIC READING TEST–FOURTH EDITION

The Standford Diagnostic Reading Test–Fourth Edition (SDRT4; Karlsen & Gardner, 1996) is intended to diagnose students' strengths and weaknesses in the major components of the reading process. There are several components that are specifically assessed: Phonetic Analysis, Vocabulary, Comprehension, and Scanning. The SDRT4 may be administered in a group or individual format. Students may be assessed with the SDRT4 from the end of grade 1 through the first semester of college. In addition to assessment of reading, the SDRT4 may be used to develop strategies for teaching reading or may be used to challenge students who are doing well.

The SDRT4 is a diagnostic test, not an achievement test, and as such it provides more detailed coverage of reading skills and places a greater emphasis on measuring the skills of low achieving students. Both norm-referenced and criterion-referenced information is available on reading skills. The normative sample was based on data collected from approximately 53,000 examinees from 1994 to 1995. The sample was found to closely match the total U.S. school enrollment statistics. The criterion-referenced scores include raw scores and Progress Indicator Cut scores. Process Indicator Cut Scores are used to classify students that have demonstrated their competence in specific areas of reading. However, Engelhard (1998) notes that these scores should be used with great caution because insufficient detail is provided on how the cut scores were set and by whom. Engelhard (1998) evaluated the reliability statistics in the SDRT4 manual and found that the use of the shorter subtests for the diagnosis of an individual's strengths and weaknesses is not recommended. No evidence for stability of scores over time is provided.

Overall, the SDRT4 is found to be a sound measure of reading. It provides adequate traditional psychometric information, clear administration directions, and scoring strategies. Teaching suggestions are also described, but the base of the interventions is not clear. Interpretation and intervention based on the SDRT4 should be done by those with specialized knowledge in clinical practices in reading.

REFERENCES

Engelhard, G. (1998). Review of the Stanford Diagnostic Reading Test, Fourth Edition. In J. C. Impara & B. S. Plake (Eds.), *The thirteenth mental measurements yearbook* (pp. 939–941). Lincoln, NE: Buros Institute of Mental Measurements.

Karlsen, B., & Gardner, E. F. (1996). *Stanford Diagnostic Reading Test–Fourth Edition.* Cleveland, OH: Harcourt Brace Jovanovich.

ELIZABETH O. LICHTENBERGER
The Salk Institute

READING

STANLEY, JULIAN C. (1918–2005)

Julian C. Stanley received his BS (1937) from what is now Georgia State University and his EdM (1946) and EdD (1950) in experimental educational psychology from Harvard University. Stanley was widely known for his work in test theory, experimental design (Campbell & Stanley, 1963), and statistics, but he was perhaps best known for his study of gifted students. From 1971, he was the director of the Study of Mathematically Precocious Youth (SMPY) and professor of psychology at Johns Hopkins University.

Stanley's interest in the intellectually talented began in 1938, a year after he became a high school science teacher while enrolled in a tests and measurements course at the University of Georgia. He pursued his career as a research

Julian C. Stanley

methodologist in education and psychology until a grant from the Spencer Foundation enabled him to create SMPY at Johns Hopkins in 1974 (Benbow & Stanley, 1983; Stanley, Keating, & Fox, 1974; Stanley, 1997).

The goals of SMPY include identifying mathematically able youngsters and enabling them to learn mathematics and related subjects faster and better than they might in the usual school curriculum. Some young people who participate in SMPY score a minimum of 700 before the age of 13 on the mathematics portion of the Scholastic Aptitude Test, a score achieved by only about 1 in 10,000 youngsters of their age group. The talent-search concept, covering the entire United States, is conducted at the Institute for the Academic Advancement of Youth (IAAY) at Johns Hopkins and in programs at Duke University, the University of Denver, and the University of Washington.

Known nationally and internationally, Stanley was a Fulbright research scholar at the University of Louvain (1958–1959) and a Fulbright-Hays lecturer in Australia and New Zealand (1974). He served as president of the American Educational Research Association (AERA) from 1965 to 1966, and was the recipient of numerous awards, including the AERA Award for Distinguished Contributions to Research in Education (1980).

REFERENCES

Benbow, C. P., & Stanley, J. C. (1983). *Academic precocity: Aspects of its development.* Baltimore: Johns Hopkins University.

Campbell, D. T., & Stanley, J. C. (1963). Experimental and quasi-experimental designs for research on teaching. In N. L. Gage (Ed.), *Handbook of research on teaching* (pp. 171–246). Chicago: Rand McNally.

Stanley, J. C. (1997). Varieties of intellectual talent. *Journal of Creative Behavior, 31,* 93–130.

Stanley, J. C., Keating, D. P., & Fox, L. H. (1974). *Mathematical talent: Discovery, description, and development*. Baltimore: Johns Hopkins University.

ANN E. LUPKOWSKI
Texas A&M University
First edition

TAMARA J. MARTIN
The University of Texas of the Permian Basin
Second and Third editions

STUDY OF MATHEMATICALLY PRECOCIOUS YOUTH

STEINART'S DISEASE (MYOTONIC DYSTROPHY)

Steinart's disease (myotonic dystrophy) appears to be caused by an autosomal dominant characteristic that results in varying degrees of mental retardation, poor muscle development, bilateral facial paralysis, and general muscular wasting. Overt myotonic dystrophy does not usually occur in early infancy. Most often, it manifests itself in late childhood or adolescence. Many children display behavioral characteristics of suspiciousness and moroseness and are asocial and submissive in treatment needs. Mental retardation is often present; although it may vary from mild to severe, it tends to be severe, particularly with early onset of the disease (Carter, 1978).

The older toddler or young child with myotonic dystrophy may have muscular weakness and wasting with psychomotor delay, drooping eyelids, and an open, drooling mouth. Cataracts are present in most individuals. High-arched palates and weak tongues are seen, as is an open, drooling mouth, even in older children. Children often have difficulty in feeding and swallowing. Abnormal curvature of the neck and back is seen. Atrophy of the extremities is often seen and clubfoot may be present. Premature baldness is also seen. Hypogonadism causes premature loss of libido or impotence in affected males. Nasal speech and articulation problems are common, as are vision problems associated with cataracts. Diabetes, heart arrhythmias, and cardiac abnormalities may be present, as well as increased incidence of diabetes mellitus (Lemeshaw, 1982).

Educational planning will often include categorical placement in classes for students with mild mental retardation; however, this disorder may not manifest itself until much later in life but then will remain constant (Tuikka, Laaksonen, & Somer, 1993). For this reason, educational placement will vary with the individual. Health problems may affect education and physical education programs. Speech services will commonly be needed, as will vision services. Orthopedic defects will often necessitate physical and occupational therapy as well as specialized adaptive educational materials. With young children having swallowing and feeding problems, an aide may be required.

REFERENCES

Carter, C. (Ed.). (1978). *Medical aspects of mental retardation*. (2nd. ed.). Springfield, IL: Thomas.

Lemeshaw, S. (1982). *The handbook of clinical types in mental retardation*. Boston: Houghton Mifflin.

Menolascino, F., & Egger, M. (1978). *Medical dimensions of mental retardation*. Lincoln: University of Nebraska Press.

Tuikka, R. A., Laaksonen, R. K., & Somer, H. V. K. (1993). Cognitive function in myotonic dystrophy: A follow-up study. *European Neurology, 33*(6), 436–441.

SALLY L. FLAGLER
University of Oklahoma

DIABETES
MENTAL RETARDATION
MUSCULAR DYSTROPHY

STEREOTYPIC BEHAVIORS

Stereotypic behaviors are variously defined in the literature. Terms are used to describe animal as well as human behaviors in developmental stages and in some abnormal or pathological situations (Berkson, 1983). Stereotyped behaviors are highly persistent and repetitious motor or posturing behaviors that seem to have little or no functional significance (Baumeister & Forehand, 1973). They are rhythmic movements that are coordinated and apparently intentional. They are repeated in the same fashion for long periods, often an hour or more at a time (Mitchell & Etches, 1977). Stereotyped movements are voluntary, brief, or prolonged habits or mannerisms that often are experienced as pleasurable (American Psychiatric Association, 1994). Stereotypic behaviors result from conditioning (in some form) and appear to be related to the achievement of homeostasis (Nijhof, Joha, & Pekelharing, 1998). Sometimes present in children of normal intelligence, they are most common among individuals with mental retardation or autism. The stereotyped behaviors, mainly seen in infancy and early childhood, may persist into adolescent and adult life, especially in institutionalized retarded persons.

The most typical movements are head rolling, head banging, and body rocking. Other rhythmic repetitive movements have been described as foot kicking, hand shaking, hand rotation, finger and toe sucking, lip biting, and tooth grinding. Nail biting is frequently associated with emotionally disturbed children. According to Sallustro and Atwell (1978) and Mitchell and Etches (1977), head rolling from side to side on the pillow occurs mainly before the infant falls asleep, but it also may be seen during sleep and while awake; it is usually encountered in early infancy up to the first 2 to 3 years of life. Head banging, seen more often in the sitting position but sometimes on hands and knees or even standing, typically starts toward the end of the first year. It sometimes follows head rolling and ceases before the age of 4 years. The child repeatedly and monotonously bangs the head against the pillow or the bars of the cot, and sometimes against a wall or the floor. This generally occurs before sleep, but it may be seen at any time of the day or night, may continue for an hour or longer, and may alternate with other rhythmic movements. Body rocking, the most frequent stereotyped behavior, is a slow, rhythmical backward and forward swaying of the trunk, usually while in the sitting position, beginning in the first year of life (Sallustro & Atwell, 1978). It can persist in normal children, but it is very common in children and adults with Down syndrome or other types of mental handicaps.

Various theories and opinions are presented in the literature regarding the origin, the mechanisms, and the significance of repetitive stereotyped behaviors. Rhythmicity is a characteristic and fundamental attribute of all life. Thelen (1979) showed in her studies of the development of normal infants during their first year of life that groups of stereotypies involving particular parts of the body or postures have characteristic ages of onset and peak performance and decline, and are highly correlated with motor development. As maturation enlarges processing capacity, repetitive behaviors are normally inhibited or incorporated into more complex behavior patterns. For many authors, the stereotypic behaviors represent a developmental disorder, as they are already seen in normal infants in relation to motor growth and maturity but they remain longer in the repertoire and persist into adolescent and adult life in mentally defective individuals. Their maintenance in some normal children might be due to personal or familial predisposition to rhythmic patterns, as head rolling and body rocking sometimes are present in one of the parents and are more frequent among other members of the family. However, the transformation of natural repetitive movements into pathological stereotypies is not clearly understood.

Many other authors believe that the movements are deliberate and purposeful, pleasurable, and self-stimulatory in character (Berkson, 1983), and that they supply compensatory satisfaction by relief of sensory monotony, body tension, discomfort, apprehension, frustration, anger, or boredom. None of the hypotheses presented explain why some of the stereotypies, like head banging and biting, are self-injurious and dangerous to the individual's well-being, while others are not (e.g., head rolling, body rocking, complex hand and finger movements).

The true significance of these movements is still unknown as to their anatomical and functional levels. Their high frequency among severely mentally disabled children suggests the failed development of cortical control and that most of these movements are probably infracortical in origin. The element of volition appears to indicate participation of the cerebral cortex in their initiation and maintenance. La Grow and Repp (1984) have reviewed various treatments and strategies used to suppress the stereotyped patterns from the behavior repertoire.

REFERENCES

American Psychiatric Association. (1994). *Diagnostic and statistical manual of mental disorders* (4th ed.). Washington, DC: Author.

Baumeister, A. A., & Forehand, R. (1973). Stereotyped acts. In N. R. Ellis (Ed.), *International review of research in mental retardation* (Vol. 6, pp. 55–96). New York: Academic.

Berkson, G. (1983). Repetitive stereotyped behaviors. *American Journal of Mental Deficiency, 88,* 239–246.

La Grow, S. J., & Repp, A. C. (1984). Stereotypic responding: A review of intervention research. *American Journal of Mental Deficiency, 88,* 595–609.

Mitchell, R. G., & Etches, P. (1977). Rhythmic habit patterns (stereotypies). *Developmental Medicine and Child Neurology, 19,* 545–550.

Nijhof, G., Joha, D., & Pekelharing, H. (1998). Aspects of stereotypic behavior among autistic persons: A study of the literature. *British Journal of Developmental Disabilities, 44*(86) 3–13.

Sallustro, F., & Atwell, C. W. (1978). Body rocking, head banging, and head rolling in normal children. *Journal of Pediatrics, 93,* 704–708.

Thelen, E. (1979). Rhythmical stereotypies in normal human infants. *Animal Behavior, 27,* 699–715.

HENRI B. SZLIWOWSKI
*Hôpital Erasme, Université
Libre de Bruxelles, Belgium*

JEANNIE BORMANS
*Center for Developmental
Problems, Brussels, Belgium*

AUTISM
MENTAL RETARDATION
SELF-INJURIOUS BEHAVIOR
SELF-STIMULATION

STEREOTYPISM

People generally are classified and fit into molds or groups that have certain attributable characteristics. With individuals with disabilities, the characteristics especially focused on are disabilities rather than abilities. Labeling an individual or fitting a person into a specific handicapped group or category according to certain characteristics has a few advantages and many disadvantages. The traditional handicapping labels are basically used to explain a medical problem or to aid in educational intervention, but the result generally is stereotyping of individuals, which may lead to misleading and inhumane side effects.

Throughout history, we can see that the treatment and attitudes toward those persons classified as different or abnormal have slowly changed (Kirk, 1972). Frampton and Gall (1955) recognized three stages: pre-Christianity, when individuals with disabilities were mistreated, neglected, or killed; the Christian era, when they were pitied and protected; and the present era. In recent years, individuals with disabilities are being accepted, educated, and integrated more and more into society.

During the early years (before present enlightenment), terms such as *idiot, mad, crazy, moron,* and *imbecile* were used to describe people who differed from the norm (Snell, 1978). These terms carried negative connotations and caused great misconceptions of what disabled individuals are really like. People were actually afraid of these individuals because of the mystery surrounding their disabilities. The fear was due partly to lack of knowledge about the causes of these deviations and partly to lack of exposure to individuals with these characteristics. At first, the disabled were put away in institutions, basements, or closets. Later, they were allowed to be kept in homes but away from schools. Even when education programs became prominent, the special education classrooms were in environments different from other children's. The first special education classrooms in regular schools were in the basement or away from the regular students.

Today, misconceptions arise from stereotyping individuals with disabilties. Although many visually handicapped individuals have no mental retardation, the term *visually handicapped* often carries the connotation that these individuals are physically disabled and severely mentally deficient (Hollinger & Jones, 1970). Goffman (1963) and Edgerton (1967) write extensively of the negative stereotypes and stigmata associated with the mentally retarded. People with cerebral palsy may have an IQ of average or above average, but their physical rigidity and slurred speech often make people talk to them as if they were unable to understand. The hearing impaired have fought against the stereotype of being deaf and dumb. People interacting with blind individuals believe they have to talk loudly in order to be heard. Learning-disabled students and students with attentional problems (Cornett-Ruiz & Hendricks, 1993) are frequently associated with the retarded even though their mental capacities are generally average or above. The emotionally disturbed are thought to be crazy or mad.

The misconceptions have caused many sociological, economic, and other types of barricades for the disabled. These individuals have been denied access to a life that is as normal as possible, not only in the physical environment but also in the social environment. Many individuals with disabilities are still isolated, laughed at, and criticized. Their problems may be increased because of added emotional stress.

We have come a long way toward bringing positive images of individuals with disabilities to the fore. The Special Olympics, media reports of accomplishments of individuals physically or mentally disabled, and improved school programs have helped to eliminate some barriers. Making the public more knowledgeable about definitions of handicapping terminology has improved public opinion. Movies or television shows about deformed or retarded individuals have switched to positive and inspiring messages. As the exceptional person becomes more prevalent in restaurants, stores, schools, and so on, the public becomes educated.

A reversal of roles would be an ideal way for the general public to learn about and relate to individuals with handicapping conditions. Spending a few hours in a wheelchair, with a blindfold on, or with mittens on, would help one to see what it is like to be disabled. It would be important for one to experience the difficulties of having the disability and to feel the stares and other negative attitudes of those more fortunate.

School intervention has changed greatly for the better. Education programs are now a great source for informing the public. Mainstreaming has helped regular classroom students to better understand special education students; mainstreaming has also helped special education students to develop feelings of belonging and self-worth. Exposure to the regular classroom student has given the special education student a model from which to learn.

If less negative labels were used, and if the educational programs were fit to the disabled individual's needs, there would be less stereotyping (Reger, Schroeder, & Uschold, 1968). It is hoped that as the positive trends continue to grow, the stigma will be replaced with understanding and acceptance.

REFERENCES

Cornett-Ruiz, S., & Hendricks, B. (1993). Effects of labeling and ADHD behaviors on peer and teacher judgments. *Journal of Educational Research, 86*(6), 349–355.

Frampton, M. E., & Gall E. D. (1955). *Special education for the exceptional.* Boston, MA: Porter Sargent.

Goffman, E. (1963). *Notes on the measurement of spoiled identity.* Englewood Cliffs, NJ: Prentice Hall.

Hollinger, C. S., & Jones, R. L. (1970). Community attitudes toward slow learners and mental retardates: What's in a name? *Mental Retardation, 8,* 19–13.

Kirk, S. A. (1972). *Educating exceptional children.* Boston: Houghton-Mifflin.

Reger, R., Schroeder, W., & Uschold, K. (1968). *Special education children with learning problems.* New York: Oxford University Press.

Snell, M. E. (1978). *Systematic instruction of the moderately and severely handicapped.* Columbus, OH: Merrill.

DONNA FILIPS
Steger, Illinois

HISTORY OF SPECIAL EDUCATION

STERN, WILLIAM (1871–1938)

William Stern, German psychologist and pioneer in the psychology of individual differences, introduced the concept of the intelligence quotient in 1912. This quotient, used to express performance on intelligence tests, is found by dividing the subject's mental age as determined by the test performance by the chronological age and multiplying by 100. In the United States, the intelligence quotient, or IQ, was used by Lewis M. Terman in his 1916 Stanford Revision of the Binet Scales.

REFERENCES

Murchison, C. (Ed.). (1961). *A history of psychology in autobiography*. New York: Russell & Russell.

Stern, W. (1914). *The psychological methods of intelligence testing*. Baltimore: Warwick & York.

PAUL IRVINE
Katonah, New York

STIGMATIZATION

See LABELING.

STIMULANT DRUGS

Stimulant drugs are a commonly used class of medications for the treatment of inattention, impulsivity, and restlessness in school-age children and adolescents, and, less often, for the treatment of narcolepsy and drowsiness or disorders of arousal in the elderly. Children and adolescents having an attention-deficit disorder (American Psychiatric Association, 1994) are the ones most often given these medications because of the significant effects of the drugs on sustained attention. In fact, stimulants are the most commonly prescribed psychotropic medications in child psychiatry (Wilens & Biederman, 1992). The drugs are so named because of their stimulation of increased central nervous system activity, presumably by way of their effects on dopamine and norepinephrine production, and reuptake at the synaptic level of neuronal functioning (Cantwell & Carlson, 1978). The drugs may also have effects on other central neurotransmitters as well as on peripheral nervous system activity. The changes in central neurotransmitter activity result in increased alertness, arousal, concentration, and vigilance or sustained attention, as well as reductions in impulsive behavior and activity or restlessness that is irrelevant to particular tasks (Barkley, 1977, 1981). While a number of substances such as caffeine fall into this class of medications, those most typically used with children and adolescents are methylphenidate (Ritalin), d-amphetamine (Dexedrine), a mixture of dextroamphetamine and racemic amphetamine salts (Adderall; Popper, 1994) and pemoline (Cylert). Despite similar behavioral effects and side effects, the mechanism of action of each of these stimulants is somewhat different, and that for pemoline is not well specified.

The stimulants are relatively rapid in their initiation of behavioral changes and in the time course over which such changes are maintained. Most stimulant drugs, taken orally, are quickly absorbed into the bloodstream through the stomach and small intestine and pass readily across the blood-brain barrier to affect neuronal activity. Behavioral changes can be detected within 30 to 60 minutes after ingestion and may last between 3 and 8 hours, depending on the type of stimulant and preparation (regular or sustained release) employed. Traces of medication and their metabolites in blood and urine can be detected up to 24 hours after ingestion, perhaps corresponding to the clinical observation of persisting side effects after the desired behavioral effects are no longer noticeable.

Approximately 70 percent or more of children over 5 years of age, adolescents, and young adults display a positive behavioral response to the stimulants. Children below age 3 are much less likely to respond well to medication, and the drugs have not been approved by the Food and Drug Administration for children younger than 6 years. The best predictor of a positive response is the degree of inattention before treatment, while that for a poor response is the presence and severity of pretreatment anxiety and emotional disturbance (Barkley, 1976; Loney, 1986; Taylor, 1983).

The medications are taken one to three times per day, with some children taking them only on school days while others remain on medication throughout the week. Medication is often discontinued during summer vacations from school to permit a rebound in appetite and growth, which may have been mildly suppressed during treatment. Children having more severe, pervasive developmental disorders such as autism or severe behavioral disorders, however, may remain on medication throughout the year (Aman, 1996). The average length of treatment with stimulants is typically 3 to 5 years, but this may increase in the future because of reports of equally positive effects with adolescents and young adults having significant inattention, impulsivity, and restlessness (Woods, 1986).

The most commonly experienced side effects are diminished appetite, particularly for the noon meal, and insomnia, although these are often mild, diminish within several weeks of treatment onset, and are easily managed by reductions in dose where problematic. Increases in blood pressure, heart rate, and respiration may occur, but they are typically of little consequence (Hastings & Barkley, 1978). Other side effects of lesser frequency are sleeplessness (Day & Abmayr, 1998); irritability, sadness or dysphoria; and proneness to crying, especially during late afternoons, when the medication is "washing out" of the body (Cantwell & Carlson, 1978). Some children experience heightened activity levels during this washout phase. Headaches and stomachaches are infrequently noted and, like all side effects, appear to be dose related. Temporary suppression of growth in height and weight may be noted in some children during the first 1 to 2 years of treatment with stimulants, but there appear to be few lasting effects on eventual adult stature. Between 1 and 2 percent of children and adolescents may experience nervous tics while on stimulant medication, but these diminish in the majority of cases with reduction in dose or discontinuation of medication. A few cases of Tourette syndrome (multiple motor tics, vocal tics, and, in some cases, increased utterance of profanities) have been reported after initiation of stimulant medication (Barkley, 1987). Children with a personal or family history of motor/vocal tics should use these drugs only with caution because of the possible emergence or exacerbation of their tic conditions, observed in more than 50 percent of such children.

The medications appear to improve fine motor agility, planning, and execution, as well as reaction time, speech articulation (in children having mild delays in fine motor control of speech), and handwriting, in some children. Increases in academic productivity, short-term memory, simple verbal learning, and drawing and copying skills frequently are noted, but little, if any, change is seen on tests of intelligence, academic achievement, or other complex cognitive processes (Barkley, 1977). Despite generally positive behavioral improvements in most children with attention-deficit/hyperactivity disorder taking stimulants, these drugs have shown little, if any, significant, lasting effect on the long-term outcome of such children in late adolescence or young adulthood once medication has been discontinued.

REFERENCES

Aman, M. G. (1996). Stimulant drugs in the developmental disabilities revisited. *Journal of Developmental & Physical Disabilities, 8*(4), 347–365.

American Psychiatric Association. (1994). *Diagnostic and statistical manual of mental disorders* (4th ed.). Washington, DC: Author.

Barkley, R. (1976). Predicting the response of hyperactive children to stimulant drugs: A review. *Journal of Abnormal Child Psychology, 4*, 327–348.

Barkley, R. (1977). A review of stimulant drug research with hyperactive children. *Journal of Child Psychology & Psychiatry, 18*, 137–165.

Barkley, R. A. (1981). *Hyperactive children: A handbook for diagnosis and treatment.* New York: Guilford.

Barkley, R. A. (1987). Tic disorders and Tourette's syndrome. In E. Mash & L. Terdal (Eds.), *Behavioral assessment of childhood disorders* (2nd ed.). New York: Guilford.

Cantwell, D., & Carlson, G. (1978). Stimulants. In J. Werry (Ed.), *Pediatric psychopharmacology.* New York: Brunner/Mazel.

Day, H. D., & Abmayr, S. B. (1998). Parent reports of sleep disturbances in stimulant-medicated children with attention-deficit/hyperactivity disorder. *Journal of Clinical Psychology, 54*(5), 701–716.

Hastings, J., & Barkley, R. (1978). A review of psychophysiological research with hyperactive children. *Journal of Abnormal Child Psychology, 7*, 413–447.

Loney, J. (1986). Predicting stimulant drug response among hyperactive children. *Psychiatric Annals, 16*, 16–22.

Popper, C. W. (1994). The story of four salts. *Journal of Child & Adolescent Psychopharmacology, 4*(4), 217–223.

Taylor, E. (1983). Drug response and diagnostic validation. In M. Rutter (Ed.), *Developmental neuropsychiatry* (pp. 348–368). New York: Guilford.

Wilens, T. E., & Biederman, J. (1992). The stimulants. *Psychiatric Clinics of North America, 15*(1), 191–222.

Woods, D. (1986). The diagnosis and treatment of attention deficit disorder, residual type. *Psychiatric Annals, 16*, 23–28.

RUSSELL A. BARKLEY
University of Massachusetts
Medical Center

ATTENTION-DEFICIT/HYPERACTIVITY DISORDER
DOPAMINE
RITALIN
TOURETTE SYNDROME

STIMULUS CONTROL

When an event, such as the ring of an alarm clock or the smell of smoke, is observed to increase the probability of a behavior—rising from bed or checking the stovetop—the response is said to be under stimulus control of the antecedent stimulus. Such responsiveness to subtle cues in the environment is imperative for survival. Stopping at red lights, selecting clothing appropriate to the weather, and entering the correct restroom in public buildings require that behavior be sensitive to the surrounding environment. Many of the responses critical to personal and social success are learned by observing parents or other students in school, but when relevant behaviors have not yet been learned, they cannot be effectively influenced by cues in the environment. Teaching such behaviors involves manipulating social and physical contexts to increase successful behavior and make unwanted behavior less likely.

B. F. Skinner suggested that stimuli that immediately precede a response and are present during reinforcement acquire control over the future occurrence of the response. His laboratory experiments demonstrated that specific physical properties of the environment, such as the intensity of light or the pitch of sound, became predictive of certain outcomes for responding, and responding then followed the presentation of those particular stimuli. Skinner highlighted two processes through which stimuli acquire control over behavior: induction and discrimination (Skinner, 1953). When induction occurs, other stimuli present during the reinforcement acquire control over behavior. This is frequently referred to as stimulus generalization, and it is important to survival. Stopping should occur, for example, at street lights that are bright red, dull red, attached to a yellow signpost, or attached to a chrome installment. Discrimination may be said to be the opposite process, where a learner's behavior comes under the control of sharply defined gradients. A child learns to call his father, who has a beard, "Daddy," but soon learns that not all men with beards should be addressed in the same manner.

Generalization and discrimination work together in the formation of concepts, or stimulus classes (Keller & Schoenfeld, 1950). A child learns that apples are red and later that a red ball is not an apple. To teach the concept of redness, a teacher may position a red and a green apple beside one another and ask the child to point to the red apple. The teacher would reinforce only the correct response. Several examples, followed by trials in which yellow and red apples are presented side by side, lead to discrimination. Next, the teacher may show the child many dissimilar objects that are red, such as fire trucks, pillows, and stoplights. The different stimulus properties of these items help to generalize the concept of redness and form a stimulus class for the set of stimuli with common characteristics.

Behavior may be influenced by stimuli that immediately precede reinforced responses, or by contextual variables that alter the value of reinforcers. Changes in the environment that alter the momentary effectiveness of a reinforcer and simultaneously alter the probable frequency of behavior that has preceded the reinforcement are referred to as motivating operations (MOs; Laraway, Snycerski, Michael, & Poling, 2003). When a child has not seen his schoolmates all weekend, the consequence of having time to chat with friends reinforces getting to school early. Not seeing friends all weekend is an MO that has an establishing effect on the reinforcing value of promptly getting to school. Correspondingly, having a headache has an abolishing effect on the reinforcing qualities of social interaction. An effective arrangement of MOs to facilitate learning in the classroom could, for example, involve teaching a child with autism new words 1 hour before lunch with carrot slices offered to reinforce appropriate responses. Skillful assessment of MOs that are present in a learner's life, such as not having gotten enough sleep or having eaten too much lunch, makes acquiring stimulus control by the arrangement of social and physical characteristics of the environment a matter of practice based on evidence rather than routine.

Several strategies for presenting cues and contexts to increase learning have been empirically validated. Presenting or removing environmental prompts that have stimulus control over desired behavior is one noted strategy. O'Neill, Blanck, and Joyner (1980) altered the physical appearance of trash cans at a university stadium to increase their use by fans. A lid resembling a baseball cap placed over the cans that, when lifted, exposed the word "Thanks" was demonstrated to be twice as effective as the unmodified cans. Motivating operations can be arranged so that desirable behaviors are more reinforcing. Researchers who found that hard academic tasks were an MO for aggressive behavior during the following recess period broke academic tasks into smaller chunks and interspersed easier tasks with more difficult ones to decrease problem behaviors (Horner, Day, Sprague, O'Brien, & Heathfield, 1991). Altering the effort required for engaging in targeted activities is another noted strategy. Vollmer, Marcus, and Ringdahl (1995) discussed two boys whose self-injurious behaviors resulted in escape from demanding tasks. When the boys were given the opportunity to take frequent breaks they were more cooperative during activities than when they were asked to remain on task. Inversely, a person with disabilities who engaged in disruptive behaviors while working at a supermarket was given a magazine to look at. The magazine diverted the worker's attention from stimuli that had previously occasioned disruptive behavior, and because it occupied his hands, disruptive behavior became more difficult to engage in (Kemp & Carr, 1995).

Stimulus control is a central aspect of learning that can be facilitated by careful attention to physical and social aspects of the environment. Arranging antecedents that augment generalization, discrimination, and concept formation sets the occasion for a learner to use relevant social behaviors. Making use of MOs such as meal schedules and socialization patterns creates the context in which learning is most likely to occur. Assessing situations that cannot be altered and making environmental accommodations makes engaging in maladaptive behaviors unnecessary. Such procedures for presenting cues and contexts that acquire stimulus control over behavior are well established and empirically validated practices that aid learners in developing skills crucial for success.

REFERENCES

Horner, R. H., Day, H. M., Sprague, J. R., O'Brien, M., & Heathfield, L. T. (1991). Interspersed requests: A non-aversive procedure for reducing aggression and self-injury during instruction. *Journal of Applied Behavior Analysis, 24,* 265–278.

Keller, F. S., & Schoenfeld, W. N. (1950). *Principles of psychology.* New York: Appleton-Century-Crofts.

Kemp, D. C., & Carr, E. G. (1995). Reduction of severe problem behavior in community employment using an hypothesis-driven multicomponent intervention approach. *Journal of the Association for Persons with Severe Handicaps, 20,* 229–247.

Laraway, S., Snycerski, S., Michael, J., & Poling, A. (2003). Motivating operations and terms to describe them: Some further refinements. *Journal of Applied Behavior Analysis, 36,* 407–414.

O'Neill, G. W., Blanck, L. S., & Joyner, M. A. (1980). The use of stimulus control over littering in a natural setting. *Journal of Applied Behavior Analysis, 13,* 370–381.

Skinner, B. F. (1953). *Science and human behavior.* New York: Free Press.

Vollmer, T. R., Marcus, B. A., & Ringdahl, J. E. (1995). Non-contingent escape as treatment for self-injurious behavior maintained by negative reinforcement. *Journal of Applied Behavior Analysis, 28,* 15–26.

THOMAS G. SZABO
Western Michigan University

STIMULUS DEPRIVATION

Stimulus deprivation refers to an increase in reinforcer effectiveness that occurs following a reduction in the availability of or access to that reinforcing event. The effectiveness of reinforcers, especially of primary reinforcers such as food, depends greatly on the deprivation state of the individual. Using edible reinforcers with a student who has just returned from lunch probably will not be as effective as using the same reinforcers immediately prior to lunch, when the student is more likely to be in a state of deprivation for food. Most stimulus events serve as effective reinforcers only if the individual has been deprived of them for a period of time prior to their use. In general, the longer the deprivation period, the more effective the reinforcer (Martin & Pear, 1983).

The magnitude or amount of a reinforcer required to change behavior is less when the individual is partially deprived of the event (Kazdin, 1980). For example, students who are temporarily deprived of teacher attention may require less attention to maintain behavior than students who have frequent access to teacher attention. If a potential reinforcer is provided in limited quantities, thus creating a partial state of deprivation, that event is more likely to maintain its effectiveness as a reinforcer.

A state of deprivation may be created intentionally by the educator to increase the value of reinforcing events. This procedure is especially valuable with events that previously were effective reinforcers but temporarily show a satiation effect. Using the principle of deprivation, the reinforcer is withheld or reduced in availability for a period of time as a means of increasing the state of deprivation. If free time, listening to music, or a particular edible item shows satiation effects, the teacher may wish to reduce or remove it for a period of time. As students become deprived, the reinforcer can once again be introduced with increased effectiveness.

Ethical and legal issues should be considered prior to use of a deprivation procedure. Major objections typically focus on deprivation of essential primary reinforcers (e.g., food, water, shelter, human contact) on the basis that it constitutes a violation of basic human rights. As noted by Kazdin (1980), however, deprivation is a natural part of human existence. All people are, in some ways, deprived by society of self-expression in such areas as free speech and sexual behavior. Certainly, special education students who demonstrate academic and behavioral difficulties frequently are deprived of access to employment or other economic opportunities as a result of their characteristics. Thus the negative effects of social deprivation that special education students normally experience as a result of their deficits must be weighed against any temporary negative effects associated with stimulus deprivation used as a treatment strategy (Baer, 1970). A decision to use deprivation, or any other aversive technique, requires careful consideration of the kind of deprivation, the duration of the program, the availability of alternative treatment strategies, and the demonstrable benefits resulting from its use (Kazdin, 1980). As a precautionary measure when using a deprivation procedure, an individual should never be completely deprived of the reinforcing event for a lengthy period of time.

Fortunately, intentional deprivation of reinforcers usually is not necessary, as the natural deprivation that occurs in the course of an individual's daily activities often is sufficient to increase reinforcer effectiveness. Since children in the classroom, for example, do not have unlimited access to free time, they normally experience a mild form of deprivation during the course of a school day. As another example, when using small amounts of edible reinforcers to increase appropriate responding, the only deprivation required may be the natural deprivation that occurs between meals. Thus a variety of events may serve as effective reinforcers simply as a result of natural deprivation without the introduction of more formal deprivation procedures.

REFERENCES

Baer, D. M. (1970). A case for the selective reinforcement of punishment. In C. Neuringer & J. L. Michael (Eds.), *Behavior modification in clinical psychology.* New York: Appleton-Century-Crofts.

Kazdin, A. E. (1980). *Behavior modification in applied settings* (Rev. ed.). Homewood, IL: Dorsey.

Martin, G., & Pear, J. (1983). *Behavior modification: What it is and how to do it* (2nd ed.). Englewood Cliffs, NJ: Prentice Hall.

CHRISTINE L. COLE
University of Wisconsin at Madison

BEHAVIOR MODIFICATION
OPERANT CONDITIONING
STIMULUS SATIATION

STIMULUS GENERALIZATION

Stimulus generalization can be defined as a set of conditions with similar properties that all begin to occasion a specific response. Stimulus generalization is often thought of as the opposite of stimulus discrimination. If tight stimulus control is achieved, then little stimulus generalization can occur. B. F. Skinner discussed stimulus generalization and stimulus control in the following manner: When a response is reinforced under certain conditions the response will most likely occur under very similar conditions. However, due to generalization, other conditions with only some similar properties can also begin to occasion the response (Skinner, 1974). Stimulus generalization was often thought of as a passive process, resulting from poor discrimination training. However, therapeutic behavior change is often dependent on stimulus generalization and needs to be understood as more than a passive process (Stokes & Baer, 1977). Often when training new responses it will be necessary for those responses to generalize to other stimuli, such as settings and individuals.

In 1977, Stokes and Baer summarized the research on stimulus generalization and found that almost half of the applied literature used a method of examining generalization through "train and hope." This method consisted of training on a specific response and then noting any other generalization that co-occurred. The method was labeled "train and hope" because researchers using this method would train one response and then hope that it would generalize to other untrained conditions. In this method no specific training for generalization occurred. Stokes and Baer suggest that behavior analysts should *not* assume that generalization will occur without direct teaching. Furthermore, the authors state that there needs to be more research on generalization and how to specifically train for generalization.

Stokes and Osnes (1989) continued the research of Stokes and Baer (1977) by discussing stimulus generalization as it relates to function. Stokes and Osnes state that there are two important questions that must be asked when assessing stimulus generalization: did the behavior occur in generalized situations, and what are the functional variables that account for the generalization. In their paper, the authors reformulated the original tactics proposed by Stokes and Baer to offer 12 strategies for programming generalization. All 12 strategies were organized into three general principles: exploit current functional contingencies, train diversely, and incorporate functional mediators. The first category, exploit current functional contingencies, refers to teaching behaviors that are likely to come into contact with natural contingencies. These contingencies can occur without the direct presence of a change agent (i.e., an adult). The next category, training for diversity, refers to training in a less rigid format. Typical discrimination training consists of rigid training with tight stimulus control. In order to program for generalization, a less rigid format may be beneficial, such

as training with multiple exemplars as well as nonexemplars. Multiple-exemplar training consists of teaching the individual multiple examples of correct responding. For example, when teaching a child to make social initiations, training should take place in multiple settings (e.g., school, the park). An additional way to train to diversity is to make antecedents and consequences less discriminable. This can be achieved by delaying the consequences and changing reinforcers. The final category, incorporating functional mediators, refers to incorporating a mediating stimulus that occurs between training and the behavior. There are several different ways that mediators can be incorporated into the training session. One example of incorporating mediating stimuli is the use of self-monitoring materials, such as schedules or self-monitoring forms.

In recent years behavior analytic approaches to treatment for developmental disabilities and autism spectrum disorders have begun to assess and program for generalization using the recommendations described by Stokes and Osnes. For example, Taylor (2001) suggests that when teaching children with autism social skills, generalization will need to be specifically programmed. Taylor recommends using multiple peers and conducting training in several different settings. Training should also involve multiple-exemplar training and teaching the children skills that will contact naturally occurring reinforcers.

Several other professionals in the field have also acknowledged the need for programming for generalization (Anderson, Taras, & Cannon, 1996; Maurice, Green, & Foxx, 2001). For example, Heflin and Alberto (2001) make several recommendations for programming generalization and maintenance when teaching children with autism. The authors suggest that the use of multiple cues, people, settings, and materials can lead to increased generalization skills, especially when teaching in the classroom context.

In summary, stimulus generalization takes place when a response begins to occur in the presence of an untrained stimulus. Through the last 30 years stimulus generalization has emerged as an important behavioral process that needs to be considered as an independent principle. The view of stimulus generalization as a passive process is no longer an extensive enough account for behavior change. Within teaching and training situations it is now common practice to account for, as well as specifically program for, stimulus generalization.

REFERENCES

Anderson, S., Taras, M., & Cannon, B. (1996). Teaching new skills to young children with autism. In C. Maurice, G. Green, & S. Luce (Eds.), *Behavioral interventions for young children with autism: A manual for parents and peers* (pp. 181–193). Austin, TX: PRO-ED.

Heflin, J. L., & Alberto, P. A. (2001). Establishing a behavioral context for learning for students with autism. *Focus on Autism and Other Developmental Disabilities, 16,* 93–101.

Maurice, C., Green, G., & Luce, S. (2001). *Behavioral interventions for young children with autism: A manual for parents and peers.* Austin, TX: PRO-ED.

Stokes, T., & Baer, D. (1977). An implicit technology of generalization. *Journal of Applied Behavior Analysis, 10,* 349–367.

Stokes, T., & Osnes, P. (1989). An operant pursuit of generalization. *Behavior Therapy, 20,* 337–355.

Taylor, B. (2001). Teaching peer social skills to children with autism. In C. Maurice, G. Green, & R. Foxx, (Eds.), *Making a difference: Behavioral interventions for autism* (pp. 83–161). Austin, TX: PRO-ED.

PAIGE B. RAETZ
THOMAS SZABO
BRITT L. WINTER
Western Michigan University

STIMULUS SATIATION

Stimulus satiation refers to the reduction in reinforcer effectiveness that occurs after a large amount of that reinforcer has been obtained (usually within a short period of time). Thus an event that initially shows reinforcing qualities may become ineffective or even aversive for a period of time if experienced too frequently or excessively. Teacher praise may be effective the first few times if it is provided in the morning, but may gradually diminish in value with additional use during the day. Treats and certain activities may be highly reinforcing if used sparingly but may lose their effectiveness if used frequently. The special educator should be sensitive to the principle of satiation and provide alternative reinforcing events when loss of effectiveness is noted (Gardner, 1978).

Satiation is especially common with primary reinforcers such as food. These reinforcers, when provided in excessive amounts within a short period, may lose their reinforcing properties relatively quickly. To prevent or delay satiation, only a small amount of the reinforcer should be provided at any one time. Satiation of primary reinforcers is usually temporary, as these events regain their reinforcing value as deprivation increases.

Secondary reinforcers such as praise, attention, and recognition are less likely than primary reinforcers to be influenced by satiation effects. The category of secondary reinforcers called generalized reinforcers is least-susceptible to satiation. This is due to the fact that the reinforcers themselves (e.g., tokens, grades, money) can be exchanged for a variety of other reinforcing events called back-up reinforcers. Thus satiation of generalized reinforcers is not likely to occur unless the individual becomes satiated with the items or events offered as back-up reinforcers. The greater the number and range of back-up reinforcers available, the less likelihood that satiation will occur (Kazdin, 1980). This would suggest that teachers consider the use of tokens, exchangeable for a wide variety of back-up reinforcers, when tangible events are required to ensure effective learning and behavior (Gardner, 1978).

The principle of satiation may also be used as an intervention tactic to reduce the value of events that appear to serve as reinforcers for maladaptive behavior. In a stimulus satiation procedure, the individual is provided with a reinforcing event with such frequency or in such large quantities that the event loses its reinforcing qualities for a period of time; the result is that the behavior maintained by that reinforcer is weakened. In a frequently cited example, Ayllon (1963) used a stimulus satiation procedure with a hospitalized psychiatric patient who hoarded large numbers of towels in her room. Although many efforts had been made to discourage hoarding, these had proved to be unsuccessful, and the staff had resorted to simply removing on a regular basis the towels she had collected. With the stimulus satiation procedure, the staff provided her with large numbers of towels without comment. After a few weeks, when the number of towels in her room reached 625, she began to remove a few, and no more were given to her. The patient engaged in no towel hoarding during the subsequent year.

The purpose of such a stimulus satiation procedure is to reduce or remove the reinforcing qualities of the event serving to maintain the maladaptive behavior. In the Ayllon study (1963) this loss of reinforcer effectiveness was reflected in the patient's comments: "Don't give me no more towels. I've got enough . . . Take them towels away. . . . Get these dirty towels out of here" (p. 57). Apparently, as the number of towels increased to an excessive level, they were no longer reinforcing and even became aversive to her.

Although long-term maintenance of behavior change was obtained in this case, the effects of stimulus satiation procedures typically are temporary. This is especially true if the reinforcer is highly valuable to the individual. Educators can enhance the effects of a satiation procedure by ensuring that, during the interim period in which the maladaptive behavior is absent or of low strength, other more appropriate replacement behaviors are taught and strengthened (Gardner, 1978).

REFERENCES

Ayllon, T. (1963). Intensive treatment of psychotic behaviour by stimulus satiation and food reinforcement. *Behaviour Research & Therapy, 1,* 53–61.

Gardner, W. I. (1978). *Children with learning and behavior problems: A behavior management approach* (2nd ed.). Boston: Allyn & Bacon.

Kazdin, A. E. (1980). *Behavior modification in applied settings* (Rev. ed.). Homewood, IL: Dorsey

CHRISTINE L. COLE
University of Wisconsin at Madison

APPLIED BEHAVIOR ANALYSIS
BEHAVIOR MODIFICATION
STIMULUS DEPRIVATION

STRABISMUS, EFFECT ON LEARNING OF

Strabismus, also called heteropia, is a visual condition in which the two eyes are not parallel when viewing an object. While one eye is fixed on an object, the other eye will be directed elsewhere. Strabismus can be classified in two ways. The first concerns the angle of separation. In concomitant strabismus, the angle of separation is fixed; in noncomitant strabismus the angle between the eye that is fixed and the deviant eye varies. Strabismus also can be classified by whether the visual paths of the two eyes converge or diverge (Harley & Lawrence, 1977).

The effect of strabismus on learning is closely tied to its age of onset. If it occurs later in childhood (Flax, 1993), after other visual reflexes have developed, it can result in double vision (diplopia), which can be stressful and lead to learning disabilities. Lipton (1971) noted significant correlations between strabismus and neurotic traits, character disorders, and learning problems. Haskell (1972), on the other hand, showed no relationship between strabismus and academic achievement.

If the onset of strabismus occurs before the age of 2, the effects are not as severe because other visual reflexes are not as developed. However, early onset of strabismus can lead to the development of ambliopia, a condition in which the brain suppresses the signals coming from the deviant eye. If not corrected, the brain can permanently lose the ability to process a 20/20 image from this eye.

Some form of strabismus occurs in approximately 5 percent of all children. The percentage increases to 40 to 50 percent for children with cerebral palsy; it is noted in as many as 60 percent of the children who are visually impaired at birth as a result of their mother's having contracted rubella during pregnancy.

Strabismus can be corrected through lenses if it is detected early in a child's life. Freeman, Nguyen, and Jolly (1996) suggest that amblyopia and strabismus deviation are the major components of visual acuity loss and should be reduced by whatever means are available. Additionally, some doctors recommend eye exercises as a way to correct the condition. This recommendation is controversial. Eden (1978) notes that strabismus often starts early in life, before the child is capable of following any rigorous exercise schedule. Once the child is capable of following such a schedule, permanent visual damage may already have occurred. In school, close work should be limited for students with strabismus, and these students should be given frequent rest periods.

REFERENCES

Eden, J. (1978). *The eye book.* New York: Viking.

Flax, N. (1993). The treatment of strabismus in the four to ten year old child. *Child and Adolescent Social Work Journal, 10*(5), 411–416.

Freeman, A. W., Nguyen, V. A., & Jolly, N. (1996). Components of visual acuity loss in strabismus. *Vision Research, 36*(5), 765–774.

Harley, R. K., & Lawrence, G. A. (1977). *Visual impairment in the schools.* Springfield, IL: Thomas.

Haskell, S. H. (1972). Visuoperceptual, visuomotor, and scholastic skills of alternating and uniocular squinting children. *Journal of Special Education, 6,* 3–8.

Lipton, E. L. (1971). Remarks on the psychological aspects of strabismus. *Sight-Saving Review, 4,* 129–138.

THOMAS E. ALLEN
Gallaudet College

AMBLIYOPIA
BLIND
CATARACTS

STRAUSS, ALFRED A. (1897–1957)

Alfred A. Strauss was born in Germany and received his medical degree and subsequent training in psychiatry and neurology there. He left Germany in 1933, became visiting professor at the University of Barcelona, and helped to establish Barcelona's first child guidance clinics. In 1937 Strauss joined the staff of the Wayne County (Michigan) School, where he served as research psychiatrist and director of child care. In 1947 Strauss founded the Cove School in Racine, Wisconsin, a residential institution that gained an international reputation for its pioneering work with

Alfred A. Strauss

brain-injured children. Strauss served as president of the school until his death.

Strauss made major contributions in the areas of diagnosis and education of brain-injured children. He developed tests for diagnosing brain injury. His studies of children without intellectual deficit who showed characteristics of brain injury in learning and behavior resulted in the first systematic description of a new clinical entity, minimal brain dysfunction. His 1947 book, *Psychopathology and Education of the Brain-Injured Child,* written with Laura Lehtinen, was the major guide for many of the numerous school programs for minimally brain-injured children that came into existence during the 1950s and 1960s.

REFERENCES

Gardiner, R. A. (1958). Alfred A. Strauss, 1897–1957. *Exceptional Children, 24,* 373.

Lewis, R. S., Strauss, A. A., & Lehtinen, L. E. (1960). *The other child.* New York: Grune & Stratton.

Strauss, A. A., & Kephart, N. C. (1955). *Psychopathology and education of the brain-injured child* (Vol. 2). New York: Grune & Stratton.

Strauss, A. A., & Lehtinen, L. E. (1947). *Psychopathology and education of the brain-injured child* (Vol. 1). New York: Grune & Stratton.

PAUL IRVINE
Katonah, New York

BIRTH INJURIES

STRAUSS SYNDROME

The term *Strauss syndrome* was coined by Stevens and Birch (1957) to describe an expanded set of behavioral characteristics of children who could not learn and did not easily fit into other classification systems. It also extended the work of a leading pioneer in the field, Alfred Strauss. Strauss's ideas regarding the education of brain-injured, perceptually handicapped children were presented in works coauthored first with Laura Lehtinen (1947) and later with Newell Kephart (1955).

The term *Strauss syndrome* was introduced to describe the brain-injured child who evidenced (1) erratic and inappropriate behavior on mild provocation; (2) increased motor activity disproportionate to the stimulus; (3) poor organization of behavior; (4) distractibility of more than an ordinary degree under ordinary conditions; (5) persistent hyperactivity; and (6) awkwardness and consistently poor motor performance (Stevens & Birch, 1957).

Despite the importance of the works of Strauss et al., it became apparent that their description of the brain-injured child pertained only to a certain portion of the total group

having neurogenic disorders of learning. Major objections to the term *brain-injured child* were presented by Stevens and Birch (1957). They concluded that:

1. The term is an etiological concept and does not appropriately describe the symptom complex. This is important because the condition that prevails is viewed in terms of symptoms rather than etiology.

2. The term is associated with other conditions, some of which have no relation to the symptom complex commonly referred to as brain injury.

3. The term does not help in the development of a sound therapeutic approach.

4. The term is not suited for use as a descriptive one because it is essentially a generic expression, the use of which results in oversimplification. (p. 349)

It is now considered archaic.

REFERENCES

Stevens, G., & Birch, J. (1957). A proposal for clarification of the terminology used to describe brain-injured children. *Exceptional Children, 23,* 346–349.

Strauss, A., & Kephart, N. (1955). *Psychopathology and education of the brain-injured child* (Vol. 2). New York: Grune & Stratton.

Strauss, A., & Lehtinen, L. (1947). *Psychopathology and education of the brain-injured child* (Vol. 1). New York: Grune & Stratton.

CECILIA STEPPE-JONES
North Carolina Central University

BRAIN DAMAGE/INJURY
ETIOLOGY
LEARNING DISABILITIES
LESIONS
MBD SYNDROME

STRENGTH MODELS OF REMEDIATION

See REMEDIATION, DEFICIT-CENTERED MODELS OF.

STREPHOSYMBOLIA

Strephosymbolia is a Greek term that literally means "twisted symbol." Originally used by Samuel T. Orton, strephosymbolia is most commonly used in discussions regarding dyslexia. Orton and others noticed that when certain children read, they often reverse letters, syllables, or words. These children see all parts of a word, but not in the accepted order. So, instead of "pebbles," a strephosymbolic child might see "pelbbse" (Johnson, 1981). This twisting of reading material is viewed as a primary symptom of dyslexia (Clarke, 1973).

Orton believed that strephosymbolia resulted from a failure to establish cerebral dominance in the left hemisphere of the brain (Lerner, 1985). The reversals that resulted from the lack of cerebral dominance were due to failure to erase memory images from the nondominant side of the brain (Kessler, 1980). These memory images were projected to the dominant side of the brain as mirror images, resulting in the reversals of letters and/or words (Kessler, 1980).

Currently, Orton's theory has little credibility, as there has been no substantiation that mirror images are projected onto the brain (Kessler, 1980). Mercer (1983) notes that these difficulties are referred to as severe reading disabilities and are treated according to the specific difficulty.

REFERENCES

Clarke, L. (1973). *Can't read, can't write, can't talk too good either.* New York: Walker.

Johnson, C. (1981). *The diagnosis of learning disabilities.* Boulder, CO: Pruett.

Kessler, J. W. (1980). History of minimal brain dysfunction. In H. E. Rice & E. D. Rice (Eds.), *Handbook of minimal brain dysfunction: A critical review.* New York: Wiley.

Lerner, T. (1985). *Learning disabilities: Theories, diagnosis and teaching strategies* (4th ed.). Boston: Houghton Mifflin.

Mercer, C. D. (1983). *Students with learning disabilities* (2nd ed.). Columbus, OH: Merrill.

JOHN R. BEATTIE
University of North Carolina at Charlotte

DYSLEXIA
READING DISORDERS

STRESS AND INDIVIDUALS WITH DISABILITIES

Stress results when physical and psychological demands on an individual exceed personal coping skills. Stress is activated when a threat to security, self-esteem, or safety is perceived. Schultz (1980) suggests that stress is often triggered by environmental interactions, which may be more problematic for children with disabilities than for non-disabled ones. Children with disabilities may also develop stress reactions to personal thoughts.

In regard to the development of stress, Schultz has suggested a pattern of (1) occurrence of an event, (2) internal assignment of the meaning of the event, and (3) occurrence of internal and external responses to the event depending on the assigned meaning.

Rutter (1981) suggests that resilience is demonstrated by young people who succeed despite stress, but that children who have handicapping conditions may be constitutionally less resilient. Particularly stressful periods for children with disabilities include school entry, change of school, and last years of school. The uncertainties present during these periods are exacerbated because of the disabled child's lack of resilience (Kershaw, 1973).

Low-achieving individuals demonstrate more stress than their better-achieving peers. Lower-functioning students with disabilities are subject to more stress in childhood than higher-functioning individuals (Westling, 1986). This increased stress may be due to social rejection and parental overprotection concurrent with the children's reduced capacity for coping with various situations.

Mainstreaming and inclusive practices may produce increased social stress in the student with disabilities. Tymitz-Wolf (1984) analyzed mildly mentally disabled students' worries about mainstreaming as related to academic performance, social interactions, and the transitions inherent in split placement. A range of worries were reported in all three areas, with worries concerning transitions being the most prevalent.

Schultz (1980) contends that stress-management programs for disabled students should emphasize instruction in adaptive coping skills, including relaxation training. Relaxation training has been used to decrease stress in learning-disabled students (Hegarty & Last, 1997; Omizo, 1981).

In addition, it has been found that parental support is very important and can be enhanced by the school providing parent support and parent support training for students (Volenski, 1995).

REFERENCES

Hegarty, J. R., & Last, A. (1997). Relaxation training for people who have severe/profound and multiple learning disabilities. *British Journal of Developmental Disabilities, 43*(85), 122–139.

Kershaw, J. D. (1973). *Handicapped children in the ordinary school: Stresses in children.* New York: Crane & Russak.

Omizo, M. M. (1981). Relaxation training and biofeedback with hyperactive elementary school children. *Elementary School Guidance & Counseling, 15*(4), 329–332.

Rutter, M. (1981). Stress, coping, and development: Some issues and some questions. *Journal of Child Psychology & Psychiatry, 22,* 323–356.

Schultz, E. (1980). Teaching coping skills for stress and anxiety. *Teaching Exceptional Children, 13*(3), 12–15.

Tymitz-Wolf, B. (1984). An analysis of EMR children's worries about mainstreaming. *Education & Training of the Mentally Retarded, 19,* 157–168.

Volenski, L. T. (1995). Building support systems for parents of handicapped children: The parent education and guidance program. *Psychology in the Schools, 32*(2), 124–129.

Westling, D. L. (1986). *Introduction to mental retardation.* Englewood Cliffs, NJ: Prentice Hall.

ANNE M. BAUER
University of Cincinnati

SELF-CONCEPT

STRONG INTEREST INVENTORY

The Strong Interest Inventory (SVIB-SCII, Fourth Edition; Hansen & Campbell, 1985) assesses an individual's interests in occupations, hobbies, leisure activities, and school subjects. The test has a long history, with its first edition, the Strong Vocational Interest Blank (SVIB), being published over 70 years ago. There have been major changes since the SVIB, most notably a gender equity process that began in 1971. Also, a theoretical framework, Holland's hexagonal model of career types was incorporated into the test. The most recent revision occurred in 1985, and with it came 17 new vocational-technical occupational groups, six newly emerging professional occupations, and updated norms.

The SVIB-SCII is a paper-and-pencil measure in which the respondent is asked to indicate "Like," "Dislike," or "Indifferent" to the items. The test takes an average of 30 minutes to complete and was designed for use with adults and 16- to 18-year-olds with a 6th grade reading ability. The SVIB-SCII is machine scored, and responses are compared to the interests of people in a wide variety of jobs. The test yields five types of information: scores on 6 General Occupational Themes, 23 Basic Interest Scales, and 207 Occupational Scales. Additionally, there are 2 Special Scales (Academic Comfort and Introversion-Extroversion), and Administrative Indexes (validity scales). Interpretive information includes a profile with an optional interpretive report.

The psychometric properties of the SVIB-SCII are excellent. Over 48,000 people taken from 202 occupational samples were used to construct the Occupational Scales. The fourth edition of the *Manual for the SVIB-SCII* describes the reliability, validity, and sampling procedures for all the scales in detail.

The SVIB-SCII is easy to administer and provides easily understood interpretive results. Critiques of the inventory praise its outstanding interpretive information and excellent psychometric properties (Busch, 1995). One issue with the test is the authors' failure to report response rates for the occupational samples; response rates can affect the representativeness of the sample and thus the predictive validity of the scales (Busch, 1995; Worthen & Sailor, 1995). However, despite the concern, the SVIB-SCII has been described as "by far the best available interest inventory" (Worthen & Sailor, 1995).

REFERENCES

Busch, J. C. (1995). In J. C. Conoley & J. C. Impara (Eds.), *The twelfth mental measurements yearbook.* Lincoln, NE: Buros Institute of Mental Measurements.

Hansen, J. C., & Campbell, D. P. (1985). *Manual for the Strong Interest Inventory* (4th ed.). Stanford, CA: Stanford University Press.

Worthen, B. R., & Sailor, P. (1995). In J. C. Conoley & J. C. Impara (Eds.), *The twelfth mental measurements yearbook.* Lincoln, NE: Buros Institute of Mental Measurements.

DEBRA Y. BROADBOOKS
*California School of
Professional Psychology*

HABILITATION
VOCATIONAL REHABILITATION COUNSELING

STRUCTURE OF INTELLECT

J. P. Guilford (1967), in his work *The Nature of Human Intelligence,* developed a model of intelligence based on his factor analysis of human intellect. The structure of intellect theory (SI) grew out of experimental applications of the multivariate method of multiple-factor analysis. The basic research was carried out on a population of young adults but successive investigations have substantiated Guilford's initial findings with subject samples ranging in age from 5 to 15 years. Implications from this theory and its concepts have led to many new interpretations of already known facts of general significance in psychology.

The major aim of the structure of intellect theory is to give the concept of intelligence a firm, comprehensive, and systematic theoretical foundation. A second aim is to put intelligence within the mainstream of general psychological theory. For his frame of reference, Guilford has chosen what he terms a morphological, as opposed to hierarchical, model. His model, which he also refers to as the "three faces of intellect," includes three categories along with their subclassifications. The three dimensions are content, referring to types of information that are discriminable by the individual; products, the outcomes of intellectual operations; and operations, referring to the primary kinds of intellectual activities or processes.

The model or cube is a three-dimensional diagram. The operations dimension is broken down into five subclassifications: evaluation, convergent production, divergent production, memory, and cognition. The six types of products are units, classes, relations, systems, transformations, and implications. The four types of content are figural, symbolic, semantic, and behavioral. The complete schema is diagrammed as an array of 120 (5 × 4 × 6) predicted cells of intellectual abilities. The 120 types of abilities are derived from the intersection of the three-way classification system. Of the 120 discrete factors, at least 82 have been demonstrated; others are still under investigation.

Although Guilford's model has not been widely used, it has pointed to a theory that has been lacking from the beginning of the era of mental testing—to give the concept of intelligence a firm, comprehensive, and systematic theoretical foundation. Guilford maintains that a firm foundation must be based on detailed observation; that the theory itself should include all aspects of intelligence; and that the result must be systematic, embracing numerous phenomena within a logically ordered structure. The outcome is his structure of intellect.

REFERENCE

Guilford, J. P. (1967). *The nature of human intelligence.* New York: McGraw-Hill.

CECELIA STEPPE-JONES
*North Carolina Central
University*

**INTELLIGENCE
INTELLIGENCE TESTING**

STUDENT STYLES QUESTIONNAIRE

The Student Styles Questionnaire (SSQ; Oakland, Glutting, and Horton, 1996), a 69-item self-report measure of temperament, assesses four bipolar temperament styles displayed by children ages 8 through 17: extroversion-introversion, practical-imaginative, thinking-feeling, organized-flexible. Its theoretical structure is based on Jung's typology theory of personality (Jung, 1921, 1946) and is consistent with the dimensions on the Myers-Briggs Type Indicator (Myers & McCaulley, 1985).

Extroversion-introversion styles address sources from which people derive energy. Those with an extroverted preference generally draw energy from others and their environments, while those with introverted preferences generally draw energy from themselves through reliance on solitude and personal time. Practical-imaginative styles address qualities on which people rely to acquire and store information. Those with practical styles generally rely on their five senses and what worked previously, while those with imaginative styles generally rely on theory and broader generalizations. Thinking-feeling styles address preferences

for forming judgments. Those with thinking preferences generally rely on their thoughts and value logic over sentiment, while those with feeling preferences generally rely on their feelings and subjective judgments. Organized-flexible styles address when one makes decisions. Those with organized styles generally make decisions as early as possible, while those with flexible styles often prefer to postpone decisions as long as possible.

The purposes of the SSQ are to identify talent, adjust for possible personal weaknesses, enhance personal and social understanding, identify preferred learning styles, promote educational development (Horton & Oakland, 1997), identify students with special needs, explore prevocational interests, and facilitate research and evaluation.

The SSQ was normed on 7,902 children and youths ages 8 through 17 nationally stratified by age, gender, race/ethnicity, geographic area, and school type. Test-retest reliability coefficients, examined over 7 months, ranged from .67 (practical-imaginative) to .80 (extroverted-introverted) for the four dimensions, with a mean of .74. Estimates of internal consistency are in the high .90s.

Factor analyses support the four-factor model (Oakland et al., 1996; Stafford & Oakland, 1996a, 1996b). Approximately 40 studies examined the construct validity of the SSQ (Oakland et al., 1996). Additional studies provide support for the equivalence of SSQ constructs for children of various ages, three racial-ethnic groups (African American, Anglo-Americans, and Hispanic-Americans), and gender (Stafford & Oakland, 1996a, 1996b). The temperament patterns of youths as measured by the SSQ and Myers-Briggs Type Indicator are consistent (Oakland et al., 1996). Studies have examined temperament patterns exhibited by children who are gifted academically (Oakland, Joyce, Horton, & Glutting, 2000), are blind (Oakland, Banner, & Livingston, 2000), and display conduct and oppositional defiant disorders (Joyce & Oakland, 2005); relationships between children's temperament and vocational interests (Oakland, Stafford, Horton, & Glutting, 2001); and differences in achievement associated with learning and teaching styles (Horton & Oakland, 1997).

Oakland and international colleagues are conducting various cross-national studies that examine the development of temperament in children and youths. Current published studies focus on Australia (Oakland, Faulkner, & Bassett, 2005), Hungary (Katona & Oakland, 2000), People's Republic of China (Oakland & Lu, 2006), and Costa Rica (Oakland & Mata, in press). SSQ data on children in Brazil, Gaza, Greece, Iran, Israel, Nigeria, Romania, South Africa, South Korea, and Zimbabwe have been acquired and are being prepared for publication.

REFERENCES

Horton, C., & Oakland, T. (1996). *Classroom applications booklet.* San Antonio, TX: Psychological Corporation.

Horton, C., & Oakland, T. (1997). Temperament-based learning styles as moderators of academic achievement. *Adolescence, 32,* 131–141.

Joyce, D., & Oakland, T. (2005). Temperament differences among children with conduct disorders and oppositional defiant disorders. *The California School Psychologist, 10,* 125–136.

Jung, C. G. (1921). *Psychological type.* New York: Harcourt, Brace, & Co.

Jung, C. G. (1946). *Psychological type.* (H. G. Baynes, Trans.). New York: Harcourt. (Original work published 1921)

Katona, N., & Oakland, T. (2000). The development of temperament in Hungarian children. *Hungarian Journal of Psychology, 1,* 17–29.

Myers, I. B., & McCaulley, M. (1985). *Manual: A guide to the development and use of the Myers-Briggs type indicator.* Palo Alto, CA: Consulting Psychological Press.

Oakland, T., Banner, D., & Livingston, R. (2000). Temperament-based learning styles of visually-impaired children. *Journal of Visual Impairment and Blindness,* January, 26–33.

Oakland, T., Faulkner, M., & Bassett, K. (2005). Temperament styles of children from Australia and the United States. *Australian Educational and Developmental Psychologist, 19,* 35–51.

Oakland, T., Horton, C., & Glutting, J. (1996). *Student styles questionnaire.* San Antonio, TX: Psychological Corporation.

Oakland, T., Joyce, D., Horton, C., & Glutting, J. (2000). Temperament-based learning styles of identified gifted and nongifted students. *Gifted Child Quarterly, 44,* 183–189.

Oakland, T., & Lu, L. (2006). Temperament styles of children from the People's Republic of China and the United States. *School Psychology International, 27*(2), 192–208.

Oakland, T., & Mata, A. (in press). Temperament styles of children from Costa Rica and the United States. *Journal of Psychological Types.*

Oakland, T., Stafford, M., Horton, C., & Glutting, J. (2001). Temperament and vocational preferences: Age, gender and racial-ethnic comparisons using the Student Styles Questionnaire. *Journal of Career Assessment, 9*(3), 297–314.

Stafford, M., & Oakland, T. (1996a). Racial-ethnic comparisons of temperament constructs for three age groups using the Student Styles Questionnaire. *Measurement and Evaluation in Counseling and Development, 19*(2), 100–110.

Stafford, M., & Oakland, T. (1996b). Validity of temperament constructs using the Student Styles Questionnaire: Comparisons for three racial-ethnic groups. *Journal of Psychoeducational Assessment, 14,* 109–120.

JACK R. DEMPSEY
University of Florida

STUDY OF MATHEMATICALLY PRECOCIOUS YOUTH

The Study of Mathematically Precocious Youth (SMPY) was officially begun on September 1, 1971, by Julian Stanley.

Stanley had become intrigued by a 13½-year-old boy who scored extremely well on several standardized mathematics tests. A fear that students such as this one might fail to be identified and appropriately served led Stanley to devise the SMPY at Johns Hopkins University.

The SMPY is geared to the top 1 to 3 percent of mathematics students in U.S. junior high schools (Johnson, 1983). These students often display swift and comprehensive reasoning, an inclination to analyze mathematical structure, a tendency to deal in the abstract, and an untiring approach to working on mathematics (Heid, 1983). Indeed, students accepted into SMPY are so mathematically advanced that they must score at least 700 on the math portion of the Scholastic Aptitude Test (SAT-M) before their 13th birthday (Stanley & Benbow, 1983). Allowances are made for those students who are over 13 years of age. They must score an additional 10 points on the SAT-M for each month of age over 13 years. For example, a student who is 13 years, 2 months, must score at least 720 on the SAT-M before being considered for the SMPY (Stanley & Benbow, 1983).

Once the students have been selected, the goal of the program is to accelerate learning in mathematics. Stanley and Benbow (1982) note that there is no sense in allowing precocious students to languish in slow-paced math classes. Math classes, they feel, should be taught according to individual students' abilities and achievements. Consequently, precocious students should spend less time in math classes, allowing for potential concentration on related topics such as physics (Tursman, 1983). Additionally, by spending less time in math class, mathematically precocious students would spend less time in school. This would allow them to take college courses while still in high school and to enter college at an earlier age (Stanley & Benbow, 1982). This is a goal of SMPY and is strongly emphasized by Stanley as a way to get these students quickly into the work force (Stanley, 1997).

The SMPY is essentially a summer program. Students are identified, evaluated, and selected for the program throughout the year. Once selected, students participate in an 8-week program, meeting 1 day a week for slightly less than 5 hours per day. Throughout the instruction, the student-teacher ratio never exceeds 1:5 (Stanley, 1980). All instructors are former SMPY graduates and usually range in age from 13 to 20. During this approximately 35-hour program, students will typically demonstrate mastery of material 2 school years beyond where they began (Stanley, 1980).

To achieve such dramatic results, SMPY uses a "diagnostic testing followed by prescriptive instruction" method of instruction (Stanley, 1980; Stanley & Benbow, 1983). An evaluation determines what the student does not know. The instructors then help the student learn the information without taking an entire course (Stanley & Benbow, 1982).

REFERENCES

Heid, M. K. (1983). Characteristics and special needs of the gifted students in mathematics. *Mathematics Teacher, 76,* 221–226.

Johnson, M. L. (1983). Identifying and teaching mathematically gifted elementary school children. *Arithmetic Teacher, 30,* 55–56.

Stanley, J. C. (1980). On educating the gifted. *Educational Researcher, 9,* 8–12.

Stanley, J. C. (1997). Varieties of intellectual talent. *Journal of Creative Behavior, 31*(2), 93–119.

Stanley, J. C., & Benbow, C. P. (1982). Educating mathematically precocious youth: Twelve policy recommendations. *Educational Researcher, 11,* 4–9.

Stanley, J. C., & Benbow, C. P. (1983). SMPY's first decade: Ten years of posing problems and solving them. *Journal of Special Education, 17,* 11–25.

Tursman, C. (1983). Challenging gifted students. *School Administrator, 40,* cover, 9–10, 12.

JOHN R. BEATTIE
University of North Carolina at Charlotte

ACCELERATION OF GIFTED CHILDREN
ADVANCED PLACEMENT PROGRAM
GIFTED AND TALENTED CHILDREN

STUTTERING

Fluency disorders typically are characterized by atypical rates and rhythms of speech, repetitions, and excessive tension and struggle when speaking. The best known and probably least understood fluency disorder is stuttering. Stuttering is somewhat paradoxical in that, while it is relatively easy to identify when listening to speech, it is somewhat difficult to define (Hartman, 1994). Stuttering typically is characterized as an abnormally high occurrence of involuntary stoppages, repetitions, or prolongations in the utterance of short speech.

Stuttering occurs universally and among individuals who differ by age, race, culture, socioeconomic status, occupation, and intelligence. Research has examined neurophysiological, psychological, social, and linguistic influences on stuttering. Stuttering is more common in males than females and often runs in families, implying biological and genetic predispositions (Guitar, 1998). Further, children who are overly dependent, have an excessive need for approval, and have low tolerance for frustration are more likely to stutter. However, the exact cause of stuttering remains unknown and is likely to differ from person to person.

When referred for a stuttering evaluation, the person often is seen by a speech/language pathologist. This professional conducts an evaluation of speech and language development and considers age of onset, family history, and diagnostic criteria for this disorder. No single measure is used to accurately diagnose stuttering. Most often a speech pathologist will include a battery to assess qualities of speech including repetitions, prolongations, blocks, interjections, and restrictions in spontaneous speech and oral reading. Speech/language pathologists also may identify a need for intervention through information obtained from teachers and parents and nonverbal signs of struggle such as eye, head, and body movements.

Individuals often encounter secondary behaviors resulting from stuttering. These behaviors may include undue physical strain and effort while speaking, and avoidance of particular situations, words, sounds, or other situations that may elicit stuttering. These secondary behaviors may become more problematic than the stuttering itself.

Stuttering can affect an individual at any age. However, the onset of stuttering occurs before age 10 in 98 percent of cases, is most likely to occur between ages 2 and 7, and is rarely retained after puberty. Accordingly, this onset coincides with a period of rapid acquisition and expansion of speech and language skills.

Approximately 5 percent of North Americans have stuttered at one time in their lives, whereas only 1 percent stutter at any given time (Mansson, 2000; Yairi & Ambrose, 1999). Normal development and growth account for many cases of recovery without any professional treatment.

Stuttering modification therapy is a popular speech-language technique in treating this population. This approach focuses on the person's attitudes and feelings about stuttering while concurrently helping the person stutter in a more relaxed way in an attempt to make their speech sound more normal. Stuttering modification therapy is based on the idea that feelings of anticipation, anxiety, and expectation contribute to stuttering.

Fluency shaping therapy is a behavioral therapy that focuses on developing fluency. The goal of fluency shaping therapy is to slow the pace of speech, which may result in controlled fluency or spontaneous recovery. Other forms of therapy focus on eliminating avoidances or utilize group therapy with other children who stutter to provide a comfortable environment for speech practice. Approaches also may focus on coping, relaxation techniques, and/or handling teasing from other students. However, no single treatment has emerged as the most effective.

REFERENCES

Guitar, B. (1998). *Stuttering: An integrated approach to its nature and treatment* (2nd ed.). Baltimore: Williams & Wilkins.

Hartman, B. T. (1994). *The neuropsychology of developmental stuttering.* San Diego, CA: Singular Publishing Group.

Mansson, H. (2000). Childhood stuttering: Incidence and development. *Journal of Fluency Disorders, 25,* 47–57.

Yairi, E., & Ambrose, N. G. (1999). Early childhood stuttering I: Persistency and recovery rates. *Journal of Speech, Language, and Hearing Research, 42,* 1097–1112.

ERIC ROSSEN
University of Florida

SPEECH THERAPY

SUBSTANCE ABUSE

Substance abuse is often said to be one of the major public health concerns in this country. The term *substance abuse* describes abusive or harmful use of any substance. A drug is any substance that crosses from the bloodstream into the brain and that somehow changes the way the brain is functioning. By this definition, some common substances such as alcohol, nicotine, and even caffeine are considered "drugs." Although caffeine, nicotine, and alcohol are by far the most common drugs in the United States, some other drugs of abuse include marijuana, cocaine, amphetamines ("speed"), heroin and other opiates, hallucinogens (LSD, psilocybin mushrooms, peyote), depressants (barbiturates, benzodiazepines, or "downers"), and prescription drugs. In recent years, the development of "designer" drugs and newer chemical compounds has gotten a good deal of media attention. Such substances as the "date rape drugs," including Rohypnol and GHB, have been gaining in popularity in recent years. Although the use and abuse of these drugs are not nearly as prevalent as some other substances, they are causing some alarm within the community of substance-abuse treatment professionals.

Many drugs are synthesized in a laboratory. Some of the synthetic, or man-made, drugs include prescription drugs such as tranquilizers, barbiturates, sedatives, narcotics, pain medications, and some hallucinogens (LSD). Although some of these drugs are indeed chemical substances, others—such as marijuana, opium, peyote, psilocybin mushrooms, and coca leaves—are natural, organic compounds. Further, some organic plants may be chemically processed to make them more usable to the human body. For example, opium and coca leaves can be processed into heroin and cocaine, respectively (Maisto, Galizio, & Connors, 1995).

Substance abuse is not a recent phenomenon. Evidence indicates that the production of beer began in ancient Egypt as early as 5,000 BCE. Within this country alone, the use and abuse of various substances has reached epidemic proportions at a number of different periods. Tobacco use by Native Americans was apparent long before the arrival of Europeans in the Americas. In the nineteenth century, morphine and opium were commonly available without a prescription. With the invention of the hypodermic needle in 1840, morphine became even more common for use as a pain medication, fueling a higher prevalence of morphine addiction. Amphetamine, inhalant, hallucinogen, and marijuana use have all been prevalent at different times during our history. Alcohol was prohibited at one time in the United States because of its detrimental effects, only to be legalized and taxed several years later. Although many people consider alcohol prohibition to have been a failure in terms of an overall method of drug control, it did lead to a marked decrease in alcohol use. Lawsuits against the major tobacco companies and efforts to curb tobacco use in the United States may lead to decreases in tobacco use (Maisto et al., 1995).

The effects of different substances depend on a number of biological and psychological factors. Of course, the type of drug that is being used will affect people's experience. Individuals' biological characteristics, such as weight, gender, and initial sensitivity to a substance, may affect their reaction to a particular substance (Maisto et al., 1995). The setting in which the substance is used also affects how an individual will experience the effect of the substance (Maisto et al., 1995). Finally, people's expectations or beliefs about how the substance will affect them play a role in their reaction to a particular substance (Goldman, Brown, & Christiansen, 1995).

Although neither necessary nor sufficient for a diagnosis of substance abuse or dependence, tolerance and withdrawal symptoms are key indicators of problematic use or addiction. Tolerance and withdrawal symptoms may indicate that the individual's body has become dependent on the drug. Tolerance basically means that the individual's body has become accustomed to the substance, such that larger and larger amounts of the substance are required to produce the same effect. Tolerance is generally developed through repeated exposure to a particular substance. However, some substances with similar actions may have what is known as cross-tolerance, in which an individual who has developed a high tolerance for a particular substance may also have a high tolerance for other, similar substances, even if the substance has not actually been used. Regular use of most substances results in tolerance, at least to some degree.

Depending on the particular substance, abrupt cessation of the substance after a high tolerance has developed may result in withdrawal symptoms. Withdrawal symptoms from any particular drug are experienced most commonly as the direct opposite of the initial effect of the substance and can be psychological, physiological, or both, depending on the substance. Substances such as marijuana and hallucinogens cause no marked physical withdrawal symptoms, but abrupt cessation of use may result in psychological distress that may be severe. Other substances, especially compounds like alcohol, barbiturates, tranquilizers, and some pain medications, cause severe physical pain as well as psychological distress. Although withdrawal from some substances leads to serious enough consequences, such as severe distress, pain, and impairment in functioning, withdrawal from other substances may lead to seizures, coma, and even death.

In addition to experiencing tolerance and withdrawal, many users may become preoccupied with a substance, focusing much of their time and attention on finding, purchasing, and using it. Many people experience craving, or an intense desire to use the substance, when they stop using. Furthermore, some users become so preoccupied with using a substance that they are unable to function in their normal everyday lives.

A number of variations of substance abuse are included in the *Diagnostic and Statistical Manual of Mental Disorders,* fourth edition (*DSM-IV;* American Psychiatric Association, 1994). Criteria are specified in *DSM-IV* for substance intoxication, withdrawal, abuse, and dependence. The major criterion for diagnosis of substance abuse according to the *DSM-IV* is "a maladaptive pattern of substance use manifested by recurrent and significant adverse consequences related to the repeated use of substances." A child or adolescent who is abusing a substance may show a number of behavior changes, including failure to complete school work, marked decreases in academic performance, behavior problems at school and home, problems with the legal system, fighting, arguing, and problems with peers. Substance dependence, by contrast, is more severe than substance abuse. According to the *DSM-IV,* substance dependence is indicated by at least three of the following symptoms: marked tolerance, withdrawal symptoms, using more of the substance than was intended, inability to control or stop using, a desire to stop using, disruption in normal everyday functioning and activities, and continuing to use the substance even after knowing that the use is causing physical or psychological problems. Note that while tolerance and withdrawal are typical hallmarks of addiction, these criteria are neither necessary nor sufficient to indicate substance dependence. One of the reasons that these criteria are not necessary for a diagnosis of substance dependence is the fact that some substances, such as marijuana and most hallucinogens, cause few marked physiological withdrawal symptoms. Thus, substance dependence may be indicated by a disruption in functioning in a number of areas of an individual's life (American Psychiatric Association, 1994).

Although many people assume that the highest rates of substance abuse are in adults, the highest rates of heavy alcohol use and of marijuana use are in those aged 18–25 years (American Psychiatric Association, 1994; U.S. Department of Health and Human Services, 1993). The initial substance use that may eventually lead to abuse or dependence generally begins in adolescence. Adolescents who show symptoms of abuse or dependence are less likely to complete school than those who do not (American Psychiatric Association, 1994). Therefore, and obviously, educators and health professionals need to pay particular attention to the problem of substance abuse in adolescence and young adulthood.

Apparently, little research is available on substance abuse in children enrolled in special education programs. One study on the possible association between special education status and substance abuse yielded alarming results. Gress and Boss (1996) surveyed students from grades 4–12 and found differences in substance use between students in special education and noncategorical classes, especially for students in intermediate (4–6) and junior high (7–8) grades. Some of the most striking differences were found between students in the intermediate grades. For instance, 20 percent of severely behaviorally disabled but only 2.3 percent of noncategorical students used marijuana. Interestingly, whereas a high percentage of students with severe behavioral disabilities and specific learning disabilities used alcohol, amphetamines, and inhalants, a lower percentage of students with developmental disabilities used these substances than did noncategorical students. The authors suggest that substance abuse among students in special education programs is related to several factors, including unmet needs for attachment and close relationships, difficulty establishing a "self-identity," a need to have a certain image within the eyes of their peers, and a need for immediate gratification. Common to all children, these factors may be especially important to students in special education who want to fit in. Gress and Boss (1996) suggest that students with serious disabilities may lack some of the necessary internal skills to deal with unmet needs. Risk of substance abuse may increase as a result of psychological, emotional, and social problems related to their specific disabilities (Gress & Boss, 1996).

Since substance use begins to be a problem for many people when they are children and adolescents, many educators and substance abuse professionals focus on prevention of substance use and abuse in this population. A number of different models are in place for prevention of substance use with children and teenagers. One that has gained recent popularity is a social norms approach, in which prevention campaigns are designed to change people's attitudes about social norms regarding substance use. Other methods of substance abuse prevention efforts geared toward children and adolescents include restricting the availability of particular substances, drink/drug refusal training, providing substance-free activities, mentoring programs, values clarification, and the development of appropriate stress management and social skills (Maisto et al., 1995).

Many different treatment methods exist to help people with substance abuse problems. Formal counseling or psychological treatment is available for individuals with substance abuse problems in inpatient, outpatient, and day treatment facilities, depending on the needs of the individual. Many people choose to attend self-help groups, such as Alcoholics Anonymous, Narcotics Anonymous, Women for Sobriety, or Rational Recovery.

Important to note is that although many people in the United States experience substance abuse problems, many others are affected by another person's substance abuse. Many children are affected by the substance abuse of their parents, siblings, extended family members, or friends. Educators should be familiar with issues related to substance abuse and be able to listen nonjudgmentally to the concerns of their students. When a child is experiencing difficulty as a result of either his or her own substance abuse or that of another person, the child should have access to a school counselor, psychologist, or social worker who can provide counseling and resources for the student.

REFERENCES

American Psychiatric Association. (1994). *Diagnostic and statistical manual of mental disorders* (4th ed.). Washington, DC: Author.

Goldman, M., Brown, S., Christiansen, B., & Smith, G. (1991). Alcoholism and memory: Broadening the scope of alcohol-expectancy research. *Psychological Bulletin, 110,* 137–146.

Gress, J., & Boss, M. (1996). Substance abuse differences among students receiving special education services. *Child Psychiatry and Human Development, 26,* 235–236.

Maisto, S., Galizio, M., & Connors, G. (1995). *Drug use and abuse.* Orlando, FL: Harcourt Brace College Publishers.

U.S. Department of Health and Human Services (USDHHS). (1993). *Alcohol and health.* Rockville, MD: Author.

PAMELA M. RICHMAN
ALISON SHANER
University of North Carolina at Wilmington

CHEMICALLY DEPENDENT YOUTH
DRUG ABUSE

SUBSTANTIA NIGRA

The substantia nigra houses the cell bodies of dopamine containing neurons that project to the striatum (putamen and caudate nucleus). This the so-called nigrostriatal pathway is the major dopamine pathway in the brain. The substantia nigra is a midbrain structure and is darkly pigmented, hence its name (i.e., black substance or black body). The nigrostriatal pathway is an important pathway in the extrapyramidal motor system, which controls background movement. Because of the importance of dopamine in the regulatory control of motor as well as emotional functioning, the nigrostriatal system has been implicated in a variety of neurobehavioral disorders (Andreasen, 1984). In particular, a breakdown of normal functioning of the dopaminergic system has been strongly implicated in schizophrenia (Andreasen, 1984). Also, other lines of investigation have suggested that dopamine plays a role in hyperactivity and attention-deficit disorder (Shaywitz, Shaywitz, Cohen, &

Young, 1983) and Rett syndrome (Segawa, 1997). The motor maladroitness frequently seen in learning-disabled children may be related in some fashion to basal ganglia/nigrostriatal irregularities (Duane, 1985; Rudel, 1985). The prototype neurologic disorder with primary substantia nigra involvement, and hence dopamine loss, is Parkinson's disease (Kolb & Whishaw, 1985).

REFERENCES

Andreasen, N. C. (1984). *The broken brain.* Cambridge, England: Harper & Row.

Duane, D. (1985). Written language underachievement: An overview of the theoretical and practical issues. In F. H. Duffy & N. Geschwind (Eds.), *Dyslexia: A neuroscientific approach to clinical evaluation.* Boston: Little, Brown.

Kolb, B., & Whishaw, I. Q. (1985). *Fundamentals of human neuropsychology.* New York: Freeman.

Rudel, R. G. (1985). The definition of dyslexia: Language and motor deficits. In F. H. Duffy & N. Geschwind (Eds.), *Dyslexia: A neuroscientific approach to clinical evaluation.* Boston: Little, Brown.

Segawa, M. (1997). Pathophysiology of Rett syndrome from the standpoint of early catecholamine disturbance. *European Child & Adolescent Psychiatry, 6*(1), 56–60.

Shaywitz, S. E., Shaywitz, B. A., Cohen, D. J., & Young, J. G. (1983). Monoaminergic mechanisms in hyperactivity. In M. Rutter (Ed.), *Developmental neuropsychiatry.* New York: Guilford.

ERIN D. BIGLER
Brigham Young University

DOPAMINE
PUTAMEN

SUBTEST SCATTER

Subtest scatter refers to the variability of an individual's subtest scores. The highs and lows of the profile indicate strengths and weaknesses on specific subtests. Differences between composite scores for an individual also are termed scatter. While the term *subtest scatter* may be aptly applied to any multiple subtest battery of basic skills, reading achievement, adaptive behavior, or other tests, the term has been popularized by its association with intellectual assessment. Exactly what role scatter has in diagnosing and differentiating among populations has not been determined. Is scatter a valid indicator for diagnostic purposes, or is it limited to identifying a subject's abilities and achievements in various areas? The believers in the significance of scatter have developed several diagnostic schemes that can be used to differentiate among populations.

Kaufman (1994) points out that scatter, significant differences in abilities measured by the Wechsler Intelligence Scale for Children (WISC-III), occurs frequently in the normal population. On the basis of this finding, he emphasizes the importance of being certain that the intersubtest variability is indeed rare in comparison with that of normal children before associating the scatter with abnormality. However, certain characteristic scatter has been consistently found for specific groups. Low scores on arithmetic, coding, information, and digit span subtests of the WISC-III have been shown to characterize the performance of many groups of learning-disabled children. This has been refuted (Dumont & Willis, 1995). It has been concluded, however, that learning disabilities are more likely to be indicated by intraindividual differences than by set profiles.

Scatter has been applied to problems other than learning disabilities. Different types of mental deficiencies have been described in terms of scatter (Roszkowski & Spreat, 1982). Organically caused mental deficiency exhibited more scatter in Wechsler Adult Intelligence Scale (WAIS) scores than environmentally caused deficiency, but not to a significant degree. Greater scatter may be linked to lower-functioning individuals. Large amounts of scatter on intelligence tests can also be associated with high degrees of maladaptive behaviors (Roszkowski & Spreat, 1983) and social-emotional problems (Greenwald, Harder, & Fisher, 1982). Thus scatter can be associated with behavioral, emotional, and organic disorders, as well as with the more commonly thought of learning disabilities.

There may be evidence linking scatter to various disorders, but it is questionable whether it is strong enough to warrant its use as a diagnostic tool. The greatest portion of the evidence says no (Kavale & Forness, 1984). Subtest scatter may be useful in specifying particular strengths and weaknesses of an individual's performance and in educational intervention planning. Caution is needed with interpretation of scatter and profile analysis, and flexibility is recommended when selecting tests for a particular population (Kamphaus, 1985). Recently developed tests of intelligence argue against interpreting subtest-level scatter and instead focus on various composite indexes (e.g., Reynolds & Kamphaus, 2003).

REFERENCES

Bannatyne, H. (1971). *Language, reading, and learning disabilities.* Springfield, IL: Thomas.

Decker, S. A., & Corley, R. P. (1984). Bannatyne's "genetic dyslexic" subtype: A validation study. *Psychology in the Schools, 21,* 300–304.

Dumont, R., & Willis, J. O. (1995). Intrasubtest scatter on the WISC-III for various clinical samples vs. the standardization sample: An examination of the WISC folklore. *Journal of Psychoeducational Assessment, 13*(3), 271–285.

Greenwald, D. F., Harder, D. W., & Fisher, L. (1982). WISC scatter and behavioral competence in high-risk children. *Journal of Clinical Psychology, 38,* 397–401.

Kamphaus, R. W. (1985). Perils of profile analysis. *Information / Edge: Cognitive Assessment & Remediation, 1,* 1–4.

Kaufman, A. S. (1994). *Intelligence testing with the WISC-III.* New York: Wiley.

Kavale, K. A., & Forness, S. (1984). A meta-analysis of the validity of Wechsler scale profiles and recategorizations: Patterns or parodies? *Learning Disability Quarterly, 7,* 136–156.

Reynolds, C. R., & Kamphaus, R. W. (2003). *Reynolds intellectual assessment scales.* Odessa, FL: Psychological Assessment Resources.

Roszkowski, M., & Spreat, S. (1982). Scatter as an index of organicity: A comparison of mentally retarded individuals experiencing and not experiencing concomitant convulsive disorders. *Journal of Behavioral Assessment, 4,* 311–315.

Roszkowski, M., & Spreat, S. (1983). Assessment of effective intelligence: Does scatter matter? *Journal of Special Education, 17,* 453–459.

Lisa J. Sampson
Eastern Kentucky University

FACTOR ANALYSIS
INTELLIGENCE
INTELLIGENT TESTING

SUICIDE

Suicide describes the act of intentionally killing oneself, whereas the term *parasuicide* refers to an unsuccessful or uncompleted suicide attempt (Kauffman, 2005). Suicide is the third leading cause of death for persons aged 15–24, with only accidents and homicides resulting in more deaths for this age group (Jensen, 2005). Data from 1992 indicated that children, youths, and young adults in this age group accounted for approximately 16 percent of all recorded suicides (Centers for Disease Control and Prevention, 1995). Cimbolic and Jobes (1990) write that adolescent males have a higher suicide rate than adolescent females; however, adolescent females have a higher parasuicide rate. The difference between parasuicide rates for females and suicides in males is a function of the method used, with males typically using more lethal means (e.g., firearms, hanging). Due to the stigmatizing effect of suicide, it is believed that the actual rate of suicide may be 2 to 3 times higher than what is officially reported (Guetzloe, 1991).

Suicide is a result of a complex interaction between environmental, social, psychological, and biological factors. Kauffman (2005) writes:

> The many complex factors that contribute to children's and adolescents' suicidal behavior include major psychiatric problems, feelings of hopelessness, impulsivity, naïve concepts of death,

substance abuse, social isolation, abuse and neglect by parents, family conflict and disorganization, a family history of suicide and parasuicide, and cultural factors, including stress caused by the educational system and attention to suicide in the mass media. Youth with emotional and behavioral disorders, especially those who use alcohol or illicit drugs, are a particularly high risk of suicidal behavior. (p. 400)

Information on the rate of suicidal behavior in children and youths who receive special education services is sparse. Guetzloe (1987, 1991) writes that evidence of a specific psychiatric disorder (e.g., mood disorder, depression, bipolar disorder, conduct disorder, psychosis) and other disabilities (e.g., developmental disabilities, deafness, physical and/or orthopedic disabilities, cerebral palsy) may contribute to suicidal ideation and possibly be overlooked by educators and care providers. For example, Peck (1985) reviewed all suicides of children and youths under the age of 15 that occurred in Los Angles County over a 3-year period ($n = 14$). Fifty percent of the sample had a documented learning or behavioral disability (i.e., hyperactivity, perceptual disorders, or dyslexia). In one particular case, Peck wrote that a student who committed suicide had received adequate educational support for his learning disability, but very little attention was given to his general feelings of unhappiness and frustration, which, in retrospect, placed him in a category of needing immediate mental health support.

McBride and Siegel (1997) investigated the role that learning disabilities played in adolescent suicides by researching spelling and handwriting errors found on suicide notes. Data from this study suggested that nearly 90 percent of the 27 suicide notes reviewed showed significant spelling and handwriting deficits. The spelling and handwriting errors were judged to be similar to those of students who have identified learning disabilities. The authors concluded that "there is evidence that children and adolescents with unrecognized, poorly treated, or untreated learning disabilities are at a higher risk of developing secondary behavior problems and psychiatric disorders than those who received adequate intervention. In the present study . . . none of the adolescents who committed suicide had been identified as learning disabled or were receiving special education help" (pp. 657–658). Interestingly, Kauffman (2005) writes that performance in school can be a factor in adolescent suicide, with an increase in suicides and parasuicide occurring in the spring term, when performance indicators, such as grades and graduation, receive greater attention.

Awareness, prevention, and intervention are critical features of successful suicide intervention programs. Jensen (2005) describes a prevention strategy that includes four steps: (1) focusing on improving services for students who are depressed and/or feeling hopeless (i.e., observation, identification, and intervention services); (2) elimination of access to lethal means of killing oneself (e.g., guns, knives, ropes, medication); (3) provision of comprehensive adult support for at-risk individuals; and (4) limiting access to media coverage that glamorizes or publicizes suicide. Educators should familiarize themselves with local resources (policies, curricula, assessments, counseling, and mental health support) that might be needed if a student is considered a risk for suicide. Specific guidelines for working with a person who has expressed suicidal feelings or thoughts include (1) taking all suicide threats seriously, (2) focusing on establishing communication with the person of concern, (3) providing emotional support, and (4) seeking immediate assistance from trained professionals (Kauffman, 2005).

In summary, suicide is the third leading cause of death in children and youths. A review of the literature suggests that students with disabilities may be at higher risk for suicidal ideation, especially students with depression, mood disorders, or undiagnosed disabilities. Educators have the responsibility to increase awareness, prevention, and intervention activities at their schools and should know how to access local resources and expertise should they encounter a student who has expressed suicidal thoughts or feelings. Guidelines for working with students who have expressed suicidal ideations include taking all threats seriously, establishing communication, providing emotional support, and seeking immediate assistance from a trained professional.

REFERENCES

Centers for Disease Control and Prevention. (1995). Suicide among children, adolescents, and young adults—United States, 1980–1992. *Morbidity and Mortality Weekly Report, 44*(15), 289–308.

Cimbolic, P., & Jobes, D. A. (1990). Youth suicide: The scope of the problem. In P. Cimbolic & D. A. Jobes (Eds.), *Youth suicide: Issues, assessment, and intervention* (pp. 3–8). Springfield, IL: Charles C. Thomas.

Guetzloe, E. C. (1989). *A special educator's perspective on youth suicide: What the educator should know.* ERIC Clearinghouse on Handicapped and Gifted Children, Council for Exceptional Children.

Guetzloe, E. C. (1991). *Suicide and the exceptional child* (Report No. E508). Reston, VI: ERIC Clearinghouse on Disabilities and Gifted Education. (ERIC Document Reproduction Service No. ED340152)

Jensen, M. M. (2005). *Introduction to emotional and behavioral disorders: Recognizing and managing problems in the classroom.* Upper Saddle River, NJ: Pearson Merrill Prentice Hall.

Kauffman, J. M. (2005). *Characteristics of emotional and behavioral disorders of children and youth* (8th ed). Upper Saddle River, NJ: Pearson Merrill Prentice Hall.

McBride, H. E. A., & Siegel, L. S. (1997). Learning disabilities and adolescent suicide. *Journal of Learning Disabilities, 30,* 652–659.

Peck, M. L. (1985). Crisis intervention treatment with chronically and acutely suicidal adolescents. In M. L. Peck, N. L. Farberow,

& R. E. Litman (Eds.), *Youth suicide* (pp. 112–122). New York: Springer.

RANDALL L. DE PRY
*University of Colorado at
Colorado Springs*

SULLIVAN, ANN

See MACY, ANN SULLIVAN.

SULLIVAN PROGRAMMED READING

The Sullivan Programmed Reading system comprises an individualized programmed workbook approach to teaching reading to students in grades 1 through 3. The sequence of the 3-year system extends from Reading Readiness through Series III, with diagnostic prescriptive teaching aids and student activities that are designed to optimize individual pacing. Pupils systematically progress from letter discrimination to word recognition or to reading sentences and stories. The first 10 weeks of the program are spent in the development of a basic vocabulary and the acquisition of skills that are necessary for the use of programmed material. This part of the series is teacher directed or oriented and must be done as a class or group. Afterward, the program allows each pupil to progress according to his or her own rate of learning. The pupil is provided with a minimal amount of information, a problem is posed, a response is solicited, and the response is corrected or reinforced. The child makes the response, then checks his or her answer against the correct response that is revealed as a slider moves down the page to reveal the next frame (Hafner & Jolly, 1972; Moyle & Moyle, 1971; Scheiner, 1969; Sullivan Associates, 1968).

The Reading Readiness and Programmed Readers Series I, II, and III provide sequential instruction in consonants, vowels, sight words, punctuation, suffixes, contractions, possessives, capitals, and comprehension. Placement tests indicate at which point in the series to enter a pupil who begins in the system after first grade. The Programmed Reading Program comprises 23 levels, with one book per level. Pupils progress through each book and are expected to pass an end-of-book test before proceeding to the next book. A total of 3,266 words are introduced in the complete program (Hafner & Jolly, 1972; Sullivan Associates, 1968).

The following components of the Sullivan Associates system may be ordered as kits or separately. Reading Readiness consists of two kits, each of which contains two full-color, 72-page Big Books, two comprehensive teacher guides, two hour-long tape cassettes, a set of Webster-masters, and a wire easel and alphabet strips. On completion of the prereading stage, the child should master (1) the names of letters; (2) how to write letters; (3) the sounds that represent letters; (4) left-to-right sequencing; (5) the concept that words are formed from groups of letters; and (6) the ability to read the words *yes* or *no* in sentences. Series I, II, and III Programmed Readers Books 1 to 23 provide logical linguistic progression, constant reinforcement, colorful art, and stimulating story content. By the end of the eighth book in Series I, 14 vowels and 23 consonant classes will have been mastered; in addition, children will know approximately 450 words phonetically and 10 sight words. On completion of Series III, 25 more vowels and consonant classes, a total of 3,200 new words, and 40 more sight words will have been mastered.

Two sets of seven filmstrips that are primarily designed to introduce the readers to new words supplement Books 1 to 14. Each filmstrip reviews material from the previous level and presents new vocabulary and characters. Three sets of Activity Books reinforce ideas provided by the programmed series through cutout patterns for characters, puppets, and games. Webstermasters allow duplications to supplement each series of programmed readers. Read and Think Series are provided for Series I and II and are to be read after completion of the programmed text to motivate children to read for enjoyment. Achievement tests (criterion-referenced) measure student progress in terms of predetermined behavioral objectives for each series. There is an item-by-item analysis of the skills tested and specific remediation for each item that is missed. Word cards and response booklets allow pupils to write their answers using a wax pencil or crayon, making the tests reusable. Teachers' guides are organized by book, skill, and unit. An overview of decoding and comprehension information, and a listing of the sound-symbol and vocabulary progression and content summary, are outlined. Each grade also contains a reading aloud, dictation, creative writing, and test section for each book level, and specific item-by-item instructions for both with remediative recycling options (Sullivan & Associates, 1968). For uses with exceptional children, see Lerner (1985).

REFERENCES

Hafner, L., & Jolly, H. (1972). *Patterns of teaching reading in the elementary school.* New York: Macmillan.

Lerner, J. (1985). *Learning disabilities: Theories, diagnosis and teaching strategies* (4th ed.). Dallas: Houghton Mifflin.

Moyle, D., & Moyle, L. (1971). *Modern innovations in the teaching of reading.* London: University of London Press.

Scheiner, L. (1969). *An evaluation of the Sullivan Reading Program (1967–1969) Rhoads Elementary School.* Washington, DC: U.S. Department of Health, Education and Welfare. (ERIC Document Reproduction Service ED 002 362)

Sullivan Associates. (1968). *Sullivan Associates programmed reading, Sullivan Press.* New York: McGraw-Hill.

FRANCES T. HARRINGTON
Radford University

READING DISORDERS
READING REMEDIATION

SUMMER SCHOOL FOR INDIVIDUALS WITH DISABILITIES

Extended-year programs for individuals with disabilities have been a highly debated issue for many years. The position of many individuals is that extended school year programs are needed for disabled students to prevent the loss of existing skills, accelerate the acquisition of new skills, and provide recreational programming and respite care for the parents. There are several main questions for which there are no appropriate answers: (1) Do extended school year programs accomplish instructional objectives, and, if so, how much? (2) If students do learn something, is it additive to what is learned during the school year? (3) Do students without extended school years lose skills, or do they increase maladaptive (i.e., irritant) responding? (4) Do students without extended school years catch up to students who do experience extended school year programming and thus negate the effect of the extended year? (5) If students with extended school years do have additive learning, is the cost effectiveness of that learning acceptable? (6) What types of extended school years (e.g., school, school plus recreational, recreational, short programs, long programs) have what types of effects, and what are the desired effects (e.g., retention, gain, degree of gain)? (7) What are the "do-ability" variables? (E.g., What teachers and aides will be involved? Is burnout an issue? Who will supervise?) (8) How will documentation be provided? (9) Is there student burnout?

There are some other questions that do have answers. First, do disabled students have a right to a public education? Public Law 94-142 and Section 504 of the Rehabilitation Act of 1973, have defined the right of children with disabilities to a free appropriate public education. Second, do specific classes of disabled students have a right to an extended school year? The courts have substantiated the right of specific classes of disabled children to extended (over 180-day) school year programs in a number of court cases (e.g., *Armstrong* v. *Kline,* 1979). Additional cases are currently pending throughout the United States. Therefore, while there is growing educational and legal support for extended-year programming, many questions still need to be addressed.

Empirical support for the current policy on extended-year programs for individuals with disabilities is difficult to find in the literature. Browder, Lentz, Knoster, and Wilansky (1984) found that the primary methodology for determining both eligibility for and effectiveness of extended-year programs was the subjective judgments of teachers and parents (Bahling, 1980; McMahon, 1983). This information, while not surprising, does not provide empirical support for extended school year programming. Ellis (1975a) studied the effects of a summer program on possible regression of 16 multihandicapped blind children and found that none of the students had regressed in eight target skill areas (e.g., communication skills). In a second study, Ellis (1975b) examined the skill levels of 145 physically and neurologically handicapped students and found a significant improvement in skill areas for the summer program participants. In contrast, Edgar, Spence, and Kenowitz (1977), in a study that examined the findings of 18 summer programs, found that the data (e.g., teacher observations, rating scales) did not strongly support the premise that such programs facilitated the maintenance of skills. However, these results are possible when there is not a coherence between the school year objectives and those of the summer program. Therefore, there are conflicting data concerning the effectiveness of extended-year programming in either maintaining or extending the learning repertoire of students with disabilities.

Zdunich (1984) reported on data gathered on extended-year programs in Canada. This study examined the effects of four types of summer programming (short programs, high-structure, low-structure, and medium-structure programs). A control group that received no summer programming was also used in the study. While the study's sample size was relatively small (overall $n = 186$), its results were interesting. First, the study found that maladaptive behaviors had been significantly reduced only in the high- and medium-structure programs and that students in the other conditions increased maladaptive responding. Second, skill development (e.g., communication, self-help, fine motor skills) was significantly greater in high- and medium-structure programs. Other types of summer experiences showed relative maintenance of skills with some small amount of skill regression. In addition, the skill acquisition data held constant over the following academic year. The study also examined many variables related to each of these two major concerns. It should provide a substantial increase in our database on the educational and social impact of extended school year programming.

REFERENCES

Bahling, E. (1980). *Extended school year program, Intermediate Unit #5, June–August, 1980.* Paper presented at the annual international convention of Council for Exceptional Children, Philadelphia. (ERIC Document Reproduction Service No. 208 609)

Browder, D. M., Lentz, F. E., Knosten, T., & Wilansky, C. (1984). *A record based evaluation of extended school year eligibility practice.* Unpublished manuscript.

Edgar, E., Spence, W., & Kenowitz, L. (1977). Extended school year for the handicapped: Is it working? *Journal of Special Education, 11,* 441–447.

Ellis, R. S. (1975a). Summer pre-placement program for severely multihandicapped blind children. *Summer 1975, Evaluation Report.* New York City Board of Education. (ERIC Document Reproduction Service No. ED136489)

Ellis, R. S. (1975b). Summer education program for neurologically and physically handicapped children. *Summer 1975, Evaluation Report.* New York City Board of Education. (ERIC Document Reproduction Service No. ED136489)

McMahon, J. (1983). Extended school year programs. *Exceptional Children, 49,* 457–460.

Zdunich, L. (1984). *Summer programs for the severely handicapped.* Edmonton, Alberta, Canada: Alberta Education.

LYLE E. BARTON
Kent State University

TUTORING

SUPERVISION IN SPECIAL EDUCATION

Current emphasis in special education is on the employment of a program administrator specifically for exceptional children. Other titles used are special education director and supervisor of exceptional children's programs. For most states, the administrator or director of special education must have an academic degree at the master's level in the education of exceptional children or a related field. Owing to the nature of the position, it is also helpful if this person completes the requirements for a supervisor's or administrator's certificate in addition to the master's degree in special education. The educational program for the preparation of exceptional children's program administrators is basically the same as for preparing general school administrators. The major difference in their preparation is in the specific exceptional children's program content requirement.

The exceptional children's program administrator has been identified by the North Carolina Division for Exceptional Children as

one who plans, develops, coordinates, supervises, administers, and evaluates the effectiveness of local educational agency's educational programs. The program administrator provides guidance and leadership to all exceptional children program personnel. The role is performed under the general supervision of the superintendent or designee. The program administrator maintains a cooperative relationship with principals, other school personnel, other related service agencies, and parents. The administrator is responsible for maintaining the program within local, state, and federal guidelines, rules, regulations, and laws which govern exceptional children.

Program administrators should have competencies in the administration of exceptional children's programs, including assessment; planning and implementing programs; budgeting; communicating with parents, central office staff, principals, other service providers, and state and local agencies; staff development; and program evaluation. Another area of expertise necessary for program administrators is the application of school law administration of exceptional children's programs. This includes knowledge of legislation about the handicapped as it relates to IDEA other state and federal statutes; confidentiality guidelines; due process procedures; procedures for auditing and evaluating compliance; authority of the hearing officer; and schools' responsibility for various placements, transportation, suspension and expulsion, related services, competency tests, and evaluations.

Program administrators should be well versed in supervision of instruction centered around personnel management. They should be able to interview and select qualified exceptional children's teachers, observe and evaluate teachers to identify teaching strengths and weaknesses, and develop professional growth plans for teachers and support staff. The administrator should be able to design instructional units that specify performance objectives, instructional sequences, learning activities, and materials and evaluation processes, and prepare an educational plan that includes curriculum content and level, activities, alternative teaching strategies, and evaluation of learning outcomes (Sage & Burrello, 1994). The program administrator should also be able to evaluate the quality, utility, and availability of learning resource materials.

REFERENCES

Comprehensive system of personnel development report. (1984, August). Raleigh: Division for Exceptional Children, North Carolina Department of Public Instruction.

Competencies and guidelines for approved teacher education programs. (1983, September). Raleigh: Division for Exceptional Children, North Carolina Department of Public Instruction.

Sage, D. D., & Burrello, L. C. (1994). *Leadership in educational reform: An administrator's guide to changes in special education.* Baltimore: Brookes.

CECELIA STEPPE-JONES
North Carolina Central University

ADMINISTRATION OF SPECIAL EDUCATION
POLITICS AND SPECIAL EDUCATION

SUPPORTED EMPLOYMENT

Supported employment is a vocational alternative that has been described in rules published by the U.S. Department of Education in the *Federal Register* (June 18, 1985) as "paid work in a variety of integrated settings, particularly regular work sites, especially designed for severely handicapped individuals irrespective of age or vocational potential." Traditionally, individuals with severe disabilities have been served in day activity centers in which the intended goal is to prepare these clients for vocational rehabilitation services and, ultimately, employment. However, this readiness model of service delivery has not prepared these individuals successfully for vocational rehabilitation services or employment. Supported employment provides employment opportunities to those individuals with mental and physical disabilities so severe that they are not eligible for vocational rehabilitation services.

Supported employment (Will, 1985) includes four characteristics that differentiate it from vocational rehabilitation services and traditional methods of providing day activity services. First, the service recipients are those typically served in day activity centers who do not have the potential for unassisted competitive employment and thus are ineligible for vocational rehabilitative services. Second, ongoing support, which is unavailable in a traditional day activity program, as well as supervision and ongoing training is involved. Supported employment is not designed to lead to unassisted competitive work as are vocational rehabilitation programs. Third, the employment focus of supported employment provides the same benefits typically obtained by people from work (e.g. income, security, mobility, advancement opportunities, etc.). It does not seek to identify and teach prerequisite skills and behaviors needed for employment as is usually done in day activity centers. Last, there is flexibility in support strategies to assist individuals with severe disabilities in obtaining and maintaining employment. This may include the provision of a "job coach" by a community agency. The coach provides training and supervision at an individual's work site, direct support to employers to offset training and special equipment costs, or salary supplements to coworkers who provide regular assistance in the performance of personal care activities while at work.

Federal initiatives have provided the impetus for the development of supported employment programs. These programs vary according to client characteristics, community resources, and employment opportunities. Options for supported employment are flexible owing to the wide range of community jobs and the variety of ways to provide support to individuals with severe disabilities (McCarthy, Everson, Moon, & Barcus, 1985). The features common to various supported employment program options are emphasis on paid employment, ongoing support and training that enables individuals with severe disabilities to get and keep a job, and social integration in which these individuals are provided with opportunities to work and interact with coworkers, supervisors, and other nondisabled individuals (Mark, O'Neill, & Jensen, 1998; Password, 1985). Examples of four supported employment options are enclaves, mobile work crews, specialized industrial programs, and supported competitive employment. A brief discussion of each follows.

An enclave is an industry-based option that relies on private and public-sector cooperation to create an organizational structure that supports the employment of individuals with severe disabilities. While a wide range of alternatives is possible with this service model, an enclave is a group of individuals with disabilities who are provided training and support by a third-party public organization among nonhandicapped workers in a private company. Rhodes and Valenta (1985) describe the ideal enclave as having the following characteristics. Enclave employees are located in physical proximity to coworkers and represent approximately 1 percent of the total workforce. Enclave employees perform the same work, have the same work routines (work hours, breaks, lunch), and are supervised in the same manner as their nonhandicapped coworkers. They are employed by the host company and arrive at work via car pools with coworkers or public or company transportation. Finally, the support organization maintains low visibility and intervenes only when necessary to maintain and support employment.

Mobile work crews are community-based employment groups that usually involve four to six individuals and a crew supervisor working together on various job sites (Bourbeau, 1985). As the title indicates, these work crews operate out of a vehicle and move from one work site to the next. The work performed by the crews is specific to community needs any may entail a variety of jobs such as janitorial work or grounds maintenance (Bourbeau, 1985). Since the job site is in the community, integration and interaction are fostered (interaction with people in the community, eating in community restaurants, etc.).

Another supported work option is described by O'Bryan (1985), the benchwork model. This model was developed at the University of Oregon in 1973 as a small, nonprofit business and since has been replicated at 17 sites. The benchwork model shares many features and constraints with traditional sheltered workshops, although it is designed for persons with more severe disabilities. The major differences are the size and location of the operation. Only 15 individuals with severe or profound disabilities are employed. The location in the community close to stores and restaurants provides the opportunity for regular participation in the surrounding community. Training in skills that relate to a typical working day are provided with the major foci on those skills necessary to experience the regular daily, weekly, and monthly rhythms of the community. One of the major constraints, however, is that job security, benefits, and integration depend on the organization's commercial success.

The fourth option, a supported competitive employment program, has been defined by Wehman (1985) as real work at the federal minimum wage at a job with predominantly nondisabled workers. The provision of specialized assistance in locating an appropriate job, intensive job-site training, and permanent ongoing support at the level required by the individual are components of this option.

Supported work options have been initiated at state and local levels to meet the vocational needs of individuals with severe disabilities. The purpose of these work options is to provide these individuals with real work opportunities and the support necessary for them to keep their jobs. Supported work has been found to be cost-effective (McCoughvin, Ellis, Rusch, & Heal, 1993). The assumption is that all persons, regardless of the severity of their disabilities, have the ability to work as long as appropriate, ongoing services are provided.

REFERENCES

Bourbeau, P. E. (1985). Mobile work crews: An approach to achieve long-term supported employment. In P. McCarthy, J. Everson, S. Moon, & M. Barcus (Eds.), *School-to-work transition for youth with severe disabilities* (pp. 151–166). Richmond: Rehabilitation Research and Training Center, Virginia Commonwealth University.

Mark, D., O'Neill, C. T., & Jensen, R. (1998). Quality in supported employment: A new demonstration of the capabilities of people with severe disabilities. *Journal of Vocational Rehabilitation, 11*(1), 83–95.

McCarthy, P., Everson, J., Moon, S., & Barcus, M. (Eds.). (1985). *School-to-work transition for youth with severe disabilities.* Richmond: Rehabilitation Research and Training Center, Virginia Commonwealth University.

McCoughvin, W. B., Ellis, W. K., Rusch, F. R., & Heal, L. W. (1993). Cost-effectiveness of supported employment. *Mental Retardation, 31*(1), 41–48.

O'Bryan, A. (1985). The specialized training program (STP) benchwork model. In P. McCarthy, J. Everson, S. Moon, & M. Barcus (Eds.), *School-to-work transition for youth with severe disabilities* (pp. 183–194). Richmond: Rehabilitation Research and Training Center, Virginia Commonwealth University.

Password. (1985, Autumn). *Office of Special Education and Rehabilitative Services (OSERS) News in Print, 1*(1), 2.

Rhodes, L. E., & Valenta, L. (1985). Enclaves in industry. In P. McCarthy, J. Everson, S. Moon, & M. Barcus (Eds.), *School-to-work transition for youth with severe disabilities* (pp. 129–149). Richmond: Rehabilitation Research and Training Center, Virginia Commonwealth University.

Wehman, P. (1985). Supported competitive employment for persons with severe disabilities. In P. McCarthy, J. Everson, S. Moon, & M. Barcus (Eds.), *School-to-work transition for youth with severe disabilities* (pp. 167–182). Richmond: Rehabilitation Research and Training Center, Virginia Commonwealth University.

Will, M. (1985, Autumn). Supported employment programs: Moving from welfare to work. *Office of Special Education and Rehabilitative Services (OSERS) News in Print, 1*(1), 8–9.

EILEEN F. MCCARTHY
University of Wisconsin at Madison

TRANSITION
VOCATIONAL REHABILITATION COUNSELING

SURROGATE PARENTS

The Individuals with Disabilities Education Act (IDEA) included parental participation as a major component in the educational planning for children with disabilities. The purpose of including parents was to ensure that the rights of the child and the parents are protected. This component of IDEA officially recognized the parents as a crucial and viable force in the life of their child and required their input in the educational planning and decision-making process. However, there are instances when a disabled child's parents, for various reasons, are unable to represent him or her in the educational decision-making process. This is when the public agency responsible for educating the child appoints a surrogate parent. According to federal regulations, a surrogate parent is appointed when (1) no parent can be identified; (2) the public agency, after reasonable efforts, cannot discover the whereabouts of a parent; or (3) the child is a ward of the state under the laws of that state (*Federal Register,* 1977, p. 42496).

Surrogate parents are individuals who are responsible for ensuring that the disabled child receives a free appropriate education in the least restrictive environment. The surrogate parents' role is limited to the educational needs of the child. However, more and more grandparents are taking on this role (Rottenberg, 1996). Specifically, the role of the surrogate parents, based on the federal regulations, relates to

(1) The identification, evaluation, and educational placement of the child. . . .
(2) The provision of a free appropriate education to the child. . . .
The public agency may select a surrogate parent in any way permitted by state law. The public agencies shall insure that a person selected as surrogate has no interest that conflicts with the interests of the child he or she represents; and has knowledge and skills that ensure adequate representation of the child. The person who is appointed as a surrogate parent cannot be an employee of the public agency that is directly involved in the education and care of the child. (*Federal Register,* 1977, p. 42496)

Shrybman (1982, pp. 267–268) listed the following rights of surrogate parents:

1. Review all written records regarding the child's education

2. Take part in the evaluation and development of the individual education plan (IEP)

3. Reject, accept, or recommend changes in the IEP

4. Request and/or initiate a second evaluation

5. Initiate mediation, hearing, or appeals procedures

6. Receive legal help at no cost if such assistance is necessary in the furtherance of the surrogate's responsibilities

7. Monitor the child's program

8. Recommend changes in the pupil's placement

9. Take advantage of all the rights afforded to natural parents in the special education decision-making process

Each state is required to develop specific requirements for the selection of the surrogate parents. Once the need has been proven by the local agency, the criteria and responsibilities are specifically defined. A surrogate parent does not have to be a professional person; however, it is important that the surrogate have a general knowledge of state and federal laws relating to the disabled. In addition, knowledge of the rules and regulations of the public school system and specific information about the child's disability and educational needs are crucial areas. The state is responsible for education and training of the surrogate parent to ensure adequate representation of the child.

The surrogate parent has many responsibilities that must be understood and explained by the local agency. Knowledge of these responsibilities are essential if the educational needs of the child are to be met in the least restrictive environment. A surrogate parent may be dismissed from his or her role if the local agency determines that the roles and responsibilities outlined by federal and state regulations have been neglected, or the well-being of the child is at risk. Shrybman (1982) listed the responsibilities of surrogate parents of children with disabilities: to attend any training program the local agency offers; to be sure there are no areas of interest that conflict with their responsibilities to the child; to be involved in identification, evaluation, program development, initial placement, review placement, and reevaluation; to be knowledgeable of the child's educational needs, wishes, and concerns; to maintain confidentiality of all records; to be aware of support provided by human services in the community; and to be sure the child is receiving special education in the least restrictive environment.

REFERENCES

Federal Register. (1977). Washington, DC: U.S. Government Printing Office.

Rothenberg, D. (1996). *Grandparents as parents: A primer for schools.* (ERIC Digest No. ED401044)

Shrybman, J. A. (1982). *Due process in special education.* Rockville, MD: Aspen.

JANICE HARPER
*North Carolina Central
University*

INDIVIDUALS WITH DISABILITIES EDUCATION IMPROVEMENT ACT
PARENT EDUCATION

SURVIVAL SKILLS

Survival skills are essential components of functional teaching. Many educators use the terms survival skills and functional teaching synonymously. Heward and Orlansky (1984) define functional skills as skills that are "frequently demanded in a student's natural environment" (p. 340). Cassidy and Shanahan (1979) suggest the term survival emphasizes the need to develop skills that will help individuals to attain personal goals and social responsibilities. A few examples of survival skills include balancing a checkbook, riding a bus, completing a job application, reading a menu, and shopping for groceries (Alcantara, 1994). Survival skills have also been extended to self-management skills in the classroom (Synder & Bambara, 1997).

Sabatino (1982) emphasized the importance of the functional curriculum model to prepare the handicapped youth for a vocational career. Examples of survival skills from this model include a word list from a driver's manual, social skills training, and using technical terms to understand career information. McDowell (1979) further stressed the need for adolescents with disabilities to exhibit specific behaviors to help them function successfully in today's society and on the job. These behaviors include showing respect for others, demonstrating good manners, knowing when certain behaviors are appropriate, and learning to accept and follow directions.

Sabatino and Lanning-Ventura (1982) state that there is an important question that must be addressed by teachers of educationally disabled students at the secondary level. When should the educational program focus on survival skills and not on overcoming educational disabilities? The answer to this question should be based on the individual characteristics of the student. However, functional teaching is most appropriate when the chances for academic gains are limited.

An essential component of survival skills in the area of reading is selection of materials. Cassidy and Shanahan (1979) identified the three basic criteria for selection as relevance, necessity, and frequency. Relevance implies considering the student's age, current level of functioning, and geographical area when selecting materials. In terms of geographical area, using materials such as a phone book or a bus schedule from a student's hometown is more appropriate than using commercial materials. Necessity suggests selecting materials that are representative of tasks required in the real world. Frequency deals with the number of times the student will deal with the materials selected. Activities such as reading menus and container labels occur often in the real world.

Potential strengths of the functional curriculum model identified by Alley and Deshler (1979) include the following: (1) students are equipped to function independently, at least over the short term, in society; (2) students may be better prepared to compete for specific jobs on graduation from high school; and (3) instruction in the functional curriculum may have particular relevance for the high school junior or senior who is severely disabled (p. 50).

REFERENCES

Alcantara, P. R. (1994). Effects of videotape instructional package on purchasing skills of children with autism. *Exceptional Children, 61*(1), 40–55.

Alley, G., & Deshler, D. (1979). *Teaching the learning disabled adolescent: Strategies and methods.* Denver: Love.

Cassidy, J., & Shanahan, T. (1979). Survival skills: Some considerations. *Journal of Reading, 23,* 136–140.

Heward, H. L., & Orlansky, M. D. (1984). *Exceptional children.* Columbus, OH: Merrill.

McDowell, R. L. (1979, May). *The emotionally disturbed adolescent* (PRISE Reporter, No. 3) (pp. 1–2). King of Prussia: Pennsylvania Resource and Information Center for Special Education.

Sabatino, D. A. (1982). An educational program guide for secondary schools. In D. A. Sabatino & L. Mann (Eds.), *Diagnostic and prescriptive teaching.* Rockville, MD: Aspen.

Sabatino, D. A., & Lanning-Ventura, S. (1982). Functional teaching: Survival skills and tutoring. In D. A. Sabatino & L. Mann (Eds.), *Diagnostic and prescriptive teaching.* Rockville, MD: Aspen.

Synder, M. C., & Bambara, L. M. (1997). Teaching secondary students with learning disabilities to self-manage classroom survival skills. *Journal of Learning Disabilities, 30*(5), 534–543.

JANICE HARPER
*North Carolina Central
University*

DAILY LIVING SKILLS
FUNCTIONAL INSTRUCTION
FUNCTIONAL SKILLS TRAINING

SWEDEN, SPECIAL EDUCATION IN

Access to equivalent education for all is the basic principle guiding Swedish education from child care to young adulthood. In accordance with this principle, pupils in need of special support are not to be treated in a differential manner, and their rights are not explicitly or separately defined. However, an emphasis is placed on the schools' obligation to attend to all pupils' needs. Thus, special education support is integrated as much as possible into the framework of regular education. National goals set up by the government are combined with a remarkably high degree of local responsibility. Municipalities are free to use collected taxes and state funding for whatever services and systems are judged to be best for their respective areas. Many municipalities delegate budgets directly to individual schools. The municipalities, schools, individual staff, and pupils formulate concrete goals that are appropriate for their own environment and make their own plans for the activities necessary in order to attain the national goals.

The current curriculum for compulsory school (grades 1–9) does not use the word or concept *mainstreaming,* but promotes the view that all pupils are to be educated in regular classes. If this is not possible, the school must indicate very clearly why other educational options for a pupil should be considered. This is an important pedagogic guideline governing school organization and operation. Earlier debates focused upon prerequisites for integration. Currently, however, the focus has shifted toward the need for the justification of segregated options, if such options are under consideration. For all pupils in need of special support, an action plan of provision must be worked out by their teachers in consultation with the pupils themselves, their parents, and specialist support teachers. This plan, which identifies needs, and the provisions for meeting them, must be continuously evaluated. All teachers educated in the new teaching training program from 2001 onward are educated in special needs education to better prepare them to meet the needs of all pupils within regular education. The intention is that specialists of special needs education are educated to advise teachers and to cooperate with the managers of schools to ensure that the needs of all pupils are met.

A special program exists for pupils with severe learning disabilities and mental retardation. This was previously the responsibility of the regional counties, but since 1996 it has been delegated to the local school board in each municipality. The special program is now closely linked to or integrated into regular school activities. A basic principle of governmental policy concerning disability is that children and young people with disabilities must be offered education in their own municipality in order that they may continue to live at home.

By 2001, special schools and institutions had ceased to exist, with the exception of regional schools for deaf children in need of instruction in sign language. The former special schools and institutions have developed into resource centers, financed by government money. Their responsibilities are competence development and consultant support to schools attended by pupils with severe disabilities.

The educational goals decided by the government are expressed in three national curricula, one for preschools, one for compulsory schools, and one for upper secondary schools. The curricula are partly consistent in order to make these activities a homogeneous system. The municipalities and their schools are responsible for finding ways of attaining these goals, evaluating the efforts, and improving the work. The government supports the municipalities and their schools in their strivings to provide and develop the quality of their internal activities. The Swedish National Agency for Education is the central administrative authority for the Swedish public school system as well as for preschool activities. It defines goals in order to administrate, informs in order to influence, and reviews in order to improve. Regardless of the method, however, the focus is always on the assertion of the right of each individual to knowledge and personal development. A government mandate from 2003 states that all activities for which local and independent school authorities are responsible will be reviewed by the agency. The overall goal is "to design and carry out the educational inspection to ensure that every pupil in each school obtains the best possible education." Special guidelines stress that schools shall give high priority to the fulfillment of the pupils' special needs. The Swedish Agency for School Improvement is responsible for general support to schools within nationally prioritized areas and support for the local development of improvement work.

The Swedish Institute for Special Needs Education is a nationwide authority for coordination of state support for special needs education and provides cost-free distribution of information and knowledge about special needs in education. All measures are aimed at enhancing the expertise within the municipal authorities.

In Sweden 73 percent of women work part time or full time outside their homes. This is the highest figure in Europe and explains why as many as 76 percent of children aged 1–5 spend 4–10 hours each day in child care at preschool, where parents pay a subsidized fee depending on income. Since 2003, all children aged 4–5 have been offered free schooling for at least 525 hours per year. The provision is mandatory for the municipalities. Most child care centers are organized in groups of 15–20 children with two to three preschool teachers. All children in need of special support should, as far as possible, receive their daily care within their ordinary child care group by means of special supervision to the regular staff or by extra personnel. There are special groups only for children with deafness or autism.

School is compulsory for children between ages 7 and 16. Children can start school at age voluntarily, which most children have since 1999. According to the national curriculum, all compulsory education is organized in a way such that individual solutions are possible for all pupils, thereby strengthening the pupils' influence and personal responsibility and taking into account all pupils' needs and individuality. The majority of pupils in need of special educational support are educated in general basic compulsory classes. In order to meet these pupils' special needs, teachers are regularly given consultations by a specialist teacher. An assistant to the teacher may work with a pupil for longer or shorter periods within the framework of the larger group's activities. As an exception, a pupil may leave the larger group for limited periods to work with a specialist teacher within the same organization, either individually or in a group for pupils with similar needs. The underlying principle is that the goals pertaining to any specific subject shall be achieved by each pupil but that the ways to attain these goals and the time utilized may vary. At grades 5 and 9 national compulsory tests are conducted in the subjects of mathematics, English, and Swedish. These tests are the basis for individual evaluations as well as for school plans and national comparisons. The aim is that every child shall pass in these subjects. However, about 10 percent do not achieve this and are restricted in their choice of further education. Grades or written comments are not allowed to be given to pupils until grade 8 of compulsory school. Until then, developmental talks are held each term by the teacher with each pupil and parents attending.

An increasing number of students (98 percent) continue their education and go on to upper secondary schools, which are free of charge. Upper secondary education is divided into 17 national 3-year programs, which offer a broad general education and basic eligibility to continue studies at the postsecondary level, even for students with disabilities and learning difficulties. Consequently, special needs have also become important issues at this level, and pupils have the same right to special support as in compulsory schools. Those pupils who have not been able to reach the goals of the compulsory school and hence are not eligible to apply to a national program may attend an individual one. In this all pupils have their own study plan, and it is possible to combine school with employment. The national programs for the severely learning disabled, which are 4 years in length, are especially oriented toward vocational training.

Within 2 years, about 50 percent of the students continue to study at the postsecondary level. Most universities and postsecondary schools are state-run and free of charge. The Equal Treatment of Students at Universities Act of 2001 aimed at making higher education, both entry and study, more accessible in all respects for people with disabilities. The Service for Students with Disabilities gives support to students with permanent disabilities, including dyslexia, neuropsychological problems, and documented psychiatric disorders. The support can consist of assistance with note taking, mentorship, sign language interpretation, and individual guidance. The Swedish Library of Talking Books and Braille produces course literature at the university level.

The Habilitation Services Department organized within the health services is regulated by two pieces of legislation, the Disabled Persons Support and Service Act and the Health and Medical Services Act, which guarantee free of charge certain forms of support for persons with developmental disabilities (i.e., physical disabilities, mental retardation, autism, or related conditions), persons who have major or chronic disabilities requiring extensive support, and persons with serious learning difficulties or those who have suffered brain damage during growth or adulthood. These acts require habilitation centers to provide counseling and other forms of personal support. However, the intention is not to replace but to supplement the other services provided by the municipality or county health care departments. The services include several experts who make assessments and provide medical treatments as well as educational, social, and psychological support in close consultation with the individual person, the family, and other resources in society.

The Assistive Technology Services incorporate collective and broad medical and technical expertise for children and adults with physical disabilities, speech impairment, and cognitive difficulties. These services are all free of charge and well developed.

The task of the disability ombudsman is to monitor the basic human rights of persons with disabilities. This involves dealing with complaints, providing legal advice, and providing information. There are several very active parents' movements engaged in the promotion of the rights of children with different kinds of special needs.

The identification and investigation of individual needs for special support take place in a variety of ways. From birth to compulsory school there are regular health checks for all children, with an attendance rate of about 99 percent. A very large proportion of children attend organized child care, and hence the need for special support can in many cases be identified before the child attains school age. Health services and to some extent psychologists are available for consultation with child care and school staff and with pupils and parents. During the last decade Swedish psychologists have shown an increasing interest in endeavoring to understand the possible neuropsychological bases of learning disabilities and behavior problems. This has resulted in an emphasis being placed on a neuropsychological approach to assessment. Although a diagnosis is often necessary in order to allocate resources, it is emphasized that learning disabilities constitute a heterogeneous diagnostic entity. To a varying extent, learning disabilities may accompany other diagnoses, ranging from mental retardation, attention-deficit/hyperactivity disorder (ADHD) and nonlanguage learning disability to primary psychiatric problems such as anxiety, depression, and posttraumatic stress disorder. In some children dyslexia, dyscalculia, or unspecified learning disability constitutes the prevailing problem. Due to the

acceptance of the concepts of multifinality and equifinality, a problem is regarded to have very different explanations, backgrounds, and consequences, thus requiring different modes of intervention. In order to gain an understanding of the characteristics that differentiate any given child from other children having the same diagnosis, neuropsychological assessment is considered to be a valuable tool. Such assessment is achieved by the administration of an extensive test battery supplemented with tests of attention, language, memory, perception, visuo-spatial abilities, and learning. An analysis of behavioral and emotional problems is accomplished by interview, observation, and self-rating questionnaires. In addition, parent and teacher ratings of child behavior are obtained. This approach allows an understanding of the individual's array of strengths and weaknesses, thereby enabling the psychologist not only to describe specific deficits but also to perform the essential task of identifying those areas in which the abilities are intact and thus may be used as beneficial compensatory strategies.

As a complement to this description of the state of the art of special education in Sweden, it may be appropriate to mention some current issues that merit attention. Although in some respects it is beneficial, the decentralized educational system also has disadvantages. Insofar as there are no resources earmarked for special education, this must be financed within the frameworks of regular school budgets. It is clearly apparent that in times of economic recession the differences between more and less economically strong local municipalities and schools tend to increase, jeopardizing the fulfillment of some pupils' special needs. It has also been observed that the decentralization process has affected the way in which special education has been defined. Thus, the inclusion of pupils into special programs for those with severe learning disabilities has remarkably increased, which in the long run could create obstacles regarding future studies and working opportunities.

Some pupils do not receive sufficient support (Swedish Agency of Education, 2003). A large group consists of pupils described as shy, quiet, and reluctant to take the initiative. Also, those who act out are sometimes overlooked. In these cases it is not a question of their receiving insufficient support; rather, their unruliness can conceal problems that the school has not been able to identify, which results in their being given the wrong kind of support. Schools seldom have the time or the opportunity to make thorough analysis of the underlying reasons for a pupil's behavior. Measures taken about pupils are often based on vague assumptions and preconceived ideas. The behavior itself must be dealt with, in order to make the pupil behave as normally as possible. Although neuropsychological assessments are in great demand, the number of educational psychologists qualified to meet these demands is very low. In Europe, the number of educational psychologists per 1,000 pupils varies between 0 and 2. In Sweden this figure is 0.3. Swedish psychologists are well educated and licensed, but thus far there is no legislation stipulating the number of educational psychologists that should be available in the schools, because this is the responsibility of each municipality to decide.

In the report it also emerged that second-generation immigrants constitute the largest proportion of pupils in need of more support than they receive. The proportion of inhabitants with immigrant and often refugee backgrounds reaches 30 percent or more in several Swedish municipalities; in some schools the proportion of immigrant-background pupils can reach 80 percent to 85 percent. Many of these children have deficits in their mother tongue as well as in their Swedish language skills, sometimes in combination with psychological problems. This situation places challenging demands on special education. Although the policy for immigrant pupils has been to provide free of charge teaching of their mother tongue in addition to Swedish, a critical discussion of whether this is beneficial for children with learning disabilities is ongoing.

Since the 1990s there has been a trend toward the creation of an increasing number of independent schools, a process facilitated by means of a school capitation allowance system. The proportion of pupils attending independent schools has doubled since the year 2000. However, there is a continuing concern that segregation and differences in quality between schools may increase as an effect of school choice, perhaps with negative long-term consequences for scholastic equality.

The tendency to implement new methods without quality assurance and a general negligence as to whether the fundamental changes in the educational system during the last decade have had an effect on the field of special education pose critical concerns.

Although the overall picture in some respects is complicated and problematic, Sweden might still be considered in the vanguard of special education development in inclusive education, thus making the further development of policy and practice intriguing and worthy of attention.

REFERENCE

Swedish Agency for School Improvement. (2005). *Pupils who need support but do not receive enough*. Report No. U04:075. Stockholm: Liber Distribution.

EVA TIDEMAN
Lund University

SWITZERLAND, SPECIAL EDUCATION IN

Education in Switzerland

Switzerland is a confederation of 26 cantons, which include 2,929 political municipalities. The cantons are autonomous states. Their population varies from 14,100 to 1,178,800 citizens. For further statistic key data, refer to the Internet (http://www.admin.ch/bfs/).

Switzerland does not have national school/educational legislation. The cantons remain the highest authority in this area, except for certain fields of vocational education. Article 69 of the Swiss Federal Constitution specifies the responsibilities of the 26 cantons for an adequate, sufficient, and free compulsory education. Compulsory education (preschool, primary school, lower secondary school) is subordinate to the Cantonal Departments of Public Education. Each canton is highly independent with regard to school administration and organization, which leads to an extreme decentralization of the school authority in Switzerland. Only few institutions on the tertiary level (e.g., universities, advanced vocational training, higher vocational schools) are administered and supported by the federal government. The federal government also promotes and supports the cooperation and coordination between the cantons.

Figure 1 is a diagram of the basic structure of the various cantonal school systems. It reveals the differences in the organization of the primary and the secondary level of compulsory education. In some cantons the decision for secondary school has to be made much earlier than in others, and depending on the canton, education on the lower secondary level lasts for 3, 4, or 5 years. On the lower secondary level, schools in most cantons provide three to four streams for pupils with different abilities and competences.

Common to all 26 educational systems are:

- *The basic structure:* pre-school (kindergarten), primary level, lower secondary level. The possibilities for educational courses on the upper secondary level, as well as on the tertiary level, depend on the size of the respective canton.

- *The compulsory education:* For all children between 6 to 7 years and 15 to 16 years, school attendance is compulsory on the primary and on the lower secondary level. Preschool is mandatory only in some cantons, but on a national level, children attend kindergarten almost without exception. Depending on the canton, preschool lasts one to two years.

- *The beginning of the school year:* All over Switzerland, the school year begins in late summer.

According to the constitution, the Swiss Conference of Cantonal Directors of Education has to guarantee a minimal intercantonal coordination. Members of the conference are the cantonal directors of education and/or other responsible representatives. The conference employs a few collaborators on a full-time basis, but mostly it mandates numerous commissions to prepare and elaborate different papers and documents. The Conference of Cantonal Directors of Education cannot promulgate any laws, it can only elaborate recommendations on behalf of the cantons.

The cantonal autonomy, mentioned above, has some clear

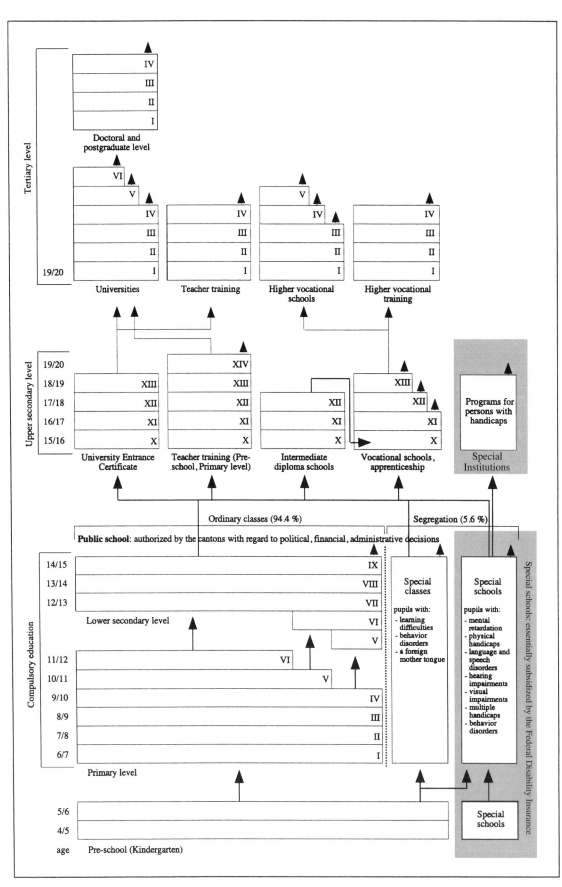

Figure 1 Diagram of the system of education in Switzerland

advantages in the field of education. On one hand, it preserves the political and cultural diversity. One example is the Romansch speaking part of Switzerland: In a country with a strictly centralistic government, Romansch would probably not have become one of the official languages at school and it would have died out sooner or later. On the other hand, it is questionable whether this strong decentralization is really necessary and whether it is still appropriate at the start of the twenty-first century. How is it useful to maintain a special department of education for as small units as some of the Swiss cantons? And how can school reforms be effected on a Swiss level if federalism is of such high importance? It often takes years to come to an agreement on a Swiss level, even for simple reforms like the beginning of the school year or the 5-day school week.

Such examples emphasize the difficulty to effect more extensive reforms such as the integration of children with special needs, reforms that can hardly be realized in a federalistic state like Switzerland.

The Education of Children with Special Educational Needs

Preschool Level

Small children with disabilities and/or developmental problems are taken care of by early childhood special education services. Early education of children with special needs can be extended from birth to kindergarten, special kindergarten, or the start of school. The most common kind of early childhood interventions are the mobile education programs: They take place at the child's home where the specialist works with the child and the family in their usual environment once or twice a week. In some cases, early childhood education programs take place in institutions or a clinic where the child lives. Most services are staffed with professionals with a degree in special education; some services also employ other specialists such as speech therapists, physiotherapists, or specialists for the education of children with sensory impairments. Costs for early childhood special education are borne to a great extent by federal disability insurance. Cantons, municipalities, or other public or private responsible bodies contribute according to specific agreements.

Compulsory Education Level

If children need special help, they usually attend a special class (tied to the regular school) or a special school (managed partly by private organizations and partly by the canton, subsidized by federal disability insurance). Thus, children with special educational needs are mostly segregated from the regular school (see Figure 1). Actually, 5.6 percent of all school-age children are schooled in classes with a special curriculum (Bundesamt für Statistik, 1997). A good number

of children in regular classes, special classes, and special schools get additional support and assistance from itinerant support services (between 10 percent to 20 percent, depending on the area in which they live). These services mostly provide psychological counseling, speech/language and psychomotor therapy. School services also include school medical service, school dental service, vocational counseling, and support teaching for immigrant children with a foreign mother tongue. Over the past 25 years, an increasing trend toward the integration of children with special educational needs into the regular school system can be observed; in some cantons, a restricted kind of integration is already practiced. As mentioned above, special schooling embraces all the school- and education-oriented endeavours for children and youths with special needs. On the compulsory education level, this function is assumed by special classes and special schools.

Special classes are small classes which contain no more than 12 children with relatively minor disabilities (learning difficulties, mild emotional disturbances, and mild sensory and speech/language disorders). Due to the structure and the grouping of these classes, they practice segregation, although they are mostly located in public schools and are under the political and financial authority of the Cantonal Departments of Education. Apart from the special classes for children with learning difficulties, many cantons also provide special classes for pupils with behavior disorders, speech/language impairments, physical handicaps, or a foreign native language. According to their special concept and the group of pupils, such classes should be taught by special teachers with a degree in special education. Unlike the regular classes, special classes are not homogeneous with regard to the age of their pupils. Depending on the number of pupils, they are grouped on four levels, which cover the compulsory education span: introduction classes or lower level, middle level, upper level, and vocational classes on the lower secondary level.

Special schools are open to all children with severe sensory, physical, and/or mental handicaps who benefit from federal disability insurance. They hold their own school facilities, mostly connected to a residential home. Special schools are managed partly by private organizations and funds under cantonal authority and partly by the canton, and they are subsidized by federal disability insurance (IV). Special schools are relatively autonomous. IV-supported special schools are classified as follows: special schools for children and youths with severe emotional and behavior disorders, with mental and multiple handicaps, with physical handicaps, with severe visual and hearing impairments, and with specific speech/language impairments. Not all these types of special schools are run by every canton, but there are contractual agreements for intercantonal cooperation.

Most cantons have their own legal provisions for their special classes and special schools. Due to its high financial commitment, the federal disability insurance has an important influence on the organization and the development of the special schools to which almost 2.5 percent of all Swiss pupils are referred.

Postschool Level

This level is particularly dominated by vocational training, although part of the vocational education already takes place on the secondary level I. On the lower secondary school level, programs include early vocational exposure/choice, vocational counseling, and vocational preparation courses. Schools on this level maintain close cooperation with vocational guidance services.

After their compulsory education, a good part of those exiting special classes take up vocational training (apprenticeship), or they enter an individualized vocational program that takes into account the trainee's difficulties and problems. The vocational training runs on a dual basis: The young people are trained in practical work in a particular enterprise 3 to 4 days a week, and 1 to 2 days a week they go to a vocational training school, where they attend general education classes as well as specific classes referring to their professional field. The training ends with a federal diploma. Some young persons with minor disabilities do not go through vocational training, but they might work on their parents' farms or carry out some unskilled work.

Young people who have difficulties training for a job in the free market because they suffer from physical handicaps (visual or—rarely—hearing impairments) get their training in specialized institutions. Many of the youths with mental retardation are occupied in sheltered workshops. On their way toward professional life, young persons with disabilities are supported by professionals of the vocational guidance services, run by the federal disability insurance. For further information on special education in Switzerland refer to Bürli (1993).

A Challenge for Educational Policy: The Integration of Children with Special Educational Needs into Regular Classes

Except for the integration of the increasing number of immigrant children within the Swiss educational system, the integration of children with special educational needs is one of the most difficult and intriguing challenges for school authorities in Switzerland. Looking back on the educational policy of the past years, the Swiss school authorities have made many efforts to establish and develop a highly differentiated network of special schools and special classes. Toward the end of the 1970s, this differentiation reached its high actual standard.

Integration is defined as the common schooling and education of handicapped and nonhandicapped pupils in ordinary classes of the public school system, with an adequate support for the children with special educational needs. This definition does not include the school settings that only practice a more or less close cooperation between special classes and ordinary classes, even if both types of classes are located under the same roof, which may allow regular interactions between handicapped and nonhandicapped pupils. Real integration is characterized by common instruction of all pupils.

How Has Integration Been Implemented up to This Day?

Most of the pupils with special educational needs in regular classes in Switzerland are children with speech and language disorders. The schooling of this category of pupils in ordinary classes should rather be seen as nonsegregation than integration. Despite their special therapeutic needs, these pupils have never been systematically segregated. In Switzerland, pupils with specific, as well as complex, speech and language disorders usually remain in their regular classes, because the Swiss public school system can provide a dense network of special logopedic support. Only about 5 percent to 10 percent of the children with speech and language disorders are referred to a special school. Most of them suffer not only from speech/language impairments, but also from behavior disorders and/or learning difficulties.

The most remarkable development toward mainstreaming can be observed in the field of learning difficulties. About 25 years ago, pupils with learning difficulties could remain in their ordinary class for the first time. Besides the instruction based on the regular curriculum they did get special assistance by a support teacher. In 1995, approximately 300 Swiss schools practiced this kind of integration. About 8 percent to 12 percent of all pupils with learning difficulties were integrated in ordinary classes. This seems to be quite a low quota, but with regard to Swiss standards it can be considered a rather high proportion (Bless, 1995, p. 61–64).

Pupils with a foreign native language attend ordinary classes in most Swiss cantons. Usually, they get special support for improving their knowledge of the standard school language. Several cantons with a high population density run special classes for these pupils, but they aim to integrate them in ordinary classes as soon as possible. But despite these integrative tendencies, the statistics plainly show a growing number of pupils with a foreign mother tongue in special classes (Kronig, 1996).

Pupils with physical handicaps or with hearing and visual impairments are integrated on a small scale. Two preconditions are essential for their mainstream placement. On one hand, these pupils have to be able to achieve the academic standard of their class without a differentiation of the regular curriculum. On the other hand, the schools have to be able to make available the necessary therapeutic support on their premises.

Despite the limited attempts to implement integration in Switzerland, several encouraging projects have been initiated lately. Some special schools apply new methods: They provide support for pupils with special educational needs who attend ordinary schools. For example, the staff of a special school support several mentally handicapped children attending the kindergarten of their residential area. One special school for pupils with hearing and language impairments did transform its division for the hearing impaired into a support and advisory center. They closed down their special classes, integrated the pupils in ordinary classes, and granted them systematic regular support. These individual cases should not be overvalued, but they can give signals for further attempts.

A look back on the evolution of mainstreaming in Switzerland proves that two conditions are essential for integration:

1. *Integration must not cause any further expenses.*
   The federal disability insurance (IV) is of high importance for the development of integration. The IV has an impeding influence on all integrative efforts, as it only subsidizes education of pupils with special educational needs in special schools and classes. As IV contributes largely to school tuition, board, and lodging, the cantons—which are responsible for the schooling and education of mentally handicapped children—are not interested in integrating these pupils. However, some of the enactments of IV make it possible to provide an integrative pedagogic and therapeutic care for pupils who need speech therapy, psychomotor therapy, or training in hearing and lip-reading. As long as integrative measures do not cause any further expenditures, the cantons are willing to back them up. If integrative measures exceed regular expenses, the cantons stop such efforts. For example, the integration of pupils with learning difficulties does not cause any problems because the cantons finance both ordinary classes and special classes (see Figure 1); therefore it does not matter in what classes these pupils are schooled. Pupils with speech and language impairments can be mainstreamed, because IV pays for their special support without having these pupils referred to a special school.

2. *Integration must not disturb the regular teaching in the classroom.*
   As long as classroom instruction can be accomplished in its regular way, integration is accepted. As soon as teachers have to individualize their lessons beyond a certain degree, integration does not have a good chance. For instance, pupils with hearing impairments and additional severe learning difficulties are rarely taught in ordinary classes, because integrating these children asks for a high degree of differentiation and individualization.

How Can the Actual and the Future Development of Integration Be Assessed?

If we take into consideration the amount of integrated pupils, we can observe neither a slowdown nor a standstill. If we consider the categories of pupils who are integrated into mainstream education, integration seems to have come to a standstill, because many groups of children with special educational needs—particularly the mentally handicapped pupils—are excluded from integrative schooling. As long as the financial conditions and structures for the disabled in Switzerland are not fundamentally changed, true and real integration—that means common education and schooling of all children—will never be possible. Only a basic reorganization of the financial system can open the way to school reforms which aim at integration in the true sense of the word.

The following determinants do or may obstruct a further reorganization of the Swiss system of education in favor of true integration:

- A political system with 26 autonomous ministries of education is not very flexible with regard to a reorganization of the educational system within a useful period.
- On an all-Swiss level, there is no strong political will to support integration.
- Financial resources set a limit to integration. The structures of financing the disabled in Switzerland have been drawn up in view of segregation. They corroborate the segregation of the disabled, and they place at a disadvantage all the cantons that strive for an extensive integration.
- Unlike the advocates for integration, the special schools can rely on an efficient lobby. Most of the boards of directors of special schools can count on the honorary support of popular politicians and of other well-known personalities of regional or cantonal importance.
- Generally, the attitude of the majority of teachers towards integration is rather ambivalent. Basically, teachers recommend and support integrative ideas and efforts, but when it comes to realizing such ideas and efforts, they are rather cautious and reserved.
- Compared to Germany, Austria, or other countries, Switzerland does not have any serious parents' movement in favor of the handicapped.

An extensive evaluation of integrative trends and tendencies within the Swiss educational system cannot be restricted to listing and classifying specific cases of realized integration. Such an approach to integration is liable to consider only one specific aspect of the reality. Another important aspect is the constant study of the relevant statistic data (Bundesamt für Statistik, 1997). Contrary to the widespread view of numerous politicians and professionals or specialists in the field of education, the Swiss educational system has become more and more intolerant towards children with specific educational needs. Figure 2 shows a continuous increase of segregated children since the school year 1983/84 (4.26 percent). In 1995/96, their number equaled 5.63 percent. It is remarkable that the number of segregated children increases parallel to the beginning and intensifying discussion on integration.

How can this increasing quota of segregated pupils be explained? Up to the mid-1990s no special schools and few special classes had been closed down, despite all integrative efforts. Thus, special institutions remain an option for the education of children with special needs. It is true that more and more of these children are integrated into the regular schools, but, on the other hand, the loss of such children is offset by segregating other groups of pupils, mostly children of immigrant families (see Figure 3).

Special classes and schools are still used—or misused—to normalize the regular school. But over the past years, the segregation policy has changed. Actually, more immigrant children are referred to special classes, which initially had been set up for children with minor disabilities.

To sum up the latest developments in the field of special

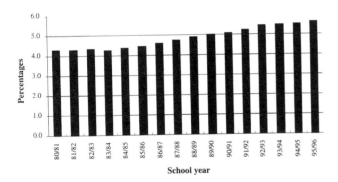

Figure 2 Percentage quota of segregated pupils in special classes and schools from 1980/81 to 1995/96, calculated on the basis of the total number of pupils of the primer and the lower secondary level (compulsory education).

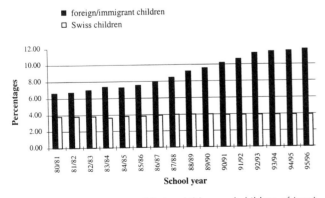

Figure 3 Percentage quota of Swiss children and children of immigrant families in special classes and schools from 1980/81 to 1995/96, calculated on the basis of the total number of pupils in compulsory education.

education, we notice that the schools have considerable trouble managing the growing diversity of their pupils. Despite the intensified discussion on integration of the past years, our schools are still not apt to more integration. On the contrary, they have even become more intolerant of children who do not comply with their standards.

REFERENCES

Bless, G. (1995). *Zur Wirksamkeit der Integration. Forschungsüberblick, praktische Umsetzung einer integrativen Schulform, Untersuchungen zum Lernfortschritt.* BernStuttgart-Wien: Haupt-Verlag.

Bless, G. (1997). *Integration in the ordinary school in Switzerland.* In Organization for Economic Cooperation and Development (OECD). *Implementing inclusive education.* Paris: OECD.

Bundesamt für Statistik. (1997). *Schülerinnen, Schüler und Studierende 1995 / 96.* Bern, Switzerland: Bundesamt für Statistik (BFS).

Bürli, A. (1993). *Special education in Switzerland.* Aspects 50. Lucerne: Edition SZH. Swiss Institute for Special Education.

Kronig, W. (1996). *Besorgniserregende Entwicklungen in der schulischen Zuweisungspraxis bei ausländischen Kindern mit Lernschwierigkeiten.* Vierteljahresschrift für Heilpädagogik und ihre Nachbargebiete (VHN).

Organization for Economic Cooperation and Development (OECD). (1997). *Education at a glance 1997: OECD indicators.* Paris: Author.

GÉRARD BLESS
University of Fribourg

WESTERN EUROPE, SPECIAL EDUCATION IN

SYDENHAM'S CHOREA

Sydenham's chorea is more commonly known as St. Vitus' Dance, but it also may be called minor chorea, rheumatic chorea, or acute chorea. It is generally regarded as an inflammatory complication of rheumatic fever, tonsillitis, or other infection; it also can be associated with pregnancy (chorea gravidarum). The condition is most prevalent in young girls between the ages of 5 and 15 and more common in temperate climates during summer and early fall. The condition has declined substantially in recent years owing to a similar decline in rheumatic fever. It is characterized by involuntary choreic movements throughout the body and occurs in about 10 percent of rheumatic attacks.

Choreic movements are rapid, purposeless, short lasting, and nonrepetitive. The movements usually begin in one limb and flow to many different parts of the body; they may resemble athetoid cerebral palsy. Fidgety behavior, clumsiness, dropping of objects, facial grimacing, awkward gait, and changes in voice or slurred speech are common symptoms that may occur at onset. A month or more may pass before medical attention is sought because these symptoms initially may be mild. Anxiety, irritability, and emotional instability also may occur because of the uncontrolled movements. The involuntary motions disappear during sleep and occasionally are suppressed by rest, sedation, or attempts at voluntary control. Sydenham's chorea is nonfatal, and recovery usually occurs within 2 to 6 months. Recurrence may happen two or three times over a period of years in almost one third of the people affected.

Differential diagnosis depends on ruling out other causes through history and laboratory studies. There are no characteristic laboratory abnormalities, and pathologic studies suggest scattered lesions in the basal ganglia, cerebellum, and brain stem. No deficits in muscle strength or sensory perception are found during neurologic examination. The course of the impairment is variable and difficult to measure because of its gradual diminution.

There is no specific treatment, but some medications (phenobarbital, diazepam, perphenazine, or haloperidol) can be effective in reducing chorea. In most situations, the person with Sydenham's is encouraged to return to school or work, even if residual symptoms continue. In severe cases, protection from self-injury by using restraints may be necessary. The prognosis for recovery is variable but the condition inevitably subsides. Reassurance that the condition is self-limiting and eventually will decline without residual impairment is in order for people with Sydenham's, their families, teachers, and classmates. Behavioral problems, mild motor abnormalities, and poor performance in psychometric testing have been reported after the chorea dissipates. It is important that affected individuals receive Therapeutic Support (Moore, 1996).

REFERENCES

Berkow, R. (Ed.). (1982). *Merck manual* (14th ed.). Rahway, NJ: Merck, Sharp, & Dohme Research Laboratories.

Bird, M. T., Palkes, H., & Prensky, A. L. (1976). A follow-up study of Sydenham's chorea. *Neurology, 26,* 601–606.

Fahn, S. (1985). Neurologic and behavioral diseases. In J. Wyngaarden & L. Smith, Jr. (Eds.), *Cecil textbook of medicine* (17th ed., pp. 2074–2075). Philadelphia: Saunders.

Magalini, S., & Scarascia, E. (1981). *Dictionary of medical syndromes* (2nd ed.). Philadelphia: Lippincott.

Merritt, H. H. (1979). *A textbook of neurology* (6th ed.). Philadelphia: Lea & Febiger.

Moore, D. (1996). Neuropsychiatric aspects of Sydenham's chorea: A comprehensive review. *Journal of Clinical Psychiatry, 57*(9), 407–414.

Nuasieda, P. A., Grossman, B. J., Koller, W. C., Weiner, W. J., & Klawans, H. L. (1980). Sydenham's chorea: An update. *Neurology, 30,* 331–334.

Daniel D. Lipka
*Lincoln Way Special Education
Regional Resources Center*

**CHOREA
HUNTINGTON'S CHOREA**

SYNAPSES

The synapse is the structure that mediates the effects of a nerve impulse on a target cell, permitting communication among nerve cells, muscles, and glands. It is a synapse that joins the terminal end of an axon of one neuron with the dendrites or cell body of another. The synapse was first described by Sir Charles Sherrington in 1897. The word itself means "connection."

Messages arrive at the synapse in the form of action potentials. Synaptic potentials are triggered by action potentials; they in turn trigger subsequent action potentials, continuing the neural message on to its destination. While action potentials vary in frequency, they do not vary in form or magnitude. It is the synaptic potential that is responsible for variance in the nervous system.

The synaptic terminals on the end tips of axons take on various forms such as ball-like endings (boutons), nobs, spines, and rings. These terminals almost, but not quite, make contact with a part of another neuron (usually a dendrite or occasionally an axon or cell body). The space between the terminal of one neuron and the other neuron is called the synaptic cleft. This cleft is miniscule, typically on the order of about 200 angstroms. Transmission time across the synaptic cleft is approximately .3 to 1.0 msec.

Synaptic transmission can be electrical or chemical, although the former is uncommon in the mammalian brain (Gazzaniga, Steen, & Volpe, 1979). With chemical transmission, one cell, the presynaptic, secretes molecules that cross a synaptic cleft and join with a postsynaptic cell. The presynaptic cell endings contain mitochondria and synaptic vesicles that hold various neurotransmitters. The neurotransmitter substances are released in tiny packettes called quanta. These substances can serve excitatory or inhibitory purposes, and not all are currently identified. However, major excitatory neurotransmitters include acetylcholine, noradrenalin, seratonin, and dopamine. Important inhibitory transmitters include gamma-aminobutric acid (GABA) and glutamate. Specific receptor molecules that receive these neurotransmitters have been identified on the postsynaptic cell.

Synapses generally are classified as axiodendritic or axiosomatic. The typical pattern is axiodendritic; this pattern occurs when an axon meets a dendrite. Somewhat less common is the axiosomatic pattern, in which an axon meets a cell body.

REFERENCES

Barr, M. D. (1979). *The human nervous system: An anatomic viewpoint* (3rd ed.). New York: Harper & Row.

Gazzaniga, M., Steen, D., & Volpe, B. T. (1979). *Functional neuro-science.* New York: Harper & Row.

DANNY WEDDING
Marshall University

DENDRITES
DOPAMINE

SYNTACTIC DEFICIENCIES

See CHILDHOOD APHASIA; LANGUAGE DISORDERS EXPRESSIVE; LANGUAGE DISORDERS.

SYSTEMS OF CLASSIFICATION

A system of classification can be developed in an effort to identify individuals as members of one of the major handicapping conditions (e.g., learning disabilities), or it may be used to provide a subclassification within a major area of exceptionality (e.g., Down syndrome as a subcategory of mental retardation). Contemporary special education services rely heavily on the classification of general handicapping conditions and, to a lesser extent, on subclassifications.

The historical origins of the use of classification systems are dominated by two events. First, special education represents a unique educational development derived from the discipline of psychology. As such, it emerged in light of that discipline's intense interest in the measurement and study of individual differences. Subsequent refinements in measurement, including the development of classification systems based on reliable individual differences, were transferred to special education practice in the first part of the twentieth century. A second related influence arose from the attempts of early special educators to provide a science of treatment. That is, the study of individual differences led to the acceptance of a nosological orientation in treatment. Long practiced in medicine, the nosological orientation presumes that disorders can be isolated with reference to etiology, that etiology can ultimately be treated, and that subsequent cases can be similarly addressed (i.e., treatment proceeds from symptom to diagnosis of etiology to specification of treatment). In this approach, the development of a precise system of classification and subclassification is essential.

Possibly the most influential classification system now in effect is that provided within Individuals with Disabilities Education Act. Ysseldyke and Algozzine (1984) indicate that through this legislation, the U.S. Department of Education recognizes 11 categories of exceptionality, although some states recognize more or less categories. In most states, the categories represent an effective determinant of service: If

an individual is not a member of the specified handicapping condition, services are not mandated. Thus, systems of classification, and related entry procedures, are essential in the selection process that ultimately determines entrance to special education.

A number of subclassification systems exist within the broad categories of exceptionality. Most of these attempt to suggest, if not prescribe, the general course of diagnosis and treatment. Two well-known systems typify this approach. The *Diagnostic and Statistical Manual of Mental Disorders* (fourth edition; *DSM-IV*) is a psychiatrically derived classification system for use with children and adults with emotional disorders. The *DSM-IV* is the standard classification system within mental health facilities in the United States, though it has far less official influence in public education. In the *DSM-IV*, disorders are grouped into five major divisions (intellectual, behavioral, emotional, physical, and developmental). Each division is further partitioned into specific disorders as defined by rigid diagnostic criteria. Individuals thus receive codes that indicate the diagnosed handicaps. Recent criticisms suggest that this system is archaic and needs to be redefined. Psychiatric classification of personality disorders, for example, could be classified in terms of severity and subtype (Tyrer, 1996).

A second classification system is used in the diagnosis and treatment of mental retardation. The American Association on Mental Deficiency classification system (Grossman, 1983) is based on a number of factors, including intelligence and adaptive behavior. In this system, the degree of retardation is specified as mild, moderate, severe, or profound. The intent of the system is clearly to specify training and structural support needs.

It is erroneous to conclude that these two well-accepted classification systems are acceptable to all agencies, that alternatives are nonexistent, or that particular systems are not revised over time. For example, the *DSM-IV* is in the fourth substantially revised edition and tends not to be used in schools; alternatives such as Quay's (1964) system are often favored. Nor is there a paucity of systems. MacMillan (1982) reports at least 10 systems were used in the twentieth century with the mentally retarded. Of these, four are now in common use. Clearly, classification systems are modified in response to the influence of social pressures, research bases, and professional opinions.

A number of theoretical and pragmatic pitfalls are evident in current classification systems. Three are particularly germane. First, the fact that multiple classification systems exist and are endorsed by various agencies creates opportunities for classification and service provision irregularities. Second, there is question as to whether behavioral diagnostic techniques possess the necessary reliability and validity to provide precise classification; error in measurement and misassignment to categories is possible (Salvia & Ysseldyke, 1985). Third, the significance of classification systems based on etiology may prove to be less important to the behavioral than the medical sciences. That is, treatment links have generally not been established between etiological diagnosis and behavioral treatment. Such links may prove difficult or impossible to achieve (Neisworth & Greer, 1975).

Despite these criticisms, classification systems remain an important consideration for special education. Kauffman (1977) provided a rationale for the continuation of attempts to classify behavior: Classification is a fundamental aspect of any developing science of behavior; classification is of importance in organizing and communicating information; and classification systems, if scientifically investigated, may ultimately assist in the prediction of behavior and offer insights into the preferred method of treatment. As noted by Kauffman (1977), the alternative to continued development of classification systems is "an educational methodology that relies on attempts to fit interventions to disorders by random choice, intuition, or trial and error" (p. 27).

REFERENCES

American Psychiatric Association. (1994). *Diagnostic and statistical manual of mental disorders* (4th ed.). Washington, DC: American Psychiatric Association.

Grossman, H. J. (Ed.). (1983). *Manual on terminology and classification in mental retardation* (3rd ed.). Washington, DC: American Association on Mental Deficiency.

Kauffman, J. M. (1977). *Characteristics of children's behavior disorders*. Columbus, OH: Merrill.

MacMillan, D. L. (1982). *Mental retardation in school and society* (2nd ed.). Boston: Little, Brown.

Neisworth, J. T., & Green, J. G. (1975). Functional similarities of learning disabilities and mild retardation. *Exceptional Children, 42*, 17–21.

Quay, H. C. (1964). Dimensions of personality in delinquent boys as inferred from factor analysis of case history data. *Child Development, 35*, 479–484.

Salvia, J., & Ysseldyke, J. E. (1985). *Assessment in special and remedial education* (3rd ed.). Boston: Houghton Mifflin.

Tyrer, P. (1996) New ways of classifying personality disorder. *Psychiatrist, 7*(1), 43–48.

Ysseldyke, J. E., & Algozzine, B. (1984). *Introduction to special education*. Boston: Houghton Mifflin.

TED L. MILLER
University of Tennessee

DIAGNOSTIC AND STATISTICAL MANUAL OF MENTAL DISORDERS
LEARNER TAXONOMIES

SYSTEM OF MULTICULTURAL PLURALISTIC ASSESSMENT

The System of Multicultural Pluralistic Assessment (SOMPA; Mercer & Lewis, 1979) was designed to provide a compre-

hensive measure of the cognitive abilities, perceptual-motor abilities, sociocultural background, and adaptive behavior of children ages 5 through 11 years. It employs three models of assessment and attempts to integrate them into a comprehensive assessment: (1) the medical model, defined as any abnormal organic condition interfering with physiological functioning; (2) the social system model, determined principally from labeling theory and social deviance perspectives taken from the field of sociology, which attempts to correct the "Anglo conformity" biases of the test developers who have designed IQ tests for the last 90 years; and (3) the pluralistic model, which compares the scores of a child with the performance levels of children of a similar ethclass (that is, the same demographic socioeconomic, and cultural background) correcting for any score discrepancies with the white middle class. English- and Spanish-language versions of the scale are available.

The SOMPA is a complex and somewhat innovative system of assessment designed to ameliorate much of the conflict over assessment in the schools. The senior author, Mercer, a sociologist, conceptualized SOMPA in the late 1960s and early 1970s from her work in sociology's labeling theory and her sociological surveys and studies of mental retardation, particularly mild mental retardation, as a sociocultural phenomenon. The SOMPA has been extensively reviewed and debated (Humphreys, 1985; Nuttall, 1979; Reynolds, 1985; Reynolds & Brown, 1984; Sandoval, 1985). Unfortunately, presentation of the SOMPA for clinical application as opposed to pure research appears to have been premature. Major conceptual and technical issues pertaining to the scale have not been resolved adequately, even considering that a complete resolution of most of these issues is not possible. As a result, the SOMPA has contributed to the controversy over assessment practices in the schools rather than moved the field closer to a resolution. Even though controversy frequently can be stimulating to a discipline, in many ways, SOMPA has polarized the assessment community.

One of the major conceptual problems of the SOMPA centers around its primary underlying assumption. Mercer developed the SOMPA in response to her acceptance of the cultural test bias hypothesis. Briefly stated, this hypothesis contends that all racial, ethnic, socioeconomic, or other demographically based group differences on mental tests are due to artifacts of the tests themselves and do not reflect real differences. According to Mercer and Lewis, this is due to the extent of Anglocentrism (degree of adherence to white middle-class values, norms, and culture) apparent in most, if not all, mental measurements. In accepting this hypothesis as fundamentally correct, Mercer relies primarily on the mean differences definition of bias, which states that any differences in mean levels of performance among racial or ethnic groups on any mental scale is prima facie evidence of bias. The principal purpose of the SOMPA is to remove this bias by providing a correct estimate of intellectual abilities, an estimated learning potential (ELP). While adding a "correction factor" to the obtained IQs of disadvantaged children is not a new idea, the SOMPA corrections are unique in their objectivity and in having a clearly articulated, if controversial, basis. The corrections are based on the child's social-cultural characteristics and equate the mean IQs of blacks, whites, and Hispanics with varying other cultural characteristics such as family structure and degree of urban acculturation.

Unfortunately for the SOMPA, its underlying assumption that mean differences among sociocultural groups indicate cultural bias in tests is the single most rejected of all definitions of test bias by serious psychometricians researching the cultural test bias hypothesis (Jensen, 1980; Reynolds, 1982). The conceptual basis for the SOMPA is far more controversial than it appears in the test manuals and is indeed open to serious question. If other approaches to the cultural test bias hypothesis had demonstrated the existence of bias, then the need for a resolution to the problem such as proposed by Mercer would remain tenable. However, the large body of evidence regarding the cultural test bias hypothesis, gathered primarily over the last decade, has failed to substantiate popular claims of bias in the assessment of native-born ethnic minorities. For the most part, the psychometric characteristics of well-designed and carefully standardized tests of intelligence such as the Wechsler scale have been shown to be substantially equivalent across ethnic groups (Jensen, 1980; Reynolds, 1982).

If this argument is dismissed and Mercer's contentions regarding test bias accepted, other serious conceptual issues remain. The ELP, a regression-based transformation of Wechsler IQs, is said to provide a good estimate of the child's innate intelligence or potential to profit from schooling. Such a claim is difficult to support under any circumstances. It is unlikely that we will ever be able to assess innate ability since environment begins to impact the organism at the moment of conception. We are left only with the possibility of observing the phenotypic construct. Furthermore, as of this writing, no evidence exists relating ELP to any other relevant criteria (Reschly, 1982).

Others have noted substantial agreement in criticisms of the SOMPA ELP, particularly regarding its construct validity (Humphreys, 1985; Reschly, 1982). Humphreys (1985) argues that

> Estimated learning potential is a thoroughly undesirable construct. Many people want to hear and believe the misinformation furnished by ethclass norms, but this is dangerous for it solves no real problems. It is conceivable, of course, that several generations from now black and Hispanic performance on standard tests of intelligence and achievement might equal the white majority. In this limited sense, ethclass norms might not misinform, but an inference that requires 50 years or more to validate helps little in dealing with today's children. They need higher scores on measures of reading, listening, writing, computing, mathematics, and science, not ethclass IQs. (p. 1519)

The ELP may in fact be misleading and result in a denial of special education services to children who are seriously at risk of academic failure or already experiencing such failure. As Reschly has stated, "All of the direct uses of ELP at present and in the foreseeable future are questionable" (p. 242). Equally controversial, even in Mercer's home field of sociology, is labeling theory, another important concept in the establishment of the need for a system like SOMPA. If we accept the contention that false negatives are more desirable than false positives in the diagnosis of mental retardation, a check on the utility function tells us that it would most likely be best to diagnose no children as mentally retarded since the incidence in Mercer's model in particular is far less than 3 percent.

Technical problems are also evident in the development and application of the concept of ELP. As noted, the ELP is a regression-based transformation of Wechsler IQs to a scale with a mean of 100 and standard deviation of 15 independent of a child's sociocultural characteristics. These transformations are made on the basis of the SOMPA sociocultural scales. Based on data derived during the norming of the SOMPA, regression equations were derived for determining the ELP. The stability of these regression equations and their generalizability to children outside the standardization sample have been called into question. Since the SOMPA was not normed on a stratified random sample of children nationwide, but rather on a sampling restricted to California, generalizability studies received some priority on the measure's publication. Regression equations derived from samples from other states, notably Texas and Arizona, have not been at all similar to the original equations; even the multiple R between the various sociocultural variables and Wechsler IQ varies substantially (i.e., from .30 to .60 in some cases) across states and across ethnic groups (Reschly, 1982). Given the state of contemporary applied psychometrics and the sophisticated normative sampling of such scales as the Wechsler series and the recent Kaufman Assessment Battery for Children, the failure to provide an adequate standardization sample for the SOMPA is inexcusable and not characteristic of the publisher.

The reliability of the ELP will also be dependent to a large extent on the stability of the sociocultural scales from which the corrections to the obtained Wechsler IQs are derived. The stability of these scores has been seriously questioned in at least one study. Over a 4-year period, Wilkinson and Oakland (1983b) report test-retest correlations that range from .39 to the high .90s across scales. Within scales and across demographic groupings such as race, sex, and socioeconomic status, the correlations also vary considerably, pointing up the real possibility of bias in the SOMPA. Apparently the ELP can change dramatically for individual children over a 4-year period (given that half of the stability coefficients reported for the SOMPA sociocultural scales are below .80), a result that seems antithetical to the entire concept of the ELP.

Stability of other SOMPA scales that should be relatively stable has also been questioned. The SOMPA health history inventory shows test-retest reliability coefficients minus ranging from –.08 (!) to .96. Considerable differences are evident within scales across demographic groupings as well. The trauma scale shows a stability coefficient of .23 for males and .74 for females (Wilkinson & Oakland, 1983a). Prepostnatal scores show a stability of .78 for whites and .96 for blacks, a scale that should remain highly stable since the SOMPA begins at age 5 years.

These are but a few of the conceptual and technical issues plaguing the SOMPA. Much work was needed on the SOMPA prior to its presentation for practical application, work that was not done. The conceptual issues in particular needed clarification.

On another level, the SOMPA must be questioned as an assessment system for children especially. The SOMPA is designed primarily as a means of providing a fairer scheme of classifying children into diagnostic categories. It has clearly not been validated adequately for this purpose. However, a more far-reaching concern to the clinician working with children experiencing school failure is the development of programs for the habilitation of learning. The SOMPA provides no real clues to the development of such interventions. This is especially damaging to practical applications of the SOMPA because it requires a substantial investment of professional time to be properly administered. The commitment of so much time and effort to an assessment system that does not provide considerable help with the development of individual educational programs cannot be justified in any kind of cost-benefit analysis. The emphasis on prevention-intervention-habilitation is more in keeping with the needs of the field.

The SOMPA cannot be recommended for use at this time. Its conceptual, technical, and practical problems are simply too great. Nevertheless, it was an innovative, gallant effort at resolving the conflict over assessment practices in the schools. Although widely used in the first several years after publication, the SOMPA quickly disappeared from the repertoire of most school psychologists and is now antiquated.

REFERENCES

Humphreys, L. G. (1985). Review of System of Multicultural Pluralistic Assessment. In J. V. Mitchell (Ed.), *Ninth mental measurements yearbook*. Lincoln, NE: Buros Institute.

Jensen, A. R. (1980). *Bias in mental testing*. New York: Free Press.

Mercer, J., & Lewis, J. (1979). *System of Multicultural Pluralistic Assessment*. New York: Psychological Corporation.

Nuttall, E. V. (1979). Review of System of Multicultural Pluralistic Assessment. *Journal of Educational Measurement, 16*, 285–290.

Reschly, D. J. (1982a). Assessing mild mental retardation: The influence of adaptive behavior, sociocultural status, and prospects for nonbiased assessment. In C. R. Reynolds & T. B. Gutkin (Eds.), *The handbook of school psychology*. New York: Wiley.

Reynolds, C. R. (1982b). The problem of bias in psychological assessment. In C. R. Reynolds & T. B. Gutkin (Eds.), *The handbook of school psychology*. New York: Wiley.

Reynolds, C. R. (1985). Review of System of Multicultural Pluralistic Assessment. In J. V. Mitchell (Ed.), *Ninth mental measurements yearbook*. Lincoln, NE: Buros Institute.

Reynolds, C. R., & Brown, R. T. (Eds.). (1984). *Perspectives on bias in mental testings*. New York: Plenum.

Sandoval, J. (1985). Review of System of Multicultural Pluralistic Assessment. In J. V. Mitchell (Ed.), *Ninth mental measurements yearbook*. Lincoln, NE: Buros Institute.

Wilkinson, C. Y., & Oakland, T. (1983a, August). *Stability of the SOMPA's health history inventory*. Paper presented to the annual meeting of the American Psychological Association, Anaheim, CA.

Wilkinson, C. Y., & Oakland, T. (1983b, August). *Stability of the SOMPA's sociocultural modalities*. Paper presented to the annual meeting of the American Psychological Association, Anaheim, CA.

CECIL R. REYNOLDS
Texas A&M University

ADAPTIVE BEHAVIOR
CULTURAL BIAS IN TESTING
MERCER, JANE R.
VINELAND ADAPTIVE BEHAVIOR SCALES–SECOND EDITION

T

TACHISTOSCOPE

The tachistoscope, or t-scope, is an instrument for presenting visual stimuli for very brief times at a controlled level of illumination (Stang & Wrightsman, 1981). The t-scope may be a self-contained unit or mounted on a slide projector.

Often the goal of tachistoscopic presentation is to determine the threshold at which subjects verbally report recognition of a stimulus. Research using the tachistoscope also has been carried out concerning the existence of subliminal perception where stimuli are said to affect behavior below the conscious threshold of perception.

Reading involves very briefly viewing words; the tachistoscopic task was broadly assumed to mimic the requirements faced by skilled readers. Despite questions of the applicability of t-scope research to everyday reading tasks, a variety of components of reading have been examined in the presence of varying speeds of presentation and levels of illumination. The threshold of word recognition can be determined and models of skilled reading can be constructed (Carr & Pollatsek, 1985; Gough, 1984; Mewhort & Campbell, 1981). The performance of skilled and disabled readers can be compared to determine the differences that might be diagnostically significant (Pirozzolo, 1979).

REFERENCES

Carr, T., & Pollatsek, A. (1985). Recognizing printed words: A look at current models. In D. Besner, T. G. Waller, & G. E. Mackinnon (Eds.), *Reading research: Advances in theory and practice* (Vol. 5, pp. 2–82). Orlando, FL: Academic.

Gough, P. B. (1984). Word recognition. In P. D. Pearsen (Ed.), *Handbook of reading research* (pp. 225–291). New York: Longman.

Mewhort, D. J. K., & Campbell, A. J. (1981). Toward a model of skilled reading performance: An analysis of performance in tachistoscopic tasks. In G. E. Mackinnon & T. G. Waller (Eds.), *Reading research: Advances in theory and practice* (Vol. 1.3, pp. 39–118). New York: Academic.

Pirozzolo, F. J. (1979). *The neuropsychology of developmental reading disorders.* New York: Praeger.

Stang, D., & Wrightsman, L. (1981). *Dictionary of social behavior and social research methods.* Monterey, CA: Brooks-Cole.

LEE ANDERSON JACKSON, JR.
University of North Carolina at Wilmington

PERCEPTUAL SPAN

TAIWAN, SPECIAL EDUCATION IN

Historical Overview

The early development of special education in Taiwan has its root in the tenets of Confucianism: "education for all" and "instruction by potential." In this context, efforts are made both by government agencies and private sectors to ensure that all exceptional individuals are entitled to a right to appropriate education. The protocol of educational alternatives for students with disabilities in Taiwan can be traced back to the late years of the nineteenth century. Interestingly, early attempts to educate the individuals with disabilities were inaugurated by the clergy. To illustrate, the first special day school (built in 1886 for children who are deaf and mute) was funded by English churches and staffed by ministers. This day school served as a catalyst for establishment of similar facilities throughout the island. Public schools did not provide special education programs until 1961, when the Dong-Men elementary school of Taipei developed the first self-contained class of its kind for children with emotional disturbances.

Educational programs for children with mental retardation (MR) have played a major role in the development of special education within the public schools. Actually, special education and classes for students with MR were considered one and the same. The confusion was attributed to overemphasis on developing programs for MR children and the lack of programs for other exceptional children and youth, which in turn was associated with the overrepresentation of students with mental retardation.

Few efforts had been organized before the 1980s to fight for the rights of populations with disabilities. The stimulus for increased public interest in and governmental attention to the welfare of people with disabilities is attributed in part to political parties and academic scholars who had their advanced studies abroad. In the late 1970s as the major opposition political party emerged, the rights movement for people with handicaps became overwhelming. The outcome has been passage of the Special Education Act of 1984 and similar legislation, plus significant changes in schools and communities.

The Special Education Act of 1984 provides the framework for special education policies and its regulations delineate a broad guideline for criteria for the identification, placement, and delivery of educational services for children with special needs. Specifications of the regulations include classroom organization, instructional objectives, and teaching methods and materials. Much of the impetus for the laws passed in the 1980s stems from issues surrounding education of children with MR, including (a) the assumed negative impact of labels, (b) expansion of special class placement, and (c) excessive reliance on single assessment measures—primarily the intelligence test.

In each locality, the Ministry of Education develops a Special Education Coordination Committee in charge of programming and monitoring of enforcement of laws and regulations associated with special education. The local government designates the Identification, Placement and Consultation Committee (IPC) to deal with special education practices in schools. The revised Special Education Act of 1997 is characterized by an addition of zero rejects to the array of special services and an extension of children from school-aged to preschool. Specifically, public schools are now open by law to all children and youths with disabilities aged 3 to 18.

Current Status

Currently, each county develops the IPC Committee. Homeroom teachers refer students with special needs. Referral is delivered to the committee, which initiates assessments and makes the final decision. The committee also recommends (based on the least-restrictive principle) the placement options ranging from regular classes to institutions. Children with disabilities come in the following categories: mental retardation, visual impairments, hearing impairments, language disorders, physical handicaps, health impairments, behavioral disorders, learning disabilities, and multiple handicaps. The current policy mandates that students with mild disabilities are placed in the regular classes with resource room services; those with moderate impairments are placed in the self-contained classes; and those with severe and profound handicaps are recommended to special schools and institutions respectively.

To reduce stigmatization to the minimum, schools have long adopted terms with educational implications. The *wisdom-developing* designation, for example, is used to refer to education associated with MR, *illumination-developing* designation for visual impairments, and *love-developing* for physical handicaps. Thus, not only do we have *Taipei Wisdom-Developing School* and *Tainan Illumination-Developing School*, but in the regular school there are *audition-developing* classes for students with hearing impairments.

Prospectus

Many educational problems of exceptional children and youth can be prevented or minimized through the provision of comprehensive services. The revised Special Education Act of 1997 applies to handicapped individuals ages 3–18. Many more special needs children are eligible for special education services. The role of the public school has been extended both in the nature of services and the ages of students served. Identification of exceptional children and high-risk children as infants or preschoolers has become a widespread practice, and early childhood programs designed to enhance development of the handicapped and prepare them for school have been demonstrated to be effective. Several metropolitan cities have already mandated the provision of preschool programs for children with disabilities. Career programs designed specifically for post-junior-high adolescents are under assessment across the island and the programs are gaining in popularity. Community resources are being applied to help young adults with handicaps establish themselves as active members of the community.

While full inclusion is in practice in the West, it appears that Taiwan has a long way to go yet. Quite against the worldwide trend of normalization, special day schools are recently flourishing in Taiwan. There were only two special day schools here for children with MR in 1980, but in 10 years, eight new schools have been added to the list, at the increase rate of one school each year. A few more are either on blueprints or under construction.

It is hoped that the Office of Special Education will be soon established both in central and local governments to coordinate policies and practices in special education. Many issues in the field of special education in Taiwan remain unresolved, but the prospect is promising, with the government starting to play the key role in setting the stage for further development.

REFERENCES

Ministry of Education. (1984). *Special Education Act.* Taiwan: Author.

Ministry of Education. (1997). *Revised Special Education Act.* Taiwan: Author.

JENGIYH DUH
*National Taiwan Normal
University*

TALENTED CHILDREN

See SPECIFIC TALENT, E.G., ACADEMICALLY TALENTED CHILDREN.

TALKING BOOKS

Talking books are books recorded on vinyl disks or, more often the case in recent years, on cassette tapes that are used principally by the visually impaired. These modified records are played on special talking book machines and recorded on modified machines as well. Talking books and the modified recorders are available to all visually impaired students registered through the American Printing House for the Blind. Severely reading impaired students with a diagnosis of dyslexia may also qualify for the use of talking books.

STAFF

AMERICAN PRINTING HOUSE FOR THE BLIND

TASH

Formerly the Association for Persons with Severe Handicaps, TASH is an international advocacy association of people with disabilities, their family members, other advocates, and professionals working toward a society in which inclusion of all people in all aspects of community is the norm. The organization is comprised of members concerned with human dignity, civil rights, education, and independence for all individuals with disabilities. Creating, disseminating, and implementing programs useful for the education and independent lifestyles of persons who are severely handicapped is a primary objective of TASH.

Formed in 1975, TASH is a membership-supported, not-for-profit association with chapters in 34 states and members in 35 countries. Current membership includes professionals, paraprofessionals, parents, and medical and legal personnel. The organization's mission is to stretch the boundaries of what is possible through building communities in which no one is segregated and everyone belongs, forging new alliances that embrace diversity, advocating for opportunities and rights, and eradicating injustices and inequities. In addition, TASH strives to actively support research, disseminate knowledge and information, and support progressive legislation and litigation. Promoting excellence in services and inclusive education for all individuals is another aim of the association.

TASH seeks to promote the full participation of people with disabilities in integrated community settings that support the same quality of life available to people with disabilities. This task is accomplished through its facilitation of training in best practices, systems change, Americans with Disabilities Act (ADA), and Individuals with Disabilities Education Act (IDEA). TASH also strives to provide information, linkage with resources, legal expertise, and targeted advocacy. The organization accomplishes its work by disseminating information via a monthly newsletter covering current disability-related issues and a quarterly academic journal containing cutting-edge research. TASH also sponsors an annual conference and topical workshops, and advocates on behalf of people with disabilities and their families through building grassroots coalitions.

TASH'S central office is located at 29 W. Susquehanna Avenue, Suite 210, Baltimore, Maryland, 21204. The association can be reached via telephone (410-828-8274), fax (410-828-6706), TDD (410-828-1306), e-mail (info@tash.org), or by visiting TASH's web site at www.tash.org

TAMARA J. MARTIN
*The University of Texas of the
Permian Basin*

TASK ANALYSIS

Task analysis is a teaching strategy that encompasses the breaking down and sequencing of goals into teachable subtasks. Moyer and Dardig (1978) noted it is a critical component of the behavioral approach and it serves a dual role in the instruction of learners with disabilities. First, it serves an effective diagnostic function by helping teachers pinpoint a student's individual functioning levels on a specific skill or task. Second, it provides the basis for sequential instruction, which may be tailored to each child's pace of learning. A thorough task analysis results in a set of subtasks that form the basic steps in an effective program. In essence, task analysis is both an assessment and a teaching tool (Ysseldyke & Elliott, 1999).

Task analysis has been acclaimed to be an effective strategy for the mildly disabled learner (Bateman, 1974; Siegel, 1972; Tawney, 1974). Gold (1976) applied this technique to the education of severely handicapped learners with great success and Williams, Brown, and Certo (1975) stated that task analysis is critical to teachers of severely disabled learners, since programmatic steps must be sequenced with precision and care.

According to Mithaug (1979), the procedures that define task analysis have evolved from Frederick Taylor's work measurement studies and Frank and Lillian Gilbreth's motion studies conducted in the late 1800s. Motion analysis was the precursor of today's task analysis, although many elements critical to motion analysis have not been included in the educational applications of task analysis. The term task analysis came into increasing use during the 1950s, whenever tasks were identified and examined for their essential components within the workplace. This foreshadowed subsequent applications of task analysis to teach individuals with disabilities in the late 1960s.

Guidelines for designing and implementing task analysis programs have been suggested (Moyer & Dardig, 1978; Siegel, 1972). These are:

Limit the scope of the main task

Write subtasks in observable terms

Use terminology at a level understandable to potential users

Write the task in terms of what the learner will do

Focus attention on the task rather than the learner

In choosing a method of task analysis, Moyer and Dardig (1978) noted that all tasks, whether from the psychomotor, cognitive, or affective domains, can be broken down into simple units of performance. However, there is no foolproof strategy for selecting the appropriate method of analysis for a given task. It is helpful first to identify the domain of the learning task and then to apply the appropriate task analysis procedure. They suggest several possible methods of task analysis that may be adopted by the special education teacher:

1. Watch a master perform. This requires watching and writing down all the steps that are required to perform the task as it is performed by someone adept at it.

2. In a variation of the first method, have the teacher perform the task, making note of the required steps. Sometimes this is difficult in that performing the task may interfere with recording the steps.

3. Work backward from the terminal objective, making note of the required steps.

4. Brainstorm. This entails writing down all the component steps without regard to order. Then, once all steps have been identified, arrange them into some logical order.

5. Make the conditions under which the task is completed progressively more simple. As the learner gains proficiency, slowly change the simplified conditions (e.g., trace name; gradually remove the model: dark model, light model, dotted model, etc.).

The ability to analyze tasks, a skill that can be acquired by any teacher, enables the detection of trends in a student's performance and the modification of task components during an instructional session (Junkala, 1973). Thus it is an extremely effective instructional method and diagnostic tool in special education.

REFERENCES

Bateman, B. D. (1974). Educational implications of minimum brain dysfunction. *Reading Teacher, 27,* 662–668.

Gold, M. C. (1976). Task analysis of a complex assembly task by the retarded blind. *Exceptional Children, 43,* 78–84.

Junkala, J. (1973). Task analysis: The processing dimension. *Academic Therapy, 8*(4), 401–409.

Mithaug, D. E. (1979). The relation between programmed instruction and task analysis in the pre-vocational training of severely and profoundly handicapped persons. *AAESPH Review, 4*(2), 162–178.

Moyer, J. R., & Dardig, J. C. (1978). Practical task analysis for special educators. *Teaching Exceptional Children, 11*(1), 16–18.

Siegel, E. (1972). Task analysis and effective teaching. *Journal of Learning Disabilities, 5,* 519–532.

Tawney, J. W. (1974). *Task analysis.* Unpublished manuscript, University of Kentucky.

Williams, W., Brown, L., & Certo, N. (1975). Basic components of instructional programs for the severely handicapped students. *AAESPH Review, 1*(1), 1–39.

Ysseldyke, J., & Elliott, J. (1999). Effective instructional practices: Implications for assessing educational environments. In C. R. Reynolds & T. B. Gutkin (Eds.), *The handbook of school psychology* (3rd ed.). New York: Wiley.

EILEEN F. MCCARTHY
University of Wisconsin at Madison

BEHAVIOR MODIFICATION
BEHAVIORAL ASSESSMENT
BEHAVIORAL OBJECTIVES

TAT

See THEMATIC APPERCEPTION TEST.

TAXONOMIES

Taxonomy is the science of systematics. It incorporates the theory and practice of classification, or sorting and ordering significant similarities and differences among members of a system to facilitate precise communication about members, enhance understanding of the interrelationships among members, and suggest areas where additional relationships might be discovered. Early attempts to design taxonomies date back to the third century BC and Aristotle's efforts to classify animals as warm- or cold-blooded. Theophrastus, Aristotle's pupil, concentrated on a system for sorting plants. In the eighteenth century in Sweden, Linnaeus designed a classification system for botany that has served as a basis for almost all subsequent systems.

Among the more commonly used taxonomies today are the Library of Congress and Dewey Decimal systems for the classification of books and the taxonomies developed for the classification of plants and animals. The latter contains categories that permit the identification of individual organisms according to species, genus, family, order, class, phylum, and kingdom.

In the late 1940s, members of the American Psychological Association who were concerned about the problems of precise communication among college examiners and researchers involved in testing and curriculum development began work on the classification of educational objectives. The result was the preparation of taxonomies of educational objectives or intended student outcomes in the cognitive, affective, and psychomotor domains (Bloom, 1956; Harrow, 1972; Krathwohl, Bloom, & Masia, 1964). The major classes in these three taxonomies are presented in Figure 1. All three reflect an emphasis on the intended outcomes of instruction and the student behaviors that would demonstrate achievement of each outcome.

Stevens (1962) developed a taxonomy for special education that focuses on physical disorders. He observed that classification systems then in use were typically based on a medical model with an emphasis on disease, etiology, and symptomatology. His intent was to improve communication regarding educationally relevant attributes or somatopsychological or body disorders and the special education procedures students with such disorders might require. Stevens stressed the differences among the terms *impairment, disability,* and *handicap* and provided for attributes that carried significance for planning special education programs. Figure 2 lists Stevens' classes.

In 1980 the World Health Organization (WHO) published its *International Classification of Impairments, Disabilities, and Handicaps.* This publication relates consequences of disease to circumstances in which disabled persons are apt to find themselves as they interact with others and adapt to their physical surroundings. The purpose of WHO's efforts, which are summarized in Figure 3, was to prepare a

1. *Somatopsychological variants*
   1.1 Handicap
   1.2 Disability
   1.3 Impairment
2. *Educationally significant attributes of somatopsychological disorders*
   2.1 Nature of condition
   2.2 Nature of therapeutic process
   2.3 Psychological aspects
   2.4 School considerations
   2.5 Cultural considerations
   2.6 Etc.
3. *Special education procedures*
   3.1 Modification of laws
   3.2 Finance
   3.3 Instructional modifications
   3.4 Noninstructional services
   3.5 Administrative modifications
   3.6 Ancillary services
   3.7 Etc.

Figure 2 Taxonomy in special education for children with body disorders (Stevens, 1962).

Cognitive Domain
  1. Knowledge
  2. Comprehension
  3. Application
  4. Analysis
  5. Synthesis
  6. Evaluation
Affective Domain
  1. Receiving/attending
  2. Responding
  3. Valuing
  4. Organization
  5. Characterization
Psychomotor Domain
  1. Reflex movement
  2. Basic fundamental movement
  3. Perceptual abilities
  4. Physical abilities
  5. Skilled movements
  6. Nondiscursive movements

Figure 1 Taxonomies of educational objectives for the cognitive, affective, and psychomotor domains (Bloom, 1956; Harrow, 1972; Krathwohl, Bloom, & Masia, 1964).

Impairments
  1. Intellectual
  2. Other psychological
  3. Language
  4. Aural
  5. Ocular
  6. Visceral
  7. Skeletal
  8. Disfiguring
  9. Generalized, sensory, and other
Disabilities
  1. Behavior
  2. Communication
  3. Personal care
  4. Locomotor
  5. Body disposition
  6. Dexterity
  7. Situational
  8. Particular skill
  9. Other activity restrictions
Handicaps
  Survival roles
  1. Orientation
  2. Physical independence
  3. Mobility
  4. Occupational
  5. Social integration
  6. Economic self-sufficiency
  Other handicaps
  7. Other handicaps

Figure 3 WHO classification of impairments, disabilities, and handicaps (WHO, 1980).

taxonomy that would ease the production of statistics regarding the consequences of disease, facilitate the collection of statistics useful in planning services, and permit storage and retrieval of information about impairments, disabilities, and handicaps (WHO, 1980). Diagnosis, a useful precursor to treatment, is a form of taxonomic classification (e.g., see Kamphaus, Reynolds, & McCammon, 1999).

Ultimately, taxonomies should be comprehensive, improve communication, stimulate thought, and be accepted by professionals in the field for which they were designed (Bloom, 1956). Whether the taxonomies available for special educators lead to the achievement of these goals remains to be seen, but without taxonomies as a guide, communication would be surely impaired (Kamphaus et al., 1999).

REFERENCES

Bloom, B. S. (Ed.). (1956). *Taxonomy of educational objectives: The classification of educational goals: Handbook I. Cognitive domain.* New York: McKay.

Harrow, A. J. (1972). *A taxonomy of the psychomotor domain: A guide for developing behavioral objectives.* New York: McKay.

Kamphaus, R. W., Reynolds, C. R., & McCammon, C. (1999). Roles of diagnosis and classification in school psychology. In C. R. Reynolds & T. B. Gutkin (Eds.), *The handbook of school psychology* (3rd ed.). New York: Wiley.

Krathwohl, D. R., Bloom, B. S., & Masia, B. B. (1964). *Taxonomy of educational objectives: Classification of educational goals: Handbook II. Affected domain.* New York: McKay.

Stevens, G. D. (1962). *Taxonomy in special education for children with body disorders.* Pittsburgh: Department of Special Education and Rehabilitation, University of Pittsburgh.

World Health Organization (WHO). (1980). *International classification of impairments, disabilities, and handicaps.* Geneva, Switzerland: Author.

MARJORIE E. WARD
The Ohio State University

BLOOM, BENJAMIN S.
SYSTEMS OF CLASSIFICATION

TAY-SACHS DISEASE

Tay-Sachs disease is a lysosmal storage disorder that is characterized by the absences of the enzyme Hexosaminidase (Hansis & Grifo, 2001). The deficiency allows harmful quantities of a fatty substance, called GM2 ganglioside, to build up in the tissues and nerve cells of the brain. This buildup results in a progressive deterioration of the central nervous system and in a loss of visual functions (Branda, Tomczak, & Natowicz, 2004; Hansis & Grifo, 2001). This genetic disorder is transmitted by an inherited autosomal recessive gene that is found more frequently among people of Jewish and European origin (Branda et al., 2004; Kaback & Desnick, 2001; Risch, 2001). Approximately one in 250 people are carriers of the Tay-Sachs disease; 1 in every 27 people of Jewish ancestry in the United States are carriers (National Institutes of Health, 2005).

Tay-Sachs syndrome manifests itself in infants between the ages of 4 to 8 months. Initial signs include a loss of peripheral vision, an abnormal startle response, cherry red spots on the retinas, a delay in psychomotor development, and a gradual regression in learned abilities (i.e., the loss of the ability to sit up; Filho & Shapiro, 2004; Hansis & Grifo, 2001; National Institutes of Health, 2005). In later stages of the disease children experience recurrent seizures, diminishing mental function, blindness, and eventually paralysis (Filho & Shapiro, 2004; National Institutes of Health, 2005). Death generally occurs before the age of six (Gravel et al., 2001). In addition to the infantile form of Tay-Sachs disease there are much rarer late onset forms with similar symptoms that are caused by varying residual enzyme activity (Gravel et al., 2001). Treatment is limited to managing the symptoms of the disease with proper nutrition, anticonvulsant medications used to suppress seizures, and other techniques used to maintain an open airway (National Institutes of Health, 2005). Genetic screening has resulted in a 90 percent reduction in the annual incidences of Tay-Sachs disease that are reported in North America (Kaback & Desnick, 2001).

REFERENCES

Branda, K., Tomczak, J., & Natowicz, M. (2004). Heterozygosis for Tay-Sachs and Sandhoff diseases in Non-Jewish Americans with ancestry from Ireland, Great Britain, or Italy. *Genetic Testing, 8,* 174–180.

Filho, J., & Shapiro, B. (2004). Tay-Sachs disease. *Archaeological Neurological, 61,* 1466–1468.

Gravel, R. A., Kaback, M. M., Proia, R. L., Sandhoff, K., Suzuki, K., and Sukuzi, K. (2001). The Gm2 gangliosides. In C. R. Scriver, A. L. Beaudet, W. S. Sly, & D. Valle (Eds.), *Metabolic and molecular bases of inherited diseases* (8th ed., Vol. 1, pp. 3827–3876). New York: McGraw-Hill.

Hansis, C., & Grifo, J. (2001). Tay-Sachs disease and preimplantation genetic diagnosis. *Advances in Genetics, 44,* 22–28.

Kaback, M., & Desnick, R. (2001). Tay-Sachs disease: From clinical description to molecular defect. *Advances in Genetics, 44.*

National Institutes of Health. (2005). *Tay-Sachs disease.* Retrieved September 3, 2005, from http://www.ninds.nih.gov/disorders/taysachs/taysachs.htm

Risch, N. (2001). Molecular epidemiology of Tay-Sachs disease. *Advances in Genetics, 44,* 42–51.

BRANDI KOCIAN
Texas A&M University

CONGENITAL DISORDERS
GENETIC COUNSELING
GENETIC TESTING
GENETIC TRANSMISSIONS

TEACCH

Treatment and Education of Autistic and related Communication handicapped CHildren (TEACCH) is a unique program offering comprehensive services, research, and professional training for autistic children of all ages, and their families, in the state of North Carolina. TEACCH is a division of the psychiatry department of the University of North Carolina School of Medicine, Chapel Hill.

The program was founded in 1966 by Eric Schopler and Robert J. Reichler as a research project supported in part by the National Institute of Mental Health. Its purpose was to investigate the following misconceptions about autism: (1) that the syndrome is primarily an emotional disorder that causes children to withdraw from their hostile and pathological parents; (2) that these parents are educationally privileged and from an upper social class; and (3) that autistic children had potential for normal or better intellectual functioning. The research results clarified these misconceptions by demonstrating that autism is a developmental disability rather than an emotional illness; that parents come from all social strata and, like their children, are the victims rather than the cause of this disability; and that in spite of peak skills, mental retardation and autism can and do coexist.

These empirical research findings led to the development of the TEACCH program based on the following principles:

1. Parents should be collaborators and cotherapists in the treatment of their own children.
2. Treatment should involve individualized teaching programs using behavior theory and special education.
3. Teaching programs should be based on individualized diagnosis and assessment.
4. Implementation should be by psychoeducational therapists or teachers who function as generalists rather than specialists in a technical field such as physical therapy or speech therapy. Treatment outcome is evaluated according to the interaction between improved skills and environmental adjustments to deficits.

The TEACCH program provides comprehensive services, including professional training and research efforts that are integrated with clinical services. Training is provided for various specialists, including teachers, psychologists, psychiatrists, pediatricians, speech pathologists, and social workers. The main emphasis is on the involvement of parents in all facets of the program directed toward adjustment in all areas of the child's life—home, school, and the community.

Home adjustment is facilitated at five regional TEACCH centers, each located in a city housing a branch of the state university system to facilitate both research and training. The centers' main function is to provide diagnosis and individualized assessment involving family and school. Parents are trained to function as cotherapists using behavior management and special education techniques. The centers' staff provide professional training and consultation.

School adjustment is fostered through special education classrooms in the public schools that include four to eight children with a teacher and an assistant teacher. These classrooms (about 54 currently) are under TEACCH direction according to individual school contracts. TEACCH functions often include hiring teachers, intensive in-service training of teachers, diagnosis and placement of children, and ongoing classroom consultation for behavior problems and special curriculum issues.

Community adaptation is facilitated through parent groups. Each center and class has a parent group affiliated with the North Carolina Society for Autistic Adults and Children, and a chapter of the National Society. The main goal of this collaboration is to improve community understanding of the client's special needs and to develop new and cost-effective services. In recent years, this involved services for the older age group, including group homes, respite care, summer camps, vocational training, social skills training, and the development of a learning-living community program.

The outcome studies of various TEACCH services have shown that autistic children learn better in a structured setting, and that with appropriate training, parents become effective in teaching and managing their own children. Such gains carry over into the home situation. Moreover, when the North Carolina rate of institutionalized autistic children is compared with the rate reported from other states and countries, it is less than one-fifth, demonstrating that a strong community support program can improve the quality of life for handicapped children and adults at a fraction of the cost incurred by institutional warehousing.

Eric Schopler
University of North Carolina at Chapel Hill

AUTISM
FILIAL THERAPY
JOURNAL OF AUTISM AND DEVELOPMENTAL DISORDERS

TEACHER BURNOUT

Increased public demands on education have produced additional pressures and stresses on teachers. Needle, Griffin,

Svendsen, and Berney (1981) report that teaching ranks third in the hierarchy of stressful professions. Studies conducted by teachers' unions and other educational agencies support the notion that many teachers are currently "burning out" (Cichon & Koff, 1980; Wilson & Hall, 1981). Special educators in particular may be at high risk for burnout and its consequences (Bradfield & Fones, 1985).

Burnout has been defined in a variety of ways in the literature during its nearly 10-year history (Gold, 1985). Weiskopf (1980) defines burnout by its relationship to six categories of stress often found at the teaching workplace. They include work overload, lack of perceived success, amount of direct contact with children, staff-child ratio, program structure, and responsibility for others. Freudenberger (1974) and Maslach (1977) find the general theme of burnout to be "emotional and/or physical exhaustion resulting from the stress of interpersonal contact." It can be viewed as a gradual process with stages ranging from mild to severe (Spaniol & Caputo, 1979).

Burnout seems to affect people working in the human social services professions particularly because of the degree of intimacy that they experience with their clients and the extended period of time that they work with them. Moreover, many of the recipients of human services do not respond to the efforts of professionals, causing disillusionment and frustration (Pines & Maslach, 1977). This may be particularly true for special education teachers because of the unique nature of their teaching responsibilities (Bradfield & Fones, 1985).

Many causes for burnout in the helping professions have been proposed. In education, occupational burnout may arise from the failure of the work environment to provide the teacher with the support and encouragement needed and expected (Needle et al., 1981). Bensky et al. (1980) point out that often teachers are not given clearly defined job descriptions and receive additional job responsibilities for which they are unprepared or to which they are unaccustomed. Role ambiguity, if not clarified as part of the education process, is likely to lead to an increase in job-related stress and dissatisfaction (Coates & Thoresen, 1976; Greenberg & Valletutti, 1980). Many teachers have cited violence, vandalism, disruptive students, inadequate salaries, lack of classroom control, lack of job mobility, and fear of layoffs as reasons for burnout (Gold, 1985).

The effects of burnout vary from individual to individual depending on such variables as personality, age, sex, and family history. Physiological manifestation may include such reactions as migraine headaches, ulcers, diarrhea, muscle tension, and heart disease. Emotional manifestations include such reactions as depression, anxiety, irritability, and nervousness. Behavioral manifestations generally include excessive smoking or overeating (American Academy of Family Physicians, 1979).

The ways in which teachers may manifest specific responses to burnout on the job is cause for concern. Spaniol and Caputo (1979) have formulated a list of symptoms that may indicate that a teacher is experiencing burnout: a high level of absenteeism, lateness for work, a low level of enthusiasm, decline in performance, lack of focus, a high level of complaints, lack of communication, and a lack of openness to new ideas.

The implications of teacher burnout are grave and broadly based. They include the individual's own personal dissatisfaction, his or her family's unhappiness, chronic health problems, problems with colleagues and school administrators, and, ultimately, ineffective teaching. Sparks and Ingram (1979) reported that the teachers from whom students learn the most are reasonable, relaxed, enthusiastic, and interested in their students. Teachers who are consistently feeling stressed have been described as irritable, tense, humorless, depressed, self-involved, and unable to perform their job well. In general, Needle et al. (1981) found that job stress affects the classroom environment, the teaching/learning process, and the attainment of educational goals and objectives.

To reduce the possibility of teacher burnout, teachers must be provided with knowledge and information on effective methods of coping with stress in the environment. One popular method has been involvement in stress management workshops (Betkouski, 1981). These workshops have been effective in providing teachers with strategies for coping with stress such as forming support groups, reviewing exercise and nutrition patterns, developing hobbies and interests outside the work environment, and practicing relaxation techniques (Shannon & Saleeby, 1980). The prevention of burnout in teaching, however, must first and foremost involve a serious commitment to improving the quality and circumstances under which teachers work.

REFERENCES

American Academy of Family Physicians. (1979). *A report on the lifestyles / personal health in different occupations: A study of attitudes and practices.* Kansas City, KS: Research Forecasts.

Bensky, J., Shaw, S. F., Gouse, A. S., Bates, H., Dixon, B., & Beane, W. (1980). Public law 94-142 and stress: A problem for educators. *Exceptional Children, 47*(1), 24–29.

Betkouski, M. (1981, March). On making stress work for you: Strategies for coping. *Science Teacher, 48,* 35–37.

Bradfield, R. H., & Fones, D. M. (1985). Stress and the special teacher: How bad is it? *Academic Therapy, 20*(5), 571–577.

Cichon, D. J., & Koff, R. H. (1980, March). Stress and teaching. *National Association of Secondary School Principals Bulletin,* 91–103.

Coates, T. J., & Thoresen, C. E. (1976). Teacher anxiety: A review with recommendations. *Review of Educational Research, 46,* 159–184.

Freudenberger, H. J. (1974). Staff burn-out. *Journal of Social Issues, 30*(1), 159–165.

Gold, Y. (1985). Burnout: Causes and solutions. *Clearinghouse, 58,* 210–212.

Greenberg, S. F., & Valletutti, P. J. (1980). *Stress and the helping professions.* Baltimore: Brookes.

Maslach, C. (1977). Job burnout: How people cope. *Public Welfare, 36,* 61–63.

Needle, R., Griffin, T., Svendsen, R., & Berney, M. (1981). Occupational stress: Coping and health problems of teachers. *Journal of School Health, 51,* 175–181.

Pines, A., & Maslach, C. (1977, April). *Detached concern and burnout in mental health professions.* Paper presented at the 2nd National Conference on Child Abuse and Neglect, Houston, TX.

Shannon, C., & Saleeby, D. (1980). Training child welfare workers to cope with burnout. *Child Welfare, 59*(8), 463–468.

Spaniol, L., & Caputo, J. (1979). *Professional burnout: A personal survival kit.* Boston: Human Services Associates.

Sparks, D., & Ingram, M. J. (1979). Stress prevention and management: A workshop approach. *Personnel & Guidance Journal, 59,* 197–200.

Weiskopf, P. A. (1980). Burn-out among teachers of exceptional children. *Exceptional Children, 47*(1), 18–23.

Wilson, C. F., & Hall, L. L. (1981). *Preventing burnout in education.* La Mesa, CA: Wright Group.

MARSHA H. LUPI
*Hunter College, City University
of New York*

TEACHER EFFECTIVENESS
TEACHER EXPECTANCIES

TEACHER CENTERS

A teacher center (TC) represents a centralized setting that facilitates teacher development, in-service programs, and the exchange of ideas (Hering, 1983). Initially, TCs were funded directly with federal dollars. The basis for this funding was the passage in 1976 of PL 94-482. Approximately 110 TCs were directly supported by the federal government. However, as noted by Edelfelt in 1982, "The categorical assignment of funds for teacher centers . . . [was] terminated in the fiscal year 1982 federal budget" (p. 393). The majority of TCs have continued as a result of their funding from other local and state sources. Their continuation supports the contention that the original concepts that premised their initiation are still valid.

A primary factor that led to the origination of TCs in the United States in the mid-1970s was the interest of teachers in being in charge of their own in-service training and to keep up with new educational trends and curricular concepts. The idea was that TC in-service programs were to depart from the traditional and standard in-service programs; for example, one-time sessions on a given topic such as discipline or learning activities for the talented and gifted. In contrast, the intent of established TC in-service

programs was to be innovative and to influence professional development; those goals are still desirable today.

Another of the original precepts was that TCs would have a full-time director who was both an administrator and a teacher. The director would then become the nucleus of a governing board that was to consist of local citizens. Boards with an efficient mix of leadership, inspiration, and idealism were and are in a position to effectively institute needed changes. Weiler (1983) has outlined a blueprint for the establishment of new TCs that make needed changes possible.

Researchers (Commission on Reading, 1984; Committee on Education and Labor, 1984; Kozal, 1984; Tunley, 1985; Zorinsky, 1985) estimate that 12 to 18 percent of the teenage and adult population groups are functionally illiterate. There are 25 to 40 million Americans who are disabled with depressed literacy skills in the primary academic areas of reading, writing, and arithmetic. This instructional need is one that active TCs can legitimately embrace through the initiation of planned in-service programs that retrain teachers to be more efficient in their instruction.

Beyond the need for TC to endorse direct instructional intervention to improve the efficiency of classroom instruction, Hering (1983) identified a composite of five major functions that TCs can attend to: (1) assist teachers in their more immediate awareness of changes in instructional knowledge as it appears in educational literature; (2) assist teachers to be more efficient in meeting the social educational goals of students that society expects its nation's schools to attend to; (3) assist teachers to be more effective in their classrooms in attending to their students' developmental and remedial instructional needs; (4) assist teachers in achieving increased social and psychological competence; and (5) assist teachers as a faculty group to be more responsible to the needs of the group.

The history of TCs (Edelfelt, 1982) has had its share of developmental setbacks. However, as Hering (1983) has pointed out, TCs that work toward a quality program of instruction for all students will simultaneously attain from the community and the school board recognition of the worth and the work of teachers. Teacher centers that are influential in achieving quality instruction for any one group or classification of students have the probability of doing the same for any other group or classification of students, including the special education student.

REFERENCES

Commission on Reading. (1984). *Becoming a nation of readers.* Washington, DC: U.S. Department of Education.

Committee on Education and Labor. (1984). *Illiteracy and the scope of the problem in this country.* Washington, DC: U.S. Government Printing Office.

Edelfelt, R. A. (1982, September). Critical issues in developing teacher centers. *Education Digest, 48,* 28–31.

Hering, W. M. (1983). *Research on teachers' centers: A summary of fourteen research efforts.* Washington, DC: National Institute of Education.

Kozal, J. (1984). *Illiterate America.* Garden City, NY: Doubleday.

Tunley, R. (1985, September). America's secret shame. *Reader's Digest,* 104–108.

Weiler, P. (1983, September). Blueprint for a teacher center. *Instructor, 93,* 146–148.

Zorinsky, E. (1985). The National Commission on Illiteracy Act. *Congressional Record, 131*(41). Washington, DC: U.S. Government Printing Office.

ROBERT T. NASH
University of Wisconsin at Oshkosh

INSERVICE TRAINING OF SPECIAL EDUCATION TEACHERS INSTRUCTIONAL MEDIA/MATERIALS CENTER

TEACHER EDUCATION AND SPECIAL EDUCATION

Teacher Education and Special Education is the official journal of the Teacher Education Division (TED) of the Council for Exceptional Children (CEC). The purposes of *Teacher Education and Special Education* are to support goals of the TED, and to stimulate thoughtful consideration of the critical issues that are shaping the future of teacher education.

The journal is published four times a year and the first issue of each volume is a potpourri issue that includes articles dealing with a wide range of topics. The second issue focuses on either preservice, in-service, or doctoral preparation. The third issue focuses on a topic of timely interest in personnel preparation. The last issue focuses on research and/or evaluation activities related to personnel preparation.

REBECCA BAILEY
Texas A&M University

COUNCIL FOR EXCEPTIONAL CHILDREN

TEACHER EFFECTIVENESS

Over the last several decades, field-based studies have been conducted on the teaching process that related specific teaching behaviors to student achievement outcomes. The results of the early studies (Anderson, Evertson, & Brophy, 1979; Crawford et al., 1978; Fisher et al., 1978; Good & Grouws, 1977, 1979; Stallings, Needles, & Strayrook, 1979) were that there is a common set of process variables that can be observed or documented in effective teachers across grade and subject areas. It is further indicated that less effective teachers do not demonstrate these same behaviors to the appropriate degree. Continued research demonstrated clearly that teachers do make a difference in children's lives, especially with regard to classroom learning (see review by Gettinger & Stoiba, 1999).

The body of this research clearly speaks to a technology of teaching, making it increasingly clear that teachers and what they do are important determinants of student achievement. We know that effective teachers (1) optimize academic learning time; (2) reward achievement in appropriate ways; (3) use interactive teaching practices; (4) hold and communicate high expectations for student performance; and (5) select appropriate units of instruction. There are, of course, exceptions to these and other principles, and as such, teachers need to be adaptable. The research does not say that there is one best system of teaching but rather that the teacher must constantly be analyzing the feedback from students and performance data and making decisions to modify the instruction. Therefore, the findings from the teacher effectiveness studies and related research should be reviewed as road maps with the teacher constantly making decisions regarding the best route to pursue and sometimes alter the selected route based on new information. In general, the literature strongly addresses the need to train teachers as accurate decision makers. It is not level of effort or the aspiration to teach well that differentiates effective instruction; it is rather knowledge, skill, and confidence (Elmore et al., 1996).

Changing teachers' behaviors has not been found to be as difficult a task as first believed (Good, 1979). Studies have examined the amount of intervention needed to create a change that will affect teacher effectiveness (Coladarci & Gage, 1984; Good, 1979; Mohlman, Coladarci, & Gage, 1982). Coladarci and Gage (1984) found that there is a lower limit in regard to how little can be done while still achieving a meaningful change in behavior. Periodic direct observation of teachers appears to be one component that facilitates adoption of the practices. An enthusiastic presentation of the information to the teachers and a spirit of support for the practices also appear to be important. Mohlman et al. (1982) found that teacher acceptance of change to the use of effective teaching practices was based on (1) teaching recommendations being stated in explicit, easily understood language; (2) a philosophical acceptance of the suggested practice on the part of the teacher; and (3) teachers' perceived view of the cost in terms of time and effort and a belief that the investment in time and effort was worth the payoff in expected student achievement.

Mohlman et al. (1982) also found that teacher acceptance of the innovations is more important than understanding of the innovations. One other finding from the research is that teachers who were trained in effective teaching practices either by workshop, summaries, or workbooks are much more likely to use these practices in their classrooms than teachers who were not provided with such information.

Various authors have separated the major components of effective teaching practices into different configurations. One possible organization places these practices under the domains of management, decision making, time utilization, and instruction, all of which interact with each other and result in the development of a supportive classroom climate. These domains and their subdomains are based on the experimental and correlational research reported regularly in journals on studies involving instructional strategies.

Effective teachers use effective classroom management. Effective classroom management means (1) organizing the physical classroom to minimize disruptions; (2) establishing teaching rules and procedures and adhering to those rules and procedures; and (3) anticipating problem situations and having action plans to prevent problems or deal with them when they occur. Effective teachers have a strong command of their subject matter and a keen awareness of how children think and learn (Elmore et al., 1996).

Management has repeatedly been demonstrated as a critical element of effective teaching in major studies, including *The First Grade Reading Group Study* (Evertson et al., 1981) and *The Study of a Training Program in Classroom Organization and Management for Secondary School Teachers* (Fitzpatrick, 1982). Management includes the establishment and teaching of rules and procedures, specification of consequences, physical organization of the classroom, and behaviors on the part of the teacher that prevent disruptive behavior. Good room management eliminates potential distractions for students and minimizes opportunities for students to disrupt others. Students' desks are arranged so that students can easily see instructional displays and visuals and so that students can be easily monitored by the teacher. Students are seated so as to eliminate "action zones." These zones are created when students select seating locations. There is a tendency in self-selection for high-ability learners to sit together in the front and low-ability students to sit at the back or side. The more effective teacher will intermingle with these students. When hand raisers are spread throughout the room, it will enable the teacher to spread his or her attention more evenly and become sensitized to low responders.

Rules govern student behaviors such as talking and respect for property. Effective teachers have only three to six rules stated in generic language. These are posted and taught through examples to students at the beginning of the school year. Merely posting rules is less effective than posting and teaching the rules. Established procedures and routines are time-saving mechanisms. When procedures are established, students know when to use the bathroom, how to head papers, how to distribute and collect assignments,

how to ask for help, and so on. Without such established procedures, time is lost in explanations, or students disrupt the classroom by not knowing the procedures.

Consistency in enforcing the rules is a hallmark of effective teachers. Effective teachers have a hierarchy of consequences they follow to maintain the rules. Eye contact, moving closer to a student, or a pointed finger might be the first level of intervention. Withholding a privilege, assigning detention, conferencing with a student, or having a student restate a broken rule might be the second level. Contacting parents, behavioral contracting, or outside assistance might constitute the third level. In all cases, the teacher should remain calm when enforcing a rule.

Prevention of problems is largely brought about by advanced planning. A teacher can help prevent behavior problems by staying in close proximity to students while frequently teaching and monitoring them. A teacher should plan positive comments that can be used with students to establish a positive mood. Finally, a teacher should formulate plans to handle hypothetical disciplinary situations.

One major reason why management is such a critical variable in the teaching process is because of its relationship to instructional time. Instructional time is highly related to academic achievement. Walberg's (1982) review of studies involving time and achievement found correlation ranges from .13 to .71 with a median of .41. Ninety-five percent of the 25 studies reviewed as "time-on-learning" reported positive effects. Instructional time is lost for members of a class where students are disruptive, procedures are not readily available for teaching, and students do not understand the behavioral expectations of the teacher.

Decision making is generally an unobservable phenomenon, but the products of the decision are observable. Teachers regularly make decisions on content, time allocations, pacing, grouping, and class activities. If the content is not taught, then students generally do not learn. The literature uses the term "opportunity to learn" when describing this phenomenon. According to Berliner (1985), teachers make content decisions based on (1) the amount of effort required to teach the subject, (2) the perceived difficulty for the students, and (3) the teacher's personal feelings of enjoyment. In making content decisions, knowledge of the subject discipline appears to be of importance. The teacher's philosophy also enters into content decisions. Research from teacher effectiveness studies shows wide variability between the subject matter content covered by teachers of the same subject and grade.

Time allocation decisions involve time allotted across the school day and within a curriculum area. Observational studies on teacher behavior indicate that less than 1 percent of the time available in reading classes focuses on the teaching of reading comprehension (Pearson & Gallagher, 1983). Fisher et al. (1978) found some teachers of the same grade level allocated 16 minutes of instruction in math each day while others were allocated 51 minutes. The basic principle that evolves from this data is that teachers' time allocation decisions can affect students' opportunity to learn.

Pacing involves the rate at which a teacher covers the course or subject material. The more material that is covered, the more opportunity to learn is given; hence, each student attains a higher achievement level. The corollary to the pacing principle is that students need to be learning the material at the pace that is followed. More effective teachers solicit regular feedback from students by frequent tests and questioning; they use that information to gauge the pace of the instruction. Sometimes the textbooks impose a pace. Why do students learn to spell 20 new words each week? Because the textbooks are set up to teach 20 words a week. Some students could learn 40, others only 10. Teachers need to be aware of how materials may put limitations on pacing.

If grouping is to be done, the teacher must base the grouping on objective criteria related to a valid achievement measure and must frequently reassess the value of the grouping. A problem inherent in grouping is the possible increased gap that can be created among different groups based on a difference in pacing. Grouping decisions cannot be taken lightly, and alternatives to grouping and differential pacing might be explored by teachers prior to a grouping decision. Teachers need to understand the consequences of grouping decisions as reflected in subsequent student achievement.

Appropriate use of time is a third component in a teaching effectiveness model. Research by Stallings et al. (1979), and Walberg (1979), and many others has revealed that time use is more important than time per se. Time can be conceptualized according to the activities being conducted. Berliner (1984) has identified the following components of time: allocated time, engaged time, time related to outcome, and academic learning time. Academic learning time (ALT) is most related to student achievement. The key is to increase the amount of ALT within the time allocated for instruction. Strategies related to room arrangement, minimizing transition time, and teaching material at the conceptual level of students all need to be addressed to increase ALT. Research on effective teachers reveals that they plan the use of their school day, allocate a greater percent of the school day to the basic subjects, and teach in groups so that students can get more instructional time. They spend 50 percent of their reading periods actually engaged in reading instruction. They use short periods of time (not over 30 seconds) to assist individual students with problems in seat work. They circulate among the students doing seat work to ensure a high degree of on-task behavior.

Most research on teacher effectiveness has been done with students in the elementary grades; some has been done at the junior high or secondary level. All have come to similar conclusions about effective teaching (Lightfoot, 1981; Stallings, 1981). MacKinzie (1983) has noted, however, that while the core principles are the same, their expression in actual practice are different. High-school faculties are content specialists who hold little investment in basic skills.

Teaching strategies are the final component of the model. They represent a wide variety of specific procedures. These strategies are based on basic principles of learning and the interaction of those principles with student characteristics. Teaching requires knowledge, explanation, elaboration, and clarification. Sequence, order, modeling, appropriate practice, goal setting, basic concept development, feedback, questioning, and a host of procedures and learning principles can be collapsed under this heading. The critical feature is to train teachers in the effective use of these procedures and in making decisions on when to best use each.

Effective teachers practice effective instruction a large percentage of the day. Instruction requires explanation, demonstration, and clarification. Effective instruction requires that material be explained and reviewed so that new material can be linked to old. Using demonstration and practice while focusing attention on the relevant dimension of a concept is a teaching art. The science of instruction followed by effective teachers is comprised of modeling, questioning, providing prompts and cues, providing feedback, and providing opportunities to practice newly learned skills. Students in classes taught by effective teachers know the goals and the expectations of the teachers for meeting those goals. Finally, research substantiates that effective teachers are people who believe they can make a difference in student achievement.

REFERENCES

Anderson, L. M., Evertson, C. M., & Brophy, J. E. (1979). An experimental study of effective teaching in first-grade reading groups. *Elementary School Journal, 79,* 193–222.

Berliner, D. C. (1984). The half-full glass: A review of research in teaching. In P. L. Hosford (Ed.), *Using what we know about teaching.* Alexandria, VA: Association for Supervision and Curriculum Development.

Caladarci, T., & Gage, N. L. (1984). Effects of minimal intervention on teacher behavior and student achievement. *American Educational Research Journal, 21*(3), 539–555.

Crawford, et al. (1978). *An experiment on teacher effectiveness and parent assisted instruction in the third grade* (3 vols.). Stanford, CA: Center for Educational Research at Stanford.

Elmore, R., Peterson, P., & McCarthey, S. (1996). *Restructuring in the classroom: Teaching, learning, and school organization.* San Francisco: Jossey-Bass.

Emmer, E., Evertson, C., Sanford, J., Clements, B., & Worsham, M. (1982). *Organizing and managing the junior high classroom.* Austin: Research and Development Center for Teacher Education, University of Texas.

Evertson, C., Emmer, E., Clements, B., Sanford, J., Worsham, M., & Williams, E. (1981). *Organizing and managing the elementary school classroom.* Austin: Research and Development Center for Teacher Education, University of Texas.

Fisher, et al. (1978). *Teaching behaviors, academic learning time, and student achievement: Final report of Phase III-B, Beginning Teacher Evaluation Study (Technical Report V-1)*. San Francisco: Far West Regional Laboratory for Educational Research and Development.

Fitzpatrick, K. (1981). *Successful management strategies for the secondary classroom.* Downers Grove, IL.

Gettinger, M., & Stoiba, K. (1999). Excellence in teaching: Review of instructional and environmental variables. In C. R. Reynolds & T. B. Gutkin (Eds.), *The handbook of school psychology* (3rd ed.). New York: Wiley.

Good, T., & Grouws, D. (1977). Teaching effects: A process-product study in fourth-grade mathematics classrooms. *Journal of Teacher Education, 28,* 49–54.

Good, T. L. (1979). Teacher effectiveness in the elementary school: What we know about it. *Journal of Teacher Education, 30,* 52–64.

Good, T. L., & Grouws, D. A. (1979). The Missouri mathematics effectiveness project. *Journal of Educational Psychology, 71,* 355–382.

Lightfoot, S. L. (1981). Portraits of exemplary secondary schools: Highland Park. *Daedalus, 110*(4), 59–80.

Mackinzie, D. E. (1983). Research for school improvement: An appraisal of some recent trends. *Educational Researcher, 12*(4), 5–17.

Mohlman, G., Caladarci, T., & Gage, N. L. (1982). Comprehension and attitude as predictors of implementation of teacher training. *Journal of Teacher Education, 33,* 31, 36.

Pearson, P. D., & Gallagher, M. C. (1983). The instruction of reading comprehension. *Contemporary Educational Psychology, 8,* 317–344.

Stallings, J. A. (1981). *What research has to say to administrators of secondary schools about effective teaching and staff development.* Paper presented at the Conference Creating the Conditions for Effective Teaching, Center for Educational Policy and Management, Eugene, OR.

Stallings, J., Needles, M., & Strayrook, N. (1979). *The teaching of basic reading skills in secondary schools, Phase I and Phase II.* Menlo Park, CA: Stanford Research Institute.

Walberg, H. J. (1979). *Educational environments and effects: Evolution, policy, and productivity.* Berkeley, CA: McCutchon.

Walberg, H. J. (1982). What makes schooling effective? A synthesis and a critique of three national studies. *Contemporary Education: A Journal of Reviews, 1*(1), 22–34.

Robert A. Sedlak
University of Wisconsin at Stout

TEACHER BURNOUT
TEACHER EXPECTANCIES
TEACHING STRATEGIES

TEACHER EXPECTANCIES

The general area of teacher expectancies involves investigating the effects of teachers' perceptions, beliefs, or attitudes about their students. Rosenthal and Jacobson (1968) tested kindergarten through fifth-grade children and then randomly identified some of them by telling their teachers that they had the greatest potential to show significant academic achievement over the school year. Results demonstrating that these children made significantly greater IQ gains than the control groups were interpreted to suggest that the teachers' expectations for the higher potential children influenced their teaching interactions with them, positively affecting the children's learning, as manifested in the higher scores. These results and interpretations were rejected by some owing to methodological flaws (e.g., the failure to measure the teachers' changed expectations and their teaching interactions). Later studies (Hall & Merkel, 1985) failed to replicate these results and indicated that teachers base their expectations for the most part on criteria relevant to academic performance and that they do not bias children's education.

With respect to the disabled student, teacher expectations have been discussed mostly in conjunction with the effects of labeling. Within this field, there is a fear that children's special education labels will cause teachers, parents, and others to lower their expectations for these children's academic and social development. The term *self-fulfilling prophecy* has been used to describe teachers' expectations and resulting instructional interactions that reinforce disabled children to act in a manner consistent with the stereotypical characteristics of their handicap. There is the possibility that these children will have difficulty in learning because "they are disabled," and may master skills only up to a level popularly ascribed to their disability. This self-fulfilling prophecy, then, might lower teachers' and others' expectations for disabled children, lower the children's expectations for themselves, and significantly limit the educational opportunities for them because they are not exposed to more advanced work or complex learning situations.

The research investigating teacher expectancies with individuals with disabilities has been inconclusive. While some studies have demonstrated that labels do affect teacher perceptions and expectations of exceptional children, others have shown no significant negative effects. MacMillan (1977) appropriately concludes:

> Although it [the evidence] does not demonstrate convincingly that calling attention to people with [for example] intellectual deficiencies by giving them special attention is always a bad thing, the controversy over labeling should make us all more sensitive to its potential hazards. (p. 245)

Hobbs (1975), who coordinated a national study on the effect of labels and their resulting expectancy effects, similarly noted no simple solution to the issues as long as labels are required for entrance into special education programs and for the reimbursement of federal and state funds to finance these programs. What appears necessary are ways to minimize the potential expectancy effect of labels while permitting their continued use in the field.

REFERENCES

Hall, V. C., & Merkel, S. P. (1985). Teacher expectancy effects and educational psychology. In J. B. Dusek (Ed.), *Teacher expectancies* (pp. 67–92). Hillsdale, NJ: Erlbaum.

Hobbs, N. (1975). *The future of children*. San Francisco: Jossey-Bass.

MacMillan, D. L. (1977). *Mental retardation in school and society*. Boston: Little, Brown.

Rosenthal, R., & Jacobson, L. (1968). *Pygmalion in the classroom*. New York: Holt, Rinehart, & Winston.

HOWARD M. KNOFF
University of South Florida

PYGMALION EFFECT

TEACHING AND CONSULTATION

Consultation as one of the methods of delivering services to exceptional children was recognized by Reynolds (1962) in his Hierarchy of Services for Special Education Services. In this hierarchy, it was recognized that the majority of students classified as exceptional should and could be served in general education classrooms with consultation being one of the support services. Deno (1970) also recognized the teacher consultant as part of a "cascade of services." Kirk and Gallagher (1979) indicated that to facilitate mainstreaming, school systems might provide consultation services to regular teachers in the form of special education teachers, psychologists, social workers, and medical personnel. They go on to indicate that consultants are available to regular teachers when they have questions about a child or when they need advice concerning special materials and methods of instruction. Thomas, Correa, and Morsink (1995) provide an extensive look at the historical and legal foundations of consultation, collaboration, and teaming in special education beginning with the Deno model.

A number of definitions of and terms for consultation have been formulated. The terms include triadic process (Tharp, 1975), developmental and problem-centered consultation (Bergan, 1977), and collaborative problem solving (Medway, 1979). In special education, Idol, Paolucci-Whitcomb, and Nevin (1986) defined collaborative consultation as "an interactive process that enables people with diverse expertise to generate creative solutions to mutually defined problems." Dettmer, Thurston, and Dyck (1995) defined school consultation and the role of the consultant as an "activity in which professional educators and parents collaborate within the school context by communicating, cooperating, and coordinating their efforts as a team to serve the learning and behavioral needs of students." It also is important to note what consultation is not. Pryzwansky (1974) pointed out that consultation should not be an "expert" providing some type of prescription. Other cautions include one for a distinction between a medical model and a behavioral approach and one for the differences between consultation and counseling and consultation and collaboration.

Three of the most popular models of consultation in special education are triadic, organizational, and behavioral. In the triadic model there is a target (person with problem), a mediator (person with means to influence change), and a consultant (person with knowledge to mobilize mediator's influence.) Thomas et al. describe the collaborative consultation model of Idol et al. as an extension of the triadic model in which the target is the student with a problem, the mediator is the general education teacher, and the consultant is the special educator or other professional. Organizational consultation focuses on interactions, interrelationships, shared decision making, and communication skills. The emphasis is on change with an organization or group. The consultant's role is primarily that of facilitator. Behavioral consultation emphasizes student behavior change. This model uses direct observation, identification of target behavior for change, and data-based interventions and assessment. Gutkin and Curtis (1982) identified characteristics present in the majority of consultation models they reviewed. These include indirect service delivery, consultant-consultee relationship, coordinate status, involvement of consultee in the consultation process, consultee's right to reject consultant suggestions, voluntary nature of consultation, and confidentiality.

The process of consultation is summarized by Thomas et al. in eight steps, which are listed below:

1. Establishing the relationship
2. Gathering information
3. Identifying the problem
4. Stating the target behavior
5. Generating interventions
6. Implementing interventions
7. Evaluating the interventions
8. Withdrawing from the consultative relationship

A concept closely related to consultation is teaming. Teams within special education are generally thought of as organized groups of professionals from different disciplines. Their common goal is cooperative problem solving. Combining collaboration and teamwork builds on the strengths of both approaches. Teaming models include the multidisciplinary team, the interdisciplinary team, and the transdisciplinary team. The multidisciplinary team concept evolved from the medical model, in which experts in various fields shared their observations and generally reported them to one person. The interdisciplinary team is similar to the multidisciplinary team, but generally the team members evaluate a child and meet to share their observations. The transdisciplinary team model is a combination of the two previously mentioned and attempts to reduce fragmentation. It is viewed as an education/treatment model that integrates assessment, program goals, and objectives from various disciplines. Its characteristics, according to Lyon and Lyon (1980), are a joint team and professional development approach and implementation of role release. Orelove and Sobsey (1991) identify other characteristics as an indirect therapy approach, multiple lines of communication, and integration of services.

Consultation, collaboration, teaming, and family involvement have been stressed in special education (especially since the passage of PL 94-142), and these concepts have been strengthened with each amended or reauthorized version of this law. Teachers and other school personnel are recognizing the importance of shared decision making as the needs of children become increasingly complex. The emphases on effective schools, total quality management, site-based management, comprehensive schools, and inclusion are providing the impetus for a model combining the salient features of previously identified consultation, collaboration, and teaming approaches. Thomas et al. proposed such a model, which they describe as interactive teaming. Interactive teaming is defined as a mutual or reciprocal effort among and between members of a team to provide the best possible educational program for a student. This model has ten elements drawn from previous research of models and programs with interactive teaming components. These are the elements which must be present for the model to be effective.

Legitimacy and autonomy

Purpose and objectives

Competencies of team members and clarity of roles

Role release and role transitions

Awareness of the individuality of team members

Process of team building

Attention to factors that affect team functioning

Leadership styles

Implementation procedures

Commitment to common goals

Consultation in special education has evolved from the concept of a professional sharing expertise with a regular classroom teacher to one of the special educator being a member of a team in which all individuals have critical roles.

REFERENCES

Bergan, J. R. (1977). *Behavioral consultation.* Columbus, OH: Merrill.

Deno, E. (1970). Special education as developmental capital. *Exceptional Children, 37,* 229–237.

Dettmer, P., Thurston, L. P., & Dyck, N. (1995). *Consultation, collaboration, and teamwork for students with special needs.* Boston: Allyn & Bacon.

Gutkin, T. B., & Curtis, M. J. (1982). School-based consultation. In C. R. Reynolds & T. B. Gutkin (Eds.), *The handbook of school psychology.* New York: Wiley.

Idol, L., Paolucci-Whitcomb, P., & Nevin, A. (1986). *Collaborative consultation.* Rockville, MD: Aspen Systems Corporation.

Kirk, S. A., & Gallagher, J. J. (1972). *Educating exceptional children* (2nd ed.). Boston: Houghton Mifflin.

Kirk, S. A., & Gallagher, J. J. (1979). *Educating exceptional children* (3rd ed.). Boston: Houghton Mifflin.

Kirk, S. A., & Gallagher, J. J. (1983). *Educating exceptional children* (4th ed.). Boston: Houghton Mifflin.

Lyon, S., & Lyon, G. (1980). Team functioning and staff development: A role release approach to providing integrated educational services for severely handicapped students. *Journal of the Association for the Severely Handicapped, 5,* 250–263.

Medway, F. J. (1979). How effective is school consultation? A review of recent research. *Journal of School Psychology, 17,* 285–292.

Orelove, F. P., & Sobsey, D. (1991). *Educating children with multiple disabilities: A transdisciplinary approach* (2nd ed.). Baltimore: Brookes.

Pryzwansky, W. W. (1974). A reconsideration of the consultation model for delivery of school-based psychological services. *Journal of Orthopsychiatry, 44,* 579–583.

Reynolds, M. C. (1962). A framework for considering some issues in special education. *Exceptional Children, 29,* 147–169.

Tharp, R. G. (1975). The triadic model of consultation: Current considerations. In C. A. Parker (Ed.), *Psychological consultation: Helping teachers meet special needs.* Reston, VA: Council for Exceptional Children.

Thomas, C. C., Correa, V. I., & Morsink, C. V. (1995). *Interactive teaming: Consultation and collaboration in special programs* (2nd ed.). Englewood Cliffs, NJ: Merrill.

ELEANOR BOYD WRIGHT
CAROL CHASE THOMAS
University of North Carolina at Wilmington

TEACHING EXCEPTIONAL CHILDREN

Teaching Exceptional Children (*TEC*) is a professional journal that is a joint production of the Council for Exceptional Children Information Center and the Instructional Materials Centers Network for Handicapped Children and Youth. It was first published in 1968 and now has a circulation of 55,000.

TEC's objective is "to disseminate practical and timely information to classroom teachers working with exceptional children and youth." Published quarterly the journal deals with various topic areas such as practical classroom procedures for use with the gifted and handicapped, educational-diagnostic techniques, evaluation of instructional material, new research findings, and reports of educational projects in progress.

The *TEC* is designed to garner feedback from readers and allow for professional input through features such as "The Teacher Idea Exchange," "Questions and Answers," "Teacher Write In," and "Letters to the Editor."

Information concerning subscriptions or manuscripts should be referred to Publication for Council for Exceptional Children, 1920 Association Drive, Reston, VA, 22091.

RICK GONZALES
Texas A&M University

COUNCIL FOR EXCEPTIONAL CHILDREN

TEACHING: INCLUSION AND CO-TEACHING

Co-teaching is a form of instruction in which a general education teacher and special education teacher work together in an inclusive classroom consisting of students with and without disabilities. Typically, the types of students with disabilities found in a co-teaching environment are students considered to have mild disabilities (i.e., learning, behavioral, and speech/language disabilities). Because students with mild disabilities bring a number of general and specific weaknesses to classrooms that may be structurally rigid and where information may be poorly organized, too abstract, uninteresting, and assumes a great deal of prior knowledge, a teacher who specializes in learning processes is a critical support.

Two issues emerge, however: (1) How do teachers teach together to facilitate more successful learning by students with and without disabilities?, and (2) What kinds of teacher and student outcomes can be expected?

What Does Research Say about Co-Teaching?

The literature on co-teaching or collaborative instruction has primarily described barriers to collaboration (e.g., Johnson, Pugach, & Hammittee, 1988; Phillips & McCullough, 1990), types of collaborative relationships (e.g., Bauwens, Hourcade, & Friend, 1989; Dettmer, Thurston, & Dyck, 1993), and a variety of collaborative skills and roles (e.g., Friend & Cook, 1992a; Knackendoffel, Robinson, Deshler, & Schumaker, 1992), and provided little data on the instructional dynamics of two teachers teaching students with and without disabilities or the performance of the students in inclusive classes (e.g., Idol, Nevin, & Paolucci-Whitcomb, 1994; Reeve & Hallahan, 1994).

In one of the few existing data-based reports on co-teaching, Hudson (1990) described gains for one group of elementary children with and without mild disabilities in grade-point average, achievement test scores, number of academic objectives mastered, adaptive behavior ratings, peer status, and school attendance when they were enrolled in two classrooms employing the Class-Within-a-Class Model for collaborative teaching. Schulte, Osborne, and McKinney (1990) discovered that students with mild disabilities who received some instruction from the special education teacher in general education settings made greater overall gains on a standardized achievement test as compared to students receiving resource room support for one period per day, and as compared to students in the general education classroom where consultation was only provided by the general education teacher. There were no significant differences on a criterion-referenced test, however.

Another study on collaborative instruction in an elementary setting provided negative results. Zigmond and Baker (1990) observed teachers and students with learning disabilities in inclusive classrooms where a combination of collaborative instruction and consultation took place. They concluded that the types of support and kinds of instruction by teachers were essentially "business as usual." Students did not make significant gains on a standardized achievement test, they earned lower grades, and curriculum-based measures showed only minimal progress. Boudah, Schumaker, and Deshler (1997) found that teachers could learn to teach together, but that teacher change translated to only minimal change in student engagement and use of learning strategies. Students also continued to perform poorly on unit tests and quizzes.

Descriptions from these and other studies indicate several other characteristics of co-teaching. Many co-teaching relationships are arranged by building administrators (Boudah et al., 1997). Perhaps because of such arrangements and little training, the special education teacher also typically functions in one of two roles: (1) provider of indirect services to students through consultation with the general education teacher (e.g., Peck, Killen, & Baumgart, 1989; Tindal, Shinn, Walz, & Germann, 1987); or (2) provider of at least some direct services within general education classrooms, but primarily or exclusively to students with disabilities and with apparently few interactions between the two teachers (e.g., Givens-Olge, Christ, & Idol, 1991; Hudson, 1990). Thus, in the second role, the special education teacher functions more like an instructional aide than a specialist or teacher of at least equivalent instructional status. In addition, many collaboratively taught classes may include a large number of students with disabilities and thus operate like "low-track" classes (Boudah & Knight, 1999). Such efforts then may lead to ceiling effects on teacher instructional change and student performance (Boudah et al., (1997).

What Might Co-Teaching Look Like?

The keys to two teachers working in the same classroom are the interactions between the teachers as well as the interactions between the teachers and students (Boudah et al., 1997). Thus, there are several possible models for co-teaching (e.g., Bauwens & Hourcade, 1997; Burrello, Burrello, & Friend, 1996). Some of the models may be called (a) teach and circulate or observe, (b) station teaching, (c) alternative teaching, and (d) team teaching.

In the first model (*teach and circulate or observe*), one teacher would present the content material (e.g., a lesson on the geography of France), and the other teacher would circulate among the students to assist as needed, or collect observation data on student behavior and performance. Teachers might use *station teaching* in order to individualize support for groups of students. For instance, one teacher may need to reteach material to one group of students who were absent the previous day, the other teacher may need to review material for a group with learning disabilities, and another group of students may work independently on an assignment. In *alternative teaching,* a small group of students might sit with one teacher in a corner of the room for additional review, reteaching, enrichment, or help completing an assignment or test.

Team teaching is more dynamic. During class instruction, teachers function in two primary roles: presenter and enhancer. During whole group instruction, the *presenter* presents content information such as facts, rules, concepts, and themes in a subject area such as social studies, math, science, or English. Meanwhile, the *enhancer* arbitrates between students and the content material being presented in class. For instance, in one instructional sequence, a science teacher might talk about a specific concept while the special education teacher simultaneously summarizes the most important points by writing bulleted statements on the chalkboard; later, the special education teacher might talk about another part of the science concept while the science teacher elaborates by providing some specific examples or an analogy. The sequence may finish with both teachers functioning as enhancers, one prompting students to summarize a chronology of facts or events while the other interjects by prompting students to predict what would happen if a different order of events had occurred. Therefore, while the presenter teaches *what* to learn, the enhancer, in essence, teaches *how* to learn the material (Boudah et al., 1997).

At least initially, the general education teacher may function in the presenter role more often, and the special education teacher commonly may function in the enhancer role. This is for obvious reasons: the general education teacher is likely to be more knowledgeable about the content being presented, and the special education teacher's strength is usually related to teaching skills or strategies for learning. Eventually, however, the general education

teacher and the special education teacher may function equally as presenter and enhancer, and both teachers may function as presenter or enhancer at any given time during a lesson. Thus, through this kind of instructional process, the special education teacher and general education teacher can complement and support each other, like partners who are dancing together (Adams, Cessna, & Friend, 1992).

In summary, in co-teaching, both teachers should be actively engaged in teaching students. Both teachers should monitor and enhance student understanding of information and concepts presented in class. Teachers can help each other expand and clarify information and concepts, teach strategies, and enhance, rather than "water down," content. Either teacher can provide whole group or individualized instruction, and both teachers are responsible for managing student behavior and evaluating performance.

Where Do Teachers Start?

As with any method for delivering instructional services to students with disabilities, it is important to focus first on the needs of individual students and decide which students would benefit from co-teaching in inclusive classes. This may not include every student or even every student with a particular disability classification. Once those decisions have been made, clustering a small number of students with disabilities in an inclusive class may not only be instructionally effective, but also may be a more efficient way for special education teachers to serve students.

In addition, co-teaching is often a change in the typical operations of a school. Therefore, co-teachers need to build their plans and schedules with the principal. In order to set up successful experiences, teachers also should be allowed to decide who will teach together. Special education teachers who are trying to facilitate inclusion may need to target general education teachers who may have some special education experience, background, and/or exposure. These teachers are most likely to understand the needs of students with disabilities and be adaptable to instructional change.

Next, co-teachers may want to conduct observations in each others' classes so that they become familiar with their partner's teaching styles and routines. Observations can provide opportunities to think about appropriate co-teaching models and ways to modify and adapt instructional methods. Co-teachers also may find that it is worthwhile to pilot one class for a period of time, develop a relationship, plan as a team, teach as a team, and evaluate team performance before committing to co-teaching for a longer period of time.

Co-teachers should seek out training experiences on specific collaborative skills as well as ways of building shared expectations. Committing to a regular team planning time can also help clarify expectations. Team planning and organization also should lead to more dynamic teaching in the classroom.

School restructuring efforts often highlight coordination and collaboration as important dimensions of the delivery of educational services for children in a broad array of programs including gifted education, English as a Second Language (ESL), Chapter 1 (Association for Supervision and Curriculum Development, 1991), as well as special education. Such integration of services necessarily requires the collaboration of those assigned to work with such a diversity of students. Co-teaching is one way for teachers to collaborate in order to provide a free and appropriate education to some students with disabilities in general education classrooms.

REFERENCES

Adams, L., Cessna, K., & Friend, M. (1992, October). *Co-teaching: Honoring uniqueness and creating unity.* Presentation made at the Annual Conference of the Council for Learning Disabilities, Kansas City, MO.

Association for Supervision and Curriculum Development. (1991). *Resolutions 1991.* Washington, DC.

Bauwens, J., & Hourcade, J. J. (1997). Cooperative teaching: Pictures of possibilities. *Intervention in School and Clinic, 33*(2), 81–85, 89.

Bauwens, J., Hourcade, J. J., & Friend, M. (1989). Cooperative teaching: A model for general and special education integration. *Remedial and Special Education, 10,* 17–22.

Boudah, D. J., Schumaker, J. B., & Deshler, D. D. (1997). Collaborative instruction: Is it an effective option for inclusion in secondary classrooms? *Learning Disability Quarterly, 20*(4), 293–316.

Burrello, L. C., Burrello, J. M., & Friend, M. (Producers). (1996). *The power of 2: Making a difference through co-teaching* [Film]. Indiana University Television Services and Elephant Rock Productions. (Available from CEC Resources, Association Drive, Reston, VA)

Dettmer, P., Thurston, L. P., & Dyck, N. (1993). *Consultation, collaboration, and teamwork for students with special needs.* Boston: Allyn & Bacon.

Friend, M., & Cook, L. (1992a). *Interactions: Collaboration skills for school professionals.* New York: Longman.

Givens-Olge, L., Christ, B. A., & Idol, L. (1991). Collaborative consultation: The San Juan Unified School District project. *Journal of Educational and Psychological Consultation, 2*(3), 267–284.

Hudson, F. (1990). *Research reports for Kansas City, Kansas public schools division of special education on CTM-collaborative teaching model at Stony Point South Elementary School, 1989–90.* Kansas City: University of Kansas Medical Center, Department of Special Education.

Idol, L., Nevin, A., & Paolucci-Whitcomb, P. (1994). *Collaborative consultation* (2nd ed.). Austin, TX: PRO-ED.

Johnson, L. J., Pugach, M. C., & Hammittee, D. J. (1988). Barriers to effective special education consultation. *Remedial and Special Education, 9,* 41–47.

Knackendoffel, E. A., Robinson, S. M., Deshler, D. D., & Schumaker, J. B. (1992). *Collaborative problem solving: Team teaching series.* Lawrence, KS: Edge Enterprises.

Peck, C. A., Killen, C. C., & Baumgart, D. (1989). Increasing implementation of special education instruction in mainstream preschools: Direct and generalized effects of nondirective consultation. *Journal of Applied Behavior Analysis, 2*(2), 197–210.

Phillips, V., & McCullough, L. (1990). Consultation-based programming: Instituting the collaborative ethic in schools. *Exceptional Children, 56,* 291–304.

Reeve, P. T., & Hallahan, D. P. (1994). Practical questions about collaboration between general and special educators. *Focus on Exceptional Children, 26*(7), 1–12.

Schulte, A. C., Osborne, S. S., & McKinney, J. D. (1990). Academic outcomes for students with learning disabilities in consultation and resource programs. *Exceptional Children, 57*(2), 162–171.

Tindal, G., Shinn, M. R., Walz, L., & Germann, G. (1987). Mainstream consultation in secondary settings: The Pine County model. *Journal of Special Education, 21,* 94–106.

Zigmond, N., & Baker, J. (1990). Mainstream experiences for learning disabled students (Project MELD): Preliminary report. *Exceptional Children, 57*(2), 176–185.

Daniel J. Boudah
Texas A&M University

INCLUSION

TEACHING STRATEGIES

Teaching strategies are those activities that are conducted by a teacher to enhance the academic achievement of students. A teaching strategy is based on a philosophical approach that is used in conjunction with a learning strategy. Teachers generally choose a particular approach based on their educational background and training, their personal beliefs, the subject being taught, the characteristics of the learner, and the degree of learning required.

Training backgrounds of special educators can range from the behavioral to the process-oriented. Teachers with behavioral backgrounds will use approaches that are task specific and focus on observable behaviors. Those coming from a process background are more inclined to follow approaches that focus on underlying processes. They try to treat the hypothesized cause of the problem or deficit rather than the observable behavior. Approaches such as perceptual-motor training or cognitive training may be followed by teachers with process orientations. Perceptual-motor training approaches are controversial and have questionable effectiveness in regard to academic achievement (Arter & Jenkins, 1979; Kavale & Forness, 1999; Sedlak & Weener, 1973). Cognitive training approaches focus on thinking skills and learning how to learn rather than specific content skills. The research on this approach is promising. Examples of behavioral approaches are direct instruction and applied behavior analysis. These approaches focus on identifying the specific content to be taught and teaching that content in a systematic fashion using a prescribed system of learning strategies. There are also subject-specific approaches. For example, in reading, some of the different approaches available are the linguistics approach, phonics, sight word, Fernald, multisensory, language experience, and the neurological impress method. These approaches focus on the organization of the materials needed for instruction and also prescribe, in some cases, specific strategies to be used.

In addition to an approach, the application of a learning strategy to a situation is needed to create a teaching strategy. A learning strategy becomes a teaching strategy when the teacher systematically plans, organizes, and uses a learning strategy with a student to achieve a specific outcome. In many texts, these learning strategies are referred to as generic strategies or principles of instruction. These strategies generally are used in conjunction with a particular phase of learning (e.g., acquisition, retention, or transfer), or for a particular type of learning (e.g., discrimination, concept, rule, problem solving). Generic strategies used for the acquisition phase include giving instruction (verbal, picture, modeling or demonstration, reading), revealing objectives to the learner, providing appropriate practice on a skill, providing feedback to the learner, organizing material into small steps and in sequential order, checking on student comprehension through questions, and offering positive and negative examples of concepts. However, it is also important for students to learn to teach others through the development of their own strategic and skillful processing of information (Alexander & Murphy, 1999).

The generic strategies that can be used to maintain skills already acquired are overlearning, reminiscence, and spaced review. To teach for transfer, multiple examples of the application of the skill or concept are needed, along with teaching the skill with the appropriate cues in the setting in which it is to be practiced. Gradually fading artificial cues and relying on natural cues in the environment is another strategy used by teachers to facilitate transfer. Some other examples of teaching strategies are the use of mnemonics, peer teaching, assigned homework, graded homework, cooperative learning, mediated instruction, and computer-assisted instruction. In strategies such as these, a variety of learning strategies are organized and used.

REFERENCES

Alexander, P., & Murphy, P. (1999). What cognitive psychology has to say to school psychology. In C. R. Reynolds & T. B. Gutkin (Eds.), *The handbook of school psychology* (3rd ed.). New York: Wiley.

Arter, J. A., & Jenkins, J. R. (1979). Differential diagnosis—Prescriptive teaching: A critical appraisal. *Review of Educational Research, 49,* 517–555.

Kavale, K., & Forness, S. (1999). The effectiveness of special education. In C. R. Reynolds & T. B. Gutkin (Eds.), *The handbook of school psychology* (3rd ed.). New York: Wiley.

Sedlak, R. A., & Weener, P. (1973). Review of research on the Illinois Test of Psycholinguistics Abilities. In L. Mann & D. Sabatino (Eds.), *The first review of special education.* Philadelphia: JSE.

ROBERT A. SEDLAK
University of Wisconsin at Stout

**ABILITY TRAINING, EARLY EFFORTS IN
APPLIED BEHAVIOR ANALYSIS
DIRECT INSTRUCTION
MNEMONICS
TEACHER EFFECTIVENESS**

TECHNIQUES: A JOURNAL FOR REMEDIAL EDUCATION AND COUNSELING

Techniques originated in July 1984 with Gerald B. Fuller and Hubert Vance as coeditors. The journal provides multidisciplinary articles that serve as an avenue for communication and interaction among the various disciplines concerned with the treatment and education of the exceptional individual and others encountering special problems in living. The orientation is primarily clinical and educational, and reflects the various types of counseling, therapy, remediation, and interventions currently employed. The journal does not mirror the opinion of any one school or authority but serves as a forum for open discussion and exchange of ideas and experiences.

The specific sections in *Techniques* represent the following content areas:

1. *Educational and Psychological Materials.* This section helps the professional to keep current by evaluating, critiquing, comparing, and reviewing educational, counseling, and psychological materials (e.g., programs, kits) that are being proposed or used in applied settings.

2. *Research Studies.* This section offers empirical research, case studies, and discussion papers that focus on specific counseling, therapy, and remediation techniques that cut across various disciplines.

3. *Practical Approaches in the Field.* This section provides a description of hands-on techniques or approaches that the author(s) have used and found to be successful within their field.

4. *Parent Education.* This section provides comprehensive treatment of such topics as disruptive children and youths, single-parent families, reconstituted

families, and prevention and treatment of child abuse and neglect.

5. *Bibliotherapy.* This is a compilation of books that are useful for the child and parent as well as the practitioner. The topics are practical and address such issues as divorce, self-concept, and drug abuse.

6. *What's New in the Field.* This section provides current information in the areas of remedial programs and counseling techniques, and includes reviews of current software programs.

GERALD B. FULLER
Central Michigan University

TECHNOLOGY FOR INDIVIDUALS WITH DISABILITIES

If there is one word that summarizes the impact of technology in the last 25 years, it is zeitgeist, the spirit of the time. The inculcation of silicon chips and microprocessors into our everyday lives irrevocably changed us from an industrial society to an informational society (Toffler, 1982). If disabled persons are to function fully in this society, they must have access to the myriad technologies that can improve communication, information processing, and learning. While technological advances are making inroads in the reduction of the impact of motoric, sensory, and cognitive disabilities, the real potential is yet to be met. The following section is an introduction to some of the technologies that are currently affecting the lives of disabled persons. It also offers an overview of some of the technologies that have yet to fulfill their promise.

The computer is second only to the printing press in its impact on the way in which humans acquire and distribute information. As computers are reduced in size and cost, their impact is multiplied geometrically. The computer has two characteristics that are particularly significant for disabled individuals: (1) as hardware decreases in size, it generally increases in capacity; and (2) the more sophisticated computers become, the easier they are to use. These characteristics are very important for individuals with disabilities in several respects. First, as computers become smaller, they also become more portable. For example, hand-held computers can be attached to wheelchairs to improve mobility. Second, as computers become easier to use, they are more accessible to the disabled. For example, reducing the number of keystrokes required to perform certain computer functions has greatly facilitated their use.

Microprocessor-based technology facilitates communication in two ways: as a compensatory device for sensory disabilities and as an assistive device for individuals whose physical impairments make communication difficult. Examples of compensatory devices include talking computer terminals that can translate text into speech (Stoffel, 1982); special adaptive devices for computers that can provide visual displays of auditory information by translating sound into text (Vanderheiden, 1982); and Cognivox, an adaptive device for Apple personal computers that combines the capabilities of voice recognition and voice output (Murray, 1982).

For individuals with motoric disabilities, communication aids have been developed that allow them to operate computers with single-switch input devices. These devices may be as simple as game paddles and joysticks or as sophisticated as screen-based optical headpointing systems. Keyboard enhancers and emulators help individuals with restricted movement by reducing the number of actuations necessary for communication. For example, Minispeak is a semantic compaction system that can produce thousands of clear, spoken sentences with as few as seven keystrokes (Baker, 1982). Adaptive communication devices can also be linked with computers to help the disabled control their living environments (e.g., by running appliances, answering the telephone, or adjusting the thermostat).

The term telecommunication means communication across distance. It is a means of storing text and pictures as electronic impulses and transmitting them via telephone line, satellite, coaxial and fiber optic cables, or broadcast transmission. Telecommunication offers several advantages over traditional means of communication. First, telecommunication is relatively inexpensive when spread across time and users. Also, telecommunicating helps alleviate the problems associated with geographic remoteness or the isolation imposed by limited mobility. Information-gathering and dissemination need not be limited to schools. It can occur in the home or office; a local area network (LAN) can link several computers or terminals to a computer with expanded memory. Such a system permits several operators to use the same software and data simultaneously. A wide-area network links computers from distant geographic regions. Examples of this networking capability can be found in several states where all of the local agencies are linked to the state agency. Statewide systems greatly reduce the time and paperwork necessary for compliance with special education legislation.

SpecialNet is another example of a wide-area network. Subscribers use it primarily to access electronic bulletin boards and to send messages through electronic mail. Electronic bulletin boards function much the same as traditional corkboards found in most schools. Users can post messages to obtain information, or they can read messages to find out the latest information about a given topic. For example, the employment bulletin board on SpecialNet posts vacancies in special education and related services. The Request for Proposals (RFP) bulletin board has information on the availability of upcoming grants and contracts. The exchange bulletin board is for users to post requests for information. Electronic mail, as the name implies, is a system whereby computer users can send and receive messages through their computers. On the SpecialNet system, each subscriber is given a special name that identifies his or her mailbox; with the aid of word processing and telecommunication software, users can send short or long documents in a matter of seconds.

In addition to capabilities offered by electronic bulletin boards and electronic mail, individuals with telecommunication hookups have access to information from large electronic libraries that store, sort, and retrieve bibliographic information. For example, the Educational Resources Information Center (ERIC), operated by the Council for Exceptional Children, is the largest source of information on handicapped and gifted children. Other important sources of information are the Handicapped Exchange (HEX), which contains information on handicapped individuals, and ABLEDATA, which is a catalog of computer hardware, software, and assistive devices for individuals with disabilities.

Another important form of telecommunication is teletext, a one-way transmission to television viewers. Teletext uses the vertical blanking interval (VBI), the unused portion of a television signal, to print information on television screens. Applications of teletext include news headlines, weather forecasts, and information on school closings. Closed captioning is a form of teletext that allows hearing-impaired individuals to see dialogue (JWK International, 1983). Experiments are now under way to use teletext to transmit instructional material. Broadcasters can transmit public domain software into homes and schools that have computers and special transmission decoding devices.

A videodisk is a tabletop device that is interfaced with a monitor to play video programs stored on 12-inch disks. When interfaced with a computer, the videodisk becomes interactive, and thus becomes a powerful instructional tool. Part of the videodisk's power comes from its storage capacity; it can hold 54,000 frames of information, including movies, filmstrips, slides, and sound. When combined with the computer's branching capacity, videodisks allow students to move ahead or go back according to the learner's needs. Information can also be shown in slow motion or freeze frame. One of the earliest educational videodisks was the First National Kidisc, a collection of games and activities for children. The California School for the Deaf in Riverside also developed a system to use the videodisk to teach language development and reading. With this system, students use light pens to write their responses on the screen (Wollman, 1981). In the past, videodisk technology has been very expensive because of the cost in developing the disks. Now, however, educators and other service providers can have customized disks made at relatively low cost.

Artificial intelligence refers to the use of the computer to solve the same types of problems and to make the same kinds of decisions faced by humans (Yin & Moore, 1984). Be-cause scientists do not fully understand how humans solve problems and make decisions, they have debated whether true artificial intelligence is possible. So far, the closest they have come is the development of expert systems, natural systems, and machine vision. Expert systems are computer programs that use knowledge and inference strategies to solve problems. The systems rely on three kinds of information: facts, relations between the facts, and methods for using the facts to solve problems (D'Ambrosio, 1985). An example of an expert system is Internist, which makes medical diagnoses. Natural language processing is the use of natural speech to communicate with computers and to translate foreign language texts. Machine vision takes advantage of sensory devices to reproduce objects on the computer screen. These technological applications, like many others, offer potential benefits to disabled individuals, but their use for physical or cognitive prostheses hinges on the commitment of vast resources for their development.

A robot is a device that can be programmed to move in specified directions and to manipulate objects. What distinguishes a robot from other technologies and prosthetic devices is its capacity for locomotion. Robotic arms can pick up and move objects, assemble parts, and even spray paint. Robots of the future will not only be able to move, they will also be able to sense the environment by touch, sight, or sound. More important, the robot will be able to acquire information, understand it, and plan and implement appropriate actions (Yin & Moore, 1984). While robots offer great potential as prosthetic devices for the disabled, their current use is limited primarily to research and manufacturing. To some extent, robots are being used in classrooms to teach computer logic.

Specific technologies are in use today in special education classrooms for nearly all categories of disabling conditions, including communication disorders, health impairments, hearing impairments, visual impairments, and students with learning disabilities in particular (e.g., see Cartwright, Cartwright, & Ward, 1995). Technology is growing most rapidly in areas where it was first used and seems to have the greatest impact on quality of life issues in the sensory impairments and communication disorders. Computer-aided instruction is on the rise as well, especially with children with learning disabilities, but is a latecomer. As recently as 1990, the major textbook in learning disabilities (Myers & Hammill, 1990) makes no mention of technology for learning disability interventions.

REFERENCES

Baker, B. (1982). Minispeak: A semantic compaction system that makes self-expression easier for communicatively disabled individuals. *Byte, 7,* 186–202.

Cartwright, P., Cartwright, C., & Ward, M. (1995). *Educating special learners* (4th ed.). Boston: Wadsworth.

D'Ambrosio, B. (1985). Expert systems—Myth or reality? *Byte, 10,* 275–282.

JWK International. (1983). *Teletext and videotex* (Contract No. 300-81-0424). Washington, DC: Special Education Programs Office.

Murray, W. (1982). The Cognivox V10-1003: Voice recognition and output for the Apple II. *Byte, 7,* 231–235.

Myers, P., & Hammill, D. (1990). *Methods for learning disorders* (4th ed.). Austin, TX: PRO-ED.

Pfaehler, B. (1985). Electronic text: The University of Wisconsin experience. *T.H.E. Journal, 13,* 67–70.

Stoffel, D. (1982). Talking terminals. *Byte, 7,* 218–227.

Toffler, A. (1982). *The third wave.* New York: Bantham.

Vanderheiden, G. (1982). Computers can play a dual role for disabled individuals. *Byte, 7,* 136–162.

Wollman, J. (1981). The videodisc: A new educational technology takes off. *Electronic Learning, 1,* 39–40.

Yin, R. K., & Moore, G. B. (1984). *Robotics, artificial intelligence, computer simulation: Future applications in special education.* Washington, DC: U.S. Department of Education.

ELIZABETH MCCLELLAN
Council for Exceptional Children

COMPUTER USE WITH STUDENTS WITH DISABILITIES
ROBOTICS
ROBOTICS IN SPECIAL EDUCATION
SPECIALNET

TECSE

See TOPICS IN EARLY CHILDHOOD SPECIAL EDUCATION.

TEGRETOL

Tegretol (carbamazepine) is an anticonvulsant medication indicated for the treatment of various types of seizure disorders. In addition, Tegretol may also be prescribed for the treatment of manic-depressive disorders, resistant schizophrenia, rage outburst, or alcohol withdrawal management (Shannon, Wilson, & Stang, 1995).

Tegretol should be taken with food to minimize gastric irritation. All individuals need to be advised to take sustained released Tegretol as a whole tablet and never crush or chew the pill. Tegretol must be taken at regular intervals during the day and exactly as ordered by the physician (Deglin & Vallerand, 1999). Abrupt discontinuation may result in severe seizure activity and is not recommended (Shannon et al., 1995). Possible side effects include dizziness or drowsi-

ness, and those starting treatment should take great care to avoid operating any machinery or driving a vehicle until their response to Tegretol is analyzed (Deglin & Vallerand, 1999). Since photosensitivity reactions also may occur, excessive sunlight should be avoided and sunscreen protection routinely used (Shannon et al., 1995).

Tegretol may cause breakthrough bleeding in women taking oral contraceptives (McKenry & Salerno, 1998). Women should be instructed to use other birth control methods as Tegretol may interfere with the effectiveness of their oral contraceptives. Tegretol is also excreted in breast milk and is not recommended in nursing mothers (McKenry & Solerno, 1998). Tegretol, along with other anticonvulsant medications such as phenytoin, (Dilantin), valproic acid (Depakene/Depakote), primidone (Mysoline), and phenobarbitol, appears to have teratogenic effects, and prenatal exposure to multiple ones appears to increase risk to the fetus (Jones, 1997). Women with seizure disorders who are at risk for pregnancy should be tested to determine if medication can be suspended if they have been seizure free for 2 years or at least maintained on a low dose. The conflict between potentially adverse effects of seizures on mother and fetus and medication on the fetus may be difficult to resolve.

An individual taking Tegretol should be advised that a medical alert identification card, bracelet, or necklace should be with the person at all times to alert health care providers of the medications that the person is taking as well as any pertinent medical history (Skidmore-Roth & McKenry, 1997). With any continuous medication regime, school personnel should be notified of this medication and any other health related concerns (Wong, 1995).

REFERENCES

Deglin, J., & Vallerand, A. (1999). *Davis's drug guide for nurses* (6th ed.). Philadelphia: F. A. Davis.

Jones, K. L. (1997). *Smith's recognizable patterns of human malformation* (5th ed.). Philadelphia: W. B. Saunders.

McKenry, L., & Salerno, E. (1998). *Pharmacology in nursing* (20th ed.). St. Louis, MO: Mosby-Year Book.

Shannon, M., Wilson, B., & Stang, C. (1995). *Govoni & Hayes drugs and nursing implications* (8th ed.). Norwalk, CT: Appleton & Lange.

Skidmore-Roth, L., & McKenry, L. (1997). *Mosby's drug guide for nurses* (2nd ed.). St. Louis, MO: Mosby-Year Book.

Wong, D. (1995). *Whaley & Wong's nursing care of infants and children* (5th ed.). St. Louis, MO: Mosby-Year Book.

KARI ANDERSON
University of North Carolina at Wilmington

ABSENCE SEIZURES
ANTICONVULSANTS
GRAND MAL SEIZURES

TELECOMMUNICATION DEVICES FOR THE DEAF

Telecommunication devices for the deaf (TDDs or TTYs) make communication available to the hearing-impaired population by providing video or printed modes of communication. Using a modem, or acoustic coupler, a TDD user types out a message to another user. This message either moves across a video display screen or is typed on a roll of paper. In this fashion, conversations can be held and information exchanged.

TDDs use a regular or slightly modified keyboard. Some special terminology is used to facilitate ease of transmission. GA, for go ahead indicates to one user that the other is waiting for a reply. SK, for stop keying, denotes the completion of a conversation. Often a Q is typed to imply a question.

The number of TDDs in public and private use is increasing rapidly. Public service agencies such as libraries, schools, and airlines are using TDDs to enable the hearing-impaired population to use their services (Low, 1985). Police and fire departments use TDDs to ensure the safety of hearing-impaired individuals. The TDD has been hailed as a great contributor to the independence of hearing-impaired persons.

REFERENCE

Low, K. (1985). Telecommunication devices for the deaf. *American Libraries, 16,* 746–747.

MARY GRACE FEELY
School for the Deaf

DEAF
ELECTRONIC TRAVEL AIDS

TELECOMMUNICATIONS SYSTEMS IN SPECIAL EDUCATION

The use of telecommunication technology for special education mirrors the explosion of technology in society. In the same way that commercial electronic network services such as Compu-Serve and The Source have become widely known to the general public, SpecialNet is an e-mail service and information source specifically for special educators. Similarly, transformation of the telephone system from copper to fiber optic wire facilitates rapid data transmission for any use, including perhaps transfer of data on special education students as they move from district to district.

Certain types of telecommunication technologies (e.g., computer-assisted instruction) delivered over telephone lines from a central location, as in the University of Illinois'

PLATO system, are being made obsolete as modifications are made for computers, thus reducing the costs of instruction delivery. Other technologies involving electronic memory and telephone transmission are expanding, notably ABLE-DATA, a bibliographic source of information on assistive devices for the disabled.

Telecommunications technology, currently in a period of rapid change, may transform special education practice in much the same way that it is transforming communication worldwide. However, in contrast to other technologies developed specifically for the disabled, special education will benefit from technological advances for all citizens. Thus the average modern family may use a computer and modem as a link to specialized news sources, stock quotes and discount brokers, specialized electronic news services, targeted mailboards, or e-mail. Disabled persons, using the same systems, may communicate with other persons with similar interests, scan specialized information sources, work in competitive employment from their homes, and avail themselves of services provided for all citizens. Special educators in public schools and higher education may use telecommunications for much the same purposes, targeting their efforts toward the acquisition of information from rapidly expanding specialized information networks.

JAMES W. TAWNEY
Pennsylvania State University

COMPUTER-ASSISTED INSTRUCTION
ELECTRONIC TRAVEL AIDS

TEMPERAMENT

Individual differences in temperament have been recognized for centuries. The Greeks talked of four basic dispositions, Kretschmer (1925) and Sheldon (1942) related personality to body types, and Eysenck (1967) linked constitutional and personality variables. Yet, the notion of constitutional contributions to behavior received only limited formal attention from American psychologists and educators until relatively recently. Major impetus to the study of temperament has come from the work of psychiatrists Alexander Thomas and Stella Chess and their colleagues (Thomas & Chess, 1977; Thomas, Chess, Birch, Hertzig, & Korn, 1963), but independent support for the notion of temperament may be found in pediatric and psychiatric research (Carey, 1981, 1982, 1985a; Graham, Rutter, & George, 1973; Rutter, 1964; Rutter, Tizard, & Whitmore, 1970), in longitudinal studies of development (Lerner & Lerner, 1983; Werner & Smith, 1982), in research on infants (Bates, 1980, 1983; Rothbart & Derryberry, 1981) and on child-family interactions (Dunn & Kendrick, 1982; Hinde, Easton, Meller, & Tamplin, 1982; Stevenson-Hinde & Simpson, 1982), in twin studies (Goldsmith & Gottesman, 1981; Matheny, Wilson, & Nuss, 1984; Wilson, 1983; Wilson & Matheny, 1983), and in work in behavioral genetics (DeFries & Plomin, 1978; Plomin, 1982; Torgersen, 1982). Temperament is an important area of concern from both research and applied perspectives. Its relevance to special education and the development and adjustment of children with disabilities is increasingly recognized.

Definitions

Although intuitively appealing, temperament has somewhat different definitions, depending on the investigator. Thomas and Chess (1977) view temperament as a stylistic variable. They consider that temperament describes how an individual behaves, not what an individual does or how well he or she does it. Thomas and Chess identified nine dimensions of temperament or behavioral style: activity level, adaptability, approach/withdrawal, attention span and persistence, distractibility, intensity of reaction, quality of mood, rhythmicity (regularity), and threshold of responsiveness. The dimensions were derived in part from Thomas and Chess's clinical observations, and were formalized in major longitudinal research, the New York Longitudinal Study (NYLS). In Thomas and Chess's view, these temperamental variations are, in part, constitutional in base.

The constitutional or biological anchoring of temperament is apparent in other definitions. Buss and Plomin (1975, 1984) propose that to be considered a temperament, a behavioral predisposition must meet criteria of developmental stability, presence in adulthood, adaptiveness, and presence in animals, and must have a genetic component. They define four dimensions that, in their view, meet these criteria: emotionality, activity, sociability, and impulsivity. Rothbart and Derryberry (1981), based primarily on their studies of human infants, suggest that temperament is best conceptualized as individual differences in reactivity and regulation that are presumed to be constitutionally based. Their formulation emphasizes arousal (or excitability) and the neural and behavioral processes that regulate or modulate it, a formulation consistent with that of Strelau (1983). Goldsmith and Campos (1986) adopt a somewhat different perspective, defining temperament as individual variation in emotionality, including differences in the primary emotions of fear, anger, sadness, pleasure, and so forth, as well as in a more general arousal; they consider both temperament and intensive parameters. It should be noted that a major definitional issue relates to distinctions between temperament and personality (Goldsmith & Campos, 1982; Rutter, 1982). Many investigators consider temperament a constitutional and genetic component of personality. This view is well reflected in the definition that emerged from the 1980 New Haven Temperament Symposium: "Temperament

involves those dimensions of personality that are largely genetic or constitutional in origin, exist in most ages and in most societies, show some consistency across situations, and are relatively stable, at least within major developmental areas" (Plomin, 1983, p. 49). Thus, despite differences in specific components and in emphases, there is some consensus that temperament is an individual difference that has its basis in biological or constitutional makeup, has some stability across setting and time, and is linked to differences in behavioral or expressive styles (Bouchard, 1995).

Measurement

Adequacy of measurement has been a persistent problem for researchers of temperament (Hubert, Wachs, Peters-Martin, & Gandour, 1982; Plomin, 1982; Rothbart, 1981; Rothbart & Goldsmith, 1985; Rutter, 1982). Rothbart and Goldsmith (1985) note that the three most commonly used data-gathering techniques for infant temperament studies are questionnaires, home observations, and laboratory observations. With older children there has been reliance primarily on parent, caretaker, or teacher reports gathered through interviews or questionnaires. Measures designed for use with adults (Burks & Rubenstein, 1979; Guilford & Zimmerman, 1949; Lerner, Palermo, Spiro, & Nesselroade, 1982) are usually self-report formats. In addition to issues of psychometric adequacy of scales, individual investigators have developed measuring instruments and techniques that are consistent with their own conceptualizations of temperament. Thus scales differ in the number of dimensions identified and in the content of those dimensions. As an example, the Thomas and Chess scale taps nine dimensions; the Buss and Plomin (EASI) scale taps four. Similarly, behavior observations in natural and laboratory settings vary according to project and investigator. The consequence has been continuing concern about constructs and measures (Baker & Velicer, 1982; Bates, 1980, 1983; Plomin, 1982; Rothbart, 1981; Thomas, Chess, & Korn, 1982; Vaughn, Deinard, & Egeland, 1980; Vaughn, Taraldson, Crichton, & Egeland, 1981). Given the importance of Thomas and Chess's influence on this field, and the relevance of their work to clinical and educational practice, their questionnaires will be described in more detail.

Thomas and Chess developed a Parent Temperament Survey (PTS) and a Teacher Temperament Survey (TTS). The PTS contains 72 items, 8 for each of the 9 hypothesized dimensions of temperament. The TTS, similar in format, contains 64 items (the dimension of rythmicity is not included). Items were selected to describe behavioral expressions of the various temperament dimensions (e.g., "When first meeting new children, my child is bashful"; from the TTS: "Child will initially avoid new games and activities, preferring to sit on the side and watch"). Items are rated 1 (hardly ever) to 7 (almost always). Dimensional scores (means of the items in each dimension) are assumed to be independent. Factor studies and qualitative analyses within the NYLS suggested three temperamental constellations that described two-thirds of the sample: the easy child, characterized as regular or rhythmic, positive in approach to new stimuli, adaptable to change, and mild or moderately intense and positive in mood; the difficult child, described as irregular, negative in response to new stimuli, low or slow in adaptability, and intense, often negative in mood; and the slow-to-warm-up child, viewed as mildly intense in reactivity, slow to adapt, but given time, positive in involvement.

A number of investigators have modified the PTS and TTS but have maintained Thomas and Chess's conceptual framework. Keogh, Pullis, and Cadwell (1980, 1982) reduced both parent and teacher scales to 23 items each, and identified simpler factor structures. The three primary factors in the TTS were task orientation, personal-social flexibility, and reactivity, an essentially negative factor. The PTS yielded two multidimensional factors and two single-dimension factors: social competence and reactivity, and mood and persistence. These factors are generally consistent with those identified by Windle and Lerner (1985) in their life span research and with those defined by Martin and his colleagues (Martin, 1984a; Paget, Nagle, & Martin, 1984) in work with schoolchildren. Also working within the Thomas and Chess framework, Carey, Fox, and McDevitt (1977) have done extensive scale development. Their questionnaires cover infancy through the elementary school years and include the Infant Temperament Questionnaire (ITQ; Carey, 1970; Carey & McDevitt, 1978), the Toddler Temperament Scale (Fullard, McDevitt, & Carey, 1978), the Behavioral Styles Questionnaire (McDevitt & Carey, 1978), and the Middle Childhood Temperament Questionnaire (Hegvik, McDevitt, & Carey, 1982). These instruments are similar in format, describe behaviors that are age and setting appropriate, and have good reliability and internal consistency. Each scale contains approximately 100 items and requires about 30 minutes for a parent to complete. Thus there are a number of instruments designed to capture parents' and teachers' views of children's temperamental characteristics. Despite their clinical appeal and usefulness, many of the questionnaires have been challenged on a number of counts: lack of independence of items and dimensions, item unreliability or bias, unknown factorial organization across developmental periods, or situational specificity of behaviors. Clearly, there are real and continuing uncertainties in the measurement of temperament that mandate caution in interpreting temperament findings. Yet, there is also considerable consistency of findings across studies and approaches, which argues for the robustness of temperament variables.

Clinical Applications

There are increasing numbers of reports of the importance of temperament in pediatric and psychiatric settings. Pedia-

tricians Carey (1981, 1985a, 1985b, 1985c) and Weissbluth (1982, 1984; Weissbluth et al.; Weissbluth, Brouillette, Kiang, & Hunt, 1985; Weissbluth & Green, 1984) emphasize that temperament is an influence on children's development and adjustment, specifically linking infants' temperamental characteristics to a variety of pediatric problems (e.g., colic, sleep difficulties). In recent work, Carey (1985b) suggests that temperament may also be viewed as an outcome or consequence of various clinical conditions, for example, pre-, post-, and perinatal conditions or insults. From psychiatric and psychological perspectives, there has also been a continuing interest in temperament as a predisposing factor for behavioral and emotional or adjustment problems (Barron & Earls, 1984; Cameron, 1977; Chess & Korn, 1970; Earls, 1981; Graham et al., 1973; Rutter, 1964; Thomas & Chess, 1977; Thomas, Chess, & Birch, 1968). Maziade et al., (1985) found difficult temperament predicted psychiatric diagnosis in later childhood, and Kolvin, Nichol, Garside, Day, and Tweddle (1982) reported relationships between temperament and aggression in clinic-referred boys. Although the processes linking temperament and problems in behavior and adjustment are not yet explicit, there appears to be enough evidence to infer a relationship.

Educational Applications

The formal application of temperament constructs to educational practice is relatively recent but is growing. As part of the NYLS, Gordon and Thomas (1967) reported that children's temperament influenced teachers' estimates of their school abilities, and Carey, Fox, and McDevitt (1977) identified relationships between parents' ratings of children and adjustment in school. A number of investigators report relationships between temperamental patterns and academic performance in school (Chess, Thomas, & Cameron, 1976; Hall & Cadwell, 1984; Hegvik, 1984, 1986; Keogh, 1982a; Keogh & Pullis, 1980; Lerner, 1983; Lerner, Lerner, & Zabski, 1985; Martin, 1984b, 1986; Martin, Nagle, & Paget, 1983; Pullis, 1979; Pullis & Cadwell, 1982; Skuy, Snell, & Westaway, 1985). It should be noted that in general, there are nonsignificant or marginally significant relationships between temperament and cognitive ability as indexed by IQ (Keogh, 1982a, 1982c; Pullis, 1983), although Martin (1985) identified moderate and significant relationships between temperament attributes of adaptability, approach/withdrawal, and persistence and IQ in a sample of grade 1 pupils. Overall, the evidence suggests that temperament and cognitive ability are partially independent contributors to educational achievement.

In addition to achievement in academic content, there is considerable evidence to suggest that temperamental variations are related to children's personal and social adjustment in school. Billman (1984), Carey et al. (1977), Chess et al. (1976), Feuerstein and Martin (1981), Hall and Keogh (1978), Keogh (1982a, 1982b, 1982c), Kolvin et al. (1982),

Lerner (1983), Lerner et al. (1985), Martin (1985), Paget et al. (1984), Terestman (1980), and Thomas and Chess (1977) have linked children's temperament and behavior and adjustment problems. The impact of temperament may be particularly powerful where children have other handicapping or problem conditions (Keogh, 1982c), although there are temperamental differences within groups of handicapped children (Hanson, 1979). Field and Greenfield (1982) suggest that temperament patterns may be associated with particular handicapping conditions, and Chess, Korn, and Fernandez (1971) report a high number of behavior disorders related to difficult temperament patterns in a group of young congenital rubella children; the latter findings were consistent with the relationship between temperament and behavior problems in a group of mentally delayed children (Chess & Korn, 1970). In a series of ongoing studies, (Keogh, Bernhemier, Pelland, and Daley, 1985) confirmed links between developmentally delayed children's temperament and their behavior problems and adjustment. Lambert and Windmiller (1977) found strong correlations between selected temperament attributes and hyperactivity in a large group of at-risk elementary school children. There also is some tentative evidence linking temperament to adjustment and achievement problems of learning-disabled pupils (Keogh, 1983; Pullis, 1983; Scholom & Schiff, 1980).

Temperament may contribute to school achievement and adjustment in several ways (Keogh, 1986) and is related to intellectual performance (Brebner & Stough, 1995). It may be a factor in a generalized response set; that is, some temperaments may fit well with the complex and changing demands of school whereas others do not. Temperament may affect a child's specific preparation for learning by allowing activity and attention to be modulated and directed easily and quickly. Temperament may interact with particular subject matter to facilitate or impede learning. Individual differences in temperament are also significant contributors to children's personal-social adjustment in school. Intuitively, at least, interpersonal problems have a strong foundation in child-peer and child-teacher interactions. Thus, personal style, or temperament, may be a major factor in problem behavior. If the relationship between children's temperament and their achievement and behavioral adjustment in school is considered within Thomas and Chess's "goodness of fit" notion, then both child characteristics and setting or task demands and conditions must be taken into account. Goodness of fit has important implications for identification, diagnosis, intervention, and treatment.

REFERENCES

Baker, E. H., & Velicer, W. F. (1982). The structure and reliability of the Teacher Temperament Questionnaire. *Journal of Abnormal Child Psychology, 10*(4), 531–546.

Barron, A. P., & Earls, F. (1984). The relation of temperament and social factors to behavior problems in three-year-old children. *Journal of Child Psychology & Psychiatry, 25*(1), 23–33.

Bates, J. E. (1980). The concept of difficult temperament. *Merrill-Palmer Quarterly, 26*(4), 299–319.

Bates, J. E. (1983). Issues in the assessment of difficult temperament: A reply to Thomas, Chess, and Korn. *Merrill-Palmer Quarterly, 29*(1), 89–97.

Billman, J. (1984, October). *The relationship of temperament traits to classroom behavior in nine year old children: A follow-up study.* Paper presented at the Conference on Temperament in the Educational Process, St. Louis, MO.

Bouchard, T. (1995). Longitudinal studies of personality and intelligence. In D. Saklofske & M. Zeidner (Eds.), *International handbook of personality and intelligence.* New York: Plenum.

Brebner, J., & Stough, C. (1995). Theoretical and empirical relationships between personality and intelligence. In D. Saklofske & M. Zeidner (Eds.), *International handbook of personality and intelligence.* New York: Plenum.

Burks, J., & Rubenstein, M. (1979). *Temperament styles in adult interaction: Application in psychotherapy.* New York: Brunner/Mazel.

Buss, A. H., & Plomin, R. (1975). *A temperament theory of personality development.* New York: Wiley.

Buss, A. H., & Plomin, R. (1984). *Temperament: Early developing personality traits.* Hillsdale, NJ: Erlbaum.

Cameron, J. R. (1977). Parental treatment, children's temperament, and the risk of childhood behavioral problems: Initial temperament, parental attitudes, and the incidence and form of behavioral problems. *American Journal of Orthopsychiatry, 48,* 140–147.

Carey, W. B. (1970). A simplified method for measuring infant temperament. *Journal of Pediatrics, 77,* 188–194.

Carey, W. B. (1981). The importance of temperament-environment interaction for child health and development. In M. Lewis & L. A. Rosenblum (Eds.), *The uncommon child.* New York: Plenum.

Carey, W. B. (1982a). Clinical use of temperament data in pediatrics. In R. Porter & G. M. Collins (Eds.), *Temperament differences in infants and young children* (pp. 191–205). London: Pitman.

Carey, W. B. (1985a). Clinical use of temperament data in pediatrics. *Developmental & Behavioral Pediatrics, 6*(3), 137–142.

Carey, W. B. (1985b). Interactions of temperament and clinical conditions. In M. Wolraich & D. K. Routh (Eds.), *Advances in developmental and behavioral pediatrics* (Vol. 6, pp. 83–115). Greenwich, CT: JAI.

Carey, W. B. (1985c). Temperament and increased weight gain in infants. *Development & Behavioral Pediatrics, 6*(3), 128–131.

Carey, W. B., Fox, M., & McDevitt, S. C. (1977). Temperament as a factor in early school adjustment. *Pediatrics, 60*(4), 621–624.

Carey, W. B., & McDevitt, S. C. (1978). Revision of the Infant Temperament Questionnaire. *Pediatrics, 61,* 735–739.

Chess, S., & Korn, S. (1970). Temperament and behavior disorders in mentally retarded children. *Archives of General Psychiatry, 23,* 122–130.

Chess, S., Korn, S., & Fernandez, P. (1971). *Psychiatric disorders of children with congenital rubella.* New York: Brunner/Mazel.

Chess, S., Thomas, A., & Cameron, M. (1976). Temperament: Its significance for early schooling. *New York University Education Quarterly, 7*(3), 24–29.

DeFries, J. C., & Plomin, R. (1978). Behavioral genetics. *Annual Review of Psychology, 29,* 473–515.

Dunn, J., & Kendrick, C. (1982). Temperamental differences, family relationships, and young children's responses to change within the family. In R. Porter & G. M. Collins (Eds.), *Temperamental differences in infants and young children* (pp. 87–105). London: Pitman.

Earls, F. (1981). Temperament characteristics and behavior problems in three-year-old children. *Journal of Nervous & Mental Disease, 169,* 367–387.

Eysenck, H. J. (1967). *The biological basis of personality.* Springfield, IL: Thomas.

Feuerstein, P., & Martin, R. P. (1981, April). *The relationship between temperament and school adjustment in four-year-old children.* Paper presented at the annual meeting of the American Educational Research Association, Los Angeles.

Field, T., & Greenberg, R. (1982). Temperament ratings by parents and teachers of infants, toddlers, and preschool children. *Child Development, 53,* 160–163.

Fullard, W., McDevitt, S. C., & Carey, W. B. (1978). *The Toddler Temperament Scale.* Unpublished manuscript, Temple University, Philadelphia.

Goldsmith, H. H., & Campos, J. J. (1982). Toward a theory of infant temperament. In R. M. Emde & R. J. Harmon (Eds.), *The development of attachment and affiliative systems* (pp. 161–193). New York: Plenum.

Goldsmith, H. H., & Campos, J. J. (1986). Fundamental issues in the study of early temperament: The Denver twin temperament study. In M. E. Lamb & A. L. Brown (Eds.), *Advances in developmental psychology* (pp. 231–283). Hillsdale, NJ: Erlbaum.

Goldsmith, H. H., & Gottesman, I. I. (1981). Origins of variation in behavioral style: A longitudinal study of temperament in young twins. *Child Development, 52,* 91–103.

Gordon, E. M., & Thomas, A. (1967). Children's behavioral style and the teacher's appraisal of their intelligence. *Journal of School Psychology, 5*(4), 292–300.

Graham, P., Rutter, M., & George, S. (1973). Temperamental characteristics as predictors of behavior disorders in children. *American Journal of Orthopsychiatry, 43*(3), 328–339.

Guildford, J. P., & Zimmerman, W. (1949). *The Guildford-Zimmerman Temperament Survey.* Beverly Hills, CA: Sheridan Supply.

Hall, R. J., & Cadwell, J. (1984, April). *Temperament influences on cognition and achievement in children with learning disabilities.* Paper presented at the annual conference of the American Educational Research Association, New Orleans, LA.

Hall, R. J., & Keogh, B. K. (1978). Qualitative characteristics of educationally high-risk children. *Learning Disability Quarterly, 1*(2), 62–68.

Hanson, M. J. (1979). A longitudinal description study of the behaviors of Down's syndrome infants in an early intervention program. *Monographs of the Center on Human Development.* Eugene: University of Oregon.

Hegvik, R. L. (1984, October). *Three year longitudinal study of temperament variables, academic achievement, and sex differences.* Paper presented at the Conference on Temperament in the Educational Process, St. Louis, MO.

Hegvik, R. L. (1986, May). *Temperament and achievement in school.* Paper presented at the sixth occasional Temperament Conference, Pennsylvania State University.

Hegvik, R. L., McDevitt, S. C., & Carey, W. B. (1982). The middle childhood temperament questionnaire. *Developmental & Behavioral Pediatrics, 3,* 197–200.

Hinde, R. A., Easton, D. F., Meller, R. E., & Tamplin, A. M. (1982). Temperamental characteristics of 3–4 year olds and mother-child interactions. In R. Porter & G. M. Collins (Eds.), *Temperamental differences in infants and young children* (pp. 66–86). London: Pitman.

Hubert, N. C., Wachs, T. D., Peters-Martin, P., & Gandour, M. J. (1982). The study of early temperament: Measurement and conceptual issues. *Child Development, 53,* 126–132.

Keogh, B. K. (1982a). Children's temperament and teachers' decisions. In R. Porter & G. M. Collins (Eds.), *Temperamental differences in infants and young children* (pp. 269–279). London: Pitman.

Keogh, B. K. (1982b). *Temperament and school performance of preschool children* (Technical report, Project REACH). Los Angeles: University of California.

Keogh, B. K. (1982c). Temperament: An individual difference of importance in intervention programs. *Topics in Early Childhood Special Education, 2*(2), 25–31.

Keogh, B. K. (1983). Individual differences in temperament: A contribution to the personal-social and educational competence of learning disabled children. In J. D. McKinney & L. Feagens (Eds.), *Current topics in learning disabilities* (pp. 33–55). Norwood, NJ: Ablex.

Keogh, B. K. (1986). Temperament and schooling: What is the meaning of goodness of fit? In J. V. Lerner & R. M. Lerner (Eds.), *New directions for child development: Temperament and social interaction in infants and children.* San Francisco: Jossey-Bass.

Keogh, B. K., Bernheimer, L., Pelland, M., & Daley, S. (1985). *Behavior and adjustment problems of children with developmental delays* (Technical report). Los Angeles: University of California, Graduate School of Education.

Keogh, B. K., & Pullis, M. E. (1980). Temperamental influences on the development of exceptional children. In B. K. Keogh (Ed.), *Advances in special education: Vol. 1. Basic constructs and theoretical orientations* (pp. 239–276). Greenwich, CT: JAI.

Keogh, B. K., Pullis, M. E., & Cadwell, J. (1980). *Project REACH* (Technical report). Los Angeles: University of California.

Keogh, B. K., Pullis, M. E., & Cadwell, J. (1982). A short form of the Teacher Temperament Questionnaire. *Journal of Educational Measurement, 29*(4), 323–329.

Kolvin, I., Nicol, A. R., Garside, R. F., Day, K. A., & Tweddle, E. G. (1982). Temperamental patterns in aggressive boys. In R. Porter & G. M. Collins (Eds.), *Temperamental differences in infants and young children* (pp. 252–268). London: Pitman.

Kretschmer, E. (1925). *Physique and character.* New York: Harcourt.

Lambert, N. M., & Windmiller, M. (1977). An exploratory study of temperament traits in a population of children at risk. *Journal of Special Education, 11*(1), 37–47.

Lerner, J. V. (1983). The role of temperament in psychosocial adaptation in early adolescents: A test of a "goodness of fit" model. *Journal of Genetic Psychology, 143,* 149–157.

Lerner, J. V., & Lerner, R. M. (1983). Temperament and adaptation across life: Theoretical and empirical issues. In P. B. Baltes & O. G. Brim (Eds.), *Lifespan development and behavior* (Vol. 5). New York: Academic Press.

Lerner, J. V., Lerner, R. M., & Zabski, S. (1985). Temperament and elementary school children's actual and rated academic performance: A test of a "goodness of fit" model. *Journal of Child Psychology and Psychiatry, 26,* 125–136.

Lerner, R. M., Palermo, M., Spiro, A., & Nesselroade, J. (1982). Assessing the dimensions of temperamental individuality across the life-span: The dimensions of temperament survey (DOTS). *Child Development, 53,* 149–160.

Martin, R. P. (1984a). *The Temperament Assessment Battery* (TAB). Athens: University of Georgia, Department of School Psychology.

Martin, R. P. (1984b, October). *A temperament model for education.* Paper presented at the Conference on Temperament in the Educational Process, St. Louis, MO.

Martin, R. P. (1985, July). *Child temperament and educational outcomes: A review of research.* Paper presented at the Symposium on Temperament, Leiden, the Netherlands.

Martin, R. P. (1986, May). *Context influences on the expression of temperament.* Paper presented at the sixth occasional Temperament Conference, Pennsylvania State University.

Martin, R. P., Nagle, R., & Paget, K. (1983). Relationships between temperament and classroom behavior, teacher attitudes, and academic achievement. *Journal of Psychoeducational Assessment, 1,* 377–386.

Matheny, A. P., Jr., Wilson, R. S., & Nuss, S. M. (1984). Toddler temperament: Stability across settings and over ages. *Child Development, 55,* 1200–1211.

Maziade, M., Caperaa, P., Laplante, B., Boudreault, M., Thivierge, J., Cote, R., & Boutin, P. (1985). Value of difficult temperament among 7-year-olds in the general population for predicting psychiatric diagnosis at age 12. *American Journal of Psychiatry, 142*(8), 943–946.

McDevitt, S. C., & Carey, W. B. (1978). The measurement of temperament in 3–7 year old children. *Journal of Child Psychiatry & Psychology, 19*(3), 245–253.

Paget, K. D., Nagle, R. J., & Martin, R. P. (1984). Interrelationships between temperament characteristics and first-grade teacher-student interactions. *Journal of Abnormal Child Psychology, 12*(4), 547–560.

Plomin, R. (1982). Behavioral genetics and temperament. In R. Porter & G. M. Collins (Eds.). *Temperamental differences in infants and young children* (pp. 155–167). London: Pitman.

Plomin, R. (1983). Childhood temperament. In B. B. Lahey & A. E. Kazdin (Eds.), *Advances in clinical child psychology* (Vol. 6, pp. 45–92). New York: Plenum.

Pullis, M. E. (1979). *An investigation of the relationship between children's temperament and school adjustment.* Unpublished doctoral dissertation, University of California, Los Angeles.

Pullis, M. E. (1983). *Temperament influences of teachers' decisions in regular and mainstreamed classes.* Paper presented at the meeting of the American Educational Research Association, New York.

Pullis, M. E., & Cadwell, J. (1982). The influence of children's temperament characteristics on teachers' decision strategies. *American Educational Research Journal, 19*(2), 165–181.

Rothbart, M. K. (1981). Measurement of temperament in infancy. *Child Development, 52,* 569–578.

Rothbart, M. K., & Derryberry, D. (1981). Development of individual differences in temperament. In M. E. Lamb & A. L. Brown (Eds.), *Advances in developmental psychology* (Vol. 1, pp. 37–86). Hillsdale, NJ: Erlbaum.

Rothbart, M. K., & Goldsmith, H. H. (1985). Three approaches to the study of infant temperament. *Developmental Review, 5,* 237–260.

Rutter, M. (1964). Temperament characteristics in infancy and the later development of behavior disorders. *British Journal of Psychiatry, 110,* 651–661.

Rutter, M. (1982). Temperament: Concepts, issues and problems. In R. Porter & G. C. Collins (Eds.), *Temperamental differences in infants and young children* (pp. 1–19). London: Pitman.

Rutter, M., Tizard, J., & Whitmore, K. (1970). *Education, health, and behavior: Psychological and medical study of childhood development.* New York: Wiley.

Scholom, A., & Schiff, G. (1980). Relating infant temperament to learning disabilities. *Journal of Abnormal Child Psychology, 8,* 127–132.

Sheldon, W. (1942). *The varieties of temperament: A psychology of constitutional differences.* New York: Harper.

Skuy, M., Snell, D., & Westaway, M. (1985). Temperament and the scholastic achievement and adjustment of black South African children. *South African Journal of Education, 5*(4), 197–202.

Stevenson-Hinde, J., & Simpson, A. E. (1982). Temperament and relationships. In R. Porter & G. M. Collins (Eds.), *Temperamental differences in infants and young children* (pp. 51–65). London: Pitman.

Strelau, J. (1983). *Temperament-personality-activity.* New York: Academic Press.

Terestman, N. (1980). Mood quality and intensity in nursery school children as predictors of behavior disorder. *American Journal of Orthopsychiatry, 50,* 125–138.

Thomas, A., & Chess, S. (1977). *Temperament and development.* New York: Brunner/Mazel.

Thomas, A., Chess, S., & Birch, H. G. (1968). *Temperament and behavior disorders in children.* New York: New York University Press.

Thomas, A., Chess, S., Birch, H. G., Hertzig, M., & Korn, S. (1963). *Behavioral individuality in early childhood.* New York: New York University Press.

Thomas, A., Chess, S., & Korn, S. J. (1982). The reality of difficult temperament. *Merrill-Palmer Quarterly, 28*(1), 1–20.

Torgersen, A. M. (1982). Influence of genetic factors on temperament development in early childhood. In R. Porter & G. M. Collins (Eds.), *Temperamental differences in infants and young children* (pp. 141–154). London: Pitman.

Vaughn, B., Deinard, A., & Egeland, B. (1980). Measuring temperament in pediatric practice. *Journal of Pediatrics, 96,* 510–514.

Vaughn, B., Taraldson, B., Crichton, L., & Egeland, B. (1981). The assessment of infant temperament: A critique of the Carey

Infant Temperament Questionnaire. *Infant Behavior & Development, 40,* 1–17.

Weissbluth, M. (1982). Plasma progesterone levels, infant temperament, arousals from sleep, and the sudden infant death syndrome. *Medical Hypotheses, 9,* 215–222.

Weissbluth, M. (1984). Sleep duration, temperament, and Conners' ratings of three-year-old children. *Developmental & Behavioral Pediatrics, 5*(3), 120–123.

Weissbluth, M., Brouillette, R. T., Kiang, L., & Hunt, C. E. (1982). Clinical and laboratory observations: Sleep apnea, sleep duration and infant temperament. *Journal of Pediatrics, 101*(2), 307–310.

Weissbluth, M., & Green, O. C. (1984). Plasma progesterone concentrations and infant temperament. *Developmental & Behavioral Pediatrics, 5*(5), 251–253.

Weissbluth, M., Hunt, C. E., Brouillette, R. T., Hanson, D., David, R. J., & Stein, I. (1985). Respiratory patterns during sleep and temperament ratings in normal infants. *Journal of Pediatrics, 106*(4), 688–690.

Werner, E. E., & Smith, R. S. (1982). *Vulnerable, but invincible: A longitudinal study of resilient children and youth.* New York: McGraw-Hill.

Wilson, R. S. (1983). The Louisville twin study: Developmental synchronies in behavior. *Child Development, 54*(2), 298–316.

Wilson, R. S., & Matheny, A. P. (1983). Assessment of temperament in infant twins. *Developmental Psychology, 19,* 172–183.

Windle, M., & Lerner, R. M. (1985). *Reassessing the dimensions of temperamental individuality across the life span: The Revised Dimensions of Temperament Survey* (DOTS-R). Unpublished manuscript, Johnson O'Connor Research Foundation, Chicago.

BARBARA KEOGH
*University of California,
Los Angeles*

ATTENTION-DEFICIT/HYPERACTIVITY DISORDER
BODY IMAGE
LEARNED HELPLESSNESS
PERSONALITY ASSESSMENT
TEACHER EXPECTANCIES

TERATOGEN

The word teratogen drives from the Greek *teras,* signifying a marvel, prodigy, or monster; thus, by definition, a teratogen is an agent that causes developmental malformations or monstrosities (Duke-Elder, 1963). The causes can be environmental, genetic, multifactorial, maternal-fetal, or unknown. Environmental agents include drugs and similar agents (e.g., alcohol, anticonvulsants, LSD), hormones, infections (e.g., cytomegalic inclusion disease, influenza, mumps, rubella, syphilis, toxoplasmosis), radiation, mechanical trauma, hypotension (low blood pressure),

vitamin deficiency or excess (hypervitaminosis A), and mineral deficiency (zinc). Genetic causes include chromosomal abnormality (e.g., Down syndrome, trisomy 13) and various hereditary patterns—sporadic, dominant, recessive, and polygenetic. Maternal-fetal interactions are exemplified by advanced maternal age and maternal hypothyroidism. Finally, a variety of dysmorphic syndromes are undetermined as to etiology. Many congenital abnormalities may be detected prior to birth. The primary means for such diagnosis has been through amniocentesis. Additionally, imaging systems such as ultrasonography demonstrate relatively gross abnormalities late in development (Spaeth, Nelson, & Beaudoin, 1983).

The timing of development helps to clarify the spectrum of associated malformations. Injuries prior to the fifteenth day of gestation affect development of primary germ layers; such abnormalities are usually so global that survival of the fetus is unusual. Between weeks two and seven, insults cause major abnormalities that affect whole organ systems. Following the first trimester (the period of differentiation of organ detail and organ interrelationship), abnormalities tend to be more limited and specific. While timing of embryonic or fetal insult relates closely to manifest anomaly, certain substances may cause varying malformations, though the time of insult is constant.

REFERENCES

Duke-Elder, S. (1963). *System of ophthalmology: Vol. III, Part 2. Congenital deformities.* St. Louis, MO: Mosby.

Spaeth, G. L., Nelson, L. B., & Beaudoin, A. R. (1983). Ocular teratology. In T. D. Duane & E. A. Jaeger (Eds.), *Biomedical foundations of ophthalmology* (Vol. 1, pp. 6–7). Hagerstown, MD: Harper & Row.

GEORGE R. BEAUCHAMP
Cleveland Clinic Foundation

CENTRAL NERVOUS SYSTEM
GENETIC VARIATIONS
THALIDOMIDE

TERMAN, LEWIS M. (1877–1956)

Lewis M. Terman received his PhD in education and psychology from Clark University, where he studied under G. Stanley Hall. Experienced as a schoolteacher, principal, and college instructor, in 1910 he joined the faculty of Stanford University, where he served as head of the psychology department from 1922 until his retirement in 1942.

With an interest in mental tests dating from his graduate studies at Clark University, Terman became a leading figure in the newly born testing movement, developing

Lewis M. Terman

dozens of tests during his career. The best known and most widely used of his tests were the Stanford-Binet tests of intelligence, which he adapted from the Binet-Simon Scale of Intelligence in 1916 and revised in 1937. He also developed the Army Alpha and Beta tests (the first group intelligence tests) for use in classifying servicemen during World War I. With the publication of the Stanford-Binet tests in 1916, Terman introduced the term intelligence quotient (IQ), a term that quickly became a part of the general vocabulary.

In 1921 Terman initiated the first comprehensive study of gifted children. His staff tested more than 250,000 schoolchildren to identify 1,500 with IQs above 140. This sample of boys and girls was studied intensively and followed up periodically in a study that continues today. Terman found that, contrary to the popular belief at the time, children with high IQs tend to be healthier, happier, and more stable than children of average ability. In addition, they are more successful in their personal and professional lives. Terman, who can be credited with founding the gifted child movement, used his findings to promote the provision of special educational programs for able students.

REFERENCES

Fancher, R. E. (1985). *The intelligence men.* New York: Norton.

Hilgard, E. (1957). Lewis Madison Terman: 1877–1956. *American Journal of Psychology, 70,* 472–479.

Murchison, C. (Ed.). (1961). *A history of psychology in autobiography.* New York: Russell & Russell.

PAUL IRVINE
Katonah, New York

STANFORD-BINET INTELLIGENCE SCALE

TERMAN'S STUDIES OF THE GIFTED

In 1911, while at Stanford University, Lewis M. Terman began a systematic collection of data on children who achieved exceptionally high scores on the Stanford-Binet Intelligence Test. In the early 1920s, working with Melita Oden, he administered the Stanford-Binet test to students referred to by teachers as being "highly intelligent." Studies of their traits and the extent to which they differed from unselected normal children were begun in 1925.

Terman's subjects were in a 1,500-child sample (800 boys and 700 girls) that was in the top 1 percent of the school population in measured intelligence; that is, they possessed tested IQs of 140 or higher (Terman & Oden, 1925).

Terman and Oden (1951) summarized the characteristics of the students in their gifted sample as (1) slightly larger, healthier, and more physically attractive; (2) superior in reading, language usage, arithmetical reasoning, science, literature, and the arts; (3) superior in arithmetical computation, spelling, and factual information about history and civics (though not as markedly as in the areas covered in (2); (4) spontaneous, with a variety of interests; (5) able to learn to read easily, and able to read more and better books than average children; (6) less inclined to boast or overstate their knowledge; (7) more emotionally stable; (8) different in the upward direction for nearly all traits.

Follow-up studies in 1947, 1951, and 1959 were completed to obtain a comparison between promise and performance. Follow-up studies by other authors have obtained less "perfect" findings, in that not all of the subjects were found to be geniuses in the sense of transcendent achievement in some field (Feldman, 1984). More recent studies have supported Terman's findings on emotional stability (Schlowinski & Reynolds, 1985), spontaneity, and creativity in play (Barnett & Fiscella, 1985), and reading aptitude (Anderson, Tollefson, & Gilbert, 1985).

The entire set of data sources for Terman's original group is maintained in closed files at Stanford University. It is estimated that less than half of the coded responses of this source of data have been transferred to tabulation sheets.

REFERENCES

Anderson, M. A., Tollefson, N. A., & Gilbert, E. C. (1985). Giftedness and reading: A cross sectional view of differences in reading attitudes and behavior. *Gifted Child Quarterly, 29*(4), 86–189.

Barnett, L. A., & Fiscella, J. (1985). A child by any other name. . . . A comparison of the playfulness of gifted and non-gifted children. *Gifted Child Quarterly, 29*(2), 61–66.

Feldman, D. H. (1984). A follow-up of subjects scoring about 180 IQ in Terman's "Genetic Studies of Genius." *Exceptional Children, 50*(6), 518–523.

Schlowinski, E., & Reynolds, C. R. (1985). Dimensions of anxiety among high IQ children. *Gifted Child Quarterly, 29*(3), 125–130.

Sears, P. S. (1979). The Terman genetic studies of genius, 1922–1972. In A. H. Passow (Eds.), *The gifted and talented.* Chicago: National Society for the Study of Education.

Terman, L. M., & Oden, M. H. (1925). *Genetic studies of genius: Mental and physical traits of a thousand gifted children.* Stanford, CA: Stanford University Press.

Terman, L. M., & Oden, M. H. (1951). The Stanford studies of the gifted. In P. A. Witty (Ed.), *The gifted child.* Boston: D. C. Heath.

ANNE M. BAUER
University of Cincinnati

GIFTED CHILDREN
GIFTED CHILDREN AND READING

TEST ANXIETY

Test anxiety is such a universal phenomenon that it hardly requires general definition. In school, on the job, or for various application procedures, tests are required. Performance on a test can impact negatively on the test-taker. Thus an essential component for an anxiety arousal state exists when the individual is placed in a test-taking situation. Test situations are specific and thus present an opportunity to investigate the nature of anxiety.

Test anxiety is usually regarded as a particular kind of general anxiety. Ordinarily, it refers to the variety of responses—physiological, behavioral, and phenomenal (Sieber, 1980)—that accompany an individual's perceptions of failure. The person experiencing test anxiety often has a fear of failure as well as a high need to succeed. Both the fear of failure and the drive for success may be internalized. In some instances, either may seem more of a desire on the part of the test-taker to please a parent or other significant individual. Regardless of the originating causes of test anxiety, it can be a debilitating state of arousal.

One of the major challenges for theorists and researchers on test anxiety is to ascertain why anxiety appears to motivate some persons yet limits seriously the performance of others. Findings from several researchers suggest that the individual's expectations of success or failure on a test are strongly correlated to the development of test anxiety (Heckhausen, 1975; Weiner, 1966). For example, it may be argued that those who are low in motivation to succeed attribute failure to a lack of ability whereas those who are high in motivation to succeed see failure as emanating more from a lack of effort. Heckhausen (1975) cites data showing that those persons with a high fear of failure tend to attribute success more to good luck than those persons with a high expectation of success. Thus, for those who expect to succeed, anxiety may be more of a motivating force than for those who fear failure. For the latter group, initial anxiety may become a debilitating form of test anxiety.

Another avenue of investigation seeks to understand the affective value of test-taking in the context of its social significance. For some persons, test anxiety is heightened if it occurs where there is an observer of the test-taking performance (Geen, 1979; Geen & Gange, 1977). Test anxiety may then be heightened if there are judges, monitors, or others with whom the test-taker must interact. Some persons may, therefore, find an oral or observed performance type of test more anxiety producing than a written test. For such persons, it appears that test anxiety is more a response to their need for and perceptions of social approval than it is to an internalized need to demonstrate competence.

In summary, much of the available research and numerous self-reports suggest that test anxiety is a recurring problem for children and adults. Moreover, test anxiety often appears to inhibit the usual maximal level of performance of the individual. Thus if a test situation is to be used as an effective means of assessing human potential, it is important that we understand more fully the origin of test anxiety as well as its impact on individual performance.

REFERENCES

Dew, K. M. H., Galassi, J. P., & Galassi, M. D. (1984). Math anxiety: Relation with situational test anxiety, performance, physiological arousal, and math avoidance behavior. *Journal of Counseling Psychology, 31,* 480–583.

Geen, R. G. (1979). The influence of passive audiences on performance. In P. Paulus (Ed.), *The psychology of group influence.* Hillsdale, NJ: Erlbaum.

Geen, R. G., & Gange, J. J. (1977). Drive theory of social facilitation: Twelve years of theory and research. *Psychological Bulletin, 84,* 1267–1288.

Heckhausen, H. (1975). Fear of failure as a self-reinforcing motive. In I. G. Sarason & C. D. Spielberger (Eds.), *Stress and anxiety* (Vol. 2). Washington, DC: Hemisphere.

Sieber, J. E. (1980). Defining test anxiety: Problems and approaches. In I. G. Sarason (Ed.), *Test anxiety: Theory, research, and applications.* Hillsdale, NJ: Erlbaum.

Weiner, B. (1966). The role of success and failure in the learning of easy and complex tasks. *Journal of Personality & Social Psychology, 3,* 339–344.

BERT O. RICHMOND
University of Georgia

ANXIETY
STRESS AND INDIVIDUALS WITH DISABILITIES

TEST EQUATING

Test equating is a technique for making the characteristics of two tests similar or identical, if possible, so that an individual's scores on the two tests mean the same thing.

This process is accomplished currently through statistical means. There are two different problems associated with test equating. One is the problem of equating scores on two tests that were designed to be of the same difficulty, for the same kind of student, with the same content. This is called horizontal equating. The other problem is how to equate tests that were designed for different populations, often younger and older students, in which the content overlaps. In this case, one test will be hard for the younger students and the other will be quite easy for the older. This is called vertical equating.

Horizontal equating, while by no means completely solved as a statistical problem, is the better developed and studied of the two. The problem is best stated as follows: For a student with ability A, the relative placement of his or her score on test 1 is identical to the relative score on test 2 if the two tests have been perfectly equated. Mathematically, the two frequency distributions must be equal in normalized form. This means that a youngster's score on test 1 is the same number of standard deviations from the mean and exceeds the same percent of other scores as on test 2. There are three major techniques for achieving horizontal equating.

The first method of horizontal equating is called the equipercentile method. It is the most widely used and seems to be the most robust method under a variety of conditions. Simply put, observed score distributions are matched for percentile points. That is, the score at the first percentile point in test 1 is equated to the score at the first percentile point for test 2. This is done for all percentile points up to 99 or perhaps 99.9. There is a smoothing of the equated scores so that there are no abrupt jumps in scores from one percentile to the next. This procedure has been shown by Petersen, Marco, and Stewart (1982) to be not as good as linear equating, the next technique covered, in which the tests are similar and linear in relationship to each other. When there is a nonlinear relationship between the tests, the equipercentile technique is superior. This case is not common.

Linear equating is the application of a straight line equation of the form $Y = aX + b$. The parameters are functions of the means and standard deviations of the two tests (Braun & Holland, 1982). Not surprisingly, it works best when there is just a simple linear relation between true test scores.

The third technique for equating tests horizontally consists of a number of related techniques grouped under the heading item-characteristic curve (ICC) techniques. These techniques generally make somewhat stronger assumptions about the nature of the test and the test-taker than do the other two methods. They are based on a model that allows estimation of a test-taker's ability. $T1$ on test 1 and $T2$ on test two. These two scores then are equated, and the observed score from which they have been estimated can be calculated. Thus we can begin with either test, estimate the student's underlying ability on the test, and use that ability

score on the other test to calculate an equivalent observed score. Since the procedure works both ways, it is hoped that the tests give similar results between calculated and actual observed scores. In general, such procedures have proven inferior to linear or equipercentile methods for large-scale standardized tests, which are carefully constructed. The ICC methods may be better for smaller, experimentally oriented tests, but their restriction to large samples makes this a rare usage.

Vertical equating is a more difficult problem, conceptually and statistically. The primary techniques used have been based on ICC models. They have not proven satisfactory to date. If two tests are given to a student, one that is hard for him or her and one that is easy (or easier), the ICC methods tend to overpredict ability score on the easy test and underpredict it on the hard test (Kolen, 1981).

REFERENCES

Braun, H. I., & Holland, P. W. (1982). Observed-score test equating: A mathematical analysis of some ETS equating procedures. In P. W. Holland & D. B. Rubin (Eds.), *Test equating* (pp. 9–49). New York: Academic.

Kolen, M. J. (1981). Comparison of traditional and item response theory methods for equating tests. *Journal of Educational Measurement, 19,* 279–293.

Petersen, N. S., Marco, G. L., & Stewart, E. E. (1982). A test of the adequacy of linear score equating models. In P. W. Holland & D. B. Rubin (Eds.), *Test equating* (pp. 71–135). New York: Academic.

VICTOR L. WILLSON
Texas A&M University

MEASUREMENT

TEST FOR AUDITORY COMPREHENSION OF LANGUAGE–THIRD EDITION

The Test for Auditory Comprehension of Language–Third Edition (TACL-3; Carrow-Woolfolk, 1999) is an individually administered measure of receptive spoken language that assesses a subject's ability to understand the following categories of English language forms: Vocabulary, Grammatical Morphemes, and Elaborated Phrases and Sentences.

The TACL-3 consists of 142 items, divided into three subtests.

> *Vocabulary:* Assessing the literal and common meanings of word classes (nouns, verbs, adjectives, and adverbs) and of words that represent basic percepts and concepts

Grammatical Morphemes: Assessing the meaning of grammatical morphemes (prepositions, noun number and case, verb number and tense, noun-verb agreement, derivational suffixes) and the meaning of pronouns, tested within the context of a simple sentence

Elaborated Phrases and Sentences: Assessing the understanding of syntactically based word relations and elaborated phrase and sentence constructions, including the modalities of single and combined constructions (interrogative sentences, negative sentences, active and passive voice, direct and indirect object), embedded sentences, and partially and completely conjoined sentences

It uses the popular point-to-the-picture-of-the-word-I-say technique. This simple procedure eliminates the external influences that are present in a less structured format. At the beginning of each subtest the phrase "Show me" is used to introduce each stimulus item. The examiner begins at the first item in each of the three subtests and stops when the examinee has three consecutive correct responses. Each item is composed of a word or sentence and a corresponding picture plate that has three full-color drawings. One of the three pictures for each item illustrates the meaning of the word morpheme or syntactic structure being tested. The other two pictures illustrate either two semantic or grammatical contrasts of the stimulus, or one contrast and one decoy. The examiner reads the stimulus aloud and directs the subject to point to the picture that he or she believes best represents the meaning of the item. No oral response is required on the part of the examinee. The test takes approximately 15 to 30 minutes to administer.

All scoring is dichotomous: 1 for correct and 0 for incorrect. Correct responses are noted in the profile examiner's record book as A, B, or C.

Percentile ranks, standard scores, and age equivalents are available for children ages 3:0 through 9:11. The TACL-3 provides a variety of norm comparisons based on a standardization sample of 1,102 children, relative to socioeconomic factors, ethnicity, gender, and disability that are the same as those estimated for the year 2000 by the U.S. Bureau of the Census. Studies have shown the absence of gender, racial, disability, and ethnic bias. Reliability coefficients are computed for subgroups of the normative sample (e.g., individuals with speech disabilities, African Americans, European Americans, Hispanic Americans, females) as well as for the entire normative group.

Earlier editions of the TACL were reviewed extensively; references for the newest edition of this instrument are unavailable because of its recent publication date. A review of the TACL-R by Schmitt (1987) concluded that the instrument can be considered both a valid and a reliable test for determining an individual's knowledge of the test's constructs. Bankson (1989) reported that the TACL-R could

be particularly useful as part of a comprehensive language evaluation of children referred for language disorders. Haynes (1989) felt the test was a well-designed and psychometrically sound instrument for evaluating limited aspects of comprehension.

REFERENCES

Bankson, N. W. (1989). Review of the Test for Auditory Comprehension of Language–Revised. In J. C. Conoley & J. J. Kramer (Eds.), *The tenth mental measurements yearbook* (pp. 822–824). Lincoln: Buros Institute of Mental Measurements, University of Nebraska Press.

Carrow-Woolfolk, E. (1999). *Test for Auditory Comprehension of Language–Third Edition.* Austin, TX: PRO-ED.

Haynes, W. O. (1989). Review of the Test for Auditory Comprehension of Language–Revised. In J. C. Conoley & J. J. Kramer (Eds.), *The tenth mental measurements yearbook* (pp. 824–826). Lincoln: Buros Institute of Mental Measurements, University of Nebraska Press.

Schmitt, J. F. (1987). *Test critiques.* Vol. VI. Austin, TX: PRO-ED. Retrieved June 14, 2004, from http://www.med.unc.edu/wrkunits/syllabus/distedu/childas/publish/refsupp/tac13.pdf

RON DUMONT
Fairleigh Dickinson University

AUDITORY PROCESSING

TEST OF ADOLESCENT AND ADULT LANGUAGE–THIRD EDITION

The Test of Adolescent and Adult Language–Third Edition (TOAL-3; Hammill, Brown, Larsen, & Wiederholt, 1994) is a revision of the Test of Adolescent Language originally published in 1981 and revised in 1987. The TOAL-3 has extended the norms to include 18- through 24-year-old persons enrolled in postsecondary education programs. This improvement required that the name of the test be changed to indicate the presence of the older population in the normative sample.

The TOAL-3 is used to assess the linguistic aspects of listening, speaking, reading, and writing of adolescents and adults. The TOAL-3 consists of eight subtests that combine to create the Overall Language Ability, as well as 10 composite quotients: Listening, the ability to understand the spoken language of other people; Speaking, the ability to express one's ideas orally; Reading, the ability to comprehend written messages; Writing, the ability to express thoughts in graphic form; Spoken Language, the ability to listen and speak; Written Language, the ability to read and write; Vocabulary, the ability to understand and use words in communication; Grammar, the ability to understand and generate syntactic and morphological structures; Receptive Language, the ability to comprehend both written and spoken language; and Expressive Language, the ability to produce written and spoken language.

The Overall Language Ability quotient and the other 10 composite quotients have a mean of 100 and a standard deviation of 15.

The normative sample exceeded 3,000 persons in 22 states and three Canadian provinces. It was representative of the U.S. population according to 1990 U.S. census percentages for region, gender, race, and residence; the sample is stratified by age. Unfortunately, the normative data were collected from only a subset of the entire young adult population. Specifically, approximately 70 percent of individuals 18 to 25 years old were described as those "who seek some form of post-secondary education following their years in high school" (Hammill et al., 1994, p. 47). It may be assumed that individuals who seek postsecondary education have better language abilities than those who do not. Moreover, young adults with a history of speech or language impairments do not pursue postsecondary education as often as do their peers without such impairments (Felsenfeld, Broen, & McGue, 1994; Records, Tomblin, & Freese, 1992). Thus, young adults who might have scored in the lower portion of the full range of language performance were unfortunately excluded from the TOAL-3 normative sample, thereby restricting the range of scores (particularly low scores) included in the norms.

All reliability coefficients exceed .80. Content, criterion-related, and construct validity have been thoroughly studied. Correlations between the TOAL-3 and other tests of language (TOLD-I:2, PPVT, DTLA-3, TOWL-2) show a considerable relationship. The TOAL-3 is also related to IQ and age. The provision of a factorial analysis has enhanced the construct validity of the test. Studies showing the absence of racial and gender bias have been added. Most important, the TOAL-3 scores distinguished dramatically between groups known to have language problems and those known to have normal language. In addition, the TOAL-3 scores distinguished between groups known to have language problems and those known to have normal language. Evidence is also provided to show that TOAL-3 items are not biased with regard to race or gender.

Most reviewers have praised the test's statistical properties, theoretical base, and clearly written manual (McLoughlin & Lewis, 1990; Roberts & Mather, 1998; Shapiro, 1989; Stinnett, 1992; Williams, 1985). Several reviewers, however, think the test is too long, yields too little useful information, and has old normative data (Richards, 1998; MacDonald, 1998).

REFERENCES

Felsenfeld, S., Broen, P. A., & McGue, M. (1994). A 28-year follow-up of adults with a history of moderate phonological disorder: Educational and occupational results. *Journal of Speech and Hearing Research, 37,* 1341–1353.

Hammill, D., Brown, L., Larsen, S. & Wiederholt, L. (1994). *Test of Adolescent Language, third edition* (TOAL-3). Austin: PRO-ED.

Johnson, C. J., Taback, N., Escobar, M., Wilson, B., & Beitchman, J. H. (1999). Local norming of the Test of Adolescent/Adult Language–3 in the Ottawa Speech and Language Study. *Journal of Speech, Language, & Hearing Research, 42,* 761–766.

MacDonald, J. (1998). Review of the Test of Adolescent Language–Third Edition. In J. C. Impara & B. S. Plake (Eds.), *The thirteenth mental measurements yearbook* (pp. 1018–1019). Lincoln: Buros Institute of Mental Measurements, University of Nebraska Press.

McLoughlin, J. A., & Lewis, R. B. (1990). *Assessing special students* (3rd ed.). Columbus, OH: Merrill.

Records, N. L., Tomblin, J. B., & Freese, P. R. (1992). The quality of life of young adults with histories of specific language impairment. *American Journal of Speech-Language Pathology, 1,* 44–54.

Richards, R. A. (1998). Review of the Test of Adolescent Language–Third Edition. In J. C. Impara & B. S. Plake (Eds.), *The thirteenth mental measurements yearbook* (pp. 1019–1021). Lincoln: Buros Institute of Mental Measurements, University of Nebraska Press.

Roberts, R., & Mather, N. (1998). Test review: Test of Adolescent and Adult Language–Third Edition (TOAL-3). *Journal of Psychoeducational Assessment, 16,* 75–83.

Shapiro, D. A. (1989). Review of the Test of Adolescent Language–2. In J. C. Conoley & J. J. Kramer (Eds.), *The tenth mental measurements yearbook* (pp. 828–830). Lincoln: Buros Institute of Mental Measurements, University of Nebraska Press.

Stinnett, T. A. (1992). Test reviews. *Journal of Psychoeducational Assessment, 10,* 182–189.

Williams, R. T. (1985). Review of the Test of Adolescent Language. In J. V. Mitchell (Ed.), *The ninth mental measurements yearbook* (pp. 1549–1551). Lincoln: Buros Institute of Mental Measurements, University of Nebraska Press.

RON DUMONT
Fairleigh Dickinson University

JOHN O. WILLIS
Rivier College

TEST OF EARLY MATHEMATICS ABILITY–THIRD EDITION

The Test of Early Mathematics Ability–Third Edition (TEMA-3; Ginsburg & Baroody, 2003) measures the mathematics abilities of children between the ages of 3:0 and 8:11 years. The test measures informal and formal (school-taught) concepts and skills in the following areas: numbering skills, number comparison facility, numeral literacy, mastery of number facts, calculation skills, and understanding of concepts. It has two parallel forms, each containing 72 items. The items of the instrument were chosen based on existing research and national norms. Almost every item is linked to an empirical research study. The items are sequenced in order of increasing difficulty.

The TEMA-3 standardization sample was composed of 1,219 children. The characteristics of the sample approximate those in the 2001 U.S. Census. The results of the test, which takes approximately 20 minutes to administer, may be reported as standard scores (M = 100, SD = 15), percentiles, and age or grade equivalents. Reliabilities are in the .90s; validity has been experimentally established. Also provided is a book of remedial techniques (Assessment Probes and Instructional Activities) for improving skills in the areas assessed by the test. Numerous teaching tasks for skills covered by each TEMA-3 item are included. After giving the test, the examiner decides which items need additional assessment information and uses the book to help the student improve his or her mathematical skills.

A separate Probes guide (Ginsburg, 2003) provides a series of follow-up questions to be used after the standard testing to examine children's methods of solution and their "zone of proximal development" with respect to key items failed during standard administration. For each item, the Probes session begins with reworded questions designed to determine if the child did not understand the original question. A strategy question then follows to identify the child's method of solution (e.g., "Tell me what you are thinking about this problem"). Next, a justification question is asked (e.g., "Can you prove to me that 2 and 2 is 5?"). Finally, the examiner gives a hint (e.g., "How about using your fingers to count?") to determine whether the child can solve the problem with some adult assistance. Conducting this sequence of questioning may reveal the source of the child's difficulty, which could directly inform a teacher's instruction or a clinician's intervention.

REFERENCES

Ginsburg, H. P. (2003). *Assessment probes and instructional activities for the Test of Early Mathematics Ability–3.* Austin, TX: PRO-ED.

Ginsburg, H. P., & Baroody, A. J. (2003). *The Test of Early Mathematics Ability: Third Edition.* Austin, TX: PRO-ED.

RON DUMONT
Fairleigh Dickinson University

JOHN O. WILLIS
Rivier College

TEST OF EARLY READING ABILITY–THIRD EDITION

The Test of Early Reading Ability–Third Edition (TERA-3; Reid, Hresko, & Hammill, 2002) measures the actual reading ability of young children. The test consists of three subtests: Alphabet (29 items) measures knowledge of the alphabet and its uses; Conventions (21 items) measures knowledge of the conventions of print; and Meaning (30 items) measures the construction of meaning from print.

There are five identified purposes of the TERA-3: (1) to identify children who are below their peers in reading development; (2) to identify strengths and weaknesses of individual children; (3) to document progress as a result of early reading intervention; (4) to serve as a measure in reading research; and (5) to serve as one component of a comprehensive assessment. To their credit, the authors clearly state that the TERA-3 is not to be used as a sole basis for instructional planning.

Each subtest has a mean of 10 and a standard deviation of 3. An overall Reading Quotient is computed using all three subtest scores. Performance is reported as a standard score (M = 100; SD = 15); percentile rank is provided. Age equivalents and grade equivalents are also given, although the authors provide cautionary remarks about their use in the manual. The TERA-3 has two alternate, equivalent forms. Answers receive a score of 1 for correct or 0 for incorrect, and expected answers are clearly indicated in the examiner's record booklet.

The TERA-3 was standardized on a relatively small stratified national sample of 875 children. These children were well matched on several critical demographics projected by the U.S. Bureau of the Census for 2000. Normative data are given for every 6-month interval. Both internal consistency and test-retest reliability are reported in the test manual. Reliability is consistently high across all three types of reliability studied. All but 2 of the 32 coefficients reported approach or exceed .90.

REFERENCE

Reid, D., Hresko, W., & Hammill, D. (2002). *Test of Early Reading Ability–third edition* (TERA-3). Austin: PRO-ED.

RON DUMONT
Fairleigh Dickinson University

JOHN O. WILLIS
Rivier College

TEST OF EARLY WRITTEN LANGUAGE–SECOND EDITION

The Test of Early Written Language–Second Edition (TEWL-2; Hresko, Herron, & Peak, 1996) measures early writing ability in children from ages 3:0 to 10:11. It consists of 57 untimed items, presented in developmental sequence, which assess the use of conventions, linguistics, and conceptualization. The Basic Writing subtest requires responses to specific items (spelling, capitalization, punctuation, sentence construction, and metacognitive knowledge), while the Contextual Writing subtest depends on the authentic assessment (story format, cohesion, thematic maturity, ideation, and story construction) of a writing sample. Subtests may be given independently or combined to provide a Global Writing Quotient.

The Basic Writing Subtest requires the administrator to establish a starting point for the child using suggested beginning items provided in the manual. Items for young students, for example, require them to draw a picture of a favorite TV character and tell about him or her, identify writing instruments, indicate directionality of printed text, and write their name. Older students are asked to construct sentences from haphazardly presented words, combine sentences, identify writing conventions, and complete similar tasks. These items, scored 1 or 0, are recorded in an individual profile record booklet.

The Contextual Writing Subtest requires the child to write a story about a visual stimulus. For younger students a simple scene is used; older students respond to a more complete scenario (e.g., a detailed playground scene). With the aid of a key, the student's story is scored on a 0–3 scale for 14 specific criteria including sentence structure, ideation, thematic maturity, structure, sequence, use of dialogue, cohesion, and elaboration. Unlike many published writing tests, the TEWL-2 gives the student the opportunity to review and edit the story prior to scoring.

The test can be used as a diagnostic device for children ages 4:0 to 10:11 and as a research tool for children 3:0 to 3:11.

Three quotients (Basic Writing, Contextual Writing, and Global Writing) are provided, each based on a mean of 100 and a standard deviation of 15. Percentile ranks, age equivalents, standard score quotients, and normal curve equivalents are also provided. The TEWL-2 norms represent more than 1,400 children from 33 states. Normative information generally conforms to population characteristics for gender, race, ethnicity, geographic region, and residence (urban/rural) relative to the 1990 U.S. Census data. Internal consistency and reliability coefficients all exceed .90. Substantial content description procedures, criterion prediction procedures, and construct identification procedures are presented.

The materials are well prepared; the manual is particularly useful, especially for scoring the Contextual Writing Subtest. Administering both tests is relatively time consuming, but as the measure is to be used diagnostically with at-risk students only, large numbers should not be involved. The provision of comparable forms permits the alternate form's use in assessing the impact of any interventions.

The TEWL-2 possesses an excellent conceptual framework and content-appropriate tasks. However, assessing a student's writing abilities from one sample of expressive writing using a single stimulus may impose serious limitations on the scope, and probably on the quality and dependability, of the diagnostic information generated by the task.

REFERENCES

Hresko, W. P., Herron, S. R., & Peak, P. K. (1996). *Test of Early Written Language, Second Edition.* Austin, TX: PRO-ED.

Hurford, D. P. (1998). Review of the Test of Early Written Language, Second Edition. In J. C. Impara & B. S. Plake (Eds.), *The thirteenth mental measurements yearbook* (pp. 1027–1030). Lincoln: Buros Institute of Mental Measurement, University of Nebraska Press.

Trevisan, M. S. (1998). Review of the Test of Early Written Language, Second Edition. In J. C. Impara & B. S. Plake (Eds.), *The thirteenth mental measurements yearbook* (pp. 1027–1030). Lincoln: Buros Institute of Mental Measurement, University of Nebraska Press.

RON DUMONT
Fairleigh Dickinson University

JOHN O. WILLIS
Rivier College

TEST OF LANGUAGE DEVELOPMENT–PRIMARY, THIRD EDITION

The Test of Language Development–Primary, Third Edition (TOLD-P:3; Newcomer & Hammill, 1997) is an individually administered, norm-referenced test for use with children ages 4 years 0 months to 8 years 11 months. This test takes approximately 1 hour and is composed of nine subtests that measure different components of spoken language. Picture Vocabulary, Relational Vocabulary, and Oral Vocabulary assess the understanding and meaningful use of spoken words. Grammatic Understanding, Sentence Imitation, and Grammatic Completion assess differing aspects of grammar. Word Articulation, Phonemic Analysis, and Word Discrimination are supplemental subtests that measure the abilities to say words correctly and to distinguish between words that sound similar. Each subtest contains sample items and between 14 and 30 test items presented orally by the examiner. Children must either point (Picture Vocabulary and Grammatic Understanding) or respond orally to each subtest. The TOLD-P:3 provides scores in the form of standard scores, percentile ranks, and age equivalents for interpretation.

The TOLD-P:3 was standardized in 1996 on a sample of more than 1,000 children in 28 states representative of the U.S. population. An additional 519 children were administered the test for use in reliability and validity studies. The sample was stratified by age and was found to be representative of the nation's school-age population as reported in the *Statistical Abstract of the United States* (U.S. Bureau of the Census, 1990) regarding gender, race, ethnicity, family income, education of parents, and disability. Test reliability, which was investigated by the coefficient alpha and test-retest methods, is high enough to warrant the use of the test with individual children. Content validity was established by relating the test's contents to the individuals' actual language and by item analysis. Criterion-related validity was established by correlating subtests with two commonly used tests (Bankson Language Test, Second Edition, and the Comprehensive Scales of Student Abilities). Construct validity was determined by studying the relationship of TOLD-P:3 to age, IQ, and school achievement, as well as by factor analysis of the scores. The TOLD-P:3 scores distinguish between groups of children who have language problems (mental retardation, learning disability, reading disability, speech delay, and articulation problems) and those who do not. Reliability and validity studies were computed separately for minority and disability groups, as well as the general population.

REFERENCES

Bell, S. K. (2000). Test review: Test of Language Development–Primary, third edition. *Journal of Psychoeducational Assessment, 18,* 167–176.

Newcomer, P. & Hammill, D. (1997). *Test of Language Development–Primary, third edition.* Austin: PRO-ED.

RON DUMONT
Fairleigh Dickinson University

JOHN O. WILLIS
Rivier College

LANGUAGE DISORDERS

TEST OF MEMORY AND LEARNING

The Test of Memory and Learning (TOMAL; Reynolds & Bigler, 1994) is a comprehensive battery of 14 memory and learning tasks (10 core subtests and 4 supplementary subtests) designed to assess persons ages 5 years 0 months through 19 years 11 months. Five subtests form the Verbal Memory Index, while five more form the Nonverbal Memory Index. Additional subtests for each index are available as additions to the core subtests. Four measures of delayed recall, given 30 minutes after the start of testing, permit the comparison of performance across time. Also included with the TOMAL are directions for computing five supplementary indexes (Attention/Concentration, Sequential Recall, Free Recall, Associative Recall, and Learning). Finally, normative tables are provided on the Supplementary Analysis forms so that a person's learning and retention curves can

be drawn and compared. To provide greater flexibility to the clinician, a set of four purely empirically derived factor indexes representing Complex Memory, Sequential Recall, Backward Recall, and Spatial Memory have been made available as well.

Subtests include Memory-for-Stories (MFS), Facial Memory (FCM), Word Selective Reminding (WSR), Visual Selective Reminding (VSR), Object Recall (OBR), Abstract Visual Memory (AVM), Digits Forward (DSF), Visual Sequential Memory (VSM), Paired Recall (PRC), Memory-for-Location (MFL), Manual Imitation (MIM), Letters Forward (LSF), Digits Backward (DSB), and Letters Backward (LSB). These subtests systematically vary the mode of presentation and response so as to sample verbal, visual, motoric, and combinations of these modalities in presentation and in response formats. The TOMAL subtests are scaled to the familiar metric of mean equaling 10 and a standard deviation of 3 (range 1 to 20). Composite or summary scores are scaled to a mean of 100 and standard deviation of 15.

Test material includes two booklets containing the stimuli for subtests; Facial Memory chips; Visual Selective Reminding test board; Delayed Recall cue card set; protocols for test including separate Supplementary Analysis forms; and the examiner's manual.

Administration time for the Core Battery (10 subtests) is approximately 45 minutes, while the entire battery (10 core subtests, 4 alternative subtests, and 4 recall subtests) takes approximately 60 to 75 minutes. Directions for each subtest are contained on the protocol pages, so the manual is not needed during administration. The Facial Memory, Paired Recall, Digits Backward, and Letters Backward subtests are the only subtests to provide unscored teaching tasks. Teaching items are also allowable on a number of other subtests, but only after the person has attempted an item and received a score of 0.

The TOMAL was standardized on 1,342 people selected as representative of the U.S. 1990 population estimates. Fifteen different age groups were divided by geographic area (17 states), race, gender, and ethnic group. Socioeconomic status (SES) was determined on the basis of the test site chosen. The sample was also stratified by urban versus rural residence. The size of the 15 sample ages tested ranged from a low of 42 at age 18 to a high of 163 at age 11.

Internal reliabilities for the TOMAL are generally high, ranging from a low of .56 to a high of .98. Of the four core indexes, all but Delayed Recall have reliabilities in the .90s. Delayed Recall averages .85 across all ages. Each of the five supplementary indexes has reliability estimates in the .90s. Of the 14 core subtests, 9 have an average reliability in the .90s, while the remaining 5 are in the .80s. Delayed recall subtests generally had lower reliabilities than did the other subtests.

Test-retest reliability coefficients for the core and supplementary indexes ranged from .81 to .92. The 14 subtest reliabilities averaged .81. Average test-retest reliability for

3 of the 14 subtests was found to be in the .70s. Two of these subtests, Facial Memory and Abstract Visual Memory, are primary subtests of the Nonverbal Memory Composite.

The TOMAL scores correlate approximately .50 with measures of intelligence and achievement, indicating that the TOMAL is related to but not the same as the measures. Measures of intelligence typically correlated with one another in the .75 to .85 range while correlating with measure of achievement in the .55 to .65 range.

Since publication of the TOMAL, several studies have provided evidence of convergent and divergent validity of the TOMAL subtests as measures of various aspects of memory by examining patterns of correlations among TOMAL subtests and the Rey Auditory Verbal Learning Test and the Wechsler Memory Scale–Revised.

REFERENCES

Bigler, E. D., & Adams, W. V. (2001). Clinical neuropsychological assessment of child and adolescent memory with the WRAML, TOMAL, and CVLT-C. In A. S. Kaufman & N. L. Kaufman (Eds.), *Specific learning disabilities and difficulties in children and adolescents: Psychological assessment and evaluation* (pp. 387–429). New York: Cambridge University Press.

Dumont, R., Whelley, P., Comtois, R., & Levine, B. (1994). Test of Memory and Learning (TOMAL): Test review. *Journal of Psychoeducational Assessment, 12,* 414–423.

Lowther, J. L., & Mayfield, J. (2004). Memory functioning in children with traumatic brain injuries: A TOMAL validity study. *Archives of Clinical Neuropsychology, 19,* 89–104.

Reynolds, C. R., & Bigler, E. (1994). *Test of memory and learning.* Austin: PRO-ED.

RON DUMONT
Fairleigh Dickinson University

JOHN O. WILLIS
Rivier College

TEST OF NONVERBAL INTELLIGENCE– THIRD EDITION

The Test of Nonverbal Intelligence–Third Edition (TONI-3; Brown, Sherbenou, & Johnsen, 1998) was created as a language-free measure of intelligence, aptitude, abstract reasoning, and problem solving for persons ages 6:0 through 89:11. It does not require the subject to read, write, speak, or listen. The test is entirely nonverbal and does not involve much movement more than a point, nod, or other symbolic gesture indicating a response decision. It is particularly useful for individuals who are deaf, language disordered (both expressive and receptive), non-English speaking, or culturally different, and those with conditions resulting from mental retardation, developmental disabilities, au-

tism, cerebral palsy, stroke, traumatic brain injury, or other neurological impairment.

The two equivalent forms of the TONI-3 make it ideal for use in situations dependent upon pre- and posttesting. Each form contains 45 items arranged to become progressively more difficult. Raw scores are converted to percentile ranks and to deviation quotients that have a mean of 100 and a standard deviation of 15 points.

The abstract/figural subject matter of the test ensures that each item presents a novel problem. There are no words, numbers, familiar pictures, or symbols within the test. The drawings in the Picture Book have been significantly improved in the TONI-3.

The test was normed in 1995 and 1996 on a sample of 3,451 people whose demographic characteristics matched those of the 1990 U.S. Census for both school-age and adult populations. The normative group was stratified by age across the variables of geographic region, gender, race, urban/rural residence, ethnicity, and presence of a disabling condition, as well as family income and educational level achieved by the adult participants and parents of minor participants.

Close to 20 years of research established the test's reliability and validity. The manual reports extensive research, including the authors' own and those studies conducted by independent investigators since the original test was first published in 1980. Substantial validity data are also reported, documenting the TONI-3's relationship to other measures of intelligence, achievement, and personality; its efficiency in discriminating groups appropriately; its factor structure; and other important estimates of test validity for samples of children, adolescents, and adults.

REFERENCES

Brown, L. (2003). Test of Nonverbal Intelligence: A language-free measure of cognitive ability. In R. Steve McCallum (Ed.), *Handbook of nonverbal assessment.* (pp. 191–221). New York: Kluwer Academic/Plenum.

Brown, L., Sherbenou, R. J., & Johnsen, S. K. (1997). *Test of Nonverbal Intelligence–Third edition, examiner's manual.* Austin, TX: PRO-ED.

Brown, L., Sherbenou, R. J., & Johnsen, S. K. (1998). *Test of Nonverbal Intelligence–Third edition.* Austin-PRO-ED.

RON DUMONT
Fairleigh Dickinson University

JOHN O. WILLIS
Rivier College

TEST OF PHONOLOGICAL AWARENESS

The Test of Phonological Awareness (TOPA; Torgesen & Bryant, 1994) measures young children's awareness of the individual sounds in words. The TOPA Kindergarten version (measuring same and different beginning sounds) can be used to identify children in kindergarten who may profit from instructional activities to enhance their phonological awareness in preparation for reading instruction. The Early Elementary version (measuring same and different ending sounds) can be used to determine if first- and second-grade students' difficulties in early reading are associated with delays in development of phonological awareness.

The elementary version assesses final sounds of words. This is a 20-item test, comprising two subtests, and is administered in large groups, in small groups (six to eight students), or individually. In the kindergarten version, items on the first subtest require students to compare the initial sound of a stimulus word to the initial sounds of three response choices and identify the response choice with the same sound. Items of the second subtest are structured similarly except that students identify the response choice with a different initial sound. At the early elementary level, the two subtests are structured in the same manner except that students identify final sounds. At the beginning of the second semester of kindergarten, students scoring in the lowest quartile are deemed at risk for poor reading development. For first- and second-grade students scoring below the lowest 15th percentile, reading problems are deemed likely due to phonological deficits.

Both versions can be administered either individually or to groups of children. The test has been standardized on a large sample of children (857 from kindergarten, 3,654 from elementary grades) representative of the population characteristics reported in the U.S. Census. The TOPA Kindergarten version does not have national representation, but the Early Elementary version does. The TOPA Kindergarten sample was gathered from 10 schools, while the TOPA Early Elementary was gathered from 38 schools.

Raw scores are calculated by adding the number of items answered correctly. The manual states that the three main types of scores obtained are raw, standard, and percentile scores. Percentiles and standard scores are obtained based on the student's raw score. The manual also provides conversions for stanines and normal curve equivalents.

The manual provides information to generate percentiles and a variety of standard scores. Internal consistency reliabilities range from .89 to .91 at different ages. Evidence of content, predictive, and construct validity also is provided in the manual.

Long (1998) finds the TOPA test format simple and reports that administration should be completed rapidly in most instances. McCauley (1998) feels that the TOPA makes a substantial contribution to the group assessment of phonological awareness in young school-age children. She states that evidence of reliability and validity is generally quite adequate.

REFERENCES

Dohan, M. (1996). The Test of Phonological Awareness: A critical review. *Journal of Speech-Language Pathology & Audiology, 20*, 22–26.

Long, S. H. (1998). Review of the Test of Phonological Awareness. In J. C. Impara & B. S. Plake (Eds.), *The thirteenth mental measurements yearbook* (pp. 1049–1050). Lincoln: Buros Institute of Mental Measurements, University of Nebraska Press.

McCauley, R. (1998). Review of the Test of Phonological Awareness. In J. C. Impara & B. S. Plake (Eds.), *The thirteenth mental measurements yearbook* (pp. 1050–1052). Lincoln: Buros Institute of Mental Measurements, University of Nebraska Press.

Torgesen, J. K., & Bryant, B. R. (1994). *Test of Phonological Awareness.* Austin: PRO-ED.

RON DUMONT
Fairleigh Dickinson University

JOHN O. WILLIS
Rivier College

TEST OF READING COMPREHENSION– THIRD EDITION

The Test of Reading Comprehension–Third Edition (TORC-3; Brown, Hammill, & Wiederholt, 1995) comprises eight subtests grouped under either the General Reading Comprehension Core, which yields a Reading Comprehension Quotient, or the Diagnostic Supplements. The General Reading Comprehension Core includes General Vocabulary (the understanding of sets of vocabulary items that are all related to the same general concept), Syntactic Similarities (the understanding of meaningfully similar but syntactically different sentence structures), Paragraph Reading (the ability to answer questions related to story-like paragraphs), and Sentence Sequencing (the ability to build relationships among sentences, both to each other and to a reader-created whole).

Four Diagnostic Supplements subtests are available for use in a more comprehensive evaluation of relative strengths and weaknesses. Three of the subtests are measures of content-area vocabulary in mathematics, social studies, and science. The final subtest, Reading the Directions of Schoolwork, measures the student's understanding of written directions commonly found in schoolwork.

Raw scores can be converted into standard scores, grade-equivalent scores, age-equivalent scores, and percentiles. The TORC-3 was standardized on 1,962 students from 19 states between 1993 and 1994. Data are provided supporting test-retest and internal consistency reliability. Information on the normative sample of students is provided by geographic region, gender, residence, race, ethnicity, and disabling condition stratified by age and keyed to the 1990

U.S. census data. Criterion-related and content validity has been updated and expanded, and test-retest reliability has been reworked to account for age effects. Studies also have been added showing the absence of gender and racial bias.

REFERENCE

Brown, V., Hammill, D., & Wiederholt, J. L. (1995). *Test of Reading Comprehension—Third edition.* Austin: PRO-ED.

RON DUMONT
Fairleigh Dickinson University

JOHN O. WILLIS
Rivier College

TEST OF SILENT WORD READING FLUENCY

The Test of Silent Word Reading Fluency (TOSWRF; Mather, Hammill, Allen, & Roberts, 2004) is a standardized, norm-referenced measure of a student's ability to recognize printed words accurately and efficiently. Its two parallel record forms can be used by classroom teachers, reading specialists, school psychologists, or other education professionals with some training in standardized test administration. Students are presented with rows of words ordered by reading difficulty with no spaces between them (e.g., onatdimhowcarblue). Students draw a line between the boundaries of as many words as possible within a 3-minute time period (e.g., on/at/dim/how/car/blue). The test should not be administered to students with known hand-eye coordination problems.

The estimated administration time is 5 minutes, and the test can be given in both individual and group formats (Zhou, 2005). A student's raw score (the number of words correctly identified) can be converted to standard, percentile, age-equivalent, or grade-equivalent scores. The TOSWRF is intended to provide a quick and efficient method for identifying students who are struggling with reading, not to be the sole measure for making eligibility or placement decisions. It also can be used as a research tool and to monitor reading progress.

The TOSWRF was normed on approximately 3,590 students, ages 6:6 through 17:11, residing in 34 states (Mather et al., 2004). The sample was representative of U.S. Census data in terms of geographic region, gender, race, ethnicity, and parents' educational background. Nineteen percent of the sample included children with exceptionalities, including learning and language disorders, emotional disturbances, or hearing impairment. No urban-rural comparisons were presented (Zhou, 2005). The reliability between Forms A and B exceeds .70 for all groups based on gender, race, ethnicity, disability, and identification as gifted. Test-retest reliability

coefficients exceeded .80 for all groups except ages 15 to 17, for whom correlations were in the .70s (Mather et al., 2004). Words were selected from a graded word frequency list to help measure content validity. TOSWRF results were compared to subtests of the Test of Word Reading Efficiency, Woodcock Reading Mastery Test–Revised, and the Woodcock-Johnson Psycho-Educational Battery–Revised Tests of Achievement to address concurrent validity. Correlations ranged from .42 to .78. Tests of construct validity showed that TOSWRF results increased with age. Subgroups of male, female, American Indian, Asian American, Hispanic American, African American, European American, and gifted students performed in the average range. Validity data suggest that the TOSWRF can accurately predict general reading ability and correctly identifies children with and without reading problems.

The TOSWRF is a reliable and valid screener of reading fluency through its test of word identification and speed. Distractions or student corrections while taking this test may result in underestimating a student's word recognition ability. However, questionable results can be checked for reliability through a brief administration of the alternate form. The TOSWRF may be useful to identify students struggling with decoding, to monitor students' reading progress, and as a research tool for students from the elementary to high school years.

REFERENCES

Mather, N., Hammill, D. D., Allen, E. A., & Roberts, R. (2004). *Test of Silent Word Reading Fluency.* Austin, TX: PRO-ED.

Zhou, L. (2005). Test review: Test of Silent Word Reading Fluency. *Communiqué, 33.*

JEFFREY DITTERLINE
University of Florida

TEST OF VARIABLES OF ATTENTION

The Test of Variables of Attention (TOVA; Greenberg, 1989/1996) is an individually administered visual continuous performance test designed primarily for diagnosing children with attentional disorders and for monitoring the effectiveness of medication in treating attentional disorders. The TOVA requires neither language skills nor recognition of letters or numbers. The task is relatively simple: One of two easily discriminated visual stimuli (a small square adjacent to the top of a larger square or a small square adjacent to the bottom of a larger square) is presented for 100 milliseconds at 2-second intervals, and the subject is required to click a button whenever the specific target appears but to inhibit responding whenever the nontarget appears. There are two conditions during the test: (1) infrequent presentation of targets, designed to measure attention; and (2) frequent presentation of targets, designed to measure impulsivity.

Seven scores are obtained on the TOVA: errors of omission, errors of commission, mean correct response time, variability, anticipatory responses, multiple responses, and postcommission response time. The TOVA kit provides a manual to aid in interpretation of test results and the test itself provides computerized test interpretations. The TOVA kit also provides two videotapes that demonstrate how the TOVA may be used to screen for attention-deficit/hyperactivity disorder (ADHD), to predict response to medication, and to monitor the psychopharmacological treatment.

The manual provides normative data on 1,590 subjects, at 15 different ages separated by sex. The norms are not stratified, and little, if any, information is provided about the makeup of these children and adults. No breakdowns for socioeconomic levels, geographic regions, education levels, or race information are provided. There is no evidence in the manual that the normative sample includes (or for that matter, excludes) special education students or children on stimulant medication. Above age 20, there are very few males in the norming tables. For ages above 19 the numbers in the norming sample age groups drop considerably, from an average of 168 subjects per group (age 4 to 19) to 36 subjects per group (age 20–80+). Still, the norm sample is impressive for a test not published by a major company.

The evidence for test-retest reliability is based on a study (no citation is provided) that reports no significant differences between testing for a randomly selected group of normal children, ADHD subjects, and learning disabled (LD) normal adults. The validity data are not adequate for the TOVA. There is question about the content validity of the measure (i.e., whether a small sample of behaviors is a valid estimate of characteristic behavior for the individual), as a very limited research base is provided (Hagin & Dellabella, 1998).

In terms of providing an accurate assessment of the presence or absence of ADHD, the TOVA produces fairly high rates of misclassification (15 percent false positive rate and 28 percent false negative rate; Stein, 1998). Overall the technical characteristics of reliability and validity are not adequately provided in the TOVA manual (Hagin & Dellabella, 1998; Stein, 1998). The TOVA can be used as part of a diagnostic battery for purposes of diagnosing attentional disorders, but this should be done with caution until more normative information is available (Stein, 1998).

REFERENCES

Chae, P. K., Kim, J. H., & Noh, K. S. (2003). Diagnosis of ADHD among gifted children in relation to KEDI–WISC and T.O.V.A. performance. *Gifted Child Quarterly, 47,* pp. 192–201.

Chae, P. K. (1999). Correlation study between WISC-III scores and *TOVA* performance. *Psychology in the Schools, 36,* 179–185.

Forbes, G. B. (1998). Clinical utility of the Test of Variables of Attention (*TOVA*) in the diagnosis of attention-deficit/hyperactivity disorder. *Journal of Clinical Psychology, 54,* 461–476.

Greenberg, L. (1986). *Test of variables of attention.* San Diego: Universal Attention Disorders.

Hagin, R. A., & Dellabella, F. (1998). Review of the Test of Variables of Attention. In J. C. Impara & B. S. Plake (Eds.), *The thirteenth mental measurements yearbook* (pp. 1058–1060). Lincoln, NE: Buro Institute of Mental Measurements.

Stein, M. B. (1998). Review of the Test of Variables of Attention. In J. C. Impara & B. S. Plake (Eds.), *The thirteenth mental measurements yearbook* (pp. 1060–1062). Lincoln, NE: Buros Institute of Mental Measurements.

RON DUMONT
Fairleigh Dickinson University

JOHN O. WILLIS
Rivier College

TEST OF WORD FINDING–SECOND EDITION

Test of Word Finding–Second Edition (TWF-2; German, 2000) assesses an important expressive vocabulary skill. An examiner can diagnose word-finding disorders by presenting five naming sections: Picture Naming (Nouns), Picture Naming (Verbs), Sentence Completion Naming, Description Naming, and Category Naming. The TWF-2 includes a special sixth comprehension section that allows the examiner to determine if errors are a result of word-finding problems or are due to poor comprehension. The instrument provides formal and informal analyses of two dimensions of word finding: speed and accuracy. The formal analysis yields standard scores, percentile ranks, and grade standards for item response time. The informal analysis yields secondary characteristics (gestures and extra verbalization) and substitution types. Speed can be measured in actual or estimated item response time.

The TWF-2 was developed to be administered to children. Three forms are provided: a preprimary form for preschool and kindergarten children, a primary form for the first and second grades, and an intermediate form for the third through sixth grades.

The TWF-2 uses four different naming sections to test a student's word-finding ability. Picture Naming (Nouns) assesses a student's accuracy and speed when naming compound and one- to four-syllable target words. Sentence Completion Naming assesses a student's accuracy when naming target words to complete a sentence read by the examiner. Picture Naming (Verbs) assesses a student's accuracy when naming pictures depicting verbs in the progressive and past tense forms. Picture Naming Categories assesses a student's accuracy and speed when naming objects and the distinct categories to which they belong.

Five supplemental analyses are provided to allow the examiner to gain critical information to enhance the interpretation of a student's test performance and help formulate a word-finding intervention plan. Three of the informal analyses (Phonemic Cueing Procedure, Imitation Procedure, and Substitution Analysis) probe the nature of students' word-finding errors. The two other analyses (Delayed Response Procedure and Secondary Characteristics Tally) contribute to interpreting students' Word-Finding Quotient.

Standard scores and percentile ranks are provided. The instrument was nationally standardized on 1,836 individuals from 26 states. Characteristics of the sample matched the national population in 1997. Reliability coefficients for typical-performing students and students with word-finding difficulties exceeded .84. Correlations between TWF-2 and other tests of vocabulary showed a considerable relationship.

REFERENCE

German, D. (2000). *Test of Word Finding–Second edition.* Austin: PRO-ED.

RON DUMONT
Fairleigh Dickinson University

JOHN O. WILLIS
Rivier College

TEST OF WORD READING EFFICIENCY

The Test of Word Reading Efficiency (TOWRE; Torgesen, Wagner, & Rashotte, 1999) is an individually administered timed test of word-reading efficiency in the English language for children and adults ages 6:0 to 24:11. This test is a measure of an individual's ability to pronounce printed words fluently and accurately. The test focuses on two main abilities: the ability to sound out words with quickness and accuracy and the ability to recognize familiar words as whole units or sight words. The goal of the TOWRE is to quantify an individual's level of skill with regard to word identification. Research shows that this is critical for ultimate reading success.

The test consists of two subtests, each with alternate forms. The Sight Word Efficiency (SWE) subtest assesses the number of real printed words that can be identified accurately within 45 seconds. There is a total of 104 words in subtest one; however, not all testees will finish the list within the allotted time. The Phonetic Decoding Efficiency (PDE) subtest measures the number of printed nonwords that can be pronounced accurately within 45 seconds. This test has 63 nonwords. When only one test form is given, the test should take about 5 minutes, including directions and practice items. Implementing both forms can take between 7 and 8 minutes to complete.

Forms A and B for both subtests are of equal difficulty. The tester first administers the practice items to the individual. If both forms are given, directions may be omitted for the second form. After the practice items are completed, test takers are asked to read the list of words or nonwords printed on the card as quickly as possible. If they cannot read a word, they may skip it and go to the next word. They must stop reading after 45 seconds. Each test taker starts at the first word regardless of age. There are no basals or ceilings for this test.

Test descriptions and history, testing and scoring procedures, standardizations, and statistics can be found in the examiner's manual. Normative tables used for scoring purposes can be found in the appendix of the examiner's manual. Test responses and scores are recorded on profile or examiner record booklets that are included with the test (separate forms for Form A and Form B).

Standardization data for the TOWRE were collected from fall 1997 to spring 1998. The sample consisted of 1,507 individuals from 30 states. The sample was not a complete representation of the current population at the time. The geographic distribution of adults was uneven, there was a lack of representation of Native Americans for children and adults, and the Hispanic population was underrepresented for the school-age child.

The alternate-form reliability coefficients computed from standard scores for the TOWRE (total word reading) ranged from .94 to .98. The alternate-form reliability for subtest one ranged from .86 to .97 and from .91 to .97 for subtest two. Test-retest reliability among all forms and age groups for the TOWRE ranged from .82 to .97. Concurrent validity was examined by looking at the correlations between the TOWRE and other reading tests. The correlation between the phonemic decoding efficiency subtest and the work attack subtest of the Woodcock Reading Mastery Tests–Revised (WRMT-R) was .85, and the correlation between sight word efficiency subtest and the word identification subtest of the WRMT-R was .89.

Predictive validity was examined by looking at the correlations between the TOWRE and the Gray Oral Reading Tests–Third Edition (GORT). The correlation between the sight word efficiency subtest and the GORT ranged from .75 to .87, and the correlation between the phonemic decoding efficiency subtest and the GORT ranged from .47 to .68. These correlations show that the TOWRE can be a strong predictor of reading ability. Its predictive validity is much higher than that of the WRMT-R.

The TOWRE appears to be a reliable and valid test of word-reading efficiency. The easy administration and short testing time also add to its appeal. However, this test was not normed using the Native American population or using an accurate representation of Hispanic children. This should be taken into consideration when choosing this testing tool.

REFERENCE

Rashotte, C. A., Torgesen, J. K., & Wagner, R. K. (1999). *Examiner's manual for the Test of Word Reading Efficiency*. Austin, TX: PRO-ED.

RON DUMONT
Fairleigh Dickinson University

JOHN O. WILLIS
Rivier College

TEST OF WRITTEN LANGUAGE–THIRD EDITION

The Test of Written Language–Third Edition (TOWL-3; Hammill & Larsen, 1996) was designed to (1) identify students who perform significantly more poorly than their peers in writing and who as a result need special help, (2) determine a student's particular strengths and weaknesses in various writing abilities, (3) document a student's progress in a special writing program, and (4) conduct research in writing.

The TOWL-3 contains eight subtests (with two equivalent forms, A and B) that measure a student's writing competence through both essay-analysis (spontaneous) formats and traditional test (contrived) formats. The TOWL-3 is untimed. Using a pictorial prompt, the student writes a passage that is scored on Contextual Conventions (capitalization, punctuation, and spelling), Contextual Language (vocabulary, syntax, and grammar), and Story Construction (plot, character development, and general composition). The contrived subtests (Vocabulary, Spelling, Style, Logical Sentences, and Sentence Combining) measure word usage, ability to form letters into words, punctuation, capitalization, ability to write conceptually sound sentences, and syntax. Composite quotients are available for overall writing, contrived writing, and spontaneous writing.

The TOWL-3 was standardized on a 26-state sample of more than 2,000 public- and private-school students in grades 2 through 12. These students have the same characteristics as those reported in the 1990 *Statistical Abstract of the United States*. The normative sample is stratified and representative relative to gender, residence, region, disabling condition, and income and education of parents.

Composite quotients are available for overall writing, contrived writing, and spontaneous writing. Percentiles, standard scores, and age and grade equivalents are provided. Internal consistency, test-retest with equivalent forms, and interscorer reliability coefficients approximate .80 at most ages, and many are in the .90s. The validity of the TOWL-3 was investigated, and relevant studies are described in the manual, which has a section that provides suggestions for assessing written language informally and that gives numerous ideas for teachers to use when reme-

diating writing deficits. In addition, the TOWL-3 is shown to be unbiased relative to gender and race and can be administered to individuals or small groups. Because two equivalent forms (A and B) are available, examiners can evaluate student growth in writing using pretesting and posttesting that is not contaminated by memory.

As a diagnostic and formative evaluation tool, it is most useful in identifying students who are performing substantially below their peers. The TOWL-3 contains a strong conceptual model of writing and good evidence of validity and subtest reliability, although it may be "too difficult for younger students (7- and 8-year-olds)." Scoring and interpretation procedures are also a bit complex and time consuming.

REFERENCES

Bucy, J. E., & Swerdlik, M. E. (1998). Review of the Test of Written Language–Third Edition. In J. C. Impara & B. S. Plake (Eds.), *The thirteenth mental measurements yearbook* (pp. 1031–1032). Lincoln, NE: Buros Institute of Mental Measurements.

Geist, E. A., & Boydston, R. C. (2002). The effect of using written retelling as a teaching strategy on students' performance on the TOWL-2. *Journal of Instructional Psychology, 29,* 108–118.

Hammill, D., Torgesen, J. K., & Wagner, R. K. (1996). Test of Written Language–Third edition. Austin: PRO-ED.

Hansen, J. B. (1998). Review of the Test of Written Language–Third edition. In J. C. Impara & B. S. Plake (Eds.), *The thirteenth mental measurements yearbook* (pp. 1070–1072). Lincoln, NE: Buros Institute of Mental Measurements.

RON DUMONT
Fairleigh Dickinson University

JOHN O. WILLIS
Rivier College

TESTS IN PRINT

Tests in Print (Buros, 1961, 1974; Mitchell, 1983; Murphy, Conoley, & Impara, 1994) are volumes that provide a comprehensive index of commercially available educational and psychological tests in English-speaking countries. The volumes contain descriptive information about each test (e.g., the age or grade levels for which the test is designed, author, publishing company, scale scores); literature related to the specific test; an index to all reviews of the test in previous Buros *Mental Measurement Yearbooks;* and references to test descriptions and related literature cited in previous *Test in Print* volumes.

The most current, *Tests in Print IV* (Murphy et al., 1994), contains thousands of descriptions of commercially available tests; references for specific tests; an alphabetical listing of test names, a directory of publishers with addresses, and an index to their tests; a title index showing both in print and out-of-print tests since previous listings; a name index for test authors, reviewers, and authors of references; and a classified subject index for quickly locating tests in particular areas.

REFERENCES

Buros, O. K. (1961). *Tests in print.* Highland Park, NJ: Gryphon.

Buros, O. K. (1974). *Tests in print II.* Highland Park, NJ: Gryphon.

Mitchell, J. V., Jr. (1983). *Tests in print III.* Lincoln, NE: Buros Institute of Mental Measurements.

Murphy, L. L., Conoley, J. C., Impara, J. C. (1994). *Tests in print IV.* Lincoln, NE: Buros Institute of Mental Measurements.

JANE CLOSE CONOLEY
University of Nebraska
First edition

ELIZABETH O. LICHTENBERGER
The Salk Institute
Second edition

BUROS MENTAL MEASUREMENTS YEARBOOK

TEST-TAKING BEHAVIOR

Psychoeducational testing is invaluable for identifying a student's strengths, limitations, and those conditions under which he or she learns best. The results of testing assist in describing behaviors, making diagnoses, estimating prognoses, assisting in intervention planning and evaluation, and in other ways. A student's behavior during testing often affects the quality of the test results. Thus, observations as to whether a student is cooperative, talkative, attentive, or interested and motivated are important because his or her test behavior affects the validity of the test data and can have important personal consequences. Several behavior qualities that can influence student performance have been identified (Oakland, Glutting, & Watkins, 2005).

Examiners should provide a comfortable, distraction-free testing environment to promote examinee attention and concentration. Receptive language qualities such as listening and expressive language skills, including oral expression, are important because modifications in test use may be necessary when a child exhibits language deficits or is not fluent in English. Examiners must be aware of physical and motor qualities that may adversely impact test performance. A child's gross muscle control impacts the assessment of adaptive behavior, and fine motor control is important for writing and other test items requiring physical manipulations. Good rapport between the examiner and child is important for establishing trust, cooperation, and promoting more valid results. The examiner should smile frequently, talk with the child before testing, and reinforce the child's efforts. A child's personal readiness for being tested includes sufficient rest, adequate food, alertness, attention, and concentration. A child's motivation to engage in and sustain testing activity over time is important for ensuring personal readiness and maintaining good rapport. A child's temperament (e.g., extroversion or introversion) and learning styles also may impact test performance. These and other factors should be considered when assessing test behavior and judging the quality and validity of testing results.

Although informal observations during testing are important, formal rating scales may be more useful for assessing a student's test session behaviors and test performance. International research results show that among young children aged at least 3.5 years in Finland, refusal to test was associated with compromised neuropsychological and linguistic test scores. Test refusal is thought to reflect a child's underlying skills deficits and attempts to avoid failure rather than the display of noncompliant or oppositional behavior (Mäntynen, Poikkeus, Abonen, Aro, & Korkman, 2001). Other international results show that among 10- to 12-year-old Turkish children, test session behaviors indicating avoidance, inattentiveness, and uncooperativeness were associated with test performances on the Wechsler Intelligence Scale for Children–Revised (Oakland, Gulek, & Glutting, 1996).

Freedom from distractibility and processing speed scores from the Wechsler Intelligence Scales for Children–Third Edition are not lower for children who display inappropriate test-taking behaviors (Oakland, Broom, & Glutting, 2000). Thus, examiners are not advised to rely on test score profiles from intelligence tests when judging test-taking behaviors. Children with Attention-Deficit/Hyperactivity Disorder compared to matched controls tend to display more inattentive, avoidant, and uncooperative behaviors, thus depressing the magnitude of children's IQs (Glutting, Robins, & de Lancey, 1997). An understanding of test session behaviors allows an examiner to decide whether testing results accurately reflect a child's cognitive abilities. This information helps educational professionals identify important qualities not measured by the test, understand thought processes used in a child's responses, discuss the child's qualities with teachers and parents, and make necessary interventions and modifications in the type and intensity of instruction.

REFERENCES

Glutting, J. J., Robins, P. M., de Lancey, E. (1997). Discriminant validity of test observations for children with attention deficit/hyperactivity. *Journal of School Psychology, 35,* 391–401.

Mäntynen, H., Poikkeus, A., Abonen, T., Aro, T., & Korkman, M. (2001). Clinical significance of test refusal among young children. *Child Neuropsychology, 7,* 241–250.

Oakland, T., Broom, J., & Glutting, J. (2000). Use of freedom from distractibility and processing speed to assess children's test-taking behaviors. *Journal of School Psychology, 38,* 469–475.

Oakland, T., Glutting, J., & Watkins, M. W. (2005). Assessment of test behaviors with the WISC-IV. In A. Profitera, D. H. Saklofske, & L. G. Weiss (Eds.), *WISC-IV clinical use and interpretation: Scientist practitioner perspectives* (pp. 435–463). San Diego, CA: Elsevier Academic Press.

Oakland, T., Gulek, C., & Glutting, J. (1996). Children's test-taking behaviors: A review of literature, case study, and research on Turkish children. *European Journal of Psychological Assessment, 12,* 240–246.

JEFFREY DITTERLINE
University of Florida

TEST ANXIETY

TEST-TEACH-TEST PARADIGM

The Test-Teach-Test Paradigm (TTT-P) is representative of an instructional concept that is similar to the concept of teaching students how to read by using the phonics approach. To conceptualize the TTT-P, we need to review some other terms: direct instruction, model-lead and test, criterion assessment, criterion instruction, and appropriate practice.

Fundamentally, the TTT-P represents an instructional sequence. The portrayal that follows (Nash, 1985) is an adaptation of the instructional sequencing suggested by Bateman (1971) and Engelmann and Bruner (1969). In the course of this portrayal, some of the other terms referred to above will be employed. The instructional concept and postures of both Bateman and Engelmann are regarded by many as representing a kind of pioneering methodology of the 1970s that distinguished special educational instruction from regular education.

A. *The initial testing part of the TTT-P*

   In a reading test with beginning second-grade students, all of the students misread the word *blew.*

B. *The teaching part of the TTT-P*

   1. The teacher begins by saying, "We are going to learn to read the word *blew* by use of sounds using a simultaneous multisensory instructional procedure."

   2. Next, the teacher directs the students to copy down the word that has been written out on the blackboard in front of the students.

   3. Then the teacher models for the students what it is that they are to do.

      a. The teacher states that this word has three sounds. The teacher says the sounds, /b/, /l/, and /ew/, and simultaneously underlines each of them while doing so, *b l ew.*

      b. Next, the teacher, using a lead, says, "We, all of us, will now individually underline the three sounds that this word has—simultaneously saying the sound of the letter or letters as we do so." The teacher and the students all together and in an audible voice do so, *b l ew.*

      c. The teacher, using an intervening test, says, "Your turn—reunderline each sound saying each sound out loud as you do so." The students do so, *b l ew.*

      d. Next, the teacher, using another model, says, "I will now loop and say in an audible voice the sounds in this word, *b l ew.*"

      e. Then, using another lead, the teacher says, "We will now all together loop and say the sounds in this word." Students and teacher do so, *b l ew.*

      f. Next, the teacher, using another intervening test, says, "Your turn, now all by yourself you loop and say out loud the sounds in this word." The students do so, *b l ew.*

      g. The teacher, using another lead, says, "We will now underline and say the word rapidly." The teacher and the students do so, *b l ew.*

      h. Then the teacher, using another intervening test, says, "Your turn—now all by yourself, you are to underline and say the word rapidly." The students do so, *b l ew.*

      i. Last, the teacher says, "All of you have just read the word *blew* correctly."

C. *The test part of the TTT-P*

   This last phase of step in the TTT-P is the simplest part to do and can be attended to in a number of ways. Using our example word, a teacher could offer repeated appropriate practice experiences in reading this particular word.

   The process of the TTT paradigm as exemplified can be replicated across any and all instruction, be it initial or advanced, and across any and all tasks, with spelling as one of the more obvious ones. In the course of doing so, the teacher will automatically be involved with these initial concepts (Nash, 1986):

   1. Direct instruction: The precise identification of what the student is to learn and how he or she is going to do so.

   2. Model-lead-and test: While carrying out any given bit of instruction, the teacher can model what the student is to do and simultaneously follows this with a lead (i.e., doing the task with the student). At this point, the teacher can employ a simple test of what it is that the student knows.

   3. Criterion assessment (CA): Both of the test parts of the TTT-P are examples of CA. The first part

tests what it is the teacher is to teach if the student fails the test; the second test of the TTT-P is simply a reaffirmation and check on what the teacher intended to teach.

4. Criterion instruction (CI): The teaching part of the TTT-P represents CI because there is an intended 1:1 correlation between the first test and the subsequent needed instruction.

5. Appropriate practice. In the execution of the instruction associated with the TTT-P, the teacher will be implementing the model-lead-test concept automatically and involving the student in the necessary practice.

Instruction that implements the concepts reviewed is instruction that guarantees student success. These patterns can be repeated as often as student errors dictate.

REFERENCES

Bateman, B. D. (1971). *The essentials of teaching.* Sioux Falls, SD: Adapt.

Engelmann, S., & Brunder, E. (1969). *Distar reading.* Chicago: Science Research.

Nash, R. T. (1985). Remediation courses. Project Success, University of Wisconsin-Oshkosh. Unpublished raw data.

Nash, R. T. (1986). *Manual for remediating the reading and spelling deficits of elementary, secondary and post-secondary students.* Flossmoor, IL: Language Prescriptions.

ROBERT T. NASH
University of Wisconsin at Oshkosh

DIAGNOSTIC-PRESCRIPTIVE TEACHING

TEXT-TO-SPEECH

Text-to-speech refers to a media format generated by a hardware or software system that will render digital textual information (such as text contained in a word processing document or web page) into audio format using a speech synthesis program. Most text-to-speech systems work in conjunction with personal computers. Prior to the advent of internal soundcards on computers, text-to-speech was accomplished by using hardware-based external speech synthesis devices. Such devices have fallen out of favor as increasingly capable and powerful soundcards have become standard equipment on most personal computers. With the exception of specialized text-to-speech devices, such as embedded text-to-speech on Braille embossers, refreshable Braille, and note taking devices, most text-to-speech is accomplished using software programs.

Text-to-speech is a media format rather than a specific technology. As such, there are multiple applications. In the disability realm, text-to-speech is commonly used by people with visual and cognitive impairments. For people with visual impairments, software technologies such as screen magnification programs and screen readers frequently combine text-to-speech with other media formats such as screen magnification and refreshable Braille displays to produce a powerful multi-modal presentation of information. In the area of learning disabilities, text-to-speech is frequently combined with other software utilities such as word prediction, homophone identification, audible spell checking, and sometimes voice recognition to produce a formidable composition suite.

Closely related to text-to-speech technology are scanning and optical character recognition (OCR) technologies. Since text-to-speech can only be rendered from digital textual information, scanners and OCR programs can be used to convert printed documents into digital ones. The documents can then be "read" by text-to-speech technology.

The quality of text-to-speech has increased dramatically in recent years. In 2004, AT&T developed a set of high-quality consumer text-to-speech fonts termed AT&T Natural Voice fonts (AT&T, 2005). These 16-bit fonts are compatible with both Microsoft and Macintosh speech operating system interfaces. Commercial examples of text-to-speech are routinely used in voice automation systems like technical and customer support. For example, text-to-speech technology can be used to present a menu to the user while voice recognition technology may be used to navigate the menu.

REFERENCE

AT&T. (2005). *AT&T Natural Voices.* Retrieved October 12, 2005, from http://www.naturalvoices.att.com/

DAVID SWEENEY
Texas A&M University

COMPUTER USE WITH STUDENTS WITH DISABILITIES
TECHNOLOGY FOR INDIVIDUALS WITH DISABILITIES

THALIDOMIDE

Thalidomide was among the first drugs for which teratogenicity was established. A teratogen is a chemical agent that can cross the placenta and cause congenital malformations. Effective as a sedative and a tranquilizer, thalidomide is an example of a teratogen that had positive effects on the mother but devastating consequences for the embryo. Even after decades of study, the mechanism by which thalidomide causes deformities is not understood (T. J., 1999).

Teratogenicity became suspected with the birth of a relatively large number of babies with phocomelia (seal-flipper limbs) and a variety of other deformities in Europe in the late 1950s and early 1960s. Phocomelia is a condition in which arms and/or legs are drastically shortened or absent and fingers/toes extend from the foreshortened limbs or the trunk. Thalidomide was widely distributed in Europe, where it is estimated to have affected over 7,000 individuals. It was withdrawn from the market in late 1961 before it passed Food and Drug Administration approval in the United States (Moore, 1982). Teratogenicity was unusually high; over 90 percent of women who took thalidomide during a particular period in pregnancy had infants with some type of defect (Holmes, 1983).

Thalidomide is the only drug whose timing of harmful effects has been well-established, causing defects only if taken by the mother when the embryo was 34 to 50 days old; earlier or later consumption had no adverse effects (Holmes, 1983). Individual defects can be traced to particular days when the mother took the drug. The specificity of the embryo's age for thalidomide effects provides a particularly dramatic example for a critical period.

The particular complex of effects is sometimes termed the thalidomide syndrome (Landau, 1986). Phocomelia is the most common and pronounced sign, but absent or deformed ears and digits are common, and malformations of forehead, heart, and digestive system occasionally occur. Generally, overall intelligence is unaffected, but some language deficits have been reported (Holmes, 1983; Landau, 1986; Moore, 1982). Because thalidomide has teratogenic but not mutagenic qualities, thalidomide-syndrome individuals would be expected to have normal children.

Despite the horrific consequences of prenatal exposure to thalidomide, research on its potential benefits began again shortly after it was withdrawn from the market. In 1964, thalidomide was given to a patient with leprosy because of evidence of the drug's antiinflammatory benefits; within days the patient's symptoms subsided and stayed reduced with continued use of thalidomide (Blakeslee, 1998). It has received FDA approval for use in treatment of leprosy, and may be of benefit in treatment of a number of other diseases, including brain and other forms of cancer, inflammatory disease, and autoimmune disorders. Thalidomide is now being used experimentally with AIDS, and appears to relieve symptoms such as oral ulcers and severe weight loss. Some research suggests that thalidomide may inhibit HIV replication (Blaney, 1995). Thalidomide has been said to be nontoxic among those taking the drug; researchers have yet to find a lethal dose (Blakeslee, 1998).

However beneficial, thalidomide remains a major human teratogen and therefore its use must be carefully monitored in order to avoid any recurrence of the severe malformations seen in children whose mothers were some of thalidomide's first users.

REFERENCES

Blakeslee, D. (1998). Thalidomide. *Journal of the American Medical Association* [HIV/AIDS Information Center]. Retrieved November 15, 1998, from http://www.ama-assn.org/special.hiv .newsline.briefing.thalido.htm

Blaney, C. (1995). Second thoughts about thalidomide. *Medical Sciences Bulletin.* Retrieved from http://pharminfo.com/pubs .msb/thalidomide.html

Holmes, L. B. (1983). Congenital malformations. In R. E. Behrman & V. C. Vaughn (Eds.), *Nelson textbook of pediatrics* (12th ed.) Philadelphia: Saunders.

Landau, S. I. (1986). *International dictionary of medicine and biology.* New York: Wiley.

Moore, K. L. (1982). *The developing human* (3rd ed.). Philadelphia: Saunders.

T. J. (1999, Feb 20). Theorizing about the dark side of thalidomide. *Science News, 155*(8), 124–125.

ROBERT T. BROWN
AIMEE R. HUNTER
University of North Carolina at Wilmington

EARLY EXPERIENCE AND CRITICAL PERIODS
ETIOLOGY
TERATOGENS

THEIR WORLD

Their World is the annual publication of the Foundation for Children with Learning Disabilities (FCLD). The FCLD was founded in 1977 and began publication of *Their World* in 1979. The publication is presented each year at FCLD's annual benefit in New York City. *Their World* is a public awareness vehicle, intended to educate the public about learning disabilities generally while emphasizing the accomplishments of the learning disabled. *Their World* publishes real-life stories about the way families cope with learning-disabled children. *Their World* supports after school, summer, athletic, and creativity programs as a support network for the learning disabled and their families. The publication is distributed to over 75,000 parents, educators, legislators, and professionals each year.

CECIL R. REYNOLDS
Texas A&M University

FOUNDATION FOR CHILDREN WITH LEARNING DISABILITIES

THEMATIC APPERCEPTION TEST

The Thematic Apperception Test (TAT) is a projective assessment instrument developed by Henry Murray (1938) as a means of investigating his theory of personality. Designed for use with subjects ages 7 and older, TAT has become one of the most widely used assessment techniques. The test materials consist of 31 black and white pictures depicting characters in various settings. Each picture is designed to elicit particular themes or conflicts. Subsets of pictures (typically 8 to 10) are selected for administration depending on the individual's age and sex and the nature of the presenting problem. Subjects are asked to tell a story about each picture as it is presented. Typical instructions stress that subjects use their imagination and include in their response a description of what the characters in the scene are doing, thinking, and feeling, the preceding events, and the outcome. Responses are recorded verbatim by the examiner. An inquiry is usually conducted after all pictures have been presented.

The TAT has also been presented in group form; this requires the subject to provide written responses. Murray and others (Groth-Marnat, 1984) have devised scoring systems for TAT; however, in clinical practice, such systems are rarely used (Klopfer & Taulbee, 1976). Variations on the TAT include the Children's Apperception Test and the Senior Apperception Test (Bellack, 1975), which include stimulus materials believed to be more relevant to children and the elderly, respectively.

REFERENCES

Bellack, L. (1975). *The TAT, CAT and SAT in clinical use* (3rd ed.). New York: Grune & Stratton.

Groth-Marnat, G. (1984). *Handbook of psychological assessment.* New York: Van Nostrand Reinhold.

Klopfer, W. G., & Taulbee, E. S. (1976). Projective tests. In M. R. Rosenzweig & L. W. Porter (Eds.), *Annual review of psychology, 17,* 543–567.

Murray, H. A. (1938). *Explorations in personality.* New York: Oxford University Press.

ROBERT G. BRUBAKER
Eastern Kentucky University

EMOTIONAL DISORDERS
PERSONALITY ASSESSMENT

THEORY OF ACTIVITY

The theory of activity is a general theoretical paradigm for psychological and developmental research that has its historical roots in work carried out in the Soviet Union between 1925 and 1945 by L. S. Vygotsky, A. R. Luria, A. N. Leont'ev, and their colleagues (Leont'ev 1978, 1981; Minick, 1985; Wertsch, 1981, 1985). Activity theory is among the most important intellectual forces in contemporary Soviet

psychology, providing a unifying conceptual framework for a wide range of psychological theory, research, and practice. As a consequence of linguistic, political, and conceptual barriers, however, it was only in the late 1970s that psychologists and social scientists in Western Europe and the United States began to become aware of activity theory.

The theory of activity is the product of an effort by Vygotsky's students and colleagues to extend the theoretical framework Vygotsky had developed between 1925 and his death in 1934. Vygotsky had been concerned with two fundamental limitations in the psychological theories of his time. First, he felt that many psychologists had underestimated or misrepresented the influence of social and cultural factors on human psychological development. He was particularly concerned with the failure to clarify the mechanisms of this influence. Second, Vygotsky felt that the disputes between the traditional psychology of mind and the behaviorist theories that were emerging in the 1920s reflected a widespread tendency in psychology and philosophy to represent mind and behavior in conceptual isolation from one another rather than as connected aspects of an integral whole (Davydov & Radzikhovskii, 1985; Minick, 1987). Vygotsky's work and the subsequent emergence of activity theory were attempts to develop a theoretical paradigm that would overcome these limitations in existing theory.

A central premise of the theory of activity is that human psychological development is dependent on a process in which the individual is drawn into the historically developed systems of social action that constitute both society and the life of the mature adult. Within this framework, psychological development or change is dependent on the individual's progressively more complete participation in social life. Modes of organizing and mediating cognitive activity are mastered and the relationship to the external world of objects and people is defined in this process.

Three additional characteristics of activity theory are also extremely important to any effort to understand it. First, the concepts, constructs, and laws that provide the basic content of psychological theory developed within this framework and that determine how psychological characteristics and their development are conceptualized are represented and defined in such a way that a connection is consistently maintained between psychological characteristics and the organization of social action (Minick, 1985). For example, Leont'ev (1978) defines personality as a system of hierarchically related goals and motives that derives its structure from (1) the objective relationships among the actions that constitute the social system; (2) the objective relationships among the actions that constitute the life of the individual; and (3) the subjective relationships among these actions that are defined by the individual's values and beliefs. With this approach to the definition of scientific constructs in psychology, it becomes impossible to conceptualize the psychological characteristics of the individual or the laws of psychological functioning and development apart from the organization of concrete social systems and the individual's place in them (Minick, 1985). This can be contrasted with theoretical frameworks in which key constructs are defined in ways that conceptually isolate the psychological (e.g., reversible operations, traits, or associative networks) and the social (e.g., social roles, social norms, social organization).

Second, the goal-oriented action serves as the central analytic object in activity theory (Davydov & Radzikhovskii, 1985; Leont'ev, 1978; Zinchenko, 1985). To analyze psychological characteristics and psychological processes in connection with socially organized action systems, one has to identify an appropriate analytic unit for the development of theory and research. As a basic unit both of the psychological life of the individual and of the organization of society, the goal-oriented action has assumed this role in activity theory.

Third, the theory of activity is based on a schema that emphasizes the importance of considering three levels of analysis in studying the goal-oriented action and the psychological processes that function and develop in connection with it (Leont'ev, 1978). At the level of activities, general yet socially and culturally defined motives are considered. For example, there are important differences in the organization of actions and goals in western systems of formal schooling and in more traditional apprenticeship systems. In formal schooling, education and learning are the motives that provide the general organizing framework for concrete goal-oriented actions. In apprenticeship, these motives are subordinated to the economic motives connected with the production of products for use or sale. At the level of operations, the impact of the object world on the way an action is carried out is considered. Under different conditions, a single set of motives may lead to the emergence of different concrete goals or to different ways of performing actions in order to realize those goals. This system of analytic levels (i.e., activity-motive, action-goal, and operation-condition) has provided activity theory with a useful framework for analyzing psychological functioning and development without losing sight of its connections with the physical and social environment in which it occurs.

As a general perspective on psychology and psychological development, the theory of activity has had an important impact on theory and practice in the broad domain of special education in the Soviet Union. While a detailed discussion of the nature of this impact is impossible in this context, a useful illustration is available in the English translation of a volume by Alexander Meshcheryakov in which he reviews his work with deaf and blind children (Meshcheryakov, 1979).

REFERENCES

Davydov, V. V., & Radzikhovskii, L. A. (1985). Vygotsky's theory and the activity-oriented approach in psychology. In J. V. Wertsch (Ed.), *Culture, communication, and cognition: Vygotskian perspectives* (pp. 35–65). New York: Cambridge University Press.

Leont'ev, A. N. (1978). *Activity, consciousness, and personality.* Englewood Cliffs, NJ: Prentice Hall.

Leont'ev, A. N. (1981). *Problems of the development of mind.* Moscow: Progress Publishers.

Meshcheryakov, A. N. (1979). *Awakening to life: Forming behavior and the mind in deaf-blind children.* Moscow: Progress Publishers.

Minick, N. (1985). *L. S. Vygotsky and Soviety activity theory: New perspectives on the relationship between mind and society.* Unpublished doctoral dissertation, Northwestern University, Evanston, IL.

Minick, N. (1987). *The development of Vygotsky's thought. Introduction to L. S. Vygotsky, Collected works: Problems of general psychology* (Vol. 1). New York: Plenum.

Vygotsky, L. S. (1987). Thinking and speech. In V. V. Davydov (Ed.), *L. S. Vygotsky, Collected works: General Psychology Vol. 1* (N. Minick Trans.). New York: Springer.

Wertsch, J. V. (Ed.). (1981). *The concept of activity in Soviet psychology.* New York: Sharpe.

Wertsch, J. V. (1985). *Vygotsky and the social formation of mind.* Cambridge, MA: Harvard University Press.

Zinchenko, V. P. (1985). Vygotsky's ideas about units for the analysis of mind. In J. V. Wertsch (Ed.), *Culture, communication, and cognition: Vygotskian perspectives* (pp. 94–118). New York: Cambridge University Press.

NORRIS MINICK
Center for Psychosocial Studies,
The Spencer Foundation

VGOTSKY, LEV S.
ZONE OF PROXIMAL DEVELOPMENT

THERAPEUTIC COMMUNITY

The therapeutic community as a model for psychosocial rehabilitation was developed following World War II by Maxwell Jones, a psychiatrist, in Great Britain. This approach developed out of Jones's experience in working with soldiers on a psychiatric unit who had suffered emotional trauma and with persons with personality problems. Jones's approach was a reaction to the traditional psychiatric hospital practice that produced dependent patients who needed resocialization in addition to treatment of their illness if they were to be discharged. He believed the hospital could be purposefully employed as a significant therapeutic milieu by facilitating full social participation by the patients (Main, 1946). Providing appropriately organized social environments, rather than just psychotherapeutic or medical approaches, was the method of effecting change in patients. Jones's work was significant for the development of social psychiatry, in which emphasis is placed on the environmental sources of stress that cause persons to learn maladaptive ways of coping rather than on illness or deviancy, the traditional psychiatric emphases.

Jones initially presented the principles and practices of the therapeutic community in *Social Psychiatry: A Study of Therapeutic Communities* (1952), but the book was limited in detail. A clearer explication of the underlying themes that guided and shaped the social interactions in the therapeutic community was provided by R. N. Rapoport, an anthropologist, in *Community as Doctor* (1960). Themes identified by Rapoport were those of (1) democratization—an equal sharing among community members of the power in decision making about community affairs; (2) permissiveness—the toleration of a wide degree of behavior from members of the community; (3) communalism—the free exchange of information and observations among all members of the community, including patients and staff; and (4) reality confrontation—the continuous presentation to the patients of interpretations of their behavior from the perspective of other members of the therapeutic community.

The principal social methods used in the therapeutic community were the discussion of events that occurred within the context of frequent community group meetings by all community members; the facilitation of exchange of information among members of the community; the development of relationships between staff and clients that emphasized their status as peers in learning through interacting with each other; the provision of frequent situations in which patients could learn more adaptive ways to cope with problematic situations by interacting with community members; and the continued examination by community members, especially staff members, of their roles to find more effective ways of functioning.

The ideology of the therapeutic community was never completely operationalized, and some found it extremely difficult to implement (Manning, 1975). Rapoport (1960) offered reasons for the difficulty in implementing Jones's ideology and explanations of why later therapeutic movements used many but not all of the principles. First, there were limits set by the local community on the extremes in democracy or permissiveness that would be tolerated; second, communalism encouraged communication in groups rather than between individuals; third, conflicts arose between ideological themes such as when excessively dominant behavior is permissively tolerated but might be anti-democratic; and fourth, there was an unresolved conflict between the rehabilitation goals that required the hospital to approximate the conditions of life outside the hospital and the treatment goals that required different conditions for the recovery of the patient than those in which the problems developed. About the same time that development of therapeutic communities was taking place, psychotropic medications were introduced into psychiatric practice. This resulted in the obscuring of the effects of the therapeutic community as psychotropic medications were often used with persons who were also in therapeutic communities. In addition, no satisfactory study of the efficacy of the therapeutic community as a treatment approach was ever conducted, though it had wide support among mental health clinicians.

The therapeutic community as developed by Jones declined from the period of the late 1950s (Manning, 1975). Other therapeutic community movements have developed that serve persons with drug, alcohol, and social adjustment problems, and persons in correctional settings. These movements have developed some distinctive characteristics in their approach to treatment but have been greatly influenced by the work of Jones.

REFERENCES

Jones, M. (1952). *Social psychiatry: A study of therapeutic communities.* London: Tavistock.

Main, T. F. (1946). The hospital as a therapeutic institution. *Bulletin of the Menniger Clinic, 10,* 66–70.

Manning, N. (1975). What happened to the therapeutic community. In K. Jones & S. Baldwin (Eds.), *The yearbook of social policy in Britain.* London: Routledge & Kegan Paul.

Rapoport, R. N. (1960). *Community as doctor.* London: Tavistock.

HAROLD HANSON
PAUL BATES
Southern Illinois University

COMMUNITY RESIDENTIAL PROGRAMS
PSYCHONEUROTIC DISORDERS
SOCIAL BEHAVIOR OF INDIVIDUALS WITH DISABILITIES

THERAPEUTIC RECREATION

See RECREATION, THERAPEUTIC.

THINK ALOUD

Think Aloud is a cognitive behavior modification program designed to improve social and cognitive problem-solving skills in young children. Based on the pioneering work of Meichenbaum, Goodman, Shure, and Spevak, and tied to theory regarding development of self-control, Think Aloud was conceived as a training program to decrease impulsivity, encourage consideration of alternatives, and plan courses of action. It emphasizes the use of cognitive modeling as a teaching tool in which teachers model their own strategies for thinking through problems. Students are then encouraged to "think out loud" while systematically approaching each problem through asking and answering four basic questions: What is my problem? How can I solve it? Am I following my plan? How did I do?

The original small group (two to four students) program (Camp & Bash, 1985) was tested on 6- to 8-year-old boys identified as hyperaggressive by teachers. In the hands of trained teachers, improvement in cognitive impulsivity was demonstrated across several trials, as was improvement in prosocial classroom behavior. Although significant decreases in aggressive behavior were also observed, this was not significantly more than observed in attention-control groups. A refresher course 6 to 12 months after the original program supported previously developed skills and led to significant decreases in hyperactivity and increases in friendliness.

With some demonstrated success in altering thinking and behavior patterns in aggressive boys in the small group situation, the authors reasoned that a more "dilute" program such as found in a large classroom should benefit a broader range of children with mild to moderate deficits in social and cognitive problem skills. In addition, availability of a classroom version of the program would help regular classroom teachers to support skills learned in the small group program. Consequently, they began in 1976 to build Think Aloud Classroom Programs spanning grades 1 to 6 (Bash & Camp, 1985a, 1985b; Camp & Bash, 1985).

Development and study of these programs was supported in part by ESEA Title IV grants to the Denver public schools. Few of the classroom program studies could be conducted with random assignment to experimental or traditional teaching programs. However, within limitations imposed by a nonequivalent control group design, children in the Think Aloud classrooms improved on measures of both social and cognitive problem-solving skills more than children in nonprogram classrooms at all grade levels. Cognitive differences between children in the Think Aloud classroom programs and comparison children were most reliable for the program for grades 1 and 2 and the program for grades 5 and 6. Differences in social problem-solving skills were reliable at all grade levels. The classroom programs can easily be adapted for use in an individual or tutorial program to intensify and individualize the experience. The materials now provide challenge to children over a broad range of developmental levels, making them suitable for special education classrooms as well as regular classrooms, for some middle school children, and for children with special needs for social skills training or assistance in curbing impulsivity.

REFERENCES

Bash, M. A. S., & Camp, B. W. (1985a). *The Think Aloud Classroom Program for Grades 3 and 4.* Champaign, IL: Research.

Bash, M. A. S., & Camp, B. W. (1985b). *The Think Aloud Classroom Program for Grades 5 and 6.* Champaign, IL: Research.

Camp, B. W., & Bash, M. A. S. (1985). *The Think Aloud Classroom Program for Grades 1 and 2.* Champaign, IL: Research.

STAFF

CAMP, BONNIE
IMPULSE CONTROL

THINKING CENTERS

See CREATIVE STUDIES PROGRAM.

THORAZINE

Thorazine is the trade name for the generic antipsychotic agent chlorpromazine. Though Thorazine was among the first synthesized drugs that were found effective in the control of behavioral symptoms associated with psychotic disorders, it is no longer as widely prescribed as it was 30 years ago. However, Thorazine is still used as a benchmark against which new antipsychotic agents are compared in terms of frequency of side effects and efficacy. Thorazine is of the drug class phenothiazine and tends to produce the classic panorama of side effects associated with the phenothiazine group.

In addition to use as a major tranquilizer with psychotic individuals, Thorazine also is used in emergency situations to limit the effects of LSD and to control prolonged behavioral reactions after intoxication with other hallucinogens. One of the major criticisms of Thorazine as a therapeutic agent has been its reported abuse as a chemical restraint (Leavitt, 1982).

In use with children, several cautions must be considered: children are more likely to show side effects; dose-related attentional problems can develop and thus create interference in learning (Seiden & Dykstra, 1977); and seizures may be potentiated in children with a preexisting seizure disorder (Bassuk & Schoonover, 1977).

REFERENCES

Bassuk, E. L., & Schoonover, S. C. (1977). *The practitioner's guide to psychoactive drugs.* New York: Plenum Medical.

Leavitt, F. (1982). *Drugs and behavior.* New York: Wiley.

Seiden, L. S., & Dykstra, L. A. (1977). *Psychopharmacology: A biochemical and behavioral approach.* New York: Van Nostrand Reinhold.

ROBERT F. SAWICKI
*Lake Erie Institute of
Rehabilitation*

STELAZINE

THORNDIKE, EDWARD L. (1847–1949)

E. L. Thorndike was an early theorist and writer who applied psychology to education. He was educated at Wesleyan, Harvard, and Columbia universities, with most of his professional career spent at Teachers' College, Columbia University. He is best known for his contributions to learning theory (Thorndike, 1905, 1931, 1932, 1935, 1949) and intellectual assessment (Thorndike, 1901, 1926, 1941).

Thorndike's major contribution to learning theory, termed the Law of Effect, is well known as a basic behavioral principle. The Law of Effect states: "any act which in a given situation produces satisfaction becomes associated with that situation, so that when the situation occurs, the act is more likely to recur also" (Thorndike, 1905, p. 203). His theory of connectionism was cognitively oriented, and viewed both physical and mental acts as involving the establishment of neural pathways. Learning was viewed as taking place when pathways were established through repetition.

Thorndike's measurement interests were diverse, as reflected by his famous dictum, "If anything exists, it exists in some amount. If it exists in some amount, it can be measured" (Thorndike, 1926, p. 38). His multifactored approach to measurement viewed intelligence as comprising abstract, mechanical, and social abilities. Intellectual assessment to Thorndike also involved the dimensions of attitude, breadth, and speed (i.e., level of difficulty, number of tasks, and rate of completion, respectively). This multifactored approach was in contrast to the approach of others of his time, who viewed intelligence as a general or unitary factor. Thorndike developed many tests, especially college entrance and achievement tests.

REFERENCES

Thorndike, E. L. (1901). *Notes on child study.* New York: Macmillan.

Thorndike, E. L. (1905). *The elements of psychology.* New York: Seiler.

Thorndike, E. L. (1926). *The measurement of intelligence.* New York: Teacher's College, Columbia University.

Thorndike, E. L. (1931). *Human learning.* New York: Century.

Thorndike, E. L. (1932). *Fundamentals of learning.* New York: Columbia University.

Thorndike, E. L. (1935). *The psychology of wants, interests and attitudes.* New York: Appleton-Century.

Thorndike, E. L. (1940). *Human nature and social order.* New York: Macmillan.

Thorndike, E. L. (1941). Mental abilities. *American Philosophical Society, 84,* 503–513.

Thorndike, E. L. (1949). *Selected writings from a connectionist's psychology.* New York: Appleton-Century-Crofts.

Thorndike, E. L., Bregman, E. O., Cobb, M. V., & Woodyard, E. (1925). *The measurement of intelligence.* New York: Columbia University.

Thorndike, E. L., & Lorge, I. (1944). *The teacher's wordbook of 30,000 words.* New York: Teacher's College, Columbia University.

JOSEPH D. PERRY
Kent State University

MEASUREMENT

THOUGHT DISORDERS

In the diagnosis of a psychiatric illness, it is common to evaluate disturbances in the following areas: consciousness, emotion, motor behavior, perception, memory, intelligence, and thinking (Ginsberg, 1985). Disorders in thinking, although most commonly associated with Schizophrenia, may also occur in paranoid disorders, affective disorders, organic mental disorders, or organic delusional syndromes such as those owed to amphetamine or phencyclide abuse (*Diagnostic and Statistical Manual of Mental Disorders,* fourth edition [*DSM-IV*], 1994). Schizophrenic patients, however, tend to show more severe and specific forms of thought disorders, and may continue to show some degree of idiosyncratic thinking when not in the acute phase of the disease (Ginsberg, 1985). According to *DSM-IV* (1994), at some point, Schizophrenia always involves delusions, hallucinations, or certain disturbances in the form of thought most often expressed by the patient in disorganized speech. A thought disorder is but one of the criteria needed for a diagnosis of Schizophrenia; the illness is also characterized by disorganization in perceptions, communication, emotions, and motor activity. The term thought disorder encompasses a large array of dysfunctions, including disturbances in the form of thought, structure of associations, progression of thought, and content of thought.

Disturbances in Form of Thought

Thinking in a healthy individual occurs in a rational, orderly way. A thought might be stimulated by unconscious or conscious impulses, affective cues, or biological drives, yet the thinking process itself is directed by reason and results in a reality-oriented conclusion. As characterized by Ginsberg (1985), disturbances in the form of thought result in sequences that are no longer logical. In formal thought disorders, thinking is characterized by loosened associations, neologisms, and illogical constructs. In illogical thinking, thinking contains erroneous conclusions or internal contradictions. In dereism, there is mental activity not concordant with logic or experience. In autistic thinking, thinking gratifies unfilled desires but has no regard for reality (p. 500).

Disturbances in Structure and Progression of Associations

In *DSM-IV*, these disturbances are included under the Form of Thought category. However, as described by both Ginsberg (1985) and Kolb (1968), a division of this category is warranted. In a healthy individual, each separate idea is logically linked with ideas both preceding and following that idea. This progression occurs in a coherent fashion and at a relatively steady, moderate rate of speech. In severe cases of disorder, however, speech becomes so disjointed as to be incomprehensible. It then includes:

1. Flight of ideas—an extremely rapid progression of ideas with a shifting from one topic to another so that a coherent whole is not maintained and considerable digression occurs from the beginning to the ending of the story. There is generally some association between thoughts (e.g., a single word in one sentence will lead to a following sentence). Flight of ideas is associated with a lack of goal-directed activity and with heightened distractibility and an accelerated inner drive. A patient might respond to the question, "What is your name?" with, "My name is David. David was in the *Bible* which is a religious document written many years ago. I feel that religion leads to persecution for many important citizens as a result of their beliefs which have been well thought out; however, thought is a very abstract concept as might be noted of music and art."

2. Clang associations—similar to flight of ideas. With clang associations, the stimulus that prompts a new thought is a word similar in sound, but not in meaning, to a new word.

3. Retardation—speech becomes slow and labored; often a lowered tone of voice is used. The patient may relate that his or her thoughts come slowly or that it is very difficult to concentrate or think about a topic.

4. Blocking—an unconscious interruption in the train of thought to such an extent that progression of thought comes to a complete halt. This is usually temporary, with thought processes resuming after a short time.

5. Pressure of speech—an excessive flow of words to such an extent that it becomes difficult to interrupt the speaker.

6. Perseveration—an occurrence in which the patient uses the same word, thought, or idea repeatedly, often in response to several different questions. One patient, when being diagnosed with the Rorschach Inkblot Test, responded to all 10 separate cards, "That looks like a man's genitals. Why are you showing me all these pictures of the same thing?"

7. Circumstantiality—the patient is eventually able to relate a given thought or story, but only after numerous digressions and unnecessary trivial details. This occurs largely in persons who are not able to distinguish essential from nonessential details. It is often observed in persons of low intelligence, in epileptics, and in cases of advanced senile mental disorder.

8. Neologism—when entirely new words are created by the patient.

9. Word salad—an incoherent mixture of words and phrases.

10. Incoherence—similar to word salad, the difference being that incoherence is generally marked by illogically connected phrases or ideas. Word salad generally consists of illogically connected single words or short phrases. A patient speaking incoherently may state, "Yes, this is the great reason for truth and validity as you must know and we all must know in times of need all great men who have an interest in greatness, perhaps, yes, cold is a very nice color, but, not inconsequentially as we have every reason to believe that our President is for better or worse, no, yesterday."

11. Irrelevant answer—an answer that has no direct relevance to the question asked.

12. Derailment—gradual or sudden deviation in one's train of thought without blocking.

Disturbances in Content of Thought

The most common disturbance in the content of thought involves a delusion, which is an idea or system of beliefs that is irrational, illogical, and with little or no basis in fact. In normal, healthy individuals, fantasy, daydreaming, rationalization, or projection can be used as effective ways to handle stress. Delusions appear to be an exaggerated form of this type of thinking. Delusions, however, are indicative of severe psychopathology in that they are patently absurd, and the patient cannot be argued out of his or her beliefs despite overwhelming evidence refuting the delusions. There are several different types of delusions, based on the specific thought content:

1. Delusions of grandeur—belief that an individual is special, important, or in some way superior to others. In many instances the patient may actually believe that he or she is someone else (e.g., God).

2. Delusions of reference—belief that innocent remarks or actions of someone else are directed exclusively at the patient. One hospitalized patient explained that whenever carrots were served at dinner, it meant that she was to take two baths that night; whenever ham

was served, it meant that she was to avoid speaking to anyone until the following day.

3. Delusions of persecution—the belief that others are spying on, plotting against, or in some way planning to harm the patient.

4. Delusions of being controlled—the belief that one's thoughts and actions are imposed by someone else. Similar to this are thought broadcasting (the belief that one's ideas are broadcast to others); thought insertion (the belief that ideas are being inserted into one's head); and thought withdrawal (the belief that ideas are being removed from one's head).

Other less common delusions include self-accusation, sin, guilt, somatic illness, nihilism, religiosity, infidelity, and poverty (*DSM-IV*, 1994; Ginsberg, 1985; Kolb, 1968; MacKinnon & Michels, 1971).

Several theories have been advanced to account for the existence of thought disorders. The more psychogenic of these theories point to inadequate ego functioning, such that the patient creates his or her own reality to cope with overwhelming stress and anxiety. Biological theories view thought disorders as being genetically transmitted. Research in this area has focused on chemical neurotransmitters such as dopamine; it found differing levels of such chemicals in disturbed and healthy individuals. The effectiveness of drug therapy in treating thought disorders lends credence to biological theories. Other theories such as learning, cognitive, and family approaches are more environmentally based, and hold that persons with thought disorders may learn maladaptive ways of thinking or acting in response to live circumstances or unhealthy family situations (Worchel & Shebilske, 1983).

REFERENCES

American Psychiatric Association. (1994). *Diagnostic and statistical manual of mental disorders* (4th ed.). Washington, DC: Author.

Ginsberg, G. (1985). The psychiatric interview. In H. Kaplan & B. Sadock (Eds.), *Comprehensive textbook of psychiatry / IV* (Vol. 1, pp. 500–501). Baltimore: Williams & Wilkins.

Kolb, L. (1968). *Noye's modern clinical psychiatry* (7th ed.). Philadelphia: Saunders.

MacKinnon, R., & Michels, R. (1971). *The psychiatric interview*. Philadelphia: Saunders.

Worchel, S., & Shebilske, W. (1983). *Psychology: Principles and applications*. Englewood Cliffs, NJ: Prentice Hall.

FRANCES F. WORCHEL
Texas A&M University

DIAGNOSTIC AND STATISTICAL MANUAL OF MENTAL DISORDERS (DSM IV) EMOTIONAL DISORDERS

THREE-TIER MODEL

With the current movement to the use of Response to Instruction (RTI) and mandates of No Child Left Behind (NCLB), the three-tier model is a layered instructional based on primary, secondary, and tertiary intervention principles (Good, Kame'enui, Simmons, & Chard, 2002). As an approach to academic goal attainment (i.e., learning to read), the three-tier model applies these levels of intensity to classrooms and student performance in targeted academic skills (Vaughn, 2002; Vaughn, Linan-Thompson, & Hickman, 2003). The primary level, or Tier 1, is comprised of the core instructional program that is provided to all students with the assumption that this program addresses key components of academic skills. For example, in reading, it would be expected that the core instructional program would address phonemic awareness, phonics, fluency, vocabulary, and comprehension. At key points in the instructional process, data-based decision making or assessment occurs. This involves collection of data on all students with results of the assessment used to identify those students who evidence gaps in instructional areas and need to move into Tier 2. Tier 2 involves the provision of secondary or supplementary instruction to address the deficits of students identified with the large-scale assessment, as well as follow-up and monitoring. Tier 2 may include problem-solving teams (comparable to prereferral teams) with the teams providing ongoing support and consultative services to the classroom teacher (e.g., Kovaleski, 2003) or it may involve small group instruction or tutoring (Texas Reading Organization, n.d.). As students are able to meet benchmark criteria, they are discontinued from the supplemental program and return to Tier 1. Those students who still do not reach appropriate benchmarks as a result of interventions at Tier 2 move into Tier 3 for more intensive and individualized assessment and intervention, possibly through special education (Berninger, 2002; Texas Reading Organization, n.d.). The movement through the three tiers is intended to be dynamic with students moving from Tier to Tier as they do or do not meet established benchmarks (Vaughn, 2002; Vaughn & Fuchs, 2003).

With increased emphasis on group application and delivery of instruction (as opposed to an individualized, special education delivery model), implementation of the three-tier model requires significant changes in service delivery at a systems level (Denton & Fletcher, 2003; Shapiro, 2000). Most of the recent research on the three-tier model has been with reading instruction in the primary grades (e.g., Berninger, 2002; Vaughn et al., 2003). Additional research to determine which instructional programs at Tier 1 and Tier 2 are empirically supported or evidence based not only in reading, but in other academic areas is needed. Some work has been done in math (e.g., Fuchs et al., 2005) and in written expression (Berninger, 2002). Further, the research needs to expand beyond primary grades; the change in developmental level of the child and conceptual level of what is required, as well as the changes in contextual demands as students progress from elementary to middle school to high school, require replication of evidence-based instruction at varying levels for differing instructional goals. Finally, research to demonstrate the generalizability of evidence-based instruction across culturally and linguistically diverse groups is needed (e.g., Vaughn, Mathes, Linan-Thompson, & Francis, 2005).

REFERENCES

Berninger, V. (2002). Best practices in reading, writing, and math assessment intervention links: A systems approach for schools, classrooms, and individuals. In A. Thomas & J. Grimes (Eds.), *Best practices in school psychology IV* (pp. 851–865). Bethesda, MD: National Association of School Psychologists.

Denton, C., & Fletcher, J. (2003). Scaling reading interventions. In B. Foorman (Ed.), *Preventing and remediating reading difficulties: Bringing science to scale* (pp. 445–463). Baltimore: York.

Fuchs, L. S., Compton, D. L., Fuchs, D., Paulsen, K., Bryant, J. D., & Hamlett, C. L. (2005). The prevention, identification, and cognitive determinants of math difficulty. *Journal of Educational Psychology, 97,* 493–513.

Good, R. H., Kame'enui, E. J., Simmons, D. S., & Chard, D. J. (2002). *Focus and nature of primary, secondary, and tertiary prevention: The CIRCUITS model* (Tech. Rep. No. 1). Eugene: University of Oregon, College of Education, Institute for the Development of Educational Achievement.

Kovaleski, J. F. (2003, December). *Secondary interventions in a three tier model: Program features and system issues.* Paper presented at the National Research Center on Learning Disabilities Responsiveness-to-Intervention Symposium, Kansas City, MO.

Shapiro, E. (2000). School psychology from an instructional perspective: Solving big, not little problems. *School Psychology Review, 29,* 560–572.

Texas Reading Organization. (n.d.). *Levels of intervention.* Retrieved February 21, 2006, from http://www.texasreading.org/3tier/levels.asp

Vaughn, S. (2002). *A 3-tier model for preventing / reducing reading disabilities.* Retrieved February 21, 2006, from http://www.utsystem.edu/everychild/presentations/SVaughnPDF9-09-02.pdf

Vaughn, S. R., & Fuchs, L. S. (2003). Redefining learning disabilities as inadequate response to instruction: The promise and potential problems. *Learning Disabilities Research & Practice, 18,* 137–146.

Vaughn, S., Linan-Thompson, S., & Hickman, P. (2003). Response to instruction as a means of identifying students with reading/learning disabilities. *Exceptional Children, 69,* 391–409.

Vaughn, S., Mathes, P. G., Linan-Thompson, S., & Francis, D. J. (2005). Teaching English language learners at risk for reading disabilities to read: Putting research into practice. *Learning Disabilities Research & Practice, 20,* 58–67.

Cynthia A. Riccio
Texas A&M University

EMPIRICALLY SUPPORTED TREATMENT
LEARNING DISABILITIES
LEARNING DISABILITIES, PROBLEMS IN DEFINITION OF
RESPONSE TO INSTRUCTION

TICS

Tics are recurrent, rapid, abrupt movements and vocalizations that represent the contraction of small muscle groups in one or more parts of the body. Motor tics may include eye blinking, shoulder shrugging, neck twisting, head shaking, or arm jerking. Vocal tics frequently take the form of grunting, throat clearing, sniffing, snorting, or squealing. These abnormal movements and sounds occur from once every few seconds to several times a day, with varying degrees of intensity. Although tics are involuntary, they often can be controlled briefly. However, temporary suppression results in a feeling of tension that can be relieved only when the tics are allowed to appear. Tics increase with anxiety and stress and diminish with intense concentration (Shapiro & Shapiro, 1981). The prevalence for tic disorders is 1.6 percent or about 3.5 million individuals in the United States. Boys are affected more frequently than girls (Baron, Shapiro, Shapiro, & Ranier, 1981).

The *Diagnostic and Statistical Manual of Mental Disorders,* fourth edition, delineates three major tic disorders that are based on age of onset, types of symptoms, and duration of the condition: transient tic disorder, chronic motor tic disorder, and Tourette syndrome (American Psychiatric Association, 1994). Familial studies suggest that these classifications may not represent distinct disorders but, rather, reflect a continuum of severity of the same disorder (Golden, 1981). The transient tic disorder or "habit spasm" is the mildest and most common of the disorders. Symptoms develop during childhood or adolescence and usually are observed in the face, head, or shoulders. Vocal tics are uncommon. Tic frequency, as well as intensity, generally fluctuates during the course of the disorder. Such childhood tics are transient and benign, disappearing after several months to 1 year.

Symptoms of the chronic motor tic disorder, which appear either in childhood or after the age of 40, are similar to those associated with the transient tic disorder. Vocalizations develop infrequently. When they are present, they tend to be grunts or other noises caused by contractions of the abdomen or diaphragm. The severity, intensity, and type of involuntary movement persist unchanged for years.

Tourette syndrome, the most severe condition, is differentiated from the other tic disorders by the presence of both motor and vocal tics and a pattern of symptoms that waxes and wanes as the tics slowly move from one part of the body to another. Complex movements such as jumping and dancing are often exhibited. Not always present, but confirmatory of Tourette syndrome, are echolalia (repetition of words or phrases spoken by others), palilalia (repetition of one's own words), coprolalia (involuntary swearing), echopraxia (imitation of the movement of others), and copropraxia (obscene gesturing). Although the nature and severity of these symptoms vary over time, the disorder rarely remits spontaneously and usually remains throughout life (Shapiro, Shapiro, Bruun, & Sweet, 1978).

REFERENCES

American Psychiatric Association. (1994). *Diagnostic and statistical manual of mental disorders* (4th ed.). Washington, DC: Author.

Baron, M., Shapiro, A. K., Shapiro, E. S., & Rainer, T. D. (1981). Genetic analysis of Tourette syndrome suggesting major gene effect. *American Journal of Human Genetics, 33,* 767–775.

Golden, G. S. (1981). Gilles de la Tourette's syndrome. *Texas Medicine, 77,* 6–7.

Shapiro, A. K., & Shapiro, E. S. (1981). The treatment and etiology of tics and Tourette syndrome. *Comprehensive Psychiatry, 22,* 193–205.

Shapiro, A. K., Shapiro, E. S., Bruun, R. D., & Sweet, R. D. (1978). *Gilles de la Tourette's syndrome.* New York: Raven.

MARILYN P. DORNBUSH
Atlanta, Georgia

ECHOLALIA
ECHOPRAXIA
TOURETTE SYNDROME

TIME ON TASK

The amount of time that students spend on task has been an issue that concerns teachers in all fields, not just those involved with special education. Squires, Huitt, and Segars (1981) have identified three measures of student involvement that may be used to determine time on task. The first, allocated time, is simply the amount of time that is planned for instruction. Obviously, students will probably not be on task for the entire time that has been allocated. The second measure, which addresses this observation, is known as engagement rate. It is defined as the percent of allocated time that students actually attend to the tasks they are assigned. The third measure, engaged time, is the number of minutes per day students spend working on specific academic or related tasks; it is an integration of allocated time and engagement rate. Stallings and Kaskowitz (1974) found that, given certain maximum time limits based on a child's age and the subject matter at hand, engaged time is the most important variable that is related to student achievement. Given this finding, many researchers have focused on increasing time on task.

As an example, Bryant and Budd (1982) used self-instruction training with three young children who had difficulties in attending to task in kindergarten or preschool. The researchers trained the children to verbalize five separate types of self-instruction: (1) stop and look; (2) ask questions about the task; (3) find the answers to the questions posed in (2); (4) give instructions that provide guidance; and (5) give self-reinforcement for accomplished tasks. The results indicated an increase in on-task behavior for two of the children and, when used in combination with an unintrusive classroom intervention of reminders and stickers, all three of the children exhibited marked increases in their engaged time.

A somewhat different approach to the study of on-task behaviors was undertaken by Whalen et al. (1979), who examined the effects of medication (Ritalin) on the on- and off-task behaviors of children identified as hyperactive. They found clear differences in a maladaptive direction in the behaviors of their subjects who had been diagnosed as hyperactive under placebo conditions when compared with peers who had no diagnoses of hyperactivity. However, while the authors acknowledged that the medication did result in more on-task and prosocial behaviors in many of their subjects, they cautioned against a wholesale reliance on medications since many long-term effects had not yet been studied. Rather, the researchers felt that careful study of all variables in individual situations (e.g., teacher tolerance, cost effectiveness, environmental adaptations) must be undertaken when making treatment decisions.

REFERENCES

Bryant, L. E., & Budd, K. S. (1982). Self-instruction training to increase independent work performance in preschoolers. *Journal of Applied Behavior Analysis, 15,* 259–271.

Squires, D., Huitt, W., & Segars, J. (1981). Improving classrooms and schools: What's important. *Educational Leadership, 39,* 174–179.

Stallings, J. A., & Kaskowitz, D. (1974). *Follow through classroom observation evaluation, 1972–1973.* Menlo Park, CA: Stanford Research Institute.

Whalen, C. K., Henker, B., Collins, B., Finck, D., & Dotemoto, S. (1979). A social ecology of hyperactive boys: Medication effects in structured classroom environments. *Journal of Applied Behavior Analysis, 12,* 65–81.

ANDREW R. BRULLE
Wheaton College

ATTENTION-DEFICIT/HYPERACTIVITY DISORDER
ATTENTION SPAN

TIME-OUT

Time-out has been used in public school settings since the 1970s and has both popular and scientific connotations.

The popular use of this term generally refers to the removal of a student from a situation due to noncompliance, disruption, or other types of problem behavior (Maag, 1999). Time-out is also a specific behavioral strategy, grounded in applied behavior analysis, which is more correctly titled *time-out from positive reinforcement* (Alberto & Troutman, 2006). Cooper, Heron, and Heward (1987) define time-out as "the withdrawal of the opportunity to earn positive reinforcement or the loss of access to positive reinforcers for a specified period of time, contingent upon the occurrence of a behavior; the effect is to reduce the future probability of that behavior" (p. 440). This definition describes a procedure that uses a technique called extinction. Extinction is broadly defined as withholding reinforcement. As noted, the intended effect of this procedure is to decrease a problem behavior. Therefore, time-out falls under the category of a punishment-oriented behavior reduction strategy. However, it is notable that specific aversives are not directly applied; only that positive reinforcement is removed for a designated period of time contingent upon a problem behavior (Sulzer-Azaroff & Mayer, 1991). Educators and psychologists have several options if they choose to use time-out, including removing the reinforcement from the student or removing the student from access to the reinforcement (Zirpoli, 2005). Three time-out procedures that meet this criterion include (1) nonseclusionary time-out, (2) exclusionary time-out, and (3) seclusionary time-out.

Nonseclusionary time-out is a technique where the student's access to specific reinforcers (or all reinforcement) occurs for a specified period of time in the setting where the problem behavior was demonstrated. A benefit of this procedure is that the student can remain in the instructional or target setting instead of being removed due to the problem behavior. Examples of nonseclusionary time-out include (a) asking a student to put his or her head down on his or her desk; (b) removal of materials, teacher attention, or access to the teacher or other adults for a specified period of time; (c) removal from activities, including use of contingent observation where the student is allowed to watch the activity and observe more appropriate responses by peers, but is not allowed to participate; and (d) visual or facial screening for students with more severe problem behavior, such as stereotypy (Alberto & Troutman, 2006).

Exclusionary time-out is a technique where the student is physically removed from an activity or environment that she or he finds reinforcing for a specified period of time (Zirpoli, 2005). Examples of exclusionary time-out include placing a student in the hallway or in a designated time-out area and/or moving a student to a study carrel or corner of the classroom contingent upon a targeted problem behavior (Maag, 1999).

Seclusionary time-out is the most restrictive method employed and involves placing the student in a seclusion or time-out room for a specified period of time. Cooper et al. (1987) write that "a time-out room is any room outside the individual's normal educational or treatment environment that is devoid of positive reinforcers and in which the individual can be safely placed for a temporary period of time" (p. 445). Seclusionary time-out has been used for behaviors such as verbal and physical aggression and property destruction (Alberto & Troutman, 2006).

Zirpoli (2005) writes that time-out can be misused or applied inappropriately, thereby exposing the student to unintended effects or harm. A common misuse of this procedure is when an educator prolongs the time that the student is in time-out by exceeding the actual amount of time that is necessary to reduce the problem behavior. As a general guideline, time in seclusionary time-out should be calculated as one minute for each year of age, not to exceed 12 minutes total (Colorado Department of Education, 2000). Another common misapplication of this procedure occurs when educators fail to recognize that some students engage in problem behavior with the intent to be removed from an instructional activity that they perceive as aversive, thus putting the teacher in a position of inadvertently reinforcing escape-maintained problem behavior. Finally, removal of the student from instructional tasks may negatively affect current and future educational performance, thus underscoring the importance of using proactive and preventative instructional methods before resorting to the use of punishment-oriented strategies.

Educators that use time-out should always adhere to district, state, and national policies, including receiving training for the correct use of time-out procedures and keeping accurate records for each episode that requires a time-out (Maag, 1999). Moreover, every effort should be made to continually evaluate the effect of the time-out procedure on student behavior and to pair the program with reinforcing activities and verbal reinforcement when the student is meeting previously taught academic and behavioral expectations (Zirpoli, 2005). For students with chronic or persistent problem behavior a functional behavioral assessment should be conducted and a behavior intervention plan developed and implemented.

In conclusion, time-out from positive reinforcement is a behavior reduction technique that is used contingent upon an inappropriate behavior. Time-outs are organized under two categories—techniques that remove reinforcement from the student (nonseclusionary time-out) and techniques that remove the student from access to reinforcement (exclusionary and seclusionary time-outs). Educators should always attempt to match the intensity of the time-out procedure with the intensity of the problem behavior. Because time-out is a behavior reduction technique, educators have the added responsibility of ensuring that this procedure serves a legitimate educational function and meets all district, state, and national guidelines (Alberto & Troutman, 2006). In addition, use of any behavior reduction strategy should always be paired with instructionally based strategies that are both proactive and preventative (see School-wide Positive Behavior Support) by explicitly teaching students appropriate replacement responses as part of an ongoing effort to provide a continuum of positive behavioral interventions and supports. For students who have either targeted or intensive/individualized behavior support needs, a functional behavioral assessment and implementation of a behavior intervention plan is recommended (Sugai et al., 2000).

REFERENCES

Alberto, P. A., & Troutman, A. C. (2006). *Applied behavior analysis for teachers* (7th ed.). Upper Saddle River, NJ: Pearson Merrill Prentice Hall.

Colorado Department of Education. (2000). *Guidelines for the use of non-exclusionary and exclusionary time-out with youth 3–21 years old receiving public education services.* Denver: Author. Retrieved October 28, 2005, from http://www.cde.state.co.us/spedlaw/download/TimeOutGuidelines.pdf

Cooper, J. O., Heron, T. E., & Heward, W. L. (1987). *Applied behavior analysis.* New York: Macmillan.

Maag, J. W. (1999). *Behavior management: From theoretical implications to practical applications.* San Diego, CA: Singular.

Sugai, G., Horner, R. H., Dunlap, G. Hieneman, M., Lewis, T. J., Nelson, C. M., et al. (2000). Applying positive behavioral support and functional behavioral assessment in schools. *Journal of Positive Behavioral Interventions, 2,* 131–143.

Sulzer-Azaroff, B., & Mayer, G. R. (1991). *Behavior analysis for lasting change.* Fort Worth, TX: Harcourt Brace College.

Zirpoli, T. J. (2005). *Behavior management: Applications for teachers* (4th ed.). Upper Saddle River, NJ: Pearson Merrill Prentice Hall.

RANDALL L. DE PRY
*University of Colorado at
Colorado Springs*

**BEHAVIOR MODIFICATION
CLASSROOM MANAGEMENT
DISCIPLINE**

TIME SAMPLING

Time sampling is an intermittent means of recording behavior by observing the subject at certain prespecified times and recording his or her behavior in a manner prescribed by the time sampling method in use. According to Arrington (1943), the major impetus to developing various time sampling procedures was provided by the National Research Council between 1920 and 1935. The council, which controlled many research fund allocations, had become concerned because the diary records typically used in research on the behavior of children were neither comparable nor exact. This group began to encourage research that used quantifiable and rep-

licable methods of data collection. One of the first researchers to accept the challenge was F. L. Goodenough (1928), whose technique involved dividing an observation session into a series of short intervals and recording whether or not the target behavior occurred during each of those intervals. Other researchers in child development and psychology (e.g., Arrington, 1932; Bindra & Blond, 1958; Olson, 1929; Parten, 1932) adopted and refined these procedures.

In more recent times, a common terminology has developed that defines the various types of time sampling methods. In a landmark study, Powell et al. (1977) discussed three different types of time sampling procedures: (1) whole interval recording, (2) partial interval recording, and (3) momentary time sampling. In all of these procedures, the observation session is divided into a series of intervals. When the intervals are equal, the procedure is known as fixed interval (e.g., every 30 seconds). When the interval lengths are assigned at random but still average to the desired length (e.g., on the average, every 30 seconds), the procedure is known as variable interval.

In whole interval time sampling, the behavior is scored as having occurred only if it has endured for the entire interval; in partial interval time sampling the behavior is recorded as having occurred if it occurs at all (even for an instant) during the interval. In the technique known as momentary time sampling (MTS), the data collector records what behavior is occurring exactly at the end of each interval.

Repp et al. (1976) demonstrated conclusively that partial interval time sampling was not an accurate means of recording behaviors when frequency was the dimension of interest. Powell et al. (1977) conducted a study on the accuracy of all of these procedures and concluded that, when used to estimate the duration of a behavior, whole interval time sampling generally provided an underestimate while partial interval recording provided an overestimate. Momentary time sampling procedures both over- and underestimated the true duration of the behavior but, when averaged, provided the most accurate measure. The researchers felt that MTS interval lengths as long as 60 seconds could be used to collect accurate data. In an extension of this study, Brulle and Repp (1984) demonstrated that MTS procedures provide an accurate estimate of the duration of the behavior when averaged, but that each data entry, even when intervals are as short as 30 seconds, is subject to considerable error. They recommended that only very short intervals be used if averages are not acceptable.

The Student Observation Scale (SOS) of the Behavior Assessment System for Children is an example of a standardized time-sampling procedure that uses a fourth approach successfully. The SOS employs brief intervals, and at the end of each, the examiner/observer records all behaviors occurring at any time during the 3-second observation (Reynolds & Kamphaus, 1992). After recording, behavior is again observed, and the process is repeated for a 15 minute total time sample.

REFERENCES

Arrington, R. E. (1932). Interrelations in the behavior of young children. *Child Development Monographs*, No. 8.

Arrington, R. E. (1943). Time sampling in studies of social behavior: A critical review of techniques and results with research suggestions. *Psychological Bulletin, 40,* 81–124.

Bindra, D., & Blond, J. (1958). A time-sample method for measuring general activity and its components. *Canadian Journal of Psychology, 12,* 74–76.

Brulle, A. R., & Repp. A. C. (1984). An investigation of the accuracy of momentary time sampling procedures with time series data. *British Journal of Psychology, 75,* 481–488.

Goodenough, F. L. (1928). Measuring behavior traits by means of repeated short samples. *Journal of Juvenile Research, 12,* 230–235.

Olson, W. C. (1929). A study of classroom behavior. *Journal of Educational Psychology, 22,* 449–454.

Parten, M. B. (1932). Social participation among preschool children. *Journal of Abnormal Social Psychology, 57,* 243–269.

Powell, J., Martindale, B., Kulp, S., Martindale, A., & Bauman, R. (1977). Taking a closer look: Time sampling and measurement error. *Journal of Applied Behavior Analysis, 10,* 325–332.

Repp, A. C., Roberts, D. M., Slack, D. J., Repp, C. F., & Berkler, M. S. (1976). A comparison of frequency, interval, and time-sampling methods of data collection. *Journal of Applied Behavior Analysis, 9,* 501–508.

Reynolds, C. R., & Kamphaus, R. W. (1992). *Behavior assessment system for children.* Circle Pines, MN: American Guidance Service.

ANDREW R. BRULLE
Wheaton College

BEHAVIOR ASSESSMENT SYSTEM FOR CHILDREN
BEHAVIOR CHARTING
BEHAVIOR MODIFICATION
BEHAVIORAL ASSESSMENT

TOFRANIL

Tofranil is the proprietary name for the drug Imipramine, which primarily is used in the treatment of major depression and nocturnal enuresis. It has been suggested that Tofranil may be useful in the treatment of school phobia (Hersov, 1985).

Though Tofranil has proved to be an effective treatment for major depression in adults (American Medical Association, 1983), its use with children is questionable. Shaffer (1985) reports that there have been few well-designed studies of the effectiveness of Tofranil and childhood depression. In one reported study in which Tofranil was compared double blind with a placebo, a 60 percent response rate was reported in both groups. In adults, Tofranil has a mild sedative effect that serves to lessen anxiety, though it is not intended to be used for this symptom. It has been suggested that it is this anxiety effect that may be helpful in a multi-disciplinary approach toward school refusal (Hersov, 1985). In the 1990s, use of Tofranil declined in favor of selective serotonin reuptake inhibitors, such as Prozac and Zoloft.

In children, Tofranil is most frequently used to ameliorate nocturnal enuresis. Numerous studies have demonstrated Tofranil's effectiveness in decreasing nighttime enuresis in most children (Shaffer, Costello, & Hill, 1968). The effect is seen rapidly, and almost always within the first week of treatment (Williams & Johnston, 1982). Unfortunately, research also has suggested that once the medication is withdrawn, many of these children begin wetting again. The effects of long-term treatment have not been studied (Shaffer, 1985). The relapse rate following cessation of the drug compares unfavorably with the withdrawal of the pad and bell procedure. The mode of action of Tofranil in decreasing nocturnal enuresis is not understood. An adverse side effect of Tofranil may be increased restlessness, agitation, and confusion.

REFERENCES

American Medical Association (AMA). (1983). *AMA drug evaluations* (5th ed.). Philadelphia: Saunders.

Hersov, L. (1985). School refusal. In M. Rutter & L. Hersov (Eds.). *Child and adolescent psychiatry: Modern approaches* (2nd ed., pp. 382–399), St. Louis, MO: Blackwell Scientific.

Shaffer, D. (1985). Enuresis. In M. Rutter & L. Hersov (Eds.), *Child and adolescent psychiatry: Modern approaches* (2nd ed., pp. 465–481). St. Louis, MO: Blackwell Scientific.

Shaffer, D., Costello, A. J., & Hill, I. D. (1968). Control of Enuresis with Imipramine. *Archives of diseases in childhood, 43,* 665–671.

Williams, D. I., & Johnston, J. H. (1982). *Pediatric urology* (2nd ed.). London: Butterworth Scientific.

GRETA N. WILKENING
Children's Hospital

DEPRESSION, CHILDHOOD AND ADOLESCENT ENURESIS

TOKEN ECONOMY

A token economy refers to a system in which conditioned reinforcers (e.g., token or point) are (a) contingently delivered following engagement in a target behavior and (b) can be exchanged for preferred items/events. A token economy involves the delivery of a stimulus (i.e., token) that can be exchanged for other preferred items (backup reinforcer). Token deliveries acquire the function of a conditioned or secondary reinforcer, meaning they are paired with and effective in accessing a backup reinforcer, and thus become associated with an increase in the future probability of a target behavior occurring. The backup reinforcer is either a primary (unconditioned) reinforcer, that is, a reinforcer that is biologically or innately of value to an individual, or it is other conditioned reinforcers (Miller, 1997). Tokens may be considered generalized reinforcers if multiple backup reinforcers are available for exchange.

Token economies are practical because they (a) are generally employed by everyday caregivers and practitioners (Leslie, 1996), (b) provide an alternative to the regular delivery of primary and highly-valued conditioned reinforcers (Miller, 1997), and (c) are effective in increasing a wide range of target behaviors (Alberto & Troutman, 2003). Martella, Nelson, and Marchand-Martella (2003) note, however, that token economies are a contrived system of reinforcement and that skills reinforced through token economies in certain environments may not occur in others. Additionally, gradually fading the use of tokens is necessary to ensure that behavior change is maintained without the regular delivery of reinforcers.

Research

Research spanning multiple domains and content areas has been conducted evaluating the use of token economies. The first and most influential studies regarding token economies were directed by Teodoro Ayllon and Nathan Azrin, who in 1965 empirically evaluated the implementation of a token economy in a hospital psychiatric ward. Tokens were delivered by hospital staff contingent upon client's engaging in a range of work-related behaviors. Results indicated that when tokens were delivered contingently, work-related behavior improved substantially for a majority of clients (Leslie, 1996). In another example, DeLuca and Holborn (1992) rewarded the bicycling behavior of boys with points that could be exchanged for preferred items. The bicycling behavior of the participants doubled in many cases after the point system was implemented.

Fox, Hopkins, and Anger (1987) were successful in reducing work time lost due to injuries and the number of accidents and injuries at two open-pit mine sites, following institution of a token economy. The costs associated with implementing the token economy were much lower than costs associated with injuries and lost work time, and results were maintained over several years. McLaughlin and Malaby (1972) found that a token economy implemented in a general education classroom was effective in increasing the assignment completion rate of students in the classroom.

Token economies have doubtlessly affected myriad areas of behavior research and practice (Alberto & Troutman, 2003; Miller, 1997) and have been successfully employed (a) in special and general education classrooms, homes, clinics, and group home facilities (Alberto & Troutman, 2003); (b) for individuals (Luiselli, 1996) and groups (Adair & Schneider, 1993); and (c) across a wide range of behaviors, including social skills (Rasing, Coninx, Duker, & Van Den Hurk, 1994), self-care skills (Ayllon & Azrin, 1965), and academic skills (McGinnis, Friman, Carlyon, 1999).

Guidelines for Implementation

A token economy can be set up in a number of ways, but involves a few principal steps. Instituting a token economy requires (a) determining the target behavior, (b) selecting tokens, (c) identifying what will be offered as backup reinforcers and the number of tokens required to receive backup reinforcers, and (d) creating a system to record token deliveries (Sulzer-Azaroff & Mayer, 1991). Also, before implementing a token economy, careful instructions to explain and teach the rules, process, and requirements of the system to both implementers and those who will participate in the system are necessary.

Check marks, poker chips, stickers, smiley faces, and stamps are common objects and symbols used as tokens, and may be stored in a receptacle or printed on a sheet of paper and eventually counted (Alberto & Troutman, 2003). In a classroom, teachers or instructional assistants may deliver tokens, prompt students to deliver tokens to themselves, or teach students to evaluate their own behavior or the behavior of others and deliver tokens accordingly. To ensure counterfeiting does not occur, hard-to-obtain objects or marked/initialed tokens should be used.

Back-up reinforcers are likely to be most effective when (a) a variety of choices are available, (b) individuals can choose their own reinforcers, (c) reinforcers are immediately available after earning all tokens, and (d) the reinforcer delivered appropriately corresponds to the amount of effort required to earn tokens. These suggestions are especially important considerations for younger individuals or individuals with disabilities. Additionally, for such populations, tokens may also need to be delivered immediately after a target behavior occurs. Use of tangible tokens may be the best choice for younger children and those with severe disabilities, as they allow individuals to easily see the accumulation or removal of tokens. Finally, tokens may also need to be exchanged on a more frequent basis for younger children and those with disabilities.

A response cost procedure is commonly employed in token economies (Martella et al., 2003). Specifically, when individuals engage in undesired behavior, a specified number of tokens may be removed from their possession. However, Sulzer-Azaroff and Mayer (1991) suggest maintaining a positive balance of tokens to avoid negative side effects associated with "owing" more tokens than have been earned. These side effects might include social withdrawal, aggression, and reduced probability of desired behavior.

The development of a plan to systematically fade token

systems is essential. Pairing token deliveries with more naturally occurring rewards, such as praise and other social reinforcers, will ensure sustained behavior change when tokens are gradually faded. Additionally, lengthening the time between occurrences of target behaviors and token deliveries, increasing the number of tokens required to exchange for preferred items, and providing tokens on an intermittent basis will be useful strategies to incorporate when planning to fade token systems (Sulzer-Azaroff & Mayer, 1991).

Case Examples

Example 1

"Felix" is a 6-year-old child with difficulties staying in his seat. To address this concern, a timer is placed on Felix's desk. If at the end of a random interval of time Felix has remained in his seat, he can put a marble (token) into a cup on his desk. At the end of class, if Felix earns three or more marbles he can play with designated toys or draw at his desk for 5 minutes (backup reinforcer).

Example 2

"Mrs. Garcia" is a ninth-grade teacher who is having trouble keeping her students from talking out in class without raising their hand. Mrs. Garcia implements a point system in which a line (denoting a point) is written on the chalkboard when a student raises his or her hand to speak. At the end of class, if more than 25 points are accumulated, students can either choose to have 10 minutes of computer time, play board games, or contribute the points toward a larger pool of points. When the students earn 200 points, they can have a class popcorn and movie party or a pizza party.

Example 3

"Mr. Horace" is concerned that his students are frequently tardy to his class and not in their seats when the bell rings. Mr. Horace decides to give an index card to each student in the class. When a student is on time to class he stamps his or her point card. At the end of the school week, if students have earned four or more stamps they can pick a prize from a prize box.

REFERENCES

Adair, J., & Schneider, J. (1993). Banking on learning: An incentive system for adolescents in the resource room. *Teaching Exceptional Children, 25*(2), 30–34.

Alberto, P. A., & Troutman, A. C. (2003). *Applied behavior analysis for teachers* (6th ed.). Upper Saddle River, NJ: Merrill Prentice Hall.

Ayllon, T., & Azrin, N. H. (1965). The measurement and reinforcement of behavior of psychotics. *Journal of Applied Behavior Analysis, 8,* 357–383.

DeLuca, R. V., & Holborn, S. W. (1992). Effects of a variable-ratio reinforcement schedule with changing criteria on exercise in obese and nonobese boys. *Journal of Applied Behavior Analysis, 25,* 671–679.

Fox, D. K., Hopkins, B. L., & Anger, W. K. (1987). The long-term effects of a token economy on safety performance in open-pit mining. *Journal of Applied Behavior Analysis, 20,* 215–224.

Leslie, J. C. (1996). *Principles of behavioral analysis.* The Netherlands: Harwood Academic Publishers.

Luiselli, J. (1996). Multicomponent intervention for challenging behaviors of a child with pervasive developmental disorder in a public school setting. *Journal of Developmental and Physical Disabilities, 8,* 211–219.

Martella, R. C., Nelson, J. R., & Marchand-Martella, N. E. (2003). *Managing disruptive behavior in the schools: A schoolwide, classroom, and individualized social learning approach.* Boston: Allyn & Bacon.

McGinnis, J. C., Friman, P. C., & Carlyon, W. D. (1999). The effect of token rewards on "intrinsic" motivation for doing math. *Journal of Applied Behavior Analysis, 32,* 375–379.

McLaughlin, T. F., & Malaby, J. (1972). Intrinsic reinforcers in a classroom token economy. *Journal of Applied Behavior Analysis, 5,* 263–270.

Miller, L. K. (1997). *Principles of everyday behavior analysis* (3rd ed.). Pacific Grove, CA: Brooks/Cole.

Rasing, E., Coninx, F., Duker, P., & Van Den Hurk, A. (1994). Acquisition and generalization of social behaviors in language-disabled deaf adolescents. *Behavior Modification, 18,* 411–442.

Sulzer-Azaroff, B., & Mayer, G. R. (1991). *Behavior analysis for lasting change.* Fort Worth, TX: Holt, Rinehart, and Winston.

SARAH FAIRBANKS
GEORGE SUGAI
University of Connecticut

APPLIED BEHAVIOR ANALYSIS
BEHAVIOR MODIFICATION
BEHAVIOR THERAPY
CONDITIONED REINFORCEMENT

TONIC NECK REFLEX, ASYMMETRICAL

See ASYMMETRICAL TONIC NECK REFLEX.

TOPICS IN EARLY CHILDHOOD SPECIAL EDUCATION

Topics in Early Childhood Special Education (TECSE) is a refereed, quarterly journal publishing articles on timely issues in early childhood special education. Three issues per year are topical; one is nontopical. The topical issues address an identified problem, trend, or subject of concern and importance to early intervention. Persons interested in services provided to infants, toddlers, and preschoolers who display developmental delays and disabilities and the families of such youngsters will find *TECSE* informative. *TECSE* has been published continuously since 1981. PRO-ED, Inc. purchased the journal from Aspen Press in 1983.

Judith K. Voress
PRO-ED, Inc.

TOPICS IN LANGUAGE DISORDERS

Topics in Language Disorders, an interdisciplinary journal that is published quarterly, addresses topics within the general fields of language acquisition, language development, and language disorders. Contributors include speech and language pathologists, psycholinguists, pediatricians, neurologists, and special educators, especially remedial reading and learning disabilities teachers. This journal originated in 1980 to meet the need for published interactions across professional boundaries on specific topics.

As the title implies, each journal presents a variety of issues surrounding one topic. A guest editor is responsible for soliciting manuscripts; in doing so, he or she seeks equality among disciplines as well as several views. Both clinical and educational application are sought with balance between theory and practice.

Members of the American Speech and Hearing Association may earn continuing education credits by reading each volume and responding to the questions at the end of the volume. Responses are then submitted to the address included in the journal.

Anne Campbell
Purdue University

TORCH COMPLEX

TORCH complex is a phrase used by some authors (e.g., Nahmias & Tomeh, 1977; Thompson & O'Quinn, 1979) to group a set of maternal infections whose clinical manifestations in children are so similar that differentiation among them on the basis of those symptoms alone may not be possible. TORCH stands for *TO*xoplasmosis, *R*ubella, *C*ytomegalovirus, and *H*erpes. Generally speaking, with the exception of herpes, the infections have only mild and transitory effects on the mother, but through pre- or perinatal transmission, they may produce severe and irreversible damage to offspring. The major manifestations are visual and auditory defects and brain damage, which may result in mental retardation. The infections generally destroy already

formed tissue rather than interfering with development; infants are frequently born asymptomatic, but gradually develop symptoms in the early years of life.

Although the major symptoms of the members of the TORCH complex are similar, the detailed symptoms, mechanisms of action, and times of major action differ.

REFERENCES

Nahmias, A. J., & Tomeh, M. O. (1977). Herpes simplex virus infections. In A. M. Rudolph (Ed.), *Pediatrics* (16th ed.). Englewood Cliffs, NJ: Prentice Hall.

Thompson, R. J., & O'Quinn, A. N. (1979). *Developmental disabilities.* New York: Oxford University Press.

Robert T. Brown
University of North Carolina at Wilmington

CYTOMEGALOVIRUS
HERPES SIMPLEX I AND II
RUBELLA
TOXOPLASMOSIS

TORRANCE, ELLIS PAUL (1914–2003)

Ellis Paul Torrance earned his AA at Georgia Military College in 1936, his BA at Mercer University in 1940, his MA at the University of Minnesota in 1944, and his PhD at the University of Michigan. He served as professor of educational psychology and as department chairman at the University of Georgia until he retired in 1984.

Torrance was widely recognized for his voluminous contributions to the field of creative, gifted, and future education. At the heart of his philosophy was the impetus to change the goals, needs, and concepts in education. Future

Ellis Paul Torrance

educational institutions need to cultivate not only learning, but thinking. As a means of teaching versatility in thinking, Torrance reconceptualized and refined sociodrama as a group creative problem-solving technique. In addition, his efforts to identify gifted people from different cultures and all ages produced the Torrance Tests of Creative Thinking (TTCT). He has also produced Thinking Creatively in Action and Movement (TCAM), Sounds and Images, What Kind of Person are You?, the Creative Motivation Scale, and Style of Learning and Thinking (SOLAT).

Torrance contributed to over 2000 publications and over 40 books, including *Guiding Creative Talent, Education and the Creative Potential, Creative Learning and Teaching, Gifted, and Talented Children in the Regular Classroom,* and *Making the Creative Leap Beyond.* He directed 118 doctoral dissertations and 39 masters' theses.

Torrance and his late wife Pansy were the founders of the Future Problem Solving Program (1974), which teaches problem-solving skills to thousands of children in America and abroad. His many honors and awards include being appointed Alumni Foundation Distinguished Professor in 1973, being awarded a grant by the Japan Society for the Promotion of Science to study creativity and creative instruction within Japanese educational institutions, and receiving the Life Creative Achievement Award from the American Creativity Association in 1994.

REFERENCES

Torrance, E. P. (1962). *Guiding creative talent.* Englewood Cliffs, NJ: Prentice Hall.

Torrance, E. P. (1963). *Education and the creative potential.* Minneapolis: University of Minnesota.

Torrance, E. P., & Safter, H. T. (1998). *Making the creative leap beyond.* Buffalo, NY: Creative Education Foundation.

Torrance, E. P., & Sisk, D. A. (1965). *Gifted and talented children in the regular classroom.* Buffalo, NY: Creative Education Foundation.

STAFF

CREATIVITY TESTS
TORRANCE CENTER FOR CREATIVE STUDIES

TORRANCE CENTER FOR CREATIVE STUDIES

The Torrance Center for Creative Studies is a research center dedicated to investigations of the development of creative potential. Its research and development program honors and builds on the legacy of Ellis Paul Torrance, a native Georgian and a University of Georgia Alumni Foundation distinguished professor emeritus. This legacy is best reflected in the following statement:

In almost every field of human achievement, creativity is usually the distinguishing characteristic of the truly eminent. The possession of high intelligence, special talent, and high technical skills is not enough to produce outstanding achievement. . . . It is tremendously important to society that our creative talent be identified, developed, and utilized. The future of our civilization—our very survival—depends upon the quality of the creative imagination of our next generation. (Torrance, 1959, p. 1)

Torrance, a pioneer in research on the identification and development of creative potential, is best known for his work in the development and refinement of the Torrance Tests of Creative Thinking (TTCT), the most widely used tests of creativity in the world.

The goals of the research and instructional program of the Torrance Center are to investigate and evaluate techniques and procedures for assessing creative potential and growth; to develop, apply, and evaluate strategies that enhance creative thinking; and to facilitate national and international systems that support creative development.

Four components—assessment, development, education, and evaluation—provide the organizational structure for the research and instructional programs of the center. Each component has been designed to contribute research that verifies and expands our understanding of creativity as a major ingredient in the development of human ability and that carries out the further development of instructional and evaluation technology to enhance the development of that ability.

Research on instruments and procedures to assess creative potential and to evaluate creative growth form the basis of the assessment component. Research on tests developed by Torrance, including validity studies, refinement of administration and scoring procedures, and interpretation of test results, and on the effects of strategies to develop creative ability, are coordinated through the center in conjunction with Scholastic Testing Service, the publishers of the Torrance tests and the Georgia Studies of Creative Behavior.

Two programs to investigate and evaluate techniques that facilitate or inhibit creative thinking and to determine the nature of systems and activities that support and encourage creative growth form the basis of the development component. The Future Problem Solving Program (FPS), founded in 1974 by E. Paul and J. Pansy Torrance, involves a deliberately interdisciplinary approach to studying and solving problems. It was motivated by a belief that we have reached a point in civilization at which education must devote a considerable part of the curriculum to helping students enlarge, enrich, and make more accurate their images of the future (Torrance, 1980). The FPS program is now international. Its headquarters are at St. Andrews College, Laurinburg, North Carolina. Anne Crabbe is the director. The Georgia FPS program is coordinated through the Torrance Center.

A major program initiative of the Torrance Center is the Torrance Creative Scholars Program. This program provides educational services to those individuals who score in the top 1½ percent of the national population on the TTCT, verbal and/or figural. The program is consistent with Torrance's assertions (1984) that

a common characteristic of people who have made outstanding social, scientific, and artistic contributions has been their creativity. Since we are living in an age of increasing rates of change, depleted natural resources, interdependence, and destandardization, there are stronger reasons than ever for creatively gifted children and adults to have a fair chance to grow. We must find these "world treasures" and give them support so that they can give society those things it so desperately needs.

A unique aspect of the Torrance Creative Scholars Program is its use of a mentoring component. This component provides a year-round mentoring network for the creative scholars. Individuals selected by Torrance are designated Torrance creative scholar-mentors; they provide mentoring services to the scholars in a variety of ways. These mentors are also eligible to become Torrance creative scholars and to receive the services of the program.

Scoring and validation of scores on the TTCT for the Torrance Creative Scholars Program are coordinated through Scholastic Testing Service. Programs and services are developed and implemented through the Torrance Center.

The third component, education, provides training for educators interested in creativity. This component operates in conjunction with the degree programs (master's, sixth year, and doctoral) offered through the department of educational psychology at the University of Georgia. Training programs offered through the center include the Torrance Center Summer Creativity Institute, the Challenge Program for preschool through fifth graders, and the Visiting Scholars Program for national and international scholars. In addition, there is the annual E. Paul Torrance Lecture and the library and archives donated to the university by Torrance. A future goal of the Torrance Center is to endow an E. Paul Torrance Research Professor Chair. The final component, evaluation, focuses on quantitative and qualitative evaluations of assessment techniques, educational strategies, and support systems for the various programs of the center.

The Torrance Center for Creative Studies was formally established at the University of Georgia in the spring of 1984 by Mary M. Frasier. It is located in the Department of Educational Psychology, College of Education, University of Georgia, Athens, GA 30602.

REFERENCES

Torrance, E. P. (1959). *Understanding creativity in talented students.* Paper prepared at the Summer Guidance Institute Lecture Series on Understanding the Talented Student, University of Minnesota.

Torrance, E. P. (1980). Creativity and futurism in education. *Retooling Education, 100,* 298–311.

Torrance, E. P. (1984). *The search for a nation's treasure* (Keynote address). St. Louis, MO: National Association for Gifted Children.

MARY F. FRASIER
University of Georgia

CREATIVITY
CREATIVITY TEST
TORRANCE, ELLIS PAUL

TORRANCE TESTS OF CREATIVE THINKING

The Torrance Test of Creative Thinking (TTCT) is composed of two tests designed to examine creativity. The Torrance Test of Creative Thinking–Verbal (TTCT-V) examines a variety of verbal aspects, and the Torrance Test of Creative Thinking–Figural (TTCT-F) explores figural aspects of creative thinking. Both versions were originally developed in 1966 by E. Paul Torrance and associates, and were renormed in 1974, 1984, 1990, and 1998. Each has two parallel forms, A and B. To date, the TTCT has been translated into 35 languages. The tests are accompanied by separate Technical and Norms manuals for both the Verbal and Figural forms, separate scoring guides for each form, and a review of research on the TTCT.

The TTCT-V may be administered to first graders through adults and requires 40 minutes to administer. The TTCT-F may be administered to kindergartners through adults and requires 30 minutes to administer. The TTCT-V uses six word-based activities to assess mental fluency, flexibility, and originality by asking participants to ask questions, improve products, and "just suppose." The TTCT-F consists of three activities, each of which requires 10 minutes to complete: picture construction, picture completion, and repeated figures of lines or circles. These picture-based activities assess mental fluency, originality, elaboration, abstractness of titles (i.e., titles given to drawings), and resistance to premature closure (i.e., the ability to continually process and consider the variety of information given in responses). In addition to these five norm-referenced measures are thirteen criterion-referenced measures, or "creative strengths": emotional expressiveness, storytelling articulateness, movement or action, expressiveness of titles, synthesis of incomplete figures, synthesis of lines or circles, unusual visualization, internal visualization, extending or breaking boundaries, humor, richness of imagery, colorfulness of imagery, and fantasy.

The TTCT-F may be scored using a "streamlined" scoring procedure that provides standardized scores for both the listed mental characteristics and the accompanying creative strengths. The TTCT-V may be scored using the provided norms, standardized scores, and national percentiles provided in the Manual for Scoring and Interpreting Results and the Technical Supplement. Scoring takes approximately 20 minutes per participant per form, and requires attention to detail, practice, and careful study of the manual; a scoring service is also provided by the publisher.

The TTCT-F was normed on a sample of 88,355 students from 42 states; the streamlined scoring norms were based on a sample of 55,600 from 37 states. (Geographic differences were reported by grouping the states sampled into the four regions used by the U.S. Department of Commerce, the National Assessment of Educational Progress, and the National Education Association.) The TTCT-V was normed on a sample of 37,327 students. In addition, one has the option of choosing age-related norms or grade-related norms for both children and adults.

Extensive information on validity is provided in the TTCT Manual. With regards to predictive validity, TTCT scores have been significantly correlated with creative achievement in 9-month, 7-year, 22-year, and 40-year longitudinal studies (Millar, 2002; Torrance & Wu, 1981). The TTCT-F manual of 1998 provides a range between .89 and .94 for the internal reliability of the items in the creative index; the interrater reliability for the test is reported to be above .90. Test-retest reliabilities and alternate-form reliabilities range from .59 to .97.

REFERENCES AND ADDITIONAL INFORMATION

Chase, C. I. (1985). Review of the Torrance Tests of Creative Thinking. In J. V. Mitchell Jr. (Ed.), *The ninth mental measurements yearbook* (pp. 1631–1632). Lincoln: Buros Institute of Mental Measurements, University of Nebraska.

Clapham, M. M. (1998). Structure of figural forms A and B of the Torrance Tests of Creative Thinking. *Educational & Psychological Measurement, 58,* 275–283.

Cramond, B. (1993). The Torrance Tests of Creative Thinking: From design through establishment of predictive validity. In R. F. Subotnik & K. D. Arnold (Eds.), *Beyond Terman: Contemporary longitudinal studies of giftedness and talent* (pp. 229–254). Norwood, NJ: Ablex.

Cramond, B., Matthews-Morgan, J., Torrance, E. P., & Zuo, L. (1999). Why should the Torrance Tests of Creative Thinking be used to assess creativity? *Korean Journal of Thinking & Problem Solving, 9,* 77–101.

Heausler, N. L., & Thompson, B. (1988). Structure of the Torrance Tests of Creative Thinking. *Educational and Psychological Measurement, 48,* 463–468.

Millar, G. W. (2002). *The Torrance kids at mid-life: Selected case studies of creative behavior.* Westport, CT: Ablex.

Rosenthal, A., DeMers, S. T., Stilwell, W., Graybeal, S., & Zins, J. (1983). Comparison of interrater reliability on the Torrance Test of Creative Thinking for gifted and non-gifted students. *Psychology in the Schools, 20,* 35–40.

Runco, M. A., & Albert, R. S. (1985). The reliability and validity of ideational originality in the divergent thinking of academically gifted and nongifted children. *Educational and Psychological Measurement, 45,* 483–501.

Swartz, J. D. (1988). Torrance Tests of Creative Thinking. In D. J. Keyser & R. C. Sweetland (Eds.), *Test critique* (Vol. 7, pp. 619–622). Kansas, MS: Test Corporation of America, a subsidiary of Westport Publisher.

Torrance, E. P., & Wu, T. (1981). A comparative longitudinal study of the adult creative achievements of elementary school children identified as highly intelligent and as highly creative. *Creative Child and Adult Quarterly, 6,* 71–76.

Torrance Center for Creative Studies: http://www.coe.uga.edu/torrance/training.html

Torrance Tests of Creative Thinking, including a detailed critique: http://www.arches.uga.edu/~kyunghee/portfolio/ttct.html

Treffinger, D. J. (1985). Review of the Torrance Tests of Creative Thinking. In J. V. Mitchell Jr. (Ed.), *The ninth mental measurements yearbook* (pp. 1632–1634). Lincoln: Buros Institute of Mental Measurements, University of Nebraska.

RON DUMONT
Fairleigh Dickinson University

JOHN O. WILLIS
Rivier College

GIFTED AND TALENTED CHILDREN
INSIGHT (IN THE GIFTED)
TORRANCE, ELLIS PAUL

TORSIONAL DYSTONIA

The term "dystonia" was first used by H. Oppenheim in 1911 to denote the coexistence of muscular hypotonia and hypertonia. Since that time, the term has been used to describe a symptom of abnormal muscle contraction, a syndrome of abnormal involuntary movements, and a disease that has either a genetic or ideopathic origin. Torsional dystonia is commonly referred to as a progressive disorder characterized by slow, twisting movements that ultimately may result in bizarre, twisting postures of the extremities or trunk. Some causes of torsional dystonia are identifiable while other causes remain unknown, making classification of the condition difficult.

The disorder has a gradual onset, beginning between the ages of 5 and 15, and commonly involves the foot or leg. Torsional dystonia may spread to several parts or all of the body, but the condition is not present during sleep.

Contractures or permanent muscle shortening and joint deformity ultimately occur. Hereditary forms of torsional dystonia are more common than ideopathic forms; one hereditary form is found most often in Ashkenazic Jews. The diagnosis of dystonia is based on clinical signs because diagnostic laboratory or biopsy findings are not known. The symptoms suggest dysfunction in the extrapyramidal system, since temporary drug-induced symptoms have occurred from medications that have a known effect on the basal ganglia of the extrapyramidal system.

Treatment of torsional dystonia generally has been disappointing. Medications such as diazepam (Valium), carb-amazepine (Tegretol), haloperidol, and, in some cases, levodapa or anticholinergic drugs have been helpful in reducing the severity of the symptoms; but none of these medications has been consistently effective. Various neurosurgical or biofeedback procedures have resulted in isolated improvement but consistent benefits have not been achieved through these approaches.

REFERENCES

Berkow, R. (Ed.). (1982). *The Merck manual* (14th ed., p. 1363). Rahway, NJ: Merck, Sharp, & Dohme.

Fahn, S. (1985). The extrapyramidal disorders. In J. Wyngaarden & L. Smith, Jr. (Eds.), *Cecil textbook of medicine* (17th ed., pp. 2077–2078). Philadelphia: Saunders.

Fahn, S., & Roswell, E. (1976). Definition of dystonia and classification of the dystonic states. In R. Eldridge & S. Fahn (Eds.), *Advances in neurology* (Vol. 14, pp. 1–5). New York: Raven.

Magalini, S., & Scarascia, E. (1981). *Dictionary of medical syndromes* (2nd ed.). Philadelphia: Lippincott.

Marsden, C. D. (1976). Dystonia: The spectrum of the disease. In M. D. Yahr (Ed.), *Basal ganglia* (pp. 351–365). New York: Raven.

Marsden, C. D., Harrison, M. J. G., & Bundey, S. (1976). Natural history of idiopathic torsion dystonia. In R. Eldridge & S. Fahn (Eds.), *Advances in neurology* (Vol. 14, pp. 177–187). New York: Raven.

Zeman, W. (1976). Dystonia: An overview. In R. Eldridge & S. Fahn (Eds.), *Advances in neurology* (Vol. 14, pp. 91–101). New York: Raven.

DANIEL D. LIPKA
*Lincoln Way Special Education
Regional Resources Center*

PHYSICAL ANOMALIES
PHYSICAL DISABILITIES

TOTAL COMMUNICATION

The expression total communication can be used in the general sense of communication through all possible channels, not only vocal (including verbal) communication, but also communication provided by such other means as mimicry, gestures, and so on. Recently, total communication has been used mainly in a more restricted field, namely the education of deaf children. It presents itself not as a method, but as "a philosophy incorporating the appropriate aural, manual, and oral methods of communication in order to ensure effective communication with and among hearing impaired persons" (Garretson, 1976, p. 300). It advocates the use of various modes of communication, such as speech (which should not be neglected, as the deaf live among a majority of hearing people), written language (reading and writing), sign language, finger spelling, pantomime, and so on.

In recent years, methods of teaching deaf children applying this philosophy have been used in a steadily increasing number of schools in the United States and in Europe. These schools gave up the oral method that had prevailed since the end of the nineteenth century, mainly in Europe, where the resolutions of the International Congress held in Milan in 1880 were accepted and recommended almost unanimously (Lane, 1980).

According to the defenders of total communication, the oral approach, including lip reading, gives unsatisfactory results as far as linguistic and cognitive development are concerned (Conrad, 1979). It is argued that even if the hearing loss is discovered early, poor parent-infant communication delays the acquisition of language considerably and irretrievably, except with children whose residual hearing is sufficient to make communication possible. Ensuing education in specialized institutions is slower and less differentiated than with hearing children and, instead of reducing the gap, increases the retardation of the deaf children.

Total communication advocates the use of signing as the most appropriate mode of early communication between parents and hearing-impaired children. The double exposure to sign and speech (about 9 out of 10 deaf children have hearing parents) should allow partially hearing children equipped with appropriate audiological aids to be educated together with their hearing peers; children whose residual hearing is insufficient should be educated through a wide network of activities, of which "spoken language, finger spelling, signing, and written language constitute the linguistic core. Being capable of consistent transmission and internal symbolization of linguistic signals, these are the media of special relevance to linguistic and cognitive growth" (Evans, 1982, p. 91).

Evans (1982) shows three problematic issues for total communication: (1) the way the linguistic competence in sign language, with its own lexical, morphological, and syntactic characteristics, is to be transferred to linguistic competence in the spoken language of the community in which the deaf person is living; (2) the necessity for a specific training or recycling of teachers in total communication; and (3) the role of the (hearing) parents, who being confronted suddenly with the deafness of their baby, are obliged to learn the sign language in which they are going to communicate with the child in a very short time.

The philosophy of total communication remains unaltered in a variant in which the exposure to speech and sign is replaced by cued speech. The deaf child is taught to perceive the spoken language through a combination of residual hearing, lip reading, and a limited number of disambiguating signs near the speaker's face (Cornett, 1967).

Opponents of total communication think that signing may prove harmful and impede the acquisition of a spoken language and that too much time spent on teaching signs (finger spelling, etc.) could be used more appropriately to teach the spoken language. They stress the fact that some deaf children, albeit a minority, educated through the oral method succeed in obtaining a satisfactory level in spoken language perception and production.

REFERENCES

Conrad, R. (1979). *The deaf schoolchild: Language and cognitive functioning.* London: Harper & Row.

Cornett, O. (1967). Cued speech. *American Annals of the Deaf, 112,* 3–13.

Evans, L. (1982). *Total communication: Structure and strategy.* Washington, DC: Gallaudet College Press.

Garretson, M. D. (1976). Total communication. In R. Frisina (Ed.), A bicentennial monograph on hearing impairment: Trends in the U.S.A. *Volta Review, 78.*

Lane, H. (1980). A chronology of the oppression of sign language in France and the United States. In H. Lane & F. Grosjean (Eds.), *Recent perspectives on American sign language.* Hillsdale, NJ: Erlbaum.

S. De Vriendt
*Vrije Universiteit Brussel,
Belgium*

AMERICAN SIGN LANGUAGE
DEAF EDUCATION

TOURETTE SYNDROME

Tourette syndrome is a child-onset neurological disorder characterized by involuntary movements or vocalizations, otherwise known as tics, and occurs in approximately .04 to .4 percent of the population (Peterson et al., 2001; Singer & Walkup, 1991). Symptoms are evident before age 18, and are seen most commonly between the ages 2 and 15. Males are two to five times more likely than females to be diagnosed with this disorder (American Psychiatric Association, 1994). Signs of Tourette syndrome first are seen in frequent, repetitive, meaningless, and rapid tics of the limbs, arms, and/or face (e.g., eye blinking). The tics occur in bouts and generally are seen daily or every other day. Over time, tics can become more complex, resulting

in multiple motor movements. Further, the course of the disorder is characterized by symptom waxing and waning, whereby displaying periods of remission that may last from weeks to years.

Verbal tics usually are seen in the form of throat clearing, coughing, grunting, shouting, or barking. Like motor tics, verbal tics may become more complex over time, whereby grunts turn into words, and words turn into phrases. The verbal tics may be characterized by echolalia, palilalia, or coprolalia. Echolalia, most commonly seen in children with autism, is the repetition of words and phrases made by others. Palilalia is the repetition of one's own word. Coprolalia is the involuntary utterance of obscene words or phrases.

Tourette syndrome appears to be genetic (American Psychiatric Association, 1994). Associated features often include attentional problems (e.g., Attention Deficit Disorder, Attention-Deficit/Hyperactivity Disorder), behavioral problems (e.g., Oppositional Defiant Disorder), Obsessive-Compulsive Disorder, sleep disorders, and learning disabilities (American Psychiatric Association, 1994). Neuroleptics (e.g., pimozide, haloperidol) have been found to be somewhat effective in the treatment of Tourette syndrome. However, adverse side effects may prompt many patients to cease its use in treatment (Chappel et al., 1995).

REFERENCES

American Psychiatric Association. (1994). *Diagnostic and statistics manual of mental disorders* (4th ed.). Washington, DC: Author.

Chappell P. B., Leckman, J. F., & Riddle, M. A. (1995). The pharmacologic treatment of tic disorders. *Child and Adolescent Psychiatric Clinics of North America, 4,* 197–216.

Peterson, B. S., Pine, D. S., Cohen, P., & Brook, J. S. (2001). Prospective, longitudinal study of tic, obsessive-compulsive, and attention-deficit/hyperactivity disorders in an epidemiological sample. *Journal of the American Academy of Child and Adolescent Psychiatry, 40,* 685–695.

Singer, H. S., & Walkup, J. T. (1991). Tourette syndrome and other tic disorders: Diagnosis, pathophysiology, and treatment. *Medicine, 70,* 15–32.

Jason Gallant
University of Florida

ECHOLALIA
ECHOPRAXIA
TICS
TOURETTE SYNDROME ASSOCIATION

TOURETTE SYNDROME ASSOCIATION

The Tourette Syndrome Association, a voluntary nonprofit organization, was founded for the purpose of assisting individuals with Tourette syndrome, their families, friends, and concerned professionals. The primary objectives of the association include disseminating information regarding symptomatology and treatment of Tourette syndrome and raising funds to encourage and support scientific research into the nature and causes of the disorder.

In an effort to promote understanding of Tourette syndrome, the organization publishes quarterly newsletters, pamphlets, medical reprints, and films, and publicizes the disorder in newspapers, magazines, radio, and television. It provides support groups at a regional level for sharing current information about research, treatment, and management of Tourette syndrome. Information may be obtained from the Tourette Syndrome Association, Bell Plaza Building, 42-40 Bell Boulevard, Bayside, NY, 11361.

MARILYN P. DORNBUSH
Atlanta, Georgia

TICS
TOURETTE SYNDROME

TOXOPLASMOSIS

Toxoplasmosis is caused by an intracellular protozoan, Toxoplasma gondii, which is transmitted via the blood to the prenatal fetus. This congenital infection causes Mild to Severe Mental and Motor Retardation. The largest number of newborns will be asymptomatic in the neonatal period so they must be observed for ocular and central nervous system disability. The newborn with symptomatic toxoplasmosis will present at birth with one or more of the following: head abnormalities (large or small), cerebral calcifications, brain damage, muscle spasticity, convulsions and seizures, visual and hearing impairments, and eye infections. An enlarged liver and spleen, which cause an extended abdomen, are often present. Rashes and jaundiced skin may be seen in infants. Motor impairment as a result of brain damage may be seen. Prognosis is poor; death occurs in 10 to 15 percent but a high percentage of children have neuromotor defects, seizure disorders, Mental Retardation, and damaged vision (Behrman, 1977; Carter, 1978).

Many children with toxoplasmosis may need to be placed in a fairly restrictive setting because of Mental Retardation and visual, hearing, and motor impairments. Children often need self-help skills training (including feeding and toileting) from an early age. Related services may be required for speech, vision, and hearing deficits. Physical and occupational therapy may also be needed. Since a variety of health problems may be present, a medical consultation will probably be needed. Team placement and management will be necessary for adequate educational programming.

REFERENCES

Behrman, R. (Ed.). (1977). *Neo-natal-perinatal diseases of the fetus and infant* (2nd ed.). St. Louis, MO: Mosby.

Carter, C. (Ed.). (1978). *Medical aspects of mental retardation* (2nd ed.). Springfield, IL: Thomas.

Hunt, M., & Gibby, R. (1979). *The mentally retarded child: Development, training and education* (4th ed.). Boston: Allyn & Bacon.

SALLY L. FLAGLER
University of Oklahoma

FUNCTIONAL SKILLS TRAINING
MENTAL RETARDATION

TOY LENDING LIBRARIES

Toy libraries, occasionally named a Toybrary, are lending libraries with a broad range of toys, learning materials, and equipment appropriate for young children. Many traditional public libraries offer a toy section that includes puzzles, games, stuffed animals, blocks, and so on, that can be checked out and taken home by children and adults. However, the real growth in toy lending libraries is a part of the increasing need for child care outside the traditional home setting. Toy lending libraries and resource centers are becoming more common across the country as childcare needs and services grow and as people become more interested and involved in meeting the needs of children and those who care for them. Such libraries allow the various child-care programs in a specific geographic area to pool their resources and share equipment, as well as to exchange ideas and information. These libraries are particularly useful to people in isolated areas or those who work alone. When these libraries limit their use to certified daycare providers, they may also serve as a motivating force that results in a greater pool of licensed and certified daycare providers.

Types of equipment typically found in such libraries include recreational equipment, sand and water play sets, transportation equipment, farm and animal sets, blocks and other manipulatives, housekeeping materials, make believe materials, infant toys, puzzles, perception, alphabet, and math materials, and large and small motor toys. Funding for toy lending libraries comes from a number of sources. The most common would be government (national, state, or local) grants, foundation awards, local United Ways, and dues from members. Special groups such as state groups (Councils for Exceptional Children) have also been known to provide start-up funds for such libraries.

DENISE M. SEDLAK
United Way of Dunn County,
Menomonie, Wisconsin

DAY-CARE CENTERS
PLAY

TRACE MINERALS

Trace minerals are minerals found in very small quantities in the human body but having significant relationships to certain metabolic events necessary for normal function. Severe deficiencies of trace minerals can result in a variety of handicaps, including orthopedic and learning disabilities. Some minerals and their relative levels in the body affect memory and attention as well. An overabundance or improper metabolism of some minerals also may produce problems. Depending on the particular mineral and the chronicity of the deficiency (or oversupply), mineral-related handicaps may or may not be reversible, though all are treatable to a large extent.

STAFF

ETIOLOGY
NUTRITIONAL DISORDERS

TRAINING FOR EMPLOYMENT IN TRADITIONAL SETTINGS

Students with mild or moderate disabilities can be educated or trained to succeed as adult workers in many vocations. The vocational program that prepares handicapped students will be similar to regular vocational education; however, unique components should be evidenced.

All vocational preparation programs should begin with an assessment phase. Students' job interests, abilities, and readiness will be evaluated. For many special education students, this assessment procedure will be their first directed opportunity to examine their own capabilities and limitations as they relate to employment (Weisgerber, 1978).

The assessment phase should be comprehensive in order to provide information that will help the instructors and students to set appropriate vocational goals. Also, adequate assessment data will ensure that the subsequent training program will be effective. Specific job skills capabilities should be identified, as well as appropriate interpersonal relationship skills. More workers with disabilities are dismissed from their employment because of lack of social skills than lack of job skills (Weisgerber, Dahl, & Appleby, 1981).

The primary goal of the training phase of a vocational program for students with disabilities will be to prepare them for successful employment. To accomplish this goal, several components must be integrated into the total program (Weisgerber et al., 1981).

The faculty responsible for these programs must continually be aware of the limitations and capabilities of the students and the employment community. Job analyses that include data concerning vocational opportunities, employers attitudes toward individuals with disabilities, and the community's receptivity to accommodating individuals with disabilities should be conducted periodically.

An amicable relationship among special education teachers, vocational education faculty, and community employers will facilitate successful employment of graduates with disabilities. Teachers who are knowledgeable about their students' work abilities can be effective advocates for these students when they are seeking employment.

Vocational training programs should use technology to assist their students in increasing their abilities and reducing the effects of their handicapping conditions. Familiarity with new devices will enable the faculty to share this knowledge with prospective employers to promote employment of students with disabilities in traditional settings.

Securing realistic work sites either at school or in businesses and factories will increase the effectiveness of a special education vocational program. By practicing specific job skills that will be used in a vocation, students will not have to be retrained when they become employed, saving the employers time and money.

Teachers who advocate employment of students with disabilities should have expertise in the area of adaptations for job sites. Alteration of the work place and occasionally the work routine may enable the worker with disabilities to become more productive. In these instances, it is the environment that is handicapping rather than the physical or mental limitations of the worker (Wade & Gold, 1978).

REFERENCES

Wade, M. G., & Gold, M. W. (1978). Removing some of the limitations of mentally retarded workers by improving job design. *Human Factors, 20,* 339–348.

Weisgerber, R. A. (Ed.). (1978). *Vocational education: Teaching the handicapped in regular classes.* Reston, VA: Council for Exceptional Children.

Weisgerber, R. A., Dahl, P. R., & Appleby, J. A. (1981). *Training the handicapped for productive employment.* Rockville, MD: Aspen.

JONI J. GLEASON
University of West Florida

HABILITATION
VOCATIONAL EDUCATION

TRAINING IN THE HOME

Literature relating to child development frequently states that parents and other family members are the primary teachers of infants and young children. A great deal of the teaching and learning of young children in the home occurs during everyday activities such as watching TV and completing daily chores. As a result of the parents' role in teaching and socializing young children, it is essential to include the family and the home environment in any intervention plan for young children at risk (Fallen & Umansky, 1985). According to Cartwright, Cartwright, and Ward (1995) many children with disabilities tend to have problems generalizing from the specific teaching setting to other settings. Therefore, an advantage of home-based training is that many opportunities are available for the parents to apply learning to life activities.

One home-based approach to early education is the Portage project. This project was designed to meet the needs of young children in rural Wisconsin. Emphasis was placed on the skills of parents in teaching their disabled children. A teacher would visit the home and provide the parents with the necessary materials, written instructions, and forms for record keeping. Some of the basic assumptions that this project was developed around are that parents are concerned about their children and want them to develop to their maximum potential; that parents can, with assistance, learn to be effective teachers; that the socioeconomic and educational levels of the parents are no indication of the willingness to help or the amount of gains the children will achieve; and that precision teaching maximizes the chances of success for children and parents. Research has shown that when parents are involved in their children's treatment and education, children do better. The family is considered the most effective system for fostering the development of the child (Shearer, 1974).

On the other hand, there are some educators who strongly suggest that parents should leave teaching of academics to the schools. Lerner (1981) states that when learning-disabled children are tutored by their parents, it makes the children feel stressed. This is because there is a good chance that the children will feel like failures in front of the most important people in their lives. This stress tends to have a negative effect on the parent-child relationship. Lerner emphasized that parents should concentrate on teaching children domestic tasks and helping them develop a good self-image. Barsch (1969) feels that parents do not have the patience to teach their children. He lists several reasons why parents should not teach academics. They include the following:

1. Parents lack essential teaching skills.
2. The parent-child instructional session often results in frustration and tension for both members.
3. Most parents and children wish that academics could be accomplished during the school day.
4. Most teachers do not have the time to guide the parents.

5. When both the home and school stress academics, the child finds little rest.
6. Parents differ greatly in their competence as teachers.
7. Parents may feel guilty if they do not find the time to tutor their child regularly.

It has been established that some parents can successfully tutor their children. Therefore, the parents' decision to tutor or not should be made on an individual basis. According to Kronick (1977), a major question that should be addressed in terms of whether to tutor or not is whether tutoring can be accomplished without depriving any family member of resources that assist in maintaining a well-balanced life. If the parents decide to teach their children at home, Lovitt (1977) has suggested four guidelines for parents. They should establish a specific time each day for the tutoring sessions; keep sessions short; keep responses to the child; and keep a record.

REFERENCES

Barsch, R. H. (1969). *The parent teacher partnership*. Reston, VA: Council for Exceptional Children.

Cartwright, G. P., Cartwright, C. A., & Ward, M. E. (1995). *Educating special needs learners* (4th ed.). Boston: Wadsworth.

Fallen, N. H., & Umansky, W. (1985). *Children with special needs* (2nd ed.). Columbus, OH: Merrill.

Kronick, D. (1977). A parent's thoughts for parents and teachers. In N. G. Haring & B. Bateman (Eds.), *Teaching the learning disabled child*. Englewood Cliffs, NJ: Prentice Hall.

Lerner, J. W. (1981). *Learning disabilities: Theories, diagnosis and teaching strategies* (3rd ed.). Boston: Houghton Mifflin.

Lovitt, T. C. (1977). *In spite of my resistance . . . I've learned from children*. Columbus, OH: Merrill.

Shearer, M. S. (1974). A home based parent training model. In J. Grim (Ed.), *First chance for children: Training parents to teach: Four models* (Vol. 3, pp. 49–62). Chapel Hill: Technical Assistance Development System, North Carolina University.

JANICE HARPER
*North Carolina Central
University*

**FAMILY RESPONSE TO A CHILD WITH DISABILITIES
HOMEBOUND INSTRUCTION
HOMEWORK
TUTORING**

TRAINING SCHOOLS

Training schools were an intricate part of the larger multipurpose residential facilities known as the "colony plan" that were established in the late 1800s. These schools served children and adolescents who were not considered eligible for public school education because of their unique educational needs.

The evolvement of the training school concept was based on earlier work by Samuel Gridley Howe (1801–1876). Howe's Perkin School for the Deaf (1848) led to the development of other self-contained schools (e.g., Massachusetts School for Idiots and Feeble-Minded Youth, 1855). Although Howe's 10-bed unit was the first residential facility established, it was not until 1848 that the first large facility, the Syracuse Institution of the Feeble-Minded was developed. Harvey B. Wilbur (1820–1883), a physician, became the first superintendent of this facility. Like Howe, Wilbur was very much influenced by the philosophy and principles of Edward Seguin; he placed a great deal of emphasis on education.

Although institutions for exceptional individuals were initially viewed as beneficial by many throughout history, their purpose, programs, and administration changed drastically. The small homelike educational establishment was replaced by the larger, overcrowded, and underfinanced multipurpose facility that would typify institutions for generations to come.

Initially, training schools in institutions were intended to serve school-aged exceptional needs children and adolescents. As years passed, it became increasingly clear that individuals who reached the age limit for school programming had few choices for continued educational services. Typically, these adults were sent to almshouses or other similar institutions.

Though educational programs continued in institutions, there was a growing emphasis on vocational training. Most of the basic operations in running these large facilities were the sole responsibility of the individuals who resided at the facility. Therefore, skills that were taught to the residents had a direct application toward the continued function of the institution.

By 1890 the school facilities of the 1850s evolved into larger facilities intended to serve four distinct groups of residents. The colony plan was developed to serve (1) the teachable portion of a school-attending group, (2) the helpless, deformed, epileptic, and unteachable, (3) the male adults who had reached school age but were unable to become self-supportive, and (4) the female adults who at that time needed close supervision. The colony plan included training schools as well as an industrial, custodial, and farm department.

As early as the 1860s, however, advocacy of education in public schools was being heard. Although it is difficult to determine precisely when the first public school special education program was initiated, credit is usually given to the public school system of Providence, Rhode Island. An auxiliary school for 15 mentally retarded students opened in December 1896 (Woodhill, 1920). By 1898 the city of Providence established three more auxiliary schools and one special education classroom in a public school.

Other cities soon followed Providence's example. By the turn of the century, special education provisions for the mentally retarded shifted from total residential training schools to generally accepted, though not always implemented, education in public school systems.

REFERENCES

Kanner, L. (1964). *A history of case and study of the mentally retarded.* Springfield, IL: Thomas.

Scheerenberger, R. C. (1983). *The history of mental retardation.* Baltimore: Brookes.

Woodhill, E. (1920). Public school clinics in connection with a state school for the feeble-minded. *Journal of Psycho Asthenics, 25,* 14–103.

MICHAEL G. BROWN
*Central Wisconsin Center for the
Developmentally Disabled*

**HISTORY OF SPECIAL EDUCATION
HUMANISM AND SPECIAL EDUCATION**

TRANQUILIZERS

The term tranquilizer is a superordinate that may be applied to two general classes of psychoactive drugs: antipsychotic agents (major tranquilizers) and antianxiety agents (minor tranquilizers). Both major and minor tranquilizers produce sedative effects, though to different degrees. Minor tranquilizers tend to produce fewer neurotoxic side effects, but appear to be more likely candidates for abuse (Blum, 1984). The following table summarizes the two groups of tranquilizers.

The major tranquilizers were developed in an attempt to humanize the treatment of psychotic individuals, who were being given long-term treatment in psychiatric hospitals. The drugs were developed based on observations of related agents that produced calming effects on wild animals. Like the minor tranquilizers, the major tranquilizers have not been found to be physically addictive. Abrupt withdrawal, however, has been reported to induce insomnia, anxiety, and gastrointestinal symptoms (Brooks, 1959; see Table 1).

In terms of the general public, the minor tranquilizers are more familiar and also show more pervasive, popular use. The benzodiazapines are often used to reduce the effects of chronic stress, tension, and emotional discomfort. Valium was at one time the most prescribed drug in the United States, with 75 percent of the prescriptions being issued by nonpsychiatrists (Blum, 1984).

In addition to more general stress-reducing effects, Valium is also a drug of abuse. Dosages of 100 to 500 mg produce intoxication (Patch, 1974). Valium also is used by

Table 1 Tranquilizers

Major	Minor
Phenothiazines	*Benzodiazapines*
Thorazine (Chlorpromazine)	Valium (Diazepam)
Stelazine (Trifluoperazine)	Librium (Chlordiazepoxide)
Mellaril (Thioridazine)	Dalmane (Flurazepam)
Prolixin (Fluphenazine)	Tranxene (Chlorazepate)
Thioxanthenes	*Meprobamate*
Navane (Thiothixene)	
Butyrophenones	
Haldol (Haloperidol)	

substance abusers to deal with the frightening effects of a "bad trip" after hallucinogen (e.g., LSD) ingestion or to diminish the hangover effects after amphetamine intoxication (Blum, 1984). Therapeutically, Valium has been found to produce symptomatic relief for tension and anxiety states, free-floating agitation, mild depressive symptoms, fatigue, and short-term treatments of insomnia (Katzung, 1982). In addition, benzodiazepines have been used as adjuncts in the treatment of seizure disorders, since administration tends to raise the seizure threshold (Katzung, 1982). Valium also has been used to relieve skeletal muscle spasms, whether induced by local reactions or trauma, and spasticity secondary to upper motor neuron disorders (Blum, 1984).

Effects commonly reported owing to drug sensitivity or to intoxication include anticholinergic effects. In addition, lethargy, headache, slurred speech, tremor, and dizziness also have been reported (Blum, 1984). Paradoxical reactions including acute periods of increased excitability, increased anxiety, hallucinations, insomnia, rage, and increased muscle spasticity also have appeared in the literature (Blum, 1984). Though severe overdose of Valium is uncommon, symptoms include somnolence, confusion, coma, and blunted reflexes (Blum, 1984). The minor tranquilizers have not been found to be physically addictive; however, habituation (psychosocial accommodation to the effects of the drugs) has been reported frequently.

REFERENCES

Blum, K. B. (1984). *Handbook of abusable drugs.* New York: Gardner.

Brooks, G. W. (1959). Withdrawal from neuroleptic drugs. *American Journal of Psychiatry, 115,* 931.

Katzung, B. G. (1982). *Basic and clinical pharmacology.* Los Altos, CA: Lange Medical.

Patch, V. D. (1974). The dangers of diazepam: A street drug. *New England Journal of Medicine, 190,* 807.

ROBERT F. SAWICKI
*Lake Erie Institute of
Rehabilitation*

MELLARIL

THORAZINE

TRANSDISCIPLINARY MODEL

Originally conceived by Hutchison (1974), the transdisciplinary model is one of several team approaches for the delivery of educational and related services to students with disabilities. The other team models are the multidisciplinary model and the interdisciplinary model. In a multidisciplinary model, team members maintain their respective discipline boundaries with only minimal, if any, coordination, collaboration, or communication (McCormick, 1984). The interdisciplinary model differs from the multidisciplinary model in that there is some discussion among the involved professionals after their individual assessments have been completed and at least an attempt to develop a coordinated service delivery plan. However, the programming recommendations are often not realistic. The teacher may not have the skills to implement the recommendations or the authority to arrange for their provision (Hart, 1977). Another problem is the lack of provision for follow-up and feedback in the interdisciplinary model.

The transdisciplinary model is the only one of the three models to adequately address the issue of coordinated service delivery. This model suggests specific procedures for sharing information and skills among professionals and across discipline boundaries. It is differentiated from the other models by its emphasis on coordination, collaboration, and communication among the involved discipline representatives and its advocacy of integrated services.

The transdisciplinary model assumes the following: (1) joint functioning (team members performing assessment, planning, and service delivery functions together; (2) continuous staff development (commitment to expansion of each team member's competencies); and (3) role release (sharing functions across discipline boundaries; Lyon & Lyon, 1980). The professional makeup of a transdisciplinary team varies depending on the needs of the student. It may include few or many professionals, but whenever possible they coordinate their assessment procedures and plan as a group for the student's daily programming.

Transdisciplinary team members are accountable for seeing that the best practices of their respective disciplines are implemented (McCormick & Goldman, 1979). However, their responsibility does not stop there. They are also responsible for monitoring program implementation, training others if necessary, and revising programs when evaluation data indicate that the procedures are not working. The teacher is usually coordinator and manager of team processes so that there is no duplication of efforts or splintering of services.

REFERENCES

Hart, V. (1977). The use of many disciplines with the severely and profoundly handicapped. In E. Sontag, J. Smith, & N. Certo (Eds.), *Educational programming for the severely and profoundly handicapped.* Reston, VA: Council for Exceptional Children, Division of Mental Retardation.

Hutchison, D. (1974). *A model for transdisciplinary staff development* (United Cerebral Palsy: Technical Report No. 8).

Lyon, S., & Lyon, G. (1980). Team functioning and staff development: A role release approach to providing integrated educational services for severely handicapped students. *Journal of the Association for Severely Handicapped, 5*(3), 250–263.

McCormick, L. (1984). Extracurricular roles and relationships. In L. McCormick & R. Schiefelbusch (Eds.), *Early language intervention.* Columbus, OH: Merrill.

McCormick, L., & Goldman, R. (1979). The transdisciplinary model: Implications for service delivery and personnel preparation for the severely handicapped. *AAESPH Review, 4*(2), 152–161.

LINDA MCCORMICK
University of Hawaii, Manoa

ITINERANT SERVICES
MULTIDISCIPLINARY TEAM

TRANSFER OF TRAINING

Transfer of training, also referred to as stimulus generalization or generalization, takes place when a behavior that has been reinforced in the presence of one stimulus event occurs in the presence of different but similar stimuli. Using the behavior analytic S > R > C paradigm, the emphasis of this learning construct is on (1) the characteristics of the events that precede a behavior, and (2) the relationship of these characteristics to the occurrence of the behavior under similar stimulus conditions.

From this viewpoint, increasing similarities in events that precede a behavior result in an increased likelihood of stimulus generalization. Conversely, there is a decreased likelihood of the trained behavior occurring as these preceding events become more dissimilar. Applied to educational programming, the influence of these similarities might be beneficial or problematic. Thus a student may be trained to respond to questions asked by an adult male teacher by raising his or her hand. If this student responds likewise in other classroom settings to questions asked by female adults, a beneficial transfer of training has occurred. However, if the student responds to his father's inquiry, "Why are you late?" by raising his or her hand, the transfer of training that has taken place might be viewed as potentially problematic.

This example highlights some of the problems that relate to transfer of training and also touches on the fundamental role of this learning explanation in the educational process. Almost without exception, students are exposed to information and material with specific stimulus characteristics or in specific stimulus settings. Traditionally, this stimulus-specific training is assumed to automatically transfer to similar stimulus events. The accuracy of this assumption is highly questionable when teaching the learner with exceptional needs. As the severity of an individual's learning problems increases, so does the need for implementation of more specific interventions that are geared toward systematically promoting transfer of training.

A variety of approaches and procedures have been applied in order to increase the positive transfer of training. These attempts have been effective to varying degrees in achieving this purpose. Specific recommendations for achieving transfer of training have been offered by Martin and Pear (1983) and Stokes and Baer (1977). These recommendations include (1) training the skills in the situation where the behavior is to occur, (2) presenting a variety of stimulus events, (3) programming common stimulus characteristics across settings, and (4) training with sufficient examples.

Training the skill in the situation where it is expected to occur addresses the relationship between the training efforts extended to develop a student's skills in one setting and the implicit desire to have that student perform those skills in another setting. The use of this tactic requires the development of as many similarities as possible between the two settings, or actual skill training in the targeted situation. Therefore, if a student is being taught to locate the correct restroom using international door symbols, as much of the training as possible should take place in similar (analogue) or actual (in vivo) settings.

Another technique for promoting transfer of training is the presentation of a variety of stimulus events. Also referred to as training loosely, this tactic involves providing the student with a wide variety of stimuli to allow practicing of the response under different but similar conditions. Accordingly, training situations might involve different trainers, differing verbal requests, and so on, each serving as a stimulus event for the same desired student response.

Programming of common stimuli is another tactic used to promote transfer of training. Alternatively referred to as the "don't teach basketball with a football" technique, this procedure focuses on the establishment of stimulus bridges between the training setting and the goal environment. Thus students are taught to respond to the materials, statements, or other stimulus events that will actually be present in the goal environment.

The final tactic suggested by these authors involves the presentation of representative stimulus events during training. In contrast to teaching a student to respond by presenting all possible stimulus options (e.g., every possible configuration of the word poison), the emphasis of "training sufficient examples" is on the use of stimulus events that encourage responses to example stimuli. Application of this technique in teaching a student to respond to teacher greetings might involve training the student to say "hi" to one teacher and priming generalization of the response by rewarding the student's response to another teacher.

The effectiveness of education to a large extent relates to the amount of training that is transferred from one stimulus event to another similar event or setting. With the exceptional learner, this transfer must often be directly encouraged. For a comprehensive explanation of transfer of training and related teaching considerations, the reader is referred to texts by Sulzer-Azaroff and Mayer (1977) and Alberto and Troutman (1977).

REFERENCES

Alberto, P. A., & Troutman, A. C. (1977). *Applied behavior analysis for teachers: Influencing student performance.* Columbus, OH: Merrill.

Stokes, T. F., & Baer, D. M. (1977). An implicit technology of generalization. *Journal of Applied Behavior Analysis, 10,* 349–367.

Sulzer-Azaroff, B., & Mayer, G. R. (1977). *Applying behavior-analysis procedures with children and youth.* New York: Holt, Rinehart, & Winston.

J. Todd Stephens
University of Wisconsin at Madison

GENERALIZATION

TRANSFORMATIONAL GENERATIVE GRAMMAR

In 1957 Noam Chomsky revolutionized the field of English grammar and research with the publication of the book *Syntactic Structures.* Chomsky, considered the father of the theory of transformational grammar, proposed a finite set of operations (called transformations) that produce (or generate) sentences of infinite number and variety without producing nonsentences. These operations are acquired during the first few years of life through exposure to conversation rather than through formal study. They are internalized by the speaker without his or her being aware of or able to state them.

Chomsky's theory describes the language people do use rather than the language they ought to use (Cattell, 1978). It focuses on competence, the ideal speaker-listener's complete command of language, as opposed to performance, the actual use of language in concrete situations as affected by imperfection and inconsistency. Unlike the traditional grammarian who deals with sentence form, or surface structure, Chomsky distinguishes between surface structure and its underlying meaning or deep structure. This is the level at which grammatical relationships are preserved. By way of

example, Quigley, Russell, and Power (1977) present the sentences "John is easy to please" and "John is eager to please." These two sentences are identical to one another in surface structure but completely different in deep structure. Muma (1978) elaborates by pointing out that the sentence "I bes here" (nonstandard dialect) is not inferior to the sentence "I am here" (standard dialect), as both are identical at the deep structure level.

Deep structures are turned into surface structures through transformations that expand, delete, and reorder sentence constituents, or component parts. These operations may be applied to all sentences without changing their meanings. Examples of transformations applied to the sentence "boys like girls" would include question (do boys like girls?), negation (boys don't like girls), and passive voice (girls are liked by boys; Quigley et al., 1977).

Transformational grammarians view the sentence as a hierarchical organization of constituents. By applying a series of rewriting rules of increasing specificity, it is possible to analyze sentence structure, working backward through the derivation of a sentence to discover the initial transformational rule by which it was generated. These rewriting rules enable linguists to describe sentences pictorially using tree diagrams. Crystal, Fletcher, and Gorman (1977) point out that the easiest and best known of these rules is represented by the formula S Æ NP + VP, or rewrite the sentence as a noun phrase and a verb phrase.

Transformational generative grammar has been applied successfully to research into language function (Dever, 1971), language development and delay, dialectic differences, and ESL studies (Quigley et al., 1977). Its detractors have noted that the distinction between language competence and performance is minimal at best when dealing with individuals with language disorders (Crystal et al., 1977). Akmajian, Demers, and Harnish (1980) note that Chomsky's model has been challenged at every level, resulting in numerous changes since the mid-1960s.

REFERENCES

Akmajian, A., Demers, R. A., & Harnish, R. M. (1980). *Linguistics: An introduction to language and communication.* Cambridge, MA: MIT Press.

Cattell, N. R. (1978). *The new English grammar.* Cambridge, MA: MIT Press.

Chomsky, N. (1957). *Syntactic structures.* The Hague: Mouton.

Chomsky, N. (1965). *Aspects of the theory of syntax.* Cambridge, MA: MIT Press.

Crystal, D., Fletcher, P., & Gorman, M. (1977). *The grammatical analysis of language disability: A procedure for assessment and remediation.* London: Arnold.

Dever, R. B. (1971). The case for data gathering. *Journal of Special Education, 5,* 119–126.

Muma, J. R. (1978). *Language handbook: Concepts, assessment, intervention.* Englewood Cliffs, NJ: Prentice Hall.

Quigley, S. P., Russell, W. K., & Power, D. J. (1977). *Linguistics and deaf children.* Washington, DC: Alexander Graham Bell Association.

SUSAN SHANDELMIER
Eastern Pennsylvania Special Education Regional Resources Center

CHOMSKY, NOAM
LANGUAGE DISORDERS
LINGUISTIC DEVIANCE

TRANSITION

Transition is the process of changing from one condition or place to another; it is common to individuals at various times throughout their lives. Transition from preschool to school environments as well as transition from school to postschool environments present problems for the young child and the adolescent. For individuals with special needs who are graduating or leaving school, this process is frequently more difficult than for others. The entitlement to a free appropriate public education may not necessarily culminate in opportunities for employment, integration into the community, or adult services. In recognition of the concerns of parents, educators, and service providers regarding the futures of students with disabilities leaving publicly supported education programs, a national priority on transition from school to work for all individuals with disabilities was announced by the Office of Special Education and Rehabilitation Services (OSERS) in 1983. The need for transitional services and the provision of some degree of financial support for these activities are addressed in PL 98-199, the Education for All Handicapped Children Amendments, and in IDEA.

Will (1984) has defined transition from school to work as "an outcome-oriented process encompassing a broad array of services and experiences that lead to employment" (p. 2). Transition refers to the period between school and work, and transitional services encompass both ends of a continuum between educational and adult services. The transition period includes the high school years, postsecondary services, and the first few years of employment. The goal of transition is meaningful paid employment and successful community functioning for individuals with disabilities. To obtain this goal, a restructuring and rethinking of the roles and responsibilities of various agencies at the federal, state, and local levels is necessary so as to ensure appropriate, nonduplicated services delivery (Vocational Transition, 1986).

The transition from school to work and adult life requires careful, systematic preparation and planning in the secondary school; cooperative support of interagency teams on graduation; and awareness and support of multiple employment options and services as needed by the community and professionals.

Generally, the difficulty in transition to postsecondary environments increases with the severity of the disability. Wilcox and Bellamy (1982) include the prevention of institutionalization in their definition of transition. They have suggested guidelines for effective transition of the more severely handicapped; these include using a case management approach to develop a comprehensive transition plan that is individualized, starts in the last years of school, has links with adult services, is locally designed, and ensures continuity of services without interruption. Preparation for the next environment should be stressed, as well as advocacy and family preparation.

Transition services may be grouped into three classes that reflect the nature of the public services used to provide support as the passage is completed: (1) transition with no special services—vocational technical schools and work experience; (2) transition with time-limited services—vocational rehabilitation, Job Training Partnership Act; and (3) transition with ongoing services—supported work environments for individuals with severe disabilities (Will, 1984).

Finally, one of the major issues surrounding transition is the lack of information about the status of special education graduates. Hasazi et al. (1985) cited the need to develop a body of data regarding the employment status of these individuals for use as a basis for future planning regarding transition activities.

REFERENCES

Hasazi, S. B., Gordon, L. R., & Roe, C. A. (1985). Factors associated with the employment status of handicapped youth exiting high school from 1979 to 1983. *Exceptional Children, 51,* 455–469.

Vocational transition: A priority for the '80s. (1986). *Project-Tie, 1*(1).

Wilcox, B., & Bellamy, G. T. (1982). *Design of high school programs for severely handicapped students.* Baltimore: Brookes.

Will, M. (1984). *OSERS programming for the transition of youth with disabilities: Bridges from school to working life.* Washington, DC: Office of Special Education and Rehabilitative Services.

EILEEN F. MCCARTHY
University of Wisconsin at Madison

VOCATIONAL EDUCATION
VOCATIONAL REHABILITATION COUNSELING

TRANSITION PLANNING FOR CULTURALLY AND LINGUISTICALLY DIVERSE STUDENTS

National concern for transition issues began in the 1980s. Transition was addressed in the Education of the Handicapped Act Amendments of 1983 and Madeline Will, former assistant secretary for special education and rehabilitative services, Office of Special Education and Rehabilitative Services, issued a policy paper regarding transition from school to work. As transition became a national priority, transition programs and models for transition were developed and evaluated across the country. Transition programs focus on employment, residential, transportation, and recreational issues. Components of model programs include functional curricula, integrated school services, community-based instruction, comprehensive individual transition plans, interagency cooperation, and follow-up of students. In addition to including these components, successful programs provide early planning and early experiences in competitive employment for their students. Parent involvement and student self-determination are considered critical aspects of successful transition planning.

Components of Transition Planning

Transition planning involves decision-making about major life considerations related to employment, education, residence, and recreation/leisure activities. Students' vocational aptitude and interests are assessed to help provide guidance in career planning. Typically, these decisions are made by the student him or herself, his or her family, educators, and adult service agency personnel in the transition planning meeting. The transition planning team works together to set goals, which the student will work to attain during his or her secondary education. That aspects of transition planning might differ when working with culturally and linguistically diverse students is a relatively new concept.

Assessment

It is important to note that assessment results, which are used in transition planning, may not be valid for culturally and linguistically diverse students or for students with disabilities. Therefore, professionals must use caution in making decisions based on results of these assessments. According to Szymanski (1994), assessment that is not culturally valid can disempower culturally diverse students in the transition process. When possible, it is recommended that authentic assessment be used, to ensure that valid information is used to make important life decisions (Harry et al., 1995).

Self-Determination

Increasingly, individuals with disabilities are being encouraged to take charge of their own lives; this is referred to as self-determination. In some schools, with guidance from educators, students are conducting their own transition planning meetings. In encouraging students from culturally and linguistically diverse backgrounds to be more self-

determined, it is critical to understand their unique family characteristics. Families either facilitate or impede student self-determination (Morningstar, Turnbull, & Turnbull, 1995), and this effect is often culture related. If educators encourage a student to have a goal of independently living in an apartment, but his or her family believes that their role is to care for their child for his or her life-span, conflict will occur. Parents are a member of the transition planning team and their support is necessary for successful transition to occur; parent values and beliefs also greatly influence their children's vision of the future (Morningstar et al., 1995). Finally, if the purpose of self-determination is to help students "to intentionally create experiences in their lives that are consistent with their unique beliefs, needs, and preferences," cultural and linguistic backgrounds need to be respected (Field, Martin, Miller, Ward, & Wehmeyer, 1998, p. 143).

Parent Involvement

In planning a student's transition from school to work, the involvement of the student and his or her parents can impact the success of the plan. Although parents have the right to participate, actual parent participation in the special education process is very limited (Gartner & Lipsky, 1987). In addition to being limited, participation decreases as the age of the child increases (Cone, Delawyer, & Wolfe, 1985; Salisbury & Evans, 1988). In a survey of parents of 129 graduates of high school special education programs, only 34 percent of the parents perceived themselves as being actively involved in their child's school program; 43 percent perceived themselves as somewhat involved (attending meetings, etc.) and 23 percent perceived that they were not involved at all (Haring, Lovett, & Saren, 1991). This limited involvement could reflect a lack of effort on the part of school personnel, or a choice made by the parents. In addition, it is common for Hispanic families to defer all educational decisions to "experts" in the school (Lynch & Stein, 1987); this is a sign of respect, rather than an indication of disinterest. While there are differing opinions regarding the need for parent involvement, there are definite benefits, such as providing input regarding their years of experience with the child, providing continuity to the child's program, setting appropriate goals for the child, and serving as an advocate for the child. Professionals need to empower parents from culturally diverse backgrounds by showing them the value of their input in making decisions for their child.

Participation has been found to differ according to ethnicity of parents (Stein, 1983; Lynch & Stein, 1987). Hispanic parents, while satisfied with their level of involvement, are less able to be involved in their child's education program and participate less actively. Both Hispanics and African Americans are less aware of services included in the Individual Education Program (IEP) than are Anglos; however, African Americans participate more actively than do Hispanics in the IEP development and assessment process. Major barriers identified in preventing Hispanic parents from participating in their child's program were work and lack of bilingual communication.

According to Turnbull and Turnbull (1982), for various reasons parents may choose not to be involved in educational decision making for their child with disabilities. They maintain that parents should not be expected to have the equivalent of a master's level training in special education. While some parents choose to be actively involved in their children's special education, some prefer to leave the educational decisions to the educational specialists. The individual needs of the parents need to be considered as well as the individual needs of the child. Professional roles should not be forced upon parents (Allen & Hudd, 1987). Parents should be given an opportunity to be informed of educational goals and objectives and allowed to participate to the degree they choose, but parental involvement should not be mandatory (Turnbull & Turnbull, 1982; MacMillan & Turnbull, 1983).

When schools do involve parents in their children's special education, often the emphasis is on obtaining signatures for documentation that required procedures were followed (Shevin, 1983). In a survey of 145 special education teachers, while 51 percent viewed the IEP meeting as an opportunity for parent involvement, 44.3 percent perceived it as merely a formality (Gerber, Banbury, Miller, & Griffin, 1986). Although legal mandates are being followed, the intent of the law is not followed if parents and/or students do not understand because of cultural or language barriers. At the same time, parents often lack the confidence to persist in their efforts to formulate their children's educational programs (Shevin, 1983). Parents not only need to be given the opportunity to be involved in educational planning for their children with disabilities, they need to be informed.

Even when professionals involve parents according to the law, often their participation is perceived as less valuable. Parents receive the message that their input is given a lower priority than that of professionals (Harry, Allen, & McLaughlin, 1995). Parents from linguistically different backgrounds may use different terms to identify and/or describe their child's characteristics, while they may be perceived as not accepting the child's limitations, thus devaluing their input in the eyes of professionals; often the difference is merely in the language used to describe the disability (Harry, 1992b). It is important to remember that although parents may interpret their child's disability differently, they still may be very perceptive regarding the disability and can be important contributors to educational planning.

Parent Education

For parents to become active members of their children's transition planning teams, education and training regard-

ing transition issues will have to be provided. In a survey of parents of students with severe disabilities, only 65 percent of the 203 respondents reported having received any information about postschool services available in their community (McDonnell, Wilcox, Boles, & Bellamy, 1985). Without this information, parents cannot effectively plan for their children's transitions. A survey of parents of young adults with mild disabilities revealed that parents were hindered in providing support for transition by a lack of information regarding issues such as knowledge of vocational abilities and limitations, potential employment opportunities for their children, and postsecondary services available (Tilson & Neubert, 1988). It is particularly important to provide information in the parents' dominant language; language usage and professional jargon are often a barrier to parent participation (Congress, 1997).

Setting Goals

In setting goals, educators must remember that norms differ across cultures (Harry et al., 1995); terms such as "work" and "independent living" are culturally-based, and families may interpret these terms differently than professionals in schools. Parents can be very effective members of their children's educational planning team; however, sensitivity to cultural differences must be considered when presenting different options within these three domains. According to Kelker et al. (1986), parents can serve various roles in transition planning, including providing information, sharing values and concerns about the student, helping to set priorities, acting as case manager, serving as an advocate for services, and providing role models. Again, professionals need to consider the cultural background and values of each family when recommending roles for them to take. It is also necessary to avoid assuming that parents are aware of the transition options within the community; individuals from culturally diverse backgrounds may be less knowledgeable than their Anglo counterparts in certain areas (Lynch & Stein, 1987).

Goodall and Bruder (1986) maintain that parents are the ultimate advocates and case managers, as they are "the one constant in a lifetime of changing services and providers" (p. 23). After the students leave high school, the parents will be responsible for them obtaining the necessary services; parental involvement in transition planning, therefore, is critical. Problems may occur in transition planning when parents' goals and aspirations are different from the potential of the child as perceived by professional educators. For example, educators may aspire for their students' competitive employment, independent living, and integrated leisure activities. However, in a close-knit Hispanic family, the parents may wish for their child to stay at home, unemployed, participating in the community as a member of their family only (Lynch, 1992).

Opportunities for persons in rural areas are limited.

This includes Native Americans who live on reservations. Transition planning will be more challenging for these students because there will not be the same array of services available to facilitate transition. The distance between the family's residence and the nearest services may result in families refusing services, even though educators believe the services to be in the best interest of the child. It is important for the educator to be aware that this refusal is a result of a cultural difference rather than an uncaring attitude about the child.

Increasing Parent Involvement

Increasing parent involvement in special education can result in positive outcomes (Boone, 1992). This may be accomplished by scheduling meetings beyond school hours, conducting meetings at a neutral site, providing additional opportunities for parental input to educational planning, providing follow-up telephone calls after meetings, and introducing parents to support groups (Gress & Carroll, 1985). At meetings, there should be enough time to allow parents and educators to share and discuss ideas (Witt, Miller, McIntyre, & Smith, 1984).

Parents can also be involved in the implementation of their children's education plans (Izzo, 1987); in teaching functional living goals, educators can discuss with parents which skills or competencies will be stressed at school and which will be taught at home by parents. Parents can be invited and encouraged to visit job sites and vocational training programs (Lehmann, Deniston, & Grebenc, 1989). Parents who are aware of what is occurring in their child's education will be able to be more involved with their child.

Stein (1983) offers the following suggestions for increasing involvement of Hispanic parents:

- conduct meetings and present school communications in the language of the home;
- encourage families to ask questions, offer suggestions, and provide information about their child;
- train bilingual parent facilitators to assist parents in becoming partners;
- consider and respect cultural differences and similarities, while also opening discussions about the consequences of such differences and similarities;
- do not expect parents to permeate the "walls" of the school but to open the doors wider and encourage parents to come in;
- help teach parents how to participate in their children's special education program by explaining clearly and accurately parental rights and responsibilities as well as available educational processes and services;
- provide necessary transportation and child-care services when parent participation at a school meeting is required; and

- frequently survey the Hispanic community and work with Hispanic community agencies to develop strategies to more actively involve Hispanic citizens. (p. 438)

Although these suggestions are particular to the involvement of Hispanic parents, they apply in general to any parent of a different culture or ethnicity. Lynch and Stein (1987) recommend the following for involving families of diverse cultural backgrounds:

- conduct a study of parent involvement to determine the differences and needs within the community;
- develop a concise position paper which addresses the importance of parental involvement in special education decision making;
- develop grant applications which support the hiring and training of parents from various cultural groups to become liaisons between the school system and other parents;
- work with other community groups and organizations to provide training about special education programs and services to individuals in the various cultural communities who have direct contact with families;
- develop training packages for parents from diverse cultures about special education programs, services, and processes;
- provide inservice education to school personnel which describes cultural and linguistic differences and sensitizes all school staff to the values and beliefs of the families whom they serve; and
- continue to recruit and hire school personnel who represent a wide range of cultural and linguistic backgrounds. (p. 110)

Awareness and sensitivity to cultural diversity and the involvement of representatives of different cultures in developing strategies to increase parent involvement within their cultures can be as effective for other groups as well as Hispanics.

Parents need to be empowered with knowledge regarding the transition process and postsecondary options for their children with disabilities to improve services available through adult agencies, as well as specific training in implementing their children's transition plans (Lehmann et al., 1989). McDonnell and Hardman (1985) report that for parents to be successfully involved in transition planning, they need information regarding the components of effective high school programs, the characteristics of adult service programs, criteria for evaluating postschool service programs, potential service alternatives, and the status of services in the local community. They suggest that schools can provide this information through conducting inservice training sessions for parents and through the development of a transition planning guide for parents.

Guidelines for Transition Planning

Although broad generalizations regarding different cultures have been presented, it is extremely important to recognize that each student and his or her family have unique characteristics all their own and there is no "recipe" for transition planning based on an individual's ethnic background. For example, one might assume that Asian-American families have high expectations for their children and would steer their child toward a scientific or technological career. This is a stereotype that will not hold true for all Asian-American families. What is important is to be aware that different families have different values and goals for their individual members. In assisting students from culturally and linguistically diverse backgrounds as they transition from school to work, it is essential that educators seek to know each student and his or her family individually and take their values, goals, and so on into consideration. Harry and colleagues (1995) claim that "shared cultural, educational, social, and linguistic experiences allow parents and professionals to proceed more directly to special education matters" (p. 102). The following general guidelines will facilitate the understanding of each family's unique culture (U.S. Department of Education, 1997; Greene, 1996; Harry et al., 1995; Harry, 1992a, 1992c; Inger, 1992; Lynch, 1992).

1. Home visits can be a valuable means for developing understanding of a family's culture and background. They offer the added advantage of meeting a family on their own turf, in comfortable surroundings. To develop a collaborative relationship with a family, educators must understand the family's perspective.

2. Ask, rather than assume, what language is spoken in the home and by what members of the family. Also, ascertain the literacy level of different family members. Take this information into consideration in all communications with the family.

3. Providing written material is not enough; it needs to be discussed verbally and explained. The transition process needs to be explained, and written materials used as a reminder, not a primary source. The most successful approach in communicating is face-to-face, in a person's native language.

4. Parent involvement, particularly in attending meetings, can be greatly enhanced by flexibility in accommodating parents' schedules, providing transportation, and altering the site of the meetings. Important information should be presented in the parents' dominant language. Positive interactions should be fostered at all meetings to ensure continued participation.

5. There is a need for improved communication regarding parent training meetings. Input from parents needs to be obtained to determine why parents do not attend and why they seem to perceive that the districts are lacking in this area. Communication can then be improved.

6. Districts need to provide inservice meetings for special education teachers to familiarize them with aspects related to the cultural diversity of the students they serve. Teachers or special education personnel responsible for transition need to have more intensive sessions specifically related to transition; however, all teachers need to be familiar with the process and know how to direct parents' questions.

7. Finally, transition councils and parent advisory groups can be effectively used to develop the transition process and facilitate collaboration between professionals and culturally and linguistically diverse families. Obtaining input from those with whom the district will be working in transition planning and service provision is a very effective way to encourage their involvement.

REFERENCES

Allen, D. A., & Hudd, S. S. (1987). Are we professionalizing parents? Weighing the benefits and pitfalls. *Mental Retardation, 25*(3), 133–139.

Boone, R. (1992). Involving culturally diverse parents in transition planning. *Career Development for Exceptional Individuals, 15*(2), 205–221.

Cone, J. D., Delawyer, D. D., & Wolfe, V. V. (1985). Assessing parent participation: The parent/family involvement index. *Exceptional Children, 51*(5), 417–424.

Congress, E. P. (Ed.). (1997). *Multicultural perspectives in working with families.* New York: Springer.

Field, S., Martin, J., Miller, R., Ward, M., & Wehmeyer, M. (1998). *A practical guide for teaching self-determination.* Reston, VA: Council for Exceptional Children.

Gartner, A., & Lipsky, D. K. (1987). Beyond special education: Toward a quality system for all students. *Harvard Educational Review, 57*(4), 367–385.

Gerber, P. J., Banbury, M. M., Miller, J. H., & Griffin, H. C. (1986). Special educators' perceptions of parental participation in the individual education plan process. *Psychology in the Schools, 23*(2), 158–163.

Goodall, P., & Bruder, M. B. (1986). Parents & the transition process. *Exceptional Parent, 16*(2), 22–28.

Greene, G. (1996). Empowering culturally and linguistically diverse families in the transition planning process. *Journal for Vocational Special Needs Education, 19*(1), 26–30.

Gress, J. R., & Carroll, M. E. (1985). Parent-professional partnership and the IEP. *Academic Therapy, 20*(4), 443–449.

Haring, K. A., Lovett, D. L., & Saren, D. (1991). Parent perceptions of their adult offspring with disabilities. *Teaching Exceptional Children, 23*(2), 6–10.

Harry, B. (1995). Developing culturally inclusive services for individuals with severe disabilities. *JASH, 20*(2), 99–109.

Harry, B. (1992a). *Cultural diversity, families, and the special education system.* New York: Teachers College Press.

Harry, B. (1992b). Making sense of disability: Low-income, Puerto Rican parents' theories of problems. *Exceptional Children, 59*(1), 27–40.

Harry, B. (1992c). Restructuring the participation of African-American parents in special education. *Exceptional Children, 59*(2), 123–131.

Harry, B., Allen, N., McLaughlin, M. (1995). Communication versus compliance: African-American parents' involvement in special education. *Exceptional Children, 61*(4), 364–377.

Inger, M. (1992). Increasing the school involvement of Hispanic parents. ERIC Clearinghouse on Urban Education. (*ERIC Digest Number 80,* 24–25)

Izzo, M. V. (1987). Career development of disabled youth: The parents' role. *Journal of Career Development, 13*(4), 47–55.

Kelker, K., Mcrae, T., Faught, K., Allard, G., Hagen, M., & Offner, R. (1986). *Planning for transition: An implementation guide for administrators and teachers.* Billings: Montana Center for Handicapped Children.

Lehmann, J. P., Deniston, T., & Grebenc, R. (1989). Counseling parents to facilitate transition: The difference parents make. *Journal for Vocational Special Needs Education, 11*(3), 15–18.

Lynch, E. W., & Stein, R. C. (1987). Parent participation by ethnicity: A comparison of Hispanic, Black, and Anglo families. *Exceptional Children, 54*(2), 105–111.

Lynch, P. S. (1992). Parents' perceptions of their involvement in planning the transition from school to work for their children with disabilities in Texas. Unpublished manuscript.

Macmillan, D. L., & Turnbull, A. P. (1983). Parent involvement with special education: Respecting individual preferences. *Education and Training of the Mentally Retarded, 18*(1), 4–9.

McDonnell, J., & Hardman, M. (1985). Planning the transition of severely handicapped youth from school to adult services: A framework for high school programs. *Education and Training of the Mentally Retarded, 10*(1), 17–21.

McDonnell, J., Wilcox, B., Boles, S. M., & Bellamy, G. T. (1985). Transition issues facing youth with severe disabilities: Parents' perspective. *Journal for the Association for Persons with Severe Handicaps, 10*(1), 61–65.

Morningstar, M. E., Turnbull, A. P., & Turnbull, H. R. (1995). What do students with disabilities tell us about the importance of family involvement in the transition from school to adult life? *Exceptional Children, 62*(3), 249–260.

Shevin, M. (1983). Meaningful parental involvement in long-range educational planning for disabled children. *Education and Training of the Mentally Retarded, 10*(1), 17–21.

Stein, R. C. (1983). Hispanic parents' perspectives and participation in their children's special education program: Comparisons by program and race. *Learning Disability Quarterly, 6*(4), 432–438.

Szymanski, E. M. (1994). Transition: Life-span and life-space considerations for empowerment. *Exceptional Children, 60*(5), 402–410.

Tilson, G. P., & Neubert, D. A. (1988). School-to-work transition of mildly disabled young adults. *Journal for Vocational Special Needs Education, 11*(1), 33–37.

Turnbull, A. P., & Turnbull, H. R. (1982). Parent involvement in the education of handicapped children: A critique. *Mental Retardation, 20*(3), 115–122.

U.S. Department of Education. (1997). *Nineteenth annual report to Congress on the Implementation of the Individuals with Disabilities Education Act.* Washington, DC: Author.

Witt, J. C., Miller, C. D., McIntyre, R. M., & Smith, D. (1984). Effects of variables on parental perceptions of staffings. *Exceptional Children, 51*(1), 27–32.

PAT LYNCH
BROOKE DURBIN
Texas A&M University

CULTURALLY/LINGUISTICALLY DIVERSE STUDENTS

TRANSPORTATION OF STUDENTS WITH DISABILITIES

Transportation of students with disabilities is usually viewed as an administrative requirement to ensure access to public education. It is seldom viewed as an opportunity to teach students community mobility skills. However, community mobility is the dynamic concept within the issue of transportation of handicapped students. The ability of an individual to participate independently or semiindependently in all aspects of community life (e.g., domestic, recreational, vocational) is dependent on community mobility (Wehman, Renzaglia, & Bates, 1985). Community mobility refers to movement from one place to another within a particular setting and travel between two community locations. The concept of community mobility was originally developed in program practice and literature related to working with visually handicapped individuals. In this literature, community mobility is referred to as orientation and mobility training.

For visually impaired individuals, orientation and mobility training has long been a well-respected component of the curriculum. As the rights of all citizens to participate in the least restrictive environment have been acknowledged, the concept of community mobility has been broadened to include the physically disabled, mentally retarded, emotionally disturbed, and other special education consumers. Assurances for meeting the basic transportation needs to and from school have been established within PL 94-142 for all special education students. However, the transportation needs of students with disabilities are complex.

The ability of a person to be independently mobile is

dependent on several factors. One of the primary factors that influences the degree of mobility attained by individuals with disabilities is the opportunity for travel from one place to another. Opportunity for mobility can be restricted by both physical and attitudinal barriers. In many communities, extensive physical modifications have been made, including construction of ramps, widening of doorways, installment of elevators, cutting out of curbs, and purchase of lift buses. Although these modifications have removed many barriers to independent mobility, obstacles still exist in all communities. Realistically, many of these obstacles are not going to be eliminated. Some of these obstacles are outside of the control of engineers and educators (e.g., weather conditions, natural terrain). Since mobility obstacles are likely to remain in every community, efforts must be directed toward teaching individuals to overcome these problems. By combining environmental changes with specific instruction programs, handicapped citizens are provided easier access as well as more skills for traveling independently within their communities. Community mobility training programs should reflect this dual concern for improving physical accessibility and training skills that compensate for various environmental barriers.

Attitudinal barriers can severely restrict a person's chances for learning independent mobility skills in an even more devastating way than physical obstacles. These barriers result from a combination of overprotectiveness and lowered expectations. Parents and professionals have contributed to this problem. According to Perske (1972), "such overprotection endangers the client's human dignity, and tends to keep him from experiencing the risk taking of ordinary life which is necessary for normal growth and development" (p. 29).

Overprotectiveness and lowered expectations can combine to present attitudinal barriers that severely limit a person's opportunity to acquire independent living skills. However, the development of responsible and effective community mobility training programs can alleviate fears and concerns regarding safety and consequently raise the expectations of parents and professionals for independent living by handicapped individuals. The development of such programs will significantly increase the opportunity an individual will have to acquire independent living skills.

More community mobility training programs have begun to emphasize the functional relationship between public transportation and access to community services. For example, Sowers, Rusch, and Hudson (1979) used systematic training procedures to teach a severely retarded adult to complete the following 10-behavior sequence to ride the city bus to and from work: (1) cross controlled intersections, (2) cross unmarked intersections, (3) use bus tickets, (4) walk to bus, (5) identify the correct bus, (6) board, (7) ride, (8) depart, (9) transfer, and (10) walk to work. Further, Marholin, O'Toole, Touchette, Berger, and Doyle (1979) taught four moderately and severely retarded adults to use public bus transportation to travel between a public institution and various community locations for shopping and eating in a restaurant.

The responsibility of public schools for transporting students with disabilities to and from school programs must be expanded to include greater sensitivity to the unique community mobility needs of individual students. In meeting these responsibilities, educators should promote the development of a normalized repertoire of transportation skills. At a basic level, this could involve assistance that enables handicapped students to use the same transportation system in association with their nondisabled peers. At a more complex level, this would require a commitment to teaching a variety of mobility skills that would enhance a person's ability to access community activities throughout his or her lifetime.

REFERENCES

Marholin, D., Touchette, P., Berger, P., & Doyle, D. (1979). I'll have a big mac, large fries, large coke, and apple pie—of teaching adaptive community skills. *Behavior Therapy, 10,* 236–248.

Perske, R. (1972). The dignity of risk. In W. Wolfensberger (Ed.), *The principle of normalization in human services.* Toronto, Ontario: National Institute on Mental Retardation.

Sowers, J., Rusch, F. R., & Hudson, C. (1979). Training a severely retarded young adult to ride the city bus to and from work. *AAESPH Review, 4,* 15–22.

Wehman, P., Renzaglia, A., & Bates, P. (1985). *Functional living skills for the moderately and severely handicapped.* Austin, TX: PRO-ED.

PAUL BATES
Southern Illinois University

ELECTRONIC TRAVEL AIDS
MOBILITY INSTRUCTION
TRAVEL AIDS FOR INDIVIDUALS WITH DISABILITIES

TRAUMATIC BRAIN INJURY AND SCHOOL REENTRY

Traumatic brain injury (TBI) involves a physical injury to the brain caused by an external force, resulting in diminished consciousness or coma (Stratton & Gregory, 1994). There are two types of traumatic brain injuries: open and closed head injuries. Open head injuries occur when an object (e.g., a bullet or shell fragment) penetrates the skull and produces damage to the brain. The damage tends to be localized about the path of the penetrating object (Lezak, 1995). In contrast, closed head injuries are more common than open head injuries and are more likely to produce diffuse damage (Begali, 1992). A blow to the head without penetrating the skull is an example of a closed head injury.

In closed head injuries, the direct impact causes the brain, which is floating in cerebrospinal fluid within the skull, to strike the inside of the skull in one or more places. The movement of the brain within the skull causes shearing and tearing of nerve fibers and contusions (i.e., bruising; Lezak, 1995). In addition to the primary effects (e.g., the bruising, shearing, tearing), secondary effects are often present in the form of brain swelling and hemorrhaging. The secondary effects compound the damage, resulting in a wide variety of neural structures being affected (Stratton & Gregory, 1994). As a result, diversity in behavioral sequelae (i.e., consequences) in TBI patients is the norm rather than the exception. Impairments in cognition, language, memory, attention/concentration, conceptual functions, abstract reasoning, judgment, academic achievement or new learning, and perception have been reported in traumatic brain injured children and adolescents. Motor and sensory deficits have also been noted along with behavioral and socioemotional problems (Begali, 1992). For additional information on the sequelae associated with TBI, see the entry on traumatic brain injury in children.

Head injury is a common occurrence among children and adolescents. It is the leading cause of death and disability in children (Begali, 1992). Approximately one million children in the United States experience a head injury each year (Research and Training Center in Rehabilitation and Childhood Trauma, 1993). Of these one million, 165,000 children and adolescents are hospitalized with a traumatic brain injury yearly (National Information Center for Children and Youth with Disabilities [NICCYD], 1993). Although most of these children and adolescents will enjoy a substantial recovery, 16,000 to 20,000 of these individuals will have moderate to severe injuries producing long-term effects (Clark & Hostetter, 1995).

Children with TBI are not new to the schools; however, the number of severely injured children surviving and returning to schools has grown. Sophisticated medical technology has resulted in an increased survival rate among children following a traumatic brain injury (Rapp, 1999). Federal law mandates that these children are to be served by the schools; however, educators and parents often lack the knowledge on how to best serve these students (Blosser & DePompei, 1991).

In 1990, traumatic brain injury was added to the list of eligibility categories under the Individuals with Disabilities Education Act (IDEA). IDEA, or Public Law 101-476, is the major special education law in the United States. PL 101-476, now PL 105-17, defines a traumatic brain injury as:

> An acquired injury to the brain caused by an external force, resulting in total or partial functional disability or psychosocial impairment, or both, that adversely affects a child's educational performance. The term applies to open or closed head injuries resulting in impairments in one or more areas, such as cognition; language; memory; attention; reasoning; abstract thinking; judgment; problem-solving; sensory, perceptual and motor abilities; psychosocial behavior; physical functions; information processing; and speech. The term does not apply to brain injuries that are congenital or degenerative, or injuries induced by birth trauma. (*Federal Register,* 1992, p. 44802)

According to the federal law, children and adolescents who experience a brain injury resulting from internal as opposed to external trauma are excluded from this definition and services. In other words, children whose injuries are caused by internal events, such as brain tumors, cerebral vascular accidents, exposure to environmental toxins, or central nervous system infections cannot be served under the TBI category, but may be eligible for services under another special education category (e.g., Other Health Impaired). Some states, however, have opted to identify, classify, and serve a broader range of children whose injuries are the result of either external or internal trauma (Rapp, 1999). State rules and regulations should be consulted to determine whether children whose brain injury is the result of internal trauma are eligible for services under the TBI category.

To be eligible for services under the TBI category of IDEA, children's educational performances must be adversely affected by their injury. For those individuals with TBI who are not eligible for special education and related services under IDEA, Section 504 of the Vocational Rehabilitation Act of 1973, a civil rights law, may provide sufficient services and protections in the general education classroom. Section 504 outlines the school district's responsibility to provide educational accommodations and related services to allow disabled students to have equal access to all publicly funded programs available to their nondisabled peers. In either case, the federal law is quite clear. Children with TBI who are eligible under IDEA or Section 504 must be served. Thus, plans must be developed and services implemented in order to successfully reintegrate these children into the classroom following their injury.

A number of resources must be mobilized and activities planned and implemented prior to a child's return to school to ensure successful school reentry, including assignment of a case manager, formation of a school or interdisciplinary team, inservice training for school personnel, family education, peer education, notification to the State's Vocational Rehabilitation Office, and collaboration among the systems (home, school, hospital/rehabilitation unit). Successful school reintegration is dependent upon collaboration and open communication among the family, school, and hospital/rehabilitation systems. Open communication is imperative in all stages of recovery. Information exchanged should begin immediately following the injury, when the child is first admitted to the hospital (Clark, 1997); however, controversy exists as to which system is responsible for making the initial contact. Haak and Livingston (1997) suggest the school should take the initiative and contact the parents to obtain permission to contact the medical facility. Opening communication channels helps ensure that the child will be appropriately served.

The school should appoint a representative (i.e., a case manager), who is knowledgeable about TBI, to serve as a liaison among the different systems. The case manager's role should be to establish and maintain communication and coordinate services among the systems on behalf of the child. The case manager should relay information to the school from the hospital regarding the severity of the child's injury, current behavior, medication management (Clark, 1997), progress, and expected discharge and school reentry dates (Haak & Livingston, 1997). Through the case manager, assessment results and the hospital/rehabilitation unit's recommendations can be forwarded to the school. The case manager provides the medical facility, on the other hand, with information from the school regarding the child's educational history, any preinjury assessment results, classroom assignments, and the school's progress in preparing for the child's reentry (Clark, 1997); for example, removal of architectural barriers, if needed. The case manager also communicates with the parents to obtain information about the child's current status and any problems the child may be experiencing.

Family education is also critical to a child's successful school reentry. The child's family needs to receive general information on TBI and TBI sequelae. They also need to be informed about the child's specific needs (e.g., educational needs) and abilities. Medical professionals and the case manager can help educate the family in these areas. Medical professionals can also provide the family with information on TBI and TBI sequelae, whereas the case manager can provide the family with information on IDEA and Section 504. The child's family needs to know what services are available in a school district, eligibility criteria to receive these services, process to obtain these services, and child and family's rights in relation to these services under the federal law (Ylvisaker, Hartwick, & Stevens, 1991).

Inservice training is another essential activity needed to facilitate a child's successful reentry back into the school setting. Common reactions of school personnel about a child preparing to return to school are either sheer panic or overconfidence. Panic may result because of the school personnel's lack of knowledge on how best to serve the child, whereas the staff's overconfidence may be based on the assumption that the child is fully recovered and educational programming can begin where it had abruptly ended at the time of the accident. These reactions are typical, but unnecessary (Rapp, 1999). Inservice training can inform and address the issues and concerns of the school staff. Inservice training conducted by an individual with expertise on TBI (e.g., a rehabilitation professional) can provide general information about TBI and TBI sequelae. The professional with expertise on TBI should provide information on the specific needs and abilities of the child as well (Ylvisaker

et al., 1991). Information about intervention strategies that may be beneficial to the child in and outside the classroom should also be included (Clark, 1997).

Besides inservice training, in-class meetings should be held between the case manager and the child's peers to educate classmates about TBI and discuss the child's condition and possible changes in his/her behavior (e.g., changes in personality). A discussion with the student's classmates about the child with his/her permission (Ylvisaker et al., 1991) may help peers to develop a better understanding of the situation and support for the student.

The state's Office of Vocational Rehabilitation should also be contacted in the likelihood that a child with TBI will need their services in order to obtain employment upon graduation from high school. Many vocational rehabilitation offices have tracking systems. Notification results in the youth's name being entered into the vocational rehabilitation system for future services. In addition, the school counselor and vocational liaison specialist for the school district should be made aware of the need to develop community-based work experiences for the child. On-site training will help the individual with TBI develop work skills needed to succeed in a competitive employment market (Ylvisaker et al., 1991).

Before the child with TBI is discharged from the medical facility, the formation of a school or interdisciplinary team is needed to develop a plan for school reentry. The team is composed of a variety of professionals, the child's parents, and the child. The team usually consists of a general education teacher, special education teacher, case manager, school psychologist, parent, and student. Other team members may include a neuropsychologist, counselor, rehabilitation specialist, speech pathologist, physical therapist, and occupational therapist. The team's composition is dependent upon the child's needs (Clark, 1997). The team develops a tentative plan consisting of accommodations and intervention strategies and addresses the possibility that special education and related services will be needed.

Transitions from the medical facility to home and from home to school, along with the injury and its aftermath, are stressful periods for most children with TBI and their families. Guidelines exist to assist families with these transitions (e.g., Cohen, Joyce, Rhoades, & Welks, 1985). For example, Cohen et al. provide guidelines to help families and school personnel determine when a child is ready to return to school and will benefit from the school experience. According to Cohen and colleagues, a child is ready to return to school when he/she is able to attend for 10–15 minutes at a time, tolerate 20–30 minutes of classroom stimulation, function in a group setting, follow simple directions, engage in meaningful communication, and demonstrate some degree of learning. These guidelines are means of helping families reduce the stress associated with the transitions.

For the child with TBI, the transition and return to school can be very stressful and upsetting. The return to school highlights the losses in cognitive abilities, academic skills, physical functioning, and changes in behavior. These losses and changes can be demoralizing to the child and make the child a target of misperceptions. An increase in risk-taking behavior (Begali, 1992), social isolation, and withdrawal may result. Classmates' understanding and support are essential during these critical periods.

The transition from home to school can result in parental frustration and stress as well. In her review, Begali (1992) reported that common parental frustrations have been found, including lack of teacher understanding about TBI, reduced parental contact with support networks, inappropriate class placements, and social isolation of the child. For the family of a child with TBI, the injury and recovery process never occur in an interpersonal vacuum. Brain injury affects both the child and his or her family (Haak & Livingston, 1997). The family may have difficulty accepting their child's limitations and possible changes in personality. Moreover, financial difficulties, injury to other family members, and weariness may exist as the result of the accident. Schools can assist the family in the aftermath of TBI by empowering the family to play an active role in their child's education, teaching the family about TBI, and offering support and counsel. Family stress and frustration highlights the importance of developing a school reintegration plan and the value of having a knowledgeable and well-prepared school staff (Begali, 1992).

When a child with TBI returns to school, questions arise concerning the most appropriate placement for the child to receive his or her education. Not all children with TBI will require special education. Some students will need only monitoring in the classroom with slight adjustments made in the curriculum based on teacher observations. Others, on the other hand, will require special education and related services. To receive these services, a student must be "educationally diagnosed" (Begali, 1992). In other words, an evaluation needs to be conducted to determine a child's eligibility for special education.

Assessment plays a prominent role in determining eligibility and treatment of traumatic brain injured children and adolescents (Begali, 1992). Assessment results provide invaluable information and help determine educational placement, related services, and instructional goals. Psychoeducational, ecological, neuropsychological, and neurological evaluations should be conducted and results should be integrated in order to determine appropriate accommodations and modifications needed in the school environment to provide optimal learning experiences for children and adolescents with TBI. Standardized testing supplemented with testing of the limits and process procedures will provide invaluable information for designing appropriate accommodations and interventions (Kaplan, 1988).

A standard psychoeducational evaluation consists of an intelligence test, achievement test, and behavioral rating scales (Rapp, 1999). A psychoeducational evaluation can predict future learning potential and learning disabilities;

however, children and adolescents with TBI are more likely to have problems with attention or concentration, memory, new learning, problem solving, and socioemotional behavior, which will not be appropriately assessed using only a standard psychoeducational battery (Rapp, 1999; Reitan & Wolfson, 1992). Therefore, other evaluation procedures are needed.

In contrast, a neuropsychological evaluation assesses a broad range of brain-behavior relationships, current cognitive strengths and weaknesses, and new learning. Educational and vocational program goals can be developed based on these assessment results. Neuropsychological evaluations and neurological evaluations, consisting of physical assessments conducted by medical specialists, should be used to augment standard psychological assessments (Goldstein, 1984). A neuropsychological evaluation should be conducted before the child reenters school and reevaluations should be conducted frequently during the first year (Rapp, 1999). Begali (1992) recommends conducting a reevaluation every 3 to 6 months for the first 2 years postinjury. Following the first or second year postinjury, reevaluations should be conducted before major school transitions, when new problems arise, or when lack of educational progress is reported (Rapp, 1999).

Ecological evaluations consist of observations of children or adolescents in a variety of settings. Students with TBI usually have difficulty monitoring and regulating their own behavior in the real world, generalizing skills and abilities, and cognitive organization. Formal testing cannot assess these skills with any degree of accuracy, nor does formal testing have any resemblance to the real world or classroom environment. Thus, observations complement formal testing. Observations of children and adolescents with TBI provide a means of monitoring these students' progress and evaluating educational programs and interventions (Rapp, 1999). Observations should be conducted on a frequent basis.

Informal testing such as curriculum-based and criterion-based assessment is also recommended. Curriculum-based and criterion-based assessment may be used to guide instructional efforts and provide feedback. Program deficiencies can be identified and revisions of instructional objectives can be made. The main point to remember in the assessment of children with TBI is that frequent formal and informal testing will be needed to monitor these children's progress, as these children can recover substantial cognitive, physical, and behavioral functioning in short periods of time (Clark, 1997).

If a child is found to be eligible for special education based on assessment results and other relevant information, the individualized education program (IEP) team, the members of the school, or interdisciplinary team will develop an IEP. The IEP is a document stating the educational goals and objectives and specific educational and related services that will be provided. The IEP is required to address the child's current level of educational performance in the areas affected by the disability (Clark, 1997). This requirement can be a challenge to the IEP team, as dramatic changes are seen in individuals with TBI during the first 3 months of recovery (Lezak, 1995). Thus, constant review and updating of educational goals and objectives is needed to keep pace with the child's recovery. A review of the IEP within 3 months of its implementation is recommended. After the initial review, the IEP should be reviewed periodically thereafter (Clark, 1997). For those who do not qualify for special education and related services under IDEA, but do qualify for services under Section 504, the school's 504 team will need to develop a plan to ensure that children with TBI are adequately served as well.

Because of the dramatic changes seen in children with TBI during the recovery process and the fact that no two traumatic brain injuries are alike, educational programs for children with TBI must be individualized, flexible, and delivered in a timely manner. Educational programs for children with TBI should ensure that professional training, instructional methods, and program practices parallel the state-of-the-art in head trauma rehabilitation. Quality educational programs should include the following options: environmental control, low student-to-teacher ratio, individualized and intensive instructional techniques (Begali, 1992), flexible class scheduling, and community-based experiences.

Some children with TBI need a more controlled environment in the schools, such as a self-contained placement. Common characteristics found among children with TBI are their limited ability in interpreting environmental cues and responding to these cues in socially appropriate ways (Wood, 1990), hypersensitivity and hyposensitivity to sensory stimuli (Savage & Wolcott, 1994), and difficulty remembering class schedules and organizing their materials. Temporary placement in a self-contained classroom may provide these individuals with the time needed to develop coping strategies to interact appropriately and to handle the less predictable and more demanding general educational environment (Begali, 1992).

Flexible class scheduling is another mark of a quality educational program for children and adolescents with TBI. Children with TBI often lack the stamina needed to attend school on a full-time basis when they first return. Shortened school days and reduction in class load and number of classes may be needed to combat fatigue. Appointments with specialists, such as an occupational or physical therapist, may need to be scheduled into the school day as well. Thus, the actual time spent in the classroom may be very limited upon initial reentry (Begali, 1992).

Small classes where the student-to-teacher ratio is low may be beneficial to some children with TBI, especially those with severe head injuries. In these smaller classes, children with TBI can receive more intensive training, closer supervision, and more frequent feedback. In addition, distractions in these classes are more likely to be held to a minimum in comparison to the larger regular education classes (Begali, 1992).

Individual and intensive instructional opportunities are other key features of quality education programs for children with TBI. Children with TBI may need individual instruction or additional instructional assistance due to cognitive impairments, problems with new learning, loss of specific skills, or behavioral problems. Remediation, compensation, and accommodation strategies may be helpful in addressing these children's difficulties. For learned maladaptive behaviors, changes in the environment and setting clear limits may be beneficial. Accommodation strategies are often the initial intervention methods used when children with TBI return to the classroom. Remediation of specific lost skills is also an appropriate strategy to use with children with TBI. Practice, repetition, and more time to relearn specific lost skills are examples of remediation strategies. Teaching compensatory strategies is another set of intervention methods that may be used to circumvent cognitive impairments. With compensatory strategies, such as the use of mnemonics, new ways of performing and learning tasks are acquired (Rapp, 1999). To maximize instructional time, limits on transitional time and extracurricular classes may be set. Attendance in an extended school program during the summer months, if eligible, may be helpful in preventing regression in learning. Due to the rapid changes in cognitive, physical, and behavioral skills and abilities, dynamic and responsive instructional approaches tailored to the individual will be required (Begali, 1992). For additional information on more specific intervention strategies to use with students with TBI, see the entry on traumatic brain injury in children.

Community-based work experience is another indicator of a quality educational program for children with TBI. In 1990, IDEA required school districts to provide students in special education with transitional services. Children with TBI who are in special education and are 14 years of age or older qualify for these services. Participation in community-based work experiences occurs during the school day. These students go to work sites located in their community to receive on-the-job training. These work experiences are arranged to help students develop good work skills, work habits, and social skills needed in today's competitive employment market. The goal of the school-to-work experience is for students to develop the skills needed to obtain meaningful employment and to have independent living opportunities upon graduation (Haak & Livingston, 1997).

School reentry is a challenging experience for the student, family, and school. At present, limited information exists on school reentry programs for children with TBI. In addition, empirical research demonstrating the effectiveness of school reentry programs for children with TBI is lacking. Collaboration among the systems (home, school, medical, and community) and drawing upon the technical expertise of these resources are needed in order to assist these children on their road to recovery.

REFERENCES

Begali, V. (1992). *Head injury in children and adolescents.* Brandon, VT: Clinical Psychology Publishing Company.

Blosser, J. L., & DePompei, R. (1991). Preparing education professionals for meeting the needs of students with traumatic brain injury. *Journal of Head Trauma Rehabilitation, 6*(1), 73–82.

Clark, E. (1997). Children and adolescents with traumatic brain injury: Reintegration challenges in educational settings. In E. D. Bigler, E. Clark, & J. E. Farmer (Eds.), *Childhood traumatic brain injury: Diagnosis, assessment, and intervention.* Austin, TX: PRO-ED.

Clark, E., & Hostetter, C. (1995). *Traumatic brain injury: Training manual for school personnel.* Longmont, CO: Sopris West.

Cohen, S., Joyce, C., Rhoades, K., & Welks, D. (1985). Educational programming for head injured students. In M. Ylvisaker (Ed.), *Head injury rehabilitation: Children and adolescents* (pp. 383–411). San Diego: College-Hill Press.

Diamond, R. (1987). Children and head injury. In A. Thomas & J. Grimes (Eds.), *Children's needs: Psychological perspectives.* Washington, DC: National Association of School Psychologists.

Federal Register. (1992, September 9). Individual with Disabilities Education Act (IDEA). U.S. Department of Education Regulations. Washington, DC: U.S. Government Printing Office.

Goldstein, G. (1984). Neuropsychological assessment. In G. Goldstein & M. Hersen (Eds.), *Handbook of psychological assessment* (pp. 181–211). New York: Pergamon.

Haak, R. A., & Livingston, R. B. (1997). Treating traumatic brain injury in the school: Mandates and methods. In C. R. Reynolds & E. Fletcher-Janzen (Eds.), *Handbook of clinical child neuropsychology* (2nd ed., pp. 482–505). New York: Plenum.

Kaplan, E. (1988). A process approach to neuropsychological assessment. In T. Boll & B. K. Bryant (Eds.), *Clinical neuropsychology and brain function: Research, measurement, and practice* (pp. 129–167). Washington, DC: American Psychological Association.

Lezak, M. D. (1995). *Neuropsychological assessment* (3rd ed.). New York: Oxford.

National Information Center for Children and Youth with Disabilities (NICCYD). (1993). *Traumatic brain injury.* Fact sheet number 18 (FS 18). Washington, DC: Author.

Rapp, D. L. (1999). Interventions for integrating children with traumatic brain injuries into their schools. In C. R. Reynolds & T. B. Gutkin (Eds.), *The handbook of school psychology* (3rd ed., pp. 863–884). New York: Wiley.

Reitan, R. M., & Wolfson, D. (1992). *Neuropsychological evaluation of older children.* South Tucson, AZ: Neuropsychology Press.

Research and Training Center in Rehabilitation and Childhood Trauma (1993). *National Pediatric Trauma Registry.* Boston: Tufts University School of Medicine, New England Medical Center.

Savage, R. C., & Wolcott, G. F. (Eds.). (1994). *Educational dimensions of acquired brain injury.* Austin, TX: PRO-ED.

Stratton, M. C., & Gregory, R. J. (1994). After traumatic brain injury: A discussion of consequences. *Brain Injury, 8*(7), 631–645.

Wood, R. L. (1990). Neurobehavioral paradigm for brain injury rehabilitation. In R. Wood (Ed.), *Neurobehavioral sequelae of traumatic brain injury* (pp. 3–17). New York: Taylor & Francis.

Ylvisaker, M., Hartwick, P., & Stevens, M. (1991). School reentry following head injury: Managing the transition from hospital to school. *Journal of Head Trauma Rehabilitation, 6,* 10–22.

PATRICIA A. LOWE
University of Kansas

CECIL R. REYNOLDS
Texas A&M University

TRAUMATIC BRAIN INJURY AND SPECIAL EDUCATION SERVICES

Traumatic brain injury (TBI) involves an insult to the brain, not of a degenerative or congenital nature, but caused by an external physical force of sufficient magnitude producing a diminished or altered state of consciousness and/or associated neurological or neurobehavioral dysfunction (Begali, 1992). Mild to severe structural or physiological changes in the neural tissue of the brain resulting from TBI may cause transient to permanent changes in behavior (Begali, 1992; Savage & Wolcott, 1994). Tissue abnormalities and neural damage resulting from TBI may be due to the direct impact following an accident involving the head or may be due to secondary effects (i.e., secondary damage or metabolic changes) associated with the trauma (Begali, 1992).

TBIs may be classified into two types, open and closed head injuries. Open head injuries involve the penetration of the skull and brain by a foreign object. The agents commonly responsible for open head injuries include bullets, shell fragments, knives, rocks, and blunt instruments. Gunshot wounds account for the majority of open head injuries, although knife and scissor wounds are frequently reported as well (Ward, Chisholm, Prince, Gilmore, & Hawkins, 1994). Open head injuries result in an increased risk of infection, bleeding, and seizures, as bone fragments or shattered pieces of shells or bullets penetrate the brain (Rapp, 1999). Primary damage, however, tends to be localized about the path of the penetrating object. As a result, cognitive losses and changes in behavior due to the localized damage are relatively circumscribed and predictable. Depending on the location of the injury, open head injuries may result in specific intellectual impairments and behavioral changes, memory deficits, slower information processing, attention and concentration difficulties, and changes in the ability to deal with everyday cognitive demands (Begali, 1992).

Closed head injuries, on the other hand, are more common and more diffuse in comparison to open head injuries (Lezak, 1995). Closed head injuries result from a direct impact to the brain, such as a blow to the head, without penetration of the skull. There are three types of closed head injuries (Reynolds, pers. comm., June 6, 1997) produced by two mechanical factors, namely, direct contact forces and inertial forces (Begali, 1992; Katz, 1992). An acceleration injury occurs when an individual's head accelerates too quickly (e.g., when a child's head is hit with a baseball bat). In an acceleration injury, the child's skull, which surrounds the brain (a gelatin-like substance supported and floating in cerebrospinal fluid), compresses against the brain and forces the brain to move to the opposite side of the initial point of impact where the brain hits the inside of the skull again. The point of initial impact is called the coup, whereas the secondary point of impact, orthogonal to the plane (i.e., opposite side) of the initial point of impact, is called the counter coup. Damage to the brain in an acceleration injury occurs at both the coup and counter coup, with more severe damage at the coup.

In contrast, a deceleration injury occurs when an individual's head decelerates or stops too quickly (e.g., when an adolescent's head strikes an immovable or stationary object, such as a car's dashboard during a motor vehicle accident). Under these circumstances, the brain moves forward and strikes the inside of the skull (coup) and then moves in the opposite direction (backwards) and strikes the inside of the skull again (counter coup). In a deceleration injury, brain damage is more severe at the site of the counter coup than the coup.

A pinball injury is a third type of closed head injury. A pinball injury may also occur during a motor vehicle accident when the individual's head strikes the dashboard and then the individual is thrown from the vehicle and lands on the ground, hitting the side of his/her head. A pinball injury results in multiple points of impact producing damage at a number of coup and counter coup sites.

Coup and counter coup damage is the product of direct contact forces. Inertial forces, on the other hand, generate other types of injuries, such as shearing and tearing of nerve fibers. Shearing and tearing of nerve fibers occur in acceleration, deceleration, and pinball closed head injuries. Shearing and tearing result from brain movement and rotation of the brain within the skull. Tearing injuries are likely to occur when nerve fibers projecting from the base of the brain are stretched to their limit, resulting in their snapping or tearing. In contrast, shearing injuries may occur, for example, when association fibers, which connect different areas of the brain together, scrape against the bony ridges of the inside of the skull. This scraping movement results in the removal of layers of association fibers.

Brain damage typically occurs in two stages, namely, the primary and second injury. The primary injury is the damage that occurs at the time of the injury, whereas the second injury results from the damage incurred from the primary injury (Lezak, 1995). Primary injuries in closed head injuries include skull fractures, concussions, contusions, and shearing and tearing injuries. A skull fracture is a crack in the cranium (i.e., the skull) surrounding the brain. The skull fracture may vary in size or severity. A contusion occurs

when the brain strikes the inside of the skull (i.e., a coup or counter coup), resulting in bruising of the brain. Blood vessels may also rupture during the accident or shortly thereafter, causing extensive bleeding. Bleeding within the cranium is dangerous and possibly fatal, as the blood accumulates in this case surrounding the brain with no place to go. As a result, pressure mounts inside the cranium. This pressure can be fatal. In contrast, a concussion occurs when the brain strikes the inside of the skull, resulting in a period of confusion or loss of consciousness. A variety of primary injuries are possible when a closed head injury occurs. Thus, each closed head injury is unique and is dependent upon the physical characteristics of the insult and the movement of the brain within the skull (Begali, 1992).

Secondary damage or the second injury develops after the insult in either an open or closed head injury. Secondary complications include (a) edema (brain swelling due to an increase in fluid content); (b) infarction (loss of brain tissue due to blood deprivation); (c) increased cranial pressure (buildup of pressure in the cranium); (d) hypoxia (oxygen deprivation); (e) hemorrhage (rupture of blood vessels in the brain); (f) hematoma (collection of blood in the brain tissue); and/or (g) infection (Pang, 1985). Secondary damage may also result from metabolic change (North, 1984), damage to the pituitary gland and hypothalamus, electrolyte disturbance (a chemical imbalance in the blood), and/or hyperventilation (excessive breathing; Pang, 1985).

Head injury is a common occurrence among children and adolescents; however, prevalence rates and incidence of TBI have been difficult to ascertain, as incongruities in classification procedures and methodological weaknesses in epidemiological studies have been reported (Lehr, 1990). It has been estimated that more than one million children in the United States sustain a mild to severe traumatic brain injury each year (Research and Training Center in Rehabilitation and Childhood Trauma, 1993). Researchers have estimated that 10 out of every 100,000 children die as a result of brain injury yearly (Luerssen, 1991). Pediatric patients account for approximately 40 percent of the TBI cases reported on an annual basis, which translates, based on different estimates, into 200,000 to 600,000 TBI child and adolescent cases each year that come to the attention of medical professionals (Brandstater, Bontke, Cobble, & Horn, 1991; Crouchman, 1990). The majority of these TBI cases occur in youth between the ages of 15 and 19 years due to automobile accidents (Farmer & Peterson, 1995). Many of these individuals will require educational support once they return to school. Approximately 50 percent of the children and adolescents who sustain a traumatic brain injury need educational support during the first year following their injury (Donders, 1994). It is estimated that 8 to 20 percent of the special education population is believed to have suffered a traumatic brain injury (Savage, 1991).

Gender differences have also been reported. Males are twice as likely as females to sustain a traumatic brain injury at all ages, except in infancy and the senior years of life (Lezak, 1995). This gender differential is found to be the greatest during the peak trauma years, the 15–24 year age range (Naugle, 1990), when males are four times more likely than females to suffer an injury (Vernon-Levett, 1991). Males also tend to sustain more severe brain injuries than females, with the male to female mortality ratio being 4:1 (Frankowski, Annegers, & Whitman, 1985).

The external forces that produce TBIs tend to vary with the age of the individual (Farmer & Peterson, 1995; Goldstein & Levin, 1990). Infants, toddlers, and preschoolers are more likely to acquire TBIs due to falls, physical abuse, and vehicular accidents (Rapp, 1999). Physical abuse, such as shaken baby or thrown infant syndrome, is the leading cause of traumatic brain injury among infants. Sixty-six percent of the infants who are physically abused sustain a brain injury as a result of the abuse (Bruce & Zimmerman, 1989). Falls, on the other hand, are the major source of TBI among children under age five and account for more than 50 percent of the injuries in the toddler and preschool population (Kraus et al., 1984). After age 5, pedestrian and bicycle injuries increase, with motor vehicle accidents, falls, recreation and sports injuries, and assaults contributing to the rate of injury (Mira, Tucker, & Tyler, 1992). Not surprisingly, adolescents and young adults are at the greatest risk of any age group for acquiring TBIs (Savage & Wolcott, 1994), primarily through motor vehicle accidents but also from sports injuries and assaults (Rapp, 1999). During adolescence, the combination of increased risk-taking behaviors and learning how to drive often lead to an increase in motor vehicle accidents. Automobile accidents account for three deaths and 260 injuries among children and adolescents each day (Brain Injury Association, 1997). Overall, moving vehicle accidents and falls are the major causes of head trauma (Lezak, 1995). Moreover, the risk of sustaining a brain injury increases dramatically with each successive TBI an individual experiences (Brain Injury Association, 1997).

There are many factors that influence the outcomes of traumatic brain injury in children: child, family, medical, school, and community factors (Farmer, 1997). A level of influence within these factors either increases the risk of poor outcomes, or creates a buffer or offers protection, and thus maximizes optimal outcomes. For example, child factors can serve as either risk or protective factors that influence TBI outcomes. Child factors include preinjury characteristics, age/developmental stage at onset, type and persistence of impairments, postinjury adjustment, and severity of injury. Type and persistence of impairments are determined by the nature of the injury, such as a closed versus open head injury, and the location and severity of the injury (Warzak, Mayfield, & McAllister, 1998). Postinjury adjustment, on the other hand, is dependent upon the child and family's coping resources and the child's social acceptance by others (Wade, Taylor, Drotar, Stancin, & Yeates, 1996). Preinjury

characteristics include genetics and the child's preexisting medical, behavioral, and affective status. Harrington (1990) reported that children with TBI with above-average intelligence, academic skills, and social skills tend to have a better prognosis than those individuals with TBI with below average skills. Students with TBI, however, are more likely to have preexisting academic problems and prior behavioral problems in comparison to their classmates (Farmer, Clippard, Wieman, Wright, & Owings, 1997).

Another potential differentiating factor that influences TBI outcomes is the age of onset or the child's developmental stage at the time of the injury. The relationship between age of onset and recovery from brain injury, however, is complex and is not well understood (Dalby & Obrzut, 1991). Early research suggested a high degree of plasticity in the brains of young children (i.e., children's brains had the ability to compensate for some injuries by reorganizing neural function). In other words, a young child's brain was thought to be more resilient in response to injury, as other brain structures spared of injury assumed the function of the damaged areas (Farmer & Peterson, 1995). Subsequent studies, however, have indicated young children's superior recovery from head trauma cannot be presumed (Farmer, 1997). In fact, recent studies have found just the opposite (i.e., more unfavorable outcomes) in younger children who have experienced a brain injury in the areas of language development (Ylvisaker, 1993), attention (Kaufmann, Fletcher, Levin, Miner, & Ewing-Cobbs, 1993), intellectual and behavioral functioning (Michaud, Rivara, Jaffe, Fay, & Dailey, 1993), and problem solving (Levin et al., 1994).

Preliminary evidence suggests preschool children may be at greatest risk (Farmer & Peterson, 1995). Disruption of primary skills (e.g., sensory, motor, language, behavioral, social skills) in early childhood may result in changes in learning, such as the order, rate, and level of learning, and development of higher order skills, such as self-regulation of behavior and planning ability (Farmer, 1997). In addition, some research (e.g., Lehr & Savage, 1990) suggests early brain injury may result in delayed, late-onset effects in which a child who appears to be fully recovered shows a marked decline in functioning over time.

Brain injury severity is another factor that influences TBI outcomes. Severity is medically diagnosed using the terms mild, moderate, and severe. Classification of brain injury severity is based on three critical factors. These three critical factors include an individual's level of consciousness, degree of posttraumatic amnesia experienced, and physical findings. In general, severity of head trauma serves as a good prognosticator of behavioral and neuropsychological outcomes (Kreutzer, Devany, Myers, & Marwitz, 1991), with more long-lasting changes in physical, cognitive, and behavioral functioning occurring with more severe TBI cases (Fay et al., 1993; Jaffe et al., 1993). Although children and adolescents who sustain severe TBIs are more likely to experience chronic effects, individual differences must be taken into account. Some individuals with severe head injuries have not encountered significant disability, whereas some children and adolescents with mild brain injuries have symptoms that cause significant and lasting impairments (Farmer, 1997; Fay et al., 1993).

Diminished or altered level of consciousness is one of the most commonly used indicators of brain trauma. The Glasgow Coma Scale (GCS; Teasdale & Jennett, 1974) is a means of assessing an individual's level of consciousness following a brain injury. The GCS is routinely used to measure the degree and duration of altered consciousness within 24 hours of the trauma and to periodically monitor changes in consciousness during the early stages of recovery (Teasdale & Jennett, 1974). A GCS score is obtained through observing, evaluating, and summarizing the patient's best-rated responses, ranging from 1 to 6 in motor movements, 1 to 5 in verbal functioning, and 1 to 4 in eye movements. Possible scores range from 3 to 15. Coma is diagnosed when there is no eye opening, inability to obey commands, and inability to speak. One critical limitation of the GCS, however, is its development and use almost exclusively with adults and older adolescents. Thus, the clinical utility of the GCS with the younger child population is questionable, as the presentation of coma differs across young children and adults (Lehr, 1990). In response to the limited utility of the GCS, alternative measures for use with comatose pediatric patients have been developed, such as the Children's Coma Scale (CCS; Raimondi & Hirschauer, 1984). The CCS has been used to assess the level of consciousness in infants and toddlers up to age 3. Possible scores range from 3 to 11 and are not interchangeable with the GCS. The CCS, however, has its limitations as well, as the predictive validity of this scale has not been examined due to limited use (Lehr, 1990).

The degree of posttraumatic amnesia (PTA) is another indicator of brain injury severity. Posttraumatic amnesia refers to the period of time when an alert individual who has experienced a brain injury has "persistent difficulties retaining new information" (Farmer & Peterson, 1995, p. 233). Estimates of brain injury severity based on PTA duration vary from less than 5 minutes to more than 4 weeks (Bigler, 1990). PTA duration correlates well with GCS ratings, with the exception of extreme GCS scores (Bigler, 1990), as PTA duration typically lasts four times longer than the period of unconsciousness or coma (Lezak, 1995). Children's Orientation and Amnesia Test (Ewing-Cobbs, Levin, Fletcher, Miner, & Eisenberg, 1989) or structured parent interviews (Rutter, Chadwick, Shaffer, & Brown, 1980) have been used to assess PTA in children. PTA is difficult to assess in young children, as children's memories are less reliable and accurate than adults. As a result, PTA is usually not assessed and reported in children under the age of 9 (Lehr, 1990).

A third indicator of injury severity is gauged by examining physical findings through a variety of medical procedures. Physicians conduct neurological examinations to assess sensory deficits, reflexes, and the motor system. Medical professionals also use a variety of technologically advanced medical procedures to assess the degree of damage sustained. Computerized tomography, magnetic resonance imagery, functional magnetic resonance imagery, single-photon emission computer tomography, positron emission tomography, regional cerebral blood flow, and brain electrical activity mapping have proven to be useful, some procedures more than others (Lezak, 1995), in evaluating the severity of injury.

Although assessment of the level of brain injury severity has its limitations, the three critical factors (i.e., level of consciousness, duration of posttraumatic amnesia, and physical findings) offer a means of predicting TBI outcomes. A mild brain injury has been defined as a GCS score of 13 to 15, which suggests little or no impairment in speaking and motor and eye movement. A PTA of less than 1 hour occurs and no known structural damage to the brain is evident (Binder, 1986). Approximately 75 to 90 percent of all head trauma falls into this category (Alves & James, 1985). Students who sustain a mild brain injury often make good academic recovery but may experience attention and concentration difficulties, fatigue, and deficits in retaining new information. Deficits following a mild TBI tend to be subtle but may have considerable impact on social, familial, academic, and occupational functioning (Lezak, 1995). The term "walking wounded" used to describe these individuals seems appropriate, as the effects of the disability often go unnoticed (Wade et al., 1996). Clusters of symptoms in affective, social, cognitive, somatic, and sensory areas may persist following a mild TBI (Warzak et al., 1998).

Moderate brain injury has been defined as a GCS score of 9 to 12 and a PTA duration of 1 to 24 hours (Bigler, 1990). Eight to ten percent of all head injuries fall into this category (Lezak, 1995). An individual with a GCS score of 9 to 12 is able to open his or her eyes, flex his or her muscles, and speak intelligibly, but is unable to sustain a conversation. Significant residual impairments often result due to the trauma. Persistent headaches, memory deficits, and difficulties with adaptive living skills have been reported (Lezak, 1995; Warzak et al., 1998). If frontal lobe damage is sustained (i.e., damage to the anterior portion of the brain), more impulsive behavior and temper outbursts or affective muting may be exhibited, whereas damage to the temporal lobe, located near the middle to top half of one's ears, may result in a true learning disorder. Planning ability and self-monitoring are frequently compromised as well. Students who have experienced a moderate brain injury may require special education and related services.

A severe head injury has been defined as a GCS score of 3 to 8 and a PTA duration of more than 24 hours (Bigler, 1990). When an individual has a GCS of 3 to 8, the ability to open one's eyes, obey commands, or utter recognizable words may be absent. Fewer than 10 percent of head trauma victims fall into the severely injured category (Lezak, 1995).

Attention deficits, behavioral slowing (i.e., both mental processing and response), memory impairments, diminished awareness of one's deficits, and impaired reasoning and verbal fluency are common (Mitiguy, Thompson, & Wasco, 1990). Insight and empathy may be compromised as well. Perseverative behavior may be displayed. Moreover, planning ability and ability to choose among alternatives may be impaired. Acting-out behavior and apathy may be exhibited and social isolation is common (Lezak, 1995). Students who experience a severe brain injury will require a variety of special services. These individuals are highly unlikely to return to the general education classroom without considerable support (Warzak et al., 1998).

Children and adolescents with TBI represent a heterogeneous group with regard to neurobehavioral characteristics and outcomes. These individuals may display a wide variety of difficulties or deficits. The difficulties or deficits may occur in one or more of the following areas: physical functioning, cognitive functioning, behavioral control, and socioemotional functioning.

Physical sequelae (i.e., consequences) associated with traumatic brain injury in children and adolescents include motor deficits, sensory deficits, speech/language dysfunction, seizure disorders, postconcussive syndrome, and fatigue. Motor deficits vary in degree depending upon the site and extent of the damage to the brain. Deficits range from fine volitional movements to severe paralysis. Motor deficits may include hemiplegia (paralysis on one side of the body), hemiparesis (weakness affecting one side of the body), hypotonicity (low muscle tone of trunk and extremities), rigidity, spasticity, tremors, ataxia (inability to coordinate voluntary muscles), and apraxia (problems in planning and executing sequential movement; Begali, 1992; Savage & Wolcott, 1994). Prognosis for a full motor recovery is relatively good in TBI patients and is better than a prognosis for full cognitive recovery. Recovery of motor functions in TBI accidents follows a predictable course with lower limb functioning returning sooner and more completely than upper limb functioning, and proximal (trunk) movements returning sooner and more completely than distal (extremity) movements. Moreover, children with TBI may lose functional use of their dominant hand and will need to learn how to write and perform various hand activities with their nondominant hand. Recovery and refinement of balance reactions or proper weight shifting and control may not occur, however, until after youngsters are discharged to their homes and schools. Thus, physical rehabilitation may be needed in the school setting (Begali, 1992).

Sensory impairments associated with TBI vary in degree depending on the extent of damage to the brain. Sensory deficits may include visual field deficits (i.e., restriction of an individual's field of vision), squinting, defects in color vision, double vision, and tracking disorders (Begali, 1992). Reduced auditory acuity and impaired ability to taste or smell have also been reported (Savage & Wolcott, 1994).

Hypersensitivity and hyposensitivity to sensory stimuli have been noted as well (Begali, 1992; Savage & Wolcott, 1994).

Speech/language dysfunction may occur with TBI. Dysarthia characterized by poor phonation skills, hypernasality, poor articulation, slow rate of speech, and monotonic speech is found in some children and adolescents following TBI. Apraxia and aphasia may also result from brain injury. Apraxia involves the inability to execute preplanned, purposeful sequences for oral communication, whereas aphasia results in partial or complete impairment in language comprehension. Aphasic individuals are able to comprehend one or two words or short phrases rather than lengthy discourse (Begali, 1992).

Epilepsy may also occur following a traumatic brain injury. Penetrating head injuries are more likely to produce epilepsy than closed head injuries (Lezak, 1995). Approximately 5 percent of children and adolescents who experience a closed head injury will develop epilepsy within 4 years after the injury (Begali, 1992). Seizures are more likely to occur in children under 5 years of age or children who have a severe injury. Seizures usually appear in the first few weeks of recovery after the head trauma. Seizures may have a delayed onset as well and begin approximately 3 months after the injury (Hauser & Hersdorffer, 1990). On the other hand, individuals who experienced a TBI and have had seizures in the past but have been seizure-free for 3 years can be 95 percent certain that they will not experience another seizure (Parker, 1990). Antileptic drugs, such as phenytoin, phenobarbital, carbamazepine, and valproate have been prescribed; however, these medications do have negative side effects. Negative side effects vary depending on the medication used and the individual. Side effects include sedation, speech disturbances, dizziness, and cognitive impairment (Bagby, 1991).

Besides seizures, a head injury, and specifically a mild head injury, may result in postconcussive syndrome. Approximately 50 percent of individuals who experience a mild traumatic brain injury report symptoms associated with a postconcussive syndrome 3 or more months after the injury (Rutherford, 1989). Fatigue, dizziness, headache, and memory deficits are the most common symptoms (Edna & Cappelen, 1987). The syndrome tends to remit with time; however, 4 percent of the individuals who experience this syndrome report persistent memory problems and 20 percent report persistent headaches 1 year after the injury (Wilberger, 1993). Students with postconcussive syndrome may be viewed as lacking in motivation or being noncompliant or defiant in the school setting, when in reality they have attention, concentration, and memory problems.

Chronic fatigue and hypersensitivity to noise are complications that often occur as a result of head trauma (Lezak, 1995). Chronic fatigue prevents individuals with TBI from functioning at their premorbid pace. Shortened school days and reduced course loads are often implemented to combat fatigue. On the other hand, hypersensitivity to noise may produce stress in children with TBI. Certain times of the school day may be overtaxing to these children, such as lunchtime or recess. Thus, reintegration into the more stimulating or hectic parts of the school day must be done gradually.

Cognitive deficits are among the most common sequelae of TBI (Lezak, 1995); however, the pattern of impairment will vary from individual to individual (Crosson, 1992). Intelligence, attention/concentration, language functions, memory, abstract reasoning and judgment, academic achievement and new learning, visual-motor skills, and perception are highly susceptible to dysfunction (Begali, 1992).

A direct relationship between the severity of TBI and degree of cognitive/intellectual impairment has been reported (Oddy, 1993). Drops of 10 points in mean verbal IQ and 30 points in performance IQ on intelligence tests have been noted in children with severe head injuries (Chadwick, Rutter, Shaffer, & Shrout, 1981). Children and adolescents with TBI show more pronounced and persistent deficits in performance IQ than in verbal IQ. As a result, individuals who have experienced a brain injury are more likely to have difficulties learning new skills and solving problems than performing well-learned skills or retrieving factual information. Viewed another way, visual-perceptual and visual-motor skills are less likely to recover fully in comparison to verbal abilities in children with TBI (Begali, 1992). Location of the injury, however, has an effect, as verbal and academic skills tend to be more impaired following left hemisphere damage, whereas visuospatial skills tend to be more impaired following right hemisphere lesions (Wilkening, 1989).

Attention and concentration difficulties are common problems among children and youth following a traumatic brain injury (Lezak, 1995). A poor attention span is not conducive to school learning and is related to a slower rate of information processing (van Zomeren & Brouwer, 1994). Difficulties with sustained attention, selective attention, switching attention, and divided attention have been reported (Haak & Livingston, 1997). These attention difficulties contribute to a variety of cognitive problems including memory, learning, language problems, and social interactions. Off-task behavior is common among these individuals, especially in unstructured classroom settings (Begali, 1992).

Significant expressive and receptive language deficits may follow a severe closed head injury, with expressive language abilities being more affected than receptive (Wilkening, 1989). Two-thirds of the individuals with language deficits, however, recover fully or at least improve to the point where only word-finding or word-naming ability is impaired (Begali, 1992). Verbal fluency, reading comprehension, and writing may also be affected (Lezak, 1995). The speed and ease of verbal production (fluency) and reading comprehension may be hindered. Moreover, students, es-

pecially younger students, may struggle with their writing as they are unable to recall letter-form movements, how to spell words correctly, or put words together to form sentences (Ewing-Cobbs & Fletcher, 1990). Auditory comprehension may be impaired as well in either a global or selective manner. Specifically, comprehension of classes of words may be affected, such as colors or prepositions (Begali, 1992). Moreover, conversational skills, which require the integration and interplay of linguistic, cognitive, and social skills, are highly susceptible to disruption following TBI in children (Russell, 1993).

Memory disorders are the most common and persistent sequelae of traumatic brain injury (Levin, 1985). When memory deficits persist, these deficits interfere with academic progress. Deficits in new learning or recent memory are more likely to be affected than rote memory. During the early stages of recovery, long-term memory or memory for earlier events return first, followed by memory for events occurring closer to the time of the injury (Lezak, 1995). Retrograde amnesia, a loss of memory for events preceding the injury, may also occur if an individual is rendered unconscious by the head trauma (Begali, 1992). Overall, memory following TBI may be less complete and show less improvement than other cognitive skills.

Conceptual functions, abstract reasoning, and judgment may also be impaired as a result of head trauma. Children who have experienced a mild to severe brain injury or have experienced diffuse damage tend to do poorly on measures of abstract thinking (Lezak, 1995). These individuals have difficulty distinguishing relevant from irrelevant material and essential from nonessential detail. Children and adolescents may have difficulty categorizing and generalizing information or applying rules, such as social rules or rules associated with grammar or mathematics. They may misinterpret social cues, make inappropriate remarks, or miscommunicate their intentions (Begali, 1992).

Academic achievement or new learning may also be affected by head injuries. Inconsistency in academic proficiency has been reported (Begali, 1992). Children with TBI may perform new learned skills accurately one day but are unable to perform the skills correctly the next day. For example, the steps learned to perform long division with precision are forgotten when the child is required to perform the task again on another occasion.

Visual-motor and visual-perceptual problems are also common among children and adolescents who have experienced a brain injury. Visual-motor and visual-perceptual difficulties may include problems with directions, misperceptions, and configural distortions (Lezak, 1995). The ability to attend to detail and part-to-whole conceptualization is likely to be poor. Visual-motor dexterity tends to be slow as well.

Behavioral and socioemotional difficulties are common sequelae following TBI in children and adolescents. These difficulties may be the most prominent features associated with the injury (Oddy, 1993). The behavioral and socio-emotional disturbances often exist as premorbid characteristics or tendencies that are exacerbated in response to the injury (Lezak, 1995). Although a well-defined pattern of behavioral and socioemotional difficulties does not exist, there are certain constellations of problems that occur more frequently than others (Haak & Livingston, 1997). Begali (1992) and Savage & Wolcott (1994) reported increases in overactive/hyperactive behavior, impulsivity, aggression, agitation/frustration, disinhibition, oppositional behavior, dependency, and lack of motivation among children and adolescents following TBI. Psychological adjustment difficulties have also been noted, including emotional lability (mood swings), anger, anxiety, withdrawal, and depression. Children and adolescents with TBI may experience difficulty in reading social cues and have poor interpersonal skills. Self-esteem issues may arise as these individuals become aware of or recognize the changes and deficits associated with their injury.

As noted, severity of the injury is related to cognitive deficits; however, the relationship between injury severity and behavioral adjustment is more complex and less understood (Ewing-Cobbs & Fletcher, 1990). Besides severity of the injury and premorbid characteristics, type of damage, site and laterality of lesion, age of onset, gender (Begali, 1992), family adaptation (Wade et al., 1996), and environmental factors influence behavioral outcomes (Farmer & Peterson, 1995).

Initial recovery following a traumatic brain injury tends to occur in a predictable series of stages, ranging from a coma to more purposeful and appropriate behavior (Farmer & Peterson, 1995). An eight-stage scale, the Rancho Los Amigos Level of Cognitive Functioning Scale (Hagen, Malkmus, & Durham, 1981), is used in rehabilitation settings to describe an individual's progress during the early stages of recovery. Children with more severe brain injuries are found at the lower levels of this scale and usually progress more slowly than individuals with less severe head injuries. Individual differences in recovery rates, however, must be taken into consideration, with some individuals recovering more rapidly and others remaining indefinitely at earlier stages of recovery. Attainment of the highest level on the Rancho Los Amigos scale does not necessarily indicate a full recovery to premorbid levels of functioning. Thus, students at each stage of recovery will need support and assistance from the schools.

Recovery from a TBI typically occurs most rapidly during the first 6–12 months following injury. Many children continue to show improvement in abilities 18–36 months postinjury. In some cases, progressive improvement has been observed beyond the 36-month postinjury mark (Boyer & Edwards, 1991).

In 1990, the Individuals with Disabilities Education Act (IDEA), Public Law 101-476 (PL 101-476), the main special education law in the United States, added traumatic brain injury as a separate eligibility category. Under this law, children with TBI whose educational performance is adversely affected by their disability are entitled to receive appropriate special education and related services necessary to meet their individual needs. According to PL 101-476, now PL 105-17, TBI is defined as follows:

> Traumatic brain injury means an acquired injury to the brain caused by an external physical force, resulting in total or partial functional disability or psychosocial impairment, or both, that adversely affects a child's educational performance. The term applies to open or closed head injuries resulting in impairments in one or more areas, such as cognition; language; memory; attention; reasoning; abstract thinking; judgment; problem-solving; sensory, perceptual and motor abilities; psychosocial behavior; physical functions; information processing; and speech. The term does not apply to brain injuries that are congenital or degenerative, or brain injuries induced by birth trauma. (*Federal Register,* 1992, p. 44802)

IDEA requires the child's brain injury to be caused by an external physical force, not internal trauma (e.g., a stroke, a brain tumor), in order for the student to meet eligibility requirements. Professionals continue to debate the appropriateness of excluding children whose brain injuries are the result of internal trauma. Some states, however, have opted to identify and classify a broader range of children and adolescents whose injuries are the result of either an external physical force or internal trauma (Rapp, 1999). Thus, a significant amount of variability exists across states regarding educational policy and eligibility criteria for students with TBI (Katsiyannis & Conderman, 1994). State rules and regulations should be consulted to determine whether children whose brain injuries are the result of internal trauma are eligible for services under the TBI category or the more generic IDEA category of Other Health Impaired (OHI).

Whatever the etiology, children with brain injuries whose educational performance is adversely affected by their injuries are entitled to an evaluation to assess eligibility for special education. If eligible for special education and related services under the TBI or OHI category, an individualized educational program (IEP) must be developed. The purpose of the IEP is to specify the student's short- and long-term educational needs.

For those individuals with TBI who are not eligible for special education and related services under IDEA, Section 504 of the Vocational Rehabilitation Act of 1973, a civil rights law, may provide sufficient services and protections in the school setting. Section 504 outlines the school district's responsibility to provide educational accommodations and related services to enable disabled students to have equal access to all publicly funded programs available to their nondisabled peers. Through a written plan, the school's 504 team outlines the educational accommodations and related services necessary, so a disabled student will be able to access and benefit from his or her educational program.

Assessment plays a prominent role in determining eligibility and in the treatment paradigm of traumatic brain injured children and adolescents (Begali, 1992). Assessment results provide invaluable information and help determine educational placement, related services, and instructional goals. Psychoeducational evaluations, ecological evaluations, neuropsychological evaluations, and neurological evaluations should be conducted and results should be integrated in order to determine appropriate accommodations and modifications needed in the school environment to provide optimal learning experiences for children and adolescents with TBI. Standardized testing supplemented with testing of the limits and process procedures will provide invaluable information for designing appropriate accommodations and interventions (Kaplan, 1988).

A standard psychoeducational evaluation consists of an intelligence test, achievement test, and behavioral rating scales (Rapp, 1999). A psychoeducational evaluation can predict future learning potential and learning disabilities under normal circumstances; however, children and adolescents with TBI are more likely to have deficits in attention and concentration (Kaufmann, Fletcher, Levin, Miner, & Ewing-Cobb, 1993), retaining and retrieving new learning (Jaffe et al., 1993), organization and problem solving (Levin et al., 1988), and changes in behavior (Deaton, 1994), which will not be appropriately assessed using only a standard psychoeducational battery (Reitan & Wolfson, 1992). A psychoeducational evaluation may be appropriate and useful, however, in determining whether a student has lost any previous learned information (Rapp, 1999).

In contrast, a neuropsychological evaluation assesses a broad range of brain-behavior relationships, current cognitive processes, and new learning. Individual strengths and weaknesses can be identified, and degree of deficits approximated. Educational and vocational program goals can be developed, and practical implications of brain injury upon everyday functioning can be assessed. Neuropsychological evaluations as well as neurological evaluations, consisting of physical assessments conducted by medical specialists, should be used to augment standard psychological assessments (Goldstein, 1984). A neuropsychological evaluation should be conducted before the child reenters school and reevaluations should be conducted frequently during the first 18–24 months following the injury (Rapp, 1999). Begali (1992) recommends conducting a reevaluation every 3 to 6 months for the first 2 years postinjury. Following the first or second year postinjury, reevaluations should be conducted before major school transitions, when new or different problems arise, or lack of educational progress is reported (Rapp, 1999).

Ecological evaluations consist of observations of children or adolescents in a variety of settings. Students with TBI usually have difficulty monitoring and regulating their own behavior in the real world, generalizing skills and abilities, and cognitive organization. Formal testing conducted in a structured setting cannot assess with any degree of accuracy any difficulties in the aforementioned areas nor does formal testing have any resemblance to the real world or classroom environment. Thus, real world observational assessments complement formal testing. Observations of children and adolescents with TBI provide a means of monitoring these students' progress and evaluating the appropriateness of educational programs and interventions developed for these individuals (Rapp, 1999). Observations should be conducted on a frequent basis.

Informal testing such as curriculum-based and criterion-based assessment is also recommended. Curriculum-based and criterion-based assessment may be used to guide instructional efforts and provide feedback. Program deficiencies can be identified and revision of instructional objectives may be made based on the results of frequent informal testing in the classroom.

In the classroom, a child or adolescent with TBI can be a real challenge. Educators may feel stymied in their efforts to reintegrate the child or adolescent with TBI into the school setting. Educational success for a child with TBI depends not only on the child but also on the teacher who is knowledgeable about brain injury, has a feeling of self-efficacy or self-competence in the classroom, and fosters a positive teacher-student relationship with the child (Farmer & Peterson, 1995).

Many schools have adopted home-school consultation models to address the educational needs of children with TBI. In home-school consultation (e.g., Conjoint Behavioral Consultation; Sheridan, Kratochwill, & Bergen, 1996), a consultant (i.e., a school psychologist) works with consultees (i.e., teachers and parents) to address the difficulties encountered by the child. Through collaborative consultation, parents and the school engage in a mutual process that leads to a reorganization around the child who has a brain injury. An empowerment model is adopted where parents take an active and central role in the educational programming for their child, including programs to meet their child's academic, social, emotional, behavioral, and vocational needs. Parents and school personnel share equally in the identification and prioritization of issues to be addressed through individual interventions. Parents and teachers along with school specialists develop and implement intervention strategies to address the issues of concern. The child's progress is monitored and modifications are made when needed. Continued dialogue between the school and home is encouraged to ensure the best possible treatment regimen for the child (Conoley & Sheridan, 1997).

Classroom placement is one of the first questions raised when a child with TBI is discharged from the hospital or rehabilitation unit. School placement may range from participation in the regular education classroom with no special supports to residential placement, depending on the child's age and learning needs (Savage, 1991). Initially, a self-contained classroom may be needed to prevent overstimulation and to increase teacher contact. Shorter school days and a reduced workload may also be needed to offset fatigue (Farmer & Peterson, 1995).

Limited research exists on the best instructional methods to use with traumatic brain injured children. Thus, sound teaching practices used with other disabled learners is what is currently recommended for use with this heterogeneous group of learners (Begali, 1992). Systematic and structured programs and compensatory training are recommended. Direct instruction in the students' most intact sensory modality is suggested to optimize children's learning. Tape recording of materials or duplicates of other students' notes may be helpful when poor note-taking skills exist. To monitor progress in learning, assignment notebooks reviewed on a regular basis by teachers and parents may also be helpful. Extended deadlines, breakdown of tasks into smaller units, reduced workload, and alternate means of assessment may need to be implemented. Establishment of routine in the classroom is extremely important and will be required, as TBI children need consistency (D'Amato & Rothlisberg, 1997). For reading recovery, material should be presented initially in a vertical format with a gradual transition to a horizontal presentation. Graph or lined paper turned sideways is suggested for youngsters who are having difficulties with mathematical computations due to visual-spatial or graphomotor difficulties. Multiple-choice formats or matching formats are recommended for students with memory problems, whereas oral exams are suggested for children with problems in written expression (Begali, 1992).

As noted earlier, attention/concentration difficulties affect a number of children with TBI. A variety of intervention strategies have been suggested to address attention/concentration difficulties, including environmental modifications, behavioral approaches, direct retraining approaches, biofeedback training, metacognitive and self-regulatory strategies (Mateer, Kerns, & Eso, 1997) and stimulant medication (Begali, 1992). Perhaps the simplest approach to help children with TBI attend in the classroom is to make environmental modifications. Environmental modifications may be as simple as having preferential seating arrangements, cueing/redirecting a child when off task, or presenting information in smaller units with multiple repetition. Behavioral approaches to increase attending may involve the implementation of a response-cost program in which privileges are taken away for lack of attending. Examples of direct retraining approaches are computer-based activities, pencil and paper exercises, and other manipulatives to allow children to practice and exercise a variety of attention-dependent skills or processes. Self-monitoring, on the other hand, falls under the rubric of self-regulatory strategies where children monitor their own attending behaviors.

A variety of strategies have also been suggested to remedy memory deficits. Memory deficits are one of the major cognitive sequelae associated with traumatic brain injuries. Internal strategies such as mnemonics, verbal strategies, and visual imagery may prove to be beneficial. External aids may also be helpful, as they may be used to extend or supplement the internal storage mechanisms. Examples of external aids include computer-based systems, paging systems, electronic organizers, and memory notebooks (Mateer et al., 1997). Direct instruction that is presented in a logical and unambiguous format using behavioral techniques, such as task analysis, modeling, shaping, reinforcement of appropriate responses, and continuous assessment have proven to be effective with a wide range of learners, including students with TBI (Colvin, 1990).

Motor deficits, sensory deficits, language/speech difficulties, and perceptual problems have also been reported as common sequelae of traumatic brain injured children. Computer-assisted training, paper and pencil cancellation tasks, mazes, visual closure worksheets, and eye-hand retraining techniques may be useful in addressing perceptual problems (Begali, 1992). In contrast, strategies to address language-processing problems may include pairing verbal with written instructions, avoiding figurative language, providing ample time to process information, and varying one's voice and intonation when repeating instructions (Blosser & DePompei, 1989). Direct remediation of specific language/speech deficits or compensatory training may also be needed. Consultation with medical specialists, however, may be the best strategy to use to address sensory deficits. Likewise, consultation with physical and occupational therapists is recommended to address motor deficits.

Social functioning may be impaired when individuals experience a brain injury. TBI can interfere with social functioning for a variety of reasons, including poor communication skills, limited mobility, decreased social cognition, and aggressive behavior. Social skills training and group activities such as cooperative learning activities may be beneficial in helping children with TBI to improve their social competency and acceptance by peers (Farmer & Peterson, 1995).

Behavioral sequelae following TBI are diverse. Both externalizing (e.g., aggression, noncompliance, anger outbursts) and internalizing (e.g., anxiety, depression) behaviors have been reported (Begali, 1992). Intervention strategies to address externalizing behaviors in the classroom environment include public posting of classroom rules and applying appropriate consequences for compliant and noncompliant behavior. Other classroom management strategies that have proven effective in reducing externalizing behaviors include teacher reprimands, precision requests, and time out. Effective use of teacher praise, on the other hand, can increase the frequency of appropriate behaviors (Kehle, Clark, & Jenson, 1997).

The predominant psychological issue faced by children and adolescents with TBI and their families is loss (Begali, 1992). The family may mourn the loss of the individual they once knew (Lezak, 1995). In other words, personality changes often accompany a traumatic brain injury. The child or members of the child's family may display shock, denial, grief, depression, and anxiety as a result of the changes. Thus, education about TBI, individual counseling for the child, family support and advocacy, and/or family therapy for the entire family, including siblings, may be needed to help the child and family cope with the changes that have occurred in the aftermath of the injury (Conoley & Sheridan, 1997).

A traumatic brain injury can be devastating not only to the child but also to the child's family. Following traumatic brain injury, a child's reintegration into the school setting can be a challenging experience. Comprehensive assessment and intervention strategies are needed to enhance the child's outcome in all areas of functioning. Collaboration among parents, educators, hospital/rehabilitation staff, and community members is needed in order to help these children and adolescents achieve independence, reach their academic potential, and lead satisfying and quality lives (Farmer & Peterson, 1995).

REFERENCES

Alves, W. M., & James, J. A. (1985). Mild brain injury: Damage and outcome. In D. P. Beck & J. T. Povlishock (Eds.), *Central nervous system trauma: Status report–1985*, Washington, DC: National Institutes of Health.

Bagby, G. (1991). Advances in anticonvulsant therapy. *Headlines, 2–5, 7–8.*

Begali, V. (1992). *Head injury in children and adolescents.* Brandon, VT: Clinical Psychology Publishing Company.

Bigler, E. D. (1990). *Traumatic brain injury.* Austin, TX: PRO-ED.

Binder, L. M. (1986). Persisting symptoms after mild head injury: A review of the postconcussive syndrome. *Journal of Clinical and Experimental Neuropsychology, 8*(4), 323–346.

Blosser, J., & DePompei, R. (1989). The head injured student returns to school: Recognizing and treating deficits. *Topics in Language Disorders, 9*(2), 67–77.

Boyer, M. G., & Edwards, P. (1991). Outcome 1 to 3 years after severe traumatic brain injury in children and adolescents. *Injury, 22*(4), 315–320.

Brain Injury Association. (1997). *Pediatric brain injury* [fact sheet]. Alexandria, VA: Author.

Brandstater, M. E., Bontke, C. F., Cobble, N. D., & Horn, L. J. (1991). Rehabilitation in brain disorders: Specific disorders. *Archives of Physical Medicine and Rehabilitation, 72,* S332–S340.

Bruce, D. A., & Zimmermann, R. A. (1989). Shaken impact syndrome. *Pediatric Annals, 18,* 482–494.

Chadwick, O., Rutter, M., Shaffer, D., & Shrout, P. E. (1981). A prospective study of children with head injuries: IV. Specific cognitive deficits. *Journal of Clinical Neuropsychology, 3,* 101–120.

Colvin, G. (1990). Procedures for preventing serious acting-out behavior in the classroom. *Direct Instruction Newsletter, 9,* 27–30.

Conoley, J. C., & Sheridan, S. M. (1997). Pediatric traumatic brain injury: Challenges and interventions for families. In E. D. Bigler, E. Clark, & J. E. Farmer (Eds.), *Childhood traumatic brain injury: Diagnosis, assessment, and intervention* (pp. 177–189). Austin, TX: PRO-ED.

Crosson, B. A. (1992). *Subcortical functions in language and memory.* New York: Guilford.

Crouchman, M. (1990). Head injury: How community pediatricians can help. *Archives of Diseases in Children, 65,* 1286–1287.

Dalby, P. R., & Obrzut, J. E. (1991). Epidemiological characteristics and sequelae of closed head-injured children and adolescents: A review. *Developmental Neuropsychology, 7,* 35–68.

D'Amato, R. C., & Rothlisberg, B. A. (1997). How education should respond to students with traumatic brain injury. In E. D. Bigler, E. Clark, & J. E. Farmer (Eds.), *Childhood traumatic brain injury: Diagnosis, assessment, and intervention* (pp. 213–237). Austin, TX: PRO-ED.

Deaton, A. V. (1994). Changing the behaviors of students with acquired brain injuries. In R. C. Savage & G. F. Wolcott (Eds.), *Educational dimensions of acquired brain injury* (pp. 257–275). Austin, TX: PRO-ED.

Donders, J. (1994). Academic placement after traumatic brain injury. *Journal of School Psychology, 32,* 53–65.

Edna, T. H., & Cappelen, J. (1987). Late post-concussional symptoms in traumatic head injury. An analysis of frequency and risk factors. *Acta Neuropsychologica, 86,* 12–17.

Ewing-Cobbs, L., & Fletcher, J. M. (1990). Neuropsychological assessment of traumatic brain injury in children. In E. D. Bigler (Ed.), *Traumatic brain injury* (pp. 107–128). Austin, TX: PRO-ED.

Ewing-Cobbs, L., Levin, H. S., Fletcher, J. M., Miner, M. E., & Eisenberg, H. M. (1989). Posttraumatic amnesia in head-injured children: Assessment and outcome. *Journal of Clinical and Experimental Neuropsychology, 11,* 58.

Farmer, J. E. (1997). Epilogue: An ecological systems approach to childhood traumatic brain injury. In E. D. Bigler, E. Clark, & J. E. Farmer (Eds.), *Childhood traumatic brain injury: Diagnosis, assessment, and intervention* (pp. 261–275). Austin, TX: PRO-ED.

Farmer, J. E., Clippard, D. S., Wiemann, Y. L., Wright, E., & Owings, S. (1997). Assessing children with traumatic brain injury during rehabilitation: Promoting school and community reentry. In E. D. Bigler, E. Clark, & J. E. Farmer (Eds.), *Childhood traumatic brain injury: Diagnosis, assessment, and intervention* (pp. 33–62). Austin, TX: PRO-ED.

Farmer, J. E., & Peterson, L. (1995). Pediatric traumatic brain injury: Promoting successful school reentry. *School Psychology Review, 24*(2), 230–243.

Fay, G. C., Jaffe, K. M., Polissar, N. L., Liao, S., Martin, K. M., Shurtleff, H. A., Rivara, J. B., & Winn, H. R. (1993). Mild pediatric traumatic brain injury: A cohort study. *Archives of Physical Medicine and Rehabilitation, 74,* 895–901.

Federal Register. (1992, September 9). Individuals with Disabilities Education Act (IDEA), U.S. Department of Education Regulations. Washington, DC: U.S. Government Printing Office.

Frankowski, R. F., Annegers, J. F., & Whitman, S. (1985). Epidemiological and descriptive studies: Part I. In D. Becker & J. T.

Povlishock (Eds.), *Central nervous system trauma: Status report* (pp. 33–45). Bethesda, MD: National Institutes of Health, National Institute of Neurological and Communicative Disorders and Stroke.

Goldstein, F. C., & Levin, H. S. (1990). Epidemiology of traumatic brain injury: Incidence, clinical characteristics, and risk factors. In E. D. Bigler (Ed.), *Traumatic brain injury* (pp. 51–67). Austin, TX: PRO-ED.

Goldstein, G. (1984). Neuropsychological assessment. In G. Goldstein & M. Hersen (Eds.), *Handbook of psychological assessment* (pp. 181–211). New York: Pergamon Press.

Haak, R. A., & Livingston, R. B. (1997). Treating traumatic brain injury in the school: Mandates and methods. In C. R. Reynolds & E. Fletcher-Janzen (Eds.), *Handbook of clinical child neuropsychology* (2nd ed., 482–505). New York: Plenum.

Hagen, C., Malkmus, D., & Durham, P. (1981). *Rancho los amigos: Levels of cognitive functioning.* Downey, CA: Professional Staff Association.

Harrington, D. (1990). Educational strategies. In M. Rosenthal, E. Griffith, M. Bond, & J. E. Miller (Eds.), *Rehabilitation of the adult and child with traumatic brain injury* (2nd ed., pp. 476–492). Philadelphia: Davis.

Hauser, W. A., & Hesdorffer, D. C. (1990). *Epilepsy: Frequency, causes and consequences.* Landover, MD: Epilepsy Foundation of America.

Jaffe, K. M., Fay, G. C., Polissar, N. L., Martin, K. M., Shurtleff, H., Rivara, J. B., & Winn, H. R. (1993). Severity of pediatric traumatic brain injury and neurobehavioral recovery at one year—A cohort study. *Archives of Physical Medicine and Rehabilitation, 74,* 587–595.

Kaplan, E. (1988). A process approach to neuropsychological assessment. In T. Boll & B. K. Bryant (Eds.), *Clinical neuropsychology and brain function: Research, measurement, and practice* (pp. 129–167). Washington, DC: American Psychological Association.

Katsiyannis, A., & Conderman, G. (1994). Serving students with traumatic brain injury: A national survey. *Remedial and Special Education, 15,* 319–325.

Katz, D. I. (1992). Neuropathology and neurobehavioral recovery from closed head injury. *Journal of Head Trauma Rehabilitation, 7,* 1–15.

Kaufmann, P. M., Fletcher, J. M., Levin, H. S., Miner, M. E., & Ewing-Cobbs, L. (1993). Attentional disturbance after pediatric closed head injury. *Journal of Child Neurology, 8,* 348–353.

Kehle, T. J., Clark, E., & Jenson, W. R. (1997). Interventions for students with traumatic brain injury: Managing behavioral disturbances. In E. D. Bigler, E. Clark, & J. E. Farmer (Eds.), *Childhood traumatic brain injury: Diagnosis, assessment, and intervention* (pp. 135–152). Austin, TX: PRO-ED.

Kraus, J. F., Black, M. A., Hessol, N., Ley, P., Rokaw, W., & Sullivan, C. (1984). The incidence of acute brain injury and serious impairments in a defined population. *American Journal of Epidemiology, 119,* 186–201.

Kreutzer, J. S., Devany, C. W., Myers, S. L., & Marwitz, J. H. (1991). Neurobehavioral outcome following brain injury. In J. S. Kreutzer & P. H. Wehman (Eds.), *Cognitive rehabilitation for persons with traumatic brain injury: A functional approach.* Baltimore: Brookes.

Lehr, E. (1990). Incidence and etiology. In E. Lehr (Ed.), *Psychological management of traumatic brain injuries in children and adolescents* (pp. 1–98). Rockville, MD: Aspen.

Lehr, E., & Savage, R. (1990). Community and school integration from a developmental perspective. In J. Kreutzer & P. Wehman (Eds.), *Community integration following traumatic brain injury* (pp. 301–310). Baltimore: Brookes.

Levin, H. S. (1985). Outcome after head injury: Part II. In D. Becker & J. T. Povlishock (Eds.), *Central nervous system trauma: Status report* (pp. 281–303). Bethesda, MD: National Institutes of Health, National Institute of Neurological and Communicative Disorders and Stroke.

Levin, H. S., High, W. M., Ewing-Cobbs, L., Fletcher, J. M., Eisenberg, H. M., Miner, M. E., & Goldstein, F. C. (1988). Memory functioning during the first year after closed head injury in children and adolescents. *Neurosurgery, 22,* 1043–1052.

Levin, H. S., Mendelsohn, D., Lilly, M. A., Fletcher, J. M., Culhane, K. A., Chapman, S. B., Harward, H., Kusnerik, L., Bruce, D., & Eisenberg, H. M. (1994). Tower of London performance in relation to magnetic resonance imaging following closed head injury in children. *Neuropsychology, 8,* 171–179.

Lezak, M. D. (1995). *Neuropsychological assessment* (3rd ed.). New York: Oxford.

Luerssen, T. G. (1991). Head injuries in children. *Neurosurgery Clinics of North America, 2,* 399–410.

Mateer, C. A., Kerns, K. A., & Eso, K. L. (1997). Management of attention and memory disorders following traumatic brain injury. In E. D. Bigler, E. Clark, & J. E. Farmer (Eds.), *Childhood traumatic brain injury: Diagnosis, assessment, and intervention* (pp. 153–175). Austin, TX: PRO-ED.

Michaud, L. J., Rivara, F. P., Jaffe, K. M., Fay, G., & Dailey, J. L. (1993). Traumatic brain injury as a risk factor for behavioral disorders in children. *Archives of Physical Medicine and Rehabilitation, 74,* 368–375.

Mira, M. P., Tucker, B. F., & Tyler, J. S. (1992). *Traumatic brain injury in children and adolescents: A sourcebook for schools.* Austin, TX: PRO-ED.

Mitiguy, J. S., Thompson, G., & Wasco, J. (1990). *Understanding brain injury: Acute hospitalization.* Lynn, MA: New Medico.

Naugle, R. I. (1990). Epidemiology of traumatic brain injury in adults. In E. D. Bigler (Ed.), *Traumatic brain injury.* Austin, TX: PRO-ED.

North, B. (1984). *Jamieson's first notebook of head injury* (3rd ed.). London: Butterworths.

Oddy, M. (1993). Head injury during childhood. *Neuropsychological Rehabilitation, 3,* 301–320.

Pang, D. (1985). Pathophysiologic correlations of neurobehavioral syndromes following closed head injury. In M. Ylvisaker (Ed.), *Head injury rehabilitation: Children and adolescents* (pp. 3–71). San Diego, CA: College-Hill Press.

Parker, R. S. (1990). *Traumatic brain injury and neuropsychological impairment: Sensorimotor, cognitive, emotional and adaptive problems of children and adults.* New York: Springer-Verlag.

Raimondi, A. J., & Hirschauer, J. (1984). Head injury in the infant and toddler. *Child's Brain, 11,* 12–35.

Rapp, D. L. (1999). Interventions for integrating children with traumatic brain injuries into their schools. In C. R. Reynolds & T. B. Gutkin (Eds.), *The handbook of school psychology* (3rd ed., pp. 863–884). New York: Wiley.

Reitan, R. M., & Wolfson, D. (1992). *Neuropsychological evaluation of older children*. South Tucson, AZ: Neuropsychology Press.

Research and Training Center in Rehabilitation and Childhood Trauma. (1993). *National pediatric trauma registry*. Boston: Tufts University of Medicine, New England Medical Center.

Russell, N. K. (1993). Educational considerations in traumatic brain injury: The role of the speech-language pathologist. *Language, Speech, and Hearing Services in the Schools, 24,* 267–275.

Rutherford, W. H. (1989). In H. S. Levin, H. M. Eisenberg, & A. L. Benton (Eds.), *Mild head injury*. New York: Oxford University Press.

Rutter, M., Chadwick, O., Shaffer, D., & Brown, G. (1980). A prospective study of children with head injuries: I. Design and methods. *Psychological Medicine, 10,* 633–645.

Savage, R. C. (1991). Identification, classification, and placement issues for students with traumatic brain injuries. *Journal of Head Trauma Rehabilitation, 6*(1), 1–9.

Savage, R. C., & Wolcott, G. F. (Eds.). (1994). *Educational dimensions of acquired brain injury*. Austin, TX: PRO-ED.

Sheridan, S. M., Kratochwill, T. R., & Bergen, J. R. (1996). *Conjoint behavioral consultation: A procedural manual*. New York: Plenum.

Teasdale, G., & Jennett, B. (1974). Assessment of coma and impaired consciousness: A practical scale. *Lancet, 2,* 81–84.

VanZomeren, A. H., & Brouwer, W. H. (1994). *Clinical neuropsychology of attention*. London: Oxford University Press.

Vernon-Levett, P. (1991). Head injuries in children. *Critical Care Nursing Clinics of North America, 3,* 411–421.

Wade, S. L., Taylor, G., Drotar, D., Stancin, T., & Yeates, K. O. (1996). Childhood traumatic brain injury: Initial impact on the family. *Journal of Learning Disabilities, 29*(6), 652–661.

Ward, J. D., Chisholm, A. H., Prince, V. T., Gilman, C. B., & Hawkins, A. M. (1994). Penetrating head injury. *Critical Care Nursing Quarterly, 17,* 79–89.

Warzak, W. J., Mayfield, J., & McAllister, J. (1998). Central nervous system dysfunction: Brain injury, postconcussive syndrome, and seizure disorder. In T. S. Watson & F. Gresham (Eds.), *Handbook of child behavior therapy* (pp. 287–309). New York: Plenum.

Wilberger, J. E. (1993). Minor head injuries in American football: Prevention of long term sequelae. *Sports Medicine, 15,* 338–343.

Wilkening, G. N. (1989). Techniques of localization in child neuropsychology. In C. R. Reynolds & E. Fletcher-Janzen (Eds.), *Handbook of clinical child neuropsychology* (pp. 291–310). New York: Plenum.

Ylvisaker, M. (1993). Communication outcome in children and adolescents with traumatic brain injury. *Neuropsychological Rehabilitation, 3,* 367–387.

PATRICIA A. LOWE
University of Kansas

CECIL R. REYNOLDS
Texas A&M University

TRAUMATIC BRAIN INJURY IN CHILDREN

Incidence and Problems

Traumatic brain injury (TBI) in children remains as a major health problem and has been reported to be the leading cause of death between the ages of 2 to 44 (Hay, 1967). Actual incidence records are only available for those with more severe injuries who sought medical treatment, but it is estimated that approximately 15,000 suffer severe traumatic brain injury in the United States each year (Di Scala et al., 1991). Severe TBI produces many observable changes, and even more changes in a child's cognitive functions. In less severe TBI, or later in the recovery, the child may appear to be functioning normally, but subtle cognitive deficits may remain that influence behavior in diffuse ways or that remain unnoticed until later stages of development are reached.

Assessment of the nature and extent of the consequences of TBI in children is more difficult and challenging than with adults, yet effective treatment and remediation requires an objective appraisal of cognitive strengths and weaknesses. Underestimating the capacity of recovery may lead to delayed rehabilitation with efforts aimed at the consequences of the injury rather than at preventative therapy (Stover & Zeiger, 1976). On the other hand, underestimating the extent of the impairment may lead to excessive stress or difficulty in emotional adjustment (Taylor et al., 1995). Clearly, even mild head injury can become a significant disruptive event to a child and his or her family unless the consequences are properly evaluated and effective rehabilitation is instituted.

Development and Time to Recovery

For a time it was generally believed that TBI sustained early in life was associated with less deleterious effects (Kennard principle). Children were thought to have a more resilient nervous system since they appear to recover more rapidly than adults, experience less persistent symptoms (Black et al., 1969), and seldom report postconcussion symptoms (Rutter et al., 1983). However, this notion is at best only partially accurate (Bolter & Long, 1985). Recent research has suggested that the likelihood of residual cognitive deficits is greater with early injury (Max et al. 1997; Taylor & Alden, 1997).

Children can "grow out" of some early deficits, but not others. In some cases, dysfunction may only appear later in the course of development (Goldman, 1971, 1972, 1974; Teuber & Rudel, 1962; Wrightson et al., 1995). For example, damage to the immature frontal lobes of a young child may not produce behavioral manifestations until much later in development when those cortical areas would normally assume functional prominence (Russell, 1959). It is likely that the effects of head injury in children combine with other functions in their development and may have widespread effects (Korkman, 1980). Age is only one variable of importance in determining the extent of recovery. In addition to age, one must consider location, nature, and the extent of the injury in order to determine the effects of the injury upon subsequent behavior.

Severity of Injury

The pathophysiology of brain injury is similar in children and adults. Severity of injury is usually measured by duration of coma and/or posttraumatic amnesia (PTA), although both are difficult to assess in younger children (Leigh, 1979). As a general guide, children experiencing coma of over 7 days seldom recover to their preinjury level. Even coma of less than 7 days or PTA of less than 3 weeks is usually associated with permanent cognitive impairment (Stover & Zeiger, 1976).

Cognitive Consequences

After severe head injury, obviously impaired physical functions tend to improve rapidly, whereas cognitive dysfunction may resolve less quickly. Head injury frequently affects intelligence, memory, speech, language, and other functions. The effects upon cognitive functions are pervasive during the first 6 months following injury (Levin & Eisenberg, 1979). Later in recovery, the effects are often characterized by slowed information processing, poor problem solving ability, impulsivity, distractibility, and poor stress tolerance with irritability and emotional lability. In addition, researchers have documented memory impairment, decreased visuospatial processing (Lord-Maes & Obrzut, 1996), and decreased attentional shift (Ewing-Cobbs et al., 1998). Common behavioral symptoms also include hyperkinesis (32 percent), discipline problems (10 percent), and lethargy (87 percent; Black, 1969), as well as ADHD (Max et al., 1998). These effects are observed in school performance and in neuropsychological testing. More important is the finding that children suffering even mild head trauma, with little or no coma and/or PTA, demonstrate attenuated cognitive abilities.

Children are undergoing significant developmental changes and even mild TBI can cause developmental setbacks leading to immature behaviors. Such damage may cause a loss of previously mastered skills and compromise future ability for the acquisition of new skills.

Emotional and Social Factors

In addition to physical impairment and cognitive dysfunction, the brain injured child is at risk for the development of emotional problems (Max et al., 1998). The risks are greater in those with low premorbid IQ, from a low socioeconomic class, or from broken homes (Rutter et al., 1983). Preinjury

family environment has also been shown to affect recovery (Yeates et al., 1997). Survivors of TBI are at a greater risk of developing psychiatric disorders as well, which is positively correlated with injury severity (Max et al., 1997, 1998).

Assessment Strategies

Proper assessment strategies leading into the development and enactment of an individually tailored intervention plan are critical in facilitating the successful reentry of the brain injured child into his or her premorbid environment. These assessment strategies focus on cognitive, emotional, and environmental factors that interact and shape subsequent behavior. Initial assessment should focus on the neuropsychological consequences of the injury. This assessment examines the relationship between the functioning of the brain and the cognitive processing abilities exhibited by the child. This assessment of cognitive abilities, coupled with a consideration of the type and severity of injury, developmental factors, and emotional functioning of the child, affords a view of basic strengths and weaknesses in cognitive functioning, which can serve to identify initial intervention strategies.

Repeated neuropsychological assessments are not necessary in most cases. Rather, a psychoeducational assessment should be of greater value later in recovery. Aptitude and achievement tests are not sensitive to the impact of a brain injury on functioning immediately following a TBI. However, they become critical components later in the assessment process for evaluating the impact of the child's processing strengths and weaknesses on school performance. The comparison of performance on aptitude and achievement tests given before and after the injury is valuable in evaluating changes in the child's ability to acquire and retain new information.

The child's emotional functioning and reaction to the environment in daily life is another key component of the assessment process. Observation of the child at home, within class, while interacting with peers, and so on is most likely to add to an understanding of the child's problems within these environments. Other assessment strategies include interviewing and utilizing scales of adaptive and emotional functioning. Evaluation of the appropriateness of the child's environment to his or her level of cognitive ability, emotional functioning, and behavioral control is needed.

Intervention Strategies

Examination of interacting cognitive, emotional, and environmental factors should be considered in the development of treatment plans. Traditional behavior management strategies may be helpful, but not completely adequate, for aiding the recovery of function in children with TBI. Because individuals with TBI often exhibit impaired concentration and memory and also have a low tolerance for frustration, environmental considerations must be made. Children with TBI should be afforded less distracting and more structured environments for study. Allowing children more time to complete their tasks can combat slowed processing. The lowered stamina of a child with TBI can be accommodated by providing frequent breaks and shortening the school day. The child's reentry into the normal school situation should be a gradual process. Care should be taken to insure that he or she is working at a level that will produce some successes. Resources such as special education and speech/language specialists should be utilized as needed. Additionally, consideration of emotional functioning should determine the need for psychological intervention. The reader is referred to a more extensive discussion of an ecological model of assessment and intervention (Farmer & Peterson, 1995; Long & Ross, 1992; Sbordone & Long, 1996).

REFERENCES

Black, P., Jeffries, J. J., Blumer, D., Wellner, A., & Walker, A. E. (1969). The posttraumatic syndrome in children. In A. E. Walker, W. F. Caveness, & M. Critchley (Eds.), *Late effects of head injury* (pp. 142–149). Springfield, IL: Thomas.

Bolter, J. F., & Long, C. J. (1985). Methodological issues in research in developmental neuropsychology. In L. C. Hartlage & C. F. Telzrow (Eds.), *The neuropsychology of individual differences* (pp. 41–59). New York: Plenum.

Di Scala, C., Osberg, J. S., Gans, B. M., Chin, L. J., & Grant, C. C. (1991). Children with traumatic head injury: Morbidity and postacute treatment. *Archives of Physical Medicine and Rehabilitation, 72,* 662–666.

Ewing-Cobbs, L., Prasad, M., Fletcher, J. M., Levin, H. S., Miner, M. E., & Eisenberg, H. M. (1998). Attention after pediatric traumatic brain injury: A multidimensional assessment. *Child Neuropsychology, 4*(1), 35–48.

Farmer, J. E., & Peterson, L. (1995). Pediatric traumatic brain injury: Promoting successful school reentry. *School Psychology Review, 24*(2), 230–243.

Goldman, P. S. (1971). Functional development of the prefrontal cortex in early life and the problem of neuronal plasticity. *Experimental Neurology, 3,* 366–387.

Goldman, P. S. (1972). Developmental determinants of cortical plasticity. *Acta Neurobiologica Experimentalis, 32,* 495–511.

Goldman, P. S. (1974). An alternative to developmental plasticity: Heterology of CNS structures in infants and adults. In D. Stein, J. Rosen, & N. Butters (Eds.), *Plasticity and recovery of function in the central nervous system* (p. 109). New York: Academic.

Hay, R. (1967). Head injuries. *Canadian Medical Association Journal, 97,* 1364–1368.

Korkman, M. (1980). An attempt to adapt methods of Luria for diagnosis of cognitive deficits in children. Convention paper INS, San Francisco, CA.

Kraus, J. F. (1995). Epidemiological features of brain injury in children: Occurrence, children at risk, causes and manner of injury, severity, and outcomes. In S. H. Broman & M. E. Michel (Eds.), *Traumatic head injury in children* (pp. 22–39). New York: Oxford University Press.

Leigh, D. (1979). Psychiatric aspects of head injury. *Psychiatric Digest,* 21–34.

Levin, H. S., & Eisenberg, H. M. (1979). Neuropsychological impairment after closed head injury in children and adolescents. *Journal of Pediatric Psychology, 4,* 389–402.

Long, C. J., & Ross, L. K. (1992). *Handbook of head trauma: Acute care to recovery.* New York: Plenum.

Lord-Maes, J., & Obrzut, J. E. (1996). Neuropsychological consequences of traumatic brain injury in children and adolescents. *Journal of Learning Disabilities, 29*(6), 609–617.

Max, J. E., Arndt, S., Castillo, C. S., Bokura, H., Robin, D., Lindgren, S. A., Smith, W. L., Sato, Y., & Mattheis, P. J. (1998). Attention-deficit hyperactivity symptomatology after traumatic brain injury: A prospective study. *Journal of the American Academy of Child and Adolescent Psychiatry, 37*(8), 841–847.

Max, J. E., Koele, S. L., Smith, W. L., Sato, Y., Lindgren, S. D., Robin, D. A., & Arndt, S. (1998). Psychiatric disorders in children and adolescents after severe traumatic brain injury: A controlled study. *Journal of the American Academy of Child and Adolescent Psychiatry, 37*(8), 832–840.

Max, J. E., Lindgren, S. D., Knutson, C., Pearson, C. S., Ihrig, D., & Welborn, A. (1997). Child and adolescent traumatic brain injury: Psychiatric findings from a pediatric outpatient specialty clinic. *Brain Injury, 11*(10), 699–711.

Russell, W. R. (1959). *Brain, memory, learning: A neurologist's view.* Oxford, England: Clarendon.

Rutter, M., Chadwick, O., & Shaffer, D. (1983). Head injury. In M. Rutter (Ed.), *Developmental neuropsychiatry* (pp. 83–111). New York: Guilford.

Rutter, M., Chadwick, O., Shaffer, D., & Brown, G. (1980). A prospective study of children with head injuries: I. Design and methods. *Psychological Medicine, 10,* 633–645.

Rutter, M. D. (1981). Psychological sequelae of brain damage in children. *American Journal of Psychiatry, 138,* 1533–1544.

Sbordone, R. J., & Long, C. J. (1996). *Ecological validity of neuropsychological testing.* Delray Beach, FL: St. Lucie.

Stover, S. L., & Zeiger, H. E. (1976). Head injury in children and teenagers: Function/recovery correlated with the duration of coma. *Archives of Physical Medicine and Rehabilitation, 57,* 201–205.

Taylor, H. G., & Alden, J. (1997). Age-related differences in outcome following childhood brain insults: An introduction and overview. *Journal of the International Neuropsychological Society, 3,* 555–567.

Taylor, H. G., Drotar, D., Wade, S., Yeates, K., Stancin, T., & Klein, S. (1995). Recovery from traumatic brain injury in children: The importance of the family. In S. H. Broman & M. E. Michel (Eds.), *Traumatic head injury in children* (pp. 188–216). New York: Oxford University Press.

Teuber, H. L., & Rudel, R. G. (1967). Behavior after cerebral lesions in children and adults. *Developmental Medicine and Child Neurology, 4,* 3–20.

Wrightson, P., McGinn, V., & Gronwall, D. (1995). Mild head injury in preschool children: Evidence that it can be associated with a persistent cognitive defect. *Journal of Neurology, Neurosurgery, and Psychiatry, 59*(4), 375–380.

Yeates, K. O., Taylor, H. G., Drotar, D., Wade, S. L., Klein, S., Stancin, T., & Schatschneider, C. (1997). Preinjury family environment as a determinant of recovery from traumatic brain injuries in school-age children. *Journal of the International Neuropsychological Society, 3*(6), 617–630.

CHARLES J. LONG
JOY O'GRADY
MICHELLE RIES
University of Memphis

TRAVEL AIDS, ELECTRONIC

See ELECTRONIC TRAVEL AIDS.

TRAVEL AIDS FOR INDIVIDUALS WITH DISABILITIES

The United States Department of Justice provides a guide to disability rights and laws to ensure equal opportunities for people with disabilities. Encompassed within this document are guidelines for access to public transportation, public accommodation, and air carriers (Disability Rights Section, 1996). America adheres to these guidelines and provides disabled travelers with various options for traveling. Numerous opportunities for accessible travel by car, boat, train, or airplane are available to those with handicaps. Airlines have made themselves more accessible by arranging for an aisle seat (many of which have removable arms for easier access), notifying the crew that a special needs traveler will be on board, and meeting special requests such as dietary needs or supplemental oxygen. Wheelchairs may be gate-checked for easier accessibility as they will be the first items offloaded at the traveler's destination or at any change of planes. Travelers with disabilities should ask the airlines or their travel agent to make reservations for the most direct route and to allow ample time to change planes if necessary.

Train travel is another option for the travelers with disabilities. Amtrak provides information and details about station accessibility along its routes. Train aisles are narrow, so wheelchair access may be limited. However, often meals are served at the person's seat. Conductors give hearing-impaired travelers necessary announcements in writing. Guide dogs travel free, and most trains are equipped with signs in braille.

Avis Rent-a-Car and Hertz Car Rental companies offer hand-control cars if reserved well in advance. Other car companies also have vehicles to offer special needs clients, including wheelchair-accessible vans.

If traveling by ship, the travelers with disabilities should check accessibility before making a reservation. Most major cruise lines have handicapped accessible cabins and public areas, but some small ships have limited access. The special needs traveler should check with each ship to find out what provisions have been made for the disabled and if specific needs can be met.

Quick travel answers can be found from sources, such as *Fodor's Great American Vacations for Travelers with Disabilities* (1994). The internet also provides multiple sites providing travel information and answering specific questions. Project Action (1999) has a comprehensive database with city and state listings of accessible travel options. National 800 numbers are listed on the Project Action web site with public transportation, airport transportation, hotel shuttles, private bus, and even tour companies' information links. Information can be located online.

Access Amtrak
60 Massachusetts Ave
Washington, DC 20002

American Foundation for the Blind
Travel Concessions for Blind Persons
15 W. 16th Street
New York, NY 10011

Centers for the Handicapped, Inc.
10501 New Hampshire Avenue
Silver Spring, MD 20903 (301-445-3350)

Diabetes Travel Service
349 E. 52nd Street
New York, NY 10022

INTERMEDIC
777 Third Avenue
New York, NY 10007

International Association for Medical Assistance
    for Travelers
350 5th Avenue, Suite 5620
New York, NY 10001

National Easter Seals Society
Information Center
230 W. Monroe St.
Chicago, IL 60606

Society for the Advancement of Travel for the
    Handicapped (SATH)
"The United States Welcomes Handicapped Visitors"
(cassette or braille available)
5014 42nd Street, NW
Washington, DC 20016 (202-966-3900)

Travel Tips for the Handicapped
U.S. Travel Service
Department of Commerce
Washington, DC 20230

Wheelchair Wagon Tours
P.O. Box 1270
Kissimmee, FL 32741 (305-846-7175)

Whole Person Tours
137 W. 32nd Street
Bayonne, New Jersey 07002 (201-858-3400)

REFERENCES

Fodor's great American vacations for travelers with disabilities. (1994). New York: Fodor's Travel Publications.

Project Action. (1999). http://projectaction.org/paweb/index.htm

Reamy, L. (1978). *Travel ability.* New York: Macmillan.

Rosenburg, M. (1985, August 25). Aid for handicapped traveler grows. *Minneapolis Star and Tribune.*

U.S. Department of Justice. (1996). *Disability rights section.* Retrieved from http://www.pueblo.gsa.gov/cic_prog/disability-law/disrits.html

SUE A. SCHMITT
University of Wisconsin at Stout
First edition

KARI ANDERSON
University of North Carolina at Wilmington
Second edition

TREACHER-COLLINS SYNDROME

See NATIONAL ORGANIZATION OF RARE DISORDERS.

TREATMENT ACCEPTABILITY

Treatment acceptability is a form of social validation that asks consumers how they feel about treatment methods prior to treatment. "Judgments of acceptability are likely to embrace evaluation of whether treatment is appropriate for the problem, whether treatment is fair, reasonable, and intrusive, and whether treatment meets with conventional notions about what treatment should be" (Kazdin, 1980, p. 259). The most basic assumption of the acceptability hypothesis is that the acceptability of a treatment method will influence the overall efficacy of the treatment. Methods that consumers feel are the most acceptable will be more effective than methods that are judged to be unacceptable. As Wolf (1978) stated, "If the participants don't like the treatment then they may avoid it, or run away, or complain loudly. And thus, society will be less likely to use our technology, no matter how potentially effective and efficient it might be" (p. 206).

Research efforts in treatment acceptability have followed the same general procedures. Subjects receive written, audio, oral, or audiovisual descriptions of problem behaviors and procedures for treating the problem behaviors. Then the subjects answer a number of questions designed to assess how acceptable the treatment is for improving the problem behavior. A number of scales of similar format have been developed for assessing treatment acceptability in different target populations. The Treatment Evaluation Inventory (TEI; Kazdin, 1980) has 15 questions scored on a seven-point Likert scale used with children and adults. The TEI requires subjects to make judgments about how acceptable an intervention is, how suitable the intervention is, how much the intervention is liked, and so on. The Intervention Rating Profile (IRP; Witt & Martens, 1983) has 20 questions scored on a six-point Likert scale; the questions were specifically written to assess teachers' acceptability judgments of interventions in classroom situations. The IRP has been used to delineate a number of treatment variables that affect teachers' acceptability ratings (Turco, Witt, & Elliott, 1985; Witt, Elliott, & Martens, 1984). The Children's Intervention Rating Profile (CIRP; Elliott et al., 1986) has seven questions scored on a six-point Likert-scale. The CIRP has been used by a number of researchers (Elliott et al., 1986; Turco & Elliott, 1986; Turco et al., 1985) to assess children's treatment acceptability.

REFERENCES

Elliott, S. N. (1986). Children's ratings of the acceptability of classroom interventions for misbehavior: Findings and methodological considerations. *Journal of School Psychology, 24,* 23–35.

Elliott, S. N., Witt, J. C., Galvin, G. A., & Moe, G. L. (1986). Children's involvement in intervention selection: Acceptability of interventions for misbehaving peers. *Professional Psychology: Research and Practice, 17,* 235–241.

Kazdin, A. E. (1980). Acceptability of alternative treatments for deviant child behavior. *Journal of Applied Behavior Analysis, 13,* 259–273.

Turco, T. L., & Elliott, S. N. (1986). Assessment of students' acceptability of teacher-initiated interventions for classroom misbehaviors. *Journal of School Psychology, 24,* 277–283.

Turco, T. L., Elliott, S. N., & Witt, J. C. (1985). Children's involvement in treatment selection: A review of theory and analogue research on treatment acceptability (pp. 54–62). *Monograph on Secondary Behavioral Disorders.* Reston, VA: Council for Exceptional Children.

Turco, T. L., Witt, J. C., & Elliott, S. N. (1985). Factors influencing teachers' acceptability of classroom interventions for deviant student behavior (pp. 46–53). *Monograph on Secondary Behavioral Disorders.* Reston, VA: Council for Exceptional Children.

Witt, J. C., Elliott, S. N., & Martens, B. K. (1984). Factors affecting teachers' judgments of the acceptability of behavioral interventions: Time involvement, behavior problem severity, and type of intervention. *Behavior Therapy, 15,* 204–209.

Witt, J. C., & Martens, B. K. (1983). Assessing the acceptability of behavioral interventions. *Psychology in the Schools, 20,* 570–577.

Wolf, M. M. (1978). Social validity: The case for subjective measurement or how applied behavior analysis is finding its heart. *Journal of Applied Behavior Analysis, 11,* 203–214.

Timothy L. Turco
Louisiana State University

Stephen N. Elliott
University of Wisconsin at Madison

TEACHER EFFECTIVENESS
TEACHER EXPECTANCIES

TRENDS IN REHABILITATION AND DISABILITY

Introduction

The purpose of this article is to introduce and explore four models of disability: the traditional model, medical model, social model, and integrative model (Seelman, 2002). The four models often appear in sequential stages in the history of many industrialized countries. With the exception of the integrative model, the knowledge base for each model tends to exclude that of the other models. Throughout this article, the models are illustrated by corresponding policies, practices, and research, using country-based examples mainly from the United States and, to a lesser extent, Japan. These models have implications for professional education and training of people with disabilities. Conclusions and recommendations will therefore address professional education and training people with disabilities as well as international and country-based policies, practices, research, and collaboration.

Trends

A number of international trends illustrate the importance of reexamining disability models that are operative in countries and international organizations. The first trend involves conflict between health professionals who identify with the medical model and people with disabilities who identify with the social model. Throughout the world, people with disabilities, who have formed a Disability Movement, are criticizing the medical model of disability and demanding greater participation in decision making (Basnett, 2001). The introduction of the World Health Organization's International Classification of Functioning, Disability and Health in 2001 suggests that a more integrative model may be emerging within the international community (WHO, 2001). The integrative model adjusts for some of the criticisms of the other models and is already influential in country-based policy, practice, research, and professional training.

The second trend involves technology. Increasingly, access to technology is associated with human rights as reflected in the Americans with Disabilities Act of 1990, the proposed United Nations Convention on the Rights of People with Disabilities, and the World Summit on the Information Society. Policies, practices, and research in universal design and design for all are examples of this trend. Human rights and technology are associated with demands to make mainstream systems and products, such as communication systems, transportation systems, and cell phones, accessible. However, accessibility features in mainstream systems and products may be regarded as "social add-ons"—not competitive in the global marketplace. Human rights and technology are also associated with policies, practices, and research in special or assistive technology for individuals (e.g., wheelchairs, hearing aids). Interface problems for individuals with disabilities and technology and interfaces between specialized and mainstream technology have generated interest among researchers. The Trace Research and Development Center at the University of Wisconsin is one of a number of centers that conduct research on interfaces.

A third trend involves rehabilitation research itself. To justify payment, rehabilitation researchers across disciplines are called upon to show evidence of outcomes, efficacy, and effectiveness of assistive technology (Fuhrer, 2001). A fourth trend involves the struggles of social welfare program administrators to keep benefit programs solvent while serving growing numbers of people with disabilities, especially older people. Countries are adopting a mix of social welfare, civil rights, and other policies to address disability issues (Van Oorscot & Hvinden, 2001; Zeitzer, 2002). Countries are struggling to contain costs of public welfare systems, but have often failed to adopt policies that may defer, lessen, or negate the need for expensive institutionalization, such as accessible mainstream systems and products. Finally, the fifth trend is poverty—a barrier to the support of disability programs in developing countries where the majority of people with disabilities live. Many cultures continue to use a traditional model of disability. In the absence of scientific and health infrastructures, disability policy and practices may be based almost exclusively on culture and religion (Barnes & Mercer, 2003; Coleridge, 1993; Ingstad & Whyte, 1995).

Models of Disability

Four models of disability are explored in this section: the traditional model, medical model, social model, and integrative model. The following factors are considered for each model: (a) knowledge base, (b) roles, (c) rules and relationships, (d) temporal and spatial parameters, and (e) bias. Corresponding policies, practices, and research are identified for each model.

The Traditional Model

The traditional model is based on culturally and religiously determined knowledge, views, and practices. Depending on cosmology, social organization, and other factors, cultures show a broad range of perspectives that place people with disabilities on a continuum from human to nonhuman. For example, some cultures practice infanticide, rejecting the humanity of disabled infants. The roles people with disabilities may assume within a given culture range from participant to pariah (Barnes & Mercer, 2003; Ingstad & Whyte, 1995). When persons with disabilities are devalued, they may be perceived as demonic or unfortunate, and often take on the role of an outcast (Coleridge, 1993). The bias of the traditional model is cultural relativity. Objective, scientifically based knowledge is not associated with this model.

Across cultures, people with disabilities have been valued differently. In his presidential address before the American Association of Physical Medicine and Rehabilitation, Thomas E. Strax, MD, made the following observation:

> From the beginning of time, humankind has wrestled with the paradox of what to do with people with disabilities. In ancient times, they were simply put to death. They were a burden on the tribe. In ancient Greece, there were two cities. Sparta removed the weak and the elderly for the good of the rest. In Athens, the warrior class protected the weak. (Strax, p. 943, 2003)

The Medical Model

The medical model is based on scientific views and practice, typically in the medical and health knowledge base. The "problem" is located within the body of the individual with a disability. The context of the medical model is the clinic or institution. Persons with disabilities assume the role of patient, a role that may be of either short-term or long-term duration depending on several factors, including the individuals' condition, policies related to institutionalization and community supports, and professional and social attitudes about disability. Authority lies with professionals. The bias of the model is the biomedical perception of normalcy and the narrow band of legitimate knowledge, usually medical and health related. Explanation of disability is reduced to the impairment level. The perspective of the person with a disability and social factors are not routinely within the knowledge base of the medical model.

Worst and Best Practices

In the West during the twentieth century, examples of worst and best medical research practices for people with disabilities can illustrate the strengths and weaknesses of the medical model. Worst practice examples can be drawn from most countries and regions.

- Willowbrook Experiments, United States: This study was designed to follow the natural progression of a disease—in this case viral hepatitis. Children with disabilities were intentionally infected with the virus and then studied during the progression of the disease. A particularly disturbing aspect of the research was that it was reviewed and approved by the New York State Departments of Mental Hygiene, Mental Health, the Armed Forces Epidemiological Board, and the New York University School of Medicine, in addition to the Willowbrook School. Although parental consent was given, the consent was based upon the school's declaration that there was room for new students at the school only in the experimental unit (http://members.aol.com/bercar/caramain.htm).

- The Holocaust and People with Disabilities: There is evidence to show that people with disabilities were systematically exterminated and were the subjects of medical experiments during the World War II Nazi period in Germany (*Forgotten Crimes: The Holocaust and People with Disabilities*, 2001).

Most countries and international organizations also have many examples of best practices within the medical model. These include:

- Breakthroughs in biomedical and technological sciences and clinical applications that have saved lives and extended the lifespan of individuals with disabilities (National Institute on Disability and Rehabilitation Research, 1999)

- Research policy reform (http://ohrp.osophs.dhhs.gov/irb/irb_guidebook.htm)

- International Classification of Impairments, Disabilities and Handicaps (ICIDH; WHO, 1980)

After the second World War, the international community adopted reforms and provided guidelines for research. These policies include the Nuremberg Code of 1947, the United Nations Universal Declaration of Human Rights of 1948, and the World Medical Association's Declaration of Helsinki of 1964. Later, some countries began to adopt policies such as institutional review boards to protect research subjects.

The influential ICIDH, which identified the cause of disability within the individual, was adopted by many users, including policy makers (social security benefits, employment, occupational health), demographers, epidemiologists and statisticians (surveys), and health planners (utilization, resources). Even before the adoption of the ICIDH, health professionals created policy and designed surveys and utilization practices within the medical model. Throughout the twentieth century, countries adopted general social welfare and health policies (which usually included people with disabilities) as the first stage in a series of disability policies that would later include general and specialized education, employment, and accessibility policies for disabled people. Examples of social welfare and health policy include Japan's Social Insurance System developed in 1922 and the Social Security Act adopted in the United States in 1935 (Miyatake, 2000).

Measurement Tools

Development and use of research measurement tools, such as the Functional Independence Measure (FIM), and concepts such as the normal curve reinforced the medical model. These tools were designed to measure impairment at the body level with the goal of curing the cause of the impairment—or at least minimizing performance difficulties. The test sites are usually clinics, rehabilitation centers, or other controlled sites. The distance walked is a key component of the health-related quality of life measure for the FIM. The measure focuses on the independent function of the person without contextual supports.

Professional Training

The knowledge base used to educate health professionals is rigorous and routinely limited to medicine and the health sciences. Therefore, health professionals may develop a view of disability that differs substantially from the reality of many disabled people. The following is a quotation from a medical doctor, before he became disabled and afterward:

> [I began] to examine his nervous system . . . felt a sense of horror come over me. You can't feel anything here on your shoulder? You can't move your legs? I next met this man in a spinal cord unit in 1985 as I was pushed to the computer next to him in occupational therapy. A few months earlier, I had severed my cervical spinal cord playing rugby and I was a quadriplegic—slightly more impaired than was my former patient. Now, 15 years after becoming disabled, I find myself completely at home with the concept of . . . being me. Now I know that my assessment of the potential quality of life of severely disabled people was clearly flawed. (Basnett, p. 45, 2001)

Disabled people may develop a view of health care that is very different from the one held by professionals. While professionals may view people with disabilities as patients, people with disabilities often accept their disabilities and move away from the patient role to resume life roles of worker, student, and parent within the community.

Legacy of the Medical Model

The medical model is based on a narrow range of views and practices involving health and welfare. Research and research tools are useful for medical purposes but not as useful for social purposes, such as measuring accessibility and participation. Professional education and training, to the extent that it has not incorporated information about quality of life and accessibility, has resulted in a "dual perspective" situation. Therefore, there is a widening gap of understanding between professionals and patients who are at some stage of transformation and recovery (Gabard & Martin, 2003).

The Social Model

The social model is based on knowledge of the experience and views and practices of people with disabilities. The model locates the problem within society, rather than within the individual with a disability. From the perspective of the social model, disability is conceived more as diversity in function or the result of discrimination in policies, practices, research, training, and education. Individuals with disabilities are the authorities. They assume a range of roles—especially the advocate role—to pursue full expression of educational and employment opportunities and citizenship. Rules are determined within a framework of choice and independent living with strong support from organized disability communities. The biases of the social model include: limiting the causes of disability either exclusively or mainly to social and environmental policies and practices, or advancing perceptions of disability in mainly industrialized countries that emphasize individual rights rather than advancing broader economic rights that may reflect the needs of impoverished developing countries (Albrecht, Seelman, & Bury, 2001; Barnes & Mercer, 2003).

Policies and Practices

While retaining health and welfare policies of the first stage of disability policy, countries are in various stages of transition from the medical model to the social model. International organizations, some industrialized countries, and some developing countries have adopted second and third stage policies and practices of special laws in education, employment, civil rights, and accessibility. The United Nations began adopting disability human rights declarations in the 1970s in support of the principle of normalization of the lives of people with disabilities. Most countries in the second stage of disability policy have adopted special education and employment policies such as Japan's School Education Law of 1947 and the Individuals with Disabilities Education Act of 1975 in the United States, which involved civil rights and mainstreaming of most children with disabilities (Statistical Abstracts, 2003). Japan and the United States are among countries that have adopted special employment-related laws, such as Japan's Human Resources Development Promotion Law of 1969 and the U.S. Rehabilitation Act of 1973, which also involved civil rights (Ministry of Labor, 1999).

Most of these laws provided services that were controlled by professionals. In the third stage, some countries began to move from special needs policies to a civil rights policy such as the Americans with Disabilities Act of 1990 in the United States. Others continued with a health, welfare, special education, and special employment approach and often added policies to make buildings and information more accessible (Heyer, 2000).

Measurement Tools

The social model perspective incorporates research that examines problems of quality of life, user satisfaction, participation, and accessibility of various domains of the environment. The perspective also examines problems of participation of people with disabilities in the research process, including survey research. Researchers have explored methods to interview people with disabilities in survey research. Section 508 of the U.S. Rehabilitation Act as amended in 1998 may require federal electronic-based surveys to be accessible to people with disabilities, not only in the collection of survey data, but also in the analysis and reporting stages. New research tools have emerged to measure quality of life and satisfaction, including the Quebec User Evaluation of Satisfaction with Assistive Technology and the Psychosocial Impact of Assistive Devices Scale (Cook & Hussey, 2002; Scherer, 2002). Researcher David Gray has been involved in the development of measures of the environment. Gray changes the outcome measure from capacity to participation, which focuses on the individual's ability to function in his or her own environment. Although people with disabilities may score low in clinical tests of capacity, they may participate in many life activities including work, education, and family and community life.

A number of the Rehabilitation Engineering Research Centers (RERCS) of the National Institute on Disability and Research (NIDRR) have developed assistive technologies and universal design products that have increased participation of people with disabilities. For example, the RERC on Universal Design and the Built Environment has developed a squat toilet and a visitable house.

Research efforts have also worked toward the development of accessible communication devices. Title IV of the Americans with Disabilities Act charged the telephone companies with a provision of interstate and intrastate telephone relay services that will provide deaf, hard-of-hearing, and speech-impaired persons with telephone service functionally equivalent to service for hearing persons. The private sector has competed for contracts to develop and manage relay services. The CapTel System can be used by people with some degree of hearing loss because it works like a telephone but also displays every word the caller says during the conversation.

Researchers have also modeled stages of change in orga-

nizations as they move toward accessibility. The Center for Rehabilitation Sciences & Technology at the University of Wisconsin at Milwaukee developed a model called A3. The A3 model conceptualizes stages in which organizations meet the needs of people with disabilities, focusing on the physical and virtual environment, consumer products, services, and systems. The A3 Model includes three elements: advocacy, accommodation, and accessibility. The advocacy stage has the following characteristics:

- minimal anticipation of needs
- reactive to "complaints"
- sometimes the person with the disability advocates
- other times someone else advocates for the person with the disability
- people with disabilities receive a different "product" than people without disabilities

The next stage is accommodation. Characteristics of accommodation include the following:

- anticipation of needs
- prepared to meet needs
- "complaints" are reduced as there is a system in place
- people with disabilities still receive a different "product" than people without disabilities
- likely requires additional time, money, effort, etc.

The third stage is accessibility. Characteristics of accessibility are:

- proactive
- recognition that better design can reduce the need for individual accommodation
- everybody receives the same "product"
- people with disabilities do not require additional time, money, effort, etc.

Education and Training

The social model is based on a knowledge base of experiences of individuals with disabilities living in society. Adoption of the social model has led to demands to educate and train architects, designers, engineers, and lawyers, as well as people with disabilities.

Engineers have begun to receive clinical training. The University of Pittsburgh School of Health and Rehabilitation Sciences provides training in the Center for Assistive Technology and the University of Pittsburgh School of Law has launched a Disability Law curriculum. A number of universities, including the University of Pittsburgh, have added a Disability Studies curriculum.

The Integrative Model

The Integrative Model has a broad knowledge base ranging from medicine to literature that is informed by the experiences of people with disabilities. The Integrative Model is "under construction." From the integrative perspective, individuals with disabilities have many roles, including citizen and patient. There are a number of evolving policies and practices that are representative of this model. Some of them are represented in the World Health Organization International Classification of Functioning, Disability and Health; the U.S. Institute of Medicine's *Enabling America: Assessing the Role of Rehabilitation Science and Engineering;* and the *NIDRR Long-Range Plan* (Brandt & Pope, 1997; National Institute on Disability and Rehabilitation Research, 1999; WHO, 2001).

Policies and Practices

While retaining general health, welfare, special education, and employment policies and practices of the first and second stages, countries are in various stages of transition to a civil rights approach and related universality of design applications in systems and markets. International organizations, such as the World Health Organization, have developed a more universal approach to disability. The following interpretation of the ICF illustrates its universality and integrative characteristics (Schneider, 2001):

Universal model	—*not a minority model*
Integrative model	—*not merely medical or social*
Interactive model	—*not linear progressive*
Parity	—*not etiological causality*
Inclusive	—*contextual, environment, & person*
Cultural applicability	—*not western concepts alone*
Operational	—*not theory driven alone*
Life span coverage	—*not adult driven (children, elderly)*
Human functioning	—*not merely disability*

The components of the ICF encourage a broad and integrative classification. The three components of the ICF are body components, activities and participation, and environment. ICF researchers will be challenged to identify the relationships among the components.

The Disability Movement is pressing a number of international organizations for conventions and statements of principle committed to full integration of people with disabilities in society. The United Nations is being pressed to adopt a convention on the rights of people with disabilities.

The World Summit on the Information Society is being pressed to adopt a section on disability within the draft Declaration of Principles. Many of these initiatives have precedent in U.S. law. The Americans with Disabilities Act of 1990 (ADA) recognizes the full civil rights of people with disabilities. The ADA also provides assistive technology and accessibility of communications with important roles in the realization of rights and opportunities. The United States has regulated the communications industry to assure access. The original Communications Act of 1934 recognized universal access for all people in the United States. In 1996, the new Telecommunications Act was amended to include rules requiring telecommunications manufacturers and service providers to make their products and services accessible to people with disabilities, if readily achievable. The United States has also created market incentives to motivate industry to make its systems and products accessible. As Section 508 of the Rehabilitation Act requires, the United States government constitutes a large market for accessible technology and employs the federal procurement system to purchase it. Section 508 requires access to electronic and information technology provided by the federal government. The law applies to all federal agencies when they develop, procure, maintain, or use electronic and information technology. Federal agencies must ensure that technology is accessible to employees and members of the public with disabilities to the extent it does not impose an "undue burden." Section 508 speaks to various means for disseminating information, including computers, software, and electronic office equipment. It applies to, but is not solely focused on, federal pages on the Internet or the World Wide Web. It does not yet apply to web pages of private industry.

Measurement Tools and Principles

Disability is not inherent in measurement tools designed with the integrative model in mind. Psychological, social, and environmental factors must be incorporated into assessments that are based on an integrative model. Assessment measures that are consistent with the integrative model assume a real world context of school, family, and employment. Health service performance measures should be based on consumer outcomes. Some measures of disability may be disability specific in which case they may change the perception of the capability of the individual.

Researchers at the RERC at the University of Buffalo have developed a prototype database on anthropometry of wheelchair users. Researchers at the Department of Rehabilitation Sciences and Technology, School of Health and Rehabilitation Sciences have developed a Virtual Reality Tele-Rehabilitation System for Analyzing the Accessibility of the Physical Environment.

Education and Training

The ICF has become a useful framework on which to base coursework for individuals across a wide number of fields, including the health professions, social work, psychology, and Disability Studies. Over 30 ICF-related courses have been identified in universities in the United States and Canada. For example, the University of Pittsburgh Department of Occupational Therapy has adopted the ICF as the foundation for curriculum design.

Conclusions, Opportunities, and Challenges

In the international area, the following policy, research, and practice opportunities and challenges exist:

- monitor U.N. Implementation of the Standard Rules and enact a U.N. Disability Human Rights Convention
- incorporate a statement on accessibility for people with disabilities into the World Summit on the Information Society draft principles
- support developing countries in provision of programs and participation for people with disabilities
- develop the ICF measures for social and environmental factors so that assessment measures assume a real world context of school, family, and employment
- base health service performance on consumer outcomes
- generate global marketplace incentives and standards to support universal design, usability, and accessibility in product design and sale
- add disability to surveys of health, income, employment, and education

In addition to the aforementioned, the domestic area provides the following opportunities and challenges:

- commit public and private research and development funding to technological inclusion of people with disabilities
- promote technological inclusion by linking technology policy to civil rights
- monitor research policies to protect people with disabilities in research conducted abroad with domestic research funding
- create a government marketplace for usable and accessible systems and products

In the practice area, the following opportunities and challenges exist:

- promote science, technology, and education and training opportunities for people with disabilities
- integrate the perspective of people with disabilities and social and environmental factors into curricula
- broaden the range of disciplines that address disability to include engineers, designers, and lawyers

- adopt the ICF as a framework to develop health-related professional education

In research, the following opportunities and challenges exist:

- develop measures of social factors and environmental domains
- develop accessible survey research process and questions about social behavior and environmental accessibility
- develop evidence-based practice
- develop assistive technology outcome measures

Opportunities for collaboration exist: Develop strategies based on the Tokushima Agreement among Japan, the United States, Australia, and Europe.

REFERENCES

Barnes, C., & Mercer, G. (2003). *Disability*. Cambridge, UK: Polity Press.

Basnett, I. (2001). Health care professionals and their attitudes toward decisions affecting disabled people. In G. L. Albrecht, K. D. Seelman, & M. Bury (Eds.), *Handbook of disability studies* (pp. 450–467). Thousand Oaks, CA: Sage.

Brandt, E. N., & Pope, A. M. (Eds.). (1997). *Enabling America: Assessing the role of rehabilitation science and engineering.* Washington, DC: National Academy Press.

Coleridge, P. (1993). *Disability, liberation and development.* United Kingdom and Ireland: Oxfam.

Cook, A. M., & Hussey, S. M. (2002). *Assistive technologies: Principles and practices* (2nd ed.). St. Louis, MO: Mosby.

Forgotten crimes: The holocaust and people with disabilities. (2001). Oakland, CA: Disability Rights Advocate.

Fuhrer, M. J. (2001). Assistive technology outcomes research: Challenges met and yet unmet. *American Journal of Physical Medicine & Rehabilitation, 80*(7), 523–535.

Gabard, D. L., & Martin, M. M. (2003). *Physical therapy ethics.* Philadelphia: F. A. Davis Co.

Ingstad, B., & Whyte, S. R. (Eds.). (1995). *Disability culture.* Los Angeles: University of California.

Ministry of Labor. (1999). *Employment and its promotion of disabled persons in Japan: A guide to employment for employers and disabled persons.* Prefectural Governments, Japan Association for Employment of the Disabled.

Miyatake, G. (2000). *Social security in Japan* (Vol. 17). Tokyo: Foreign Press Center.

National Institute on Disability and Rehabilitation Research. (1999). *NIDRR long-range plan.* Washington, DC: National Institute on Disability and Rehabilitation Research, U.S. Department of Education.

Scherer, M. J. (Ed.). (2002). *Assistive technology: Matching device and consumer for successful rehabilitation.* Washington, DC: American Psychological Association.

Schneider, M. (2001, June). *Participation and environment in the ICF and measurement of disability: Classification, assessment, surveys and terminology.* Paper presented at the World Health Organization United Nations Meeting on Measurement of Disability, New York.

Seelman, K. D. (2002, October 24). *Disability studies and the disciplines: Bridges and chasms.* Paper presented at the Invest in Disability Week, Ann Arbor, Michigan.

Strax, T. E. (2003). Consumer, advocate, provider: A paradox requiring a new identity paradigm. *Archives of Physical Medical Rehabilitation, 84,* 943–945.

U.S. Bureau of the Census. (2003). *Statistical abstracts of the United States.* Washington, DC: Author.

Van Oorscot, W., & Hvinden, B. (2001). *Disability policies in European countries.* Dordrecht, The Netherlands: Kluwer Law International.

World Health Organization (WHO). (2001). *International classification of functioning, disability and health.* Geneva: Author.

World Health Organization (WHO). (1980). *International classification of impairments, disabilities, and handicaps.* Geneva: Author.

Zeitzer, I. (2002). The challenges of disability pension policy: Three Western European case studies of the battle against the numbers. In E. Fultz & R. Marcus (Eds.), *Reforming worker protections: Disability pensions in transformation.* Budapest, Hungary: International Labor Organization.

KATHERINE D. SEELMAN
University of Pittsburgh

ANNUAL REPORT TO CONGRESS ON THE IMPLEMENTATION OF THE INDIVIDUALS WITH DISABILITIES EDUCATION ACT, TWENTY-FIFTH EXECUTIVE SUMMARY OF DEMOGRAPHY OF SPECIAL EDUCATION

TRIARCHIC THEORY OF INTELLIGENCE

See INTELLIGENCE, TRIARCHIC THEORY OF.

TRICHORHINOPHALANGEAL SYNDROME

Trichorhinophalangeal syndrome is a relatively rare hereditary condition that is traced to a defect on chromosome 8. Children born with this disorder have thin, sparse hair; thick, heavy eyebrows along the bridge of the nose, thinning out toward the distal portions of their faces; a pear-shaped or bulbous nose; large eyes; thin upper lip; small and/or extra teeth; small jaw; and a horizontal groove under their chin. These children are short in stature and have thin fingernails. Abnormalities of the skeletal system, including short, stubby fingers and toes, are common. Problems in bone growth appear around age 3 or 4 years and persist and worsen until adolescent growth is completed. Degenerative hip disease may develop in the young adult and senior years (Rudolph, 1991; Jones, 1988).

Trichorhinophalangeal syndrome comes in two forms: Types I and II, with Type II more severe than Type I. Besides the degree of severity, other distinguishing characteristics of Type II include a smaller head circumference and susceptibility to upper respiratory infections. Moreover, these children have Mild to Moderate Mental Retardation and delayed onset of speech. Children with Type I are usually of normal intelligence. Some children with Type II may have a hearing loss. Standard treatment for the syndrome is symptomatic and supportive. Surgery may be performed to correct limb and extremity abnormalities. Genetic counseling may also be helpful (Thoene, 1992).

For children who are mentally retarded or speech delayed, it will be important to begin services through an Early Childhood Intervention (ECI) program. Based on the child's progress and development, he/she may continue to require additional support through special education or speech therapy.

REFERENCES

Jones, K. L. (Ed.). (1988). *Smith's recognizable patterns of human malformation* (4th ed.). Philadelphia: Saunders.

Rudolph, A. M. (1991). *Rudolph's pediatrics—19th edition.* Norwalk, CT: Appleton & Lange.

Thoene, J. G. (Ed.). (1992). *Physician's guide to rare diseases.* Montvale, NJ: Dowden.

JOAN MAYFIELD
Baylor Pediatric Specialty Service

PATRICIA A. LOWE
University of Kansas

TRICHOTILLOMANIA

Trichotillomania is a low-incidence disorder (occurring in less than 1 percent of pediatric referrals) of self-injurious behavior that consists of pulling out one's hair; it is often accompanied by trichophagia, subsequent eating of the hair. The etiology of trichotillomania is unknown, but it has long been held to be of a psychoanalytic or Freudian nature. It occurs most often in conjunction with a major psychological or psychiatric disorder, particularly Schizophrenia and lower levels of Mental Retardation, though it also occurs with narcissistic personality disorders. In special education programs, it is most often encountered among mentally retarded populations. Incidences of Trichotillomania have also been reported in conjunction with episodes of child abuse. Incidence is generally greater in females than males.

A variety of treatment approaches have been attempted

with this unusual disorder, including psychoanalysis, traditional psychotherapies, hypnotherapy, and a variety of operant and other behavior modification techniques. Generally, the earlier the age of onset, the greater the likelihood of successful treatment (Sorosky & Sticker, 1980). Behavioral techniques appear to be the most successful methods of treating Trichotillomania and trichophagia, particularly when competing responses can be developed, although success has been reported with a variety of techniques and the role of spontaneous remission is not known. Sources of treatment information include Azrin and Nunn (1973), Bayer (1972), and Mannino and Delgado (1969).

Some recent animal research suggests that a variety of self-injurious behaviors, including Trichotillomania and trichophagia, may, in some cases, be of neurological origin. Relationships to damage of cells around the substantia nigra have been suggested.

REFERENCES

Azrin, N. H., & Nunn, R. G. (1973). Habit reversal: A method of eliminating nervous habits. *Behavior Research & Therapy, 11,* 619–628.

Bayer, C. A. (1972). Self-monitoring and mild aversion treatment of trichotillomania. *Journal of Behavior Therapy & Experimental Psychiatry, 3,* 139–141.

Mannino, F. C., & Delgado, R. A. (1969). Trichotillomania in children: A review. *American Journal of Psychiatry, 4,* 229–246.

Sorosky, A. D., & Sticker, M. B. (1980). Trichotillomania in adolescence. *Adolescent Psychiatry, 8,* 437–454.

CECIL R. REYNOLDS
Texas A&M University

SELF-INJURIOUS BEHAVIOR

TRISOMY 18

As indicated by its name, trisomy 18 is a congenital disease owed to the presence of three chromosomes 18 instead of two. Trisomy 18 symptomatology was first described by Edwards et al. (1960); therefore, the term Edwards syndrome is sometimes used instead of trisomy 18. As in many autosomal trisomies, severe polymalformations are observed. Moreover, affected patients show many common features, so that trained physicians are able to diagnose the syndrome on clinical inspection. Generally, trisomy 18 newborns are postmature (42 weeks of pregnancy), but nevertheless show a birth weight below 2,500 g (Hamerton, 1971); hydramnios (too much amniotic fluid) is the rule. An elongated skull with prominent occiput is noted, together with microcephaly. Micrognatia (small mandible), low-set ears, short neck, short sternum, prominent abdomen with umbilical hernia, and narrow hips are usual findings. The extremities are also characteristic: fingers are in forced flexion, very difficult to unfold, and deviated so that the third one is recovered by the second and the fourth. Arches are present in most, if not all, fingers. These dermatoglyphic configurations are rare in normal people or in those with other chromosome diseases. Clubfoot is frequent, and the big toe is in dorsiflexion. Internal malformations include severe congenital heart anomalies in more than 95 percent of all cases, either intraventricular, septal defects or patent ductus arteriosus. Indeed, premature death can be related to these heart defects. Failure to thrive is the rule and, despite palliative treatment, death occurs in a mean time of 70 days (Hamerton, 1971). Developmental retardation is always observed, but accurate testing is difficult.

From a cytogenetic point of view, standard trisomy 18 concerns more than 80 percent of all cases. Mosaicism trisomy 18/normal cell line occurs in less than 10 percent of patients; survival may be longer and symptomatology less severe. Trisomy 18 from a transmitted translocation by one of the parents is rare. Incidence is situated around 1 in 10,000 births (Hook & Hamerton, 1977). This is much less than in trisomy 21; the symptoms are more severe, and many affected embryos are spontaneously aborted early in pregnancy. Interestingly, 80 percent of all newborn cases are female, suggesting a strong lethality in the male. Some authors (Conen & Erkman, 1966) have also reported on a different survival rate depending on whether the baby is a girl (294 days) or a boy (96 days). Maternal age is above average (32 years), but the relationship is not as clear, as in trisomy 21. In the presence of a small fetus showing few movements and severe hydramnios, it may be profitable to have a late prenatal diagnosis, during the seventh or eighth month of pregnancy. This may avoid a caesarean section for the mother.

REFERENCES

Conen, P. E., & Erkman, B. (1966). Frequency and occurrence of chromosomal syndromes. II. E-trisomy. *American Journal of Human Genetics, 18,* 387–398.

Edwards, J. H., Harnden, D. G., Cameron, A. H., Crosse, V. M., & Wolff, O. H. (1960). A new trisomic syndrome. *Lancet, 1,* 787–790.

Hamerton, J. L. (1971). *Human cytogenetics* (Vol. 2). New York: Academic.

Hook, E. B., & Hamerton, J. L. (1977). The frequency of chromosome abnormalities detected in consecutive newborn studies—Differences between studies—Results by sex and by severity of phenotypic involvement. In E. B. Hook & I. A. Porter (Eds.), *Population cytogenetics—Studies in human.* New York: Academic.

L. KOULISCHER
Institut de Morphologie
Pathologique, Belgium

GENETIC COUNSELING

TRISOMY 21

Trisomy 21 or Down syndrome is a combination of birth defects characterized by Mental Retardation, abnormal facial features, heart defects, and other congenital disorders. Approximately 1 in 800 to 1 in 1,000 infants is born with this disorder (March of Dimes, 1997). Trisomy 21 occurs in all races and economic levels; however, incidence is highest among Caucasians. Over 250,000 individuals with Trisomy 21 (March of Dimes, 1997) live in the United States. Life expectancy and quality of life has greatly increased over the past 20 years due to improved treatment of related complications and better developmental educational programs (Ball & Bindler, 1999). Mortality rates for infants with Trisomy 21 and congenital heart defects remain high at 44 percent. However, overall life expectancy among adults has improved to over 55 years (March of Dimes, 1997).

The cause of Trisomy 21 is unknown. A number of theories including genetic predisposition, radiation exposure, environmental factors, viruses, and even infections have been proposed (Wong, 1995). Trisomy 21 does result from an aberration in chromosome 21 in which three copies instead of the normal two occur due to faulty meiosis (nondisjunction) of the ovum or, sometimes, the sperm. This results in a karyotype of 47 chromosomes instead of the normal 46. The incidence of nondisjunction increases with maternal age and the extra chromosome originates from the mother about 80 percent of the time (Wong, 1995). Mothers over the age of 35 years are at the greatest risk for rearrangement of their chromosomes and their risk of having a child with Trisomy 21 increases greatly with age. At age 35, the risk is calculated to be 1 in 385 births, at age 40, the risk increases to 1 in 106 births, and at age 49, the risk of having a baby with Trisomy 21 is 1 in 11 (Wong, 1995). Prenatal testing through amniocentesis or chorionic villus identifies Trisomy 21 (March of Dimes, 1997). Both procedures carry a risk of infection and miscarriage. Genetic counseling is available for couples with a known family history of genetic birth defects and is also indicated for mothers over the age of 35 (March of Dimes, 1997).

The physical signs of Trisomy 21 are apparent at birth. The newborn is lethargic and has difficulty eating. Trisomy 21 newborns have almond-shaped eyes with epicanthal folds, a protruding tongue, a small mouth, a single palmar crease (simian crease), small white spots on the iris of the eye (Brushfield spots), a small skull, a flattened bridge across the nose, a flattened profile, small and low-set ears, and a short neck with excess skin (Wong, 1995). Slowed growth and development are characteristic of this syndrome, especially in speech formation. Other physical abnormalities include dry, sensitive skin with decreased elasticity, short stature, broad hands and feet, abnormal fingerprints, and hypotonic limbs (Ball & Bindler, 1999). Premature dementia similar to Alzheimer's disease usually occurs during the fourth decade of life, and an increase in leukemia, diabetes mellitus, thyroid disorders, and chronic infections are all common in individuals with Trisomy 21 (Wong, 1995).

The degree of mental retardation with Trisomy 21 varies greatly and ranges from mild to profound. Although children with Trisomy 21 can usually do most things that any child can learn to do (walking, talking, dressing, self-feeding, and toileting), they develop at a slower rate and at a later age (March of Dimes, 1997). The exact age of achievement of developmental milestones and skills cannot be predicted. However, early intervention programs beginning in infancy encourage these special children to reach their greatest potential.

Special education programs are available around the country with many children fully integrated into regular classroom situations (March of Dimes, 1997). The future for special children with Trisomy 21 is brighter than 20 years ago. Many will learn to read, write, take care of themselves, and hold partially supported employment while living semi-independently in group homes (March of Dimes, 1997).

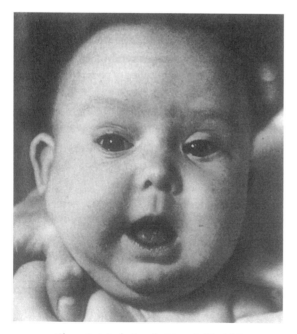

Characteristic facies of a trisomic 21 child

REFERENCES

Ball, J., & Bindler, R. (1999). *Pediatric nursing: Caring for children* (2nd ed.). Stamford, CT: Appleton & Lange.

March of Dimes. (1997). *Down syndrome: Public education information sheet.* Retrieved from http://www.noah.cuny.edu/prenancy/march_of_dimes/birth_defects/downsynd.html

Wong, D. (1995). *Whaley & Wong's nursing care of infants and children* (5th ed.). St. Louis, MO: Mosby-Year Book.

KARI ANDERSON
University of North Carolina at Wilmington

DOWN SYNDROME
GENETIC COUNSELING

TUBERCULOSIS

See CHRONIC ILLNESS IN CHILDREN.

TUBEROUS SCLEROSIS

Tuberous sclerosis is an inherited disorder transmitted as an autosomal dominant trait with variable penetrance affecting the skin, brain, retina, heart, kidneys, and lungs. It belongs to the group of diseases called phakomatoses, characterized by malformations, the presence of birthmarks, and the tendency to tumor formation in the central nervous system, skin, and viscera. The estimated frequency of occurrence is 1 per 30,000 live births (Berg, 1982). About 25 percent of the patients are sporadic owing to new mutations.

Tuberous sclerosis is a protean disorder chiefly manifested by epilepsy, mental deficiency, and cutaneous lesions. Convulsions are the most frequent initial symptom (up to 88 percent), presenting often in early life as infantile spasms (about 70 percent), usually between the fourth and sixth months of life. The convulsions later become generalized grand mal epilepsy and focal or akinetic seizures (Gomez, 1979; Hunt, 1983; Jeavons & Bower, 1964; Pampiglione & Moynahan, 1976). Mental Retardation, when present, is usually severe; one-third of the patients may have normal intelligence (Gomez, 1979). Only 12 to 15 percent of affected subjects are free of epilepsy and Mental Retardation. The cutaneous lesions are multiple. Adenoma sebaceum is the characteristic sign of the disease. It appears in the face between 1 and 5 years of age (usually after 4 years), starting as a macular rash over the cheeks in a butterfly appearance, then increasing in size and covering the nose, lips, and chin with a granular aspect. Those adenoma named Pringle's are seldom absent but they may grow very slowly. Hypopigmented leaf-shaped spots called white or achromatic spots or depigmented nevi are the most frequent sign in up to 95 percent of cases (Hunt, 1983); they are disseminated over the trunk and the limbs and are present at birth (Gold & Freeman, 1965), but they increase in number during the first 2 years of life. They appear more numerous under Wood's light and may be demonstrable in clinically asymptomatic parents. Shagreen patches are thickenings of skin best seen in the lumbos-acral region. Periungueal fibroma (Koenen tumors) are more often present on the toes than on the fingers and appear after the first decade and in adults; they may be the only sign in parents of an affected child.

The pathology in the nervous system shows the presence of cortical malformations, variable in size (called tubers), that contain neurons, astrocytic nuclei, and giant cells. The tubers also can be located in the subependymal area and contain calcium deposits that can be identified on X-rays or CAT scans. They may grow into the ventricles, interfering with cerebral spinal fluid circulation, blocking the foramen of Monro or the aqueduct of Sylvius, and producing hydrocephalus and signs of raised intracranial pressure. Tumors can also be present in the heart, the lungs, and the kidneys, but they can be discovered easily by ultrasound examination showing angiomyolipoma or even cystic tumors (Avni et al., 1984). The examination of the ocular fundus may reveal tumoral lesions at the nerve head or about the disk, even in the absence of vision complaints.

Diagnosis of the disease is based on the association of epilepsy, Mental Retardation, and skin lesions. It can be made very early in life on the presence of infantile spasms and achromatic spots in correlation with the cerebral calcifications seen on CAT scans of the brain (Lee & Gawler, 1978).

REFERENCES

Avni, E. F., Szliwowski, H., Spehl, M., Lelong, B., Baudain, P., & Struyven, J. (1984). Renal involvement in tuberous sclerosis. *Annales de Radiologie, 27,* 2–3, 207–214.

Berg, B. O. (1982). Neurocutaneous syndromes. In K. F. Swaiman, & F. S. Wright (Eds.), *The practice of pediatric neurology.* New York: Mosby.

Gold, A. P., & Freeman, J. M. (1965). Depigmented nevi: The earliest sign of tuberous sclerosis. *Pediatrics, 35,* 1003–1005.

Gomez, M. R. (1979). Clinical experience at the Mayo Clinic. In M. R. Gomez (Ed.), *Tuberous sclerosis* (pp. 16–20). New York: Raven.

Hunt, A. (1983). Tuberous sclerosis: A survey of 97 cases. *Developmental Medicine and Child Neurology, 25,* 346–357.

Jeavons, P. M., & Bower, B. D. (1969). Infantile spasms. *Clinics Developmental Medicine, 15,* London: Sime/Heinemann.

Lee, B. C., & Gawler, J. (1978). Tuberous sclerosis. Comparison of computed tomography and conventional neuroradiology. *Radiology, 127*(2), 403–407.

Pampiglione, G., & Moynahan, E. I. (1976). The tuberous sclerosis: Clinical and EEG studies in 100 children. *Journal Neurology Neurosurgery & Psychiatry, 39,* 666–673.

HENRI B. SZLIWOWSKI
*Hôpital Erasme, Université
Libre de Bruxelles, Belgium*

TURKEY, SPECIAL EDUCATION IN

Turkey has a centralized education system. The Ministry of Education has an Office of Special Education that monitors all special education services in Turkey. These special education services are regulated by the new Special Education

Law (KHK/573), which replaced the old law in 1997. Basic principles of special education, as cited in the new Special Education Law, are as follows:

1. All special needs individuals should be provided special education services according to their interests, desires, sufficiencies, and abilities.
2. Special education should be started as early in one's life as possible.
3. Special education services should be planned and administered without segregating the special needs individuals from their social and physical environments to the greatest extent possible.
4. Priority should be given to educating special needs individuals with other individuals (i.e., in regular education environments) by considering their educational performances and modifying the instructional goals, contents, and processes.
5. Collaboration should be made with other organizations and institutions providing rehabilitation services in order to prevent the interruption of services.
6. Individualized education plans should be developed and education programs should be individualized for special needs individuals.
7. Families should be encouraged to take part in every process of special education actively.
8. Opinions of nongovernment organizations of special needs individuals should be considered in developing special education policies.
9. When planning special education services, elements should be included to facilitate special needs individuals' interactions with and adaptation to society.

There are guidance and research centers affiliated with the Office of Special Education in every major town to monitor the local special education services in Turkey. Main responsibilities of the guidance and research centers are as follows:

- to accept referrals from schools and conduct assessments
- to identify special needs individuals
- to place identified individuals in regular or special education environments
- to follow-up the special needs individuals
- to conduct inservice training to education personnel

There are 99[1] guidance and research centers all around Turkey at present. Personnel of these centers include special education teachers as well as counselors, which total 606 at press time.

There are various placement alternatives for special needs students in Turkey. Until 1997, most special needs students were placed in special schools or special classes where available; they were integrated in regular classes when special education placement was not available. In a sense, special students used to be integrated whenever they did not have a chance to be segregated. However, the new Special Education Law has a principle mandating integration to be considered as the preferred option for special needs students. Hence, this principle is expected to facilitate special education placements according to the "least restrictive environment" concept.

The number of special needs students from various disability categories enrolled in special schools, special classes, and regular classes in 1997–98 in Turkey is 31,215. When all special needs students are considered, it is observed that 41 percent of them are educated in special schools, 26 percent of them are educated in special classes, and 33 percent of them are educated in regular classes.

The total number of students enrolled in elementary and secondary education programs is 11,355,736 (according to the records of the Ministry of Education). These data show that 0.3 percent of all students are special needs students. This means that the percentage of special needs children receiving special education services is rather low in Turkey.

The new Special Education Law mentions the need for special education support services for the integrated special needs students. Integration was started in Turkey without providing any support services to the integrated students and/or to their teachers. Therefore, integration did not prove to be a successful placement for many special needs students in the past. Now that special education support services are considered in the Special Education Law, regular schools are expected to have support personnel for providing services such as teacher consultations, inclass support, or resource room services when necessary.

Special education is a rather new and rare professional discipline in Turkey. Special education teacher training programs exist in only three universities: Abant Izzet Baysal University, Anadolu University, and Gazi University. The oldest of these programs, Anadolu University Special Education Teacher Training Program, started to graduate special education teachers in 1987. Thus, many teachers working with special needs students were originally trained as regular teachers and completed special education certificate programs, which are no longer offered.

Special education teacher training programs offer BA degrees in three special needs categories: developmental disabilities, hearing impairments, and visual impairments. Teacher training programs for the developmentally delayed have a behavioral orientation and emphasize direct instruction for teaching concepts and skills. Teacher training programs for the visually impaired aim to equip their students with knowledge necessary for teaching partially sighted and blind students. In teacher training programs for the hearing impaired, the auditory-oral approach is followed.

Most of the graduates of special education teacher training programs apply to the Ministry of Education to be appointed as a special education teacher in a school or a guidance and research center, and some graduates choose to work in private schools. The total number of teachers working in special schools and special classes is 2,653 at present, 435 of which are special education teachers.

Regarding special education research in Turkey, in addition to the quantitative methodologies, single-subject and qualitative research methodologies are two popular trends of the past few years. Although these research methodologies differ remarkably in terms of philosophical orientations as well as data collection/data analysis procedures, both are perceived to be very appropriate for improving special education knowledge and practices. Accordingly, the number of research projects, theses, and dissertations conducted qualitatively or by single-subject designs is increasing considerably in Turkey.

NOTES

[1]All quantitative data are obtained from the Office of Special Education except where indicated.

GONAL KIRCAALI-IFTAR
Anadolu University

EASTERN EUROPE, SPECIAL EDUCATION IN
WESTERN EUROPE, SPECIAL EDUCATION IN

TURNBULL, ANN P. (1937–   )

An Alabama native, Ann P. Turnbull received her BSEd from the University of Georgia, her MEd from Auburn University in 1971, and her EdD from the University of Alabama. Her formal education emphasized special education of children

Ann P. Turnbull and H. R. Turnbull

with Mental Retardation, and early practical experience was gained as a teacher of children with Mild Mental Retardation at schools in La Grange, Georgia (1968–1970). She is currently codirector of the Beach Center on Families and Disability and a professor in the department of special education at The University of Kansas.

Turnbull's research focuses on family systems and family-centered services, and includes programmatic implementation of policy requirements associated with PL 94-142. Parental involvement in educational decision making and the development of a conceptual framework for family research and intervention based on family systems theory has been a major interest of Turnbull. Her focus on policy issues includes exploring government-provided services for enhancing the ability of families to provide care for their members with disabilities.

In 1988, Turnbull was a Joseph P. Kennedy, Jr. Policy Fellow working with the U.S. House of Representatives Select Committee on Children, Youth, and Families, and in 1990 she was selected as one of three women from the international field of Mental Retardation to receive the Rose Fitzgerald Kennedy Leadership Award. Among her many leadership roles in professional and family organizations, she has served as chair of the family committee for the International League of Societies for Persons with Mental Handicaps and member of the board of directors of the American Association on Mental Retardation. She is currently a member of the board of directors of Zero to Three of the National Center for Clinical Infant Programs and the Autism National Committee. Turnbull was inducted as a member of The University of Kansas Women's Hall of Fame in 1994.

She is a reviewer for the journal *Exceptional Children* and the *Journal of the Association for Persons with Severe Handicaps*. She is assistant editor of the *Journal of Positive Behavior Interventions*. She was the vice president of the American Association on Mental Retardation for 2001–2002, and president of that association from 2003–2004. She was a member of the National Advisory Board, National Center on Family Support from 2000–2001, and a member of the National Advisory Board, Ready to Learn Initiative, Public Broadcasting System in 2001.

Turnbull has been the principal investigator on over 20 federally funded research grants, and has authored and coauthored 25 books and many more articles, chapters, and monographs. Her books include *Cognitive Coping, Families, and Disability* (1993); *Exceptional Lives: Special Education in Today's Schools* (1995); and *Families, Professionals, and Exceptionality: Collaborating for Empowerment* (1997).

REFERENCES

Turnbull, A. P., Patterson, J. M., Behr, S. K., Murphy, D. L., Marquis, J. G., & Blue-Banning, M. J. (Eds.). (1993). *Cognitive coping, families, and disability.* Baltimore: Brookes.

Turnbull, A. P., & Turnbull, H. R. (1997). *Families, professionals, and exceptionality: Collaborating for empowerment* (3rd ed.). Columbus, OH: Merrill/Prentice Hall.

Turnbull, A. P., Turnbull, H. R., Shank, M., & Leal, D. (1998). *Exceptional lives: Special education in today's schools.* Columbus, OH: Merrill/Prentice Hall.

E. Valerie Hewitt
Texas A&M University
First edition

Tamara J. Martin
The University of Texas of the Permian Basin
Second edition

Rachel M. Toplis
Falcon School District 49, Colorado Springs, Colorado
Third edition

TURNBULL, H. RUTHERFORD (1937–   )

H. Rutherford Turnbull received his BA in political science from Johns Hopkins University in 1959 and his LLB/JD from the University of Maryland Law School in 1964. He later attended Harvard Law School, earning his LLM in the Urban Studies program in 1969. As the father of an adult son with Mental Retardation and Autism, Turnbull has specialized in law and public policy affecting persons with mental and developmental disabilities. He is currently codirector of the Beach Center on Families and Disability and professor of special education and courtesy professor of law at The University of Kansas.

Turnbull concentrates his research and training in four areas: special education law and policy, mental disability law and policy, public policy analysis, and ethics as related to disability policy and service provision. His initial work in the areas of special education law and rights of institutionalized persons led him to concentrate on issues that define and redefine the concepts of consent, least restriction, and parent participation in the education of children with disabilities. His work with policymakers and professional caregivers has focused on issues concerning the treatment of infants with disabilities and the restructuring of Medicaid financing of residential and other services for persons with Mental Retardation.

Turnbull's service in elected and appointed leadership includes president of the American Association on Mental Retardation (1985–1986), director of The Association for Retarded Citizens of the United States (1981–1983), chairman of the American Bar Association Commission on Mental and Physical Disability Law (1992–1995), and

trustee of the Judge David Bazelon Mental Health Law Center (1993–1997). He served as chairman of the Judge David Bazelon Center for Mental Health Law in the years 2001, 2002, and 2003.

Since developing his specialization in the mid-1970s while professor of public law and government at the Institute of Government of The University of North Carolina in Chapel Hill (1969–1980), Turnbull has authored over 125 articles, book chapters, monographs, technical reports, reviews, and commentaries related to disability issues. His major works include *Consent Handbook* (1978), *Free Appropriate Public Education: Law and the Education of Children with Disabilities* (1997), and *Exceptional Lives: Special Education in Today's Schools* (1998). He has been "of counsel" on amicus briefs in two disability cases heard by the United States Supreme Court as well as author and draftsman of North Carolina's special education law and limited guardianship law and PL 100-407, Assistive Technology for Individuals with Disabilities Act of 1988.

Turnbull was recognized in *Who's Who in America* from 1995 to 2003. His honors include the National Public Service Award of the International Council for Exceptional Children (1996) and the National Leadership Award of the American Association on Mental Retardation (1997).

REFERENCES

Turnbull, H. R. (1978). *Consent handbook.* Washington, DC: American Association on Mental Retardation.

Turnbull, H. R. (1997). *Free appropriate public education: Law and the education of children with disabilities* (Rev. ed.). Denver, CO: Love.

Turnbull, A. P., Turnbull, H. R., Shank, M. S., & Leal, D. J. (1998). *Exceptional lives: Special education in today's schools.* Columbus, OH: Merrill/Prentice Hall.

Tamara J. Martin
The University of Texas of the Permian Basin

Rachel M. Toplis
Falcon School District 49, Colorado Springs, Colorado

TURNER SYNDROME

Turner syndrome (TS) is a genetic disorder characterized by a complete or partial loss of one of the X chromosomes. TS affects approximately 1 out of 2,500 female live births; however, in rare cases males have been affected and share similar features seen in females (Rovet, 2004). This syndrome is characterized by skeletal, lymphatic, and reproductive abnormalities and recent advances indicate brain structure abnormalities. Improvements in hormone understanding has allowed for treatment of some of the related deficits historically associated with TS.

TS was first described in the early 1800s, but more thoroughly described by Turner in the 1930s as characterized by sexual infantilism, short stature, abnormality of elbow formation, and webbing of the neck (Turner, 1938). Polani, Lessof, and Bishop (1956) first linked TS to the X chromosome due to an increased incidence of colorblindness found in the TS population. Monosomy is accountable for approximately 50 percent of all cases, followed by Mosaicism (30 percent), and the remaining associated with various deletions, rearrangements, or translocations (Jacobs et al., 1997). The differences in genetic abnormalities account for the variability seen in the physical and cognitive expressions of the syndrome (Rovet, 2004).

In addition to those characteristics initially described by Turner, distinctive physical features associated with TS are short stature and low production of female sex hormones resulting in the lack of estrogen production, lower androgen levels, and the lack of ova (Bishop et al., 2000). TS has been associated with a smaller fourth digit metacarpal and high arched palate that contributes to feeding difficulties (Rovet, 2004). Further cranial deformations contribute to a higher incidence of ear canal infections (Stenberg, Nylen, Windh, & Halcrantz, 1998). Deficits in lymph clearance result in fetal demise and complications. TS has been connected with renal abnormalities, cardiac abnormalities, pigmented nevi, thyroid dysfunction, impaired glucose tolerance, hypertension, and nail dysplasia (Lippe, 1991; Miyabara, Suzumori, Yonemitsu, & Sugihara, 1997).

Brain structure analysis using neuroimaging has recently identified abnormalities in the parietal lobes, reduced volume of the hippocampus, caudate, lenticular, and thalamic nuclei (Murphy et al., 1993). These findings lend support to associated symptoms characterized by deficits in long-term memory, executive processing deficits, and visuo-spacial deficits. Genetic studies have identified the area of the X chromosome responsible for many of the physical and cognitive deficits seen in TS (Zinn et al., 1998). Verbal ability tends to be normally distributed; however, performance abilities tend to two standard deviations below the mean (Bishop et al., 2000; Garron, 1977). Deficits can also be seen in math associated skills as well as memory (Bishop et al.).

Special education practitioners should be aware of the wide distribution of characteristics associated with TS. Recent hormone replacement therapy has allowed for treatment resulting in normal stature and less obvious physical expressions of the syndrome (Rovet, 2004). Full psycho-educational evaluations and neuropsychological evaluations should take place to determine learning deficits and strengths due to the variability in expression. Not all of those who express mosaic genetic makeup or undergo hormone replacement therapy will be sterile; however, therapy surrounding issues of sterility should be addressed when appropriate.

REFERENCES

Bishop, D., Canning, E., Elgar, K., Morris, E., Jacobs, P., & Skuse, D. (2000). Distinctive patterns of memory function in subgroups of females with Turner syndrome: Evidence for imprinted loci on the X-chromosome affecting neurodevelopment. *Neuropsychologia, 38,* 712–721.

Garron, D. C. (1977). Intelligence among persons with Turner's syndrome. *Behavior Genetics, 7,* 147–152.

Jacobs, P., Dalton, P., James, R., Mosse, K., Power, M., et al. (1997). Turner syndrome: A cytogenetic and molecular study. *Annals of Human Genetics, 61,* 471–483.

Lippe, B. (1991). Turner syndrome. *Endocrinology Metabolism Clinicians of North America, 20,* 121–152.

Miyabara, S., Suzumori, K., Yonemitsu, N., & Sugihara, H. (1997). Developmental analysis of cardiovascular system of 45, X fetuses with cystic hygroma. *American Journal of Medical Genetics, 68,* 135–41.

Murphy, D. G. M., DeCarli, C., Daly, E., Haxby, J. V., Aleen, G., et al. (1993). W-chromosome effects on female brain: A magnetic resonance imaging study of Turner's syndrome. *Lancet, 342,* 1197–2000.

Polani, P. E., Lessof, M. H., & Bishop, P. M. F. (1956). Colourblindness in "ovarian agenesis" (gonadal dysplasia). *Lancet, 2,* 118–119.

Rovet, J. (2004). Turner syndrome: A review of genetic and hormonal influences on neuropsychological functioning. *Child Neuropsychology, 10*(4), 262–269.

Stenberg, A. E., Nylen, O., Windh, M., & Halcrantz, M. (1998). Otological problems in children with Turner's syndrome. *Hearing Research, 124,* 85–90.

Turner, H. (1938). A syndrome of infantilism, congenital webbed neck, and cubitus valgus. *Endocrinology, 23,* 566.

Zinn, A., Tonk, V., Chen, Z., Flejter, W., Gardner, A., Guerra, R., et al. (1998). Evidence for a turner syndrome locus or loci at p11.2–p22.1 *American Journal of Human Genetics, 63,* 1757–1766.

MICHELLE T. BUSS
Texas A&M University

GENETIC COUNSELING
GENETIC TESTING
GENETIC TRANSMISSION
KLINEFELTER SYNDROME
MOSAICISM

TUTORING

Tutoring is a method of instruction in which one or a small group of students (tutees) receive personalized and individualized education from a tutor. Tutoring is widely used with students of all ages and all levels of ability. However, in elementary and secondary schools, it is most often used as an adjunct to traditional classroom instruction: (1) to provide remedial or supplementary instruction to students who have difficulty learning by conventional methods, including mainstreamed, handicapped children; (2) to provide students with increased opportunities to actively participate in the learning process and receive immediate feedback; and (3) to help relieve the classroom teacher of instructional and noninstructional duties.

In most cases, tutoring is provided to students by someone other than the regular teacher. This may be an adult who volunteers or is paid, a college student, a programmed machine or computer, or, in many cases, another student. The term peer tutoring is used when children serve as tutors to others close to their age who are functioning at a lower level. The term cross-age tutoring is used when older children or adolescents work with tutees who are several years younger than themselves.

The practices of peer and cross-age tutoring were recorded as early as the first century AD by Quintilian in the *Institutio Oratoria*. However, the practice was not formalized and instituted on a widespread basis until the late-eighteenth century by Andrew Bell in India and later by William Lancaster in England. Tutoring was standard practice in the one-room schoolhouses of America until graded classes helped reduce the heterogeneity of student ability. Renewed interest in children teaching children began in the early 1960s because of shortages in professional teachers. Educators argued that disadvantaged children might learn more from a peer than from an adult. Several large-scale tutoring programs in New York City, Washington, DC, Chicago, Michigan, and California were successful (Allen, 1976).

Since 1970, numerous research studies and anecdotal reports have documented the benefits of tutoring for both the tutee and the tutor. Both have been found to benefit in terms of increases in achievement, school attitudes, peer acceptance, and self-image (Devin-Sheehan, Feldman, & Allen, 1976). Successful outcomes of tutoring have been reported for nondisabled tutees, tutees in special education including the moderately retarded, and those with aggressive behavior disorders (Maher, 1982).

Research further indicates that the effectiveness of tutoring depends greatly on how it is organized and structured and the nature of the relationship between the tutor and tutee. Some guidelines for developing a successful tutoring program follow.

Tutors must be carefully selected, trained, and supervised. Prospective tutor recruits must be dependable, responsible, and knowledgeable in the skill to be taught. They must be trained in tutoring skills (e.g., praising, task analysis, direct instruction, communication) and be provided with specific materials. A designated tutor supervisor must be available. Tutors and tutees should be matched carefully so that they have good rapport and work together conscientiously. Contracts are helpful in spelling out the responsibilities of each. If possible, tutoring should be held twice weekly for at least 30 minutes each session over a minimum of 10 weeks. The program should be continually monitored to determine its effectiveness. Meetings should be scheduled separately with the tutors and tutees to discuss any problems.

Extensive descriptions of tutorial procedures can be found in Allen (1976) and Ehly and Larsen (1980). The use of disabled students as tutors for the nondisabled has been discussed by Osguthorpe (1984).

REFERENCES

Allen, V. L. (1976). *Children as teachers: Theory and research on tutoring.* New York: Academic.

Devin-Sheehan, L., Feldman, R. S., & Allen, V. L. (1976). Research on children tutoring children: A critical review. *Review of Educational Research, 46,* 355–385.

Ehly, S. W., & Larsen, S. C. (1980). *Peer tutoring for individualized instruction.* Boston: Allyn & Bacon.

Maher, C. A. (1982). Behavioral effects of using conduct problem adolescents as cross-age tutors. *Psychology in the Schools, 10,* 360–364.

Osguthorpe, R. T. (1984). Handicapped students as tutors for nonhandicapped peers. *Academic Therapy, 19,* 473–483.

FREDERIC J. MEDWAY
University of South Carolina

TEACHING STRATEGIES

TWINS

Twins may pose a number of educational problems because of their close relationship and their strong attachment to one another. For instance, they often show language delay. Because they are content with each other's company and consequently socialize less with other children and adults than singletons, they tend to be less influenced by the linguistic environment (Luchsinger, 1961). Indeed, they may develop a jargon that enables them to communicate with one another but that is incomprehensible to others. This private idiom is called cryptophasia. Cryptophasia is not a language sui generis (as some have thought it was), but a sort of pidgin based on the language of the adults (Lebrun, 1982). Despite reduced vocabulary and absence of grammar, it makes communication possible between the twins; they have so many affinities that they can understand one another with just a few words. To improve the twins' language command, speech therapy may be necessary. Moreover, it may be desirable to separate them part of the day so that they can learn to socialize.

REFERENCES

Lebrun, Y. (1982). Cryptophasie et retard de langage chez les jumeaux. *Enfance* (3), 101–108.

Luchsinger, R. (1961). Die Sprachentwicklung von ein- und zweiengen Zwillingen und die Vererbung von Sprachstörungen in den ersten drie Lebensjahren. *Folia Phoniatrica* (13), 66–76.

YVAN LEBRUN
*School of Medicine, Brussels,
Belgium*

ZYGOSITY

U

ULCERS AND CHILDREN WITH DISABILITIES

While little empirical evidence exists to substantiate the relationship between ulcers and handicapped conditions, it appears that children with disabilities may be more predisposed to ulceration than their nondisabled peers. Kim, Learman, Nada, and Thompson (1981) found that 5.4 percent of the residents in a large institution for mentally retarded children had peptic ulcers.

Other factors often associated with handicapping conditions also appear to lead to ulceration. For example, ulcers are more likely to occur in children with lower IQs (Christodoulou, Garigoulos, Poploukas, & Marinopoulou, 1977; Kim et al., 1981). Additionally, ulcers occur more often in children who are withdrawn and less likely to express their feelings or frustrations (Chapman & Loeb, 1967; Christodoulou et al., 1977), similar to some emotionally disabled children. Finally, children who come from extended family situations (e.g., divorced or separated parents) are more likely to have ulcers, a factor that has been shown to be more likely to occur in children with disabilities than in their nondisabled peers (Beattie & Maniscalco, 1985).

Particular types of ulcers, particularly ulcerative colitis, may result in growth retardation and cosmetic problems that may lead to eligibility for services under the IDEA (Gillman, 1994; McClung, 1994).

REFERENCES

Ackerman, S. H., Manaker, S., & Cohen, M. I. (1981). Recent separation and the onset of peptic ulcer disease in older children and adolescents. *Psychosomatic Medicine, 43,* 305–310.

Beattie, J., & Maniscalco, G. (1985). Special education and divorce: Is there a link. *Techniques, 1,* 342–345.

Chapman, A. H., & Loeb, D. G. (1967). Psychosomatic gastrointestinal problems. In I. Frank & M. Powell (Eds.), *Psychosomatic ailments in childhood and adolescence.* Springfield, IL: Thomas.

Christodoulou, G. N., Gargoulas, A., Poploukas, A., & Marinopoulou, A. (1977). Primary peptic ulcers in childhood: Psychosocial, psychological and psychiatric aspects. *Acta Psychiatrica Scandinavica, 56,* 215–222.

Gillman, J. (1994). Inflammatory bowel diseases: Psychological issues. In R. Olsen, L. Mullins, J. Gillman, & J. Chaney (Eds.), *Pediatric psychology.* Boston: Longwood.

Kim, M., Learman, L., Nada, N., & Thompson, K. (1981). The prevalence of peptic ulcer in an institution for the mentally retarded. *Journal of Mental Deficiency Research, 25,* 105–111.

McClung, H. (1994). Inflammatory bowel diseases: Medical issues. In R. Olsen, L. Mullins, J. Gillman, & J. Chaney (Eds.), *Pediatric psychology.* Boston: Longwood.

Mylander, M. (1982). *The great American stomach book.* New Haven, CT: Tichnor & Fields.

JOHN R. BEATTIE
University of North Carolina at Charlotte

ANTISOCIAL BEHAVIOR
DIVORCE AND SPECIAL EDUCATION
EMOTIONAL DISORDERS

ULTIMATE INSTRUCTION FOR THE SEVERE AND PROFOUNDLY RETARDED

The criterion of ultimate functioning (Brown, Nietupski, & Hamre-Nietupski, 1976) refers to a method of prioritization that may be used in developing programs for the severely or profoundly disabled learner. Although the type of handicapping condition may vary, this program development philosophy has most often been applied to individuals who have been classified as mentally retarded.

Use of this type of rationale to develop curricula for such persons extends from three major assumptions (Brown et al., 1976). First, the exceptional needs learner should be taught skills that increase the student's independence in and access to less restrictive environments. Second, transfer of training, response generalization, and response maintenance cannot be assumed to occur with such learners. Third, programming efforts with the severely or profoundly handicapped learner should address the wide variety of individual learning characteristics of this group. Thus application of the criterion of ultimate functioning in developing curricula for these students requires that the skills and behaviors taught to such individuals should relate directly to the behaviors that will be expected of them in nonschool environments.

Brown et al. (1976) developed the concept of the criterion of ultimate functioning in response to inadequacies of educational programs that had been generated based on alternative curriculum philosophies. With the severely or profoundly disabled learner, these philosophies have often been either developmental or nontheoretical in nature (Haring & Bricker, 1976).

The developmental approach to curriculum delineation reflects adherence to a stage or hierarchical explanation of learning. From this perspective, the skills that are taught the severely or profoundly disabled learner are dictated by the normal pattern of development that often takes place with the nondisabled child. Moving from the simple to the complex, the skills that are taught in developmentally oriented curricula might include teaching a student to vocalize before teaching words or teaching visual orientation before teaching word recognition. Proponents of a developmental approach to education feel that the simpler tasks must be mastered before the more complex skills are taught. Actual applications of a developmental orientation to the education of the severely or profoundly exceptional learner have often been criticized because of their inflexibility (e.g., "John is stabilized at the preoperational level") and lack of direct relationship to the teaching of immediately relevant skills (e.g., teaching object use through picture matching).

An alternative approach that has been used to develop curricula for the severely or profoundly disabled learner has been referred to as nontheoretical (Haring & Bricker, 1976). This orientation develops curriculum content based on teacher-specified individual needs of the student. The emphasis of these types of programs has been on the use of specific methodologies that effectively teach the student new and increasingly complex skills. These skills do not reflect a particular developmental progression but instead are those skills that are relevant for the student as decided by the teacher. Although the emphasis on methodological consistency apparent in curricula of this type has often led to impressive skill acquisition, these skills have, at times, reflected teacher priorities that are not necessarily consistent with the best interests of the student (e.g., sitting quietly but not necessarily completing a task).

In response to the potential limitations of these curriculum development approaches, the criterion of ultimate functioning (Brown et al., 1976) suggests teaching skills that are (1) relevant to student needs in light of individual learning characteristics; (2) immediately useful in terms of the environment(s) in which the student functions; and (3) able to increase the independence and ability of the student to attain access to more normative social environments. The teaching methods that are used from this perspective are based on specific analysis of the skills of the student and the requirements of the environment. Differences between these two assessment areas become the teaching objectives.

The criterion of ultimate functioning, used as a rationale for curriculum development with the severely or profoundly disabled learner, breaks with the traditional developmental curriculum orientation. The skills that are taught are directly relevant in terms of the environments in which the student does, or is expected to, function. Building on techniques that emphasize specific analysis of student behaviors and environmental requirements, this approach systematically teaches the exceptional needs student skills that increase independence in and access to less restrictive settings. In contrast with the nontheoretical approach mentioned previously, this focus on independence and normative (chronologically age-appropriate) environments reflects a view of the student as an integral part of society. Theoretically, the degree to which the student might access social environments is a direct function of teaching the skills necessary for effective adaptation to those environments. Accordingly, the skills that are taught address not only the immediate relevance of learning experiences but also the long-term relevance of such skills.

REFERENCES

Brown, L., Nietupski, J., & Hamre-Nietupski, S. (1976). The criterion of ultimate functioning. In M. A. Thomas (Ed.), *Hey! Don't forget about me*. Reston, VA: Council for Exceptional Children.

Haring, H., & Bricker, D. (1976). *Overview of comprehensive services for the severely / profoundly handicapped*. New York: Grune & Stratton.

J. TODD STEPHENS
University of Wisconsin at Madison

CURRICULUM FOR STUDENTS WITH SEVERE DISABILITIES PROFOUNDLY RETARDED

UNITED CEREBRAL PALSY

United Cerebral Palsy (UCP) is a national voluntary association comprised of state and local affiliates and the national organization, United Cerebral Palsy Associations (UCPA), which is headquartered in New York City. A governmental affairs office is located in Washington, DC. Local affiliates provide direct services to individuals with cerebral palsy and their families, including special education, transitional services, and community living facilities. State affiliates coordinate the programs of local affiliates, provide services to areas not covered by locals, and work with agencies at the state level to further UCP goals. United Cerebral Palsy Associations assists state and local affiliates by formulating national policies on which affiliates are organized, managed, and supported. It also represents the UCP on a national level.

There are five district offices: UCP of Northeast in New

York City; UCP of Midwest in Des Plaines, Illinois; UCP of southwest in Dallas, Texas; UCP of Western in Burlingame, California; and UCP of Southeast in East Point, Georgia. United Cerebral Palsy Associations' district offices were established to bring national services closer to affiliates and to transmit affiliate needs quickly to the national organization.

The UCP began as a parent group organized to improve services and educational programming for children with cerebral palsy. One of the first formal units was the Association for Cerebral Palsy, established in 1942 in California. In 1946, a parent group formed the New York State Association for Cerebral Palsy. These groups, along with others like them, evolved into a national agency that provides advocacy for legislative efforts, research and training, and direct services to clients. On August 12, 1948, the national organization was established as the National Foundation for Cerebral Palsy, a nonprofit membership corporation located in New York City. On August 12, 1949, the corporate name was changed to United Cerebral Palsy Associations, Inc. By 1952, more than 100 affiliates were linked with the national organization. As of September 1983, there were 228 local affiliates and 46 state affiliates.

UCPA works in many ways to generate new programs and services. In representing UCP in national affairs, UCPA cooperates with federal government agencies that administer programs that affect individuals with cerebral palsy. In addition, UCPA articulates UCP's positions on national issues such as national health services and transportation for people with disabilities. The UCPA develops model services for people with disabilities that are designed to be replicated in local communities (Cohen & Warren, 1985). The UCPA also supports national standards for the conduct of community programs. Through the UCP Research and Educational Foundation, UCPA promotes research into the causes of cerebral palsy, means of prevention, training of medical and allied personnel, and biomedical technology to improve mobility and communication. In addition, UCPA supports professional education by granting clinical fellowships and student traineeships and by running conferences and institutes. The UCPA uses national communications media to educate the public about cerebral palsy and to raise funds (e.g., public service messages are contributed to UCPA by television networks, radio and press syndicates, and national magazines). Public education and information materials are available from UCPA.

REFERENCES

Cohen, S., & Warren, R. (1985). *Respite care: Principles, programs, and policies.* Austin, TX: PRO-ED.

Nielsen, C. (1978). *The cerebral palsy movement and the founding of UCPA, Inc.* Unpublished manuscript.

United Cerebral Palsy Associations. (1983). *Annual report 1983.* New York: Author.

United Cerebral Palsy Association. (undated). *Meet your national organization.* New York: Author.

CAROLE REITER GOTHELF
Hunter College, City University of New York

ADVOCACY FOR CHILDREN WITH DISABILITIES CEREBRAL PALSY

UNITED KINGDOM, SPECIAL EDUCATION IN THE

See ENGLAND, SPECIAL EDUCATION IN.

UNITED STATES DEPARTMENT OF EDUCATION

The United States Office of Education, a precursor to the current federal Department of Education, was created by an act of Congress in 1867. Its original mission was to collect and disseminate information on the condition of education in the states and U.S. territories. According to Campbell et al. (1975), the Office of Education was responsible for establishing a system to identify and advance promising educational practices in school districts throughout the country.

During the nineteenth and early twentieth centuries, the Office of Education was located within the U.S. Department of the Interior. In 1939 the office was transferred to the jurisdiction of the Federal Security Agency. Its final home prior to achieving Cabinet level (departmental) status was with the U.S. Department of Health, Education, and Welfare (1953–1980).

Public Law 96-88, passed by Congress and signed by President Carter in 1979, created the U.S. Department of Education. The new department assumed all of the functions previously assigned to the Office of Education, and also included education-related programs and functions previously administered by other entities within HEW such as rehabilitation. Soll (1984) suggests that the rapid proliferation of social programs and the political mobilization of various educational constituencies combined to stimulate the creation of a Cabinet-level Department of Education.

Although exercising a modest role in American education during its first century of existence, the federal-level education agency has assumed an increasingly important role in administering national education initiatives. Recently (since the mid-1960s), the federal Office (now Department) of Education has been charged with (1) the collection and dissemination of educationally relevant national data; (2) the support of educational research; and (3) the financial and technical support of programs in compensatory education, special education, rehabilitation, higher education, vocational and adult education, and student financial assistance. According to the Department of Education's web site, the 2006 fiscal year budget for all activities administered by the U.S. Department of Education was approximately $72.8 billion.

REFERENCES

Campbell, R. F., Cunningham, L. L., Nystrand, R. O., & Usdan, M. D. (1975). *The organization and control of American schools.* Columbus, OH: Merrill.

Soll, C. D. (1984). The creation of the Department of Education. In R. J. Stillman (Ed.), *Public administration: Concepts and cases* (3rd ed., pp. 370–377). Boston: Houghton Mifflin.

GEORGE JAMES HAGERTY
Stonehill College
Second edition

KIMBERLY APPLEQUIST
University of Colorado at Colorado Springs
Third edition

OFFICE OF SPECIAL EDUCATION AND REHABILITATIVE SERVICES
POLITICS AND SPECIAL EDUCATION

UNIVERSAL DESIGN

Everywhere, people are talking about universal design (UD). A recent Internet search of the *Dallas Morning News,* the *New York Times,* and the *Los Angeles Times* revealed more than 140 articles that included the phrase "universal design." A Google web search of the same phrase revealed more than 230,000 matches on the web. Universal design has been developed and adopted in an attempt to make all products and environments accessible or usable by the full range of individuals desiring to use them. Universal design was first introduced as an architectural concept associated with providing access to buildings and facilities for individuals having a variety of abilities and disabilities. Initially, private and public facilities had few provisions for individuals with disabilities and, consequently, utilization and access was somewhat limited. Early attempts at providing adequate accessibility usually consisted of efforts such as adding wooden ramps and custom elevators to stairways, adding specialized handrails, widening doorways, and so forth. These efforts obviously involved retrofitting changes to existing structures. Universal design principles, on the other hand, advocate the initial design of facilities to accommodate as many people as possible regardless of age, ability, or situation. Due to the functionality of the design, everyone may benefit from the increased usability factors. For example, while ramps were initially provided for disability access, they have universal benefits and are used everyday for the convenience of individuals delivering equipment, pulling wheeled computer bags, or pushing strollers. Similar benefits are experienced by the everyday use of automatic door openers. By designing these features into the initial structures they are even more useful, less obtrusive, more economical, and more aesthetic. Similar benefits can be experienced in the design of telephones, electronics, utensils, tools, and so on. Today's computer operating systems have similar usability features intended for disabled individuals but which offer added features for everyone, such as screen magnification features used in teaching situations. Consequently, everyone benefits from the awareness and expertise that universal design has brought to the creation of today's products and environments.

Ron Mace is credited with coining the term "universal design" (cited in Pisha & Coyne, 2001). The earliest reference to the term in the literature was found in a bibliography of resources authored by Brown and Vargo (1993), which listed a pamphlet entitled "Universal Design: Housing for the Life Span of All People" (Mace, 1988). Mace became a principal investigator for the Center for Universal Design at the University of North Carolina in 1989, where he continued his work in accessible architecture (Center for Universal Design, 1997a). In 1997, Mace and his group published the most definitive model of UD thus far delineated—"The Seven Principles of Universal Design" (Center for Universal Design, 1997c). Ron Mace died on June 29, 1998 (Center for Universal Design, 1997a), but the Center continues to provide information and leadership in this area (see Center for Universal Design at N.C. State University, IDEA Center at The University at Buffalo, & Universal Design Educator's Network, 2004).

The early definitions of UD are remarkably similar. Brown and Vargo (1993) defined UD as the design of a building, product, or environment so that it can be used by all people. In 1996, Lozada also defined UD in architectural terms: "The idea behind universal design is building a home that is equipped to accommodate someone with special needs but at the same time is not inconvenient for the average person who may not have a disability" (p. 18). It is interesting to note that Lozada used the double negative "not inconvenient" to describe the benefits of UD to people without disabilities. This phrase created emphasis on the benefits of UD to people *with* disabilities. Mace and his colleagues at the Center for Universal Design subtly changed the emphasis in their definition which stated:

> Universal design is the design of products and environments to be usable by all people, to the greatest extent possible, without the need for adaptation or specialized design. . . . The intent of universal design is to simplify life for everyone by making products, communications, and the built environment more usable by as many people as possible at little or no extra cost.

Universal design benefits people of all ages and abilities (Center for Universal Design, 1997c¶1).

What was striking about this definition was that "disability" had been taken out of it. There was no longer a demarcation between the two populations. Even so, authors would—and still do—continue to associate UD with disability access.

One of the first areas that UD would be applied was technology integration. Early work at the Center for Universal Design had applied the seven principles to industrial and electronic engineering in devices such as kiosks and mobile telephones. Numerous product designers and industrial engineers had embraced UD concepts in the design of their products (see Center for Universal Design, 2004).

However, a schism between *product engineering* intended for people without disabilities and *rehabilitation engineering* intended for those with disabilities would appear in the literature. For the most part, early publications considered UD an extension of assistive technology and rehabilitation engineering (Brown & Vargo, 1993; Burgstahler et al., 1997; Lozada, 1996; McGuinness, 1997). This is a theme that continues today (Hitchcock & Stahl, 2003; McGuire et al., 2003; Scott et al., 2003), though some theorists (Rose & Meyer, 2002; Stahl, 2004) have more broadly applied UD, and question the utility of drawing such a distinction since the stated objective of UD is to design environments that include everyone.

In keeping with the disability theme, much of the research referencing concepts of UD has focused on assistive technology; that is, the application of technology to accommodate people with disabilities. Fichten et al. (2001) completed a fairly large study of assistive technology integration in the higher education environment. They concluded that institutions generally have a poor plan to integrate assistive technology into the campus environment. Faculty often did not have basic knowledge of how assistive technologies worked. Subsequently, faculty inadvertently adopted instructional materials and methods that prevented access to the curriculum. This violated the UD principle of perceptible information in that it prevented effective communication (instruction) regardless of ambient conditions or sensory abilities. Fichten et al. also concluded that assistive technology had many benefits in the educational environment, but also could create barriers to learning. Their work put the application of UD to assistive technology squarely in the purview of future researchers.

An area receiving special attention with regard to universal design is that of web page accessibility. Like buildings, accessibility features were initially added to existing web sites as individuals discovered problems encountered by viewers with sensory or motor disabilities. Various standards and agencies have been established to help ensure that web sites are designed to accommodate the widest range of individuals regardless of age, ability, or situation. Examples include the W3C Web Content Accessibility Guidelines (WCAG) 2.0 and the Center for Applied Special Technology's (CAST) Bobby software that examines web pages and "notes technical or design issues that may present barriers to persons with disabilities who access the site." (Cooper, 1999)

Universal design concepts in education have led to concepts such as Universal Design for Learning. CAST has proposed Universal Design for Learning (UDL; Center for Applied Special Technology, 2005), a design feature that provides a blueprint for creating flexible goals, methods, materials, and assessments that accommodate learner differences by creating educational materials that provide multiple approaches to meet the needs of diverse learners. As with architecture and product development, the potential benefits are experienced by all individuals who interact with the materials, not just by those with disabilities.

REFERENCES

Brown, D. S., & Vargo, J. (1993). Bibliography of resources on universal design. *Journal of Rehabilitation, 59*(3), 8–11.

Burgstahler, S., Comden, D., & Fraser, B. (1997). Universal design for universal access: Making the Internet more accessible for people with disabilities. *Alki, 13*(3), 8–9.

Center for Applied Special Technology. (2005). *What is Universal Design for learning?* Retrieved September 15, 2005, from http://cast.org/udl/

Center for Universal Design. (1997a). *Design pioneer and visionary of universal design.* Retrieved April 21, 2004, from http://www.design.ncsu.edu/cud/center/history/ronmace.htm

Center for Universal Design. (1997b). *The principles of universal design, version 2.0.* Retrieved April 22, 2004, from http://www.design.ncsu.edu/cud/univ_design/princ_overview.htm

Center for Universal Design. (1997c). *What is universal design?* Retrieved April 21, 2004, from http://www.design.ncsu.edu/cud/univ_design/ud.htm

Center for Universal Design. (2002). *Guidelines for use of the principles of universal design.* Retrieved May 4, 2004, from http://www.design.ncsu.edu:8120/cud/univ_design/use_guidelines.pdf

Center for Universal Design. (2004). *Resources.* Retrieved April 22, 2004, from http://www.design.ncsu.edu/cud/resources/resources.htm

Center for Universal Design at N.C. State University, IDEA Center at The University at Buffalo, and Universal Design Educator's Network. (2004). *Universal design education online.* Retrieved May 4, 2004, from http://www.udeducation.org/

Cooper, M. (1999). *Universal design of a web site.* Technology and Persons with Disabilities Conference Proceedings, California State University, Northridge.

Fichten, C. S., Asuncion, J. V., Barile, M., Genereux, C., Fossey, M., Judd, D., et al. (2001). Technology integration for students with disabilities: Empirically based recommendations for faculty. *Educational Research and Evaluation: An International Journal on Theory and Practice, 7*(2–3), 185–221.

Hitchcock, C., & Stahl, S. (2003). Assistive technology, universal design, universal design for learning: Improved learning opportunities. *Journal of Special Education Technology, 18*(4), 45–52.

Lozada, M. (1996). Easy living: Universal design housing. *Vocational Education Journal, 71*(2), 18–21, 58.

Mace, R. (1988). Universal design: Housing for the life span of all people [Pamphlet]. Rockville, MD: U.S. Department of Housing and Urban Development.

McGuinness, K. (1997). Beyond the basics. *American School & University, 69*(11), 39–40, 42.

McGuire, J. M., Scott, S. S., & Shaw, S. F. (2003). Universal design for instruction: The paradigm, its principles and product for enhancing instructional access. *Journal on Postsecondary Education and Disability, 17*(1), 10–20.

Pisha, B., & Coyne, P. (2001). Smart from the start: The promise of universal design for learning. *Remedial and Special Education, 22*(4), 197–203.

Rose, D. H., & Meyer, A. (2002). *Teaching every student in the digital age: Universal design for learning.* Alexandria, VA: Association for Supervision and Curriculum Development.

Scott, S. S., Loewen, G., Funckes, C., & Kroeger, S. (2003). Implementing universal design in higher education: Moving beyond the built environment. *Journal on Postsecondary Education and Disability, 16*(2), 78–89.

Stahl, S. (2004). *Universal design for learning.* Unpublished manuscript.

DAVID SWEENEY
RONALD ZELLNER
Texas A&M University

COMPUTERS IN HUMAN BEHAVIOR
COMPUTER USE WITH STUDENTS WITH DISABILITIES

UNIVERSAL NONVERBAL INTELLIGENCE TEST

The Universal Nonverbal Intelligence Test (UNIT; Bracken & McCallum, 1998) is an individually administered instrument designed for use with children and adolescents ages 5:0 through 17:11. It is intended to provide a fair assessment of intelligence for those who have speech, language, or hearing impairments, different cultural or language backgrounds, those who are unable to communicate verbally, and those with mental retardation, autism, giftedness, and learning disabilities.

The UNIT measures intelligence through six culture-reduced subtests that combine to form two Primary Scales (Reasoning [RQ] and Memory [MQ]), two Secondary Scales (Symbolic [SQ] and Nonsymbolic [NQ]), and a Full Scale (FSIQ). Each of the subtests (Symbolic Memory, Cube Design, Spatial Memory, Analogic Reasoning, Object Memory, and Mazes) are conducted using eight reasonably universal hand and body gestures, demonstrations, scored items that

do not permit examiner feedback, sample items, corrective responses, and transitional checkpoint items to explain the tasks to the examinee. The entire process is nonverbal but does require motor skills for manipulatives, paper and pencil, and pointing.

Three administrations are available for use depending on the reason for referral. These are an Abbreviated Battery containing two Subtest Scores (10 to 15 minutes), the Standard Battery containing four Subtest Scores (30 minutes), and the Extended Battery containing six Subtest Scores (45 minutes).

Standardized through a carefully generated stratified random sampling plan, the UNIT resulted in a sample that closely matched the U.S. population according to the 1995 U.S. Census. Normative data were collected from a thorough nationwide sample of 2,100 children and adolescents, ranging in age from 5:0 through 17:11. An additional 1,765 children and adolescents were added to the standardization sample to participate in the reliability, validity, and fairness studies. This gives a total of 3,865 participants across the variables of age, sex, race, Hispanic origin, region, community setting, classroom placement, special education services, and parental educational achievement.

Technical qualities appear to be quite strong. Reliabilities are high for both standardization and clinical samples. Validity studies show strong concurrent validity with many other measures of intelligence. The UNIT has also been acknowledged as a moderately good predictor of academic achievement. Discriminant validity evidence is cited, demonstrating that the UNIT differentiates between those with mental retardation, learning disabilities, speech-language impairments, and giftedness. Some concern has been raised about the criterion-related validity and the factor analysis for minority and clinical samples (Young & Assing, 2000), but overall this test is a theoretically and psychometrically sound measure of nonverbal intelligence.

REFERENCES

Athanasiou, M. S. (2000). Current nonverbal assessment instruments: A comparison of psychometric integrity and test fairness. *Journal of Psychoeducational Assessment, 18,* 211–229.

Bracken, B. A., & McCallum, R. S. (1998). *Universal Nonverbal Intelligence Test, examiner's manual.* Itasca, IL: Riverside.

Caruso, J. C., & Witkiewitz, K. (2001). Memory and reasoning abilities assessed by the Universal Nonverbal Intelligence Test: A reliable component analysis (RCA) study. *Educational & Psychological Measurement, 61,* 5–22.

Drossman, E. R., & Maller, S. J. (2001). Core profiles of school-aged examinees in the national standardization sample of the Universal Nonverbal Intelligence Test. *School Psychology Review, 20,* 567–579.

Farrell, M. M., & Phelps, L. (2000). A comparison of the Leiter-R and the Universal Nonverbal Intelligence Test (UNIT) with children classified as language impaired. *Journal of Psychoeducational Assessment, 18,* 268–274.

Fives, C. J., & Flanagan, R. (2002). A review of the Universal Nonverbal Intelligence Test (UNIT): An advance for evaluating youngsters with diverse needs. *School Psychology International, 23,* 425–448.

Maller, S. J. (2000). Item invariance in four subtests of the Universal Nonverbal Intelligence Test across groups of deaf and hearing children. *Journal of Psychoeducational Assessment, 18,* 240–254.

Maller, S. J., & French, B. F. (2004). UNIT factor invariance across deaf and standardization samples. *Educational and Psychological Measurement, 64,* 647–660.

Plake, B. S., & Impara, J. C. (Eds.). (2001). *The fourteenth mental measurements yearbook.* Lincoln, NE: Buros Institute of Mental Measurements.

Young, E. L., & Assing, R. (2000). Test review: The Universal Nonverbal Intelligence Test (UNIT). *Journal of Psychoeducational Assessment, 18,* 280–288.

RON DUMONT
Fairleigh Dickinson University

JOHN O. WILLIS
Rivier College

INTELLIGENCE TESTING

V

VAKT

VAKT is a multisensory method of instruction that uses visual, auditory, kinesthetic, and tactile senses to reinforce learning (Richek, List, & Lerner, 1983). Unlike most other teaching strategies, the VAKT method emphasizes the kinesthetic sensory input provided by tracing and the tactile sensory input provided through varying textures of stimuli. The VAKT method is based on the principle that some children learn best when redundant cues are provided through many sensory channels (Mercer & Mercer, 1985). During instruction, the student sees the stimulus, listens to the teacher pronounce the stimulus, and then traces the stimulus over some textured material (e.g., sandpaper, corduroy, Jello). Thorpe and Sommer-Border (1985) contend that the kinesthetic-tactile component increases students' attention to the task. Under VAKT instruction conditions, students are more likely to attend selectively to distinctive features of the target letters and words. In addition, they tend to persevere or stay on task for longer periods of time at higher rates of engagement.

Many variations in the types of sensory activities have been devised. Depending on the style of learning of individual students, emphasis may be on one sensory channel over another. Some students may need more involved sensory experiences. More potent stimulation may be provided by such activities as tracing stimuli in sand trays, cornmeal, or Jello. Other activities include tracing in air, tracing in air while blindfolded, and tracing over raised stimuli of varying textures. Since the activities used with the VAKT method are time consuming, it has been recommended they be used particularly in cases of severe learning deficits (Richek et al., 1983). However, VAKT activities can be used with milder deficits or even everyday learning.

Two instructional systems used for teaching word recognition that highlight the VAKT methodology are the Fernald method (Fernald, 1943) and the Gillingham method (Gillingham & Stillman, 1968). The Fernald method combines the VAKT methods with a whole-word, language experience approach; the Gillingham method combines VAKT with a synthetic phonics approach.

The Fernald method consists of four learning stages through which students must pass. Each stage has specific procedures for teaching word recognition. As the student passes through the sequential stages, instruction entails less use of the kinesthetic and tactile senses. Words are chosen by the student for study based on stories generated by the student and written down by the teacher. This language experience approach is used to maintain student interest. Stage one emphasizes tracing and writing from memory individual words selected by the student. The teacher writes down a selected word on a large card and pronounces it while writing. Next, the student traces over the word with one or two fingers while saying the word. Word tracing is repeated until the student believes that the word can be written accurately from memory. The student now writes the word without looking at it and pronounces it while writing. If the word is written correctly from memory, it is stored in a word bank. If the student cannot write the word, the tracing procedure is repeated (Richek et al., 1983).

Stage two learning is initiated when the teacher believes that the student no longer needs to trace words for learning. Instruction differs from stage one in two ways: the words are presented on smaller cards and tracing is eliminated. As in stage one, words are selected from student-generated stories. A selected word is printed on a card; the student looks at it and says the word. The student then attempts to write the word from memory (Richek et al., 1983).

During stage three, the student begins to read from textbooks. Students can read from any material that they desire. Words are selected from the text, but are no longer written on cards. Instead, the student looks at the word in the text, says the word, then writes it down from memory (Richek et al., 1983).

Stage four is characterized by the student being able to read a word in context, say it, and remember it without having to write it. The student is taught to decode unknown words by associating them with known words or by using contextual cues. The student writes down for further review the words that he or she cannot figure out using these means (Richek et al., 1983).

The Gillingham method is a highly structured phonics approach that uses the VAKT methods to enhance learning. The method is based on the work of Orton (1937) dealing with the relationship between cerebral dominance and reading and language disorders. A series of associative processes are used to link the names and sounds of phonemes with their written symbols. Six fundamental associations are used in instruction: (1) visual-auditory (V-A), (2) auditory-visual (A-V), (3) auditory-kinesthetic (A-K), (4) kinesthetic-auditory

(K-A), (5) visual-kinesthetic (V-K), and (6) kinesthetic-visual (K-V; Mercer & Mercer, 1985).

Instruction begins with the student learning letters and their sounds. Letter names are taught by the teacher showing the student a letter and saying the name (V-A). The student then repeats the letter name (A-K). The sounds of letters are taught next using the same procedures. The teacher prints the letter and explains its formation. The student then traces over the letter, copies the letter, and writes the letter from memory (A-K; K-A). The next stage involves reading words. The first set of words contains the vowels (V) a and i and consonants (C) b, g, h, j, k, n, p, and t. Sound blending is taught using letter patterns such as CVC, CVCe, etc. After a basic set of words is learned, words are combined into simple sentences and stories from which the student reads. Instruction proceeds with extensive use of spelling and dictation exercises (Mercer & Mercer, 1985; Richek et al., 1983).

REFERENCES

Fernald, G. M. (1943). *Remedial techniques in basic school subjects.* New York: McGraw-Hill.

Gillingham, A., & Stillman, B. (1968). *Remedial teaching for children with specific disability in reading, spelling, and penmanship.* Cambridge, MA: Educator's.

Mercer, C. D., & Mercer, A. R. (1985). *Teaching students with learning problems* (2nd ed.). Columbus, OH: Merrill.

Orton, S. T. (1937). *Reading, writing, and speech problems in children.* New York: Norton.

Richek, M. A., List, L. K., & Lerner, J. W. (1983). *Reading problems: Diagnosis and remediation.* Englewood Cliffs, NJ: Prentice Hall.

Thorpe, H. W., & Sommer-Border, K. (1985). The effect of multisensory instruction upon the on task behavior and word reading accuracy of learning disabled children. *Journal of Learning Disabilities, 18,* 279–286.

LAWRENCE J. O'SHEA
University of Florida

FERNALD METHOD
GILLINGHAM-STILLMAN ALPHABETIC APPROACH
MULTISENSORY INSTRUCTION

VALETT DEVELOPMENTAL SURVEY OF BASIC LEARNING ABILITIES

The Valett Developmental Survey of Basic Learning Abilities was developed in 1966 by Robert E. Valett. The survey is designed to emphasize the use of psychoeducational diagnosis and evaluation to ascertain specific learning and behavioral problems in children ages 2 to 7 (Valett, 1967). A total of 53 learning behaviors that may appear in a deficit form have been grouped under seven major areas of learning as follows: motor integration and physical development (e.g., "Throw me the ball"); tactile discrimination (e.g., "Put your hand in the bag and find the spoon"); auditory discrimination (e.g., "Say, we are going to buy some candy for mother"); visual motor coordination (e.g., "Draw me a picture like this"); visual discrimination (e.g., "Show me one like this"); language development and verbal fluency (e.g., "What burns?"); and conceptual development (e.g., "Give me two pennies"). A graded range of one to four items for a particular age level constitutes a 233-task survey. Each of the seven major areas is operationally defined and arranged developmentally in ascending order of difficulty (Southworth, Burr, & Cox, 1980; Valett, 1967; Mann, 1972; Roger, 1972). The instrument, educational rationale for remedial programming, and remedial materials are presented in a loose-leaf workbook format that are number-keyed to the major areas and subtasks (Mann, 1972; Valett, 1966). Scoring is based on correct, incorrect, or partial development. The range of developmental levels and strengths and weaknesses are noted for the purpose of planning remedial programming (Southworth et al., 1980). Program suggestions that relate directly to the 53 learning behaviors are provided by Valett's (1968) *Psychological Resource Program.*

REFERENCES

Buros, O. K. (1972). *The seventh mental measurements yearbook.* Highland Park, NJ: Gryphon.

Johnson, S. K., & Marasky, R. L. (1980). *Learning disabilities* (2nd ed.). Boston: Allyn & Bacon.

Mann, L. (1972). Review of the Valett Developmental Survey of Basic Learning Abilities. In O. Buros (Ed.), *The seventh mental measurements yearbook.* Highland Park, NJ: Gryphon.

Mitchell, J. V. (1983). *Tests in print III: An index to tests, test reviews and the literature on specific tests.* Lincoln: University of Nebraska Press.

Roger, R. A. (1972). Review of the Valett Developmental Survey of Basic Learning Abilities. In O. Buros (Ed.), *The seventh mental measurements yearbook.* Highland Park, NJ: Gryphon.

Southworth, L. E., Burr, R. L., & Cox, A. E. (1980). *Screening and evaluation in the young child: A handbook of instruments to use from infancy to six years.* Springfield, IL: Thomas.

Valett, R. E. (1966). *The Valett Developmental Survey of Basic Learning Abilities.* Palo Alto, CA: Consulting Psychologist Press.

Valett, R. E. (1966). A psychoeducational profile of basic learning abilities. *Journal of School Psychology, 4,* 9–24.

Valett, R. E. (1967). A developmental task approach to early childhood education. *Journal of School Psychology, 2,* 136–147.

Valett, R. E. (1968). *Psychological resource program.* Belmont, CA: Fearson.

FRANCES HARRINGTON
Radford University

REMEDIAL INSTRUCTION

VALIDITY, TEST

Psychological and educational tests are used quite frequently in special education to help make important decisions regarding the educational and social programming of students. Scores on such tests may be used to help districts make predictions about performance on a statewide writing benchmark exam, help Student Study Teams decide if a child has serious depression that requires immediate treatment, or help administrators know if students will succeed in the workforce after graduation. The penultimate concept associated with these dimensions of testing is *validity*, which concerns the accuracy and soundness of specific *interpretations* of a test score. Fundamental to the issue of validity is the degree of empirical and theoretical support for making evaluative judgments about a person from the particular score(s) received on a test (Salvia & Ysseldyke, 2004). To wit, validity is not the property of a test but rather the *meaning* assigned to the test scores (Messick, 1995).

When special educators attempt to derive meaning about or make inferences from test scores, it should be based on (1) the balance of evidence supporting the meaning of the scores, (2) the relevance of the scores to the particular applied purpose and utility in the applied setting, (3) the credibility and value implications of score interpretation and implications for action, and (4) the evidence and arguments that make clear the functional value of testing, including its intended and unintended social consequences (Messick, 1980, 1989a, 1989b). Validity is an inductive summary of existing evidence for, and potential consequences of, score interpretation and use; although supporting evidence may come from numerous quantitative as well as qualitative sources, keep in mind that validity is a unitary concept (Messick, 1989a, 1989b) that is deeply embedded and fused within the system of science.

Measurement and Theory

Science seeks to predict and explain the world around us, and in so doing, must engage in precise measurement and must have an explanatory framework or theory from which to attribute meaning to observed or latent variables. In order to weigh the truthfulness of those scientific explanations, the scientist must start by *validating* their measurement systems and establishing rules for assigning numbers to attributes. Once measurement rules are laid down, different examiners, using the same procedures, will be more likely to arrive at the same score for a student. Formulating such procedures is critical to what is known as the *standardization* of an instrument. When instruments are standardized, the numbers assigned to attributes enables the user to report events in finer details instead of in vague generalities. Standardization, then, enables the user to communicate more clearly and opens the door for other scientists to verify or validate constructs as well. Although standardization is a key internal requirement for any measurement system to be considered useful, it is a procedural concept related to its reliability (Salvia & Ysseldyke, 2004).

It is one thing to establish the standardization and reliability of a measurement system, but the scores must also contribute to our understanding and appreciation of real-life phenomenon. High reliability does not necessarily guarantee that a test will be practical and meaningful. For example, if a score on a measure of social competence is indexed to nothing but itself, it has no meaning; for scores to be meaningful, they must be tied to other scores or variables existing within a larger network of data related to social competence. When there is a confirmatory relationship with other important dimensional variables then the validity of the instrument (or score) is established. This networked relationship among scores is at the heart of a theory, enabling scientists to explore and interpret the meaning of something.

Theory allows scientists to answer the question of "why" certain relationships exist among variables. When one unpacks a theory, they will find a nomological network of constructs, hypotheses, and operational definitions or measures (Cronbach & Meehl, 1955). Constructs are related to other constructs by hypotheses. Hypotheses are the proposed interpretations of events. Constructs interconnected by one or more hypotheses provide the beginnings for a theory of the primary construct. Theories need to be translated into observable events or processes, made visible by operational definitions or measures. Once theories become more specified, they can then be tested by collecting data. When observed relationships correspond to the hypothesized relationships among the constructs, then one can be reasonably satisfied that the theory has gained utility for understanding the phenomena under study. Not only is utility gained, but so is an increased ability to infer that the operational definitions of the constructs were appropriate; that is, the measures used in this theory-building process actually represented or reflected the constructs they were designed to measure. Therefore, if a measure or test accurately captures the construct it was designed to, then *construct validity* is obtained. Tests and test validation flow through the scientific process of theory development and make convenient operational definitions of often invisible attributes of human behavior. For an excellent description of the scientific process of theory validation and constructing nomological networks, the reader is directed to the work of Gerald Patterson and colleagues from the Oregon Social Learning Center (Patterson & Bank, 1986; Patterson, Reid, & Dishion, 1992).

Types of Evidence for Validity

The preceding summary of scientific inquiry and theory development highlights the validation process whereby latent variables are given their validity. When researchers or evaluation entrepreneurs develop testing or assessment tools for public use, they must apply certain standards for ensuring their quality (American Psychological Association, American Educational Research Association, & National Council on Measurement in Education, 1999). Quality assurance can be demonstrated in several ways: by its (1) content validity, (2) criterion validity, and (3) construct validity. "Face" validity is often mentioned in assessment situations but is not an appropriate kind of validity evidence; suffice it to say that face validity is the degree to which a measure looks like it measures what it is supposed to, and is related more to issues of social rapport or public acceptability as opposed to technical aspects of measurement (Nevo, 1985; Salvia & Ysseldyke, 2004). Measures of Attention-Deficit/Hyperactivity Disorder, for example, often have strong face validity.

Content validity deals with the appropriate degree to which test items, questions, or tasks represent the whole domain of knowledge or behaviors that constitute that trait. At its core, content validity is a sampling issue where a sample is drawn from a larger population or universe of potential items defining that trait or behavior (Gregory, 2004). Since one cannot sample all possible items, test developers hope to generalize or make inferences from the smaller to larger sample. Item sampling needs to be broad and representative before valid inferences of the construct can be made. Evidence for content validity usually comes from the subjective judgment of those designing the test or from experts who are familiar with the content area under validation and can rate the appropriateness of those items or tasks. The subjective, opinion-based portion then gives way to statistical procedures that help describe the internal homogeneity of the test's item structure, usually reported by coefficient alpha or Kuder-Richardson-Formula-20 correlational procedures. The test's item intercorrelations can then be factor analyzed to determine how many dimensions or traits are needed to explain test performance. That is, is there one general factor trait or several subfactors that best fits what the test is measuring? The process of content validation is the first step toward establishing construct validity because of how much time, consideration, and comprehensive defining goes into the construct underlying the test.

Criterion-related validity refers to whether the trait being measured by the test is related to some external behavior or measure of interest. In other words, can the measurement system predict a person's status or performance on some other criterion? For example, how well does a score on an IQ test predict future success in school as measured by grades, acceptance to college, or SAT scores? Two subtypes of criterion validity exist: (1) *predictive validity,* which examines the relationship between a score collected today and then on some future criterion score, and (2) *concurrent validity,* which examines the relationship between predictor and criterion variables collected at the same time. The primary

difference between these two subtypes has to do with the timing of when predictor and criterion data are collected.

Generally speaking, criterion-related validity helps elaborate which direction and to what extent predictor and criterion variables might or might not reflect the same trait. For example, if one is evaluating an intelligence test that purportedly measures fluid and crystallized abilities, one would want a predictor variable such as a full-scale IQ to show a strong, positive relationship with criterion SAT scores. Conversely, one would not want or be particularly interested in establishing that the IQ also measures and predicts anxiety, since the construct of anxiety may not be part of the predicted underlying nomological network of one's theory of intelligence. However, if one did want to convince others that the anxiety trait is not being measured, then scores on the IQ test (the predictor) would hopefully be uncorrelated with other anxiety measures or behaviors (the criterion). Evidence for supporting criterion-related validity generally comes from mean score differences between/among groups or populations of interest, and/or from correlational data (Cronbach & Meehl, 1955). As mentioned earlier, criterion-related validity also requires demonstrating that test scores are uncorrelated with theoretically unrelated variables; that is, while one desires predictor-criterion test scores to converge and support one's theory/construct, zero or low and nonsignificant correlations between predictor-criterion variables also helps support independence from other traits. If for some reason two seemingly unrelated traits do correlate, then one needs to detect if it is because the traits are being measured the same way (i.e., due to method variance) and not because the predictor and criterion variables actually measure the same trait. This complex process is known in the research literature as *convergent and discriminant validity* as validated by the *multitrait-multimethod matrix*. For a fuller discussion of this theoretical validation process, see Campbell and Fiske (1959).

Construct validity relates to whether the test or assessment system accurately measures the construct it was intended to measure. Construct validity is more than just about a correlation coefficient or saying that a test can now be used because it contains a certain *amount* of construct validity; rather, it rests on a program of research that continually seeks to gather a variety of evidence from abundant sources that lend support to a theory and its underlying nomological network of constructs, hypotheses, and operational definitions (Cronbach & Meehl, 1955; Gregory, 2004). Construct validity is regarded as the unifying concept that glues all types of validity together (Messick, 1995). Evidence such as test homogeneity, appropriate developmental changes consistent with theoretical predictions, group differences that are theory consistent, intervention effects that are theory consistent, correlations with other related and unrelated tests, logical and compelling arguments, and factor analysis of test scores are all potential evidence for supporting construct validity (Gregory, 2004; Messick, 1995).

While all research scientists are in the business of validating constructs (i.e., construct validity), the name that is perhaps most associated with the concept is Samuel Messick (cf. Messick, 1980, 1989a, 1989b, 1995), whose writings cover the philosophy, values, ethics, social consequences, and actions of assessment. Whereas construct validity was once seen as a last resort for supporting a test (Barrett, 1992), Messick's work has moved it to the forefront, where it is now the foundational basis for all test validation because it involves doing good science in order to understand both predictor and criterion variables and their interaction. The notion of construct validity has had its fair share of critics, who describe it as a vapid utopian doctrine that is conceptually confusing and inherently difficult to translate into practical steps for research and application (Barrett, 1992; Gregory, 2004). Nevertheless, in this day and age of test proliferation and the focus on "cash validity" over good science, special educators need to be concerned about selecting measurement tools with solid construct validity because the potential social, legal, and political consequences of misusing such decision tools are enormous (Gregory, 2004; Messick, 1995). The current industry around marketing assessment tools to public education has made it all the more important for school districts to allocate as much time critically evaluating the validity of purchased assessment tools as they do evaluating students with those tools. Using poorly validated tests undermines the accuracy and soundness of test score interpretations and could potentially lead special educators away from making effective educational judgments for children. However, when special educators demand clear evidence of validity, it ultimately benefits the professional reputation of special education itself.

REFERENCES

American Psychological Association, American Educational Research Association, & National Council on Measurement in Education. (1999). *Standards for educational and psychological tests.* Washington, DC: AERA.

Barrett, G. V. (1992). Clarifying construct validity: Definitions, processes, and models. *Human Performance, 5*(1&2), 13–58.

Campbell, D. T., & Fiske, D. W. (1959). Convergent and discriminant validation by the multitrait-multimethod matrix. *Psychological Bulletin, 56,* 81–105.

Cronbach, L. J., & Meehl, P. E. (1955). Construct validity in psychological tests. *Psychological Bulletin, 52,* 281–302.

Gregory, R. J. (2004). *Psychological testing: History, principles, and applications* (4th ed.). Boston: Allyn & Bacon.

Messick, S. (1980). Test validity and the ethics of assessment. *American Psychologist, 35,* 1012–1027.

Messick, S. (1989a). Meaning and values in test validation: The science and ethics of assessment. *Educational Researcher, 18*(2), 5–11.

Messick, S. (1989b). Validity. In R. L. Linn (Ed.), *Educational measurement* (3rd ed., pp. 12–103). New York: Macmillan.

Messick, S. (1995). Validity of psychological assessment: Validation of inferences from persons' responses and performances as scientific inquiry into score meaning. *American Psychologist, 50,* 741–749.

Nevo, B. (1985). Face validity revisited. *Journal of Educational Measurement, 22,* 287–293.

Patterson, G. R., & Bank, L. (1986). Bootstrapping your way in the nomological thicket. *Behavioral Assessment, 8,* 49–73.

Patterson, G. R., Reid, J. B., & Dishion, T. J. (1992). *A social interactional approach, vol. 4: Antisocial boys.* Eugene, OR: Castalia Publishing.

Salvia, J., & Ysseldyke, J. E. (2004). *Assessment in special and inclusive education* (9th ed.). Boston: Houghton Mifflin.

ROLLEN C. FOWLER
Eugene 4J School District,
Eugene, Oregon

NORMAL CURVE EQUIVALENT RELIABILITY

VALIUM

Valium (diazepam) may be used for the management of anxiety disorders or for the short-term relief of the symptoms of anxiety. Valium may be useful in the symptomatic relief of acute agitation, tremor, impending or acute delirium tremens, and hallucinosis. It also is used for the relief of skeletal muscle spasms or for spasticity caused by upper motor neuron disorders such as cerebral palsy; thus, it may be used for some children in special education classes. In some cases, it also may be used as an adjunct in status epilepticus and severe recurrent epileptic seizures. It has a central nervous system depressant effect, and is thought to act on parts of the limbic system, the thalamus, and hypothalamus. Side effects may include drowsiness, fatigue, and ataxia, with less frequent reactions of confusion, depression, headache, hypoactivity, and slurred speech.

A brand name of Hoffman-LaRoche, Inc., Valium is available in tablets of 2, 5, and 10 mg and in 2 ml and 5 ml ampuls for injection. Recommended dosages for children over 6 months of age is .04 to .2 mg/kg, not to exceed a .6 mg/kg within an 8-hour period, with gradual increase of dosage as needed and tolerated. Oral administration to children should be at .12 to .8 mg/kg per 24 hours divided into 6 to 8 hour doses. Oral solution is 1 and 5 milligrams per ml. in the injectable form, dosages of up to 5 mg for children under 5 years of age and up to 10 mg for children over 5 years of age. The half-life varies from 20 to 80 hours.

Overdosage may produce somnolence, confusion, or coma, and withdrawal symptoms such as convulsions, cramps, and tremor may occur following abrupt discontinuance.

The antidote for overdose is Romazicon. For the reversal of sedation .2 mg IV per 15 to 20 minutes is used with the maximum of 3 mg in one hour. Valium is contraindicated if patient is taking sodium oxybate.

Contraindications/Cautions: Acute angle glaucoma, alcohol intoxication, CNS depression, caution if psychosis, caution if impaired pulmonary function, caution if under 6 months old, impaired liver function, and in elderly patients.

REFERENCES

Epprocrates Rx Pro Version 7.50. (2006). Washington, DC: King Guide Publications.

Physician's desk reference. (1984). Oradell, NJ: Medical Economics.

LAWRENCE C. HARTLAGE
Evans, Georgia
First edition

LOLETA LYNCH-GUSTAFSON
California State University, San Bernardino
Third edition

ANXIETY
ANXIETY DISORDERS

VALPROIC ACID

Valproic acid is the recommended nonproprietary name for dipropylacetic acid. The common (proprietary) name for this drug is Depakene. Valproic acid is an anticonvulsant mood stabilizer. Anticonvulsant mood stabilizers are now frequently used in combination with antipsychotic drugs (APDs) in treating both schizophrenia and bipolar disorder (Ichikawa, Chung, Dai, & Meltzer, 2005). In the United States and Europe, the sodium salt of dipropylacetic acid is used. In South America, the magnesium salt of dipropylacetic acid is also marketed. Valproic acid is effective in the treatment of absence seizures as well as epilepsy. It is considered of some use in the treatment of myoclonic seizures and in tonic-clonic seizures (Dreifuss, 1983). It is also used to treat certain forms of bipolar cyclothymia, and may be used with ADHD children who are unresponsive to or have problems with stimulant medication.

Side Effects: Weight gain, tremor, and transient hair loss are commonly reported. Importantly, valproic acid has minimal neurological adverse effects (sedation, ataxia, impairment of cognitive function) compared with other antiepileptic drugs, a finding that may be of particular relevance in many patients with epilepsy. The major side effects reported are drowsiness, gastrointestinal discomfort, and changes in appetite. The Committee on Drugs of the American Academy of Pediatrics lists valproic acid as having minimal effects on cognitive functioning. The most significant and rare side effect of valproic acid is hepatic failure.

REFERENCES

Dreifuss, F. E. (1983). How to use valproate. In P. L. Morselli, C. E. Pippenger, & J. K. Penry (Eds.), *Antiepileptic drug therapy in pediatrics* (pp. 219–227). New York: Raven.

Ichikawa, J., Chung, Y., Dai, J., & Meltzer, H. (2005). Valproic acid potentiates both typical and atypical anti-psychotic-induced prefrontal cortical dopamine release. *Brain Research, 1052*(1), 56–62.

Speilberg, S. S. (1985). Behavioral and cognitive effects of anticonvulsant therapy. *Pediatrics, 76,* 644–646.

Simon, S., & Penry, J. K. (1975). Sodium di-N-propylacetate (DPA) in the treatment of epilepsy. *Epilepsia, 16,* 549–573.

GRETA WILKENING
Children's Hospital
First edition

LOLETA LYNCH-GUSTAFSON
California State University, San Bernardino
Third edition

ANTICONVULSANTS
DEPAKENE

VALUES CLARIFICATION

Values clarification, an approach to moral instruction used with both disabled and nondisabled pupils, stems from the humanistic education movement of the 1960s. Students trained in values clarification are taught to investigate the facts pertinent to a moral issue and to examine their feelings in a systematic manner. Values clarification teaches students the process of obtaining values and encourages them to explore personally held values and examine how they affect their decision-making processes (Casteel & Stahl, 1975). Rather than defining values in terms of good or bad, students learn to see values as guiding principles that affect choices. Critics of this approach have argued that values cannot be taught from a relativist position, and have questioned the appropriateness of using schools as settings for the teaching of values. As a result, values clarification started to lose its popularity as an educational force by the late 1970s (Brummer, 1984).

Raths, Harmin, and Simon (1978) outlined a seven-step process common to many values clarification curricula: (1)

students are helped to examine and choose from alternative opinions; (2) they are assisted in weighing these alternatives in a thoughtful manner; (3) students are helped to see the value of making a free choice; (4) students are encouraged to prize their choices; (5) they are provided with an opportunity to publicly acclaim their chosen values; (6) students are encouraged to act on their choices; and (7) they are helped to establish behavior patterns that are consistent with their chosen values.

Students who are exposed to values clarification training become better consumers of information by learning to ask appropriate questions. Junell (1979) states that students' involvement and identification are heightened when values are taught in the context of an emotionally charged environment. As they develop their ability to integrate factual content with emotional responses, the trained students come to understand how they assign meaning and values to problems.

Values clarification activities might include rank ordering of preferential activities, sensitivity training, and listening skills development. Simulations are commonly employed to provide students with practice in values application. Social or philosophical dilemmas, based on real or hypothetical issues, are often presented as problems to be solved. Lockwood (1976) discusses the efficacy of using examples from other cultures when devising materials. The issues may be discussed in large or small groups, and students are encouraged to invoke their social decision-making skills in developing possible solutions.

Special education students are often faced with value decisions relating to their disabilities. For example, vocational programs for special education students may rule out certain academic options. The disabled adolescent, limited in career opportunity, needs to explore the implications of vocational choices. Values clarification can help these youngsters to pick appropriate career directions and to learn decision-making principles necessary for adequate socialization at the work place (Miller & Schloss, 1982).

Some emotionally disturbed and learning-disabled children have been found to act without carefully considering the implications of their behaviors (Miller & Schloss, 1982). Values clarification provides a structure within which behaviorally disturbed children may find consistency. Thompson and Hudson (1982) found values clarification effective in reducing the maladaptive behavior of emotionally disturbed children. These children were also reported to be happier and less anxious.

Values clarification has also been used to help regular education students accept mainstreamed handicapped pupils. Simpson (1980) trained students to examine the effects of social influence and group affinity, and found that it eased the mainstreaming transition for both disabled and nondisabled students. Future research might focus on the long-range effects of values education on the attitudes of the general population toward individuals with disabilities.

REFERENCES

Brummer, J. J. (1984). Moralizing and value education. *Educational Forum, 48*(3), 263–276.

Casteel, J. D., & Stahl, R. J. (1975). *Value clarification in the classroom: A primer.* Santa Monica, CA: Goodyear.

Junell, J. S. (1979). *Matters of feeling: Values education reconsidered.* Phi Delta Kappa Foundation.

Lockwood, A. L. (1976). *Values education and the study of other cultures.* Washington, DC: National Educational Association.

Miller, S. R., & Schloss, P. J. (1982). *Career-vocational education for handicapped youths.* Rockville, MD: Aspen Systems.

Raths, L. E., & Harmin, M., & Simon, S. B. (1978). *Values and teaching.* Columbus, OH: Merrill.

Simpson, R. L. (1980). Modifying the attitudes of regular class students toward the handicapped. *Focus on Exceptional Children, 13*(3), 1–11.

Thompson, D. G., & Hudson, G. R. (1982). Value clarification and behavioral group counseling with ninth grade boys in a residential school. *Journal of Counseling Psychology, 29,* 394–399.

GARY BERKOWITZ
Temple University

CONSCIENCE, LACK OF IN INDIVIDUALS WITH DISABILITIES
MORAL REASONING

VAN DIJK, JAN (1937–)

Jan van Dijk is world known for his work with rubella deaf-blind children. In 1958 he became a teacher of normal prelingual profoundly deaf children at the Institute for the Deaf, St. Michielsgestel, the Netherlands. His interest in the deaf-blind department led him to study at the Perkins Institute for the Blind, Watertown, Massachusetts, where he received the Inis Hall Award for his thesis. He continued his studies in education and special education at the Catholic University of Nijmegen and completed his doctoral program with the publication of *Rubella Handicapped Children* (1982), an extensive study of rubella children in Australia. Van Dijk continues his work at the institute as the director of the Deaf-Blind School and the Dyspraxic Deaf School. For his important contributions to the education of deaf-blind children, he received the Ann Sullivan Award in 1974. Van Dijk is currently with the Institute for the Deaf in St. Michielsgestel, Netherlands (van Dijk, Carlin, & Hewitt, 1991).

Educational programming begins with a differential diagnosis for each child, not only for appropriate placement within the nine schools at the institute, but also to determine the child's learning style. This diagnosis is accomplished through the clinical use of such instruments as the Test of Development of Eupraxia in Hands and Fingers in Young Children, Test for Finger Eupraxia for Intransitive Movements, Bergs-Lezine Test for Imitation of Simple Gestures, Rhythm Test of Hand and Mouth for Prelingually Deaf Preschool Children, Finger Block Test, Hiskey Nebraska Test for Learning Aptitude, Reynell-Zinkin Scales, Denver Developmental Screening Test, and an adaptation of the Rimland Diagnostic Checklist for Behavioral Disturbed Children (van Dijk, 1982).

The guiding principle of the method is that the child is in the central position. The teacher "follows" the child and "seizes," in a natural way, what the child is trying to express. In order to do this, a close attachment or bond must be developed between child and teacher so that the teacher can be sensitive to the slightest nuance of the child's expression. This guiding principle precludes the use of a teacher-developed curriculum. Rather, the curriculum develops from the child's interests and desires. As the environment responds, the child feels the sense of mastery or competency necessary to reach out into the world.

Because the deaf-blind child is deprived of the organizing senses of vision and hearing, the world appears chaotic and meaningless. Meaning is developed by ordering and structuring the child's day in place and time, and with people. At first, the activities are similar to those of normal mother-child activities. The teacher creates enjoyable situations that encourage the child to initiate activities. The child learns it is nice to do something together with someone else. Initially, he or she may need to be taken through the activities passively (resonance). Then the child begins to move together with the adult (coactive movement) until the activity is done successively rather than together (imitation).

As the child's day becomes ordered around activities of interest, ideas are formed. The child anticipates events and may express this anticipation through "signal behavior" or body language. As the teacher responds, the child realizes that these signals produce a positive reaction. They then form the child's idiosyncratic lexicon known and responded to by all adults associated with the child. Drawings and objects are also used to represent, or signal, activities (objects of reference). Gradually the drawings and objects become more and more abstract until the child is ready to use formal symbolic language systems.

The special quality of the van Dijk method is that language is not taught as a labeling process, but as a social interaction between two people having a conversation about objects, activities, and emotions of mutual interest. Results with this method may not be as immediate as with a stimulus-response program, for example. It may be several years before the child develops signal behavior. However, there is a possibility of reaching high levels of language performance. Although this method has been developed primarily for deaf children who have language potential based on a differential diagnosis, professionals working with the severely and profoundly disabled are seeing value in it for their populations as well (Sternberg, Battle, & Hill, 1980).

REFERENCES

Hammer, E. (1982). The development of language in the deaf-blind multihandicapped child: Progression of instructional methods. In D. Tweedie & E. Shroyer (Eds.), *The multihandicapped hearing impaired: Identification and instruction.* Washington, DC: Gallaudet College Press.

Sternberg, L., Battle, C., & Hill, J. (1980). Prelanguage communication programming for the severely and profoundly handicapped. *Teacher Education & Special Education, 3,* 224–233.

van Dijk, J. (1982). *Rubella handicapped children.* Lisse, the Netherlands: Swets & Zeitlinger.

van Dijk, J. (1986). An educational curriculum for deaf-blind multihandicapped persons. In D. Ellis (Ed.), *Sensory impairments in mentally handicapped people.* San Diego, CA: College Hill.

van Dijk, J., Carlin, R., & Hewitt, H. (1991). *Persons handicapped by rubella: Victors and victims—A follow-up study.* Amsterdam, the Netherlands: Swets & Zeitlinger.

van Uden, A. (1977). *A world of language for deaf children. Part I: Basic principles.* Lisse, the Netherlands: Swets & Zeitlinger.

Visser, T. (1985). A development program for deaf-blind children. *Talking Sense, 31*(3), 6–7.

PEARL E. TAIT
Florida State University

RUBELLA
THEORY OF ACTIVITY

VAN RIPER, CHARLES (1905–1991)

A native of Champion, Michigan, Charles Van Riper received both his BA in 1926 and MA in 1930 from the University of Michigan, and his PhD in 1934 from the University of Iowa. His degrees were in speech pathology and psychology. He was a professor in the department of speech pathology and audiology of Western Michigan University. He also was the director of the Speech and Hearing Clinic at that university since 1936.

One of the premier authorities in the field of speech correction, Van Riper contributed to the theory and correction of stuttering and developed methods for understanding, evaluating, and altering speech behavior. In 1978 the sixth edition of his textbook *Speech Correction: Principles and Methods,* was published.

Van Riper was concerned with involving the family in the therapy of any child with a speech problem. He believed that parents who know what they are doing are frequently better speech therapists than formally trained therapists. He began his book *Your Child's Speech Problems* (1961) with the statement that "once parents understand what the speech problem (of their child) is and what should be done, they can do great deeds" (p. xi).

A member of Phi Beta Kappa, Van Riper received the honors of the Association of the American Speech and Hearing

Association. He has been included in *Leaders in Education, Who's Who in the South and Southwest,* and *American Men and Women of Science.*

REFERENCES

Van Riper, C. (1961). *Your child's speech problems.* New York: Harper & Row.

Van Riper, C. (1978). *Speech correction: Principles and methods* (6th ed.). Englewood Cliffs, NJ: Prentice Hall.

E. Valerie Hewitt
Texas A&M University

SPEECH AND LANGUAGE DISABILITIES
SPEECH DISORDERS

VELO-CARDIO-FACIAL SYNDROME (SHPRINTZEN SYNDROME)

Velo-cardio-facial syndrome (VCFS) is considered to be among the most prevalent microdeletion syndromes (Pulver et al., 1994). It has a prevalence rate of 1 individual per 2,000 to 4,500 live births (Tézenas Du Montcel, Mendizabal, Aymé, Lévy, & Philip, 1996). Individuals with VCFS are commonly described as having distinctive facial features, including a cleft palate, long face, and prominent nose; heart abnormalities; learning problems (Eliez & Feinstein, 2004; Murphy, Jones, Griffiths, Thompson, & Owen, 1998); mental retardation; hypernasal speech (Eliez & Feinstein); and an increased risk for a variety of mental illnesses, including bipolar disorder (Carlson et al., 1997) and schizophrenia (Pulver et al.).

The first published accounts of VCFS were by Sedláčková (1967), who reported finding many patients with facial abnormalities and hypernasal speech. VCFS started gaining the attention of the scientific community through the article by Shprintzen et al. (1978) reporting on the common characteristics found in 12 patients at the "Center for Cranio-Facial Disorders (CCFD) of Montefiore Hospital and Medical Center" (p. 56). VCFS received its name in this article.

The purpose of this paper is to provide a brief overview of the current knowledge of VCFS. Discussion will begin with the physical and behavioral manifestations of VCFS. This will be followed by a discussion of its etiology, detection and assessment, and developmental course. Discussion will conclude by discussing interventions commonly used to treat VCFS.

Physical and Behavioral Manifestations of VCFS

Many physical and behavioral characteristics are associated with VCFS. Shprintzen (2000) listed over 185 clinical features of individuals diagnosed with VCFS. Although an exhaustive list of features is not feasible, this section will cover the most commonly cited traits. These traits will be grouped into seven categories: physical features/medical impairments, chromosomal abnormalities, brain structure abnormalities, cognitive impairments, language difficulties, motor impairments, and behavioral/psychological impairments.

Eliez and Feinstein (2004) stated that over 100 physical abnormalities and medical conditions are linked to VCFS. Common physical characteristics include long a face, prominent nose, flattened cheeks, cleft secondary palate (Eliez & Feinstein), broad nasal bridge, overbite, mild fusion of the eyebrows, thick scalp hair, and narrow folds of the eyelids (Shprintzen et al., 1978). Other physical characteristics include below-average height with "slender hands and digits" (Eliez & Feinstein, p. 123). Medical conditions common to individuals with VCFS include hypothyroidism and cardiac abnormalities (Eliez & Feinstein).

Chromosomal abnormalities are generally present with VCFS. Most individuals with VCFS have a "*de novo* 3 Mb deletion at chromosome 22q11.2" (Eliez & Feinstein, 2004, p. 126). Edelmann et al. (1999) reported finding large variability in the location and deletion size. This deletion has been passed onto the children of VCFS individuals in some cases.

Several brain structure abnormalities are common in individuals with VCFS. These individuals commonly have 11 percent reductions in total brain volume (Eliez, Schmitt, White, & Reiss, 2000). This reduction usually consists of cerebral atrophy (Chow et al., 1999), with a reduction of both white and gray matter (Antshel, Kates, Roizen, Fremont, & Shprintzen, 2005; Eliez et al., 2001). Gray matter reductions are most prominent in the left hemisphere (Eliez, Schmitt, et al., 2000; Kates et al., 2001), including the left parietal lobe (Eliez, Schmitt, et al., 2000). Both temporal lobes have been found to have reduced volumes (Eliez et al., 2001). Eliez et al. (2001) found that temporal lobe volume appears to diminish with age among individuals with VCFS. Individuals with VCFS also have been found to have reduced hippocampus volumes compared to those without this disorder (Eliez et al., 2001). Individuals with VCFS have been found to have larger basal ganglia (Eliez, Barnea-Goraly, Schmitt, Liu, & Reiss, 2002), ventricles (Chow et al., 1999), Sylvian fissues (Bingham et al., 1997), and frontal lobes (Eliez, Schmitt, et al., 2000) than normal controls.

Several cognitive impairments are associated with VCFS. Henry et al. (2002) compared a sample of 19 adults with VCFS to a sample matched for gender, age, and IQ. They discovered deficits in planning, problem solving, visual perception, abstract thought, and social thought. Van Amelsvoort et al. (2004) found that individuals with VCFS and schizophrenia had "deficits in response inhibition, sustained attention and perceptual sensitivity" (p. 229) in comparison to participants without comorbid schizophrenia. Additionally, individuals with VCFS have been shown to have a higher prevalence of mental retardation (Eliez, Palacio-espasa, et al., 2000; Feinstein et al., 2002) than those without VCFS.

A common finding among children with VCFS is a statistically significant performance over verbal IQ discrepancy (Moss et al., 1999; Swillen et al., 1999). This finding has been used as evidence of a nonverbal learning disability among many individuals with VCFS (Swillen et al., 1999). This trend, however, does not appear to hold true for individuals with comorbid schizophrenia (van Amelsvoort et al., 2004).

Individuals with VCFS commonly experience language difficulties at a greater rate than those without VCFS (Feinstein, Eliez, Blasey, & Reiss, 2002; Moss et al., 1999; Shprintzen et al., 1978). Individuals with VCFS typically exhibit delayed language acquisition and difficulties in social interactions (Eliez, Palacio-Espasa, et al., 2000). Eliez, Palacio-Espasa, et al. discovered that children with VCFS tend to display deficits in initiating interactions with others. These children also displayed deficits in symbolic play (Eliez, Palacio-Espasa, et al.).

Several motor impairments are common to those with VCFS. Swillen et al. (1999) found that many children with VCFS displayed deficient psychomotor skills, which were more pronounced when asked to complete tasks requiring complex motor skills. Gross motor deficits were also found, with poorer performance in the left hand as opposed to the right.

Several behavioral and psychological impairments are associated with VCFS. Common behavioral problems include impulsivity, social withdrawal (Eliez, Palacio-Espasa, et al., 2000; Papolos et al., 1996), and attention problems (Eliez, Palacio-Espasa, et al.). Attention-Deficit/Hyperactivity Disorder is commonly found among individuals diagnosed with VCFS (Papolos et al.). Impairments of thought and mood include anxiety, flat affect (Papolos et al.), high rates of Obsessive-Compulsive Disorder, Bipolar Disorder (Papolos et al.), and schizophrenia (Murphy, Jones, & Owen, 1999).

Etiology of VCFS

VCFS is one of the few disorders with a relatively clear etiology; however, there is still a lot to be learned about the development of this disorder. VCFS is a congenital, dominant, autosomal condition (Eliez, Schmitt, et al., 2000). Scambler et al. (1992) discovered that the majority of patients with VCFS had a 22q11.2 chromosomal microdeletion. As a result, VCFS has more recently been termed 22q11.2 deletion syndrome (Scambler et al.). Because of this link, VCFS has been thought of as a prime disorder for studying the contribution of genetic factors to brain development across a lifespan (Eliez & Feinstein, 2004). The etiology of VCFS will be discussed in four categories: deletion, genes, enzymes, and brain structure.

Chromosomal microdeletion is thought to be a causal factor for VCFS. The genetic mutation thought to result in VCFS is linked to the twenty-second chromosome. The q11.2 region of chromosome 22 is thought to be "one of the most mutable regions in the entire human genome" (Antshel et al., 2005, p. 8). The deletion occurs during gametogenesis (Edelmann et al., 1999). Then a subsequent rearrangement occurs during synapsis (Antshel et al.). A series of homologous "DNA low copy repeats (LCR)" (Antshel et al., p. 9) exist in the normal break points for the proximal and distal ends of the deletion. As a result of these homologous LCRs, these regions may misalign, causing a distal LCR of one chromatid to align with the proximal LCR of the other chromatid. Consequently, one copy ends up with two 22q11.2 segments, and the other has none. Antshel et al. stated, "this type of interchromosomal recombination event resulting in a loss of 22q11.2 in the resulting sperm or egg is by far the most common mechanism for the deletion" (p. 9).

Alternately, an interchromosomal rearrangement may occur in which there is a repetition of the proximal LCR. This causes the 22q11.2 region to loop over itself, effectively splicing out information contained between the breaking points (Antshel et al., 2005). Antshel et al. estimated that this phenomenon occurs in 10 percent or less of all cases. Both methods result in the loss of some genetic material due to the deletion. The discussion that follows will be on specific deleted or affected genes that may be related to the symptomology of VCFS.

Several genes are thought to contribute to VCFS. Yamagishi, Garg, Matsuoka, Thomas, and Srivastava (1999) discovered that the UFD1L gene plays a major role in the prenatal development of the brain, palate, heart, and frontonasal regions. Because of its existence on the 22q11.2 section, the absence of this gene may account for many of the abnormalities in these areas. Abnormalities in brain structure associated with VCFS may also be related to the ES2 and GSCL genes, which have been shown to be involved in the embryogenesis of mice brains (Gottlieb et al., 1997).

Saito et al. (2001) looked into the SNAP29 gene that maps onto the 22q11 chromosome. The SNAP29 gene is thought to inhibit transmission in the superior cervical ganglion regions (Li et al., 2000); therefore, it is a possible contributor to the psychopathology experienced in individuals with 22q11 deletions. Saito et al. found that all individuals with 22q11 deletions with either bipolar disorder or schizoaffective disorder had 3 Mb deletions (which included the SNAP29 gene). Only one case of VCFS with schizophrenia had a 1.5 Mb deletion. Thus, the size of the 22q11 deletion and the SNAP29 gene may be a determining factor in the development of psychopathology in individuals with VCFS.

Several enzymes contribute to the development of VCFS. Individuals diagnosed with VCFS have been found to be homozygous for the catechol-o-methyltransferase gene (COMT; Lachman et al., 1996); therefore, individuals with VCFS have the least COMT enzyme activity of any identifiable group of people. Because COMT is important for neurotransmitter function, individuals with VCFS have been prime participants for study of the genetic basis of psychopathology (Carlson et al., 1997). The association between COMT activity and psychopathology is still unclear, due to contradictory findings in the research literature (Eliez & Feinstein, 2004); therefore, the role of COMT in the etiology of various mental disorders requires further study.

Brain structure abnormalities are also thought to cause VCFS. Research into the effects of microdeletion on these disorders provides some evidence of a direct link between the deletion site and specific psychological symptoms. E. W. C. Chow et al. (1999) argued that the majority of the brain structure abnormalities in VCFS are similar to those reported in patients with schizophrenia. Bassett and Chow (1999, p. 887), for example, argued that "a 22qDS subtype could serve as a neurodevelopmental model for schizophrenia." Brain abnormalities found in adults with schizophrenia and VCFS include "T2 weighted white matter bright foci (BF), 90 percent; developmental midline anomalies, 45 percent; cerebral atrophy or ventricular enlargement, 54 percent; mild cerebellar atrophy, 36 percent; skull base abnormalities, 55 percent; and minor vascular abnormalities, 36 percent" (Chow et al., p. 1436). The superior temporal gyrus abnormalities may be of particular interest in the study of schizophrenia because of its location at the auditory cortex (Pandya, 1995). Structural abnormalities in this part of the brain have been associated with reports of auditory hallucinations (Barta, Pearlson, Powers, Richards, & Tune, 1990).

Although some research shows a link between VCFS and a diagnosis of schizophrenia, other research questions if the link is direct, or if the strength of this link is misleading. Papolos et al. (1996) argued that most cases are better classified as Bipolar Disorder, with some cases fitting the criteria for Schizoaffective Disorder. Feinstein et al. (2002) argued that because of the high prevalence of psychopathology in other individuals with learning disabilities, mental retardation, or developmental language disorders, it is unclear whether the high rates of psychopathology in persons with VCFS are caused by these factors or directly from VCFS. In their prospective study of children and adolescents, Feinstein et al. compared differences in the rates of psychopathology between individuals with VCFS and individuals with developmental delays and mental retardation. They found no statistically significant differences between groups.

Detection and Assessment of VCFS

Because of the specific chromosomal deletion associated with VCFS, the presence of this disorder can be tested for at infancy (Eliez & Feinstein, 2004). One of the more common methods to determine the presence of VCFS is to look for the 22q11.2 deletion through the Fluorescent In Situ Hybridization (FISH) method (Eliez, Palacio-Espasa, et al., 2000). The FISH method has been termed "the gold standard for diagnosis of VCFS" (L. Y. Chow, Garcia-Barcelo, Wing, & Waye, 1999, p. 761). It should be noted that VCFS is just one of several phenotypes associated with 22q11 deletion syndrome.

Although the FISH method is accurate in diagnosing VCFS, it may be impractical to have every newborn undergo this scrutiny. A more practical course uses the FISH method to screen for VCFS in individuals with behavioral and physical manifestations associated with VCFS (Gothelf et al., 1999). Swillen et al. (1999) stated that speech problems and/or cardiac abnormalities typically spur professionals to look for a 22q11.2 deletion. Because of the widespread acceptance of the FISH method, some studies only include those diagnosed with this method, "to increase diagnostic certainty" (Feinstein et al., 2002, p. 313).

One way to detect VCFS is to notice developmental delay. Developmental delay is commonly associated with VCFS. Shprintzen (2000) argued that because the common facial features of individuals with VCFS are not markedly abnormal, and many of its manifestations are behavioral (not present at birth), many individuals are not diagnosed in childhood. Developmental delays have been noted to lead professionals to refer individuals for assessment for VCFS; however, developmental delays may be attributed to other health problems typical of those with VCFS, delaying the detection of VCFS (Antshel et al., 2005). Eliez, Palacio-Espasa, et al. (2000) suggest that because of the common developmental problems in language development and tendency for social withdrawal, children assessed for VCFS should also be evaluated for autism.

VCFS may be detected by observing that an individual has learning difficulties. Because of the prevalence of learning difficulties in individuals with VCFS, individuals with learning disabilities who have additional VCFS symptoms should be assessed for VCFS. At two hospitals for individuals with learning disabilities, Murphy et al. (1998) looked for patients with VCFS. They looked for individuals who also had a psychotic disorder, family history of a psychotic disorder, stereotypical facial malformations, or congenital heart disease. Out of 265 patients, they selected 74 for testing using this criteria. Of the 74 patients selected, 22 were found to have a 22q11 deletion.

A diagnosis of schizophrenia is another factor that could be used to detect VCFS. High numbers of individuals with VCFS develop schizophrenia. Some individuals with schizophrenia may have other symptoms that make them good candidates for VCFS screening. Karayiorgou et al. (1995) looked for the presence of a 22q11.2 deletion in a random sample of patients with schizophrenia. Out of that sample, they found two individuals with VCFS, representing a substantially higher prevalence than in the larger population. Gothelf et al. (1997) selected individuals with schizophrenia, palate abnormalities, and heart defects for assessment for microdeletions. Of the 20 patients with schizophrenia, they found 3 had VCFS. A similar study was conducted with 15 adults with schizophrenia who were selected for testing based on possessing two of the five qualifying criteria. Of these 15, 10 tested positive for VCFS (Bassett & Chow, 1999).

Developmental Course of VCFS

The developmental course of individuals with VCFS has been well documented. At birth, many infants with VCFS experience failure to thrive (74 percent), heart malformations (76 percent), and lower respiratory problems (65 percent; Shprintzen, 2000). Scherer, D'Antonio, and Kalbfleisch (1999) found that, as toddlers, developmental delays can be seen in individuals with a 22q11.2 deletion. They also stated that physical abnormalities, such as a cleft lip and palate, can also be seen at this age. Most toddlers with VCFS experience delays in receptive and expressive language, and mild delays in gross motor ability (Gerdes et al., 1999; Golding-Kushner, Weller, Shprintzen, 1985; Swillen et al., 1999). Eliez, Palacio-Espasa, et al. (2000, p. 112) studied four children with VCFS under the age of 5 and found "marked delay in motor development, a delay in language acquisition, intellectual functioning in the mentally retarded to borderline range in three out of four subjects, and attention difficulties." They also found "deficits in initiating relationships and in symbolic play . . . [and] a trend toward interruption in their train of thought" (p. 112). Scherer et al. (1999) found that the IQs of toddler to preschool children with VCFS ranged from mild/moderate mentally retarded to near average range.

During middle childhood, children with VCFS experience marked improvements in some aspects of their development. They often improve in language, reading of words, spelling, and speech (Golding-Kushner et al., 1985); however, difficulties with language formulation, understanding verbal abstractions, higher-order comprehension (Golding-Kushner et al.), and vocabulary (Gerdes et al., 1999) tend to persist. Eliez and Feinstein (2004, p. 124) stated that "speech almost invariably remains hypernasal." In middle childhood, 94 percent of individuals with VCFS showed evidence of a learning disability or mental retardation (Cohen, Chow, Weksberg, & Bassett, 1999). In their review of literature, Eliez and Feinstein (2004) concluded that there was no prospective data on the developmental outcomes of individuals with VCFS into adulthood.

Individuals with VCFS are more likely to develop psychological impairments. The first psychological impairments associated with children known to have VCFS are separation or generalized anxiety (Shprintzen, 2000). Usiskin et al. (1999) reported that children with VCFS account for 6.4 percent of all cases of childhood-onset schizophrenia. Approximately 64 percent of children and adolescents have been found to meet the criteria for bipolar disorder (Papolos et al., 1996). This trend appears to only increase into adulthood. Shprintzen, Goldberg, Golding-Kushner, and Marion (1992) found that approximately 20–30 percent of individuals with VCFS over 16 years old also received a

diagnosis of schizophrenia. Murphy et al. (1999) discovered that 30 percent of their sample of 50 adults with VCFS had a psychotic disorder.

Individuals with VCFS are more likely to develop brain structure abnormalities. Eliez and Feinstein (2004) stated that:

> A review of most of the available neuroimaging studies of children with VCFS would suggest that there is an early alteration of the parietal lobe and cerebellum, and that the decrease of temporal lobe gray matter and hippocampus can be observed only in adults. (p. 130)

Alterations of white matter are thought to "be due to delays in myelin development, disturbances in organization or density of axons within the cerebral cortex, or alterations in the cellular structure of white matter" (Antshel et al., 2005, p. 11). Glaser et al. (2002) argued that individuals with an inherited 22q11.2 microdeletion from their mothers have an accelerated loss in gray matter. This accelerated loss leads to significantly less overall gray matter volume and subsequent cognitive impairments (Glaser et al.). Because of the decrease in gray matter with age, Chow, Zipursky, Mikulis, and Bassett (2002, p. 212) stated that individuals with VCFS may follow "an abnormal or deteriorating neurodevelopmental course."

Interventions Used to Treat VCFS

Little is written on the treatment of individuals with VCFS; however, some guidelines can be drawn based on what is known about this disorder from the research literature. Compton (2004) suggested that individuals with high susceptibility for schizophrenia should be considered for preventative interventions. Gladston and Clarke (2005) suggested the use of clozapine to treat psychotic symptoms that may be a result of VCFS. Gothelf et al. (1999) discovered that a sample of individuals with VCFS who also had psychosis did not respond well to neuroleptic drugs; however, two of their patients showed a reduction of psychotic symptoms with clozapine. Based on these findings, they suggested the use of clozapine for other individuals with VCFS and psychosis. Because of the learning and speech difficulties associated with VCFS, those with this disorder may benefit from academic remediation services and speech therapy. Because of Golding-Kushner et al.'s (1985) findings that individuals with VCFS have difficulties with higher-order thinking, including the use of abstractions, these individuals may respond best to clear directions that use concrete examples.

VCFS is the most common microdeletion syndrome. This disorder has many physical and behavioral manifestations, including specific facial features, cardiac abnormalities, learning difficulties, and speech problems. VCFS is almost always caused by a 22q11.2 deletion. Because of the clear etiology of this disorder, VCFS has served as a model to understand other disorders, such as nonverbal learning disabilities and schizophrenia. VCFS can be detected through the FISH method, with priority in screening given to individuals with developmental delays, learning difficulties, or schizophrenia. Many studies have provided information on the developmental course of VCFS; however, few studies have given information on the effects of VCFS through adulthood. Because of the lack of research on treatment, more studies need to be conducted to disseminate knowledge of how to best help individuals with this disorder.

REFERENCES

Antshel, K. M., Kates, W. R., Roizen, N., Fremont, W., & Shprintzen, R. J. (2005). 22q11.2 deletion syndrome: Genetics, neuroanatomy and cognitive/behavioral features. *Child Neuropsychology, 11,* 5–19.

Barta, P. E., Pearlson, G. D., Powers, R. E., Richards, S. S., & Tune, L. E. (1990). Auditory hallucinations and smaller superior temporal gyral volume in schizophrenia. *American Journal of Psychiatry, 147,* 1457–1462.

Bassett, A. S., & Chow, E. W. C. (1999). 22q11 deletion syndrome: A genetic subtype of schizophrenia. *Biological Psychiatry, 46,* 882–891.

Bingham, P. M., Zimmerman, R. A., McDonald-McGinn, D., Driscoll, D., Emanuel, B. S., & Zackai, E. (1997). Enlarged Sylvian fissures in infants with interstitial deletion of chromosome 22q11. *American Journal of Medical Genetics (Neuropsychiatric Genetics), 74,* 538–543.

Carlson, C., Papolos, D., Pandita, R. K., Faedda, G. L., Veit, S., Goldberg, R., et al. (1997). Molecular analysis of velo-cardio-facial syndrome patients with psychiatric disorders. *American Journal of Human Genetics, 60,* 851–859.

Chow, E. W. C., Mikulis, D. J., Zipursky, R. B., Scutt, L. E., Weksberg, R., & Bassett, A. S. (1999). Qualitative MRI findings in adults with 22q11 deletion syndrome and schizophrenia. *Biological Psychiatry, 46,* 1436–1442.

Chow, E. W. C., Zipursky, R. B., Mikulis, D. J., & Bassett, A. S. (2002). Structural brain abnormalities in patients with schizophrenia and 22q11 deletion syndrome. *Biological Psychiatry, 51,* 208–215.

Chow, L. Y., Garcia-Barcelo, M., Wing, Y. K., & Waye, M. M. Y. (1999). Schizophrenia and hypocalcaemia: Variable phenotype of deletion at chromosome 22q11. *Australian and New Zealand Journal of Psychiatry, 33,* 760–762.

Cohen, E., Chow, E. W. C., Weksberg, R., & Bassett, A. S. (1999). Phenotype of adults with the 22q11 deletion syndrome: A review. *American Journal of Medical Genetics, 86,* 359–365.

Compton, M. T. (2004). Considering schizophrenia from a prevention perspective. *American Journal of Preventative Medicine, 26,* 178–185.

Edelmann, L., Pandita, R. K., Spiteri, E., Funke, B, Goldberg, R., Palanisamy, N., et al. (1999). A common molecular basis for rearrangement disorders on chromosome 22q11. *Human Molecular Genetics, 8,* 1157–1167.

Eliez, S., Barnea-Goraly, N., Schmitt, J. E., Liu, Y., & Reiss, A. L. (2002). Increased basal ganglia volumes in velo-cardio-facial syndrome (deletion 22q11.2). *Biological Psychiatry, 52,* 68–70.

Eliez, S., Blasely, C. M., Schmitt, E. J., White, C. D., Hu, D., & Reiss, A. L. (2001). Velocardiofacial syndrome: Are structural changes in the temporal and mesial temporal regions related to schizophrenia? *American Journal of Psychiatry, 158,* 447–453.

Eliez, S., & Feinstein, C. (2004). Velo-cardio-facial syndrome (deletion 22q11.2): A homogeneous neurodevelopmental model for schizophrenia. In M. S. Keshavan, J. L. Kennedy, & R. M. Murray (Eds.), *Neurodevelopment and schizophrenia* (pp. 121–137). New York: Cambridge University Press.

Eliez, S., Palacio-Espasa, F., Spira, A., Lacroix, M., Pont, C., Luthi, F., et al. (2000). Young children with velo-cardio-facial syndrome (CATCH-22). Psychological and language phenotypes. *European Child & Adolescent Psychology, 9,* 109–114.

Eliez, S., Schmitt, J. E., White, C. D., & Reiss, A. L. (2000). Children and adolescents with velocardiofacial syndrome: A volumetric MRI study. *American Journal of Psychiatry, 157,* 409–415.

Feinstein, C., Eliez, S., Blasey, C., & Reiss, A. L. (2002). Psychiatric disorders and behavioral problems in children with velocardiofacial syndrome: Usefulness as phenotypic indicators of schizophrenia risk. *Biological Psychiatry, 51,* 312–318.

Gerdes, M., Solot, C., Wang, P. P., Moss, E., LaRossa, D., Randall, P., et al. (1999). Cognitive and behavior profile of preschool children with chromosome 22q11.2 deletion. *American Journal of Medical Genetics, 85,* 127–133.

Gladston, S., & Clarke, D. J. (2005). Clozapine treatment of psychosis associated with velo-cardio-facial syndrome: Benefits and risks. *Journal of Intellectual Disability Research, 49,* 567–570.

Glaser, B., Mumme, D. L., Blasey, C., Morris, M. A., Dahoun, S. P., Antonarakis, S. E., et al. (2002). Language skills in children with velocardiofacial syndrome (deletion 22q11.2). *Journal of Pediatrics, 140,* 753–758.

Golding-Kushner, K. J., Weller, G., & Shprintzen, R. J. (1985). Velo-cardio-facial syndrome: Language and psychological profiles. *Journal of Craniofacial Genetics and Developmental Biology, 5,* 259–266.

Gothelf, D., Frisch, A., Munitz, H., Rockah, R., Aviram, A., Mozes, T., et al. (1997). Velocardiofacial manifestations and microdeletions in schizophrenic inpatients. *American Journal of Medical Genetics, 72,* 455–461.

Gothelf, D., Frisch, A., Munitz, H., Rockah, R., Laufer, N., Mozes, T., et al. (1999). Clinical characteristics of schizophrenia associated with velo-cardio-facial syndrome. *Schizophrenia Research, 35,* 105–112.

Gottlieb, S., Emanuel, B. S., Driscoll, D. A., Sellinger, B., Wang, Z., Roe, B., et al. (1997). The DiGeorge syndrome minimal critical region contains a *goosecoid*-like (GSCL) homeobox gene that is expressed early in human development. *American Journal of Human Genetics, 60,* 1194–1201.

Henry, J. C., van Amelsvoort, T., Morris, R. G., Owen, M. J., Murphy, D. G. M., & Murphy, K. C. (2002). An investigation of the neuropsychological profile in adults with velo-cardio-facial-syndrome (VCFS). *Neuropsychologia, 40,* 471–478.

Karayiorgou, M., Morris, M. A., Morrow, B., Shprintzen, R. J., Goldberg, R., Borrow, J., et al. (1995). Schizophrenia susceptibility associated with interstitial deletions of chromosome 22q11. *Proceedings of the National Academy of Sciences in the USA, 92,* 7612–7616.

Kates, W. R., Burnette, C. P., Jabs, E. W., Rutberg, J., Murphy, A. M., Grados, M., et al. (2001). Regional cortical white matter reductions in velocardiofacial syndrome: A volumetric MRI analysis. *Biological Psychiatry, 49,* 677–684.

Lachman, H. M., Morrow, B., Shprintzen, R., Veit, S., Parsia, S. S., Faedda, G., et al. (1996). Association of codon 108/158 catechol-o-methyltransferase gene polymorphism with the psychiatric manifestations of velo-cardio-facial syndrome. *American Journal of Medical Genetics (Neuropsychiatric Genetics), 67,* 468–472.

Li, T., Ball, D., Zhao, J., Murray, R. M., Liu, X., Sham, P. C., et al. (2000). Family-based linkage disequilibrium mapping using SNP marker haplotypes: Application to a potential locus for schizophrenia at chromosome 22q11. *Molecular Psychiatry, 5,* 77–84.

Moss, E. M., Batshaw, M. L., Solot, C. B., Gerdes, M., McDonald-McGinn, D. M., Driscoll, D. A., et al. (1999). Psychoeducational profile of the 22q11.2 microdeletion: A complex pattern. *Journal of Pediatrics, 134,* 193–198.

Murphy, K. C., Jones, L. A., Owen, M. J. (1999). High rates of schizophrenia in adults with velo-cardio-facial syndrome. *Archives of General Psychiatry, 56,* 940–945.

Murphy, K. C., Jones, R. G., Griffiths, E., Thompson, P. W., & Owen, M. J. (1998). Chromosome 22q11 deletions: An under-recognized cause of idiopathic learning disability. *British Journal of Psychiatry, 172,* 180–183.

Pandya, D. N. (1995). Anatomy of the auditory cortex. *Revue Neurologique, 151,* 486–494.

Papolos, D. F., Faedda, G. L., Veit, S., Goldberg, R., Morrow, B., Kucherlapati, R., et al. (1996). Bipolar spectrum disorders in patients diagnosed with velo-cardio-facial syndrome: Does a hemizygous deletion of chromosome 22q11 result in bipolar affective disorder? *American Journal of Psychiatry, 153,* 1541–1547.

Pulver, A. E., Karayiorgou, M., Wolyniec, P. S., Lasseter, V. K., Kasch, L., Nestadt, G., et al. (1994). Sequential strategy to identify a susceptibility gene for schizophrenia: Report of potential linkage on chromosome 22q12–q13.1: Part 1. *American Journal of Medical Genetics (Neuropsychiatric Genetics), 54,* 36–43.

Saito, T., Guan, F., Papolos, D. F., Rajouria, N., Fann, C. S. J., & Lachman, H. M. (2001). Polymorphism in SNAP29 gene promoter region associated with schizophrenia. *Molecular Psychiatry, 6,* 193–201.

Scambler, P. J., Kelly, D., Lindsay, E., Williamson, R., Goldberg, R., Shprintzen, R., et al. (1992). Velo-cardio-facial syndrome associated with chromosome 22 deletions encompassing the DiGeorge locus. *The Lancet, 339,* 1138–1139.

Scherer, N. J., D'Antonio, L. L., & Kalbfleisch, J. H. (1999). Early speech and language development in children with velocardiofacial syndrome. *American Journal of Medical Genetics (Neuropsychiatric Genetics), 88,* 714–723.

Sedláčková, E. (1967). The syndrome of the congenitally shortened velum: The dual innervation of the soft palate. *Folia Phoniatrica, 19,* 441–450.

Shprintzen, R. J. (2000). Velo-cardio-facial syndrome: A distinctive behavioral phenotype. *Mental Retardation and Developmental Disabilities, 6,* 142–147.

Shprintzen, R. J., Goldberg, R., Golding-Kushner, K. J., & Marion, R. W. (1992). Late-onset psychosis in the velo-cardio-facial syndrome. *American Journal of Medical Genetics, 42,* 141–142.

Shprintzen, R. J., Goldberg, R. B., Lewin, M. L., Sidoti, E. J., Berkman, M. D., Argamaso, R. V., et al. (1978). A new syndrome involving cleft palate, cardiac anomalies, typical facies, and learning disabilities: Velo-Cardio-Facial Syndrome. *Cleft Palate Journal, 15,* 56–62.

Swillen, A., Vandeputte, L., Cracco, J., Maes, B., Ghesquière, P., Devriendt, K., et al. (1999). Neuropsychological, learning and psychosocial profile of primary school aged children with the velo-cardio-facial syndrome (22q11 deletion): Evidence for a nonverbal learning disability? *Child Neuropsychology, 5,* 230–241.

Tézenas Du Montcel, S., Mendizabal, H., Aymé, S., Lévy, A., & Philip, N. (1996). Prevalence of 22q11 microdeletion. *Journal of Medical Genetics, 33,* 719.

Usiskin, S. I., Nicholson, R., Krasnewich, D. M., Yah, W., Lenane, M., Wudarsky, M., et al. (1999). Velocardiofacial syndrome in childhood-onset schizophrenia. *Journal of the American Academy of Child & Adolescent Psychiatry, 38,* 1536–1543.

van Amelsvoort, T., Henry, J., Morris, R., Owen, M., Linszen, D., Murphy, K., et al. (2004). Cognitive deficits associated with schizophrenia in velo-cardio-facial syndrome. *Schizophrenia Research, 70,* 223–232.

Yamagishi, H., Garg, V., Matsuoka, R., Thomas, T., & Srivastava, D. (1999). A molecular pathway revealing a genetic basis for human cardiac and craniofacial defects. *Science, 283,* 1158–1161.

GORDON D. LAMB
Texas A&M University

VELOPHARYNGEAL INADEQUACY

Velopharyngeal inadequacy (VPI) is an inclusive term which refers to deficiencies in structure or function of the velopharyngeal mechanism. Such deficiencies result in loss of control of nasal resonance in speech. This can significantly affect intelligibility and may also cause swallowing dysfunction. The velopharyngeal mechanism includes the velum (soft palate) and posterior and lateral walls of the uppermost portion of the pharynx. The role of the velopharyngeal mechanism is to perform a sphincter-like maneuver which can disconnect the upper airway (nasopharynx and nasal cavities) from the vocal tract by forming a tight seal. The sphincter can also relax to allow the free flow of air or sound into the nasal area. This action produces the differentiation of oral speech sounds such as the vowels and most consonants from nasal sounds such as n, m, and -ing in English. Another commonly used generic term is velopharyngeal dysfunction (VPD).

One problem area subsumed under VPI is anatomical

structure anomalies, termed velopharyngeal insufficiency. In this case, there may be a lack of tissue in the velum which means it is too small to make contact with the posterior pharyngeal wall, thus compromising the seal necessary for disconnecting the nasal area. Another structural problem may involve interference from or loss of tonsilar tissue. Large palatine tonsils can obstruct the movements of the velum or lateral pharyngeal walls. In addition, pharyngeal tonsils (adenoids) can temporarily reduce the distance to be covered by velar elevation and their disappearance, due to surgery or maturation, may reveal a latent velar insufficiency. Finally, oral surgery techniques used to correct craniofacial deficiencies (e.g., maxillary advancement) may increase the diameter of the velopharyngeal portal beyond the capability of the existing velopharyngeal mechanism.

VPI also encompasses the term velopharyngeal incompetence. This term describes physiological dysfunction affecting movement of the velum or pharyngeal walls. The muscle fibers in these structures can be misdirected so that appropriate movement, such as medial motion in the lateral pharyngeal walls or elevation of the velum, is impossible. Muscle pairs may be asymmetric or asynchronous in their contraction response. Nervous supply to the muscles may be deficit, resulting in paralysis or paresis (weakness).

Velopharyngeal inadequacy can also describe the mislearning of the nasal/oral balance of specific speech sounds that occurs in the presence of hearing impairment and deafness. In addition, idiosyncratic phonological development or dialectical differences can also produce nonstandard nasal resonance patterns during speech.

Differential diagnosis of this condition involves perceptual and acoustic analysis of speech, examination of oral motor structures and functions and visualization of the velopharyngeal mechanism using videofluoroscopy and/or endoscopy. VPI can be reduced or corrected with surgical or behavioral intervention. Determination of the best treatment options for an individual can best be made by consulting a Cleft Palate Team that includes surgical and speech-language pathology professionals.

REFERENCES

Johnson, A. F., & Jacobson, B. H. (Eds.). (1998). *Medical speech-language pathology: A practitioner's guide.* New York: Thieme.

Shprintzen, R. J., & Bardach, J. (1995). *Cleft palate speech management: A multidisciplinary approach.* St. Louis, MO: Mosby.

STAFF

VENEZUELA, SPECIAL EDUCATION IN

Venezuela's 25 million inhabitants, 60 percent of whom are younger than 29, are largely urban and located in the densely populated northern coastal region. Despite its rich natural and economic resources, poverty among its people continues to increase. In 2003, 61 percent of its population was considered to be impoverished. In 2001, 907,694 Venezuelans, 3.7 percent of its population, had special educational needs (Instituto Nacional de Estadística, 2003).

Special education began in 1930 as a private philanthropic initiative. In the 1950s a medical model was employed that focused on deficiencies and provided rehabilitation services. In 1973, the Department of Exceptionality within the Education Ministry was founded. In 1975 the Special Education Office was created to assume responsibility for designing, supervising, evaluating, controlling, and providing follow-up services consistent with national policy. Each of the country's 23 states has its own Department of Special Education responsible for implementing national policies. In turn, local schools and agencies are responsible for implementing state policies.

In 1994, a political reorientation process began, one designed to promote the principle of equality of educational conditions and opportunities for all and to promote a comprehensive educational model for people with special needs in light of their individual needs (Cumbre Mundial de la Infancia, 1990). In 1999, this process was incorporated within the National Constitution (Artículo 81, Constitución de la República Bolivariana de Venezuela, 1999).

Special education is a branch of the country's educational system (Ley Orgánica de Educación, 1980) that is guided by the principles and purposes that govern regular education while maintaining an interdependent relationship with regular education. Special education is organized by age groups: ages 0 through 5, 6 through 15, and above 15 (Acuerdo de Santiago, 1996; Ministerio de Educación, Cultura y Deportes, 2003).

Since 1997, the Educational Comprehensive Attention Model has guided special education services. The needs of people with special educational needs are reviewed using a holistic model that considers an individual's strengths and weaknesses in light of biological, psychological, and social qualities. Interdisciplinary professional teams are responsible for providing special programs for persons from conception through adulthood. Strategic special education policies are the provision of comprehensive educational attention (in schools and special education services) and the promotion of educational mainstreaming of children with special needs within the regular education system and other branches of the education system.

Attempts are made to serve persons who are classified as displaying mental retardation (through institutes of special education), hearing and visual deficiencies (through special education units), physical impairments (through rehabilitation and hospital units), learning disabilities (through learning disabilities centers, psychoeducational units, and integrated classrooms), and autism (through centers for persons with autism; Universidad Pedagógica Experimental Libertador, 1998; Ministerio de Educación, Cultura y Deportes, 2001). Various support programs exist, including prevention and early identification (through centers of child development), language (through centers for language rehabilitation), education and work (through labor educational workshops), and social integration (through social integration programs in regular schools).

Conditions in Venezuela have prevented the attainment of its special education goals. Some examples follow. Mainstreaming and integration have not been widely implemented. Few people with special education needs are served. For example, during the 2002–2003 school year, 11 percent of the population with special education needs received services (101,577 out of 907,694): 0.09 percent of those presented with autism ($n = 888$), 0.48 percent with hearing deficiencies ($n = 4,432$), 0.17 percent with visual deficiencies ($n = 1,587$), 6.72 percent with learning disabilities ($n = 61,060$), 0.14 percent with physical impairments ($n = 1,322$), 0.12 percent with cerebral palsy ($n = 1,111$), 1.89 percent with mental retardation ($n = 1\,7,190$), 0.33 percent with language disorders ($n = 2,999$), 0.03 percent who are talented and gifted ($n = 329$), and 1.09 percent considered to be at risk ($n = 9,969$; Ministerio de Educación, 2004). Little is known about the quality of special education services. Efforts are needed to coordinate regular and special education curriculum. Undergraduate teacher education programs need to focus on preparing special educators (Duran & Montenegro, 2000), and other training programs are needed to prepare human resource personnel (Moreno, 2003). Efforts to obtain a stronger commitment from society to implement prevention programs and to enable families, schools, and the community to access needed services are needed.

Venezuela is making some progress in its efforts to improve special education resources. Some examples follow. The importance of special education is receiving more public attention and support. There seems to be a growing recognition as to the importance of adapting a holistic, biopsychosocial vision of each person that considers his or her strengths and limitations (Article 81, Constitución de la República Bolivariana de Venezuela, 1999; Article 22, Ley Orgánica para la Protección del Niño y del Adolescente, 2000). During the 1998 Social Development Summit held in Lima, Peru, Venezuela reported having accomplished its beginning goals of promoting integrated education (Oficina Central de Coordinación y Planificación-Cordiplan, 1998) albeit with limited national coverage. Venezuela has participated in international summits and meetings that addressed equal opportunities and respect for diversity.

Some research projects have begun in an attempt to promote integrative, sequential, and interdisciplinary policies (León, 2003). These projects also may help promote social integration and social and personal accomplishments in accord with the potential of each child, adolescent, or adult with special educational needs. There is growing support for eliminating the duality between regular and special education national programs.

REFERENCES

Acuerdo de Santiago. (1996). *Seguimiento de las Metas de la Infancia.* Santiago, Chile: UNICEF.

Campagnaro, S. (1999). La integración o inclusión. Nueva modalidad educativa para eliminar el dualismo entre educación especial y educación regular. *Cuaderno de Educación, 2,* 119–125.

Constitución de la República de Bolivariana de Venezuela. (1999). Artículo 81.

Duran, M., & Montenegro, L. (2000). El docente venezolano de aula regular de cara al nuevo milenio y su formación en el área de educación especial. In T. Shea & A. Bauer (Eds.), *Educación Especial- un enfoque ecológico.* Mexico City, México: McGraw Hill.

Instituto Nacional de Estadística. (INE). (2003). *Censo 2001.* Caracas, Venezuela: Author

Ley Orgánica de Educación. (1980). Gaceta Oficial de la República de Venezuela No. 2.635. Julio 9.

Ley Orgánica para la Protección del Niño y del Adolescente. (2000). Gaceta Oficial de la República de Venezuela No. 5.266. Octubre 2.

León, C. (2003). *Estudio descriptivo comparativo y relacional del Desarrollo Infantil Integral en una muestra de niñas y niños de diferentes edades, niveles socioeconómicos y regiones del país.* Unpublished PhD dissertation. Universidad Católica Andrés Bello, Caracas, Venezuela.

Ministerio de Educación. (1997). *Jornadas de Reorientación Político Conceptual de la Modalidad de Educación Especial.* Caracas, Venezuela: noviembre.

Ministerio de Educación, Cultura y Deportes. (2001). *Guía técnica y pedagógica de la modalidad educación especial para el curso 2001–2002.* Dirección de Educación Especial.

Ministerio de Educación, Cultura y Deportes. (2003). *El Currículum de las Personas con Necesidades Educativas Especiales.* Presentado en la Jornada de Trabajo para la organización de la discusión curricular del año escolar 2002–2003.

Ministerio de Educación y Deportes. (2004). *Memoria y Cuenta 2003.* V. CXXVIII–No. CXXIV. Caracas, Venezuela.

Moreno, Marianela. (2003). *Informe de Investigación sobre Personal en Servicio de la Modalidad de Educación Especial.* Entregado en la Dirección de Educación Especial del Ministerio de Educación, Cultura y Deportes. Caracas, Venezuela, Noviembre.

Nuñez, Beatriz. (1999). *Conceptualización y Política de la Modalidad de Educación Especial en Venezuela. Dirección de Educación Especial.* Ministerio de Educación, Trabajo presentado en el Simposio Los Paradigmas que orientan las políticas de Educación Especial en el III Congreso Iberoamericano de Educación Especial, Foz de Iguazú, Brasil, Noviembre.

Oficina Central de Coordinación y Planificación—Cordiplan. (1998). República de Venezuela: *Informe País para la Cumbre Mundial de Desarrollo Social de Lima,* Perú.

Ordenanza para la educación, el desarrollo e integración de personas con discapacidad. Gaceta Municipal. República Bolivariana de Venezuela. Estado Miranda. Municipio Baruta. 2 de Octubre de 2001.

Reglamento de la Ley Orgánica de Educación, Gaceta Oficial de la Republica Bolivariana de Venezuela No. 36.787. 15 de Septiembre de 1999.

Universidad Pedagógica Experimental Libertador (UPEL). (1998). *Conceptualización y política de la atención educativa de las personas con necesidades especiales.* Serie Publicaciones Interinstitucionales, Caracas. Fundación UPEL-IMPM. UPEL.

UNESCO. (1999). *Informe Final III Reunión Regional de Directores de Educación Especial, I Reunión Regional de los Consejos Nacionales de Discapacidad. Foz de Iguazú* (Brasil), 2 al 4 de noviembre 1999.

CARMEN LEÓN
MARIANELA MORENO
LOURDES MONTENEGRO
*Andrés Bello Catholic University
Caracas, Venezuela*

VERBAL DEFICIENCY

Verbal deficiency is a term with multifaceted meaning in the field of special education. It refers to the use and understanding of language and indicates abilities that are either deficient in terms of an individual's overall level of functioning or clearly below the norm for individuals of a certain age. Frequently, verbal deficiency is diagnosed when a child's verbal IQ on an individually administered intelligence measure such as the Wechsler Intelligence Scale for Children–III, is significantly lower than performance IQ (Kaufman, 1994). Verbal deficiency is also inferred from a child's relative difficulty on those portions of group administered standardized achievement tests that rely heavily on verbal skills. Parents and educators often note that a child's verbal skills are not age appropriate. A child may exhibit difficulty in following directions given orally or comprehending information presented orally. The child also may have difficulty with verbal expression. Language arts skills such as reading, composition, and spelling may be impaired. Speech pathologists working with children may use the term verbal deficiency when referring to subnormal development of language structures, verbal fluency, and knowledge of vocabulary. A verbal deficiency may have roots and causes that are primarily medical. Hearing impairment, especially if mild, can be an undetected cause of verbal deficiency. A history of chronic otitis media (middle ear inflammation) and resulting intermittent hearing loss can be a factor as well. Neurological impairment can result in deficiencies in verbal skills while leaving other areas of functioning relatively intact. Although developmentally disabled children often show depressed functioning in all areas, this possible cause must be considered when a child

presents with verbal deficiency. It is sometimes possible to infer through evaluation and testing specific developmental difficulties that lead to verbal deficiency. These include expressive or receptive language deficiencies or a central auditory processing disorder. A learning disability (as defined by failure to learn at a normal rate despite average intellectual ability) in the language arts area also can be associated with a verbal deficiency.

Emotional factors also must be considered in understanding the concept of verbal deficiency in children. Physical or emotional abuse in the home as well as specific emotional disorders can affect the development of verbal skills. Sociocultural factors, some more readily apparent than others, may also play a role in the development of verbal deficiency. Manni, Winikur, and Keller (1984) provide discussion on this topic. English may not be the child's native language and may not be spoken in the home at all. Different dialects of the English language may be spoken at home. Educational level of the adult in the home, as well as the amount of time spent with the child on verbal tasks, may affect verbal development. Chronic school absenteeism, for medical or other reasons, can result in verbal deficiency. In conclusion, a single or combination of causes may be present when a child presents with a verbal deficiency, and Sattler (1982) and Kaufman (1979, 1994) provide a more detailed discussion of the nature and causes for such.

REFERENCES

Kaufman, A. S. (1979). WISC-R research: Implications for interpretation. *School Psychology Digest, 8,* 5–27.

Kaufman, A. S. (1994). *Intelligent testing with the WISC-III.* New York: Wiley.

Manni, J. L., Winikur, D. W., & Keller, M. R. (1984). *Intelligence, mental retardation, and the culturally different child.* Springfield, IL: Thomas.

Sattler, J. M. (1982). *Assessment of children's intelligence and special abilities* (2nd ed.). Boston: Allyn & Bacon.

MELANIE L. BROMLEY
*California State University, San
Bernardino*

EXPRESSIVE LANGUAGE DISORDERS
RECEPTIVE LANGUAGE DISORDERS

VERBALISMS

Verbalisms is a term coined by Cutsforth (1932) to describe the use of words by the blind that represent terms or concepts with which the blind could not have had first-hand experience. Color words are one example. Blind children learn quickly that sighted individuals refer to green grass, blue sky, and a bright orange sun and use such terms freely in their own language although they never experience these colors. The development of verbalisms is important to the mastery of language and communication by the blind; however, the blind should also be encouraged not to rely exclusively on verbal learning.

REFERENCE

Cutsforth, T. D. (1932). The unreality of words to the blind. *Teachers Forum, 4*, 86–89.

CECIL R. REYNOLDS
Texas A&M University

BLIND

Flanagan, D. P., McGrew, K. S., & Ortiz, S. O. (1999). *The Wechsler Intelligence Scales and Gf-Gc Theory: A contemporary approach to interpretation.* Boston: Allyn & Bacon.

Hess, A. K. (2001). *Review of Wechsler Adult Intelligence Scale, Third Edition (WAIS-III).* Mental Measurements Yearbook (14th ed.) (Electronic Version).

Kaufman, A. S., & Lichtenberger, E. O. (1999). *Essentials of WISC-III and WPPSI-R assessment.* New York: Wiley.

The Psychological Corporation. (1997). *WAIS-III—WMS-III technical manual.* San Antonio: Author.

Tulsky, D. S., & Ledbetter, M. F. (2000). Updating the WAIS-III and WMS-III: Considerations for research and clinical practice. *Psychological Assessment, 12*(3), 253–262.

KATHLEEN PELHAM-ODOR
California State University, San Bernardino

VERBAL SCALE IQ

The verbal scale IQ is a standard score (with mean of 100 and a standard deviation of 15) derived from a combination of six subtests that comprise the verbal scale of the Wechsler Intelligence Scales. Every subtest on the verbal scale requires that the examinee listen to an auditorily presented verbal stimulus and respond verbally. The verbal scale IQ is a measure of general verbal skills, such as verbal fluency, ability to understand and use verbal reasoning, and verbal knowledge. It is based on both formal and informal educational opportunities, and requires understanding words, drawing conceptual similarities, and knowledge of general principles and social situations. The verbal scale IQ is interpreted as a good indicator of verbal comprehension and expressive language skills and has good test-retest reliability. It is also considered to be an indicator of "crystallized" ability or intellectual functioning on tasks calling on previous training, education, and acculturation. Auditory attention is also reflected in the score.

Because of the verbal orientation of most American schools, the verbal scale IQ is by far the best predictor of academic achievement for students. Verbal scale alone can be used with examinees who are visually or motor impaired and examinees for whom English is a second language. Examinees from low socioeconomic backgrounds or minority cultures often earn a verbal scale IQ that is lower than their actual intellectual ability. Significant differences between verbal scale IQs and performance scale IQs are helpful in detecting and diagnosing the presence of a learning or language disability.

REFERENCES

Flanagan, D. P., & Kaufman, A. S. (2004). *Essentials of WISC-IV assessment.* Hoboken, NJ: Wiley.

VERBO-TONAL METHOD

The verbo-tonal method (VTM) is primarily an auditory method for the education of deaf children. It was developed by Petar Guberina in Zagreb, Yugoslavia (Guberina, Skaric, & Zaga, 1972) and reformulated by Asp and Guberina (1981). The term verbo-tonal was first coined to characterize an original audiometric technique that measured the perception of speech segments called logatomes (hence the term *verbo*) of variable main frequency spectrum (hence the word *tonal*) from the low, such as *bru-bru,* to the high, such as *si-si.*

Guberina insists on the importance of the suprasegmental, or prosodic, features of spoken language: rhythm, pitch variations, and stress. He considers that all deaf children and adults have some hearing capacities, not only inferior but also different from those of the normally hearing. Those whose cochlear function is completely lost can still perceive speech sounds through their vibro-tactile sensitivity. For every deaf individual, therefore, it is possible to determine an optimal field (OF) for speech reception, characterized by those frequencies of the speech spectrum in which residual hearing, and/or vibro-tactile perception, are most efficient. The OF can be limited to the low frequencies (including impulses of infrasound frequency perceptible by tactile sensation) or to the high frequencies. It also can be discontinuous, consisting of two restricted frequency bands, one low, one high. Having observed that better speech perception could be achieved by amplifying only the OF frequencies and eliminating the others, Guberina devised special apparatus capable of selecting distinct frequency bands.

Besides the technical equipment, specific training procedures characterize the VTM. Individual work consists of auditory and speech training. For speech correction, particular attention is given to the analysis of faults. Following this, the therapist modifies his or her own speech to counteract the erroneous perception that has led to faulty production. Several modifications of pitch, tension, duration, phonetic context, and even phonetic structure are used. The visual channel of speech reception, lip reading, is not trained specifically.

Body rhythm is based on the concept that speech is a function of the whole body, and that appropriate macro-motricity movements involving the body will facilitate the finer micromotricity movements of speech organs. Specific movements based on the phonetic features of the various speech sounds are executed simultaneously with their utterance. The deaf child, equipped with appropriate amplification, first watches and listens to the therapist, then is asked to reproduce the associated speech and body movements with the control of the residual hearing.

Musical rhythm aims at sensitizing the deaf child to the rhythm and changing intonation pattern of normal speech, while simultaneously training him or her to perceive and reproduce every phoneme in its different positions: initial, intermediate, or terminal. This is accomplished by presenting to the child a series of comptines, each constructed with a limited number of repetitive nonsense syllables, allowing for easy identification and reproduction.

Phonetic graphism, a later adjunct to the verbo-tonal method was developed by Gladic (1982). This technique is based on coordination between the fine hand movements of painting and writing and the subtle vocal tract motricity of the speech act.

Although devised for the education of the deaf, VTM has been adapted to the rehabilitation of children with a wide variety of language and personality disorders (Asp & Guberina, 1981). First developed in Zagreb in the 1950s, VTM was shortly thereafter introduced in France. In the beginning of the 1960s, it was demonstrated in several other western European countries, the United States, Canada, and some Latin American countries. It has since developed worldwide, gaining variable degrees of acceptance among oralist-oriented educators and parents of deaf children.

REFERENCES

Asp, C., & Guberina, P. (1981). *The verbo-tonal method.* New York: World Rehabilitation Fund Monographs.

Gladic, V. A. (1982). *Le graphisme phonétique.* Brussels, Belgium: Labor.

Guberina, P., Skaric, I., & Zaga, B. (1972). *Case studies in the use of restricted bands of frequencies in auditory rehabilitation of the deaf.* Zagreb, Yugoslavia: Institute of Phonetics, Faculty of Arts.

Olivier Périer
*Université Libre de Bruxelles
Centre Comprendre et Parler,
Belgium*

DEAF
DEAF EDUCATION

VERSABRAILLE

Versabraille, a device for the blind, is a computer with a braille keyboard. In lieu of a screen, there are 20 electronic braille cells, each containing the usual six dots that can be selectively raised to form braille characters. After a period of machine familiarization, reading speed on the 20-cell display is comparable to paper braille reading rates.

One of the main advantages of this system is that it can store much braille information on small floppy disks. Furthermore, it does not necessitate any printing on paper, and makes word processing and the production of tables and charts possible.

Michel Bourdot
*Centre d'Etude et de
Reclassement, Brussels,
Belgium*

BLIND
BRAILLE

VIDEOFLUOROSCOPY

Videofluoroscopy is a method of obtaining fluorographic/radiographic and images of anatomical structure and physiological function. This procedure offers the benefits of low radiation levels, synchrony of visual and sound data for speech, and multiple viewing planes. The procedure requires an interface between common medical fluoroscopy equipment and a video recorder. The patient is observed in multiple positions to produce different views of the area of interest. A barium solution is administered to highlight soft tissue structures. The procedure is usually conducted by a team composed of a speech-language pathologist, radiologist, and an imaging technician. Two common applications of this procedure are to observe the functioning of the velopharyngeal mechanism during speech production and to track the movement of food and liquid during swallowing (Skolnick & Cohn, 1989).

Velopharyngeal inadequacy (VPI) may be suspected because an individual's speech contains inappropriate nasal resonance (i.e., hypernasality, hyponasality, assimilative nasality, cul de sac resonance). Videofluoroscopy is then used to evaluate the structure and function of the velopharyngeal mechanism while the individual produces selected speech samples which stress the valving capability of the mechanism. The information gained during this procedure aids in differential diagnosis, supports decisions regarding the efficacy of surgical or prosthetic and/or behavioral management of VPI, and can indicate the course of therapy.

Another form of the videofluoroscopy procedure, a modified barium swallow (MBS) study, can be used where neuromuscular problems have resulted in problems with swallowing. The MBS study is utilized to identify specific points of dysfunction in the upper gastrointestinal tract during eating and swallowing. The occurrence of foreign material entering the airway (aspiration) is of particular interest during the MBS study since this condition can lead to aspiration pneumonia. During this procedure, the patient is fed different consistencies and amounts of food/liquid containing a barium trace. The information gained includes how the individual is able to organize material in his or her mouth, prepare to swallow it, and how that material moves through the pharynx toward the esophagus and stomach. A treatment regimen, which can include dietary management, postural changes, and muscle stimulation, will result from an MBS study. The procedure is usually conducted by a speech-language pathologist, a radiologist, and an imaging technician, and the results are presented to a team of professionals for recommendations and followup.

REFERENCE

Skolnick, M. L., & Cohn, E. R. (1989). *Studies of speech in patients with cleft palate.* New York: Springer-Verlag.

STAFF

VIDEOTAPING IN SPECIAL EDUCATION

Videotaping is a feedback technique that has been derived from the field of interaction analysis (Amidon & Hough, 1967; Flanders, 1970; Webb, 1981). In special education, it is often used as a training system that permits special education teachers to monitor and modify their own teaching behavior (Shea, 1974). A student teacher teaches a lesson, is critiqued, shown a videotape, and reteaches the lesson (Koetting, 1985). The interaction analysis technique allows the teacher to employ various schemes for identifying units of behavior and mapping the relationships of the behaviors in time and space.

Procedurally, an observer (special education teacher, student teacher, supervisor, or principal) sits in a classroom and views a videotape. As the observer follows the flow of events, he or she identifies specific units of behavior and makes notations of their occurrences. Identification of each unit is based on a set of descriptive categories; the resultant series of notations provides the "map," which is subject to interpretation and analysis.

The use of videotaping has improved many observation problems inherent in evaluating complex interactions of the teaching-learning process. In classrooms for the emotionally handicapped, videotaping provides a method of permanently recording and stimulating teacher-pupil interactions for professional preparation. It also provides the opportunity for immediate feedback, immediate and repetitive replay,

accurate recording, and availability for analysis (Fargo, Fuchigami, & Cagauan, 1968; Haring & Fargo, 1969).

Birch (1969) demonstrated that categorizing and recording the frequency of one's own verbal behaviors may be a powerful training procedure leading to changes in recorded preservice teacher behaviors. Thomas's (1972) research supported Birch's findings that the self-monitoring procedure, viewing videotapes of one's own teaching and categorizing the behaviors observed, can have an effect on the behavior of teachers who are already teaching and who have had as many as 15 years of teaching experience.

Research also indicates that 4-minute videotape segments may provide the best, most practical diagnostic tool available to supervisors in both preservice and in-service programs (Hosford & Neuenfeldt, 1979).

Videotaping for improving target behaviors with various special education populations is reported throughout the literature. Bricker, Morgan, and Grabowski (1972) used taped recordings of cottage attendant behavior to increase the time and quality of interactions with developmentally delayed children on a ward in a residential facility. The use of commercial trading stamps as token reinforcers in combination with an on-ward training program was used. The results demonstrated increases in interaction time associated with a progressive increase in the suitability of tasks selected by the attendants across four intervention phases if training was paired with viewing the videotapes and the delivery of trading stamps.

Gilbert et al. (1982) studied the effects of a peer modeling film on anxiety reduction and skill acquisition with children with health-related disabilities who were learning to self-inject insulin. The modeling film had no effect on reducing anxiety but the girls viewing the peer modeling film showed greater skill in self-injection.

Performance training methods such as live modeling, videotaped modeling, and individual video feedback has been proven effective in altering parent-child behaviors and attitudes (O'Dell, Mahoney, Horton, & Turner, 1979; Webster-Stratton, 1981). However, these studies addressed only the short-term effectiveness of videotape training methods. Webster-Stratton (1982) studied whether changes brought about by videotape modeling are maintained over longer periods of time with 35 mothers and their 3- to 5-year-old children who exhibited inappropriate behaviors. The results of this study indicated that most of the behavioral changes noted during the short evaluation were maintained. At 1-year follow-up, mother-child interactions were significantly more positive and significantly less negative, nonaccepting, and domineering than at baseline assessment. A significant reduction in behavior problems at 1-year follow-up compared with baseline also was noted. There was a notable drop, however, in mother-child positive affect behaviors (showing lack of confidence and inability to manage problem behaviors).

The positive effects of using videotaping as a training tool for special education personnel, teachers in training, and special learners and their parents is clearly supported in the literature. The opportunity to emit behaviors and obtain feedback on performance are crucial variables of the technique.

REFERENCES

Amidon, E. J., & Hough, J. B. (Eds.). (1967). *Interaction analysis: Theory, research and application.* Reading, MA: Addison-Wesley.

Birch, D. R. (1969). *Guided self-analysis and teacher education.* Unpublished doctoral dissertation, University of California, Berkeley.

Bricker, W. A., Morgan, D. G., & Grabowski, J. G. (1972). Development and maintenance of a behavior modification repertoire of cottage attendants through tv feedback. *American Journal of Mental Deficiency, 77,* 128–136.

Fargo, C., Fuchigami, R., & Cagauan, C. A. (1968). An investigation of selected variables in the teaching of specified objectives to mentally retarded students. *Education & Training of the Mentally Retarded, 3,* 202–208.

Flanders, N. A. (1970). *Analyzing teaching behavior.* Reading, MA: Addison-Wesley.

Gilbert, B. O., Johnson, S. B., McCallum, M., Silverstein, J. H., & Rosenbloom, A. (1982). The effects of a peer-modeling film on children learning to self-inject insulin. *Behavior Therapy, 13,* 186–193.

Haring, N. G., & Fargo, G. A. (1969). Evaluating programs for preparing teachers of emotionally disturbed children. *Exceptional Children, 36,* 157–162.

Hosford, P., & Neuenfeldt, J. (1979). Teacher evaluation via videotape: Hope or heresy? *Educational Leadership, 36,* 418–422.

Koetting, J. R. (1985). *Video as a means for analyzing teaching: A process of self-reflection and critique.* Paper presented at the annual convention of the Association for Educational Communications and Technology, Anaheim, CA.

O'Dell, S. L., Mahoney, N. D., Horton, N. G., & Turner, P. E. (1979). Media assisted parent training: Alternative models. *Behavior Therapy, 10,* 103–110.

Shea, T. M. (1974). *Special education microteaching clinic: Final report* (Report No. 020533). Edwardsville: Southern Illinois University, Special Education Microteaching Clinic. (ERIC Document Reproduction Service No. ED 126 665)

Thomas, D. R. (1972). *Self-monitoring as a technique for modifying teaching behaviors.* Unpublished doctoral dissertation, University of Illinois, Urbana-Champaign.

Webb, G. (1981). An evaluation of techniques for analyzing small group work. *Programmed Learning and Educational Technology, 18,* 64–66.

Webster-Stratton, C. (1981). Videotape modeling: A method of parent education. *Journal of Clinical Child Psychology, 10,* 93–98.

Webster-Stratton, C. (1982). The long-term effects of a videotape modeling parent training program: Comparison of immediate and 1-year follow-up results. *Behavior Therapy, 13,* 702–714.

DEBORAH A. SHANLEY
*Medgar Evers College, City
University of New York*

SUPERVISION IN SPECIAL EDUCATION
TEACHER EFFECTIVENESS
TEACHER TRAINING

VINELAND ADAPTIVE BEHAVIOR SCALES, SECOND EDITION

The Vineland Adaptive Behavior Scales, Second Edition (Vineland-II; Sparrow, Cicchetti, & Balla, 2005) is an assessment of adaptive behavior, which is defined by the authors as the performance of daily activities required for personal and social sufficiency. Three forms of the Vineland-II are available: two Survey forms, which assess individuals from birth to age 90, and the Teacher Rating Form, applicable for students aged 3 through 21. The Vineland-II can be used to identify individuals who have mental retardation, developmental delays, autism spectrum disorders such as Asperger syndrome, and other impairments. Assessment with the Vineland-II can be useful for diagnosis, qualification for special programs, progress monitoring, program and treatment planning, and research.

The two Survey forms—the Survey Interview Form and the Parent/Caregiver Rating Form—assess adaptive behavior in four broad domains: Communication, Daily Living Skills, Socialization, and Motor Skills. The Survey forms differ from each other only in method of administration (interview versus rating scale). The Survey Interview Form is administered as a semistructured interview with the parent or caregiver of the individual being assessed. This interview format encourages the parent or caregiver to elaborate on his or her responses, which allows the examiner to gain additional clinical information useful for making differential diagnoses. Examiners can choose to administer the Parent/Caregiver Rating Form when a face-to-face interview is not practical. The Parent/Caregiver Rating Form is especially well suited for progress monitoring after an interview administration has been obtained. The Vineland–II Teacher Rating Form provides an additional source of data, assessing the same four domains of behaviors but focusing on readily observable behaviors exhibited in a classroom setting.

For this revision, some item content was modified to reflect the impact of cultural and technological changes on societal expectations of adaptive behavior. Items have been added to improve measurement for very young children and for adults. Additionally, the norms were extended through adulthood, enabling the examiner to identify strengths and weaknesses and age-related declines in the adaptive functioning of older adults.

The predecessor of the Vineland Adaptive Behavior Scales was the Vineland Social Maturity Scale, originally published in 1935 by Edgar A. Doll for use in the evaluation of individuals with mental retardation. In developing the Vineland SMS (Doll, 1935, 1965), Doll pioneered features that remain important aspects of the Vineland-II, including his use of the "third party" method of administration. This method does not require the participation of the individual whose adaptive behavior is being assessed, but only requires a respondent who is familiar with the individual's behavior. Use of this method produces a valid measurement of the day-to-day activities that cannot be adequately measured through direct administration of tasks, and also allows the assessment of individuals who will not or cannot perform on command in a direct administration situation, such as infants, individuals with severe or profound mental retardation, individuals with severe emotional disturbances, and individuals with physical disabilities.

Another of Doll's contributions was to highlight the critical role of measuring social competence in assessing individuals with mental retardation. Doll defined social competence as "the functional ability of the human organism for exercising personal independence and social responsibility" (Doll, 1953, p. 10); he felt that a diagnosis of mental deficiency would be incomplete without an evaluation of the individual's capacity for maintaining themselves and their affairs.

Although it was several years before the role of adaptive behavior in assessing and classifying individuals with mental retardation was widely recognized, in 1959 the American Association on Mental Retardation (AAMR) published its first official manual and formally included deficits in adaptive behavior, in addition to subaverage intelligence, as an integral part of the definition of mental retardation (Heber, 1959, 1961). That AAMR manual listed two major facets of adaptive behavior.

1. The degree to which the individual is able to function and maintain him- or herself independently.
2. The degree to which he or she meets satisfactorily the culturally imposed demands of personal and social responsibility. (Heber, 1961, p. 61)

Although modified somewhat, the major premises of Heber's definition are still evident in later editions of the AAMR manual. According to the AAMR's current requirements for a diagnosis of mental retardation, an individual must have significant limitations (two or more standard deviations below the mean of the norm population) in at least one of the three domains of adaptive behavior, and an IQ score of 70 or below (AAMR, 2002, p. 76). The onset of the disability must occur before 18 years of age. Because it provides estimates of an individual's adaptive behavior and ranking in comparison with a national normative group, the Vineland-II is well suited for use in the diagnosis and evaluation of mental retardation.

The most recent (2002) edition of the AAMR manual identifies three domains of adaptive behavior: conceptual (involving such skills as language, money concepts, and reading and writing), practical (activities of daily living, occupational skills, etc.), and social (interpersonal, responsibility, obeying laws, etc.). The content and scales of the Vineland-II are organized within a three-domain structure similar to the three areas of adaptive functioning identified by the AAMR:

- Communication (Receptive, Expressive, and Written subdomains): how an individual speaks, understands others, and uses written language;
- Daily Living Skills (Personal, Domestic, and Community subdomains): the practical skills and behaviors that are needed to take care of oneself, and
- Socialization (Interpersonal Relationships, Play and Leisure Time, and Coping Skills subdomains): the skills and behaviors that people need to get along with others and for use in leisure activities.

In addition, the Vineland-II offers a Motor Skills Domain, for assessing important physical skills in children through age 6, and an optional Maladaptive Behavior Index—a composite of internalizing, externalizing, and other types of undesirable behavior that may interfere with the individual's adaptive functioning.

Each Vineland-II domain is made up of two or three subdomains, for a total of eleven Vineland-II subdomains. Within each domain, the subdomains yield v-scale scores that sum to yield the domain composite standard scores. The four domain composite scores make up the Adaptive Behavior Composite (ABC) for individuals through age 6; for individuals aged 7 and older, the first three domain composites (minus Motor Skills) form the ABC. Available scores include subdomain v-scale scores (mean = 15, SD = 3), domains and ABC standard scores (mean = 100, SD = 15), confidence intervals, percentile ranks, stanines, and age equivalents.

The Vineland-II Survey forms were standardized on a random sample of over 3,000 individuals stratified according to sex, race/ethnicity, parental education level, and region. The manual presents three types of evidence for the reliability of the Vineland-II. Internal consistency reliabilities are in the high .70s to low .80s for the subdomains, in the mid .80s to low .90s for the domains, and in the mid .90s for the Adaptive Behavior Composite. Test-retest reliabilities are in the mid to high .80s, and interrater reliabilities are in the mid .70s. Validity evidence presented in the manual includes evidence based on content, factor structure, relationships with other measures, and clinical group data.

REFERENCES

American Association on Mental Retardation (AAMR). (1992). *Mental retardation definition, classification, and systems of supports* (9th ed.). Washington, DC: Author.

American Association on Mental Retardation (AAMR). (2002). *Mental retardation definition, classification, and systems of supports* (10th ed.). Washington, DC: Author.

Doll, E. A. (1935). A genetic scale of social maturity. *American Journal of Orthopsychiatry, 5,* 180–188.

Doll, E. A. (1953). *Measurement of social competence.* Circle Pines, MN: American Guidance Service.

Doll, E. A. (1965). *Vineland Social Maturity Scale.* Circle Pines, MN: American Guidance Service.

Grossman, H. J. (Ed.). (1973). *Manual on terminology and classification in mental retardation* (1973 rev.). Washington, DC: American Association on Mental Deficiency.

Grossman, H. J. (Ed.). (1977). *Manual on terminology and classification in mental retardation* (1977 rev.). Washington, DC: American Association on Mental Deficiency.

Grossman, H. J. (Ed.). (1983). *Classification in mental retardation* (1983 rev.). Washington, DC: American Association on Mental Deficiency.

Heber, R. F. (1959). A manual on terminology and classification in mental retardation. [Monograph suppl.]. *American Journal of Mental Deficiency.*

Heber, R. F. (1961). A manual on terminology and classification in mental retardation (2nd ed.). [Monograph suppl.]. *American Journal of Mental Deficiency.*

Sparrow, S. S., Balla, D. A., & Cicchetti, D. V. (1984). *Vineland Adaptive Behavior Scales.* Circle Pines, MN: American Guidance Service.

Sparrow, S. S., Cicchetti, D. V., & Balla, D. A. (2005). *Vineland Adaptive Behavior Scales, Survey Forms* (2nd ed.). Circle Pines, MN: AGS Publishing.

JOHN BIELINSKI
VERENA GETAHUN
AGS Publishing

ADAPTIVE BEHAVIOR
MENTAL RETARDATION
VINELAND SOCIAL-EMOTIONAL EARLY CHILDHOOD SCALES

VINELAND SOCIAL-EMOTIONAL EARLY CHILDHOOD SCALES

The Vineland Social-Emotional Early Childhood Scales (SEEC; Sparrow, Balla, Cicchetti, 1998) is designed to measure the emotional functioning of children from birth to 5 years, 11 months. The SEEC scales were derived from the Socialization domain of the Vineland Adaptive Behavior Scales. There are three scales on the SEEC: Interpersonal Relationships, Play and Leisure Time, and Coping Skills. A Social-Emotional Composite score is also available. The types of behaviors assessed include those such as paying attention, entering social situations, understanding emo-

tional expression, developing relationships, and developing self-regulatory behaviors. The scales are designed to help develop early intervention plans and to chart developmental progress in preschool and kindergarten programs.

Administration of the SEEC Scales is done via a semi-structured interview with a child's caregiver. Items are scored based on how often a child is reported to perform a certain behavior: a score of 2 indicates that the child "usually performs," a score of 1 indicates that a child "sometimes or partially performs," and a score of 0 indicates that a child "never performs." Age-based standard scores (M = 100, SD = 15), percentile ranks, and descriptive categories are obtained from the scales. The entire SEEC Scales administration time is usually 15 to 25 minutes.

The norms of the SEEC scales were computed from the normative data of the Vineland Adaptive Behavior Scales (Sparrow et al., 1998). The standardization sample was comprised of 1,200 children from birth to age 5 years, 11 months. Median internal consistency reliability coefficients for each of the scales ranged from .80 for Play and Leisure Time to .91 for Coping Skills. The median internal consistency value for the Composite was .93. Interrater reliability values ranged from .47 to .60. Validity studies reported the correlation between the SEEC Scales and the Early Development Scale of the Scales of Independent Behavior to be .63. In addition to the convergent validity information, a number of studies have indicated that the Vineland Socialization Domain differentiates between normal children and developmentally delayed children.

REFERENCE

Sparrow, S. S., Balla, D. A., & Cicchetti, D. V. (1998). *Vineland Social-Emotional Early Childhood Scales.* Circle Pines, MN: American Guidance Service.

ELIZABETH O. LICHTENBERGER
The Salk Institute

ADAPTIVE BEHAVIOR
VINELAND ADAPTIVE BEHAVIOR SCALES

VINELAND TRAINING SCHOOL

The Training School at Vineland, New Jersey, has had a long and influential role in the history of mental retardation in the United States. Originally founded in 1888 by Olin S. Garrison as a private school and institution for the "feeble-minded," the Training School maintained a reputation for high standards of care and for pioneering experimental and research work. Rather than being a medical setting, it was designed to provide care and research within a psychological-educational context.

In 1901 Edward R. Johnstone became director of the Training School, a position he held until 1943. The genesis of many of the institution's later activities was the establishment in 1902 of the Feebleminded Club by a group of interested professionals and financial backers (Doll, 1972). In 1904 Johnstone started the summer school, one of the first programs designed to provide training for teachers of the mentally retarded. This program subsequently established university affiliations, and many leaders in the field were graduates of the program. In 1913 the Department of Extension was founded to publicize findings in the field. This led in 1914 to the Committee on Provisions for the Feebleminded, which undertook the first organized efforts of national scope to promote better state laws and increased institutional care for the retarded.

In 1906 the first psychological laboratory for the study of mental retardation was established at the Training School and Henry H. Goddard was appointed director of research. It was here that Goddard did his most famous work, translating and adapting the Binet intelligence scales, helping develop World War I army tests, and conducting extensive research on mental retardation. Goddard's (1912) study of the family history of Deborah Kallikak, a resident of the institution, became one of the most widely read research projects of the day; it gave impetus to the eugenics movement.

The laboratory Goddard directed continued to be considered a center for research on mental retardation for decades after his resignation in 1918. As director of research from 1925 to 1949, Edgar A. Doll made several important contributions, the most well known of his efforts being the establishment of criteria of social functioning. In the early 1960s the Training School changed its name to the American Institute for Mental Studies and in 1981 the Elwyn Institute assumed management responsibility for the facility.

REFERENCES

Doll, E. A. (1972). A historical survey of research and management of mental retardation in the United States. In E. P. Trapp & P. Himelstein (Eds.), *Readings on the exceptional child: Research and theory* (2nd ed., pp. 47–97). New York: Appleton-Century-Crofts.

Goddard, H. H. (1912). *The Kallikak family.* New York: Macmillan.

TIMOTHY D. LACKAYE
*Hunter College, City University
of New York*

**HISTORY OF SPECIAL EDUCATION
MENTAL RETARDATION**

VISION TRAINING

Optometric visual training (vision therapy) is the art and science of developing visual abilities to achieve optimal vision performance and comfort. Training techniques are used in the prevention of the development of vision problems, the enhancement of visual efficiency, and the remediation and correction of existing visual problems.

Visual training encompasses orthoptics, which is a non-surgical method of treating disorders of binocular vision. Orthoptic techniques were used as early as the seventh century by a Greek physician, Paulus Aeginaeta, who used a mask with small perforations to correct strabismus. The mask was still in use in 1583 by George Bartisch, the founder of German ophthalmology.

In the early eighteenth century, Buffon advocated occlusion of the good eye to improve vision in the poorer eye. This was followed by Wheatstone's mirror invention of the stereoscope, which was employed to correct postoperative divergence of the eyes. Brewster modified the stereoscope, which is still in use in visual training programs today, with lenses.

In 1864 Javal founded orthoptics and demonstrated that binocular vision could be recovered with the use of a stereoscope. Orthoptics took a step forward in 1903 when Worth established a fusion theory, classified binocular vision into three grades, developed the amblyoscope, and devised the four-dot test to detect suppression. Worth, who headed up the English orthoptic school, which stressed fusional capacity, stated that the essential cause of squint is a defect of the fusional faculty. Worth believed that the weak fusion could be reeducated.

Optometric vision training techniques were developed by Arneson, who used the principle of peripheral stimulation with a circular disk of 30 inches in diameter. Patients were asked to fixate a rotating jewel on the Arneson rotator "to aid central fixation and fusion through motion." This was the first of many techniques that were developed by optometrists to modify visual behavior by changing the accommodative convergence relationship. In 1932 two optometrists, Crow and Fuog, published a series of visual training papers that introduced the concept of visual skills.

In addition, lens application, especially at the near point to enhance visual comfort, began to play an important role in the 1930s when Skeffington developed the analytical examination with a group of optometrists from the optometric extension program. Harmon further demonstrated that "appropriate lens for near point would reduce physiological stress." A plus lens is therefore prescribed as a single vision or bifocal during or after a program of optometric vision training.

The need for visual training is established with the objective and subjective findings of the visual analysis and an evaluation of the ocular motility, accommodative facility, eye teaming ability, and visual perception. The visual analysis includes a detailed ocular, medical, and genetic history followed by distance and near visual acuity determination, external evaluation of the eyes, and cover test to determine eye position. Pupillary reflexes, keratometry, objective and subjective refraction, distance and near acuity, horizontal and vertical ductions, fusional amplitudes, and accommodative tests precede any visual training therapy. Additional testing procedures evaluate suppressions, stereopsis, eye preference, macular integrity, and foveal fixation.

Visual symptoms indicating the possible need for visual training include crossed eyes, headaches, head tilt, short attention span, rubbing and constant blinking of the eyes, poor hand-eye coordination, blurring of vision, holding of books close to the eyes, double vision, word and letter reversals, covering an eye, losing the place when reading, or the avoidance of near work.

Many of the current visual training techniques developed by Brock, Nichols, Getman, MacDonald, Schrock, Kraskin, and Greenstein emphasize development of smooth eye movement skills (fixation ability). These include pursuit, the ability of the eyes to smoothly and accurately track a moving object or read a line of print, and saccadic movement, the ability to move the eyes from one object or word accurately.

Additional skills emphasized in visual training are eye-focusing skills, eye-aiming skills, eye-teaming skills (binocular fusion), eye-hand coordination, visualization, visual memory, visual imagery, and visual form perception. These techniques have been found to be effective in eliminating or reducing visual symptoms even when the visual acuity is 20/20 at distance and near on the Snellen acuity charts.

Techniques employing lenses, prisms, the steroscope, and rotator are used to align the eyes and maximize optimal visual efficiency. Visual training procedures also are used when there are overt eye turns such as those encountered in constant, intermittent, or alternating strabismus (esotropia or exotropia). Prism therapy is often used in conjunction with lens therapy in the correction of horizontal and vertical deviations of the eye.

Visual training techniques also have been used in the treatment of amblyopia, learning-related problems, and juvenile delinquency; in sports training programs; and with older adults and workers having visual difficulties on the job.

The optometrist often works on a multidisciplinary team that includes the educator, psychologist, social worker, rehabilitation specialist, orientation and mobility instructor, and child development specialist who specializes in the remediation of the child, teen, or adult with a learning disability or visual impairment. These methods are effective only if learning problems are related to vision system problems as opposed to a central processing dysfunction.

REFERENCES

American Optometric Association. (1985). *Vision therapy news backgrounder*. St. Louis, MO: Author.

Borish, I. (1970). *Clinical refraction* (3rd ed.). Chicago: Professional.

Griffin, J. R. (1982). *Binocular anomalies procedures for vision therapy* (2nd ed.). Chicago: Professional.

Harmon, D. B. (1945). *Lighting and child development*. Philadelphia: Illuminating Engineering.

Hurtt, R. N., Rasicovici, A., & Windsor, C. (1952). *Comprehensive review of orthoptics and ocular motility*. St. Louis, MO: Mosby.

McDonald, L. W. (1970). *Optometric visual training—Its history and developments*. St. Louis, MO: American Optometric Association.

Richman, J. E., Cron, M., & Cohen, E. (1983). *Basic vision therapy, A clinical handbook*. Big Rapids, MI: Ferris State Press.

Skeffington, A. M. (1946). *Visual rehabilitation, analytical optometry*. Duncan, OK: Occupational Education Programs.

Skeffington, A. M. (1959). *The role of a convex lens*. St. Louis, MO: American Optometric Association.

Von Norden, G., & Maumenee, A. E. (1967). *Atlas of strabismus*. St. Louis, MO: Mosby.

BRUCE P. ROSENTHAL
State University of New York

DEVELOPMENTAL OPTOMETRY
OPTOMETRISTS
VISUAL ACUITY
VISUAL IMPAIRMENT

VISUAL ACUITY

Visual acuity refers to the degree to which the human eye can distinguish fine detail at varying distances. It is dependent on the eye's ability to bend light rays and focus them on the retina (Cartwright, Cartwright, & Ward, 1994). Tests of visual acuity provide measures of the smallest retinal formed images distinguishable by someone's eyes. The results of such tests are influenced by such factors as the area of retina stimulated, the intensity and distribution of illumination, the amount of time of exposure, the effects of movement, and whether the visual acuity test is conducted with each of the eyes separately or both together (Duke-Elder, 1968).

Distance visual acuity is usually measured with a Snellen chart (first published in 1862) and according to Snellen's formula (based on use with this chart). In this formula, $V = d/D$, with V standing for visual acuity; d representing the distance at which test types are read on the chart; and D representing the distance at which the letters subtend an overall angle of 5 minutes on the Snellen chart (Jan, Freeman, & Scott, 1977). Thus, if at a distance (d) of 20 feet a child can identify letters on the 20 line (D) of a Snellen chart, his or her visual acuity (V) is 20/20, which is considered to be normal vision.

If a child's visual acuity is assessed as 20/200 in the better eye without correction, the child is only able to see images at a distance of 20 feet that a person with normal vision can see at 200 feet. Such a child would be classified as legally blind. Some low-vision children are able to see images at distances no farther than a few feet. If a child has a visual acuity measurement of 5/40, it means that he or she can see the 40 line (D) on the Snellen chart from a distance of 5 feet (d). Since such a rating is an equivalent of 20/160, it would also classify such a child as legally blind (Jan et al., 1977). Below measurements of 20/400, visual acuity is usually assessed by having the subject count fingers seen at short distances. LP noted for an eye examination means that the child can only perceive light.

When assessing children's visual acuity, particularly those with low vision, it is important to use visual displays with high-contrast letters and to avoid glare and visual distractions. In instances where a child has difficulty in localizing the symbols to be discriminated (e.g., when testing a child with cognitive difficulties), it may be necessary to occlude parts of the chart (Jose, 1983).

When assessing young children, those who are learning disabled, or those who have multiple handicaps that limit their ability to identify the letters on the Snellen chart, it may be necessary to use alternate methods to assess visual acuity. One of these methods, the Snellen E, requires the student to indicate the position of the E symbol (whether left, right, up, or down). Caution must be used in administering this test since a grasp of directionality and some eye-hand coordination is required to succeed; some training of the child may facilitate the application.

Other methods of approximating visual acuity include the use of an optokinetic drum, Sheridan's Stycar miniature toys, the Rosenbaum Dot Test, and the New York Lighthouse Symbol Flashcards. The last test employs three symbols, a house, an umbrella, and an apple, that conform to the sizes of the Snellen letters. The child can identify the symbols on the chart by naming them in any understandable way or by pointing to a symbol placed in front of the table where the child is seated (Faye, Padula, Padula, Gurland, Greenberg, & Hood, 1984).

In addition to testing for distance visual acuity, it is important to assess a child's near distance acuity because so many school and work-related tasks are performed at close distances. Near tasks, required in much of school learning, are usually performed from a distance of 14 to 16 inches. A major problem confronting the assessment of near vision is the lack of standardization in the types of chart systems that are currently used for this purpose. The Snellen near-point card uses the metric system to indicate close distance visual acuity. The Jaeger consists of 20 different type sizes in increasing graduations; it indicates the type sizes that the student is able to identify. The Point system uses type sizes in which one point equals 1/72 of an inch. Thus a student who can read newspaper print has a near point Snellen equivalent of 20/40, a Jaeger recording of J4-5, and a Point recording of 8; a student who can only read newspaper head-lines has a Snellen rating of 20/100, a Jaeger recording of J17, and a Point recording of 18 (Jose, 1983). A lay person may find it difficult to reconcile such diverse findings. For them to be understood by teachers and parents, the visual examiner should explain their nature and implications. Information respecting the visual acuity, both far and near, of all children, but particularly the disabled, is an essential guide for children's instruction.

REFERENCES

Cartwright, G. P., Cartwright, C. A., & Ward, M. J. (1994). *Educating exceptional learners* (4th ed.). Boston: Wadsworth.

Duke-Elder, S. A. (1968). *Systems of ophthalmology*. St. Louis, MO: Mosby.

Faye, E. E., Padula, W. V., Padula, J. B., Gurland, J. E., Greenberg, M. L., & Hood, C. M. (1984). The low vision child. In E. E. Faye (Ed.), *Clinical low vision* (pp. 437–475). Boston: Little, Brown.

Jan, J. E., Freeman, R. D., & Scott, P. (1977). *Visual impairment in children & adolescents*. New York: Grune & Stratton.

Jose, R. T. (1983). *Understanding low vision*. New York: American Foundation for the Blind.

EMILY WAHLEN
Hunter College, City University of New York

VISUAL IMPAIRMENT
VISUAL-MOTOR AND VISUAL-PERCEPTUAL PROBLEMS
VISUAL TRAINING

VISUAL EFFICIENCY

Visual efficiency, as defined by Barraga (1970, 1976, 1980, 1983), relates to a variety of visual skills including eye movements, adapting to the physical environment, attending to visual stimuli, and processing information with speed and effectiveness.

In keeping with this definition is Barraga's (1983) definition of the visually impaired child as a child whose visual impairments limit his or her learning and achievement unless there are adaptations made in the way that learning experiences are presented to the child and effective learning materials are provided in appropriate learning environments.

The basic idea behind the notion of visual efficiency is that children learn to see best by actively using their visual abilities. As applied to the visually impaired (i.e., low-vision children), this means that they should be provided with such opportunities for learning and should be taught in such ways that they learn effectively to use their residual vision. Low-vision children, without proper opportunities and training, may not be able to extract much useful information from their visual environments simply by being provided with appropriate visual environments, but they can learn to use their visual information with proper opportunities and training so that they eventually can make sense out of what were previously indistinct, uncertain visual impressions. Barraga's (1983) program to develop efficiency in visual functioning, intended for the training of low-vision children, is one that emphasizes structured training for visual efficiency.

Associated with the idea of visual efficiency is the concept of functional vision. This concept is concerned with the ways that children use their vision rather than with their physical visual limitations, although the latter improves with specific training as well (Cartwright, Cartwright, & Ward, 1994).

REFERENCES

Barraga, N. C. (1970). *Teacher's guide for development of visual learning abilities and utilization of low vision.* Louisville, KY: American Printing House for the Blind.

Barraga, N. C. (1976). *Visual handicaps and learning: A developmental approach.* Belmont, CA: Wadsworth.

Barraga, N. C. (1980). *Source book on low vision.* Louisville, KY: American Printing House for the Blind.

Barraga, N. C. (1983). *Visual handicaps and learning.* Austin, TX: Exceptional Resources.

Cartwright, G. P., Cartwright, C. A., & Ward, M. J. (1994). *Educating exceptional learners* (4th ed.). Boston: Wadsworth.

JANET S. BRAND
Hunter College, City University of New York

FUNCTIONAL VISION

VISUAL IMPAIRMENT

Godfrey Stevens, in his study on Taxonomy in Special Education for Children with Body Disorders (1962), used the term impairment to mean any deviation from the normal. Thus impairment was interpreted by many to mean disorder at the tissue level. Recently, however, visual impairment has come to mean the disability due to a medical disorder, rather than the medical disorder itself. For example, glaucoma would be the disorder; diminished eyesight would be the impairment. The term visual impairment takes on a broad meaning. In many cases it denotes visual loss other than total blindness, such as the "blind" and the "visually impaired," thereby separating the functionally blind from those who have some remaining vision. Four different categories are used to describe those with visual impairments. The term

"partially sighted" refers to a visual problem resulting in the need for special education. "Low vision" includes individuals with severe visual problems, often including the inability to read at normal distances even with the use of glasses or contact lenses. "Legally blind" refers to those individuals with less than 20/200 vision or with an extremely limited field of vision, often 20 degrees at the widest point. "Totally blind" includes those who must learn with Braille or other nonvisual means (Visual Impairments, 2004). Visual impairment has become somewhat synonymous with the term visual disability or visual handicap.

REFERENCES

Stevens, G. D. (1962). *Taxonomy in special education for children with body disorders.* Pittsburgh, PA: Department of Special Education & Rehabilitation.

Visual Impairments: A publication of the National Dissemination Center for Children with Disabilities. (2004, January). Retrieved January 1, 2006, from http://www.nichcy.org/pubs/factshe/fs13txt.htm

GIDEON JONES
Florida State University
First edition

LINDSAY HALLIDAY
California State University, San Bernardino
Third edition

VISUAL PERCEPTION AND DISCRIMINATION

VISUAL TRAINING

VISUAL-MOTOR AND VISUAL-PERCEPTUAL PROBLEMS

Many researchers have emphasized the importance of perceptual-motor skills to the development of children. Piaget and Inhelder (1956) stated that early sensory-motor experiences are basic to more advanced mental development, and Sherrington (1948) proposed that the motor system is the first neurological system to develop and the foundation for later perceptual growth. The concern for perceptual-motor development is a recurring theme in many areas of the history of special education (Lerner, 1976). While this perceptual-motor framework can be used to discuss all areas of perception that relate to motor responses—auditory, visual, haptic, olfactory, etc.—the relationships between visual-motor perception and discrimination and learning problems have received the greatest attention. The interest in visual motor perceptual problems in the United States can be traced back to the early research of Werner and Strauss (1939) and Strauss and Lehtinen (1947) with brain-damaged children. They noted that disturbances in visual perception and visual motor perceptual functioning often accompany central nervous system damage. Their work also fostered the rapid growth and development of several visual motor training programs by theorists such as Barsch, Frostig, Getman, and Kephart.

Although early researchers reported that visual-perceptual and visual-motor problems were evident in individuals with brain damage, a distinction between these two types of disturbances was not always made. While Goldstein and Scheerer (1959) considered visual-motor and visual-perceptual deficits as separate entities, Bartley (1958) viewed perception as being either experiental or motor. Some of the assessment instruments used to measure visual perception are actually visual-motor copying tasks; for example, the Bender Gestalt Test, the coding subtest of the Wechsler scales of intelligence, and the developmental test of visual motor integration, all require motor responses.

The failure to differentiate between visual-perceptual and visual-motor tasks may have far-reaching consequences. Perception is most directly tested when objects or pictures of various shapes, positions, or sizes are matched, or in some other way differentiated; it is then a task of interpreting what is seen. When the difficulty is demonstrated in a task that requires reproducing designs or spatial relationships, it is described as a visual-motor difficulty (i.e., the acts of perceiving and reproducing an object are combined). It may be possible that the child who displays a visual-motor difficulty also has a perceptual problem, although that inference cannot be made on the basis of a reproduction task. In normal development, visual perception of form precedes the visual motor reproduction of the form (Piaget & Inhelder, 1956), and copying requires skills of an order different from perceiving (Abercrombie, 1964).

Children who have visual-motor problems have difficulty coordinating their movements with what they see. Kirk and Chalfant (1984) reported that breakdowns in three areas may occur when a child displays problems in visual-motor perception and discrimination. First, a child may have problems with laterality, or lateral dominance. This type of problem becomes apparent when both sides of the body perform the same act at the same time when that is not part of the task, or when a child uses only one side of his or her body when two sides are called for. Second, a child may have a directional disability. Directional disabilities manifest themselves when the child fails to develop an awareness of basic directions such as right from left, up from down, and front from back. Very young children will have problems in directionality; this is normal during the early stages of development, but as the child matures, this problem usually corrects itself. If these difficulties continue, the child may have problems in learning. Finally, a child is said to have a breakdown in visual-motor perception when the child's development is limited to the stage where the

hand leads the eye. As visual-motor perception is refined, the eye should lead the hand.

Problems in visual-motor perception and discrimination can be seen in both academic and nonacademic tasks. In particular, visual-motor difficulties are most evident when children are involved in pencil and paper activities, play with or manipulate toys and objects, or catch or throw a ball, or when they are involved in any tasks that require good eye-hand coordination.

Many educators and psychologists have believed for years that adequate visual-motor development is directly related to academic achievement. As a result of this belief, a number of standardized tests were developed to assess children's visual-motor performance. Unfortunately, the use of these tests has not been supported by the literature. Visual-motor tests have been shown to be unreliable and theoretically or psychometrically unsound (Salvia & Ysseldyke, 1985). These inadequacies raise the question as to their usefulness, and whether they should be used in planning educational programs for children.

Despite the inadequacies of visual-motor tests, they are still being used in the schools. Advocates of visual-motor testing use these assessment instruments to diagnose brain injury, to identify children with visual-motor problems so that training programs can be established to remediate learning disabilities, and to determine the degree to which visual-motor perception and discrimination problems may be interfering with academic achievement. Some of the most common assessment devices used to measure visual-motor skills include the Bender-Gestalt Test, the Developmental Test of Visual Motor Integration, and the Purdue Perceptual Motor Survey.

The methods used in visual-motor training programs are generally developmental and emphasize the importance of early motor learning and visual-spatial development in children. While many of the advocates of visual-motor training programs have slightly different rationales for their programs, the basic perceptual-motor orientation and the recommended training activities are very similar. Barsch, Getman, Frostig, and Kephart all propose techniques for working with children with learning problems (Myers & Hammill, 1990).

One of the areas of controversy that surrounds the use of these training programs is the emphasis on training visual-motor perception processes to improve a child's skills in academic areas such as reading. Hammill and Larsen (1974) have argued that there is no evidence to support the assumption that academic learning is dependent on these types of psychological processes. However, unfortunately, both the critics and advocates of these training programs have based their arguments on highly questionable research reports (Hallahan & Kauffman, 1976). Detailed, recent meta-analyses demonstrate no real benefit to academic learning with perceptual-motor training programs (Kavale & Forness, 1999).

REFERENCES

Abercrombie, M. (1964). *Perceptual and visuo-motor disorders in cerebral palsy*. London: Heinemann.

Bartley, S. (1958). *Principles of perception*. New York: American Orthopsychiatric Association.

Goldstein, K., & Scheerer, M. (1959). Abstract and concrete behavior: An experimental study with special tests. *Psychological Monographs, 83*.

Hallahan, D., & Kauffman, J. (1976). *Introduction to learning disabilities*. Englewood Cliffs, NJ: Prentice Hall.

Hammill, D., & Larsen, S. (1974). The relationship of selected auditory perceptual skills and reading ability. *Journal of Learning Disabilities, 7,* 429–436.

Kavale, K., & Forness, S. (1999). The effectiveness of special education. In R. Reynolds & T. B. Gutkin (Eds.), *The handbook of school psychology* (3rd ed.). New York: Wiley.

Kirk, S., & Chalfant, J. (1984). *Academic and developmental learning disabilities*. Denver, CO: Love.

Myers, P., & Hammill, D. (1990). *Methods for learning disorders*. Austin, TX: PRO-ED.

Piaget, J., & Inhelder, B. (1956). *The child's concept of space*. London: Routledge & Kegan Paul.

Salvia, J., & Ysseldyke, J. (1985). *Assessment in special and remedial education* (3rd ed.). Boston: Houghton Mifflin.

Sherrington, C. (1948). *The integrative action of the nervous system*. New Haven, CT: Yale University Press.

Strauss, A., & Lehtinen, L. (1947). *Psychopathology and education of the brain injured child*. New York: Grune & Stratton.

Werner, H., & Strauss, A. (1939). Types of visuo-motor activity and their relation to low and high performance ages. *Proceedings of the American Association of Mental Deficiency, 44,* 163–168.

DEBORAH C. MAY
State University of New York at Albany

DONALD S. MAROZAS
State University of New York at Geneseo

PERCEPTION
PERCEPTUAL MOTOR DIFFICULTIES
VISUAL-MOTOR INTEGRATION

VISUAL-MOTOR INTEGRATION

Visual-motor integration, also referred to as visual-motor association, denotes the ability to relate visual stimuli to motor responses in an accurate and appropriate manner. Historically, visual-motor problems have been associated with learning disabilities and, within a diagnostic-remedial intervention model, visual-motor skills have been taught to learning disabled pupils as a prerequisite to academic skills (Lerner, 1985). This interest in visual-motor development

within the learning disabilities field can be traced to the early work of Strauss and Werner (1941), who studied the visual-motor problems of developmentally disabled students and believed that faulty visual-motor coordination was a behavioral symptom of brain damage. Werner and Strauss popularized the notion that adequate conceptual development is dependent on perceptual and motor development.

An important advocate of the magnitude of visual-motor integration to academic success is Getman. His visuomotor theory (Getman, 1965; Getman, Kane, & McKee, 1968) outlines the successive stages of visual-motor integration, including innate response, general motor systems, special motor systems, ocular motor systems, speech motor systems, visualization systems, vision or perception, and cognition. Each of these levels is conceptualized as more precise and exacting than the preceding one, with complete mastery at each stage required before completion of subsequent systems can be achieved. Therefore, within this model, academic learning must be preceded by extensive and successful motor learning. The implication is that learning disabled children need exercise in the base levels of motor and visual-motor development before academics can be addressed.

Another proponent of the relation between learning disabilities and visual-motor integration is Kephart (1960, 1971), who theorized that breakdowns may occur at three key points in the development of visual-motor coordination. A child may fail to develop (1) an internal awareness of laterality of the left and right sides of the body and their differences; (2) left-right awareness within the body, which could lead to directionality problems; and (3) visual-motor coordination at the stage when the hand leads the eye. As Getman, Kephart believes that the education of the perceptually motor-disabled child must address motoric and visual development before conceptual skills.

Several teaching programs based on visual-motor integration theory have been designed, including Getman's Developing Learning Readiness: A Visual-Motor Tactile Skills Program. This program comprises activities in six areas: general coordination, balance, eye-hand coordination, eye movement, form recognition, and visual memory. Additionally, tests addressing visual-motor integration have been developed. One widely used measure, Beery and Buktenica's Developmental Test of Visual Motor Integration (1967), which requires examinees to reproduce geometric forms, is a norm-referenced test of the degree to which visual perception and motor behavior are integrated in young children.

Visual-motor integration assessment and remediation have been the focus of research. A test of visual-motor integration, the VMI-R, was a developmental to indicate and identify a possible learning disability involving visual perception and fine-motor development (eg., hand-eye coordination). The VMI-R may be very helpful to professionals assessing children, for it will allow them to earlier and appropriately test a child's fine-motor and visual perceptual development and earlier indicate a potential learning disability. But the results of such test which seem to elucidate etiology of or instructional procedures for learning disabilities have failed to support the effectiveness of visual-motor training for improving academic learning (Kavale & Forness, 1999).

REFERENCES

Aylward, E. H., & Schmidt, S. (2001). *An examination of three tests of visual-motor integration. Journal of Learning Disabilities,* 328–330.

Beery, K. D., & Buktenica, N. A. (1967). *Developmental Test of Visual-Motor Integration student test booklet.* Chicago: Follett.

Getman, G. N. (1965). The visuomotor complex in the acquisition of learning skills. In J. Heilmuth (Ed.), *Learning disorders* (Vol. 1). Seattle, WA: Special Child.

Getman, G. N., Kane, E. R., & McKee, G. W. (1968). *Developing learning readiness: A visual-motor tactile skills program.* Manchester, MO: Webster Division, McGraw-Hill.

Kavale, K., & Forness, S. (1999). The effectiveness of special education. In C. R. Reynolds & T. B. Gutkin (Eds.), *The handbook of school psychology* (3rd ed). New York: Wiley.

Kephart, N. C. (1960). *The slow learner in the classroom.* Columbus, OH: Merrill.

Kephart, N. C. (1971). *The slow learner in the classroom* (2nd ed). Columbus, OH: Merrill.

Lerner, J. W. (1985). *Learning disabilities: Theories, diagnosis, and teaching strategies* (4th ed). Boston: Houghton Mifflin.

Strauss, A. A., & Werner, H. (1941). The mental organization of the brain injured mentally defective child. *American Journal of Psychiatry, 97,* 1194–1202.

LYNN S. FUCHS
DOUGLAS FUCHS
Peabody College, Vanderbilt University
First edition

YOLANDA TENORIO
California State University, San Bernardino
Second edition

MELANIE BROMLEY
California State University, San Bernardino
Third edition

DIAGNOSTIC PRESCRIPTIVE TEACHING
DYSLEXIA
VISUAL-MOTOR AND VISUAL-PERCEPTUAL PROBLEMS

VISUAL PERCEPTION AND DISCRIMINATION

Visual perception is a difficult concept that involves complex interactions between the individual and the environment. It is the ability to recognize stimuli and to differentiate among them (Frostig & Home, 1973). Visual perception is observing the surrounding physical world through our sense of sight (Sleeuwenhoek & Boter, 1995). Basically, visual perception and discrimination is the ability to physiologically interpret what is seen. There are a number of physiological factors that play a role in visual perception and discrimination, including sharpness of sight, range of vision, sense of color, adaptation to light and darkness, sensitivity to contrast, and eye movements, along with the environmental factors such as familiarity with the environment, weather conditions, the nature of the material (contrast and size), and task variables, also including a number of personality factors, including intelligence, character, age, concentration, and motivation (Sleeuwenhoek & Boter, 1995).

Visual-perceptual problems are concerned with disabilities that occur despite the fact that a child has physiologically healthy eyes. A child may have 20/20 visual acuity and adequate eye muscle control, and still have visual perceptual problems. These disabilities may include problems in form perception: discriminating the shapes of letters, numbers, pictures, or objects; position in space: discriminating the spatial orientation—left/right, top/bottom, etc.—of letters or words; visual closure: discriminating pictures or words with parts missing; and figure-ground discrimination: the ability to perceive a figure as distinct from the background (Hallahan, Kauffman, & Lloyd, 1985). A child who has problems with visual perception and discrimination may have difficulty in school because most academic activities require good visual-perceptual skills. In particular, the areas of math and reading will be difficult for the child who cannot distinguish between a multiplication and an addition sign, or who has difficulty discriminating pictures, letters, numbers, or words. During the early stages of a child's development, these problems are normal, but as a child matures, parents and teachers should become concerned if these difficulties persist.

The measurement of visual perception is complicated since it is tested by perceptual skills and motor skills. Tests such as the Visual Motor Gestalt Test, the coding subtest of the Wechsler Scales (WISC-III), and the Developmental Test of Visual-Motor Integration (VMI-3) all require motor responses and all are based on the assumption that the reproduced form is indicative of the individual's visual perception of the shape. However, Goldstein and Scheerer (1959) consider visual-perceptual and visual-motor deficits as separate entities. According to this perspective, if a child copies a figure incorrectly, a teacher cannot assume that the child has a visual-perceptual problem; additional information is needed. When a child copies a figure incorrectly, but can correctly select a picture of the figure from a group of choices, then there is an indication that the problem may be a visual-motor one. However, if the child selects an incorrect choice, then there is evidence that there may be a visual-perceptual difficulty (Hallahan et al., 1985). Some tests that measure visual perception and discrimination without requiring a drawing response include the Test of Visual-Perceptual Skills–Non-Motor (Revised), the Motor-Free Visual Perceptual Test (MVPT-R), the Visual Reception and Visual Closure subtests of the Illinois Test of Psycholinguistic Abilities (ITPA-Revised), the discrimination of forms and mutilated pictures subtests of the Stanford-Binet, and the Position in Space subtest of the Frostig Developmental Test of Visual Perception (DTVP-2).

REFERENCES

Frostig, M., & Home, D. (1973). *Frostig program for the development of visual perception.* Chicago: Follett.

Goldstein, K., & Scheerer, M. (1959). Abstract and concrete behavior: An experimental study with special tests. *Psychological Monograph, 83.*

Hallahan, D., Kauffman, J., & Lloyd, J. (1985). *Introduction to learning disabilities* (2nd ed). Englewood Cliffs, NJ: Prentice Hall.

Sleeuwenhoek, H. C., & Boter, R. D. (1995). Perceptual-motor performance and the social development of visually impaired children. *Journal of Visual Impairment & Blindness, 89*(4), 359–368.

DEBORAH C. MAY
State University of New York at Albany

DONALD S. MAROZAS
State University of New York at Geneseo
First edition

CHAZ ESPARAZA
California State University, San Bernardino
Third edition

BENDER-GESTALT TEST
DEVELOPMENTAL TEST OF VISUAL PERCEPTION-2
ILLINOIS TEST OF PSYCHOLINGUISTIC ABILITIES
VISUAL-MOTOR PERCEPTION AND DISCRIMINATION

VISUAL TRAINING

See VISION TRAINING.

VISUOMOTOR COMPLEX

Visuomotor complex is a term used by Getman (1965) to describe his model of the development of the visuomotor system and its relationship to the acquisition of learning skills.

This model reflects Getman's training as an optometrist by emphasizing the visual aspects of perception. It illustrates the developmental sequences that a child progresses through while acquiring visual-perceptual and motor skills, and emphasizes that each successive stage is dependent on earlier stages of development.

The six systems of learning levels in this model are (from the lowest to the highest) the innate response system, the general motor system, the special motor system, the ocular motor system, the speech-motor system, and the visualization system. These systems all contribute to vision or the perceptual event that results in cognition when many perceptions are integrated (Lerner, 1971).

This visuomotor complex requires solid learning at each level before proceeding to the next level. Getman believes that children will not succeed in educational programs if they do not have adequate experiences in the lower systems of development. A teaching program, Developing Learning Readiness: A Visual-Motor Tactile Skills Program (Getman, Kane, & McKee, 1968), is based on this model.

This visuomotor model has been criticized for simplifying learning, overemphasizing the role of vision, neglecting the role of language, speech, and feedback, and not providing empirical evidence for the theory (Lerner, 1971; Myers & Hammill, 1969).

REFERENCES

Getman, G. (1965). The visuomotor complex in the acquisition of learning skills. In J. Hellmuth (Ed.), *Learning disorders* (Vol. 1, pp. 49–76). Seattle, WA: Special Child.

Getman, G., Kane, E., & McKee, G. (1968). *Developing learning readiness: A Visual-Motor Tactile Skills Program.* Manchester, MO: Webster Division, McGraw-Hill.

Lerner, J. (1971). *Children with learning disabilities.* Boston: Houghton Mifflin.

Myers, P., & Hammill, D. (1969). *Methods for learning disorders.* New York: Wiley.

DEBORAH C. MAY
State University of New York at Albany

VISUAL PERCEPTION AND DISCRIMINATION
VISUAL TRAINING

VOCABULARY DEVELOPMENT

The knowledge of vocabulary, that is, the ability to recognize words and understand their meanings, is recognized as possibly the most important factor in being able to use and understand spoken and written language. Vocabulary knowledge is very closely associated with the ability to comprehend what is heard or read, and may be related to general intelligence and reasoning ability.

According to Harris (1970), children develop a variety of types of vocabulary knowledge in a developmental sequence. First they develop a hearing vocabulary, or the ability to respond to spoken words even before they themselves are able to use speech. For a number of years children are able to respond to more words that they hear than words that they are able to use themselves. Following the appropriate development of a hearing vocabulary, children begin to acquire emerging reading skills and a reading vocabulary—words that they are able to recognize in print and know the meanings of in context. Gradually, the developing reader is able to recognize more words in print and is able to use more words than in the speaking and writing vocabulary. Harris has explained that a child's total vocabulary involves all of the words that he or she can eventually understand and use in all the communications skills, including listening, speaking, reading, and writing.

The significance of a varied and well-developed vocabulary cannot be overemphasized, according to Johnson and Pearson (1984). They have identified and explained the reading process as a communication between an author and a reader. That communication is successful only when the reader is able to understand the author's original intent by recognizing and understanding the vocabulary that the author uses. It follows, then, that in order to be a fluent, proficient, and successful reader, it is necessary to possess a rich and varied vocabulary and word knowledge background.

General vocabulary development, and the ability to recognize words either in isolation or in context, have a common link in the diversity of words that the reader can both understand and use. Many of the words that the developing learner and reader uses and understands have been with him or her from early years; other words are learned and developed as they are used in the context of school-related activities. Therefore, while a rich experiential background during the preschool years is certainly a requisite for later vocabulary learning, much of the vocabulary development that the child experiences is accomplished in school. According to Smith and Johnson (1980), Stauffer (1969), and Johnson and Pearson (1984), a meaningful vocabulary is developed through reading- and writing-related activities in a variety of ways. These include the development of a basic sight vocabulary, various word identification strategies, including phonics, structural analysis, context clues, and instruction in understanding the deeper meanings of words. Through the activities outlined in basal reading programs, and occasionally through the use of content area materials, students are taught to use and understand synonyms, antonyms, homophones, and multiple meaning words. They also are taught to use the various resources such as dictionaries and thesauruses for determining word meaning.

One of the best ways to learn new words and what they mean is to become involved with reading and listening. Moffett and Wagner (1983) have stated that children need to become habitual readers. They must immerse themselves in a variety of reading and listening activities that will enable them to experience words in a variety of contexts and allow them to make generalizations about the meanings of words and how they may be used. Particularly during the elementary years, they argue, much of schooling must be involved with providing children with a variety of language-related situations that require them to be actively engaged in the production and reception of language in both oral and written forms. As the child becomes more engaged in reading and writing activities, preferably related to different content areas, not only is general vocabulary knowledge increased, but reasoning ability and conceptual development are enhanced.

The essence of reading and writing is communication, and the crucial variable in communication seems to be vocabulary knowledge. What distinguishes the fluent, successful reader from the poor reader seems to be a knowledge of words and what they mean. A successful and appropriate program of vocabulary development in the school, coupled with the child's preschool experiential background, may provide that key ingredient to becoming a successful language user. Johnson and Pearson (1984) give a complete and detailed account of how to provide an appropriate program of vocabulary development in school.

REFERENCES

Harris, A. J. (1970). *How to increase reading ability* (5th ed.). New York: McKay.

Johnson, D. D., & Pearson, P. D. (1984). *Teaching reading vocabulary* (2nd ed.). New York: Holt, Rinehart, & Winston.

Moffett, J., & Wagner, B. J. (1983). *Student centered language arts and reading, K-13: A handbook for teachers* (3rd ed.). Boston: Houghton Mifflin.

Smith, R. J., & Johnson, D. D. (1980). *Teaching children to read* (2nd ed.). Reading, MA: Addison-Wesley.

Stauffer, R. G. (1969). *Directing reading maturity as a cognitive process.* New York: Harper & Row.

JOHN M. EELLS
Souderton Area School District,
Souderton, Pennsylvania

INTELLIGENCE
READING
READING REMEDIATION

VOCATIONAL EDUCATION

The goal of vocational education programs is to prepare students to enter the work world. Astuto (1982) described vocational programs as focusing on the development of basic academic skills, good work habits, personally meaningful work values, self-understanding and identification of preferences, skills and aptitudes, occupational opportunities, the ability to plan and make career decisions, and the locating and securing of employment. The basic program components for vocational education are recognized as remedial basic skills, specific job training, personal and social adjustment skills, career information, modified content in subject areas, and on-the-job training. Ondell and Hardin (1981) discussed four types of occupational activities that would be part of a vocational program: paid work experience during the day, paid work experience after school hours, unpaid work observation, and in-school vocational laboratory.

From a historical perspective, the first piece of legislation to address the vocational educational needs of individuals with disabilities was the Vocational Education Act of 1963 (PL 88-210). The Educational Amendments of 1976 (PL 94-482) strengthened provisions for youths with disabilities in vocational education. According to Ondell and Hardin (1981) legislation promoting vocational education and the rights of individuals with disabilities has included the Smith-Hughes Act of 1917, which provided funds for vocational education in public schools; the Civilian Rehabilitation Act of 1920, which assigned responsibility for the administration of vocational rehabilitation to state boards of vocational education; the Vocational Rehabilitation Amendments of 1943, which expanded the 1920 act to include mentally and emotionally disabled persons; the Vocational Education Act of 1963, which provided occupational training for persons with special needs and allowed some of a state's allotment to be used in funding these programs; and the Vocational Amendments of 1968, which included more specific terminology and specified that 10 percent of the monies received by the state be set aside for the vocational education of individuals with disabilities. With these monies many specifically designed programs were started, thus expanding the area of vocational education to encompass special groups (pp. 2–3).

In the last century the U.S. economy has changed from being based almost solely in manufacturing and agriculture to one that, since the technology revolution, now provides mainly services and information. Computers and the Internet dictate new rules for the workplace, and thus also for vocational education. These trends have two implications for vocational education programs. It signals a shift in the type of requirements for the education and training fields to adequately prepare the upcoming U.S. workforce, and a shift in the levels of that education and training necessary to fulfill these new jobs (Shumer, 2001).

This has led to a new wave of policy reform that has put less emphasis on specific programs and more emphasis on reform and accountability. These new academic standards emerged with passage of the Carl D. Perkins Vocational and Applied Technology Education Act of 1990 (PL 101-392, also called Perkins II; Stone, Kowske, & Alfeld, 2004). This was one of "the most significant policy shifts in the history of federal involvement in vocational-technical education. For the first time, emphasis was placed on academic, as well as occupational skills" (Hayward & Benson, 1993, p. 3).

The most recent incarnation of the Carl D. Perkins Vocational and Technical Education Act (PL 105-332) was signed into law in 1998. Perkins III continues the theme of improving academic achievement while readying students for continued education and work. The law also reaffirms the commitment to serve special populations, increase accountability, and expand the use of technology (Rojewski, 2002). New initiatives include the need to negotiate core performance indicators. "Core performance indicators include things such as student attainment of identified academic and vocational proficiencies . . . attainment of a high school diploma or postsecondary credential; placement in postsecondary education, the military, or employment" (Lynch, 2000).

Probably one of the most important modern acts to influence vocational education for students with special needs is the 2001 No Child Left Behind Act (NCLB). NCLB requires that all students, including students with disabilities, be held to challenging content and achievement standards—that their progress is to be measured annually by assessments aligned with those high standards, and that schools and school districts are held accountable for achieving such results (www.ed.gov). Each state must meet requirements that are directly related to achievement and instruction for the full range of students with disabilities. These core principles include: statewide participation rates for students with disabilities, for purposes of measuring "Adequate Yearly Progress (AYP), must be at or above 95 percent; appropriate accommodations are provided to students with disabilities who need them; alternate assessments in reading/language arts and mathematics provided to students with disabilities who are unable to participate in the regular assessment . . . and results from those assessments must be reported. Each State must provide information on actions taken to raise achievement for students with disabilities or narrow the achievement gap and evidence that such efforts are improving student achievement" (PL 107-110, 2001). This means that states must raise achievement levels for students with disabilities. This emphasis on student achievement places more pressure on special education classes to find ways to increase academic performance. What this surmises is the reduced opportunity for students to take vocational classes due to the demands of more intensive academic classes. Vocational classes are trying to combat this by changing the curriculum to integrate more academics into the coursework.

REFERENCES

Astuto, T. A. (1982). *Vocational education programs and services for high school handicapped students*. Bloomington: Council of Administrators of Special Education, Indiana University.

Hayward, G. C., & Benson, C. S. (1993). *Vocational-technical education: Major reforms and debates 1917–present.* Washington, DC: U.S. Department of Education, Office of Vocational and Adult Education.

Lynch, R. L. (2000). *New directions for high school career and technical education in the 21st century* (Information Series No. 384). Columbus: The Ohio State University, ERIC Clearinghouse on Adult, Career, and Vocational Education.

No Child Left Behind Act of 2001, Public Law No. 107-110 (2001).

Ondell, J. T., & Hardin, L. (1981). *Vocational education programming for the handicapped.* Bloomington: Council of Administrators of Special Education, Indiana University.

Rojewski, J. W. (2002). Preparing the workforce of tomorrow: A conceptual framework for career and technical education. *Journal of Vocational Education Research, 27*(1), 7–35.

Shumer, R. (2001). A new, old vision of learning, working, and living: Vocational education in the 21st century. *Journal of Vocational Education Research, 26*(3), 261–272.

Spellings Announces New Special Education Guidelines, Details Workable, "Common-Sense" Policy to Help States Implement No Child Left Behind. (May 10, 2005). U.S. Department of Education. Retrieved January 13, 2006, from http://www.ed.gov

Stone, J. R., III, Kowske, B. J., & Alfeld, C. (2004). Career and technical education in the late 1990s: A descriptive study. *Journal of Vocational Education Research, 29*(3), 195–223.

EILEEN MCCARTHY
University of Wisconsin at Madison
First edition

MICHELLE EVANS
California State University, San Bernardino
Third edition

REHABILITATION VOCATIONAL EVALUATION

VOCATIONAL EVALUATION

Vocational evaluation is a term that encompasses the processes undertaken in determining eligibility and appropriate program plans for students entering vocational education. Specific components and processes used in vocational evaluation include assessment of skills, aptitude, interests, work behaviors, social skills, and physical capabilities (Leconte, 1985; Levinson & Capps, 1985; Peterson, 1985; Rosenberg & Tesolowski, 1982). At this time, students with disabilities and students who are disadvantaged are the main targets for vocational evaluation programs (Levinson, 1994).

The area of vocational assessment is affected by the Carl Perkins Vocational Education Act of 1984, which mandates that schools provide each handicapped or disadvantaged student who enrolls in a vocational education program an assessment of the individual's interests, abilities, and special needs with respect to the successful completion of the vocational education program (Cobb & Larkin, 1985). During 1990 the Carl Perkins Act was amended, and it became mandatory for all states to create, and to put into practice, standards and measurements that would outline student progress. These outcomes were required to have two key measurements: (1) student progress in learning and increased aptitude, and (2) evaluating job placement, or "secondary school completion" (Association for Career & Technical Education, 1995).

It is important to note that it is the local school systems that hold the responsibility for administering and upgrading existing programs (Association for Career & Technical Education, 1995). Occasionally educational agencies will reach an agreement with vocational rehabilitation agencies to conduct vocational evaluations. This is essential for schools that don't have the necessary funds to provide a vocational evaluation program for themselves. One such agency is the Hiram G. Andrews Vocational Rehabilitation Center, which implements preparation in 26 different areas (Levinson, 1994).

The terms vocational evaluation and vocational assessment are often used interchangeably. Although Leconte (1985) indicated that the Division on Career Development (DCD) of the Council for Exceptional Children (CEC) does not discriminate between vocational evaluation and vocational assessment, he differentiated between the two terms as follows: vocational assessment is an ongoing process carried out by professionals from many different disciplines, and information from vocational assessment is incorporated into a student's total educational program; vocational evaluation is an in-depth process conducted by a trained vocational evaluator, usually in a vocational evaluation center. There are different methods these administrators use in their evaluation. For instance, there are tests that measure individual performance, samples of individual work, written tests, and interviews that are normally employed (Levinson, 1994).

School personnel have not been able to agree on a term or title to represent the realm of student assessment in vocational education. When first introduced into school settings, programs were called vocational evaluation based on the service's origin in vocational rehabilitation. After PL 94-142, the service was aligned with services for special education, and different forms of evaluation were frequently referred to as vocational assessment. In essence, vocational evaluation has been delineated as a more intensive, time-limited service than vocational assessment. Although the term vocational evaluation represents the broad umbrella under which vocational assessment is subsumed, for our purposes the terms will be referred to as vocational evaluation assessment. The purposes and goals are well defined and agreed on throughout the literature. Vocational assessment is a process that can measure skills, attitudes, interests, and physical abilities. In addition, it can predict success in occupational placements and prescribe the necessary program plan needed to reach the necessary objectives. Furthermore, it can explore interests and match them with abilities while observing behavioral changes.

Levinson and Capps (1985) discussed vocational assessment as a process that yields critical information with which vocational programming decisions may be made. They include the identification of appropriate goals and instructional methods in the process. Peterson (1985) suggested six guidelines for effective vocational assessment: (1) use trained personnel: (2) develop and use locally developed work samples; (3) obtain access to a vocational evaluation center; (4) plan to develop and expand vocational assessment in phases with a team; (5) ascertain that vocational assessment is instructionally relevant and useful; and (6) ensure that the vocational assessment is used for vocational guidance and the identification of appropriate career and vocational service. Peterson (1985) stated that vocational assessment can be "a powerful tool in the education of special students" since it can provide a link between special education or Chapter 1 services and vocational education. However, it has been pointed out that the current system employed for vocational evaluation is lacking (Lowman, 1993). Therefore, the challenge to fully operationalize these services with respect to students with disabilities remains firmly in place.

REFERENCES

Association for Career & Technical Education. (1995). The Test Makers. *Vocational Education Journal, 70*(3), 30.

Cobb, R. B., & Larkin, D. (1985). Assessment and placement of handicapped pupils into secondary vocational education programs. *Focus on Exceptional Children, 17*(7), 1–14.

Leconte, P. (1985, December). *Vocational assessment of the special needs learner: A vocational education perspective.* Paper presented at the meeting of the American Vocational Association Convention, Atlanta, GA.

Levinson, E. M. (1994). Current vocational assessment models for students with disabilities. *Journal of Counseling & Development, 73,* 94–101.

Levinson, F. M., & Capps, C. F. (1985). Vocational assessment and special education triennial reevaluations at the secondary school level. *Psychology in the Schools, 22,* 283–292.

Lowman, R. L. (1993). The inter-domain model of career assessment and counseling. *Journal of Counseling & Development, 71,* 549–554.

Peterson, M. (1985, December). *Vocational assessment of special students: A comprehensive developmental approach.* Paper presented at the meeting of the American Vocational Association Convention, Atlanta, GA.

Rosenberg, H., & Tesolowski, D. G. (1982). Assessment of critical vocational behaviors. *Career Development for Exceptional Individuals, 5,* 25–37.

EILEEN MCCARTHY
University of Wisconsin at Madison
First edition

CANDACE ANDREWS
California State University, San Bernardino
Third edition

VOCATIONAL REHABILITATION COUNSELING

VOCATIONAL REHABILITATION ACT OF 1973

See REHABILITATION ACT OF 1973.

VOCATIONAL REHABILITATION COUNSELING

According to the 2006–2007 edition of the *Occupational Outlook Handbook,* "Rehabilitation counselors help people deal with the personal, social, and vocational effects of disabilities. They counsel people with disabilities resulting from birth defects, illness or disease, accidents, or the stress of daily life. They evaluate the strengths and limitations of individuals, provide personal and vocational counseling, and arrange for medical care, vocational training, and job placement. Rehabilitation counselors interview both individuals with disabilities and their families, evaluate school and medical reports, and confer and plan with physicians, psychologists, occupational therapists, and employers to determine the capabilities and skills of the individual. Conferring with the client, they develop a rehabilitation program that often includes training to help the person develop job skills. Rehabilitation counselors also work toward increasing the client's capacity to live independently" (p. 6). While this general definition is correct, the actual activities engaged in by rehabilitation counselors and the resources available to them vary considerably depending on their work setting.

Approximately 9,000 of the estimated 18,000 to 20,000 rehabilitation counselors in the United States are certified rehabilitation counselors. The prototypical rehabilitation counselor works for one of the state Department of Vocational Rehabilitation (DVR) agencies and places primary emphasis on the vocational adjustment of disabled clients who are adjudged to have the potential for gainful employment. Rehabilitation counselors also work in a wide variety of allied settings such as sheltered workshops, centers for the developmentally disabled, rehabilitation centers, Veterans' Administration programs, employment services, alcohol and drug abuse programs, halfway houses, insurance companies, and private for-profit organizations that specialize in the rehabilitation of industrially injured clients. New developments in the rehabilitation counselor's role are seen in recent movements to provide independent living skills to the severely disabled and assistance to disabled youths as they make the transition from school to the world of work.

The profession of rehabilitation counseling emerged with the passage of PL 236 (Smith-Fess Act) in 1920, which established the civilian vocational rehabilitation program in the United States. However, it was not until the passage of PL 565 in 1954 that federal funds were available to encourage formal academic training for rehabilitation personnel. There are approximately 110 rehabilitation counselor training programs accredited by the Council on Rehabilitation Education (CORE) and/or members of the National Council on Rehabilitation Education (NCRE; IDEA, 1990). Today the professional identity of the rehabilitation counselor is well established and there is consensus regarding an appropriate educational curriculum. The knowledge base and competencies for this profession are reflected in the following core subjects that are taught in most rehabilitation counselor training programs: history and philosophy of rehabilitation, vocational and personal counseling, physical disabilities, developmental disabilities, mental illness, psychosocial implications of disability, psychological testing, vocational evaluation, occupational information and employment trends, community resources, job placement, and supervised internships.

The most prominent professional organizations for rehabilitation counselors are the National Rehabilitation Association, the National Rehabilitation Counseling Association, and the American Rehabilitation Counseling Association. Within the past decade, certification procedures for rehabilitation counselors have been established through the efforts of various professional organizations. Certification is based on a combination of education, experience, and the successful completion of a national examination. While certification procedures do guarantee minimum standards of competency, they may be criticized for restricting entrance into the profession by those who are otherwise qualified but lack formal credentials. Many rehabilitation employers expect applicants to be certified, but this is by no means universal and the eventual status of certification is unclear at present.

The high social validity of rehabilitation counseling is indicated by the continuing bipartisan congressional support that rehabilitation legislation has enjoyed for over 65 years. Additional economic benefits accrue to society from the reductions in welfare, disability, and medical assistance payments after the disabled person enters the work force.

Studies of the cost effectiveness of vocational rehabilitation programs showed that the conversion of two rehabilitative day treatment programs to supported employment programs resulted in improved vocational outcomes with no increase in costs (Clark et al., 1996). In human terms, state DVR agencies rehabilitate between 300,000 and 400,000 physically challenged people per year. The dignity and self-esteem these individuals feel when they become contributing members of society cannot be measured in dollars.

REFERENCES

Bureau of Labor Statistics. (2005). *Occupational outlook handbook: 2006–2007 edition.* Washington, DC: U.S. Department of Labor.

Clark, R. E., Bush, P. W., Becker, D. R., et al. (1996). A cost-effectiveness comparison of supported employment and rehabilitative day treatment. *Administration and Policy in Mental Health, 24,* 63–77.

U.S. Congress. (1990). *Public Law 101-476: Individuals with Disabilities Education Act.* Washington, DC: Government Printing Office.

JOHN D. SEE
University of Wisconsin at Stout
First edition

CLAUDIA CAMARILLO-DIEVENDORF
Pitzer College, Claremont
Third edition

VOCATIONAL EVALUATION

VOCATIONAL VILLAGE

A vocational village is a cloistered community in which persons with and without disabilities live and work. It is often referred to as a sheltered village. There is a strong work ethic in the community. The setting is not usually designed for transition but rather as a permanent living/working arrangement for individuals with disabilities. There is usually a deep religious undertone in such villages and a majority of the time they are church sponsored. The nondisabled residents of the village are often volunteer workers who have made a long-term commitment to the village. There are also some nondisabled workers who are students working in practicum arrangements or in work-study activities. Baker, Seltzer, and Seltzer (1977) explain that

common to all sheltered villages is the segregation of the retarded person from the outside community and the implicit view that the retarded adult is better off in an environment that shelters him/her from many of the potential failures and frustrations of life in the outside community. (p. 109)

It is a delivery model that espouses the principle of separate but equal.

REFERENCE

Baker, B. L., Seltzer, G. B., & Seltzer, M. M. (1977). *As close as possible: Community residences for retarded adults.* Boston: Little, Brown.

ROBERT A. SEDLAK
University of Wisconsin at Stout

**COMMUNITY RESIDENTIAL PROGRAMS
SHELTERED WORKSHOPS**

VOICE DISORDERS (DYSPHONIA)

Aronson (1985) says that, "A voice disorder exists when quality, pitch, loudness, or flexibility differs from the voices of others of similar age, sex, and cultural group." What constitutes an abnormal voice is a relative judgment that is made by the speaker, the listener, and professionals who may be consulted. Causes of voice disorders are usually classified as either organic (physical) or functional (behavioral). Recent studies report the incidence of voice disorders in the U.S. population of school-aged children to be between 6–9 percent (Aronson, 1985). The parameters by which a voice can be judged as abnormal are considered in context. For example, a voice that is so hoarse that it distracts the listener or interferes with intelligibility can be identified as disordered and in need of treatment. The pitch of a female voice considered to be appropriate during her school-aged years may be too high for effective function as she enters the business world. The person who cannot produce a voice loud enough to be heard in a typically noisy classroom or one whose voice is so inflexible that the speaker seems emotionless may also be identified as abnormal. In some cases, such abnormal voice symptoms indicate the presence of an underlying illness which is in need of medical diagnosis and treatment. If a hoarse voice quality exists for an extended period of time (i.e., longer than two weeks), it could indicate the presence of a mass lesion in the larynx (voice box) which could be benign or malignant. An inability to alter pitch or loudness to convey meaning could signal a neuromuscular problem associated with incipient neurological disease. An inappropriately high pitch, used habitually, might point to endocrine dysfunction or to psychosocial issues which require attention (Colton & Casper, 1990).

Evaluation and treatment of voice disorders requires the combined efforts of the speech-language pathologist and an otolaryngologist (ENT). These professionals will examine the physical status of the larynx, velopharyngeal mechanism, and supporting respiratory system and will analyze the voice both perceptually and acoustically to determine if a clinically significant disorder exists. They will then attempt to identify the etiological factors underlying any abnormalities and prescribe a course of treatment. Often, the first choice for treatment is behavioral modification to eliminate factors contributing to the voice disorder and to establish good vocal hygiene. Less frequently, voice problems require physical management which might include medication, for example, in allergy therapy, or a more invasive treatment, such as surgery.

REFERENCES

Aronson, A. (1985). *Clinical voice disorders.* New York: Thieme.

Colton, R. H., & Casper, J. K. (1990). *Understanding voice problems.* Baltimore: Williams & Wilkins.

STAFF

SPEECH

VOLTA REVIEW, THE

The Volta Review was founded in 1898. It is published four times a year, with a monograph issue in September. The publication is a product of the Alexander Graham Bell Association for the Deaf, a nonprofit organization founded by Alexander Graham Bell in 1890 that serves as an information center for people with hearing impairment. Bell believed that people with hearing losses could be taught to speak and, through lip reading, could learn to understand others.

Only articles devoted to the education, rehabilitation, and communicative development of individuals with hearing impairment are published by *The Volta Review.* The target audience includes teachers of the hearing impaired; professionals in the fields of education, speech, audiology, language, otology, and psychology; parents of children with hearing impairments; and adults with hearing impairments. The articles are peer-reviewed for possible publication and vary in length, and the journal includes advertisements as well as illustrations. Topics include issues related to hearing impairment such as language development, parental concerns, medical/technical and psychosocial issues, teaching, and computers.

REBECCA BAILEY
Texas A&M University
First edition

TAMARA J. MARTIN
The University of Texas of the Permian Basin
Second edition

DEAF
DEAF EDUCATION

VOLUNTARY AGENCIES

Voluntary agencies are organizations that use volunteers to serve on decision-making boards or to provide services for the community. Volunteers are members of a community whom, without the expectation of pay, offer their time to benefit agencies that serve particular groups in an area. Volunteers on agency governing boards make decisions on the purchase of property and capital equipment, organizational policy, specific human services that will be available in the community, allocation of funds to other agencies (United Way, foundations, etc.) or within their own agency, and fund-raising.

Approximately 84 million Americans serve as volunteers in such agencies each year (Shtulman, 1985). According to the Current Population Survey (CPS), about 83.9 million Americans served as volunteers in 2001, resulting in an estimated 239 billion dollars worth of work (Independent Sector, 2001). Women have provided a large portion of volunteer service but the entry of large numbers of women into the work force has limited their availability for volunteer service. However, an increasingly active senior citizen population is providing a pool of dependable, dedicated volunteers. Additionally, volunteering rates have increased in younger Americans from 2002–2003, with teenagers, on average, volunteering more often than other age groups (Helms, 2004). Another developing source is through the workplace. Some firms make it possible for their employees to have released time for community service; these firms say that this "loaned executive" program contributes to a better workforce through the opportunity for workers to apply or develop skills, a lower rate of absenteeism, and increased productivity (United Way, 1985).

REFERENCES

Helms, S. (2004). *Youth volunteering in the states: 2002 and 2003.* University of Maryland: The Center for Information & Research on Civic Learning & Engagement. Retrieved from http://www .civicyouth.org/PopUps/FactSheets/FS_Vol_state.pdf

Independent Sector. (2001). *Giving and volunteering in the United States 2001.* Retrieved January 15, 2006, from http://www .independentsector.org

Shtulman, J. (1985). *A question and-answer session on voluntarism.* Holyoke, MA: Transcript-Telegram.

United Way. (1985). *Volunteer notes.* Alexandria, VA: Author.

DENISE M. SEDLACK
United Way of Dunn County,
Menomonie, Wisconsin
First edition

THOMAS NEISES
California State University, San
Bernardino
Third edition

ADVOCACY FOR CHILDREN WITH DISABILITIES
LIBRARY SERVICES FOR INDIVIDUALS WITH DISABILITIES

VON RECKLINGHAUSEN, FRIEDRICH (1833–1910)

Friedrich von Recklinghausen, a German pathologist, was a major contributor to the development of pathological anatomy as a branch of medicine. He is best known for his description, in 1863, of neurofibromatosis, or von Recklinghausen's disease, characterized by multiple small tumors affecting the subcutaneous nerves. The disease is hereditary and is associated with mental retardation.

REFERENCES

Talbott, J. H. (1970). *A biographical history of medicine.* Orlando, FL: Grune & Stratton.

von Recklinghausen, F. (1962). Multiple fibromas of the skin and multiple neuromas. In E. R. Long (Trans.), *Selected readings in pathology* (2nd ed.). Springfield, IL: Thomas.

PAUL IRVINE
Katonah, New York

NEUROFIBROMATOSIS
MENTAL RETARDATION

VYGOTSKY, LEV S. (1896–1934)

Lev S. Vygotsky was a Soviet psychologist and semiotician. His work had a tremendous impact on the development of psychology in the Soviet Union and is currently attracting a great deal of interest outside Russia as well (Wertsch, 1985a, 1985b).

In the West, Vygotsky is known primarily for his work on the relationship between the development of thinking and speech in ontogenesis (Vygotsky, 1962, 1978). In Vygotsky's view, the more complex forms of human thinking, memory, and attention depend on the individual's mastery of historically and culturally developed means of organizing and mediating mental activity. Vygotsky argued that words and speech are first used in social interaction to organize and mediate the mental activity of several individuals working cooperatively on a task, and that these same linguistic means are later appropriated by the individual and internalized to be used in organizing and mediating his or her mental activity when working alone on similar tasks. In this sense, Vygotsky felt that certain kinds of social interaction between children and adults (or more competent peers) can create a "zone of proximal development" that raises the level of the child's cognitive functioning in the context of social interaction and helps move the child toward the next or proximal stage of independent functioning.

For Vygotsky, however, this work was only part of a much broader program of theory and research that was concerned with the relationships between historically developed modes of social behavior and the psychological development of the individual in all its aspects (Minick, 1987). In the decade following his death, the efforts of his colleagues and students to develop this broader theoretical framework led to the emergence of what is known as the theory of activity, a theoretical and research paradigm that illuminates the work of many contemporary Russian psychologists.

Vygotsky had a lifelong interest in developing theory, research, and practical intervention techniques relevant to abnormal psychological functioning and development in both children and adults. He wrote extensively on these topics (Vygotsky, 1987) and founded several institutes that continue to play an important role in Russian work in this area. Through this work and that of colleagues and students such as A. R. Luria (Luria, 1979), Vygotsky played a central role in the development of Soviet work in this domain.

REFERENCES

Luria, A. R. (1979). *The making of mind: A personal account of Soviet psychology.* Cambridge, MA: Harvard University Press.

Minick, N. (1987). The development of Vygotsky's thought. In N. Minick (Trans.), *Introduction to L. S. Vygotsky, Collected works: Problems of general psychology* (Vol. 2). New York: Plenum.

Vygotsky, L. S. (1962). *Thought and language* (E. Hanfmann & G. Vakar, Eds. and Trans.). Cambridge, MA: MIT Press. (Original work published 1934)

Vygotsky, L. S. (1978). *Mind in society* (M. Cole, V. John-Steiner, S. Scribner, & E. Souberman, Eds.). Cambridge, MA: Harvard University Press.

Vygotsky, L. S. (1987). Thinking and speech. In V. V. Davydov (Ed.) & N. Minick (Trans.), *L. S. Vygotsky, Collected works: General psychology* (Vol. 2). New York: Plenum. (Original work published 1934)

Vygotsky, L. S. (1978). (1987). In A. V. Zaporozhets (Ed.) & J. Knox (Trans.), *L. S. Vygotsky, Collected works: The foundations of defectology* (Vol. 5) New York: Plenum.

Wertsch, J. V. (1985a). *Vygotsky and the social formation of mind.* Cambridge, MA: Harvard University Press.

Wertsch, J. V. (Ed.). (1985b). *Culture, communication, and cognition: Vygotskian perspectives.* New York: Cambridge University Press.

NORRIS MINICK
Center for Psychosocial Studies,
The Spencer Foundation

THEORY OF ACTIVITY
ZONE OF PROXIMAL DEVELOPMENT

W

WAIS-III

See WECHSLER ADULT INTELLIGENCE SCALE–THIRD EDITION.

WALLIN, JOHN EDWARD (J. E.) WALLACE (1876–1969)

J. E. Wallace Wallin, a pioneer in the fields of special education and clinical psychology, was born in Page County, Iowa on January 21, 1876 to Henry and Emma M. (Johnson) Wallin, originally from Sweden. Wallace was the third of nine children. He attended the public schools of Stanton, Iowa. On June 21, 1913, at the age of 37, he married his wife, Frances Geraldine Tinsley. The couple had two daughters, Geraldine Tinsley Wallin Sickler, born in 1919, and Virginia Stanton Wallin Obrinski, born in 1915, who also became a psychologist.

Wallin obtained his BA degree in 1897 from Augustana College in Rock Island, Illinois. He attended Yale and studied under Dr. Edward W. Scripture and George Trumbull Ladd. Scripture had done his own thesis under "the great German psychologist," Wilhelm Wundt. While at Yale, Wallin

John Edward Wallace Wallin

completed an MA degree in 1899, and a PhD in 1901. Wallin also worked as an assistant to Dr. G. Stanley Hall at Clark University in Worcester, Massachusetts. Wallin served as head of the psychology department and vice-president of the East Stroudsburg State Teachers College in Pennsylvania. While at Stroudsburg, he taught courses in physiological, child, genetic, educational, and abnormal psychology, and Mental Retardation. Wallin held numerous positions in the following years. He was the head of the department of psychology and education at the Normal Training School at Cleveland, Ohio, from 1909 to 1910, where he developed the field of special education, psychoclinical examinations, and one of the first group intelligence tests. By 1912, he established a psychoeducational clinic at the University of Pittsburgh, which was one of the first such clinics in the country. Wallin went on to become the director of numerous other clinics and special schools and affiliated with more than 25 colleges and universities (Wallin, 1955).

Outspoken, argumentative, critical, and at times cantankerous, Wallin was a crusader and a pioneer for disabled children. He was a leading advocate for the use of clinical psychology in education, especially as it relates to identification, diagnosis, and prescription for children with disabilities (P.I., 1979), and was a strong advocate for the proper training of clinicians. He worked to establish the principle that all children would benefit from an education, regardless of degree of disability, and helped to establish special classes in Western Pennsylvania, Ohio, Missouri, and Delaware. Wallin also made extensive contributions to the area of special education and the field of psychology by publishing over 30 books and 350 articles throughout his career, including psychological textbooks. He was a political activist for policies, regulations, and change to ensure appropriate education for children with special needs. He was a member of numerous professional organizations and served on many committees, such as the secretary of the committee on special education for the White House Conference on Child Health and Protection from 1929–1930. He continued to write into his 90s. Wallin died on August 5, 1969.

REFERENCES

P. I. (1979). John Edward Wallace Wallin (1876–1969). A biographical sketch. *Journal of Special Education, 13,* 4–5.

Wallin, J. E. W. (1955). *The odyssey of a psychologist: Pioneering experiences in special education, clinical psychology, and mental hygiene with a comprehensive bibliography of the author's publications.* Wilmington, DE: Author.

KIM RYAN-ARREDONDO
Texas A&M University

WATSON, JOHN B. (1878–1958)

John B. Watson developed and publicized the basic concepts of behaviorism, which in the 1920s became one of the major schools of psychological thought. Watson obtained his PhD at the University of Chicago and continued there as an instructor until 1908, when he accepted a professorship at Johns Hopkins University. Watson's behaviorism explained human behavior in terms of physiological responses to environmental stimuli and psychology as the study of the relationship between the two. Watson sought to make psychology "a purely objective experimental branch of natural science," with conditioning as one of its chief methods.

Watson's zealous environmentalism led him into some extreme positions, such as his assertion that he could train any healthy infant, regardless of its heredity, to become any type of person he might designate: "doctor, lawyer, artist, merchant-chief, and . . . even beggar-man and thief." Hyperbole aside, Watson's behaviorism was a dominant force in American psychology for decades and underlies many of today's behaviorally oriented instructional approaches. Watson eventually left the academic world, completing his career as an executive in the field of advertising.

John B. Watson

REFERENCES

Skinner, B. F. (1959). John Broadua Watson, behaviorist. *Science, 129,* 197–198.

Watson, J. B. (1919). *Psychology from the standpoint of a behaviorist.* Philadelphia: Lippincott.

PAUL IRVINE
Katonah, New York

BEHAVIOR MODIFICATION
CONDITIONING

WEB ACCESSIBILITY

Web accessibility is the degree to which a web-based resource is widely usable. Resources that have a high level of accessibility will be accessible by users regardless of the device or software used to access the resource, the functional limitations or abilities of the user, or the conditions of access (e.g., low bandwidth connections, display size). Conversely, web resources that have a low level of accessibility are not usable by a majority of users because of limitations associated with platform, information format, ability/disability, or ambient conditions. Design techniques that increase web accessibility seek to minimize these limitations, although they cannot be completely eliminated under this definition.

Since web accessibility of a specific resource is almost always situational rather than prescriptive, defining it in concrete terms is difficult. The World Wide Web Consortium (W3C), specifically the subgroup of the W3C that deals with accessibility issues (also known as the Web Accessibility Initiative, or WAI) states that "Web accessibility means that people with disabilities can perceive, understand, navigate, and interact with the web, and that they can contribute to the web. Web accessibility also benefits others, including older people with changing abilities due to aging" (W3C, 2005a). An important point to this description is that web accessibility benefits users beyond those with disabilities.

Much has been written in recent years about web accessibility, but little scholarly research has been done. Most of the available literature, much of it online, focuses on *how* to achieve Web accessibility rather than *what* it is. To this end, two well known standards have been promulgated.

Standards

The first (and most widely known) is the Web Content Accessibility Guidelines version one (WCAG1.0; W3C, 2005b). The WCAG consist of fourteen guidelines that are further broken down into 65 checkpoints. These checkpoints detail design and programming rules that guide developers in how to make web-based content accessible. Each of the checkpoints is also given a priority of one, two, or three. Priority one checkpoints are those items considered to be the most critical by the W3C. Priority two checkpoints are considered important, while priority three checkpoints are considered desirable. All of the guidelines are further sorted into two overriding themes that guide accessible design: ensuring graceful transformation (of information), and making content understandable and navigable. An example of a WCAG1.0 checkpoint is given in the following.

Guideline 1. Checkpoint 1. "Provide a text equivalent for every non-text element (e.g., via 'alt,' 'longdesc,' or in element content). *This includes:* images, graphical representations of text (including symbols), image map regions, animations (e.g., animated GIFs), applets and programmatic objects, ascii art, frames, scripts, images used as list bullets, spacers, graphical buttons, sounds (played with or without user interaction), stand-alone audio files, audio tracks of video, and video" (W3C, 1999).

Taking a cue from the W3C, the federal government (specifically the Access Board) created a subset of the original WCAG1.0 guidelines in 2000 and dubbed them the Electronic and Information Technology Accessibility Standards or, as they are more commonly known, the Section 508 standards (Access Board, 2000). These standards were based upon the existing priority one checkpoints found in the WCAG1.0 standards with several minor changes. An excellent comparison of the two standards can be found online at http://www.jimthatcher.com/sidebyside.htm (Thatcher, 2005). The 508 standards apply specifically to federal agencies' web sites, but the standards have been widely adopted by non-federal institutions as they represent a succinct and demonstrable subset of the more comprehensive (and sometimes esoteric) WCAG1.0 standards. As more and more institutions, both public and private, have written institutional web accessibility policies, the 508 standards have been instructive.

Assessment

There are a variety of accessibility "checkers" available to content developers and assessment personnel. They fall into several categories of implementation:

- Authoring Tool Checkers—These are built-in accessibility features of software applications used to develop web sites. Web authoring tools such as Dreamweaver (http://www.macromedia.com/macromedia/accessibility/) and Frontpage (http://www.microsoft.com/frontpage/using/accessibility/default.htm) provide utilities to implement accessibility features during the development phase.
- Stand-Alone Checkers—These are applications that are used during the postdevelopment phase of web site

management. Some examples are Bobby (http://www.cast.org/bobby/) and Wave (http://www.wave.webaim.org/index.jsp). Stand-alone checkers are good solutions for individual web developers that have access to the web site being checked.
- Enterprise Checkers—These are web-based applications that can check very large web sites and collect/disseminate information in a web-based format. Enterprise Checkers are good for assessing large web sites in a decentralized environment where the web content is located on a variety of servers. An example of an Enterprise Checker is WebXM (http://www.watchfire.com/products/webxm/default.aspx). Another example is UsableNet's LIFT (http://www.usablenet.com/).

There is a fairly comprehensive list of accessibility checkers located at http://www.webaim.org/products/evalandrepair/.

It is important to note that accessibility checkers cannot catch all accessibility errors. Only about 25 percent of published accessibility guidelines (when using WCAG guidelines) are automatically verifiable with accessibility checking software. The other 75 percent may be indicated by accessibility checking software, but must be verified by the author.

REFERENCES

Access Board. (2000). *Electronic and Information Technology Accessibility Standards (Section 508).* Retrieved October 10, 2005, from http://www.access-board.gov/sec508/standards.htm

Thatcher, J. (2005). *Side by side WCAG vs. 508.* Retrieved October 10, 2005, from http://www.jimthatcher.com/sidebyside.htm

World Wide Web Consortium (W3C). (1999). *Checklist of checkpoints for Web content accessibility guidelines 1.0.* Retrieved October 10, 2005, from http://www.w3.org/TR/WCAG10/full-checklist.html

World Wide Web Consortium (W3C). (2005a). *Introduction to Web accessibility.* Retrieved October 10, 2005, from http://www.w3.org/WAI/intro/accessibility.php

World Wide Web Consortium (W3C). (2005b). *WAI guidelines and techniques.* Retrieved October 10, 2005, from http://www.w3.org/WAI/guid-tech.html

DAVID SWEENEY
Texas A&M University

WECHSLER, DAVID (1896–1981)

Known primarily as the author of intelligence scales that played, and continue to play, a critical role in the lives of millions of individuals throughout the world, David

Wechsler had a humanistic philosophy about testing as a part of assessment. His professional writing includes more than 60 articles and books that emphasize the importance of motivation, personality, drive, cultural opportunity, and other variables in determining an individual's functional level.

Born in Rumania, Wechsler moved with his family of nine to New York City at age 6. At 20 he completed a BA degree at City College in 1916 and an MA the following year at Columbia University under Robert S. Woodworth. The next few years were spent with the armed forces, where Wechsler helped evaluate thousands of recruits, many of whom could not read English and who had little formal schooling. Near the end of his Army tour he studied with Charles Spearman and Karl Pearson in London and then, on a fellowship, with Henri Pieron and Louis Lapique in Paris. These studies provided the foundation for his continuous enthusiasm for the "nonintellective" components of intelligence.

While completing his PhD at Columbia in 1925, Wechsler worked as a psychologist in New York City's newly created Bureau of Child Study. After serving as secretary for the Psychological Corporation (1925–1927) and in private clinical practice (1927–1932), Wechsler became chief psychologist at New York's Bellevue Hospital, a post he held for 35 years. In that position he developed the tests that carried both his and the hospital's name in the early editions: the Wechsler-Bellevue Intelligence Scale I (1939) and Scale II (1942), the Wechsler Intelligence Scale for Children (1949), the Wechsler Adult Intelligence Scale (1955), and the Wechsler Preschool and Primary Scale of Intelligence (1967). He continued to help with the revision of his scales in retirement. The utility of the scales has warranted periodic updating by the publisher.

Wechsler believed his most important work to be his article "The Range of Human Capacities" (1980), the seminal work for his book by the same name that was published in 1935 and revised in 1971. A more popular contribution is the concept of a deviation quotient used for reporting adult intelligence test scores in place of mental age and ratio IQ used with the Binet tests for children and youths. Today nearly all cognitive ability tests use standard scores patterned after the deviation IQ.

The many honors Wechsler received from professional groups and universities around the world include the Distinguished Professional Contribution Award from the American Psychological Association (APA, 1973), similar awards from APA's Division of Clinical Psychology (1960) and Division of School Psychology (1973), and an honorary doctorate from the Hebrew University in Jerusalem.

JOSEPH L. FRENCH
Pennsylvania State University

INTELLIGENCE TESTING

WECHSLER ABBREVIATED SCALE OF INTELLIGENCE

The Wechsler Abbreviated Scale of Intelligence (WASI) is an individually administered test that measures the intelligence in clinical and nonclinical populations. The test can be administered in approximately 30 minutes to individuals between the ages of 6 and 89.

The WASI consists of four subtests: Vocabulary, Similarities, Block Design, and Matrix Reasoning. All WASI items are new and parallel to their full Wechsler counterparts. Block Design consists of a set of 13 modeled or printed two-dimensional geometric patterns that the examinee replicates within a specified time limit using two-color cubes. Matrix Reasoning is similar to the WAIS-III and WISC-IV Matrix Reasoning subtest. Similarities is parallel to the WISC-IV and WAIS-III subtests and includes low-end picture items. Vocabulary has both oral and visual presentation of words and also has picture items that were designed to extend the floor of the test. The four subtests result in a Full Scale IQ score (FSIQ) and can also be divided into Verbal IQ (VIQ) scores and Performance IQ (PIQ) scores. The PIQ score comprises the performance on Matrix Reasoning, which measures nonverbal fluid ability, and Block Design, which measures visuomotor and coordination skills. The VIQ score assesses performance on the Vocabulary and Similarities subtests of the WASI. An estimate of general intellectual ability can also be obtained from just a two-subtest administration that includes Vocabulary and Matrix Reasoning and provides only the FSIQ score.

Nationally standardized with 2,245 cases, the WASI has reliability coefficients for both the children and adolescent subtests, and FSIQs range from .81 to .98. The WASI subtests have significant correlations with the corresponding subtests of the WISC-III. Additionally, it has been evidenced that the WASI measures constructs similar to those measured by its WAIS-III counterparts.

Reviews of the WASI have been generally positive. However, Axelrod (2002) did note that for a clinical sample he examined, "the WASI did not consistently demonstrate desirable accuracy in predicting scores. . . . The results suggest that clinicians should use the WASI cautiously, if at all, especially when accurate estimates of individuals' WAIS-III results are needed" (p. 23).

REFERENCES AND ADDITIONAL INFORMATION

Axelrod, B. N. (2002). Validity of the Wechsler Abbreviated Scale of Intelligence and other very short forms of estimating intellectual functioning. *Assessment, 9,* 17–23.

Hays, J. R., & Shaw, J. B. (2003). WASI profile variability in a sample of psychiatric inpatients. *Psychological Reports, 92,* 164–166.

Plake, B. S., & Impara, J. C. (Eds.). (2001). *The fourteenth mental measurements yearbook.* Lincoln, NE: Buros Institute of Mental Measurements.

Ryan, J. J., Carruthers, C. A., & Miller, L. J. (2003). Exploratory factor analysis of the Wechsler Abbreviated Scale of Intelligence (WASI) in adult standardization and clinical samples. *Applied Neuropsychology, 10,* 252–256.

RON DUMONT
Fairleigh Dickinson University

JOHN O. WILLIS
Rivier College

INTELLIGENCE QUOTIENT
INTELLIGENCE TESTING, HISTORY OF
INTELLIGENT TESTING
STANFORD BINET INTELLIGENCE SCALE–FIFTH EDITION
WECHSLER, DAVID

WECHSLER ADULT INTELLIGENCE SCALE–THIRD EDITION

The Wechsler Adult Intelligence Scale–Third Edition (WAIS-III) is an individually administered measure of intellectual ability for ages 16 to 89. The WAIS-III contains 14 subtests, which provide a Verbal Scale IQ (VIQ), Performance Scale IQ (PIQ), and a global Full Scale IQ (FSIQ). Each of these IQ scores is a standard score with a mean of 100 and a standard deviation of 15. On the other hand, each of the 14 subtests is a scaled score with a mean of 10 and a standard deviation of 3.

The Verbal IQ is composed of six subtests: Vocabulary, Similarities, Arithmetic, Digit Span, Information, and Comprehension, Letter-Number Sequencing is a new supplementary subtest that may replace Digit Span when it has been spoiled. The Performance IQ is composed of five subtests: Picture Completion, Digit Symbol-Coding, Block Design, Matrix Reasoning, and Picture Arrangement. Symbol Search and Object Assembly are both supplementary subtests. Symbol Search may substitute for Digit Symbol-Coding when it has been spoiled. Object Assembly is an optional subtest that does not count toward the IQ or Index scores. It can be used to replace any spoiled Performance subtest, but only for individuals younger than 75 years of age. Verbal and Performance subtests alternate to maintain the examinee's interest. The WAIS-III also groups its subtests into four indexes: Verbal Comprehension (VCI), Perceptual Organization (POI), Working Memory (WMI), and Processing Speed (PSI).

The Index scores are also standard scores with a mean of 100 and a standard deviation of 15. It is not necessary to administer all subtests in order to obtain IQ and Index scores. The examiner can administer subtests according to what scores are required (IQ scores, Index scores, or both).

The administration time of the WAIS-III varies according to what subtests are given and the level of ability of the examinee. Administration of the 11 subtests required to obtain the three IQ scores range from 60 to 90 minutes, averaging about 75 minutes. Administration of the 11 subtests required for the four indexes takes approximately 60 minutes, with a range of 45 to 75 minutes. The 13 subtests needed to obtain both IQ and Index scores take about 80 minutes, ranging from 65 to 95 minutes. Object assembly takes an additional 10 to 15 minutes.

The WAIS-III was standardized on a U.S. sample of 2,450 English-speaking subjects. The normative sample was stratified by age, gender, ethnicity, geographic region, and educational level, and was consistent with the 1995 U.S. census data. This sample was divided into 13 age groups that ranged from 2 to 10 years. The sample consisted of individuals from all intellectual ability levels. For the purpose of performing item bias analyses, the WAIS-III was administered to an additional 200 African-American and Hispanic individuals without discontinue rules.

Reliability for the WAIS-III is strong. The average split-half reliability coefficients were .97 for the Verbal IQ, .94 for the Performance IQ, and .98 for the Full Scale IQ, with average coefficients for the factor indexes ranging from .88 for Processing Speed to .96 for Verbal Comprehension. Average split-half reliabilities for the subtests ranged from .70 for Object Assembly to .93 for Vocabulary. Three hundred ninety four individuals from the standardization sample were retested an average of 5 weeks after initial testing, providing test-retest data for the WAIS-III. The IQs and Indexes have test-retest reliability coefficients ranging from .88 to .96.

The four-factor structure of the WAIS-III has been validated. However, there was not strong support for the Perceptual Organization factor for the oldest age group, ages 75 to 89 (Kaufman & Lichtenberger, 1999). Criterion validity was performed by correlating the WAIS-III with the WAIS-R (Wechsler, 1981). The correlations between the two tests were high, with a correlation of .94 for the Verbal IQ, .86 for the Performance IQ, and .93 for the Full Scale IQ (Kaufman & Lichtenberger, 1999). On average, individuals obtained about 2.9 points less on the Full Scale IQ on the WAIS-III than on the WAIS-R. This is what would be expected given the Flynn effect (Flynn, 1984). In his work, Flynn found a similar pattern between the WAIS and WAIS-R.

Many improvements were made in the third edition of the WAIS, but the major features of the WAIS-R were retained. The floor of the WAIS-III IQ scores was extended down to 45 and the ceiling was extended to 155. The age range was extended to 89 years.

The norms of the test were updated and the test no longer relies on a reference group (ages 20 to 34) for calculating all scaled scores. A number of items were modified in other subtests, and the artwork was updated on Picture Completion, Picture Arrangement, and Object Assembly. Three subtests were added to the WAIS-III: Letter-Number Sequencing, Matrix Reasoning, and Symbol Search. The addition of Matrix Reasoning and Letter-Number Sequencing has enhanced the measurement of fluid reasoning and working memory (Kaufman & Lichtenberger, 1999). In addition, the WAIS-III relies less than the WAIS-R on timed performance when calculating the Performance IQ. According to Kaufman and Lichtenberger, the addition of the four index scores is the major structural change in the WAIS-III, and these four-factor indexes are helpful in interpretation. Although criticisms have been made of the WAIS-III, its strengths appear to be greater than its weaknesses (Kaufman & Lichtenberger).

REFERENCES

Donders, J., Zhu, J., & Tulsky, D. (2001). Factor index score patterns in the WAIS-III standardization sample. *Assessment, 8,* 193–203.

Flynn, J. R. (1984). The mean IQ of Americans: Massive gains 1932 to 1978. *Psychological Bulletin, 95,* 29–51.

Jeyakumar, S. L. E., Warriner, E. M., & Raval, V. V. (2004). Balancing the need for reliability and time efficiency: Short forms of the Wechsler Adult Intelligence Scale–III. *Educational & Psychological Measurement, 64,* 71–87.

Kaufman, A. S., & Lichtenberger, E. O. (1999). *Essentials of WAIS-III assessment.* New York: Wiley.

Kennedy, J. E., Clement, P. F., & Curtiss, G. (2003). WAIS-III Processing Speed Index scores after TBI: The influence of working memory, psychomotor speed and perceptual processing. *Clinical Neuropsychologist, 17,* 303–307.

Plake, B. S., & Impara, J. C. (Eds.). (2001). *The fourteenth mental measurements yearbook.* Lincoln, NE: Buros Institute of Mental Measurements.

Taub, G. E., McGrew, K. S., & Witta, E. L. (2004). A confirmatory analysis of the factor structure and cross-age invariance of the Wechsler Adult Intelligence Scale–Third Edition. *Psychological Assessment, 16,* 85–89.

Taylor, M. J., & Heaton, R. K. (2001). Sensitivity and specificity of WAIS-III/WMS-III demographically corrected factor scores in neuropsychological assessment. *Journal of the International Neuropsychological Society, 7,* 867–874.

Tulsky, D. S., & Ledbetter, M. F. (2000). Updating the WAIS-III and WMS-II: Considerations for research and clinical practice. *Psychological Assessment, 12,* 253–262.

Tulsky, D. S., Saklofske, D. H., Chelune, G. J., Heaton, R. K., Ivnik, R. J., Bornstein, R., et al. (Eds.). (2003). *Clinical interpretation of the WAIS-III and WMS-III.* San Diego, CA: Academic Press.

Wechsler, D. (1981). *Wechsler Adult Intelligence Scale—Revised.* San Antonio, TX: Psychological Corporation.

Zhu, J., Tulsky, D. S., Price, L., & Chen, H. (2001). WAIS-III reliability data for clinical groups. *Journal of the International Neuropsychological Society, 7,* 862–866.

Ron Dumont
Fairleigh Dickinson University

John O. Willis
Rivier College

INTELLIGENCE QUOTIENT
INTELLIGENCE TESTING, HISTORY OF
INTELLIGENT TESTING
WECHSLER, DAVID

WECHSLER INDIVIDUAL ACHIEVEMENT TEST–SECOND EDITION

The Wechsler Individual Achievement Test–Second Edition (WIAT-II; Wechsler, 2001) is a measure of academic achievement skills and problem-solving abilities for ages 4 through 85. Administration time varies depending on the age of the examinee and the number of subtests administered, but the test usually takes 45 minutes to complete for children in kindergarten or prekindergarten, 90 minutes for grades 1 through 6, and approximately 90 to 120 minutes for grades 7 through 16 (4-year college). An individual's performance is compared to others in the appropriate age range or grade level. Two stimulus books include information regarding appropriate starting points, reversals, discontinuation rules, and appropriate prompting and querying for each of the subtests. The WIAT-II presents one item at a time without time limits, except for the Written Expression subtest. The WIAT-II has four content areas (Reading, Mathematics, Written Language, and Oral Language) assessed using the following subtests:

Word Reading: naming letters, phonological skills (working with sounds in words), and reading words aloud from lists. Only the accuracy of the pronunciation (not comprehension) is scored.

Pseudoword Decoding: reading nonsense words aloud from a list (phonetic word attack).

Reading Comprehension: matching words to pictures, reading sentences aloud, and orally answering oral questions about reading passages. Silent reading speed is also assessed.

Spelling: written spelling of dictated letters and sounds and words that are dictated and read in sentences.

Written Expression: writing letters and words as quickly as possible, writing sentences, and writing a paragraph or essay.

Numerical Operations: identifying and writing numbers, counting, and solving paper-and-pencil computation examples with only a few items for each computational skill.

Math Reasoning: counting, identifying shapes, and solving verbally framed "word problems" presented both orally and in writing or with illustrations. Paper and pencil are allowed.

Listening Comprehension: multiple-choice matching of pictures to spoken words or sentences and replying with one word to a picture and a dictated clue.

Oral Expression: repeating sentences, generating lists of specific kinds of words, describing pictured scenes, and describing pictured activities. Content of answers is scored, but quality of spoken language is not for most items.

Depending on the subtest, items are either scored dichotomously or assigned a score of 0, 1, or 2. A composite score for reading is the total of the raw scores obtained on the word reading, reading comprehension, and pseudoword reading subtests. A composite score for written language is the total of the raw scores obtained on spelling and written expression subtests. Finally, a composite score for oral language is the total of the raw scores obtained on listening comprehension and oral expression subtests. There are qualitative descriptions for the scores: extremely low, borderline, low average, average, high average, superior, very superior. The WIAT-II also provides scoring guidelines and additional scoring examples. Optional scoring includes Reading Comprehension: Target Words; Reading Comprehension: Reading Speed; Written Expression: paragraph or essay word count; Written Expression: paragraph or essay holistic score.

The WIAT-II provides standard scores (with a mean of 100 and a standard deviation of 15), percentiles, stanines, normal curve equivalents (NCEs), and age and grade equivalents for each of the subtests. Scores are based either on the student's age (4-month intervals for ages 4 through 13, 1-year intervals for ages 14 through 16, and one interval for ages 17 through 19) or on the student's grade (fall, winter, and spring norms for prekindergarten through grade 8, full-year norms for grades 9 through 12, and separate college norms).

This measure was normed on a sample of 5,586 individuals between 4 and 85 years of age. The sample was representative of the 1998 U.S. Census data with respect to grade, age, geographic region, gender, ethnicity, and parent education level. About 8–10 percent of the sample at each grade level had either a learning disability, speech-language impairment, emotional disturbance, mild mental impairment, ADHD, or had a mild hearing impairment. About 3 percent of the population at each grade level was gifted and talented. All students spoke English. A sample of 1,069 students was given both the WIAT-II and a Wechsler Intelligence Scale so that examinees' WIAT-II scores could be compared to achievement scores predicted from their intelligence scale scores on the basis of actual test scores from the sample.

The average interitem reliability coefficients range from .80 to .98, and WIAT-II scores demonstrate adequate stability across time, ages, and grades. Studies have indicated that the subtests that are more likely to result in variability, such as Reading Comprehension, Written Expression, and Oral Expression, produce overall interrater correlations of .94, .85, and .96 respectively. Also, the pattern of correlations among the subtests provides discriminant evidence of validity. Correlation coefficients among the scores on the reading-related, mathematics, and spelling subtests of the WIAT-II and those on corresponding subtests of the WIAT, Wide Range Achievement Test–Third Edition (WRAT-3), and Differential Ability Scales (DAS) are highly consistent. Correlation coefficients between the WIAT-II and the Wechsler scales range from .25 to .82.

REFERENCES

Glutting, J. J., & McDermott, P. A. (1994). Core profile types for the WISC-III and WIAT: Their development and application in identifying multivariate IQ-achievement discrepancies. *School Psychology Review, 23,* 619–630.

Konold, T. R. (1999). Evaluating discrepancy analyses with the WISC-III and WIAT. *Journal of Psychoeducational Assessment, 17,* 24–35.

Plake, B. S., Impara, J. C., & Spies, R. A. (Eds.). (2003). *The fifteenth mental measurements yearbook.* Lincoln, NE: Buros Institute of Mental Measurements.

Ward, T. J., Ward, S. B., Glutting, J. J., & Hatt, C. V. (1999). Exceptional LD profile types for the WISC-III and WIAT. *School Psychology Review, 28,* 629–643.

Wechsler, D. (2001). *Wechsler Individual Achievement Test–Second Edition: Manual.* San Antonio, TX: Psychological Corporation.

RON DUMONT
Fairleigh Dickinson University

JOHN O. WILLIS
Rivier College

ACHIEVEMENT TESTS
WECHSLER, DAVID

WECHSLER INTELLIGENCE SCALE FOR CHILDREN–FOURTH EDITION

The Wechsler Intelligence Scale for Children–Fourth Edition (WISC-IV; Wechsler, 2003a, 2003b) is an individually administered clinical instrument for assessing the cognitive ability of children of ages 6 years 0 months through 16 years 11 months. It is composed of 15 subtests, 10 of which have been retained from the WISC-III and 5 of which are new subtests. Administration takes approximately 65–80 minutes for most children. The test provides a composite score (Full Scale IQ) that represents general intellectual ability as well as four factor index scores (Verbal Comprehension, Perceptual Reasoning, Working Memory, and Processing Speed). Each of the IQs and factor indexes are standard scores with a mean of 100 and a standard score of 15 for 33 age bands. The subtests on the WISC-IV provide scaled scores with a mean of 10 and a standard deviation of 3.

Three subtests comprise the Verbal Comprehension Index: Similarities, Vocabulary, and Comprehension. In addition, two supplementary verbal subtests, Information and Word Reasoning, are also available and may substitute for any of the other Verbal Comprehension subtests if needed. These subtests assess verbal reasoning, comprehension, and conceptualization.

Three subtests comprise the Perceptual Reasoning Index: Block Design, Picture, Concepts, and Matrix Reasoning. Picture Completion is a supplementary subtest that can be used as a substitution if necessary. These subtests measure perceptual reasoning and organization.

Two subtests comprise the Working Memory Index: Digit Span and Letter-Number Sequencing. There is also one supplementary subtest, Arithmetic, that can be used to replace either of the Working Memory subtests. These subtests measure attention, concentration, and working memory.

Two subtests comprise the Processing Speed Index: Coding and Symbol Search. Cancellation is a supplementary subtest and can be used as a substitute for either subtest of the Processing Speed Index. These subtests measure the speed of mental and graphomotor processing.

There are two manuals that accompany the WISC-IV. The Administration and Scoring Manual contains all of the information needed to administer subtests, score responses, and complete the Record Form. The Technical and Interpretive Manual contains psychometric, technical, and basic interpretive information. During revision from the WISC-III to the WISC-IV, the Stimulus Book artwork was updated to be more attractive and engaging for children. Outdated items were revised or removed and new items were incorporated to reflect more contemporary ideas and situations. The Record Form was redesigned to reduce the occurrence of administration and scoring errors, and includes an abbreviated version of the administration and scoring rules for each subtest. Administration procedures were simplified to improve the user-friendliness of the scale. Instructions to examiners are more succinct and understandable, and similar wording is used across subtests to provide consistency and clarity. There are teaching, sample, and/or practice items along with queries and prompts incorporated within every subtest that should enhance the child's understanding and retention of the subtest task.

The standardization sample for the WISC-IV included 2,200 children divided into 11 age groups ranging from 6 to 16, with 200 participants in each age group. (Note that the Arithmetic subtest was normed on only 1,100 children—100 per age). The sample was representative of the 2000 U.S. Census with respect to age, sex, race, parent education level, and geographic region.

The overall internal consistency reliability for the subtests ranges from .79 to .90. For the composite scales, the internal consistency reliability ranges from .88 to .97. The test-retest reliability ranges from .76 to .92 for the subtests and from .86 to .93 for the composite scales, with a mean time interval of 32 days. Research on the Wechsler scales

has provided strong evidence of validity based on the scales' internal structure. Intercorrelations among subtests provide initial evidence of both the convergent and discriminant validity of the WISC-IV. Evidence of criterion validity was also shown by moderate to high correlations between the WISC-IV and the WISC-III, WPPSI-III, WAIS-III, WASI, WIAT-II, CMS, and GRS.

REFERENCES

Flanagan, D. P., & Kaufman, A. S. (2004). *Essentials of WISC-IV assessment.* New York: Wiley.

Sattler, J. M., & Dumont, R. P. (2004). *Assessment of children: WISC-IV and WPPSI-III supplement.* San Diego, CA: Jerome Sattler.

Wechsler, D. (2003a). *Wechsler Intelligence Scale for Children–Fourth Edition: Administration and scoring manual.* San Antonio, TX: Psychological Corporation.

Wechsler, D. (2003b). *Wechsler Intelligence Scale for Children–Fourth Edition: Technical and interpretative manual.* San Antonio, TX: Psychological Corporation.

RON DUMONT
Fairleigh Dickinson University

JOHN O. WILLIS
Rivier College

INTELLIGENCE QUOTIENT
INTELLIGENCE TESTING, HISTORY OF
INTELLIGENT TESTING
WECHSLER, DAVID

WECHSLER MEMORY SCALE–THIRD EDITION

The Wechsler Memory Scale–Third Edition (WMS-III; Wechsler, 1997a, 1997b) is an individually administered battery of learning, memory, and working memory measures for ages 16 through 89. It is comprised of 11 subtests, with 6 primary subtests and 5 optional subtests. The primary subtests can be administered in approximately 30–35 minutes. Administration of the optional subtest will add approximately 15–20 minutes to the actual testing time. There are eight Primary Indexes that include scores from orally presented and visually presented subtests. The Immediate Memory Index, which represents overall memory performance, is comprised of the Auditory Immediate Index and Visual Immediate Index. The Auditory Delayed Index, Visual Delayed Index, and Auditory Recognition Delayed Index comprise the General Memory Index, which represents overall delayed memory performance. The Working Memory Index, a measure of one's capacity to manipulate information in short-term memory, is comprised of one auditory and one visual working memory task. There are also four Auditory Process Composites (Single-Trial Learning, Learning Slope, Retention, and Retrieval) that provide supplemental information about processes or aspects of memory when information is presented in the auditory modality.

There are two manuals that accompany the WMS-III. The Administration and Scoring Manual contains all of the information needed for administration, recording, and scoring procedures for the WMS-III subtests, indexes, and composite scores. The WAIS-III–WMS-III Technical Manual contains the psychometric, technical, and basic interpretive information for the WAIS-III and WMS-III. The two Stimulus Booklets have an easel construction that enables them to stand alone. They contain examinee pages and examiner pages, which contain administration directions. The WMS-III Record Form is designed to facilitate administration, recording, and scoring. There is space to record and score the examinee's responses to the test items for each subtest and it also provides information such as discontinue rules, time limits, and other prompts to help facilitate proper test administration. There is a four page summary section following the subtest pages that is printed on a single fold-out sheet, which can be detached from the rest of the Record Form. The layout makes it convenient to transfer subtest raw scores from the subtest pages to the Score Conversion Pages.

The WMS-III was conormed with the Wechsler Adult Intelligence Scale–Third Edition (WAIS-III), a measure of intellectual ability. As a result, comparisons can be made between intellectual ability and memory functioning. The standardization sample included 1,250 individuals for the WMS-III and 2,450 individuals for the WAIS-III between 16 and 89 years of age. The sample was representative of the 1995 U.S. Census with respect to age, sex, race/ethnicity, education level, and geographic region. Both tests yield standard scores with a mean of 100 and a standard deviation of 15 for 13 age bands.

The average internal consistency reliability across age groups for the Primary subtest scores ranges from .74 to .93, with a median reliability of .81. The average internal consistency reliability for the Primary Indexes ranges from .74 to .93, with a median reliability of .87. The test-retest reliability ranges from .62 to .82 (median = .71) for the Primary subtest scores and from .70 to .88 (median = .82) for the Primary Indexes, with a mean retest interval of 35.6 days. Evidence of concurrent validity of the WMS-III is based on its correlation with several other measures. Correlations between the Indexes of the WMS-III and WMS-R range from .15 to .73. The correlations between the WMS-III and the CMS Indexes range from .13 to .76, with the highest correlations between the auditory indexes of the WMS-III and the corresponding CMS indexes. In addition, the WIAT Reading Composite correlates with the WMS-III visual memory indexes in the .20s, and with the auditory memory indexes, ranging from the .30s to the .40s.

REFERENCES

Cole, J. C., Lopez, B. R., & McLeod, J. S. (2003). Comprehensive tables for determination of strengths and weaknesses on the WMS-III. *Journal of Psychoeducational Assessment, 21,* 79–88.

Langeluddecke, P. M., & Lucas, S. K. (2003). Quantitative measures of memory malingering on the Wechsler Memory Scale–Third edition in mild head injury litigants. *Archives of Clinical Neuropsychology, 18,* 181–197.

Langeluddecke, P. M., & Lucas, S. K. (2003). Wechsler Adult Intelligence Scale–Third Edition findings in relation to severity of brain injury in litigants. *Clinical Neuropsychologist, 17,* 273–284.

Plake, B. S., & Impara, J. C. (Eds.). (2001). *The fourteenth mental measurements yearbook.* Lincoln, NE: Buros Institute of Mental Measurements.

Wechsler, D. (1997a). *Wechsler Memory Scale–Third Edition: Administration and scoring manual.* San Antonio, TX: Psychological Corporation.

Wechsler, D. (1997b). *WAIS-III–WMS-III: Technical manual.* San Antonio, TX: Psychological Corporation.

Wilde, N. J., Strauss, E., & Chelune, G. J. (2003). Confirmatory factor analysis of the WMS-III in patients with temporal lobe epilepsy. *Psychological Assessment, 15,* 56–63.

RON DUMONT
Fairleigh Dickinson University

JOHN O. WILLIS
Rivier College

MEMORY DISORDERS
TESTS OF MEMORY AND LEARNING
WECHSLER, DAVID

WECHSLER PRESCHOOL AND PRIMARY SCALES OF INTELLIGENCE–THIRD EDITION

The Wechsler Preschool and Primary Scales of Intelligence–Third Edition (WPPSI-III; Wechsler, 2002) is an individually administered instrument that assesses cognitive functioning and global intelligence for early childhood. The WPPSI-III is widely utilized in clinical and school settings as a means to identify potential delays or intellectual giftedness in early childhood development. It is frequently used to aid in decision making for special education preschool placement. The instrument can provide information pertaining to a child's cognitive strengths and weaknesses related to language, visual-perceptual skills, visual-motor integration, and reasoning.

The instrument covers a broad age range where advances in development are typical for youngsters. Therefore, the instrument is divided into two separate batteries (the first for ages 2 years 6 months through 3 years 11 months and the second for ages 4 years through 7 years 3 months). The test consists of 14 subtests that combine into four or five composites: Verbal IQ (VIQ), Performance IQ (PIQ), Processing Speed Quotient (PSQ, for upper ages only), General Language Composite (GLC), and a Full Scale IQ (FSIQ).

The FSIQ is a general measure of global intelligence reflecting performance across various subtests within the VIQ and PIQ domains. In general, the VIQ contains subtests that measure general fund of information, verbal comprehension, receptive and expressive language, attention span, and degree of abstract thinking. The PIQ is composed of subtests that collectively assess visual-motor integration, perceptual-organizational skills, concept formation, speed of mental processing, nonverbal problem solving, and graphomotor ability.

Composite scores are derived by combining scores from selected subtests as follows:

- Ages 2:6–3.:11
  VIQ: Receptive Vocabulary, and Information
  PIQ: Block Design and Object Assembly
  GLC: Receptive Vocabulary and Picture Naming
  FSIQ: VIQ and PIQ combined
- Ages 4:0–7:3
  VIQ: Information, Vocabulary, and Word Reasoning (Comprehension and Similarities may be substituted)
  PIQ: Block Design, Matrix Reasoning, and Picture Concepts (Picture Completion and Object Assembly may be substituted)
  PSQ: Coding and Symbol Search
  GLC: Receptive Vocabulary and Picture Naming
  FSIQ: VIQ, PIQ and Coding

Note that there are guidelines when deciding to utilize a substitution in replace of a core subtest. Only one substitution is allowed for a core subtest from either VIQ or PIQ. Overall, no more than two substitutions can be made when deriving a FSIQ.

The WPPSI-III was standardized on a sample of 1,700 children who were selected as being representative of the 2000 U.S. Census data stratified on age, gender, geographic region, ethnicity, and parental education levels. The standardization sample was divided into nine age groups: eight of the groups contained 200 children, and one group (7:0–7:3 year old) consisted of 100 children.

There are age-specific starting points for each subtest as well as practice items to allow the child to become familiar with each task. Some subtests are scored as pass-fail, and others are scored based on the quality of response. The child receives full credit for all items prior to the starting point and does not receive credit for items after the discontinue rule is met. In general, the points are tabulated to formulate a raw score, which is converted into standard scores. The

instrument also includes reverse and discontinue rules to eliminate unnecessary fatigue or extended testing time. Reverse rules are designed to tap into items prior to the child's age-specific starting point to allow the examiner to extend the floor for children who experience difficulty with the first couple of items. The discontinue rules vary for each subtest but follow the same underlying principle, which governs the examiner to discontinue administration after the child fails to correctly respond to a set number of items.

Scores provided include scaled scores, standard scores, percentiles, and qualitative descriptors. All raw scores are converted to allow a child's performance to be compared to his or her same-aged peers from the normative sample. Scaled scores have a mean of 10 and a standard deviation of 3. The composite standard scores have a mean of 100 and a standard deviation of 15. Percentile ranks are used to describe the child's performance relative to the normative sample as being better than or equal to the calculated percentage. Descriptors include Extremely Low, Borderline Intellectual Functioning, Low Average, Average, High Average, Superior, and Very Superior range.

Internal consistency values for each subtest ranged from .75 to .96. The test-retest coefficients ranged from .86 to .92. The average internal consistency values and test-retest coefficients exceeded .80. Correlations were obtained comparing the WPPSI-III FSIQ with other global measures; when compared with alternate assessment instruments such as the Differential Ability Scales, Bayley Scales of Infant Development-II, and WPPSI-R, coefficients ranged from .80 to .89.

REFERENCES

Hamilton, W., & Burns, T. (2003). WPPSI-III: Wechsler Preschool and Primary Scale of Intelligence (3rd ed.). *Applied Neuropsychology, 10,* 188–190.

Lichtenberger, E., & Kaufman, A. (2004). *Essentials of WPPSI-III assessment.* Hoboken, NJ: Wiley.

The Psychological Corporation. (2002). *WPPSI-III technical and interpretive manual.* San Antonio, TX: Author.

Sattler, J. M., & Dumont, R. P. (2004). *Assessment of children: WISC-IV and WPPSI-III supplement.* San Diego, CA: Jerome Sattler.

Wechsler, D. (2002). *WPPSI-III administration and scoring manual.* San Antonio, TX: Psychological Corporation.

RON DUMONT
Fairleigh Dickinson University

JOHN O. WILLIS
Rivier College

BAYLEY SCALES FOR INFANT DEVELOPMENT, SECOND EDITION
INTELLIGENCE QUOTIENT
INTELLIGENCE TESTING, HISTORY OF

INTELLIGENT TESTING
KAUFMAN ASSESSMENT BATTERY FOR CHILDREN–II
WECHSLER, DAVID

WELSH FIGURE PREFERENCE TEST

The Welsh Figure Preference Test (FPT) was developed by George Welsh in 1949, for his doctoral thesis, as a projective assessment of psychopathology. More recently, it has been used as a measure of creativity more than as a diagnostic tool for the evaluation of psychopathology.

The Welsh FPT (Welsh, 1959) consists of a booklet containing 400 black and white line drawings. Examples of items from the Welsh FPT are shown in the Figure. The scale was revised by Welsh in 1980. It is designed for use with individuals aged 6 years and up. It requires nearly an hour to complete and, despite being intended as a projective, provides objective scoring. Instructions to the test taker are simple. Individuals are asked to view each drawing and indicate on an answer sheet whether they like or dislike the drawing. The intent was to provide nonlanguage stimulus

Figure 1 Examples of "like" and "don't like" items from the Welsh Figure.

materials suitable for a wide range of individuals who could not be assessed with language-laden measures such as the MMPI, or projective measures such as the TAT, requiring extensive verbal expression.

The Welsh FPT can separate artists from nonartists, as can many other tests; it can also separate clinical from nonclinical populations. However, it has not been extensively researched considering its publication date. Welsh (1986) contends that the Welsh FPT is useful as a measure of creativity; it has been used in creativity research since at least 1965. Its uses in creativity research seem well established at this time, but its validity as a measure of psychopathology is questionable.

REFERENCES

Welsh, G. S. (1949). *A projective figure-preference test for diagnosis of psychopathology: I. A preliminary investigation.* Doctoral thesis, University of Minnesota, Minneapolis.

Welsh, G. S. (1959). *Welsh Figure Preference Test.* Palo Alto, CA: Consulting Psychologists.

Welsh, G. S. (1980). *Welsh Figure Preference Test, revised edition.* Palo Alto, CA: Consulting Psychologists.

Welsh, G. S. (1986). Positive exceptionality: The academically gifted and the creative. In R. T. Brown & C. R. Reynolds (Eds.), *Psychological perspectives on childhood exceptionality: A handbook.* New York: Wiley-Interscience.

CECIL R. REYNOLDS
Texas A&M University

CREATIVITY

WERNER, HEINZ (1890–1964)

Heinz Werner received his PhD from Vienna University in 1914 with highest honors. Perhaps the beginning of his scholarly career began when he read about the evolution of animals, man, and the cosmos. He became increasingly interested in philosophy and psychology while at the University of Vienna. His work in the field of psychological phenomena is relevant to psychologists, educators, anthropologists, students of animal behavior, and scholars investigating aesthetic phenomena.

His contributions to the field have been many. He has published over 15 books and monographs and more than 150 articles within a 50-year period. His principal publications include *Comparative Psychology of Mental Development* (1940) and *Developmental Processes: Heinz Werner's Selected Writings* (1978). His selected writings include his general theory and perceptual experiences in Volume I; Volume II focuses on cognition, language, and symbolization.

Werner was a great teacher and researcher, and he inspired others to follow his example in the search for understanding of psychological phenomena. His theory was interdisciplinary because all of his developmental principles apply to all the life sciences. He founded an Institute for Human Development at Clark University in 1958. This institute made Clark an "international center directed toward the developmental analysis of phenomena in all the life sciences" (Werner, 1978). Werner's contributions to the field of developmental psychology are steadily gaining recognition.

REFERENCES

Werner, H. (1940). *Comparative psychology of mental development*. New York: Harper & Brothers.

Werner, H. (1978). *Developmental processes: Heinz Werner's selected writings*. New York: International Universities Press.

REBECCA BAILEY
Texas A&M University

WERNICKE'S APHASIA

Wernicke's aphasia is one of several subdivisions of fluent aphasia. This is the first type of aphasia described, and it is one in which the localization description still holds true in terms of the symptoms correlating with damage to particular location in the brain. Those possessing communicative deficits consistent with Wernicke's aphasia have pathology in the dominant superior temporal gyrus. A lesion in the superior posterior temporal is obligatory for Wernicke's aphasia.

Major language characteristics of Wernicke's aphasia are defective auditory comprehension; disturbed reading and writing; defective repetition of words and sentences with speech, that is incessant at normal prosody with a rapid rate; good articulation but paraphasic speech, containing semantic and literal paraphasias and possible extra syllables added to words (Graham-Keegan & Caspari, 1997; Hegde, 1994). Other types of fluent aphasia include:

Transcortical Sensory

Here, the lesion is most frequently in the temporoparietal region but the precise Wernicke's area is spared. Damage to the posterior portion of the middle temporal gyrus is often seen; with some cases, the angular gyrus and visual and auditory association cortex are also involved.

Major language characteristics are very similar to those of Wernicke's aphasia with the difference being that in transcortical sensory aphasia repetition is intact (this skill is impaired in Wernicke's).

Conduction

This rare disorder is also called central aphasia. The neuroanatomical basis is very controversial, but consistent with the newer model of viewing the brain as a total system whose symptoms from impairment reflect impairments not only in specific locations within the brain but also in pathways and synergistic interactions. The most frequent theory of location of damage for this type of fluent aphasia is damage to the supramarginal gyrus and the arcuate fasciculus that connects Broca's area with Wernicke's area.

The major distinguishing language characteristic of conduction aphasia is severe impairment in repetition (repetitions may contain added or deleted phonemes); function words are more difficult to repeat. Individuals with conduction aphasia may comprehend problems in repeating sentences.

REFERENCES

Chapey, R. (1994). *Language intervention strategies in adult aphasia* (3rd ed.). Baltimore: Williams & Wilkins.

Graham-Keegan, L., & Caspari, I. (1997). Wernicke's aphasia. In L. L. LaPointe (Ed.), *Aphasia and related neurogenic language disorders* (pp. 42–62). New York: Thieme.

Hegde, M. (1994). *A coursebook on aphasia and other neurogenic language disorders*. San Diego, CA: Singular.

SHEELA STUART
George Washington University

APHASIA
DYSPHASIA
LANGUAGE DISORDERS

WESTERN EUROPE, SPECIAL EDUCATION IN

Current special education practices in Europe differ from country to country and from region to region in any particular country. These practices have been strongly influenced by the affluence of particular European nations and their social welfare outlook. While Spain and Portugal are concerned about their children and youth with disabilities, the funds and services available to them are far less than in Scandinavia.

The nature of special education funding and services also varies from country to country, depending on political structures and traditions. The degree of political-educational centralization plays an important role. In France, national authority is likely to be more strongly felt in the education of individuals with disabilities than in West Germany, where the federal government has little or no authority in public schools, and where financial support and the provision of services for special education are likely to vary from one region to another. Generally, the most comprehensive financial support for services to the handicapped, at all ages, has been in Scandinavia.

Curriculum

Special education curriculum in Western Europe has not been as narrowly academic as in the United States. Traditionally, Western European special education has been more responsive to the extra-academic aspects of special education. The graphic arts, music, and social and vocational experiences are more often woven into the disabled child's daily activities. Thus, music therapy for disabled students has received widespread support (Pratt, 1983), and the educational usefulness of toy libraries has been widely recognized (deVincentis, 1984). Theater programs for children with Mental Retardation, motor disabilities, and cerebral palsy have received acclaim (Cohen, 1985). Excursions and travel are considered important educational experiences. The quality of relationships between teachers and pupils is strongly emphasized.

Europeans may be becoming more Americanized in their special education outlooks in that a more instructionally directed focus appears to be emerging. American influences are also revealed in European movements toward noncategorical types of special education, often in the face of previously accepted, and often complicated, categorical models (as in the Netherlands). European attention to integration of special education with general education has also been influenced by American practices, albeit in European terms (Organization for Economic Cooperation and Development [OECD], 1985a, 1985b). Even though Europeans have led the way in assisting the transition of handicapped youths into the world of work, American efforts in this area have influenced their practices considerably.

Early Intervention

The most pervasive and effective interventions with Western European handicapped children, prior to their enrollment in formal educational programs, are medically related. Most European nations provide mandatory health screening and reporting for young children, as well as free medical services. In Austria, a multidisciplinary team headed by a social pediatrician steps in as soon as a child has a problem. Indeed, as soon as a child is officially identified as being disabled, the child's parents begin receiving a disability pension. In France, early intervention begins with the compulsory screening of all infants at birth and again at 2 years. Interdisciplinary teams operate out of "early medico-social activity centers to provide therapies, education, and support in home and natural environments" (Zucman, 1985). However, day care of a more educational nature also can be observed. In Switzerland, a disabled child's involvement with itinerant educational services begins at an early age (even at birth) and continues, when needed, until the child's integration into school (Pahud & Besson, 1985).

Preschool

Preschool special education had its beginnings in Germany, where Froebel was the first educator to formalize it on a public basis. Current preschool special education in Western Europe varies from nation to nation. For example, different nations have different beginning ages for compulsory education, so that even the definition of preschool education varies. Also, the Europeans have traditionally favored parents as the main educators of their children, particularly when young. The social welfare underpinnings of such states as Sweden have been very supportive of parents who remain at home with their young, offering them paid leave from employment. Countries such as Italy have made remarkable advances in integrating preschoolers into regular education programs.

Least Restrictive Environment and Mainstreaming

Modern-day principles of least restrictive environment and mainstreaming originated with the Bill of Rights for the mentally retarded and the principle of normalization in Scandinavia. Both concepts strongly influenced much of Western Europe. Thus the notion of integrating students with disabilities into the main body of education was well on its way, even without American influences. Indeed, reforms in this respect were begun in Norway in 1920 (Booth, 1982). Nevertheless, the United States can take credit for institutionalizing the ideas of least restrictive environment and mainstreaming, and for offering models for the Europeans to adopt. The degree to which the principles of least restrictive environment have prevailed has differed from country to country.

In Denmark, special education is an integral part of regular education within a sophisticated range of educational services. In fact, administrative integration of services for the disabled with those for the nondisabled was passed into law on January 1, 1979, on the premise that disabled individuals should receive services in the same way as the nondisabled (Juul, 1980). Italy's Law 517/1977 has gone far beyond general recommendations for implementation of least restrictive environments to providing procedural plans for implementing the education of exceptional students within regular classrooms (Strain, 1985). On the other hand, in West Germany, where responsibility for the education of the disabled was traditionally assumed by religious and voluntary organizations, terminology for such education was originally couched in the language of segregation. Public school teachers were unfamiliar with the education of children with special needs, and it was difficult for the teachers to prepare to work with the disabled. This meant some hesitancy in certain European nations with respect to mainstreaming; however, mainstreaming has moved forward at a steady pace overall.

Transition

European efforts in transition education have been in the vanguard in many respects (Booth, 1982; OECD, 1981, 1985a, 1985b), with significant efforts being made to help exceptional youths and young adults to move into the world of work. The Netherlands has been noteworthy for providing sheltered workshops for more involved exceptional youths and adults while supervising more able ones who are actively employed in the open market. Again, the social welfare outlook in nations such as the Netherlands, which even purchases paintings from artists unable to sell their works, conditions Western European attitudes toward the handicapped. In France, the Union Nationale des Association de Parents d'Enfants Inadaptes, which operates hundreds of schools for moderately to severely handicapped children and youths, has a strong vocational emphasis in its curriculum. It also has operated the Centres d'Aide pour Travail to aid in the employment of the disabled. In Austria an organization called Jugend am Werk (Youth at Work), which originated with the idea of providing shelter and work to disadvantaged youths, went on to provide vocational training centers, sheltered workshops, and residential centers for the handicapped. Unfortunately, the employment picture in most European countries has been dismal over the past decade, with high unemployment rates for nondisabled workers. Opportunities for the handicapped to work in the normal marketplace have been significantly reduced as a consequence.

The Educateur Movement

Educateurs are special types of teacher/child-care workers who are competent to work with maladapted young people, including disabled youths. They are trained in nonacademic subjects such as sports, acting, arts and crafts, and other leisure-time activities. They teach vocational subjects, supervise vocational placements, work with families, schools, and communities, and act as advocates for their student clients. The educateur profession is well established in France, with numerous colleges providing rigorous training. The educateur movement has spread across much of Western Europe. It has also influenced Canadian services. In the United States, Project Re-Ed was a variant of the educateur model. In European nations, there have been adaptations according to national and local needs. Similar professions have emerged under different names with somewhat different identities and functions. In West Germany the educateurs are called erziehers; in the Netherlands they are identified as orthopedagogues; and in Scandinavia they are milieu therapists.

Therapeutic Communities

The Europeans have also been noted for their creation of therapeutic communities. Professionals and lay people critical of traditional government and professional roles in serving the disabled and the ill have been instrumental in fostering these.

In Great Britain, psychiatrists Laing and Cooper created a therapeutic home at Kingsley Hall, London. They viewed mentally ill individuals as victims of home and society, and saw hospitals as degrading and dehumanizing for them (1971). Laing's views of the causes of mental illness have altered over the years. His perceptions that mental hospitals dehumanize and often harm their residents, and that relationships between professionals and their clients on a day-to-day personal basis may be the best way to help the latter, have been increasingly shared by others.

In France the movement toward therapeutic communities following World War II began in earnest with the work of Jean Vanier (Wolfensberger, 1973) in the movement called l'Arche (place of refuge). Vanier built a small community in Trosly-Breuil, France, where mentally handicapped and nonhandicapped adults could live and work together as families. Vanier's work has inspired the creation of other similar facilities across France and elsewhere.

Most important in the therapeutic community movement has been the anthroposophic movement. This was inaugurated at the turn of the twentieth century by Rudolf Steiner, an Austrian philosopher and educator. The inspirations of the anthroposophic movement led to the creation of the Waldorf method and Waldorf schools. The Waldorf method, while originally intended for normal children, was found also to be applicable to exceptional children. Anthroposophic education is developmental in orientation, and multifaceted. It emphasizes art, bodily movement, music, community involvement, and work. Anthroposophic schools have sought to integrate therapy with education and to engage in therapies that find their expression in art, drama, role playing, and so on. Anthroposophic schools serving the disabled are now numerous in Great Britain and on the continent. Originally oriented toward the mentally retarded and multiply handicapped, they have recently expanded to serve the emotionally disturbed as well.

Particularly noteworthy within the anthroposophic movement has been the Camphill movement. This was begun in the early 1940s by Karl Konig, an Austrian-psychiatrist who came to Scotland to escape Nazi persecution. Inspired by anthroposophic philosophy, which views an individual's inner personality as remaining whole and intact despite the nature and degree of that individual's disabilities, Konig created a special village in the vicinity of Aberdeen, Scotland, in which mentally retarded villagers and normal coworkers could live and work together. The original Camphill movement has spread considerably since that time, both in Europe and the United States. Some settlements serve children, while others serve adults. The orientation of the Camphill settlements, which are self-contained communities, is contrary to modern-day notions of least restrictive environment. Nevertheless, they offer a remarkable combination of care and opportunity for self-fulfillment to many handicapped individuals.

Minority Disabled

Changed immigration policies and intensive industrialization during the postwar period saw an influx of millions of immigrants or "guest workers" from Africa, Asia, and less affluent European nations into Western Europe. Today, there are second and third generations of these minorities in most Western European nations. With some exceptions, there has been difficulty in integrating them. Decreases in employment opportunities in Western Europe have meant increased hardships and alienation for many (e.g., Turks in Germany, Arabs in France, Indians and Pakistanis in Great Britain). The children of such families constitute a large proportion of underprivileged and disadvantaged students in Western Europe. Elevated levels of handicaps and school failure are the consequence. At the same time, such students, because of their alienated status, are less likely to benefit from benign European attitudes toward the handicapped. It should be observed that the Dutch have been particularly accepting of such minority populations.

Professional Preparation

There is considerable variation in the professional preparation of special education teachers in Europe. In some countries, there appear to be few special requirements. In others, licensure or certification requirements are demanding. In certain countries, there are likely to be differences from one region to another. Germany has traditionally been interested in experimenting with different training models. In England and Wales, more systematic training was instituted as a consequence of the Warnock Report. Switzerland has a number of different teacher institutes, each of which has a special orientation to the cantons that they serve. The Institut des Science de l'Education, at Geneva, associated with the name of Piaget, has been known for its research into the cognitive processes of handicapped students; it is a national training resource. Switzerland's Zentralstelle fur Heilpadagogik coordinates the efforts of its various teacher training centers in respect to special education. In several countries, specialization in special education is entirely on the graduate level. Some countries (e.g., Scotland) require that candidates for special education training have at least 1 year of teaching in regular education. In France, theoretical studies and practicum requirements are distinguished from each other.

Voluntary Agencies

As in the United States, voluntary organizations have a significant place with respect to assisting handicapped students. They run preschool centers, schools, sheltered workshops, group homes, and hospitals. They even provide professional training. In West Germany the largest of these is the Catholic Caritas. There is also Lebenshilfe, the National Association of Parents and Friends of the Mentally Handicapped, which operates day-school nurseries, sheltered workshops, and hostels. In Switzerland, an umbrella organization called Pro Infirmis coordinates the work of other organizations serving the disabled. It provides a comprehensive educational program as well, publishes books and brochures, and offers consultations for children and adults. In Austria, the Save the Children Society assists children with special needs in homes and rehabilitation centers. It also offers help in times of crisis. In Great Britain, voluntary agencies work closely with public authorities. In Scandinavia, the Norwegian Red Cross has created special schools and vocational rehabilitation centers; after making them viable, it turns them over to the government.

Auxiliary Services

Widespread, comprehensive, and effective support services for students with disabilities are likely to be obtained in most of the nations of Western Europe. For one thing, these nations have broad-based national health insurance systems combining private and public institutions into an easily accessible network of services (Massie, 1985). Many of the medical and ancillary medical services that disabled children require are obtainable through such government-supported services.

REFERENCES

Booth, T. (1982). *Special need in education.* Stratford, England: Open University Educational Enterprises.

Cohen, H. U. (1985). "Var Teater": A Swedish model of children's theatre for participants with disabilities. *Children's Theatre Review, 34.*

deVincentis, S. (1984, April). *Swedish play intervention for handicapped children.* Paper presented at the annual convention of the Council for Exceptional Children, Washington, DC.

Juul, K. D. (1979). European approaches and innovations in serving the handicapped. *Exceptional Children, 44,* 322–330.

Juul, K. D. (1980). Special education in Western Europe and Scandinavia. In L. Mann & D. A. Sabatino (Eds.), *The fourth review of special education.* New York: Grune & Stratton.

Juul, K. D. (1984, April). *Toy libraries for the handicapped.* Paper presented at the annual convention of the Council for Exceptional Children, Washington, DC.

Juul, K. D., & Linton, T. E. (1978). European approaches to the treatment of behavior disordered children. *Behavior Disorders, 3,* 232–249.

Kugel, F. B., & Wolfensberger, W. (Eds.). (1968). *Changing patterns of residential services for the mentally retarded.* Washington, DC: President's Committee on Mental Retardation.

Linton, T. E. (1971). The educateur model: A theoretical monograph. *Journal of Special Education, 5,* 155–190.

Massie, R. K. (1985). The constant shadow: Reflections on the life of a chronically ill child. In N. Hobbes & J. M. Perrin (Eds.), *Issues in the care of children with chronic illness*. San Francisco: Jossey-Bass.

Organization for Economic Cooperation and Development (OECD). (1981). *Integration in the school*. Washington, DC: Author.

Organization for Economic Cooperation and Development (OECD). (1985a). *Integration of the handicapped in secondary schools: Five case studies. The Education of the handicapped adolescent: II*. Washington, DC: Author.

Organization for Economic Cooperation and Development (OECD). (1985b). *Handicapped youth at work: Personal experiences of school-leavers: The education of the handicapped adolescent: III*. Paris: Centre for Educational Research and Innovation.

Oyer, H. J. (1976). *Communication for the hearing handicapped. An international perspective*. Baltimore: University Park Press.

Pahud, D., & Besson, F. (1985, Summer). Special education in Switzerland: Historical reflections and current applications. *Journal of the Division of Early Childhood, 9*, 222–229.

Pratt, R. R. (Ed.). (1983). *The International Symposium on Music in Medicine, Education, and Therapy for the Handicapped*. Lanham, MD: University Press of America.

Strain, P. (1985). A response to preschool handicapped in Italy: A research based developmental model. *Journal of the Division for Early Childhood, 29*, 269–271.

Tarnapol, L., & Tarnapol, M. (1976). *Reading disabilities: An international perspective*. Baltimore: University Park Press.

Taylor, E. J. (1980). *Rehabilitation and world peace*. New York: International Society for Rehabilitation of the Disabled.

Taylor, W. W., & Taylor, I. W. (1960). *Special education of physically handicapped children in Western Europe*. New York: International Society for the Welfare of Cripples.

Wolfensberger, W. (1964). General observations on European countries. *Mental Retardation, 2*, 331–337.

Wolfensberger, W. (1973). *A selective overview of the work of Jean Vanier and the movement of L'Arche*. Toronto, Canada: National Institute of Mental Retardation.

Zucman, E. (1985). Early childhood programs for the handicapped in France. *Journal of the Division for Early Childhood, 9*, 237–245.

DON BRASWELL
*Research Foundation, City
University of New York*

BELGIUM, SPECIAL EDUCATION IN
EASTERN EUROPE, SPECIAL EDUCATION IN
ENGLAND, SPECIAL EDUCATION IN
FRANCE, SPECIAL EDUCATION IN

WHELAN, RICHARD J. (1931–)

Born in Emmett, Kansas, Richard J. Whelan received his BA (cum laude) from Washburn University in 1955 with

Richard J. Whelan

majors in history, political science, psychology, and education. By 1957, he completed all requirements for a MA in history, with concentrations in American, European, and Far Eastern history at the University of Kansas. In 1966, he received the EdD from the University of Kansas with concentrations in special education (emotional and behavior disorders), educational psychology and research. He is currently licensed as a social studies and psychology teacher as well as a teacher of students with emotional and behavior disorders. He also holds licenses as a special education supervisor/coordinator, director of special education, and school psychologist. The Supreme Court of the State of Kansas has certified him as a mediator and an approved trainer of mediators. He also serves as a special education administrative hearing officer and hearing officer trainer for the Kansas State Board of Education. In addition, he is a special education hearing officer for the Bureau of Indian Affairs. During the Korean War, he served as an Instructor of Electronics, Computers, and Power Control Systems at the U.S. Army Radar and Guided Missile School.

Whelan's earliest professional experiences were at the Southard School of the Menninger Clinic where he served as a recreational therapist, child care worker, teacher, and Director of Education. At the University of Kansas and University of Kansas Medical Center, he has held academic appointments in psychiatry, pediatrics, and special education. His administrative posts have included chairperson of the Department of Special Education, dean of a Graduate Division, Dean of the School of Education, and Director of Education for the University Affiliated Program at the Medical Center. Since 1968, he has held the chair for the Ralph L. Smith Distinguished Professor of Child Development. From 1972 to 1974, he served as director of the Division of Personnel Preparation in the Bureau of Education for the Handicapped (now Office of Special Education and Rehabilitation Services) in the Department of Health, Education, and Welfare.

Whelan has held numerous board memberships and serves as a consultant to psychiatric hospitals, universities, government agencies, schools, and other education related organizations. During his career, Whelan has served on seven publication boards, and has held offices in state and national professional organizations. He was chairperson of the Evaluation Training Consortium, a nationwide evaluation training project funded by the U.S. Office of Education. He was a founder and officer of the Kansas Federation of the Council for Exceptional Children. He is a member of Phi Kappa Phi, and has been recognized by Leaders in Education, Who's Who in America, and Outstanding Educators of America. He has received several service awards including the Award for Leadership in Behavior Disorders from the Midwest Symposium Organization.

Whelan has contributed over 100 publications, including *Emotional and Behavioral Disorders: A 25 Year Focus* (1998) and *Educating Students with Mild Disabilities: Strategies and Methods* (Meyen, Vergason, & Whelan, 1998). His professional preparation included extensive experiences in psychoanalysis, psychoeducational and applied behavior analysis theories, and interventions. He emphasized experimental research designs and precise measurement in his own research, as well as in the classes he taught for graduate students. More importantly, he believes that the best teachers of professionals are the children they serve: "They will let you know if you are doing it correctly." Whelan put this belief into practice while teaching and while directing a psychoeducational clinic for children with disabilities and their families at the University of Kansas Medical Center.

Whelan retired from the University of Kansas, Special Education Department in 2000 after 37 years of service.

REFERENCES

Whelan, R. J. (Ed.). (1998). *Emotional and behavioral disorders: A 25 year focus.* Denver: Love.

Meyen, E. L., Vergason, G. A., & Whelan, R. J. (Eds.). (1998). *Educating students with mild disabilities: Strategies and methods.* Denver: Love.

STAFF

OFFICE OF SPECIAL EDUCATION AND REHABILITATIVE SERVICES

WHOLE WORD TEACHING

The term *whole word teaching* has been used as the label for two different approaches to beginning reading instruction. Mathews (1966) in *Teaching to Read: Historically Considered* describes the first approach as a "words-to-letters"

method that was introduced into reading instruction in Germany in the eighteenth century and later brought to the United States.

The development of the words-to-letters method was motivated by dissatisfaction with the ABC method, the prevailing method of reading instruction since the invention of the Greek alphabet. Critics of the ABC method did not disagree with its underlying philosophy that mastery of the alphabet and syllables (combinations of vowels and consonants such as *ba, bē,* bu) were prerequisite skills for learning to read. However, they took issue with the procedures used to teach those skills, namely, years of drill, which they described as senseless, tortuous, desperately dull work. The method that eventually evolved presented beginning readers with whole words in their total form followed by an analysis of the sounds and letters. This was an analytic approach to teaching the alphabet, whereas the ABC method was a synthetic approach under which students were taught to combine syllables into words only after having mastered their pronunciation as isolated units.

Mathews (1966) refers to the second approach that has been called whole word teaching as a "words-to-reading" method. This method, commonly called the "look-and-say" method, also had its roots in Germany and may have been used by some teachers in the United States as early as the 1830s. Horace Mann, a strong advocate of the method, is often credited with having brought about its widespread use (Betts, 1946). However, according to Mathews (1966), it was Francis Parker, the first widely known practitioner of the look-and-say method, who played a far more significant role in its initiation. Under his leadership as superintendent of schools in Quincy, Massachusetts (1875–1878), and later as principal of Cooke County Normal School, Illinois (1883–1899), students were taught to read 150 to 200 words in the context of sentences and stories before being introduced to the sounds of letters. The teaching of names of letters was delayed for at least 2 years so that they would not be confused with the sounds of letters. While Parker's schools were widely acclaimed, it is doubtful that the look-and-say method would have gained the foothold it did had he not become closely associated with John Dewey, head of the departments of philosophy, psychology, and pedagogy at the University of Chicago.

When Parker was appointed director of the School of Education at the university in 1900, the two joined forces. Although Dewey was not interested in developing a methodology for teaching children to read, he thoroughly agreed with Parker's educational philosophy and adopted the look-and-say method strongly advocated by Parker. In this way, the look-and-say method came to occupy a prominent place in a new system of education (advocated by Dewey) to which the adjective progressive was applied (Mathews, 1966). As the influence of the progressive education movement grew, so did the use of the look-and-say approach to reading. During the first 2 decades of the twentieth century, it became firmly entrenched in elementary reading programs and remained so until the mid-1950s, when Rudolf Flesch (1955) captured the growing public alarm over what was happening in the nation's elementary schools in his book *Why Johnny Can't Read*. Flesch challenged the prevailing practice in beginning reading instruction that emphasized a look-and-say approach. He advocated a return to a phonic approach using existing research as support for his position.

Flesch's book led to a great deal of public debate, which in turn spawned numerous research efforts to identify the best method(s) for beginning reading instruction. Among these were 27 U.S. Office of Education grade 1 studies and a study funded by the Carnegie Corporation of New York (Chall, 1967).

REFERENCES

Betts, E. A. (1946). *Foundations of reading instruction.* New York: American Book.

Chall, J. (1967). *Learning to read: The great debate.* New York: McGraw-Hill.

Flesch, R. (1955). *Why Johnny can't read and what you can do about it.* New York: Harper & Brothers.

Mathews, M. M. (1966). *Teaching to read: Historically considered.* Chicago: University of Chicago Press.

MARIANNE PRICE
*Montgomery County
Intermediate Unit,
Norristown, Pennsylvania*

PHONOLOGY
READING DISORDERS
READING REMEDIATION

WIDE RANGE ACHIEVEMENT TEST–THIRD EDITION

The Wide Range Achievement Test–Third Edition (WRAT-3; Wilkinson, 1993) is an instrument used to measure the development of basic academic skills in the areas of reading, spelling, and arithmetic for ages 5 through 75. There are two alternate test forms, the Blue and Tan version, providing three subtests that may be given in any order: (1) reading (recognizing and naming letters and pronouncing printed words), (2) spelling (writing names, letters, and words from dictation), and (3) arithmetic (counting, reading number symbols, computing oral problems). For the Reading subtest, the phonetic guide for each reading item is printed on the test form and the individual being tested reads from the Reading Card included with the materials. The instructions for each test and the correct answers for items are located in the manual, though there is also an optional Spelling Card. Administration time varies depending on the age and ability of the examinee, but usually takes between 15 to 30 minutes to complete and approximately 5 minutes to score. The Blue and Tan forms may be administered together

in order to provide a more comprehensive analysis of the individual's skills.

This measure was normed in 1992 and 1993 on a sample of 4,433 individuals between 5 and 75 years of age. The sample was representative of the 1990 U.S. census data with respect to age, geographic region, gender, ethnicity, and socioeconomic level. The WRAT-3 yields standard scores (mean of 100 and standard deviation of 15), grade scores (kindergarten to 12th grade), absolute scores, percentiles, and normal curve equivalents.

The internal consistency of the items on the WRAT-3 ranges from .85 to .95 over the nine WRAT-3 subtests, and coefficient alpha scores for the three combined tests range from .92 to .95. Test-retest reliability ranges from .91 to .98. Content validity was measured by the Rasch statistic of item separation, and the highest separation score possible was found for each test of the WRAT-3. Moderate positive correlations have been demonstrated with the Full Scale Score on the WISC-III and higher correlations were noted with the Verbal score. Weaker correlations have been demonstrated with the WRAT-3 and other standardized group tests of achievement, and the authors have stated that this is the result of significant differences in the test formats. Studies have indicated moderate to strong correlations with the Kaufman Functional Academic Skills Test (K-FAST), the Woodcock-McGrew-Werder Mini-Battery of Achievement (MBA), and the Kaufman Brief Intelligence Test (K-BIT; Klimczak et. al, 2000; Flanagan et al., 1997). Also, strong correlations, ranging from .72 to .98, have been demonstrated between the WRAT-3, K-BIT, and Peabody Picture Vocabulary Test–Revised (PPVT-3) for adults with developmental disabilities (Powell et al., 2002).

REFERENCES

Conoley, J. C., & Impara, J. C. (Eds.). (1995). *The twelfth mental measurements yearbook.* Lincoln, NE: Buros Institute of Mental Measurements.

Flanagan, D. P., McGrew, K. S., Abramowitz, E., Lehner, L., Untiedt, S., Berger, D. & Armstrong, H. (1997). Improvement in academic screening instruments? A concurrent validity investigation of the K-FAST, MBA, and WRAT-3. *Journal of Psychoeducational Assessment, 15,* 99–112.

Klimczak, N. C., Bradford, K. A., Burright, R. G., & Donovick, P. J. (2000). K-FAST and WRAT-3: Are they really different? *Clinical Neuropsychologist, 14,* 135–138.

Powell, S., Plamondon, R., & Retzlaff, P. (2002). Screening cognitive abilities in adults with developmental disabilities: Correlations of the K-BIT, PPVT-3, WRAT-3, and CVLT. *Journal of Developmental & Physical Disabilities, 14,* 239–246.

Wilkinson, G. S. (1993). *Wide Range Achievement Test–Third Edition: Administration manual.* Wilmington, DE: Wide Range, Inc.

RON DUMONT
Fairleigh Dickinson University

JOHN O. WILLIS
Rivier College

ACHIEVEMENT TESTS

WIDE RANGE ASSESSMENT OF MEMORY AND LEARNING–SECOND EDITION

The Wide Range Assessment of Memory and Learning–Second Edition (WRAML-2; 2003) is an individually administered clinical instrument designed to measure an individual's learning and memory functions for school-age children to adults. Specifically, the test assesses an individual's ability to actively learn verbal and visual information. Moreover, the WRAML-2 allows for the acquisition of new learning, in addition to the assessment of both delayed and immediate recall.

Administration time varies depending on the age and ability of the examinee, but the Core Battery takes less than 1 hour to complete. A Screening Battery consisting of four subtests from the Core Battery affords a basic indication of memory functioning. This Screening Battery correlates well with the total scale, and can be given in approximately 10–15 minutes. Several subtests are included to supplement the Core Battery, thus allowing the examiner to add supplementary indices and subtests to facilitate qualitative analyses when necessary. The test should be administered by a trained clinician under the direct supervision of a psychologist experienced in the administration of testing.

The Core Battery consists of six subtests, and each subtest yields a norm-referenced score. The WRAML-2 Core Battery is comprised of two Attention-Concentration, two Verbal, and two Visual subtests—yielding an Attention-Concentration Index, a Verbal Memory Index, and a Visual Memory Index. These subtests collectively yield a General Memory Index. In addition, a new Working Memory Index has been added, and is comprised of the Symbolic Working Memory and Verbal Working Memory subtests. Also, four new recognition subtests have been added. They are the Design Recognition, Picture Recognition, Story Memory Recognition, and Verbal Recognition subtests. Since the last edition, the designs on the Design Memory cards have been changed and an additional Design Card has been added. In addition, the Picture Memory subtest includes new and contemporary full-color scenes, and the Story Memory subtest provides new stories and has been updated and lengthened to accommodate adults.

Standard scores (M = 100, SD = 15), scaled scores (M = 10, SD = 3), and percentiles can be obtained from all of the indices, and allow the examiner to make age-based comparisons of performance. Age equivalents are provided for the child and preadolescent age groups.

The WRAML-2 is normed for children and adults aged 5–90 years. The norm sample was formed using a national stratified sampling technique, controlling for such variables as age, education level, race, religion, and sex. A good amount of detail is included in the administration manual concerning the representativeness of the norming samples.

The administration manual also contains a good deal of information concerning the psychometric aspects of the test. Alpha reliabilities for the Core Battery Verbal Memory Index, Visual Memory Index, and Attention-Concentration Index are .92, .89, and .86 respectively. The Alpha Reliability for the General Index is .93.

REFERENCES AND ADDITIONAL INFORMATION

Clark, R. M. (1992). Review of the Wide Range Assessment of Memory and Learning. In O. K. Buros (Ed.), *The eleventh mental measurements yearbook* (pp. 1034–35). Highland Park, NJ: Gryphon.

Dewey, D., Kaplan, B. J., Crawford, S. G., & Fisher, G. C. (2001). Predictive accuracy of the Wide Range Assessment of Memory and Learning in children with attention deficit hyperactivity disorder and reading difficulties. *Developmental Neuropsychology, 19,* 173–189.

Luo, X., & Li, X. (2003) Memory and learning ability of children with ADHD. *Chinese Mental Health Journal, 17,* 188–190.

Medway, F. J. (1992). Review of the Wide Range Assessment of Memory and Learning. In O. K. Buros (Ed.), *The eleventh mental measurements yearbook* (pp. 1034–35). Highland Park, NJ: Gryphon.

Putzke, J. D., Williams, M. A., & Glutting, J. J. (2001). Developmental memory performance: Inter-task consistency and base-rate variability on the WRAML. *Journal of Clinical & Experimental Neuropsychology, 23,* 253–264.

Williams, J., & Haut, J. S. (1995). Differential performances on the WRAML in children and adolescents diagnosed with epilepsy, head injury, and substance abuse. *Developmental Neuropsychology, 11,* 201–213.

Whitaker, D. P., & Brim, S. (2000). Review of the Wide Range Assessment of Memory and Learning. *Journal of Psychoeducational Assessment, 18.*

RON DUMONT
Fairleigh Dickinson University

JOHN O. WILLIS
Rivier College

WIDE RANGE ASSESSMENT OF VISUAL MOTOR ABILITIES

The Wide Range Assessment of Visual Motor Abilities (WRAVMA; Adams & Sheslow, 1995) provides a Visual-Motor Integration Composite resulting from separate subtest assessments of Fine-Motor, Visual-Spatial, and Visual-Motor abilities. These three areas can be measured individually or in combination.

Administration time for each subtest of the WRAVMA takes about 4–10 minutes. The Fine-Motor (peg board) test has the individual insert as many pegs as possible into a waffled, roughly square peg board. The examinee has 90 seconds to complete this task. Norms are provided for both dominant and nondominant hands. In the Visual-Spatial (matching) test, the child is asked to mark the option that goes best with the standard presented. Correct selection depends on visual-spatial skills such as perspective, orientation, rotation, and size discrimination. The Visual-Motor (drawing) subtest requires children to copy designs that are developmentally arranged to increase in difficulty. The manual supplies examples of acceptable and unacceptable responses for the 24 drawing items, as well as justifications for each. The test booklets are colorful and appealing.

Performance on the subtests can be interpreted both qualitatively and quantitatively to create a more complete evaluation of visual-motor abilities. Scaled scores, standard scores, age equivalents, and percentiles may be obtained for each subtest.

The WRAVMA was normed on a representative sample of over 2,600 children, ages 3–17, stratified according to gender, geographic region, socioeconomic standing, and race/ethnic group. This sample reflected the 1990 U.S. Census data.

Reliability measures of the three subtests show internal consistency coefficients exceeding .90 and test-retest reliability coefficients ranging from .81 to .91. Construct validity is supported by item separations of .99. Concurrent validity varies from .67 for the WRAVMA Visual-Spatial Test with the Motor Free Visual Perception test, to .81 for the WRAVMA Fine-Motor Test with the Grooved Pegboard, and .87 for the WRAVMA Visual-Motor test with the Beery-Buktenica Developmental Test of Visual-Motor Integration (VMI).

REFERENCES

Adams, W., & Sheslow, D. (1995). *Wide Range Assessment of Visual Motor Abilities.* Wilmington, DE: Wide Range.

Plake, B. S., & Impara, J. C. (Eds.). (2001). *The fourteenth mental measurements yearbook.* Lincoln, NE: Buros Institute of Mental Measurements.

RON DUMONT
Fairleigh Dickinson University

JOHN O. WILLIS
Rivier College

WIEACKER SYNDROME

Wieacker syndrome, also known as apraxia, involves the inability to execute familiar voluntary movements. A child with Wieacker syndrome is physically able to perform motor acts and has a desire to perform the acts, but is unable to perform the movements upon request (Merck, 1987). When motor movement does occur in a child with this syndrome, the movement is often uncontrolled, unintentional, inappropriate, and clumsy.

Selective apraxias do exist. For example, a child with constructional apraxia is unable to draw, whereas a child with oculomotor apraxia is unable to move his or her eyes (Thoene, 1992).

Apraxia results from a lesion in the neural pathways of the brain associated with the memory of learned patterns (Merck, 1987). The lesion may be due to a stroke, head injury, dementia, congenital malformation of the central nervous system, or metabolic or structural disease (Merck, 1987; Thoene, 1992).

Physical and occupational therapy is recommended to help a child with apraxia to relearn voluntary movements. If apraxia is a symptom of another disorder, treatment of the primary disorder is required (Thoene, 1992).

REFERENCES

Merck manual of diagnosis and therapy. (1987). (15th ed.). Rahway, NJ: Merck & Co.

Thoene, J. G. (Ed.). (1992). *Physician's guide to rare diseases.* Montvale, NJ: Dowden.

JOAN MAYFIELD
Baylor Pediatric Specialty Service

PATRICIA A. LOWE
University of Kansas

WILBUR, HERVEY BACKUS (1820–1883)

Hervey Backus Wilbur, physician and educator, established the first school for mentally retarded children in the United States when he took a group of retarded children into his home in Barre, Massachusetts, in 1848. With the published accounts of the educational work of Edouard Seguin to guide him, Wilbur fashioned out of his own experience a system of teaching that was successful to a degree not previously thought possible.

In 1851, the New York State legislature established an experimental residential school for mentally retarded children, the second state school for the mentally retarded in the United States, with Wilbur as superintendent. Residential schools were opened in a number of other states during the next few years, many of them patterned after the New York School. This school, over which Wilbur presided until his death, is today the Syracuse Developmental Center.

Wilbur was a founder and the first vice president (with Edouard Seguin as president) of the Association of Medical Officers of American Institutions for Idiotic and Feeble-

Minded Persons, now the American Association on Mental Retardation. He produced numerous pamphlets and articles dealing with the care and treatment of mentally retarded persons.

REFERENCES

Godding, W. W. (1883). In memoriam: Hervey Backus Wilbur. *Journal of Nervous & Mental Diseases, 10,* 658–662.

Scheerenberger, R. D. (1983). *A history of mental retardation.* Baltimore: Brookes

PAUL IRVINE
Katonah, New York

ADAPTIVE BEHAVIOR SCALES

WILD BOY OF AVEYRON

The Wild Boy of Aveyron—or Victor, as he later came to be known—first was noticed by a group of peasants who witnessed him fleeing through the woods of south central France. He was spotted on subsequent occasions digging up turnips and potatoes or seeking acorns. He was captured in the forest of Aveyron, France, by three hunters in July 1799. It was determined that the boy was about 11 or 12 years of age, was unable to speak, and had been living a wild existence. He was taken to the Institution of Deaf Mutes in Paris and was assigned to the care of Jean Itard.

Itard, a young French physician, believed that this wild creature was physiologically normal and that his intellectual deficiencies were due to a lack of "appropriate sensory experiences in a socialized environment" (Scheerenberger, 1983). Itard was convinced that with an adequate training program, Victor would show great intellectual development and could be transformed from a savage to a civilized being. Because Victor's intellectual deficiencies were not seen as physiologically based, but were attributed to isolation and social and educational neglect, this was viewed as an opportunity to substantiate the effectiveness of educational methods being developed at the time (Maloney & Ward, 1979).

Over the next 5 years, Itard worked intensively with Victor and established a sequence of educational activities designed to teach him speech, self-care, and manners; and to develop his intellectual functions and emotional faculties. Itard employed socialization techniques and sensory training methods much like those he had used with deaf children (Robinson & Robinson, 1965).

Victor's progress was sometimes frustratingly slow, despite Itard's affection, effort, and ingenuity. Still, the doctor made tremendous gains in his 5 years of work with the boy, later documenting this in great detail (Kirk & Gallagher, 1979). Victor accomplished a great deal: he was able to recognize objects, identify letters of the alphabet, and comprehend the meaning of many words (Maloney & Ward, 1979). However, he never learned to speak, and Itard felt his program of instruction had failed. The physician decided to terminate the program after 5 years of intensive work with Victor.

Itard's experiences with the Wild Boy of Aveyron are particularly notable since his work was the first documented, systematic attempt to teach a handicapped person. Although his attempts to make the boy "normal" failed, Itard did make significant gains, and showed that even a severely disabled individual could make great improvements with training.

REFERENCES

Kirk, S. A., & Gallagher, J. J. (1979). *Educating exceptional children* (3rd ed.). Boston: Houghton Mifflin.

Maloney, M. P., & Ward, M. P. (1979). *Mental retardation and modern society.* New York: Oxford University Press.

Robinson, H. B., & Robinson, N. M. (1965). *The mentally retarded child.* New York: McGraw-Hill.

Scheerenberger, R. C. (1983). *A history of mental retardation.* Baltimore: Brookes.

KATHLEEN RODDEN-NORD
GERALD TINDAL
University of Oregon

HISTORY OF SPECIAL EDUCATION
ITARD, JEAN MARC

WILL, MADELEINE C. (1945–   )

Madeleine C. Will obtained her BA in 1967 from Smith College and her MA in 1969 at the University of Toronto, Canada. As assistant secretary for special education and rehabilitative services in the U.S. Department of Education from 1983 to 1989, Will held the highest-ranking federal position for the advocacy of individuals with disabilities. During her tenure, she was responsible for the programs in the department's Office of Special Education, the Rehabilitation Services Administration, and the National Institute for Handicapped Research—the three units comprising the Office of Special Education and Rehabilitative Services. She supervised education department programs serving 4.5 million disabled children and 936,000 adults with disabilities. Committed to the belief that federal programs must not be administered on the basis of concepts that underestimate the potential contribution of disabled citizens, Will was responsible for the initiation of transition and supported work

Madeleine C. Will

models that strive to direct those with disabilities toward independent living and meaningful employment.

Will has written extensively on the topic of special education, its successes, failures, and recommendations for improvements (Will, 1984, 1986, 1988). She is a strong advocate of a more cohesive, less fragmented system: what she terms a *partnership* between special education and regular education to improve service delivery to all students. For students with learning problems in regular classrooms, she proposes increased time for instruction, support systems for teachers, principal-controlled programs and resources at the building level, and new instructional approaches.

Will has advocated for individuals with disabilities in numerous ways, including her service as chair of the Government Affairs Committee of the Montgomery County Association for Retarded Citizens in 1979 and member of the Government Affairs Committee of the National Association for Retarded Citizens. Additionally, from 1974 to 1976, she assisted in the development and operation of a program integrating preschoolers with disabilities into two nursery schools in Montgomery County, Maryland.

REFERENCES

Will, M. C. (1984). Let us pause and reflect—but not too long. *Exceptional Children, 51*(1), 11–16.

Will, M. C. (1986). Educating children with learning problems: A shared responsibility. *Exceptional Children, 52*(5), 411–415.

Will, M. C. (1988). Educating students with learning problems and the changing role of the school psychologist. *School Psychology Review, 17*(3), 476–478.

TAMARA J. MARTIN
*The University of Texas of the
Permian Basin*

OFFICE OF SPECIAL EDUCATION AND REHABILITATIVE SERVICES

See NATIONAL ASSOCIATION OF RETARDED CITIZENS

WILLIAMS SYNDROME

Williams syndrome (Williams, Baratt-Boyes, & Lowe, 1961) is a rare autosomal genetic disorder that affects 1:25,000 live births. It occurs in all ethnic groups, affects males and females equally, and has been reported internationally (Pober & Dykens, 1993). The disorder is associated with facial dysmorphology, renal and cardiovascular abnormalities, statural deficiencies, characteristic dental malformation, and infantile hypercalcaemia and hyperacusis (McKusick, 1988). A microdeletion of genes on chromosome 7q11.23 has been identified in 98 percent of the individuals with Williams syndrome. The missing region typically includes the ELN gene, which is thought to account for the vascular and connective tissue abnormalities (Ewart, Jin, Atkinson, Morris, & Keating, 1994). The other phenotypic characteristics are most likely linked to the adjacent 16 or more genes that are part of the standard deletion in Williams syndrome (Mervis, Morris, Bertrand, & Robinson, 1999; Tassabehji et al., 1999).

Williams syndrome belongs to a group of conditions that are not characterized by a single behavior anomaly (Flint & Yule, 1994). However, certain characteristics are sufficiently frequent to suggest that their origin lies in a common biological disorder. Characteristics may include psychiatric disorders (e.g., symptoms of anxiety, hyperactivity, and preoccupations) as well as an outgoing social nature, an exuberant enthusiasm, a sense of the dramatic, overfriendliness, inappropriate interpersonal behaviors including indiscriminate affection, a short attention span, sleep disturbance, and hyperacusis (sensitivity to noise; Einfeld, Tonge, & Florio, 1997; Williams Syndrome Association, 2002).

Since individuals with Williams syndrome often have a short attention span and tend to be highly distractible, teachers of students with Williams syndrome may want to implement the following strategies: flexibility in requirements for time spent working, frequent breaks in work time, a high-motivation curriculum, minimal distractions, rewards for attending behaviors, and, when possible, redirection around off-task behaviors, allowing some degree of choice for the child in terms of activity, and working in small groups. In addition, since individuals with Williams syndrome often have a heightened sensitivity to sounds (hyperacusis), teachers of students with Williams syndrome may want to implement these strategies: provide warning just before predictable noises when possible (e.g., fire drills, hourly bells), allow the child to view and possibly initiate the source of bothersome noises (e.g., turn the fan on and off, see where the fire alarm is turned on), make tape recordings of the sounds and encourage the child to experiment with the recording (e.g., playing it louder/softer; Williams Syndrome Association, 2002).

Persons with Williams syndrome frequently show an abnormal interest in strangers (Mervis et al., 1999). Adolescents and adults with Williams syndrome often approach strangers to engage them in conversation. Displayed photographs of unfamiliar faces were shown to young adults and their judgments were recorded as to how friendly and approachable they found the faces to be (Bellugi, Adolphs, Cassady, & Chiles, 1999). Individuals with Williams syndrome offered significantly more positive ratings of faces than others of the same chronological age or mental age.

Individuals with Williams syndrome have a distinctive cognitive profile. Their IQ scores typically range between 40 and 100, with a mean of 60 (Lenoff, Wang, Greenberg, & Bellugi, 1997; Levitin & Bellugi, 1998). Although their verbal intellectual abilities are below average, they are typically higher than their visual conceptual intellectual abilities (Mervis et al., 1999). Children and adolescents with Williams syndrome generally display severely deficient spatial abilities (Bellugi, Marks, Bihrle, & Sabo, 1993; Bellugi, Poizner, & Klima, 1989; Bihrle, 1990; Mervis et al., 1999), especially on visual-motor tasks (Beery & Buktenica, 1967; Elliot, 1990). Their mathematics skills also are deficient (Pagon, Bennett, LaVeck, Stewart, & Johnson, 1987), along with difficulty performing activities that require knowledge of number, space, substance, weight, and quantity (Bellugi, Klima, & Wang, 1996).

Since individuals with Williams syndrome typically have a nonverbal learning disorder, there are several recommended learning strategies that teachers of students with Williams syndrome can implement. For example, in reading comprehension, ensure that decoding skills have been mastered first (the student must be able to read words accurately before he or she can understand meaning). Typically, a phonics-based reading curriculum is most effective. Teach reading comprehension skills directly (e.g., making inferences and deductions, understanding cause and effect). Develop self-questioning techniques to monitor comprehension. Teach students that they must interact with the text. Encourage verbalization of strategies to enable students to internalize comprehension strategies (who, what, why, where, and when). Teach the organization and structure of paragraphs and teach signal words indicating transitions. In terms of vocabulary development, make concrete associations for unknown words whenever possible. Be "child centered" (e.g., use words they encounter in their own reading, define words they want to know, work from known associations and understandings). Encourage students to verbalize and paraphrase their understandings. Work toward a depth in understanding; do not let them slide by with surface understandings. Connect words into meaningful semantic categories and teach multiple meanings. Build semantic maps or webs. Highlight morphological rules and patterns; directly teach prefixes, roots, and suffixes. Finally, in the area of writing, provide brief daily practice to improve handwriting rate and legibility. Teach the student to use verbal self-directions to guide those practices. Address posture, position of hand and paper, grasp of pencil, and directions for forming individual letters. Teach keyboarding and word processing skills to the student at a young age. Focus on only one aspect of writing at a time (e.g., prewriting, writing, and editing). Hold expectations for rate and volume of written products based on the student's demonstrated abilities. Teach transitional words. Teach organizational patterns for writing paragraphs, then, for longer works, such as essays, provide a purpose and structure for writing (Williams Syndrome Association, 2002).

Music often holds special interest and affinity in persons with Williams syndrome. However, this interest has been recognized only recently (Reis, Schader, Milne, & Stephens, 2003). For some, music can help overcome obstacles. For example, some children have overcome acute sensitivity to loud noises in order to engage in dancing in which music is playing at levels that would otherwise bring them to tears (Williams Syndrome Association, 2002). Even though individuals with Williams syndrome have motor problems, including coordination, these problems are less apparent when playing musical instruments (Levitin & Bellugi, 1998). However, their affinity for music may be stronger than their musical ability (Williams Syndrome Association, 2002).

Williams syndrome is caused by a genetic/chromosomal defect and thus has no cure. However, early diagnosis can provide a better understanding of problems that may arise, leading to a more successful life for the child and relief and support for the parents. Medical conditions of individuals with Williams syndrome need to be monitored regularly by a physician who specializes in this disorder as well as by general practitioners and health visitors (Williams Syndrome Foundation, 2004).

REFERENCES

Beery, K. E., & Buktenica, N. A. (1967). *Developmental test of visual motor integration.* Cleveland, OH: Modern Curriculum Press.

Bellugi, U., Adolphs, R., Cassady, C., & Chiles, M. (1999). Towards the neural basis for hypersociability in a genetic syndrome. *Neuroreport, 10,* 1–5.

Bellugi, U., Klima, E. S., & Wang, P. P. (1996). Cognitive and neural development: Clues from genetically based syndromes. In D. Magnussen (Ed.), *The life-span development of individuals: Behavioral, neurobiological, and psychological perspectives* (pp. 223–43). The Nobel Symposium. New York: Cambridge University Press.

Bellugi, U., Marks, S., Bihrle, A., & Sabo, H. (1993). Dissociations between language and cognitive functions in Williams syndrome. In D. Bishop & K. Mogford (Eds.), *Language devel-*

opment in exceptional circumstances (pp. 177–89). Hillsdale, NJ: Erlbaum.

Bellugi, U., Poizner, H., & Klima, E. S. (1989). Language, modality and the brain. *Trends in Neurosciences, 10*, 380–388.

Bihrle, A. M. (1990). *Visuospatial processing in Williams and Down syndrome.* Unpublished doctoral dissertation, University of California and San Diego State University.

Einfield, S. L., Tonge, B., & Florio, T. (1997). Behavioral and emotional disturbance in individuals with Williams syndrome. *American Journal on Mental Retardation, 102*(1), 45–53.

Elliot, C. D. (1990). *Differential ability scale.* San Diego, CA: Harcourt, Brace, Javanowich.

Ewart, A. K., Jin, W., Atkinson, D., Morris, C. A., & Keating, M. T. (1994). Supravalvular aortic stenosis associated with a deletion disrupting the elastin gene. *Journal of Clinical Investigation, 93*, 1071–1077.

Flint, J., & Yule, W. (1994). Behavioral phenotypes. In M. Rutter, E. Taylor, & L. Hersov (Eds.), *Child and adolescent psychiatry: Modern approaches* (3rd ed., pp. 666–89). Oxford, England: Blackwell Scientific Publications.

Lenoff, H. M., Wang, P. P., Greenberg, F., & Bellugi. (1997). Williams syndrome and the brain. *Scientific American, 277*, 68–73.

Levitin, D. J., & Bellugi, U. (1998). Musical abilities in individuals with Williams syndrome. *Music Perception, 15*, 357–389.

McKusick, V. (1988). *Mendelian inheritance in man: Catalog of autosomal dominant, autosomal recessive and X-linked phenotypes.* Baltimore: Johns Hopkins University Press.

Mervis, C. B., Morris, C. A., Bertrand, J., & Robinson, B. F. (1999). Williams syndrome: Findings from an integrated program of research. In H. Tager-Flsuberg (Ed.), *Neurodevelopmental disorders* (pp. 65–110). Boston: MIT Press.

Pagon, R., Bennett, F., LaVeck, B., Stewart, K., & Johnson, J. (1987). Williams syndrome: Features in late childhood and adolescence. *Pediatrics, 80*(1), 85–91.

Pober, B. R., & Dykens, E. M. (1993). Williams syndrome: An overview of medical, cognitive, and behavioral features. *Mental Retardation, 5*, 929–943.

Reis, S., Schader, R., Milne, H., & Stephens, R. (2003). Music & minds: Using a talent development approach for young adults with Williams syndrome. *Council for Exceptional Children, 69*(3), 293–313.

Tassabehji, M., Metcalfe, K., Karmiloff-Smith, A., Carette, M. J., Grant, J., Dennis, N., et al. (1999). Williams syndrome: Use of chromosomal microdeletions as a tool to dissect cognitive and physical phenotypes. *American Journal of Human Genetics, 64*, 118–125.

Williams, J. C. P., Baratt-Boyes, B. G., & Lowe, J. B. (1961). Supravalvular aortic stenosis. *Circulation, 24*, 1311–1318.

Williams Syndrome Association. (2002). http://www.williams-syndrome.org/forteachers/musicandws.html

Williams Syndrome Foundation. (2004). http://www.williams-syndrome.org.uk/about_ws/treatment.htm

KRISTA SCHWENK
University of Florida

INFANTILE HYPERCALCEMIA

WILLOWBROOK CASE

The Willowbrook case, or *New York State Association for Retarded Children v. Carey,* was litigation tried by Judge Orrin Judd in which the conditions in the Willowbrook State School in New York State were challenged. Specific charges included widespread physical abuse, overcrowded conditions and understaffing, inhumane and destructive conditions, extended solitary confinement, and lack of therapeutic care. Brought on behalf of more than 5,000 residents of the Willowbrook State School, this class-action suit is recognized as a landmark in protection from harm litigation.

During a series of Willowbrook trials, witnesses appeared and provided court testimony documenting the inhumane conditions and the physical, mental, and emotional deterioration of residents. On April 21, 1975, the New York Civil Liberties Union, the Legal Aid Society, the Mental Health Law Project, and the U.S. Department of Justice announced that the parties to the Willowbrook litigation had agreed on a consent judgment that would resolve the suit. This consent decree, which was approved on May 5, 1975, established standards in 23 areas to secure the constitutional rights of the Willowbrook residents to protection from harm.

This consent decree, which was to be implemented within 13 months or less, identified duty ratios of direct-care staff to residents of one to four during waking hours for most residents, and required an overall ratio of one clinical staff member for every three residents. The decree prohibited seclusion, corporal punishment, degradation, medical experimentation, and routine use of restraints. It established the primary goal of Willowbrook as the preparation of residents for development and life in the community, and it mandated individual plans for the residents' education, therapy, care, and development.

Additionally, the decree required (1) 6 hours of programmed activity each weekday; (2) nutritionally adequate diets; (3) dental services; (4) 2 hours of daily recreational activities; (5) adaptive equipment as needed; (6) adequate clothing; (7) continually available physicians; (8) contracted services with an accredited hospital; (9) an immunization program; (10) compensation for voluntary labor in accordance with minimum wage laws; and (11) correction of health and safety hazards.

Another set of requirements to be implemented, but not subject to the 13-month timetable, included reduction in the number of Willowbrook beds, establishment of 200 new community placements, increased funding to Willowbrook, creation of a review panel to oversee implementation of standards of the consent decree, initiation of a consumer advisory board composed of parents and relatives of residents, community leaders, residents, and former residents, and creation of a professional advisory board.

This Willowbrook case promoted improvements in the lives of the Willowbrook residents, focused public attention on the conditions of institutionalized individuals, and, as with other landmark cases, affected many similar cases.

DOUGLAS FUCHS
LYNN S. FUCHS
Peabody College, Vanderbilt University

DEINSTITUTIONALIZATION
HUMANISM AND SPECIAL EDUCATION
MENTAL RETARDATION

WILSON'S DISEASE

See KAYSER-FLEISCHER RING

WITMER, LIGHTNER (1867–1956)

Lightner Witmer established the world's first psychological clinic at the University of Pennsylvania in 1896, an event that marked the beginning not only of clinical psychology but also of the diagnostic approach to teaching. Previously director of the psychological laboratory at the University of Pennsylvania, where he succeeded James McKeen Cattell, Witmer moved psychology from the theoretical concerns of the laboratory to the study of learning and behavior problems of children in the classroom. Proposing a merging of the clinical method in psychology and the diagnostic method in teaching, Witmer developed an interdisciplinary approach to education, his clinic provided training for psychologists, teachers, social workers, and physicians. He formed special classes that served as training grounds for teachers from across the nation and as models for many of the special classes that were

Lightner Witmer

established in the early part of the twentieth century. Anticipating special education's strong influence on mainstream education, Witmer suggested that learning-disabled children would show the way for the education of all children.

REFERENCES

Watson, R. I. (1956). Lightner Witmer: 1867–1956. *American Journal of Psychology, 69,* 680.

Witmer, L. (1911). *The special class for backward children.* Philadelphia: Psychological Clinic.

PAUL IRVINE
Katonah, New York

WOLF-HIRSCHHORNE SYNDROME

Wolf-Hirschhorne syndrome, also known as Wolf Syndrome or 4p-Syndrome, is a genetic disorder resulting from a defect in chromosome 4. The incidence rate of Wolf-Hirschhorne syndrome is 1 out of 50,000 births (Thoene, 1992). The syndrome occurs more often in females than males by a ratio of 2:1. Approximately one-third of the children who are born with the syndrome die in the first 2 years of life as a result of either cardiac failure or bronchopneumonia (O'Brien & Yule, 1995).

Primary features of the disorder include low birth weight, deficient or low muscle tone, physical and Mental Retardation, and a very small head. Prominent facial characteristics are also found in this syndrome, such as cleft lip, cleft palate, downturned mouth, small jaw, low-set ears, high forehead, and beak-like nose. Squinting of the eyes is another common feature. Heart and kidney problems and seizures occur in approximately 50 percent of the children with this disorder. In some cases, reconstructive surgery is needed to address facial abnormalities.

In schools, special education may be needed to address learning disabilities. Due to delayed psychomotor development and speech/communication abilities, physical therapy, occupational therapy, and speech services will be needed (O'Brien & Yule, 1995). Vocational services may be helpful. Genetic counseling may also be beneficial (Thoene, 1992).

REFERENCES

O'Brien, G., & Yule, W. (Eds.). (1995). *Behavioral phenotypes.* London: Mac Keith Press.

Thoene, J. G. (Ed.). (1992). *Physician's guide to rare diseases.* Montvale, NJ: Dowden.

JOAN MAYFIELD
Baylor Pediatric Specialty Service

PATRICIA A. LOWE
University of Kansas

WOLFENSBERGER, WOLF P. J. (1934–   )

Born and raised in Germany in the period just before and during World War II, Wolf P. J. Wolfensberger studied in the United States. He earned a BA in philosophy from the now-defunct Siena College of Memphis, Tennessee. He subsequently pursued graduate training in psychology and education at St. Louis University, during which time he became a naturalized U.S. citizen in 1956, and received his MA in psychology in 1957. Wolfensberger continued his studies of psychology and special education, earning his PhD in these fields in 1962 from George Peabody College for Teachers (now Peabody College, Vanderbilt University).

Wolfensberger was mentored by two widely known psychologists while an intern: Walter Klopfer, the famous personality psychologist, at the Norfolk (Nebraska) State Hospital; and Jack Tizard, while Wolfensberger was a post-doctoral research fellow in Mental Retardation at Maudsley Hospital (the University of London teaching hospital) in England. Following the latter experience, Wolfensberger became a Mental Retardation research scientist at the Nebraska Psychiatric Institute (1964–1971), where he eventually rose to the rank of associate professor of medical psychology in the departments of psychiatry and pediatrics. For 2 years (1971–1973), he was a visiting scholar at the Canadian National Institute on Mental Retardation, with a joint faculty appointment at York University. From 1973 to 1992, Wolfensberger served as a professor in the Division of Special Education and Rehabilitation at Syracuse University, and from 1992 to the present, he has been a research professor in the School of Education there. At the same time, he has been the director of the Syracuse University Training Institute for Human Service Planning, Leadership and Change Agentry (Wolfensberger, pers. comm., June 9, 1998).

A prolific writer and researcher, Wolfensberger has devoted nearly his entire career to social advocacy for better life conditions for and high-quality services to people with disabilities. He has been one of the major proponents, arguably *the* major proponent, of the principle of normalization, in 1983 designing Social Role Valorization, focusing on the relation between social roles and consequences, as the successor to this concept. His instruments (PASS and PASSING) for evaluating services in terms of normalization and Social Role Valorization criteria have been used worldwide. Additionally, Wolfensberger is the originator of the Citizen Advocacy scheme, which promotes one-to-one advocacy for people with handicaps and is used throughout the English-speaking world. Many other advocacy-related schemes have borrowed this concept (Wolfensberger, pers. comm., June 9, 1998).

In 1991, Wolfensberger's work in the area of normalization was recognized by a Delphi panel of experts as the most influential work in the field of Mental Retardation in the United States during a 50-year period. He continues the work he began in the 1970s, conducting training workshops for human services personnel and the families of individuals with disabilities, and serves as an advocate in 11 different countries. Wolfensberger has also spoken and written against the growing legitimization of "deathmaking" of all sorts of unwanted and devalued people (Wolfensberger, 1994).

REFERENCES

Kugel, R., & Wolfensberger, W. (Eds.). (1968). *Changing patterns in residential services for the mentally retarded.* Washington, DC: President's Committee on Mental Retardation.

Wolfensberger, W. (1972). *The principle of normalization in human services.* Toronto, Canada: National Institute on Mental Retardation.

Wolfensberger, W. (1980). Research, empiricism, and the principle of normalization. In R. J. Flynn & K. E. Witsch (Eds.), *Normalization, social integration, and community services,* Baltimore: University Park Press.

Wolfensberger, W. (1994). A personal interpretation of the mental retardation scene in light of the "Signs of the Times." *Mental Retardation, 32,* 19–33.

Wolfensberger, W., & Zauha, H. (Eds.). (1973). *Citizen advocacy and protective services for the impaired and handicapped.* Toronto, Canada: National Institute on Mental Retardation.

CECIL R. REYNOLDS
Texas A&M University
First edition

TAMARA J. MARTIN
The University of Texas of the Permian Basin
Second edition

NORMALIZATION

WOOD, M. MARGARET (1931–   )

M. Margaret (Peggy) Wood began in special education as an NDEA fellow at the University of Georgia where, following the awarding of her BA in elementary education in 1953 from Goucher College, she earned her MEd (special education) in 1960. Wood immediately followed the MEd with an EdD, awarded with distinction in 1963 from the University of Georgia with a major in special education and a minor in psychology. Wood then did postdoctoral study at the Hillcrest Residential Treatment Center in Washington, DC. From 1964 to 1969, Wood was director of the teacher preparation program for teachers of emotionally disturbed students in the division for exceptional children at the University of Georgia. It was during this time that her view of therapeutic approaches to children in the schools ma-

M. Margaret Wood

tured and she began to work in earnest toward developing a psychoeducational approach to these children's problems. This approach has become known widely as developmental therapy.

In 1970 Wood received funding for the establishment of the Rutland Center for Severely Emotionally Disturbed Children; she directed the center until 1974. Developmental therapy, as practiced at the Rutland Center under Wood's direction, became a model approach to the provision of special education services to emotionally disturbed children in the public schools. More than 250 developmental therapy centers have been established in schools worldwide, though nearly all are in North and South America. Wood has continued her active interest in developmental therapy but has focused on research and dissemination activities since 1974, when she became project director of a federally sponsored model in-service training program. Wood was promoted to the rank of professor in the division for exceptional children at the University of Georgia in 1977.

Wood has more than 50 scholarly publications to her credit, most dealing with some aspect of developmental therapy, and has authored or edited six books (Wood, 1975, 1982; Williams & Wood, 1977). Wood is best known as the originator of developmental therapy, a major innovation in public school delivery of special education services to severely emotionally disturbed children. Wood has a significant reputation as a mentor and many well-known professionals have studied with her and practiced developmental therapy at the Rutland Center.

REFERENCES

Williams, G. H., & Wood, M. M. (1977). *Developmental art therapy.* Baltimore: University Park Press.

Wood, M. M. (Ed.). (1975). *Developmental therapy.* Baltimore: University Park Press.

Wood, M. M. (1982). Developmental therapy: A model for therapeutic intervention in the schools. In C. R. Reynolds & T. B. Gutkin (Eds.), *The handbook of school psychology.* New York: Wiley.

CECIL R. REYNOLDS
Texas A&M University

DEVELOPMENTAL THERAPY

WOODCOCK DIAGNOSTIC READING BATTERY

The Woodcock Diagnostic Reading Battery (WDRB; Woodcock, 1997) is a set of carefully engineered (Woodcock, 1992) tests for clinical measurement of reading achievement and important abilities related to reading. Test development, item calibration, scaling, cluster composition, and interpretation were accomplished through the Rasch single-parameter logistic test model (Rasch, 1960; Wright & Stone, 1979), and stepwise multiple regression analysis. Continuous-year norming, based on a nationally representative sample of 6,026 individuals ranging in age from 4 to 95 years, produced highly accurate normative data—10 points at each grade level and 12 points at each age level for school-aged individuals.

The WDRB is comprised of six tests from the WJ-R Tests of Cognitive Ability (Woodcock & Johnson, 1989) and four tests from the WJ-R Tests of Achievement (Woodcock & Johnson, 1989). The tests were combined into one format to be "more useful to those who are reading specialists and researchers" (Rudman, in press). That is, one short battery of tests includes (1) tests of basic reading and reading comprehension skills, (2) important reading-related tests (phonological awareness and oral comprehension), and (3) reading aptitude tests.

The reading tests include Letter-Word Identification, Passage Comprehension, Word Attack, and Reading Vocabulary. The phonological awareness tests include Incomplete Words and Sound Blending. The oral comprehension tests are Oral Vocabulary and Listening Comprehension.

Four tests comprise the Reading Aptitude cluster: Memory for Sentences, Visual Matching, Sound Blending, and Oral Vocabulary. These tests are based on tasks that are statistically and logically associated with proficiency in reading, but are uncontaminated with reading content. The median correlation between the WDRB Reading Aptitude cluster and Broad Reading achievement clusters is .78.

The Reading Aptitude cluster in this battery is particularly notable in that it makes a valid aptitude measure available to a wide array of specialists who might otherwise not be trained to administer an intellectual ability test. Because the aptitude tests were conormed with the achievement tests, actual discrepancy norms are available. Use of conormed tests is the most accurate and valid method for determining the presence and severity of an aptitude/achievement discrepancy (McGrew, 1994). This is because the discrepancy norm calculation procedure fully accounts for regression to the mean (McGrew et al., 1991). (Practitioners who use separately normed instruments for aptitude/achievement discrepancy analysis do not possess actual data for both the predictor and criterion variables from the same sample of subjects.)

A reading performance model, included in the examiner's manual, helps examiners interpret the reading-related abilities. An individual's phonological awareness exerts a major influence on his or her decoding or basic reading skills. His or her oral comprehension exerts a major influence on reading comprehension. When these related tests are administered in conjunction with the reading achievement tests, examiners can obtain a better picture of why an individual has a reading problem.

Administration time is approximately 50 to 60 minutes for all 10 tests. A wide range of scores are available, notably age and grade equivalents, standard scores, percentile ranks, and instructional zones. Rudman (in press) seemed particularly impressed by the associated *Scoring and Interpretive Program for the Woodcock Diagnostic Reading Battery* (Schrank & Woodcock, 1978). He said "The narrative reports are remarkably smooth and do not read as most computer narratives normally do" (p. 8).

The reliability and validity characteristics of the WDRB are very good and meet basic technical requirements for both individual placement and programming decisions. Repeated-measures reliability (for individuals retested 1 to 17 months after initial testing) is extremely high (McArdle and Woodcock, in press), especially for the learned abilities, such as Letter-Word Identification (.92) and Passage Comprehension (.82). The median test stability over this wide range of time for all 10 tests is .81. Rudman (in press) described this as "a surprising picture of stability of traits." Concurrent validity evidence is established through moderate to strong correlations between the WDRB and measures of cognitive abilities, achievement, and language proficiency, including the Peabody Individual Achievement Test (Dunn & Markwardt, 1970), the Wechsler Intelligence Scale for Children–Revised (Wechsler, 1974), the Stanford-Binet Intelligence Scale–Fourth Edition (Thorndike, Hagen, & Sattler, 1986), the Kaufman Intelligence Battery for Children (Kaufman & Kaufman, 1983), the Kaufman Tests of Educational Achievement (Kaufman & Kaufman, 1985), the Basic Achievement Skills Individual Screener (Psychological Corporation, 1983), the Wide Range Achievement Tests–Revised (Jastak & Wilkinson, 1984), and the Mini-Battery of Achievement (Woodcock, McGrew, & Werder, 1994). Construct validity evidence is presented via a pattern of increasing scores with age.

REFERENCES

Dunn, L. M., & Markwardt, F. C. (1970). *Peabody Individual Achievement Test*. Circle Pines, MN: American Guidance Service.

Jastak, S. R., & Wilkinson, G. S. (1984). *Wide Range Achievement Test–Revised*. Wilmington, DE: Jastak.

Kaufman, A. S., & Kaufman, N. L. (1983). *Kaufman Assessment Battery for Children*. Circle Pines, MN: American Guidance Service.

Kaufman, A. S., & Kaufman, N. L. (1985). *Kaufman Tests of Educational Achievement*. Circle Pines, MN: American Guidance Service.

McArdle, J., & Woodcock, R. W. (1997). Modeling components of change from time-lagged test-retest data. *Psychological Methods, 2*(4), 403–435.

McGrew, K. S. (1994). *Clinical interpretation of the Woodcock-Johnson Tests of Cognitive Ability–Revised*. Boston: Allyn & Bacon.

McGrew, K. S., Werder, J. K., & Woodcock, R. W. (1991). *WJ-R Technical Manual*. Itasca, IL: Riverside.

Psychological Corporation. (1983). *Basic Achievement Skills Individual Screener*. San Antonio, TX: Author.

Rasch, G. (1960). *Probabilistic models for some intelligence and attainment tests*. Copenhagen, Denmark: Danish Institute for Educational Research.

Rudman, H. C. (in press). Review of the Woodcock Diagnostic Reading Battery. In *The fourteenth mental measurements yearbook*. Lincoln: University of Nebraska Press.

Schrank, F. A., & Woodcock, R. W. (1998). *Scoring and interpretive program for the Woodcock Diagnostic Reading Battery*. Itasca, IL: Riverside.

Thorndike, R. L., Hagen, E. P., & Sattler, J. M. (1986). *Stanford-Binet Intelligence Scale–Fourth Edition*. Itasca, IL: Riverside.

Wechsler, D. (1974). *Wechsler Intelligence Scale for Children–Revised*. San Antonio, TX: Psychological Corporation.

Woodcock, R. W. (1992, April). *Rasch technology and test engineering*. Invited presentation to the American Educational Research Association annual conference, San Francisco.

Woodcock, R. W. (1997). *Woodcock Diagnostic Reading Battery*. Itasca, IL: Riverside.

Woodcock, R. W., & Johnson, M. B. (1989). *Woodcock-Johnson–Revised Tests of Achievement*. Itasca, IL: Riverside.

Woodcock, R. W., & Johnson, M. B. (1989). *Woodcock-Johnson–Revised Tests of Cognitive Ability*. Itasca, IL: Riverside.

Woodcock, R. W., McGrew, K. S., & Werder, J. K. (1994). *Mini-Battery of Achievement*. Itasca, IL: Riverside.

Wright, B. D., & Stone, M. H. (1979). *Best test design*. Chicago: MESA Press.

FREDRICK A. SCHRANK
Olympia, Washington

WOODCOCK-JOHNSON III TESTS OF ACHIEVEMENT

The WJ III measures a great many aspects of academic achievement with a wide variety of relatively brief tests. Many of these achievement tests can be used with the WJ III Tests of Cognitive Abilities to assess a student's abilities on many specific Cattell-Horn-Carroll (CHC) *Gf-Gc* "cognitive factors." Examiners are permitted to select the tests they need to assess abilities in which they are interested for a particular student.

The WJ III Tests of Achievement provide interpretive information from 22 tests to measure cognitive performance.

- Reading
  Letter-Word Identification: naming letters and reading words aloud from a list.
  Reading Fluency: speed of reading sentences and answering "yes" or "no" to each.
  Passage Comprehension: orally supplying the missing word removed from each sentence or very brief paragraph (e.g., "Woof," said the _____, "biting the hand that fed it.").
  Word Attack: reading nonsense words (e.g., plurp, fronkett) aloud to test phonetic word attack skills.
  Reading Vocabulary: orally stating synonyms and antonyms for printed words and orally completing written analogies (e.g., elephant : big :: mouse : _____).
- Written Language
  Spelling: writing letters and words from dictation.
  Writing Fluency: writing simple sentences, using three given words for each item, and describing a picture, as quickly as possible for 7 minutes.
  Writing Samples: writing sentences according to directions. Many items include pictures; spelling does not count on most items.
  Editing: orally correcting deliberate errors in typed sentences.
  Spelling of Sounds: written spelling of dictated nonsense words.
  Punctuation and Capitalization: formal writing test of these skills.
- Mathematics
  Calculation: involves arithmetic computation with paper and pencil.
  Math Fluency: speed of performing simple calculations for 3 minutes.
  Applied Problems: oral math "word problems," solved with paper and pencil.
  Quantitative Concepts: oral questions about mathematical factual information, operations signs, and so on.
- Oral Language
  Story Recall: The student answers oral questions about stories that were dictated to the student.
  Understanding Directions: The student follows oral directions to point to different parts of pictures.
  Picture Vocabulary: The student points to named pictures or names pictures.
  Oral Comprehension: the student provides antonyms or synonyms to spoken words and completes oral analogies (e.g., elephant is to big as mouse is to _____)
- Supplemental
  Story Recall—Delayed: the student answers questions about the stories heard earlier.
  Sound Awareness: rhyming, deletion, substitution, and reversing of spoken sounds.
  Academic Knowledge: oral questions about factual knowledge of science, social studies, and humanities.

The WJ III provides raw scores that are converted, using age- or grade-based norms, to Standard Scores, Percentile Ranks, W-scores, age and grade equivalents (AE and GE), relative proficiency index (RPI), Instructional Ranges, and Cognitive-Academic Language Proficiency (CALP) levels. All score transformation is performed through the use of the computer program (WJ III Compuscore). The program also can generate several "discrepancy" analyses: intraability discrepancies (intracognitive, intraachievement, and intraindividual) and ability achievement discrepancies (predicted achievement versus achievement, general intellectual ability versus achievement, and oral language ability versus achievement).

The WJ III was normed on 8,818 children and adults (4,783 in grades kindergarten through 12) in a well-designed national sample. The same persons also provided norms for the WJ III tests of academic achievement, so the ability and achievement tests can be compared directly and cognitive and achievement tests can be combined to measure CHC factors. The technical manual provides extensive coverage of reliability and validity areas. The median reliability coefficient alphas for all age groups for the standard battery of the WJ III ACH for tests 1 through 12 ranged from .81 to .94. For the Extended battery, median coefficients ranged from .76 to .91. The reliability scores for the WJ III meet or exceed standards. The median cluster reliabilities are mostly .90 or higher, and the individual test reliabilities are mostly .80 or higher, and can be used for decision-making purposes with support from other sources. The technical manual presents a considerable amount of evidence supporting the validity of scores from the test, noting that the earlier versions of the battery have also been shown to have validity. The WJ III ACH content is similar to that of other achievement tests. Growth curves of cluster scores illustrate expected developmental progressions. Extensive data focus on validity evidence from confirmatory factor analyses of test scores from participants aged 6 to adult. The internal correlations of the entire battery are consistent with relations between areas of achievement and between areas of achievement and ability clusters.

REFERENCES

Mather, N., & Jaffe, L. (2002). *Woodcock-Johnson III: Reports, recommendations, and strategies.* New York: Wiley

Mather, N., Wendling, B. J., & Woodcock, R. W. (2001). *The essentials of WJ III tests of achievement assessment.* New York: Wiley.

Plake, B. S., Impara, J. C., & Spies, R. A. (Eds.). (2003). *The fifteenth mental measurements yearbook.* Lincoln, NE: Buros Institute of Mental Measurements.

RON DUMONT
Farleigh Dickinson University

JOHN O. WILLIS
Rivier College

WOODCOCK-JOHNSON III TESTS OF COGNITIVE ABILITIES

Unlike many individual ability tests, the Woodcock-Johnson III Tests of Cognitive Abilities (WJ III COG; Schrank, Flanagan, Woodcock, & Mascolo, 2001) are explicitly designed to assess a student's abilities on many specific Cattell-Horn-Carroll (CHC) *Gf-Gc* cognitive factors, not just a total score or a few factors. The General Intellectual Ability (GIA) score of the WJ III is based on a weighted combination of tests that best represent a common ability underlying all intellectual performance. Examiners can get a GIA (Std) score by administering the first seven tests in the Tests of Cognitive Abilities or a GIA (Ext) score by administering all 14 cognitive tests. Each of the cognitive tests represents a different broad CHC factor. A Brief Intellectual Ability (BIA) score is available that takes about 10 to 15 minutes to administer and is especially useful for screenings and reevaluations. The BIA score is derived from three cognitive tests: Verbal Comprehension, Concept Formation, and Visual Matching. Examiners are permitted to select the tests they need to assess abilities in which they are interested for a particular student.

The WJ III Tests of Cognitive Abilities provides interpretive information from 20 tests to measure cognitive performance.

- Comprehension-Knowledge (*Gc*)
  Verbal Comprehension: Naming pictures, giving antonyms or synonyms for spoken words, and completing oral analogies.
  General Information: Answering "where" and "what" factual questions.

- Long-Term Retrieval (*Glr*)
  Visual-Auditory Learning: The student is taught rebus symbols for words and tries to read sentences written with the symbols.
  Retrieval Fluency: The student tries to name as many things as possible in 1 minute in each of three specified categories (e.g., fruits).

- Visual Processing (*Gv*)
  Spatial Relations: The student tries to select by sight alone, from many choices, the fragments that could be assembled into a given geometric shape.
  Picture Recognition: The student is shown one or more pictures and tries to identify it or them on another page that includes several similar pictures.

- Auditory Processing (*Ga*)
  Sound Blending: The student tries to identify dictated words broken into separate sounds.
  Auditory Attention: The student tries to recognize words dictated against increasingly loud background noise.

- Fluid Reasoning (*Gf*)
  Concept Formation: For each item, the student tries to figure out the rule that divides a set of symbols into two groups.
  Analysis-Synthesis: The student tries to solve logical puzzles involving color codes similar to mathematical and scientific symbolic rules.

- Processing Speed (*Gs*)
  Visual Matching: As quickly as possible for 3 minutes, the student circles two identical numbers in each row of six numbers.
  Decision Speed: As quickly as possible for 3 minutes, the student tries to find the two pictures in each row that are most similar conceptually (e.g., sundial and stopwatch).

- Short-Term Memory (*Gsm*)
  Numbers Reversed: The student repeats increasingly long series of dictated digits in reversed order.
  Memory for Words: The student tries to repeat dictated random series of words in order.

- Additional Tests
  Incomplete Words: The student attempts to recognize words dictated with some sounds omitted. This is an additional measure of *Ga*.
  Auditory Working Memory: The student tries to repeat randomly dictated words and numbers (e.g., cow 9 up 3 5) with the words first and then the numbers in the order they were dictated. This test also measures *Gsm*, working memory, or division of attention.
  Visual-Auditory Learning—Delayed: The student tries again to read sentences written with the rebuses

learned in Visual-Auditory Learning. There are norms from half an hour to 8 days. This is an additional measure of *Glr*.

Rapid Picture Naming: The student tries to name simple pictures as quickly as possible for 2 minutes. This test measures *Gs* and naming facility or Rapid Automatized Naming (RAN).

Planning: The student traces a complex, overlapping path without lifting the pencil, retracing any part of the path, or skipping any part. *Gf* and *Gv* are involved in this test.

Pair Cancellation: The student scans rows of pictures and tries, as quickly as possible for 3 minutes, to circle each instance in which a certain picture is followed by a certain other picture (e.g., each cat is followed by a tree). This test also measures *Gs*.

The WJ III provides raw scores that are converted, using age- or grade-based norms, to Standard Scores, Percentile Ranks, W scores, age and grade equivalents (AE and GE), relative proficiency index (RPI), Instructional Ranges, and Cognitive-Academic Language Proficiency (CALP) levels. All score transformation is performed through the use of the computer program (WJ III Compuscore). The program can also generate several "discrepancy" analyses: intraability discrepancies (intracognitive, intraachievement, and intraindividual) and ability achievement discrepancies (predicted achievement versus achievement, general intellectual ability versus achievement, and oral language ability versus achievement).

The WJ III was normed on 8,818 children and adults (4,783 in grades kindergarten through 12) in a well-designed national sample. The same persons also provided norms for the WJ III tests of academic achievement, so the ability and achievement tests can be compared directly and cognitive and achievement tests can be combined to measure CHC factors. The technical manual provides extensive coverage of reliability and validity areas. The median reliability coefficient alphas for all age groups for the standard battery of the WJ III COG for tests 1 through 10 ranged from .81 to .94. For the extended battery, median coefficients ranged from .74 to .97. The reliability scores for the WJ III meet or exceed standards. The median cluster reliabilities are mostly .90 or higher, and the individual test reliabilities are mostly .80 or higher and can be used for decision-making purposes with support from other sources. The manual presents considerable evidence supporting the validity of scores from the test, noting that the earlier versions of the battery have also been shown to have validity. Test content on the WJ III COG has emerged from previous versions, is similar to the content found on other well-established cognitive measures, or is based on sound experimental instruments.

REFERENCES

Mather, N., & Jaffe, L. (2002). *Woodcock-Johnson III: Reports, recommendations, and strategies.* New York: Wiley

Plake, B. S., Impara, J. C., & Spies, R. A. (Eds.). (2003). *The fifteenth mental measurements yearbook.* Lincoln, NE: Buros Institute of Mental Measurements.

Rizza, M. G., McIntosh, D. E., & McCunn, A. (2001). Profile analysis of the Woodcock-Johnson III Tests of Cognitive Abilities with gifted students. *Psychology in the Schools, 38* (Special issue: New perspectives in gifted education), 447–455.

Schrank, F. A., Flanagan D. P., Woodcock R W., & Mascolo, J. T. (2001). *Essentials of WJ III Cognitive Abilities assessment.* New York: Wiley.

RON DUMONT
Farleigh Dickinson University

JOHN O. WILLIS
Rivier College

ACHIEVEMENT TESTS
CRITERION-REFERENCED TESTS

WOODCOCK LANGUAGE PROFICIENCY BATTERY–REVISED

The Woodcock Language Proficiency Battery–Revised (WLPB-R; Woodcock, 1991; Woodcock & Muñoz-Sandoval, 1995) is designed to provide an overview of a subject's language skills in English (or Spanish), to diagnose language abilities, to identify students for English as a second language instruction, and to plan broad instructional goals for developing language competencies. The instrument is appropriate for individuals aged 2 to over 90 years of age. For interpretive purposes, each WLPB-R provides cluster scores for Broad Language Ability (English or Spanish), Oral Language Ability, Reading Ability, and Written Language Ability. When the entire battery is used, the WLPB-R provides a procedure for evaluating the strengths and weaknesses among an individual's oral language, reading, and written language abilities. When both the English and Spanish forms are administered, examiners can obtain information about language dominance and relative proficiency in each language.

The WLPB-R oral language tests measure linguistic competency, semantic expression, expressive vocabulary, and verbal comprehension/reasoning. The WLPB-R reading tests measure the ability to identify sight vocabulary, to apply structural analysis skills, and comprehend single-word stimuli and short passages. The written language tests assess a broad range of writing tasks. These include tasks measuring the ability to produce simple sentences with ease, writing increasingly complex sentences to meet varied demands, and other tasks measuring punctuation, capitalization, spelling, word usage, and the ability to detect and correct errors in spelling, punctuation, capitalization, and word usage in written passages.

Administration time varies depending on the purposes of the assessment and the number of tests administered (20 minutes to over 1 hour). A wide variety of interpretive scores are available, including age and grade equivalents, instructional ranges, standard scores, and percentile ranks.

The English form was standardized on more than 6,300 individuals ranging in age from 2 to over 90. Lehmann (1995), who reviewed the WLPB-R primarily from a psychometric perspective, commented favorably on the development of continuous (gathered throughout the school year), rather than interpolated, norms. The Spanish form was standardized on more than 2,000 native Spanish-speaking subjects. The Spanish form uses equated U.S. norms for interpretive purposes.

Internal consistency reliability coefficients and standard errors of measurement (SEMs) were calculated for all tests and clusters and are reported in the *WLBP-R Examiner's Manual*. Reliabilities are generally in the high .80s and low .90s for the individual tests, and in the mid .90s for the clusters. Test-retest reliability, interrater reliability, and alternate forms reliability statistics are also reported. All provide evidence that scores from the WLPB-R are reliable. Poteat (1995) said that "the profusion of reliability data varies but generally the WLPB-R appears to have satisfactory to excellent reliability" (p. 416).

The manual also presents evidence of concurrent validity as established through moderate to strong correlations between the WLPB-R and other measures of cognitive abilities, achievement, and language proficiency. Poteat (1995) said that "it is difficult to summarize these very diverse data very succinctly, but the WLPB-R is positively correlated to measures of language development and ability" (p. 416). Intercorrelations among WLPB-R tests are also presented in the manual, providing adequate evidence of construct validity. In addition, a study by Schrank, Fletcher, and Alvarado (1996) provides evidence that the WLPB-R tests are good measures of cognitive-academic language proficiency (CALP; Cummins, 1984). The study by Schrank et al. (1996) also showed that the WLPB-R correlated highly with language performance in the classroom. This additional validity evidence was recommended in the review by Poteat (1995).

REFERENCES

Cummins, J. (1984). *Bilingualism and special education: Issues in assessment and pedagogy*. Austin, TX: PRO-ED.

Lehmann, I. J. (1995). Review of the Woodcock Language Proficiency Battery–Revised. *The twelfth mental measurements yearbook* (pp. 1118–20). Lincoln: University of Nebraska Press.

Poteat, G. M. (1995). Review of the Woodcock Language Proficiency Battery–Revised. *The twelfth mental measurements yearbook* (pp. 1120–21). Lincoln: University of Nebraska Press.

Schrank, F. A., Fletcher, T. V., & Alvarado, C. G. (1996). Comparative validity of three English oral language proficiency tests. *Bilingual Research Journal, 20*(1), 55–68.

Woodcock, R. W. (1991). *Woodcock Language Proficiency Battery–Revised, English Form*. Itasca, IL: Riverside.

Woodcock, R. W., & Muñoz-Sandoval, A. (1995). *Woodcock Language Proficiency Battery–Revised, Spanish Form*. Itasca, IL: Riverside.

FREDRICK A. SCHRANK
Olympia, Washington

NONDISCRIMINATORY ASSESSMENT WOODCOCK-JOHNSON PSYCHOEDUCATIONAL TEST BATTERY

WOODCOCK-MUÑOZ FOUNDATION

The Woodcock-Muñoz Foundation (WMF) is a private, nonprofit operating foundation that supports the advancement of contemporary cognitive assessment based on the Cattell-Horn-Carroll (CHC) theory of human cognitive abilities (McGrew, 2005). The foundation engages in programs of instructional support to graduate-level professional preparation programs, research concerning the abilities of individuals with diagnosed exceptionalities, and closely related educational and research projects.

The foundation promotes contemporary practices in the assessment of cognitive abilities internationally through a variety of programs that provide support for instructional materials that are important to graduate training programs in cognitive assessment, research into the cognitive profiles of individuals with diagnosed exceptionalities (learning problems, neuropsychological conditions, behavioral and psychiatric problems, and giftedness), and the advancement of effective clinical assessment practices and the dissemination of research findings through direct professional development opportunities.

The foundation's external and internal research programs facilitate a bridge between CHC theory and applied cognitive assessment practices. The foundation's external research program focuses on the investigation of profiles of cognitive abilities of individuals with diagnosed exceptionalities and the relations between subject demographic characteristics, cognitive abilities, and academic achievement. Collaborative research, particularly with early career professionals, is actively encouraged. The foundation's internal research program consists of three primary projects. The Clinical Data Base Project has as its purpose the development and analysis of a rich and evolving clinical subject cognitive ability database. The Human Cognitive Abilities Project has as its purpose the investigation of the structure and organization of human cognitive abilities via secondary analysis of historical and contemporary data sets. The International Cognitive Assessments Project has as its purpose the development of a small number of noncommercial, contemporary cognitive assessment instruments for specific populations in Eastern Europe, based on need.

REFERENCE

McGrew, K. S. (2005). The Cattell-Horn-Carroll Theory of Cognitive Abilities: Past, present, and future. In D. P. Flanagan & P. L. Harrison (Eds.), *Contemporary intellectual assessment* (2nd ed., pp. 136–81). New York: Guilford.

FREDRICK A. SCHRANK
Olympia, Washington

KEVIN S. MCGREW
St. Joseph, Minnesotta

WOODCOCK READING MASTERY TESTS–REVISED

Available in two forms, the Woodcock Reading Mastery Tests–Revised (WRMT-R; Woodcock, 1987) is an individually administered test designed to assess a variety of reading abilities of individuals between the ages of 4 and 75. The WRMT-R is useful in various settings, such as instructional placement, individual program planning, and progress evaluation (Cohen & Cohen, 1994). The test consists of six subtests, including Visual-Auditory Learning, Letter Identification, Word Identification, Word Attack, Word Comprehension, and Passage Comprehension. Visual-Auditory Learning involves learning several unfamiliar visual symbols representing words. Letter Identification assesses an individual's ability to identify by name or sound the letters of the alphabet. Word Identification requires the test taker to read words ranging in difficulty. Word Attack evaluates the ability to pronounce nonsense words using phonic skills. Word Comprehension is comprised of antonyms, synonyms, and analogies. Finally, Passage Comprehension is designed to evaluate reading comprehension skills. From these subtests, five cluster scores are obtained: Readiness, Basic Skills, Reading Comprehension, Total Reading-Full Scale, and Total Reading-Short Scale. Percentile ranks, grade and age equivalent scores, instructional ranges, and strengths and weaknesses can also be obtained. Depending on the form used, administration time ranges from 30 to 60 minutes.

The WRMT-R was recently renormed, and is now referred to as the Woodcock Reading Mastery Test–Revised/Norma-

tive Update (WRMT-R/NU; Woodcock, 1997) The examiner's manual for the WRMT-R/NU offers information regarding technical aspects such as norming, reliability, and validity. The WRMT-R/NU was normed using approximately 3,700 subjects; however, new norms were not collected for subjects in grades 13–16 or ages 23 and older. Subjects were randomly selected using a stratified sampling method based on variables such as geographic region, community size, sex, and so on from 1994 U.S. census data. Split-half reliability coefficients of the original WRMT-R ranged from .34 to .98, and ranged from .87 to .89 in the WRMT-R Normative Update. Content and concurrent validity were described. However, the authors do not substantiate the content validity of the WRMT-R, although they report using "outside experts" and experienced teachers. Concurrent validity was established with comparisons to such tests as Iowa Tests of Basic Skills, Peabody Individual Achievement Test–Revised, KeyMath–Revised, and Kaufman Test of Educational Achievement.

In comparing the original WRMT-R norms with those from the 1997 update, it appears that there is little change in the level of performance of students who are average to above average for their grade or age (Woodcock, 1997). However, the performance of students who are below average appears to have declined. The result of these changes is that where student performance has improved, the WRMT-R/NU standard scores and percentiles will be lower than on the original norms, and conversely, where performance has declined, WRMT-R/NU standard scores and percentiles will be higher (Woodcock, 1997).

The WRMT-R has been revised several times. An atheoretical development of this test allows for the test to be applied to many clinical and remedial settings. However, several problems with this scale exist. Cooter (1989) reported that the WRMT-R assesses reading "in fragments rather than holistically." In addition, reliability and validity data is limited. The authors report data on WRMT-R split-half reliability and establish validity in a questionable fashion (Compton, 1990). In addition, the reliability of WRMT-R individual subtests for grade 11 and above do not appear to be consistent with the reported norms of other age groups (Cohen & Cohen, 1994).

REFERENCES

Cohen, S. H., & Cohen, J. (1994). Review of the Woodcock Reading Mastery Tests–Revised. In D. J. Keyser & R. C. Sweetland (Eds.), *Test critiques: Volume X*. Austin, TX: PRO-ED.

Compton, C. (1990). *A guide to 85 tests for special education*. Belmont: Fearon/Janus.

Cooter, R. (1989). Review of the Woodcock Reading Mastery Tests–Revised. In J. C. Conoley & J. J. Kramer (Eds.), *The tenth mental measurements yearbook*. Lincoln: University of Nebraska Press.

Woodcock, R. W. (1987). *Woodcock Reading Mastery Tests–Revised*. Circle Pines, MN: American Guidance Service.

Woodcock, R. W. (1997). *Woodcock Reading Mastery Tests–Revised/Normative Update.* Circle Pines, MN: American Guidance Service.

DARIELLE GREENBERG
*California School of
Professional Psychology*

WOODCOCK-JOHNSON PSYCHOEDUCATIONAL BATTERY

WOODS SCHOOLS

The Woods Schools, located in Langhorne, Pennsylvania, was established in 1913 to provide educational and training programs for students with development delays, retardation, brain damage, and learning disabilities. The school is primarily a residential facility that features group home life in small cottages with an intensive staff ratio that provides for direct care and services to meet the individual needs of students. The school provides for day and residential students on a coed basis.

The school programs offer a wide range of educational experiences to students who are severely disabled and who require therapeutic services. Vocational training is provided. Students are trained in a wide range of vocational exploration experiences that establish appropriate work habits, basic working skills, and prevocational experiences that lead to job training. Remedial services, tutorial instruction, and therapeutic services are designed to meet the individual needs of students as they progress through the programs.

REFERENCE

Sargent, J. K. (1982). *The directory for exceptional children* (9th ed.). Boston: Porter Sargent.

PAUL C. RICHARDSON
Elwyn Institutes

VOCATIONAL EDUCATION

WORD BLINDNESS

Congenital word blindness, word blindness, dyslexia, developmental dyslexia, specific dyslexia, developmental alexia, visual aphasia, and strephosymbolia are all terms that have on some occasions been used interchangeably in the special education literature (Evans, 1982; Orton, 1937; Wallin, 1968) to indicate a child's inability to learn to read. Developmental dyslexia was defined by Critchley (1964) as a specific difficulty in learning to read, often of genetic origin, which existed in spite of good general intelligence, and without emotional problems, brain damage, or impairments of vision or hearing. Ford (1973) defined congenital word blindness or dyslexia as the inability of a child to learn the meaning of graphic symbols.

Although literature is available from as early as the 1800s (Kussmaul, 1877), there is no clear agreed upon cause for this problem. Causes that have been hypothesized ranged from maternal and natal factors, ophthalmological factors, cerebral dominance issues, and minor neurological impairments, to genetic issues (Critchley, 1964). Clemesha (1915) attributed word blindness to a congenital defect or deficiency in the brain or to some pathological process. Heitmuller (1918) felt that developmental alexia or word blindness was a developmental defect of the visual memory center for the graphic symbols of language. Orton (1937) postulated that dyslexic symptoms were the result of mixed dominance, which he called motor integrating abilities. His theory attributed reading reversals to the possibility that the mirrored counterparts of words located in the dominant hemisphere were stored in the subdominant hemisphere; therefore, children without a clearly established dominant hemisphere would have confusion with learning to read words. He also believed that this difficulty in establishing dominance was inherited. DeHirsch (Hallahan & Cruickshank, 1973) postulated a central nervous system dysfunction or developmental lag as the cause of word blindness. She believed "that both delayed cerebral dominance and language disorders may reflect a maturational dysfunction" (p. 106).

Although there continues to be a lack of consensus on which terminology to use, as well as on the meaning of the terms chosen, the literature is clearly divided between the medical (those professionals who are looking for a cause) and the educational (those professionals who are more interested in determining a means to remediate the problem). The medically oriented group is more likely to see word blindness or dyslexia as an inability to learn to read owing to a central nervous system dysfunction or brain damage, while the educationally oriented group is more likely to describe this group as children who are having trouble learning to read. There are other distinctions between the medical and educational professions. Educators are more concerned with the developmental sequence of reading skills; the medical community is concerned with disabilities in language and speech, motor development, and perception. Educators differentiate between reading problems of children and adults, and make a distinction between maturational lag and a central nervous system dysfunction. Educators do not see one easy way of remediating but base remediation on intensive diagnostic information related to the specific skills that individual children are missing, the child's best modality for learning, the appropriate materials, and so on. Educators are less likely to recommend individuals treatment, but work within the entire school population to improve reading instruction for all children (Lerner, 1971). One final distinction between the two groups of professionals is that the medically oriented research has been conducted most often by physicians in Europe, while the educational research has been done by educators, psychologists, and reading specialists in the United States. DeHirsch, a language pathology theorist and psychiatrist (Hallahan & Cruickshank, 1973), has done extensive research in the area of dyslexia and has been greatly responsible for the integration of research from both of these groups.

Specific behavioral characteristics that may be present in children who have been diagnosed as word blind include a general clumsiness or spatial disorientation, minor sensory disorders, difficulty in eye control, defects in body image, confusion of right and left, faulty estimates of spatial and temporal categories, difficulty in interpreting the meaning of facial expressions, difficulty in arithmetic skills, difficulty with processing of complex linguistic verbalizations, difficulty with formulation, a tendency for cluttering, disorganized verbal output, hyperactivity, and difficulty with figure-group concepts (Critchley, in Franklin, 1962; DeHirsch, 1952).

Heller (1963) described screening criteria for detecting word blindness in school-aged children. These criteria include normal intelligence, normal vision and hearing, marked reduction in reading and spelling ability, discrepancy between reading and other abilities, inability to read by the sight method, ability to learn to read by auditory repetition, and evidence of dissociation of visual word-image from acoustic word-image. Remediation techniques traditionally have emphasized the phonetic approach (Hinshelwood, 1917; Holt, 1962; Miles, 1962; Orton, 1937), with training occurring in individualized sessions. A more individualized eclectic approach was hypothesized by Naidoo (1972) and DeHirsch (Hallahan & Cruickshank, 1973), with emphasis on evaluating each student's strengths and weaknesses and devising an individualized program based on the results. Specific remediation techniques have been well developed by Wagner (1976).

The Word Blind Centre for Dyslexic Children was established in 1962 in London, England, by the Invalid Children's Aid Association (ICAA; Naidoo, 1972). It was in operation from 1962 to 1970; its goals were both research and the treatment of dyslexic children. The ICAA has been responsible, since 1963, for the publication of the *Word Blind Bulletin*. In the United States, the National Advisory Committee on Dyslexia and Related Reading Disorders was created by the Secretary of Health, Education and Welfare (HEW) in 1968. Its purpose was to investigate, clarify, and resolve the controversial issues surrounding dyslexia. The committee determined that the term dyslexia served no useful educational purpose. It recommended the creation of an Office of Reading Disorders within HEW to improve reading instruction for all children who were experiencing difficulty in reading (*Report to the Secretary of the Department of Health, Education and Welfare,* 1969).

REFERENCES

Clemesha, J. C. (1915). Congenital word blindness or inability to learn to read. *Journal of Ophthalmology Oto-Laryngoloy, 9*(1), 1–6.

Critchley, M. (1962). In A. W. Franklin (Ed.), *Word-blindness or specific developmental dyslexia.* Proceedings of a conference called by the Invalid Children's Aid Association. London: Pitman.

Critchley, M. (1964). *Developmental dyslexia.* London: Heinemann Medical.

DeHirsch, K. (1952). Specific dyslexia or strephosymbolia. *Folia Phoniatrica, 4,* 231–248.

DeHirsch, K. (1973). In D. P. Hallahan & W. M. Cruickshank (Eds.), *Psychoeducational foundations of learning disabilities.* Englewood Cliffs, NJ: Prentice Hall.

Evans, M. M. (1982). *Dyslexia: An annotated bibliography. Contemporary problems of childhood #5.* Westport, CT: Greenwood.

Fisher, J. H. (1905). Case of congenital word-blindness (inability to learn to read). *Ophthalmic Review, 20,* 315–318.

Ford, F. R. (1973). Developmental word blindness and mirror writing. In *Diseases of the nervous system in infancy, childhood, and adolescence* (6th ed.). Springfield, IL: Thomas.

Franklin, A. W. (Ed.). (1962). *Word-blindness or specific developmental dyslexia.* Proceedings of a conference called by the Invalid Children's Aid Association. London: Pitman.

Hallahan, D. P., & Cruickshank, W. M. (1973). *Psychoeducational foundations of learning disabilities.* Englewood Cliffs, NJ: Prentice Hall.

Heitmuller, G. H. (1918). Cases of developmental alexia or congenital word blindness. *Washington Medical Annual, 17,* 124–129.

Heller, T. M. (1963). Word-blindness—A survey of the literature and a report of twenty-eight cases. *Pediatrics, 31*(4), 669–691.

Hinshelwood, J. (1917). *Congenital word-blindness.* London: H. K. Lewis.

Holt, L. M. (1962). In A. W. Franklin (Ed.), *Word-blindness or specific developmental dyslexia.* Proceedings of a conference called by the Invalid Children's Aid Association. London: Pitman.

Kussmaul, A. (1877). Word-deafness—Word blindness. In A. H. Buck & H. von Ziemssen (Eds.), *Diseases of the nervous system, and disturbances of speech. Vol. 14 of Cyclopaedia of the Practice of Medicine.* New York: Wood.

Lerner, J. W. (1971). *Children with learning disabilities* (2nd ed.). Boston: Houghton Mifflin.

Miles, T. R. (1962). In A. W. Franklin (Ed.), *Word-blindness or specific developmental dyslexia.* Proceedings of a conference called by the Invalid Children's Aid Association. London: Pitman.

Naidoo, S. (1972). *Specific dyslexia: The research report of the ICAA Word Blind Centre of Dyslexic Children.* London: Pitman.

Orton, S. T. (1937). *Reading, writing, and speech problems in children.* New York: Norton.

Orton, S. T. (1966). *Word-blindness in school children and other papers on strephosymbolia (specific language disability—dyslexia) 1925–1946.* Pomfret, CT: Orton Society.

Report to the Secretary of the Department of Health, Education, and Welfare. (1969, August). Washington, DC: National Advisory Committee on Dyslexia and Related Disorders.

Wagner, R. F. (1976). *Helping the word blind: Effective intervention techniques for overcoming reading problems in older students.* West Hyzck, NY: Center for Applied Research in Education.

Wallin, J. E. W. (1968). Congenital word blindness (dyslexia) in children. *Journal of Education, 151*(1), 36–51.

SUSANNE BLOUGH ABBOTT
*Bedford Central School District,
Mt. Kisco, New York*

CONGENITAL WORD BLINDNESS, HISTORY OF
DYSLEXIA
READING DISORDERS
READING REMEDIATION

WORDS IN COLOR

Words in Color is a one-to-one sound-symbol approach to teaching reading that was devised in 1957 by Caleb Gattegno. Gattegno, a scientist, approached the problems of reading as he did the problems of mathematics and physics. He introduced the concept of temporal sequence into reading methodology (Gattegno, 1970) and proposed that our language is coded into a series of sounds that, when uttered in sequence, produce wholes that we call words. The timing of the sounds in sequence is essential learning for correct pronunciation (Aukerman, 1971). Words in Color is based on the premise that reading is a process of decoding printed symbols and translating them into sounds and words. Color is used in the initial stage of reading to help the learner make an association between the symbol and the sound.

In the Words in Color program, there are 21 charts of letter sounds, letters in combination, and word families. Included on these charts are the 47 distinct sounds of American English in 280 different instances of letters and letter combinations. In beginning reading instruction, the child looks at the colored charts of words, then writes the same letters or words in black and white and reads what he or she has written. The names of the letters are not used, only the sounds and colors. In Words in Color the vowels are taught as sound-symbol shapes. The learner's attention is focused on the shape of the letter and how it relates in shape to the other vowels.

Gattegno introduced his Words in Color program as a novel approach to teaching reading. He asserted that, "illiteracy can be wiped out at a far smaller cost than any wild dreamer has ever dreamed. [He is] prepared to do the computation if asked" (Gattegno, 1970). Results of research studies on the Words in Color program are mixed (Aukeman, 1971). Some studies have shown positive results (DeLacy,

1973) but Gattegno is far from reaching his goal of wiping out illiteracy with the Words in Color program.

REFERENCES

Aukerman, R. C. (1971). *Approaches to beginning reading.* New York: Wiley.

DeLacy, E. (1973). Clinical reading cases—Some speculations concerning sequence in colour and look-and-say. *Slow Learning Child, 20*(3), 160–163.

Gattegno, C. (1969). *Towards a visual culture.* New York: Outerbridge Dienstfrey.

Gattegno, C. (1970). The problem of reading is solved. *Harvard Educational Review, 40*(2), 283–286.

NANCY J. KAUFMAN
*University of Wisconsin at
Stevens Point*

READING DISORDERS
READING REMEDIATION

WORKFARE

Workfare is a term that was coined in the 1980s to describe welfare reform efforts that require able-bodied Aid to Families with Dependent Children (AFDC) parents to work in public service projects in exchange for monthly benefits. These unpaid jobs were typically at the city or county level and involved entry-level positions in clerical, human services, or park maintenance work. The majority of the participants were single females with children over the age of 6.

In 1981 the Reagan administration proposed a mandatory national workfare program, but Congress, reluctant to endorse such sweeping legislation in the absence of empirical evidence, instead passed the 1981 Omnibus Budget Reconciliation Act. This 1981 legislation encouraged, but did not require, the states to implement workfare programs as part of their welfare reform initiatives. By 1985, 37 states were experimenting with some type of workfare (Work-Not-Welfare, 1985). In most cases, workfare was but one small component in a broader employment effort that might include career planning, vocational training, high school equivalency courses, job placement services, child-care vouchers, transportation assistance, and on-the-job training with subsidies to employers. The states were allowed to use Federal Work Incentive Program funds in these reform initiatives.

As the states began to generate their own welfare reform models compatible with local philosophies and resources, it became clear that there were widely different approaches being tried across the country. This diversity provided social researchers with an unprecedented natural laboratory in which to study different systems. The most thorough research on workfare was conducted by the Manpower Demonstration Research Corporation (MDRC) of New York City. In 1982, with financial help from the Ford Foundation, this nonprofit research group began a 4-year comparative study of welfare reform in 11 different states. The following generalizations and quotations were taken from MDRC's report on the first three study sites (February, 1986): San Diego, California; Baltimore, Maryland; and two counties in Arkansas:

1. The studied states are increasing the employment of welfare recipients and, in some cases, reducing the costs of welfare.

2. The states place more emphasis on job search activities than on workfare activities and workfare "has not turned out to be either as punitive as its critics feared or as praiseworthy as its advocates claimed."

3. The findings indicate that the public service jobs are generally valued by both the participants and their supervisors, and are not considered "make work" activities.

4. In most cases, the participants already possess the necessary entry-level skills before they begin their jobs, so the workfare experience does not contribute to new vocational skills development.

5. Supervisors report that participants' productivity and attendance are as good as that of most other paid employees.

6. The majority of the participants agree that the work requirement is fair. Many feel positive about the work they do, and feel that they are making a contribution.

Undoubtedly, the most widely reported success story in work welfare reform comes from the state of Massachusetts, where 20,000 welfare recipients were placed in jobs (States Refocus, 1985). This program, which was voluntary and did not have the punitive quality often associated with workfare, reported that 86 percent of its first-year beneficiaries were still off welfare after 12 months. This represented savings to the state of over $60 million. This was not a controlled experiment so it is not clear how much of Massachusetts' success was due to other variables such as general economic recovery.

In California another approach, which has the overwhelming support of both conservatives and liberals, is being tried. This approach will make participation mandatory with "strict provisions for cutting off payments to those who do not participate, and a large-scale effort to make sure that those who do will get adequate training and job-placement services" (Work for Welfare, 1985).

In conclusion, workfare is being tried in numerous settings and has wide emotional appeal because of its logical connection with such concerns as the federal deficit and the poverty cycle of AFDC families. However, a final accounting of workfare and related strategies will not be available for a number of years so it would seem prudent for policy makers to heed the advice of Manpower Demonstration Research Corporation (1986) when it says, no one model—including workfare—is at this point recommended for national replication.

REFERENCES

Gueron, J. (1986). *Work initiatives for welfare recipients: Lessons from a multi-state experiment.* New York: Manpower Demonstration Research.

States refocus welfare, with eye on "real" jobs. (1985, October 28). *U.S. News & World Report.*

Work for welfare. (1985, October 7). *Time.*

Work-not-welfare effort encounters the deficit. (1985, July 19). *Wall Street Journal.*

JOHN D. SEE
University of Wisconsin at Stout

REHABILITATION
SOCIOECONOMIC STATUS

WORLD FEDERATION OF THE DEAF

The World Federation of the Deaf (WFD) was founded in 1951. It consists of 83 members representing the languages of English, French, and Italian. Its central office is in Rome, Italy. The WFD is a collection of associations of the deaf from various countries. These national or international organizations encompass societies and bodies acting for the deaf, health, social, and educational groups related to the aims of the federation, professionals involved with deafness or performing special assignments for the federation, and parents and friends of the deaf. Through social rehabilitation of deaf individuals, the WFD is a leader in the fight against deafness.

Among its services, the federation makes available social legislation concerning the deaf as well as statistical data. It also serves as consultant to the World Health Organization and UNESCO. The WFD sustains a library and bestows awards for merit and special achievement in education and social rehabilitation of the deaf. The federation holds commissions in the areas of communication, arts and culture, pedagogy, psychology, medicine, audiology, social and vocational rehabilitation, and spiritual care. The federation publishes a journal triannually entitled *Voices of Silence,* in addition to the *Proceedings of International Congresses and Meetings* and a dictionary.

MARY LEON PEERY
Texas A&M University

WORLD HEALTH ORGANIZATION

WORLD HEALTH ORGANIZATION

The World Health Organization (WHO) is a specialized agency of the United Nations with primary responsibility for international health matters and public health. Created in 1948, it comprises of delegates representing member states and is attended by representatives of intergovernmental organizations and nongovernmental organizations in official relationships with WHO. Assemblies are held annually, usually in Geneva.

The official functions of WHO are varied; they include (1) directing and coordinating authority on international health work; (2) assisting governments in strengthening health services; (3) furnishing technical assistance and emergency aid; (4) stimulating and advancing work to eradicate or control epidemic, endemic, and other diseases; (5) promoting improved nutrition, housing, sanitation, recreation, economic, and working conditions, and other aspects of environmental hygiene; (6) encouraging cooperation among scientific and professional groups that contribute to the advancement of health; (7) promoting material and child health and welfare, and fostering the ability to live harmoniously in a changing total environment; (8) fostering activities in the field of mental health; (9) working for improved standards of teaching and training in health, medical, and related professions; (10) studying and reporting on administrative and social techniques affecting public health and medical care from preventive and curative perspectives; and (11) assisting in developing informed public opinion on health matters.

Several WHO activities relate directly to diagnostic and classificatory issues in special education. First, WHO produces key writings concerning the use of health statistics and undertakes psychiatric epidemiology devoted to comparative research on mental disorders. Second, WHO compiles the International Classification of Diseases (ICD), a statistical classification of diseases; complications of pregnancy, childbirth, and the puerperium; congenital abnormalities; accidents, poisonings, and violence; and symptoms and ill-defined conditions. The ICD has been adapted for use as a nomenclature of diseases, with mental disorders constituting one major category. Subsumed in this category are classifications along with operational definitions of handicapping conditions.

Several other systems are tied to the ICD, including the *Diagnostic and Statistical Manual (DSM)* as well as the *Grossman Manuals on Terminology and Classification* of the American Association on Mental Retardation. Third, the Mental Health Unit of WHO has implemented an intensive program to acquire systematic data on variables in diagnostic practice and use of diagnostic mental disorder terms. This has resulted in a multiaxial scheme for the classification of childhood mental disorders, with three main axes: clinical psychiatric syndromes, individual intellectual levels of functioning regardless of etiology, and associated physical, organic, and psychosocial factors in etiology.

DOUGLAS FUCHS
LYNN S. FUCHS
Peabody College, Vanderbilt University

WORLD REHABILITATION FUND

The World Rehabilitation Fund, also known as the International Exchange of Experts and Information in Rehabilitation (IEEIR), seeks to identify, "import," disseminate, and promote the use of innovative rehabilitation and special education knowledge from other countries. Information about unique programs, practices, and research, as well as the policies of other nations, is sought for dissemination to professionals in the United States.

The IEEIR program is substantially supported by the Office of Special Education and Rehabilitation Services (OSERS) of the U.S. Department of Education. It is an out-growth of the National Institute of Handicapped Research (NIHR, an OSERS division) mandate to facilitate the use of selected ideas and practices generated in other countries. Selection of knowledge or problem areas to guide the program staff are set jointly by OSERS, NIHR, and IEEIR staffs.

The IEEIR engages in the awarding of fellowships, the publication of monographs, and the dissemination of information. The fellowship program enables qualified U.S. experts to study and report on either special education or rehabilitation developments in other lands. This group includes rehabilitation and special education faculty, researchers, and administrators. Other specialists such as rehabilitation engineers, physicians, psychologists, independent living leaders, and consumer advocates also participate.

Overseas experts with substantial qualifications germane to the priorities set for the United States are identified and commissioned to prepare monographs for publication by the IEEIR program. Five monographs a year are commissioned.

To facilitate dissemination efforts, fellows commit themselves to reporting their observations and recommendations to their peers in relevant journals and at professional meetings. Since one of the criteria for selecting fellows is the degree to which they are centers of influence within their fields, IEEIR expects that they will influence not only students and researchers, but also practitioners and administrators. The communication skills and past record of a fellow are key considerations in awarding fellowships.

In addition to the reports they submit, fellows are expected to report their experiences and observations to professional meetings and other interested groups. Publication in professional journals is also encouraged. Both U.S. fellows and foreign monograph authors may be invited to present their findings at conferences designed for U.S. specialists to keep them abreast of innovations and new ideas.

The World Rehabilitation Fund headquarters is located at 400 East 34th Street, New York, NY 10016. Information on specific programs and monographs available may be requested from this office.

DIANE E. WOODS
World Rehabilitation Fund

WORLD HEALTH ORGANIZATION

WRAT-III

See WIDE-RANGE ACHIEVEMENT TEST—THIRD EDITION.

WRITING AS EXPRESSIVE LANGUAGE

Since written expression is the most complex and the last form of language to be achieved, it can best be explained from a perspective that considers the influence of linguistic and cognitive abilities as well as the uniqueness of this expressive mode. The interrelatedness of language skills has been conceptualized by Myklebust (1965) in terms of a hierarchical construct that suggests that listening, speaking, reading, and writing develop in a progression that is ascendable and reciprocal. Implicit to this theory is the premise that competency at each rung of the language ladder is prerequisite to success at the next. Credibility for this paradigm has been provided by many researchers, including Loban (1976), who longitudinally followed a group of students from kindergarten through twelfth grade and found a positive relationship of achievement among the language arts. Children who were judged to be good listeners and speakers in kindergarten were the same students who later excelled in reading and writing, retaining their status as superior language users throughout their school careers. Conversely, children who did not begin their schooling with oral language competence continued to be evaluated as below average in all language skills.

The concept that achievement in written forms is influenced by development in preceding forms has been easier to verify than the nature of the reciprocity that occurs among the linguistic functions. Wolf and Dickinson (1985) described the development of oral and written language systems as being profoundly interactive in that growth in each mode results in cognitive processing changes that exert influence in a cyclical manner. For example, these researchers noted that early phonological and metalinguistic development in oral language affects the acquisition of reading skills; in turn, achievement in the reading form influences perspectives of listening, speaking, and writing. Wolf and Dickinson further explained that written expression with its emphasis on refining alters one's cognitive orientation to speaking and reading. Thus it appears that written expression can be thought of as a shaper or enhancer of other linguistic forms.

Another complicating factor to understanding the relationship among language processes concerns the consideration that changes occur as development unfolds. Kroll (1981) has proposed a developmental model for examining the relationship between speaking and writing. This model describes four principal associations between these two expressive forms: the first phase is termed separate and involves the preparation for writing (the learning of technical skills required to produce the written symbols for speech); the second phrase involves consolidation of oral and written language (the understanding that writing is similar to talk written down); the third phase focuses on differentiation of oral and written language (awareness that talking is more casually conversational than the formality of writing); and the fourth stage addresses the systematic integration of speaking and writing (the knowledge that a wide range of different forms can be used in both speaking and writing depending on the context, audience, and purpose of the communication). Although Kroll admitted that this model presents an oversimplification of the interaction that occurs, it is nonetheless helpful for explaining broad outlines of development.

For the handicapped population, the acquisition of written expression is typically problematic. Difficulties that inhibit achievement in this skill can occur in each or all of the preceding forms; a child who has oral language deficits and/or reading problems will, in all likelihood, have deficiencies in written expression also. However, instruction in writing should not be postponed until competency in the other modes has been achieved. It is much more viable to simultaneously teach all language skills in a holistic manner that will encourage growth through reciprocity.

Phelps-Gunn and Phelps-Terasaki (1982) have described written expression from a multidimensional framework that considers the dynamics involved in effective writing. They have developed a Total Writing Process Model for identifying and remediating deficits. This model addresses problems with form, content, and structure; pragmatic abilities for audience and mode; and proofreading. This instructional plan appears to be extremely comprehensive and may prove to be an effective method for remediating writing deficits.

REFERENCES

Kroll, B. M. (1981). Developmental relationships between speaking and writing. In B. M. Kroll & R. J. Vann (Eds.), *Exploring speaking-writing relationships: Connections and contrasts* (pp. 32–54). Urbana, IL: National Counsel of Teachers of English.

Loban, W. (1976). *Language development: Kindergarten through grade twelve.* Urbana, IL: National Counsel of Teachers of English.

Myklebust, H. R. (1965). *Development and disorders of written language* (Vol. 1). New York: Grune & Stratton.

Phelps-Gunn, T., & Phelps-Terasaki, D. (1982). *Written language instruction.* Rockville, MD: Aspen.

Wolf, M., & Dickinson, D. (1985). From oral to written language: Transition in school years. In J. B. Gleason (Ed.), *The development of language* (pp. 227–76). Columbus, OH: Merrill.

PEGGY L. ANDERSON
*University of New Orleans,
Lakefront*

WRITING ASSESSMENT
WRITING REMEDIATION

WRITING ASSESSMENT

Competence in writing requires the mastery and automation of a vast array of skills. To ensure that these skills develop in an efficient and efficacious manner, it is generally believed that assessment should be included as an integral part of disabled students' writing programs. This belief is primarily based on the assumption that information from the assessment process should make it possible for teachers to more readily determine a student's writing strengths and weaknesses, individualize instruction, monitor writing performance, and evaluate the effectiveness of the composition program.

The assessment of disabled students' writing should focus on both the written product and the process of writing (Graham, 1982). There are a host of procedures for evaluating the various attributes embodied in the written product; the most popular of these will be reviewed at length. Relatively few techniques, however, are available for examining the process by which students compose. The most common procedures include: (1) observing and, in some instances, timing the various activities and behaviors that the student engages in during the act of writing; (2) interviewing students about their approach to writing and questioning them about their reasons for particular composing behaviors; and (3) asking students to verbally report what they are thinking while they write. Regrettably, the reliability and validity of these procedures have not been adequately established and the results from such assessments may, as many critics have suggested, yield a distorted picture of the writing process (Humes, 1983).

Both formal and informal assessment procedures have been used to examine the relative merits and/or shortcomings of disabled students' writing. The most frequently used standardized test is the Test of Written Language (TOWL). According to the authors (Hammill & Larsen, 1983), this instrument "can be used to ascertain the general adequacy of a product written by a student and to determine specific proficiency in word usage, punctuation and capitalization (style), spelling, handwriting, vocabulary, and sentence production" (p. 5). The TOWL consists of six subtests. Scores for three of these subtests (vocabulary, thematic maturity, and handwriting) are derived from a spontaneous sample of writing. The remaining word usage, spelling, and style subtests employ a contrived format; for example, a student's proficiency in word usage is determined by a sentence completion activity. Although the TOWL appears to have a sound theoretical basis and to be reasonably valid and reliable, there is some question as to the value of the vocabulary and thematic maturity scores (Williams, 1985).

A second standardized test that has been used with disabled students is the Picture Story Language Test (PSLT; Myklebust, 1965). The PSLT has been used as a writing achievement test, a diagnostic instrument, and a research tool for studying the development and disorders of written language. In using this test, a student writes a story in response to a picture and the resulting composition is scored in terms of productivity (number of words, sentences, and words per sentence), correctness (word usage, word endings, and punctuation), and meaning (actual content conveyed). Although the PSLT has been widely used with disabled students, serious questions regarding the validity and reliability of the instrument have been raised (Anastasiow, 1972).

Informal assessment procedures have been used to assess a variety of factors ranging from story quality to writing mechanics. Not surprisingly, the quality of students' writing has proven to be the most difficult factor to define and measure. Probably the oldest measure of writing quality is the holistic method. With this method, an examiner makes a single overall judgment on the quality of a student's writing (Mishler & Hogan, 1982). Each paper is read at a fairly rapid pace and the examiner attempts to weigh the various factors (content, organization, grammar.) in roughly equal proportions. The examiner's overall impression is quantified on a Likert-type scale, ranging from poor to high quality. To increase accuracy and reliability, most holistic scoring systems include representative examples of specific scores.

A more complex procedure for determining the quality of a student's writing is the analytic method. With this method, the student's paper is analyzed and scored on the basis of several different factors such as ideation, grammar, and spelling (Moran, 1982). The scores for each of these factors are then averaged to produce a single grand score. Although the analytic method may provide more useful information for instructional purposes, it is much more time-consuming than the holistic method.

A relatively recent development in the measurement of writing quality is the primary trait scoring method. With this procedure, different scoring systems are developed for different writing tasks. For a task such as writing a short story, the examiner would decide ahead of time what traits should be evaluated and what types of response will be considered appropriate and inappropriate for each trait. For example, for a short story one of the primary traits might be the introduction and development of the protagonist (Graham & Harris, 1986). Consequently, stories that adequately present and develop the leading character would receive credit for this trait.

It must be pointed out that measures of writing quality can be influenced by a variety of factors (Graham, 1982). One prominent source of variability involves the writer. Students often evidence considerable variation in their writing quality from one assignment to the next. Writing performance also can be influenced by the popularity of the proctor, the intended audience, teacher directions, and so on. An additional source of variability resides in the examiner. There is considerable evidence that grades assigned to student's papers tend to be unreliable. Fortunately, the consistency with which examiners score writing quality can be improved if the following guidelines and recommendations are followed: (1) examiners should receive considerable practice and training in using the intended scoring procedure; (2) the writing task should be highly structured and the assigned topic should be interesting; (3) identifying factors such as name, grade, and date should be removed from each paper; and (4) papers should not be graded for lengthy periods of time or in noisy or distracting environments.

A number of procedures have been used to evaluate the various elements embodied in the written products. Writing fluency has typically been assessed by examining total number of words written, average sentence length, and number of words written per minute. Vocabulary diversity has been measured by counting the occurrence of particular vocabulary items such as adjectives or adverbs and by computing the corrected type/token ratio (number of different words divided by the square root of twice the number of words in the sample) or the index of diversification (average number of words that appear between each occurrence of the most frequently used word in a composition). Proficiency with the mechanics of writing is generally determined by tabulating the occurrence of a particular behavior (e.g., spelling errors), while syntactic maturity is often defined in terms of the average length of T-units (main clause plus any attached or embedded subordinate clauses).

It is important to note that students' knowledge of their writing performance can be a powerful motivator and have a potent effect on learning. Nevertheless, the value of circling every misspelled word, writing "AWK" above every clumsy wording, or red-marking each deviation from standard English is questionable. Intensive evaluation may have little or no effect on writing improvement and may, in fact, make students more aware of their limitations and less willing to write (Burton & Arnold, 1963). Feedback on the positive aspects of a student's composition, in contrast, can have a facilitative effect on writing performance (Beaven, 1977). It also is desirable to dramatize a student's success through the use of charts, graphs, verbal praise, and so on.

REFERENCES

Anastasiow, N. (1972). Review of the Picture Story Language Test. In O. K. Buros (Ed.), *Seventh mental measurement yearbook.* Highland Park, NJ: Gryphon.

Beaven, M. (1977). Individualized goal setting, self-evaluation, and peer evaluation. In C. Cooper & L. Odell (Eds.), *Evaluating writing: Describing, measuring, judging.* Urbana, IL: National Council of Teachers of English.

Burton, D., & Arnold, L. (1963). *The effects of frequency of writing and intensity of teacher evaluation upon high school students' performance in written composition.* (Research Report No. 1523). Tallahassee, FL: USOE Cooperative.

Graham, S. (1982). Composition research and practice: A unified approach. *Focus on Exceptional Children, 14,* 1–16.

Graham, S., & Harris, K. (1986). *Improving learning disabled students' compositions via story grammars: A component analysis of self-control strategy training.* Paper presented at the American Educational Research Association, San Francisco.

Hammill, D., & Larsen, S. (1983). *Test of Written Language.* Austin, TX: PRO-ED.

Humes, A. (1983). Research on the composing process. *Review of Educational Research, 53,* 201–216.

Mishler, C., & Hogan, T. (1982). Holistic scoring of essays: Remedy for evaluating the third R. *Diagnostique, 8,* 4–16.

Moran, M. (1982). Analytic evaluation of formal written language skills as a diagnostic procedure. *Diagnostique, 8,* 17–31.

Myklebust, H. (1965). *Development and disorders of written language.* New York: Grune & Stratton.

Williams, R. (1985). Review of Test of Written Language. In J. V. Mitchell (Ed.), *Ninth mental measurement yearbook.* Lincoln: University of Nebraska Press.

STEVE GRAHAM
University of Maryland

WRITING REMEDIATION

WRITING DISORDERS

While research on writing disorders in context is limited, the sources of difficulty emerge when they are considered within a framework or model of writing. Writing is a complex cognitive activity (Hayes & Flower, 1980) that requires writers to coordinate and regulate the use of task-specific strategies during three overlapping and recursive writing stages (i.e., prewriting, drafting, revising). During prewriting, task-specific strategies focus on planning and organizing. Writers generate and select writing topics, decide on a purpose for writing, identify the audience, generate and gather ideas about the topic, and organize the ideas into a network or structural plan (e.g., text structure such as story narrative, compare/contrast, sequence). During drafting, task-specific strategies involve the activation of the structural plan, translation of ideas into printed sentences, fleshing out of placeholders in the plan with details, and signaling of relationships among the elements of the plan. During monitoring and revising, task-specific strategies pertain to evaluation and analysis. The writer reads the draft to see whether the objectives concerning audience, topic, purpose, and structure have been achieved, and applies correction strategies to portions of the text that fail to meet expectations.

Though these task-specific strategies are necessary, they are not sufficient for skilled writing. A second domain involves the execution of these strategies. Metacognitive knowledge is the executive or self-control mechanism that helps writers activate and orchestrate activities in each of the writing stages. Metacognitive knowledge includes the ability to self-instruct or direct oneself in the writing stages, to monitor strategy use, and to modify or correct strategy use on the basis of outcomes. Without metacognitive knowledge, writers fail to access writing strategies and monitor their use even when the strategies are in their behavioral repertoire.

A third domain includes the mechanical skills that make writing a fluent process. This domain involves writers' knowledge of rules related to spelling (orthographic knowledge), writing conventions (punctuation, capitalization), and language (syntactic knowledge). These skills are of primary importance to writers in the stage of final revision in light of the importance of legibility to the audience. In addition, for the successful strategic employment of these skills, writers must not only acquire mechanical skills, they must acquire the task-specific strategies and metacognitive knowledge governing their use. For example, writers who lack task-specific strategies may not know how to rehearse or study spelling words to improve recall, whereas writers who lack metacognitive knowledge may learn to accurately spell words for the weekly spelling test, but fail to accurately spell or monitor their spelling of the same words in written compositions. Skillful writers not only acquire the mechanical means to produce text, they acquire the cognitive tools that help them know when and how to use those means, how to monitor their use, and how to correct errors when they occur.

According to this model of writing, writing disorders may result from one of several causes (Walmsley, 1983). First, writing disorders may emanate from a lack of understanding of task-specific strategies. For example, disabled writers with task-specific strategy deficits in the use of specific organizational structures may have trouble employing a relevant text structure that can guide them in planning, organizing, drafting, and monitoring their ideas. Second, writing disabilities may result from deficiencies in metacognitive knowledge. Such writers may have learned strategies but fail to activate them in the appropriate situations. Third, impairments in related cognitive processes may affect writing performance. Specifically, inadequate or delayed development in listening, speaking, or reading may affect writing performance since these processes share a common language base and rely on similar strategic processes involving the communication and comprehension of ideas. Finally, the failure to acquire specific rule-governed principles in spelling, grammar, and writing conventions can detrimentally affect the mechanics of writing, writing fluency, and overall comprehensibility.

More is known about the specific disabilities of students in the domain of writing mechanics than is known about disabilities in the use of task-specific strategies or metacognitive knowledge. Several studies confirm that disabled learners commit more punctuation and capitalization errors than nondisabled learners (Myklebust, 1973; Poplin et al., 1980; Poteet, 1978). These deficiencies have been observed in terms of students' ability to rewrite sentences containing punctuation and capitalization errors and to generate error-free compositions. Even greater performance differences between disabled and nondisabled students have been found on measures of spelling accuracy (Myklebust, 1973; Poplin et al., 1980; Poteet, 1978). Furthermore, disabled learners have deficiencies in their ability to apply task-specific strategies involving the study of spelling words (Foster & Torgesen, 1983) and in their application of metacognitive knowledge to detect and correct spelling errors (Deshler, 1978). However, several studies suggest that strategy and metacognitive deficits may be ameliorated with training. For example, research suggests that spelling deficits can be partly overcome by the teaching of task-specific strategies involving procedures for studying spelling words (Graham & Freeman, 1985; Nulman & Gerber, 1984), and for spelling novel words by analogy to known words (Englert, Hiebert, & Stewart, 1985). Likewise, metacognitive deficiencies involving the monitoring, detection, and correction of spelling errors or mechanical errors may be remediated with self-instructional training that directs students to reread and correct errors (Schumaker et al., 1982).

Mechanical aspects involving syntactic skills also have been studied, but the results are more equivocal. On tasks that require students to produce the correct syntactic form (e.g., subject-verb agreement, plurals) in incomplete sentences, disabled writers perform significantly lower than nondisabled writers (Poplin et al., 1980). On the other hand, on measures of syntactic complexity based on the average length of sentences and clauses produced by students, several studies have reported no qualitative differences in the presence of certain syntactic structures or the complexity of sentences (Moran, 1981; Nodine, Barenbaum, & Newcomer, 1985; Poteet, 1978). At the same time, several studies have found quantitative differences in students' written productions: Disabled writers produced significantly fewer sentences and fewer total words (Myklebust, 1973; Nodine et al., 1985; Poteet, 1978). Thus performance seems to be delimited less by students' syntactic inadequacies than by difficulties in knowing how to generate ideas and how to sustain thoughts about a topic.

Though mechanical skills are important, they are not the barrier to proficient writing once thought (Walmsley, 1983). The teaching of mechanical skills does not necessarily improve the quality of compositions, and young writers do not need to master the mechanics of writing before being introduced to writing. Instead, writers' knowledge of task-specific strategies in the actual composing process may be a more critical determinant of writing success. Of particular importance in the domain of composing strategies is students' awareness of text structures. Text structures are specific organizational schemes internalized by writers that describe the elements that should be included and how they should be ordered. There are different text structures for different writing purposes. For example, stories usually consist of five major elements: a setting (i.e., main character, time, place), a problem confronting the main character, the main character's response to the problem, the outcome of the response, and the story's conclusion. Similarly, expository materials contain structures such as compare/contrast, problem/solution, and chronological sequence. Knowledge of these structures influences the ability of writers to successfully plan, generate, organize, compose, and monitor their ideas.

Nodine et al. (1985) conducted one of the few studies examining children's use of a story structure in written compositions. A group of learning-disabled, reading-disabled, and normally achieving students were asked to write a story about three related pictures. The results suggested that learning-disabled (LD) students differed from both reading-disabled and normally achieving students in their ability to produce a tale that was storylike. Almost half of the LD students failed to generate a story that met story structure expectations. Furthermore, LD students were less aware of potential confusions caused by unrelated or inexplicable events in their compositions. Similar deficits in structural awareness have been reported in studies examining students' knowledge of expository text structures (Wong & Wilson, 1984).

The domain important to both the successful use of task-specific strategies and mechanical skills in composing is metacognitive knowledge. Metacognitive knowledge includes the abilities to self-instruct, self-monitor, self-correct, and self-regulate the writing process. Several studies suggest that disabled learners have serious deficiencies in their ability to activate previously learned strategies and to self-instruct or self-monitor during text production and comprehension (Bos & Filip, 1984; Wong, 1985). That these problems are attributable to metacognitive knowledge is suggested by two studies that indicate that the training of self-control processes improves composing and organizational abilities. Wong and Sawatsky (1984), for example, taught LD students to elaborate on or finish an initial sentence stem (e.g., The tall man helped the woman) by employing a five-step self-control procedure that helped students determine the writing purpose, draft a response, and monitor their writing. Following training, the sentence elaborations of students significantly improved. Similarly, Wong and Wilson (1984) trained LD students to organize scrambled passages by applying a five-step self-instructional procedure. The ease with which students were trained suggested that the LD children may have had some rudimentary idea about passage organization, but it was either incompletely developed or not spontaneously activated by the students. Since students readily benefited from self-control training, the results suggested that metacognitive strategies were similarly inactive or incomplete.

In summary, the literature suggests that several deficiencies may impede students' writing performance. Deficiencies in spelling, grammar, and writing conventions have been reported—though these may not be the barriers to writing success as much as students' lack of task-specific strategies and metacognitive knowledge. Research is still needed to determine the impact of other elements of the writing process (e.g., audience, prior knowledge) on performance in each of the writing stages. However, it is certain that writing competence will be associated not only with the acquisition of efficient strategies pertaining to the use of each element, but with the metacognitive knowledge that helps the writer know when and how to use the element in planning, drafting, monitoring, and revising compositions.

REFERENCES

Bos, C. S., & Filip, D. (1984). Comprehension monitoring in learning disabled and average students. *Journal of Learning Disabilities, 17,* 229–233.

Deshler, D. D. (1978). *Psychoeducational aspects of learning-disabled adolescents.* In L. M. Mann, L. Goodman, & T. L. Wiederholt (Eds.), *Teaching the learning-disabled adolescent.* Boston: Houghton Mifflin.

Englert, C. S., Hiebert, E. H., & Stewart, S. R. (1985). Spelling unfamiliar words by an analogy strategy. *Journal of Special Education, 19,* 291–306.

Englert, C. S., & Thomas, C. C. (1987). Sensitivity to text structure in reading and writing: A comparison of learning disabled and non-handicapped students. *Learning Disability Quarterly, 10,* 93–105.

Hayes, J. R., & Flower, L. S. (1980). Writing as problem solving. *Visible Language, 14,* 388–399.

Foster, K., & Torgesen, J. K. (1983). The effects of directed study on the spelling performance of two subgroups of learning disabled students. *Learning Disability Quarterly, 6,* 252–257.

Graham, S., & Freeman, S. (1985). Strategy training and teacher- vs. student-controlled study conditions: Effects on LD students' spelling performance. *Learning Disability Quarterly, 8,* 267–274.

Moran, M. R. (1981). Performance of learning disabled and low achieving secondary students on formal features of a paragraph-writing task. *Learning Disability Quarterly, 4,* 271–280.

Myklebust, H. R. (1973). *Development and disorders of written language. Vol. 2. Studies of normal and exceptional children.* New York: Grune & Stratton.

Nodine, B. F., Barenbaum, E., & Newcomer, P. (1985). Story composition by learning disabled, reading disabled, and normal children. *Learning Disability Quarterly, 8,* 167–179.

Nulman, J. A. H., & Gerber, M. M. (1984). Improving spelling performance by imitating a child's errors. *Journal of Learning Disabilities, 17,* 328–333.

Poplin, M. S., Gray, R., Larsen, S., Barikoski, A., & Mehring, T. (1980). A comparison of components of written expression abilities in learning disabled and non-learning disabled students at three grade levels. *Learning Disability Quarterly, 3,* 46–53.

Poteet, J. A. (1978). *Characteristics of written expression of learning disabled and non-learning disabled elementary school students.* Muncie, IN: Ball State University. (ERIC Document Reproduction Service No. ED 1590830)

Schumaker, J. B., Deshler, D. D., Alley, G. R., Warner, M. M., Clark, F. L., & Nolan, S. (1982). Error monitoring: A learning strategy for improving adolescent academic performance. In M. W. Cruickshank & J. W. Lerner (Eds.), *Coming of age: Vol. 3. The best of ACLD.* Syracuse, NY: Syracuse University Press.

Walmsley, S. A. (1983). Writing disability. In P. Mosenthal, L. Tamor, & S. A. Walmsley (Eds.), *Research on writing: Principles and methods.* New York: Longman.

Wong, B. Y. L. (1985). Metacognition and learning disabilities. In D. L. Forrest-Pressley, G. E. MacKinnon, & T. G. Waller (Eds.), *Metacognition, cognition and human performance: Vol. 2. Instructional practices* (pp. 137–80). New York: Academic.

Wong, B. Y. L., & Sawatsky, D. (1984). Sentence elaboration and retention of good, average and poor readers. *Learning Disability Quarterly, 7,* 229–236.

Wong, B. Y. L., & Wilson, M. (1984). Investigating awareness of and teaching passage organization in learning disabled children. *Journal of Learning Disabilities, 17,* 477–482.

CAROL SUE ENGLERT
Michigan State University

WRITING ASSESSMENT
WRITING REMEDIATION

WRITING REMEDIATION

The writing difficulties exhibited by many students with disabilities necessitate the development and use of instructional procedures aimed at improving writing competence, particularly in terms of disabled students' functional writing skills. The remediation of disabled students' writing difficulties, however, has not received much attention in either the research literature or in school settings. Leinhardt, Zigmond, and Cooley (1980) found, for example, that disabled students may spend less than 10 minutes a day generating written language. Although there are many possible reasons why writing remediation appears to receive a limited amount of time and emphasis in handicapped students' instructional programs, teacher attitudes and backgrounds may be the key factors in determining the quantity and quality of writing instruction for these students. According to Graham (1982), many teachers do not enjoy writing and are not prepared to teach composition. Furthermore, many special education teachers may feel that writing is not a critical skill for their students and may choose to spend their instructional time teaching what they consider to be more important skills (e.g., reading, arithmetic).

For the most part, writing instruction for disabled students has drawn heavily on techniques used with normally achieving youngsters. One commonly recommended instructional procedure has been to use a phase approach. This approach emphasizes the various stages of the composition process (prewriting, writing, and revising) and is designed to develop security in the use of these stages. In a phase approach described by Silverman et al. (1981), the teacher first structures the writing process with prewriting activities that involve thinking, experiencing, discussing, and interacting. The student and the teacher then develop a series of questions that are used to guide the writing process. During the revising stage, the teacher critiques the student's writing and they jointly revise the student's paper. Although empirical support for this particular model or other phase approaches is limited, this writing procedure does stress the development of two important skills: thinking as a preliminary facet of composing and revision of the initial draft of the written product. In addition, a phase approach to writing may be especially suitable for disabled students since it helps reduce cognitive strain by taking a large complex problem such as writing and breaking it down into smaller subproblems.

Another traditional approach that has been used to teach specific writing skills to disabled students is modeling. With this approach, students may be asked to imitate a specific type of sentence pattern, a well-known style of writing, a certain type of paragraph, and so on. There are two basic approaches to modeling. One approach stresses strategy explanation and model illustration; the other emphasizes problem solving. With the former, a student may be asked to mimic a specific type of paragraph (e.g., topic sentence located at the start of the paragraph) following an examination and analysis of several examples that are representative of the style to be emulated. The latter can be illustrated by examining a procedure developed by Schiff (1978). With this procedure, examples of a particular type of paragraph are selected. Sentences for each paragraph are then written on a separate strip of paper and their order randomized. Students rearrange the sentences in each paragraph and compare their arrangements with the original model. At present, it is impossible to draw any definitive conclusions on the relative effectiveness of these procedures, as there is virtually no research that examines them.

A great deal of attention has been directed at teaching disabled students information about language and writing with the aim of promoting the correct use of structure, form, and language. One of the most consistently held beliefs in the history of writing instruction is that the teaching of grammar and usage is critical to the development of writing competence. Formal grammar, however, is difficult to master and knowledge of grammatical concepts does not appear to be necessary for the skillful use of written language (Blount, 1973). This is not meant to imply that teachers should not attend to disabled students' use of structure or form in their writing or that these skills cannot be improved. Rather, improvement of usage and form "may be more effectively achieved through direct practice of desirable forms when the need arises" (Graham, 1982, p. 6).

An interesting alternative to traditional writing approaches is the use of procedures that seek to minimize or circumvent disabled students' poor writing skills. The most commonly used alternative is dictation. Traditionally, dictation has involved having a student furnish the content or ideas orally while the teacher or a peer structures the form the material takes on paper. The conventional dictation process can be adapted by using a tape recorder as an aid to organizing content (i.e., ideas are taped and later written and edited by the student). In some instances, dictation is employed as a temporary aid and its use diminishes as the student becomes more adept at the mechanics of writing. Dictation may represent a viable alternative for students with adequate oral language skills who have been unable, after years of intensive instruction, to automate and integrate basic writing skills.

A recent alternative to traditional writing instruction approaches is the cognitive-behavior modification (CBM) procedure. Typically CBM training involves teaching students to regulate task-specific and metacognitive strategies through processes such as self-instruction, self-assessment, and self-reinforcement (Harris, 1982). For example, Harris and Graham (1985) reported a CBM composition training procedure that significantly increased learning-disabled students' use of verbs, adverbs, and adjectives and resulted in higher-quality story ratings. Further, generalization and maintenance probes taken up to 14 weeks after training yielded positive results. The CBM training regimen in this study included skills training (instruction on specific task-appropriate strategies), metacognitive training (instruction in the self-regulation of those strategies), and instruction

concerning the significance of such activities. In a second study, Graham and Harris (1986) found that CBM procedures also could be used to improve the overall structure of learning-disabled students' compositions through the use of a story grammar strategy. Training procedures were similar to those in the first study; however, strategy training consisted of instruction in story grammar elements: setting, goal(s), action(s), emotional responses, and ending.

Educators also have attempted to improve disabled students' writing skills by further refining or developing their reading, oral language, and thinking skills. Since reading, writing, thinking, and language skills are interrelated, it is assumed that intensive and generalized instruction in an area such as oral language, for example, will have an indirect and positive effect on a student's writing ability (Groff, 1978). Although these skills may be interrelated, they do not necessarily function in an interactive and supportive way. Generalized instruction in an area such as reading or oral language appears to be of limited value in the immediate improvement of a student's writing (Graham, 1982).

A recent development in the teaching of writing to students with disabilities has been the advent of the computer, particularly the word processor. The word processor, with its various capabilities for storing and editing texts, has the potential to both strengthen and significantly change the nature of writing instruction. The word processor and other technological advances should not, however, be viewed as a cure-all for disabled students' writing problems. MacArthur and Graham (1986), for instance, found no major differences between handwritten stories and those composed on a word processor, even though the learning-disabled students in their study had considerable experience using the computer.

Additional instructional recommendations for teaching writing to students with disabilities have been summarized by Graham (1982). These include (1) providing students with plenty of opportunities to write and exposing them to a variety of practical and imaginative assignments; (2) having writing assignments, whenever possible, serve a real purpose and be directed at an authentic audience; (3) having a pleasant and encouraging composition program; and (4) deemphasizing writing errors.

REFERENCES

Blount, N. (1973). Research on teaching literature, language, and composition. In R. Travers (Ed.), *Second handbook of research on teaching*. Chicago; Rand McNally.

Graham, S. (1982). Composition research and practice: A unified approach. *Focus on Exceptional Children, 14,* 1–16.

Graham, S., & Harris, K. (1986). *Improving learning disabled students' compositions via story grammars: A component analysis of self-control strategy training*. Paper presented at the American Educational Research Association, San Francisco.

Groff, P. (1978). Children's oral language and their written composition. *Elementary School Journal, 78,* 181–191.

Harris, K. (1982). Cognitive behavior modification: Application with exceptional students. *Focus on Exceptional Children, 15,* 1–16.

Harris, K., & Graham, S. (1985). Improving learning disabled students' composition skills: Self-control strategy training. *Learning Disability Quarterly, 8,* 27–36.

Leinhardt, G., Zigmond, N., & Cooley, W. (1980). *Reading instruction and its effects.* Paper presented at the American Educational Research Association, Boston.

MacArthur, C., & Graham, S. (1986). *LD students' writing under three conditions: Word processing, dictation, and handwriting.* Paper presented at the American Educational Research Association, San Francisco.

Schiff, P. (1978). Problem solving and the composition model: Reorganization, manipulation, analysis. *Research in the Teaching of English, 12,* 203–210.

Silverman, R., Zigmond, N., Zimmerman, J., & Vallecorsa, A. (1981). Improving written expression in learning disabled students. *Topics in Language Disorders, 1,* 91–99.

STEVE GRAHAM
KAREN R. HARRIS
University of Maryland

WRITING ASSESSMENT
WRITING DISORDERS

WYATT v. STICKNEY

The case of *Wyatt v. Stickney* established constitutionally minimum standards of care; in the last 2 decades, *Wyatt* has been credited with establishing the legal precedent for a constitutional right to treatment for involuntarily committed mentally ill patients. Directly addressing Alabama's state institutions for the mentally ill and mentally retarded, this case represented a landmark federal judicial intervention in the mental institutions of a sovereign state, and signaled dozens of *Wyatt*-type "right to treatment" lawsuits in nearly every part of the country.

As a result of the unrefuted "atrocities" documented in *Wyatt* (1972), the "shocking" and "inhumane" conditions in New York's Willowbrook State School for the Mentally Retarded (1973), and 25 other suits involving the U.S. Justice Department (1979), congressional legislation for financial assistance and a "Bill of Rights" for institutionalized persons were enacted.

Only six decisions based on the Wyatt case have ever been published in the law reports (1971–1981), although it is cited in over 200 judicial decisions and is the subject of numerous law reviews and other professional journal articles.

Ricky Wyatt was one of about 5,000 mental patients at Bryce State Hospital, Tuscaloosa, the same hospital estab-

lished in 1861 through the urging of the advocate Dorothea Dix. Stonewall B. Stickney was a psychiatrist and the chief administrative officer of Alabama's Mental Health Board. The case was filed initially by 99 of 100 dismissed staff members plus Ricky Wyatt's aunt and other guardians on October 23, 1970. The plaintiff employees alleged that this reduction in staff would deprive patients at Bryce of necessary treatment and sued for reinstatement. Stickney had released over 100 of the 1,600 employees at Bryce owing to reduced state cigarette tax revenues allocated to the department, while redirecting the limited funds to community mental health services. Stickney believed in preventing institutionalization.

The employee plaintiffs withdrew their reinstatement claim prior to Judge Frank M. Johnson's initial reported decision on March 12, 1971. The court found that more than 1,500 geriatric patients and about 1,000 mentally retarded patients were involuntarily committed at Bryce for reasons other than being mentally ill, and were receiving custodial care but not treatment.

Judge Johnson ordered the development and implementation of adequate treatment standards and a report within 6 months; he requested the U.S. departments of Justice and Health, Education, and Welfare, as "friends of the court," to assist in evaluating the treatment programs and standards. On August 12, 1971, the court allowed the request. All involuntary patients from Partlow State School and Hospital in Tuscaloosa, housing nearly 2,500 mental retardates with segregated facilities for blacks, and Searcy Hospital in Mount Vernon, a formerly all-black hospital for the mentally ill, were to be included in the class suit. Defendants filed the court-directed report on September 23, 1971, and Judge Johnson ruled on December 10, 1971, allowing the state 6 months to correct three basic deficiencies. He called for "a humane psychological and physical environment, . . . qualified staff in numbers sufficient to administer adequate treatment, and . . . individualized treatment plans." Following additional testimony, briefs, and standards proposed by "the foremost authorities on mental health in the United States," the parties agreed to standards that mandated a "constitutionally acceptable minimum treatment program" for the mentally ill at Bryce and Searcy as ordered by the court on April 13, 1972.

Judge Johnson also ruled, in a supplemental order issued the same day, that unrebutted evidence of the "hazardous and deplorable inadequacies in the institution's operations at Partlow was more shocking than at Bryce or Searcy." He said that "The result of almost 50 years of legislative neglect has been catastrophic; atrocities occur daily"; Judge Johnson published these findings (1972):

> A few of the atrocious incidents cited at the hearing in this case include the following: (a) a resident was scalded to death by hydrant water; (b) a resident was restrained in a strait jacket for 9 years in order to prevent hand and finger sucking; (c) a

resident was inappropriately confined in seclusion for a period of years, and (d) a resident died from the insertion by another resident of a running water hose into his rectum. Each of these incidents could have been avoided had adequate staff and facilities been available.

Judge Johnson ordered the defendants to (1) implement the standards for adequate habilitation for the retarded at Partlow; (2) establish a human rights committee; (3) employ a new administrator; (4) submit a progress report to the court within 6 months; and (5) pay attorneys' fees and costs to the plaintiffs.

The defendants appealed both decisions to the Fifth Circuit Court of Appeals in May 1972. The review court, on November 8, 1974, upheld the constitutional right to treatment concept and ruled that the federal judicially determined standards did not violate the state's legislative rights.

REFERENCE

Civil rights of the institutionalized. Report of the Committee on Judiciary United States Senate on S.10 together with minority and additional views. (1979). Washington, DC: U.S. Government Printing Office.

LOUIS SCHWARTZ
Florida State University
First edition

KIMBERLY F. APPLEQUIST
University of Colorado at Colorado Springs
Third edition

HISTORY OF SPECIAL EDUCATION
PHILOSOPHY OF EDUCATION FOR INDIVIDUALS WITH DISABILITIES

X

X-LINKED DOMINANT INHERITANCE

The consequences of the presence of a recessive gene on one X chromosome are well known. X-linked dominant inheritance, however, follows a different pattern. First, males and females can show the trait equally, and, if a pathologic gene is concerned, patients of both sexes are affected. Second, if a male carrier of the dominant trait "A" marries a homozygous recessive female "aa," all his daughters will exhibit the trait "A" (they are heterozygous "Aa," having received one X from the "aa" mother and the paternal X with "A"), and all his sons will show the trait "a" (they have received the X chromosome from their mothers and the recessive "a" behaves like a dominant). This mode of transmission, from father to daughter, is in fact so characteristic that, when it is observed, the presence of an X-dominant gene is almost demonstrated. Only a few rare diseases are known to be X-linked dominants. X-linked dominant inherited diseases, though rare, result in a variety of handicapping conditions. Not all genetic disorders need result in disabilities, however. Proper care during pregnancy and throughout life can avoid many natural consequences of genetic disorders.

L. KOULISCHER
Institut de Morphologie
Pathologique, Belgium

CONGENITAL DISORDERS
ETIOLOGY
GENETIC COUNSELING
X-LINKED RECESSIVE INHERITANCE

X-LINKED RECESSIVE INHERITANCE

It is well known that the same gene may present different forms, called alleles. All alleles are located at a fixed place of a chromosome, the locus. In any person, only two alleles are present, one at each locus of the same chromosome pair. One of the two alleles originates from the father, the other from the mother. Alleles can be either dominant (usually represented by a capital letter: "A"), or recessive (represented by a small letter: "a"). As indicated by its name, the dominant form prevails over the recessive one. This means that the carrier of "Aa" (heterozygote) will show the character "A," the recessive "a" being masked. To express itself, "a" must be in the homozygote state "aa." This happens when two "Aa" heterozygotes marry: 25 percent of all their children will be "aa."

This general rule does not apply to the sex chromosomes. In the XX female, only one X is active in any cell, the other one being inactivated (Lyon, 1961). In a heterozygote female "Aa," the gene "A" will express itself in half of the cells, and "a" in the other half. Most often, the fact that the normal allele is active in half of the cells is enough to determine normal characteristics. For instance, if a woman is a carrier of the recessive mutation responsible for blindness for the red color (daltonism), half of the cells of her retina will be blind for red, but the others not and this will be sufficient to give almost normal color vision. The male has an XY sex chromosome set: only one X, transmitted by the mother, is present. The Y chromosome is very small and has only a few genes.

Any boy has a 50 percent chance to inherit one of the two maternal Xs. If he receives the X with a normal dominant allele, there will be no problem. If he receives an X with a recessive abnormal allele from an heterozygous mother, all his cells (not half of them, as in his mother) will be affected. The gene "a" alone, although recessive, behaves like a dominant (e.g., in the case of daltonism, he will be blind to the red). In short, an X-linked recessive gene is transmitted by the mother to half of her sons. If the gene determines a disease, half of the male progeny will be affected, the mother herself being apparently normal. Moreover, half of her daughters will be "normal carriers" and thus will be at risk of having half of their sons affected. When an affected male marries, all his children will be normal. The boys receive their X chromosome from the normal mother and the girls are heterozygous (the problem concerns their future children). Only the exceptional and seldom reported marriage of a heterozygous woman "Aa" with an affected man "a" can produce affected "aa" homozygous females.

The striking fact in this sort of X-linked recessive pedigree is that only males are affected (black squares). Inversely, when a family is found with only males presenting a disease, the transmission of an X-linked recessive gene is likely. According to McKusick (1983), there are at present

115 confirmed and 128 possible X-linked genes. It is not possible to cite them all in this entry. The most commonly known recessives are those associated with hemophilia, agammaglobulenemia and other immunological diseases, eye diseases including colorblindness, ocular albinism, and some forms of cataract, a few deafness syndromes, Lesch-Nyhan syndrome (Mental Retardation, spastic cerebral palsy, choreoathetosis, uric acid urinary stones, and self-destructive biting of fingers and lips), muscular dystrophy, myopathy, and testicular feminization.

Mental deficiency and X-linked recessive genes deserve special comment. It is well known that more boys than girls show Mental Retardation. This suggests an excess of X-linked recessive diseases. Often, Mental Retardation is associated with other symptoms to form a syndrome (e.g., Lesch-Nyhan syndrome). A newly discovered disease is Mental Retardation, macroorchidism, and elongated face associated with the presence of a fragile site on the X-chromosome, known as the Xq28 fragile site, observed in 1 out of 2,000 male births. Fryns (1984) has published a review of 83 families ascertained through 83 index patients. He summarizes the problems raised by this particular chromosome anomaly: In one-third of the families, pedigree data were consistent with X-linked recessive inheritance in the other two-thirds, the presenting symptom was familial Mental Retardation with a mentally retarded mother, or Mental subnormality with hyperkinetic behavior. Even the transmission through a normal asymptomatic X-fragile male carrier seemed likely in four families. Although more data are still necessary, at present the fragile Xq28 syndrome appears to be an important cause of X-linked Mental Retardation, with the advantage that carriers can be detected by means of relatively simply cytogenetic techniques.

From a preventive point of view, it is important first to diagnose correctly any X-linked disease with Mental Retardation, and to detect the normal heterozygote mothers at risk. This is not always possible, but it is a new area of research and it is hoped, with the help of biochemistry and molecular DNA analysis, to prevent in the near future the birth of affected males.

REFERENCES

Fryns, J.-P. (1984). The fragile X syndrome. A study of 83 families. *Clin. Genet., 26,* 497–528.

Lyon, M. F. (1961). Gene action in the X-chromosome of the mouse. (Mus musculus). *Nature, 190,* 372–373.

L. Koulischer
Institut de Morphologie
Pathologique, Belgium

CONGENITAL DISORDERS
GENETIC COUNSELING
X-LINKED RECESSIVE INHERITANCE

X-RAYS AND DISABILITIES

Irradiation of the developing fetus during the early stages of development as a consequence of maternal X-rays is now clearly recognized as a potential cause of later physical and cognitive abnormalities. There may be dramatic effects associated with irradiation that are clearly recognized at birth. There may be other, more subtle effects appearing at later ages, such as reduced head size. Pioneer studies on the subject were done by Zappert (1926), Murphy (1929), and Goldstein (1930; Berg, 1968).

Clinical X-rays are a major source of the radiation absorbed by the human body during any particular year. It has been estimated that people on the average absorb less than 4 rads a year and that half of this is from medical X-rays (e.g., upper gastrointestinal series, abdominal X-rays, dental and chest X-rays). This does not include treatment for cancer, during which ranges somewhere between 30 and 250 rads have been observed (Batshaw & Perrett, 1981).

Though the potential dangers to the fetus from X-ray radiation were recognized before World War II, the dangers of radiation were most dramatically brought into focus by the events of that war. It was found that there was a direct relationship between the distance of a pregnant woman from the point of impact of the atomic bombs at Hiroshima and Nagasaki and the degree of damage suffered by her unborn child. Women who survived the bomb explosion but were within a half-mile of it were found to have miscarriages, while there was an extremely high incidence of microcephalic children born to those who were 1¼ miles away (Wood, Johnson, & Omiri, 1967). Still farther away, there was no clear evidence of cognitive or physical damage to the children that were later born, but some 20 years later, as adults, they had a high incidence of leukemia (Miller, 1968).

One major study of pregnant women who were receiving cobalt treatments for cancer discovered that 20 out of 75 of the infants born to them had definitive central nervous system abnormalities. Sixteen of these were microcephalic (Copper & Cooper, 1966). The corroboration of these findings in later studies has resulted in caution and forbearance on the part of physicians with respect to the use of X-rays with pregnant women. Normally, women should not have abdominal X-rays more than 2 weeks after the last period. X-rays during the first trimester are discouraged on any but the most necessary grounds. X-rays as diagnostic tests, such as those once carried out to establish fetal size, have been replaced with less invasive procedures like ultrasound. Indeed, there has been recent evidence suggesting that some of the more subtle kinds of handicaps (e.g., those associated with learning disabilities) may be the consequences of X-ray use.

On the positive side it should be observed that X-rays have played a role in assisting in the assessment of handicapped individuals. Thus X-rays of the bone structures of hands and wrists have provided estimates of carpal ossification in cases where delayed maturation has been suspected. X-rays also are essential for the diagnosis of various physical problems and deformities (e.g., dislocations, fractures, internal injuries, congenital defects). Computerized axial tomography (CAT) has revolutionized medical diagnosis. While X-rays by themselves can show only the length and width of a bodily organ, the CAT scan can also reveal depth. Significant contributions to our understanding of learning disorders have been made by CAT scans (Mann & Sabatino, 1985).

REFERENCES

Batshaw, M. L., & Perrett, Y. M. (1981). *Children with handicaps.* Baltimore: Brookes.

Berg, J. M. (1968). Aetiological aspects of mental subnormality: Pathological factors. In A. M. Clarke & A. D. B. Clarke (Eds.), *Mental deficiency.* New York: Free Press.

Cooper, G., & Cooper, J. B. (1966). Radiation hazards to mother and fetus. *Clinical Obstetrics & Gynecology, 9,* 11.

Mann, L., & Sabatino, D. A. (1985). *Foundations of cognitive processes in remedial and special education.* Rockville, MD: Aspen.

Miller, R. W. (1968). Effects of ionizing radiation from the atomic bomb on Japanese children. *Pediatrics, 72,* 1483.

Wood, J. W., Johnson, K. G., & Omiri, Y. (1973). In utero exposure to the Hiroshima atomic bomb. An evaluation of head size and mental retardation: Twenty years after. *Pediatrics, 39,* 385.

LESTER MANN
*Hunter College, City University
of New York*

**CAT SCAN
NEURAL EFFICIENCY ANALYZER**

X-RAY SCANNING TECHNIQUES

The history of X-ray scanning techniques of the brain is eloquently outlined in the text by Oldendorf (1980). Up until the advent of CAT (computed axial tomography) scanning in 1973, the image of the brain could only be grossly inferred by either bony abnormalities of the skull as seen on routine skull X-rays or by a technique (pneumoencephalography) in which air was introduced into the brain ventricles (either directly or via spinal puncture). The resultant shadowy contrast between ventricle, brain, and bone would permit some visualization of major cerebral landmarks sufficient to detect some types of gross structural pathology (e.g., hydrocephalus, tumor). However, the technique of pneumoencephalography had significant morbidity risks and was invasive. The pneumoencephalogram has been replaced by CAT scanning.

An historical predecessor of CAT scanning was the radio-active isotope scan (based on differences in rate of absorption of radioactive particles in normal and abnormal brain tissue), which began clinical use in 1947 and continued until the advent and clinical implementation of CAT scanning. The CAT and other neuroimaging techniques have essentially replaced the radioactive isotope scan. This is also the case with routine cerebral arteriography, which used to be the only way to visualize blood vessels of the neck and head; it has been replaced in large part by digital subtraction angiography (DSA). The DSA is an X-ray scanning technique that uses a computer program to "subtract" background tissue in the X-ray image that is not of the same density as blood vessels. Comparisons of these techniques, sample figures, and a more complete discussion of their diagnostic usefulness are presented in Bigler (1988).

Positron emission tomography (PET) is a technique that permits the mapping of brain metabolism by using radioactive-labeled glucose or oxygen. Based on different metabolic rates, an image of the major cerebral structures can be obtained with specific indication of which brain areas were using the most glucose or oxygen (e.g., the brain area most involved in a particular task while PET scanning was being done).

REFERENCES

Bigler, E. D. (1988). *Diagnostic clinical neuropsychology* (2nd ed.). Austin: University of Texas Press.

Oldendorf, W. H. (1980). *The quest for an image of brain.* New York: Raven.

ERIN D. BIGLER
Brigham Young University

**CAT SCAN
NUCLEAR MAGNETIC RESONANCE**

XYY SYNDROME

XYY syndrome, or Polysomy Y, is a rare chromosomal genetic syndrome where males have an extra Y chromosome, becoming XYY instead of the normal XY sex chromosome (males) or XX (females; Cure Research, n.d.). XYY syndrome usually does not cause abnormal physical features or medical conditions. Typically XYY males are taller than average (about 6'2") and may experience severe acne (Contact a Family, 2002). Puberty occurs at the expected time; sex organs and secondary sex characteristics develop normally (Nielson, 2005). Because of the lack of distinct physical or medical features, the condition often only is detected during genetic analysis for other reasons (The Real Facts Contributions Company, n.d.).

Currently there is no known cause of the mutation that leads to the formation of the XYY syndrome (Nielson, 2005). XYY is not inherited and occurs randomly (Genetics Home Reference, 2005). The frequency of XYY is difficult to ascertain due to statistical differences between studies, as well as the fact that genetic testing is not necessarily done on all males who have the syndrome. It may be as common as 1 in 900 or as rare as 1 in 1,500, or even 1 in 2,000 (O'Neil, 2005).

Early studies of the XYY syndrome led to the erroneous conclusion that these men were genetically predisposed to antisocial, aggressive behavior, below-average intelligence, and homosexuality (O'Neil, 2005); these early myths have been disproved (Merck, 2005). Although males with XYY often have intellectual ability in the average range, their overall ability tends to be 10 to 15 points lower than their siblings (Yale New Haven Health, n.d.). Some XYY males experience learning difficulties; others experience delayed speech development and behavior problems. These difficulties can be overcome with appropriate interventions by parent, teacher, and speech language pathologist (when necessary) working together cooperatively (Nielson, 2005).

REFERENCES

Contact a Family. (2002). *XYY syndrome.* Retrieved September 4, 2005, from http://www.cafamily.org.uk.Direct.x15.html

Cure Research. (n.d.). *Introduction: Jacobs syndrome.* Retrieved September 4, 2005, from http://www.cureresearch.com/j/jacobs_syndrome/intro.htm.

Genetics Home Reference. (2005). *47, XYY syndrome.* Retrieved September 4, 2005, from http://ghr.nlm.nih.gov.condition=47xxysyndrome

Merck & Co. Inc. (2005). *The Merck manual of diagnosis and therapy.* [Electronic version]. Whitehouse, NJ: Author. Retrieved September 4, 2005, from http://www.merck.com

Nielson, J. (2005). *XYY males and orientation.* Retrieved September 4, 2005, from http://www.aadk/TURNER/ENGELSK/XYY.HTM

O'Neil, D. (2005). *Sex chromosome abnormalities.* Retrieved September 4, 2005, from http://anthro.palomar.edu/abnormal/abnormal_5.htm

The Real Facts Contribution Company. (n.d.). *XYY.* Retrieved September 4, 2005, from http://www.therfcc.org/xxy-127569.html

Yale New Haven Health. (n.d.). *XYY syndrome.* Retrieved September 4, 2005, from http://yalenewhavenhealth.org/library/healthguide/en-us/illnessconditions/topic

JOSEPH D. PERRY
Kent State University
First edition

LATANYA HENRY
Texas A&M University
Third edition

CHROMOSOMES, HUMAN ANOMALIES, AND CYTOGENETIC ABNORMALITIES
GENETIC COUNSELING

Y

YALE, CAROLINE A. (1848–1933)

Caroline A. Yale, teacher and principal at Clarke School for the Deaf in Northampton, Massachusetts, from 1870 to 1922, was a leading figure in the development of educational services for the deaf in the United States. She developed a system for teaching speech to the deaf and was a founder, with Alexander Graham Bell and others, of the American Association to Promote the Teaching of Speech to the Deaf. At Clarke School, she organized a teacher-education department that was responsible for the training of large numbers of student teachers. Through her teacher-training activities and numerous publications, Yale was a major contributor to the acceptance of instruction in speech as an essential element in the education of deaf children.

REFERENCES

Taylor, H. (1933). Caroline Ardelia Yale. *The Volta Review, 35,* 415–417.

Yale, C. A. (1931). *Years of building.* New York: Longmans, Green.

PAUL IRVINE
Katonah, New York

BELL, ALEXANDER GRAHAM (1847–1922)
DEAF EDUCATION

YEAR-ROUND SCHOOLS

The concept and use of year-round schools for special and general education has developed, in part, as a result of changing expectations and roles of public education in the community (Hanna, 1972). The traditional answer to the question of school responsibility was simple: Transmit the heritage, or at least that part of it considered to be important, to the educated person. The traditional school said, in effect, fit children and youths into the fixed curriculum of academic subjects. If they do not care, or in the case of many exceptional students, cannot cope with it, that is unfortunate. In the cases of many exceptional students, traditional education models forced them out or openly expelled them if attendance laws permitted. In other cases, students were tracked into vocational education or home economics. More progressive educators organized schools around a child-centered orientation in order to more effectively stimulate student interest, provide for the exploration and expression of those interests, and, therefore, assist in desirable personality growth (Olsen & Clark, 1977).

A system embracing year-round schooling is able to affirm the central values of the earlier concepts while providing programming in light of the school's basic responsibility to help improve the quality of living in the local community or region. The traditional school curriculum is still almost standard practice (Ysseldyke & Algozzine, 1983). The approach involved in year-round schools, however, provides curriculum flexibly structured about the enduring life concerns of humans everywhere. These concerns, with their attendant problems, are those of earning a living, communicating ideas and feelings, enjoying recreation, and finding some measure of self-identity.

REFERENCES

Hanna, P. (1972). What thwarts the community education curriculum? *Community Education Journal,* (May, 27–30).

Olsen, E. G., & Clark, P. A. (1977). *Life-centering education.* Midland, MI: Pendell.

Ysseldyke, J., & Algozzine, B. (1983). *Introduction to special education.* Boston: Houghton Mifflin.

CRAIG D. SMITH
Georgia College

EXTENDED SCHOOL YEAR FOR STUDENTS WITH DISABILITIES
LICENSING AND CERTIFICATION OF SCHOOLS
SUMMER SCHOOL FOR INDIVIDUALS WITH DISABILITIES

YOUNG CHILDREN'S ACHIEVEMENT TEST

The Young Children's Achievement Test (YCAT) is an individually administered measure designed to determine early academic abilities and document educational progress. Its main purpose is to help identify young children who are at risk for school failure. The test was designed for English-speaking preschoolers, kindergartners, and first-graders (ages 4:0 through 7:11). The YCAT yields an overall Early Achievement Standard Score and individual subtest standard scores for the following five subtests: General Information, Reading, Mathematics, Writing, and Spoken Language. The YCAT allows for flexibility in administration because the subtests can be administered in any order or be given independent of each other. A variety of scores are reported for both the subtests and composite score, including standard scores (with a mean of 100 and standard deviation of 15), percentiles, and age equivalents.

The YCAT materials include an examiner's manual, picture book, examiner record booklets, and student response forms. The examiner record booklet indicates multiple examples of correct responses, which facilitates the scoring process. Items are either scored as correct (1) or incorrect (0), and there are approximately 20 items per subtest.

The YCAT was normed on 1,224 children. The sample was representative of the U.S. population as reported in 1997 by the U.S. Bureau of the Census. Overall, the YCAT appears to be a reliable measure. Test-retest reliability was calculated over a 2-week period and ranged from .97 to .99. Interrater reliability ranged from .97 to .99 for the individual subtests. Internal consistency as measured by Cronbach's coefficient alpha ranged from .74 to .92, with the majority of subtest values in the mid-to-high .80s. The Early Achievement Composite Score yielded high internal consistency values of .95 to .97.

REFERENCE

Plake, B. S., Impara, J. C., & Spies, R. A. (Eds.). (2003). *The fifteenth mental measurements yearbook.* Lincoln, NE: Buros Institute of Mental Measurements.

RON DUMONT
Fairleigh Dickinson University

JOHN O. WILLIS
Rivier College

YSSELDYKE, JAMES EDWARD (1944–   )

James Edward Ysseldyke, noted educator, psychologist, and researcher, was born in Grand Rapids, Michigan, in 1944. He received his BA in 1966 in psychology and biology from Western Michigan University, and both his MA in 1968 and PhD in 1971 in school psychology from the University of Illinois, where he studied with T. Ernest Newland. He is currently professor of educational psychology at the University of Minnesota, teaching primarily in school psychology

James Edward Ysseldyke

and also in special education, and since 1991, he has been director of the National Center on Educational Outcomes at the university. Ysseldyke is the former director of the University of Minnesota Institute for Research in Learning Disabilities, and is presently codirector of the Minnesota Center for Reading Research.

Much of Ysseldyke's work has been concentrated in the area of special education assessment. He and his colleagues have investigated the relationship of psychometric properties of tests, particularly reliability and validity, to the decision-making process in multidisciplinary team meetings (Poland, Thurlow, Ysseldyke, & Mirkin, 1982). Ysseldyke's work in this area has indicated that, in many instances, decisions on eligibility for special education and programming are made prior to the official team meeting, with test data having little or no effect on the process. Similarly, he has found little correlation between the results of a child's standardized tests and the child's subsequent classroom placement (Ysseldyke, Algozzine, Richey, & Graden, 1982). These findings have encouraged additional detailed research on the issue.

Ysseldyke has recently noted the exclusion of students with disabilities in significant numbers from state and national data collection programs, thus precluding the evaluation of these students in terms of educational outcomes (Vanderwook, McGrew, & Ysseldyke, 1998). He has also coauthored, with Bob Algozzine, a book with instructional approaches for teachers of special needs students, *Special Education: A Practical Approach for Teachers* (1995). Ysseldyke is perhaps best known to students of special education, however, for his highly successful text coauthored with John Salvia, *Assessment in Special and Remedial Education* (1985).

REFERENCES

Poland, S. F., Thurlow, M. L., Ysseldyke, J. E., & Mirkin, P. K. (1982). Current psychoeducational assessment and decision-making practices as reported by directors of special education. *Journal of School Psychology, 20,* 171–179.

Salvia, J., & Ysseldyke, J. E. (1985). *Assessment in special remedial education.* Boston: Houghton Mifflin.

Vanderwood, M., McGrew, K. S., & Ysseldyke, J. E. (1998). Why we can't say much about students with disabilities during education reform. *Exceptional Children, 64*(3), 359–370.

Ysseldyke, J. E., & Algozzine, B. (1995). *Special education: A practical approach for teachers* (3rd ed.). Boston: Houghton Mifflin.

Ysseldyke, J. E., Algozzine, B., Richey, L., & Graden, J. (1982). Declaring students eligible for learning disability services: Why bother with the data? *Learning Disability Quarterly, 5,* 37–44.

E. VALERIE HEWITT
Texas A&M University
First edition

TAMARA J. MARTIN
The University of Texas of the Permian Basin
Second edition

COUNCIL FOR EXCEPTIONAL CHILDREN INSTITUTES FOR RESEARCH ON LEARNING DISABILITIES

YUNIS-VARON SYNDROME

Yunis-Varon Syndrome is a rare genetic disorder caused by an autosomal recessive gene. Children with Yunis-Varon Syndrome have skeletal ectodermal tissue (e.g., nails and teeth) and cardiorespiratory defects. Skeletal defects include complete or partial absence of the shoulder blades, digital abnormalities (i.e., absence of or underdeveloped thumbs, big toes, and fingertips), and abnormal growth of the bones of the cranium (i.e., the skull). These children have abnormally large hearts and respiratory difficulties, along with feeding problems, which can be life-threatening, especially in infancy (National Organization for Rare Disorders [NORD], 1997). In fact, neonatal death is a significant feature of Yunis-Varon Syndrome (Lapeer & Fransman, 1992).

Other physical features of this disorder include abnormal or unusual facial characteristics. Children with this syndrome have sparse or no eyebrows and eyelashes, thin lips, and excessively small jaws. These children are also short in stature due to pre- and postnatal growth retardation (NORD, 1997).

Twelve cases of the syndrome have been reported in the literature, which suggests a rare disorder and/or a high mortality rate associated with the disorder. Children who have survived the infancy period have been reported to have additional problems, including bilateral hearing loss, spinal defects, and impacted teeth (Lapeer & Fransman, 1992). Special education support services, such as speech services, may be helpful, especially if a hearing loss is evident.

REFERENCES

Lapeer, G. L., & Fransman, S. L. (1992). Hypodontia, impacted teeth, spinal defects, and cardiomegaly in previously diagnosed case of the Yunis-Varon syndrome. *Oral Surgery, Oral Medicine, and Oral Pathology, 73*(4), 456–460.

National Organization for Rare Disorders (NORD). (1997). *Yunis-Varon syndrome.* New Fairfield, CT: Author.

PATRICIA A. LOWE
University of Kansas

JOAN W. MAYFIELD
Baylor Pediatric Specialty Service

Z

ZEAMAN, DAVID (1921–1984)

After receiving his PhD from Columbia University in experimental psychology in 1948, David Zeaman embarked on a lifelong career developing and elaborating on an attention theory of retardate discriminative learning. In the early 1950s, he conducted pilot studies specializing in animal learning with his wife, Betty House, at the Mansfield State Training School in Connecticut. They thought that the techniques developed for studying animal behavior could be adapted for retarded children with low ability to speak or understand language. That early work proved promising, leading to funding by the National Institute of Mental Health for a project that lasted 20 years. The Mansfield State School administrative provided space for a permanent laboratory that is still in existence.

The initial target behavior for Zeaman and House's research was a discriminative learning task disguised as a candy-finding game. Early results convinced them that the deficiency they observed in retarded subjects was due to attentional deficits rather than slow learning. They developed a mathematical attention model with the basic assumption that discriminative learning requires a learning chain of two responses: attending to the relevant dimension and approaching the correct cue of that dimension.

Their approach to retardation was to look for changes in parameter values of the model related to intelligence. The parameter that was most affected by level of intelligence turned out to be the initial probability of attending to the colors and forms that were the relevant dimensions of the tasks. Later work related this finding to three factors: (1) breadth and adjustability of breadth of attention—subjects of higher intelligence can attend to more dimensions at once and can narrow attention when necessary; (2) dimensionality of the stimulus—subjects of low intelligence are likely to attend to stimuli holistically rather than analytically; and (3) fixed as well as variable components of attention such that strong dimensional preferences interfere with learning—salience of position cues in retardates slows learning about colors, forms, sizes, and other aspects of stimuli. A history of research and theory development from the first publication of the model in 1963 to 1979 can be found in Ellis's *Handbook of Mental Deficiency* (1963).

Zeaman served as editor of the *Psychological Bulletin* and as associate editor of *Intelligence*. He received many awards and honors from organizations, such as the American Psychological Association and the National Institute of Mental Health.

REFERENCE

Zeaman, D., & House, B. J. (1963). The role of attention in retardate discrimination learning. In N. R. Ellis (Ed.), *Handbook of mental deficiency: Psychological theory and research*. New York: McGraw-Hill.

STAFF

HOUSE, BETTY
ZEAMAN-HOUSE RESEARCH

ZEAMAN-HOUSE RESEARCH

David Zeaman and Betty House, along with other researchers located primarily at the University of Connecticut and the Mansfield Training School, have contributed substantial research on attention theory to the literature on Mental Retardation. Though more than 100 years of psychological and educational research on attention has concluded that the process is multifactorial (Alabiso, 1972), the Zeaman-House, and later Fisher-Zeaman, focus on selective attention has provided several learning theories useful in understanding and teaching mentally retarded persons.

Using a series of simple visual discrimination tasks, Zeaman and House found that plotting of individual, rather than averaged, group responses produced learning curves that differed significantly from traditional learning curves. The former curves stayed around the chance (50 percent) correct level, then jumped quickly to 100 percent accuracy. Prior to plotting individual data with backward learning curves, the expectation would have been for a gradual, incremental curve from chance to the 100 percent correct level. This discontinuity caused these researchers to postulate two processes, one controlling the length of the first part of the curve, and one determining the rapid jump to correct problem solution. Mentally retarded learners in the 2- to 4-year mental age range performed more poorly on these tasks than children of normal intelligence at comparable mental ages. Also, Zeaman and House determined that, among mentally retarded subjects, IQ was a more accurate predictor of better discrimination, independent of mental age (Robinson & Robinson, 1976).

The two-stage or two-phase discrimination learning process proposed by Zeaman and House (1963) suggests an early attention phase during which the plotted learning curve is essentially horizontal, indicating chance-level responses. During this phase, the subject has not discovered the relevant stimuli of an object and is randomly attending to various stimulus dimensions. The second phase of the discrimination process involves attention to relevant stimulus dimensions, leading to rapid improvement in learning (Mercer & Snell, 1977).

Because mentally retarded subjects produced chance-level curves of longer initial duration (yet also demonstrated steeply sloped curves comparable to subjects with higher mental ages), Zeaman and House (1963) argued that the inefficient learning of mentally retarded persons was, at its core, a function of their attention. This finding was important because it suggested that the actual learning potential of mentally retarded persons was not defective, and that interventions could be devised to improve attention and discrimination. The differences observed between slower-learning mentally retarded persons and faster or normal learners were based more on the time it took to learn to attend to relevant stimuli than to select the relevant cue itself (Zeaman & House). The work by Zeaman and House in the area of attention and discrimination learning led to studies of other relevant variables such as transfer of training, stimulus factors (e.g., size, position, color, shape), novelty and oddity learning, and the effects of reward characteristics.

Later, their attention theory was expanded to include examinations of the relationship of retention to attention and learning. Ten years after publication of the earlier work, Fisher and Zeaman (1973) noted that although the attention deficits that affect learning in mentally retarded persons are amenable to manipulation and improvement, the retention limitations attributable to the reduced cognitive capacity of such subjects may not be so flexible. Both the earlier and more recent work by Zeaman, House, and their colleagues have generated considerable productive research by others. These latter focuses, many of which suggest implications for education and training of mentally retarded learners, include work on the number of stimulus dimensions employed, reward and incentive conditions, and transfer and oddity learning.

REFERENCES

Alabiso, F. (1972). Inhibitory functions of attention in reducing hyperactive behavior. *American Journal of Mental Deficiency, 77*, 259–282.

Fisher, M. A., & Zeaman, D. (1973). An attention-retention theory of retardate discrimination learning. In N. R. Ellis (Ed.), *The international review of research in mental retardation* (Vol. 6). New York: Academic.

Mercer, C. D., & Snell, M. E. (1977). *Learning theory research in mental retardation: Implications for teaching.* Columbus, OH: Merrill.

Robinson, N. M., & Robinson, H. B. (1976). *The mentally retarded child: A psychological approach.* New York: McGraw-Hill.

Zeaman, D., & House, B. J. (1963). The role of attention in retardate discrimination learning. In N. R. Ellis (Ed.), *Handbook of mental deficiency.* New York: McGraw-Hill.

JOHN D. WILSON
Elwyn Institutes

HOUSE, BETTY
ZEAMAN, DAVID

ZERO INFERENCE

Zero inference is a term that refers to the instructional needs of individuals with severe disabilities (Brown, Nietupski, & Hamre-Nietupski, 1976). Typically, teachers of nonhandicapped students teach a series of core skills using a variety of materials (e.g., counting using wooden cubes). It is assumed that these students will then learn strategies, roles, and concepts necessary to the use of such core skills in other natural settings. It cannot be inferred that severely disabled students can be taught critical skills in an artificial (i.e., nonnatural) setting using artificial materials and be expected to perform the same skills in more natural settings.

Because of the nature of their mental, physical, or emotional problems, severely disabled students often need educational, social, psychological, or medical services that are beyond those offered in classes for nondisabled students. Educational needs are notable in that some students with severe handicaps may have severe language or perceptual-cognitive deficits. They may fail to attend to even pronounced social stimuli and may lack even the most rudimentary forms of verbal control (U.S. Office of Education, 1975). Severely disabled students may have the need for intensive instruction in areas including social behavior, communication skills, personal care, mobility and ambulation skills, academic and cognitive behaviors, and vocational skills (Wehman, Renzaglia, & Bates, 1985). Many of the skills required for adaptive performance in postschool environments will need to be taught to severely disabled students because of the nature of their performance and cognitive deficits. Such instruction is referred to as the zero-degree inference strategy.

Characteristics of the zero-degree inference strategy of instruction include the belief that no inferences can be made about training a student to perform at a skill level that he or she will be able to use in postschool settings. In order for severely disabled students to generalize skills taught in more natural (i.e., nonschool) settings, strategies must be used to ensure that generalization will occur (Stokes & Baer, 1977). Training across multiple settings, materials, and trainers may be included in instruction of students with severe disabilities. General case programming (Horner, Sprague, & Wilcox, 1982), in which common characteristics of several materials or settings are assessed in an effort to teach students a strategy that can be used in a variety of postschool settings, may be used. Additionally, techniques of systematic instruction, including data-based instruction and assessment of student progress, are necessary to ensure the acquisition of usable skills on the part of severely disabled learners (Lynch, McGuigan, & Shoemaker, 1977).

Employing training techniques including generalization or general case strategies and systematic instruction will ensure the acquisition of skills that can be used by severely disabled students in all necessary environments. Teachers who make zero inferences regarding student performance will be more likely to see success in student performance across situations requiring similar skills.

REFERENCES

Brown, L., Nietupski, J., & Hamre-Nietupski, S. (1976). Criterion of ultimate functioning. In M. A. Thomas (Ed.), *Hey, don't forget about me!* Reston, VA: Council for Exceptional Children.

Horner, R. H., Sprague, J., & Wilcox, B. (1982). General case programming for community activities. In B. Wilcox & G. T. Bellamy (Eds.), *Design for high school programs for severely handicapped students* (pp. 61–68). Baltimore: Brookes.

Lynch, V., McGuigan, C., & Shoemaker, S. (1977). Systematic instruction: Defining the good teacher. In N. Haring (Ed.), *An inservice program for personnel serving the severely handicapped.* Seattle: Experimental Education Unit, University of Washington.

Stokes, T. F., & Baer, D. M. (1977). An implicit technology of generalization. *Journal of Applied Behavior Analysis, 10,* 349–367.

U.S. Office of Education. (1975). *Estimated number of handicapped children in the United States, 1974–75.* Washington, DC: Bureau of Education for the Handicapped.

Wehman, P., Renzaglia, A., & Bates, P. (1985). *Functional living skills for moderately and severely handicapped individuals.* Austin, TX: PRO-ED.

CORNELIA LIVELY
University of Illinois, Urbana-Champaign

SELF-CONTAINED CLASS
SELF-HELP TRAINING
TRANSFER OF TRAINING

ZERO-REJECT

The term *zero-reject* identifies a policy of providing to all children with handicapping conditions a free, appropriate, and publicly supported education. The constitutional foundation of zero-reject is the Fourteenth Amendment, which guarantees that no state may deny any person within its "jurisdiction the equal protection of the laws." The courts have interpreted this to mean that no government may deny public services to a person because of his or her unalterable characteristics (e.g., sex, race, age, disability). Advocates of children with handicaps claimed that these children have the same rights to education as children who are not disabled. If a state treats children with disabilities differently (e.g., by denying them the opportunity to attend school, by inappropriately assigning them to a special education program), then it is denying them "equal protection of the laws" on the basis of their unalterable characteristics.

In 1975 Congress noted that over one million children with disabilities in the United States were being denied an appropriate public education, and passed PL 94-142, the Education of All Handicapped Children Act, which specified that no child with a handicapping condition (aged 3 to 21) could be excluded from school by recipients of federal funds for the education of children with disabilities. Zero-reject, the mandate to include all children in public schools and to provide an appropriate education for them, represented a new responsibility for public school systems at the time. The policy of zero-reject has remained strong throughout the revisions to PL 94-142, which include the 1990 passage of the Individuals with Disabilities Education Act (IDEA), and the 1997 Amendments to the IDEA.

The law promotes the zero-reject policy by requiring the schools to provide an education that would be meaningful to the child when he or she leaves school, particularly in facilitating the movement of qualified individuals with disabilities into mainstream employment. State education agencies have the responsibility of ensuring the policy of zero-reject, but the rule applies to the state, each school district, private schools, and state-operated programs such as schools for students with visual or hearing impairments.

Judicial interpretation of the zero-reject rule has included the order that students whose behavior is caused by their disability may not be expelled or suspended. The courts have also ordered, under the zero-reject policy, that students with contagious diseases may not be excluded from public education with other students unless there is a high risk that other students will be infected (Turnbull, Turnbull, Shank, & Leal, 1995).

REFERENCE

Turnbull, A. P., Turnbull, H. R., Shank, M., & Leal, D. (1995). *Exceptional lives: Special education in today's schools.* Englewood Cliffs, NJ: Prentice Hall.

CAROLE REITER GOTHELF
Hunter College, City University of New York
First edition

DONNA WALLACE
The University of Texas of the Permian Basin
Second edition

EQUAL PROTECTION
FREE APPROPRIATE PUBLIC EDUCATION
INDIVIDUALS WITH DISABILITIES EDUCATION
    IMPROVEMENT ACT OF 2004 (IDEIA)

ZIGLER, EDWARD (1930–   )

Edward Zigler received his BA in history from the University of Missouri at Kansas City in 1954 and his PhD in psychology from the University of Texas, Austin in 1958. He is currently Sterling Professor of Psychology at Yale University, Director of the Bush Center in Child Development and Social Policy, and head of the psychology section of the Child Study Center.

Named by President Carter to chair the fifteenth anniversary Head Start Committee in 1980, Zigler was a member of the National Planning and Steering Committee for Head Start and was appointed to Head Start's first National Research Council. He was also the first director of the Office of Child Development and Chief of the U.S. Children's Bureau.

The essence of Zigler's work has been the systemic evaluation of experiential, motivational, and personality factors in the behavior of mentally retarded persons, and the demonstration of how these factors (delineated by experimental results) affect retarded children's performance. He also proposed a classification system for Mental Retardation along two axes: one, individuals would be ordered by IQ and on the other, by organic, familial, and/or undifferentiated etiologies. Zigler believes that beyond any doubt, many of the reported differences between retarded and nonretarded persons of the same MA are a result of motivational and emotional differences that reflect variations in experiential histories (Blatt & Morris, 1984).

Zigler has authored and coauthored over 300 publications in the field including: *Familial Mental Retardation: A continuing dilemma* (1967), and, with D. Balla, *The Social Policy Implications of a Research Program on the Effects of Institutionalization on Retarded Persons* (1977).

The recipient of many awards and honors, Zigler's current research interests are cognitive and social-emotional development in children (particularly those with Mental Retardation), motivational determinants of children's performance, and the applicability of developmental theory to the area of psychopathology.

REFERENCES

Blatt, B., & Morris, R. J. (1984). *Perspectives in special education personal orientations.* Glenview, Illinois: Scott, Foresman.

Zigler, E. (1967). Familiar mental retardation: A continuing dilemma. *Science, 155,* 292–298.

Zigler, E., & Balla, D. (1977). The social policy implications of a research program on the effects of institutionalization on retarded persons. In P. Mittler (Ed.), *Research to practice in mental retardation* (Vol. 1, pp. 267–281). Baltimore: University Park Press.

ELAINE FLETCHER-JANZEN
*University of Colorado at
Colorado Springs*

HEAD START

ZONE OF PROXIMAL DEVELOPMENT

Zone of proximal development (ZPD) is a concept developed by Vygotsky (1978) that refers to a range of performance that includes the child's current independent performance level as well as the level that the child could perform with the collaboration with an adult or more competent peer. The ZPD is a concept important to learning in general. If the child is approached below the zone, boredom and lessening of motivation could occur. If the child is approached above the zone, frustration can occur. Alternatively, approaching the child within the upper range of the zone facilitates participation and can maximize benefit to the child (e.g., Gray & Feldman, 2004). Maximizing the approach to the upper range of the zone of proximal development is important in extending the range. The adult must have knowledge of the child's interests, strengths, and weaknesses as well as understanding of the best methods that will move the child to more advanced levels of cognitive development (Minick, 1988).

This process of approach and guidance is referred to as scaffolding. The process by which the individual progresses from his or her initial independent learning level to being able to problem-solve independently at what was previously attainable only with assistance is facilitated by scaffolding procedures. With scaffolding or assistance, the individual navigates the learning needed to be able to attain a higher level of understanding. The scaffolding process may involve joint problem-solving or prompting with the adult gradually decreasing his or her support in the process (Wood, Bruner, & Ross, 1976). While his theory and the principles associated with it originated many years ago, popularity of the concepts wax and wane along with the emphasis on the sociocultural influences of learning and development (Kozulin, 2004).

ZPD is most often considered with regard to its application to dynamic assessment as an alternative to standard psychometric testing. With dynamic assessment, the focus is not on the level of independent functioning, but rather on identifying the ZPD in which the child can function with assistance (Chaiklin, 2003). Learning potential or emergent psychological functions are seen as equally as important as what has already been mastered and a variety of techniques have been developed for assessment of ZPD (see Lidz & Gindis, 2003).

REFERENCES

Chaiklin, S. (2003). The zone of proximal development in Vygotsky's analysis of learning and instruction. In A. Kozulin, B. Gindis, V. Ageyev, & S. Miller (Eds.), *Vygotsky's educational theory in cultural context* (pp. 39–64). Cambridge, MA: Cambridge University Press.

Gray, P., & Feldman, J. (2004). Playing in the zone of proximal development: Qualities of self-directed age mixing between adolescents and young children at a democratic school. *American Journal of Education, 110*(2), 108–146.

Kozulin, A. (2004). Vygotsky'z theory in the classroom: Introduction. *European Journal of Psychology of Education, XIX,* 3–7.

Lidz, C., & Gindis, B. (2003). Dynamic assessment of the evolving cognitive functions in children. In A. Kozulin, B. Gindis, V. Ageyev, & S. Miller (Eds.), *Vygotsky's educational theory in cultural context* (pp. 293–357). Cambridge: Cambridge University Press.

Minick, N. (1988). The zone of proximal development and dynamic assessment. In C. S. Lidz (Ed.), *Foundations of dynamic assessment.* New York: Guilford.

Vygotsky, L. S. (1978). *Mind in society.* Cambridge, MA: Harvard University Press.

Wood, D. J., Bruner, J. S., & Ross, G. (1976). The role of tutoring in problem-solving. *Journal of Child Psychology and Psychiatry, 172,* 89–100.

CONSTANCE J. FOURNIER
CYNTHIA A. RICCIO
Texas A&M University

LEARNING POTENTIAL
LEARNING POTENTIAL ASSESSMENT DEVICE
THEORY OF ACTIVITY
VYGOTSKY, LEV S.

Z SCORES, IN DETERMINATION OF DISCREPANCIES

Since the passage of PL 94-142 (Education for all Handicapped Children Act of 1975) several measurement discrepancy models have been recommended in the measurement and special education literature for defining a child as learning disabled (Berk, 1984; Boodoo, 1985; Reynolds et al., 1984; Willson & Reynolds, 1985). These models are all used to estimate the difference between a child's aptitude and achievement, and to determine whether such a difference constitutes a severe discrepancy. The models recommended for use involve the use of standard scores. Under each model, a true discrepancy between a subject's aptitude and achievement is estimated using the subject's standard score on the respective aptitude and achievement test. Many of the standardized aptitude and achievement measures used for individualized testing are normed using the standard score scale with a mean ($\overline{X}$) of 100 and a standard deviation (S) of 15.

An alternative scale that simplifies the statistical formulas used in the discrepancy models for assessing a severe discrepancy is the Z score scale (Hopkins & Stanley, 1981). This scale has a mean of 0 and a standard deviation of 1 and has the advantage of representing the scores directly in standard deviation units. The following illustrates its use with the Simple Difference Model. Under this model, a difference is defined as [Aptitude (X) – Achievement (Y)] with the standard deviation of this difference, S_D, given by

$$S_D = (S_X^2 + S_Y^2 - 2r_{XY}S_X S_Y)^{1/2}$$

where r_{XY} is the correlation between X and Y. The standard error of estimate of a difference, SE, is given by

$$SE = [S_X^2(1 - r_{XX'}) + S_Y^2(1 - r_{XY'})]^{1/2}$$

where $r_{XX'}$, $r_{YY'}$, are the reliabilities of X and Y respectively.

Using the Z score scale, each of the aptitude and achievement scores is converted to the corresponding Z score using

$$Z_X = \frac{X - \overline{X}}{S_X}$$

and

$$Z_Y = \frac{Y - \overline{Y}}{S_Y}$$

Then, a simple difference is ($Z_X - Z_Y$). The standard deviation of this difference is

$$S_D = (2 - 2r_{XY})^{1/2}$$

where r_{XY} is the correlation between X and Y, and the standard error of estimate is given by

$$SE = (2 - r_{XX'} - r_{YY'})^{1/2}$$

REFERENCES

Berk, R. A. (1984). *Screening and diagnosis of children with learning disabilities.* Springfield, IL: Thomas.

Boodoo, G. M. (1985). A multivariate perspective for aptitude-achievement discrepancy in learning disability assessment. *Journal of Special Education, 18,* 489–499.

Hopkins, K. D., & Stanley, J. C. (1981). *Educational and psychological measurement and evaluation* (6th ed.). Englewood Cliffs, NJ: Prentice Hall.

Reynolds, C. R., Berk, R. A., Boodoo, G. M., Cox, J., Gutkin, T. B., Mann, L., Page, E. B., & Willson, V. L. (1984). *Critical measurement issues in learning disabilities.* Report of the USDE, SEP Work Group on Measurement Issues in the Assessment of Learning Disabilities.

Willson, V. L., & Reynolds, C. R. (1985). Another look at evaluating aptitude-achievement discrepancies in the diagnosis of learning disabilities. *Journal of Special Education, 18,* 477–488.

GWYNETH M. BOODOO
Texas A&M University

DISCREPANCY FROM GRADE
LEARNING DISABILITIES, SEVERE DISCREPANCY ANALYSIS IN

ZYGOSITY

Zygosity is twinning that may result in monozygotic (MZ), or identical twins, and dizygotic (DZ), or fraternal twins. The cause of MZ twinning remains unknown while the cause of DZ twinning is largely the result of multiple ovulation (Groothuis, 1985). Placentation helps to explain zygosity of twins, where dichorionic placentas take place in all DZ pairs and in about 30 percent of MZ twins. Monochorionic placentas occur only with MZ twins (Siegel & Siegel, 1982). A twin birth occurs in approximately 1 in 80 pregnancies. For women who already have given birth to twins, the incidence of having a second set rises to 1 in 20. The incidence of MZ twins is 3.5 per 1,000 live births independent of race and maternal age. With maternal age DZ twinning increases. It is slightly more frequent in blacks and most unusual in Asians (Groothuis, 1985; Siegel & Siegel, 1982).

Twinning is of relevance to special education personnel because there are increased risks for medical, psychological, developmental, and educational problems. Twin pregnancies have been associated with higher rates of such symptoms as nausea and vomiting. The greatly increased mortality of twins at birth (i.e., 15 percent) has been attributed to the high prematurity rate (i.e., 60 percent) in terms of both gestation time and birth weight. Twins also experience a higher rate of such perinatal problems as entangling of cords, prolapsed cords, hypoxia anemia, respiratory distress syndrome, and jaundice. These risks are generally higher for MZ twins and the second born of both MZ and DZ twins (Young et al., 1985). Twins also experience congenital anomalies such as heart disease, cleft lip, and cleft palate about twice as frequently as children of single births.

There is a general consensus that twins experience higher rates of developmental and behavioral problems than the general population. Like the medical difficulties, these risks are generally more severe for MZ and second-born twins. During the preschool years, problems are focused in such areas as verbal and motor development, discipline, sharing, toilet training, separation, and individual needs. Many of the problems continue for school-aged twins with classroom assignments, school avoidance, peer relations, and academic performance as special concerns. During adolescence, the identity crisis could be exacerbated for twins who have not resolved separation and individuation issues earlier. Regarding school-related abilities, the degree of impairment has been found to be dependent on birth problems and illness as antecedents (Matheny, Dolan, & Wilson, 1976). Moreover, Matheny et al. reported that twins in comparison with the general population have higher rates of learning disabilities and social immaturity. Siegel and Siegel (1982) point out that IQ deficits are questionable, especially when antecedent and environmental factors are controlled.

Typical recommendations for management and guidance follow: (1) Encourage parents to avoid emphasizing similarities; (2) separate twins at school as soon as possible but delay if problems are encountered; (3) establish individual expectations for school performance; and (4) give psycho-education assessment to twins with early medical problems. Parents are referred to the National Mother of Twins Club for information and resources.

REFERENCES

Groothuis, J. R. (1985). Twins and twin families. A practical guide to outpatient management. *Clinics in Perinatology, 12,* 459–474.

Matheny, A. P., Dolan, A. B., & Wilson, R. S. (1976). Twins with academic learning problems: Antecedent characteristics. *American Journal of Orthopsychiatry, 46,* 464–469.

Siegel, S. J., & Siegel, M. M. (1982). Practical aspects of pediatric management of families with twins. *Pediatrics in Review, 4,* 8–12.

Young, B. K., Suidan, J., Antoine, C., Silverman, F., Lustig, I., & Wasserman, J. (1985). Differences in twins: The importance of birth order. *American Journal of Obstetrics and Gynecology, 151,* 915–921.

JOSEPH D. PERRY
Kent State University

SIBLINGS OF INDIVIDUALS WITH DISABILITIES
TWINS